Handbook of
SOCIAL
PROBLEMS

Handbook of

SOCIAL PROBLEMS

A Comparative International Perspective

Edited by

George Ritzer

University of Maryland

SAGE Publications
International Educational and Professional Publisher
Thousand Oaks ■ London ■ New Delhi

For information:

Sage Publications, Inc.
2455 Teller Road
Thousand Oaks, California 91320
Email: order@sagepub.com

Sage Publications Ltd.
6 Bonhill Street
London EC2A 4PU
United Kingdom

Sage Publications India Pvt. Ltd.
B-42, Panchsheel Enclave
Post Box 4109
New Delhi 110 017 India

Printed in the United States of America

Library of Congress Cataloging-in-Publication Data

Handbook of social problems: A comparative international perspective / edited by George Ritzer.
    p. cm.
Includes bibliographical references and index.
ISBN 0-7619-2610-0 (cloth)
    1. Social problems. 2. Social problems—United States. I. Ritzer, George.
HN28.H29 2004
361.1—dc22

                               2003015883

This book is printed on acid-free paper.

03   04   05   06   10   9 8 7 6 5 4 3 2 1

Acquisitions Editor:	Jerry Westby
Editorial Assistant:	Vonessa Vondera
Production Editor:	Denise Santoyo
Copy Editors:	Barbara Coster, Carla Freeman
Typesetter:	C&M Digitals (P) Ltd.
Indexer:	Teri Greenberg
Cover Designer:	Ravi Balasuriya

CONTENTS

PREFACE

As near as I can tell, this is the first Handbook in the area of social problems since Erwin Smigel's (1971) *Handbook on the Study of Social Problems.* It strikes me as odd that there has been such a long hiatus between Handbooks in this area, since there are a number of reasons to think that there would have been several of them in the intervening years.

First, and most important, we are dealing with some of the most significant issues not only in sociology and the social sciences but in the social world in general. Given the importance of *all* the topics covered in this volume, one would have thought there would have been a number of Handbooks like this one.

Second, any given social problem changes, sometimes dramatically, over time, and there is a continuing need to update what we know about each of them. In the realm of drugs (not even deemed worthy of a chapter in the Smigel volume), for example, concern about LSD might have loomed large several decades ago, but drugs like crack cocaine (cocaine was first used in this way in the late 1970s) and Ecstasy (first banned in 1985) could not have been considered sources of social problems, since they either did not exist, at least as we know them today, or were not deemed illegal. To take another example, while terrorism was thought of as a social problem several decades ago, large-scale terrorism in the United States was not so considered until September 11, 2001.

Third, a mountain of research has appeared on every social problem in the intervening period, and the state of our knowledge of each is radically different today than it was three decades ago. For example, in Howard Kaplan's essay in this volume (Chapter 32) on mental illness (interestingly, Kaplan also wrote the essay on this topic in the Smigel *Handbook*), the vast majority of the references are post-1971 and therefore could not have influenced his previous overview of the state of our knowledge of mental illness as a social problem. The wide-scale use of certain drugs to treat various mental illnesses has only come into existence in recent years, and therefore studies of their use and impact are relatively recent and could not have appeared in the previous essay.

Fourth, while some social problems are timeless (crime, war, inequalities of various sorts), many have receded in importance, and perhaps even disappeared, and others have become much more important and, in some cases, have come into existence for the first time in the years since the publication of the Smigel volume. In terms of those that have grown less important, global nuclear war (Chapter 20 in this volume) stands out, at least from the American (and Russian) perspective, because of the end of the cold war and the Soviet Union. Nonetheless, these countries and many others have continued to engage in wars, and national security is, if anything, a more central concern. In addition, premarital sex (Chapter 30) is no longer seen as the threat it once was, and mental illness (Chapter 32) garners, probably wrongly, much less public attention. Furthermore, issues like homosexuality (again, Chapter 30) are no longer seen as social problems by most scholars and laypeople as well. The Smigel volume devoted a chapter to religion as a social problem, while that topic is not dealt with here (although problems like religious conflict and the current scandals in the Catholic church indicate that problems remain).

Among those social problems that have grown more important, or at least have come to be considered more important, gender inequality (Chapter 10), terrorism (Chapter 21), technology (Chapter 24), and risk and safety (Chapter 26) are among the most obvious.

Most striking are the issues that were not considered social problems only a few decades ago. While globalization (Chapter 23) certainly existed, and was producing problems for many less developed nations, there was little awareness of it, and certainly of it as a problem, in the early 1970s. Much the same thing could be said about consumption (Chapter 14), although there were those visionaries like Thorstein Veblen, John Kenneth Galbraith, and Jean Baudrillard who anticipated the current concern with consumption-related problems. Most obvious is the fact that AIDS and the Internet, among other phenomena, did *not* exist three decades ago and hence could not have been considered as either social problems or potential sources of them.

Then, within long-term problem areas, there are specific problems that are of relatively recent vintage. For example, new forms of terrorism (Chapter 21) have come on the scene, and some forms of sexual behavior (e.g., unprotected sex with those one does not know well) are now considered major social problems.

Thus, the point is that because of all of these changes in social problems, and innumerable others, there is a great need for a *Handbook of Social Problems* three decades after the publication of the last one.

However, the greatest difference between this Handbook and its predecessor is that this one has an explicit comparative international perspective and is not restricted to the use of American experts on social problems (the contributors to the Smigel *Handbook* were, save one, all at American universities and the book was concerned with American social problems). The world has grown much smaller in the last several decades and it is impossible to restrict ourselves to the American context in discussing social problems (and virtually everything else). As a result, research on social problems is increasingly international and comparative. All the social problems discussed in this book, and it may well be that *all* social problems, whether or not they are touched on here, are international in character and must be discussed in that context.

For example, take the issue of ecological problems (Chapter 6) that know no international borders. In Ulrich Beck's famous formulation, many ecological problems produced by developed countries like the United States have a profound impact on many other nations, but they may eventually have a boomerang effect on the developed nation(s) that caused the problem(s). Drugs (Chapter 29) and children (and adults) engaged in the international sex trade (Chapter 31) criss-cross the world with increasing frequency and rapidity. Whether or not they cross national borders, there are many social problems that are common to nations in many parts of the world. For example, inequality (Chapters 7, 8, and 10) is a problem everywhere, as are problems relating to health (Chapter 17) and the health care delivery system (Chapter 18). In terms of health-related issues, nothing illustrates the need for a comparative international perspective more than the recent global outbreak of SARS (Severe Acute Respiratory Syndrome). Thus, not only is there a need for a Handbook offering an overview of social problems, but such a Handbook *must*, given the realities of the contemporary world, have a comparative international perspective.

There are more pragmatic reasons for the publication of this Handbook, at least as far as the scholars and teachers who are its intended audience are concerned. For a scholar who studies a particular social problem, it is likely that this volume offers an overview of that topic within the broad context of social problems, as well as in relationship to many other closely related problems. Since so many of these topics overlap and interpenetrate, most scholars will not only be interested in overviews that deal with their focal interests but also of allied topics and issues.

For the many faculty members and graduate students who teach courses on social problems, this book is designed to offer a handy and up-to-date reference resource that should prove to be an invaluable aid in preparing lectures and discussions on a wide array of social problems. Each chapter provides a knowledge base that is much more wide-ranging and complete, and is far more up-to-date, than the information offered in basic textbooks in the field. Furthermore, it allows those teachers who do not already do so to give their courses on social problems a much needed comparative international perspective. My hope and guess is that this volume will become a much used resource for those who teach social problems, one that never is out of reach for very long while the course is under way.

Most of the textbooks in the field are, as one would expect, targeted at the undergraduate and would be inappropriate at the graduate level. Thus, this volume, written by professionals for professionals, makes an excellent text for a graduate-level course on social problems.

Although social problems as a distinct field and course are most developed in the United States, this volume, given its international focus, should be of use throughout the world. It is my hope that it will spur more interest globally in this topic and that it will lead to the development of courses devoted to social problems in many nations. Encompassed under this broad heading are a number of monumental problems that deserve attention not only individually but also taken together as a whole, composed of a number of closely related and interrelated problems. Given the increasingly globalized nature

of the world in general, and social problems in particular, it seems natural that the study of social problems and courses devoted to them will become global as well.

I would like to thank the authors of the various essays in this volume for their efforts. While Smigel admitted that his volume was published without key essays because several authors were unable to meet their commitments, *all* the essays that were intended to be included in this volume are found here. In a few cases, the authors are different from those who originally agreed to write the essays in question. In other cases, coauthors have been added along the way. Nevertheless, this is the volume I originally envisioned, and it is being brought out on schedule and in a timely manner. Needless to say, this could not have occurred without the diligence of the authors represented here.

As with a number of recent projects, I could not have done this without the help of Todd Stillman, who managed innumerable tasks and details with his usual great skill and aplomb. Finally, thanks to Jerry Westby and the rest of the Sage team for having the vision to see the merit of this project and for supporting it so well.

George Ritzer

REFERENCE

Smigel, Erwin O., ed. 1971. *Handbook on the Study of Social Problems*. Chicago, IL: Rand McNally.

INTRODUCTION

1

SOCIAL PROBLEMS

A Comparative International Perspective

GEORGE RITZER

University of Maryland

The international and comparative nature of the essays in this volume lead to a concern with, among many other things, the relationship between social problems and degree of societal development and affluence. There are at least four interrelated issues involved in this relationship.

The first, and most obvious, is that less developed and less affluent societies are more likely to experience a wide range of social problems, and to a greater degree, than more developed and affluent societies. Relatedly, the poor in any society, developed or not, are more likely to experience social problems than the affluent. While many of the chapters in this volume make this point in various ways, I discuss it last in this introductory chapter because it is so well known and obvious. The focus of this chapter is on some less well known and sometimes counterintuitive ideas about the relationship between social problems and degree of societal affluence.

Second is the idea that affluence causes, or at least brings with it, a series of social problems that do not exist, at least to the same degree, in less affluent societies. This issue is made clear in Ulrich Beck's (1992) discussion of the risk society (see, also, Tulloch, this volume). For example, it is only affluent countries that can afford large numbers of a wide range of technologies (automobiles, air conditioners, nuclear power plants, etc.), and these technologies play a major role in the production of many problems, most notably air pollution, the widening of the hole in the ozone layer, the greenhouse effect, and many others.

While these create difficulties for affluent countries, it is also true that they simultaneously create problems for less affluent countries around the

Author's Note: I would like to thank Mike Ryan for many useful contributions to this essay.

world. As Beck puts it, poverty attracts risk. Thus, virtually everyone throughout the world will suffer from the increasing size of the hole in the ozone layer, although it is caused primarily by the affluent nations of the world. However, the affluent nations can also afford to take actions to mitigate, or solve, many of these problems, while poor nations have no choice but to live with, and suffer from, their adverse consequences. Nonetheless, it remains the case that affluence brings with it problems (e.g., storage of nuclear waste) that are not found in poor nations or at least do not affect them to the same degree (although rich nations often try to pawn such problems off on poor ones).

A third, and related, issue, suggested especially by Yearley (this volume) in his essay on ecological problems, is the fact that it is only with affluence that certain things can come to be imagined as social problems. Thus, it is not just that affluence itself creates problems, but it is only with affluence that people come to conceive of certain things as problems. To put it another way, what is conceived as a social problem in an affluent society would not be so considered in a less developed one.

One of the areas in which this is most obvious is excessive consumption (see the essay by Goodman). For virtually all societies throughout history, and even most societies today (as well as parts of affluent societies), the problem has been inadequate consumption. That is, in most societies, the problem has been insufficient consumption of, for example, food, with the result that a large portion of the population is undernourished or malnourished. In fact, there are currently about a billion people in the world who suffer from malnutrition (Nestle 2002). In contrast, in affluent societies, especially the United States, Western Europe, and Japan, excessive consumption— "hyperconsumption" (Ritzer 2001:155–7)—of food (and virtually everything else) has come to be defined as a social problem. It is almost inconceivable to think of people in the less developed nations of the world thinking of too much consumption, of food or anything else, as a problem.

A fourth issue discussed in this chapter is the increasing vulnerability of affluent societies to social problems. There is no question that affluence brings with it certain problems (e.g., air pollution), although it is important to remember that it also is associated with the ability to solve or mitigate them (e.g., technologies that reduce air pollution) as well as other, perennial, social problems (e.g., poverty, at least for the majority of the population). However, what is much less noticed is the fact that the more affluent the society, the more vulnerable it is to certain new social problems (whether or not they are created by developed societies). That is, the very affluence of a society makes it vulnerable to problems that would not be social problems in poorer societies.

This is related to a concept in postmodern theory known as *the strength of the weak* (Baudrillard [1983] 1990; Genosko 1992, 1994). That notion will prove important in the ensuing discussion, as will its converse—coined here for the first time—*the weakness of the strong*. As we will see, the latter idea is reflected in the fact that the weak (in this case, weak—less developed, poor—nations) are impervious to many social problems that are highly costly, if not crippling, to strong (developed and affluent) nations. This is not to say that the weak are not faced with overwhelming social problems, many of them traceable directly to the fact that they are weak. It is also not to say that the strength of a powerful nation does not serve as protection against many social problems. However, both of the preceding points are well-known and frequently discussed in the social sciences and the popular media. What is not so immediately obvious and not so well-known is the greater imperviousness of weak nations to some social problems and, more important, the greater vulnerability of strong nations to at least some of them. This is well illustrated by the events of September 11, 2001, the effect of those terrorist attacks, and their aftermath.

SEPTEMBER 11: THE VULNERABILITY OF HIGHLY DEVELOPED, AFFLUENT SOCIETIES

Among the many things that were made clear by the terrorist attacks of September 11 is the vulnerability of a highly developed and affluent society like the United States to social problems that are far less likely to exist in less affluent societies. This is particularly clear when the situation in the United States is contrasted to that of the ostensible sources of the terrorism, the Taliban and Al-Qaeda. Yes, the Taliban were ousted from power in Afghanistan and Al-Qaeda and, along with its leader, Osama bin Laden, were forced to flee. However, it is unlikely that day-to-day lives of most Afghans, especially their economic lives, were much affected by these political changes. Impoverished Afghans suffered little in the way of economic losses from the American "invasion," since they had so little to lose.[1] The small farmers, shepherds, or small shopkeepers spread thinly through Afghanistan were not tightly integrated with each other, let alone the overall Afghan economy, with the result that what happened in places like Kabul had little economic impact on the remote and thinly populated areas that define the country.

In contrast, while the terrorist attack did not force George W. Bush to flee (unless it was his brief detour to an air base in Colorado in the immediate aftermath of the attack), it cost the United States dearly, and the costs continue to mount. These extraordinary costs are traceable to the vulnerabilities of a highly complex and tightly integrated economy and society. The most obvious cost was the loss of about 3,000 lives and billions of dollars of property at the site of the World Trade Center and its environs, as well as at the Pentagon.[2] But far more costly, at least in terms of dollars, was the aftermath of the attack—lost business in and around New York and Washington (and many other places in the United States and throughout the world), the precipitous decline in the airline business, which, among other things, forced the huge carrier—United—into bankruptcy (other airlines preceded it and still others are likely to file for bankruptcy in the future). Tourist and convention business in New York and Washington, D.C., and many other locales underwent a steep decline and have yet to recover fully. Business at many hotels and restaurants suffered badly. Most generally, the economy (and the stock market), which might have begun to recover in late 2001 or early 2002, was plunged further into a recession that continues into mid-2003. In the aftermath of the attack, uncountable sums have been, and will be, expended on increased security of every

conceivable type. The war in Afghanistan was costly, but it pales in comparison to the 2003 war against Iraq (undertaken, at least in part, because of Iraq's ostensible links to terrorism), for which the down payment was about $80 billion, and that cost is likely to skyrocket in the postwar period (it is estimated that the cost could be $1 trillion, or even more).

Overall, we are probably talking in terms of several trillion dollars of costs directly and indirectly linked to September 11. The plain fact is that few, if any, other countries could experience losses of such magnitude *and* afford to pay the costs associated with them. It is the wealth of the United States that makes it vulnerable to such losses and to being led into such enormous expenditures to cope with the problems stemming from September 11. In other words, the costs of September 11 are only a problem because the United States is wealthy enough to experience, and to pay for, them. Thus, the portion of the Pentagon destroyed in the attack was rebuilt almost instantaneously, and planning is already well under way for reconstructing the area around the World Trade Center. In contrast, it is unlikely that much of significance that was destroyed in Afghanistan has been rebuilt, or will be rebuilt soon, because there are few, if any, funds available for such projects.[3] More generally, the cost of the war against the Taliban was far less costly to Afghanistan in dollar terms (absolutely, and perhaps even relatively) than the attack on the World Trade Center was to the United States.[4]

The public cost of September 11 is mirrored at the individual level in the United States. For example, fear of terrorism (see Martin, this volume) and advice from the Department of Homeland Defense has recently led many people to rush out and spend hundreds of dollars each on things like duct tape and plastic sheeting to seal their windows and doors in the event of a chemical or biological attack. Large numbers of people clearly need to be quite affluent in order to afford such expenditures to deal with an eventuality that is highly unlikely to affect them (especially if they live in places like Rapid City, South Dakota, or Taos, New Mexico). In contrast, once again, Afghans could afford to do little or nothing to protect themselves against the American "invasion."

Furthermore, all of this money spent by the federal government, states, municipalities, and individuals will create innumerable problems down the line—taxes will need to be raised (or at least tax cuts reduced), innumerable local, state, and federal programs will go unfunded or have their support slashed, and individuals will suffer a wide array of negative consequences from their own outlays to protect themselves as well as from cuts in government expenditures and therefore in government services. Of course, some will benefit. Defense contractors will experience a boom as a result of the wars with Afghanistan and especially Iraq; all of those munitions used, and equipment worn out or destroyed, must be replaced. Oil prices might go down because a regime friendlier to the United States is put in place in Iraq, but in the short run before the war, oil (and gasoline) prices rose precipitously, with negative consequences for just about everyone in the United States (an exception would be those associated with the oil and gasoline industries). Also experiencing gains will be those industries engaged in the production of a wide range of protective gear and the provision of protective services for individuals and corporations.

In its efforts to build a coalition for the war with Iraq, the Bush administration had great difficulty in finding nations that were willing to participate (Great Britain was the main exception). There are many reasons why other nations were unwilling to participate, but one is certainly the economic cost and the problems that would flow from expenditures associated with such an undertaking. That is, once again, only the most affluent could afford a war like the one against Iraq; no other nation in the world today could have afforded to undertake a war like that fought by the United States against Iraq.[5] Thus, no other nations could have caused, or experienced, the problems associated with such a war (see Roxborough, this volume).

Contrast the September 11 attacks on the World Trade Center to a hypothetical terrorist attack on the largest structures in Kabul (you could select innumerable other cities throughout the less well-developed world and make much the same point). There are no skyscrapers in Kabul into which jet passenger planes could be flown, it would not cost much to rebuild the largest buildings in Kabul were they to collapse, and relatively few lives would be lost in these smaller buildings. The impact on the economy of Afghanistan would be negligible, since the economy itself is very small and, in any case, it (and the larger society) is not tightly integrated. What happens in one part of Kabul would have little relationship to trade and business in other parts of the city, let alone the country. The tourist, airline, and hotel business in Kabul, already negligible, would not be affected to any great degree. No expensive counterattacks would be mounted by the Afghan government because there would be no money or equipment to undertake them. And individual Afghans would take no countermeasures, since they would not be helpful to most and, in any case, few could afford things like duct tape and plastic sheeting, which in any case would probably be unavailable.

Thus, the above illustrates the greater vulnerability of affluent societies to various social problems. It demonstrates the weakness of affluent societies: the weakness of the strong. The general conclusion is that a highly advanced, complex infrastructure is more vulnerable, easier to disrupt, and with far greater negative consequences than a less developed, simple infrastructure. For example, if terrorists were able to find a way to cripple America's power grid, it would cause untold difficulties for the nation and a large proportion of its citizens. Then there is the increasing reliance of Americans on the Internet, with the result that a significant disruption in it caused by hostile hackers would have a crippling effect on a wide range of things, especially the economy. To take another example, the dependency of the United States on oil-producing nations, because of its enormous number of automobiles, makes it highly vulnerable to increases in the price, or disruptions in the flow, of oil. This list could be extended almost indefinitely, but the central point is abundantly clear. The contrast, of course, is once again a less affluent and developed nation like Afghanistan, where life would be little affected and associated costs would be minimal if its power grid, Internet service, or gasoline supply were to be disrupted. After all, relatively few Afghans have electric power, a computer and Internet provider, or an automobile.

It is also the case that the technological marvels created by affluent societies can, in some cases, be used as highly effective weapons against them. Of course, the best-known example of this is the use, by the terrorists, of huge American passenger jets loaded with fuel as, in effect, piloted and highly explosive rockets. On September 11, such weapons proved capable of doing the unthinkable—bringing down the Twin Towers and turning them into a massive rubble heap. Apparently, the only weapons the hijackers used to gain control of the airplanes were simple and primitive box cutters. The terrorists had no weapons of their own that could have accomplished such devastating destruction; the weapons were provided, quite conveniently, by the United States. The point is that the wealthy nations produce the weapons capable of disrupting, if not destroying, themselves; weak nations produce and have few such weapons of their own.

SOCIAL PROBLEMS CAUSED BY AFFLUENCE

Affluent societies are not only uniquely vulnerable to various social problems, their affluence also causes an array of social problems. One specific example is high rates of obesity and the adverse consequences for health and health care that flow from it.

One reflection of America's unprecedented affluence is the fact that most people consume more food than they need, and this is reflected in estimates that in 2000, over 64 percent of Americans were overweight (body mass index—BMI—over 25), 30.5 percent were obese (BMI over 30), and 4.7 percent were severely obese (BMI over 40).[6] Furthermore, all evidence points to a dramatic increase in all three categories in recent years. Between 1976 and 2000, the percentage of those in the overweight category grew from 46 to 64.5; the obese from 14.4 to 30.5; and among the severely obese the increase was from 2.9 percent in 1994 (no figures from 1976 were available on this category) to 4.7 percent in 2000. There is no disputing the fact that the numbers are large and growing and that being overweight, especially being obese or severely obese, is unhealthy, with a number of diseases more common (heart disease, stroke, diabetes) and with life span shortened, often dramatically. Furthermore, the percentage of those in the overweight and obese categories is far greater in the United States than in all other countries, most notably the similarly affluent countries of Western Europe. (However, it is worth noting that even there, the percentages in these categories is increasing dramatically and may eventually approach those of the United States. In fact, overall in 2000 the number of those overweight throughout the world matched, for the first time, those who were undernourished [Nestle 2002:16].)

While there is no question that obesity is a problem in itself, and the cause of many other social problems (especially health-related problems of various types—see essays by Cockerham and Twaddle), it is important to remember that most people throughout history (and in less developed nations today) would have dearly loved to be able to gain weight, if not be overweight, and the consumption of a greater number of calories would have saved many who died from malnutrition.

Interestingly, in the United States, being overweight and obese is *not* positively correlated with social class. In fact, overall, those of lower socioeconomic status are *more* likely to be overweight and obese than those in higher social classes (O'Beirne 2003). Using educational level as a surrogate for social class, in 2000, 26.1 percent of those with less than a high school diploma were obese, whereas 15.2 percent of those with a college degree were obese (American Obesity Association 2002). Interestingly, the entire social class difference stems from the fact that women in the lower classes are about 50 percent more likely to be obese than women in the higher classes, while there is little difference among men in terms of obesity across social classes (U.S. Department of Health and Human Services 2001). Thus, we have a great democratization in terms of "fatness." It used to be (and still is, in less developed countries) that, in the main, one had to have some wealth in order to become fat. Now, the poor, at least in the United States, can also become fat. Indeed, they have a greater likelihood of being overweight and obese—and suffering the wide array of associated problems.

However, it is worth remembering that those considered poor in the United States today are comparatively affluent relative to the poor in much of the rest of the world, to say nothing of throughout history. Thus, even among the poor in America today, obesity as a social problem (and as a cause of many other social problems) is associated with (comparative) affluence. However, the more general point is that it is only with affluence that the excessive consumption of food—and much else—can come to be a social problem.

Another, even more specific, example of problems caused by affluent countries, this time affecting less developed nations, comes from the ability of affluent nations, especially the United States, to afford to purchase huge numbers of computers and to replace them with great regularity. It is estimated that more than 40 million computers became obsolete in 2001 alone; between 1997 and 2007 the total will be perhaps as high as 500 million (Goodman 2003). Why is this a problem? Well, it turns out that many of the components of computers are dangerous (when left in landfills, heavy metal can seep into drinking water), and the issue (like that of nuclear waste) is what to do with them. How can they be disposed of without posing a threat to the American population? The answer, not surprisingly, is to dump them on less affluent nations and let them cope with the problems created by large numbers of obsolete computers.

While there are laws against it, "e-waste" is finding its way into China, India, and Pakistan. There, poorly paid workers break down the computers (and other hardware such as monitors and printers) in order to extract elements that have some value—bits of copper and gold, for example. However, there are dangerous elements in this e-waste:

> Glass from monitors contains lead, which afflicts the nervous system and harms children's brains. Batteries and switches contain mercury, which damages organs and fetuses. Motherboards contain beryllium, the inhalation of which can cause cancer. . . . Near a riverbank that has been used to break down and burn circuit boards, a water sample revealed levels of lead 190 times as high as the drinking water standard set by the World Health Organization. (Goodman 2003:A18)

Thus, problems created by the ability of wealthy individual Americans, as well as well-heeled American corporations, to upgrade computers with great regularity and in great quantities has created problems that have been exported to less affluent nations. Said the head of a company that buys discarded computers and ships them overseas as waste, "I could care less where they go. . . . My job is to make money" (Goodman 2003:A18).

Similar problems exist, or will come into existence, with technological advances in other areas in the United States and other affluent societies. For example, as high-definition televisions become increasingly affordable and popular, old cathode ray sets—containing lots of lead—will become obsolete. And, when the flat-panel monitors that have recently come into vogue become obsolete, the mercury in them will cause problems, undoubtedly for those in less developed nations who were never able to afford them in the first place. The people in these countries often recognize the danger, but do the work because having no income is even more deadly.

DEFINING CERTAIN ISSUES AS SOCIAL PROBLEMS

Another aspect of the weakness of the strong is the fact that problems that would not be considered problems in other societies come to be defined as such in affluent nations. Some examples discussed in this volume exist in the realm of consumption (Goodman), the media (Kellner), and mental illness (Kaplan). For example, it is only in affluent societies that such consumption-related problems as the increasing hegemony of the fast-food restaurant (Ritzer 2000), the disenchantment associated with "cathedrals of consumption" like megamalls and casino-hotels (Ritzer 1999), the high cost of credit card debt (Manning 2000; Ritzer 1995), and, more generally, the commodification of everything can be considered as social problems. Similarly, while those in affluent societies worry about the nature and quality of that which is available in the media, those in less developed societies are concerned about their lack of access to the media, including the offerings (e.g., soap operas, reality TV) that are so criticized by intellectuals in affluent societies. In the realm of mental illness, while those in affluent societies are concerned about deinstitutionalization and the proper medication for those labeled as mentally ill, in less affluent societies such people are likely to be seen as little more than somewhat unusual members of society. Deinstitutionalization is not a problem, since there were few, if any, institutions in the first place. Medication is not an option, since most, if not all, psychotropic drugs are far too expensive for those in these societies. Tonry (this volume) discusses the adverse effect of imprisonment on prisoners, their families, and their communities. While this might be, or become, a worry in developed countries, it is doubtful that less affluent nations will concern themselves with this issue, let alone undertake costly actions to deal with it. Of course, this list could be extended greatly, but the central point is that it is often the case that that which is defined as a social problem in affluent, developed societies is not so defined in poor, less developed societies.

Relatedly, the ability of the rich nations to create technologies to diagnose and perhaps deal with social problems leads them to define various matters as problems that would not be so defined in poor nations. For example, some years ago, and to some extent continuing to this day, the radon levels in or near people's homes came to be defined as a social problem in part because of the creation of "radon detectors" capable of measuring such levels. Radon came to be defined as a social problem by many home owners, and some homes were renovated extensively in order to reduce or eliminate the problem. Furthermore, some people sold homes, perhaps at unduly low prices, because of high radon levels, and buyers backed off on purchasing homes that had high levels of radon. In contrast, it is highly unlikely that radon would be considered a social problem in, say, Kabul and elsewhere throughout Afghanistan. There are far more pressing problems, especially where one's next meal is going to come from.

This point is most easily illustrated in the area of health and illness. Many threats to health only become recognized when technologies are developed—almost always in highly developed nations—to diagnose and treat them. For example, GERD (gastroesophageal reflux disease, usually described colloquially as heartburn) only came to be defined as a significant health problem in the United States (and other developed countries) with the development of endoscopy as a widely used tool to diagnose

GERD by inspecting the esophagus for damage. Furthermore, without a method of treatment, there was little point in diagnosing the problem, since little could be done about it. However, early diagnosis became more important with the development of a new class of drugs, such as Prilosec, Prevacid, and more recently Nexium, capable of suppressing stomach acid and therefore greatly reducing the possibility of damage to the esophagus caused by acid reflux. Prior to these developments, people thought of "heartburn" as a nuisance to be endured or treated symptomatically with antacids of various types. However, today heartburn has come to be seen by many in the United States and other developed nations (with the help of the major drug companies and their ubiquitous advertisements for drugs like Nexium) as a major health risk and a potential cause of serious health problems like Barrett's disease and the accompanying higher (but not high) risk of esophageal cancer.

Of course, among the poor in developed countries, and in many less developed countries, heartburn continues to be defined as largely a nuisance. Concern about it is overwhelmed by far larger and more pressing problems. Few are going to be able to afford endoscopies, and the technology is likely to be low on the list of needs in such areas and nations. Furthermore, even if a diagnosis was possible and made, few would be able to afford the high cost of the "cure"—Nexium is a very expensive medication that only well-off (or insured)[7] members of affluent societies can afford.

NEVERTHELESS, THE POOR SUFFER MORE FROM SOCIAL PROBLEMS

While to this point this chapter has emphasized the weakness of the strong—the social problems that plague affluent, developed countries—the overwhelming conclusion to be derived from the chapters in this volume is that it is the poor countries, and the poor in affluent nations, who suffer most from a wide range of social problems. However, as the following overview, based on many of the chapters in this volume, shows, there are also important exceptions to this generalization.

• Population problems (Desai) are certainly largely the province of less developed and less prosperous nations. Indeed, the problems stem, at least in part, from the lack of development and prosperity, and they contribute to an exacerbation of those difficulties. Furthermore, in developed and well-off nations, it is the poor who cause and suffer from population problems to an excessive degree.

• Problems associated with economic inequality (Babones and Turner) are, by definition, closely linked to level of development, with inequality being a far greater problem in developed nations than in less developed countries. This is true if for no other reason than the fact that such a large proportion of the population in less developed countries is poverty stricken. Thus, they are likely to be more worried about survival than about the relatively few who are far better off than they are. Of course, economic inequality is a social problem in both developed and less developed nations. However, we can also look at economic inequality among and between nations, and in this sense it is the less affluent nations that, by definition, suffer more from such inequality than developed countries.

• There is far more variability from nation to nation on racial and ethnic inequality than on economic inequality (Feagin and Batur; Hall; Persell, Arum, and Seufert). Thus, racial conflict is a major issue in the highly developed United States as well as a number of less developed nations (Brazil is an example discussed by Feagin and Batur). In contrast, ethnic conflict is a comparatively minor matter in the United States, but not long ago it was a major issue in the former Yugoslavia and may become a larger issue in Iraq as the possibility of confrontation between Shiites, Sunnis, and Kurds increases with the end of the regime of Saddam Hussein.

• Although gender inequality (Wharton) is a major issue in well-heeled and developed countries like the United States and the nations of Europe, women have far greater problems in many less developed countries, where they are far more oppressed and suffer from a wide range of obscenities such as clitorectomies.

• Large urban areas (Kim and Gottdiener) are associated with a wide range of problems everywhere in the world, but those problems (especially those associated with overurbanization) are greatly exacerbated in the large cities of the less developed world such as Mexico City, Calcutta, and Nairobi.

• While work-related problems (Sullivan) exist throughout the world, their nature differs depending on level of development. While those in developed countries worry about the quality of their work and their work lives, those in less developed countries are more concerned about the absence of work and the economic problems that accompany the lack of a job and an income.

• Similarly, family problems (Berardo and Shehan) are nearly universal, but the nature of the problems differs greatly in terms of our central concern here. Thus, the quality of family life may be an issue in developed countries, but the ability simply to sustain a family of any type with limited economic means is a far greater problem in less developed nations, as well as in the poorer areas of developed nations.

• AIDS (Lichtenstein) is a horrendous social problem and creates innumerable other problems wherever it is found (and it is found almost everywhere), but its prevalence is closely tied to a lack of development and affluence (as are many other health problems [Cockerham]; it is also the case that the availability and quality of medical services is lowest in the least developed and poorest countries [Twaddle]). While the disease first attracted attention in the United States, it is now a far greater problem in the poverty-stricken nations of Africa and Southeast Asia. In the United States today, AIDS is disproportionately a problem for the lower classes. Also relevant here are economic differences in access to medications that can greatly mitigate the effects of AIDS and lengthen life significantly. Thus, because those drugs are very expensive, relatively well-to-do (or at least well-insured) members of affluent societies can afford them, but the poor everywhere, especially in less developed countries, have virtually no chance of acquiring them (although there are some signs that drug companies are being forced to become more responsive to this issue).

- Genocide (Smith) has certainly occurred in developed nations (the most infamous example occurred, of course, in Nazi Germany), but it is more likely in less developed areas (the Turkish genocide committed against Armenians, the effort by the Tutsis to exterminate the Hutus in Burundi, etc.).

- As is the case with many other issues discussed in this volume, globalization (Boli) and its problems are closely associated with the level of development of a nation. Indeed, most of the issues and protests surrounding globalization involve the view that it is the developed nations that profit most from globalization, while the less developed nations gain relatively little and may even be net losers in the process (Stiglitz 2002). Another aspect of globalization is pointed up by Goode's analysis of the drug problem. In this case, most of the developed world's drugs come from less developed nations in various parts of the world. As Goode puts it, "The poorer an area, society, or community, the greater the likelihood that the production, trafficking, and sale of illegal drugs will flourish."

- Advanced technologies (Webster and Erickson) create social problems for less developed nations primarily because they can afford few, if any, of them. Thus, for example, in the war with Iraq in 2003, the Iraqi army had no chance against the technologically sophisticated American (and to a lesser extent British) army. However, advanced technology creates problems for developed nations, and this has been discussed above in terms of the weakness of the strong.

- The whole issue of the global digital divide as it relates to the Internet (Drori) is another matter that closely tracks a nation's level of development (as well as differences within a nation). It is quite clear that the richest nations dominate the Internet and access to it, while the incapacities of those in less developed nations in this regard represent serious problems for the denizens of those nations.

- I have already briefly discussed the issue of risk (Tulloch) and the idea, closely related to the theme of this section and volume, that poverty attracts risk. The converse is also the case, with the wealthy and wealthy nations experiencing risk not only directly but also as a result of what Beck (1992) calls the "boomerang effect."

- Matters are somewhat different in the case of the related problems of crime (Tonry), juvenile delinquency (Stafford), and drug abuse (Goode). These are greater problems, or at least are perceived as such, in the most developed nations, especially the United States. It is sometimes hard to tell whether they are greater problems there, or whether the United States, because of its affluence, can better afford to define these things as problems and then seek to deal with them. For example, does the enormous number of people in America's prisons (Tonry reports that the number of people in American prisons per 100,000 populations is 5 to 12 times higher than other Western nations, and the disparity is undoubtedly greater when the rates for less developed nations are considered) reflect a higher crime rate than in less developed nations? Or, is it a reflection of the ability to afford large police forces to catch criminals, extensive court systems to process them, and extremely expensive prisons to house them? Less developed nations may have as great, or even more pervasive, problems with crime, but their crimes may go unreported and unpublicized and criminals may not be apprehended, tried, and incarcerated simply because the infrastructure needed to accomplish such objectives is too expensive.

- Sexual problems (Plummer) are interesting from this perspective since, again, it is likely that only developed countries can afford to have, or at least recognize, many of them. Of course, the whole idea of what, if anything, is a sexual problem has been called into question in recent years. Thus, the activism of, for example, homosexuals, primarily in developed nations, as well as the work of a number of scholars on such issues (most notably Michel Foucault), has led to a dramatic decline in developed countries of the sense in the general population that homosexuality is a social problem (but that is not to say that homosexuals do not continue to face serious problems in developed nations). Interestingly, in this case, it may be that homosexuality is more likely to be considered a problem by the general population in less developed nations because they have not had such social movements or been as exposed to the literature on homosexuality and sexuality more generally.

• A more specific social problem is the global sex trade, especially the role of children in it (Davidson). In this case, it is clear that less developed nations (e.g., Thailand) are central destinations for those (usually from affluent nations) interested in participating in the global sex trade. Furthermore, those same nations are the sources of people, including children, who are exported, often unwillingly, to developed countries to be used there in the sex business.

• There are obviously disabled people throughout the world, but disability (Albrecht) is less of a social problem in less developed nations (even though there are likely *more* disabled persons in such areas) primarily because they can afford to do little about it. It is just one of the many adverse realities that those in such nations are forced to endure. For example, Albrecht points out that "Persons with spinal cord injuries, for example . . . usually do not have the resources and medical care to survive for years after injury, so not many of them can be counted as disabled in resource-constrained nations." In contrast, disability is a far greater problem, or at least is perceived as such, by those in well-off nations, again largely because they have a far greater ability to take actions that will ameliorate the problem and make life better for those (like those with spinal cord injuries) who are disabled.

• Finally, while affluent nations are certainly not immune to corruption (LaFree and Morris), they seem to have been better able to afford, and to develop, better methods of limiting and controlling it. In contrast, corruption seems rampant in less developed nations in part because of the inability to afford such countermeasures. Furthermore, it may be that corruption is greater in less developed nations because of their comparative poverty. That is, those in positions of power have greater economic need (although corruption is certainly not restricted to economic gain) to take advantage of opportunities to enrich themselves than their counterparts in more affluent nations. Thus, according to LaFree and Morris, "8 of the 10 nations that have the

highest levels of perceived corruption . . . are classified as low income by the World Bank (Bangladesh, Nigeria, Uganda, Indonesia, Kenya, Cameroon, Azerbaijan, and Tanzania), and the remaining 2 nations (Ukraine and Bolivia) are classified as low-middle income." In contrast, "Not a single one of the 28 high-GNP nations was classified as having high levels of perceived corruption."

Thus, while there are important exceptions, it comes as no surprise that most social problems cause greater difficulties in poor, less developed nations than they do in well-to-do, developed countries.

CONCLUSION

Overall, the point of this introduction and, more generally, this handbook is to demonstrate the importance and utility of looking at, and thinking about, social problems from a comparative international perspective. There are a large number of common problems across many nations, but there are also important differences among and between these nations in what is a social problem. It is important that we gain a better and more systematic understanding of both these similarities and differences, as well as their causes.

NOTES

1. Although what they lost may have been large compared to the relatively meager quantity of material phenomena (money, materiel, infrastructure, etc.) that they possessed.

2. We have no solid numbers on the cost of the war to Afghanistan in terms of lives lost and adverse economic consequences. In percentage terms, it is possible that such costs were even higher in Afghanistan, at least in the immediate aftermath of the war. However the lack of integration of Afghanistan's comparatively undeveloped economy served to limit the economic cost in the longer term, whereas the tightly integrated character of the U.S. economy exacerbated the problem and the cost. Indeed, the American economy continues to suffer badly from September 11 and its aftermath.

3. Iraq is different, since the United States wanted to demonstrate that it could not only conquer Iraq and topple Saddam Hussein but also rebuild the country.

4. Or consider the fact that in the Iraq war of 2003, the United States often used highly sophisticated weapons that cost far more than the buildings they were being used to destroy.

5. Of course, many nations chose not to participate, or to oppose the war, on moral grounds.

6. These statistics are provided by the American Obesity Association (2002) and are compiled mainly from a number of official government sources. Nestle (2002) offers slightly more conservative figures, but they are a bit dated. While the numbers here are not terribly reliable, there is no question that large numbers of Americans are overweight and that their numbers are increasing.

7. And, of course, such insurance exists only in affluent nations.

REFERENCES

American Obesity Association. 2002. Retrieved from www.obesity.org/subs/fastfacts/aoafactsheets.shtml.

Baudrillard, Jean. [1983] 1990. *Fatal Strategies.* New York: Semiotext(e).

Beck, Ulrich. 1992. *Risk Society: Towards a New Modernity.* London, England: Sage.

Genosko, Gary. 1992. "The Struggle for an Affirmative Weakness: de Certeau, Lyotard and Baudrillard." *Current Perspectives in Social Theory* 12:179–94.

——. 1994. *Baudrillard and Signs: Signification Ablaze.* London, England: Routledge.

Goodman, Peter. 2003. "China Serves as Dump Site for Computers." *Washington Post,* February 24, pp. A1, A18.

Manning, Robert. 2000. *Credit Card Nation.* New York: Basic Books.

Nestle, Marion. 2002. *Food Politics: How the Food Industry Influences Nutrition and Health.* Berkeley, CA: University of California Press.

O'Beirne, Kate. 2003. "Poor and Fat: A Special Problem in America." *National Review* 55:2.

Ritzer, George. 1995. *Expressing America: A Critique of the Global Credit Card Society.* Thousand Oaks, CA: Pine Forge.

——. 1999. *Enchanting a Disenchanted World: Revolutionizing the Means of Consumption.* Thousand Oaks, CA: Pine Forge.

——. 2000. *The McDonaldization of Society.* Thousand Oaks, CA: Pine Forge.

——. 2001. *Explorations in the Sociology of Consumption: Fast Food, Credit Cards and Casinos.* London, England: Sage.

Stiglitz, Joseph. 2002. *Globalization and Its Discontents.* New York: W. W. Norton.

U.S. Department of Health and Human Services. 2001. *The Surgeon General's Call to Action to Prevent and Decrease Overweight and Obesity.* Rockville, MD: U.S. Department of Health and Human Services, Public Health Service, Office of the Surgeon General.

THEORETICAL ISSUES IN THE STUDY OF SOCIAL PROBLEMS AND DEVIANCE

JOEL BEST

University of Delaware

Social problems and deviance are concepts so familiar that, at first, it seems that their meaning must be obvious. Courses in these topics have long been among the most widely offered and most popular in the undergraduate sociology curriculum. And yet, both terms turn out to be slippery, hard to define, and of uncertain value in sociological theorizing. This chapter explores these problems by tracing the evolution in sociological thinking about social problems and deviance.

The term *social problem* emerged in the nineteenth century (Schwartz 1997). Originally, it was singular; "*the* social problem" referred to the complicated, conflicted relationship between labor and capital in recently industrialized societies. But, by the century's end, it became plural; commentators now recognized that there were many social problems, and it was understood that they fell—albeit not exclusively—within sociology's domain.

As a concept, social problem had one great advantage, and one glaring flaw. The advantage was that the term seemed familiar and most people thought they understood what it meant; the flaw was that it proved almost impossible to define social problem in any analytically satisfactory way. From the beginning, sociologists used the term primarily as a course title; generations of undergraduates took courses called "Social Problems," but sociologists' analyses rarely made serious use of the concept.

Compared with *social problem*, the term *deviance* has a much shorter history (Best 2004). Sociologists began writing about deviance after World War II. At least at first, deviance seemed to have a workable, agreed upon definition, although this soon came into question. Like social problems, deviance remains the subject of a common undergraduate course, but its theoretical value has become disputed.

THE SEARCH FOR AN OBJECTIVE DEFINITION OF SOCIAL PROBLEM

At first glance, the meaning of *social problem* seems evident. In the commonsensical use of the term, social problems are all those phenomena, such as crime, racism, poverty, and overpopulation, that pose problems for society. Historically, this is how the undergraduate social problems course has used the term. One 1929 survey of sociology departments found that about half of those responding had social problems courses; the 13 subjects treated most frequently were "Poverty, Crime, the Family, Race Problems, Immigration, Divorce, Population, Standards of Living, Disease, Labor Problems, Wages, Accidents, and Child Problems" (Reinhardt 1929:384). Twenty-five years later, a review of social problems textbooks found that the nine most frequently covered problems were "crime, delinquency, mental disorders, race conflict, family breakdown, alcoholism, unemployment, sex offenses, [and] political corruption" (Herman 1954:106). The list has continued to evolve, but the format of the social problems course has not: the first week's lectures and the textbook's first chapter offer some definition of social problem; the remaining lectures and chapters then address crime, racism, and other social problems, one by one. Typically, there is next to no effort to relate these various topics to one another, or to the concept of social problem.

Sociologists have had considerable difficulty agreeing on a more formal definition of social problems; one early critic noted: "The phrase . . . is one of those much used popular expressions which turn out to be incapable of exact definition" (Case 1924:268). Typically, however, sociologists define social problems as harmful social conditions that become a focus of concern and an object of reform efforts. Such definitions are called objectivist, in that they imply that conditions can be recognized as social problems through the application of some objective standard for measuring harm, that they share some identifiable qualities that fit the definition. This objectivist approach transcends many of sociology's classic theoretical divides. Thus, Robert K. Merton (1961) offers a functionalist interpretation: "The first and basic ingredient of a social problem consists of any substantial discrepancy between socially shared standards and actual conditions of social life. . . . [T]he study of social problems requires sociologists to attend to the dysfunctions of patterns of behavior, belief, and organization" (pp. 701, 731). In contrast, consider this definition

from Eitzen and Baca Zinn's (2000) conflicted-oriented text:

(1) [S]ocietally induced conditions that cause psychic and material suffering for any segment of the population, and (2) acts and conditions that violate the norms and values found in society. The distribution of power in society is the key to understanding these social problems. The powerless, because they are dominated by the powerful, are likely to be thwarted in achieving their basic needs. . . . In contrast, the interests of the powerful are served. (P. 10)

These definitions emphasize predictably different aspects of social life—functionalism's "socially shared standards" or conflict theory's "distribution of power"—but both suggest that social problems have distinctive qualities that set them apart from other, nonproblematic conditions within society.

Objectivist definitions face at least three serious challenges. The first is that they must be very broad, and therefore vague. Lists of social problems tend to encompass phenomena as different as acts and experiences of single individuals (such as suicide and mental illness) and global phenomena (such as globalization or global warming). The challenge confronting any definition is obvious: what exactly do suicide and global warming—to say nothing of crime and racism and all of the other chapter topics in the typical social problems text—have in common? What objective qualities do they share?

A second challenge is historical: the lists of social problems change. After 1970, few social problems texts dared to ignore sexism, but earlier books had given gender issues little attention. Similarly, we can anticipate that more and more textbooks published in the near future will feature a chapter on globalization. If social problems can be defined according to objective criteria, why do lists of social problems change? Surely there was sexism before 1970 and globalization before 2000. Why weren't they identified as social problems by textbook authors?

The third challenge is practical: social problem has not proved to be a particularly useful concept for sociological analysis. Precisely because the category was so diverse, because the phenomena that it encompassed had so little in common, social problems rarely became the focus for either theoretical writings or empirical research. At first glance, this may seem to be a ridiculous claim. After all, a very large share of sociological work is about crime, racism, and other topics considered social problems; bibliographies for some of these topics feature thousands of entries. Haven't there been hundreds of concepts, such as alienation, anomie, class conflict, cultural lag, deviance, dysfunction, and social disorganization, that focus on social problems? Surely the literature on social problems is vast.

But such arguments miss the point. To be sure, sociologists have written extensively about many of the phenomena that are considered social problems, but they have written very little about social problems as such, or even about those social phenomena *as* social problems. If Spector and Kitsuse (1977) exaggerated when they asserted "there is not and never has been a sociology of social problems" (p. 1), they were not far off the mark. The concept of social problem was too broad and too vague to be useful. There have been remarkably few efforts to devise general theories of social problems. After all, what sort of theory might be expected to account for suicide, crime, racism, and global warming? And how could analysts frame empirical research that could hope to address such a diffuse concept?

The difficulties posed by the concept were apparent surprisingly early. Theoretical articles about social problems generally were rare, and many of those that did appear criticized the logical flaws in objectivist definitions (Case 1924; Fuller and Myers 1941; Waller 1936). Other sociologists viewed the study of social problems as a throwback to their discipline's early ties to social work: social problems research was tainted as being applied, whereas true sociology was a form of pure science, and therefore more prestigious (Rose 1971). When the Society for the Study of Social Problems (SSSP) was established, its first president, Ernest W. Burgess (1953), argued that one of its purposes was "to bridge the gap (which seems to be widening instead of closing) between sociological theory and the study of social problems" (p. 2).

In principle, broad theoretical frameworks might seem to offer ways of thinking about social problems. Functionalism, for example, might argue that social problems are dysfunctional (except, of course, when they serve latent functions), or conflict theory might insist that social problems—like all other social arrangements—are products of conflicting class interests. Horton (1966) contrasted order and conflict theories of social problems, but without identifying specific sources in which either was fully articulated. In fact, such efforts at theoretical statements were rare—probably because the variation within the broad category of social problems made it virtually impossible to develop plausible generalizations. Rather than presenting fully articulated theories of social problems, sociologists identified "perspectives" centered on concepts such as social disorganization or value conflicts that might be applied in the analyses of the various specific conditions called problems (Rubington and Weinberg 2003).

In other words, the term *social problem* has been associated with sociology since the late nineteenth century, but its use as a concept has been more pedagogical than analytic. In the United States, courses called "Social Problems" became standard entry-level offerings, and most books entitled *Social Problems* have been written as textbooks for those courses. There were few—and no especially influential—theories about social problems as a general category of phenomena, nor was there any agreed upon definition of the term. This also seems to be true for social problems studies in other countries: at least in Japan (Ayukawa 2000) and Canada and other English-speaking nations, social problems textbooks and courses adopt the familiar problem-by-problem organization; the chapters written by foreign scholars for collections about social problems in India (Sakena [1961] 1978) and Africa (Rwomire 2001) focus on particular phenomena defined as problems while glossing over the broader nature of social problems (the same approach was adopted by American scholars writing in a volume on Soviet social problems [Jones, Connor, and Powell 1991]); and even the book in hand, for all its emphasis on international coverage, addresses problems one by one. Rather than discussing social problems in general, sociologists have almost always preferred to study and theorize about crime, racism, and other particular phenomena considered social problems.

Nor did this change when SSSP began publishing the journal *Social Problems*. Neither the association nor the journal were founded upon a precise, agreed upon definition of social problems. Almost without exception, the papers presented at the annual SSSP conferences and the articles published in the journal dealt with particular problems—such as crime, or even specific types of crime—rather than with social problems as a whole. The field of social problems did not begin to achieve intellectual coherence until the 1970s.

THE EMERGENCE OF DEVIANCE

The history of deviance as a sociological concept is rather different than that of social problems. Whereas social problem was a familiar, albeit ill-defined concept, sociologists only began to speak of deviance after World War II. To be sure, there was a long history of interest in—and theorizing about—suicide, crime, delinquency, mental illness, drug addiction, and other behaviors that would eventually be considered forms of deviance. They were all considered instances of social pathology or social problems, but of course those broader categories also included other phenomena, such as racism and poverty, that usually would not be classified as deviant. There was, during the first half of the twentieth century, no distinctive classification for what would be called deviance.

The concept of deviance had its origin in the statistical concept of deviation. The discovery that many measured phenomena assumed an approximately normal distribution around some mean led to measures of dispersion, such as the standard deviation. Social scientists began using the term *deviation* as a metaphor to describe differences from what was typical. For example, in the 1920s, the new science of intelligence testing identified statistical standards for normal intelligence, and those at the extremes of the distribution—particularly the low-scoring "feebleminded," but also high-scoring "geniuses"—became "mental deviates" (Witty and Lehman 1928). Similarly, Fuller and Myers (1941) used the term when they defined a social problem as "an actual or imagined deviation from some social norm cherished by a considerable number of persons"

(p. 25). Near mid-century, "sex deviate" enjoyed some popularity as a term for homosexuals and others whose behavior, again, was thought to vary from the norm. As late as 1951, when Edwin Lemert published *Social Pathology*—the first fully articulated statement of what would become the labeling perspective—he began by defining deviation in statistical terms: "[W]e are interested in . . . how human beings differ and deviate from the central tendencies or average characteristics of populations in which they are found and in which they interact" (p. 27). It is important to appreciate the implications of this word choice: both *deviation* and *deviate* conjured visions of scientific objectivity, of a measurable distance from some statistical norm.

Metaphorically speaking, breaking rules that most people obeyed could be seen as a form of behavioral deviation. But, while deviation retained its technical meaning within statistics, characterizing some behavior as deviant gave the term additional, moral connotations. If deviation referred to rulebreaking (or deviant) behavior, then what made an act deviant was not simply that it varied from what was typical, but that it violated some norm. This shift in emphasis is apparent in Robert K. Merton's "Social Structure and Anomie" (1938)—undoubtedly the most influential work on deviance to appear in the first half of the twentieth century. Merton identifies his topic as nonconformity—"deviations from prescribed patterns of conduct" (p. 672). At a couple of places, he refers to these violations as "deviate behavior," as well as "antisocial behavior" and "aberrant conduct." However, Merton was less interested in defining deviant behavior than in extending Durkheim's idea of anomie, by locating it within culture and social structure.

Merton's basic argument has become familiar: any culture articulates goals for society's members, while the social structure provides an approved set of institutionalized means for achieving those goals. Individuals who accept both the approved goals and the approved means are conformists—they conform to society's expectations (e.g., individuals may work hard [approved means] to earn the money needed to get ahead [approved goal]). However, there are other possible responses: innovators accept the approved goals but reject the means (say, by turning to crime to steal the money to get ahead); ritualists reject the goals but embrace the means (Merton says little about this option); retreatists reject both the goals and the means (e.g., dropping out of society and into drug dependence or mental illness); while rebels simultaneously accept and reject both goals and means by trying to subvert the current system and promote some alternative social arrangements. While Merton's analysis was theoretical, he makes occasional reference to several types of "deviate behavior" including crime, mental illness, and vice.

It would be another 10 years before sociologists began speaking of "deviance." The new word belonged to the era of Grand Theory (Talcott Parsons [1948] was one of the first to use it). The impulse was to recognize underlying patterns, similarities among what might seem on the surface to be diverse phenomena. Deviance was defined as rulebreaking, the violation of some social norm. (Although Durkheim [(1895) 1982] spoke only of "crime," his observations that rule violations marked societal boundaries and thereby affirmed the social order provided a conceptual foundation for the new term.) Deviance encompassed—at least—crime, delinquency, suicide, homosexuality and other forms of sexual misbehavior, drug addiction, and mental illness; all of these, analysts argued, violated laws, religious commandments, or at least informal expectations for normal behavior. Most sociologists had not followed Durkheim's lead: while there were already substantial sociological literatures on each of these topics, they had not previously been analyzed as one phenomenon—deviance.

This vision of deviance as rulebreaking belonged within the Durkheimian, functionalist tradition of emphasizing societal consensus. Societies had shared norms and sanctioned those who broke the rules. Sociologists could recognize these general patterns and, by doing so, might be better able to understand specific forms of deviant behavior, such as criminality. It is no accident that deviance emerged as a sociological concept when it did—during the postwar years when structural functionalism had its greatest influence. In 1957, Marshall Clinard published *Sociology of Deviant Behavior,* the first textbook devoted to the new term. Rulebreaking seemed to offer a simple, straightforward, objective definition of deviance.

THE RISE AND FALL OF LABELING THEORY

By the early 1960s, however, critics challenged rulebreaking's adequacy as a definition of deviance. Howard S. Becker's *Outsiders* (1963) became the emblematic statement for what would be called labeling theory. Becker's basic point was that deviance could not be defined by any objective quality, such as rulebreaking behavior. It was too easy to identify instances where individuals were sanctioned when they had not actually broken any rules (witchcraft prosecutions became a favorite example of this), as well as instances of rulebreaking that were not treated as deviance (e.g., studies showing that middle-class adolescents could get away with behavior that would have gotten lower-class youths arrested [Chambliss 1973]). Deviance could not be simply equated with rulebreaking. Rather, Becker (1963) argued, what mattered was societal reaction: "[D]eviance is *not* a quality of the act the person commits, but rather a consequence of the application by others of rules and sanctions to an 'offender.' The deviant is one to whom that label has successfully been applied; deviant behavior is behavior that people so label" (p. 9).

This call to shift the focus from offenders to social control was heeded by other analysts who began to examine the creation of rules, the designation (or labeling) of particular acts as rule violations, the way social control agents processed designated deviants, and the ways individuals responded to being labeled. These studies were often grouped together as labeling theory, although the designation was too grand. There was no integrated theory of labeling deviance. Rather, different analysts associated with the labeling school located their own work in very different theoretical traditions— Durkheimian (Erikson 1966), Weberian (Gusfield 1963), Marxian (Chambliss 1964), phenomenological (Kitsuse 1962), and so on. What the studies considered to reflect labeling theory had in common was a critical approach: they usually adopted qualitative methods and inductive reasoning; and they tended to portray deviants sympathetically while being more critical of social control agents. Many of the early labeling studies appeared in *Social Problems* (which Becker edited from 1961 through 1964). SSSP, which had been organized in opposition to the American Sociological Association, provided an organizational base for labeling's critique of mainstream sociology. By the late 1960s, the labeling perspective began to spread abroad; in particular, a new generation of critical English sociologists began adopting it (Cohen 1971).

Defining deviance in terms of societal reaction did not delineate the concept's domain with any precision. *Outsiders* devoted a good deal of attention to jazz musicians—a perfectly legal occupation—although Becker (1963) argued: "[T]heir culture and way of life are sufficiently bizarre and unconventional for them to be labeled outsiders" (p. 79). Erving Goffman's *Stigma* (1963), another influential labeling statement, added to the confusion. Perhaps all deviants were stigmatized, but were all the stigmatized deviant? Goffman explicitly indicated that racial minorities were stigmatized, but few sociologists seemed eager to treat race as deviance. It was all very well to define deviance in terms of societal reaction, but which sorts of reactions distinguished deviance? It was not clear that labeling's definition could stand close inspection.

Although labeling theory claimed the spotlight during the early 1960s, it soon attracted critics of its own. By the mid-1970s, labeling had come under attack from at least four rival theoretical orientations. First, the resurgence of *conflict theory* led to charges that labeling theory failed to appreciate and criticize elites' involvement in deviance. Conflict theorists argued that social control was a tool of elite interests, that elites managed the creation of rules and controlled the agencies that enforced them. This enabled elites to define efforts by the powerless to resist domination as deviant, so that the entire social control apparatus served to maintain the status quo and thereby preserve elite privilege. In this critique, labeling theorists stood accused of ignoring the political significance of deviance and social control. Further, conflict theorists charged that the labeling perspective overlooked elite actions—ranging from white-collar crime and corruption, to economic and political domination—that should be considered deviant. This was an influential critique, in part because it portrayed labeling theory, which had been presented as a worldly, radical critique of mainstream sociology, as itself naive and conservative (Gouldner 1968; Liazos 1972; Taylor, Walton, and Young 1973).

Second, the emergence of *feminism* led to claims that labeling theory, like most sociology, ignored the interests and concerns of women. Here, the most troubling criticism was that labeling theory was insensitive to women's victimization. Social control agents sought to sanction deviants who, labeling suggested, could be seen as either relatively powerless victims, or as clever trickster heroes who outwitted the more powerful forces of social control. Indeed, labeling theorists often studied "crimes without victims" that could be analyzed in these terms (Schur 1965). In contrast, feminists drew attention to women's victimization, especially via rape and domestic violence, and they charged that labeling theory's sympathetic treatment of deviants ignored these serious problems (Millman 1975; Rodmell 1981).

A third, related critique reflected the emergence of *identity politics* within both society and sociology. During the 1970s, identity-based social movements began emerging; noteworthy were the movements among gays and lesbians and the disabled. Both homosexuality and disability had routinely been classified as forms of deviance, but activists now argued that these designations were inappropriate. Advocates of gay liberation, for example, insisted that homosexuals should be viewed as a minority group, analogous to a racial or religious minority. Just as the civil rights movement had struggled to gain equal rights for African Americans, so should the gay rights movement demand equality for gays and lesbians. Thus, classifying homosexuality as deviance was an offensive distraction; for these critics, what should have been at issue was not the morality of breaking rules, or the reaction of the societal majority, but the politics of gaining rights. Identity politics was important because it characterized the sociology of deviance as misguided, as just one more barrier to victims of discrimination achieving full equality. Like the criticism of conflict theorists, the feminist and identity politics critiques condemned labeling theory—which had defined itself as championing the vulnerable—for being allied with the powerful and neglecting the claims of the weak (Humphreys 1972; Scotch 1988).

Finally, *mainstream sociology*—which had been the target of labeling's critique—in turn leveled its own attack against labeling theory. Its principal critiques were (1) that labeling focused on a very narrow set of questions about societal reaction and, in the process, ignored some of the oldest and most important research topics in the study of deviance, such as trying to identify the causes of deviance, and (2) that labeling's descriptions of deviance and social control were, if not empirically wrong, at least distorted versions of what deviants and social control agents did. Labeling's sudden rise to prominence in the 1960s had taken mainstream sociologists by surprise. In general, they did not attempt to counter labeling's central theoretical claim—that deviance could not be defined except in terms of societal reaction. Rather, they finessed the issue by translating the labeling approach into testable hypotheses (e.g., regarding the degree to which racial minorities were disadvantaged in social control processing), and tested them. Those tests often offered only weak support for the labeling perspective (Gove 1975).

By the mid-1970s, all four of these attacks had been mounted, and the sociology of deviance was in considerable confusion. The original consensus—that deviance could be objectively defined as rulebreaking—had been disrupted by labeling's critique that deviance could only be defined in terms of subjective societal reactions. But, in turn, labeling's critics challenged that position for acquiescing to a social system that maintained political, social, and economic inequities, for ignoring the victimization of women, for overlooking the political rights of minorities, and for promoting a narrow and incorrect vision of social control. In the face of these varied attacks, the sociology of deviance became fragmented, and at least some sociologists fled the field of deviance into the emerging sociology of social problems.

SOCIAL PROBLEMS: THE CONSTRUCTIONIST STANCE

The familiar critique that objectivist definitions of social problems were inherently inadequate paralleled labeling's argument that deviance could only be defined in terms of subjective reactions. But the labeling theorists had gone beyond simply criticizing mainstream sociology and offering a subjectivist definition of deviance; they had developed a body of theoretical and empirical work based on the insight that societal reaction was central to understanding deviance. With labeling's example in mind, during the 1970s, sociologists began trying to develop a coherent theory of social problems based on recognizing that the only thing all social problems had in common was their designation as social problems.

Although there were competing formulations (Blumer 1971; Mauss 1975), the most influential version of this approach was that of Spector and Kitsuse (1977). They defined social problems as "the activities of individuals or groups making assertions of grievances and claims with respect to some putative conditions" (p. 75). This was a radical reformulation. Objectivist definitions of social problems had centered on the characteristics of problematic social conditions; most analysts had assumed that it was some feature of those conditions that distinguished social problems from other phenomena. Even critics of the objectivist mainstream, Spector and Kitsuse argued, had been reluctant to commit to a subjectivist approach; they had invariably focused their own research on social conditions, rather than definitions. Now, conditions were dismissed as merely "putative," and the analyst's focus was redirected to the activities—the claimsmaking—through which people designated social problems. The previously unanswerable question—"What do the various phenomena (suicide, overpopulation, etc.) labeled social problems have in common?"—that had bedeviled every effort to develop a coherent sociology of social problems now had an answer: the only thing those phenomena have in common is that they are labeled social problems. That is, if there was to be a sociology of social problems, it would have to be rooted in the study of claimsmaking, rather than conditions.

This new approach was called constructionist because it concerned the social construction of social problems. (The expression *social construction* spread widely, particularly among qualitative sociologists, following the publication of Berger and Luckman's *The Social Construction of Reality* [1966].) Typically, constructionist researchers presented case studies that examined how some social problem became a focus for concern; for example, Pfohl (1977) argued that pediatric radiologists played a key role in calling attention to the "battered child syndrome" during the 1960s. Such studies were guided by such research questions as Who made the claims about this social problem, and why did they do so? What was the nature of those claims? and What reactions did those claims produce among the press, the public, and policymakers? Soon dozens, then hundreds of analyses were added to a literature on the construction of social problems. Particularly during the perspective's emergence, constructionist research tended to be concentrated in the journal *Social Problems,* which, just as it ad supported labeling's emergence, now seemed eager to provide a forum for a fledgling theory of social problems; however, as constructionism evolved, work began to appear in a wide range of venues, including sociology's flagship journals (e.g., Hilgartner and Bosk 1988).

Constructionism's great accomplishment was that, for the first time, one could argue that there was a substantial sociology of social problems. Earlier studies of crime, racism, and so on had failed to find a useful analytic foundation in objectivist definitions of social problems, and therefore failed to generate analyses of the larger category of social problems. However, constructionists began to develop studies of the strengths and weaknesses of different sorts of claimsmakers, the relative effectiveness of different sorts of claims, and so on. They framed their research questions and interpreted their findings in terms of social problems generally.

Still, constructionism had its critics. Most mainstream sociologists, who had been accustomed to using social problems as a title for the undergraduate course, dismissed constructionism for shifting the focus away from social conditions (and, therefore, the problem-by-problem organization long favored by lecturers and textbooks). Pressed by constructionism's example, there were even efforts to devise objectivist social problems theories, although these have yet to inspire researchers (Jamrozik and Nocella 1998). Most social problems courses continued to fit the familiar mold, undisturbed by critiques of the logical flaws in objectivist definitions, or by the emergence of constructionist research. Some sociologists misunderstood the new approach, and equated it with a sort of *vulgar constructionism*; that is, they assumed that social constructionists analyze the creation of fanciful, nonexistent social problems. In this view, crime and racism *are* social problems, while UFO abductions or satanic ritual abuse are social constructions. (Constructionists abetted this misunderstanding. They often favored studying moral panics and other dubious claims, precisely because these examples laid bare the process of social construction.)

However, the most significant critique of constructionist studies of social problems came from within the phenomenological tradition (Woolgar and Pawluch 1985). They argued that constructionists depended on a form of analytic hocus-pocus; on the one hand, constructionists insist that all knowledge is socially constructed, yet, on the other hand, constructionists routinely privilege some knowledge as true, while dismissing other knowledge as mere claims. Woolgar and Pawluch referred to this process as *ontological gerrymandering.* For example, a constructionist analyst might ask why feminists were able to construct rape—long a common crime—as a major problem in the 1970s. In framing this question, the analyst tacitly assumes that the condition (i.e., the actual nature and incidence of rape) was more or less unchanged, while attributing any increased concern about rape to the feminists' claimsmaking. Thus, Woolgar and Pawluch argued, constructionism is built upon a logical inconsistency: analysts may assert that all knowledge is socially constructed, but they in fact divide knowledge into that which goes uncontested and the claims that are considered problematic.

The issue of ontological gerrymandering split constructionists. Some viewed the critique as devastating. They came to be called *strict constructionists* because they argued that social problems analysts ought to strictly avoid making any assumptions about objective reality. For example, Ibarra and Kitsuse (1993) suggested that sociologists of social problems should stop referring to social conditions, and focus only upon "condition categories," that is, upon the language (or categories) used to construct social problems. However, removing themselves one step further from the phenomena considered social problems was no solution, because language is itself embedded in society, so that whatever words analysts choose carry their own assumptions about reality (Best 1993).

Most constructionists adopted a position of *contextual constructionism* (Best 1995). That is, they viewed Woolgar and Pawluch's critique as a useful warning that analysts needed to be aware of the assumptions they made. However, they argued that it remained legitimate to interpret claims within their contexts. For instance, if claimsmakers announced that drug use was out of control, analysts could place those claims within their context (e.g., What was known about the level of drug use that provided a basis for the claims?). Where strict constructionism threatened to force sociologists into an infinite regress, moving ever further away from the phenomena that were labeled social problems, contextual constructionism allowed them to continue studying the process of claimsmaking. It was no contest.

Two other developments paralleled the emergence of constructionist analyses in the 1970s. The first involved other sociologists of deviance who focused on the process of *medicalization* (Conrad and Schneider 1992). Medicalization was the process of redefining deviance in medical terms, of adopting the language of disease, symptom, treatment, and so on. Scientific advances and increased professionalism led to increased prestige for medical authorities during the course of the twentieth century, and they in turn claimed authority over a growing domain of phenomena. Medical terminology was applied to many forms of deviance, such as juvenile delinquency, alcoholism, and poor school performance. Medicalization became a familiar way of constructing social problems, and analysts of medicalization and social problems construction often invoked each other's work.

The second development involved the revival of *social movements* as a sociological specialty. As late as 1960, many sociologists viewed social movements as aberrant arrangements that attracted the socially marginal, and researchers focused on understanding why some individuals came to join movements. However, the growing visibility of the civil rights movement and other campaigns that had sociologists' sympathies led to the emergence of new theoretical approaches to studying movements, such as resource mobilization and framing processes. Rather than trying to understand what might lead some people to join social movements, sociologists

began studying the conditions under which movements might succeed. These efforts—particularly studies of how movements framed, or articulated, their grievances—overlapped with constructionist analyses; claimsmaking was often the work of social movement activists (Benford and Snow 2000).

As the body of constructionist work expanded, so did statements of constructionist theory (Hilgartner and Bosk 1988; Loseke 2003). The process was largely inductive. The typical constructionist research project was a case study that sought to explain how and why some social problem came to public attention, and the growing body of case studies served as a foundation for generalizations that might, in turn, raise new questions that could inspire further research. Because constructionism developed within American sociology, most early case studies focused on some problem's recent rise to national visibility in the United States. However, as the constructionist orientation spread, analysts began examining other sorts of cases, such as constructions of social problems in the historical past (Fine 1997) or in specific localities (Mann 2000). In particular, studies situated in other countries began to appear; some of these were the work of analysts based in the United States (e.g., Jenkins's [1992] study of British moral panics), but foreign scholars also began examining the construction of social problems in their own nations, particularly in Japan (Ayukawa 2000), Canada (Mann 2000), and England (Furedi 1997). More recently, analysts have begun to move beyond single case studies, into comparative analyses (such as Linders's [1998] analysis of abortion claims in the United States and Sweden) and studies of the diffusion of social problems claims across national borders (Best 2001).

Similarly, research and theoretical writing began to focus on particular processes, including the rhetoric of claimsmaking, mass media dissemination of claims, policy making, and social problems work. Social problems work refers to the application of social problems constructions, often during interpersonal interaction (Holstein and Miller 1993). For instance, after claimsmaking led to the recognition of domestic violence as a social problem and after new policies (e.g., establishing additional shelters for abused women) emerged, it remained necessary for individual social control agents to construct particular situations as instances of the larger social problem. Thus, workers in shelters must determine whether prospective clients are victims of domestic abuse, and they must further help the clients define themselves in those terms (Loseke 1992). Such studies, of course, derived from earlier labeling analyses of social control agents processing deviants. While the typical constructionist case study examines a national claimsmaking campaign, social problems construction can also be viewed as a process that occurs within microsociological, interpersonal interaction.

The expression *social construction* spread across many disciplines after 1980 and, in the process, took on very different meanings (Guillory 2002; Hacking 1999). Particularly within the humanities, the term became associated with postmodern theory and political critiques. The fact that the same term, *social construction*, was being used by people making a wide range of theoretical assumptions led to considerable confusion. Denunciations of constructionism often equate it with nihilistic critiques of science and other knowledge. It is important to understand that sociologists of social problems meant something very different when they used the term.

Constructionism flourished as an approach to social problems, in part, because it lacked competition. The obstacles to developing a coherent objectivist definition of social problems meant that other sociologists had never developed social problems as a focus for research, so constructionists had the field largely to themselves. However, it is not enough to merely insist that social problems are socially constructed and to continue to produce case studies demonstrating how the process occurred in this or that instance. Theoretical perspectives that do not continue to grow begin to wither. Whether the constructionist perspective will remain a useful research focus will depend upon researchers finding ways to extend it. Sociologists have linked constructionism to sociological studies of medicine, science, mass media, social movements, political sociology, or diffusion, and the perspective is increasingly borrowed by scholars in other disciplines, such as political science, communication, and public health (Rochefort and Cobb 1994; Winett 1998). Such connections offer the best hope of extending sociology's only general theory of social problems.

THE DECLINE OF DEVIANCE

For some sociologists of deviance, the shift to constructionist studies of social problems offered an escape from the various critiques of labeling theory mounted in the 1970s. However, other sociologists continued to write about deviance. In a few cases, they sought to develop alternative, general theories of deviance. Some proponents of conflict theory, for example, seemed interested in exploring deviance, but suggestions that, say, armed robbery might better be viewed as political action rather than deviance, while false advertising should be recognized as deviant, threatened to so dramatically alter the domain of deviance that few other analysts seemed eager to adopt this approach (Liazos 1972). Similarly, social learning theory sought to apply the perspective of behaviorism to the study of deviance (Akers 1998), while control balance theory (Tittle 1995) attempted to integrate several theoretical approaches into a single framework. There was even a call for the sociology of deviance to return to its earliest principles, to define deviance as moral lapses (Henderschott 2002). At least initially, none of these approaches attracted wide interest or acceptance among students of deviance.

For the most part, sociologists of deviance seemed to prefer finessing the larger theoretical issues raised by labeling theory and its critics, to discuss deviance without committing themselves to a precise definition of the term. This was most easily accomplished by focusing on theoretical issues within the general topic of deviance: examining the social psychology or social organization of deviance; discussing deviant transactions or deviant careers; or linking the study of deviance to other subjects of current sociological interest, such as emotion (Braithwaite 1989; Katz 1988), gender (Schur 1984), the life course (Sampson and Laub 1992), or discourse (Hall et al. 1978). Case studies continued to appear, especially in the journal *Deviant Behavior,* often dealing with relatively exotic forms of deviance, such as rodeo groupies (Gauthier and Forsyth 2000). Although there were exceptions, such as the volumes by Adler and Adler (2003) and Rubington and Weinberg (2002), many deviance textbooks downplayed the importance of theoretical coherence, in favor of a series of loosely related chapters concerned with different forms of deviance—crime, mental illness, and so on. It became, in short, common to write and teach about deviance without actually committing to a particular definition of deviance.

Deviance had become a standard term within the sociological lexicon. For example, a discussion of early corporate takeovers—a legal, albeit frowned-upon business transaction—calls them "deviant" (Hirsch 1986). However, even these casual references were declining. JSTOR (the name is short for journal storage) offers a full-text database for major academic journals; a search for articles containing the word *deviance* published in the discipline's flagship journals—the *American Sociological Review,* the *American Journal of Sociology,* and *Social Forces*—reveals that usage of the term peaked in the 1970s and declined through the 1980s and 1990s (Best 2004). There was a growing sense that deviance was no longer an area of active, cutting-edge scholarship. Colin Sumner published his book *The Sociology of Deviance: An Obituary* in 1994, and other critics began arguing over the proposition that deviance was "dead" (Goode 2002; Hendershott 2002; Miller, Wright, and Dannels 2001). Although the fact that deviance was both a familiar term and institutionalized as a popular undergraduate course meant that the reports of its demise may have been premature, it was no longer the lively focus for intellectual work that it had been between 1950 and 1975.

Sociologists of deviance had never developed a strong organizational base to support their specialty. They had no distinctive professional organization: the American Sociological Association had dozens of specialized sections, but none for deviance; nor did the SSSP have a division devoted to the topic. There were, however, numerous professional societies dedicated to the study of specialized topics within deviance. Students of crime, for instance, could present their papers at meetings of an ASA section, an SSSP division, the American Society of Criminology, the Academy of Criminal Justice Sciences, and a host of regional organizations as well as groups devoted to studying homicide and other subspecialties within criminology. Similarly, *Deviant Behavior,* the only journal devoted to the topic, appeared relatively late (in 1981); published by a commercial press, rather than a scholarly

society, it lacked the circulation and visibility of many other journals. The absence of a strong organizational base did nothing to discourage analysts' shift away from studying deviance.

Many sociologists turned away from studying deviance in general, in favor of research on specialized topics within the larger category of deviance. In a sense, that represented a reversion to the favored research topics before deviance emerged as a concept, when sociologists had studied crime, delinquency, mental illness, and the like separately. Of course, this specialized research had never stopped, but, while deviance was a fashionable concept, sociologists envisioned these specialized studies as somehow falling within the broader category of deviance. Now they were more often content to locate their work within some specialty.

In particular, criminology enjoyed a great revival after 1980, aided by both the emergence of criminal justice as a separate academic discipline and the influx of substantial additional funding for research on crime and criminal justice. As personal computers became increasingly powerful, and as statistical software packages became increasingly easy to use, the criminological literature—like that in sociology more generally—became characterized by ever more sophisticated methods and statistics. These provided tools for reformulating and testing established criminological theories.

For example, classical criminology viewed offenders as motivated by short-run self-interests; from this perspective, strong social controls were needed to constrain criminality. This approach was revived as *control theory,* which argued that it was not crime that demanded explanation, but individuals' failure to commit crimes. Theorists argued that law-abiding behavior had its roots in childhood socialization toward self-control and in the controlling effect of ties to family, school, work, and respectable friends (Gottfredson and Hirschi 1990; Sampson and Laub 1993). Similarly, Merton's (1938) "Social Structure and Anomie," which saw blocked opportunities as the root of deviance, evolved into *strain theory,* which identified a variety of circumstances that might lead individuals to define their opportunities as blocked, and a variety of ways they might respond to those obstacles, including angry reactions that led to criminal behavior (Agnew 1992). Experiencing blocked opportunities, of course, reflected social structure; advantaged individuals—those who had more social capital (Hagan and McCarthy 1997)—were less likely to experience strain and turn to crime.

Control theory and strain theory had their roots in functionalist sociology, but critical, conflict interpretations also flourished. These focused on differential power—elites' ability to shape the laws and their enforcement, and criminality as acts of the powerless that, if not overtly political, at least had political implications. Many of the most influential theoretical statements of the conflict approach dated from the 1970s (Quinney 1977; Taylor et al. 1973; Turk 1969). While these theorists offered an expansive, macrosociological vision, the researchers who sought to test those theories required data that might be subjected to sophisticated statistical analyses; as a result, they tended to concentrate on narrow research questions for which data sets might be assembled, such as examining whether the criminal justice system favored whites and the middle and upper classes.

Still other criminologists focused on the geography of crime. *Routine activity theory* emphasized that crime depended on locating vulnerable targets; places that offered more of these opportunities would attract crime (Cohen and Felson 1979). For example, as more women entered the workforce, residences were less likely to be occupied during the daytime, making burglary more attractive. Perhaps the most heavily publicized criminological theory at the end of the twentieth century was *broken windows theory* (Kelling and Coles 1996). Here, the argument was that minor forms of disorder, such as an unrepaired broken window, signaled a neighborhood's tolerance for trouble and attracted criminals who believed they could operate with impunity. This approach attracted public attention when authorities in New York City claimed that cracking down on disorder had led to dramatic reductions in crime rates during the 1990s. However, crimes also fell in cities that had not adopted broken-windows policing, and researchers who studied the decline in crime concluded that rising economic prosperity probably had more effect on crime rates than police policies (Karmen 2000; Taylor 2001). The most careful empirical analysis suggested that, while disorder and crime were correlated, both had their

roots in neighborhood poverty and were affected by collective efficacy (residents' sense that people can and do try to exert control over a neighborhood) (Sampson and Raudenbush 1999).

This is by no means a complete list. Criminologists entertained a variety of other theoretical approaches—social learning theory, rational choice theory, feminist theory, even sociobiology. At the beginning of the twenty-first century, criminology had become a complex, thriving specialty, the scene of considerable intellectual activity. Yet, it is remarkable that, although it would not have been difficult to generalize from much of this criminological work to the broader topic of deviance—after all, control theory, strain theory, and conflict theory had previously served as influential perspectives within the study of deviance, and approaches such as routine activity theory or broken windows theory could have been easily extended to cover more than criminality—few analysts chose to take this step. It seemed much easier to develop and debate ideas within the narrower confines of criminology than to try to extend the same ideas into the contested realm of deviance. In general, most criminologists accepted that the criminal law defined the boundaries of their field, whereas the definition and domain of deviance remained disputed.

Criminology was by no means unique. Parallel developments occurred in specialties centered on other forms of deviance: specialties such as substance abuse, mental illness, suicide, homosexuality, and disability all extended their institutional bases during the last quarter of the twentieth century; they expanded the number and size of their professional associations, journals, research centers, and funding agencies. In short, the literature addressing most of the topics that might be subsumed under the broad heading of deviance continued to grow and grow, even as sociologists made less and less use of the term *deviance*. Sociologists continued to have a great deal to say about crime, mental illness, and so on, but they seemed increasingly reluctant to address the general topic of deviance.

THE IMPORTANCE OF DEFINITIONS

Both social problems and deviance are generalizing concepts, intended to draw attention to underlying similarities among what might otherwise seem to be diverse, unrelated phenomena. Of course, this is a central form of sociological thought—many key concepts, including status, role, and social change, have this generalizing quality; identifying and exploring patterns of previously unrecognized similarities is one of the things that distinguishes the sociological perspective from common sense. But such concepts can only advance our thinking to the degree that their definitions are coherent (they must make sense) and useful (generalization must offer some analytic advantage).

Definitional issues have bedeviled analysts of both deviance and social problems. In general, sociologists have substituted commonsense understandings—as revealed in the standard method of organizing textbooks and undergraduate courses—for precise definitions. That is, both deviance and social problems usually have been defined in terms of lists of the phenomena they include. Deviance, an examination of textbooks' tables of contents reveals, includes crime, mental illness, drug abuse, and so on, while social problems covers crime, racism, poverty, and the like. Both lists feature phenomena considered troubling: deviance is often thought of as troubling behavior, while social problems are considered troubling social conditions.

As a pedagogical device, a means of getting undergraduates to think about topics of contemporary concern, courses in social problems and deviance may be defensible. This week's lectures about crime may disabuse students of folk stereotypes, and teach them something about the sorts of questions sociologists ask, and the sorts of answers they favor. And next week's topic—say, racism in the social problems class, or mental illness in the deviance course—may offer similarly helpful information.

But this pedagogical framework falls short of a sociological theory of social problems or deviance. Mainstream sociology has preferred to pretend that some sort of objectivist stance is possible, that social problems are social conditions that share some qualities, or that all deviance involves rulebreaking. Subjectivist critics have found it easy to challenge the mainstream's arguments; instead, they argue, social problems and deviance must be understood as subjective categories—as, respectively, social constructions or labels.

These subjectivist critiques have had differing impacts. Within the sociology of social problems, constructionism continues to thrive, in large part because it has no rival. The concept of social problem has never been the foundation for extensive sociological theorizing and research by analysts adopting other perspectives. They continue to study specific social problems from any of the available theoretical perspectives—functionalism, conflict theory, feminism, and so on—so that we have many studies of the causes of delinquency, patterns of racial inequality, and the like, but few nonconstructionist analyses of social problems in general. Constructionists—a relatively small group made up of primarily qualitative sociologists—currently have the field of social problems theory to themselves.

The situation among sociologists of deviance is rather different. At least when the concept first emerged in the 1950s, analysts hoped that it could be the basis for systematic theorizing, based, presumably, on the notion of rulebreaking. Labeling's critique called that possibility into question, but, in turn, labeling's approach came under attack. While some sociologists continue to write about deviance, there is evidence that the concept has become less popular and that researchers increasingly choose to frame their work in terms of specialized subjects, such as criminology.

Sociologists are unlikely to develop general theories of either social problems or deviance until they can resolve the definitional issues that underpin discussions of both concepts.

REFERENCES

Adler, P. A. and P. Adler, eds. 2003. *Constructions of Deviance.* 4th ed. Belmont, CA: Wadsworth.

Agnew, R. 1992. "Foundation for a General Strain Theory of Crime and Delinquency." *Criminology* 30:47–87.

Akers, R. L. 1998. *Social Learning and Social Structure: A General Theory of Crime and Deviance.* Boston, MA: Northeastern University Press.

Ayukawa, J. 2000. "The Sociology of Social Problems in Japan." *American Sociologist* 31 (Fall):15–26.

Becker, H. S. 1963. *Outsiders.* New York: Free Press.

Berger, P. L. and T. Luckmann. 1966. *The Social Construction of Reality.* New York: Doubleday.

Benford, R. D. and D. A. Snow. 2000. "Framing Processes and Social Movements." *Annual Review of Sociology* 26:611–39.

Best, J. 1993. "But Seriously Folks: The Limitations of the Strict Constructionist Interpretation of Social Problems." Pp. 129–47 in *Reconsidering Social Constructionism,* edited by J. A. Holstein and G. Miller. Hawthorne, NY: Aldine de Gruyter.

——. 1995. "Constructionism in Context." Pp. 337–54 in *Images of Issues,* 2nd ed., edited by J. Best. Hawthorne, NY: Aldine de Gruyter.

——, ed. 2001. *How Claims Spread: Cross-National Diffusion of Social Problems.* Hawthorne, NY: Aldine de Gruyter.

——. 2004. *Deviance: Career of a Concept.* Belmont, CA: Wadsworth.

Blumer, H. 1971. "Social Problems as Collective Behavior." *Social Problems* 18:298–306.

Braithwaite, J. 1989. *Crime, Shame and Reintegration.* New York: Cambridge University Press.

Burgess, E. W. 1953. "The Aims of the Society for the Study of Social Problems." *Social Problems* 1:2–3.

Case, C. M. 1924. "What Is a Social Problem?" *Journal of Applied Sociology* 8:268–73.

Chambliss, W. J. 1964. "A Sociological Analysis of the Law of Vagrancy." *Social Problems* 12:46–67.

——. 1973. "The Saints and the Roughnecks." *Society* 11:24–31.

Clinard, M. B. 1957. *Sociology of Deviant Behavior.* New York: Rinehart.

Cohen, L. E. and M. Felson. 1979. "Social Change and Crime Rate Trends." *American Sociological Review* 44:588–608.

Cohen, S., ed. 1971. *Images of Deviance.* Harmondsworth, England: Penguin.

Conrad, P. and J. W. Schneider. 1992. *Deviance and Medicalization.* 2nd ed. Philadelphia, PA: Temple University Press.

Durkheim, E. [1895] 1982. *The Rules of Sociological Method.* New York: Free Press.

Eitzen, D. S. and M. Baca Zinn. 2000. *Social Problems.* 8th ed. Boston, MA: Allyn & Bacon.

Erikson, K. T. 1966. *Wayward Puritans.* New York: Wiley.

Fine, G. A. 1997. "Scandal, Social Conditions, and the Creation of Public Attention." *Social Problems* 44:297–323.

Fuller, R. C. and R. R. Myers. 1941. "Some Aspects of a Theory of Social Problems." *American Sociological Review* 6:24–32.

Furedi, F. 1997. *Culture of Fear.* London, England: Cassell.

Gauthier, D. K. and C. J. Forsyth. 2000. "Buckle Bunnies." *Deviant Behavior* 21:349–65.

Goffman, E. 1963. *Stigma.* Englewood Cliffs, NJ: Prentice Hall.

Goode, E. 2002. "Does the Death of the Sociology of Deviance Claim Make Sense?" *American Sociologist* 33 (Fall):107–18.

Gottfredson, M. R. and T. Hirschi. 1990. *A General Theory of Crime.* Stanford, CA: Stanford University Press.

Gouldner, A. W. 1968. "The Sociologist as Partisan: Sociology and the Welfare State." *American Sociologist* 3:103–16.

Gove, W. R., ed. 1975. *The Labelling of Deviance.* New York: Wiley.

Guillory, J. 2002. "The Skoal Affair and the History of Criticism." *Critical Inquiry* 28:470–508.

Gusfield, J. R. 1963. *Symbolic Crusade.* Urbana, IL: University of Illinois Press.

Hacking, I. 1999. *The Social Construction of What?* Cambridge, MA: Harvard University Press.

Hagan, J. and B. McCarthy. 1997. *Mean Streets: Youth Crime and Homelessness.* Cambridge, England: Cambridge University Press.

Hall, S., C. Critcher, T. Jefferson, J. Clarke, and B. Roberts. 1978. *Policing the Crisis: Mugging, the State, and Law and Order.* London, England: Macmillan.

Hendershott, A. 2002. *The Politics of Deviance.* San Francisco, CA: Encounter.

Herman, A. P. 1954. "The Disproportionate Emphasis on Description in Social Problem Texts." *Social Problems* 1:105–109.

Hilgartner, S. and C. L. Bosk. 1988. "The Rise and Fall of Social Problems." *American Journal of Sociology* 94:53–78.

Hirsch, P. M. 1986. "From Ambushes to Golden Parachutes." *American Journal of Sociology* 91:800–37.

Holstein, J. A. and G. Miller. 1993. "Social Constructionism and Social Problems Work." Pp. 151–72 in *Reconsidering Social Constructionism,* edited by J. A. Holstein and G. Miller. Hawthorne, NY: Aldine de Gruyter.

Horton, J. 1966. "Order and Conflict Theories of Social Problems as Competing Ideologies." *American Journal of Sociology* 71:701–13.

Humphreys, L. 1972. *Out of the Closets: The Sociology of Homosexual Liberation.* Englewood Cliffs, NJ: Prentice Hall.

Ibara, P. R. and J. I. Kitsuse. 1993. "Vernacular Constituents of Moral Discourse." Pp. 25–58 in *Reconsidering Social Constructionism,* edited by

J. A. Holstein and G. Miller. Hawthorne, NY: Aldine de Gruyter.

Jamrozik, A. and L. Nocella. 1998. *The Sociology of Social Problems.* Cambridge, England: Cambridge University Press.

Jenkins, P. 1992. *Intimate Enemies.* Hawthorne, NY: Aldine de Gruyter.

Jones, A., W. D. Connor, and D. E. Powell, eds. 1991. *Soviet Social Problems.* Boulder, CO: Westview.

Karmen, A. 2000. *New York Murder Mystery.* New York: New York University Press.

Katz, J. 1988. *Seductions of Crime.* New York: Basic Books.

Kelling, G. L. and C. M. Coles. 1996. *Fixing Broken Windows: Restoring Order and Reducing Crime in Our Communities.* New York: Free Press.

Kitsuse, J. I. 1962. "Societal Reaction to Deviant Behavior." *Social Problems* 9:247–56.

Lemert, E. M. 1951. *Social Pathology: A Systematic Approach to the Theory of Sociopathic Behavior.* New York: McGraw-Hill.

Liazos, A. 1972. "The Poverty of the Sociology of Deviance." *Social Problems* 20:103–20.

Linders, A. 1998. "Abortion as a Social Problem." *Social Problems* 45:488–509.

Loseke, D. R. 1992. *The Battered Woman and Shelters.* Albany, NY: State University of New York Press.

———. 2003. *Thinking About Social Problems.* 2nd ed. Hawthorne, NY: Aldine de Gruyter.

Mann, R. M. 2000. *Who Owns Domestic Abuse? The Local Politics of a Social Problem.* Toronto, Canada: University of Toronto Press.

Mauss, A. L. 1975. *Social Problems as Social Movements.* Philadelphia, PA: Lippincott.

Merton, R. K. 1938. "Social Structure and Anomie." *American Sociological Review* 3:672–82.

———. 1961. "Social Problems and Sociological Theory." Pp. 697–737 in *Contemporary Social Problems,* edited by R. K. Merton and R. A. Nisbet. New York: Harcourt, Brace & World.

Miller, J. M., R. A. Wright, and D. Dannels. 2001. "Is 'Deviance' Dead?" *American Sociologist* 32:43–59.

Millman, M. 1975. "She Did It All for Love: A Feminist View of the Sociology of Deviance." Pp. 251–79 in *Another Voice,* edited by M. Millman and R. M. Kanter. Garden City, NY: Anchor.

Parsons, T. 1948. "The Position of Sociological Theory." *American Sociological Review* 13:156-71.

Pfohl, S. J. 1977. "The 'Discovery' of Child Abuse." *Social Problems* 24:310–23.

Quinney, R. 1977. *Class, State, and Crime.* New York: McKay.

Reinhardt, J. M. 1929. "Trends in the Teaching of 'Social Problems' in Colleges and Universities in the United States." *Social Forces* 7:379–84.

Rochefort, D. A. and R. W. Cobb. 1994. *The Politics of Problem Definition.* Lawrence, KS: University Press of Kansas.

Rodmell, S. 1981. "Men, Women, and Sexuality: A Feminist Critique of the Sociology of Deviance." *Women's Studies International Quarterly* 4:145–55.

Rose, A. M. 1971. "History and Sociology of the Study of Social Problems." Pp. 3–18 in *Handbook on the Study of Social Problems,* edited by E. O. Smigel. Chicago, IL: Rand McNally.

Rubington, E. and M. S. Weinberg, eds. 2002. *Deviance.* 8th ed. Boston, MA: Allyn & Bacon.

———, eds. 2003. *The Study of Social Problems.* 6th ed. New York: Oxford University Press.

Rwomire, A., ed. 2001. *Social Problems in Africa.* Westport, CT: Praeger.

Saksena, R. N., ed. [1961] 1978. *Sociology, Social Research and Social Problems in India.* Westport, CT: Greenwood.

Sampson, R. J. and J. H. Laub. 1992. "Crime and Deviance in the Life Course." *Annual Review of Sociology* 18:63–84.

———. 1993. *Crime in the Making: Pathways and Turning Points through Life.* Cambridge, MA: Harvard University Press.

Sampson, R. J. and S. W. Raudenbush. 1999. "Systematic Social Observation of Public Spaces." *American Journal of Sociology* 105:603–51.

Schur, E. M. 1965. *Crimes Without Victims.* Englewood Cliffs, NJ: Prentice Hall.

———. 1984. *Labeling Women Deviant.* New York: Random House.

Schwartz, H. 1997. "On the Origin of the Phrase 'Social Problems.'" *Social Problems* 44:276–96.

Scotch, R. K. 1988. "Disability as the Basis for a Social Movement." *Journal of Social Issues* 44:159–72.

Spector, M. and J. I. Kitsuse. 1977. *Constructing Social Problems.* Menlo Park, CA: Cummings.

Sumner, C. 1994. *The Sociology of Deviance: An Obituary.* Buckingham, England: Open University Press.

Taylor, I., P. Walton, and J. Young. 1973. *The New Criminology.* London: Routledge & Kegan Paul.

Taylor, R. B. 2001. *Breaking Away from Broken Windows.* Boulder, CO: Westview.

Tittle, C. R. 1995. *Control Balance: Toward a General Theory of Deviance.* Boulder, CO: Westview.

Turk, A. T. 1969. *Criminality and Legal Order.* Chicago, IL: Rand McNally.

Waller, W. 1936. "Social Problems and the Mores." *American Sociological Review* 1:922–33.

Winett, L. 1998. "Constructing Violence as a Public Health Problem." *Public Health Reports* 113: 498–507.

Witty, P. A. and H. C. Lehman. 1928. "An Interpretation of the Heredity Background of Two Groups of Mental Deviates." *American Journal of Sociology* 34:316–29.

Woolgar, S. and D. Pawluch. 1985. "Ontological Gerrymandering." *Social Problems* 32:214–27.

Methodological Issues in the Study of Social Problems

Norman K. Denzin

University of Illinois, Urbana-Champaign

Yvonna S. Lincoln

Texas A&M University

Given that the logic of privatization . . . shapes archetypes of citizenship, [and] manages our perceptions of what constitute the "good society" . . . it stands to reason that new ethnographic research approaches must take global capitalism not as an end point of analysis, but as a starting point.

(Kincheloe and McLaren 2000:304)

My abhorrence of neoliberalism helps to explain my legitimate anger when I speak of the injustices to which the ragpickers among humanity are condemned. It also explains my total lack of interest in any pretension of impartiality. I am not impartial, or objective. . . . [This] does not prevent me from holding always a rigorously ethical position.

(Freire 1998:22)

Our discussion of the methodological issues involved in the study of social problems and deviance moves in four directions at the same time. We first locate ourselves within social problems theory. We then offer a brief history of the field of qualitative inquiry and its relationship to the study of social problems. A sequence of historical moments is presented. These moments are connected to capitalism's three major phases in the twentieth century (Jameson 1991:400–12). Third, we identify five basic methodological and paradigmatic approaches to social problems inquiry—positivism, postpositivism, critical theory, constructivism, and participatory models (Guba and Lincoln 2000:164). We briefly compare and contrast these frameworks in terms of their ontologies, epistemologies, and methodological stances. We move, fourth, to the present, analyzing a set of recurring methodological, moral, and ethical issues in social problems inquiry, including the crises of representation, legitimation, vocality, and ethics.

In our discussion, we borrow from Kong, Mahoney, and Plummer (2002:244), who speak of queering the interview, of deconstructing the intertextual discourses that surround the use of the interview as a research tool in the study of same-sex experiences. In queering social problems inquiry, we, like Kong, Mahoney, and Plummer, challenge traditional methodological approaches to the study of deviance. At the same time, drawing on critical race theory, we want to bring race and gender into this discourse. We believe that the methodological tools of the social sciences create racialized, gendered subjects. These subjects are frequently racialized and gendered, sometimes made deviant, as they are being defined through the eyes of the white male researcher (Dunbar, Rodriguez, and Parker 2002:284).

In advancing our position, we see ourselves "working the hyphens," that is, reinventing spaces and places between self and other in social problems and deviance research (Fine 1994:71). In working the hyphens, we want to self-consciously unpack "notions of scientific neutrality, universal truths, and researcher dispassion" (Fine 1994:70–1). We invite readers to imagine how traditional models of social problems inquiry can be unsettled, challenged, asking how "we can braid critical and contextual struggle back into our texts" (Fine 1994:71). With Fine, we want to challenge the "complicity of researchers in the construction of [deviant] others" (p. 71). We want to imagine transgressive possibilities, asking how interpretive inquiry can advance the goals of radical democracy, goals that apply equally to all persons, regardless of handicap, sexual orientation, race, gender, class, or ethnicity. We begin with traditions, history, and definitions.

TRADITIONS

Within the sociological community there is a long and distinguished tradition involving the critical, qualitative study of social problems and deviance (Conrad 1997; Gubrium and Holstein 2002:10; Nichols 2003). A commitment to ethnographic field methods, including interviewing, participant observation, life story and oral history construction, is a basic focus of this tradition (Becker 1970:107; Denzin 2001:x). In sociology, the work of the "Chicago School" in the 1920s and 1930s firmly established this connection between deviance and life history, ethnographic, and case study methodology (Becker 1970). In anthropology, during the same time period, Boas, Mead, Bennedict, Bateson, Evans-Pritchard, Radcliffe-Brown, and Malinowski charted the outlines of the fieldwork method, wherein the observer went to a foreign setting to study the customs and habits of another society and culture (see Rosaldo 1989:25–45 for a critique of this tradition).

Within the critical, social science community there is an equally complex tradition that locates the study of deviance and social problems in the complex moral, cultural, economic, and political apparatuses of the neoliberal capitalist state and its systems of citizenship and governmentality (Gubrium and Holstein 2002:8). From this vantage point, deviance and social problems exemplify issues involving the regulation of persons and their morality (Conrad 1997:39).

Our chapter is informed by these two traditions, and two others as well. In *The Sociological Imagination,* C. Wright Mills (1959) challenged scholars in the human disciplines to develop a point of view and a methodological attitude that would allow them to examine how the private troubles of individuals, which occur within the immediate world of experience, are connected to public issues and the public responses to these troubles (see also Agger 2000:265; Lemert 1997:161). Mills's sociological imagination was biographical, interactional, and historical. For him social problems always occurred within a specific historical and ideological moment. Mills wanted to bend the structures of capitalism to the ideologies of radical democracy (Agger 2000:265; Lemert 1997:161). We build on Mills.

Finally, we draw on recent developments within the field of qualitative inquiry. Over the last three decades there has been an explosion in the field of qualitative research. Critical qualitative inquiry is part of that explosion. Indeed it is part of a larger reformist movement that began in the 1960s (Denzin and Lincoln 2000a:x; Schwandt 2000:189). The interpretive and critical paradigms, in their several forms, are central to this movement, as are complex epistemological and ethical criticisms of traditional social science research.

Some term this the seventh moment of inquiry (Denzin and Lincoln 2000b:2, 12; see below). This is a period of ferment and explosion. It is defined by breaks from the past, a focus on previously silenced voices, a turn to performance texts, and a concern with moral discourse, with critical conversations about democracy, race, gender, class, nation, freedom, and community (Lincoln and Denzin 2000:1048).

In the seventh moment, at the beginning of the twenty-first century, there is a pressing demand to show how the practices of critical, interpretive qualitative research can help change the world in positive ways. It is necessary to examine new ways of making the practices of critical qualitative inquiry central to the workings of a free democratic society. These are some of the issues that we attempt to address in this chapter.

History and Definitional Issues

Qualitative research is a field of inquiry in its own right. It cross-cuts disciplines, fields, and subject matter.[1] A complex, interconnected family of terms, concepts, and assumptions surround the term. These include the traditions associated with positivism, poststructuralism, and the many qualitative research perspectives/lenses, and the methods connected to cultural and interpretive studies.

In North America, qualitative research operates in a complex historical field that cross-cuts seven historical moments. These seven moments overlap and simultaneously operate in the present. We define them as the traditional (1900–1950); the modernist, or golden age (1950–1970); blurred genres (1970–1986); the crisis of representation (1986–1990);

postmodern, a period of experimental and new ethnographies (1990–1995); postexperimental inquiry (1995–2000); and the future, which is now (2000–). The future, the seventh moment, is concerned with moral discourse, with a reunion of science and art, with the development of sacred textualities. The seventh moment asks that the social sciences and the humanities become sites for critical conversations about democracy, race, gender, class, nation, freedom, and community.

Successive waves of epistemological theorizing move across these seven moments. The traditional period is associated with the positivist, foundational paradigms. The modernist or golden age and blurred genres moments are connected to the appearance of postpositivist arguments. At the same time, a variety of new interpretive, qualitative perspectives were taken up, including hermeneutics, structuralism, semiotics, phenomenology, cultural studies, and feminism.[2] In the blurred genre phase, the humanities became central resources for critical, interpretive theory, and the qualitative research project broadly conceived. The researcher became a *bricoleur* learning how to borrow from many different disciplines.

The blurred genres phase produced the next stage, the crisis of representation. Here researchers struggled with how to locate themselves and their subjects in reflexive texts (Bruner 1993; Clough 1998). A kind of methodological diaspora took place, a two-way exodus. Humanists migrated to the social sciences, searching for new social theory, new ways to study popular culture and its local, ethnographic contexts. Social scientists turned to the humanities, hoping to learn how to do complex structural and poststructural readings of social texts. The line between a text and a context blurred. In the postmodern, experimental moment, researchers continued to move away from foundational, and quasi-foundational, criteria (Schwandt 1996). Alternative evaluative criteria were sought: those that were evocative, moral, critical, and based on local understandings (Lincoln 2000).

North Americans are not the only scholars struggling to create postcolonial, nonessentialist, feminist, dialogic, performance texts; texts informed by the rhetorical, narrative turn in the human disciplines (Delamont, Coffey, and Atkinson 2000). This international work troubles the traditional distinctions between science, the humanities, rhetoric, literature, facts, and fictions. As Atkinson and Hammersley (1994) observe, this discourse recognizes "the literary antecedents of the ethnographic text, and affirms the essential dialectic" (p. 255) underlying these aesthetic and humanistic moves.

Moreover, this literature is reflexively situated in multiple, historical, and national contexts. It is clear that America's history with qualitative inquiry cannot be generalized to the rest of the world (Atkinson, Coffey, and Delamont 2001). Nor do all researchers embrace a politicized, cultural studies agenda that demands that interpretive texts advance issues surrounding social justice and racial equality.

Lopez (1998) observes that "there is a large-scale social movement of anticolonialist discourse" (p. 226), and this movement is evident in the emergence of African American, Chicano, Native American, Aboriginal, and Maori standpoint theories. These theories question the epistemologies of Western science that are used to validate knowledge about indigenous peoples. Maori scholar Russell Bishop (1998) presents a participatory and participant perspective (Tillman 1998:221) that values an embodied and moral commitment to the research community one is working with. This research is characterized by the absence of a need to be in control (Bishop 1998:203; Heshusius 1994). Such a commitment reflects a desire to be connected to and to be a part of a moral community. The goal is compassionate understanding (Heshusius 1994).

These understandings are only beginning to enter the literature on social problems. As they do, a blurring of the spaces between the hyphens that join researchers and those studied occurs. Definitions of social problems are thereby made more problematic.

Queering Social Problems Inquiry

In the context of discussing the study of same-sex experience, Kong et al. (2002) present compelling historical evidence to support the conclusion that *"the sensibilities of interviewing are altered with the changing social phenomena that constitute 'the interviewee'"* (p. 240, italics in original). Reviewing the interviewing of gays in North America and Europe over the past 100 years, they trace a movement from a "highly positivist mode of research

through one where the boundaries become weaker, and on to a situation where interviewing has been partially deconstructed" (p. 240).

They distinguish three historical moments, traditional, modernizing, and postmodern. Their analysis contrasts the three periods in terms of assumptions about interviewers, gays, lesbians, questions asked, approaches taken, wider cultural discourses, and politics. In the traditional period, interviewers are presumed to be objective and heterosexual, closeted in the modern period, and out in the postmodern moment. Same-sex experiences are approached clinically, in terms of pathologies in the traditional period, while they are normalized in the postmodern period, where disease discourses give way to talk of liberation, politics, and postmodern ethics.

Kong et al. (2002:254) offer three conclusions relevant to our arguments in this chapter. Interviewing gays and lesbians today is very different from interviewing them at the end of the nineteenth century. With the arrival of postmodern understandings, new forms of interviewing and new kinds of findings and understandings are appearing. A form of reflexive, radical historicity should now be a part of all interpretive inquiry. Equally important, any form of inquiry, such as the interview, is itself a cultural form, in which questions and answers become self-validating.

Reading History

We draw several conclusions from this brief history, noting that it is, like all histories, somewhat arbitrary. First, each of the earlier historical moments is still operating in the present, either as legacy, or as a set of practices that researchers continue to follow or argue against. The multiple, and fractured, histories of qualitative research now make it possible for any given researcher to attach a project to a canonical text from any of the above-described historical moments. Multiple criteria of evaluation compete for attention in this field. Second, an embarrassment of choices now characterizes the field of qualitative research. There have never been so many paradigms, strategies of inquiry, or methods of analysis to draw upon and utilize. Third, we are in a moment of discovery and rediscovery, as new ways of looking, interpreting, arguing, and writing are debated and discussed. Fourth, the qualitative research act can no longer be viewed from within a neutral, or objective, positivist perspective. Class, race, gender, national origin, language, and ethnicity shape the process of inquiry, making research a multicultural, pluricultural, and sometimes multilingual process.

QUALITATIVE RESEARCH AS PROCESS

Any definition of qualitative research must work within this complex historical field. Qualitative research means different things in each of these moments. Nonetheless, an initial, generic definition can be offered.

Qualitative research is multimethod in focus, involving an interpretive, naturalistic approach to its subject matter. This means that qualitative researchers study things in their natural settings, attempting to make sense of, or interpret, these things in terms of the meanings people bring to them. Qualitative research involves the studied use and collection of a variety of empirical materials—case study, personal experience, introspection, life story, interview, observational, historical, interactional, and visual texts as well as material objects—which describe routine and problematic moments and meanings in individuals' lives.

Three interconnected, generic activities define the qualitative research process. They go by a variety of different labels, including theory, method and analysis, ontology, epistemology, and methodology. *Behind these three terms stands the personal biography of the gendered researcher who speaks from a particular class, racial, cultural, and ethnic community perspective.* The gendered, multiculturally situated researcher approaches the world with a set of ideas, a framework (theory, ontology), which specifies a set of questions (epistemology), which are then examined (methodology, analysis) in specific ways. That is, empirical materials bearing on the question are collected and then analyzed and written about. Every researcher speaks from within a distinct interpretive community, which configures, in its special way, the multicultural, gendered components of the research act. This community has its own historical research traditions, which constitute a

distinct point of view. This perspective leads the researcher to adopt particular views of The Other who is studied. At the same time, the politics and the ethics of research must also be considered, for these concerns permeate every phase of the research process.

Resistances to Qualitative Studies

The academic and disciplinary resistances to qualitative research illustrate the politics embedded in this field of discourse. The challenges to qualitative research are many. Qualitative researchers are called journalists, or soft scientists. Their work is termed unscientific, or only exploratory, or entirely personal and full of bias. It is called criticism and not theory, or it is interpreted politically, as a disguised version of Marxism, or humanism (see Huber 1995; also Denzin 1997:258–61 for a review).

These resistances reflect an uneasy awareness that its traditions commit one to a critique of the positivist or postpositivist project. But the positivist resistance to qualitative research goes beyond the "ever-present desire to maintain a distinction between hard science and soft scholarship" (Carey 1989:99). The positive sciences (physics, chemistry, economics, and psychology, for example) are often seen as the crowning achievements of Western civilization, and in their practices it is assumed that "truth" can transcend opinion and personal bias (Carey 1989:99). Qualitative research is seen as an assault on this tradition, whose adherents often retreat into a "value-free objectivist science" (Carey 1989:104) model to defend their position. They seldom attempt to make explicit, and critique, the "moral and political commitments in their own contingent work" (Carey 1989:104).

Positivists further allege that the so-called new experimental qualitative researchers write fiction, not science, and that they have no way of verifying their truth statements. Ethnographic poetry, and fiction, signal the death of empirical science, and there is little to be gained by attempting to engage in moral criticism. These critics presume a stable, unchanging reality that can be studied with the empirical methods of objective social science. The province of qualitative research, accordingly, is the world of lived experience, for this is where individual belief and action intersect with culture. Under this model, there is no preoccupation with discourse and method as material interpretive practices that constitute representation and description. Thus is the textual, narrative turn rejected by the positivists.

The opposition to positive science by the postpositivists, and the poststructuralists, is seen, then, as an attack on reason and truth. At the same time, the positive science attack on qualitative research is regarded as an attempt to legislate one version of truth over another.

This complex political terrain defines the many traditions and strands of qualitative research: the British and its presence in other national contexts; the American pragmatic, naturalistic, and interpretive traditions in sociology, anthropology, communications, and education; the German and French phenomenological, hermeneutic, semiotic, Marxist, structural, and poststructural perspectives; feminist studies, African American studies, Latino studies, queer studies, studies of indigenous and aboriginal cultures. The politics of qualitative research create a tension that informs each of the above traditions. This tension itself is constantly being reexamined and interrogated, as qualitative research confronts a changing historical world, new intellectual positions, and its own institutional and academic conditions.

We turn now to a brief discussion of the major differences between qualitative and quantitative approaches to research.

QUALITATIVE VERSUS QUANTITATIVE RESEARCH

The word *qualitative* implies an emphasis on processes, and meanings, that are not rigorously examined, or measured (if measured at all), in terms of quantity, amount, intensity, or frequency. Qualitative researchers stress the socially constructed nature of reality, the intimate relationship between the researcher and what is studied, and the situational constraints that shape inquiry. Such researchers emphasize the value-laden nature of inquiry. They seek answers to questions that stress *how* social experience is created and given meaning. In contrast, quantitative studies emphasize the measurement and analysis of causal relationships between variables, not processes. Proponents claim that their work is done from within a value-free framework.

Research Styles: Doing the Same Things Differently?

Of course, both qualitative and quantitative researchers "think they know something about society worth telling to others, and they use a variety of forms, media and means to communicate their ideas and findings" (Becker 1986:122). Qualitative research differs from quantitative research in five significant ways (Becker 1996). These points of difference turn on different ways of addressing the same set of issues.

1. *Uses of positivism and postpositivism.* First, both perspectives are shaped by the positivist and postpositivist traditions in the physical and social sciences. These two positive science traditions hold to naive and critical realist positions concerning reality and its perception. In the positivist version, it is contended that there is a reality out there to be studied, captured, and understood, while the postpositivists argue that reality can never be fully apprehended, only approximated (Guba 1990:22). Postpositivism relies on multiple methods as a way of capturing as much of reality as possible. At the same time, emphasis is placed on the discovery and verification of theories. Traditional evaluation criteria like internal and external validity are stressed, as is the use of qualitative procedures that lend themselves to structured (sometimes statistical) analysis.

Historically, qualitative research was defined within the positivist paradigm, where qualitative researchers attempted to do good positivist research with less rigorous methods and procedures. Some midcentury qualitative researchers (Becker et al. 1961) reported participant observations findings in terms of quasistatistics. As recently as 1999 (Strauss and Corbin 1999), two leaders of the grounded theory approach to qualitative research attempted to modify the usual canons of good (positivistic) science to fit their own postpositivist conception of rigorous research.

Flick (1998:2–3) usefully summarizes the differences between these two approaches to inquiry. He observes that the quantitative approach has been used for purposes of isolating "causes and effects, . . . operationalizing theoretical relations, . . . [and] measuring and . . . quantifying phenomena, . . . allowing the generalization of finding" (p. 3). But today, doubt is cast on such projects: "Rapid social change and the resulting diversification of life worlds are increasingly confronting social researchers with new social contexts and perspectives, . . . traditional deductive methodologies . . . are failing, . . . thus research is increasingly forced to make use of inductive strategies instead of starting from theories and testing them. . . . [K]nowledge and practice are studied as local knowledge and practice" (p. 2).

2. *Acceptance of postmodern sensibilities.* The use of quantitative, positivist methods and assumptions has been rejected by a new generation of qualitative researchers who are attached to post-structural, postmodern sensibilities. These researchers argue that positivist methods are but one way of telling a story about society or the social world. They may be no better, or no worse, than any other method; they just tell a different kind of story.

This tolerant view is not shared by everyone. Many members of the critical theory, constructivist, poststructural, and postmodern schools of thought reject positivist and postpositivist criteria when evaluating their own work. They see these criteria as being irrelevant to their work, and contend that it reproduces only a certain kind of science—a science that silences too many voices. These researchers seek alternative methods for evaluating their work, including verisimilitude, emotionality, personal responsibility, an ethic of caring, political praxis, multivoiced texts, dialogues with subjects, and so on.

3. *Capturing the individual's point of view.* Both qualitative and quantitative researchers are concerned about the individual's point of view. However, qualitative investigators think they can get closer to the actor's perspective by detailed interviewing and observation. They argue that quantitative researchers are seldom able to capture the subject's perspective because they have to rely on more remote, inferential empirical materials.

4. *Examining the constraints of everyday life.* Qualitative researchers are more likely to confront and come up against the constraints of the everyday social world. They see this world in action and embed their findings in it. Quantitative researchers abstract from this world and seldom study it directly. They seek a nomothetic or etic science based on probabilities derived from the study of large numbers of randomly selected cases. These kinds of statements stand above and outside the constraints of everyday life. Qualitative researchers, on the other hand, are committed to an emic, ideographic, case-based position, which directs their attention to the specifics of particular cases.

5. *Securing rich descriptions.* Qualitative researchers believe that rich descriptions of the social world are valuable, while quantitative researchers, with their etic, nomothetic commitments, are less concerned with such detail. They are deliberately unconcerned with such descriptions because such detail interrupts the process of developing generalizations.

These five points of difference described above (uses of positivism, postmodernism, capturing the individual's point of view, examining the constraints of everyday life, securing thick descriptions) reflect commitments to different styles of research, different epistemologies, and different forms of representation. Each work tradition is governed by a different set of genres, each has its own classics, its own preferred forms of representation, interpretation, and textual evaluation. Qualitative researchers use ethnographic prose, historical narratives, first-person accounts, still photographs, life history, fictionalized facts, and biographical and autobiographical materials, among others. Quantitative researchers use mathematical models, statistical tables, and graphs, and usually write in an impersonal, third-person prose.

WORKING THE HYPHEN—THE OTHER AS RESEARCH SUBJECT

From its turn-of-the-century birth in modern, interpretive form, qualitative research has been haunted by a double-faced ghost. On the one hand, qualitative researchers have assumed that qualified, competent observers could with objectivity, clarity, and precision report on their own observations of the social world, including the experiences of others. Second, researchers have held to the belief in a real subject, or real individual, who is present in the world and able, in some form, to report on his or her experiences. So armed, the researchers could blend their own observations with the self-reports provided by subjects through interviews, life story, personal experience, and case study documents.

These two beliefs have led qualitative researchers across disciplines to seek a method that would allow them to record their own observations accurately while also uncovering the meanings their subjects brought to their life experiences. This method would rely upon the subjective verbal and written expressions of meaning given by the individuals studied, these expressions being windows into the inner life of the person. Since Dilthey ([1900] 1976), this search for a method has led to a perennial focus in the human disciplines on qualitative, interpretive methods.

Recently, as noted above, this position and its beliefs have come under assault. Poststructuralists and postmodernists have contributed to the understanding that there is no clear window into the inner life of an individual. Any gaze is always filtered through the lenses of language, gender, social class, race, and ethnicity. There are no objective observations, only observations socially situated in the co-created or temporally conjoined worlds of the observer and the observed. Research participants, or individuals, are seldom able to give full explanations of their actions or intentions; all they can offer are accounts, or stories, about what they did and why. No single method can grasp the subtle variations in ongoing human experience. Consequently, qualitative researchers deploy a wide range of interconnected interpretive methods, always seeking better ways to make more understandable the worlds of experience that have been studied.

Interpretive Paradigms

All qualitative researchers are philosophers in that "universal sense in which all human beings . . . are guided by highly abstract principles"

(Bateson 1972:320). These principles combine beliefs about *ontology* (What kind of being is the human being? What is the nature of reality?), *epistemology* (What is the relationship between the inquirer and the known?), and *methodology* (How do we know the world, or gain knowledge of it?) (see Guba and Lincoln 2000). These beliefs shape how the qualitative researcher sees the world and acts in it. The researcher is "bound within a net of epistemological and ontological premises which—regardless of ultimate truth or falsity—become partially self-validating" (Bateson 1972:314).

The net that contains the researcher's epistemological, ontological, and methodological premises may be termed a *paradigm* (Guba 1990:17), or interpretive framework, a "basic set of beliefs that guides action" (Guba 1990:17). All research is interpretive, and guided by a set of beliefs and feelings about the world and how it should be understood and studied. These beliefs may be taken for granted, only assumed, while others are highly problematic and controversial. Each interpretive paradigm makes particular demands on the researcher, including the questions that are asked and the interpretations that are brought to them.

At the most general level, four major interpretive paradigms structure qualitative research: positivist and postpositivist, constructivist-interpretive, critical (Marxist, emancipatory), and feminist-poststructural. These four abstract paradigms become more complicated at the level of concrete specific interpretive communities. At this level, it is possible to identify not only the constructivist but also multiple versions of feminism (Afrocentric and poststructural),[3] as well as specific ethnic, Marxist, and cultural studies paradigms.

Table 3.1 presents these paradigms and their assumptions, including their criteria for evaluating research and the typical form that an interpretive or theoretical statement assumes in the paradigm.[4]

The *positivist* and *postpositivist paradigms* work from within a realist and critical realist ontology, objective epistemologies, and rely upon experimental, quasiexperimental, survey, and rigorously defined qualitative methodologies (see Atkinson et al. 2001; Becker 1996; Becker et al. 1961). The *constructivist paradigm* assumes a relativist ontology (there are multiple realities), a subjectivist

Table 3.1   Interpretive Paradigms

Paradigm/Theory	Criteria	Form of Theory	Type of Narration
Positivist-Postpositivist	Internal, external validity	Rationalistic, logical-deductive Grounded	Scientific report
Constructivist	Trustworthiness, credibility, transferability, confirmability	Substantive-formal, Ethnographic fiction	Interpretive case studies, essays, stories, experimental writing
Feminist/Afrocentric	Lived experience, dialogue, caring, emotion, praxis, accountability, race, class, gender, reflexivity	Critical, Standpoint	Essays, stories, experimental writing
Ethnic	Afrocentric, lived experience, dialogue, caring, accountability, race, class, gender, language	Standpoint, Critical, Historical	Essays, fables, dramas [**deconstructions, historical analyses**]
Marxist	Emancipatory, critical theory, falsifiable, dialogical, race, class, gender [**dialectic**]	Historical, Economic, Class-Bound	[**Historical,**] economic, sociocultural analyses
Cultural Studies	Cultural practices, praxis, social texts, subjectivities [**genders**]	Social criticism [**deconstruction, poststructural analyses**]	Cultural theory-as-criticism
Queer Theory	Reflexivity, deconstruction	Social criticism, historical analyses	Theory-as-criticism, Autobiography

epistemology (knower and subject co-create understandings), and a naturalistic (in the natural world) set of methodological procedures (Guba and Lincoln 2000; Schwandt 1996). Findings are usually presented in terms of the criteria of grounded theory. Terms like *credibility, transferability, dependability*, and *confirmability* replace the usual positivist criteria of internal and external validity, reliability, and objectivity.

Feminist, ethnic, Marxist, cultural studies, and queer theory models privilege a materialist-realist ontology, that is, the real world makes a material difference in terms of race, class, and gender (Guba and Lincoln 2000; Olesen 2000). Subjectivist epistemologies and naturalistic methodologies (usually ethnographies) are also employed. Empirical materials and theoretical arguments are evaluated in terms of their emancipatory implications. Criteria from gender and racial communities (e.g., African American) may be applied (emotionality and

feeling, caring, personal accountability, dialogue). *Poststructural feminist theories* emphasize problems with the social text, its logic, and its inability to ever fully represent the world of lived experience (Clough 1998; Fine 1994; Gergen and Gergen 2000; Olesen 2000; Richardson 2000). Positivist and postpositivist criteria of evaluation are replaced by other terms, including the reflexive, multivoiced text that is grounded in the experiences of oppressed people.

The *cultural studies and queer theory paradigms* are multifocused, with many different strands drawing from Marxism and feminism and the postmodern sensibility (Agger 2000; Kong et al. 2002). There is a tension between a humanistic cultural studies that stresses lived experiences, and a more structural cultural studies project that stresses the structural and material determinants (race, class, gender) of experience. The cultural studies and queer theory paradigms use methods strategically, that is, as resources for understanding and for producing resistances to local structures of domination. Such scholars may do close textual readings and discourse analysis of cultural texts, as well as local ethnographies, open-ended interviewing, and participant observation. The focus is on how race, class, and gender are produced and enacted in historically specific situations.

Bridging the Historical Moments: Into the Present

Two theses have organized our discussion to this point. First, in its relationship to the field of social problems inquiry, the history of qualitative research is defined more by breaks and ruptures than by a clear, evolutionary, progressive movement from one stage to the next. These breaks and ruptures move in cycles and phases, so that what is passe today may be in vogue a decade from now. Just as the postmodern, for example, reacts to the modern, someday there may well be a neomodern phase that extols Malinowski and the Chicago school and finds the current poststructural, postmodern moment abhorrent.

Our second assumption builds on the tensions that now define qualitative social problems research. There is an elusive center to this contradictory, tension-riddled enterprise, which seems to be moving further and further away from grand narratives and single, overarching ontological, epistemological, and methodological paradigms. This center lies in the humanistic commitment of the researcher to always study the world from the perspective of the interacting individual. From this simple commitment flows the liberal and radical politics of qualitative social problems research. Action, feminist, clinical, constructionist, ethnic, critical, and cultural studies researchers are all united on this point. They all share the belief that a politics of liberation must always begin with the perspective, desires, and dreams of those individuals and groups who have been oppressed by the larger ideological, economic, and political forces of a society, or a historical moment.

This commitment defines an ever-present, but always shifting center in the discourses of qualitative research. The center shifts and moves, as new, previously oppressed, or silenced voices enter the discourse. Thus, for example, feminists and ethnic researchers have articulated their own relationship to the postpositivist and critical paradigms. These new articulations then refocus and redefine previous ontologies, epistemologies, and methodologies, including positivism and postpositivism.

These two theses suggest that only the broad outlines of the future can be predicted, as the field confronts and continues to define itself in the face of four fundamental issues.

The first and second issues are what we have called the crises of representation and legitimation. These two crises speak, respectively, to the other and their representations in our texts and to the authority we claim for our texts and for ourselves, as social scientists and authors. Third, there is the continued emergence of a cacophony of voices speaking with varying agendas from specific gender, race, class and ethnic, and third world perspectives.

Fourth, throughout its history, qualitative social problems research has been defined in terms of shifting scientific, moral, sacred, and religious discourses. Since the Enlightenment, science and religion have been separated, but only at the ideological level, for in practice religion and the sacred have constantly informed science and the scientific project. The divisions between these two systems of meaning are becoming more and more blurred. Critics increasingly see science from within a magical, shamanistic framework (Rosaldo 1989:219). Others are moving science away from its empiricist foundations and closer to a critical, interpretive project that stresses morals and moral standards of evaluation (Clough 1998:136–7; Schwandt 2002: 39–58, 137–70).

Three understandings shape the present moment:

1. The qualitative researcher is not an objective, authoritative, politically neutral observer standing outside and above the text (Bruner 1993:1);

2. The qualitative researcher is "historically positioned and locally situated [as] an all-too-human [observer] of the human condition" (Bruner 1993:1);

3. Meaning is "radically plural, always open, and . . . there is politics in every account" (Bruner 1993:1).

The problems of representation and legitimation flow from these three understandings.

The Crisis of Representation

As indicated, this crisis asks the questions, "Who is The Other? Can we ever hope to speak authentically of the experience of The Other, or An Other? And if not, how do we create a social science that includes The Other?" The short answer to these questions is that we move to including The Other in the larger research processes that we have developed. For some (Kincheloe and McLaren 2000), this means participatory, or collaborative, research and evaluation efforts. These activities can occur in a variety of institutional sites, including clinical, educational, and social welfare settings.

For still others (Bishop 1998; Heshusius 1994), it means a form of liberatory investigation wherein The Others are trained to engage in their own social and historical interrogative efforts, and then are assisted in devising answers to questions of historical and contemporary oppression, which are rooted in the values and cultural artifacts that characterize their communities.

For still other social scientists (Dunbar et al. 2002; Richardson 2000), it means becoming coauthors in narrative adventures. And for still others, it means constructing what are called "experimental," or "messy," texts, where multiple voices speak, often in conflict, and where readers are left to sort out which experiences speak to their personal lives (Denzin 1997). For still others, it means presenting to the inquiry and policy community a series of autohistories, personal narratives, lived experiences, poetic representations, and sometimes fictive or fictional texts, which allow The Other to speak for herself or himself. The inquirer or evaluator becomes merely the connection between the field text, the research text, and the consuming community in making certain that such voices are heard (Atkinson and Hamersley 1994; Bruner 1993; Delamont et al. 2000). Sometimes, increasingly, it is The Institutionalized Other who speaks, especially as The Other gains access to the knowledge-producing corridors of power and achieves entrée into the particular group of elites known as intellectuals and academics or faculty.

The point is that both The Other and more mainstream social scientists recognize that there is no such thing as unadulterated truth, that speaking from a faculty, an institution of higher education, or a corporate perspective automatically means that one speaks from a privileged and powerful vantage point—and that this vantage point is one to which many do not have access, either by dint of social station or education.

Judith Stacey (1988) speaks of the difficulties involved in representing the experiences of The Other about whom texts are written. Writing from a feminist perspective, she argues that a major contradiction exists in this project, despite the desire to engage in egalitarian research characterized by authenticity, reciprocity, and trust. This is so because actual differences of power, knowledge, and structural mobility still exist in the researcher-subject relationship. The subject is always at grave risk of manipulation and betrayal by the ethnographer (p. 23). In addition, there is the crucial fact that the final product is too often that of the researcher, no matter how much it has been modified or influenced by the subject. Thus, even when research is written from the perspective of The Other, for example, women writing about women, the women doing the writing may "unwittingly preserve the dominant power relations that they explicitly aim to overcome" (Bruner 1993:23).

The Author's Place in the Text

The feminist solution clarifies the issue of the author's place in the interpretations that are written. This problem is directly connected to the problem of representation. It is often phrased in terms of a false dichotomy, that is, "the extent to which the personal self should have a place in the scientific scholarly text" (Bruner 1993:2). This false division between the personal and the ethnographic self rests on the assumption that it is possible to write a text that does not bear the traces of its author. Of course, this is incorrect. All texts are personal statements.

The correct phrasing of this issue turns on the amount of the personal, subjective, poetic self that is in fact openly given in the text. Bruner (1993) phrases the problem this way: "The danger is putting the personal self so deeply back into the text that it completely dominates, so that the work becomes narcissistic and egotistical. No one is advocating ethnographic self-indulgence" (p. 6). The goal is to openly return the author to the text in a way that does "not squeeze out the object of study" (p. 6).

Stacey (1988) reviews the many ways to openly return the author to the qualitative research text. Fictional narratives of the self may be written (Bruner 1993). Performance texts can be produced (Denzin 1997). Dramatic readings can be given. Field interviews can be transformed into poetic texts, and poetry, and short stories and plays can be written (Richardson 2000). The author can engage in a dialogue with those studied. The author may write through a narrator, "directly as a character . . . or through multiple characters, or one character may speak in many voices, or the writer may come in and then go out of the [text]" (Bruner 1993:6).

The Crisis of Legitimation

It is clear that critical race theory, queer theory, and feminist arguments are moving further and further away from postpositivist models of validity and textual authority. This is the *crisis of legitimation* that follows the collapse of foundational epistemologies. This so-called crisis arose when anthropologists and other social scientists addressed the authority of the text. By the authority of the text we reference the claim any text makes to being accurate, true, and complete. At the same time, the authority of the author is called into question. Is a text faithful to the context and the individuals it is supposed to represent? Does the text have the right to assert that it is a report to the larger world that addresses not only the researcher's interests but also the interests of those studied.

This is not an illegitimate set of questions, and it affects all of us and the work that we do. And while many social scientists might enter the question from different angles, these twin crises are confronted by everyone.

THE CRISIS OF VOCALITY: NEW AND OLD VOICES COPING WITH THE PRESENT

A variety of new and old voices, critical theorists, feminists, and ethnic scholars, have also entered the

present situation, offering solutions to the crises and problems that have been identified above. The move is toward pluralism, and many social scientists now recognize that no picture is ever complete, that what is needed is many perspectives, many voices, before we can achieve deep understandings of social phenomena, and before we can assert that a narrative is complete.

The modernist dream of a Grand or Master Narrative is now a dead project. The postmodern era is defined, in part, by the belief that there is no single umbrella in the history of the world that might incorporate and represent fairly the dreams, aspirations, and experiences of all peoples.

Critical Theorists

The critical theorists, from the Frankfurt, to the Annales, world-systems, and participatory action research schools, continue to be a major presence in qualitative research, and they occupy a central place in social problems theory (Kincheloe and McLaren 2000). The critique and concern of the critical theorists has been an effort to design a pedagogy of resistance within communities of differences. The pedagogy of resistance, of taking back "voice," of reclaiming narrative for one's own rather than adapting to the narratives of a dominant majority, was most explicitly laid out by Paolo Freire working with adults in Brazil. His work is echoed most faithfully by a group of activist priests and scholars who are exploring what is called "liberation theology"— the joining of the Catholic Church to egalitarian ends for the purposes of overturning oppression and achieving social justice through empowerment of the marginalized, the poor, the nameless, the voiceless. Their program is nothing less than the radical restructuring of society toward the ends of reclaiming historic cultural legacies, social justice, the redistribution of power, and the achievement of truly democratic societies.

Feminist Researchers

Poststructural feminists urge the abandonment of any distinction between empirical science and social criticism (Clough 1998; Olesen 2000). That is, they seek a morally informed social criticism that is not committed to the traditional concerns or criteria of empirical science. This traditional science, they argue, rests a considerable amount of its authority on the ability to make public what has traditionally been understood to be private (Clough 1998:137). Feminists dispute this distinction. They urge a social criticism that takes back from science the traditional authority to inscribe and create subjects within the boundaries and frameworks of an objective social science. This social criticism "gives up on data collection and instead offers rereadings of representations in every form of information processing, empirical science, literature, film, television, and computer simulation" (Clough 1998:137).

Feminist philosophers (Fine 1994) note distinct problems with several of the scientific method's most basic premises: the idea that scientific objectivity is possible, the effect that that mandate for objectivity has on the subjects of research, and the possibility of conducting an unbiased science at all on behalf of the targets, subjects, and participants of our research. Liberation and feminist theologians are central to this new discourse. They ask hard questions, including "Where and what are the places of women, persons of color, the poor, the homeless, and the hungry in the church, in science, in art, and literature?"

Critical Race and Queer Theory Scholars

There is yet another group of concerned scholars determining the course of qualitative social problems research: they are critical race and queer theory scholars who examine the question of whether history has deliberately silenced, or misrepresented, them and their cultures (Dunbar et al. 2002; Kong et al. 2002).

This new generation of scholars, many of them persons of color, challenge both historical and contemporary social scientists on the accuracy, veracity, and authenticity of the latter's work, contending that no picture can be considered final when the perspectives and narratives of so many are missing, distorted, or self-serving to dominant majority interests. The result of such challenges has been twofold: one, the reconsideration of the Western canon, and two, the increase in the number of historical and scientific works that recognize and reconstruct the perspectives

of those whose perspectives and constructions have been for so long missing.

Thus have we written the present. It is a messy moment, full of multiple voices, experimental texts, breaks, ruptures, crises of legitimation and representation, self-critique, new moral discourses, and technologies. We venture now into the future, attempting to inscribe and describe the possibilities of this seventh moment.

BACK TO THE FUTURE

Recent understandings in the social sciences (Schwandt 2000, 2002) now convince us that there *is* no "God's-eye view"; there is no "voice from nowhere," no "voice from everywhere." It is not that we might elect to engage in work that is postmodern. Rather, it is that we have inherited a postmodern world, and there is no going back. We do not "choose" to be postmodern. The historical moment has chosen us.

The implications of this understanding, of this resituating of the argument, are enormous. We have come and gone in the "great Paradigm wars." The wars are over. While we were fighting, the boundaries and borders over which we were fighting were redrawn until they were meaningless. We are not free to "choose" postmodernism. It is the historical moment when the modernist epoch ends: contingent, pluralistic, ambiguous, freed (or jettisoned) from the certainties of yesterday, decentered, noisy with previously unheard voices.

Mary Gergen and Ken Gergen (2000) argue that we are already in the post "post" period—post poststructuralism, post postmodernism, an age of reconstruction. What this means for interpretive, ethnographic practices is still not clear. But it is certain that things will never again be the same. We are in a new age where multivoiced texts, cultural criticism, and postexperimental works will become more common, as will more reflexive forms of fieldwork, analysis, and intertextual representation.

Another way, then, of describing this moment in time and space is to paraphrase Thomas Berry (1978), who commented that "we are between stories. The Old Story will no longer do, and we know that it is inadequate. But the New Story is not yet in place" (p. 33). And so we look for the pieces of the Story, the ways of telling it, and the elements that will make it whole, but it hasn't come to us yet. So we are now the ultimate *bricoleurs,* trying to cobble together a story that we are beginning to suspect will never enjoy the unity, the smoothness, the wholeness that the Old Story had. As we assemble different pieces of the Story, our bricolage begins to take not one, but many shapes.

Slowly it dawns on us that there may not be one future, one "moment," but rather many; not one "voice," but polyvocality; not one story, but many tales, dramas, pieces of fiction, fables, memories, histories, autobiographies, poems, and other texts to inform our sense of liveways, to extend our understandings of The Other, to provide us with the material for "cultural critique." The modernist project has bent and is breaking under the weight of postmodern resistance to its narratives, to what Berry calls "the Old Story."

The press for a civic social science remains. We want a civic sociology—by which is meant fieldwork located not only in sociology, but rather an extended, enriched, cultivated social science embracing all the disciplines. Such a project characterizes a whole new generation of qualitative researchers: educationists, sociologists, political scientists, clinical practitioners in psychology and medicine, nurses, communications and media specialists, cultural studies workers, and a score of other assorted disciplines.

The moral imperatives of such work cannot be ignored. We have several generations of work in social science that has not only *not* solved serious human problems, but many times has only worsened the plight of those we studied. Beyond morality is something equally important; the mandates for such work come from our own sense of the human community. A detached social science frequently serves only those with the means, the social designation, and the intellectual capital to keep themselves detached. We face a choice, in the seventh moment, of declaring ourselves committed to detachment, or in solidarity with the human community. We come to know, and we come to exist meaningfully, only in community. We have the opportunity to rejoin that community as its resident intellectuals and change agents.

An interesting, and significant, concomitant to expressions of interest in a civic social science is the implied end of the commitment to the Enlightenment dualism of means and ends. We are emerging from many moments in social science where ends and means have been carefully, objectively, separated. The implications of a civic social science are far more than human solidarity. Such a social science also signals the dying of the means-ends dualism. In a civic social science, the ends of ethnography—strong, just, egalitarian communities—are reconciled with the means for achieving those ends. In the seventh moment, the means (methods) of social science are developed, refined, and cherished for their contributions to communities characterized by respectful and loving difference, social justice, and equal access to material, social, educational, and cultural capital (the ends of ethnography). Methods vie among themselves not for experimental robustness, but rather for vitality and vigor in illuminating the ways to achieve profound understanding of how we can create human flourishing.

We are also seeing an emerging dialogue around what paradigms mean, and how we learn to trust their results (Lincoln 2002). The vast array of methods, paradigms, and proposals for trustworthiness has the power to blind us to the fact that many individuals and paradigm adherents, working from very different embarkation points, have arrived at destinations quite similar. The feminists, for example, with their critical emphasis on women's ways of knowing, share many understandings with the race and ethnic theorists, who likewise argue that nondominant, subaltern ways of knowing, while different from majority, academic, or conventional scientific epistemologies, have much to offer in our understanding of the vast array and variety of human social life. Critical theorists and those who work with life history and *testimonio* forms intuitively understand that the epistemological is political, and each has similar proposals for how we might view validity, and therefore the "truth" of any account.

As a consequence, we have before us the possibility of entering into more meaningful dialogue with each other, not about how we can create a new metaparadigm, but rather about the similarities we are uncovering in our work. We see many affinities and parallels emerging from methodological reflections on fieldwork under way. If a seventh moment is yet to be charted, such dialogues among paradigm and methodological adherents might well be undertaken.

One final characteristic that marks this moment is the activity and ferment between margins and center. What was center is now decentered; what was margin and border is now taking center stage. The staggering array of new materials, new resources, new stories, new critiques, new methods, new epistemological proposals, new forms of validity, new textual improvisations, new performed interpretations all demonstrate an undeniably new, if shifting, center to this work. What was marked formerly by the firm and rigid shapes of a Eurocentric geometry is now the fluid, shape-shifting image of chemical flux and transformation, of the symbolic dreamtimes of non-European and indigenous cultures, as margins move to the center, the center moves to the margins, and the whole is reconstituted again in some new form. The whole concept of center and margins is being transfigured by methods, methodologies, research practices, and epistemologies scarcely dreamed of a generation ago.

And as we wait, we remember that our most powerful effects as storytellers come when we expose the cultural plots and the cultural practices that guide our writing hands. These practices and plots lead us to see coherence where there is none, or to create meaning without an understanding of the broader structures that tell us to tell things in a particular way. Erasing the boundaries between self, other, and history, we seek to learn how to tell new stories, stories no longer contained within or confined to the tales of the past. And so we embark together on a new project, a project with its own as yet not fully understood cultural plots and cultural practices.

And what remains, throughout, will be the steady but always changing commitment of all qualitative social problems researchers—the commitment, that is, to study human experience and its problems from the ground up, from the point of interacting individuals who together and alone make and live histories that have been handed down to them from the ghosts of the past.

NOTES

1. Qualitative research has separate and distinguished histories in education, social work, communications, psychology, history, organizational studies, medical science, anthropology, and sociology.

2. Definitions: *Structuralism*: any system is made up of a set of oppositional categories embedded in language; *semiotics:* the science of signs of or sign systems—a structuralist project; *poststructuralism*: language is an unstable system of referents, making it impossible to ever completely capture the meaning of an action, text, or intention; *postmodernism*: a contemporary sensibility, developing since World War II, that privileges no single authority, method, or paradigm; *hermeneutics*: an approach to the analysis of texts that stresses how prior understandings and prejudices shape the interpretive process; *phenomenology:* a complex system of ideas associated with the works of Husserl, Heidegger, Sartre, Merleau-Ponty, and Alfred Schutz, including transcendental, subjectivist, existential, Marxist, and hermeneutic forms; *cultural studies:* a complex, interdisciplinary field focusing on power, politics, culture, history, context, articulation, and agency, which merges with critical theory, feminism, and poststructuralism.

3. Olesen (2000) identifies three strands of feminist research: mainstream empirical, standpoint and cultural studies, and poststructural, postmodern, placing Afrocentric and other models of color under the cultural studies and postmodern categories.

4. These, of course, are our interpretations of these paradigms and interpretive styles.

REFERENCES

Agger, Ben. 2000. *Public Sociology: From Social Facts to Literary Acts.* New York: Rowman & Littlefield.

Atkinson, Paul, Amanda Coffey, and Sara Delamont. 2001. "Editorial: A Debate about Our Canon." *Qualitative Research* 1:5–21.

Atkinson, Paul and Martyn Hammersley. 1994. "Ethnography and Participant Observation." Pp. 248–61 in *Handbook of Qualitative Research*, edited by Norman K. Denzin and Yvonna S. Lincoln. Thousand Oaks, CA: Sage.

Bateson, Gregory. 1972. *Steps to an Ecology of Mind.* New York: Ballantine.

Becker, Howard S. 1970. "The Life History and the Scientific Mosaic." Pp. 63–74 in *Sociological Work: Method and Substance,* edited by Howard S. Becker. Chicago, IL: Aldine.

Becker, Howard S. 1986. *Doing Things Together.* Evanston, IL: Northwestern University Press.

——. 1996. "The Epistemology of Qualitative Research." Pp. 53–71 in *Ethnography and Human Development,* edited by Richard Jessor, Anne Colby, and Richard A. Schweder. Chicago, IL: University of Chicago Press.

Becker, Howard S., Anselm Strauss, Blanche Geer, and Everett C. Hughes. 1961. *Boys in White.* Chicago, IL: University of Chicago Press.

Berry, Thomas. 1978. "The Old Story." *Anima* 4:31–46.

Bishop, Russell. 1998. "Freeing Ourselves from Neo-colonial Domination in Research: A Maori Approach to Creating Knowledge." *International Journal of Qualitative Studies in Education* 11:199–219.

Bruner, Edward. 1993. "Introduction: The Ethnographic Self." Pp. 1–26 in *Anthropology and Literature,* edited by Paul Benson. Urbana, IL: University of Illinois Press.

Carey, James W. 1989. *Culture as Communication.* Boston, MA: Unwin Hyman.

Clough, Patricia Ticineto. 1998. *The End(s) of Ethnography.* 2nd ed. New York: Peter Lang.

Conrad, Peter. 1997. "Presidential Address: Public Eyes and Private Genes: Historical Frames, News Constructions and Social Problems." *Social Problems* 44:139–54.

Delamont, Sara, Amanda Coffey, and Paul Atkinson. 2000. "The Twilight Years?" *International Journal of Qualitative Studies in Education* 13:223–38.

Denzin, Norman K. 1997. *Interpretive Ethnography.* Thousand Oaks, CA: Sage.

——. 2001. *Interpretive Interactionism.* 2nd ed. Thousand Oaks, CA: Sage.

Denzin, Norman K. and Yvonna S. Lincoln. 2000a. "Preface." Pp. ix-xx in *Handbook of Qualitative Research,* 2nd ed., edited by Norman K. Denzin and Yvonna S. Lincoln. Thousand Oaks, CA: Sage.

——. 2000b. "Introduction: The Discipline and Practice of Qualitative Research." Pp. 1–29 in *Handbook of Qualitative Research,* 2nd ed., edited by Norman K. Denzin and Yvonna S. Lincoln. Thousand Oaks, CA: Sage.

Dilthey, W. L. [1900] 1976. *Selected Writings.* Cambridge, England: Cambridge University Press.

Dunbar, Christopher, Jr., Dalia Rodriguez, and Laurence Parker. 2002. "Race Subjectivity and the Interview Process." Pp. 279–98 in *Handbook of Interview Research,* edited by Jaber F. Gubrium and James A. Holstein. Thousand Oaks, CA: Sage.

Fine, Michelle. 1994. "Working the Hyphens: Reinventing Self and Other in Qualitative Research." Pp. 70–82 in *Handbook of Qualitative Research,* edited by Norman K. Denzin and Yvonna S. Lincoln. Thousand Oaks, CA: Sage.

Flick, Uwe. 1998. *An Introduction to Qualitative Research.* London, England: Sage.

Freire, Paulo. 1998. *Pedagogy of Freedom.* New York: Rowman & Littlefield.

Gergen, Mary and Ken Gergen. 2000. "Qualitative Inquiry: Tensions and Transformations." Pp. 1025–48 in *Handbook of Qualitative Research,* 2nd ed., edited by Norman K. Denzin and Yvonna S. Lincoln. Thousand Oaks, CA: Sage.

Guba, Egon G. 1990. "The Alternative Paradigm Dialog." Pp. 17–30 in *The Paradigm Dialog,* edited by Egon G. Guba. Newbury Park, CA: Sage.

Guba, Egon G. and Yvonna S. Lincoln. 2000. "Paradigmatic Controversies, Contradictions, and Emerging Confluences." Pp. 163–88 in *Handbook of Qualitative Research,* 2nd ed., edited by Norman K. Denzin and Yvonna S. Lincoln. Thousand Oaks, CA: Sage.

Gubrium, Jaber F. and James A. Holstein. 2002. "From the Individual Interview to the Interview Society." Pp. 3–32 in *Handbook of Interview Research,* edited by Jaber F. Gubrium and James A. Holstein. Thousand Oaks, CA: Sage.

Heshusius, Louis. 1994. "Freeing Ourselves from Objectivity: Managing Subjectivity or Turning toward a Participatory Mode of Consciousness." *Educational Researcher* 23:15–22.

Huber, Joan. 1995. "Centennial Essay: Institutional Perspectives on Sociology." *American Journal of Sociology* 101:194–216.

Jameson, Fredric. 1991. *Postmodernism, or, the Cultural Logic of Late Capitalism.* Durham, NC: Duke University Press.

Kincheloe, Joe L. and Peter McLaren. 2000. "Rethinking Critical Theory and Qualitative Research." Pp. 279–314 in *Handbook of Qualitative Research,* 2nd ed., edited by Norman K. Denzin and Yvonna S. Lincoln. Thousand Oaks, CA: Sage.

Kong, Travis S., Dan Mahoney, and Ken Plummer. 2002. "Queering the Interview." Pp. 239–58 in *Handbook of Interview Research,* edited by Jaber F. Gubrium and James A. Holstein. Thousand Oaks, CA: Sage.

Lemert, Charles. 1997. *Postmodernism Is Not What You Think.* Boston, MA: Blackwell.

Lincoln, Yvonna S. 2000. "Varieties of Validity: Quality in Qualitative Research." Pp. 210–60 in *Higher Education: Handbook of Theory and Research,* Vol. 14, edited by John S. Smart and Corinna Ethington. New York: Agathon.

Lincoln, Yvonna S. 2002. "On the Nature of Qualitative Evidence." Paper presented at the Annual Meeting, Association for the Study of Higher Education, Sacramento, California, November 21–24.

Lincoln, Yvonna S. and Norman K. Denzin. 2000. "The Seventh Moment: Out of the Past." Pp. 1047–65 in *Handbook of Qualitative Research*, 2nd ed., edited by Norman K. Denzin and Yvonna S. Lincoln. Thousand Oaks, CA: Sage.

Lopez, Gerardo R. 1998. "Reflections on Epistemology and Standpoint Theories: A Response to 'A Maori Approach to Creating Knowledge.'" *International Journal of Qualitative Studies in Education* 11:225–31.

Mills, C. Wright. 1959. *The Sociological Imagination.* New York: Oxford University Press.

Nichols, Lawrence T. 2003. "Rethinking Constructionist Agency: Claimsmakers as Conditions, Audiences, Types and Symbols." *Studies in Symbolic Interaction: A Research Annual* 26:269–84.

Olesen, Virginia. 2000. "Feminisms and Qualitative Research at and into the Millennium." Pp. 215–56 in *Handbook of Qualitative Research*, 2nd ed., edited by Norman K. Denzin and Yvonna S. Lincoln. Thousand Oaks, CA: Sage.

Richardson, Laurel. 2000. "Writing: A Method of Inquiry." Pp. 923–48 in *Handbook of Qualitative Research,* 2nd ed., edited by Norman K. Denzin and Yvonna S. Lincoln. Thousand Oaks, CA: Sage.

Rosaldo, Renato. 1989. *Culture & Truth*. Boston, MA: Beacon.

Schwandt, Thomas A. 1996. "Farewell to Criteriology." *Qualitative Inquiry* 2:58–72.

——. 2000. "Three Epistemological Stances for Qualitative Inquiry." Pp. 189–213 in *Handbook of Qualitative Research*, 2nd ed., edited by Norman K. Denzin and Yvonna S. Lincoln. Thousand Oaks, CA: Sage.

——. 2002. *Evaluation Practice Reconsidered*. New York: Peter Lang.

Stacey, Judith. 1988. "Can There Be a Feminist Ethnography?" *Women's Studies International Forum* 11:21–7.

Strauss, Anselm and Juliet Corbin. 1999. *Basics of Qualitative Research.* 2nd ed. Thousand Oaks, CA: Sage.

Tillman, Linda C. 1998. "Culturally Specific Research Practices: A Response to Bishop." *International Journal of Qualitative Studies in Education* 11:221–4.

Social Problems and Public Policy

Tim Blackman

University of Teesside

Roberta Woods

Northumbria University

The Decline of Public Policy

An experiment is under way in Vancouver, where residents are being invited to play a computer game exploring different policy options for the development of their region. Called QUEST and inspired by the video game SimCity, it is part of the Georgia Basin Futures Project aimed at helping the public to understand alternative futures for complex and interacting ecological, social, and economic systems (see www.basinfutures.net). The game enables players to generate scenarios for the region based on options chosen from a menu of goals such as full employment, more land set aside for parks, lower housing densities, or fewer deaths from vehicle accidents. The computer works with the player's chosen options and shows how they interact, conflict, or reinforce each other when the scenario is run forward. The idea behind QUEST is to demonstrate the systemwide consequences of individual decisions, particularly the consequences for the sustainability of the system. The game's designers do not see the main challenge for sustainable development to be a lack of policy or technical tools. Instead they see the challenge to be a lack of public understanding of how choices about single issues interrelate to produce surprising outcomes, including undesired outcomes that, if known, would alter the choices previously made.

This is a dilemma that goes to the heart of public policy. Public policy often involves conflicting policy goals, short-term and long-term trade-offs, and unforeseen consequences. Despite the advance of individualism in both political and economic spheres over the past few decades, the persistence of "social problems" continues to demand a macroperspective through which the relational and emergent nature of these problems can be understood (Emirbayer 1997). Giddens (1998) has argued that there is a moral transition involved in this: "The new individualism, in short, is associated with the retreat of tradition and custom. . . . We have to make our lives in a more active way than was true of previous generations, and we need more actively to accept responsibilities for the consequences of what we do and the lifestyle habits we adopt" (pp. 36–7). Social problems such as crime, unemployment, and ill health both affect private lives and are emergent social outcomes of private choices. They are, however, beyond private action alone to solve.

Robert Reich (2001) takes up this theme in his book on American economic and social trends, *The Future of Success,* arguing that there is an increasing divergence between the public interest and the private actions of individuals. A particular problem is the sorting mechanisms fuelled by the dynamics of the new economy. Reich argues that without strong public policies these mechanisms will drive income inequalities, school segregation, and neighbourhood polarisation to points where the resulting divided and insecure society emerges as an unintended consequence on a huge and intractable scale. His concern is that the emergent nature of society needs to be more widely understood as a consequence of decisions made in everyday life by large numbers of people. The question he puts is whether the big choices about American society are made as societal choices, through democratic institutions, or as private choices through markets. He asks us to

[i]magine that several decades ago a giant genie appeared in the American sky, offering the nation a big choice: "Either you keep the economic arrangements you have now, stay working as you are, or—do I have a deal for you! By the start of the next century, some of you will be extraordinarily rich, most of you will be better off in terms of what you can buy, and the economy will balloon. But that's not all. . . . The other part of the deal I'm offering is this: Your jobs will be less secure, your incomes less predictable; there will be

wider disparities of earnings and wealth; and your society will fragment." (P. 230)

Today there seems to be less optimism that societal choices, based on a public interest that is arrived at democratically, can be made and politicians trusted with them. In the optimism of the 1960s it was possible for the Kennedy and Johnson presidencies to commit to the Great Society welfare reforms as a means, it was claimed, of achieving social integration and a better life for all. This optimism faded with the onset of world recession after the postwar boom. Political elites and the mass media in high-income Western societies asked the question, Can we afford welfare? and the New Right claimed that "excessive" and "untargeted" welfare spending was crowding out individual initiative and private enterprise (Clarke and Piven 2001).

The public interest rationale for public policy is thus under pressure from the spread of individualism and social fragmentation. This chapter discusses how both public policy and public management have become recast by these trends: the emphasis on the responsibility to find employment, rather than the right to work; on local social policy rather than national welfare states; and on containing government expenditure rather than welfare expansion. These newer individualistic, local, and managerialist approaches have in fact been shown to work in particular circumstances, and some useful initiatives have been developed, such as better targeted support for individuals, greater consultation, and improved management of large projects. But they are too often "technical fixes" and by no means always work even within their own terms. Above all, they fail to engage the public in *choices about social futures* and are insufficiently systemic to change course in a sustainable way from the societal trajectory of division and insecurity identified by Reich.

The chapter concludes by considering social problems as emergent phenomena that demand an understanding of both the key parameters that produce them and the local complexity of their dynamics, dynamics in which conventional command-and-control public bureaucracies are ill equipped to intervene. First, however, the chapter examines the state of public policy in the United States, Europe, and Japan, discussing a series of examples that progress through a consideration of the individual, the local, and the national as spheres of policy action. By considering these spheres of action in terms of possibilities for achieving change, the chapter aims to understand how policy measures can address complex social problems, drawing on the ideas of complexity theory. Complexity theory does not treat these spheres as separate. Instead, it focuses attention on how different spheres of action interact, producing outcomes that emerge and follow trajectories of change and development that gravitate towards important general qualities. Understanding these processes is crucial to the success of policy interventions.

THE INDIVIDUAL SPHERE: WELFARE-TO-WORK

In America during the 1980s, the New Right critique of social welfare focused on the image of a demoralised "underclass" of people overly dependent on state handouts. This saw an intensification of policy measures aimed at moving people into work and reducing dependency on income maintenance while maintaining the deregulated economic environment considered to be the engine of growth (Clarke and Piven 2001; Martinson and Holcomb 2002; Stoesz 2002). The underclass concept was also influential in Europe and Japan, although it was often used as a warning about pursuing U.S.-style deregulation. In Japan especially, the concept has been interpreted in terms of a shameful dependency on public assistance to be avoided if at all possible, alongside a Scandinavian-like policy commitment to maximising employment (J. Campbell 2002; Garon 2002). In Europe, there are certainly strong elements of these American and Japanese perspectives, but the less judgemental idea of "social exclusion" has come to dominate official social policy discourse in most countries.

Originating from the French concept of solidarity and the role of the state in furthering social integration, social exclusion describes the idea of a rupturing of the social bond between an individual and his or her society that can be tackled by appropriate

inclusive measures that are part of the *mainstream* of public policy making and implementation. It is a multifaceted idea spanning a range of social problems from truancy and school nonattendance to long-term unemployment. The policy responses have been equally multidimensional, from individual counselling to improved parenting or employability to cross-sectoral area-based initiatives to connect unemployed people with job opportunities or improve health status. Across all of these responses there is a common aim of "reinserting" individuals, families, or groups into a cohesive civic culture. In contrast, the underclass idea justifies policies that emphasise the "special needs" of the personally inadequate, sometimes punitively. America's post-1996 welfare reforms, for example, place considerable emphasis on benefit claimants needing to be personally responsible for finding employment, with public financial support conditional on time limits and various compliance, enforcement, and sanctioning arrangements (Martinson and Holcomb 2002). This regime coexists with the incarceration of American young men on a huge scale, disproportionately ethnic minorities, unable to sustain jobs in a deregulated labour market that generalises insecurity and division (Downes 2001). Policies of social inclusion and reinsertion stand in opposition to this growth of "a post-Keynesian state that replaces the social-welfare treatment of poverty by its penal management" (Wacquant 2001:95).

Reinsertion policies, however, have had significant lacunae, such as the inadequacy of social security benefits for those excluded from employment. Indeed, the main focus of European social inclusion policies has been on training and job subsidies aimed at reconnecting unemployed people with labour markets, albeit still generally more regulated ones than in the United States. Although the language is less harsh, the concept of social exclusion has in common with the idea of an underclass a concern with individual responsibility, especially to find employment. Targets to get more and more welfare benefit recipients into employment have been widely adopted by European states. The necessary programmes have not been cheap, and rely on various types of wage subsidy as well as some direct employment creation, mainly aimed at people whose employability is affected by disadvantages such as low skills, age, or disability. Detailed empirical studies of the European experience are now appearing, with a particularly interesting evaluation by Van Oorschot (2002) of the so-called Dutch miracle: the recent decrease in unemployment that has accompanied welfare-to-work measures during a period of strong employment growth.

Clearly the success of welfare-to-work programmes is strongly influenced by the level of job creation, as well as the willingness and feasibility of unemployed people moving to areas with better job opportunities—a particular issue in Europe where there are relatively low levels of labour mobility (Boeri, Hanson, and McCormick 2002). Van Oorschot's study considers the efficacy of welfare-to-work in the apparently favourable conditions of high employment growth. Dutch policies during the 1990s sought to change the behaviour of both unemployed people, by making benefits conditional on them improving their employability and taking up work if offered, and employers, who are often reluctant to hire them. Wage supplements, interviews, and counselling are among the measures aimed at getting the unemployed into work, including disabled claimants, while employers also receive tax reductions. In addition, it was recognised that nearly half of all social assistance claimants had very low employability due to factors such as age, caring responsibilities, or language problems. They have been targeted for "social activation" to tackle social isolation and apathy through voluntary work that exempted them from having to find employment.

Although unemployment has fallen during implementation of these measures, and many people found employment through them, Van Oorschot shows that the number of unemployed beneficiaries has been significantly lower than the growth in jobs. What has happened is that full-time jobs held by men in the industrial sector have been replaced by a larger number of part-time jobs often taken up by new labour market entrants, especially women. As a result, the total hours worked annually in the Dutch economy actually changed very little during the 1990s. Furthermore, a claimant moving onto benefits at the end of the 1990s was no more likely to move out of benefits than at the beginning of the

decade. Some policy measures conflicted with the welfare-to-work policies, such as replacing short-term disability benefits with an obligation on employers to continue paying wages, which has discouraged some employers from hiring people suspected as having health problems.

Van Oorschot concludes that the welfare-to-work programme has not cured long-term unemployment in the Netherlands but has stigmatised those who remain on benefits. In particular, he argues that it has reduced the level of social protection in Dutch society because employment growth has enabled governments to cut back the generosity of insurance benefits. If unemployment rises again, much larger numbers of Dutch employees will be dependent on inferior means-tested public assistance. The programme has therefore created the potential for a future social problem to emerge, depending on future employment scenarios.

Waddan (2003) reaches a similar conclusion about America's post-1996 welfare-to-work reforms. These have seen a dramatic fall in benefit-dependent households, again during a sustained period of economic growth. An interesting feature of the U.S. case is the variability in how the reforms have been implemented at state level so that, for example, it is apparent that there is no necessary connection between punitive measures against benefit recipients pursued in some states and reductions in benefit dependency seen in all states (Waddan 2003:26). A feature of the reforms that appears to have worked is that the time-limiting of benefits encourages people to seek work rather than eat into their time-limited welfare entitlement. However, what really matters is whether people move out of poverty. The studies that Waddan reviews have so far shown that most of those who move into work have not achieved earnings that lift them out of poverty, and some, who are neither any longer on welfare nor working, have seen their poverty deepen.

Modern social policies often individualise social problems despite their public interest rationale, in contrast to the big picture that the QUEST project is working with and that is an obvious concern for environmental sustainability. Welfare-to-work policies, for example, focus on individual employability. It is true that at an individual level, factors such as low education, ethnicity, age, or interview technique are likely to predict the risk of unemployment, regardless of the actual level of unemployment in a society, and therefore programmes that target individual needs seem sensible. But this neglects the big picture. These individual characteristics are only relevant insofar as they interact with a wider parameter value, the unemployment level. At this scale, individual factors are not likely to be important determinants of unemployment because what matters is the *level* of unemployment (Davey-Smith, Ebrahim, and Frankel 2001). Adjust this parameter value and the behaviour of individuals, and the barriers and opportunities they face, appear quite different. Thus, while welfare-to-work programmes can give a high priority to providing minimum levels of qualifications, especially for young people, and are therefore aimed at being both responsive and preventative, a key incentive for young people to gain qualifications is the prospect of good employment. These prospects still vary widely because of geographical differences in the availability of jobs.

Even in low unemployment societies, problems of poverty and inequality persist. Mackenbach et al. (2002) show that in the Nordic countries of Europe, with their long histories of relatively egalitarian social and economic policies, there are substantial inequalities in self-reported morbidity, and these are being accentuated by the general trend towards better health status being greater among higher income groups. Although they continue to comprise a distinctive social-democratic welfare regime, typified by high rates of female employment, a more equal distribution of incomes, and more universal provision of public services across all social classes, these countries have not eliminated difficult social problems (Salonen 2001). The extremes of America's racialised urban ghettoes and gated communities, or even the United Kingdom's inner-city deprivation and outer "sink" estates, are absent, but those at the bottom of the income and education scales still live more segregated lives in the most deprived housing areas, often ethnically concentrated. Social exclusion as a concept, therefore, still has relevance because social problems are not just issues of poverty.

Japan is a significant example in this respect. Its combination of high employment, generous but often unclaimed social security benefits, and the duty of family members to support each other has created a society with one of the lowest rates of poverty and welfare dependency among the world's more developed economies (Garon 2002). However, this is also now a system with considerable tensions. The increasing participation of women in employment is necessitating the replacement of their unpaid care work with funded services, and the principle of the deserving poor that underpins its public welfare provision is being challenged by the rise of social problems such as homelessness. Homelessness in particular has revealed the extent to which Japanese social policy depends on the family: much of the problem has been caused by a combination of recession since the early 1990s and the vulnerability to unemployment of able-bodied male labourers who have no family support (Ezawa 2002). In addition, the centrality of the family has been shaken by the "discovery" of child abuse and, excluding sexual abuse, of natural mothers as the main perpetrators (Goodman 2002a). A society that has prided itself on the virtual elimination of poverty is having to come to terms with social problems as public issues.

There are two aspects of the concept of social exclusion that are particularly important. Firstly, it recognises how exclusion from rights and customary standards of material comfort can be a result not just of low income but also of age, gender, geographical location, or ethnicity, conditions that often interact together and with key parameters such as the unemployment level (Burchardt, Le Grand, and Piachaud 2002). Secondly, social exclusion is a dynamic as well as a multidimensional concept. It goes beyond the statistics of poverty to capture the sense in which exclusion not only happens to some people but is done to some people by other people, whether wittingly or not. These observations—that social problems are produced by interactions between initial conditions and key parameters, and that they are consequences of actions taken by all of us—imply adopting a wider perspective than the individual with their special needs. One-to-one support is always valuable but rarely sustainable; the issue is one of a supportive social context, which has encouraged much recent attention to the state of neighbourhoods.

The Local Sphere: Polarising Neighbourhoods

For Byrne (1999), one of the most visible manifestations of social exclusion—deprived neighbourhoods—are *products of policies* that have had the effect of "promoting exclusion through space" (p. 122). In the United Kingdom, he argues, there has been an interaction between spatially targeted urban regeneration programmes and national social policy changes that, far from reintegrating poor people in these locales, has trapped them in low-paid, insecure employment with minimal social protection. This is not a process that is unique to the United Kingdom or even other liberal welfare regimes:

> The evidence is now overwhelming. It does not show that all post-industrial cities are polarized. It shows they are polarizing, and that those which are fully subject to liberalizing post-industrial capitalism are polarized. . . . This is as much a matter of ideological hegemony as of inevitable systemic tendency. (Pp.112–13)

The hegemony of liberal economics has on the whole been facilitated by policy measures rather than contained or reversed by public policies deployed as alternative instruments of control over the societal trajectories otherwise determined by liberalisation. For example, in the United Kingdom the redistributive effects of regional policies have not countered the spatial impact of cutting higher-level taxes; public policy planning and management often mimic the principles of liberal economics; and urban regeneration rarely achieves more than marginal citizen participation given the priority accorded to the needs of development capital (Hamnett 1997; Hill 2000; Newman 2001). The underlying cause of mobile capital seeking the highest return is paradoxically treated as a solution by regeneration programmes aimed at attracting private investment to "underperforming" areas. An alternative public policy response would be instead to tax this mobility and distribute the revenue to abandoned areas as an ongoing process of resource equalisation aimed at achieving comparable living standards across the space economy. Reade (1987), for example, has advocated

taxation of development value as a logical source of resources for repairing the damage caused by capital and population migration, a type of displaced feedback that could move spatial economies to much more even patterns of development. On a much larger scale, the taxation of international financial transactions has been proposed as an important tool of poverty reduction on a global scale (Townsend 2002). The common counterargument, of course, is that these interventions would impair wealth creation, but this is a further example of not modelling the social effects of policy choices.

The migration of population and capital has meant that labour market problems in deprived neighbourhoods are compounded by "concentration effects." The people left behind are increasingly coping not just with poverty but a rise in crime, drugs, antisocial behaviour, dereliction, and stigma that are widely perceived as problems for everyone, not just the residents trapped in these areas. Often there are also problems with failing public and private sector services that find it difficult to recruit staff, are insufficiently compensated for the extra costs of meeting needs in these areas, and have problems of viability due to low demand. Local job creation has often not reduced unemployment because new jobs are taken by commuters, in-migrants, or new labour market entrants (M. Campbell 2002). Social problems are diverse but largely emanate from the lack of access to employment that can sustain even average standards of living. Lone parenthood is one example. Webster (2002) shows how the dramatic rise in lone parenthood in the United Kingdom since the early 1980s, and earlier in the United States, has followed the equally large rise in male unemployment. In the main, men without jobs are not wanted as long-term partners. Echoing Van Oorschot's (2002) study, Webster also shows that British welfare-to-work policies aimed at lone parents and using in-work tax credits have had a very modest impact on lone parent employment in the worst unemployment areas, with the take-up of tax credits proportionally much higher in low-unemployment areas. This again emphasises the need not just for supply-side measures but demand-side measures that explicitly aim to close geographical inequalities in access to employment.

Other social problems closely connected with deprived neighbourhoods include drug use, smoking, and poor health. These have all been linked with stresses caused by living in these neighbourhoods (Boardman et al. 2001; Duncan, Jones, and Moon 1999; Kleinschmidt, Hills, and Elliott 1995; Marsh et al. 1999; Reijneveld 1998; Thomson, Petticrew, and Morrison 2002). Such findings have led to policy prescriptions that emphasise tackling the diminution of social capital by combining improvements to the local environment and public services with community development, individual support with accessing opportunities and building personal confidence, resident involvement, and concerted multiagency work (Lupton and Power 2002). There has been mixed success with these local interventions, and it is often unclear why some succeed while others fail. Conditions external to the neighbourhood are critical, so local action to tackle decline is likely to be necessary but not sufficient. For example, Nevin et al. (2001) show how the risk of neighbourhood abandonment in the urban centres of northwest England is associated with a combination of neighbourhood conditions *and* external factors. The key external factors are the employment level and interest rates, and these affect the rate at which residents exit to more popular areas. Large amounts of money have been spent on renewing many deprived areas only for these external factors to operate in a way that leads to continuing abandonment and ultimately demolition.

In the United States, a key goal of the federal HOPE VI program has been to spatially deconcentrate very low-income households. The program has funded the redevelopment of rundown public housing areas to create more mixed income neighbourhoods and provided either public rehousing or vouchers for private renting to many residents so that they can move to other areas. A tracking study by Buron et al. (2002) found that for most residents, their housing environment improved as a result of the program, but a substantial proportion experienced continuing problems with drug trafficking and violent crime, and about half of those who moved into private renting using the vouchers found it difficult to pay the rent. Also, while the intention was to encourage rehoused residents to participate in

new, more supportive social networks in mixed income areas, relatively little interaction with new neighbours occurred.

While neighbourhood context clearly has some effect on quality of life—particularly crime, the quality of local services, and the quality of the environment—there are few reports in the literature of neighbourhood renewal achieving any significant reduction in social inequalities, and its role as an instrument of social policy appears quite modest. Health, and especially mental health, can benefit to some extent from neighbourhood improvements, but health impact assessments have also warned against the disruptive and potentially health-damaging consequences of renewal programmes, particularly if accompanied by rent increases, and the negative health effects that may occur for residents in adjoining unimproved neighbourhoods (Hirschfield et al. 2001). Area-based programmes such as neighbourhood renewal also inevitably exclude many areas in an attempt to target resources, and in the United Kingdom this has been identified as a cause of racial and social unrest as some areas and groups are perceived to benefit while others lose out (Cantle 2001). In addition, unemployment and other types of deprivation may affect far more individuals living outside the most deprived neighbourhoods than within them. In Scotland, McLoone (2001) shows that if area-based initiatives targeted 20 percent of the most deprived postcode sectors nationally (equivalent to the U.S. zip code), only 41 percent of unemployed people and 34 percent of low-income households would be included. Over half of all postcode sectors would have to be targeted to include 80 percent of unemployed people or 74 percent of low-income households. McLoone concludes that there needs to be greater emphasis on national strategies rather than neighbourhood targeting.

Individual support regardless of neighbourhood has been shown to be effective in reducing the incidence of a range of social problems. For example, Olds et al. (1997) report results from a longitudinal study of the effect of a programme of prenatal and early childhood home visits by nurses to first-time mothers in the United States. A follow-up study when the children were 15 years old found that the intervention group of mothers was almost half as likely as a comparison group to have been identified as perpetrators of child abuse and neglect. Among women who were unmarried and on low incomes, the intervention was associated with fewer subsequent births, less use of welfare, fewer arrests, and lower levels of drug and alcohol problems compared with mothers in the nonintervention group. Clearly, individual interventions can make a difference and therefore may deny many potential beneficiaries their better outcomes if restricted to geographically defined deprived areas.

However, the model of intervention at this individual level remains one based on personal deficits. While this can appear effective, it largely works within the structures of exclusion that generate the problems that are then individualised as inadequate people unable to cope with the pressures around them. For example, given the choice between receiving home visits or a higher income, it is likely that the vast majority of mothers in the Olds et al. (1997) study would choose the latter. They are likely to make that choice out of a clear recognition that their problems are poverty-related. But a problem with this argument that it is structural causes rather than symptoms that should be tackled by public policy has been a paucity of work modelling and demonstrating the tangible effects of a structural approach.

In this respect, a recent report by Mitchell, Dorling, and Shaw (2000) is very important: it takes up this issue by deploying statistical modelling to simulate what Britain's map of the public's health would look like under different national policy scenarios. They simulate changes at a national level in income inequality, in unemployment, and in rates of childhood poverty, and model the resulting health outcomes for each of Britain's 723 local parliamentary constituencies, modelling these outcomes according to the values of these key parameters. If national taxation reduced income inequality back to its level in 1983—a fairly modest target—an estimated 7,500 lives of people aged under 65 would be saved each year because of the statistical link between premature mortality and income inequality. Further lives could be saved by ending unemployment and eradicating childhood poverty. Rather than local policies trying to moderate some of the effects of national macroeconomic and social policies, this research shows that these national policies themselves are both causes of, and therefore keys to tackling, poor health in deprived areas.

THE NATIONAL SPHERE: AGEING SOCIETIES

If we turn to what is often presented as the social problem of ageing, and the position of people for whom employment may not be an option in order to avoid social exclusion, what is the significance of public policy for their welfare? In the United States, the population is ageing but continuing to grow due to immigration; in Europe and Japan, ageing is coinciding with population decline, and this is causing particular concern about financing pensions and care services (Bermingham 2001). Clearly, this is a sphere where public policy responses need to be on a national scale. Initial conditions vary greatly across countries, and Blackman, Brodhurst, and Convery (2001) explore whether national "welfare regimes" are a useful way of understanding cross-national differences in care systems at a time when demographic change is putting all systems under pressure. State responsibility for providing health and social care for older people is greatest in the Scandinavian social-democratic welfare regimes, where political action has established universal publicly funded care as part of women's right to paid work. High levels of taxation in these high-income countries provide the resources for provision on this scale, and there is widespread political support for the services because beneficiaries span the social classes and there is no significant opportunity to exit to a private market in care. In contrast, publicly funded care services for older people are currently least developed in countries such as Italy, Greece, Ireland, and Japan, where relatives, primarily daughters and female spouses, are expected to provide this care. The role of the state has been very limited in these "familist" welfare regimes, with dependency on public or voluntary services a last resort and associated with stigma.

Both the social democratic and familist regimes are under pressure due to a declining 15- to 64-year-old population. In the social democratic regimes, this is causing labour shortages and cost inflation. In the familist regimes, it is the shrinking pool of family carers that is critical and compounded by economic and social changes associated with greater individualism, such as the eclipse of the male "family wage" by work-based wages, the growth of female education and employment aspirations, and, among older people, a trend towards living independently rather than coresiding with their adult children (Blackman et al. 2001; Izuhara 2002; Watanabe 2000). Both regime types face sharply rising government spending on care, although factors such as morbidity and disability trends, the shifting balance between formal and informal care, and future changes in unit costs of care mean there is a very substantial funnel of doubt about the extent of this future increase in demand for services and their costs (Bermingham 2001).

The key to understanding differences between welfare regime types is welfare culture, especially the very different attitudes to the respective roles of the state and the family. However, while welfare culture helps to explain cross-national differences, from a social policy perspective there is a particular concern with how well these different welfare mixes foster the inclusion of older people, a group that has tended to be neglected by the employment-focused concept of social exclusion. Giarchi (1996), for example, reveals the enclosed nature of family life for some older Italians, whom he describes as "captive within households" (p. 374), and whose disengagement from social life is actively fostered, especially in the south of Italy. Hugman (1994) cites studies that have found high levels of self-reported loneliness among older people in Greece and Poland, both countries with an apparently high degree of family centredness. Eurobarometer sample data have shown considerable cross-national disparity in the life satisfaction of older people, ranging from 68 percent in Denmark stating that they are very satisfied with their lives, to just 6 percent in Greece (Walker and Maltby 1997). Despite the family orientation of Greek society, in which older people traditionally have a central position, 36 percent in Greece said they often felt lonely. This compared with less than 5 percent in Denmark, where the great majority of older people live independently and have less contact with relatives.

Cultural factors are important in interpreting these findings, as older people in Greece are likely to have high expectations about the range and frequency of contacts they should have with their families. In general, however, older people prefer to receive the support they need to live as independently as possible in their own homes. While social care is increasingly recognised as a significant factor in achieving this independence—so that older people receive assistance in carrying out activities of daily living—pension income and health care are of critical importance. Older people are of course one group for whom in general welfare-to-work programmes are not appropriate, although the pressure of ageing populations on pensions has caused a slowing down or reversal of earlier trends to early retirement, and recently some countries have raised their statutory retirement ages. Older people are also a group that has been relatively neglected by programmes to tackle deprived neighbourhoods, despite being vulnerable to the problems of these areas, such as high crime rates and poor facilities (Scharf et al. 2002).

The significance of ageing as a social problem is associated with the fact that across the countries of the Organisation for Economic Co-operation and Development (OECD), 40 percent to 60 percent of public expenditure is sensitive to age structure (OECD 2001). As well as pensions, this includes health care and social care spending where demand is increasing sharply as more people survive into their 80s and 90s. The OECD estimates that age-related public spending will rise by 6 percent to 7 percent of GDP by 2050, a forecast that takes into account countervailing trends such as pension reform. The impact will be greatest in countries where relatively generous earnings-related pension schemes occur together with a rapid ageing trend.

The old-age dependency ratio, or the number of retired people as a proportion of the employed population, is often presented as the key to the affordability of age-related spending. Italy faces the most acute problems of all the OECD countries as its ratio increases from 29 percent in 2000 to a forecast 67 percent by 2030 (OECD 2001). By contrast, the United States—which is facing less pressure from population ageing than the OECD average—is expected to see its old-age dependency ratio rise from 22 per cent to 38 per cent over this period. While the ratio is deteriorating in all countries, countervailing trends include increasing female participation in employment, falls in unemployment, improved productivity of those in employment, and immigration. Countries have also addressed affordability by reforming pensions. As with the social security system, generally these have taken two forms: price reforms have reduced the level of benefits while volume reforms have reduced access to insurance schemes. Companies are also increasingly replacing final salary pension schemes with money purchase schemes that do not guarantee benefits. As a result, many countries now face pensioner incomes falling well behind wages and pressure to save privately for retirement.

Age-related public spending on health and social care varies considerably across countries but it is not the high-spending social-democratic welfare regimes that appear to be least sustainable. The greatest pressure is being experienced by the South European and Japanese familist regimes where the increasing participation of women in employment and smaller family sizes are limiting the scope for family care on which frail and disabled older people have overwhelmingly depended. In addition, these countries tend to have many older people receiving relatively generous pensions that have helped to provide cash for care, and the generosity of these pension systems is having to be cut back due to deteriorating dependency ratios. The response has been to start expanding the provision of home help and day care services, most dramatically in the case of Japan, where a series of three Gold Plans between 1990 and 2000 has greatly increased spending on these services and short-stay community centres and nursing homes, although provision still lags behind the United Kingdom, for example (Goodman 2002b). In Greece and Italy, many families cope by hiring an immigrant worker to live in, part of a general increase in demand for immigrant workers to take on household tasks as young educated women turn away from traditional mother and homeworker roles. Indeed, immigration is sometimes suggested as a solution to deteriorating dependency ratios in OECD countries to expand the supply of labour, but

it is unlikely that it can have any marked effect (Bermingham 2001; Boeri et al. 2002; OECD 2000). The issue is discussed further later in the chapter when considering scenario planning.

Two policy responses to the challenge of providing care in ageing societies are apparent, reflecting wider issues about affordability of welfare arising from political resistance to tax rises and concerns about the efficiency and performance of public services. The first is prevention, whereby governments are trying to identify how early intervention can prevent higher costs later on. The focus of welfare-to-work programmes on young people and the home nurse visiting programme described above are typical examples of preventative public policy. In the field of ageing, it is not just growth in the number of older people that is a significant spending driver but also rates of disability and institutionalisation. Costs can be moderated downwards substantially by measures to promote healthy ageing, prevent disability, and prevent admission to high-cost acute care and nursing institutions.

The second policy response is to increase the efficiency and effectiveness of public policies and services by more closely matching services to needs, achieving better integration between services, and making much more use of research evidence about "what works." In the field of older people's care, initiatives such as the United Kingdom's introduction of care management have been shown to achieve significant improvements in service productivity (Davies, Fernandez, and Nomer 2001). In many countries, this type of response has also involved making greater use of the private sector in a variety of ways: as sources of investment through private-public partnerships, of spare capacity to deal with demand pressures, of management expertise, and of alternative provision. Thus, new ways of working are emerging that emphasise efficiency and effectiveness in tackling social problems, especially target-setting—a new paradigm for national social policies.

SOCIAL POLICY, TARGETS, AND COMPLEXITY

Policy decisions are made by combining three factors: resources, evidence, and values. Currently, most decisions are based mainly on values and resources, although there is increasing attention paid to "evidence-based practice." It is particularly the issue of values that causes most concern when considering the efficiency and effectiveness reforms of governments attempting to contain the cost of rising welfare demands. This is currently the subject of considerable debate in the United Kingdom. At one extreme it is argued that, say, if food production can be left to private enterprise, then there is no reason why education or health care cannot be provided through private enterprise as long as this "works." At the other extreme, it is claimed that public services should be motivated not by profit but by meeting needs, and that the ethical basis of public services is compromised by commercial criteria.

These arguments are complicated by observations that private enterprise cannot function without public policy to provide a regulatory framework and tackle market failures, and that no profit-making enterprise is likely to succeed without meeting the needs of its customers. In fact, there has been an increasing blurring of any distinction between private and public services in many areas. Private providers are often commissioned to deliver public services according to the needs-based criteria, and public services are subjected to new performance management regimes that have imposed private sector practices such as cost centres and targets. There are many examples from around the world of the implications of contracting in the public services. Martinson and Holcomb (2002), for instance, show how in the case of American welfare reform, local welfare agencies now contract with numerous private and not-for-profit organisations that provide the employment services and case management that benefit payments are conditional upon. These performance-based arrangements require considerable management and monitoring, although the improved accountability achieved has generally been welcomed. But characteristic problems with performance management are also evident, such as the perverse incentive for organisations to meet their job placement targets by "creaming," or focusing on the job-ready. The response, common elsewhere, has been to expand the number of performance measures.

However, the spread of an "audit culture," with its panoply of measures and targets, is further undermining public policy and the distinctive public services ethos on which the delivery of social policies depends. This is because social problems are complex and tackling them requires flexibility and learning, which are discouraged by the command-and-control tendencies of audit cultures. While apparently a debate about management practice, this issue is in fact far more fundamental because governments are increasingly framing social problems as needing to be managed rather than solved.

Few managers of public services are now without responsibility for a set of quantitative targets that they are held accountable for achieving, although the possible dysfunctional effects of targets are well documented (Smith 1995). These include gaming, when teachers focus their efforts on students at the borderline of an exam performance measure while neglecting other students, and biasing, such as when hospitals give a lower priority to clinical need to meet waiting time targets. Consequently, success in meeting targets can lose credibility as a method for judging performance, especially if a large number of centrally dictated targets conflict with meeting local priorities. The response is often to seek better targets, and a great deal of effort has been invested in this type of work (Boyne 2002). Attempts to improve the validity of targets as measures of performance tend to lead their to overproliferation, but there are more fundamental problems with management by targets than the search for valid and reliable measures of performance. These follow from three problems connected with the inadequate theory on which the approach is conventionally based.

The first problem is that in order to hold an identifiable management accountable for performance, the system that delivers the outcome a policy objective aims for is often misspecified. Thus, a school is specified as the system for delivering examination results when the school actually comprises many systems, some achieving better results than others. Schools also have inputs from other systems, such as students' achievements in feeder schools and their material and home circumstances (Fitz-Gibbon 1996; Byrne and Rogers 1996). These all substantially influence outcomes at school level.

Examination performance is likely to vary more across subjects within schools than for all subjects across schools, and the characteristics of a school's intake are much more important than the effect of the school alone in determining its results.

Attempts to address this issue of system misspecification include "whole system" approaches. Rather than focusing on specific interventions or services, this approach looks at all the people in a defined population and implements strategies that intervene in the wider system parameters *and* the local context, both of which affect outcomes for the population. Whole system intervention is also based on "theories of change" (Pawson and Tilley 1997). Theories of change are working ideas about how change will occur as a result of the intervention, as well as what the expected outcomes will be. This contrasts with the "black box" approach to how change occurs that typifies target-setting. Indeed, O'Neill (2002) identifies how new audit regimes monitor requirements about both processes and targets, yet there is no necessary connection between conforming to process requirements and meeting the organisation's targets.

The wider system parameters that influence local outcomes demand national and increasingly international policy measures such as managing the economy at full employment or benefit/tax credit levels that lift all children out of poverty. The local context is the level of organisational interventions such as training or housing programmes tailored to local conditions. It is at this level where much effort is being expended on "joining up" initiatives and services, with whole-systems thinking influential in working towards a "postbureaucratic" local social policy (Netherlands Institute for Care and Welfare 2002). A third intermediate level of the region or city-region is also increasingly advocated as a space of strategic action for mobilising collective effort by agencies and integrating programmes within urban systems defined by networks such as travel-to-work patterns (Healey 2002).

A good account of the case for whole-systems public policy is set out in the final report of the Committee on the Quality of Health Care in America. In an important appendix, Plsek (2001) argues that public policy does not achieve its aims in many circumstances because it is delivered by organisations that apply "mechanical systems thinking" well beyond the situations where it is appropriate. Such thinking may work where there is a high degree of certainty about outcomes from actions and a high degree of agreement among the people taking the actions. Plsek gives routine surgery as an example—in this type of situation it can make sense to fully specify appropriate behaviour and reduce variation. However, there are many other situations that lie in a "zone of complexity," where there are only limited levels of certainty and agreement, and where detailed plans and controls do not make sense. Plsek's example is delivering primary care services, where there are many different models that have worked in some situations but not in others. Taking this perspective, it is clear that most public policy is in the zone of complexity.

The zone of complexity, Plsek argues, calls for interventions not by mechanical organisational systems with detailed plans and controls but by *complex adaptive systems* (CASs). A CAS comprises individual agents whose actions are interconnected and who can learn. The responses of these agents and of the environments in which they act are not mechanical and predictable but nonlinear and unpredictable in detail. Policy frameworks for complex adaptive systems need to create the conditions under which desirable outcomes are possible rather than try to prescribe agents' behaviour to achieve these outcomes. Prescription has its place, but in terms of the policy framework defining a few rules that are locally applied. Detailed action is then decentralised and this produces local variation, ideally producing the desired outcomes in a number of possible ways that are suited to local context, but also generating knowledge about good and not-so-good interventions.

As Plsek points out, these ideas are not new, although the synthesis offered by this account is new and has been identified as a new field of "complexity theory." Complexity theory focuses on interactions, especially the whole system as the causal system that produces the outcome a policy measure aims for. By only focusing on part of this system, there is a danger that important causal factors will be ignored (Örtendahl 2002). Cross-agency targets will not help if there is no mechanism that brings agencies together as part of an interacting system with inclusive thinking and learning. There is increasing recognition of whole systems in health and social care and attempts to find system solutions by, for example, creating new multiprofessional agencies and programmes (Shaw 2002). But it is still often the separate subsystems that are held accountable for performance, with their own targets.

A second theoretical problem with management by targets is that the approach assumes that the delivery system, even if treated as a whole system, is in equilibrium, so that a given input achieves a proportionate output. There seem to be few examples of this input-output equilibrium and many that suggest there is no such direct relationship. Pawson and Tilley (1997) review extensive evidence that there is no direct relationship between money spent on crime reduction initiatives and successful outcomes because local contexts vary in ways that produce quite different interactions between the extra resources and local behaviour. While there will be circumstances when additional resources produce proportionate outcomes, it seems more common for additional resources to produce disproportionately large or small outcomes, or for the outcomes to vary unpredictably. Governments largely ignore this complexity in their tendency to make better outcomes—defined, measurable, and accountable—a condition of any extra public spending, together with the associated apparatus of performance management and audit. However, the systems into which extra resources are injected are too complex for the relationship to be so direct. Governments then turn to bad theory when the systems fail: it must be poor management that is to blame, and this can be exposed using performance indicators and league tables of performance, even though evidence is beginning to accumulate that this cannot be the sole or even main reason. For instance, White (2002) shows that the local level of deprivation almost perfectly explains differences in performance between many local authorities in London; where it does not, this seems to be a consequence of imperfections in the deprivation measure. In general, performance appears to be reflecting local conditions rather than significant variations in management competence.

A third and related theoretical problem with targets when addressing complex social problems is that the state of a system is regarded as amenable to command-and-control. An intervention in the initial conditions of a system produces an outcome that depends on both these initial conditions and the subsequent interaction between the intervention and the system's self-organisation. The potential for nonlinear change is huge under these conditions, and command-and-control will not bridge the implementation gap that can result from this complexity. In some organisations, management practice has adapted by striving for alignment between the values of the organisation and those of its employees and customers so that it can work on the basis of high levels of trust and adaptability rather than command-and-control and prescription. Fitz-Gibbon (1996) concludes from a study of school effectiveness that the key to effectiveness is to feed back information on valued outcomes to those responsible, so they can make adjustments that "close in" on the outcomes. The fact that outcomes are coproduced also means that the delivery organisation is not the only part of the system. Its customers, clients, and users coproduce the outcome by bringing their own resources and behaviour into an interaction with the service provider.

COMPLEXITY AND LEARNING IN PUBLIC POLICY

Intervening in complex social problems needs less prescription of detail and more intelligent accountability through reports and inspections for a smaller number of dimensions. As Plsek (2001) identifies, paradoxically the best way to achieve complex outcomes is to work with the self-organising capacities of local agents within a set of a few simple rules, rather than adopt the mechanistic approach of designing complex policy and procedural machinery that has led to the proliferation of targets considered earlier. Plsek and Wilson (2001) suggest that these dimensions should be limited to general direction pointing, boundary setting, resource allocation, and permissions. An example would be a policy on health inequalities. The policy approach could be a

Table 4.1   Comparing Organisational Cultures

Management by Targets	*Management by Learning*
Central leadership • *Command and control hierarchy*	Distributed leadership • *Alignment and teamwork*
Rule-based decision making • *Complete, detailed specifications*	Boundaries and permissions • *Few, simple rules*
Evaluation based on audit and performance measures • *High-stake indicators often published in league tables*	Evaluation based on scanning, feedback, and learning • *Contextualised data on outcomes of concern fed back to those responsible*
Users are units of resource and statistics	Users are coproducers and evaluators

general direction pointing that all policy areas contribute on an ongoing basis to health improvement actions that narrow inequalities. The boundaries could be that actions must have a user focus (such as user participation in programme design and evaluation), that each service shares a common aim and pools resources with at least one other (for example, housing and health promotion), and that demonstrable learning occurs from information feedbacks that prioritise evaluation by users (consultation, surveys, operational data). Actions would have to keep their spending within common formula-based budgets (to take account of local conditions) with multiagency access to them. Accountability would be based on open access to information and intelligent audit with a focus on theories of change rather than black box evaluation.

If performance management of target achievement is based on bad theory, it might be expected not to work. A leading figure in the U.K.'s New Labour government, David Blunkett, was recently quoted as saying, "There is mounting frustration in government that, after nearly five years in power, the promised transformation in public services has yet to be seen. Centrally set targets have proved elusive, and even the modest pledges of the 1997 election were unexpectedly difficult to achieve" (Perkins 2002). The problem has been an approach based on the introduction of targets that have little relationship to internal local system states and little regard for the influence on performance of wider system parameters.

Organisations that attend to their internal system state, especially the knowledge of their personnel,

trust, and alignment, and scan and respond to their environments, especially with scenario modelling and anticipatory planning, are *learning organisations.* This is a term now frequently encountered in the management literature, but there has been a surprising lack of engagement in this literature with pedagogic research, which might be expected to provide some useful clues for learning organisations. Issues of trust and blame, which now feature prominently in debates about targets and performance, are also prominent in debates about good pedagogy. For example, Biggs (1999) contrasts "theory X" and "theory Y" approaches to pedagogy, with the former assuming that students cannot be trusted and the latter supporting student autonomy and, in particular, student learning. Theory X is reflected in practices such as negative reinforcement using anxiety to "motivate," time stress, blame-the-student explanations of failure, cynicism towards lecturers perceived as not believing in what they are doing, and little input by students to decisions that affect them. The parallel with bad management practices is clear. Management by targets can engender a culture of "Who is to blame and who is to be rewarded?" while management by learning aims for a culture of "What do we know and how do we find out what works?" Table 4.1 elaborates this contrast.

An increasingly widespread approach to the learning organisation in public policy is the paradigm of evidence-based policy and practice (Trinder and Reynolds 2000). This is the approach taken by Fitz-Gibbon and Tymms (2002) to school improvement. They do not reject using indicators but emphasise the need for good "tracking" systems as well as controlled experimentation to find out what practices work best: performance management then becomes a collective research enterprise. For example, Fitz-Gibbon (1996) advocates the use of confidence intervals in monitoring indicators of exam performance that compare "value added" (residuals) with predictions of exam achievement derived from regression analysis using data on prior achievement. But although Fitz-Gibbon and Tymms (2002) argue for collecting a good range of indicators, there is an issue with their methodology due to the nature of public services as complex and interacting systems. Their approach implies that the general relationship between inputs and outputs is explainable in terms of linear regression, with residuals representing exceptions—either very good or very poor performance. In fact, typically more than half of such variation remains unexplained and the relationship between inputs and outputs is nonlinear and discontinuous. Interactions complicate any direct, uniform relationships between independent and dependent variables, with outcomes emerging from these interactions in ways that are very difficult to predict. This has led Byrne (2002) to argue that focusing on relationships between variables is the wrong approach, because what matters is *cases* (or systems) and how their condition is determined by their interactions with environmental parameters that make possible a number of system states (such as good performance and bad performance).

The problem has seen both management theory and policy evaluation methodology converge on complexity theory as a new type of systems thinking (Pawson and Tilley 1997; Stacey 2000). Complex phenomena have been the subject of this chapter, as most social problems are complex. They are characterised by nonlinear interactive processes, the emergence of new phenomena, patterns of both continuous and discontinuous change, and outcomes that cannot be predicted from past trends. The organisations that intervene in complex social problems are themselves complex adaptive systems, yet, as discussed above, policy and management approaches often do not enhance this adaptability but seek instead to regulate it (Zimmerman, Lindberg, and Plsek 2001).

Complexity reveals itself over time not in terms of uniform relationships but of *transitions* in system

behaviour due to interactions with either internal or external changes. A steady state represents convergence on what is called an "attractor" when, say, all the schools in a regional education system return much the same outcomes year-on-year. But a system may shift from a steady state if a key parameter changes, such as a cut in budgets or a new policy on selection. The system might begin transforming and outcomes flip between different values, with local systems—the schools—starting to diverge into different states (a phenomenon identified by Byrne and Rogers 1996). Finally, the parameter value may change further and shift the system into chaotic behaviour so that local systems start returning different values in wholly unpredictable ways. Although a conceptual sketch, this scenario might well capture the effects on delivery organisations of increasingly cutting back their budgets. It could, for example, explain the observation made by Blackman et al. (2001) that standards of social care for older people show increasing internal variability as the national social care system becomes less well resourced.

The greatest significance of an ability to learn is in dealing with uncertainty. Uncertainty is a feature of many social problems existing in the zone of complexity. OECD governments have responded by using scenario planning. This has focused on the effects of key parameter changes on system behaviour so that possible futures can be anticipated and planned for in the long term. In scenario planning language, the key parameters are known as "drivers" and the attractors are called "outcomes" or "worlds" (S. Davies et al. 2001). The phase transitions seen in the behaviour of complex systems are modelled in scenario planning by "wild cards" that hypothesise unexpected changes with significant impacts.

Returning to the example of national policy responses to ageing discussed above, the OECD (2000) has modelled possible ageing scenarios for nine countries using two key parameters, persons aged 65 and over and the labour market participation rate, with the dependency ratio as the outcome. The importance of the second parameter, the labour market participation rate, is important not only because of its effect on dependency ratios but also because it is much more susceptible to policy action than ageing. Three scenarios are modelled, all assuming that women's labour market participation continues to increase in line with recent trends. In the first "benchmark scenario," men's participation rate is assumed to continue to fall in line with recent trends. In the second "constant scenario," men's participation rate is kept stable, and in the third "reversal scenario," it gradually returns to that of 1960. The reversal scenario is therefore likely to counteract the effect of ageing on the dependency ratio. Modelling this effect shows that it has only a modest influence, but, if instead of the dependency ratio, outcomes are modelled for the share of the total population that is employed, a considerable easing of the effects of ageing is evident. The effect depends on the level of the existing participation rate; in Japan, where existing rates are high, the effect is far less pronounced. The reversal scenario is used to justify the authors' conclusion that there is nothing inevitable about the effects of population ageing. For most countries, policy measures that increase the participation of older workers in the labour market should substantially contain the economic effects of ageing. This presents a rather different picture to the "burden of care" perspective that has driven attempts to improve the targeting of services for older people.

This conclusion, though, should be qualified by noting the possibility of phase transitions caused by wild cards. Three demographic wild cards are identified in the scenario planning literature: massive migration from the developing world into the developed world; Europe and Japan failing to take the necessary policy measures to cope with the challenges of their ageing populations; and a collapse of the sperm count, causing an even more substantial decline in population replacement rates than forecast (S. Davies et al. 2001). Although immigration has been proposed as a way of addressing Europe's and Japan's decline in working age populations, the scale of immigration that would be necessary to offset declines in the ratio of working age populations to older people is huge: for Japan, Bermingham (2001) estimates that it would need to be 9.7 million immigrants per annum! Nevertheless, large-scale immigration remains a possibility, and the implications for the culture and society of the receiving countries are also huge, so much so that Byrne (2002) uses this scenario as an example of likely phase transition, in contrast to the OECD's reversal scenario, which envisages the use of policy measures to steer countries away from critical falls in the proportion of the existing population that is employed, with no qualitative transition in the nature of their societies. Which trajectory occurs depends on how the key parameters move and the policy decisions taken. The modelling presents a policy choice between increasing the employment participation of older people and large-scale immigration, with the latter likely to have least effect but most social and political impact.

CONCLUSION

This chapter began with a discussion of public policy as representing the public interest in relation to social problems. Recent developments such as welfare-to-work, neighbourhood targeting, and efficiency measures to cope with the affordability "crisis" of ageing have eroded universalist conceptions of welfare as social protection and the moderation of inequalities through redistributive mechanisms. While there are features of these developments that "work," there is a great danger that, as the QUEST designers recognise, "society" will become less and less meaningful because the extent of individualisation in policies, practices, discourses, and information means that people can no longer "see" the society that is emerging.

Management by targets is one aspect of this problem. The alternative to command-and-control is to create conditions in an organisation that are learning-orientated and discursive, and this is what is needed in order to intervene in complex social problems. It involves reformulating targets as feedbacks, the monitoring information needed to track change. If this information is fed back continuously, it encourages constant dialogue about what it means, what the organisation is achieving, and what it should be achieving.

Table 4.2 summarises how managing complexity looks quite different to managing by targets. In these examples, the systems are defined differently and the key variables and parameters are different. Public policy based on complexity should work better than policy based on targets and the theory

Table 4.2   Comparing Performance Management and Complexity

	Examples	
	Performance Management Paradigm	*Complexity Paradigm*
System boundaries	Administrative area Hospital	Local economy Care pathway
State variables	Housing voids and units Patient throughputs	Quality of life/livability Quality of care
System parameters	Targets Budget "silos"	Permissions Pooled budgets

X tools of audit culture because it is based on developing and testing theories about why things actually happen—in pedagogic terms, deep rather than surface learning. But there is also a need to establish where things are going and where we want them to go so that rather than just responding to trends, there is an explicit effort to steer the trajectory of social and economic change. What is needed is more QUESTs that involve people in public debate about social problems and social trends. People can then engage with these problems and trends as active and informed agents taking action to achieve desired social futures. Without this, action is likely to reflect individual interests because these are tangible, rather than the collective interest that is less tangible in modern and complex market economies.

Social problems create opportunities for system transformation if they become framed as turning points (or "crises," from the Greek *krinein*, to decide) inviting choices between alternative future scenarios. For example, the response of Japanese governments to the ageing issue during the 1980s was to promote more of the same: Japan's "welfare society" ideology, based in practical terms on the role of women as unpaid carers at home. However, in the face of women's political mobilisation against the extent of this imposed role and a broad-based popular campaign, the Japanese state has been forced to introduce long-term care insurance. This has expanded socialised care from its previous focus on low-income older people without family support to the middle class. Eto (2001) observes that the untenable situation experienced by many Japanese women meant that the "strong sense of crisis they felt often transformed ordinary housewives into feminists" (p. 21), but what is also significant is that, while the familial principle remains strong in the government reforms that have been made, progressive municipal mayors in Japan have used the introduction of long-term care insurance as an opportunity to build local welfare systems. These have developed as collective responses to the social and economic trends that the crisis of family care brought into the arena of public debate and political action.

The issue, then, is the availability of means that enable people to link their private concerns and preferences with an appreciation of, and engagement with, alternative outcomes at system or societal levels. Scenario planning, for example, should not be the preserve of experts and political elites but a popular practice. There is potential for this in the growth of computer modelling in schools and colleges as a tool for students to better understand the world around them and, in particular, to discover system behaviours that are not evident at an individual level (see, for example, Colella, Klopfer, and Resnick 2001). Using models that show how social problems and trends originate and develop should help to reestablish a public sphere for public policy. Byrne (2002) calls such computer-based models "macroscopes"; these increase the scale of our perspective from the traditional community level of observation and action, which has become detached from real economic and social processes, to the system level at which markets and governments operate. The significance of initiatives such as QUEST is that they take the macroscope concept further by showing how existing policy tools are available to take social trajectories in new and different directions: futures that are chosen, rather than futures that just arrive. Reich (2001) used the image of the giant genie in the quotation at the beginning of this chapter. With the computing power, modelling expertise, and Web access now available, perhaps the scenario he describes can move beyond fantasy to a reality of reflective societies.

REFERENCES

Bermingham, J. R. 2001. "Immigration: Not a Solution to Problems of Population Decline and Aging." *Population and Environment* 22:355–63.

Biggs, J. 1999. *Teaching for Quality Learning at University.* Buckingham, England: Open University Press.

Blackman, T., S. Brodhurst, and J. Convery. 2001. *Social Care and Social Exclusion.* Basingstoke, England: Palgrave.

Boardman, J. D., B. K. Finch, C. G. Ellison, D. R. Williams, and J. S. Jackson. 2001. "Neighbourhood Disadvantage, Stress, and Drug Use Among Adults." *Journal of Health and Social Behavior* 42:151–65.

Boeri, T., G. Hanson, and B. McCormick. 2002. *Immigration Policy and the Welfare System.* Oxford, England: Oxford University Press.

Boyne, G. A. 2002. "Concepts and Indicators of Local Authority Performance: An Evaluation of the Statutory Frameworks in England and Wales." *Public Money & Management* 22:17–24.

Burchardt, T., J. Le Grand, and D. Piachaud. 2002. "Introduction." In *Understanding Social Exclusion,* edited by J. Hills, J. Le Grand, and D. Piachaud. Oxford, England: Oxford University Press.

Buron, L., S. J. Popkin, D. Levy, L. E. Harris, and J. Khadduri. 2002. *The HOPE VI Resident Tracking Study.* Washington, DC: Urban Institute.

Byrne, D. 1999. *Social Exclusion.* Buckingham, England: Open University Press.

———. 2002. *Interpreting Quantitative Data.* London, England: Sage.

Byrne, D. and T. Rogers. 1996. "Divided Spaces—Divided School: An Exploration of the Spatial Relations of Social Division." *Sociological Research Online* 1 (2). Retrieved from www.socresonline.org. uk/socresonline/1/2/3.html.

Campbell, J. C. 2002. *Japanese Social Policy in Comparative Perspective.* Washington, DC: World Bank Institute.

Campbell, M. 2002. "Beyond the Fragments? Growth, Jobs and Inclusion." In *Joined-Up Regeneration: Objective 1 and Urban Regeneration—Grasping a Unique Opportunity,* edited by Sheffield Hallam University. Sheffield, England: Sheffield Hallam University Press.

Cantle, T. 2001. *Community Cohesion: A Report of the Independent Review Team.* London, England: Home Office.

Clarke, J. and F. F. Piven. 2001. "United States: An American Welfare State?" In *International Social Policy,* edited by P. Alcock and G. Craig. Basingstoke, England: Palgrave.

Colella, V. S., E. Klopfer, and M. Resnick. 2001. *Adventures in Modeling: Exploring Complex, Dynamic Systems with StarLogo.* New York: Teachers College Press.

Davey-Smith, G., S. Ebrahim, and S. Frankel. 2001. "How Policy Informs the Evidence." *British Medical Journal* 322:184–5.

Davies, B., J. Fernandez, and B. Nomer. 2001. *Equity and Efficiency Policy in Community Care: Needs, Service Productivities, Efficiencies and Their Implications.* Aldershot, England: Ashgate.

Davies, S., B. Boland, K. Fisk, and M. Purvis. 2001. *Strategic Futures Thinking: Meta-Analysis of Published Materials on Drivers and Trends.* London, England: Cabinet Office Performance and Innovation Unit.

Downes, D. 2001. "The Macho Penal Economy: Mass Incarceration in the United States—a European Perspective." *Punishment & Society* 3:61–80.

Duncan, C., K. Jones, and G. Moon. 1999. "Smoking and Deprivation: Are There Neighbourhood Effects?" *Social Science and Medicine* 48:497–505.

Emirbayer, M. 1997. "Manifesto for a Relational Sociology." *American Journal of Sociology* 103:281–317.

Eto, M. 2001. "Public Involvement in Social Policy Reform: Seen from the Perspective of Japan's Elderly-Care Insurance Scheme." *Journal of Social Policy* 30:17–36.

Ezawa, A. 2002. "Japan's 'New Homeless.'" *Journal of Social Distress and the Homeless* 11:279–91.

Fitz-Gibbon, C. T. 1996. *Monitoring Education: Indicators, Quality and Effectiveness.* London, England: Cassell.

Fitz-Gibbon, C. T. and P. Tymms. 2002. "Technical and Ethical Issues in Indicator Systems: Doing Things Right and Doing Things Wrong." *Education Policy Analysis Archives* 10 (6). Retrieved from www.epaa. asu.eda/epaa/v10n6.

Garon, S. 2002. *Japanese Policies toward Poverty and Public Assistance.* Washington, DC: World Bank Institute.

Giarchi, G. G. 1996. *Caring for Older Europeans: Comparative Studies in 29 Countries.* Aldershot, England: Arena.

Giddens, A. 1998. *The Third Way: The Renewal of Social Democracy.* Cambridge, England: Polity Press.

Goodman, R. 2002a. "Child Abuse in Japan: 'Discovery' and the Development of Policy." In *Family and Social Policy in Japan,* edited by R. Goodman. Cambridge, England: Cambridge University Press.

———. 2002b. "Anthropology, Policy and the Study of Japan." In *Family and Social Policy in Japan,* edited by R. Goodman. Cambridge, England: Cambridge University Press.

Hamnett, C. 1997. "A Stroke of the Chancellor's Pen: The Social and Regional Impact of the Conservative's 1988 Higher Rate Tax Cuts." *Environment and Planning A* 29:129–47.

Healey, P. 2002. "On Creating the 'City' as a Collective Resource." *Urban Studies* 39:1777–92.

Hill, D. M. 2000. *Urban Policy and Politics in Britain.* London, England: Palgrave.

Hirschfield, A., D. Abrahams, R. Barnes, J. Hendley, and A. Scott-Samuel. 2001. *Health Impact Assessment: Measuring the Effect of Public Policy on Variations in Health: Final Report.* Liverpool, England: University of Liverpool Department of Civic Design and Department of Public Health.

Hugman, R. 1994. *Ageing and the Care of Older People in Europe.* Basingstoke, England: Macmillan.

Izuhara, M. 2002. "Care and Inheritance: Japanese and English Perspectives on the 'Generational Contract.'" *Ageing and Society* 22:61–77.

Kleinschmidt, I., M. Hills, and P. Elliott. 1995. "Smoking Behaviour Can Be Predicted by Neighbourhood Deprivation Measures." *Journal of Epidemiology and Community Health* 49 (Suppl. 2):S72–S77.

Lupton, R. and A. Power. 2002. "Social Exclusion and Neighbourhoods." In *Understanding Social Exclusion,* edited by J. Hills, J. Le Grand, and D. Piachaud. Oxford, England: Oxford University Press.

Mackenbach, J. P., M. J. Bakker, A. E. Kunst, and F. Diderichsen. 2002. "Socioeconomic Inequalities in Health in Europe: An Overview." In *Reducing Inequalities in Health: A European Perspective,* edited by J. Mackenbach and M. Bakker. London, England: Routledge.

Marsh, A., D. Gordon, C. Pantazis, and P. Heslop. 1999. *Home Sweet Home? The Impact of Poor Housing on Health.* Bristol, England: Policy Press.

Martinson, K. and P. A. Holcomb. 2002. *Reforming Welfare: Institutional Change and Challenges.* Assessing the New Federalism Occasional Paper No. 60, Washington, DC: Urban Institute.

McLoone, P. 2001. "Targeting Deprived Areas within Small Areas in Scotland: Population Study." *British Medical Journal* 323:374–5.

Mitchell, R., D. Dorling, and M. Shaw. 2000. *Inequalities in Life and Death.* Bristol, England: Policy Press.

Netherlands Institute for Care and Welfare. 2002. *Local Social Policy in the Netherlands.* Factsheet. Utrecht, Netherlands: NIZW.

Nevin, B., P. Lee, L. Goodson, A. Murie, and J. Phillimore. 2001. *Changing Housing Markets and Urban Regeneration in the M62 Corridor.* Birmingham, England: Centre for Urban and Regional Studies, University of Birmingham.

Newman, J. 2001. *Modernising Governance: New Labour, Policy and Society.* London, England: Sage.

OECD. 2000. *Reforms for an Ageing Society.* Paris. France: Author.

———. 2001. *Fiscal Implications of Ageing: Projections of Age-Related Spending.* Economics Department Working Paper No. 305, Paris, France: Author. Retrieved from www.oecd.org/eco/eco.

Olds, D. L., J. Eckenrode, C. R. Henderson, H. Kitzman, J. Powers, R. Cole, K. Sidora, P. Morris, L. M. Pettitt, and D. Luckey. 1997. "Long-Term Effects of Home Visitation on Maternal Life Course and Child Abuse and Neglect: Fifteen-Year Follow-Up of a Randomized Trial." *Journal of the American Medical Association* 278:680–1.

O'Neill, O. 2002. "Called to Account." Reith Lectures 2002, Lecture 3. Retrieved from www.bbc.co.uk/radi04/reitH3002/3.shtml.

Örtendahl, C. 2002. "Sweden." In *Health Targets in Europe,* edited by M. Marinker. London, England: BMJ Books.

Pawson, R. and N. Tilley. 1997. *Realistic Evaluation.* London, England: Sage.

Perkins, A. 2002. "Blunkett Speaks for Devolved Services." *The Guardian,* February 2. Retrieved from *Guardian Unlimited,* www.guardian.co.uk/uk_news/story/0,3604,643575,00.html.

Plsek, P. 2001. "Redesigning Health Care with Insights from the Science of Complex Adaptive Systems." In *Crossing the Quality Chasm: A New Health System for the 21st Century.* Committee on Quality Health Care in America, Institute of Medicine. Washington, DC: National Academy Press.

Plsek, P. E. and T. Wilson. 2001. "Complexity, Leadership, and Management in Healthcare Organisations." *British Medical Journal* 323:746–9.

Reade, E. 1987. *British Town and Country Planning.* Milton Keynes, England: Open University Press.

Reich, R. B. 2001. *The Future of Success.* London, England: William Heinemann.

Reijneveld, S. A. 1998. "The Impact of Individual and Area Characteristics on Urban Socioeconomic Differences in Health and Smoking." *International Journal of Epidemiology* 27:33–40.

Salonen, T. 2001. "Sweden: Between Model and Reality." In *International Social Policy,* edited by P. Alcock and G. Craig. Basingstoke, England: Palgrave.

Scharf, T., C. Phillipson, A. E. Smith, and P. Kingston. 2002. *Growing Older in Socially Deprived Areas: Social Exclusion in Later Life.* London, England: Help the Aged.

Shaw, V. 2002. "Trusts on the Way to Take on Kids' Services." *Local Government Chronicle,* 2 August, p. 3.

Smith, P. 1995. "On the Unintended Consequences of Publishing Performance Data in the Public Sector." *International Journal of Public Administration* 18:277–310.

Stacey, R. D. 2000. *Strategic Management & Organisational Dynamics.* Harlow, England: Prentice Hall.

Stoesz, D. 2002. "The American Welfare State at Twilight." *Journal of Social Policy* 31: 487–504.

Thomson, H., M. Petticrew, and D. Morrison. 2002. *Housing Improvement and Health Gain: A Summary and Systematic Review.* Glasgow, Scotland: Medical Research Council Social & Public Health Sciences Unit, University of Glasgow.

Townsend, P. 2002. "Human Rights, Transnational Corporations and the World Bank." In *World Poverty: New Policies to Defeat an Old Enemy,* edited by P. Townsend and D. Gordon. Bristol, England: Policy Press.

Trinder, L. and S. Reynolds, eds. 2000. *Evidence-Based Practice: A Critical Appraisal.* Oxford, England: Blackwell Science.

Van Oorschot, W. 2002. "Miracle or Nightmare? A Critical Review of Dutch Activation Policies and Their Outcomes." *Journal of Social Policy* 31:399–420.

Wacquant, L. 2001. "Deadly Symbiosis: When Ghetto and Prison Meet and Merge." *Punishment & Society* 3:95–134.

Waddan, A. 2003. "Redesigning the Welfare Contract in Theory and Practice: Just What Is Going On in the USA?" *Journal of Social Policy* 32:19–36.

Walker, A. and T. Maltby. 1997. *Ageing Europe.* Buckingham, England: Open University Press.

Watanabe, S. 2000. "The Japan Model and the Future of Employment and Wage Systems." *International Labour Review* 139:307–33.

Webster, D. 2002. "Unemployment: How Official Statistics Distort Analysis and Policy, and Why." Paper presented at the Radical Statistics Annual Conference, University of Northumbria at Newcastle, UK, 16 February. Available from david.webster @gch.glasgow.gov.uk.

White, S. 2002. "League Leaders." *Local Government Chronicle,* 19 April, pp. 12–13.

Zimmerman, B., C. Lindberg, and P. Plsek. 2001. *Edgeware: Insights from Complexity Science for Health Care Leaders.* Irving, Texas: VHA Inc.

SOCIAL PROBLEMS

5

POPULATION CHANGE

SONALDE DESAI

University of Maryland

ANATOMY OF POPULATION EXPLOSION

In 2002, the world's population was estimated to be about 6.2 billion. This reflects a fourfold increase from about 1.6 billion at the turn of the century (Gelbard, Haub, and Kent 1999), a striking contrast to the growth of the human population during the 200,000 years human beings have populated the earth. It is estimated that on the eve of agricultural revolution, the world's population was about 4 million, but grew rapidly once human societies moved from hunting and gathering to stable agriculture. By the first century A.D., the population is estimated to have been a little more than 200 million. In the following 17 centuries, the population grew steadily, although plagues and famines took their toll from time to time, with the world population approaching about a billion at the start of the industrial revolution in the mid-eighteenth century (Gelbard et al. 1999). Thus, for tens of thousands of years, the world population grew slowly, but in the last 200 years it has reached over 6 billion people. It is not surprising that the term *population explosion* has been coined to describe this phenomenon (Weeks 1999).

However, it is important to remember that in each era in which major population expansion has taken place, it has been accompanied by positive developments. During the hunting and gathering stage, a large amount of land was required to support a small population, resulting in food shortages as the population grew. However, a move from hunting and gathering to agricultural society increased the "carrying capacity" of the earth, allowing for a population expansion, as did a move from slash-and-burn agriculture to a stable intensive cropping pattern (Boserup 1976). In most recent times, the spurt of population growth began in Western Europe with the onset of the industrial revolution and spread to developing countries in the twentieth century. Much of this expansion is caused by a decline in mortality. For the United States, it is estimated that if the United States had not experienced any improvements in mortality since 1900, the population would only be half its current size; one quarter of the present population would have been born and died and the other quarter would not have been born at all (White and Preston 1996).

POPULATION CHANGE AND SOCIAL PROBLEMS

Over the past few decades, the rapid growth in population has sounded many alarms around the world. It has been argued that unchecked population growth will lead to many negative outcomes for individuals, nations, and the world. Having large families makes it difficult for parents to care for their children properly; growing populations demand more schools, hospitals, and jobs, increasing the burdens on poor nations; population growth results in environmental degradation affecting the whole world. Many developing countries have established strong family planning programs to control their population, and China has adopted a very stringent birth planning policy that requires most Chinese couples to stop after one child.[1] Developed countries are equally concerned about changing the composition of the world with a rapid population increase in poor countries, so they provide assistance to poor countries to develop family planning programs.

However, the specific ways in which population changes affect societies vary across countries, as do actions required to deal with population growth. Societies with growing economies such as the East Asian countries are better able to accommodate population growth than sub-Saharan countries with low rates of economic growth. Similarly, Costa Rica has tried to address the problem of population growth by investing in education and child health, Indonesia has set up a strong family planning program, and China and Singapore have emphasized strong sanctions against people who have too many children. While poor countries are trying to deal with problems associated with growing populations, industrial societies are trying to deal with strains of declining and aging populations.

Thus, any examination of social problems associated with population growth must start with a better understanding of different dimensions of population change and locate these trends within a broader socioeconomic landscape. This chapter examines the trends in three major factors that affect the size of national populations: mortality, fertility, and migration. By focusing on changes in these determinants of the ultimate population size in historical and cross-cultural contexts, the chapter seeks to understand the problems associated with changing fertility, mortality, and migration patterns and to trace public policy options for dealing with these problems.

MORTALITY DECLINE AND POPULATION GROWTH

Life expectancy at birth[2] in the Roman era is estimated to be around 22 years, rising to around 35 in the Middle Ages for Western Europe (Petersen 1975). Since the industrial revolution, however, life expectancy has been steadily improving, with a rapid improvement in the twentieth century. Average life expectancy at birth increased from about 40 to 45 at the turn of the century in various parts of Western Europe and in the United States to around 60 to 65 by the 1950s, and it is currently around 72 to 76. Changes in developing countries have been equally dramatic, with Indian life expectancy increasing from about 23 years in 1900 to about 39 years in 1950 and about 60 years in 1990 (Gelbard et al. 1999). This epidemiological transition in Europe and the United States has been attributed to improving nutrition (McKeown and Record 1962) and improvement in the knowledge of germ theory, resulting in a better understanding of the ways in which diseases are spread, and a consequent improvement in hygiene and sanitation (Preston and Haines 1991). In contrast to the slow mortality decline in the developed countries, developing countries have experienced a rapid drop in mortality by learning from the experiences of the developed countries and implementing vigorous public health and vaccination campaigns.

These dramatic improvements in life expectancy have been particularly effective at very young ages. In the premodern era, when life expectancy was around 20 years, nearly 53 percent of children died before reaching age 5. In contrast, in the year 2000, with average world life expectancy of 68, only about 3 percent of the children die before age 5. Even in the poorest countries of the world (such as Uganda, Zambia, and Sierra Leone), where life expectancy is around 40, the proportion of children dying before age 5 has been reduced to about 27 percent (Weeks 1999). This phenomenal decline in mortality has had a number of consequences, both positive and negative. On the one hand, by reducing mortality risks, particularly at very young ages, the mortality transition has significantly improved the quality of life, even in the poorest countries of the world. On the other hand, the mortality decline is directly responsible for the population explosion we witness today.

Societies with a high level of mortality require higher fertility to compensate for the loss of life. It is estimated that with a life expectancy of 20, an average couple must have 6.1 children for a society to replace itself, that is, attain zero population growth. As mortality declines, the replacement level fertility rate goes from 6.1 children per woman to 4.2 children, 3.3 children, and 2.1 children for life expectancy levels of 30, 40, and 68 respectively (Weeks 1999). Over the long term, most societies seem to respond to mortality decline by reducing childbearing, a phenomenon that has been described as "demographic transition" (Notestein 1953; Thompson 1930). However, while mortality decline improves the quality of life and longevity is sought after eagerly by individuals, fertility decline is far from being universally desirable and involves tremendous social changes in marriage and family building patterns. Thus, while mortality decline is ultimately accompanied by fertility decline, the pace of these two changes often varies, resulting in high levels of population growth between the two regimes, one governed by high fertility and mortality and the other governed by low fertility and mortality.

FERTILITY TRANSITION

While mortality decline is the first phase of demographic transition, a movement from the regime of "natural fertility" to that of controlled fertility is the second phase of demographic transition. The term *natural fertility* refers to the fertility patterns observed in a noncontracepting population. However, it is important to note that even pretransitional societies did not encourage situations in which people had as many children as biology permitted. Even

among the Hutterites, a socioreligious sect living near the U.S.-Canada border with the highest recorded fertility in the world, on average women only had about nine children in their lifetime. Since theoretically a woman can bear children between ages 15 and 45, a 30-year reproductive lifespan should allow for many more births, as evidenced by many women in traditional societies who have given birth 15 or more times. On the whole, even high fertility societies such as Kenya, Morocco, and Egypt in the 1950s have recorded a Total Fertility Rate (TFR)[3] of only about 6 to 7 children.

What kept the fertility rate from reaching its theoretical maximum in these noncontracepting populations? Biological as well as social forces have played an important role in curtailing fertility even in the absence of modern contraception. Long periods of breastfeeding, often as long as three years, curtailed the return of ovulation and hence increased the interval between births (Simpson-Herbert and Huffman 1981); social practices frowned upon the resumption of intercourse following birth—for example, the medieval church, influenced by the second-century anatomist Galen, ruled that couples should abstain from sexual relations until their child had been weaned (Santow 1995); in some societies like India, sexual relations in middle age are frowned upon, and shame at a "grandmother pregnancy" leads to celibacy once an oldest son or daughter has a child. Delayed marriage was quite common in many societies, and where early marriages are practiced (such as in India), the girl often resides with her parents following marriage, thereby increasing the age at effective marriage (Basu 1993). All of these factors combine to keep fertility below its theoretical maximum (Bongaarts 1975).

Fertility transition, however, involves deliberate control of childbearing on the part of individuals, quite distinct from the fertility control that involuntarily occurs due to social norms regarding breastfeeding or the appropriateness of sexual relationships under certain circumstances. In industrial and many industrializing societies, fertility transition has wrought phenomenal changes in family composition. In a space of 50 years, world fertility has fallen from a fertility rate of 5 children per woman to 2.8 children per woman, with some European countries having fertility rates of 1.2 or lower (U.N. Population Division 2001).

How do we explain when, where, and why the fertility transition takes place? Ansley Coale (1973), a noted demographer, has described three preconditions for the fertility transition:

1. *Fertility control must be within the calculus of rational choice.* This precondition goes to the heart of human behavior. Instead of assuming that the number of children one has is determined by God, individual couples must see childbearing as something that is within their conscious control.

2. *Reduced fertility must be seen as being socially and economically advantageous.* Individuals must feel that having fewer children or postponing childbearing is desirable, given their life circumstances; otherwise, they would have no reason to adopt a means of fertility control.

3. *Effective techniques of birth control must be available.* Even when individuals want to limit fertility, pregnancy can only be controlled if effective means of birth control are available. The advance of modern contraception has increased individuals' ability to control their fertility beyond anything available to people in centuries past. But even before the advent of the pill, traditional methods of contraception, including withdrawal, rhythm, and sponge, had been quite effective. However, knowledge of these methods was more easily available in some societies than in others.

Factors Shaping Fertility Transition

While these three conditions describe the basic process of fertility decline, why specific societies begin fertility transition at any given point in their history has been the subject of much debate among demographers. Three major explanations have been advanced: (1) Rational choice theories suggest that at particular junctures in history, such structural conditions as urbanization and industrialization reduce the economic advantages of having a large family; (2) ideational theories suggest that cultural rather than structural forces change how people view children and childbearing, and at a certain point in the sociocultural history of a society, children begin to be seen as a liability to personal freedom and achievement, resulting in a move from a regime of "natural fertility" to controlled fertility; and (3) theories focusing on cost and availability of contraception suggest that there is substantial unwanted fertility in any society that is curtailed when effective means of fertility control become available. Since these explanations result in totally different public policy prescriptions for fertility control, they have been the subject of considerable debate.

Structural or rational choice theories emerged with demographic transition theories (Notestein 1953; Thompson 1930), which suggested that industrialization and urbanization create a way of life that makes having more than a few children impractical. Industrialization also reduces mortality, increasing the number of surviving children and creating resource constraints on parents. These resource constraints manifest themselves in many ways, including land fragmentation, and lead parents to curtail family size. The rational choice approach received a boost with the emergence of economic theories based on new home economics (Becker 1993). Economists developed elaborate models in which children were seen as being similar to many other goods parents consumed, requiring both time and monetary input on the part of parents. The time component of child rearing became particularly important as women increasingly began to work in nonagricultural settings. As long as women worked largely on family farms or as petty traders, they could care for their children while working. This was particularly important for young children who required breastfeeding (Ho 1979; Lloyd 1991; Mason and Palan 1981). However, once they began participating in waged labor in nonagricultural settings, they lost this flexibility. Simultaneously, urbanization led to declining social support systems and availability of extended family members who could provide child care. Thus, increased demands on women's time meant that they had to make a distinct choice between work and large families (Presser 2001). Economic development also increased the costs of child rearing by increasing the educational requirements for the new labor force, making it more rational for parents to have fewer, but better educated, children rather than many children with low levels of education (Bledsoe et al. 1999).

While costs of child rearing increased, economic benefits to children declined. In rural, largely agricultural economies, children become economically productive at very young ages; in sub-Saharan Africa, it is estimated that by age seven, a child begins to produce more than he or she consumes (Caldwell 1976). However, as societies begin to urbanize and industrialize, fewer jobs are available to children, and increased educational demands also reduce the time children spend working. Consequently, costs of child rearing increase.

Economic development is also associated with an increased role of government and public mechanisms in providing a number of services formerly provided by the family. For example, the emergence of social security and pension schemes reduced parental reliance on children, particularly sons, for old age support (Demeny 1987; Livi-Bacci 2001). Improved medical technology ensured that although people lived longer, they lived healthier lives and were able to take care of themselves well into older ages (Crimmins, Saito, and Ingegneri 1997), and at the same time, nursing homes and medical professionals began replacing children as primary caretakers for the elderly. Urbanization also ensured that adult children were often separated from their rural roots and reduced extended family ties, resulting in the process of "emotional nucleation" and reducing children's willingness to support their elderly parents (Caldwell 1976).

This story of economic development, resulting in urbanization, education, women's participation in wage labor, and, consequently, increasing the conflict between consumption and having large numbers of children, seems theoretically consistent and intuitively appealing. This led many developing countries to rally behind a cry of "Development is the Best Contraceptive" at the 1974 United Nations Population Conference held in Bucharest (Finkle and Crane 1975). However, in spite of the appeal of the rational choice models, empirical evidence supporting the theory has been far from consistent.

A number of inconsistencies undermine the structural explanations. While the Western nations experienced both economic growth and fertility

decline, the timing of these changes did not always correspond with demographic transition theory. The Princeton European Fertility Project, a massive compilation of data from a large number of European countries, documented that countries like France experienced fertility decline at relatively low levels of development, while countries like England were late starters and began fertility transition at a much higher level of development (Coale 1986). An analysis of age-specific marital fertility in European populations suggests that birth order-specific fertility control, used by demographers to measure deviation from natural fertility, was largely absent before the 1880s in most countries, with the notable exception of France. Between 1880 and 1930, fertility control seems to have spread through Europe, with the onset of transition being only weakly correlated to socioeconomic factors but strongly linked to language and culture, particularly demonstrated by the difference in fertility between the Flemish and French-speaking provinces of Belgium (Cleland 2001). Moreover, several developing regions, including Sri Lanka, India, China, and Bangladesh, have entered fertility transition far earlier than their levels of economic development would predict (Bongaarts and Watkins 1996). Classic demographic transition theory argues that mortality decline is a precondition to fertility decline. However, the Princeton European Fertility project, in examining a decade-by-decade variation in fertility and mortality, found that fertility declined at dramatically different levels of mortality across different regions, and in one or two cases fertility decline began even before mortality decline (Van de Walle 1986). These findings have been interpreted to suggest that social and cultural forces play an important role in determining the onset of fertility transition by making the notion of controlled fertility as well as contraceptive use acceptable to people.

This sociocultural perspective, often called the "diffusion perspective," has significant policy implications. Unlike the rational choice perspective, which emphasizes the importance of structural changes, the diffusion perspective suggests that fertility decline can occur under varying socioeconomic conditions once people begin to understand the importance of small families and find contraceptive use acceptable. Mass communication plays an important role in this, and research shows that fertility rates are considerably lower for women who watch television regularly, even in a less developed region like Africa (Westoff and Rodriguez 1995). This would imply that national governments could act as agents of social change by utilizing mass media and other forms of communication to suggest to couples that fertility reduction could be both socially and personally beneficial. These strategies, often dubbed "Information, Education, and Communication" strategies, could be particularly useful in providing individuals with information regarding social changes that might not be immediately apparent to them from their personal experiences. For example, mortality decline and its impact on surviving family size may not be immediately apparent to couples (Montgomery and Cohen 1997), since they are unlikely to have access to mortality statistics. Providing this information may reduce fertility by making couples aware that they do not need to have a large number of children in order to ensure against potential mortality risks.

The diffusion perspective, however, is not without its critics. Hammel (1995) comes to the conclusion that language and ethnicity in Balkan fertility decline was often a proxy for other political factors. Mason (1997), following pioneering work by Davis (1963), convincingly argues that fertility control is only one possible response to structural changes. Thus, while the French may have chosen fertility control in response to structural changes, the English chose migration, with children from large families migrating to the colonies in order to reduce the burden on the land. Moreover, the Princeton European Fertility Project relied on the emergence of parity-specific fertility control as a marker of fertility transition, but families could choose to control family size more directly. Ethnographic evidence from many societies, including those in the West, shows instances of widespread infanticide, abandonment of children, neglect in the hopes that they die, fostering, adoption, and selling children into servitude or apprenticeship (Mason 1997). All of these strategies can reduce effective family size and can even provide parents with the desired age and sex composition of children. These strategies would affect family size but would not result in fertility control, thereby weakening the link between structural conditions and family size in studies like the Princeton European Fertility Project. These critiques call into question the assumption by diffusion theorists that regulation of fertility is fundamentally different in pre- and posttransitional societies, with individuals in pretransitional societies being simply governed by social rules and only beginning to make conscious decisions regarding the number of children they have, once the fertility transition takes place. This negation of individual agency in pretransitional societies is tied in to the notion that culture is a relatively rigid template affecting individual behavior, a notion increasingly challenged by anthropologists (Hammel 1990).

The third perspective argues that regardless of what leads people to want fewer children, they cannot do so unless effective contraceptives are available. Thus, instead of the adage "Development is the best contraceptive," this view argues that "although development and social change create conditions that encourage smaller family size, contraceptives are the best contraceptive" (Robey, Ruttstein, and Morris 1993). While there is much anecdotal evidence of unwanted pregnancies, demographic surveys in a large number of developing countries carried out in the 1970s and 1980s provided the first numerical estimates of the number of women who did not want any more children but were not using contraception. There are manifold reasons why couples do not use contraception, even when they do not want more children. These include lack of knowledge regarding contraceptive techniques, difficulty in obtaining contraception, high cost of contraception, side effects, partner disapproval, social unacceptability of contraception, infrequent sex, and subfecundity (Bongaarts and Bruce 1995). According to one estimate, as many as 24 percent of all births in Africa are unwanted (Bongaarts and Bruce 1995). This has provided a rationale for state-sponsored family planning programs, and it has been argued that investments in family planning programs have been important for triggering fertility decline, particularly in developing countries where fertility decline began at a far lower level of socioeconomic development. According to a project in

1990, in the absence of a current commitment to family planning programs by the world community and national governments, the population of the world could be expected to reach 14.6 billion in year 2100 instead of the 10 billion projected by World Bank data (Bongaarts, Mauldin, and Phillips 1990).

This has been dubbed the "supply side" view of fertility decline as opposed to the "demand side" view, which emphasizes social change and a resultant change in the desired number of children. The critiques of the supply side approach argue that increased availability of contraception is simply a response to an increased demand for it. Increases in income, education, urbanization, and women's participation in wage labor create conditions in which individuals desire smaller families. Once this desire to control fertility exists, individuals will find ways of doing it. If modern contraceptives are available, they will be used; otherwise, individuals will rely on traditional methods, including periodic abstinence, withdrawal, abortion, and infanticide (Pritchett 1994). Fertility transition in Western Europe and the United States was achieved mainly without any help from modern contraceptives and mainly under disapproval of the state and the religious clerics. Urban white women of native parentage in the northeastern United States in 1900 had such low fertility that they did not reproduce themselves (Sanderson 1987). They managed to achieve below replacement fertility while living under Comstock Laws, which made dissemination of contraceptive information illegal, designed precisely to prevent such "race suicide" due to the tendency of alien immigrants to outbreed the natives. In modern times, the lowest fertility is found in Spain, Italy, and Belgium—Catholic nations where the state has done relatively little to promote family planning.

Delayed marriage and nonmarriage, a response recommended by Malthus, have been an important strategy used by families to control fertility in the absence of modern contraception (Dixon 1978). Research on Ireland offers an interesting insight into this process. Following the Great Potato Famine in 1845, there was a consolidation in landholding, with a movement to raising cattle rather than intensive tillage. This demanded larger farm sizes (Jackson 1984) and led to severe land shortages. While the Irish attempted to deal with this via emigration, for those who remained the addition of a bride to a family meant a reduction in the standard of living for the groom's family, unless she brought substantial dowry. Marriage of a daughter brought with it a need to supply a dowry. Thus, postponement of marriage or nonmarriage was a strategy that many families used to conserve their standards of living. Mean age at marriage for Irish women around 1900 was about 31, and nearly 20 percent never married (Dixon 1978; Sklar 1977). These unmarried women largely ended up as nuns or spinster aunts in their brothers' homes, and some migrated to the United States (Jackson 1984). A similar control of marriage is observed in rural India in the mid-twentieth century, with informal fraternal polyandry being practiced by brothers in households to avoid family partition and land fragmentation (Das Gupta 1995).

While exploring and evaluating these different theoretical perspectives, it is important to remember two tensions facing the field of population studies:

1. The issues addressed by population studies incite popular and governmental passions, and research funding for demography has been abundant. This has been a mixed blessing. On one hand, policy interest in the field has allowed for large data-gathering projects and research centers vital to the development of a multidisciplinary field with strong data needs. On the other hand, a need to provide a quick policy fix to myriad population problems distorts the focus and channels energies into developing immediate programs and actions that governments can undertake as opposed to understanding long-term fundamental social processes.

2. Research on fertility and family formation is an important part of many disciplines, including sociology, anthropology, history, economics, and biology. Moreover, unlike many other subfields of various disciplines, the field of demography works actively to bring together individuals and perspectives from different disciplines with a focus on empirical research. The tensions inherent in any multidisciplinary field are further exacerbated by the vast geographical and historical scope of the phenomena under study.

One way of resolving the tensions associated with policy orientation may be to distinguish between the immediate programs a government can undertake and the long-term policies that shape social institutions, with the latter being of greater interest to social sciences. Policies regarding social security, child support, and child care are particularly important in this regard. Overcoming the barriers posed by the multidisciplinary nature of population studies is more challenging because it juxtaposes several dilemmas faced by social sciences, namely the contradictions between structure and agency, explaining stability as well as change, and looking for universal patterns while respecting historical and contextual specificity.

While constituting only a minority of the research on fertility, some of the most creative and synthetic frameworks in fertility studies move beyond disciplinary perspectives and attempt to deal with these challenges (Ginsburg and Rapp 1999; Greenhalgh 1990; McNicoll 1980). These studies locate themselves at the nexus of structural forces and individual agency by focusing on a diverse set of topics. These include the expansion of church, state, and capitalist interests in former Spanish, French, and Dutch colonies and the formation of sexual unions and support of children (Stoler 1989); marriage and childbearing among the poor and minority populations in the United States in the context of increasing marginalization and alienation (Edin 2000; Wilson and Neckerman 1986); and coercive state policies in China and women's negotiation of their own childbearing within these autocratic structures (Greenhalgh and Li 1995).

PROSPECTS FOR WORLD POPULATION GROWTH

It is clear that fertility decline has begun in many countries around the world. Bangladesh, once considered a country most unlikely to experience fertility decline, has experienced a rapid drop in TFR from 6.8 in the mid-1980s to 3.8 in the late 1990s (U.N. Population Division 2001). Fertility decline in northern and southern Africa is already well under way. Fertility in western Africa and parts of East Africa remains high, but even here, signs of fertility decline are evident in many countries (U.N. Population Division 2001). Although it is impossible to forecast how the pace of fertility decline will proceed, past experience indicates that unlike historical fertility transitions in Europe, once fertility begins to decline in modern times, this decline is very rapid. South Korean fertility fell from a TFR of 5.6 in the early 1960s to 1.51 in the late 1990s; even a traditional country like Egypt went from a TFR of 6.5 to 3.4 in a span of 30 years. While some demographers do not expect the fertility decline in Africa to be as rapid as in other parts of the world (Gelbard et al. 1999) due to widespread poverty, high illiteracy, and strong traditional preference for large families, even in Africa there are instances of rapid decline, such as in Kenya, where fertility fell from 7.9 to 4.6 in a period of 20 years (U.N. Population Division 2001).

Hence, the United Nations projects that world fertility will continue to decline from a present average of 2.82 children per woman to a near replacement level of 2.15 children per woman by the year 2050. Even for the least developed nations, fertility is expected to fall from a level of 5.77 at present to 2.51 by the year 2050 (U.N. Population Division 2001).

However, a decline in fertility is not tantamount to halting population growth. Two other factors will continue to increase population:

1. Mortality continues to decline without any signs that we have reached a biological maximum of life expectancy (Oeppen and Vaupel 2002). Current life expectancy at birth in developing countries is around 63, and in the poorest countries is around 51. It can reasonably be expected to increase to about 75, the current life expectancy in industrial societies. Thus, barring an escalation in the incidence of AIDS, other epidemics of global proportion, or worldwide famine, we have not yet reached the end of a mortality revolution.

2. As a result of past high fertility, many countries have a vast majority of their population below age 15. For example, while population under age 15 composes only 18 percent of industrial societies, it forms 33 percent of the population of less developed nations. These young people will soon reach childbearing age. Thus, even if fertility were to decline to

Table 5.1   Population Growth in World Regions, 1750 to 2050

Region/Country	*Population in Millions*				
	1750	*1900*	*1950*	*2000*	*2050*
World	791	1650	2521*	6055	9322
More Developed	191	539	813*	1188	1181
North America	2	82	172	310	438
Europe	163	408	547	729	603
Japan, Australia, & New Zealand	26	49	95	149	140
Less Developed	600	1111	1709	4867*	8141
Africa	106	133	221	784	2000
Asia (less Japan)	478	904	1321	3563	5335
Latin America & Caribbean	16	74	167	519	806
	Percentage of World Population				
World	100	100	100	100	100
More Developed	24	33	32*	20*	13
North America	—	5	7	5	5
Europe	21	25	22	12	6
Japan, Australia, & New Zealand	3	3	4	2	2
Less Developed	76*	67	68	80*	87
Africa	13	8	9	13	21
Asia (less Japan)	60	55	52	59	57
Latin America & Caribbean	2	4	7	9	9

Source: For population 1700–2000, Gelbard et al. (1999); for medium projections 2050, U.N. Population Division (2001).

Note: * indicates data have been rounded to the nearest whole number.

a replacement level in these countries, such a large cohort of young people reaching childbearing ages will result in an echo fertility that will keep the population growing. This phenomenon, called "population momentum," is expected to account for more than half the growth in the next century.

It is impossible to accurately forecast how large the world population will be in the next century. But the United Nations creates forecasts using various assumptions. They project that starting with a world population of 6 billion in year 2000, the world will contain 7.9 billion people if fertility declines at a rapid rate; it will be 9.3 billion if fertility declines at a moderate rate; and we will number 10.9 billion if fertility declines slowly (U.N. Population Division 2001).

BELOW REPLACEMENT FERTILITY

In addition to increasing the inhabitants of our world, population growth has also changed the geographic balance of power. As Table 5.1 indicates, between the years 1750 and 1900, the population in more developed regions, particularly North America, grew at a more rapid pace than that in less developed regions of the world. Consequently, the share of developed countries in the world population increased from 24 percent to 33 percent. However, between 1950 and 2000, population growth in developing countries has far outstripped that in the developed world, resulting in a drop of the population share of the developed world to 20 percent. If the present trends continue, according to the United Nations medium projections, by the year 2050 the developed world will contain only 13 percent of the world's people.

Extremely low fertility in industrialized societies plays an important role in this redistribution. The original demographic transition theory assumed that fertility and mortality would both decline to settle at a low level, where the society would continue to reproduce itself or would grow very slowly. However, many nations in Europe are now at below replacement-level fertility. Replacement-level fertility, defined as the level at which the population replaces itself, is about TFR of 2.1. In 2001, the TFR in many countries, such as Spain (1.2), Italy (1.3), Japan (1.3), Sweden (1.5), Portugal (1.5), Hungary (1.3), and the United Kingdom (1.7), was well below replacement. Countries with below-replacement-level fertility are largely located in Europe, but several East Asian nations, such as Taiwan, South Korea, and China, have also reached below-replacement-level fertility.

The term "Second Demographic Transition" was first used by Lesthaeghe and van de Kaa (1986) to describe changes in family formation in Western Europe since World War II. These changes involved postponement of marriage, increase in proportion remaining single, increase in cohabitation, increase in length of time living in parental home, the "baby bust," and increased fertility in cohabitational unions. Marriages as well as cohabitational unions are more likely to dissolve, and participants in these unions are less likely to remarry (Lesthaeghe 1998). Below-replacement-level fertility and fears of population decline have resulted in public concern regarding the "birth dearth" in many countries, and several governments have tried to implement policies designed to increase the birthrate.

Synthetic theories combining rational choice and ideational shift provide interesting explanations of these phenomena. A number of structural changes in Europe have changed the cost-benefit calculus of childbearing. Increasing standards of living and state welfare systems have reduced individual reliance on children as caretakers in old age (Livi-Bacci 2001). Increasing education for women and growing economic opportunities lead to increased employment for women and result in greater demands on their time (Presser 2001). At the same time, a number of cultural and ideational changes have reduced the emotional importance of children. Increased secularization has led to increased tolerance for behavior that was once perceived as deviant, particularly cohabitation, abortion, and nonmarital fertility (Lesthaeghe and Sukryn 1988). There has also been a change in the way individuals view self-actualization. Increased individuation has led to a transformation from a society in which the emphasis was on children and child rearing to a social structure in which individual achievement and self-fulfillment are valued, with children forming a part of self-fulfillment for some people and not for others. Dutch demographer Van de Kaa (1987) defines this shift as a transition from "king child" to "king pair with a child."

When we look at the below-replacement-level fertility in Europe, limits to government policies become clear. The failure of Czechoslovakian pronatalist policies provides an interesting example. Czechoslovakia adopted a number of profamily policies in the postwar era. By the mid-1960s, these became explicitly pronatalist and included a number of incentives: monthly child care subsidy, lump sum payment at the birth of each child, income tax reduction at the birth of the first child, rent reduction in government-owned housing (depending upon the number of children), and other types of subsidies (Frejka 1980). This led to an immediate rise in fertility in the early 1970s. However, in a few years these measures were taken for granted and had little or no effect on subsequent cohorts (Frejka and Ross 2001), and by 2001, Czechoslovakian TFR dipped to 1.1.

While thinking about below-replacement-level fertility in Europe, it is important to note that the United States has not followed a similar pattern. Following a postwar baby boom, U.S. fertility steadily declined between 1960 and 1990. From a high TFR of 3.5 in the early 1960s, a replacement TFR of a little over 2.0 was achieved by 1972. Fertility continued to decline, reaching a low of about 1.8 by 1978. This decline fed the fears of a European-style birth dearth, but the TFR has increased since then, reaching above 2.0 by the year 1989. It has been argued that the American fertility has remained steady around replacement level since the 1970s. The apparent move toward below-replacement-level fertility was fueled by postponement rather than elimination of childbearing, and once this postponement effect worked its way through the U.S. age structure, fertility returned to a steady rate of replacement level. Current below-replacement-level fertility for Taiwan (TFR of 1.7) is also attributable to the same postponement effect (Bongaarts and Griffith 1998)

The divergence between the United States and Europe remains puzzling. Is it real or simply a statistical artifact created by the postponement of marriage? At least one school of thought holds that European low fertility is real and not a statistical artifact (Lesthaeghe and Willems 1999). However, if these differences between the United States and Europe are real, then the question is, Can the United States be expected to move toward a European pattern or will it continue on a divergent path? While it seems likely that a fundamental shift toward what students of European fertility have termed "postmodern" or "postmaterialist" values (Van de Kaa 2001) has been occurring even in the United States, its impact seems largely limited to raising the age at which childbearing occurs, rather than the elimination of childbearing altogether. The structural conditions and societal response in the United States are quite different from Europe. First, the United States is continually replenished by immigrants who bring totally different values and usually have higher fertility than the native-born (Kahn 1994). Second, religious values still deeply affect American society, with social life largely organized around such community institutions as school and church, making it difficult for childless individuals to find a social location. It is interesting to note that even hedonistic American television serials like *Sex and the City* still hold on to the utopia of finding a committed partner and building a family.

Is Population Growth a Social Problem?

As outlined above, while fertility around the world is beginning to converge, different parts of the world face diametrically opposite demographic futures. Industrial societies, particularly European countries, are facing declining as well as aging populations. In contrast, developing countries are facing populations growing through at least the next century and are struggling to deal with an influx of young workers. Consequently, the perception of population problems differs across these two settings.

Developing countries are mired in debates that have their roots in the storm of controversy set off by the publication of *An Essay on the Principle of Population*, first published anonymously by Thomas Malthus (1798). Malthus argued that population increases geometrically and food production grows arithmetically. Thus, population growth would inevitably outstrip subsistence unless some checks were applied. Positive checks built into nature include famine and disease; preventive checks under human control include late marriage and abstinence (Malthus 1798). Malthusian arguments were intuitively appealing to many, and gathered a considerable following among political economists of the day. One of the most influential aspects of the Malthusian doctrine was a change in the way welfare institutions came to be viewed in Victorian England. In the early nineteenth century, it is estimated that nearly one in nine persons received some sort of welfare (Petersen 1979), and the tax rate needed to sustain this level of welfare was becoming highly onerous. However, until the propagation of Malthusian doctrine, most taxpayers considered it their moral duty to contribute toward the support of the poor in their parish. Malthus argued vehemently that poor relief only served to increase the number of the poor, because parents did not feel the burden of feeding their own children and would inevitably keep reproducing. His ideas, as well as the high cost of poor relief, led to the amendment of Poor Laws in 1834.

Malthusian arguments were severely criticized by humanists as well as by Marxists. Humanists resented any interference in such intensely personal decisions as marriage. Poets and writers composed many satirical ditties; Byron wrote, "Without cash, Malthus tells you take no bride. So Cash rules Love" (Petersen 1979). Underlying this discourse was an assumption that the earth was bountiful enough to support a much larger population, particularly with the opportunity to migrate to the colonies. A second line of attack on

Malthusian ideology emerged from Marxists, who argued that the impoverishment of the proletariat was to be laid at the door of the capitalist system, rather than their own proclivity for procreation. Engels, in particular, argued that Malthus did not take into account the fact that workers always produce more than they consume and that their poverty is a function of the exploitation of labor rather than their tendency to overpopulate (Engels 1944).

Echoes of these debates still permeate the discourse on population growth, albeit with some surprising twists. Neo-Malthusians continue to argue that the poverty of poor nations is a direct consequence of population growth outstripping the state's capacity to keep up with the needed investments in capital stock, schools, hospitals, and other public goods (Kelley and Schmidt 1996). These arguments have been used to justify strong state intervention in curtailing population growth. Not surprisingly, India was the first country to announce an official population policy in 1952. Indian intelligentsia had long been influenced by Malthusian perspectives. Malthus taught at the East India Company's college, training India's future administrators. These company officials were deeply influenced by Malthusian views, and their interaction with the Indian elites led to the establishment of the Malthusian League in India, thereby laying the foundation for a future government-sponsored population control program.

China and India, the two most populous countries in the world, have strong state policies for population control. China implemented a one-child policy in 1979, which has been somewhat relaxed to permit another child to rural residents with a daughter, but childbearing decisions remain circumscribed by government rules and regulations. Similarly, India flirted with a forcible sterilization program in 1976, resulting in a crippling election defeat for the then ruling party. Present-day India retains a number of antinatalist policies such as ineligibility of individuals with more than two children to stand in election in some states and ineligibility for maternity leave for third and higher-order births. However, neither India nor China found this move toward explicit population control easy to reconcile with the professed socialist (Marxist, in the case of China) ideology. In fact, at a United Nations conference on population held in Bucharest in 1974, India and China led a chorus of developing nations shunning the industrialized world's agenda for population control and supporting enhanced economic development as a prerequisite for fertility decline. Nevertheless, following this conference, both countries engaged in strong population control policies that persist to date in some form.

Social scientists, however, have been far more cautious in linking population and economic growth. A National Academy of Sciences review undertaken in 1986 (Johnson and Lee 1986), as well as a subsequent 1994 review by the Overseas Development Council (Cassen 1994), comes to the conclusion that while not to be treated with equanimity, population growth is not the overwhelming cause of affliction for developing countries that some have claimed, and certainly not the prime cause of the difficulties of development. Contrary to Malthusian expectations, increasing world population has not brought starvation in its wake; agricultural production has been able to keep pace with population growth. Technological advancement, possibly spurred by higher demand for food grains, has been quite effective in meeting increased needs. Large and widespread famines are largely a phenomenon of the past, and where they exist, they are mainly due to the ineffectiveness of the state machinery and the international system in providing relief (Dreze and Sen 1991).

A number of other areas are more likely to be negatively affected by rapid population growth. In regions where nonagricultural growth is slow and agriculture offers few jobs, overt or hidden unemployment could soar (Cassen 1994). The ever-increasing size of the student population will place greater demands on schools and classrooms and result in increasing class sizes (Kelley 1996). Population growth also increases the pressure on the environment, particularly the forests, by increasing the need for cultivable land (Pebley 1998; Rosero-Bixby and Palloni 1998). However, empirical results suggest that these relationships, while plausible, are often relatively weak. For example, most countries around the world have managed to expand primary education, even in the face of an ever-growing school-age population; at the same time, low population growth is not a sufficient condition for educational expansions. While some countries with low population growth, such as South Korea, have been extremely successful in increasing education, other countries with low population growth (such as Thailand) have only experienced modest success. Similarly, while population growth reduces pressure on forests for farmland, if it is associated with economic growth, it leads to higher consumption, which in turn has a negative effect on the environment.

A number of factors affect the strength of the relationship between population growth and economic development:

1. Economic and social development are affected far more by the nature of social and economic institutions than the sheer number of people in a nation. The East Asian economic crisis clearly documents instances where the internal political system, corruption, and global capitalism combine to decimate economies that were a decade ago seen to be shining examples of the "virtuous cycle" of reduced population growth-investments in education-economic growth.

2. Often factors that are seen as outcomes of population growth are also determinants of growth; for example, statistical studies that attempt to disentangle the cause and effect seem to find that education, economic growth, and health systems tend to have a far greater effect *on* population growth than they are to be affected *by* population growth (Johnson and Lee 1986; Kelley and Schmidt 1996).

3. Population growth seems to be associated with some medium-term positive economic impacts that offset short-term negative impacts. Improved technology and changes in institutional arrangements are particularly important. For example, one explanation of increased agricultural productivity in nineteenth-century England is the dismantling of feudal systems, which occurred under population pressure. With growing population, agricultural wages fell and rents on land increased. This destroyed the basic raison d'être of feudalism, resulting in increased owner cultivation, land improvements, and technological innovation in agriculture (North and Thomas 1970).

This brief review masks many divisions among the "neo-Malthusian" and the "revisionist" camps.

However, the following statement by a National Academy of Sciences panel seems to sum up the state of the knowledge quite well: "On balance, we reach the qualitative conclusion that slower population growth would be beneficial to economic development of developing countries" (Johnson and Lee, 1986:90). As Kelley and McGreevey (1994) point out:

This statement, arduously negotiated to obtain unanimous support by the NAS working group, exemplifies several attributes of modern economic thought on population: 1) Population growth has both positive and negative impacts (thus, "on balance"); 2) the actual size of the net impact—even whether it is strong or weak—cannot be determined based on existing evidence (thus, "qualitative"); 3) only the direction of the impact from high current growth rates can be discerned (thus, "slower," not "slow"); and, 4) the net impact varies from country to country—in most cases it will be negative, in some it will be positive, and in others it will be neutral (thus "developing countries"). (P. 112)

While a deep conviction that population explosion is harmful to human well-being seems to be faltering, there is a rise in human rights concerns regarding population policies that, in a missionary zeal to control population, trample on individual needs (Dixon-Mueller 1993). The latter results in strong protests against top-down population policies that try to influence intensely personal decisions. These protests have often been spearheaded by women, since most of the family planning programs target women rather than men. In spite of these protests and somewhat cautious findings by social scientists, governments in many developing countries remain convinced that population growth poses a major impediment to economic development. Consequently, family planning programs continue to form a cornerstone of government policies in many developing countries, and industrialized countries continue to provide substantial financial assistance for these programs.

PROBLEMS ASSOCIATED WITH FERTILITY DECLINE

Ironically, while developing country governments are mired in dealing with population growth, industrial societies have become preoccupied with the consequences of fertility decline. Mortality decline, combined with a decrease in the number of children born each year, have changed the population composition of most industrial societies. Whereas the median age in Europe was 29 in 1950, it has increased to 38 in the year 2000 and is expected to reach 49.5 by the year 2050; the median age in the United States will increase from 29.5 (1950) to 35.6 (2000) and 41 (2050). In contrast, even in the year 2050, the median age in less developed countries is expected to be around 35 (U.N. Population Division 2001). Today, in developed societies, the proportion of the elderly aged 60 and above has just surpassed that of children (19 percent vs. 18 percent), and in 2050 it is expected to be double that of children (33 percent vs. 16 percent). Thus, population aging is a major phenomenon facing the industrial world.

Taking care of this elderly population is likely to place a major strain on the society. In the United States, for example, the social security system is set up in such a way that the payroll taxes deducted from workers support the elderly. While the social security system is currently accumulating a surplus, it is estimated that with the baby boom generation retiring, and without serious restructuring, this system will be unable to care for the elderly by the year 2029. While reducing benefits and increasing payroll taxes is one alternative, continued immigration is another way by which the dependency ratio can be reduced.

INTERNATIONAL MIGRATION

International migration has always existed, but the magnitude of migration at the dawn of the twenty-first century is unlike any seen before. As of the year 2000, about 160 million people were living outside their country of birth, up from 120 million in 1990 (Martin and Widgern 2002). However, to place international migration in perspective, a majority of the more than 6 billion inhabitants of the earth live and die close to where they were born, never crossing a national border.

At present, only five countries officially welcome international migrants. About 800,000 residents are admitted annually to the United States, 200,000 to Canada, 75,000 to Australia, 65,000 to Israel, and 35,000 to New Zealand (Martin and Widgern 2002). In the United States, nearly 66 percent of the legal immigrants arrive to join their families, 13 percent arrive on employment preferences, and the rest are part of a refugee or diversity visa program (Immigration and Naturalization Service 2002). Of these, 13 percent come from Europe, 31 percent from Asia, and 38 percent come from Mexico, South and Central America, and the Caribbean. Thus, an overwhelming majority are from developing countries.

In addition to legal residents, many countries have temporary migrants who are allowed inside the country to work but cannot settle there permanently. Singapore is an interesting example. Singapore contains nearly 1 million foreigners among its 2.2 million workers. Government policy is to welcome foreign professionals, providing them with long-term residencies and allowing them to bring their families. For unskilled workers, the rules are stricter and they are not allowed to bring their families. Female workers are subjected to pregnancy tests and sent home if they become pregnant. Even marrying a Singaporean citizen does not guarantee a migrant the right to stay in Singapore.

Guest worker programs have a long history with Chinese labor imported to Malaya, Indian coolies to the West Indies, and temporary labor migrations systems in southern Africa. However, most countries have found that guest workers, once admitted, often tend to stay and form ethnic enclaves in the host nation (Castles 1986). Since migrant workers tend to come from a different ethnic and cultural background, an influx of migrants has historically been a cause of concern in almost all host countries. This issue has particularly been of concern to the European Union in recent years. Foreigners and foreign workers in Europe form about 3 percent to 9 percent of the population in most countries, but Switzerland (19 percent foreigners) and Luxembourg (36 percent foreigners) contain a much larger concentration of foreign workers. Oil-producing countries of the Middle East have also seen a significant influx of foreign workers; in 2001, foreigners were 70 percent of a workforce of 10 million in Saudi Arabia (Martin and Widgern 2002).

Illegal immigrants form a third category of migrants. These are foreigners who enter a country without inspection or who obtain entry legally but then violate the terms of their entry by overstaying or obtaining unauthorized employment. It is difficult to estimate the unauthorized workers in any country, but it is particularly difficult in the United States, given the size of this population. These estimates seem to range between 2 million and 10 million. An Urban Institute study placed this number at 8.5 million in the year 2000, considerably increased from 3 million in 1980 and 5 million in 1995 (Passel 2001).

Refugees form another important category of migrants. By one estimate, the total number of refugees is about 14.5 million, with 43 percent located in the Middle East and another 22 percent in Africa. Refugees from Afghanistan living in Pakistan formed nearly 13 percent of the total refugee pool in 2001. Refugees from Palestine and Afghanistan, at 4 million and 3.6 million respectively, are the two largest refugee populations (U.S. Committee for Refugees 2001).

Although international migration serves many individual needs, it also causes a tremendous dislocation in the lives of immigrants and their families. Immigrants often move to new societies where many of their cultural beliefs are unwelcome. Frequently they must learn a new language. Among immigrants to the United States, nearly 80 percent, about 15 million people, speak a language other than English at home (Martin and Midgley 1999). Families are often separated, with a husband moving without his wife or a mother leaving her children behind to be cared for by the grandparents. Often new immigrants are poorer than the native-born and initially suffer from a lack of social, cultural, and financial capital.

Given these social problems involved in migration, the decision to migrate is not an easy one for the migrants. Migrants move for both economic and noneconomic reasons; host countries accept them for both economic and noneconomic reasons. Lack of employment opportunities in origin countries push people out, opportunities in destination countries pull them in. War and persecution push people out, while a desire to reunite with family members lures them to destination countries. However, since the migrants are overwhelmingly from the less developed regions of the world, it seems reasonable to assume that political instability and lack of economic opportunities at home lead to migration.

CHANGING DEMOGRAPHIC FUTURES

This chapter has examined the changes in human population as well as social and economic factors leading to such changes as mortality decline, fertility decline, and migration. Population change has been one of the most significant events of the twentieth century. In the twentieth century, world population tripled, life expectancy increased considerably, prevalence of marriage in Europe and the United States declined, and family size declined in most parts of the world. These changes have had a significant impact on the way we live our lives. Today, 60-year-olds are called young-old, and most of us plan to live well into our 80s. Increasingly, instead of spending a large part of their lives in child rearing, women have fewer children and more child-free years.

One of the most common threads running through the chapter is the way in which social and economic processes are linked to population changes, both as antecedents and as consequences. The other common thread indicates the way in which the lives of people in one part of the world are linked to their neighbors in another part of this planet. Both fertility and mortality decline in developing countries has begun at a considerably lower level of socioeconomic development than the levels at which Europe began to experience mortality and fertility declines. Fertility in the United States remains above the extremely low fertility experienced by many European nations, at least partially, because of the higher family size of its immigrant population. War and persecution as well as poverty in many developing countries fuel the migration to the developed world.

NOTES

1. Rural couples are usually allowed a second child if their first child is a girl.
2. Life expectancy at birth is defined as the number of years individuals in a cohort could expect to live on

average if they experienced the prevailing age-specific mortality rates. Since likelihood of death is high in infancy and then again at older ages, life expectancy at birth is usually lower than it is at age one.

3. Total Fertility Rate (TFR) in a particular year is defined as the synthetic measure of average number of children a cohort of women would have if at each age they have children at the same rate as the women in the index year.

REFERENCES

Basu, Alaka M. 1993. "Cultural Influences on the Timing of First Births in India: Large Differences That Add Up to Little Difference." *Population Studies* 47:85–95.

Becker, Gary S. 1993. *A Treatise on the Family*. Cambridge, MA: Harvard University Press.

Bledsoe, Caroline H., John B. Casterline, Jennifer A. Johnson-Kuhn, and John G. Haaga, eds. 1999. *Critical Perspectives on Schooling and Fertility in the Developing World*. Washington, DC: National Academy of Sciences.

Bongaarts, John. 1975. "Why High Birth Rates Are So Low." *Population and Development Review* 1:289–96.

Bongaarts, John and Judith Bruce. 1995. "The Causes of Unmet Need for Contraception and the Social Content of Services." *Studies in Family Planning* 26:57–75.

Bongaarts, John and Feeney Griffith. 1998. "On the Quantum and Tempo of Fertility." *Population and Development Review* 24:271–91.

Bongaarts, John, W. P. Mauldin, and James F. Phillips. 1990. "Demographic Impact of Family Planning Programs." *Studies in Family Planning* 21:299–310.

Bongaarts, John and Susan Watkins. 1996. "Social Interactions and Contemporary Fertility Transition." *Population and Development Review* 22:639–82.

Boserup, Esther. 1976. "Environment, Population, and Technology in Primitive Societies." *Population and Development Review* 2:21–36.

Caldwell, John C. 1976. "Toward a Restatement of Demographic Transition Theory." *Population and Development Review,* 321–66.

Cassen, Robert, ed. 1994. *Population and Development: Old Debates, New Conclusions*. Washington, DC: Overseas Development Council.

Castles, Stephen. 1986. "The Guest Worker in Western Europe—An Obituary." *International Migration Review* 20:761–78.

Cleland, John. 2001. "Potatoes and Pills: An Overview of Innovation-Diffusion Contributions to Explanations of Fertility Decline." In *Diffusion Processes and Fertility Transition: Selected Perspectives,* edited by John Casterline. Washington, DC: National Academy Press.

Coale, Ansley. 1973. "The Demographic Transition." *Proceedings of the International Population Conference*, Vol. 1. Liege, Belgium.

——, ed. 1986. *The Decline of Fertility in Europe*. Princeton, NJ: Princeton University Press.

Crimmins, Eileen M., Yasuhiko Saito, and Dominique Ingegneri. 1997. "Trends in Disability-Free Life Expectancy in the United States, 1970–90." *Population and Development Review* 23:552–72.

Das Gupta, Monica. 1995. "Fertility Decline in Punjab, India: Parallels with Historical Europe." *Population Studies* 49:481–500.

Davis, Kingsley. 1963. "Theory of Change and Response in Modern Demographic History." *Population Index* 29:346–66.

Demeny, Paul. 1987. "Re-Linking Fertility Behavior and Economic Security in Old Age: A Pronatalist Reform." *Population and Development Review* 13:128–32.

Dixon, Ruth. 1978. "Late Marriage and Non-Marriage as Demographic Responses: Are They Similar?" *Population Studies* 33:449–66.

Dixon-Mueller, Ruth. 1993. *Population Policy and Women's Rights: Transforming Reproductive Choice*. Westport, CT: Praeger.

Dreze, Jean and Amartya K. Sen. 1991. *Hunger and Public Action*. Oxford, England: Clarendon.

Edin, Kathryn. 2000. "How Low Income Single Mothers Talk about Marriage." *Social Problems* 47:112–33.

Engels, Frederick. 1844. "Outlines of a Critique of Political Economy." *Deutsch-Französische Jahrbücher.*

Finkle, Jason L. and Barbara B. Crane. 1975. "The Politics of Bucharest: Population, Development, and the New International Economic Order." *Population and Development Review* 1:87–114.

Frejka, Tomas. 1980. "Fertility Trends and Policies: Czechoslovakia in the 1970s." *Population and Development Review* 6:65–93.

Frejka, Tomas and John Ross. 2001. "Paths to Subreplacement Fertility: The Empirical Evidence." *Population and Development Review* 27 (Supplement): 213–54.

Gelbard, Alene, Carl Haub, and Mary M. Kent. 1999. "World Population beyond Six Billion." *Population Bulletin* 54(1).

Ginsburg, Faye and Rayna Rapp. 1999. "The Politics of Reproduction." *Annual Review of Anthropology* 20:311–43.

Greenhalgh, Susan. 1990. "Toward a Political Economy of Fertility: Anthropological Contributions." *Population and Development Review* 16:85–106.

Greenhalgh, Susan and Jiali Li. 1995. "Engendering Reproductive Policy and Practice in Peasant China: For a Feminist Demography of Reproduction." *Signs: Journal of Women in Culture and Society* 20:601–41.

Hammel, Eugene A. 1990. "A Theory of Culture for Demography." *Population and Development Review* 16:455–85.

——. 1995. "Economics 1, Culture 0: Fertility Change and Differences in the Northwest Balkans, 1700–1900." In *Situating Fertility: Anthropology and Demographic Inquiry,* edited by Susan Greenhalgh. New York: Cambridge University Press.

Ho, Teresa J. 1979. "Time Costs of Child Rearing in the Rural Philippines." *Population and Development Review* 5:643–62.

Immigration and Naturalization Service. 2002. *Statistical Yearbook, 2000.* Retrieved from www.ins.usdoj.gov/ graphics/aboutins/statistics/IMM00yrbk/IMM2000. pdf.

Jackson, Pauline. 1984. "Women in 19th-Century Irish Emigration." *International Migration Review* 18: 1004–20.

Johnson, D. G. and Ronald D. Lee, eds. 1986. *Population Growth and Economic Development: Policy Questions.* Washington, DC: National Academy Press.

Kahn, Joan R. 1994. "Immigrant and Native Fertility during the 1980s: Adaptation and Expectations for the Future." *International Migration Review* 28:501–19.

Kelley, Allen C. 1996. "The Consequences of Rapid Population Growth on Human Resource Development: The Case of Education." In *The Impact of Population Growth on Well-Being in Developing Countries,* edited by Dennis A. Ahlburg, Allen C. Kelley, and Karen O. Mason. Berlin, Germany: Springer.

Kelley, Allen C. and William P. McGreevey. 1994. "Population and Development in Historical Perspective." In *Population and Development: Old Debates, New Conclusions,* edited by Robert Cassen. Washington, DC: Overseas Development Council.

Kelley, Allen C. and Robert M. Schmidt. 1996. "Toward a Cure for the Myopia and Tunnel Vision of the Population Debate: A Dose of Historical Perspective." In *The Impact of Population Growth on Well-Being in Developing Countries,* edited by Dennis A. Ahlburg, Allen C. Kelley, and Karen O. Mason. Berlin, Germany: Springer.

Lesthaeghe, Ron. 1998. "On Theory Development: Applications to the Study of Family Formation." *Population and Development Review* 24:1–14.

Lesthaeghe, Ron and Johan Sukryn. 1988. "Cultural Dynamics and Economic Theories of Fertility Change." *Population and Development Review* 14:1–45.

Lesthaeghe, Ron and Dirk J. Van de Kaa. 1986. "Twee Demografische Transities." Pp. 19–68 in *Bevolking, Groei En Krimp,* edited by Ron Lesthaeghe and Dirk J. Van de Kaa. Deventer, The Netherlands: Van Loghum Slaterus.

Lesthaeghe, Ron and Paul Willems. 1999. "Is Low Fertility a Temporary Phenomenon in the European Union?" *Population and Development Review* 25:211–28.

Livi-Bacci, Massimo. 2001. "Comment: Desired Family Size and the Future Course of Fertility." *Population and Development Review* 27 (Supplement):282–89.

Lloyd, Cynthia. 1991. "The Contribution of the World Fertility Surveys to an Understanding of the Relationship between Women's Work and Fertility." *Studies in Family Planning* 22:144–61.

Malthus, Thomas. 1798. *An Essay on the Principle of Population.* London, England: J. Johnson.

Martin, Philip and Elizabeth Midgley. 1999. "Immigration to the United States." *Population Bulletin* 54(2).

Martin, Philip and Jonas Widgern. 2002. "International Migration: Facing the Challenge." *Population Bulletin* 57(1).

Mason, Karen O. 1997. "Explaining Fertility Transitions." *Demography* 34:443–54.

Mason, Karen O. and V. T. Palan. 1981. "Female Employment and Fertility in Peninsular Malaysia: The Maternal Role Incompatibility Hypothesis Reconsidered." *Demography* 18:549–75.

McKeown, Thomas and R. G. Record. 1962. "Reasons for the Decline of Mortality in England and Wales during the Nineteenth Century." *Population Studies* 16:94–122.

McNicoll, Geoffrey. 1980. "Institutional Determinants of Fertility Change." *Population and Development Review* 6:441–62.

Montgomery, Mark and Barney Cohen, eds. 1997. *From Birth to Death: Mortality Decline and Reproductive Change.* Washington, DC : National Academy Press.

North, Douglass and Robert P. Thomas. 1970. "An Economic Theory of the Growth of the Western World." *Economic History Review* 23:1–17.

Notestein, Frank. 1953. "Economic Problems of Population Change." Pp. 13–31 in *Proceedings of the Eighth International Conference of Agricultural Economics.* London, England: Oxford University Press.

Oeppen, Jim and James W. Vaupel. 2002. "Broken Limits to Life Expectancy." *Science* 296:1029–31.

Passel, Jeffrey S. 2001. *Estimates of Undocumented Migrants Living in the United States: 2000.* Washington, DC: Urban Institute.

Pebley, Anne R. 1998. "Demography and the Environment." *Demography* 35:377–89.

Petersen, William. 1975. *Population.* New York: Macmillan.

——. 1979. "Malthus and the Intellectuals." *Population and Development Review* 5:469–78.

Presser, Harriet. 2001. "Comment: A Gender Perspective for Understanding Low Fertility in Post-Transitional Societies." *Population and Development Review* 27 (Supplement):177–83.

Preston, Samuel and Michael Haines. 1991. *Fatal Years: Child Mortality in Late Nineteenth-Century America.* Princeton, NJ: Princeton University Press.

Pritchett, Lant. 1994. "Desired Fertility and Impact of Population Policies." *Population and Development Review* 20:1–55.

Robey, Bryant, Shea O. Ruttstein, and Leo Morris. 1993. "The Fertility Decline in Developing Countries." *Scientific American* 269(6):60–66.

Rosero-Bixby, Luis and Alberto Palloni. 1998. "Population and Deforestation in Costa Rica." *Population and Environment* 20:149–85.

Sanderson, Warren. 1987. "Below-Replacement Fertility in Nineteenth Century America." *Population and Development Review* 13:305–13.

Santow, Gigi. 1995. "Coitus Interruptus and the Control of Natural Fertility." *Population Studies* 49:19–43.

Simpson-Herbert, Maylin and Sandra L. Huffman. 1981. "The Contraceptive Effect of Breastfeeding." *Studies in Family Planning* 12:125–33.

Sklar, June. 1977. "Marriage and Nonmarital Fertility: A Comparison of Ireland and Sweden." *Population and Development Review* 3:359–75.

Stoler, Ann. 1989. "Making Empire Respectable: Race and Sexual Morality in 20th Century Colonial Cultures." *American Ethnologist* 16:634–60.

Thompson, W. S. 1930. *Population Problems.* New York: McGraw-Hill.

U.N. Population Division. 2001. *World Population Prospects: The 2000 Revision. Vol. 1, Comprehensive Tables.* New York: United Nations.

U.S. Committee for Refugees. 2001. *World Wide Refugee Survey.* Retrieved 2002 from www.refugees.org/world/statistics/wrs01_tableindex.htm.

Van de Kaa, Dirk J. 1987. "Europe's Second Demographic Transition." *Population Bulletin* 42(1).

——. 2001. "Postmodern Fertility Preferences: From Changing Value Orientation to New Behavior." *Population and Development Review* 27 (Supplement):290–331.

Van de Walle, Francine. 1986. "Infant Mortality and the European Demographic Transition." In *The Decline of Fertility in Europe,* edited by Ansley J. Coale and Susan Watkins. Princeton, NJ: Princeton University Press.

Weeks, John R. 1999. "Population: An Introduction to Concepts and Issues." Belmont, CA: Wadsworth.

Westoff, Charles F. and German Rodriguez. 1995. "The Mass Media and Family Planning in Kenya." *International Family Planning Perspectives* 21:26–31.

White, Kevin M. and Samuel H. Preston. 1996. "How Many Americans Are Alive Because of Twentieth-Century Improvements in Mortality." *Population and Development* 22:415–29.

Wilson, William J. and Kathryn M. Neckerman. 1986. "Poverty and Family Structure: The Widening Gap between Evidence and Public Policy Issues." In *Fighting Poverty: What Works and What Doesn't,* edited by Sheldon Danziger and Daniel Weinberg. Cambridge, MA: Harvard University Press.

ECOLOGICAL PROBLEMS

STEVEN YEARLEY

University of York

SEAS OF TROUBLES

In November 2002, the *Prestige*—an ageing oil tanker registered in the Bahamas and carrying a cargo of fuel oil from Latvia—got into difficulties. As it passed the northwest coast of Spain, its hull cracked and it started to leak oil. Driven by wind and tides, it began to drift inshore. Boats sent to try to recover the damaged vessel sought to rotate it away from the main force of the damaging waves; they then began to tow it southwest out to sea. As no Spanish or Portuguese port would accept the risk of the leaking tanker, it was being taken south, apparently in the hope of finding shelter in some African port. But it soon broke up and sank, still off the Spanish coast, taking most of its cargo down with it. Subsequently, undersea photography has shown its cargo continuing to leak out, though submarine repairs are believed likely to be able to staunch that flow. Beaches and coastlines have been smothered in deposits of heavy, nonvolatile oil. Extensive international news coverage has shown how fishing boats, particularly in Galicia, have been obliged to stay in port and how local shellfish farms have been overwhelmed by the oil. The economic and social impact on nearby communities is predicted to be extreme. And, though voluntary and official agencies have tried to respond vigorously to the obvious, immediate problems, there are differences of opinion over the best way to clean up the oil. Detergents and other chemicals used to disperse the oil may have worse ecological impacts in the long run than the oil itself. At the same time, workers engaged in gathering up the oil are concerned about the adequacy of the protective equipment that they have managed to acquire: they worry about repeatedly breathing in the fumes from the beached fuel and about the consequences of exposing their skin to the potentially carcinogenic oil for prolonged periods. Consumers worry about eating shellfish in restaurants, and tourism managers are anxious about impacts on the tourist trade.

Though this is just one case of contemporary ecological problems, it exemplifies very many of the sociologically significant features of ecological problems.

- First, though the ecological impact is chiefly a problem for the Spanish authorities, the cause of the problem is complicatedly international. The oil, owned by a Russian-backed Swiss company (Crown Resources) with major offices in London, is reported to have come from the Baltic states on a Liberian tanker registered in the Bahamas and carrying a multinational crew. The oil being transported is said to have been for the Southeast Asian market. Had it not sunk so soon, it might have ended up polluting an African country's waters or port. Ecological problems frequently have an international dimension and are beyond the control of single states; the causes and the consequences of environmental problems are often geographically very remote from each other. The spatial dimension of the problem is often so wide and so complex that ecological problems commonly appear to have a global dimension.

• The industrialized world has been very slow to decrease its dependence on fossil fuels, so however much coastal communities worry about the routine traffic in oil along their shores, the economies of these countries are as reliant on oil as ever. Though some European countries, notably Germany and Denmark, have displayed a reasonable commitment to moving towards alternative energy sources, other European states and North American countries have essentially retained their reliance on fossil fuels. In some senses the reluctance to go any further with nuclear energy programs, along with moves away from more highly polluting coal, has ensured that oil dependence persists and may even increase. Ecological problems thus arise directly from the central industrial and energy policies of contemporary states and cannot be resolved by ecological policies alone. In this sense, to view these social problems primarily as ecological problems is potentially misleading.

• Worldwide shipping is regulated by international agreements; in particular, because of a series of oil-tanker accidents, there is now an agreement to build only double-hulled ships, where the cargo is contained inside a second, protective skin. This means that ruptures in the ship's hull will admit water but will not automatically allow the cargo to escape. The *Prestige* was built in the 1970s, well before this regulation came into force; some campaigners are pressing for all single-hulled tankers to be withdrawn straightaway, but their owners argue that the ships were bought in good faith and should not be scrapped before they have paid their way. No one seems prepared to pay the kind of compensation that could result in the immediate decommissioning of single-hulled boats. Older tankers such as the *Prestige* are subject to a program of regular inspections, though doubts were raised by some commentators in Spain about the regulatory history of this particular vessel. Ecological issues are negotiated in international contexts; the resulting agreements typically have long lead times, and even problems that are widely seen as urgent may wait decades for resolution.

• The disastrous sinking of the *Prestige* produced headlines around the world and resulted in large packs of press personnel converging on Galicia. The story yielded some truly dramatic photographic images, both of the nearly submerged vessel and of the foul oil-covered beaches. This sinking became part of the litany of oil spills from the *Torrey Canyon* in England (1967), the Amoco *Cadiz* in France (1978), the Exxon *Valdez* in Alaska (1989), the *Braer* off Scotland (1993), and the *Sea Empress* in Wales (1996), as well as other huge spills near Tobago and off Angola (in 1979 and 1991 respectively), which received rather less attention. But the press coverage is, in important ways, misleading. The world's oceans are pervasively contaminated with oil, but recent estimates suggest that the majority of this pollution stems from other sources than tanker wrecks, from ships routinely dumping oil to clean their tanks and from oil originally disposed of on land, in garages, and in industrial processes, for example. Spills from tankers contribute only some 12 per cent of the volume that ends up in the seas (Seager 1995:42). The mass media commonly cover ecological problems; such problems make good news stories and often yield compelling images. However, though ecological issues are in many respects more media friendly than most other social problems, media coverage is skewed towards the presentation of disasters and away from more routine forms of ecological harm, some of which may be more consequential in the longer run (see Anderson 1997:5). Moreover, coverage—as is well known—is fickle, and the story of the *Prestige* soon faded from international media.

• Oil from the *Prestige* caused a number of immediate problems for wildlife and is thought likely to have many longer-term consequences as well. Seabirds that came into contact with the heavy oil suffered because it soaked into their feathers. They could not clean themselves and the oil made them heavy; in the longer run they would suffer from ingesting it. Shellfish that lived in the intertidal zone became covered with the oil and died. Sea otters were caught in the slick. Volunteers tried to clean the affected birds and animals and to rid the beaches and coastline of as much of the oil as possible. But some of the suffering was also concentrated on fish farms, oysters and mussels in particular, kept in moored cages by local aquaculturalists. Seagoing fisherpersons also suffered, since, though they could get their boats out, the inshore fish that they usually caught would most likely be contaminated with the oil and would thus be unsaleable. This ecological problem counted nature and humans among its victims, and this demonstrates a wider point: that ecological problems are both problems of nature and problems for society. A focus on ecological issues as social problems also draws attention to the way in which the social/natural boundary is drawn. In this case the farmed shellfish occupy a liminal position as domesticated nature.

• Soon after the disaster occurred, disputes broke out over the best way to proceed in countering the problem and in beginning the process of remediation. Though the authorities had been trying to tow the ship away when it sank, some commentators suggested that the sinking was a blessing in disguise. It was argued that, once it sank to the cold depths, the dense oil would all but solidify within the ship and thus remain locked in place, causing little environmental harm (except maybe very locally) for many years. This contrasted with earlier "management" strategies that included having the British military bomb the *Torrey Canyon* in order to disperse and, with luck, burn the oil from that wreck. But "oil" is not just oil: different cargoes have different properties, depending on the density and exact chemical composition of the petroleum product being carried. Analogies were drawn and redrawn with earlier spills, depending on how similar the oil was thought

to be. On land, meanwhile, there were disputes over how dangerous the oil might be to those people who were trying to clear it away; there was also uncertainty about the best disposal options for the oil sludge that was scooped up. Ecological problems have shown themselves to be peculiarly difficult because of the complexity of knowledge required in their diagnosis and treatment. In the case of the *Braer*, the tanker that ran aground off the north of Scotland in 1993, bad weather impeded any intervention. At first this was thought to be likely to compound the disaster, since little remediation could be started. But once the bad weather subsided, the problem looked a lot less bad than had been anticipated, and the bad weather itself came to be seen as having dispersed much of the oil and lessened its impact. Even wildlife were apparently deterred by the bad weather, and there was less contamination of local fauna than had been anticipated, even though fishing for prawn and mussels was restricted for long afterwards. At the same time, the calculation of the likely impacts of ecological problems has led to courts and accountants holding minute arguments over the exact "costs" of environmental harms; the willingness of such institutions to accept valuations of nature in monetary terms has itself led to disquiet and raised anxieties about modernist strategies for the valuation of nature (see Jacobs 1994; O'Neill 1993).

Starting with one particular problem issue, we have been able to elicit several aspects of the character of ecological problems. They are commonly supranational and may be displaced from the wealthy onto the poor; they touch on the central business of industrialized, market economies; they relate to the choice of regulatory instruments and the chronic difficulties multinational bodies face in taking decisive action; many ecological problems are treated favorably by media analysts although the commonest representation of the problems may not be the most accurate one; ecological problems frequently take shape at the meeting points of society and nature; lastly, action on the environment typically requires specialist knowledge, but this knowledge may itself be contested, leading to disputatious struggles over policy. The following discussion takes up all these points.

ECOLOGICAL PROBLEMS
AS INTERNATIONAL PROBLEMS

Environmental problems had been widely recognized as having a supranational dimension from at least the 1970s onwards. In both North America and in northern Europe it was suggested that acidic emissions from power stations and from industrial smokestacks could result in ecological damage hundreds of kilometers from the source of the pollution. It was clear also that effluents dumped in watercourses could contaminate areas very remote from the source of the pollution. The Great Lakes collected U.S. and Canadian pollution and distributed it around their shores and out into the St. Lawrence Seaway (Hannigan 1995:1–2); the Rhine brought Swiss and German pollution to the Netherlands and out into the North Sea. This illustrated the way in which governments could not pass laws to clean up their countries if leading sources of pollution lay just beyond their borders. Countries varied greatly in their susceptibility to these problems. Owing to its size, the United States suffered comparatively little, though the same problems were repeated at the state level (Rabe 2000:40–2). The United Kingdom was also relatively immune, since prevailing winds swept pollution towards Continental Europe, permitting little to be delivered in return. With many land borders, small Continental European countries, by contrast, were much more subject to these difficulties. These problems received probably their most shocking exemplification in 1986 with the explosion at the Chernobyl nuclear power plant in present-day Ukraine. The cloud of radioactive material passed westwards over Europe, leaving patchy contamination in its path, most pronounced where rain washed the radioactive material to earth (Liberatore 1999). Even Ireland and Wales, at the western rim of Europe, suffered considerable contamination of farmland, and stock movements were restricted for several years afterwards. National sovereignty and governmental authority seemed to mean little if major forms of pollution and health-endangering contamination such as radioactive fallout could not be controlled.

If these processes became most publicly recognized in the countries of the North, that does not imply that they were unimportant in the developing world; they were manifest but in a rather different way. Developing countries generally face difficulties in trying to industrialize and modernize because modern manufacturing plants and infrastructures are expensive and technically complex. They either have to borrow money to fund their industrialization or they must rely on attracting investment from overseas firms. Both paths generated environmental harms.

To put it at its simplest, a country can try to make itself appealing to investors from foreign companies in a variety of ways: by offering advantageous tax schemes, by boasting of cheap labor costs, or by keeping levels of regulation beguilingly low (Yearley 1992a:157–66). Of course, companies will also be attracted to countries that have particular reserves of sought-after commodities—bauxite in Jamaica, copper in Chile, or antimony in Bolivia, for instance; under these circumstances, local authorities can apparently sometimes press for higher environmental performance standards (see Warhurst and Hughes-Witcomb 2000). A country that fails to offer benefits of the above kinds is unlikely to win much investment in its industry, given the competition between countries seeking economic advancement. Accordingly, alongside the downward pressure on wage rates and taxation levels in developing countries, there is a systematic pressure countering environmental regulation (see Michalowski and Kramer 1987). Countries that try to set their environmental standards "too high" risk deterring investment altogether. On the other hand, if countries allow their environmental standards to decline, they are likely to appeal chiefly to dirty industries, which find the costs of compliance with advanced environmental performance standards too exacting. In the 1970s and 1980s these economic forces gave rise to the situation in which dirty industries were said to be fleeing regulation in the North and relocating to the developing world (for an assessment see Leonard 1988). In the most hypocritical cases, consumers in North America and Europe could buy imported products manufactured by processes thought to be so hazardous to workers or threatening to the neighboring environment that they were outlawed in the consumers' own countries. Pollution from the industries that developing countries did manage to attract could, naturally enough, cross national boundaries itself (George 1992:24–8): extensive forest fires in Indonesia that affected air quality and even airline transport in Malaysia and Singapore in 1997–1998 and again in 2002 exemplify this point. But the greatest limitations on state sovereignty evident in much of the developing world were in relation to setting and maintaining regulatory standards rather than in relation to the uncontrollable nature of transborder pollution.

Ecological problems of other sorts were also imposed on poorer countries by the wealthy world, as the case of the *Prestige*'s short-lived diversion towards Africa graphically illustrates. In particular, the rising cost of waste disposal in the North in the final quarter of the twentieth century meant that it started to make economic sense to ship waste to developing countries for disposal. The nastier the waste, the larger the cost saving tended to be. Savings could be further enhanced if the recipient countries were unaware of—even misled about—the extent of the dangerousness of the cargoes (see Yearley 1996:72–3). In the 1980s, countries in West Africa seemed to be especially heavily targeted, since they were reasonably close to the European sources of the hazardous or unsavory wastes and because their economies were in a sufficiently weakened state that any way to earn hard currency payments seemed appealing, in the short run at least. However, the double standard in this trade was widely publicized by groups in the developing countries themselves and by environmental campaigners in the North, and most forms of unregulated waste trading were brought to an end by international agreements reached in the 1990s (Susskind 1994:32).

Over the same period, many countries opted also for the other approach to stimulating economic development: they tried to get loans or grants—often in the form of aid—to assist with the initial investment costs. In the 1970s the sources of such loans were revolutionized when Northern commercial banks began to seek new opportunities in the South (Lever and Huhne 1985). Banks are obviously in the business of making loans and living off the profits from the interest. For big Western banks, lending to Southern countries was appealing for three reasons. First, this was a relatively neglected area, so there was initially little competition in the making of loans. Second, certain Southern countries' economies—for example, Mexico's and Brazil's—were expected to grow quickly, thus yielding a good return on the loans. Third, there was a belief that countries were a special, low-risk sort of borrower; unlike individuals or even companies that might default on loans, countries would always be there. It seemed that countries simply could not go bankrupt.

The banks, notably U.S. ones, lent enthusiastically, and loans accumulated so that by the 1980s several South American countries each had debts around $100 billion and so that the total indebtedness of the third world came close to $1,000 billion (George 1988). And, effectively, these big debtors did start to go bankrupt. In their eagerness to lend, the banks had backed some very poor investments. They even lent to corrupt states, where much of the money simply disappeared. Very little of it generated enough profits to pay the interest on the loans, though the banks still demanded their repayments. In the worst cases, countries were having to use all their export earnings just to service their debts, and their populations were therefore not benefiting at all from trade or from the loans.

Through the 1980s this complex and distressing story unfolded. Three consequences are of particular importance to the present discussion. The first and pivotal consequence was the growing importance of two international financial bodies, the World Bank and the International Monetary Fund (IMF). As the commercial banks fretted over the extent of their bad debts and the indebted countries tried to work out a strategy for survival, these two bodies assumed a powerful advisory and brokerage role. Although they are both international agencies, they are dominated by Northern representatives (who, they would say, put up most of the money), and their priority was to safeguard the international monetary system and only secondarily to assist debtor nations (Stiglitz 2002:16–19). The second and third consequences followed from the strategy advocated by the World Bank and IMF. Their view was that the situation would best be fixed not by writing off debts but by encouraging debtor countries to try to meet repayments, primarily by increasing their export earnings. They should thus do more to attract investment even if that meant accepting dirty industry or building incinerators to deal with the wastes of the North. These institutions' advice thus made pollution of the underdeveloped world more likely. At the same time, earnings could be boosted by exploiting natural resources more energetically and by turning agricultural land over to export-oriented crops. This focus on increasing earnings was to be coupled with decreases in government spending, a policy that hit expenditure on such government tasks as maintaining sewerage systems, pollution monitoring, and abatement measures (Yearley 1992a:174–83). At the same time as pollution was likely to be on the increase, spending on pollution control was reduced. By the close of the twentieth century, the number of debtor countries had hardly declined. An international campaign to mark the millennium by a cancellation of debts in the world's poorest economies received some support from the industrialized world's finance ministers but has been only very slowly implemented. Despite widespread misgivings about this indebtedness and internal reforms intended to give greater priority to environmental issues in lending and funding decisions, the IMF and World Bank have become—if anything—ever firmer in their attachment to the neoliberal orthodoxy and offer only more and freer trade as the solution to the developing world's difficulties. The IMF and World Bank are now routinely treated as the ogres of the international system and as enforcers of environmental despoilation by antiglobalization protesters (thus, see Starr 2000).

Global Ecological Problems

Although the potential supranational dimension of environmental problems had long been recognized, in the 1990s many ecological problems became recast as "global" problems, indicating that their impacts and solution were not the business of single states or even geographical regions, but of the world as a whole (Dietz and Rosa 2002). Specific cases seemed to indicate that this categorization made sense. The principal concern is that over global warming. It is now widely believed, though perhaps not by the current U.S. president, that humankind's burning of fossil fuels (gasoline and coal) over the last two centuries has increased the amount of carbon dioxide (CO_2) in the atmosphere. Other gases, including chlorofluorocarbons (CFCs—synthetic compounds used for blowing insulating foams and much besides) and methane (CH_4—a gas produced in large quantities by rotting landfill and by the digestive operations of cattle), also have a greenhouse impact. All these gases share the property that, when present in the atmosphere, they absorb heat energy as it radiates away from the earth's surface into space. According to reports of the Intergovernmental Panel on Climate Change (IPCC), the more of the gases there are in the atmosphere, the better it is at insulating the earth's surface, and the warmer the biosphere will tend to become (see Houghton 1997). Two things appear to make this issue "global." First, the problem arises from emissions dispersed all over the globe. As each molecule of CO_2 stays in the atmosphere for several years on average, emissions from a British car could potentially contribute to the warming impact anywhere in the world and so on. Second, many of the anticipated consequences of global warming themselves operate at a global level. For example, it is believed that as oceans become fractionally warmer, the water will expand, leading to a rise in sea levels. This effect will be compounded by the melting of ice on the continents, since that too will swell the size of the seas. Ocean levels could rise by tens of centimeters within decades, perhaps by more than a meter over the century. And the sea will rise all over the globe. Equally, a warmer atmosphere is likely to be a more energetic atmosphere, leading to more storms and more extremes of weather. Despite widespread concern about the probable consequences of global warming, little has been achieved in the form of international agreements to counter further global-warming emissions. As noted in connection with the *Prestige*, few economies have made any progression in diminishing their oil dependence, and though several countries, largely led by EU member states, have set themselves targets for emission reductions, no one is projecting anything other than increasing worldwide CO_2 concentrations in coming decades (see the studies in O'Riordan and Jäger 1996).

Some other ecological problems shared these global characteristics. For example, as discussed later on, worry about humanly caused harm to the ozone layer led to international agreements to phase out the worst ozone-depleting chemicals (chiefly CFCs [chlorofluorocarbons], the same chemicals that also contribute to global warming), commencing in the mid-1990s. Though the manufacture of CFCs was concentrated in a few countries, there were many more countries that were users of these chemicals, and the environmental harms were as remote from the source of the pollution as in the case of global warming. The earth has just the one ozone layer and it shrouds the whole globe, albeit with far from uniform thickness. A plausible case can also be made for the so-called persistent organic pollutants (POPs), which include toxic chlorinated pesticides, polychlorinated biphenyls, furans, and dioxins; as the name POPs suggests, these molecules are very persistent and can be transported huge distances, making their threat effectively worldwide. Other environmental problems attain their global reach by the sheer repetition of local pollution (traffic fumes would be an example here) or by the worldwide distribution of ecological harms as a by-product of trade. Further problems, such as the loss of species, are rendered "global" by conceptual means, for example through the conventions by which biodiversity is assessed. Though orangutans may be endangered in Southeast Asia and tigers at risk from India to southeastern China, it is now common to regard such problems as a subset of the problem of biodiversity loss worldwide, as the study by Mazur and Lee indicates (1993:700–12).

Although the "global" label has come into prominence in the last decade, it is not clear that one can draw exact, let alone scientific, boundaries around problems that are global and those that are "merely" international or national. To label a problem as global is implicitly to suggest that everyone has an interest in overcoming that problem. And it seems that Northern institutions have been keen to monopolize control over the application of the term so that the industrialized world effectively determines which problems attain this status and which do not. Even where there is a special line of funding for "global" environmental issues (for example, through the World Bank and the United Nations), the North has been able to influence the definition and qualifying characteristics of the problems (Middleton,

O'Keefe, and Moyo 1993:202–12; Yearley 1996:77–86). The fact that the vocabulary of global interests was less prominent at the Johannesburg Earth Summit in 2002 than it had been at the Rio de Janeiro meeting 10 years before hints at the South's dissatisfaction with the apparently universal talk of global problems, when poverty and development problems were not classified as global priorities at all.

But, as mentioned in the discussion of the *Prestige* at the start of this chapter, one of the most complex aspects about environmental problems is that they are typically economic and industrial or employment issues at the same time as ecological issues. For this reason, one other enormously important influence on the recognition of the globe's environmental problems is the World Trade Organization (WTO). Like the World Bank and IMF, the WTO is a multilateral international agency intended to be concerned with world economic well-being. Formed in 1995, the WTO's function is to promote free trade; in particular it is concerned to oppose inappropriate impediments to international commerce. The neoliberal economic orthodoxy maintains that free trade tends to boost the economic well-being of all trading partners. The WTO aims to serve the world community by identifying and eliminating obstacles to such free trade and thus promoting general wealth. Signatory nations have granted the WTO power to rule on free-trade issues and to impose economic penalties on noncomplying signatory countries. The reason the WTO impacts so heavily on environmental matters is that nearly all environmental regulations are, seen in a certain light, impediments to trade. Mandatory recycling of beer bottles, for example, tends to favor home producers over the brewers of novel imported beers, since the costs of recovering the bottles will typically be higher for foreigners. Any tax breaks given to electricity production from domestic renewable sources would be economically unfair to conventional electricity generators offering to export electricity from a neighboring country. In any case referred to it, the WTO therefore has to rule on whether infringements to free trade are permissible or not.

Contrary to the assumptions of many of its critics, the WTO is not obliged to rule in favor of free trade, and against the environment, on every occasion. The countries that drew up the WTO constitution allowed various considerations to "trump" free trade; in particular, preexisting international treaties (for example, on environmental matters) have standing against the demands of unfettered trade. Moreover, the founding rules can in principle be revised and reformed so as to favor environmental protection or the advancement of human rights. New members who join gain voting rights, and it is just about possible that, in the future, the WTO could become a vehicle for environmentally progressive change. Even at present, the WTO cannot be used as a way of, for example, freeing trade in elephant tusks, since that trade is already internationally regulated by CITES (the Convention on International Trade in Endangered Species of Wild Fauna and Flora). Furthermore, the WTO did find in favor of wildlife preservation in the matter of "turtle-friendly" shrimp fishing, where the WTO appellate body stated that "trade restrictions based on production methods could be used to protect the environment and to guard natural resources outside a nation's borders" (Vogel 2000:358). Though the U.S. proposal to exclude from its market shrimp that had been caught in nets that lacked "turtle exclusion devices" was ruled against (essentially because the United States appeared to be insisting on one particular technique for protecting turtles and not on turtle protection in general), the right of the U.S. authorities (and thus others too) to hinder free trade in shrimp for ecological reasons was accepted in principle.

Finally, in this section it is worth noting that other processes can render an environmental issue global. Since the mid-1990s there has been a growing controversy, principally in Europe, about the acceptability of genetically engineered crops and products. Concerns have been voiced by campaigners and some scientists that genetically modified (GM) crops could be injurious to wildlife; others have argued that the standards for the testing of GM foodstuffs are inadequate, since they do not reflect the degree of novelty represented by these technologically transformed foods. At the start of the twenty-first century an uneasy stalemate had been reached, in which decisions about the acceptability of these crops in Europe had been postponed into the indefinite future. A new "front" was unexpectedly opened in 2002 when the U.S. Agency for International Development (USAID) announced it intended to respond to drought-induced food shortages in southern Africa by offering GM corn (maize). Some countries agreed to accept the aid on condition that the grain was milled before distribution, so as to ensure that seeds could not be saved and subsequently planted. Zambia has so far rejected the aid entirely. Leading U.S. representatives argue that opponents of GM are threatening lives in Zambia out of an irrational attachment to fears about the new crop-production techniques, while GM's opponents interpret the U.S. aid as a form of Trojan horse. Once people have consumed GM corn it is harder for policy makers to reject it in the future. In this way, a potential ecological problem-issue that had been limited chiefly to the North and to major grain-producing countries such as Argentina is now being globalized through the actions of official aid-donating agencies (for empirical analyses of developing country perspectives see Priest 2001:35–49).

CONSTRUCTING ECOLOGICAL PROBLEMS

As noted above, in the case of the *Prestige* it seems clear that the extent of media attention is not directly proportionate to the severity of the problem. Although the economic and ecological consequences of the Galician oil spill are likely to be severe, perhaps for a period of years, the routine contamination of the seas receives far less coverage than the occasional tanker wreck. Though it does not require a great deal of sociological expertise to understand why these episodic events command the lion's share of attention, there is an important broader point that the media focus (and, to some extent therefore, the resulting public gaze) has implications for cultural understandings of ecological problems (for an exploratory account see Anderson 1997:107–69). Numerous media analyses of environmental stories have been undertaken; they show that the dynamics of coverage are far from straightforward. Hansen (1993), in his study of Greenpeace, for example, finds that the campaigning group is less good at influencing the news agenda when the media topic is "saturated" than when it is relatively neglected (p. 176). Despite this complexity, several sociologists have concentrated on the question of how particular ecological problem-claims rise to prominence (Yearley 1992a).

An attempt to synthesize these claims has been made by Hannigan (1995), who suggests that six factors are "necessary for the successful construction of an environmental problem" (pp. 54–6). The factors he proposes are

1. Scientific authority for and validation of claims

2. Existence of "popularizers" who can bridge environmentalism and science

3. Media attention in which the problem is "framed" as novel and important

4. Dramatization of the problem in symbolic and visual terms

5. Economic incentives for taking positive action

6. Emergence of an institutional sponsor who can ensure both legitimacy and continuity (p. 55).

He and other authors provide illustrative material to support these assertions. For example, climate change seemed to have its popularizer in Dr. James Hansen, the NASA scientist who testified before the Senate Committee on Energy and Natural Resources in 1988 that a clear signal of humanly propelled climate change had been detected (Hempel 2000:287). Prior to his testimony, climate change had been discussed mainly in academic circles, and even environmental campaign organizations had made little of it (see Pearce 1991:284). Equally, the apparent urgency of ozone depletion seemed to be stirred by computer-generated images of the globe showing areas of ozone thinning, especially images in which regions with the most extreme depletion were shown in black—making the "hole" in the ozone starkly real (Hannigan 1995:55). In the case of climate change, the role of the World Meteorological Organization and the United Nations Environment Program as institutional sponsors for the production and continuing refinement of scientific assessments of climate change and its likely consequences have maintained the issue's visibility (for a critical reading see Boehmer-Christiansen 2003).

However, it is hard to accept Hannigan's assertion that all six factors are *necessary*. Though economic incentives were important for, among other things, phasing out the use of leaded gasoline in Europe, there are currently few economic incentives supporting the construction of climate change as an international environmental problem. Rather, it is the relative cheapness of oil and the high costs of doing away with the infrastructures that support worldwide oil dependency that, in the opinion of many, have inhibited more concerted policy actions in this area. Similarly, environmental and consumer resistance to GM crops and foodstuffs appears to be well established, and even to be growing within the United States, without the emergence of any obvious institutional sponsors. It is quite contrary, for example, to U.K. governmental opinion and to the advice of the official agency with responsibility for food safety that consumers, campaigners, and leading supermarkets (with their eyes only on consumers) persist in resisting the new food technologies. This topic can be seen as the focus of a well-documented recent study (Lowe et al. 1997), in which the authors analyzed the way in which the problem of farm pollution of river environments in rural England was "constructed." During the 1980s, farm pollution—particularly that from dairy farms—was transformed from a relatively unnoticed source of river contamination to the major scourge of water quality in Britain. At the same time, dairy farmers were transmogrified; erstwhile natural figures in the countryside, they became moral offenders threatening the environmental order. This change came about not so much because farm pollution worsened, though it probably did increase, but because farmers became subject to a new regulatory gaze and came to be judged by new moral criteria.

The key to this transformation was water privatization and the establishment of the National Rivers Authority (NRA) as an independent regulatory body. Formerly, the quality of water in rivers had been overseen by officials attached to water authorities. Their chief worries were about large-scale industrial pollution and about the connection between sewage treatment plants and water abstraction. When water was to be privatized in the U.K. in the mid-1980s, a struggle ensued concerning the regulation of water quality. Initial plans would have given the privatized companies control over regulatory activities as well, a move that was opposed by an alliance of consumer and environmentalist voices and by industry; many industrialists feared that private water-company leniency towards their own activities would lead to contaminated rivers, in turn endangering the dependable supply of adequately clean water to industry. An independent regulatory authority, the NRA, was established. However, the NRA faced a difficult early life. The water companies, many of which inherited polluting sewage treatment facilities, were given waivers permitting them to pollute until new investment had time to pay off. Industrial emissions were increasingly in compliance with existing regulations. How was the new agency to establish its significance? By conducting water quality surveys in new ways, the water regulators identified farm pollution as an important component of the threats to water quality, and indeed the largest such threat.

Environmentalists (including Friends of the Earth) and water regulators spurred each other on. Campaigners from environmental groups took the claims about farm pollution on board; they devised new strategies responding, in particular, to the idea that farm wastes threatened rivers of high wildlife value (industry tended to pollute already dirty rivers). The water regulators did not want to be outflanked by environmental campaigners, and made a point of responding to the public's reports of pollution incidents. In the midst of this regulatory activity, many farmers perceived themselves as unfairly cast in the role of environmental sinners, though they had little long-term choice but to comply with regulators' demands.

It is clear both that the construction of environmental problems is of key sociological importance and that organizations such as Friends of the Earth and Greenpeace have become extremely adept at building ecological problem-claims. But it does not seem that one can adopt quite as straightforward an approach as the one favored by Hannigan. For one thing, as Mary Douglas (1982) and other commentators have pointed out, there appears to be a broader cultural component to society's and subcultures' interpretation of natural dangers. In a Durkheimian manner, Douglas observes that societies inscribe onto the natural world their cultural anxieties so that, for example, free-market individualism in the

United States assumes that nature is robust and will bounce back whatever is thrown at it, while dissident cultures (such as those of environmentalists) assume that "risks are incurred involuntarily [and] we are all helpless victims of a fate we cannot escape and [as] risk taking unleashes irreversible destruction, humanity has no options in the future" (Douglas and Wildavsky 1982:190). Contrary to Hannigan's implicit treatment of all ecological problems as similar, Douglas's work would suggest that certain constructions of ecological problems would seem more likely to resonate with some groups in society than would others.

Recently, and writing from a more Continental European perspective, Beck (1995) as well as Giddens (1994:198–227) has made a similar point. In these authors' view, environmental concerns are only concerns about "the environment" as commonly understood in a limited sense. To explain why, we need to place contemporary environmental concerns in a broad historical context. Early modern societies, before the industrial revolution, were characterized by many worries about the external environment. Harvests and food supply, as well as freedom from flood and climatic catastrophes, depended critically on climate conditions, and societies experienced periodic problems of shortages with natural resources. During the nineteenth and early twentieth centuries the common experience was that the external environment was coming more and more under human control. Weather forecasting and understanding of the climate improved. Enhanced farming techniques seemed to free societies ever more from abject dependence on nature. And even if the degree of control over the environment was still highly limited, there was at least optimism that the control would progressively increase. The present was reasonably bright and the future brighter still.

The key recent development has been the reversal of this optimism. Critically, this reversal has happened not so much because the environment has not submitted to further controls, but because the controls themselves have caused new and unexpected harms. Control over food production seemed to be offered by industrial agrochemicals, but these turned out to be potentially harmful to consumers and to the wildlife that we had come to value. Mass generation of energy freed us from a kind of dependency on the climate by allowing buildings to be warmed or cooled as much as wished, but the nuclear power that offered to give us bountiful energy turned out to have hazards of its own (Liberatore 1999). Accordingly, a central claim is that modern environmental concern is not so much a concern about the external environment as it is an anxiety about a humanized nature; as Beck (1995) somewhat obscurely puts it, "[T]he ecological movement is not an environmental movement but a social, inward movement which utilizes 'nature' as a parameter for certain questions" (p. 55). Societies are freed from dependence on the vagaries of the weather but are now dependent for their security on the good behavior of the operators of nuclear power stations. The new GM food-production techniques currently on offer boast of a future free from anxieties about food scarcity, but leave us dependent for our food safety and environmental well-being on the adequacy of the regulatory system and the scientific testing of genetically engineered food crops (Levidow 1999). Where we feared nature, we now worry about the dependability of organizations and regulatory systems. On this view, therefore, modern environmental concern is an anxiety about the environment only in a special and rather confined sense. It is much more a concern about the trustworthiness of the people and systems that regulate newly humanized nature (Wynne 1996). It is within this context that ecological problem-claims are worked up and contested.

COMPREHENDING NATURE

Ecological problems are a peculiar form of social problem, since, though they are problems for societies, they appear to be problems in nature. As problems in the natural world—on the shores of Galicia, for example—environmental problems are therefore frequently understood and expressed in scientific terms. The threat of climate change, for example, only makes sense within the context of scientific understandings of atmospheric chemistry, solar radiation, and meteorological patterns. Common sense and everyday experience are not good guides to whether climate change is occurring. In particular, they are not good guides as to whether climate change is occurring because of releases of additional greenhouse gases or for some other reason, nor to

what the implications of climate change may be a decade or more from now. The politics and culture of environmentalism accordingly have a closer relationship with scientific expertise than most other areas of public life (Yearley 1992b)

On the face of it, one might suppose that this scientific component of environmental knowledge would tend to assist those making claims about ecological problems, since they would have scientific "facts" on their side. One might also expect that the prevalence of scientific considerations would promote agreement, since the scientific results would usher people on opposing sides of any dispute into accord. One can point to instances where the central role of scientific knowledge has had something like these favorable consequences (see Benedick 1991; Grundmann 2001). Thus, without simplifying dramatically, one can argue that members of the university-based scientific community worked out that there was a hypothetical pollution risk from substances (most notoriously CFCs) that might degrade the ozone layer. The suspected ozone depletion was then detected by scientific equipment deployed in the upper reaches of the atmosphere, and subsequently, government officials organized teams of scientific advisers to work out strategies for agreed international reductions in ozone-depleting substances (on just this interpretation see Parson 1994).

However, the relationship between science and environmental protection has not always been this straightforward. On the contrary, environmentalists have commonly seen demands for scientific "proof" used to delay or avoid action on ecological problems. For example, up to the 1990s, environmental organizations and many scientists repeatedly expressed concerns about acidic emissions from power stations, factories, and vehicles. They proposed that these gas emissions were responsible for the increasingly acid character of rainwater that appeared to be falling in neighboring regions, a few hundred kilometers away. This "acid rain" was said to be causing trees to die in large numbers and to be harming wildlife by making rivers and lakes too acidic. By and large, the attitude of the authorities was to accept that this story was possibly true. But they demanded more scientific evidence before they would take any action to curb acid emissions, since it would—they said—be irresponsible to impose costs on the power industry and on consumers without being sure that such action would have demonstrable environmental benefits. Much more recently a similar pattern of argument has surrounded debates over the environmental safety of genetically modified organisms, particularly food crops genetically engineered for resistance to weed killers or to exhibit resistance to certain insect pests. In the past, farmers have not needed special environmental authorization to plant new varieties of food crops; environmentalists argue that GM crops are different and need to be thoroughly checked for adverse consequences before they can be planted. The authorities argue that tests to date have shown the crops to be harmless and that there should be no further restriction unless undesirable side effects become manifest. In both these cases, the experience of environmental campaigners has been that demands for scientific proof have tended to be used to defend the status quo, and campaign organizations have had to adapt their techniques to meet this new challenge. Thus, far from the centrality of science ensuring that agreement is reached, science's role can sometimes appear to be that of protecting the existing state of affairs from environmental reform.

In other ways too, scientific reasoning may be used to thwart environmentalists' objectives. During the Reagan years (most of the 1980s) in the United States, industrialists challenged a series of environmental standards and regulations that had been introduced by the Environmental Protection Agency (EPA). They sought judicial review of the EPA's regulations, arguing before the courts that their industries had been unfairly treated. Using rather idealized notions of standards of scientific proof, industry representatives argued, often successfully, that the EPA's rulings had not been based on the most rigorous science (Jasanoff 1990:180–207; see also Yearley 1997). The weakening of environmental regulations that Reagan and his political allies sought was achieved as much through these indirect means as by explicit changes to the EPA and to environmental legislation.

One further dimension in which the practical weakness of science has been manifest can be demonstrated through the case of climate change. Climate change resulting from the enhanced greenhouse effect is thought by very many to be among the most severe international environmental problems. It could result in dramatic alterations in the climate with more intense storms and flooding, in rises in sea level as the seas expand and as ice melts into the oceans, and in threats to wildlife as habitats are transformed by changing weather patterns. For obvious reasons, much of the running on the diagnosis of this problem and on forecasting its implications has been made by scientific bodies. But even in this urgent and dramatic case, the involvement of scientists has not guaranteed agreement. For one thing, the necessary predictions are technically very difficult. Ordinary weather forecasting runs up against limitations after approximately one week. It is accordingly difficult to have great confidence in climate predictions that are made decades into the future. Worse still, these predictions necessarily depend on making assumptions about how the overall weather system will respond to warming; it may be that the relatively settled patterns of air and water flows that underlie current weather forecasts will themselves be altered by global temperature rises. These inherent difficulties with the business of climate prediction are compounded by other factors: for example, as climate models demand enormous computing power, the leading models are concentrated in the developed world. Lacking ownership of—and possibly even access to—these models, policy makers from countries of the South may treat the models with a certain degree of suspicion (see Boehmer-Christiansen 2003:71–85). Equally, the models need to be checked against data on climate conditions supplied from around the world, but it is hard to ensure that similar standards of data quality are observed everywhere. Sophisticated models may be fed dubious data. On balance, even though concerns about climate change are fundamentally based on appeals to science, that does not guarantee that policy makers are knowledgeable or agreed about the extent of the problem (see the studies collected in Miller and Edwards 2001, and on the strategies of greenhouse skeptics, see McCright and Dunlap 2000).

CONCLUSIONS

Ecological problems are a key and distinctive form of contemporary social problem. They are distinctive largely because of the way that they are jointly social and natural problems and because they are commonly supranational in their scale. The inability of states to address these problems comprehensively on their own leads to a need for international coordination and sometimes for global action. However, as has been shown, other aspects of international action—by governments, by firms, by multilateral agencies, and by banks—may also tend to exaggerate environmental difficulties. The recognition of their supranational character is only a very small step in their resolution. Indeed, claims about the global interest in addressing a particular issue may readily come to be seen as tendentious. Furthermore, it is impossible to separate ecological problems from other kinds of problems, problems of economic management, job creation, and resource distribution. All key environmental problems are simultaneously social problems of other sorts, and few can be solved by treating them as narrowly ecological. Even within nations, it is becoming clearer that the location of environmental harms may follow other patterns of inequality; this is the basis for recent arguments about "environmental justice" (for an overview see Ringquist 2000).

Furthermore, ecological problems are simultaneously problems in society and in the natural world. As Beck reminds us, most contemporary ecological fears are not fears of raw nature but of nature that has been already humanized, brought under more or less imperfect human "control." We may worry about the weather but we also worry about what "we" are doing to the climate system. This means that ecological problems are typically open to scientific analysis, sometimes to technological resolution. But rather than this scientific aspect leading ecological problems to be more tractable than other social problems, the reverse can sometimes be the case (Yearley 1997). Officials may use the demand for scientific proof to delay policy intervention. But even in less manipulative contexts, the people addressing a problem may have imperfect information or other reasons for scientific disagreement. In the GM case, it is the very basis for safety testing that is in dispute. For this reason, ecological problems are a prime site for examining issues around the social role of scientific expertise in the contemporary world (Yearley 1995).

REFERENCES

Anderson, Alison. 1997. *Media, Culture and the Environment.* London, England: UCL Press.

Beck, Ulrich. 1995. *Ecological Politics in an Age of Risk.* Cambridge, England: Polity Press.

Benedick, Richard E. 1991. *Ozone Diplomacy: New Directions in Safeguarding the Planet.* London, England: Harvard University Press.

Boehmer-Christiansen, Sonja. 2003. "Science, Equity, and the War against Carbon." *Science, Technology, and Human Values* 28:69–92.

Dietz, Thomas and Eugene A. Rosa. 2002. "Human Dimensions of Global Environmental Change." Pp. 370–407 in *Handbook of Environmental Sociology,* edited by Riley E. Dunlap and William Michelson. Westport, CT: Greenwood Press.

Douglas, Mary and Aaron Wildavsky. 1982. *Risk and Culture: An Essay on the Selection of Technological and Environmental Dangers.* Los Angeles, CA: University of California Press.

George, Susan. 1988. *A Fate Worse than Debt.* London, England: Penguin.

———. 1992. *The Debt Boomerang: How Third World Debt Harms Us All.* London, England: Pluto Press.

Giddens, Anthony. 1994. *Beyond Left and Right: The Future of Radical Politics.* Cambridge, England: Polity Press.

Grundmann, Reiner. 2001. *Transnational Environmental Policy: Reconstructing Ozone.* London, England: Routledge.

Hannigan, John. 1995. *Environmental Sociology: A Social Constructionist Perspective.* London, England: Routledge.

Hansen, Anders. 1993. "Greenpeace and Press Coverage of Environmental Issues." Pp. 150–78 in *The Mass Media and Environmental Issues,* edited by Anders Hansen. Leicester, England: Leicester University Press.

Hempel, Lamont C. 2000. "Climate Policy on the Installment Plan." Pp. 281–302 in *Environmental Policy,* edited by Norman J. Vig and Michael E. Kraft. Washington, DC: CQ Press.

Houghton, John. 1997. *Global Warming: The Complete Briefing.* Cambridge, England: Cambridge University Press.

Jacobs, Michael. 1994. "The Limits to Neoclassicism: Towards an Institutional Environmental Economics." Pp. 67–91 in *Social Theory and the Global Environment,* edited by Michael Redclift and Ted Benton. London, England: Routledge.

Jasanoff, Sheila. 1990. *The Fifth Branch: Science Advisers as Policymakers.* London, England: Harvard University Press.

Leonard, H. Jeffrey. 1988. *Pollution and the Struggle for the World Product.* Cambridge, England: Cambridge University Press.

Lever, Harold and Christopher Huhne. 1985. *Debt and Danger: The World Financial Crisis.* Harmondsworth, Middlesex, England: Penguin.

Levidow, Les. 1999. "Britain's Biotechnology Controversy: Elusive Science, Contested Expertise." *New Genetics and Society* 18:47–64.

Liberatore, Angela. 1999. *The Management of Uncertainty: Learning from Chernobyl.* London, England: Routledge.

Lowe, Philip, Judy Clark, Susanne Seymour, and Neil Ward. 1997. *Moralizing the Environment: Countryside Change, Farming and Pollution.* London, England: UCL Press.

Mazur, Allan and Jinling Lee. 1993. "Sounding the Global Alarm: Environmental Issues in the U.S. National News." *Social Studies of Science* 23:681–720.

McCright, Aaron M. and Riley E. Dunlap. 2000. "Challenging Global Warming as a Social Problem: An Analysis of the Conservative Movement's Counter-Claims." Social Problems 47:499–522.

Michalowski, Raymond J. and Ronald C. Kramer. 1987. "The Space between Laws: The Problem of Corporate Crime in a Transnational Context." *Social Problems* 34:34–53.

Middleton, Neil, Phil O'Keefe, and Sam Moyo. 1993. *The Tears of the Crocodile: From Rio to Reality in the Developing World.* London, England: Pluto Press.

Miller, Clark and Paul N. Edwards, eds. 2001. *Changing the Atmosphere: Expert Knowledge and Environmental Governance.* Cambridge, MA: MIT Press.

O'Neill, John. 1993. *Ecology, Policy and Politics.* London, England: Routledge.

O'Riordan, Tim and Jill Jäger. 1996. *Politics of Climate Change: A European Perspective.* London, England: Routledge.

Parson, Edward A. 1994. "Protecting the Ozone Layer." Pp. 27–73 in *Institutions for the Earth,* edited by Peter M. Haas, Robert O. Keohane, and Marc A. Levy. Cambridge, MA: MIT Press.

Pearce, Fred. 1991. *Green Warriors: The People and the Politics behind the Environmental Revolution.* London, England: Bodley Head.

Priest, Susanna Hornig. 2001. *A Grain of Truth: The Media, the Public and Biotechnology.* New York: Rowman & Littlefield.

Rabe, Barry G. 2000. "Power to the States: The Promise and Pitfalls of Decentralization." Pp. 32–54 in *Environmental Policy,* edited by Norman J. Vig and Michael E. Kraft. Washington, DC: CQ Press.

Ringquist, Evan J. 2000. "Environmental Justice: Normative Concerns and Empirical Evidence." Pp. 232–56 in *Environmental Policy,* edited by Norman J. Vig and Michael E. Kraft. Washington, DC: CQ Press.

Seager, Joni. 1995. *The New State of the Earth Atlas.* New York: Simon & Schuster.

Starr, Amory. 2000. *Naming the Enemy: Anti-Corporate Movements Confront Globalization.* London, England: Zed Books.

Stiglitz, Joseph. 2002. *Globalization and Its Discontents.* London, England: Allen Lane.

Susskind, Lawrence E. 1994. *Environmental Diplomacy: Negotiating More Effective Global Agreements.* New York: Oxford University Press.

Vogel, David. 2000. "International Trade and Environmental Regulation." Pp. 350–69 in *Environmental Policy,* edited by Norman J. Vig and Michael E. Kraft. Washington, DC: CQ Press.

Warhurst, Alyson and Nia Hughes-Witcomb. 2000. "Mining and the Environment in Latin America: The Pollution-Haven Hypothesis Revisited." Pp. 43–65 in *Industry and Environment in Latin America,* edited by Rhys Jenkins. London, England: Routledge.

Wynne, Brian. 1996. "May the Sheep Safely Graze? A Reflexive View of the Expert-Lay Knowledge Divide." Pp. 44–83 in *Risk, Environment and Modernity: Towards a New Ecology,* edited by Scott Lash. London, England: Sage.

Yearley, Steven. 1992a. *The Green Case: A Sociology of Environmental Issues, Arguments and Politics.* London, England: Routledge.

——. 1992b. "Green Ambivalence about Science: Legal-Rational Authority and the Scientific Legitimation of a Social Movement." *British Journal of Sociology* 43:511–32.

——. 1995. "The Environmental Challenge to Science Studies." Pp. 457–79 in *Handbook of Science and Technology Studies,* edited by Sheila Jasanoff, Gerald E. Markle, James C. Petersen, and Trevor Pinch. London, England: Sage.

——. 1996. *Sociology, Environmentalism, Globalization.* London, England: Sage.

——. 1997. "Science and the Environment." Pp. 227–36 in *The International Handbook of Environmental Sociology,* edited by Michael Redclift and Graham Woodgate. Cheltenham, England: Edward Elgar.

GLOBAL INEQUALITY

SALVATORE J. BABONES

University of Pittsburgh

JONATHAN H. TURNER

University of California, Riverside

T he valuable resources of the world—money, education, and quality of life—are distributed unequally within and between societies. At the top of the global stratification system are the early industrializing societies of Europe, the United States, and Canada, and select Asian societies like Japan, Singapore, and Hong Kong. At the bottom are over a billion people who live on just a dollar a day. Over the past five decades, consistent economic growth in the advanced economies of the world has led to a tripling of real income per capita at the high end of the global income distribution, while per capita income in some countries at the bottom of the distribution have hardly changed. Thus, in the gross sense of inequality as the gap between the richest and the poorest citizens of the world, global inequality has increased dramatically since World War II, continuing a macro trend of the previous hundred (Pritchett 1997) or perhaps thousand (Maddison 2001) years.

Vast inequalities have come to exist between the leading industrialized countries and the poorer countries of the world in both income and in the quality-of-life factors that income can buy. In Table 7.1, we break the countries of the world into five quintiles based on income and report median levels of life expectancy, illiteracy, and child mortality for each income quintile. For every indicator, the median result improves with every increase in income quintile. For example, infant mortality is on average 18 times higher in the typical low-income country (such as Ethiopia [103.7 per 1,000 live births], Nigeria [83.3], or Cambodia [100.2]) than in the typical high-income country (such as the United States [6.9] or Germany [4.8]). Female life expectancy is almost twice as

Table 7.1   Median Levels of Social Indicators, by per Capita Income Level Quintile (1999)

Income Quintile	Income per Capita (PPP)	Life Exp. at Birth Female (years)	Life Exp. at Birth Male (years)	Adult Il-literacy Female	Adult Il-literacy Male	Infant Mortality (per 1000 births)	Under 5 Mortality (per 1000 births)
Lowest	$880	42.8	46.8	66.7	40.7	93.3	151.0
Low	$2,339	68.12	63.2	30.2	26.1	47.3	61.5
Medium	$4,676	72.5	67.7	16.7	8.7	25.5	30.5
High	$8,354	75.2	68.8	4.5	3.2	14.5	18.0
Highest	$22,896	80.3	74.9	(0)[a]	(0)[a]	5.1	6.0

Source: World Bank (2001).

Note: a. Not reported because figure is close to zero

long in Belgium (81.2 years) as in Uganda (42.4), while even in the healthiest low-income quintile country it only reaches 61.7 years (Comoros). Leaving aside the poorest of the poor, social indicators for middle income countries are substantially worse than those for the richest ones. Countries like Jordan (GDP per capita $3,955), Peru ($4,622), and Macedonia ($4,651) are firmly in the middle of the world income distribution, yet they are major recipients of Western foreign aid for poverty and social relief. By the standards of Europe, North America, and Japan, the vast majority of the countries of the world are "poor," both in terms of income and in terms of quality of life.

A first step in understanding the magnitude of the gap between the rich and the poor on a global scale is understanding just what "poor" means in international context. Poverty measurement is a difficult task even within a society with a single currency and set of prices for commodities. Measuring global poverty necessitates the comparison of living standards and consumption levels across a wide variety of societal contexts. Work in this area by Ravallion, Dat, and Van der Walle (1991), Chen, Dat, and Ravallion (1994), and Ravallion and Chen (1997) has formed the basis for most recent estimates of global poverty levels. Drawing on this research, multilateral organizations such as the United Nations and the World Bank use several definitions of poverty in order to gauge the level of deprivation that people must endure. *Absolute poverty* is defined

as a situation where people do not have enough money for survival, with two distinct subcategories: *world poverty,* where people live on less than $365 per year, and *extreme poverty,* where individuals must live on less than $275 per year. There are over 600 million people living in such extreme poverty and many hundreds of millions at or just above the world poverty level. World poverty is also geographically concentrated; for example, the World Bank (2000) estimates that 49 percent of those in sub-Saharan Africa and 44 percent of those in South Asia live below world poverty levels.

One way to put these figures into context is to compare the living standards represented by absolute global poverty levels to those associated with the concept of poverty within nations, particularly within developed nations. No Americans or Western Europeans live in absolute poverty (as defined by the United Nations), but many people in the developed world live in *relative poverty,* meaning that they lack the resources necessary to survive as full participants in the society in which they live. Thus, according to standards set by the Census Bureau, approximately 12 percent of Americans live in poverty, but poverty in the United States is defined by a national poverty line of just over $18,000 income for a family of four, or over $4,500 per person (Proctor and Dalaker 2001). This is more than *10 times* the United Nations definition of absolute poverty. Part of this gap is due to higher costs of living in developed countries, but part of it is also due to the fact that the living standards considered necessary for full participation in society are much higher in the developed world than in developing countries.

Poverty levels, while related to inequality, are not synonymous with it. Poverty measurement concerns the comparison of income levels at the lower end of a population with norms established for that population. Inequality, by contrast, is an attribute of the entire distribution of incomes. Thus, the scale of the gap between high and middle incomes, while irrelevant or indirectly relevant for poverty measurement (through its effect on prices or on mean income levels), is directly relevant for the measurement of inequality. *Inequality* is a summary measure of the disparity between positions in an entire stratification system; correspondingly, income inequality is an attribute of the entire income distribution, generally represented by a Lorenz curve. All of the income levels represented in a population contribute to the measurement of inequality. "Zero" inequality is only attained when all members of a society live at the same level, regardless of what that level is. It could correspond to a 0 percent poverty rate or to a 100 percent poverty rate. One of the most equal societies known in modern times, judged by conventionally accepted measures such as the Gini coefficient, was China during the Cultural Revolution. Another is Luxembourg today.

Global income inequality is generally thought of as consisting of within-nation and between-nation components. However, this neat division is complicated by the fact that income—and thus inequality—is generally measured at the household level. Income stratification within and between households is not random with respect to other important sociological variables, such as age, race, and gender, the effects of which can and do stretch across national borders. For example, there is what is sometimes termed *double deprivation* in poverty rates because women and children are much more likely to be in poverty than adult males. Although the data are somewhat dated, the United Nations Commission on the Status of Women (1995) found that women constitute 60 percent of the world's population but receive just 10 percent of the income and hold only 1 percent of the world's wealth, while taking up two-thirds of all working hours. These

problems are compounded by the fact that, on the whole, the poorest populations have the highest fertility rates, ensuring that the global stratification system will remain bottom heavy with women and, especially, children. The interaction of poverty and fertility with race, education, social class, and other variables makes the formulation of comprehensive models of inequality at the national level difficult, and at the international level near impossible.

As these examples illustrate, vast inequalities exist between countries, within countries, and even within households. In this chapter, we concentrate our attention on two types of "global" inequality: comparative within-nation inequality and cross-country international inequality. Both types of inequality have been the subject of much debate in the sociological literature, though often this literature has generated more heat than light. Below, we hope to bring light to some of the more obscure methodological issues on which these debates have centered. Our goals in this article are (1) to benchmark where we stand in terms of understanding comparative levels of inequality within and between the nations of the world, (2) to review and put into perspective the emerging body of research on trends in between-country inequality, and (3) to trace some of the causes and consequences of the international variability in within-nation inequality. We conclude this chapter with some general policy guidelines for dealing with global inequality.

ASSESSING LEVELS OF INEQUALITY

By any standard, enormous levels of inequality—access to resources, both economic and noneconomic—exist within all countries. For example, in a "typical" country (based on median levels of income inequality), the poorest 20 percent of the households in a population command only 7 percent of the total income earned in the country, while the richest 20 percent of households command around 40 percent of total income (data from Deininger and Squire 1996). This implies that, in broad terms, the typical well-to-do household commands five to six times the resources of its poorer neighbors—and this despite the fact that everywhere in the world poorer households tend to be larger households. Inequality in household income levels is not the only kind of inequality that exists within a society—political and social inequalities can be equally, if not more, important—but income inequality is relatively easier to measure and to compare across countries and time periods. Income differences are also likely to reflect other forms of inequality.

Measuring Income Inequality

Many different methods of measuring inequality have been used in the scientific and journalistic literatures. Some, such as the cursory income quintile analyses used above, have simple intuitive interpretations but possess poor statistical properties. Others, such as Theil's (1967) entropy index, possess desirable measurement qualities but are difficult for the layperson to understand. Standard sources (Champernowne 1974; Champernowne and Cowell, 1998; Cowell 1995; Fields 2001) agree that there are at least four basic qualities that any inequality measure should possess:

1. Anonymity—people's specific identities should be irrelevant to the inequality measure.

2. Scale independence—the units of income (dollars, euros, etc.) and their magnitudes (mean levels) should be irrelevant to the inequality measure.

3. Population independence—two populations with a fixed ratio of people at every given income level should show the same level of inequality (doubling the number of people at every income level should leave the inequality measure unchanged).

4. Satisfaction of the "Pigou-Dalton transfer principle"—any transfer of income from a higher-income person to a lower-income one should lead to a reduction in measured inequality or at least to no change in inequality, but never an increase in inequality (and vice versa).

All summary measures of inequality in general use—highest and lowest quintile income shares, high-to-low income share ratios, the Gini (1912) coefficient, the Theil (1967) entropy index, the Atkinson (1983) coefficient—satisfy these four intuitive principles. For computational formulas for these measures and a discussion of how they relate to the four principles above, see Fields (2001, chap. 2).

Another, related way to think of inequality is through the analysis of *Lorenz curves*. The Lorenz (1905) curve is the plot of the cumulative distribution of income in a population (on the vertical axis) against the cumulative distribution of the population itself (on the horizontal axis), ranked by income level. An idealized example of a Lorenz curve is depicted in Figure 7.1. The 45-degree straight line indicates perfect equality in the distribution of income. That is, 10 percent of the population receives 10 percent of the income, 20 percent gets 20 percent of the income, and so on. The sample Lorenz curve drawn below it represents the distribution of income in a population. The greater the distance between the Lorenz curve and the 45-degree line, the greater the level of inequality in the population. For a population with a given distribution of income, any transfer of income from a higher-income person to a lower-income person, with no other changes in the income distribution, moves a portion of the Lorenz curve up and to the left, representing a reduction in inequality.

Lorenz curves represent in a single snapshot all the information contained in the population income distribution. Changes in a single country's income distribution over time can best be understood through detailed examination of changes in the Lorenz curve, rather than through reliance on a single summary statistic. For example, a change in the shape of the income distribution that raises income for the poor and the rich simultaneously, while reducing incomes in the middle, might result in no change in inequality measured using a single summary statistic, since the transfer from middle to poor reduces inequality at the same time that the transfer from middle to rich increases it. A comparison of the before-and-after Lorenz curves, however, will detect the change in the distribution of income.

Unfortunately, it is not practical to compare Lorenz curves for large numbers of countries, and summary measures for each country's level of inequality are necessary for use in further statistical modeling. Due to its long pedigree and ease of interpretation, the Gini coefficient has become the standard inequality measure used in international comparative research, and the emerging international inequality datasets report only Ginis. Conveniently, the Gini coefficient is closely tied to

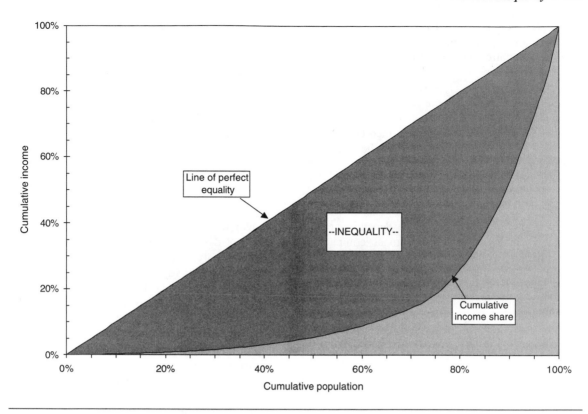

Figure 7.1   Illustration of Lorenz Curve

the Lorenz curve representation of inequality. Again referring to Figure 7.1, the Gini coefficient is the proportion of the total area under the 45-degree line that falls above the Lorenz curve. It thus runs from a low of zero (when every member of the population has the same income level, the Lorenz curve falls exactly on the 45-degree line) to a maximum of one (when one person receives all the income in the population, the Lorenz curve follows the base of the chart). Incidentally, since the area under the 45-degree line is by construction one-half, the Gini coefficient is arithmetically equal to twice the area of "inequality" marked on the chart in Figure 7.1.

One problem with the Gini coefficient is that it cannot be directly decomposed into hierarchical contributions to inequality from different sources. The critical application here is the decomposition of global inequality into within-nation and between-nation components. Of the measures mentioned above, only the Theil index possesses this property (Bourguignon 1979). So for studying cross-national comparisons of inequality in national income distributions, and for international inequality among national income levels, the Gini coefficient is generally used. For decomposing global inequality into within-nation and between-nation components, the Theil is becoming increasingly popular. The difficulty is that the Theil index is generally not reported in compilations of within-country inequality statistics. Aggregate income by quintile, however, *is* commonly reported, and software to estimate inequality measures from quintile aggregates is now freely available from the World Bank (Chen, Dat, and Ravallion 2002).

In comparative work, the choice of summary measure to use in studying a nation's income distribution is often driven by the facts of availability. Luckily, for a given distribution of income, most income inequality measures are very highly correlated (Champernowne 1974). Different indices, however, are more or less sensitive to changes in different areas of the income distribution. Assuming a lognormal distribution of income, the variance or standard deviation of the logged incomes is most sensitive to the degree of spread at the bottom of the income distribution, the Gini coefficient is most sensitive to the spread in the middle, and the Theil index is most sensitive to the spread at the top (Champernowne 1974). As a result, each measure might be more or less appropriate, depending on the research objective. For international comparative work, the Gini is probably the best measure, since it is most closely associated with the idea of the range of "typical" incomes within a country. Also, being less sensitive to dispersion at the extremes, it is perhaps more reliable where the quality of the data is low. It is certainly the most common measure found in the comparative literature.

Patterns of Inequality within Nations

Until recently, a major impediment to research on cross-national patterns of inequality was the lack of internationally comparable data on within-country inequality. In recent decades, data infrastructure improvement efforts in two distinct directions have helped to improve the situation. First, many statistical agencies around the world have worked to collect income distribution data that are directly comparable in methodology across a number of countries. Two broad cross-national efforts have been especially successful. The World Bank's Living Standards Measurement Study (LSMS) has funded or supported surveys in 33 developing countries since 1985; for several countries, comparable data are available for multiple time periods. The Luxembourg Income Study (LIS) of Luxembourg's Center for Population, Poverty, and Policy Studies, also dating from the early 1980s, brings together 25 developed-country statistical agencies in an effort to publish standardized data on income distributions. Together, these two datasets provide a reasonably indicative snapshot (and increasingly a motion picture) of income

distributions in developing and developed countries respectively.

The second trend has been toward the collation of the results of existing national income distribution studies into broadly cross-national databases. Collecting 2,621 sets of survey results from over 100 sources, scholars at the World Bank recently constructed such a database, making truly global international comparisons possible for the first time (Deininger and Squire 1996). The Deininger-Squire dataset contains reported Gini coefficients from each study, as well as income quintile data for a large subset of studies. It also includes detailed information on the source of the data, such as the type of data collected (income or expenditure), the unit of analysis (personal or household), and the coverage of the survey (national, urban, rural, etc.). This allows the proper selection of observations for truly parallel cross-country analyses. The dataset contains observations for most countries dating back to 1970, and for some countries as far back as the nineteenth century, allowing intertemporal comparisons as well.

The Deininger-Squire dataset has been used as the foundation database for a more extensive, ongoing project at the United Nations University to extend the data coverage to as many countries and time periods as possible (WIDER 2000). In Figure 7.2, we summarize the WIDER-reported inequality levels for countries in each of seven regions of the world in the 1990s. The process we used to choose which reported Gini coefficients to use in constructing Figure 7.2 (of the multiple estimates available for each country) illustrates the care that must be taken in properly using cross-national inequality datasets. Any reported Gini coefficient with full population coverage was preferred over any partially representative Gini (typically urban or rural). Gross income/expenditure was preferred over net. Then, income-based statistics were used where available before expenditure-based statistics. Where there were multiple observations at the same level of coverage and type over the period 1990 to 1999, they were averaged. The resulting breakdown of the 126 observations by Gini coefficient source can be found in the notes to Figure 7.2.

The United States, with an average Gini coefficient of around 37.9 (and rising) over the course of the

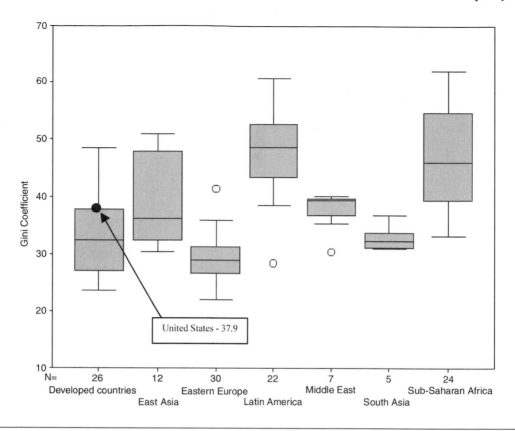

Figure 7.2   Inequality by Region of the World (*n* = 126)

Source: WIDER (2000).

Note: Data notes for Gini coefficients:

Coverage Level:

Full population	114
Partial population	12

Data Type (in order of preference used):

Income, gross	56
Monetary income, gross	1
Taxable income, gross	1
Earnings, gross	1
"Income"	4
Expenditure	44
Income, net	13
Expenditure, net	5
[BLANK]	1

decade, falls in between the world mean (38.3) and the world median (36.2). However, levels of inequality in the United States fall toward the high end of the distribution of developed countries. In general, richer countries show less inequality, as shown in Figure 7.3. In Figure 7.3, we combine the WIDER (2000)-reported Gini coefficients used above with Penn World Table (Heston, Summers,

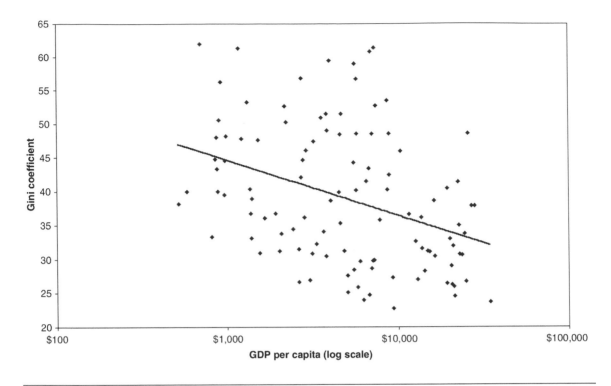

Figure 7.3   Distribution of Gini Coefficients by National Income Level ($n = 126$)

Data sources: WIDER (2000) for Gini coefficients and Penn World Table (Heston et al. 2001) for real GDP per capita at purchasing power parity (series RGDPCH).

and Aten 2001) GDP data to plot the distribution of within-country inequality by national income level. As shown in Figure 7.3, inequality generally declines with increasing national income levels (although the trend is weak compared with the total variation in inequality). This contradicts the famous Kuznets (1955) hypothesis, that inequality is similarly low in both low-income and high-income countries, and high in middle-income countries. In Kuznets's model, inequality rises when a poor country begins to grow, as workers move from the lower-income agricultural sector to the higher-income industrial sector. Maximum inequality is reached when a country is half industrialized. Full industrialization implies a return to lower inequality, now at a higher average level of income. A cross-sectional Kuznets curve—a global snapshot like Figure 7.3 but showing low inequality in the poorest countries as well as in the richest—has been observed in prior studies (Babones 2002a; Bourguignon and Morrison 1990; Jha 1996), but clearly is not observed for the 1990s. This suggests two possibilities. Either income inequality has recently risen quite dramatically in countries with low levels of income per capita (obliterating the left side of the inverted-U Kuznets curve), or the availability of data for a wider sample of countries has shown that inequality in poor countries is not as low as was previously thought.

Li, Squire, and Zou (1998) report that, in general, within-country inequality is quite stable over time. They studied trends in the 49 countries in the Deininger-Squire database that had observed Gini coefficients for at least four distinct time points over the period 1947 to 1994. Carefully adjusting for the differing Gini definitions and methodologies used in the various countries over the course of the study period, they found that 32 of the 49 countries showed no significant trend in income inequality.

Seven countries showed declining inequality, while 10 countries showed rising inequality. Even among those countries with significant trends, 10 of the 17 countries had trends that, while statistically significant, were quantitatively negligible. If it is true that levels of inequality have changed little in most countries over the past several decades, then it seems likely that prior reports of a cross-sectional Kuznets curve were clouded by sample censoring problems, rather than reflecting the true state of the data, since the data should not have changed much in recent years.

Rapidly increasing inequality, however, has been observed in two key countries in the global economy: the United States and China. In the United States, the national Gini coefficient held steady between 34.5 and 35 throughout the 1940s, '50s, and '60s. Since then, the Gini coefficient has risen noticeably to 37.9. In China, the overall picture has been the same but the trend more marked. The Gini coefficient was in the region of 27.2 at the end of the Cultural Revolution in the mid-1970s. It later rose nine points to 36.2 by the mid-1990s. While the first figure may have been artificially low due to the political climate of the times, the two-decade increase is nonetheless dramatic. Anecdotal evidence is that the increase in inequality in China is continuing, as the southern coastal regions develop while the interior of the country remains mired in poverty.

National and International Components of Inequality

As large as the gaps between rich and poor are within individual countries, even wider gaps exist between the aggregate resource levels of rich countries and those of poor countries. Among countries listed in the Penn World Table (Heston et al. 2001), the ratio of the national income per capita of richer (80th percentile) to poorer (20th percentile) countries is roughly 40:1 when income per capita for all countries is converted to dollars at market exchange rates. Thus, a typical well-to-do country such as Portugal or Taiwan has 40 times the capacity to buy goods on the world market (such as computers, wheat, or oil) as does a typical poor country, such as Kenya or Cambodia. Even when national incomes are compared in terms of local purchasing power,

the 80th:20th percentile ratio is still around 10:1. The gap between the very richest countries and the poorest is, of course, much, much wider, and this does not even account for the fact that there is a group of extremely poor countries for which data simply are not available.

One way to compare levels of within-nation inequality to levels of between-nation inequality is to construct a summary measure of inequality, such as the Gini coefficient, using the nation as the unit of analysis. Doing so presents several methodological challenges. First is the fact that each nation's income level is expressed in its own currency units. There is an active debate on the appropriate method for converting national currency units into a common unit for analysis (typically U.S. dollars); on this topic, see especially the exchange between Firebaugh (2000a) and Korzeniewicz and Moran (2000). One group of scholars (Firebaugh 1999; Schultz 1998), most closely associated with the field of economic demography, argues that national incomes should be converted to dollars using purchasing power parity (PPP) factors. The PPP exchange factor is (in broad terms) the exchange rate that would make the cost of a typical domestic consumption basket equal in the two currencies. The use of this rate in studying between-nation inequality best operationalizes the concept of inequality as the difference in domestic living standards between countries.

A second group of scholars (Babones 2002b; Korzeniewicz and Moran 1997), most closely associated with the world-systems tradition in sociology, argues that national incomes should be converted to dollars using market foreign exchange (F/X) rates. Where market exchange rates are not available (which is often the case when dealing with historical data), official exchange rates are used. The F/X rate operationalization best captures a country's economic influence on world markets and in interactions at the international level. Reinforcing this conceptualization, world-systems scholars tend to use gross national product (GNP), rather than gross domestic product (GDP), to operationalize national income. GNP represents the income available to a nation, after transfer payments such as the repatriation of profits by foreign corporations. The choice of GNP or GDP as the income variable, however, has little effect on measured inequality.

A direct application of the Lorenz curve logic underlying domestic inequality measurement to the international sphere, taking the country as the unit of analysis, would involve ranking all countries by their levels of *total* income, since global income is the sum of each nation's total income, not of each nation's income per capita. For obvious reasons, this approach is not desirable for the present purpose, since we are generally interested in differences in average living standards, not differences in the sizes of national economies. The standard treatment is to compute inequality measures (such as the Gini coefficient) using each nation's dollar income (GDP or GNP) per capita as the relevant income level and to weight each country by its population. In practice, this weighting is done by treating each country as if it represented a set of N individuals, all at income level Y, where N is the population of the country and Y is its income per capita.

On the basis of such "weighted" inequality measures, the level of between-nation inequality is much greater than the average level of within-nation inequality. In addition, F/X-based analyses yield much higher inequality estimates than do PPP-based analyses (this is due to the fact that prices are generally lower in poorer countries). In terms of Gini coefficients, between-nation inequality is roughly twice as great as average within-nation inequality (compare Figure 7.2 on page 107 with Figure 7.5 discussed below).

Several recent studies have attempted to decompose total global inequality into within-nation and between-nation components. This differs from a simple comparison of levels of within-nation and between-nation inequality that take the individual and the nation, respectively, as the unit of analysis. In a true decomposition, the objective is to score all individuals in the world on a single income inequality measure (such as the Theil index), which can be decomposed into two additive components, and then to compare the magnitudes of the within-country and between-country components. Estimates of the percentage of global inequality that is due to between-nation inequality range from 68 percent (Goesling 2001) to 83 percent (Korzeniewicz and Moran 1997). Both studies take the same basic approach of decomposing Theil indices, but differ with respect to income series, currency conversions, and specific samples used. A third study, by Schultz (1998), takes instead a regression approach. Depending on the specific operationalization, he reports a between-nation component ranging from two-thirds to four-fifths. While similar in magnitude, his results are not directly comparable to those of the other two studies, since they represent a decomposition of income variance, rather than a decomposition of Theil entropy. In any case, it is clear that the single largest factor contributing to global inequality is the wide variation in income levels across countries.

All three recent decompositions of global inequality into within-country and between-country components rely on the additivity of the two components of inequality to combine known within-country and between-country statistics into a global statistic. This is fundamentally a top-down approach. Several scholars are currently working on the complementary bottom-up problem, beginning with a simulation of the full distribution of incomes at the individual level across all countries of the world. Individual incomes can then be aggregating up into inequality measures, or used in a global Lorenz curve analysis. See Babones (2002a), Sala-i-Martin (2002), and Milanovic (2002) for more information.

TRENDS IN INTERNATIONAL INEQUALITY

The importance of between-country, or international, inequality was, of course, known long before actual estimates were made of its magnitude in relation to within-country inequality. There are two largely disjoint literatures on trends in income inequality between nations. The first, based mainly in neoclassical economics, is regression based, and concerned with the problem of convergence in income per capita across the countries of the world. In these studies, the dependent variable is economic growth, and convergence (reduction in inequality) is represented by a negative coefficient in the regression of national growth rates on national income levels. This literature is generally considered part of the growth literature, and is not discussed here. The second major literature, spanning economic history, demographics, and sociology, is concerned mainly with the change over time in measures of international inequality. The literature is largely descriptive, rather than explanatory. It is this descriptive literature that is our focus in this chapter.

We begin this section with a brief discussion of very long term trends in international inequality, followed by a review of the recent debate that has focused on trends in the past four decades. We then complement this review with our own analysis of trends in international inequality, holding the sample constant to highlight differences in measured inequality resulting strictly from differences in methodologies.

Long-Term Trends in Global Inequality

Over the past two millennia, economic inequality has increased dramatically between broad regions of the world. The principal reason for this trend is that the world is much more differentiated in terms of the level of development than it was even a few hundred years ago. Most countries were agrarian with similar levels of national income, with the large mass of their populations living at or near subsistence. Within-nation inequality varied somewhat, depending upon the capacity of elites to extract economic surplus generated by agrarian labor, but in general, agrarian societies revealed very high levels of internal inequality. Yet, across the whole range of agrarian societies, differences were comparatively small, at least by today's standards of inequality, and as a result, between-nation inequality was not dramatic.

Maddison (2001) has made GDP per capita estimates for seven wide regions of the world for four time points over the past 2,000 years. Using his GDP estimates to compute interregional Gini coefficients for the years 1, 1000, 1820, and 1998 ("international" comparisons would be meaningless over this time frame) yields the results graphed in Figure 7.4. These interregional Gini coefficients at each time period ignore any within-country variation, and represent only the differences in average income levels between the regions of the world defined by Maddison. Although the results can only be considered to be broadly indicative, the enormous increase in the scale of inequality over time can probably be taken at face value.

As Figure 7.4 indicates, even before the beginning of the industrial revolution, differences in average incomes had begun to emerge between broad areas of the world. Between the years 1000 and 1820, incomes in Western Europe and Japan grew nearly four times as fast as did incomes in the rest of the world. The nineteenth and twentieth centuries saw a continuation of this already-existing trend, with incomes in Western Europe, North America, Japan, and Australia rising more than three times faster than in the rest of the world (Maddison 2001, chap. 1).

The Debate on Recent Trends

In the grand sweep of economic history that is Maddison's focus, the direction of trends over time in income inequality are crystal clear. Recent trends, over periods of decades rather than centuries, are more difficult to discern.

Currently, there is considerable debate over whether inequality has increased or decreased over the last four decades. Korzeniewicz and Moran (1997) and Babones (2002b) report rising inequality from 1960 to 1992, whereas Schulz (1998) and Firebaugh (1999) find that inequality has remained relatively stable over this period. Meanwhile, Melchior and Telle (2001) and Goesling (2001) report falling levels of inequality. In a recent review article, Firebaugh (2000b) reaffirmed his view that between-country inequality has stabilized.

The reason behind these contradictory findings probably resides in the respective methodologies of investigators. The Korzeniewicz and Moran and Babones findings rely upon the level of the GNP evaluated at international F/X rates to determine national income, whereas Schultz and Firebaugh use GDP converted to dollars using PPP factors. Melchior and Telle also use the GDP/PPP methodology, but extend the study period into the late 1990s.

In the exchange alluded to in the previous section, Firebaugh (2000a) criticizes the uncertainty and volatility in exchange rate figures; Korzeniewicz and Moran (2000) object that the procedures for calculating purchasing power are ridden with estimation problems and heroic assumptions, including difficulties in securing sufficient numbers

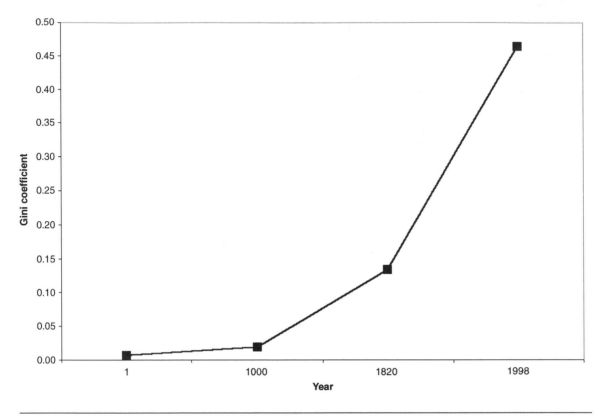

Figure 7.4   Millennial Trends in International Income Inequality, Weighted by Population (Seven World Regions)

Data source: Maddison (2001, Tables 1-1 and 1-2, pp. 27–8).

Note: Ginis are computed based on population and GNP estimates for seven regions of the world. These are Africa, Asia outside Japan, Japan, Eastern Europe, Latin America, the Western "offshoots" (United States, Canada, Australia, and New Zealand), and Western Europe. Time axis not to scale.

of benchmark countries and years as well as the inability to account for the quality of goods and services (which exchange rates would capture). In the end, it is difficult to determine conclusively that one methodology is better than the other, and it is perhaps most reasonable to consider the results from both when evaluating trends in global inequality.

RECONCILING CONFLICTING RESULTS

It is difficult to compare the various conflicting results on international inequality because they not only use different measures of national income and

different currency conversion factors, but they also use different sets of countries for which they have data available. We have replicated international inequality results for both methodologies using a common set of countries. Data are from Heston et al. (2001). We compute population-weighted inequality using F/X and PPP based upon real GDP per capita for 110 countries over the period 1960 to 1996. The results are graphed in Figure 7.5.

Our results confirm the trends generally reported in the literature. Over the entire period, the F/X-based inequality series reports much higher levels of inequality than does the PPP-based series. Trends in both series are relatively flat until around 1980, when

Figure 7.5   Population-Weighted International Inequality, F/X versus PPP Series (*n* = 110)

the trajectories diverge dramatically. After 1980, the FX-based series shows inequality rising, while the PPP-based series shows inequality declining. The close conformity of our results to those reported in the literature suggests that a range of contentious methodological issues—use of GDP versus GNP to measure national income, specifics of sample composition, choice of initial and terminal years, and so on—are not empirically relevant to the debate. The choice of currency conversion method is sufficient to account for the divergence in results. Note that the PPP conversion factors are effectively smoothed over a five-year period, which accounts for the lower annual volatility in the PPP series.

The results reported in Figure 7.5 and the discussion above and in most of the literature are for population-weighted inequality. A major difficulty in interpreting population-weighted statistics in any international comparison is that one country, China, accounts for almost 25 percent of the world's

population. Thus, to a large extent, population-weighted international inequality is just the inequality between China and the rest of the world. This leads to serious methodological problems, since it is universally accepted that economic data for China are highly suspect. The problem of estimating China's GDP is so difficult that the Penn World Table (Heston et al. 2001) devotes an entire methodological appendix to the problem. The table's PPP conversion factors, in particular, are little more than best guesses for China—China has participated in none of the benchmark price surveys that underlie the PPP methodology. While this does not justify the categorical exclusion of China from economic comparisons, it does suggest that one should be wary of the extent to which one's results depend solely on data for China. Removing China from the analyses underlying Figure 7.5 yields the trends reported in Figure 7.6.

Clearly, with China excluded, the rest of the world has seen no sustained decrease in inequality

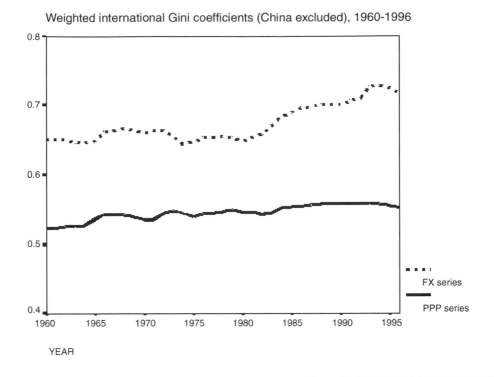

Figure 7.6   Population-Weighted International Inequality, F/X versus PPP Series (China Excluded)

over any time period, regardless of the currency conversion method chosen. Interestingly, the track of the FX series hardly changes when China is excluded, while the track of the PPP series changes dramatically, especially after 1980. It might or might not be true that rapid growth in China has led to reduced global inequality, but we can confidently assert that, excluding China, the rest of the poor countries of the world are not catching up. The trend in unweighted Gini coefficients for the same 110 countries, shown in Figure 7.7, confirms this picture. Taking the country as the unit of analysis, between-country inequality in GDP per capita has risen dramatically since 1960, by any measure. Contrasting these trends with those found for weighted inequality suggests that converging incomes in a few high-population countries (especially China) belies a general condition of strongly diverging levels of income per capita among the countries of the world.

CAUSES AND CONSEQUENCES OF DOMESTIC INEQUALITY

We have only just begun to unravel the causal web surrounding the level of within-country inequality and its correlates. Unionization and public spending are associated with, and presumably lead to, lower levels of inequality (Gustafsson and Johansson 1999). Although the direction of causality is not as certain, within-country inequality is also related to national health (Wilkinson 1996) and education (Alderson and Nielsen 1999) indicators. In both the Organization for Economic Cooperation and Development (OECD) (Gustafsson and Johansson

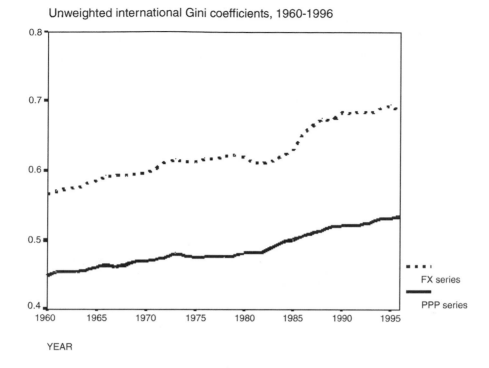

Unweighted international Gini coefficients, 1960-1996

Figure 7.7 Unweighted International Inequality, F/X versus PPP Series (*n* = 110)

1999) and the developing world (Alderson and Nielsen 1999), demographic factors are highly correlated with inequality as well.

In general, the relative lack of time series data on within-nation inequality, combined with the slow rate of change in broad societal indicators, has meant that most of the research on the causes and consequences of inequality has been based on cross-sectional samples. This is, however, changing, as data improve each year. In the next section, we highlight two important avenues of cross-national research on within-nation inequality: globalization and inequality, and inequality and economic growth.

GLOBALIZATION AND DOMESTIC INEQUALITY

Several recent studies have attempted to substantiate links between perceived trends toward the creation of a more global economy and perceived increases in income inequality. Here we say "perceived" because, as discussed above, in the broadly cross-national context, within-country income inequality has been relatively stable over time. Also, despite the received wisdom that we are every year living in a more global world, empirical evidence to this effect has been patchy (Chase-Dunn, Kawano, and Brewer 2000). Nonetheless, Alderson and Nielsen (2002) do find such a link for OECD countries. They find that longitudinal changes in inequality within specific countries are related to factors such as import penetration and investment outflow, leading to the conclusion that the deindustrialization of the OECD is leading to increasing inequality in the world's wealthiest countries. Beer and Boswell (2002) echo this result for developing nations, finding that foreign investment dependence is an important longitudinal predictor of rising inequality.

Taken together, these two studies suggest that globalization—in the form of OECD country investment in the periphery of the world economy, complemented by a returning flow of goods to the OECD—promotes inequality on both sides.

Both of these studies set out in new research directions, and their results must for now be considered preliminary. Nonetheless, they are intriguing. Interestingly, when combined with the general stability of within-country inequality, they imply the lack of a broad trend toward greater global integration, since globalization would, by their arguments, be reflected in increasing levels of within-nation inequality. An interesting alternative twist on the relationship between globalization and inequality is Bergesen and Bata's (2002) conjecture that within-nation and between-nation inequality are themselves related. They find a "synchronicity" in movements in between-nation and average within-nation inequality, which they argue are generally increasing at the same pace over time. Shocks to this trend line, however, affect between-nation and within-nation inequality in opposite directions. They hypothesize that any increase in between-nation inequality strengthens class solidarity in poorer countries, resulting in a decrease in within-nation inequality. Conversely, relatively lower (than trend) between-nation inequality is hypothesized to weaken within-country solidarity. They argue that this interaction between the two levels of inequality is evidence of the existence of a global class system.

Whether or not globalization, as a dynamic phenomenon, is related to changes in within-country inequality, it is certain that structural features of the world economy do explain a significant proportion of the cross-sectional variation in within-country inequality. Alderson and Nielsen (1999) report a positive relationship between relative dependence on foreign capital and within-nation inequality, and Gustafsson and Johansson (1999) report an association of high inequality with developing-country import penetration. It is well-known that within-nation inequality exhibits strong regional patterns (high in Latin America and Africa, low in Asia and Europe). The socialist countries of the soviet bloc and China had very low levels of income inequality under socialism and are registering massive increases in inequality as they integrate into the capitalist world economy.

Inequality and Growth

In what must surely rank as one of the most influential articles in the history of economics, Kuznets (1955) hypothesized an organic link between economic growth and changes in inequality. As discussed above, empirical evidence for the Kuznets hypothesis has not materialized. Neither has empirical support for other theoretical arguments for a link between income inequality and growth. Confirming the seminal model of Galor and Zeira (1993), Deininger and Squire (1998) do report that high initial inequality in *asset* ownership, particularly in the distribution of land ownership, tends to depress subsequent economic growth, especially income growth for the poor, but this is as close as we get. Income inequality itself seems to be inversely related to rates of investment (Alesina and Perotti 1996), though the direction of causality has not been established, and the relationship between investment and growth has recently been called into question (Babones 2002a; Barro 1997; Blomstrom, Lipsey, and Zejan 1996).

In two isolated studies using now dated inequality data, Persson and Tabellini (1994) and Alesina and Rodrik (1994) did find significant negative correlations between income inequality and growth, but newer data from Deininger and Squire (1996, 1998) have largely invalidated these findings. Persson and Tabellini purported to demonstrate that inequality was important for growth, but only in democracies, while Alesina and Rodrik argued that high inequality reduced growth through its effect on tax policies.

All in all, it seems likely that extreme inequality is not good for growth, but the relationship is probably mild. Figure 7.8 plots Penn World Table rates of economic growth in the 1990s versus circa 1990 Gini coefficients for the 96 countries for which data are available. There is a slight, but nonsignificant, quadratic trend. Clearly, any causal relationship between the two variables must be subtle and contingent.

CONCLUSIONS

Our social environment encompasses high levels of inequality, both within and between nations. Some level of within-nation inequality has certainly existed since the beginnings of nations, and before

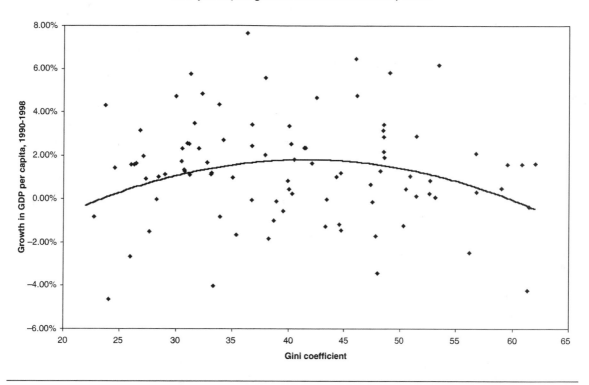

GDP per capita growth vs. Gini coefficients, 1990s

Figure 7.8   Income Inequality and Economic Growth, 1990s (*n* = 94)

that, within-society or within-tribe inequality. "For the poor shall never cease out of the land" (Deut. 15:11). Between-nation or between-region inequality is also of ancient pedigree, but attained extreme proportions only with the coming of the industrial revolution. All experts agree that international inequality rose dramatically between 1820 and 1960. There is intense debate over its trajectory since 1960, especially for the period after 1980. Whatever its trend, the existing level of between-nation inequality is high enough to account for at least two-thirds, and perhaps more, of total global (within- and between-nation) inequality. Moreover, there is some evidence that the forces of globalization in trade, investment, and the labor force are working to increase levels of within-nation inequality. Thus, even if between-nation inequality is on the

decline, total inequality may remain stable or even increase over the next several decades.

In this chapter we have focused exclusively on measures of income inequality. There are, of course, many important dimensions to global inequality besides income inequality: extreme inequalities exist both within and between nations in access to health care, levels of education, nutrition, and general quality of life. Still, income is a good indicator of what a household or a society can afford to buy, and while it may be true that "money is not everything," it can typically buy what it is not. For example, whether through government programs or market systems, high-income countries are able to allocate far greater resources to health, education, and welfare than are low-income countries. GDP per capita in India is a little over $400 per year;

according to the United Nations (2002), infant mortality in India runs 64 per 1,000 live births, 43 percent of the population is illiterate, and 69 percent of the population lives without sanitary sewerage. By comparison, GNP per capita in Mexico is over $4,000 per year; infant mortality is 28 per 1,000, the illiteracy rate is 9 percent, and only 27 percent of the population lives without sanitary sewerage. Similar comparisons hold for the correlation of income with welfare within countries.

The problems posed by the long-term persistence of high levels of within-nation and between-nation inequality are many and varied. The broad swath of the world's population living at or near biological survival levels is chronically exposed to Malthusian pressures of malnutrition and disease. If the rich countries of the world will not act to alleviate such misery out of humanitarian concern, they may be forced to act out of self-preservation. Diseases incubated within such weakened human populations do not respect national boundaries, as the global AIDS epidemic tragically demonstrates. Moreover, geopolitical and geoeconomic problems that originate in poor countries can have a profound impact on rich countries. International refugee flows, wars and civil conflicts, and international terrorism will continue to be high policy priorities for developed nations for the foreseeable future.

Thus, the persistently high level of global inequality is not only an important social problem in itself, but is also an important correlate, and potentially a predictor, of other social problems. Income inequality is probably best thought of as a general indicator for the broad level of social inequality. Despite the methodological problems inherent in comparing income surveys cross-nationally, operationalizing currency conversion factors, and combining within-country with between-country data, income is relatively well measured (compared with other unequally distributed resources), and reasonably complete time series for income for large numbers of countries exist. In the Lorenz diagram and its associated inequality measures, we also have a well-articulated framework for studying income inequality. All this makes income inequality easier to analyze than other forms of inequality, and we think it likely that most attempts to understand global inequality in the future will concentrate on income inequality.

On the other hand, we have already done most of what is possible with the existing data on income distributions, to the point where diminishing returns to additional research are already starting to set in. In its place, we see an important need for additional research on the correlation of income inequality with other forms of inequality, both within and between nations. There is a vast literature on social stratification, but we see a need for more internationally comparative work explicitly addressing how inequality affects and is affected by other social forces. Meanwhile, there is an open field for scholarship on how the level of international inequality affects the dynamics of the international state system. The first phase of research on global inequality, collating basic data and setting methodological standards for its analysis, is nearly over; the next phase, addressing issues of causality, is at hand.

REFERENCES

Alderson, Arthur S. and Francois Nielsen. 1999. "Income Inequality, Development, and Dependence: A Reconsideration." *American Sociological Review* 64:606–31.

———. 2002. "Globalization and the Great U-Turn: Income Inequality Trends in 16 OECD Countries." *American Journal of Sociology* 107:1244–99.

Alesina, Alberto and Roberto Perotti. 1996. "Income Distribution, Political Instability, and Investment." *European Economic Review* 40:1203–28.

Alesina, Alberto and Dani Rodrik. 1994. "Distributive Politics and Economic Growth." *Quarterly Journal of Economics* 109:465–89.

Atkinson, Anthony B. 1983. *The Economics of Inequality.* 2nd ed. Oxford, England: Clarendon Press.

Babones, Salvatore J. 2002a. *The International Structure of Income and Its Implications for Economic Growth, 1960–2000.* Dissertation, Department of Sociology, Johns Hopkins University.

———. 2002b. "Population and Sample Selection Effects in Measuring International Income Inequality." *Journal of World-Systems Research* 8:1–22.

Barro, Robert J. 1997. *Determinants of Economic Growth: A Cross-Country Empirical Study.* Cambridge, MA: MIT Press.

Beer, Linda and Terry Boswell. 2002. "The Resilience of Dependency Effects in Explaining Income Inequality in the Global Economy: A Cross-National Analysis, 1975–1995." *Journal of World-Systems Research* 8:30–59.

Bergesen, Albert J. and Michelle Bata. 2002. "Global and National Inequality: Are They Related?" *Journal of World-Systems Research* 8:130–44.

Blomstrom, Magnus, Robert E. Lipsey, and Mario Zejan. 1996. "Is Fixed Investment the Key to Economic Growth?" *Quarterly Journal of Economics* 111: 269–76.

Bourguignon, Francois. 1979. "Decomposable Inequality Measures." *Econometrica* 47:901–20.

Bourguignon, Francois and Christian Morrison. 1990. "Income Distribution, Development and Foreign Trade: A Cross-Sectional Analysis." *European Economic Review* 34:1113–32.

Champernowne, David G. 1974. "A Comparison of Measures of Inequality of Income Distribution." *Economic Journal* 84:787–816.

Champernowne, David G. and Frank A. Cowell. 1998. *Economic Inequality and Income Distribution.* New York: Cambridge University Press.

Chase-Dunn, Christopher K., Yukio Kawano, and Benjamin Brewer. 2000. "Trade Globalization since 1795: Waves of Integration in the World-System." *American Sociological Review* 65:77–95.

Chen, Shaohua, Gaurav Dat, and Martin Ravallion. 1994. "Is Poverty Increasing in the Developing World?" *Review of Income and Wealth* 40:359–76.

———. 2002. *POVCAL: A Program for Calculating Poverty Measures from Grouped Data.* Washington, DC: World Bank.

Cowell, Frank A. 1995. *Measuring Inequality.* 2nd ed. London, England: Prentice Hall.

Deininger, Klaus and Lyn Squire. 1996. "A New Data Set Measuring Income Inequality." *World Bank Economic Review* 10:565–91.

———. 1998. "New Ways of Looking at Old Issues: Inequality and Growth." *Journal of Development Economics* 57:259–87.

Fields, Gary S. 2001. *Distribution and Development: A New Look at the Developing World.* New York: Russell Sage.

Firebaugh, Glenn. 1999. "Empirics of World Income Inequality." *American Journal of Sociology* 104: 1597–630.

———. 2000a. "Observed Trends in Between-Nation Income Inequality and Two Conjectures." *American Journal of Sociology* 106:215–21.

———. 2000b. "The Trend in Between-Nation Income Inequality." *Annual Review of Sociology* 26:323–39.

Galor, Oded and Joseph Zeira. 1993. "Income Distribution and Macroeconomics." *Review of Economic Studies* 60:35–52.

Gini, Corrado. 1912. "Variabilita e Mutabilita: Contributo allo Studio delle Distribuzioni e Relazioni Statische." *Studi Economico-Giuridici della Universita di Caligliari* 3(2):3–159.

Goesling, Brian. 2001. "Changing Income Inequalities within and between Nations: New Evidence." *American Sociological Review* 66:745–61.

Gustafsson, Bjorn and Mats Johansson. 1999. "In Search of Smoking Guns: What Makes Income Inequality Vary over Time in Different Countries?" *American Sociological Review* 64:585–605.

Heston, Alan, Robert Summers, and Bettina Aten. 2001. *Penn World Table (PWT) Mark 6.0* (MRDF). Philadelphia, PA: Center for International Comparisons, University of Pennsylvania.

Jha, Sailesh K. 1996. "The Kuznets Curve: A Reassessment." *World Development* 24:773–80.

Korzeniewicz, Roberto Patricio and Timothy Patrick Moran. 1997. "World-Economic Trends in the Distribution of Income, 1965–1992." *American Journal of Sociology* 102:1000–39.

———. 2000. "Measuring World Income Inequalities." *American Journal of Sociology* 106:209–14.

Kuznets, Simon. 1955. "Economic Growth and Income Inequality." *American Economic Review* 45:1–28.

Li, Hongyi, Lyn Squire, and Heng-fu Zou. 1998. "Explaining International and Intertemporal Variations in Income Inequality." *Economic Journal* 108:26–43.

Lorenz, Max O. 1905. "Methods of Measuring the Concentration of Wealth." *Journal of the American Statistical Association* 9:209–19.

Maddison, Angus. 2001. *The World Economy: A Millennial Perspective.* Paris, France: OECD.

Melchior, Arne and Kjetil Telle. 2001. "Global Income Distribution 1965–98: Convergence and Marginalisation." *Forum for Development Studies* 28:75–98.

Milanovic, Branko. 2002. "True World Income Distribution, 1988 and 1993: First Calculation Based on Household Surveys Alone." *Economic Journal* 112:51–92.

Persson, Thorsten and Guido Tabellini. 1994. "Is Inequality Harmful for Growth? Theory and Evidence." *American Economic Review* 84:600–21.

Pritchett, Lant. 1997. "Divergence, Big Time." *Journal of Economic Perspectives* 11:3–17.

Proctor, Bernadette D. and Joseph Dalaker. 2001. *Poverty in the United States: 2001.* Washington, DC: U.S. Government Printing Office.

Ravallion, Martin and Shaohua Chen. 1997. "What Can New Survey Data Tell Us about Recent Changes in Distribution and Poverty?" *World Bank Economic Review* 11:357–82.

Ravallion, Martin, Gaurav Dat, and Dominique van der Walle. 1991. "Quantifying Absolute Poverty in the Developing World." *Review of Income and Wealth* 37:345–61.

Sala-i-Martin, Xavier. 2002. "The Disturbing 'Rise' of World Income Inequality." *National Bureau of Economic Research*, Working Paper 8904.

Schultz, T. Paul. 1998. "Inequality in the Distribution of Personal Income in the World: How It Is Changing and Why." *Journal of Population Economics* 11:307–44.

Theil, Henri. 1967. *Economics and Information Theory.* Amsterdam, The Netherlands: North-Holland.

United Nations. 1995. *The World's Women 1995: Trends and Statistics.* 2nd ed. New York: Author.

———. 2002. *Social Indicators.* Retrieved from unstats.un.org/unsd.

WIDER. 2000. *World Income Inequality Database.* Vol. 1.0. Tokyo, Japan: United Nations University.

Wilkinson, Richard G. 1996. *Unhealthy Societies.* London, England: Routledge.

World Bank. 2000. *Global Poverty Report (July).* New York: World Bank.

———. 2001. *World Development Indicators.* Washington, DC: World Bank.

Racism in Comparative Perspective

Joe R. Feagin

University of Florida

Pinar Batur

Vassar College

The Global Color Line: Systems of Racial Oppression

At the beginning of the twentieth century, the brilliant sociologist W. E. B. Du Bois ([1903] 1989) explained that "since 732 when Charles Martel beat back the Saracens at Tours, the white races have had the hegemony of civilization—so far that 'white' and 'civilized' have become synonymous in every-day speech." Europeans thus invented the "color line" across the globe, thereby making it such that "the problem of the twentieth century is the problem of the color line" (p. xxxi). In the process of creating this global color line, Western imperialist colonizers of distant societies racialized economic and social relations everywhere. Today,

this color line still represents the line drawn for many societies' arrangements of socioracial oppression.

Since the eighteenth century, Western rationalizations of this global color line have often defended it in terms of a racist, and often antiblack, ideology. Writing during World War II, Alan Russell (1944), a prominent European intellectual, produced a typical ideological rationale for racial oppression in *Colour, Race and Empire*: "The aversion which so many white people feel towards the negro *[sic]* races, based on aesthetic dislike, allied often to what amounts to intellectual contempt, has a parallel in the feelings which are entertained towards the 'yellow' races, but here it is not merely dislike, but almost fear, rooted in alarm at the

121

frugality, intelligence and consequent efficiency of these peoples" (p. 21).

Writing about the global color line, Du Bois ([1940] 1984) pointed out that in the process of creating this line, which was indeed an intimate part of European imperialism, numerous white-racist practices have maintained hegemony through "unconscious acts and irrational reactions unpierced by reason, whose current form depended on the long history of relation and contact between thought and idea" (p. 6). He underscores the connection between racist ideas and actions to maintain the racist system. Boldly Eurocentric and racist ideas early became basic components of capitalist ideologies and have long been integral to the establishment of European global hegemony. Thus, as European colonialism gradually created a world racist order, it often absorbed or remade already existing social inequalities, in a layering social formation that takes a number of different forms in the modern world (Batur and Feagin 1999:8–9).

Historically, institutionalized oppression of one human group by another constitutes one of the world's enduring society-level problems. It is generally in the Marxist tradition that one finds the most developed analyses of social oppression. Building in part on Adam Smith, the pathbreaking Karl Marx developed the idea that human labor is the source of great wealth generation in capitalistic societies. In a capitalistic system, class oppression takes the form of transferring productive value, wealth, generated by workers' labor to an elite of capitalists. This is a social relationship of class exploitation and oppression, yet it is by no means the only major oppression created in human societies.

In many societies, racial exploitation and oppression are as fundamental. This oppression takes the form of well-institutionalized, systemic racism with roots in European imperialism that swept the globe beginning in the fifteenth century. As with social class systems, racial class systems encompass certain key dimensions: widespread racial discrimination and related exploitation; the racialized stereotyping, ideology, and emotions that defend this oppression; the institutionalized hierarchy and inequality resulting from it; the many human and societal costs generated by oppression; and the resistance movements that develop in opposition.

Under racial oppression that developed across the globe with European imperialism and colonialism, much wealth created by workers of color was transferred to whites—most heavily to the white bourgeoisie and elites—along with other privileges of the new category defined as "race." In the first centuries of this external (and internal) colonialism, exploitation was typically done by overt enslavement and official segregation. In more recent decades, racial oppression has been accomplished by informal means. Such informal means remain effective in positioning whites as privileged and those who are not white as unjustly disadvantaged. In racist societies like those discussed below, low-wage labor by workers of color generates economic value and profits taken by (white) capitalists. Employers extract added "surplus value" from the labor done by workers of color through the coercive structures of the racist system. Accepting what Du Bois ([1935] 1992) called the "psychological wage of whiteness" (p. 700), most white workers collude in racist arrangements, benefiting by securing better-paying jobs and "white" privileges. A racist system transfers energies of, and wealth created by, the oppressed to improve the lives of most whites. Great inequality of power is part of racial oppression, as is cultural imperialism asserting the values and views of the dominant group in rationalizing oppressive arrangements. White-generated stereotypes and ideologies become pervasive, and whites periodically use violence to keep the racially subordinated group in "its place" (Young 1990:62).

In this chapter, we look beyond surface appearances of the societies selected to illustrate the global racist system and thus show the underlying realities of racial oppression, features often papered over by racial rationalizations. We urge readers to look at racial matters in dialectical terms: exploiter and exploited are in an ongoing, life-and-death struggle—a relationship with a certain stability yet much potential for change.

SOME HISTORICAL BACKGROUND

Since the fifteenth century, the expansion of Western capitalism around the globe has fostered the division of peoples according to what Europeans came to see as superior and inferior "races." This capitalistic expansion created many colonies of racially subordinated peoples, and racial hierarchy and inequality became permanent aspects of this global political-economic system. The first large groups of labor for this newly emerging capitalistic-colonialist system were laborers of color, both those enslaved and transported and indigenous peoples whose labor was stolen within their societies. By the eighteenth and nineteenth centuries, international development of Western capitalism was fostering extensive ideological racism and "scientific" racism in attempts to rationalize new forms of enslaved labor and exploitative peonage. Euro-racism's global structure was superimposing itself on major institutions of societies it invaded, thereby shaping identities and everyday experiences (Batur-VanderLippe and Feagin 1996). Reaching in some form many societies, this exploitative racialization process has persisted for more than 500 years.[1]

European imperialism began with the overseas expansion of Spain and Portugal, whose rulers sought valuable goods taken by force from indigenous peoples. In the 1400s, the ideological rationale for this often genocidal theft of goods, land, and labor was provided by Catholic popes in papal bulls echoing religious justifications for Christian crusades against Muslims in earlier centuries. Pope Alexander VI issued a bull of demarcation, resolving Spanish and Portuguese disputes. Revised by the Treaty of Tordesillas, this bull put all the world's non-Christian peoples at the disposal of colonial powers (Cox 1948:331–2; Sardar, Nandy, and Davies 1993:8–9).

Over the next several centuries, numerous European countries—especially the Netherlands, England, and France—spurred the global expansion of capitalism, in the process fostering great inequalities between colonizers and colonized. Scholars, theologians, and politicians developed theories of European (later, white) superiority and the inferiority of peoples caught in colonialism. Colonized peoples were demonized in terms of wildness, cruelty, laziness, promiscuity, and heathenism (Takaki 1990:12). The major racist intellectual of the nineteenth century, Count Joseph de Gobineau, noted thus: "[White people] are gifted with reflective energy, or rather with an energetic intelligence. . . . They have

a remarkable, even extreme love of liberty, and are openly hostile to the formalism under which the Chinese are glad to vegetate, as well as the strict despotism which is the only way of governing the Negro" (quoted in Ani 1994:272).

Over time, this European colonialism became a domination based on colonial political administration, exploitative trade, and missionary efforts to convert indigenous populations to "civilization." In Asian, African, and American societies, this domination fostered colonial administrations' oppressive rule, unequal trade, and imposition of Christianity and Western culture. Everyday life in the colonies was radically distorted and restructured, if not destroyed, by European oppressors, who controlled colonized societies politically, economically, and culturally. Exploitation of colonized peoples and their natural resources was accompanied by systematic slavery, peonage, and savage and coercive violence (Brewer 1986; Fanon 1963).

Writing in the 1930s, Du Bois ([1935] 1992), perhaps the first scholar of globalizing racism, captured the centrality of labor exploitation of peoples of color in this summary of the new colonial-capitalistic world order:

That dark and vast sea of human labor in China and India, the South Seas and all Africa; in the West Indies and Central America and in the United States—that great majority of mankind, on whose bent and broken backs rest today the founding stones of modern industry—shares a common destiny; it is despised and rejected by race and color; paid a wage below the level of decent living; driven, beaten, prisoned and enslaved in all but name; spawning the world's raw material and luxury—cotton, wool, coffee, tea, cocoa, palm oil, fibers, spices, rubber, silks, lumber, copper, gold, diamonds, leather—how shall we end the list and where? All these are gathered up at prices lowest of the low, manufactured, transformed, and transported at fabulous gain; and the resultant wealth is distributed and displayed and made the basis of world power and universal dominion and armed arrogance in London and Paris, Berlin and Rome, New York, and Rio de Janeiro.

He then added:

Here is the real modern labor problem. Here is the kernel of the problem of Religion and Democracy, of Humanity. . . . Out of the exploitation of the dark proletariat comes the Surplus Value filched from human beasts which, in cultured lands, the Machine and Harnessed Power veil and conceal. The emancipation of man is the emancipation of labor and the emancipation of labor is the freeing of that basic majority of workers who are yellow, brown and black. (Pp. 15–16)

Du Bois was perhaps the first scholar to discuss the special character of the racialized surplus value extracted from the world's non-European peoples in order to bring great wealth to Western countries.

THE UNITED STATES

From the beginning, theft of land and labor were at the heart of the European colonization of North America. As with other conquered areas, European imperialists and colonists sought to control the land and the peoples who lived there. Unlike France in Africa (see below), England (later Great Britain) populated the seized territories with large numbers of white colonists, who eventually exceeded in number the indigenous Americans. Descendants of colonists overthrew British authority and established a white-controlled state. Whites would remain in coercive control of local populations of color to the present day—generally in a highly exploitative formation similar to overseas colonialism in some ways, a formation called "internal colonialism."

The early white colonists in North America and their descendants shared the view of most European colonizers that land under indigenous control is available for their use. According to white-racist constructions, the land is "discovered" by "civilized" whites who "use the land in a productive way." Indigenous Americans who resisted land-taking were killed off or driven beyond European settlement. With few Native Americans available for labor, and an insufficient European labor supply, larger farmers and plantation owners soon opted for enslaved Africans as needed workers. Enslavement of large numbers of Africans generated much wealth for many white families. Without this labor, it is possible that there would not have been a successful American Revolution and, thus, a United States—at least in the historical time frame that it developed. As a result of this long period of exploitation and enslavement of Africans, the United States has long

had a large African-origin population, one of the world's largest.

In the mid-twentieth century, Oliver Cox (1948) was the first scholar to undertake an extended analysis of U.S. society as a racist system. Cox showed how long-term exploitation of black labor created a lasting structure of racial classes arranged in a hierarchy. White elites decided "to proletarianize a whole people—that is to say, the whole people is looked upon as a class—whereas white proletarianization involves only a section of the white people" (p. 344). This white-racist system was part of the country's foundation from earliest decades—and today remains systemic. The 1787 Constitutional Convention was composed of 55 white men, the majority with links to slaveholding, slave trading, or the financing and marketing of slave-made products in international trade. Much wealth was garnered from this system, and many nonslaveholding whites benefited from the prosperity created by this system. The American Revolution—and later European and U.S. industrial revolutions—were substantially funded by the slavery-centered economic system's substantial profits. Later on, by the 1880s and 1890s, a system of near-slavery, termed legal segregation and much like apartheid in South Africa, was developed by U.S. whites—an openly racist system abandoned only in the late 1960s. From 1619 to the present, trillions of dollars in wealth have been taken from African Americans who were enslaved, as well as from those exploited under segregation and contemporary patterns of informal discrimination—trillions that account for much of the wealth and prosperity of generations of white Americans, to the present day.

Most whites today have inherited resources from the unjust enrichment gained by ancestors from Native Americans, African Americans, and other Americans of color. For example, from 1865 to the 1930s, some 246 million acres were more or less given away by the federal government under the Homestead Act. One researcher (Williams 2000) estimates that perhaps 46 million people (almost all whites) are current beneficiaries of that discriminatory U.S. government program. Other U.S. government giveaways of major socioeconomic resources that went only to whites included major air routes, radio and television frequencies, lumber and mineral resources on federal lands, and all major government contracts and licenses until the 1960s. Until then, almost all new capital formation was in white hands, and most unions and better-paying job categories excluded black workers (Cross 1984).

Contemporary Discrimination

Systemic racism remains central. There are still high levels of white stereotyping and discrimination directed against African Americans and other Americans of color. In one 1990s survey, evaluating eight antiblack stereotypes (including "prefer to accept welfare" and have "less native intelligence"), three-quarters of whites agreed with one or more. Some 55 percent agreed with two or more (Anti-Defamation League 1993). In a 2001 survey, a majority of whites nationally applied one or more stereotyped traits to African Americans: lazy, aggressive/violent, prefer welfare, or always complaining (Bobo 2001). Anti-Latino and anti-Asian prejudice can be seen in yet other research. Thus, anthropologist Jane Hill (1995) examined whites' mocking of Spanish and Latinos. Mocking of Spanish is common in the United States and is mostly created by college-educated whites for such items as greeting cards, coffee cup slogans, children's cartoons, video games, and media cartoons. White mocking of Latino and black dialects of English shows a "general unwillingness to accept the speakers of that language and social choices they have made as viable and functional. . . . We are ashamed of them" (Lippi-Green 1997:201).

Discrimination remains widespread. One study reported that 60 percent of more than a thousand black respondents faced discrimination in their workplaces. Most with college degrees reported discrimination. Asian and Latino American workers, especially the best-educated, also reported much discrimination (Bobo and Suh 2000:527–9). A large survey of black military personnel found that many had faced racist jokes, racist comments and materials, and barriers in regard to their careers (Scarville et al. 1999:46–78). In a federal survey with thousands of housing audits in 25 metropolitan areas, black renters were estimated to have faced discrimination half the time, and homeseekers, about 59 percent of the time. Recent studies in Fresno, New

Orleans, San Antonio, Houston, Boston, and Montgomery have found rates of 58 percent to 80 percent for discrimination in rental housing for black testers and 52 percent to 78 percent for Latino testers (Feagin 2000:155–6). Recent studies indicate that bankers in many U.S. cities set interest rates on loans higher for black and Latino homeowners than for comparable whites: "Prime lenders are not serving low-income communities, communities of color, and seniors; Subprime lenders are targeting elderly and minority borrowers and communities; most subprime borrowers are stuck with loans having unjustifiable and onerous provisions; brokers and loan officers often rely on bait and switch tactics whereby key loan terms change at closing" (PR Newswire 2002).

Americans of color face discrimination in many other aspects of their lives. A National Academy of Sciences report found that black patients receive discriminatory medical care compared with whites. They are less likely to get appropriate heart surgery and diagnostic tests, and more likely to have limbs amputated when they have diabetes than comparable whites. They are much less likely to get kidney transplants (Srikameswaran 2002:F-1; Talk of the Nation 2002). Numerous research studies report discrimination for African Americans when they shop and when they come into contact with white police officers or face bail setting by white judges (Ayres 1991; Ayres and Waldfogel 1994; Forman, Williams, and Jackson 1997:231–6).

The contemporary reality of inequality in the United States can be seen in basic statistics: African Americans live shorter lives—about six to seven years less—than white Americans. On the average, African American families garner about 60 percent of the income of the average white family, and African American families average about 10 percent of the wealth of the typical white family. Today some 95 percent to 100 percent of the top positions in major economic, political, and educational organizations are still held by whites, mostly men (Feagin 2000). These dramatic inequalities demonstrate the long-term effects of 400 years of racism.

In the United States, terroristic violence involving white supremacists remains a serious problem. Not long after the 1995 bombing of an Oklahoma federal building, which killed 169 people, other bomb plots were uncovered, one targeting the Southern Poverty Law Center in Montgomery, Alabama, and two targeting federal buildings. Today, there are an estimated 441 armed antigovernment militias, many involving supremacists. An estimated 12 million whites support the sometimes violent antigovernment movement (Klanwatch Project 1996:3–5). One influential leader was the late William Pierce, a physicist who authored *The Turner Diaries,* which has reportedly sold 185,000 copies. This racist book was reported to be among those read by Timothy McVeigh, the white terrorist who bombed the Oklahoma building. After that bombing, Pierce said: "We'll see some real terrorism—planned, organized terrorism—before too long. I suspect that a growing number of exasperated, fed up Americans will begin engaging in terrorism on a scale that the world has never seen before" (quoted in Klanwatch Project 1996:38).

The Future: The Coming White Minority

The United States is a diverse and ever changing society in its racial and ethnic makeup. By the 2050s, the United States will likely be majority African, Latino, Asian, Middle Eastern, and Native American. Major challenges to contemporary white control of the country are already arising from population and related sociopolitical changes. Today, European Americans are but a minority in half of the largest 100 U.S. cities and in the states of Hawaii, New Mexico, Texas, and California. Between 2015 and 2040, they will become a statistical minority in many other states. Americans of color will gradually increase economic and political strength and will likely gain power in the struggle against racism. For whites, there seem to be two major choices in this dynamic environment. They will react by working for more extensive racial separatism, as in old South Africa. Data indicate that some whites are currently choosing guarded-gated communities, private schools, and armed militias. Some are moving to whiter areas of the country, such as the Rocky Mountain states. And some whites are building conservative coalitions with certain lighter-skinned or more Euro-assimilated Asian and Latino Americans, whom many whites treat as "honorary whites" (Feagin 2000:237–72).

Alternatively, some activists of all racial and ethnic backgrounds hope and work for another U.S. scenario. They are working for a more democratic future. In this scenario—and reality in some places—Americans of color are building effective coalitions across groups of color, together with large numbers of supportive whites. These coalitions are working to break down discriminatory barriers. They are pressing U.S. institutions to move toward true multicultural democracy for the first time in U.S. history.

France: Colonialism and Contemporary Racism

France has a long tradition of overseas colonialism. While whites in the United States have historically exploited many people of color mostly within the country, whites in France have played a major international role in colonizing areas of the globe such as the African continent. In the U.S. case, whites built up wealth by exploitation of Americans of color. In the French case, the exploitation of Africa brought great wealth to white entrepreneurs in and colonizers of Africa, as well as the French government. Du Bois ([1946] 1965) analyzed Europe's colonization process, arguing that extreme poverty in African colonies was "a main cause of wealth and luxury in Europe. The results of this poverty were disease, ignorance, and crime" (p. 37). In the African case, unjust exploitation of labor and land has long been a major source of wealth for European companies and countries.

French colonialism differed from other colonialism in that it usually took in newly colonized peoples as citizens of France. Colonial administrators propagated French culture in an attempt to assimilate colonized peoples into the French empire. Yet, they were still seen as inferior citizens. The African theorist of race, Frantz Fanon (1963), argued that European colonialism brought violence on subordinated peoples through construction of the colonial world as "good" and "evil." Through "colonial exploitation the settler paints the native as a sort of quintessence of evil" (p. 41). Viewing Europeans as good and Africans as evil has long been part of the European culture of racism. Such an ideology has been integral to racial subordination during the colonial period and subsequent postcolonial era.

Racism and Immigrants Today

In France, some racial and ethnic groups, including the Jews, have long been targets of racialized hostility and subordination. The end of overseas colonialism brought new groups of color into French society, mostly from areas once colonized by France. Today, it is estimated that one in every four French citizens has a non-French parent or grandparent (Silverman 1992). Popular and official government analyses of immigration problems focus on immigrants of color from Africa, most of whom settled in France after the 1960s Algerian War.

Many whites now see immigration in racialized terms. Surveys of the population find high levels of racist and antiimmigrant attitudes. One 2000 poll found that less than a third of the French respondents were willing to say they were "not racist." A substantial majority agreed that there were too many foreigners in the country. Six in 10 asserted there were too many Arabs—with 4 in 10 feeling there were too many black residents (Daley 2002:A4).

According to a recent United Nations report, numerous European countries are seeing a resurgence of racist-right political parties and of hate crimes. One sees the growth in influence of racist parties in France as well as in Austria, Belgium, Germany, Italy, Norway, and Australia. Racist-right parties have elected numerous members to parliaments and garnered up to a quarter of the votes in elections. Such groups are racist and attack, verbally and sometimes violently, racial, ethnic, and religious groups, especially immigrants of color (Deen 1998).

Since the 1960s, the migration of Algerians to France has made Islam the country's second religion, after Catholicism. The large number of Muslims has brought a hostile reaction from whites who fear loss of traditional culture. Intellectual and popular debates focus on immigrant conflicts with French culture rather than on racialized perceptions of whites (Johnson 1993:59; Silverman 1992:3–4). When whites view racial segregation in housing as a result of immigrants' "individual choices," they de-emphasize dynamics of institutionalized racism directed against African French groups in housing markets.

Indeed, the term *immigrant* in French (as increasingly, in English in the United States and Great Britain) is popularly used to define only those of non-European origin, and especially those of African origin. Officially, people in France are classified in terms of nationality as a "foreigner" or a "national." However, there is little popular recognition among whites that naturalized Africans are citizens of France. Contrary to racist argument, the proportion of immigrants in the population has not increased: they account for about the same proportion of the population today (7 percent) as in 1931. The overwhelming majority of those popularly classified as immigrants have lived in France for more than 10 years (Silverman 1992:3).

Since 1980, African immigration has come to the forefront of public debate among whites, pressed there by racist-right advocates like Jean-Marie Le Pen. In the 2002 presidential election, Le Pen got 6 million votes, 17 percent of the vote, putting him into the final round of the presidential election. Though he lost, his support indicates the power of racist thought and action. Le Pen's support is greatest in urban areas with sizable numbers of immigrants. Racist-right groups advocate ending African immigration, providing job priority for native-born whites, forcing Africans to return to Africa, and reimposing the death penalty. The racist-right objects to acquisition of French nationality by second-generation African French people, whose parents are criticized for attachment to home-country values (De Wenden 1991:108; Kristeva 1993:97–8). In efforts to attract conservative white voters, the French government itself has pursued repressive policies against African immigrants and their supporters (Singer 1996:19).

Today, a large antiracist association, SOS Racism, is challenging xenophobia, anti-Semitism, and racism in France. SOS Racism advocates equality of rights and giving immigrants the right to vote. SOS Racism had 50,000 followers at its inception and has attracted media attention for antiracism demonstrations attended by hundreds of thousands (Kristeva 1993:13–14). After Le Pen got into the presidential runoff in 2002, more than a million men and women protested his National Front party in cities across France.

Today, foreign-born immigrants constitute a small part of France's 60 million people. Yet they and their children are increasingly targets for attacks. Discrimination in housing, workplaces, and education is commonplace. Numerous immigrants and their children, including those with substantial education, find opportunities for better jobs blocked by discrimination. Many bars and clubs are closed to the African French. A recent report on racism by the Institute of Economic and Social Studies found that discrimination against nonwhite immigrants and citizens in the workplace is increasing: "An invisible ceiling exists in social and economic life in France that stops the rise of qualified immigrants to middle and high-level executive positions" (Godoy 2002). Even the French National Employment Agency has suggested that nonwhite immigrants seeking employment provide names that hide their African origins, for research indicates that those with European-sounding names have a better chance at employment. Much employment and housing discrimination is blatantly racist in France today (Godoy 2002).

As in the United States, violent attacks on people of African descent continue today. The most extreme form of discrimination is "Arabicide," a term some use for the many unsolved murders of Arab residents of France (Woodall 1993). Muslim communities face various other attacks on their cultural traditions. One issue is the right of Muslim girls to wear traditional head scarves in public schools. While some Muslim feminists have argued that scarves represent the influence of patriarchy, others argue that the scarves represent assertion of women's rights if voluntarily worn by women. Yet the French government interprets the increasing number of students wearing scarves in schools as an indication of the appeal of "Muslim fundamentalism" (Ibrahim 1994). Even France's President Jacques Chirac has aroused racist sentiments by accusing Algerian immigrants of being "welfare cheats" who produce children to drain the welfare system (Creamean 1996). This stereotyped notion is similar to false accusations made by whites in the United States about African Americans and immigrants of color.

As France moves into the European Union (EU), the complexities of the new Europe are now intruding. The EU stresses workers' rights, the standardization of policies in regard to minority communities, and a stable immigration policy. Racist right-wingers in France resist these policies in anti-EU movements. One survey of young people in EU countries found many to be very nationalistic (Chasan 2000; Frangoudaki 2000:355). Racist music, such as the song "Beating Up Blacks," seems to be gaining in popularity. Recently, a French television executive was fined for allowing this song to be performed on air, with lines like "Can't stand the foreigners, the darkies . . . flick on the lighters, we're going to set them on fire" ("French TV Executive" 1996:65).

In several European countries, hate crimes are on the increase. Between fall 2000 and late 2001, there were more than 406 *violent* anti-Semitic incidents in France, with 700 more in the spring of 2002. These included vandalism, shootings, and firebombing, often targeting Jewish-owned restaurants, synagogues, schools, and cemeteries. Children have been attacked as they left schools, and worshippers have been stoned after synagogue services. There is also a resurgence of neofascist groups that celebrate Adolph Hitler and the Holocaust (Southam News 2002:A6). In spring 2002, an outburst of hate crimes against Jews and other groups in France was repeated in other European countries. Responding to anti-Semitic and other racist violence in numerous countries, the EU justice and home affairs ministers issued a statement against racism and xenophobia that committed them to using the law and information exchange to fight rising racism in Europe: "The European Union strongly condemns the racist acts perpetrated in various places in the European Union in the recent weeks. At a time of acute international tension, especially in the Middle East, it is vital to preserve the spirit of harmony, entente and intercultural respect within our societies" (Spinant 2002:n.p.).

Colonialism begins by bringing oppression to distant lands, but in virtually every case, it has eventually brought oppression and conflict to the colonizing country as well, especially if the colonized migrate to the colonizing country. In the postcolonial era, institutional racism persists. Immigrants experience the violent legacy of African colonialism in the land of the colonizer.

BRAZIL: A RACIAL DEMOCRACY?

The two countries examined so far both have a long history of colonial exploitation of people of color within the country or outside. Whites in France were among the first to colonize non-European societies overseas. Whites in the United States, while beginning mostly as a colony of England, eventually liberated themselves and began their own internal and external colonial efforts targeting people of color. Numerous societies that are not predominantly white have arisen out of such colonial actions, yet have not been so fortunate as to completely free themselves from the continuing, oppressive effects of that colonialism, including economic neocolonialism. We now examine two predominantly non-European countries that were originally European colonies but have struggled to break with the effects of that horrific past.

In the Western Hemisphere, Brazil is second in population only to the United States. It has the largest African-origin population outside of Africa—more than 60 million, and, counting all people of mixed ancestry, at least half of its population. Although slavery was abolished in the nineteenth century, well-institutionalized racial discrimination still has a major impact on Afro-Brazilians today. Thus, in many restaurants, black customers are excluded; a major television show portraying a white man and black woman kissing received protests; and Afro-Brazilian service workers are expected to use the service entrance of buildings. Afro-Brazilians hold less than 3 percent of the seats in the two houses of the Brazilian legislature. Many employers routinely choose white over black applicants for better-paying jobs ("The Colours of Brazil" 1986:42). Black workers average less than half the incomes of white workers, and few are found in major corporate and political positions. Advertisements for jobs in newspapers specify "good appearance," a euphemism for "white" (Muello 2002). Forty percent of the black population works in minimum-wage jobs. And black Brazilians constitute just 1 percent of students in universities. At the University of São Paulo, only 5 of the 5,000 faculty members are black. Afro-Brazilians also make up most of the poor (Hart 1988; Whitaker 1991). This oppressive social, economic, and political situation is the legacy of European colonization and subsequent slavery and racial oppression.

Brazil was early colonized by Spain and Portugal. The emerging European textile industry consumed so much dye from Brazil that, by the end of the 1500s, 100 ships traveled regularly there. The Portuguese established sugar cane plantations. Some indigenous inhabitants were enslaved, but most were killed by the European colonizers or, as with indigenous peoples in the United States, died from European diseases. Soon, Brazil resembled the U.S. South, with large numbers of enslaved Afro-Brazilians working on plantations to produce sugar, coffee, and rubber for the expanding capitalist world market (Burns 1993:23–7, 216–17; Skidmore and Smith 1994:140). Brazil's slave population numbered about 5 million—more than half its total population—just before the abolition of slavery in 1888. Since Brazil became independent of Portugal in 1822, the country's history has been marked by recurring military intervention in politics on behalf of white elites.

Is There "Racial Democracy"?

Once slavery ended, large-scale racial inequality did not end, but has long been fiercely maintained by whites. In spite of widespread discrimination and oppression, a myth emerged that Brazil had "good" racial relations. To the present day, the majority of whites, as well as some other Brazilians, see the country as a unique "racial democracy." This notion of racial democracy usually recognizes the existence of some prejudice and discrimination, but claims that such are isolated and that Afro-Brazilians are roughly equal in society. The mainstream ideology argues that because of Brazilian exceptionalism, multicultural Brazil is not starkly divided along racial lines like the United States and South Africa (Hanchard 1994:43). By downplaying racial differences, white elites avoid addressing problems of racially based inequality in the economy, education, life expectancy, and health care.

This mythology constantly ignores persisting racial hostility and discrimination. Emerging in the nineteenth century, racist views and ideologies have remained part of Brazil's culture and influence white Brazilians' thinking about the past, present, and future. Today, the racist perspective is seen in immigration policies favoring whites, in negative attitudes to interracial marriages, and even in many Afro-Brazilians' preference for lighter skin tones. Although many light-skinned Brazilians believe that racial differences are unimportant, they and other Brazilians use more than 100 words for racial identification; "black" (*preto*) does not have the same meaning in Brazil as in the United States or South Africa. In Brazil, *preto* describes a person with mostly or all African ancestry. A racially mixed person who would likely be called black in the United States is identified in Brazil as *moreno* or mulatto, depending on the degree of African ancestry. Since "Negro" includes *pretos* and *morenos,* it is a political term for black-power movements, as in Brazil's Movimento Negro (Hanchard 1994; Sanders 1981). Despite this diverse terminology, the country's racial hierarchy is supported by strong white stereotypes that view blacks as "bad-smelling, dirty, unhygienic, ugly" and view mulattoes as "pushy and envious of whites" (Sanders 1981:2).

Not surprisingly, whiteness remains a symbol of superiority and the avenue to privilege and power, and discrimination and poverty remain widespread for Afro-Brazilians. Recently, Ms. Benedita da Silva, the first black female governor of the state of Rio de Janeiro, noted that "I go into a five-star hotel and they address me in English. That's because a well-dressed black woman simply isn't within the standard model for black Brazilians, and they assume she has to be a foreigner. So I have to tell them, 'No. I am a Brazilian'" (quoted in Rohter 2002:A4). Helio Santos, a black university professor, has underscored the contradictions in his country today: "Brazilian society discriminates against blacks at every point, but it is hidden, disguised. . . . There is an illusion of social democracy in Brazil" (quoted in Whitaker 1991:41). As in the United States, the illusion of equality serves elites' political purposes while racial discrimination remains integral to society. The promise of economic success frames the European colonizers' persisting myth that equality will come, along with prosperity, in the near future. In this sense, Brazil is similar to the United States and South Africa.

While colonial developments in Brazil and the United States were different, racial ideologies and inequalities have been similar over the long course of both countries' history. Persisting socioeconomic inequality among Brazil's racial groups sharpened between the 1960s and the 2000s as the result of so-called modernization. International companies headquartered in the United States and Europe have invested heavily in Brazil. Not surprisingly, then, Afro-Brazilians have demanded equal-opportunity legislation to secure greater access to education and employment, and developed human rights movements. As in the United States, white officials have sought to reduce commitments to rights and curtail government efforts to reduce racial inequality. During the 1988 centennial celebration of slavery's abolition, the government organized a celebration, but Afro-Brazilian groups held counter-demonstrations protesting continuing inequality and proposing a strengthening of ties between blacks in Brazil and other parts of the African diaspora (Andrews 1992:256–7; Winant 1992:173–92).

Since 5 percent of the population, mostly whites, control almost all the land, there have been major land protests. Some 50,000 rural poor marched in the late 1990s to protest the slow pace of land reform. Though he was the first Brazilian president to discuss racism as a national issue, President Fernando Henrique Cardoso was criticized for not undertaking land reforms that would confront elites (Olivier 1999). Under Cardoso's administration, visible gains have been made, mainly in the government bureaucracy, and some universities have begun to reserve positions for Afro-Brazilian students (Oliviera 1999). Another movement is that of indigenous people. Even though national censuses indicate rapid growth of the indigenous population, some of the 216 identified indigenous groups are still facing extinction. While they make up nearly 4 percent of the population, their voices have long been ignored by the white elites (Kennedy 2000:311).

The Brazilian case shows the impact of European colonialism not only on economic and political institutions but also on the creation and development of a persisting ideology of white racism. The legacy of Afro-Brazilian slavery remains a central part of Brazil's present, and thereby promises to continue to influence the country's future through the continuing dominance of systemic racism.

SOUTH AFRICA EMERGES FROM APARTHEID

Now cited as an example of how a country can liberate itself from European colonialism, contemporary South Africa is an important case to examine. South Africa was created as a country by European imperialists, not by Africans. As with North America, European colonizers constructed the country, and then constructed its mythological history in racist and exploitative terms, often viewing the land as "discovered" by whites who were allegedly the first to use it "productively."

Contrary to much European thinking, South Africa has a long and complex history. The Khoisan people were living in what is now called South Africa when the ancestors of the current Bantu-speaking black majority settled there around 300 B.C.E. The first European settlement dates to 1652, when the Dutch established a small supply station. As Dutch settlements spread, confrontations with indigenous peoples led to what Europeans call "Kaffir Wars." *Kaffir* is a degrading term (like *nigger* in the United States) that whites have long applied to black South Africans. Britain's conquest of the Cape Colony in 1806, and British settlement beginning in 1820, fueled out-migration of Dutch farmers (called "Boers") into the interior (Davidson 1991; Harris 1987; Oliver and Atmore 1989; Thompson 1985). The British imperialists abolished slavery and changed regulations on black labor, and the Boers interpreted these actions as putting the Khoisan and Bantus "on an equal footing with Christians, contrary to the laws of God and the natural distinction of race" (Worden 1994:11–12).

Early on, a white mythology about land ownership developed. Some Dutch settlers began calling themselves "Afrikaners," or the "white tribe of Africa" (Thompson 1985:76). Defending slavery, white colonizers argued that "we make the native Africans work for us in consideration of allowing them to live in our country" (Davidson 1991:269). According to the white-racist ideology, there were *no* native black South Africans prior to the arrival of

Europeans! This naïve view persists even today (Thompson 1985:70). From the beginning, many European occupiers saw colonization as a civilizing mission that justified killing, subjugation, and enslavement of indigenous peoples. European colonizers rated themselves as racially superior to Africans, whom they, like white colonizers elsewhere, considered to be animal-like, and stereotyped as "idolatrous and licentious, thieving and lying, lazy and dirty" (Thompson 1985:71).

Apartheid

Created in 1910, the Union of South Africa united British and Boer areas of the country. This united, white-controlled state imposed segregation on defined populations of "blacks" and "coloreds," the latter of mixed white-black ancestry. A 1913 Native Lands Act limited land ownership and settlement for blacks and coloreds to restricted areas. Voting rights and political representation were for whites only. As mining expanded, the racial structure of the preindustrial colonial society became part of new capitalist industry. Almost without exception, white workers held skilled and supervisory positions, while black workers were most of the unskilled workers and worked under severe conditions (Thompson 1985:111–12).

Black South Africans often drew on their home cultures to resist apartheid. Opposition to racist policies came from the African National Congress (ANC), founded in 1912 to demand voting rights, freedom of residence, and land for black Africans. White voters elected the openly racist National Party in 1948 with its platform of apartheid and commitment to complete segregation. Apartheid was a racial hierarchy where whites, a fifth of the population, ruled over the large majority of colored and black Africans. Discrimination was extensively institutionalized (Lipton 1985:14–15). The 1950 Population Registration Act established legal registration by racial group; the Group Areas Act prohibited blacks from residing outside zoned areas. White officials sought to control opposition by passing security legislation against so-called communist activities. Since the white minister of justice decided who were "Communists," this permitted the silencing of any people opposed to racist policies through imprisonment and police violence. The government took control of education from the missionary schools, creating a separate and inferior system for black Africans (Thompson 1985:295).

Black Resistance

When whites accelerated the oppressiveness of the apartheid system, those opposed increase their efforts as well, in groups like the ANC and Pan-African Congress (PAC). After the Sharpeville massacre in 1964, in which the police killed many demonstrators, Nelson Mandela and other ANC and PAC leaders were sentenced to prison (Meli 1988). Imprisonments were followed by torture and deaths of some in custody. When support of apartheid became violent, the antiapartheid movement became stronger and more violent in response. Black demonstrations resulted in hundreds of deaths of protesters at the hands of police (Diseko 1991: 40–62). During the 1970s, opposition to apartheid in black townships forced the government to search for new ways to legitimize control. Thus, the restrictions on labor organization among black workers and on multiracial political parties were lifted. In addition, the ANC was changing its emphasis from armed struggle to mass political mobilization (Barrell 1991:64–92).

Recurring differences among black, colored, and Asian South Africans were periodically used by whites to channel black anger away from white oppression. By providing for limited political participation by Asian and colored people in a 1984 constitution, the government tried to divide the nonwhite population. Demonstrations in townships were met with brutal suppression (Thompson 1985). These divide-and-conquer strategies allowed the government to continue to rule, and by accentuating racial-ethnic divisions, such governmental actions produced lasting problems for the development of a democratic South Africa to the present day.

Increases in black protests, together with an international economic boycott, put great pressure on the white leadership, especially the businesspeople disturbed by chaos and loss of profits. Soon, in 1989, the new white head of government, F. W. deKlerk, began dismantling apartheid, and in 1994, Nelson Mandela, head of the ANC, was elected to the South African presidency. This marked a dramatic shift in political power, from oppressors to oppressed, something rarely seen in human history without large-scale revolutions.

What Will the Future Bring?

In contemporary South Africa, whites are little more than a tenth of the country's 45 million people, yet they still dominate economic and certain other major institutions. One challenge is to bring democratic changes to all institutions. The new black South African government has outlawed apartheid, but the movement to socioeconomic equality has been very difficult. Racial discrimination remains institutionalized in everyday life, from the city of Pretoria—which white Afrikaner separatists see as their spiritual capital—to the rural homelands, where many Zulus resist the ANC as a continuation of oppression (Keller 1994:A1; Masland and Conteras 1994:34–7).

Today, there is substantial opposition among whites, particularly Afrikaners, to the recent economic, social, and political changes. For example, a major radio station (Radio Pretoria) broadcasts in the Afrikaans language much programming opposed to the changes in the direction of an integrated and multicultural society. As a recent press report puts it, this station offers an important, yet "unique voice for conservative Afrikaners, the white minority that oppressed blacks for decades and then resisted, sometimes violently, the transition to multiracial democracy" (Swarns 2002:A1). The station broadcasts programs of interest to conservative whites, especially Afrikaners, including much traditional music. Programs reflecting the yearning for the apartheid past are listened to by at least 100,000 whites. Feeling abandoned and alienated, these whites are disturbed about the changes in employment, with affirmative action for black Africans, and the increasing (though small) unemployment for whites. They are concerned about black Africans moving into traditionally white neighborhoods and about interracial marriages. As the station's head expressed it, "We, the Afrikaner people, opened up this country, developed this country, put this country in the front ranks of the developed countries of the world. . . . Black Africa is wiping out everything we have brought" (quoted in Swarns 2002:A1).

A key problem for the black-led government of South Africa is the fact that most of the economy is controlled by white entrepreneurs and white-controlled corporations. This situation is under great pressure for change. One spokesperson for the government, Joel Netshitenzhe, has indicated the rationale for changing this situation: "The implication of not involving the majority at all levels of the economy is that the country relies on a smaller pool of wisdom and expertise, it has a smaller middle class and employed population." He added that changes are necessary to increase aggregate demand for blacks, and if changes are not made, blacks will likely "become cynical of democracy" (quoted in Stoppard 2002:n.p.).

Historically, South Africa's gold, diamond, and platinum mines have made many whites—especially those in international corporations—very wealthy, yet the black laborers who generated that wealth have received little benefit. The new government is now determined that not only political power but also economic power be democratically controlled, if not fully redistributed. Thus, in the year 2000, the government set forth for discussion a plan providing for negotiation with white owners and executives for the transfer of the control of major industries to the black majority. In 2002, the government also started moving forward on a Minerals and Petroleum Resources Development bill. When this legislation is put into full effect, the government will become the owner of all the country's mineral resources. Since many of these resources have historically been controlled by white resources firms, this marks a major shift in ownership of the country's major resources (Cauvin 2002:W1).

One immediate-term goal is to move a third of mining assets, as well as half of new businesses, to the control of black South Africans. One way this is being done is to bring in black partners—a program called Black Economic Empowerment. At least one major firm, Anglo-Platinum, has already laid out such a plan, and others are considering them. Legislation to implement the Black Economic Empowerment policy was under way in 2003, and it has sought to provide benefits to black miners and their communities, as well as to protect the environment and provide for long-term sustainable development. Thus, one major concern of many black South Africans is to guarantee that these new partnerships actually provide economic benefits to ordinary blacks and the numerous small businesses—and not just to members of the new black middle class and elites (Stoppard 2002).

A number of black South Africans have begun to seek compensation for extreme brutality and killings that apartheid officials and programs carried out. Lawyers for a number of black plaintiffs, including relatives of those killed by apartheid regimes, have filed lawsuits seeking billions in compensation—for example, for the actions of IBM and certain Swiss, German, and U.S. banks during the apartheid era. These companies, according to the lawsuits, provided money and technology that enabled the systemic racism of apartheid to be much more effective in operation. According to the lawsuits, these companies knew that their money and products were being used in violation of human rights. Some expect the number of legitimate claims to increase to thousands of cases ("Apartheid Victims" 2002).

In June 1999, a new president was elected to replace Mandela, the ANC leader Thabo Mbeki. To this point in time, the black-led ANC has had a mixed record in political office. The ANC party has facilitated a peaceful transition from white to black political rule, and it has provided some economic help for poor black South Africans. So far, however, it has failed in its policies in reducing unemployment and stimulating regional development for the majority of the black population. President Mbeki was elected because the new opposition, called the Democratic Alliance, represents white power to many of the country's black citizens. Yet, even many black South African voters now seem to be losing hope for real economic development and prosperity ("Race about Race" 2000:5).

Frantz Fanon, a strong critic of European colonialism, once asked: "What is South Africa?" He answered his own question: "A boiler into which thirteen million blacks are clubbed and penned in by two and a half million whites" (Fanon [1952] 1967:87). Today, South Africa is changing significantly, yet whites still have by far the most economic control, and a great many black South Africans feel the country is not changing nearly fast enough. The case of South Africa reveals how European colonialism has historically operated through a trilogy of domination—administration, trade, and religion—to establish a system of white control for a very long period of time, for centuries. Well-institutionalized racism became part of most social sectors. Racial discrimination has regularly shaped the construction of racial and ethnic identities and everyday experiences. The once legally, now informally, segregated patterns of housing, education, and employment reveal persisting patterns of racist practices of white South Africans. After centuries of exploitation, the lives of the black people of southern Africa have been changed fundamentally.

CONCLUSION

Across the globe, institutionalized forms of racism have become structural realities in many non-European societies through the means of European and American overseas colonialism. This has typically operated through the means of bureaucratic administrations, exploitative trade, Christian missionary culture, and, more recently, a global media culture. European, and later U.S., colonizers rationalized this colonial expansion by defining themselves as superior modernizers of those peoples who were very "uncivilized." The construction of colonized peoples as racially inferior was fundamental to legitimizing exploitation and enslavement. Racist ideology and institutions were integral to colonialism, and white racism has remained central within colonized and colonizing countries into the current era.

The postcolonial lives of both colonized and colonizers have been scissored by conflict and violence. Across the globe, well-institutionalized racism can be seen in highly racialized stereotyping, practices, and institutions. Not surprisingly, thus, the processes of Western imperialism often forced colonized peoples to accept stereotypes of whites as superior and themselves as inferior. This pervasive ideology usually required colonized peoples to accept growing patterns of racial-ethnic inequality and continuing European and U.S. domination. For Western countries, non-European countries remain major sources of extractive resources that fuel the dynamic Western economies. Such economic neo-colonialism continues the exploitation of human beings and their natural resources and thus the

destruction of their lives, bodies, families, and cultures (Batur-VanderLippe 1992).

As we have documented, the problem of white-maintained racist systems has been a global reality now for many centuries. This has never been more true than today. The challenge for the racially oppressed is how to confront white-maintained racism effectively and on a global scale. Beginning in the late nineteenth century, several Pan-African conferences were among the first to globalize the antiracist movement. Writing in 1927, W. E. B. Du Bois summarized a statement made by the fourth Pan-African Congress. This declaration asserted the legitimate human rights of peoples of color across the globe: voting rights, education, rights to land, and economic development for the benefit of the many rather than the white few (Du Bois 1995: 670–5).

Widespread demands for economic equality, political participation, social justice, and cultural representation are still goals for those seeking an antiracist future for the planet (Batur-VanderLippe 1998). Today, an awareness of this global challenge is growing, and those involved are emphasizing the creation of new terms of human coexistence and international relations. For example, in fall 2001, some 160 countries met in Durban, South Africa, at the first World Conference against Racism, Racial Discrimination, Xenophobia, and Related Intolerance. Most governments represented there—but not including the United States, which withdrew early—agreed to a new international plan (the "Durban Declaration") for fighting racism and xenophobia in countries across the globe. This Declaration explicitly labels racist systems such as slavery a crime against humanity, and the European delegates there even agreed to an expression of regret for European involvement in slavery. This conference signaled a growing international concern with racism and xenophobia.

The unfortunate early withdrawal of the right-wing U.S. government from that conference, however, signals the great difficulties that the U.S. (then the George W. Bush) political administration had in exploring an end to racism in the United States and overseas. In the United States, South Africa, Brazil, and France, institutionalized discrimination maintained by whites continues to destroy the lives and communities of many millions of people of color. In postcolonial France, racialized thinking and practice still target French Muslims from Africa, who regularly experience the destruction of property and attacks on their culture. In South Africa and in Brazil, in spite of their quite different histories, citizens of African ancestry still face much socioeconomic stereotyping, discrimination, and oppression. In the United States, there is continuing conflict over the continuing racial oppression that is directed by many whites at various groups of Americans of color. Today, postcolonial governments still allow the discriminatory realities descending from European colonialism to continue. Their effects can be seen in persisting racial inequalities in, among other institutional areas, education, housing, business, employment, public accommodations, and health care.

From our perspective, realistic evaluations of the present and future of postcolonial societies require a deep understanding and direct confrontation of entrenched racial inequalities and a major organized struggle against these burdensome realities. Fortunately, in the few decades right after World War II, the conditions of the cold-war era facilitated the revolt of colonial societies against their European masters. Ironically, the cold war between the former Soviet Union and the United States and its European allies reshaped the political dependency of most postcolonial societies. They became their own political masters. Yet, severe and often racialized economic neocolonialism has persisted. This economic (and often cultural) neocolonialism is often an extension of the old imperialistic-capitalistic domination created in previous eras. Today, as the capitalist system re-creates itself in globalizing and neocolonial forms, it still creates or reinforces racial discrimination and inequalities that remain embedded in the societies and cultures of both former colonies and former colonizing countries (Batur and Feagin 1999).

In his brilliant book *Darkwater*, W. E. B. Du Bois (1996) reminded those of European extraction that they have not lived by their own professed morality: "The number of white individuals who are practicing with even reasonable approximation the democracy and unselfishness of Jesus Christ is so small and unimportant as to be fit subject for jest in Sunday supplements" (p. 501). Later, in the same book, Du Bois notes the changes that must eventually come in the world racial order.

Du Bois made this sage comment in relation to how the world's non-European majority viewed what is called World War I:

> But what of the darker world that watches? Most men belong to this world. With Negro and Negroid, East Indian, Chinese, and Japanese they form two-thirds of the population of the world. A belief in humanity is a belief in colored men. If the uplift of mankind must be done by men, then the destinies of this world will rest ultimately in the hands of darker nations.
>
> What, then, is this dark world thinking? It is thinking that as wild and awful as this shameful war was, it is nothing to compare with that fight for freedom which black and brown and yellow men must and will make unless their oppression and humiliation and insult at the hands of the White World cease. The Dark World is going to submit to its present treatment just as long as it must and not one moment longer. (P. 507)

As we enter the twenty-first century, most of the world's people carry the burden of the history of European and American racism in their minds. Just under 200 million people have died in genocide and mass murders over the past century, yet the human race still searches for global solutions to genocide in terms of intervention, assistance, restoration, and punishment. The Treaty of Rome, dated April 11, 2002, established an International Criminal Court. Supporters anticipate that this important court will establish a legitimate global reach in matters of war crimes, crimes against humanity, and genocide. However, the U.S. government has so far refused to sign this important international treaty. At the time of writing, the conservative U.S. (George W. Bush) administration has argued that giving the international court jurisdiction over U.S. soldiers cannot be allowed because of the U.S. American Service Members Protection Act. Indeed, this arch-conservative administration demanded that the U.S. government should have a seat on this tribunal, but will only participate in interventions of its own choosing. In this perspective, any American brought before the tribunal might testify, but could not be convicted. In July 2002, the United States also began to withdraw its commitment to another important international legal agreement, the Convention against Torture, which it had signed in 1994. The conservative U.S. administration argued that mandatory inspections of its operations would be too intrusive (Anderson 2002:7; "In This Case Might Is Right" 2002:35; "UN-nerving" 2002:3).

Crimes against humanity are global offenses. Fifty years ago, when Justice Robert Jackson of the United States made his opening statement at the International Military Tribunal in Nuremberg, set up to try German war criminals, he said: "The wrongs that we seek to condemn and punish have been so calculated, so malignant and so devastating that civilization cannot tolerate their being ignored, because it cannot survive their being repeated" (Powell 1995:52). Yet, not only have we seen these wrongs repeated—in widespread, often violent racial oppression in many countries, and in genocide from Cambodia to Kosovo to Rwanda to Chechnya—we are also witnessing the silencing of the voice of universal objection and the erosion of various governments' commitment, including recently that of the United States, to the well-being of humanity.

On April 16, 1963, the U.S. civil rights leader Dr. Martin Luther King Jr. (1964) wrote a letter from his Birmingham, Alabama, jail cell to a group of clergy who argued that King's protest actions were unwise. In the letter, King said, "I am in Birmingham because injustice is here. . . . I cannot sit idly by in Atlanta and not be concerned about what happens in Birmingham. Injustice anywhere is a threat to justice everywhere" (p. 77). Throughout the world, systemic racism continues to destroy the lives of many millions of people, along with their (and all) hopes for a better world. Only if we the people of planet earth can learn to empathize with those routinely targeted and harmed by white racism can we comprehend its destructiveness, and only if we comprehend that destructiveness can we ever develop successful strategies to fight racism both locally and globally.

NOTE

1. Portions of this article draw on and update Pinar Batur and Joe R. Feagin's (2003) "Colonialism and Post-Colonialism: The Global Expansion of Racism," pp. 356–71 in *Racial and Ethnic Relations,* by Joe R. Feagin and Clairece Booher Feagin. Upper Saddle River, NJ: Prentice Hall. Used by permission.

REFERENCES

Anderson, J. B. 2002. Unsigning the ICC. *Nation,* April 29, p. 7.

Andrews, G. 1992. "Racial Inequality in Brazil and the United States: A Statistical Comparison." *Journal of Social History* 26:234–57.

Ani, M. 1994. *Yurugu: An African-Centered Critique of European Cultural Thought and Behavior.* Trenton, NJ: Africa World Press.

Anti-Defamation League. 1993. *Highlights from an Anti-Defamation League Survey on Racial Attitudes in America.* New York: Anti-Defamation League.

"Apartheid Victims Broaden Claims to Target IBM, German Banks." 2002. *Agence France Presse*, July 1. Retrieved April 1, 2003, from Lexis-Nexis.

Ayres, I. 1991. "Fair Driving: Gender and Race Discrimination in Retail Car Negotiations." *Harvard Law Review* 104:820–30.

Ayres, I. and J. Waldfogel 1994. "A Market Test for Race Discrimination in Bail Setting." *Stanford Law Review* 46:987–1047.

Barrell, H. 1991. "The Turn to the Masses: The African National Congress' Strategic Review of 1978–1979." *Journal of South African Studies* 18:64–92.

Batur, P. and J. R. Feagin. 1999. "Racial and Ethnic Inequality and Struggle from the Colonial Era to the Present: Drawing the Global Color Line." Pp. 3–24 in *The Global Color Line: Racial and Ethnic Inequality and Struggle from a Global Perspective*, edited by P. Batur and J. Feagin. Stamford, CT: JAI Press.

Batur-VanderLippe, P. 1992. *The Discourse of Counterattack: Ethnic Movements and the Formation of Ethnic Identity.* Unpublished Ph.D. dissertation, University of Texas, Austin.

——. 1998. "Centering on Global Racism and Anti-Racism: From Everyday Life to Global Complexity." *Sociological Spectrum* 19:467–84.

Batur-VanderLippe, P. and J. R. Feagin. 1996. "Racism in the Post-Colonial World." *International Policy Review* 6:30–41.

Bobo, L. D. 2001. *Inequalities That Endure? Racial Ideology, American Politics, and the Peculiar Role of the Social Sciences.* Presented at a meeting of the University of Illinois on The Changing Terrain of Race and Ethnicity, October, Chicago, IL.

Bobo, L. D. and S. A. Suh. 2000. "Surveying Racial Discrimination: Analyses from a Multiethnic Labor Market." Pp. 527–64 in *Prismatic Metropolis: Inequality in Los Angeles*, edited by L. D. Bobo, M. L. Oliver, J. H. Johnson Jr., and A. Valenzuela. New York: Russell Sage.

Brewer, A. 1986. *Marxist Theories of Imperialism.* New York: Routledge.

Burns, E. B. 1993. *A History of Brazil.* 3rd ed. New York: Cornell Press.

Cauvin, H. E. 2002. "A Radical Overhaul for South African Mining." *New York Times,* June 4, p. W1.

Chasan, A. 2000. "Border Skirmishes: European Integration vs. Ugly Atavisms." *World Press Review,* January 2, p. 2.

"The Colours of Brazil." 1986. *The Economist,* May 10, p. 42.

Cox, O. C. 1948. *Caste, Class, and Race.* Garden City, NY: Doubleday.

Creamean, L. 1996. "Membership of Foreigners: Algerians in France." *Arab Studies Quarterly* 16:49–67.

Cross, T. 1984. *Black Power Imperative: Racial Inequality and the Politics of Nonviolence.* New York: Faulkner.

Daley, S. 2002. "France's Nonwhites See Bias in Far Rightist's Strength." *New York Times,* April 30, p. A4.

Davidson, B. 1991. *Africa in History.* New York: Collier Books.

Deen, T. 1998. "Rights: U.N. Worried over Alarming Rise in Xenophobia." Retrieved March 19, 2003, from www.oneworld.org/ips2/sept98/12_34_035.html.

De Wenden, C. W. 1991. "North African Immigration and the French Political Imaginary." Pp. 98–110 in *Race, Discourse and Power in France,* edited by M. Silverman. Brookfield, VT: Gower.

Diseko, N. 1991. "The Origins and Development of the South African Student's Movement SASM: 1968–1976." *Journal of South African Studies* 18:40–62.

Du Bois, W. E. B. [1903] 1989. *The Souls of Black Folk.* New York: Bantam Books.

——. [1940] 1984. *Dusk of Dawn: An Essay toward an Autobiography of a Race Concept.* New Brunswick, NJ: Transaction Books.

——. [1946] 1965. *The World and Africa.* New York: International Publishers.

——. [1935] 1992. *Black Reconstruction in America.* New York: Atheneum.

——. 1995. "The Pan-African Congresses." Pp. 670–5 in *W. E. B. Du Bois: A Reader,* edited by David L. Lewis. New York: Henry Holt.

——. 1996. *Darkwater.* P. 551 in *The Oxford W. E. B. Du Bois Reader,* edited by Eric Sundquist. New York: Oxford University Press.

Fanon, F. [1952] 1967. *Black Skin, White Masks.* Translated by C. Markmann. New York: Grove Weidenfeld.

——. 1963. *The Wretched of the Earth.* Translated by C. Farrington. New York: Grove Press.

Feagin, J. R. 2000. *Racist America.* New York: Routledge.

Forman, T. A., D. R. Williams, and J. S. Jackson. 1997. "Race, Place and Discrimination." Pp. 231–61 in *Perspectives on Social Problems,* edited by C. Gardner. New York: JAI Press.

Frangoudaki, A. 2000. "Reproduction of the Patterns of Interstate Power Relations in the Conceptions of 15-Year-Old Students in EU Countries: The Persistence of Prejudice." *Journal of Modern Greek Studies* 18:355.

"French TV Executive, Former TV Host Fined for Racist Song Performed on Air about Blacks." 1996. *Jet,* April 1, p. 65.

Godoy, J. 2002. "Rights-France: Anti-Immigrant and Racist Views on the Rise." *Inter Press Service.* Retrieved April 1, 2003, from Lexis-Nexis.

Hanchard, M. 1994. *Orpheus and Power: The Movimento Negro of Rio de Janeiro and São Paulo, Brazil, 1945–1988.* Princeton, NJ: Princeton University Press.

Harris, J. 1987. *Africans and Their History.* New York: Mentor.

Hart, D. 1988. "Racial Bias Entrenched." *Chronicle of Higher Education,* July 20:31–2.

Hill, Jane H. 1995. "Mock Spanish: A Site for the Indexical Reproduction of Racism in American English." University of Arizona, Tucson, Arizona. Unpublished research paper.

Ibrahim, Y. 1994. "France Bans Muslim Scarf in Its Schools." *New York Times,* September 11, p. 4.

"In This Case Might Is Right: It Looks Bad, but the U.S. Should Be Wary of the International Criminal Court." 2002. *Time,* July 15, p. 35.

Johnson, D. 1993. "The Making of the French Country." Pp. 35–61 in *The National Question in Europe in Historical Context,* edited by M. Teich and R. Porter. Cambridge, England: Cambridge University Press.

Keller, B. 1994. "Rival Visions of a Post-Apartheid Future Divide South Africa's Zulus." *New York Times,* April 4, p. A1.

Kennedy, D. 2000. "Who Are Brazil's Indigenas: Contributions of Census Data Analysis to Anthropological Demography on Indigenous Populations." *Human Organization* 59:311.

King, Martin Luther, Jr. 1964. *Why We Can't Wait.* New York: Penguin.

Klanwatch Project. 1996. *False Patriots: The Threat of Antigovernment Extremists.* Montgomery, AL: Southern Poverty Law Center.

Kristeva, J. 1993. *Countries without Nationalism.* New York: Columbia University Press.

Lippi-Green, R. 1997. *English with an Accent.* New York: Routledge.

Lipton, M. 1985. *Capitalism and Apartheid: South Africa, 1910–1984.* Totowa, NJ: Rowman & Allenheld.

Masland, T. and J. Conteras. 1994. "Ballots or Bullets." *Newsweek,* April 11, pp. 34–7.

Meli, F. 1988. *South Africa Belongs to Us: A History of the ANC.* Bloomington, IN: Indiana University Press.

Muello, P. 2002. "Black Brazilians at Last Emerging from Margins." *Associated Press, BC cycle.* Retrieved April 1, 2003, from Lexis-Nexis.

Oliver, R. and A. Atmore. 1989. *Africa since 1800.* 3rd ed. Cambridge, England: Cambridge University Press.

Oliviera, F. 1999. "A Bible and an Automatic." *Index on Censorship* 28:115–17.

Powell, B. 1995. "Lessons of Nuremberg." *Newsweek,* November 6, p. 52.

PR Newswire. 2002. "New Study of High Cost Home Lending Reveals Widespread Racial Disparities; In Response, CRC, California's Largest CRA Coalition, Calls for Further Regulation, and Support for Local Responses to Predatory Lending." Retrieved April 1, 2003, from Lexis-Nexis.

"Race About Race: South Africa's Racial Election." 2000. *The Economist,* December 9, p. 5.

Riding, A. 1994. "Mitterrand's Mistakes: Vichy Past Is Unveiled." *New York Times,* September 9, p. A4.

Rohter, L. 2002. "The Saturday Profile; From Maid to Rio Governor, and Still Fighting." *New York Times,* April 17, p. A4. Retrieved April 1, 2003, from Lexis-Nexis.

Russell, Alan G. 1944. *Colour, Race and Empire.* Port Washington, NY: Kennikat Press.

Sanders, T. 1981. "Racial Discrimination and Black Consciousness in Brazil." *American Universities Field Staff Reports* 42:n.p.

Sardar, Z., A. Nandy, and M. W. Davies. 1993. *Barbaric Others: A Manifesto on Western Racism.* London, England: Pluto Press.

Scarville, J., S. B. Button, J. E. Edwards, A. R. Lancaster, and T. W. Elig. 1999. *Armed Forces Equal Opportunity Survey.* Arlington, VA: Defense Manpower Data Center.

Silverman, M. 1992. *Deconstructing the Country: Immigration, Racism, and Citizenship in Modern France.* London, England: Routledge.

Singer, D. 1996. "Liberte, Egalite, Racisme?" *The Nation,* October 21, p. 19.

Skidmore, T. and P. Smith. 1994. *Modern Latin America.* 2nd ed. Oxford, England: Oxford University Press.

"Southam News. We Must Speak Out against Racism." 2002. *Guardian Charlottetown,* May 16, p. A6.

Spinant, D. 2002. "EU Adopts Declaration Condemning Racism." *EUObserver.com.* Retrieved April 1, 2003, from Lexis-Nexis.

Srikameswaran, A. 2002. "A Great Divide: Institutional Racism on One Side, Misinformation on the Other Mean Minorities Lag in Receiving Transplants and Heart Surgeries." *Pittsburg Post-Gazette,* July 23, p. F-1.

Stoppard, A. 2002. "Economy—South Africa: Black Empowerment Policy Worries Investors." *Inter Press Service.* Retrieved April 1, 2003, from Lexis-Nexis.

Swarns, R. L. 2002. "In a New South Africa, an Old Tune Lingers." *New York Times,* October 7, p. A1.

Takaki, R. 1990. *Iron Cages.* New York: Oxford University Press.

Talk of the Nation. 2002. "Racial Inequalities in Health Care." National Public Radio. Retrieved April 1, 2003, from Lexis-Nexis.

Thompson, L. 1985. *Political Mythology of Apartheid.* New Haven, CT: Yale University Press.

"UN-nerving: America and the United Nations." 2002. *The Economist,* July 27, p. 3.

Whitaker, Charles. 1991. "Blacks in Brazil: The Myth and the Reality." *Ebony*, February, pp. 41, 60–4.

Williams, T. 2000. *The Homestead Act: Our Earliest National Asset Policy.* Presented at the symposium of the Center for Social Development, September, St. Louis, MO.

Winant, H. 1992. "Rethinking Race in Brazil." *Journal of Latin American Studies* 24:173–92.

Woodall, Chris. 1993. "Arabicide in France: An Interview with Fausto Guidice." *Race and Class* 35:21–33.

Worden, Nigel. 1994. *The Making of Modern South Africa.* 2nd ed. Oxford, England: Blackwell.

Young, I. M. 1990. *Justice and the Politics of Difference.* Princeton, NJ: Princeton University Press.

Ethnic Conflict as a Global Social Problem

Thomas D. Hall, Lester M. Jones Professor of Sociology

DePauw University

Ethnic conflict is a complex topic, fraught with a great deal of baggage and hidden meanings, including two very thorny issues: (1) what do we mean by "conflict"; and (2) what does "ethnicity" mean. Many debates and arguments about ethnic conflict find their roots in assumed meanings for these terms and the baggage they carry with them. Sometimes the debates resolve once all parties work with the same or similar definitions. The discussions about "ethnicity" are further muddied by the historical context or contexts to which they refer. Not only have the terms varied widely in social science use (Omi and Winant 1994), but also the actual phenomena have changed over time (Hall 1984, 1998).

A great deal of recent social science writing has been directed at unpacking or deconstructing the theoretical assumptions embedded in various definitions, and even "facts." While often useful, such discussions can rapidly devolve into solipsistic musings that have little or no use in actual analysis. Yet, to ignore these issues is to invite misunderstanding by writers and readers of each other, and more significantly by social scientists of the very phenomena they are trying to comprehend. One way of escaping this morass is to include in discussions of definitions the theoretical baggage that accompanies them. This is often a very recursive process; once some definition is advanced, further investigations—theoretical and empirical—may call into question some of the assumptions upon which it was originally based, and indicate that some refinement is required. Still, definitions are tools to aid analysis, not ends in themselves. But, like all tools, they must be used cautiously, carefully, and with attention to the purpose for which they are employed.

I begin with some basic definitions that I refine in the course of this essay. I attempt to be clear about my assumptions so that readers who operate from different definitions and perspectives can still find some use in this discussion, even if they decide to transform some of it to fit their own understandings of the basic terms.

"Conflict" is an immense category for human disputes that range from relatively mild disagreements, such as the meaning of words, interpretation of events, and so on, to extremely violent attempts to eliminate another person or group of persons. Conflict can also range from blatant and overt, to very subtle and hidden. In general, lower levels of conflict are an improvement of more intense and more violent forms. Not all conflict is "bad." On occasion it can be useful to all parties, more typically to various parties differentially.

"Ethnicity" is far more complex. A basic definition might be a group of humans who share significant elements of culture and who reproduce themselves socially and biologically. Typically, they share a sense of identity, which is typically, but not always, recognized by other ethnic groups. Thus, ethnicity is socially constructed in at least two ways. First, it is reproduced through socialization processes, wherein new members—again typically through birth, but at times through various forms of capture or adoption—learn how to act as members of the group. Second, it is socially constructed by self-recognition and recognition by others. In such social construction processes, the ethnic identity may as often be a consequence of other actions, including conflicts, as it is an end in itself. In the language of statistical analysis, ethnicity can be either a dependent or independent variable. In fact, most often it is both in complex recursive social processes that shape and reshape its content and meaning.

The rub, or difficulty, in all this is the rooting of the identity in biological reproduction, which is often assumed to be "natural," "innate," or even "immutable." This generates at least two problems. First, the problem is that "race" is often assumed to be quintessentially biological, but is in fact often if not always socially constructed (Cavalli-Sforza and Cavalli-Sforza 1995; Gould 1996; Montagu 1997; Omi and Winant 1994; Smedley 1999). This is the familiar debate between "primordialist" or "essentialist" and "socially constructed" approaches to ethnicity and race. In situations where there is a widespread assumption that ethnicity is biologically rooted, typically in some aspect of phenotypical manifestation, such as skin tone, eye folds, tooth shape, hair, and so on, ethnicity has become racialized.

Thus, "race" is both a special case of "ethnicity" and a problematic one: how and why did this or that feature or constellation of features come to be seen as "racial," and why not others?

The second problem is that ethnicity is typically constructed historically. Where the historical depth is sufficient (what is sufficient is itself problematic), it can often appear "natural," "primordial," "essential," or "racial." In those times and places where humans did not move far from their home territories, there is in fact an association of phenotypical features, culture, and identity. This association, however, is not "natural" or "normal," but an artifact of relative geographical stability, which itself is historically rooted. However, ethnic groups in fact change and transmute through time, fragmenting, amalgamating, and exchanging members. Where these processes are slow, they again may appear to be racial or biological because their social and historical construction is not readily perceptible to a casual observer. Two processes are especially revealing. First is the exchange or migration of individuals or families across boundaries, even while the boundaries remain stable (Barth 1969; Haaland 1969). Indeed, Frederick Barth (1969) goes so far as to claim ethnicity is demarcated by its boundaries, not the "cultural stuff" it contains. Second is ethnogenesis, the formation of a new group from parts of other groups, or families, or individuals (for many examples, see Hill 1996). Ethnogenesis often simultaneously entails ethnocide, especially when two or more formerly distinct groups merge into a larger group. At other times, ethnogenesis is the result of one group splitting into two or more separate groups.

A problem here is that these processes are slow and often contested, sometimes violently, with a great deal of slippage back and forth along the various dimensions of change. Put alternatively, ethnic boundaries are nearly always fluid, fuzzy, and permeable. One consequence of the rise of the modern state with precisely defined geographic boundaries is that that precision has been metaphorically extended to all sorts of human groupings whose boundaries are anything but precise. Indeed, even those rare cases where ethnic boundaries do appear precise are really only a snapshot or freeze frame of larger, slower processes of continual change.

Finally, conflict itself can be ethnogenetic. Two groups, defined arbitrarily, or by the terms of a conflict if the conflict persists sufficiently long, may come to define themselves, and each other, as ethnically distinct. In the modern world (the last half millennium or so), this most often occurs with the splitting of states: Norway from Sweden, the two Germanies, Vietnams, or Koreas. As Germany illustrates, the splits can be temporary, and as Czechoslovakia illustrates, the reverse, amalgamations, can also be temporary. In premodern times, especially among nonstate societies, these processes were much more fluid in that there was little interest in precise demarcation of boundaries. None of this, however, is meant to imply that individuals were confused about who they were or their group membership(s), although they may often be contested.

ETHNIC CHANGE AND CONFLICT ARE "NORMAL"

According to Ted Gurr and Barbara Harff (1994; Gurr 1993, 2000; Harff and Gurr 1998), ethnic conflict and ethnic violence have been the leading cause of casualties in warfare over the last few decades. Wilma Dunaway (2003) argues that the rate of increase of ethnic conflict has not grown since the end of the Cold War (1991), but that ethnic conflicts have become more costly for states and for capitalist enterprises. Still, for many observers this recent prevalence of ethnic conflicts is a puzzle. My argument here is that this puzzle arises from an incorrect framing of the problem. The real puzzle is why there is not far more conflict. Following Gurr's (1993, 2000) pioneering work on ethnic conflict and his Minorities at Risk Project, there are on the order of 6,000 identifiable ethnic groups in the world today (at the beginning of the twenty-first century). Yet there are fewer than 200 recognized states in the world. That is to say that ethnic diversity is quite common, and hence at least the potential for conflict. Much of Gurr's work has been directed at uncovering the situations that make conflict more, or less, likely. I return to this issue below. For now I continue to explore this diversity issue a bit.

If ethnicity were evenly distributed (a historically rash assumption), then every state would have approximately 30 groups. Still, as of the 1980s, the number of states with 95 percent or more of the population in the largest ethnic group is quite small, 30, with half those in Europe. Furthermore, given the movement of workers and refugees, the number is probably lower in the first decade of the twenty-first century (Laczko 2000:133). In other words, the so-called nation-state is a chimera. This then raises the puzzle, Why is the ethnically pure nation-state so widely held as an ideal? The answer is complex, rooted in both recent trends and deep historical processes.

One of the consequences of modernization, democratization, industrialization, and globalization has been an increasing uniformity in ideals of how to form a state. John Meyer and colleagues (1997) argue persuasively that were a new state to form today, we could predict in considerable detail how it would be organized politically and bureaucratically. This is a consequence of an emerging global culture that has accompanied the increasing tightening of global capitalism on the world economy. Since the modern state is ideally (ideally in the Weberian sense of an ideal type) ethnically uniform, that ideal has spread as well. But this begs the question of how that ideal arose.

In order to explore this question, it is necessary to revisit the long history of human states. One of the best sources on this is William H. McNeill (1986) in his series of lectures on "Polyethnicity." Whether one follows more or less conventional world history (which is far from conventional and undergoing considerable intellectual foment; see *Journal of World History* over the last decade), or follows various accounts of long-term social change (Chase-Dunn and Hall 1997; Denemark et al. 2000; Frank and Gills 1993; Hall 1998; Lenski 1966, 1976; Nisbet 1969; Sanderson 1995, [1995] 1999), it is clear that since their first invention some 5,000 years ago, states have steadily expanded and progressively gobbled up neighboring groups, whether they be other states or any of a wide range of types of nonstate societies. Whether such expansionary conquests are a form of ethnic conflict is itself a minor puzzle. Historically, ethnic differences have not played a major role in analyses of state expansion. They have been seen as more of a side effect. Still, there is an ethnic aspect to such conquests, and especially to attempts to rebel and break loose from a conquering state.

In expanding, even those primary or autochthonous states quickly came to absorb peoples who were ethnically different. In McNeill's terms, states quickly become polyethnic, or what today might be called ethnically plural or multicultural. Early states often were not concerned with ethnic or cultural uniformity, save possibly within a narrow elite. Rather, they focused on the efficient collection of tribute, but beyond that they tolerated a great deal of pluralism. Typically, however, ethnic groups within a state were ranked hierarchically (Laczko 1990), with the ethnicity of the dominating elite at the peak. Even without a policy directed toward doing so, this created some pressure for lower-ranked groups to assimilate into or acculturate toward the dominant culture. Other factors like location and occupational specialization, crop specialization, and so on created pressures to maintain differences. The net result is that the multiethnic state is "normal" in the statistical sense, and has been for five millennia. This deepens the puzzle of the chimera of the ethnically homogeneous nation-state.

Many writers, ancient and modern, have noted that a plural or polyethnic state is more difficult to administer. Uniformities in language, measures, monetary denominations, and cultural practices for commercial exchanges make exchange much easier. Indeed, one way of overcoming these obstacles was a trade diaspora (Curtin 1984) in which members of one ethnic group moved to another state and formed an enclave with which coethnics traded. Members of the enclave then conducted exchanges with the host society. In sum, for many millennia, states maintained a dynamic balance between the pressures for uniformity and for difference, and thus stayed plural.

Following McNeill (1986), this situation began to change in the seventeenth through nineteenth centuries. Two sets of factors contributed to this. One was more or less a historical accident. As European states were consolidating out of congeries of competing petty kingdoms and merging variant dialects, the pressures from administrators and merchants for uniformity increased (Bartlett 1993; Tilly 1975, 1990). Historians writing during those times turned to ancient writings to learn how to build states. They read how the ancients bemoaned the diversity of ethnic groups (usually described as nations or peoples) as these early classical states formed. This coincidence, of reading ancients at precisely the time in their own histories that they were undergoing similar problems, reinforced their view that ethnic uniformity was vital to building a successful state.

The second factor was a change in the nature of warfare. As states in Europe became larger and as guns began to come into common use, states needed larger and larger infantries. Eventually, the need was for armies larger than what could be drawn from elite classes or mercenaries. However, arming peasants has always been dangerous. Their loyalty needed to be ensured. One means of doing so was the conceptualization of citizenship and patriotism for the fatherland or motherland. But this is nigh impossible when loyalties are to localities, such as villages or small districts. Larger identities must be built. Thus begins a process of subsuming local identities within a larger state identity, and the birth of the nation-state as an ideal.

This is the process that Benedict Anderson (1991) has called the "imagined community" and that Eugene Weber (1976) described in *Peasants into Frenchmen*. Peter Sahlins (1989) shows in some detail how these processes worked differently in the Pyrenees as the boundary between France and Spain came to be precisely defined. All these, and many other accounts, demonstrate that this national unity is a very slow process, and that it inherently entails a good deal of ethnic conflict as identities are reshaped and reformed. That is, the rise of the nation-state as an ideal is itself one of the causes of ethnic conflict. Phrased alternatively, nationalism, or patriotism, inherently generates ethnic conflict.

Intellectually, as this ideal of the nation-state came to be seen as "normal" or "natural," the persistence of ethnically distinct groups within states came to be seen as problematic. The ideal became so widely accepted as part of the modernization paradigm that many social thinkers expected ethnic conflict to decrease. Hence, its continuation, and indeed its perceived rise in recent decades, became a puzzle.

There are two levels of Eurocentrism embedded in this discussion. First, the emphasis on ethnic homogeneity clearly does emerge from the dominance of European and European-derived states in the modern world. Second, and more subtle, the relatively low attention among European and United States social scientists to ethnic processes in Asia, especially in the premodern world, may overemphasize the European versions of states in this analysis. One may consider a series of counterfactual scenarios. What if Chinese, Arab, or Indian sailors had "discovered" and colonized the Americas? Would the state today have such an emphasis on ethnic homogeneity? While fundamentally unanswerable, such a question does serve to highlight how both historical facts and the study of history may have distorted our understanding of the roles of states in ethnic conflict. One obvious remedy is more detailed, historical studies of state relations with surrounding peoples in Asia and elsewhere to develop a more robust understanding of the various roles of states and state organization (tributary, industrial, capitalist) in ethnic relations. A glimmer of an answer can be uncovered in closer examination of the history of state expansion into the territories of other peoples.

STATE EXPANSION AND ETHNIC CONFLICT

Before examining this rise in ethnic conflict further, it is necessary to reexamine state expansion, this time with a focus on interactions with nonstate societies or indigenous peoples (Hall and Nagel 2000). For a variety of reasons (that need not be examined in detail here), relations with nonstate societies, often glossed as "barbarians," have not been considered under the heading of ethnic conflict, at least not until the twentieth century, when some indigenous populations, like the first nations in North America, have come to be seen as ethnic minorities. There are at least two major differences in how these groups have related to states through time.

First, they have been more subject to pressures to assimilate, to become "civilized," that is, to take up the sedentary, agricultural life of people in state societies, including especially formal, bureaucratically

organized political structures (for cogent review see Maybury-Lewis 2000). States from China (Barfield 1989, 1990, 2001), to early Indian states (Srinivas 1996), to Rome (Wells 1999a, b), to Spain in the Americas (Hill 1996; Weber 1992; Weber and Rausch 1994), to the United States (Hoxie 1984), and to Africa (Macharia 2003) have tended to view nonstate groups as politically unorganized, or "acephalous," or without reason. States have a very difficult time dealing with the informal, charismatic, fluid organization of many nonstate societies. Consequently, they often pressured such groups to take on formal organizations or to assimilate, typically as peasants, into the state. Indigenous peoples often resisted fiercely, and not infrequently fled to hinterlands that states found undesirable or unusable. However, when they have been absorbed, and if they did take up the culture of the encroaching state, they have been destroyed as a separate ethnic group. This is ethnic conflict in the extreme, annihilating a group identity, even if the group members survive as individuals, a process labeled ethnocide.

Yet, there is a second, more subtle difference. The interactions with states, typically but not universally, have been violent and very conflictual and have had serious social structural effects far beyond the border or frontier zone of immediate fighting. Brian Ferguson and Neil Whitehead (1992 a, b) refer to this much larger zone of volatile change as the "tribal zone." Here "tribal" needs to be in quotes because it has several meanings. Often the label "tribal," like "primitive," is a not so subtle justification for confiscation of land or mineral rights or seizure of some other resource. Often it is used as justification for forced assimilation into state culture. Incidentally, this is why many indigenous peoples in the United States have insisted on changing their names, such as from Navajo Tribe to Navajo Nation. It is also why many of these same groups now insist on using their name in their own language rather than the names by which they have been known, such as Navajo Community College becoming Diné College, Sioux returning to Lakota, Nakota, or Dakota, or the League of the Iroquois to Haudenosaunee.

Even where used analytically, "tribal" is a catchall term that is no more precise than "nonstate society." Finally, even if "tribal" is precisely defined to refer to a form of social organization with semi-formal leadership, between band and chiefdom, the classification itself masks the historical nature of most such tribal organizations. Ferguson and Whitehead (1992a, b) follow the lead of Morton Fried (1967, 1975) in arguing that most "tribes" are in fact a product of intense interactions of nonstate societies with expanding states. "Tribes" may be formed by the breakup of organized chiefdoms, or the unification of groups of band societies. In short, most often they are not a "stage" in an evolutionary sequence, but a by-product of the expansion of states.

These kinds of transformations often ripple far beyond the zone of immediate contact with the expanding state. They disrupt traditional organizations and reorganize, often along new lines, the groups that exist in the "tribal zone." Among other consequences, this means that even very early, first-hand observations of "tribal" life seldom reflect some pristine condition, but rather are products of long, intensive interactions. State-level observers who are literate and leave records seldom arrive in remote areas that have not already been incorporated into the tribal zone. David Anderson (1994), in reconstructing cycling among chiefdoms in the southeastern United States by reexamining documents from the DeSoto expedition in the sixteenth century, provides an exemplary model of how to interpret such accounts to overcome the tribal zone effect. The collections compiled by Ferguson and Whitehead (1992a) and Hill (1996) provide numerous examples of these effects, although those in Hill focus on ethnogenetic effects.

Thus, a great deal of ethnic change and ethnic conflict is engendered in the tribal zone by state expansion. Furthermore, much of this conflict is invisible, or nearly so, in the historical record. The accounts in Ferguson and Whitehead (1992a), Anderson (1994), and Hill (1996) are notable precisely because they are able to penetrate this veil by an astute use of documents often in combination with archaeological evidence. A key implication of these studies is that states everywhere, throughout their five millennia of existence, have had these kinds of effects on nonstate societies. Thus, this is probably the oldest and most common form of ethnic conflict. Furthermore, it has not solely been a result of European expansion. Let me hasten to add that by this I do *not* mean to claim that European expansion and colonialism or capitalism has been somehow less devastating than has often been argued. Rather, the root of such conflicts is in the state qua state. To be sure, the form of the state—tributary, mercantile, capitalist, or industrial—shapes in profound ways these general processes, but it is stateness that is key. If one compares the accounts of early Spanish colonialism in the collections compiled by Donna Guy and Thomas Sheridan (1998a, b) or David Weber and Jane Rausch (1994) with accounts of early Rome by Peter Wells (1999a, b, 1992), Dyson (1985), Mattingly (1992), or Miller (1993), one is immediately struck by the continuities in policies and strategies, and less by the differences. Differences emerge with the rise of modern, industrial, capitalist states and derive in no small part from the vastly superior power—military, political, and economic—in comparison to indigenous peoples (see, e.g., Hall 1989). Thomas Barfield (1989, 1990, 2001) finds similarities among the states that dealt with Central Asia steppe pastoralists over several millennia.

If these types of conflicts are ruled out of consideration with respect to ethnic conflict, the universe of conflicts becomes much smaller, and much more distorted. By examining such conflicts, wider similarities and differences can emerge. Furthermore, if analysts ignore these millennia-old processes, they run a high risk of assuming that the processes occurring in the last 500 years, or even the last 100 years, are typical and normal, and thus cannot analytically separate effects of states from effects that are due to the specific type of state: tributary, mercantile, industrial, or global.

Over these five millennia, some human groups have become quite large and have destroyed or absorbed many other, smaller groups. There are a variety of ways that this can happen, with probably more variation in the consequences for indigenous groups than for formerly autonomous states. It is useful to distinguish among different fates. Detailed histories over millennia of Chinese absorption of nonstate people and of analogous processes in South Asia would no doubt yield further insights into the varieties of these processes.

Genocide, Ethnocide, and Culturicide[1]

There are many ways an ethnic or an indigenous group might be destroyed. Genocide, ethnocide, and culturicide all share an element of intentional destruction of a group. Genocide is the most familiar, and certainly the most brutal: the outright murder of all members of an identifiable descent group, or the attempt to do so. In contrast, ethnocide and culturicide involve attempts to destroy a group's identity, and/or culture, without necessarily killing individual human beings.

Ethnocide is an attempt to destroy the identity of a group. In its ideal typical form, it would entail full assimilation of individuals into the dominant group, although some cultural elements might still persist (see, e.g., Ortiz 1984, 1985). A key feature here, besides the obvious internal contradiction of destroying an identity but allowing some of its "content" to remain, is that the group, qua a group, disappears. In contrast, culturicide is an attempt to kill a culture, whether or not its members survive and whether or not they retain a separate identity (Clastres 1980; Fenelon 1997, 1998, 2002). A notorious example is that of Richard Pratt, founder of the Carlisle Indian School, whose explicit goal for the school was "to kill the Indian, but save the man" (Adams 1995). While Pratt seems seriously retrograde at the beginning of the twenty-first century, he was a humanitarian reformer in the context of the late nineteenth century, when many still called for outright genocide (Adams 1995; Hoxie 1984). Here the separate identity may survive, but the cultural content is eliminated.

Ethnocide and culturicide are somewhat overlapping processes. Each process, and indeed which process operates, is largely conditioned on the degree to which group distinctions are racialized. Obviously, to the degree that a group is marked by readily visible phenotypically distinctive features, maintenance of identity in the face of destruction of the culture is easier and more common.

Ethnocide is closely similar to the older concept of assimilation, in which one group adjusts its culture to become progressively more like that of another group. The difference is the clear intent to eliminate the group identity. Culturicide, on the other hand, does not need to destroy the identity as long as the "content" of the identity becomes nearly the same as that of the dominant group and thus subordinate to the socioeconomic goals, practices, and ideologies of those in power.

So how is it that indigenous peoples have resisted attempts at ethnocide or culturicide? One way, albeit unplanned, is by remaining small, and therefore relatively nonthreatening, at least to the point that the costs of pursuing ethnocide or culturicide have not been worthwhile. Another has been via relative isolation. This, however, is most often an accident of history—location within a region of little interest to any states or lack of resources that are seen as valuable to states. Another is building upon, or using, a recognized land base to keep the community viable.

Some forms of resistance are covert, echoing Scott's (1985) concept of "weapons of the weak." Many forms of resistance transmute forms or masquerade as something else. For instance, the events in Chiapas, Mexico, have often been cast in the light of a regional-, a peasant- (and hence a class-), or a caudillo-driven rebellion. They are less often discussed as an indigenous Mayan rebellion (but see Boswell and Chase-Dunn 2000; Collier 1999; Katzenberger 1995; McMichael 2000; Morton 2000). Movements in the United States, such as the American Indian Movement (AIM), are often seen solely in terms of localized ethnic, urban, or racial rebellions. Indigenous resisters are often far ahead of those who report about them—connected via the United Nations, a large variety of their own organizations, and the Internet (Langman, Morris, and Zalewski 2003; Smith and Ward 2000; Wilmer 1993). Anna Tsing's (1993) *In the Realm of the Diamond Queen* can be read as an account of ways in which local people, in this case Dayaks in Kalimitan, resist state incorporation. Indeed, Tsing's account and Stoler's (1995) account of plantation resistance in Sumatra or Peluso's (1992) account of forestry "management" in Java have as key components—if not the driving component—the struggle for survival of indigenous cultures, identities, organization, and economies. This applies to indigenous peoples throughout Southeast Asia (e.g., Sponsel 2000a, b; Steinberg 1987) and Asia in general (Barnes, Gray, and Kingsbury 1995). In other cases, traditional culture and organization itself is a resource that facilitates resistance and survival (Champagne 1989, 1992; Fenelon 1998). Virtually every place in the world indigenous resistance struggles continue (Gurr 1993; Hall and Fenelon 2003), even in Europe, as, for example, among the Saami (Eidheim 1969). Kurdish activities in West Asia and Miskito resistance in Nicaragua have long been noted as indigenous movements (Gurr and Harff 1994).

Another form of resistance has been conscious efforts to maintain "traditional culture" not as static and unchanging but rather as evolving according to the desires of group members resisting domination, rather than in accord with the desires or directions of outsiders. That is, "traditional culture," like all other social forms and structures, evolves and changes continuously, if sporadically and unevenly (Fenelon, 1998:27–30, 72; Smith and Ward 2000). An extension of culture maintenance is culture building. For instance, there are 33 tribal colleges in the United States (American Indian Higher Education Consortium 2000; Boyer 1997).[2] These are institutions of higher education, typically equivalents of junior colleges, run by various Native American groups. They differ from the typical U.S. junior college in the number of courses they offer that promote traditional culture, language, crafts, and customs. In some cases, language programs have been aimed at reviving or reinvigorating a language that has fallen out of use. Indeed, these are often their key missions. That is, tribal colleges are often one institutional means of preserving and enhancing "traditional cultures."

Resistance can also take the form of building other localized institutions that conform to traditional cultural values. The Diné (Navajo) have several such institutions. The Navajo Nation Police, while acting much like any other rural police force in the United States, is also culturally sensitive to Navajo traditions and works within them. More direct are the "Peacemaker Courts," which pursue resolution of disputes among Navajos through means that are in accord with Navajo concepts of harmony, avoiding the adversarial techniques of U.S. courts.[3]

Other forms of resistance are less institutionalized, but nonetheless important. Carol Ward and colleagues (2000; Baird-Olsen and Ward 2000) analyze how women among the northern Cheyenne have adapted conventional 12-step programs that address alcohol abuse or spouse abuse to Cheyenne culture, promoting Cheyenne family values. Miller (1994) and Chiste (1994) discuss the ways in which Native women are producing new feminisms within changing tribal governments. Another common institution among Native Americans in the United States is the maintenance of matrilineal family systems, including especially ownership of property. This often comes at a great price, as missionaries and bureaucratic functionaries have repeatedly attacked matrilineality as "barbaric," un-Christian, or chaotic. Native American feminism often organizes in ways that oppose more mainstream feminist movements. Typically, Native American feminists focus on issues of identity and cultural preservation as prior to more narrowly feminist concerns (Jaimes and Halsey 1992; Shoemaker 1995).

Religion can be yet another form of resistance. Maintenance of religious practices that anthropologists are wont to call shamanism, again over massive attempts to destroy these practices, asserts an entirely different way of approaching the supernatural and the sacred. Today, as New Agers have begun to practice various forms of shamanism, Indian groups have protested such attempts to appropriate Native traditions (Churchill 1994, 1996; Rose 1992).

The revival of older traditions, such as the Sun Dance (see, e.g., Fenelon 1998:114, 288–94; Jorgensen 1972), can be another form of this resistance. These revivals hark back to many revitalization movements: the Longhouse religion of the Iroquois (Wallace 1969), the Ghost Dance movement (Brown 1976; Champagne 1983; DeMallie 1982; Landsman 1979; Thornton 1981, 1986), and the Native American Church (Aberle 1982; La Barre 1964; Stewart 1987), and so on. These movements, all of which are somewhat syncretic, preserve many traditional values and have all met with some success in combating the destructiveness of incorporation into the capitalist world-system. The Longhouse religion has been a source of strength among Iroquois. The Native American Church (NAC; also known as the peyote religion) has been very successful in helping individuals recover from alcoholism. Also, NAC has won several court battles that allow members to use peyote (Iverson 1999:181–2).

All of these religious traditions are vastly different from various monotheisms found in the states of the modern world-system. Their survival and growth is an important form of resistance to the ideologies of the modern world-system and to pressures for increasing homogeneity of culture from various globalization processes.

Probably the most significant forms of resistance are the various ways that resources are managed collectively, for collective good. Here one must be careful not to read this as conventional "public goods" administration. This goes much further, in collective ownership of goods—land and livestock most commonly—that are typically individually, privately owned commodities in the capitalist world-system. Such challenges go to the heart of fundamental assumptions about capitalism, neoliberalism, and private property. Given these challenges, it is all the more surprising that stronger efforts to eliminate them have not occurred. Franke Wilmer (1993) argues persuasively that indigenous groups have succeeded in part because denial of their rights to sovereignty would entail dismantling the entire international relations regime based on the Peace of Westphalia (1648), which is the basis of the contemporary nation-state system. Sometimes too they succeed because these challenges are included or embedded in other challenges.

However, some of these forms of resistance preserve not only symbols but material practices that contradict how capitalism is practiced. They represent alternative ways of organizing human life. What is far from clear is whether these too can ultimately become "merely symbolic." Is an American Indian nation that insists on tribal sovereignty and administers resources according to principles of collective rationality, yet externally participates in a capitalist world-system according to capitalist principles, resisting globalizing capitalism, or slowly evolving into an alternative form of capitalism? Clearly, all forms of human organization are changing under the pressures of global capitalism. There is no reason to expect that indigenous groups or that ethnic groups will not experience and attempt to shape the processes of change. In many cases, the nature of those changes will not be clear for some time.

Furthermore, conflict both causes and is a consequence of these changes.

STATES, ETHNIC MINORITIES, AND GLOBALIZATION

While the analysis of globalization is controversial in many ways (e.g., Hall 2002a; Manning 1999; Sklair 2002), there have been two modern waves of globalization of trade in the late nineteenth century spilling into the early twentieth century and the late twentieth century spilling into the twenty-first century (Chase-Dunn, Kawano, and Brewer 2000; Clark 2002; McMichael 2000; Rodrik 1997). Both have generated waves of immigration (Dunaway 2003; Gabaccia 1994). Furthermore, various conflicts, many of which were ethnic in character, have generated immense numbers of refugees (Dunaway 2003; Gurr and Harff 1994; UNHCR 2003). These, in turn, create potentials for many future conflicts as immigrants are subjected to pressures to assimilate, or return home, and as refugees transform from temporary "guests" into more or less permanent residents.

These conflicts and potential conflicts differ in many ways from conflicts surrounding indigenous peoples. The key difference is that immigrants and refugees have a home state that has the potential of supporting their claims for preservation or even autonomy in the international arena. As Gurr and Harff (1994) argue, the severity of such potential conflicts is a function of the relative power of the states involved, with stronger states posing more of a threat than weaker states. Concerns over potential refugees and potential rebellions play a significant role in global politics. In early 2003, a major sticking point in negotiations between Turkey and the United States over support for the war against Iraq revolved around the roles of Kurds during and after the war. Turkey is deeply threatened by any Kurdish independence movement, since so many Kurds live in Turkey. Within Iraq, the Kurds offer potential resistance to Saddam Hussein, but are problematic in a postwar Iraq. Their useful resistance could all too easily turn into a potentially destabilizing ethnic separatist movement or movements.

Movement of peoples, either as voluntary migrants seeking improved living conditions, semivoluntary migrants pushed from their home by poor economic conditions and attracted to other areas by the promise of work, or as refugees from various conflicts—ethnic or not—are leading to increasing ethnic diversity in many states. Such movements greatly increase the number of potential conflicts.

Additional problems in understanding ethnic conflicts stem from their mutability and efforts by some leaders to "ethnicize" conflicts. Franke Wilmer (2002) among others argues persuasively that the conflicts in the former Yugoslavia were *not* rooted in ancient ethnic antagonisms, but in fact were fomented by leaders who sought deeply emotional issues around which to mobilize their followers in order to maintain or enhance their political positions. Thus, what were at root political conflicts became ethnic, and in some cases cast as racial. According to Malcolm (1994), this is why libraries, monuments, and other historical repositories so often became military targets—in order to forcibly rewrite history to coincide with current political goals.

Many observers have noted too how Europeans and European-derived settler states became vitally concerned over the former Yugoslavia, yet were loathe to become involved in the even more intense and vicious ethnic conflict that took place in Rwanda. In both cases, it is arguable, if not completely demonstrable, that the conflicts were at root political and economic, not ethnic, but quickly became ethnicized. Why that is so remains problematic, although many have speculated that race has played a major role while others argue that it is the proximity of the Balkans to Europe. In many ways, these debates are emblematic of continuing debates about the origins and causes of ethnic conflict.

CAUSES OF ETHNIC CONFLICT: CURRENT RESEARCH

Much of the older research on ethnic conflict focused on either nationalism (Connor 1994; Horowitz 1985) or ethnic competition and mobilization (Olzak 1992; Olzak and Nagel 1986; Pincus and Ehrlich 1994) or was a critique of international relations theory (Carment and James 1997). Current research on ethnic conflict can be divided into five types: (1) quantitatively based research, (2) world-systems analysis-derived research, (3) case studies, (4) studies of indigenous relations, and (5) studies that seek to bridge psychological and macrostructural approaches. In practice, these categories overlap extensively. In this very brief summary, I discuss and cite only very recent works, but ones that include extensive bibliographies to lead interested readers deeper into any or all of them.

Among the quantitative approaches, the most ambitious and global has been the work of Ted Robert Gurr and colleagues, called Minorities at Risk. In addition to works already cited (Gurr 1993, 2000; Gurr and Harff 1994; Harff and Gurr 1998), there is an elaborate Web site (www.cidcm.umd.edu/inscr/mar) maintained at the University of Maryland devoted to the project that provides links to published papers, working papers, and several datasets. While much of the Minorities at Risk Project is directed at various quantitative studies, it is extensively supplemented with case studies, especially in Gurr (2000) and Gurr and Harff (1994). While the data compiled by the project is the most comprehensive compiled in one place, it does not claim to be universal. The disclaimers and codebooks make clear the limitations of the data.

Several studies bridge the quantitative and world-systems approaches.[4] Especially intriguing is the work of Olzak and Tsutsui (1998). Using Minorities at Risk data, they show that the risk of ethnic mobilization is not uniform across peripheral areas as some world-systems analysts have argued. Rather, they show that "peripheral countries with more ties to intergovernmental organizations have significantly lower levels of ethnic violence" than those without such ties. Furthermore, those with "more memberships in international organization experience a significantly higher magnitude of ethnic nonviolent protest" (1998:691). This research robustly underscores the claims made by Gurr and Harff (1994, espec. chap. 5) and world-systems analysts that ethnic conflicts cannot be understood as strictly local phenomena, but are intimately linked to international and global processes.

Wilma Dunaway (2003) argues that while there has not been a precipitous rise in ethnic conflicts since the end of the cold war, nonetheless, ethnic conflict is becoming more and more troublesome for the entire capitalist world economy. In major part that is because it is becoming more costly, both politically in terms of creating instabilities and economically by disrupting markets and commodity chains. Of equal significance, she argues that both indigenism and ethnification are inherent contradictions in the modern world-system and that both have the potential of accelerating counter-hegemonic movements and pushing the entire system toward transformation. This article links four of the five types of research together conceptually.

Other world-systems research focuses on the antiquity of ethnic conflicts and their roles in the transformations of older, precapitalist, or pre-ca. 1500 C.E. world-systems (Hall 1998). In two articles (Hall 2000c, 2002b) I link ancient and modern patterns of ethnic conflict by examining the complex roles of frontiers in ethnic processes—transformations, ethnocide, and ethnogenesis on frontiers. I argue that frontier zones, and their attendant ethnic conflicts, have often played an important role in system transformations, suggesting that Dunaway's argument is not unique to the modern world-system.[5]

Case studies of ethnic conflict abound. As noted, Gurr (2000; Gurr and Harff 1994) argues that quantitative studies must be supplemented with detailed case studies in order to understand the nuances of ethnic conflict. Furthermore, much of the Minorities at Risk data comes from culling numerous case studies of ethnic conflicts. A combination of quantitative and case studies provides a much more robust and subtle understanding of ethnic conflicts.

As noted, several studies emphasize indigenous conflicts as a form of ethnic conflict. While much of the current research sees indigenous conflicts as a significant part of ethnic conflict, there is also an extensive literature on indigenous peoples and their struggles. Al Gedicks (1993, 2001) emphasizes environmental struggles. Fenelon and I (Hall and Fenelon 2003) argue, much like Dunaway (2003), that indigenous struggles are particularly challenging to the contemporary world-system. Also, I (Hall 2000c, 2002b) argue that frontier regions are particularly salient for studying such processes. Indeed, some of the best world-system-based case studies focus on indigenous peoples (Dunaway 1994, 1996, 2000; Faiman-Silva 1997; Fenelon 1997, 1998,

2002; Hall 1989; Hämäläinen 1998; Harris 1990; Himmel 1999; Jones 1998; Meyer 1994; Pickering 2000, 2003; Volk 2000; Ward et al. 2000). Most of these studies focus on peoples indigenous to the Americas. Smith and Ward (2000) concentrate on Australia, but without a world-systems approach. Hill (1996) focuses on South America. Alison Brysk (1996) focuses on the "internationalization of indigenous rights." In general, literature on indigenous peoples is strongly regionalized, in part due to the legacies of anthropological research and in part because of the extensive investment in time required by scholars to learn about a particular region.

Finally, there are studies that seek to bridge the psychological and the macrostructural approaches. Wilmer (2002) advances a complex thesis, at least with respect to the former Yugoslavia, that because identity is embedded in early childhood and because it is often entangled with separation anxieties of males from their mothers, ethnic identity issues carry both much more emotional baggage and have the potential under specific child-rearing practices to dichotomize and demonize "the other," thus promoting extreme violence. Her argument is far too rich and nuanced to explicate fully here, but it is one way of linking very micro and social psychological processes with much larger macro interstate and interethnic processes.

Whether or not one follows Wilmer's or others' accounts, it is clear that conflict can become ethnicized, or can even be ethnogenetic. This complicates immensely the task of sorting out whether or not ethnic conflict has increased since the end of World War II or since the end of the cold war.

Dan Chirot and Martin Seligman (2001) provide other ways to bridge the micro and macro approaches. These tend to focus on the roles of identity and its linkages to economic and political processes. Articles examine the roles of the media and the creation of a climate of fear. The collection is notable for its interdisciplinary approach to ethnic conflict. Indeed, articles in this collection fall into or straddle all of these categories, including several interesting case studies.

While there is already a rich and complex literature on ethnic conflict, much work remains to be done. Globally, coverage is far from even. Many more case studies from other regions are needed, especially from Asia. As these become available, many of the existing theoretical approaches will need to be modified, if not replaced wholesale.

Summary

Ethnic conflict is an immensely complex social phenomenon, made all the more so by the common tendency of conflicts to have many causes, some of which appear to be other than what they are, or that are intentionally manipulated by various actors. What recent events do demonstrate is that ethnicity, and race, are issues that are not disappearing and becoming less important. If anything, ethnic conflicts will remain a major source of intergroup violence in the coming decades. Yet, framed in longer historical perspectives, this is not all that surprising.

First, states have been absorbing and transforming formerly autonomous groups for millennia. To be sure, the frequency, density, intensity, and means by which these changes have occurred have changed considerably throughout history. Thus, any ethnic conflict must be analyzed and understood in its deep historical context. Second, ethnic mixing is "normal," not ethnic "purity." Third, ethnicity can be both the cause of and a consequence of conflict. Fourth, to ignore conflicts with indigenous peoples as a form of ethnic conflict misunderstands the phenomenon fundamentally.

In the shorter term, recent processes of global change, often glossed under the term *globalization*—and whether globalization is seen as a process originating in the nineteenth century, or earlier, or solely in the late twentieth century—are radically and rapidly changing the contexts under which ethnic conflict arises. In short, ethnic conflicts are no longer, if they ever were, entirely local. Rather, they are embedded in larger global, or world-systemic, processes and cannot be understood without reference to those processes.

Notes

1. This discussion draws heavily on the work of James Fenelon (1997, 1998, 2002), who developed the concept of culturicide. Clastres (1980) makes the earliest use of the term *ethnocide*, albeit not with this precise meaning.

2. Boyer (1997) actually lists 31 tribal colleges, but 2 more have opened since the report was published.

3. The foundational principle of the Peacemaker Court is *k'e*, or "respect, responsibility, and proper relationships among all people." Based upon traditional Navajo ceremonies that seek a common goal among groups of individuals, the Peacemaker Court assists disputants in the healing process by fostering a mutually beneficial agreement. See tlj.unm.edu/resources/navajo_nation/index.hm. This is well illustrated in the video *Winds of Change: A Matter of Promises* (PBS documentary, 1990).

4. Basic introductions to world-systems analysis are available in Hall (2000a, b, 2002a).

5. Brooks (2002) presents a nuanced, contrasting account of the roles of race, ethnicity, gender, and class in the exchange of captives for coerced labor in northwest New Spain/southwest United States.

References

Aberle, David F. 1982. *The Peyote Religion among the Navaho.* Chicago, IL: University of Chicago Press.

Adams, David Wallace. 1995. *Education for Extinction: American Indians and the Boarding School Experience, 1875–1928.* Lawrence, KS: University Press of Kansas.

American Indian Higher Education Consortium. 2000. *Tribal College Contributions to Local Economic Development.* Alexandria, VA: Author. Available at www.aichec.org.

Anderson, Benedict. 1991. *Imagined Communities: Reflections on the Origin and Spread of Nationalism.* London, England: Verson.

Anderson, David G. 1994. *The Savannah River Chiefdoms: Political Change in the Late Prehistoric Southeast.* Tuscaloosa, AL: University of Alabama Press.

Baird-Olson, Karen and Carol Ward. 2000. "Recovery and Resistance: The Renewal of Traditional Spirituality among American Indian Women." *American Indian Culture and Research Journal* 24 (4):1–35.

Barfield, Thomas J. 1989. *The Perilous Frontier.* London, England: Blackwell.

———. 1990. "Tribe and State Relations: The Inner Asian Perspective." Pp. 153–82 in *Tribe and State Formation in the Middle East,* edited by Philip S. Khoury and Joseph Kostiner. Berkeley, CA: University of California Press.

———. 2001. "The Shadow Empires: Imperial State Formation along the Chinese-Nomad Frontier." Pp. 11–41 in *Empires: Perspectives from*

Archaeology and History, edited by Susan E. Alcock, Terence N. D'Altroy, Kathleen D. Morrison, and Carla Sinopoli. Cambridge, England: Cambridge University Press.

Barnes, R. H., Andrew Gray, and Benedict Kingsbury. 1995. *Indigenous Peoples of Asia*. Monograph and Occasional Papers Series, No. 48. Ann Arbor, MI: Association for Asian Studies, Inc.

Barth, Frederick. 1969. *Ethnic Groups and Boundaries*. Boston, MA: Little, Brown.

Bartlett, Robert. 1993. *The Making of Europe: Conquest, Colonization and Cultural Change 950–1350*. Princeton, NJ: Princeton University Press.

Boswell, Terry and Christopher Chase-Dunn. 2000. *The Spiral of Capitalism and Socialism: The Decline of State Socialism and the Future of the World-System*. Boulder, CO: Lynne-Rienner.

Boyer, Paul. 1997. *Native American Colleges: Progress and Prospects*. An Ernest L. Boyer Project of the Carnegie Foundation for the Advancement of Teaching. Princeton, NJ: Carnegie Foundation for the Advancement of Teaching.

Brooks, James F. 2002. *Captives and Cousins: Slavery, Kinship, and Community in the Southwest Borderlands*. Chapel Hill, NC: University of North Carolina Press.

Brown, Kaye. 1976. "Quantitative Testing and Revitalization Behavior: On Carroll's Explanation of the Ghost Dance." *American Sociological Review* 41:740–4.

Brysk, Alison. 1996. "Turning Weakness into Strength: The Internationalization of Indigenous Rights." *Latin American Perspectives* 23 (2):38–57.

Carment, David and Patrick James, eds. 1997. *Wars in the Midst of Peace: The International Politics of Ethnic Conflict*. Pittsburgh, PA: University of Pittsburgh Press.

Cavalli-Sforza, Luigi Luca and Francesco Cavalli-Sforza. 1995. *The Great Human Diasporas: The History of Diversity and Evolution*. Translated by Sarah Thorne. New York: Addison-Wesley.

Champagne, Duane. 1983. "Social Structure, Revitalization Movements and State Building: Social Change in Four Native American Societies." *American Sociological Review* 48:754–63.

——. 1989. *American Indian Societies: Strategies and Conditions of Political and Cultural Survival*. Cambridge, MA: Cultural Survival.

——. 1992. *Social Order and Political Change: Constitutional Governments among the Cherokee, the Choctaw, the Chickasaw, and the Creek*. Stanford, CA: Stanford University Press.

Chase-Dunn, Christopher and Thomas D. Hall. 1997. *Rise and Demise: Comparing World-Systems*. Boulder, CO: Westview.

Chase-Dunn, Christopher, Yukio Kawano, and Benjamin D. Brewer. 2000. "Trade Globalization since 1795: Waves of Integration in the World-System." *American Sociological Review* 65:77–95.

Chirot, Daniel and Martin E. P. Seligman, eds. 2001. *Ethnopolitical Warfare: Causes, Consequences, and Possible Solutions*. Washington, DC: American Psychological Association.

Chiste, Katherine Beaty. [1994] 1999. "Aboriginal Women and Self-Government: Challenging Leviathan." *American Indian Culture and Research Journal* 18 (3):19–43; reprinted Pp. 71–90 in *Contemporary Native American Cultural Issues*, edited by Duane Champagne. Walnut Creek, CA: Altamira.

Churchill, Ward. 1994. *Indians Are Us: Culture and Genocide in Native North America*. Monroe, ME: Common Courage.

——. 1996. *From a Native Son: Selected Essays on Indigenism, 1985–1995*. Boston, MA: South End.

Clark, Robert P. 2002. *Global Awareness: Thinking Systematically about the World*. Lanham, MD: Rowman & Littlefield.

Clastres, Pierre. [1980] 1994. *The Archaeology of Violence*. Translated by Jeanine Herman. New York: Semiotext(e). (Orig.: *Recerches d'anthropologie politique*. Paris: Editions du Seuil.)

Collier, George A. with Elizabeth Lowery Quaratiello. 1999. *Basta! Land & the Zapatista Rebellion in Chiapas*. Oakland, CA: Food First Books.

Connor, Walker. 1994. *Ethnonationalism: The Quest of Understanding*. Princeton, NJ: Princeton University Press.

Curtin, Philip D. 1984. *Cross-Cultural Trade in World History*. Cambridge, England: Cambridge University Press.

DeMallie, Raymond J. 1982. "The Lakota Ghost Dance: An Ethnohistorical Account." *Pacific Historical Review* 51:385–405.

Denemark, Robert A., Jonathan Friedman, Barry K. Gills, and George Modelski, eds. 2000. *World System History: The Social Science of Long-Term Change*. London, England: Routledge.

Dunaway, Wilma A. 1994. "The Southern Fur Trade and the Incorporation of Southern Appalachia into the World-Economy, 1690–1763." *Review of the Fernand Braudel Center* 17:215–41.

——. 1996. *The First American Frontier: Transition to Capitalism in Southern Appalachia, 1700–1860*.

Chapel Hill, NC: University of North Carolina Press.

——. 2000. "The International Fur Trade and Disempowerment of Cherokee Women, 1680–1775." Pp. 195–210 in *World-Systems Reader: New Perspectives on Gender, Urbanism, Cultures, Indigenous Peoples, and Ecology,* edited by Thomas D. Hall. Lanham, MD: Rowman & Littlefield.

——. 2003. "Ethnic Conflict in the Modern World-System: The Dialectics of Counter-Hegemonic Resistance in an Age of Transition." *Journal of World-Systems Research* 9 (1):3–34. Available online at csf.colorado.edu/wsystems/jwsr.html.

Dyson, Stephen L. 1985. *The Creation of the Roman Frontier.* Princeton, NJ: Princeton University Press.

Eidheim, Harald. [1969] 1998. "When Ethnic Identity Is a Social Stigma." Pp. 39–57 in *Ethnic Groups and Boundaries,* edited by Frederik Barth. Boston, MA: Little, Brown. Reprinted by Waveland: Prospect Heights, IL.

Faiman-Silva, Sandra L. 1997. *Choctaws at the Crossroads: The Political Economy of Class and Culture in the Oklahoma Timber Region.* Lincoln, NE: University of Nebraska Press.

Fenelon, James V. 1997. "From Peripheral Domination to Internal Colonialism: Socio-Political Change of the Lakota on Standing Rock." *Journal of World-Systems Research* 3 (2):259–320. Available online at csf.colorado.edu/wsystems/jwsr.html.

——. 1998. *Culturicide, Resistance, and Survival of the Lakota (Sioux Nation).* New York: Garland.

——. 2002. "Dual Sovereignty of Native Nations, the United States, & Traditionalists." *Humboldt Journal of Social Relations* 27 (1):106–45.

Ferguson, R. Brian and Neil L. Whitehead, eds. 1992a. *War in the Tribal Zone: Expanding States and Indigenous Warfare.* Santa Fe, NM: School of American Research Press.

——. 1992b. "The Violent Edge of Empire." Pp. 1–30 in R. B. Ferguson and N. L. Whitehead, eds. *War in the Tribal Zone.* Santa Fe, NM: School of American Research Press.

Frank, Andre Gunder and Barry K. Gills, eds. 1993. *The World System: Five Hundred Years or Five Thousand?* London, England: Routledge.

Fried, Morton. 1967. *The Evolution of Political Society.* New York: Random House.

——. 1975. *The Notion of Tribe.* Menlo Park, CA: Cummings.

Gabaccia, Donna R. 1994. *From the Other Side: Women, Gender, and Immigrant Life in the U.S., 1820–1990.* Bloomington, IN: Indiana University Press.

Gedicks, Al. 1993. *The New Resource Wars: Native and Environmental Struggles against Multinational Corporations.* Boston, MA: South End.

——. 2001. *Resource Rebels: Native Challenges to Mining and Oil Corporations.* Cambridge, MA: South End.

Gould, Stephen J. 1996. *The Mismeasure of Man.* New York: Norton.

Gurr, Ted Robert. 1993. *Minorities at Risk: A Global View of Ethnopolitical Conflicts.* Washington, DC: United States Institute for Peace Press.

——, ed. 2000. *Peoples versus States: Minorities at Risk in the New Century.* Washington, DC: United States Institute of Peace Press.

Gurr, Ted Robert and Barbara Harff. 1994. *Ethnic Conflict in World Politics.* Boulder, CO: Westview.

Guy, Donna J. and Thomas E. Sheridan, eds. 1998a. *Contested Ground: Comparative Frontiers on the Northern and Southern Edges of the Spanish Empire.* Tucson, AZ: University of Arizona Press.

——. 1998b. "On Frontiers: The Northern and Southern Edges of the Spanish Empire in America." Pp. 150–66 in *Contested Ground: Comparative Frontiers on the Northern and Southern Edges of the Spanish Empire,* edited by Donna J. Guy and Thomas E. Sheridan. Tucson, AZ: University of Arizona Press.

Haaland, Gunnar. 1969. "Economic Determinants in Ethnic Processes." Pp. 53–73 in *Ethnic Groups and Boundaries,* edited by Frederick Barth. Boston, MA: Little, Brown.

Hall, Thomas D. 1984. "Lessons of Long-Term Social Change for Comparative and Historical Study of Ethnicity." *Current Perspectives in Social Theory* 5:121–44.

——. 1989. *Social Change in the Southwest, 1350–1880.* Lawrence, KS: University Press of Kansas.

——. 1998. "The Effects of Incorporation into World-Systems on Ethnic Processes: Lessons from the Ancient World for the Contemporary World." *International Political Science Review* 19:251–67.

——, ed. 2000a. *A World-Systems Reader: New Perspectives on Gender, Urbanism, Cultures, Indigenous Peoples, and Ecology.* Lanham, MD: Rowman & Littlefield.

——. 2000b. "World-Systems Analysis: A Small Sample from a Large Universe." Pp. 3–27 in *A World-Systems Reader: New Perspectives on Gender, Urbanism, Cultures, Indigenous Peoples, and Ecology,* edited by Thomas D. Hall. Lanham, MD: Rowman & Littlefield.

——. 2000c. "Frontiers, and Ethnogenesis, and World-Systems: Rethinking the Theories." Pp. 237–70 in *A World-Systems Reader: New Perspectives on Gender, Urbanism, Cultures, Indigenous Peoples, and Ecology,* edited by Thomas D. Hall. Lanham, MD: Rowman & Littlefield.

——. 2002a. "World-Systems Analysis and Globalization: Directions for the Twenty-First Century." Pp. 81–122 in *Theoretical Directions in Political Sociology for the 21st Century, Research in Political Sociology,* Vol. 11, edited by Betty A. Dobratz, Timothy Buzzell, and Lisa K. Waldner. Oxford, England: Elsevier Science.

——. 2002b. "World-Systems, Frontiers, and Ethnogenesis: Incorporation and Resistance to State Expansion." Pp. 35–66 in *Borderlines in a Globalized World: New Perspectives in a Sociology of the World-Systems,* edited by Gerhard Preyer and Mathias Bös. Boston, MA: Kluwer Academic.

Hall, Thomas D. and James V. Fenelon. 2003. "Indigenous Resistance to Globalization: What Does the Future Hold?" Pp. 173–88 in *Crises and Resistance in the 21st Century World-System,* edited by Wilma A. Dunaway. Westport, CT: Greenwood.

Hall, Thomas D. and Joane Nagel. 2000. "Indigenous Peoples." Pp. 1295–301 in *The Encyclopedia of Sociology,* Vol. 2, rev. ed., edited by Edgar F. Borgatta and Rhonda J. V. Montgomery. New York: Macmillan.

Hämäläinen, Pekka. 1998. "The Western Comanche Trade Center: Rethinking the Plains Indian Trade System." *Western Historical Quarterly* 29 (4):485–513.

Harff, Barbara and Ted Robert Gurr. 1998. "Systematic Early Warning of Humanitarian Emergencies." Working Paper, Minorities at Risk Project. Available at www.cidcm.umd.edu/projects/mar.htm.

Harris, Betty J. 1990. "Ethnicity and Gender in the Global Periphery: A Comparison of Basotho and Navajo Women." *American Indian Culture and Research Journal* 14 (4):15–38.

Hill, Jonathan D., ed. 1996. *History, Power, and Identity: Ethnogenesis in the Americas, 1492–1992.* Iowa City, IA: University of Iowa Press.

Himmel, Kelly D. 1999. *The Conquest of the Karankawas and the Tonkawas: A Study in Social Change, 1821–1859.* College Station, TX: Texas A&M University Press.

Horowitz, Donald L. 1985. *Ethnic Groups in Conflict.* Berkeley, CA: University of California Press.

Hoxie, Frederick E. 1984. *A Final Promise: The Campaign to Assimilate the Indians, 1880–1920.* Lincoln, NE: University of Nebraska Press.

Iverson, Peter. 1999. *"We Are Still Here": American Indians in the Twentieth Century.* Wheeling, IL: Harlan Davidson.

Jaimes, M. Annette with Theresa Halsey. 1992. "American Indian Women: At the Center of Indigenous North America." Pp. 311–44 in *The State of Native America: Genocide, Colonization, and Resistance,* edited by M. Annette Jaimes. Boston, MA: South End.

Jones, Kristine L. 1998. "Comparative Raiding Economies: North and South." Pp. 97–114 in *Contested Ground: Comparative Frontiers on the Northern and Southern Edges of the Spanish Empire,* edited by Donna Guy and Thomas Sheridan. Tucson, AZ: University of Arizona Press.

Jorgensen, Joseph J. 1972. *The Sun Dance Religion: Power for the Powerless.* Chicago, IL: University of Chicago Press.

Katzenberger, Elaine, ed. 1995. *First World, Ha Ha Ha! The Zapatista Challenge.* San Francisco, CA: City Lights Books.

La Barre, Weston. 1964. *The Peyote Cult.* Hamden, CT: Shoe String.

Laczko, Leslie S. 1990. "Review of McNeill's *Polyethnicity and National Unity in World History*." *Canadian Review of Sociology and Anthropology* 27 (3):426–8.

——. 2000. "Canada's Linguistic and Ethnic Dynamics in an Evolving World-System." Pp. 131–42 in *A World-Systems Reader: New Perspectives on Gender, Urbanism, Cultures, Indigenous Peoples, and Ecology,* edited by Thomas D. Hall. Lanham, MD: Rowman & Littlefield.

Landsman, Gail. 1979. "The Ghost Dance and the Policy of Land Allotment." *American Sociological Review* 44:162–6.

Langman, Lauren, D. Morris, and J. Zalewski. 2003. "Cyberactivism and Alternative Globalization Movements." Pp. 218–35 in *Crises and Resistance in the 21st Century World-System,* edited by Wilma A. Dunaway. Westport, CT: Greenwood.

Lenski, Gerhard. 1966. *Power and Privilege: A Theory of Social Stratification.* New York: McGraw-Hill.

——. 1976. "History and Social Change." *American Journal of Sociology* 82:548–64.

Macharia, Kinuthia. 2003. "Resistant Indigenous Identities in the 21st Century World-System: Selected African Cases." Pp. 189–200 in *Crises and Resistance in the 21st Century World-System,* edited by Wilma A. Dunaway. Westport, CT: Greenwood.

Malcolm, Noel. 1994. *Bosnia: A Short History.* New York: New York University Press.

Manning, Susan, ed. 1999. "Introduction [To special issue on Globalization]." *Journal of World-Systems Research* 5:137–41. E-journal available at csf. Colorado.edu/jwsr, issue 137–461.

Mattingly, D. J. 1992. "War and Peace in Roman North Africa: Observations and Models of State-Tribe Interaction." Pp. 31–60 in *War in the Tribal Zone,* edited by R. Brian Ferguson and Neil L. Whitehead. Santa Fe, NM: School of American Research Press.

Maybury-Lewis, David. 2002. *Indigenous Peoples, Ethnic Groups, and the State.* 2nd ed. Boston, MA: Allyn & Bacon.

McMichael, Philip. 2000. *Development and Social Change: A Global Perspective.* 2nd ed. Thousand Oaks, CA: Pine Forge.

McNeill, William H. 1986. *Polyethnicity and National Unity in World History.* Toronto, Canada: University of Toronto Press.

Meyer, John W., John Boli, George M. Thomas, and Francisco O. Ramirez. 1997. "World Society and the Nation-State." *American Journal of Sociology* 103:144–81.

Meyer, Melissa L. 1994. *The White Earth Tragedy: Ethnicity and Dispossession at a Minnesota Anishinaabe Reservation, 1889–1920.* Lincoln, NE: University of Nebraska.

Miller, Bruce G. [1994] 1999. "Contemporary Tribal Codes and Gender Issues." *American Indian Culture and Research Journal* 18 (2):43–74. (Reprinted pp. 103–26 in *Contemporary Native American Cultural Issues,* edited by Duane Champagne. Walnut Creek, CA: Altamira.)

Miller, David Harry. 1993. "Ethnogenesis and Religious Revitalization beyond the Roman Frontier: The Case of Frankish Origins." *Journal of World History* 4:277–85.

Montagu, Ashley, ed. 1997. *Man's Most Dangerous Myth: The Fallacy of Race.* Walnut Creek, CA: Altamira.

Morton, Adam David. 2000. "Mexico, Neoliberal Restructuring and the EZLN: A Neo-Gramscian Analysis." Pp. 255–79 in *Globalization and the Politics of Resistance,* edited by Barry K. Gills. New York: St. Martin's.

Nisbet, Robert. 1969. *Social Change and History: Aspects of the Western Theory of Development.* New York: Oxford University Press.

Olzak, Susan. 1992. *The Dynamics of Ethnic Competition and Conflict.* Stanford, CA: Stanford University Press.

Olzak, Susan and Joane Nagel, eds. 1986. *Competitive Ethnic Relations.* New York: Academic.

Olzak, Susan and K. Tsutsui. 1998. "Status in the World-System and Ethnic Mobilization." *Journal of Conflict Resolution* 42:691–720.

Omi, Michael and Howard Winant. 1994. *Racial Formation in the United States: From the 1960s to the 1990s.* 2nd ed. New York: Routledge.

Ortiz, Roxanne Dunbar. 1984. *Indians of the Americas: Human Rights and Self-Determination.* New York: Praeger.

——. 1985. "The Fourth World and Indigenism: Politics of Isolation and Alternatives." *Journal of Ethnic Studies* 12:79–105, 2:113–20.

Peluso, Nancy Lee. 1992. *Rich Forests, Poor People: Resource Control and Resistance in Java.* Berkeley, CA: University of California Press.

Pickering, Kathleen Ann. 2000. *Lakota Culture, World Economy.* Lincoln, NE: University of Nebraska Press.

——. 2003. "The Dynamics of Everyday Incorporation and Antisystemic Resistance: Lakota Culture in the 21st Century." Pp. 2001–217 in *Crises and Resistance in the 21st Century World-System,* edited by Wilma A. Dunaway. Westport, CT: Greenwood.

Pincus, Fred L. and Howard J. Ehrlich. 1994. *Race and Ethnic Conflict.* Boulder, CO: Westview.

Rodrik, Dani. 1997. *Has Globalization Gone Too Far?* Washington, DC: Institute for International Economics.

Rose, Wendy. 1992. "The Great Pretenders: Further Reflections on Whiteshamism." Pp. 403–21 in *The State of Native America: Genocide, Colonization, and Resistance,* edited by M. Annette Jaimes. Boston, MA: South End.

Sahlins, Peter. 1989. *Boundaries: The Making of France and Spain in the Pyrenees.* Berkeley, CA: University of California Press.

Sanderson, Stephen K., ed. 1995. *Civilizations and World-Systems: Two Approaches to the Study of World-Historical Change.* Walnut Creek, CA: Altamira.

——. [1995] 1999. *Social Transformations: A General Theory of Historical Development.* Expanded ed. Lanham, MD: Rowman & Littlefield.

Scott, James C. 1985. *Weapons of the Weak: Everyday Forms of Peasant Resistance.* New Haven, CT: Yale University Press.

Shoemaker, Nancy, ed. 1995. *Negotiators of Change: Historical Perspectives on Native American Women.* New York: Routledge.

Sklair, Leslie. 2002. *Globalization: Capitalism and Its Alternatives.* 3rd ed. Oxford, England: Oxford University Press.

Smedley, Audrey. 1999. *Race in North America: Origin and Evolution of a Worldview.* 2nd ed. Boulder, CO: Westview.

Smith, Claire Heather Burke and Graeme K. Ward. 2000. "Globalisation and Indigenous Peoples: Threat or Empowerment?" Pp. 1–24 in *Indigenous Cultures in an Interconnected World,* edited by Claire Smith and Graeme K. Ward. St. Leonards, NSW Australia: Allen & Unwin.

Sponsel, Leslie E. 2000a. "Identities, Ecologies, Rights, and Futures: All Endangered." Pp. 1–22 in *Endangered Peoples of Southeast and East Asia: Struggles to Survive,* edited by Leslie E. Sponsel. Westport, CT: Greenwood.

———. 2000b. *Endangered Peoples of Southeast and East Asia: Struggles to Survive.* Westport, CT: Greenwood.

Srinivas, M. N. 1966. *Social Change in Modern India.* Berkeley, CA: University of California Press.

Steinberg, David Joel, ed. 1987. *In Search of Southeast Asia: A Modern History.* Honolulu, HI: University of Hawaii Press.

Stewart, Omer C. 1987. *Peyote Religion: A History.* Norman, OK: University of Oklahoma Press.

Stoler, Ann Laura. 1995. *Capitalism and Confrontation in Sumatra's Plantation Belt, 1870–1970.* 2nd ed. Ann Arbor, MI: University of Michigan Press.

Thornton, Russell. 1981. "Demographic Antecedents of a Revitalization Movement: Population Change, Population Size, and the 1890 Ghost Dance." *American Sociological Review* 40:88–96.

———. 1986. *We Shall Live Again: The 1870 and 1890 Ghost Dance Movements as Demographic Revitalization.* New York: Cambridge University Press.

Tilly, Charles, ed. 1975. *The Formation of National States in Western Europe.* Princeton, NJ: Princeton University Press.

———. 1990. *Coercion, Capital, and European States.* Cambridge, MA: Basil Blackwell.

Tsing, Anna Lowenhaupt. 1993. *In the Realm of the Diamond Queen: Marginality in an Out of the Way Place.* Princeton, NJ: Princeton University Press.

"United Nations High Commissioner for Refugees." 2002. Retrieved from www.unhcr.org.

Volk, Robert "Skip." 2000. "'Red Sales in the Sunset': The Rise and Fall of White Trader Dominance in the United States' Navajo Reservation and South Africa's Transkei." *American Indian Culture and Research Journal* 24:69–97.

Wallace, Anthony F. C. 1969. *The Death and Rebirth of the Seneca Movement.* New York: Knopf.

Ward, Carol, Elon Stander, and Yodit Solom. 2000. "Resistance through Healing among American Indian Women." Pp. 211–36 in *A World-Systems Reader: New Perspectives on Gender, Urbanism, Cultures, Indigenous Peoples, and Ecology,* edited by Thomas D. Hall. Boulder, CO: Rowman & Littlefield.

Weber, David J. 1992. *The Spanish Frontier in North America.* New Haven, CT: Yale University Press.

Weber, David J. and Jane M. Rausch. 1994. *Where Cultures Meet: Frontiers in Latin American History.* Wilmington, DE: Scholarly Resources Inc.

Weber, Eugene. 1976. *Peasants into Frenchmen: The Modernization of Rural France, 1789–1914.* Stanford, CA: Stanford University Press.

Wells, Peter S. 1992. "Tradition, Identity, and Change beyond the Roman Frontier." Pp. 175–88 in *Resources, Power, and Interregional Interaction,* edited by Edward Schortman and Patricia Urban. New York: Plenum.

———. 1999a. *The Barbarians Speak: How the Conquered Peoples Shaped Roman Europe.* Princeton, NJ: Princeton University Press.

———. 1999b. "Production within and beyond Imperial Boundaries: Goods, Exchange, and Power in Roman Europe." Pp. 85–101 in *World-Systems Theory in Practice,* edited by P. Nick Kardulias. Lanham, MD: Rowman & Littlefield.

Wilmer, Franke. 1993. *The Indigenous Voice in World Politics: Since Time Immemorial.* Newbury Park, CA: Sage.

———. 2002. *The Social Construction of Man, the State and War: Identity, Conflict, and Violence in Former Yugoslavia.* New York: Routledge.

GENDER INEQUALITY

AMY S. WHARTON

Washington State University

Gender is a central organizing principle of social life in virtually all cultures of the world. But what is gender and how exactly is it expressed? Answers to these questions have proliferated in recent years (Hawkesworth 1997). Early theorists treated gender as strictly an individual characteristic—as an attribute of people, acquired through socialization and embedded in personality or identity. This view also tended to recognize a clear distinction between sex, defined as the biological or genetic aspects of maleness and femaleness, and gender, which represented the socially defined meanings attached to sex categories (Acker 1992). Though some still adhere to these views, most contemporary gender scholars endorse a view of gender that is more multilayered and complex (Acker 1992; Hawkesworth 1997; Ridgeway and Smith-Lovin 1999; Risman 1998). For example, Ridgeway and Smith-Lovin (1999:192) conceive of gender as a "system of social practices"; this system creates and maintains gender distinctions and it "organizes relations of inequality on the basis of [these distinctions]." In this view, the gender system involves the creation of both differences *and* inequalities.

Three features of this more recent definition are important to keep in mind. First, gender is as much a process as a fixed state. This implies that gender is being continually produced and reproduced. Stated differently, we could say that gender is enacted or "done," not merely expressed. Second, gender is not simply a characteristic of individuals, but occurs at all levels of the social structure. This is contained in the idea of gender as a "system" of practices that are far-reaching, interlocked, and exist independently of individuals. Gender thus is a multilevel phenomenon (Risman 1998). This insight enables us to explore how social processes, such as interaction, and social institutions, such as work, embody and reproduce gender. Third, this definition of gender refers to its importance in organizing relations of inequality. Whether gender differentiation must necessarily lead to gender inequality is a subject of debate. As a principle of social organization, however, gender is one critical dimension upon which social resources are distributed.

These shifts in the meanings of gender have had considerable impact on how gender inequality has been understood. While previous approaches tended to trace gender inequality to differences in the characteristics of women and men as individuals, more recent views emphasize the roles played by social interaction patterns and institutions. More important, however, by treating gender as a multi-level phenomenon, gender theory and research on inequality has had to address the ways that these levels interrelate. These interrelations play an important role in the reproduction of gender inequality and the possibilities for challenging the gender order.

One inadvertent consequence of an individualist view of gender is that women and men have often been portrayed as either villains or victims—oppressing, exploiting, or defending against each other. While inequality does not just happen, how it happens is more complex than this. Just as gender must be viewed as not simply a property of individuals, so too, gender inequality must be understood as the product of a more complex set of social forces. These may include the actions of individuals, but they are also to be found in the expectations that guide social interaction, the composition of social groups, and the structures and practices of the institutions. These forces are subject to human intervention and change, but are not always visible, known, or understood. They are subtle, may be unconscious, and are reproduced often without conscious intent or design.

This chapter begins with a brief discussion of the shift from individual to social relational and institutional accounts of gender. Next, I examine the implications of this shift for theory and research on gender inequality. In particular, I present several alternative "social relational" approaches to gender inequality, followed by a discussion of a gendered institutions perspective. In both sections I discuss some of the key research on gender inequality that has been informed by each perspective. In the final section, I briefly explore directions for future research and debate.

INDIVIDUALS, INTERACTION, AND INSTITUTIONS: CHANGING CONCEPTIONS OF GENDER

Gender theory and research can be generally divided into three broad frameworks, each with a different view of where the "sociological action" is with respect to gender. For some, this action resides mainly in individuals—their personalities, traits, emotions, or identities. Proponents of these views thus focus their attention on the individual attributes of women and men, often seeking to identify areas of gender difference.

By contrast, others argue that students of gender should focus less on individuals and more on interaction and social relations. Rather than assuming that people possess a relatively stable set of traits and abilities that they bring to organizations, social relational approaches argue that people actively construct their reactions and behaviors in response to features of the social context. The social context includes the other participants in the setting, and it includes features of the environment where the interaction takes place. From this perspective, then, gender emerges and is sustained within social relations; hence, social context—the groups and settings where people gather—plays a much greater role in these perspectives than in those with a more individualist orientation.

Understanding the power of gender in social life without reducing it to individual traits is also the aim of a gendered institutions approach. This perspective directs us to the organization, structure, and practices of social institutions. From a gendered institutions perspective, these entrenched, powerful, and relatively taken-for-granted aspects of the social world play key roles in producing and reproducing gender inequality.

While research informed by an individualist approach to gender (i.e., one that locates gender in the traits and behaviors of individuals) continues to expand, social relational and institutional perspectives have become more popular in recent years. This popularity can be seen in almost all areas of gender scholarship, including research on inequality. Rather than viewing inequalities as arising from differences in the characteristics of women and men, researchers have grown more attentive to the ways in which inequalities are produced by features of the social context. Those influenced by social relational accounts of gender have tended to focus on how the structure of social interaction perpetuates gender distinctions and gender inequality. Gendered institutions approaches, by contrast, place greater emphasis on the practices, policies, and structures of organizations themselves.

SOCIAL CONTEXT AND SOCIAL RELATIONS: THE INTERACTIONAL BASIS OF GENDER INEQUALITY

The key feature of social relational explanations of gender inequality is their recognition of the fundamental interdependence that exists between individuals, groups, and larger social units. These perspectives' roots can be found in the work of classical theorists like Marx ([1857] 1973) and Simmel ([1908] 1955), and later researchers like Blau (1977). Two kinds of social relational approaches have been especially relevant to understanding gender inequality. These include status characteristics theory and research on group composition and social networks.

While they differ in important respects, each approach views social categorization as essential to social interaction. Social categorization refers to the processes through which individuals classify others and themselves as members of particular groups. Virtually everyone agrees that sex category is an extremely important social category (Aries 1996). For some, it is *the* most important social category. There are many other social categories, however, including those based on racial or ethnic distinctions, age, ability, and so on. All of these social categories may be relevant for social interaction in particular situations and settings. Social categorization is important because it sets into motion the production of gender differences and inequality. The perspectives examined below differ somewhat in their understanding of how and why that occurs, however.

Status Characteristics Theory: The Importance of Expectations

How does social interaction help produce gender distinctions and inequalities? Status characteristics theory (also referred to as the theory of "expectation states") offers a straightforward answer to this question: As Ridgeway (1997) explains, "[G]ender becomes an important component of interactional processes because the problems of organizing interaction evoke cultural schemas that reinforce continual sex categorization" (p. 219). Because interaction requires that people orient themselves to one another, it is necessary to have some basis for categorizing others vis-à-vis oneself. In Risman's (1998) words: "Gender is something we do in order to make social life more manageable" (p. 33).

Sex categorization serves this purpose better than any other categorization system, according to Ridgeway and other status characteristics theorists. Continuing reliance on sex categorization as a way to organize interaction, however, tends to create gender expectations and stereotypes. People learn to expect certain kinds of behaviors and responses from others based on their sex category. These expectations serve as cognitive reminders of how we are supposed to behave in any given situation. Risman (1998) refers to them "as accurate folklore that must be considered in every interaction" (p. 32). People thus respond to others based on what they believe is expected of them and assume that others will do likewise.

To explain why and how categorizing others by sex produces gender expectations and inequality, these theorists introduce the idea of a status characteristic. A status characteristic is "an attribute on which individuals vary that is associated in a society with widely held beliefs according greater esteem and worthiness to some states of the attribute (e.g., being male) than others (being female)" (Ridgeway 1993:179). Gender is clearly a status characteristic, and this is true in virtually all societies. Once a characteristic like sex category has status value, it begins to shape expectations and form the basis for stereotypes.

Gender is not the only basis on which people differentially assign power and status, however. For example, age is also a status characteristic; adults are generally ascribed more status and power than children. Similarly, depending upon the particular society, racial or ethnic distinctions may also operate in this way. Furthermore, expectation states theory recognizes that multiple status characteristics may be activated in any given situation.

Status characteristics theory was developed to explain goal-oriented interaction, such as occurs in workplaces, classrooms, or in any group oriented toward a collective end. In these kinds of settings, the important expectations are those relating to performance. That is, group members assess how competent each is and how much value to attach to each other's contributions. People form their expectations about others' competence by weighing each status characteristic in terms of its relevance to the task at hand. This weighting process is not assumed to be conscious or precise; rather, expectation states theorists believe that people seek cues as to how others will perform in a particular situation and use status characteristics to assess this. These performance expectations tend to disadvantage those with lower status value (in the case of gender, women). Women are expected to be less competent than men, and their contributions are expected to be less valuable.

Status characteristics theory recognizes that the effects of gender on social interaction may vary from situation to situation. It assumes that status characteristics such as gender are more likely to be "activated" (i.e., central to people's awareness) in some situations than others. Ridgeway expects gender to be most influential when two conditions hold: the interactants are members of different sex categories, and gender is relevant to the task or purpose of the interaction.

For status characteristics theorists, a group's sex composition helps to determine how gender will shape the group's interactions. The second approach focuses explicitly on the role of sex composition. From this perspective, the meaning and impact of one's own sex category depends on the sex composition of the group. A person's own sex category is less relevant to any particular interaction than the sex category memberships of those with whom she or he is interacting.

Group Composition, Homophily, and Social Networks

Much research suggests that social ties of all types tend to be organized according to the homophily principle: Social ties tend to be between people who are similar on salient sociodemographic dimensions (Popielarz 1999). Partly, this reflects people's preferences. Homophily thus arises out of people's preference for sameness, a preference that is expressed in their interpersonal relations. McPherson, Popielarz, and Drobnic (1992) argue that the homophilous social ties experienced in everyday life are further reinforced—and

developed—in people's group memberships. As they explain, "We argue that most homophily occurs because ties are shaped by the opportunities presented to people in groups. We do not encounter people who are seriously different enough from us frequently enough for them to become social network contacts" (p. 168). Thus, individuals' access to others is mediated by the groups to which they belong; groups enable certain kinds of ties (namely, ties to similar others) while reducing the likelihood of ties to those who are dissimilar.

These ideas about the importance of homophily in social life have implications for understanding gender inequality. The social-psychological underpinnings of homophily lie in social categorization or social identity theory, perspectives that emphasize how people use social categories to classify self and others, and to guide interaction (Hogg and Abrams 1988; Tajfel 1982; Turner 1987). These theories assume that people define themselves in terms of one or more social identities, and as members of one group as compared to other groups. Categorization, in turn, engenders certain feelings and behaviors. "Otherness" (or difference) is generally associated with more negative outcomes for individuals and groups. Similarity, on the other hand, attracts; that is, people are drawn to those whose attitudes, values, and beliefs are similar to their own. Similarity may also make communication easier, thus contributing to a greater sense of trust and feeling of kinship. Conversely, difference may be threatening and communication more difficult.

Ascribed characteristics, such as sex, race, and age, often become "proxies" for similarity (or dissimilarity). Sex, race, and age are important ascribed characteristics in social life because they are easily observed and difficult to hide. The power of these characteristics also derives from the fact that sex, race, and age are highly institutionalized statuses and, hence, each is laden with layers of social meaning. This increases their value as proxies for similarity and dissimilarity, since they are believed to be reliably associated with particular characteristics.

The similarity-attraction connection implies that sex-segregated groups would be more satisfying to their members than more integrated groups. People should prefer to interact with others like themselves and feel uncomfortable, threatened, and less committed when they are in more heterogeneous groups. These issues have received significant attention from researchers and have been especially important in understanding women's and men's work experiences. For example, studies have focused on people's experiences in groups of varying sex composition. They are interested in whether people have different experiences in mixed-sex groups than in groups that contain all men or all women. In general, the similarity-attraction hypothesis assumes that both women and men would prefer settings where they were in the majority to those where they were less well represented.

These dynamics were captured in a provocative study by Tsui, Egan, and O'Reilly (1992). These researchers examined the consequences of "being different" for workers' attachment to their firms. They hypothesized that people who were more different from other members of their work groups would be less attached (e.g., less psychologically committed, more likely to be absent from work, and more likely to quit) than those who were more similar. Several forms of difference were examined, including sex, age, race, education, and tenure with the employer.

Consistent with the arguments presented above, Tsui, Egan, and O'Reilly found that being different from one's coworkers on ascribed characteristics (i.e., age, race, and sex) had negative consequences on attachment, while being different with respect to education or tenure with the employer did not have these consequences. Moreover, these authors found that whites and men—that is, those who were members of the historically dominant categories—reacted more negatively to being different than nonwhites and women. This research thus suggests that being different is difficult for people, especially when it involves difference of an ascribed characteristic, like sex.

This study is part of a large body of literature on the consequences of similarity and difference (Allmendinger and Hackman 1995; Chemers, Oskamp, and Costanzo 1995; Williams and O'Reilly 1998). Though much of this research has been conducted in the United States, the effects of demographic diversity have also been studied in other societies, such as China (Tsui and Farh 1997; Xin and Pearce 1996). While the findings are not always consistent, the results suggest that a group's demography affects both individual members and group outcomes, and that "at the micro level, increased diversity typically has negative effects on the ability of the group to meet its members' needs and to function effectively over time" (Williams and O'Reilly 1998:116). More recent research has qualified this latter finding, as studies have begun to identify the conditions under which the negative effects of difference at the individual level, or diversity at the group level, may be eliminated or reduced (Chatman et al. 1998; Flynn, Chatman, and Spataro 2001; Jehn, Northcraft, and Neale 1999). Overall, however, this line of research suggests that the social relations of difference and similarity are important in themselves, regardless of the effects of specific kinds of difference (i.e., gender, race, age).

While Tsui and colleagues (1992) focused on the reactions of those who are different from others in the group, others have examined the majority's reactions or looked at the interactions between the majority and the minority. Rosabeth Moss Kanter explored these issues in her 1977 classic, *Men and Women of the Corporation*. Kanter argued that the relative proportions of different "social types" in a group shape members' social relations. "As proportions shift," she suggests, "so do social experiences" (p. 207). Proportions have this effect because they influence how people perceive one another.

Kanter (1977) was particularly interested in what she called "skewed groups" (p. 208). In these groups, one social type is numerically dominant and the other is a very small numerical minority (e.g., 15 percent or less). Kanter's focus on this type of group stemmed from the fact that this is likely to be the situation experienced by "newcomers" to a social setting. Women who enter jobs or workplaces historically dominated by men, for example, are apt to enter as a minority of this type, as are people of color who enter jobs historically dominated by whites. Because it is unlikely that an employer would hire large numbers of women or people of color at one time, sex (and race) integration happens slowly, one or two people at a time. Members of the numerical minority in skewed groups are called tokens. For Kanter, this term is not pejorative, nor does it refer to people who are assumed to have been hired because of their sex or race. Instead, the term *token* is a neutral label, referring to those whose "social type" constitutes 15 percent or less of a group.

Being a token can be a highly stressful experience. Even if successful in terms of their overall job performance, the conditions under which tokens work are different from those of the dominant group and may be psychologically burdensome. Of course, some tokens will not experience these stresses, and some may even derive self-esteem from successfully overcoming the challenges associated with token status. Nevertheless, Kanter's point is that how people experience work is shaped in part by how many of their social type are present.

While some researchers focus on tokens, others are interested in how people's experiences differ across the full range of group types. Allmendinger and Hackman's (1995) study of symphony orchestras provides an example of this line of research. These researchers were interested in how the sex composition of a symphony orchestra affected its members' attitudes. This study examines 78 orchestras in four geographical locations, including the United States, United Kingdom, the former East Germany, and the former West Germany. Historically, women have been only a small percentage of players in professional orchestras, and this is true worldwide (Allmendinger and Hackman 1995). In this study, the percentage of women ranged from 2 percent to 59 percent.

Allmendinger and Hackman's (1995) findings are generally consistent with the similarity-attraction paradigm, though they show that it is more complicated than one might assume. For example, they found that while women were less satisfied when they were in orchestras dominated by men (i.e., 90 percent or more male) than those that were more balanced (i.e., between 40 percent and 60 percent women), they were especially dissatisfied in orchestras that contained between 10 percent and 40 percent women. Male orchestra members also were less satisfied when women were greater than 10 percent but less than 40 percent of members. These findings held true in all four countries, underscoring the power of group composition. Allmendinger and Hackman suggest that once women become a significant minority (i.e., greater than 10 percent), they

gain power and cannot be as easily overlooked by their male counterparts. In their words: "Together, these processes result in tightened identity group boundaries for both genders, increased cross-group stereotyping and conflict, less social support across gender boundaries, and heightened personal tension for everyone" (p. 453).

These studies illustrate some of the dynamics that may help perpetuate gender inequality. When men or women enter an occupation, job, or work setting that has been previously dominated by the other sex, discomfort—even hostility—may ensue. Those already employed may resent the newcomer and be unsure about how to relate to him or her. Group norms may have to be renegotiated and miscommunication may occur. The newcomer is likely to feel equally uncomfortable, cautious, and unsure about how or where she or he fits in. The discomfort on both sides may produce conflict. The newcomer may not have much incentive or desire to stay.

The dynamics surrounding women who enter jobs traditionally held by men may be very different from those occurring when men enter predominantly female jobs. Men in predominantly male jobs may perceive women as a threat to their power and status and thus may be motivated to drive them out. The forms this resistance may take range from attempts to make women uncomfortable or to refuse assistance and support, to more serious expressions of hostility and harassment, including sexual harassment.

Williams's (1989, 1995) research on men employed in predominantly female occupations, such as nursing and elementary school teaching, tells a different story. She shows that while relatively few men seek out predominantly female occupations, those who do are likely to be successful and more highly economically rewarded than their female coworkers. Williams attributes this to several factors: Because femaleness is less highly valued than maleness, women entering predominantly male occupations must struggle to fit in and demonstrate their competence. Men entering predominantly female occupations, on the other hand, carry no such burden. Maleness is positively regarded, in general, and thus men in predominantly female occupations may strive to demonstrate these qualities and preserve their distinctiveness from women.

Men are not necessarily strategic and conscious of these efforts to "do masculinity." Indeed, Williams believes that men's motives to preserve gender distinctions stem in part from deep-seated psychological processes. Nevertheless, men are likely to benefit from their token status in ways that women do not. While female tokens must prove themselves capable of doing "men's work," male tokens often find themselves on glass escalators; these are invisible and sometimes even unwanted pressures to move up in the workplace (Williams 1995).

Social Networks

The relations between group composition and gender inequality are also the focus of social network research. Network analyses are well represented in the literatures on organizations and careers (Granovetter 1974; Podolny and Baron 1997) and have been increasingly used to examine gender (and racial) differences in career dynamics and outcomes (Ibarra 1992, 1993; Ibarra and Smith-Lovin 1997; Smith-Lovin and McPherson 1993). In general, this research suggests that women and men tend to have different kinds of work-related networks and that these differences tend to be disadvantageous to women's careers.

The network literature on gender and race has generated many useful substantive findings (see Ibarra and Smith-Lovin 1997 and Smith-Lovin and McPherson 1993 for reviews). More important, however, these analyses have helped illuminate forms of inequality that are often overlooked by other frameworks. By treating networks as social resources (or social capital) (Coleman 1988; Portes 1998), network research calls attention to the instrumental importance of social ties, including the ways that these ties provide resources that can be invested or mobilized to secure other valued ends. For example, researchers have studied the ways in which social ties, as represented by personal networks, can be useful in job searches and can positively influence other occupational outcomes, such as occupational status (Hanson and Pratt 1991). Both the range (diversity) and composition (members' placement in social hierarchies) of personal networks can affect occupational attainment; more diverse networks provide greater access to information than less diverse networks, and networks that include more powerful or prestigious actors provide greater access to influence (Campbell 1988; Campbell, Marsden, and Hurlbert 1986).

By viewing networks as social resources (or "social capital"), this literature thus calls attention to the role of social relations in constraining and enabling access to power, opportunity, and other kinds of valued social goods. From this perspective, gender and other forms of inequality can be understood as a function of differences between the social relations within which individuals are embedded.

As the twenty-first century begins, the global labor force is more diverse than ever. Roughly 40 percent of the world's paid workers are women, a figure that has been increasing since the 1970s (Padavic and Reskin 2002). In the United States, as Tsui and colleagues (1992) note, "more and more individuals are likely to work with people who are demographically different from them in terms of age, gender, race, and ethnicity" (p. 549). Given these changes, it has become more important than ever to understand the consequences of homophily, social networks, and "being different" for women and men in the workplace.

Gendered Organizations and Gendered Institutions

Much of social life is organized and routine. People are employed by organizations, such as business firms or the government. They attend school and may be members of churches or voluntary associations, such as neighborhood or political groups. In fact, many of the interactions people have take place within organizations. The social practices that are associated with organizations play an especially important role in the production and reproduction of gender and gender inequality.

Institution is a somewhat more abstract and more all-encompassing concept. In simplest terms, sociologists define an institution as "an organized, established pattern," or even more simply, "the rules of the game" (Jepperson 1991:143). Institutions, then, are those features of social life that seem so regular, so ongoing, and so permanent that they are often accepted as just "the way things are." Each major social institution is organized according to what Friedland and Alford (1991) call "a central logic—a set of material practices and symbolic constructions" (p. 248). These logics thus include structures, patterns, and routines, and they include the belief systems that supply these with meaning.

Two additional aspects of institutions are important to keep in mind. First, institutions tend to be self-perpetuating and thus to take on a life of their own. This implies that there need not be—and often is not—any conscious intent on the part of participants to create or reproduce gender. In addition, because they are taken for granted, institutions tend to produce a socially shared "account" of their existence and purpose: "Persons may not well comprehend an institution, but they typically have ready access to some functional or historical account of why the practice exists. . . . Institutions are taken-for-granted, then, in the sense that they are both treated as relative fixtures in a social environment and explicated (accounted for) as functional elements of that environment" (Jepperson 1991:147). The availability of these accounts helps explain why institutions are so rarely challenged or scrutinized: People believe that their purpose and functioning are self-evident.

As this discussion reveals, institutions incorporate more of the social landscape than organizations. In fact, many institutions contain several different types of organizations. Given this, I refer to this framework as the gendered institutions approach, recognizing that it includes aspects of organizations as well.

Gendered Institutions

Acker (1992) observes that many of the institutions that constitute the "rules of the game" in American society—and, indeed, most societies—embody aspects of gender. As Acker (1992) defines it, to say that an institution is gendered means that "gender is present in the processes, practices, images and ideologies, and distributions of power in the various sectors of social life. Taken as more or less functioning wholes, the institutional structures of the United States and other societies are organized along the lines of gender. . . . [These institutions] have been historically developed by men, currently dominated by men, and symbolically interpreted from the standpoint of men in leading positions, both in the present and historically" (p. 467).

Drawing on these ideas, gender scholars suggest that the structures and practices of organizations are gendered at all levels and that these aspects of gender are analytically distinct from the effects of group composition (Britton 2000). In Steinberg's (1992) words: "Masculine values are at the foundation of informal and formal organizational structures. . . . Images of masculinity and assumptions about the gendered division of labor organize institutional practices and expectations about work performance" (p. 576). As an example of this line of argument, some research has focused on how cultural beliefs about gender infuse people's understandings of jobs, occupations, and particular work activities (Pierce 1996). By establishing certain work roles, jobs, and occupations as appropriate for one gender and off-limits to another, these cultural beliefs establish the "way things are" or a set of commonsense understandings of who should engage in what type of work.

Gendered Jobs and Gender Inequality

That jobs dominated by a particular gender come to be seen as most appropriate for that gender may seem unproblematic and inevitable, but this association is produced through a complex process of social construction. As Reskin and Roos (1990) note, virtually any occupation can be understood as being more appropriate for one sex or another "because most jobs contain both stereotypical male and stereotypical female elements" (p. 51). Nursing, for example, increasingly requires workers to be skilled in the use of complex medical technologies. Emphasizing the caring aspects of this occupation, however, allows it to be cast as an occupation particularly appropriate for women—in the United States, at least. Most jobs and occupations contain enough different kinds of characteristics that they can be construed as appropriate for *either* women or men. Indeed, jobs and occupations that are predominantly female in the West are not necessarily held by women in other parts of the world and vice versa.

For example, in Senegal and Tunisia, approximately half of all nurses are men (Anker 1998).

The gendering of work can also be seen in gender-integrated positions or in jobs that contain a minority of the other gender (Hall 1993; Williams 1989, 1995), and it applies to jobs held by men as well as those that are predominantly female (Maier 1999; Pierce 1996). For example, as a growing literature on work and masculinity has shown, many predominantly male jobs implicitly and explicitly require incumbents to display traditionally masculine behaviors, such as aggressiveness (Pierce 1996). Maier (1999:71) argues that managerial practices and organizational cultures—not merely specific jobs—embody a "corporate masculinity" that privileges individualism, competitiveness, and technical rationality.

In some situations, the work tasks may be gendered as feminine, but the worker performing them is male. Hall's (1993) study of table servers offers a useful example of these arrangements. Styles of table service are laden with gender meanings. A familial style of service, which Hall labels "waitressing," has been historically associated with women working in coffee shops and family restaurants. By contrast, "waitering" is a more formal style, usually associated with male servers in high-prestige restaurants. Hall suggests that even in sex-integrated restaurants, "work roles, job tasks, and service styles" (p. 343) continue to be gendered, such that waitering—whether performed by women or men—is more highly valued by employers and customers than is waitressing.

The gender-typing of occupations, jobs, and work tasks is not a random process, however. In particular, low-status jobs containing low amounts of power and control over others are much more likely to be gendered female than high-status jobs requiring the exercise of authority. Anker (1998) shows that three-quarters of employed women worldwide work in seven occupations: nurses, secretaries/typists, housekeepers, bookkeepers and cashiers, building caretakers and cleaners, caregivers, and sewers and tailors. Padavic and Reskin (2002) suggest that "most of these occupations appear to conform to stereotypes of women as caring, patient, nimble-fingered, skilled at household tasks, and docile" (p. 71).

Deference—or the capacity to place oneself in a "one down" position vis-à-vis others—is a characteristic demanded of low-status social groups in many circumstances. This capacity may also be expressed as "niceness" or the ability to get along. It is not surprising that when this capacity is a job requirement, women will be viewed as better qualified than men. Moreover, even when deference may not be a formal job requirement, jobs containing large numbers of women are likely to contain an informal job requirement that encourages this behavior. Conversely, jobs involving the display of authority are more likely to be gendered as male, at least in part because authority in the context of the United States is seen as a masculine characteristic.

The Worth of Jobs

An important link between the gendering of jobs and gender inequality appears when we examine the relative values attached to different kinds of work. The higher societal value placed on males and masculinity over females and femininity is reproduced within the workplace. In this setting, the relative worth of activities can be assessed economically, in the form of wages, and symbolically, in the form of status and prestige. On both counts, men and masculine activities are more highly valued than women and feminine activities.

Economists have devoted considerable attention to understanding what determines the "worth" of jobs and why some jobs pay more than others. For the most part, these scholars have emphasized the role of human capital in wage determination (see, e.g., Becker 1985; Mincer and Polachek 1974). Human capital refers to the portfolio of skills that workers acquire through various kinds of "investments" in education, training, or experience. Applied to the gender wage gap, human capital theory implies that women earn less than men because of differences in the kind and amount of human capital each has accumulated.

Feminist scholars and others argue that this provides an incomplete understanding of the gender wage gap; they have critiqued economic arguments for overlooking the many ways that social factors shape wage-setting and wage inequality (see, e.g., England and Farkas 1986; Steinberg and Haignere

Table 10.1   Gender Inequality around the World[a]

	Percentage Females in Employment Sector			Percentage Female Administrators and Managers	Gender Wage Gap[b]
	Agriculture	Industrial	Service		
Belgium	32.3	19.5	49.3	18.8	88
Denmark	20.0	25.1	54.3	19.2	85
Germany	37.2	23.4	54.0	25.8	83
Greece	42.7	21.9	40.4	22.0	71
Spain	26.0	16.1	45.7	31.9	80
France	32.4	24.2	53.1	9.4	82
Ireland	12.8	23.5	51.0	22.6	
Italy	32.7	24.3	42.4	53.3	86
Luxembourg	25.0	10.3	34.3	8.6	82
Netherlands	25.9	16.6	48.8	20.3	71
Austria	49.0	21.5	53.3	23.9	
Portugal	51.6	29.4	52.0	31.0	
Finland	32.3	24.0	59.0	25.3	83
Sweden	24.4	21.9	58.8	38.9	89
United Kingdom	25.4	22.1	54.0	32.9	76
Poland	44.5	34.8	55.0	34.7	
Slovenia	48.1	39.4	56.0	28.2	
Hungary	24.8	38.6	52.6	33.8	
Czech Republic	32.7	37.5	54.4	26.9	
Slovakia	31.3	38.2	57.3	27.4	
United States	25.3	26.3	59.3	42.7	74

Source: Table 1.2 (pp. 6–7) in T. Van Der Lippe and L. Van Dijk (2001).

a. Data on percentage of women administrators and managers from 1995; all other data from 1997.

b. Based on hourly earnings of full-time workers.

1987). In addition, researchers have suggested that institutional or structural factors, as well as individual-level factors, contribute to the gender wage gap (Roos and Gatta 1999). By focusing on these issues, the study of gender inequality and the gender wage gap has broadened from a narrow focus on individuals' human capital to a concern with social structural and institutional factors. On a more general level, interest in understanding women's earnings and work experiences has contributed to a more accurate view of labor markets. Researchers who focus only on men—especially white men—tend to "exaggerate the extent to which labor market processes are meritocratic" (Reskin and Charles 1999:384).

During the last few decades, research on the gender wage gap has proliferated. As Table 10.1 shows, men earn more than women in virtually every country in the world (Anker 1998; Blau and Kahn 1992, 2001; Padavic and Reskin 2002). Researchers' understanding of how the gender-based wage inequality occurs, how it has changed over time, and its variations among women and among men have become increasingly more complex and nuanced (Bernhardt, Morris, and Handcock 1995; Blau and Kahn 2001; England 1992; Goldin 1990). Two major themes in this work illustrate recent developments.

First, research on the gender wage gap in the United States has become increasingly attentive to issues of race and ethnicity (Browne 1999; Kilbourne, England, and Beron 1994; Tomaskovic-Devey 1993). As Reskin and Charles (1999) note, the historical tendency has been a "balkanization of research on ascriptive bases of inequality" (p. 380).

Studies of the gender wage gap, in particular, have often ignored racial and ethnic variations among women and men. Not only does this produce potentially inaccurate results, it has hindered efforts to understand the forces generating and maintaining wage inequality.

A second, emerging theme in recent studies of the gender wage gap are attempts to relate gender-based wage inequality to wage inequality more generally, as well as to other forces that are transforming the workplace, such as globalization. Wage inequality in the United States has increased in recent decades—a pattern that reflects industrial and occupational restructuring, changing labor force demographics, globalization, and political trends (Morris and Western 1999). This widening inequality not only reflects earnings differences between women and men, but also differences *among* women and *among* men (Mishel, Bernstein, and Schmitt 1999). A narrow focus on the gender wage gap misses these broader patterns of inequality. These trends are not confined to the United States, but are operating on a global scale as economic competition intensifies and employment is restructured (Blau and Kahn 2001; Walby 2000).

The Gender Segregation of Occupations and Jobs

Gender segregation is an entrenched and pervasive feature of the industrial workplace and, like other aspects of gender inequality, is a worldwide phenomenon. Women make up almost half of the paid labor force, but women and men are employed in different occupations, firms, and jobs (Bielby and Baron 1984; Cotter et al. 1995, 1997; Jacobs 1999; Reskin 1993, 1994; Reskin and Hartmann 1986; Reskin, McBrier, and Kmec 1999; Tomaskovic-Devey 1993). Large-scale, quantitative studies of occupational segregation in the United States have documented trends in segregation over time and identified factors associated with changes in segregation levels (e.g., Beller 1982; Beller and Han 1984; Cotter et al. 1995). These studies suggest that the declines in occupational segregation that took place in the 1970s appear to have leveled off in the 1990s (Jacobs 1999).

Other researchers have examined segregation cross-nationally, looking for clues as to the economic, political, and cultural factors that produce gender segregation and inequality (Charles 1992; Jacobs and Lim 1992; Roos 1985). Although occupational sex segregation is a feature of all industrial societies, its form varies widely. These variations have been traced to several factors. For example, Brinton (1993) argues that Japan's relatively low levels of occupational sex segregation as compared to the United States's reflects differences in the two countries' occupational distributions. In particular, Japan employs more people in lesser-segregated areas of agriculture and manufacturing than in more highly sex-segregated white-collar positions. In her study of occupational sex segregation in 12 industrialized countries, Roos (1985) concluded that "the United States pattern is fairly typical—large numbers of women in high-prestige clerical occupations, low-prestige professional and technical positions, and low-prestige service jobs" (p. 48).

More recent studies extend Roos's findings and suggest that a country's level of occupational sex segregation depends upon a variety of economic, social, and cultural factors. Women generally have greater access to predominantly male occupations in countries with low birthrates and strong egalitarian belief systems, while sex segregation is increased when countries have large service sectors (Charles 1992). Governmental policies relating to gender also play a role in shaping a country's level and pattern of occupational sex segregation. Chang (2000) distinguishes between "interventionist" and "non-interventionist" governments; interventionist governments actively attempt to influence women's labor force participation by passing legislation guaranteeing equal opportunity in the workplace, or by providing direct benefits to families, such as state-subsidized child care or paid family leave. Depending upon the level and type of intervention they engage in, governments help to define their country's "sex segregation regime" (Chang 2000).

This literature on occupational segregation has been supplemented in recent years by research at other levels of analysis. Bielby and Baron (1984), for example, moved segregation research from the occupation level to the job level and firm level of analysis; they showed that job segregation within firms was considerably higher than segregation at the occupational level. Tomaskovic-Devey (1993) also found extremely high levels of job segregation by gender in his study of North Carolina firms. Achatz, Allmendinger, and Hinz (2000) also reported high levels of job-level sex segregation in their study of West German organizations. Even if occupations appear gender-integrated, these studies demonstrate that women and men rarely work together, holding the same job in the same firm. A second extension of segregation research moves it in a more macro direction by focusing on labor markets—rather than jobs or occupations. Cotter et al. (1997) show that occupational integration at the local labor market level improves earnings for all women in that labor market, regardless of the gender composition of a woman's own occupation.

A Gendered Institution's View of Gender Inequality Across the Globe

A gendered institutions perspective has been particularly useful for understanding cross-national variations in gender inequality. As Buchmann and Charles (1995) argue, "If we are to understand cross-national variability in women's economic roles, it may therefore be useful to begin by identifying a set of macro-level variables that systematically influence the perceptions and actions of individual men and women. . . . Organizational and institutional factors are important in this regard, because they set the context within which men and women make educational, labor market, and/or fertility decisions" (p. 66).

Researchers have conceived of these institutional contexts in different ways. For example, Chang (2000) contends that a country's response to gender inequality generally adheres to one of four patterns: substantive egalitarian, formal-egalitarian, traditional family-centered, and economy-centered. Each pattern embodies a distinct "gender logic" that is reflected in that country's norms and state policies. Hence, rather than cross-national convergence in patterns of gender stratification, Chang suggests that gender stratification assumes different forms under different institutional regimes. Esping-Andersen's (1990, 1999) typology of Western welfare states provides another framework for an institutional analysis of gender inequality. In addition to factors such as the relative importance of the market

versus the state in shaping employment outcomes, Esping-Andersen's framework takes into account the state's and market's roles in easing family caregiving responsibilities. While gender inequality figures less explicitly into his typology than Chang's, Esping-Andersen's approach has been used extensively to examine aspects of gender inequality and women's employment across societies (van der Lippe and van Dijk 2002).

Recall that an arrangement that is highly institutionalized is one that is so taken for granted, it seems to reproduce itself. In other words, the arrangement persists without conscious intervention and effort. It thus is much more difficult to alter something that is highly institutionalized than it is to perpetuate it. As a result, highly institutionalized arrangements do not require coercion to sustain them, making participation appear voluntary and easily justifiable. The gendered aspects of state policy and the economy described above clearly fit this description; they are often unintended, taken for granted, and may operate so subtly that they are rarely scrutinized. In this respect, gender distinctions and inequalities are highly institutionalized features of the modern state and economy.

Where Do We Go From Here? Toward a Multilayered Conception of Gender and Gender Inequality

One of the most significant and ongoing contributions of feminist scholarship has been its intensive examination of the concept of gender. This examination has produced a conceptual shift over time in how gender is understood. Early feminist scholars treated gender as an attribute of individuals; gender was a role people acquired through socialization; it was "carried" into workplaces (or to schools or families), where it was then expressed in people's behaviors and beliefs. Because gender was treated as a property of people, the possibility that institutions or features of the social context could play a role in the reproduction of gender distinctions and inequalities was overlooked. Although some contemporary feminist scholars continue to view gender solely as an aspect of the person, most believe that gender is a multifaceted system of practices and relations that operates at all levels of the social world (Hawkesworth 1997; Ridgeway and Smith-Lovin 1999).

This more multilayered view of gender can be seen in many areas of feminist research, but has been most powerfully put to use in research on gender inequality in the workplace. The broadening of feminist conceptions of gender has increased the reach of feminist scholarship and expanded its influence on the social sciences. Treating gender strictly as an individual-level characteristic limits our ability to examine how gender distinctions and inequality are produced at other levels of the social order. A gendered institutions approach makes clear, however, that social structure, institutions, and interaction cannot be understood without taking gender into account.

As a multilevel system affecting individuals' identities and characteristics, patterns of social interaction, and social institutions, the gender system and the inequalities it produces shape social life in crucial ways. What are the key issues this raises for future research on gender inequality? First, as gender research becomes more social relational and institutional, social context becomes a more critical variable than in the past. This implies that we need to be less concerned with gender distinctions and inequalities per se and more concerned with understanding systematically how social contexts vary in the way these distinctions and inequalities are constituted and expressed. As this chapter shows, the relevant social contexts for understanding gender inequality range from the level of social groups engaged in interaction to organizations and institutions and societal regimes. Instead of asking whether gender differences and inequalities exist, we need to look at how their level and expression vary across social contexts (see Nelson and Bridges 1999).

One important line of research moving in this direction relates to studies exploring the effects of diversity on workers and work organizations. This research draws from Kanter's work in an important respect, as it is concerned with the ways that the demographic composition of work groups shapes interaction and behavior (Chemers et al. 1995; Ruderman, Hughes-James, and Jackson 1996). Diversity researchers, however, are not exclusively or even primarily concerned with the sex composition of groups, but are also interested in how other kinds of differences shape people's interactions on the job and their responses to work.

A significant finding emerging from these studies is that differences between people—such as those deriving from gender or race—are not always salient in the workplace. A salient characteristic is one that influences a person's perceptions and behavior in a situation, and it is one that shapes how others respond to that person (Turner 1987). While sex category is probably more salient in more situations than many other attributes of a person, diversity research suggests that it is not always an important factor in workplace social relations. For example, Chatman et al. (1998) found that a more collectivistic organizational culture that emphasizes teamwork and encourages people's sense of a shared fate can create cohesiveness even among diverse groups. Diversity researchers challenge employers in the twenty-first century to create workplaces where people who are different can work together.

Second, future research should attend to multiple levels of analysis and institutional contexts. For example, Nelson and Bridges (1999) combine the insights of a gendered organizations view with more conventional organizational theory. They use the latter to specify the conditions under which larger societal patterns of gender inequality—including those engendered by market forces—might be reduced or enhanced by particular organizational structures, policies, and practices. In this way, Nelson and Bridges argue that organizations vary in the ways that gender is institutionalized; organizations differ both in the degree to which they reinforce market-based gender inequality and the means through which they accomplish this.

Finally, researchers have become increasingly concerned with the relations between gender and other bases of distinction and stratification, such as age, race, or ethnicity, sexual orientation, or social class. A growing literature challenges the notion that women (or men) represent a homogeneous category, whose members share common interests and experiences. Theory and research seeking to describe the intersections between race, class, and gender, in particular, have proliferated, and there is increasing attention to these questions among those interested in the workplace. In the years ahead, it will be important to more systematically address how other forms of social differentiation besides gender are constructed and maintained in the workplace. Doing this requires that we overcome the "balkanization" between the literatures on racial, gender, and other forms of inequality (Reskin and Charles 1999:380) and begin to focus on "organizational systems of inequality" (Nelson and Bridges 1999:5).

CONCLUSION

As a system of social practices that produces distinctions between women and men and organizes inequality on the basis of those distinctions, gender is a powerful principle of social life. Gender thus is a complex, multilevel system that is visible throughout the social world. This complexity poses challenges for those interested in eliminating gender inequality. At the same time, gender scholars are continuing to develop new tools and insights to unravel this complexity. Their work will be as important during the twenty-first century as ever.

REFERENCES

Achatz, J., J. Allmendinger, and T. Hinz. 2000. "Sex Segregation in Organizations: A Comparison of Germany and the U.S." Presented at the American Sociological Association Annual Meeting, Washington, DC.

Acker, J. 1992. "Gendered Institutions." *Contemporary Sociology* 21:565–69.

Allmendinger, J. and J. R. Hackman. 1995. "The More, the Better? A Four-Nation Study of the Inclusion of Women in Symphony Orchestras." *Social Forces* 74:423–60.

Anker, R. 1998. *Gender and Jobs: Sex Segregation of Occupations in the World.* Geneva, Switzerland: International Labour Office.

Aries, E. 1996. *Men and Women in Interaction.* New York: Oxford University Press.

Becker, G. 1985. "Human Capital, Effort, and the Sexual Division of Labor." *Journal of Labor Economics* 17:S33-S58.

Beller, A. H. 1982. "Occupational Segregation by Sex: Determinants and Changes." *Journal of Human Resources* 17:371–92.

Beller, A. H. and K. K. Han. 1984. "Occupational Sex Segregation: Prospects for the 1980s." Pp. 91–114 in *Sex Segregation in the Workplace,* edited by Barbara F. Reskin. Washington, DC: National Academy Press.

Bernhardt, A., M. Morris, and M. S. Handcock. 1995. "Women's Gains or Men's Losses: A Closer Look at the Shrinking Gender Gap in Earnings." *American Journal of Sociology* 101:302–28.

Bielby, W. T. and J. N. Baron. 1984. "A Woman's Place Is with Other Women: Sex Segregation within Organizations." Pp. 27–55 in *Sex Segregation in the Workplace,* edited by Barbara F. Reskin. Washington, DC: National Academy Press.

Blau, F. D. and L. Kahn. 2001. "Understanding International Differences in the Gender Pay Gap." Working Paper 8200. National Bureau of Economic Research Working Paper Series. Cambridge, MA: NBER.

Blau, P. M. 1977. *Inequality and Heterogeneity.* New York: Free Press.

Brinton, M. C. 1993. *Women and the Economic Miracle: Gender and Work in Postwar Japan.* Berkeley, CA: University of California Press.

Britton, D. M. 2000. "The Epistemology of the Gendered Organization." *Gender & Society* 14:418–34.

Browne, I., ed. 1999. *Latinas and African-American Women at Work.* New York: Russell Sage.

Buchmann, M. C. and M. Charles. 1995. "Organizational and Institutional Factors in the Process of Gender Stratification: Comparing Social Arrangements in Six European Countries." *International Journal of Sociology* 25:66–95.

Campbell, K. E. 1988. "Gender Differences in Job-Related Networks." *Work and Occupations* 15:179–200.

Campbell, K. E., Peter V. Marsden, and Jeanne S. Hulbert. 1986. "Social Resources and Socioeconomic Status." *Social Networks* 8:97–117.

Chang, M. 2000. "The Evolution of Sex Segregation Regimes." *American Journal of Sociology* 105:1658–701.

Charles, M. 1992. "Accounting for Cross-National Variation in Occupational Sex Segregation." *American Sociological Review* 57:483–502.

Chatman, J. A., J. Polzer, S. Barsade, and M. Neale. 1998. "Being Different Yet Feeling Similar: The Influence of Demographic Composition and Organizational Culture on Work Processes and Outcomes." *Administrative Science Quarterly* 43:749–80.

Chemers, M. M., S. Oskamp, and M. A. Costanzo. 1995. *Diversity in Organizations.* Thousand Oaks, CA: Sage.

Coleman, J. S. 1988. "Social Capital in the Creation of Human Capital." *American Journal of Sociology* 94 (Supplement):S95–S121.

Cotter, D. A., J. DeFiore, J. M. Hermsen, B. M. Kowalewski, and R. Vanneman. 1997. "All Women Benefit: The Macro-Level Effect of Occupational Integration." *American Sociological Review* 62:714–34.

———. 1995. "Occupational Gender Desegregation in the 1980s." *Work and Occupations* 22:3–21.

England, P. 1992. *Comparable Worth: Theories and Evidence.* New York: Aldine de Gruyter.

England, P. and G. Farkas. 1986. *Households, Employment, and Gender: A Social, Economic and Demographic View.* New York: Aldine de Gruyter.

Esping-Andersen, G. 1990. *The Three Worlds of Industrial Capitalism.* Cambridge, MA: Polity Press.

———. 1999. *Social Foundations of Postindustrial Economies.* New York: Oxford University Press.

Flynn, F. J., J. A. Chatman, and S. E. Spataro. 2001. "Getting to Know You: The Influence of Personality Impressions and Performance of Demographically Different People in Organizations." *Administrative Science Quarterly* 46:414–42.

Friedland, R. and R. R. Alford. 1991. "Bringing Society Back In: Symbols, Practices, and Institutional Contradictions." Pp. 232–65 in *The New Institutionalism in Organizational Analysis*, edited by Walter W. Powell and Paul J. DiMaggio. Chicago, IL: University of Chicago Press.

Goldin, C. 1990. *Understanding the Gender Gap: An Economic History of American Women.* New York: Oxford University Press.

Granovetter, M. S. 1974. *Getting a Job.* Cambridge, MA: Harvard University Press.

Hall, E. J. 1993. "Waitering/Waitressing: Engendering the Work of Table Servers." *Gender & Society* 7:329–46.

Hanson, S. and G. Pratt. 1991. "Job Search and the Occupational Segregation of Women." *Annals of the Association of American Geographers* 81:229–53.

Hawkesworth, M. 1997. "Confounding Gender." *Signs* 22:649–85.

Hogg, M. A. and D. Abrams. 1988. *Social Identifications: A Social Psychology of Intergroup Relations and Group Processes.* London, England: Routledge.

Ibarra, H. 1992. "Homophily and Differential Returns: Sex Differences in Network Structure and Access in an Advertising Firm." *Administrative Science Quarterly* 37:363–99.

———. 1993. "Personal Networks of Women and Minorities in Management: A Conceptual Overview." *Academy of Management Review* 18:56–87.

Ibarra, H. and L. Smith-Lovin. 1997. "New Directions in Social Network Research in Gender and Organizational Careers." Pp. 359–84 in *Handbook of Organizational Behavior,* edited by S. Jackson and C. Cooper. New York: Wiley.

Jacobs, J. A. 1999. "The Sex Segregation of Occupations: Prospects for the 21st Century." Pp. 125–41 in *Handbook of Gender and Work,* edited by G. N. Powell. Thousand Oaks, CA: Sage.

Jacobs, J. A. and S. T. Lim. 1992. "Trends in Occupational and Industrial Occupation by Sex in 56 Countries, 1960–80." *Work and Occupations* 19:450–86.

Jehn, K. A., G. B. Northcraft, and M. A. Neale. 1999. "Why Differences Make a Difference: A Field Study of Diversity, Conflict, and Performance in Workgroups." *Administrative Science Quarterly* 44:741–63.

Jepperson. R. L. 1991. "Institutions, Institutional Effects, and Institutionalism." Pp. 143–63 in *The New Institutionalism in Organizational Analysis,* edited by W. W. Powell and P. J. DiMaggio. Chicago, IL: University of Chicago Press.

Kanter, R. M. 1977. *Men and Women of the Corporation.* New York: Basic Books.

Kilbourne, B. S., P. England, and K. Beron. 1994. "Effects of Individual, Occupational, and Industrial Characteristics on Earnings: Intersections of Race and Gender." *Social Forces* 72:1149–76.

Maier, M. 1999. "On the Gendered Substructure of Organization: Dimensions and Dilemmas of Corporate Masculinity." Pp. 69–93 in *Handbook of Gender and Work,* edited by G. N. Powell. Thousand Oaks, CA: Sage.

Marx, K. [1857] 1973. *Grundrisse: Foundations of the Critique of Political Economy.* Translated by Martin Nicolaus. New York: Random House.

McPherson, J. M., P. A. Popielarz, and S. Drobnic. 1992. "Social Networks and Organizational Dynamics." *American Sociological Review* 57:153–70.

Mincer, J. and S. Polachek. 1974. "Family Investments in Human Capital: Earnings of Women." *Journal of Political Economy* 82:S76-S108.

Mishel, L., J. Bernstein, and J. Schmitt. 1999. *The State of Working America, 1998–99.* Ithaca, NY: ILR Press.

Morris, M. and B. Western. 1999. "Inequality in Earnings at the Close of the Twentieth Century." *Annual Review of Sociology* 25:623–57.

Nelson, R. L. and W. P. Bridges. 1999. *Legalizing Gender Inequality.* New York: Cambridge University Press.

Padavic, I. and B. Reskin. 2002. *Women and Men at Work.* Thousand Oaks, CA: Pine Forge.

Pierce, J. 1996. *Gender Trials: Emotional Lives in Contemporary Law Firms.* Berkeley, CA: University of California Press.

Podolny, J. M. and J. N. Baron. 1997. "Social Networks and Mobility in the Workplace." *American Sociological Review* 62:673–93.

Popielarz, P. 1999. "Organizational Constraints on Personal Network Formation." *Research in the Sociology of Organizations* 16:263–81.

Portes, A. 1998. "Social Capital: Its Origins and Applications in Modern Sociology." *Annual Review of Sociology* 24:1–14.

Reskin, B. F. 1993. "Sex Segregation in the Workplace." *Annual Review of Sociology* 19:241–70.

Reskin, B. F. and C. Z. Charles. 1999. "Now You See 'Em, Now You Don't: Race, Ethnicity, and Gender in Labor Market Research." Pp. 380–407 in *Latinas and African-American Women at Work,* edited by I. Brown. New York: Russell Sage.

Reskin, B. F. and H. I. Hartmann. 1986. *Women's Work, Men's Work: Sex Segregation on the Job.* Washington, DC: National Academy Press.

Reskin, B. F., D. B. McBrier, and J. A. Kmec. 1999. "The Determinants and Consequences of Workplace Sex and Race Composition." *Annual Review of Sociology* 25:335–61.

Reskin, B. F. and P. A. Roos. 1990. *Job Queues, Gender Queues: Explaining Women's Inroads into Male Occupations.* Philadelphia, PA: Temple University Press.

Ridgeway, C. 1993. "Gender, Status, and the Social Psychology of Expectations." Pp. 175–98 in *Theory on Gender/Feminism on Theory,* edited by P. England. New York: Aldine de Gruyter.

Ridgeway, C. L. 1997. "Interaction and the Conservation of Gender Inequality." *American Sociological Review* 51:603–17.

Ridgeway, C. L. and L. Smith-Lovin. 1999. "The Gender System and Interaction." *Annual Review of Sociology* 25:191–216.

Risman, B. 1998. *Gender Vertigo.* New Haven, CT: Yale University Press.

Roos, P. A. 1985. *Gender and Work: A Comparative Analysis of Industrial Societies.* Albany, NY: State University of New York Press.

Roos, P. A. and M. L. Gatta. 1999. "The Gender Gap in Earnings: Trends, Explanations, and Prospects." Pp. 95–124 in *Handbook of Gender and Work,* edited by G. N. Powell. Thousand Oaks, CA: Sage.

Ruderman, M. N., M. W. Hughes-James, and S. E. Jackson, eds. 1996. *Selected Research on Work Team Diversity.* Washington, DC: American Psychological Association and Center for Creative Leadership.

Simmel, G. [1908] 1955. *Conflict and the Web of Group Affiliations.* New York: Free Press.

Smith-Lovin, L. and J. M. McPherson. 1993. "You Are Who You Know: A Network Approach." Pp. 223–51 in *Theory on Gender/Feminism on Theory,* edited by P. England. New York: Aldine de Gruyter.

Steinberg, R. J. 1992. "Gender on the Agenda: Male Advantage in Organizations." *Contemporary Sociology* 21:576–81.

Steinberg, R. J. and L. Haignere. 1987. "Equitable Compensation: Methodological Criteria for Comparable Worth." Pp. 157–82 in *Ingredients for Women's Employment Policy,* edited by C. Bose and G. Spitze. Albany, NY: State University of New York Press.

Tajfel, H. 1982. *Social Identity and Intergroup Relations.* Cambridge, England: Cambridge University Press.

Tomaskovic-Devey, D. 1993. *Gender and Racial Inequality at Work.* Ithaca, NY: ILR Press.

Tsui, A. S., T. D. Egan, and C. A. O'Reilly III. 1992. "Being Different: Relational Demography and Organizational Attachment." *Administrative Science Quarterly* 37:549–79.

Tsui, A. S. and J. L. Farh. 1997. "Where Guanxi Matters: Relational Demography and Guanxi in the Chinese Context." *Work and Occupations* 24:56–79.

Turner, J. C. 1987. *Rediscovering the Social Group: A Self-Categorization Theory.* New York: Basil Blackwell.

Van der Lippe, T. and L. Van Dijk. 2001. "Introduction." Pp. 1–4 in *Women's Employment in a Comparative Perspective,* edited by T. Van der Lippe and L. Van Dijk. New York: Aldine de Gruyter.

——. 2002. "Comparative Research on Women's Employment." *Annual Review of Sociology* 28:221–41.

Walby, S. 2000. "Analyzing Social Inequality in the 21st Century: Globalization and Modernity Restructure Inequality." *Contemporary Sociology* 29:813–18.

Williams, C. L. 1989. *Gender Differences at Work.* Berkeley, CA: University of California.

——. 1995. *Still a Man's World.* Berkeley, CA: University of California.

Williams, K. Y. and C. A. O'Reilly. 1998. "Demography and Diversity in Organizations." *Research in Organizational Behavior* 20:77–140.

Xin, K. R. and J. L. Pearce. 1996. "Guanxi: Connections as Substitutes for Female Institutional Support." *Academy of Management Journal* 39:1641–58.

Urban Problems in Global Perspective

Chigon Kim

University of Dayton

Mark Gottdiener

State University of New York, Buffalo

The images of the city portrayed by scholars, policy makers, planners, and artists have always been ambivalent: Cities have been praised as places of opportunity, engines of growth, agents of social justice, and habitats of cultural diversity, on the one hand, and condemned as breeding grounds of problems and strains, including poverty, homelessness, joblessness, violence, crime, pollution, and congestion, on the other (Gottdiener and Hutchison 2000). For urban residents, these contrasting images are everyday realities that are intermingled in their lived urban space and urban life: Cities are places of opportunities as well as problems.

Urban areas are produced by economic, political, and cultural forces operating at the international, national, and local levels. In the process of urban development, cities have confronted a variety of problems, which may constrain the potential of future development. Cities in different countries with different socioeconomic and political systems often face quite similar problems, although their scales, trends, or causes differ from place to place. Homelessness and crime, for example, are problems faced by urbanites in developed countries like America and Britain, as well as in cities of the less developed world. While it is important to consider the urban problems of the former, the sheer magnitude of issues and concerns confronting the latter overshadow that attention. Understanding urban problems in a global perspective, therefore, compels us to focus primarily on the crisis of urbanization confronting the developing countries. With this emphasis in place, it is important to note, however, that economic development and prosperity, such as that experienced by the developed countries, do not guarantee the elimination of urban problems, as their persistence in places like New York, London, and Paris attests.

This chapter examines urban problems in a global context. Due to the complexity of the topic, we have chosen to focus most specifically on urban poverty and inequality, racial segregation and ghettoization, inadequate housing and homelessness, and crime. In this chapter, we contextualize urban problems in the process of urbanization; delineate the link between the spatial patterns of urban development and urban problems; explain how urban problems are connected to broader economic, political, and social processes at the international, national, and local levels (e.g., global economy, state policy, land-based interest groups); discuss social consequences of urban problems; and finally address some attempts by urbanites to remedy their most pressing urban problems.

An Urbanizing World

At the turn of the twenty-first century, 2.8 billion people lived in cities, representing 47 percent of the world's population; in 1950, by contrast, fewer than 750 million people or 29 percent of the world's population were city dwellers (United Nations Centre for Human Settlements [UNCHS] 1987, 2001). By the year 2006, more than half of the world's population is projected to live in cities (UNCHS 1999). Such rapid urbanization, on a massive scale, and over a short period of time, has been propelled to a great extent by the developing countries, and almost all population growth in the near future will take place in the cities of the developing world. The number of urban residents in the developing countries has exploded from fewer than 300 million (17%) in 1950 to over 1.9 billion (40%) in the year 2000, a figure that is expected to double in the three decades to come. The share of the world's population living in urban areas of developing countries continues to soar from 12 percent in 1950 to 68 percent in 2000. By the year 2015, this figure will have reached 75 percent of the world's population, and the number of urban dwellers in developing countries will be about the same size of the current world's urban population, 2.8 billion.

The process of rapid, massive, and abrupt urbanization under way in the developing countries is unprecedented. The developed countries at large are already urbanized, with over three-quarters of their population now living in urban areas, and their rates of urban growth are low and even decreasing. Although there are wide variations between and within regions in the pace and level of urbanization, the current rates of urbanization in the developing world are five times higher than those in the developed world. Such an unprecedented nature of third world urbanization brings with it many social problems, which are more pressing among poor countries with only a very limited capacity to cope with them.

The process of urbanization in developing countries can be captured by increases in the number and size of cities. The number of large cities with more than 1 million urban population increased during the second half of the twentieth century. The number of large cities has increased from 80 in 1950 to 365 in the year 2000. This rise in large cities has been more dramatic in the developing countries, from 31 in 1950 to 242 in 2000 (UNCHS 1999). Over the last two decades, the number of large cities more than doubled in the developing world (see Table 11.1). In addition, the size of cities is also rapidly increasing. In 1950, New York was the only megacity with 10 million or more residents in the world; out of 5 megacities in 1975, 3 were in developing countries; at the outset of the twentieth century, 15 out of 19 are now in developing countries (United Nations Population Division [UNPD] 2001:6). These megacities in developing countries are expected to grow faster than those in developed countries. The rapid growth of megacities is one of the most significant transformations of urban settlement space in developing countries.

In the past, cities served as both huge magnets and containers that concentrated people and economic activities or wealth within well-defined, bounded spaces (Mumford 1961). Today, cities are expanding with a new pattern of spatial organization, marked by the growth of "multicentered metropolitan regions" (Gottdiener and Hutchison

Table 11.1 Urbanization and Urban Problems, by Region

	Urban Population, 2000		Average Annual Urban Population Increase, 1990-2000		Number of Large Cities (over 1 million)		Access to Safe Water, 1990-97	Access to Adequate Sanitation, 1990-97	Income Poverty, 1997 (less than U.S. $1 per day)		Quality of the Urban Housing Stock, 1993	
											Permanent Structure	Housing in Compliance
	Million	%	Million	%	1980	2000	%	%	Million	%	%	%
Developed countries:	946	74.7	6.4	0.70	104	123	—	—	—	—	98	97
High-income economies	667	78.3	4.7	0.73	76	90	—	—	—	—	98	97
Transitional economies	279	67.1	1.6	0.61	28	33	—	—	—	—	97	94
Developing countries:	1,944	40.3	54.7	3.30	109	242	87	75	1,320	30.0	73	63
Latin America & Caribbean	388	75.4	7.7	2.20	25	52	87	81	130	26.3	78	74
Sub-Saharan Africa	217	34.3	8.1	4.71	7	33	75	66	220	35.8	60	49
North Africa & Middle East	211	59.9	6.3	3.55	13	24	84	95	10	3.5	84	73
Asia & Pacific	1,128	33.9	32.5	3.40	64	133	92	76	960	30.9	71	59
World Total	2,890	47.4	61.0	2.37	213	365	—	—	—	—	82	75

Source: UNCHS (1999).

Note: — = data not available.

2000). In contrast to the characteristics of the traditional bounded city, the new form of settlement space can be typified by two features: It extends over a large region and it contains many separate centers, each with its own abilities to draw workers, shoppers, and residents. Not every country of the world is experiencing the new form of multicentered metropolitan growth, but all countries seem to be subjected to a process of urban development that produces gigantic cities and urbanization on a regional scale. This explosive growth implies an immense social crisis for the developing countries.

For example, a large proportion of the urban poor remain deprived of basic services such as water supply and sanitation. As shown in Table 11.1, 13 percent of the urban population in developing countries lacked access to safe water, and about twice that figure lacked access to sanitation. Access to safe water and sanitation is less widespread in sub-Saharan Africa than in any other region. Many people living in poverty are forced to purchase water from street vendors at high prices. Access to safe water is a major issue for the urban poor. In many cities, in addition, public transportation is often overcrowded, inadequate, and technically outdated. Insufficient public transport systems, coupled with deteriorating traffic conditions, mean high commuting costs for low-income households.

Before proceeding with an examination of urban problems, per se, let us briefly examine changing perspectives that have guided research in the past. We shall argue that at least some of these approaches must be used eclectically in order to understand fully the complexity of urban issues in a global context.

CHANGING PERSPECTIVES ON URBANIZATION AND URBAN PROBLEMS

Studies on urbanization and urban problems have been guided by several theoretical perspectives that tie urbanization processes to the larger ones of societal development and change. Among them, modernization/ecological theory and dependency/world-system theory stand out (Kasarda and Crenshaw 1991). More recently, the sociospatial perspective has been formulated, which synthesizes many of the positive features of previous approaches

(Gottdiener and Hutchison 2000). A main theoretical question is, What is necessary for an understanding of urbanization and urban problems in both developed and developing countries? Debates have revolved around structural determinants of urbanization, on the one hand, and the relationship between the city, its hinterland, and national and global development on the other. These theoretical perspectives emphasize different structural factors and portray different relations of cities to society. We advocate the sociospatial perspective, which enables us to encompass urbanization and urban problems as a dialectical articulation between space and society, between structure and agency, and between the global and the local.

In both developed and developing countries, the well-being of urban life is intertwined with globalization. While globalization encompasses many dimensions (see Waters 1995), the significant focus is most commonly on the economic effects in the city. This dimension can be captured by the increasing mobility of capital, the spatial concentration of command and control functions, the rise of a worldwide production system, and the intensification of competition. Economic globalization unleashes market forces that penetrate into every aspect of social life and every corner of the globe. The priority of market mechanisms is further fostered by government deregulation pursued by powerful actors, including transnational corporations (TNCs), intergovernmental organizations (e.g., GATT, WTO), and international financial institutions (e.g., IMF, World Bank). The impetus of globalization can be well epitomized as the "annihilation of space through time" or "time-space compression" (Harvey 1989a). Simply put, constraints of geographical distance are becoming less important as a result of the contemporary, computer-aided development of transportation, communication, and information technology. These changes are coupled with the unification of businesses across nation-states as a result of the ownership structure of transnational corporations and the internationalization of banking. Now worldwide corporations and worldwide banks control business.

Urban life in both developed and developing countries is increasingly linked to the operation of the global economy, as world-system theory argues (Smith 1996; Smith and Timberlake 1993). The cycle of investment, manufacturing, consumption, and profit making that leads to more investment integrates consumers and producers in a country with manufacturing, banking, and consumption activities in other countries, including the third world. As the developing countries are incorporated into the global economy, the actions of the powerful interests at the global level affect urbanization, spatial arrangement, urban organization, and urban life. Urban economies, for example, are linked across the globe and increasingly controlled by decisions made at the global level. The actions of the powerful interests, such as the opening of a plant somewhere and a closing someplace else, affect the well-being of the entire community.

Cities are the nodes and hubs of globalizing economic activities. In contrast to world-system theory, however, this role for cities does not mean that all important influences on urban development derive from the global level alone. The process of urbanization in both developed and developing countries involves a complex combination of economic, political, and social forces that are relatively independent of the global economy. Important political, economic, and social forces that account for urban change also arise from within community territory. Through their direct and indirect intervention and regulation, for example, governments provide opportunities and incentives for both business and urban residents to behave in specific ways. In addition, the nature of class structure and especially the control by urban elites through the government and military are important factors in understanding the patterns of urbanization. Urban dynamics is not exclusively a class phenomenon, however. Urban politics has a class component but cannot always be explained by that factor alone. Homeowner politics and the struggle to control over territory and its quality of life are also important political considerations (Mele 2000).

Today, many urban problems are directly or indirectly related to the effects of global market forces. First, globalization increases the inequality among cities. The city becomes a collective actor competing against other locations in order to attract capital investment. Urban governments, in collaboration and partnership with "pro-growth coalitions"

(Gottdiener 1994), play the role of entrepreneurs selling their cities to global investors (Harvey 1989b). Cities, vying for footloose capital investment, compete with each other in providing favorable conditions for capital accumulation such as incentives (e.g., tax breaks, subsidies), infrastructure, and urban services. The wealth of cities is increasingly dependent on the ability to attract outside investment. In addition, the command and control functions tend to be concentrated into a small number of global cities (Sassen 1991). The end result of this process is that there is currently a worldwide pattern of winners and losers structured by the uneven development of globalization. While some locations prosper, others are brought to ruin or neglected by the economic processes of global business interests.

In addition to the wealth inequalities among all cities around the world resulting from the global competition over investment and capital flows, globalization also has increased the fragmentation of the social fabric within cities. The recurrent waves of widespread sociospatial restructuring resulting from globalization since the 1970s, including deindustrialization and changes in the structure of employment, decentralization, the spatial transfer of value, and the spatial mismatch between job locations and worker residences, are responsible for current urban problems in both developed and developing countries. The benefits of globalization are distributed neither evenly nor at random across social groups within urban space. The economically disadvantaged include women, minorities, the young, and the old, all of whom are more vulnerable to the pressures of global market forces on employment opportunities and changes in social services. In particular, certain minority groups have experienced spatial isolation and social exclusion. In the United States and England, this effect is manifested as racial segregation and ghettoization.

In sum, understanding the causes and consequences of urban problems in both developing and developed countries requires the appreciation of factors at all levels—the global, the national, and the local. The sociospatial perspective, which incorporates aspects of the world-system approach, helps us understand the interplay of economic, political, cultural, and spatial factors associated with urban problems. The following discussion addresses those problems most pertinent to developing countries with massive population influx in cities, those problems persistent in developed countries with incessant sociospatial restructuring, and those problems common to both developing and developed societies. Among the former, the problem of overurbanization and demographic shifts from the country to the city counts as the most pertinent. Among those problems in developed countries, we discuss the concentration of urban poverty, focusing on racial residential segregation and ghettoization in the Unites States and England. Following these sections, we discuss housing problems, homelessness, and crime. We then consider attempts to alleviate urban problems through new social movements and the mobilization of city citizens.

URBANIZATION AND URBAN PROBLEMS IN THE DEVELOPING COUNTRIES

Overurbanization

The urban experience of the developed societies shows a close, positive link between industrialization, urbanization, and economic development. Cities are nodes of economic, political, and social activities. Modern cultural traits (e.g., rationality, technological innovation) and modern social institutions (e.g., education and health care systems) diffuse out from urban centers to the hinterland. Urban growth in the developed countries is balanced, with a full range of cities in the city-size hierarchy. Nonetheless, urban growth has always been a double-edged sword: Development increases consumer markets and sources of tax revenues, but at the same time, it increases the demand for infrastructure, amenities, and public services.

In contrast, the pattern and process of urban growth in the third world is characterized by overurbanization, where all the negative effects of city growth experienced by developed countries are magnified many times. The notion of overurbanization in the third world discredits a supposedly immanent link between industrialization, urbanization, and economic development. Overurbanization

is a sociospatial process of excess population concentration in urban areas beyond the capacity to provide basic services and housing infrastructure to urban dwellers. Overurbanized cities lack jobs, education, health care facilities, and other necessary resources to support their growing urban population (Bradshaw and Schafer 2000).

Urban problems related to overurbanization are alarming and increasingly serious in recent years. Overcrowding is a common urban problem in much of the developing world. The urban explosion in the developing countries continues to the point that now urban areas cannot stand any further population increase (cf. Brockerhoff 1999). Overurbanization distorts the allocation of productive resources such as labor. Regular full-time, year-round jobs are relatively rare, yet there is a massive supply of labor in overurbanized cities. Given the limited economic performance of the developing countries, it is not unusual that job creation is very slow and the rate of unemployment is very high. In addition to an abundant reservoir of surplus labor, underemployment is also a problem in third world cities, such as temporary, casual, or seasonal labor (Gugler 1982). Underutilized labor may even disguise the full magnitude of unemployment and the crisis of development.

Another aspect of overurbanization is the glaring lack of supply in the provision of urban infrastructure and collective consumption commodities, such as housing, education, and health care. The urban poor without political and economic power are spatially concentrated in the most disadvantaged areas, where they are neglected by local and national government provisions of basic services. This pattern of development not only causes but also compounds the problem of urban poverty, as we discuss more fully below.

Overurbanization is often evidenced by the presence of *primate cities.* In the developed countries such as the United States, there is an even distribution in the number of cities according to size. Such a profile constitutes "balanced" urbanization, and it provides both business and people with a variety of locational choices and urban environments. In the developing world, by contrast, the disparities among urban centers are very great. In most developing countries, one or two immense cities prominently dominate the intranational urban system. The presence of primate cities, or urban primacy, indicates "a lack of economic, political and social integration in any given system of cities" (Kasarda and Crenshaw 1991:1). The lack of balanced city-size distributions is thought to represent a symptom of underdevelopment and uneven development. Resources and values of the country, including power, wealth, social institutions, and opportunities, are excessively concentrated in these primate cities. Great disparities in regional and urban/rural socioeconomic development will also constrain future development. Overurbanization and primate city growth as urban problems can be illustrated by consideration of the demographic changes in developing countries that are markedly different from those in already developed, urbanized societies.

Demographic Shifts and the Urban Population Explosion

The demographic determinants of urban growth consist of the natural increase of urban populations, rural-to-urban migration, and the reclassification of urban territorial boundaries such as annexation. In the early stage of urbanization, urban populations grew very slowly because their high birthrate was offset by an equally high death rate. Following World War II, the introduction of modern medical techniques and preventive medicines to the developing countries resulted in a population explosion. For most of the developing countries, birthrates now greatly outstrip death rates, and overpopulation is a serious social problem. Population pressure in rural areas, coupled with limited arable land, pushes poor peasants and farmworkers to move to cities. Large cities in the developing countries thus suffer from a double population explosion: a high rate of natural increase and a high rate of rural-to-urban migration. This pattern is completely different than the one experienced by cities in developed countries.

Over the last two decades, rural-to-urban migration accounts for half of urban population increases in the third world cities; the remainder is attributed to the sustained high birthrate relative to the declining death rate (Findley 1993). Of these demographic determinants, rural-to-urban migration is responsive to adversity in rural areas and the attraction of urban areas. Push factors include population pressure, a lack of land tenure, agribusiness, and rural underdevelopment. Pull factors include wage disparities and differentials in opportunities between the rural areas and the urban areas (Firebaugh 1979). The relative contribution of migration to urban growth varies from city to city and from region to region, because the type and rate of migration depends on the initial level of urbanization and the strength of the urban economic base. However, the most common motivation of rural-to-urban migration is the prospect for better opportunity and life chances in growing cities.

The surge of rural-to-urban migration often precedes any sign of economic development, so strong is the pull of the city in most developing countries. Yet, with limited economic growth, large-scale demographic change of this type only results in overurbanization and its myriad problems, such as extreme poverty (see below). Large cities in the developing countries are commonly faced with various urban problems, including shortages of affordable housing, jobs, amenities, and basic public services. Many urban problems are closely connected with uncontrolled, explosive urban population growth. However, structural factors tied with these demographic problems are noteworthy.

First, the failure of agricultural development sufficient to sustain the quality of life has led excess population to migrate to the cities. Second, the demographic problems of the third world are compounded by the limited success of economic development. Finally, most of the developing countries share a common experience of social, economic, and political exploitation under colonialism, as world-system theory maintains. These structural factors may hinder the balanced growth of third world cities. As a result, many developing countries today possess a single, gigantic primate city that is overurbanized, or excessively populated, while retaining a relatively underurbanized interior with no large cities. The primate city remains the center for most investment and economic growth. This pattern of primate development, which is quite different than in the developed countries, compounds the problems of urban life in developing countries.

Urban Poverty and Inequality

Poverty and inequality are persistent and pervasive social problems in the urbanizing world. In the developing countries, the proportion of urban residents living in poverty is very high and the distribution of income is extremely unequal. The estimated number of poor urban residents in developing countries is well over 950 million, or 49 percent of the urban population for the year 2000 (UNCHS 1999). Between 1987 and 1998, countries with economies in transition have experienced a rapid increase in poverty, whereas the rate of poverty has declined most significantly in East Asia and the Pacific, with a slight increase after the Asian financial crisis. In Africa, a majority of urban residents have experienced deterioration in the standard of living; they are impoverished by debt crisis and the structural adjustment programs dictated by international financial institutions such as the IMF. While Africa is the poorest region, income distribution is most unequal in Latin America and the Caribbean (UNCHS 2001). In these regions, urban poverty and inequality worsened considerably during the 1980s, a period dubbed as the "lost decade" (Caldeira 1996:60).

The urbanization of poverty in the developing world is a prominent trend that gives rise to a global concern (Piel 1997). The urbanization of poverty refers to the tendency that the urban share of poverty is likely to grow in accordance with urbanization. In almost all developing countries, poverty is more pervasive in rural areas than in urban areas and most people still live in rural areas. The developing world, however, is rapidly urbanizing, and rural-to-urban migration accounts for about half of urban population growth. Destitution and the relative deprivation in rural areas are factors behind the massive migration of peasants and farmworkers toward cities. Migration, however, does not always rescue them from poverty. Migrants at large remain poor, despite moving, and poverty is becoming a primary urban problem. When the influx of population into a city exceeds its capacity to support the population, the incidence of poverty is likely to grow, although the growth rate may not be as fast as the speed of impoverishment in rural areas.

Many urban problems in the developing countries are associated with the urbanization of poverty.

Poverty-related problems include malnutrition, ill health, inadequate housing, homelessness, lack of access to education and other public services, casual work, and crime (Cairncross, Hardoy, and Satterthwaite 1990). These problems are more prevalent in urban areas than rural areas. In the developing countries, they are exacerbated by uncontrolled, rapid urban development. Cities in the developed world also have many urgent problems that remain unresolved, although they are not necessarily related to the urbanization of poverty. In the United States, for example, problems of residential segregation, discrimination in housing markets, and homelessness persist, particularly in large cities.

Poverty and poverty-related problems have disastrous effects on the conditions of living for the disadvantaged, particularly women and children in urban areas. The "feminization of poverty" is a distinct demographic trend that is more prominent in urban areas. The majority of the poor are women, representing about 70 percent of the people living in poverty over the world, and the number of women in poverty tends to increase, especially in the developing countries (Marcoux 1998). The feminization of poverty in developing countries is in part accounted for by the increase in female-headed households in urban areas. In addition to women, children are disproportionately affected by poverty and inequality: More than half of the children in the urban areas of developing countries are poor. The majority of these poor children live in slums and squatter settlements. There are also a large number of children who live on the street and who often fall prey to organized crime, drugs, and prostitution (UNCHS 1999).

The daily plight of the urban poor is usually behind the scenes until a grim episode brings it to the public eye. A recent disastrous incident was the landslide of a waste dump in Payatas, Manila, on July 11, 2000 (UNCHS 2001:xxvi). Triggered by days of heavy rain, an enormous mountain of garbage collapsed, burying a shantytown nearby where tens of thousands of scavengers earned their living by recycling the garbage. In the avalanche of rubbish, 218 people were killed and another 300 people are still believed missing. They were victims of poverty and most were refugees from rural destitution in the provinces.

SOCIOSPATIAL RESTRUCTURING AND URBAN PROBLEMS IN THE DEVELOPED COUNTRIES

While developing countries face many pressing urban problems because of the magnitude of population growth, developed countries and countries with economies in transition have never been immune to urban problems. In the United States, urban inequality and segregation are seemingly intractable issues of urban life. Based on the Multi-City Study of Urban Inequality (MCSUI), for example, a series of studies has reported persistent inequality (e.g., racial and gender differences in educational attainment, labor force participation, and earnings), labor market segmentation, and residential segregation in major cities of the United States.[1] The urban conditions of former socialist societies differed significantly from those of capitalist societies (Bradshaw and Fraser 1989; Kennedy and Smith 1989). With liberalization and the introduction of market mechanisms, however, these countries with economies in transition now face many urban problems similar to capitalist societies (Gottdiener and Hutchison 2000:271–4). Consequently, while poverty in places like the United States does not exist on a massive scale, as it does in many developing countries, that issue along with the problem of racial segregation persists in developed countries as well.

Racial Segregation and Ghettoization in the United States and England

Urban settlement space in the United States has long been characterized by residential segregation on the basis of race, especially for African Americans. Since the early wave of immigration, urban settlement space has been compartmentalized, with ethnic colonies and territories of foreign immigrants. As population shifts occur, patterns of urban settlement space are shaped and reshaped incessantly, but residential segregation by race remains intact. Residential segregation by race is severe, especially in older cities with declining populations and manufacturing bases in the Northeast and the Midwest. A recent study, based on block-level data from Census 2000, suggests persistent

and pervasive residential segregation in the United States, together with demographic and spatial variations. The levels of segregation tend to be high in large cities or in cities with large minority populations; the average levels of segregation are highest among blacks, followed by Hispanics and Asians (Frey and Myers 2002). Another study on trends in residential segregation over the last two decades shows that residential segregation among blacks and whites remains substantially high, although the segregation index of blacks from whites has declined in most metropolitan areas over the last two decades (Logan 2001).

In Britain, racial composition is less diverse than in the United States. In addition, racial minorities constitute only a small proportion of the total population. It is estimated that about 4 million racial minorities live in Britain, representing about 7 percent of the population, and about half of them live in London (Katwala 2001). Major groups include Indian, Pakistani, black Caribbean, black African, Bangladeshi, and Chinese. Racial minorities are disproportionately concentrated in major cities and large metropolitan areas. Within a city, racial minorities tend to be segregated into impoverished neighborhoods or areas of low-quality housing due in part to discriminatory practices in housing markets and economic marginalization. Notwithstanding spatial concentration and segregation, the majority of racial minorities live in mixed areas (Daley 1998). As in American cities, however, racial segregation and racial tensions are by no means trivial in British cities. Inexorable racial segregation, combined with relentless social exclusion and deprivation, leads to racial conflict and racially motivated riots. During the summer of 2001, for example, clashes between white and South Asian youths swept through the northern cities of England, including Bradford, Burnley, and Oldham.

Nowhere are the sociospatial effects of racial segregation as clear as in metropolitan areas across the United States, where racial and ethnic conflict persists as an urban problem. Although racial diversity is growing in America, the magnitude of racial residential segregation is so high that urban experiences of different racial groups are confined and constricted within the boundaries of their own fragmented social world. Individual life chances and the quality of urban life are affected by residential location, spatial arrangement, and segregation. Moreover, racial segregation has a detrimental effect on social integration at the societal level. In their study of the causes and consequences of racial segregation, researchers have delineated multiple dimensions of population clustering. Massey and Denton (1993), for example, used five measures to study patterns and contours of racial residential segregation: unevenness, isolation, clustered, concentrated, and centralized. The effects of segregation tend to intensify as each of these dimensions is accumulated and articulated in settlement space. Sharp racial segregation reinforces uneven development in urban space, generating spatial differentiation in opportunity structure and life chances. Furthermore, racial segregation in the United States is not restricted to urban settlement space. It is regionwide. Taken as a whole, suburban settlement space may be even more segregated than central cities. However, many urban problems, including concentrated poverty, joblessness, and crime, are associated with intense racial segregation in cities, rather than in the suburbs.

There is controversy over the primary cause of the growing concentration of poverty in major American cities. Whereas some researchers attribute it to racial segregation (Massey and Denton 1993), others insist that social and structural transformations over the last decades have played a major role (Wilson 1987, 1996). Proponents of the latter position, although they underline social and structural transformations, do not deny the harmful effects of racial segregation on the concentration of poverty (see, e.g., Jargowsky 1997:143). In the United States, the urban poor in major metropolitan areas are increasingly segregated into high-poverty neighborhoods, which are also increasingly divided along racial lines. A recent study shows that the number of the urban poor living in those racially segregated, high-poverty neighborhoods commonly labeled as ghettos (predominantly African American), barrios (predominantly Hispanic), and slums (mixed or white) almost doubled in recent decades, from 4 million in 1970 to 8 million in 1990 (Jargowsky 1997).

Urban racial minorities are vulnerable to structural changes in the urban economy taking place under the pressure of the global economy. In the process of deindustrialization and reindustrialization, the urban labor market has been increasingly polarized into low-skilled and rising high-skilled sectors. Deindustrialization, including plant closings and the relocation of manufacturing, has destroyed low-skilled, blue-collar jobs that were traditionally the main sources of livelihood for urban racial minorities; by contrast, the growth of high-tech, knowledge-based industries in major cities has created job opportunities for skilled workers with educational credentials. As a result of changes in the urban economic base, urban minorities have turned increasingly to the low-wage service sector.

In addition, economic restructuring has accompanied changes in the spatial organization of work. In the United States, the restructuring of settlement space since the 1950s is characterized by the general process of deconcentration (Gottdiener 1994, 2002; Gottdiener and Hutchison 2000, chap. 5). Deconcentration is a ubiquitous leveling of industries, jobs, and the labor force across space. Driven by two distinct sociospatial forces of decentralization and recentralization, deconcentration has produced spatial differentiation and fragmentation. Whereas command and control functions, finance, and other specialized producer services tend to remain in major urban centers due in part to the advantages of agglomeration economies, production, commercial activities, and other business functions have dispersed across space. The suburbanization of jobs— that is, the movement of jobs from the cities to the suburbs—is part of this broader process of deconcentration. This spatial redistribution of employment opportunities generates a growing mismatch between the suburban location of employment and minorities' residences in the inner city. If, as is the case in most American cities, public transportation is limited in scope and service, then the inner-city poor are isolated from these suburban job opportunities. Poor regional public transportation, in combination with the deconcentration of employment, reduces the probability of finding jobs for urban minorities living in impoverished inner-city neighborhoods.

The sociodemographic transformation of the inner city is another important structural factor involved in the concentration of poverty in major

American cities. Whereas deindustrialization and deconcentration have shaped contours of urban labor markets and employment opportunities, sociodemographic transformations have brought about changes in the urban class structure. The flight of whites to suburbia is clearly an important phase in this changing class structure and the crystallization of residential segregation. What is of more importance is the large-scale migration of high-income blacks and other racial minorities out of the inner-city neighborhoods. Gone with this selective out-migration are the social buffers and role models for the less affluent. Residents remaining in the impoverished inner-city neighborhoods are "the truly disadvantaged" (Wilson 1987), increasingly isolated from the mainstream.

Many studies have documented the devastating effects of living in an overwhelmingly impoverished neighborhood (for a review, see Sampson, Morenoff, and Gannon-Rowley 2002; Small and Newman 2001). The harmful "neighborhood effects" or "concentration effects" are manifold and far-reaching, including lack of quality schools, deprivation of conventional role models, inability to access jobs and job networks, and a high risk of crime and victimization. Without doubt, racial segregation is combined with the growing concentration of poverty. In parallel with growing neighborhood poverty and social isolation, these neighborhood effects on life chances grow more severe over time in many U.S. cities (Jargowsky 1997; Sampson and Wilson 1995).

GLOBALIZATION AND URBAN PROBLEMS IN DEVELOPING AND DEVELOPED COUNTRIES

Housing Problems

Urban space is highly differentiated by the quantitative and qualitative dimensions of housing conditions, such as size, location, extent of provision for basic services, and accessibility. Housing conditions are of central importance to the quality of life for everyone in settlement space. For example, residential location is tied to the provision of public services and access to employment opportunities. In most rapidly growing cities of the developing countries, housing is a critical problem precisely because

there are too few units. In Brazil, with about 36 million households in 1991, for example, the shortage reached almost 6 million; among the existing dwellings, over 10 million units needed to be repaired (UNCHS 2001:198). Developing countries are estimated to need 21 million housing units every year for this decade (2000–2010), and the figure will increase to 25 million for the following decade (2010–2020) to accommodate additional urban households (UNCHS 1999). As elsewhere, the more rapidly growing cities tend to have a higher proportion of housing shortages.

The problem of housing shortages is not confined to the developing countries. Accessibility to adequate housing is a critical issue for the urban poor in the United States and the United Kingdom. In both countries, about a third of all households still do not own their home and the rates of home ownership fell during the 1980s and increased again in the mid-1990s (UNCHS 1996:214). The rates of home ownership in central cities and growing regions are lower than the national average not only in the United States (U.S. Department of Housing and Urban Development [HUD] 1999) but also in the United Kingdom (Cambridge Econometrics 2002). The aggregated statistical figures also disguise great disparities between social groups in home ownership. The rates of home ownership among racial minorities, especially in the inner-city neighborhoods, are far below the national average, and female-headed households are less likely to be owners.

The problem of housing is not confined to the absolute number of housing deficits. A more serious problem is the quality of existing and new housing units such as substandard housing and overcrowding. In the developing countries, a very high proportion of the urban housing stock is substandard, being built on illegally occupied land with temporary materials, no authorization, and no access to basic infrastructure and services. About a quarter of the urban housing units in the developing countries are temporary structures, and more than a third of urban housing units have been constructed without compliance with local regulations (UNCHS 1999; see also Table 11.1). Overcrowding is another indicator of the quality of housing: When measured by floor area per person, urban dwellers in low-income countries occupy only a sixth of the average living space in high-income countries (UNCHS 2001:199). The severity of housing problems in growing cities of the developing world can be illustrated by the "hotbed" system in Calcutta, India, where two or three tenants rent the same bed in a room to use in turn over a 24-hour period (UNCHS 1996:217).

Given these housing conditions, informal or illegal housing is not unusual in most cities of the developing countries. For households on limited income, the possibility of owner-occupation is diminishing, and informal housing, including illegal subdivisions and sharing, becomes an important source of affordable, if not adequate, accommodation. By relying on informal housing, the urban poor may minimize costs and maximize income. Illegal subdivisions are the main source of housing supply for the urban poor, along with housing built in squatter settlements, in many cities of the developing world (Hardoy and Satterthwaite 1989). Sharing is another type of informal housing. Recent migrants arriving in a city with the help of family members, relatives, or friends tend to rely on migration networks for initial accommodation and job information (Lindert and Western 1991). The recent migrants and the urban poor settle in nonstandard, poor-quality housing usually nestled on the urban periphery where public utilities and infrastructure are typically not serviced (Peattie and Aldrete-Haas 1981). Informal settlements are not the same as squatter settlements: Although all people living in illegal settlements are commonly labeled as squatters, most are not squatters, because they occupy the land with permission or implicit approval of the landowner. Unlike squatters, informal residents are not usually threatened with eviction.[2]

The shortage of affordable housing for low-income urban households in the developing countries has resulted in a proliferation of squatter settlements or shantytowns (UNCHS 1999). Squatter settlements in some large cities are growing fast. The sheer number of urban migrants in these developing countries is too great for either the private or public sector to provide adequate housing or shelter, and thus many families end up in squatter settlements. Shantytowns have many names all over the world: *favellas* (Brazil), *bustees* (India), *barriadas* (Mexico), *problaciones* (Chile), *villas miseria* (Argentina), *bidonvilles* (Africa), *Kampungs* (South Asia). Despite different names, these squatter settlements have many features in common, including frequent public health crises, crime, crushing poverty, and no future for the next generation since few countries provide them with schools.

In the developing countries, shantytowns are large residential districts where the working class often lives. Many of the individuals who build these settlements are real estate entrepreneurs. The majority of shantytown dwellers live in rental housing (Datta 1990). The urban poor find cheap rental accommodation in shantytowns despite impoverished living conditions. Shantytowns are often the only places where the working class can find affordable housing. Informal settlements with predominantly rental accommodation are persistent in many cities of Latin America, where the demand for cheap rental accommodation far exceeds the supply and where controls on the quality of housing are negligible. These shantytowns are called *ciudades perdidas* in Mexico, *favelas de quinta* in Brazil, and *corralones* in El Salvador (UNCHS 1996:218). In general, shantytowns continue to grow because they are where the increasing numbers of poorly paid urban workers and migrants to the city can obtain shelter.

Visual images of informal settlements are bleak, and observers may assume that these are defeated, disorganized neighborhoods. Although social problems, such as limited urban services and infrastructure, persist in most informal and illegal settlements, case studies show that these are vital and viable communities. Many shantytowns possess a robust social order (Aina 1990). Their sociospatial networks give them access to jobs and some help when needed. A common conception is that life in these places is totally peripheral to the vibrancy of the urban economy. The marginality of shantytown inhabitants, however, is largely a myth (Perlman 1976). Many shantytowns support robust economies in themselves, including areas of real estate investment. They often are the location for small-business enterprises started by urban migrants. Shantytowns may also be the sites for small and medium-size factories. In addition, recent penetration of multinational corporations as part of the restructuring of the global economy has brought the support of subcontracting into the developing countries (Safa 1987). This phenomenon of vertical disintegration creates new manufacturing jobs and helps local entrepreneurs while integrating shantytowns into the global economy.

Homelessness

In many large cities of the developing countries, lack of adequate and affordable housing is quite common, and the scale of urban homelessness, when compared with the developed countries, is enormous. The number of the homeless around the world is estimated from 100 million to 1 billion, depending on its definition (UNCHS 1996:229, 2001:197). The lower-bound 100 million counts only those who have no shelter at all (i.e., houseless), and the upper-bound 1 billion includes those who are dwelling in substandard, insecure, or temporary shelters without provision for the most basic services such as safe water, sanitation, and drainage. Homelessness, measured either way, is a global problem, although the cold statistic itself does not accurately reveal the devastating condition of the homeless. For the many urban poor, sleeping in public buildings, parks, or other public space may be a part of their daily routine.

In a narrow sense, the homeless are those who cannot afford shelter by themselves. With no access to housing, they sleep outside or in public space such as streets, doorways, parks, and subways. In India, for example, the homeless are seen virtually everywhere: on pavements, in parks and unused water pipes, and under bridges (UNCHS 1996:230). Some of them are lucky enough to be accommodated in night shelters provided by local governments, voluntary organizations, or other social institutions. Persons or households under these two circumstances—sleeping rough and sleeping in night shelters—are highly visible and often stigmatized as criminals or dangerous at best. There are also a number of invisible or concealed homeless people who take advantage of housing opportunities offered by family members and friends because they cannot afford alternative accommodation by themselves (Springer 2000). Recent migrants in cities often double up with relatives and friends, thereby disguising their lack of accommodation. A large number of the concealed homeless consist also of women and children who have run away from domestic violence and sexual abuse (UNCHS 1996:230).

Although there is generally a sharp distinction in regard to the availability and quality of housing among cities in the developed and developing countries, the problem of homelessness is a growing concern in the developed countries as well. In the early 1990s, several observers pointed to the presence of apparently homeless people sitting on the city streets in the United States, although their exact number could not be counted (Applebome 1991). One observer suggested that during the decade of the 1990s, there were more people homeless than at any other time since the Great Depression of the 1930s (Blau 1992). Another estimated that on any given night, as many as 350,000 people in America were without shelter (Peroff 1987).[3] In addition, it has been noted that squatting as well as homelessness has become increasingly more common in the cities of Europe as well as the United States (Adams 1986).

Now homelessness is a growing phenomenon in Europe within countries that once possessed ambitious, publicly supported housing programs. In the 1995 report, the European Observatory on Homelessness estimated that there were 2 million homeless people in 12 member states in any one year in the early 1990s (Avramov 1995). This figure included nearly half a million homeless people in the United Kingdom, the second largest figure, followed by France, with a third of a million. Germany had the most extensive figure among member states, with an estimate of over 800,000 homeless people. The extent of homelessness varied from country to country in Europe for various reasons, including national economic situations, housing market conditions, real estate speculation, and welfare policies. This vast difference in reported homelessness among member countries, however, reflected also incompatible definitions adopted by countries (Smith 1999).

As in the United States, the problem of homelessness has gotten worse in Britain over the years. In England, for example, the number of households applying to local authorities for homeless assistance has increased from 102,650 during 1997–98 to 114,340 during 2000–01. Such statutory homelessness figures underestimate the scale of the homeless problem, because young single people and childless couples are not accepted by the local authority as being in "priority need," although they have nowhere to go. For this reason, the young homeless are increasingly visible in British cities (Smith 1999). In addition, the official figure excludes the "hidden homeless" living in temporary accommodation. *Crisis,* the homeless charity in the United Kingdom, estimates that there are still some 400,000 people stuck in temporary housing. In contrast to statutory homelessness, which is on the increase, the number of people sleeping rough on the streets has decreased by over two-thirds in the last three years (U.K. Department for Transport, Local Government and the Regions 2002). The dramatic reduction in rough sleepers is primarily attributed to government intervention and funding and the work of voluntary organizations that provide a wide range of services (Social Exclusion Unit 1998).

Most often the homeless population in both developing and developed countries consists of the unemployed, migrants, substance abusers, mentally ill people, racial and ethnic minorities, battered women, runaway youths, and street children. Among them, street children who work and live on the street are the most visible manifestation of urban poverty. However, some of the homeless sleeping in public buildings or open spaces have sufficient income to rent a room or bed. Others have homes in rural areas, but they move to cities for work temporarily during the slack season on the farm. They choose to sleep rough or in night shelters to maximize savings and to minimize costs (UNCHS 1996:230). Despite the distinct demographic profiles of the homeless, structural forces are underpinning the problem of homelessness. In many cities, the supply of adequate and affordable housing has fallen short of the demand. In the United States and some European countries, such as the United Kingdom and those of the former Soviet Union, welfare state restructuring and public assistance cuts have caused homelessness. In developing countries, the constant influx of migrants is funneled into urban areas, where there is neither a supply of "official" shelter nor full-time jobs. Under these conditions and without any improvements in the global economy, the presence of the homeless will persist in urban areas around the world.

Crime and Violence

Cities in both developed and developing countries are at a high risk of crime and violence. Urban residents, especially in large cities of the developing countries, are more exposed to crime and violence. In the developing countries, crime rates tend to increase in line with urbanization. The results of the International Crime Victim Survey (ICVS) indicate that over one in five urban residents of the developing world have experienced at least one incidence of property or violent crime during the reference year (United Nations International Crime and Justice Research Institute [UNICRI] 1995, 1998).[4] Sub-Saharan Africa has the highest rate of victimization for almost all types of crime. Violent crimes, including assault/threat and robbery, are more prevalent in Latin America, compared with other regions (Fajnzylber, Lederman, and Loayza 1998). Asian cities, by contrast, show the lowest level of crime and criminal victimization for all types of crime.

Crimes that occur in urban areas are, for the most part, violent or property-related street crimes. The occurrence of such acts is global in scope, although the nature and incidence of crime and violence vary from country to country, and from city to city. Despite differences in political, economic, and social systems, major cities around the globe face a similar problem of violent street crime (Body-Gendrot 2000). A fear of crime has become a universal urban experience for those living in large cities all over the world. Yet, urban dwellers in the developing world are more vulnerable to criminal victimization for several reasons. First of all, they are exposed to swift social changes that may further contribute to the risk of victimization, such as rapid rural-to-urban migration, squalid and overcrowded housing in slums and squatter settlements, family disruption, inadequate health and educational services, and insufficient job opportunities. In addition, costs of crime tend to be high among poor urban residents in the developing countries because of inadequate institutional coping mechanisms, including crime control and prevention measures, criminal justice systems, and social support networks.

When city dwellers speak of crime, they usually mean violent crime, which includes murder or homicide, infanticide, assault, rape, robbery, sexual abuse, and domestic violence. The definition and categories of violent crime differ from country to country, depending on cultural values and power relations (UNCHS 2001:223). A common denominator is visibility; all kinds of violent crimes are visible in cities. In recent years, urban violence has grown in most cities of the developing world in terms of the absolute number and as a proportion of all crimes. In some growing cities, for example, Tokyo and Singapore, overall violent crime has decreased, whereas in most cities of the developing world, urban violence has increased in accordance with urban growth.

Violence against women, or "gender-based violence," takes various forms, including rape, sexual abuse, domestic violence, and trafficking in women (United Nations Population Fund [UNFPA] 2000:25–30). The most common form of violence against women is domestic violence. Surveys in a variety of countries found that between a third and half (or more) of women reported being beaten by their partner (Heise, Ellsberg, and Gottemoeller 1999). Battering is the leading cause of injury to women in the United States. Women in the developing countries run the highest risk of rape and sexual abuse. A considerable proportion of victims are 15 years of age or under. Voluminous trafficking in women and girls occurs in Asian cities, where the sex industry is particularly active in connection with tourism (UNFPA 2000:29). Violence against women contributes to the increase in female homelessness in cities (UNCHS 1996:233).

Urban violence is often linked to the underground economy such as drug dealing, drug trafficking, gambling, or prostitution. Evidence shows a strong relationship between violent crime and drug use in the United States (National Institute of Justice 1990). Now the emergence of organized global crime is a new pressing threat to urban dwellers. Powerful criminal organizations operate a wide range of activities throughout the globe. The globalization of crime—that is, organized crime linked to the global criminal networks—is increasing (Castells 1998:166–205; UNCHS 2001:223). Global criminal networks are present in local streets and neighborhoods where the criminal economy thrives. Anything can be an object of transaction across borders where there is a demand and a market: drugs, weapons, illegal migrants, women, children, and body parts.

The United States has been known for the highest rate of violent crime among the developed countries (Zimring and Hawkins 1997), and now it possesses the largest per capita prison population in the world (Walmsley 2003). Tragic stories conveyed by news media daily give the impression that violent crime is rampant in cities and that the American city is a dangerous place to live or to hang out (Yanich 2001). Many people think that crime is on the increase, and cities have become more dangerous than they were in the past, but how accurate is that assessment? In the year 2000, the number of estimated victimizations was 25.9 million (Rennison 2001). This figure represents a fall in the rate of both property and violent crimes by 10 percent and 15 percent, respectively, between 1999 and 2000. The decline in violent crime is noteworthy. The level of violent crime in 2000 was the lowest since 1985 (Shaw-Taylor 2002), although recent reports on that level for the years 2001 and 2002 indicate that it is on the rise again. These up-and-down trends in official statistics and victimization surveys, however, should not be exaggerated, because self-reported data may reveal no discernible change in the rate of crime over time. In addition, if translated into probabilities, the chances of an American becoming a victim of property or violent crime are still very high, 1 in 11. Without doubt, this high likelihood of victimization increases the fear of crime among city dwellers and affects the well-being of urban areas.

To understand the nature of urban crime, it is necessary to view it as a spatial as well as a social phenomenon. In both developed and developing countries, the links between poverty, segregation, and crime are increasingly prominent (UNCHS 2001:223). Within any given city, the incidence of crime varies by neighborhood. In other words, urban space is partitioned into areas of relative safety and terror. In both developed and developing countries, crime and violence are more likely to take place within the poor marginalized urban areas (Bourguignon 2001). In the United States, crime and violence rates tend to be high in areas with a high concentration of poverty (Hagan and Peterson 1995). The demographic profiles of criminal offenders and their victims also show spatial aspects of violence and crime. Typically, criminal incidents follow the lines of class and racial segregation in the city; young, disadvantaged, minority males living in marginalized neighborhoods are the main perpetrators and also the principal victims of violence and crime (U.S. Department of Justice, Federal Bureau of Investigation 2000:215–6). Furthermore, they are at high risk for arrest and imprisonment (Hagan and Peterson 1995). Most incarcerated felons are either African American or Hispanic, and virtually all are poor. They come from the ghetto areas of the city, and their crimes usually were committed in those areas.

URBAN SOCIAL MOVEMENTS AND THE ALLEVIATION OF URBAN PROBLEMS

In this chapter, we examine urban problems in the global context, focusing on poverty and inequality, inadequate housing, homelessness, and crime. Along with increasing acknowledgment of global links, we must recognize differences existing among countries. For example, nations having the same position in the world system will display different patterns of urbanization, depending on state intervention, class structure, and other structural factors. It is unlikely, therefore, that urban problems are determined by global forces alone. National and local differences add to the complexity of urbanization and urban problems, as our sociospatial perspective suggests. Along with variations, there exist growing commonalities and links between large cities and regional agglomerations in both developed and developing countries: Evidence shows that the quality of life declines in massive metropolitan areas, especially those that are growing rapidly (Brockerhoff and Brennan 1997).

How do urban dwellers, especially the urban poor and the disadvantaged, respond to the conditions of living and the experience of everyday life? This is a critical issue often neglected in the discussions of urban problems (Gottdiener and Hutchison 2000:292–4). The urban poor and the disadvantaged are traditionally viewed as passive masses imbued with a so-called "culture of poverty" (Lewis 1966). According to this view, a culture of poverty evolves among the poor as a reaction and adaptation to their conditions of living and feelings of despair. Components of a culture of poverty include fatalism, lack of ambition, absence of a work ethic, and an alleged need for immediate gratification. These responses to the conditions of living—that is, the symptoms of poverty—become the cultural habits of the poor that are transmitted from generation to generation. The poor and the disadvantaged are also considered as parasites on the formal economy and callous to city and national political life. In this view, slums and squatter settlements lack internal social organization or cohesion and are isolated from the rest of society. This view is epitomized in the "marginality theory" of shantytown areas in developing countries (for a discussion, see Castells 1983:179–90; Perlman 1976).

This passive, "culture of poverty" view, however, does not fit urban reality today in both developing and developed countries, if we consider the ubiquity of urban social movements. Around the world, the urban poor are more likely to experience economic exploitation (e.g., subcontracting or industrial homework at a piece rate), political repression (e.g., threat of eviction), social stigma (e.g., being labeled as a "dangerous class"), and cultural exclusion (e.g., lack of education) in their everyday life and even at the street level. In this sense, they are marginalized, but they are never marginal in the social, political, economic, and cultural spheres of the larger society. They build and maintain social networks and community organizations in their neighborhoods, and they always must be reckoned with as a powerful political force. Social resources (e.g., job information, social support) constantly flow through these social networks and community organizations. They resort to self-help and coping mechanisms, organizing the household as the central unit for the production and consumption of livelihood and engaging in the informal sector. Among these and other responses of urban residents to the conditions of living, we pay particular attention to urban social movements that frequently arise in urban social settings.

Traditionally, social movements relied on local resource mobilization aimed at limited sociopolitical goals. Recent urban social movements, however, are more broad and diverse in scope, as characterized by "more conscious movements making much greater demands on the state" (Datta 1990:44). The poor and the disadvantaged have struggled against the government with demands for better health, education, and neighborhood services. Urban social movements take many forms, depending on targets and goals, such as movements for affordable housing (Castells 1983; Ramirez 1990), making squatter and shantytown settlements legal (Schneier 1990), promoting the self-governing of squatter communities (Castells 1983), and demanding greater political representation (Mabogunje 1990). Recent urban social movements are concerned with social and political effects no longer limited to local areas. As a result of organized opposition to global restructuring agents, such as the IMF or transnational corporations, urban social movements have broadened their perspectives to deal with issues that affect all levels of society.

Urban social movements emerged as central actors originally in Latin American cities during the 1960s and 1970s. Now, urban social movements are common among city dwellers in both developed and developing countries. For example, there is a growing movement of women around the world mobilizing around the issue of women's rights and empowerment. In particular, women in the developing countries play a critical role in urban politics and urban social movements (Coquery-Vidrovitch 1990). Due to fewer government services and economic contraction, women in the third world are forced to engage in various survival strategies. Women take advantage both of the informal economy and of shantytown dwellings to earn a living. The active involvement of women in urban social movements is driven by their active role in urban shantytown life.

The growing number of class-based union activities is another recent development of political struggles within the city. As manufacturing jobs have shipped to the third world, an associated rise in union activity and class struggles has resulted. Countries such as Brazil and India, for example, have formidable industrial labor forces, and with them have come active trade union movements and class-based political action. Urban social movements are different from these class-based labor movements because of their openness of participation and their

generality of interests. Various urban social movements (e.g., squatter movements, environmental movements, and women's rights movements) that spring up in cities involve new patterns of local political activity that are independent of or crosscut class relations.

Recent urban social movements are connected to the global economy and directed toward its agents of international control. In the 1970s, for example, the IMF, which controls most of the third world debt and national financing, called for structural adjustment and austerity measures among all its client countries. In turn, national governments responded by eliminating subsidies on food and other consumer goods. This placed a severe burden on households. In response to the threat of hunger and increased misery, residents of cities began rioting to protest food subsidy cutbacks (Walton 1987; Walton and Ragin 1990). The IMF riots or food riots were powerful political events that caused the fall of state regimes in many third world countries such as Liberia in 1979, Tunisia and Morocco in 1981, the Dominican Republic in 1984 and 1985, Brazil in 1983, and Chile in 1983 and 1985 (Datta 1990).

When urban social movements recede, they usually leave a strong network of nongovernmental organizations (NGOs) that play a central role in resource mobilization for the disadvantaged. Together with urban social movements, the involvement of the various NGOs is critical to urban well-being in developing countries. Under the pressure of the heavy debt burden, many third world states became less able to manage urban problems, let alone facilitate development. The waning power of third world states is attributed to debt crisis and the externally imposed constraints. The growing debt crisis and the structural adjustment measures mandated by the IMF, World Bank, and other transnational financial institutions seriously undermined the ability and authority of third world states. As states become weak and unable to allocate necessary resources to cope with growing urban problems, the role of NGOs in urban development becomes more evident.

Various NGOs fill the void created by the weakening state. Whereas the power and capacity of third world states is crumbling, the realms of civil society are growing stronger and more influential (Migdal 1988). NGOs, including churches, self-help groups, and community organizations, increasingly take over the responsibility of providing basic public services (Bratton 1989). The growing involvement of NGOs in urban development (e.g., providing housing, safe water, education, health care) ameliorates urban problems stemming from overurbanization, if they work properly. However, not all NGOs work for positive effects. Some are "aligned with foreign capital and therefore more interested in promoting profits than development" (Bradshaw and Schafer 2000:103).

At the same time, it is also easy to overemphasize the significance of these NGOs, despite their almost romanticized popularity among left-wing ideologues. When the United Nations held an international meeting of NGOs in Durban, South Africa, during the year 2001, it rapidly disintegrated into a shameful and mindless exercise in the virulent condemnation of Israel to the exclusion of addressing the terribly pressing urban problems that NGOs once engaged. The ease with which pro-Palestinian and, in some disturbing cases, openly anti-Jewish sentiments co-opted this international meeting under the auspices of the United Nations clearly implies that such local movements alone will ultimately be able to do little to alleviate the world's urban problems. For example, we note that the headquarters of most international nongovernmental organizations (INGOs) are located in the key *developed* countries of the world. In addition, there are many NGOs that advance the interests of global capital and transnational financial institutions, rather than facilitate balanced urban development. The World Bank has launched various projects in collaboration with NGOs, and its partnership with these local groups gives their leadership financial resources that are often spent without accountability as well as providing them with considerable political clout vis-à-vis other local social movements more concerned with the alleviation of urban problems. Most recently, reviews of these projects have pointed to their respective irrelevancy in the drive to improve the living conditions of the urban poor and poorly sheltered. Instead, they often foster the interests of global capital. Finally, the increasing involvement of NGOs in development initiatives undermines the power and legitimacy of third world national governments, which often have well-meaning social welfare programs of their own not tied to global interests (Ndegwa 1996).

To be sure, the urban problems of developing countries continue to grow without much relief. Poverty and overurbanization, in particular, seem intractable today. Homelessness and crime are problems that also have a significant impact on the quality of urban life in advanced industrial societies. In this chapter, we have focused on describing the most pressing urban problems and have also offered a critical evaluation of the grassroots attempts to remedy them. It is beyond the scope of this chapter to discuss possible solutions, considering the complexity of the problems themselves and their considerable variation among the countries of the world.

NOTES

1. The MCSUI was conducted in Atlanta, Boston, Detroit, and Los Angeles from 1992 to 1994. Data collected from the MCSUI contain comprehensive information about labor market dynamics, residential segregation, and neighborhood characteristics useful to understand the "contours of deepening urban inequality" (Johnson, Oliver, and Bobo 1994; for a review, see O'Connor, Tilly, and Bobo 2000).

2. Eviction is the most imminent threat, immanent in all squatter settlements. Between 1983 and 1988, for example, 720,000 people lost their homes to demolitions and redevelopments in Seoul, Korea, and 90 percent of those evicted did not obtain an apartment in the redeveloped site (Asian Coalition for Housing Rights 1989; UNCHS 1996:245).

3. In the United States, homelessness grew during the 1980s (Burt 1992). A recent estimate of the homeless in the United States amounts to 750,000 on any given night (Alston 1998).

4. Thirteen developing countries participated in the ICVS conducted during the period 1992–94 (UNICRI 1995). In 1996–97, the survey was carried out in 18 countries (UNICRI 1998). These surveys, administered by the UNICRI, focused on individuals at 16 years and older who reported being victims of crime. Samples were mainly drawn from a major city of each participating country.

REFERENCES

Adams, C. 1986. "Homeless in the Postindustrial City: Views from London and Philadelphia." *Urban Affairs Quarterly* 21:527–49.

Aina, T. A. 1990. "Shanty Town Economy: The Case of Metropolitan Lagos, Nigeria." Pp. 133–48 in *Third World Urbanization: Reappraisals and New Perspectives,* edited by S. Datta. Stockholm, Sweden: HSFR.

Alston, P. 1998. "Hardship in the Midst of Plenty." Pp. 29–31 in *The Progress of Nations.* New York: UNICEF. Retrieved October 14, 2002, from www.unicef.org/pon98/30–35.pdf.

Applebome, P. 1991. "Although Urban Blight Worsens, Most People Don't Feel Its Impact." *New York Times,* January 28, p. A20.

Asian Coalition for Housing Rights. 1989. "Evictions in Seoul, South Korea." *Environment and Urbanization* 1:89–94.

Avramov, D. 1995. *Homeless in the European Union.* Brussels, Belgium: FEANTSA.

Blau, J. 1992. *The Visible Poor: Homelessness in the United States.* New York: Oxford University Press.

Body-Gendrot, S. 2000. *The Social Control of Cities? A Comparative Perspective.* Oxford, England: Blackwell.

Bourguignon, F. 2001. "Crime as a Social Cost of Poverty and Inequality: A Review Focusing on Developing Countries." Pp. 171–91 in *Facets of Globalization: International and Local Dimensions of Development,* edited by S. Yusuf, S. Evenett, and W. Wu. Discussion Paper No. 415. Washington, DC: World Bank.

Bradshaw, Y. W. and E. Fraser. 1989. "City Size, Economic Development, and Quality of Life in China: New Empirical Evidence." *American Sociological Review* 54:986–1003.

Bradshaw, Y. W. and M. J. Schafer. 2000. "Urbanization and Development: The Emergence of International Nongovernmental Organizations amid Declining States." *Sociological Perspectives* 43:97–116.

Bratton, M. 1989. "The Politics of Government-NGO Relations in Africa." *World Development* 17:569–87.

Brockerhoff, M. 1999. "Urban Growth in Developing Countries: A Review of Projections and Predictions." *Population and Development Review* 25:757–78.

Brockerhoff, M. and E. Brennan. 1997. *The Poverty of Cities in the Developing World.* Policy Research Division, Working Paper No. 96. New York: Population Council.

Burt, M. R. 1992. *Over the Edge: The Growth of Homelessness in the 1980s.* Washington, DC: Urban Institute Press.

Cairncross, S., J. E. Hardoy, and D. Satterthwaite. 1990. "The Urban Context." Pp. 1–24 in *The Poor Die Young: Housing and Health in Third World Cities,* edited by J. E. Hardoy, S. Cairncross, and D. Satterthwaite. London, England: Earthscan.

Caldeira, T. 1996. "Building Up Walls: The New Pattern of Spatial Segregation in São Paulo." *International Social Science Journal* 147:55–66.

Cambridge Econometrics. 2002. *The Imbalance between the Growth of Household Numbers and Regional Housing Supply Will Widen Sharply in the South of England over the Next Decade.* Press Release. Retrieved November 6, 2002, from www.camecon.co.uk/whatsnew/releases/pdffiles/reg022.pdf.

Castells, M. 1983. *The City and the Grassroots: A Cross-Cultural Theory of Urban Social Movements.* Berkeley, CA: University of California Press.

———. 1998. *The Information Age: Economy, Society, and Culture.* Vol. 3, *End of Millennium.* Oxford, England: Blackwell.

Coquery-Vidrovitch, C. 1990. "A History of African Urbanization: Labor, Women and the Informal Sector—A Survey of Recent Studies." Pp. 75–89 in *Third World Urbanization: Reappraisals and New Perspective,* edited by S. Datta. Stockholm, Sweden: HSFR.

Daley, P. 1998. "Black African in Great Britain: Spatial Concentration and Segregation." *Urban Studies* 35:1703–24.

Datta, S., ed. 1990. *Third World Urbanization: Reappraisals and New Perspectives.* Stockholm, Sweden: HSFR.

Fajnzylber, P., D. Lederman, and N. Loayza. 1998. *Determinants of Crime Rates in Latin America and the World: An Empirical Assessment.* Washington, DC: World Bank.

Findley, S. E. 1993. "The Third World City: Development Policy and Issues." Pp. 1–31 in *Third World Cities: Problems, Policies, and Prospects,* edited by J. D. Kasarda and A. M. Parnell. Newbury Park, CA: Sage.

Firebaugh, G. 1979. "Structural Determinants of Urbanization in Asia and Latin America, 1950–1970." *American Sociological Review* 44:199–215.

Frey, W. H. and D. Myers. 2002. "Neighborhood Segregation in Single-Race and Multirace America: A Census 2000 Study in Cities and Metropolitan Areas." Working Paper. Washington, DC: The Fannie Mae Foundation. Retrieved October 7, 2002, from www.censusscope.org/FreyWPFinal.pdf.

Gottdiener, M. 1994. *The Production of Urban Space.* 2nd ed. Austin, TX: University of Texas.

———. 2002. "Urban Analysis as Merchandising: The 'LA School' and the Understanding of Metropolitan Development." Pp. 159–80 in *Understanding the City: Contemporary and Future Perspectives,* edited by J. Eade and C. Mele. Oxford, England: Blackwell.

Gottdiener, M. and R. Hutchison. 2000. *The New Urban Sociology.* 2nd ed. Boston, MA: McGraw-Hill.

Gugler, J. 1982. "Overurbanization Reconsidered." *Economic Development and Cultural Change* 31:173–89.

Hagan, J. and R. D. Peterson, eds. 1995. *Crime and Inequality.* Stanford, CA: Stanford University Press.

Hardoy, J. E. and D. Satterthwaite. 1989. *Squatter Citizen: Life in the Urban Third World.* London, England: Earthscan.

Harvey, D. 1989a. *The Condition of Postmodernity.* Oxford, England: Blackwell.

——. 1989b. "From Managerialism to Entrepreneurialism: The Formation of Urban Governance in Late Capitalism." *Geografiska Annaler* 71B:3–17.

Heise, L., M. Ellsberg, and M. Gottemoeller. 1999. *Ending Violence against Women.* Population Reports, Series L. No. 11. Baltimore, MD: Population Information Program, Johns Hopkins School of Public Health. Retrieved September 6, 2002, from www.jhuccp.org/pr/111edsum.stm.

Jargowsky, P. A. 1997. *Poverty and Place: Ghettos, Barrios, and the American City.* New York: Russell Sage.

Johnson, J. H., M. L. Oliver, and L. D. Bobo. 1994. "Understanding the Contours of Deepening Urban Inequality: Theoretical Underpinnings and Research Design of Multi-City Study." *Urban Geography* 15:77–89.

Kasarda, J. D. and E. M. Crenshaw. 1991. "Third World Urbanization: Dimensions, Theories, and Determinants." *Annual Review of Sociology* 17:467–501.

Katwala, S. 2001. "The Truth of Multicultural Britain." *The Observer,* November 25. Retrieved October 5, 2002, from www.observer.co.uk/race/story/0,11255,605337,00.html.

Kennedy, M. D. and D. A. Smith. 1989. "East Central European Urbanization: A Political Economy of the World-System Perspective." *International Journal of Urban and Regional Research* 13:597–623.

Lewis, O. 1966. *La Vida: A Puerto Rican Family in the Culture of Poverty.* New York: Random House.

Lindert, P. and A. van Western. 1991. "Household Shelter Strategies in Comparative Perspective: Evidence from Low Income Groups in Bamako and La Paz." *World Development* 19:1007–28.

Logan, J. 2001. *Ethnic Diversity Grows, Neighborhood Integration Lags Behind.* State University of New York, University at Albany, Lewis Mumford Center. Retrieved October 5, 2002, from www.albany.edu/mumford/census.

Mabogunje, A. 1990. "Organization of Urban Communities in Nigeria." *International Social Science Journal* 42:355–66.

Marcoux, A. 1998. "The Feminization of Poverty: Claims, Facts, and Data Needs." *Population and Development Review* 24:131–9.

Massey, D. S. and N. A. Denton. 1993. *American Apartheid: Segregation and the Making of the Underclass.* Cambridge, MA: Harvard University Press.

Mele, C. 2000. *Selling the Lower East Side: Culture, Real Estate, and Resistance in New York City.* Minneapolis, MN: University of Minnesota Press.

Migdal, J. 1988. *Strong Societies and Weak States: State-Society Relations and State Capabilities in the Third World.* Princeton. NJ: Princeton University Press.

Mumford, L. 1961. *The City in History.* New York: Harcourt Brace Jovanovich.

National Institute of Justice. 1990. *Drug Use Forecasting.* Annual Report, 1988. Washington, DC: U.S. Department of Justice.

Ndegwa, S. 1996. *The Two Faces of Civil Society: NGOs and Politics in Africa.* New York: Kumarian.

O'Connor, A., C. Tilly, and L. D. Bobo, eds. 2000. *Urban Inequality: Evidence from Four Cities.* New York: Russell Sage.

Peattie, L. and J. A. Aldrete-Haas. 1981. "'Marginal' Settlements in Developing Countries: Research, Advocacy of Policy, and Evolution of Programs." *Annual Review of Sociology* 7:157–75.

Perlman, J. E. 1976. *The Myth of Marginality: Urban Poverty and Politics in Rio de Janeiro.* Berkeley, CA: University of California Press.

Peroff, K. 1987. "Who Are the Homeless and How Many Are There." Pp. 33–45 in *The Homeless in Contemporary Society,* edited by R. Bingham, R. Green, and S. White. Beverly Hills, CA: Sage.

Piel, G. 1997. "The Urbanization of Poverty Worldwide." *Challenge* 40 (1):58–68.

Ramirez, R. 1990. "Urbanization, Housing and the (Withdrawing) State: The Production-Reproduction Nexus." Pp. 204–34 in *Third World Urbanization: Reappraisals and New Perspective,* edited by S. Datta. Stockholm, Sweden: HSFR.

Rennison, C. M. 2001. *Criminal Victimization, 2000: Changes 1999–2000 with Trends 1993–2000.* Washington, DC: U.S. Department of Justice, Bureau of Justice Statistics.

Safa, H. I. 1987. "Urbanization, the Informal Economy and State Policy in Latin America." Pp. 252–74 in *The Capitalist City,* edited by M. P. Smith and J. R. Feagin. Oxford, England: Blackwell.

Sampson, R. J., J. D. Morenoff, and T. Gannon-Rowley. 2002. "Assessing 'Neighborhood Effects': Social Processes and New Directions in Research." *Annual Review of Sociology* 28:443–78.

Sampson, R. J. and W. J. Wilson. 1995. "Toward a Theory of Race, Crime, and Urban Inequality." Pp. 37–54 in *Crime and Inequality,* edited by J. Hagan and R. D. Peterson. Stanford, CA: Stanford University Press.

Sassen, S. 1991. *The Global City: New York, London, Tokyo.* Princeton, NJ: Princeton University Press.

Schneier, G. 1990. "Latin America: A Tale of Cities." *International Social Science Journal* 125:337–54.

Shaw-Taylor, Y. 2002. "Data Watch: Changes in Violent Crime in the 100 Largest Cities of the US: 1980–2000." *Cities* 19:123–8.

Small, M. L. and K. Newman. 2001. "Urban Poverty after the Truly Disadvantaged: The Rediscovery of the Family, the Neighborhood, and the Culture." *Annual Review of Sociology* 27:23–45.

Smith, D. A. 1996. *The Third World Cities in Global Perspective: The Political Economy of Uneven Urbanization.* Boulder, CO: Westview.

Smith, D. A. and M. Timberlake. 1993. "World Cities: A Political Economy/Global Network Approach." *Research in Urban Theory* 3:181–207.

Smith, J. 1999. "Youth Homelessness in the UK: A European Perspective." *Habitat International* 23:63–77.

Social Exclusion Unit. 1998. *Rough Sleeping.* Retrieved October 5, 2002, from www.socialexclusionunit.gov .uk/publications/reports/html/rough/srhome.htm.

Springer, S. 2000. "Homelessness: A Proposal for a Global Definition and Classification." *Habitat International* 24:475–84.

U.K. Department for Transport, Local Government and the Regions. 2002. *More Than a Roof: A Report into Tracking Homelessness.* Retrieved October 7, 2002, from www.dtlr.gov.uk/information/homelessness/index.

United Nations Centre for Human Settlements (UNCHS). 1987. *Global Reports on Human Settlements.* Oxford, England: Oxford University Press.

——. 1996. *An Urbanizing World.* (Global Report on Human Settlements 1996). Oxford, England: Oxford University Press.

——. 1999. *Basic Facts on Urbanization.* Nairobi, Kenya: United Nations Centre for Human Settlements (Habitat).

——. 2001. *Cities in a Globalizing World.* (Global Report on Human Settlements 2001). London, England: Earthscan.

United Nations International Crime and Justice Research Institute (UNICRI). 1995. *Criminal Victimization of the Developing World.* Publication No. 55. Rome, Italy: UNICRI.

——. 1998. *Victims of Crime in the Developing World.* Publication No. 57. Rome, Italy: UNICRI.

United Nations Population Division (UNPD). 2001. *World Urbanization Prospects: The 1999 Revision.* New York: United Nations.

United Nations Population Fund (UNFPA). 2000. *The State of World Population 2000: Lives Together, Worlds Apart: Men and Women in a Time of Change.* New York: UNFPA.

U.S. Department of Housing and Urban Development (HUD). 1999. *The State of the Cities, 1999.* Third Annual Report. Retrieved November 6, 2002, from www.huduser.org/publications/pdf/soc99.pdf.

U.S. Department of Justice, Federal Bureau of Investigation. 2000. *Crime in the United States 2000: Uniform Crime Reports.* Washington, DC: U.S. Government Printing Office. Retrieved August 12, 2002, from www.fbi.gov/ucr/00cius.htm.

Walmsley, R. 2003. *World Prison Population List.* 4th ed. London, England: U.K. Home Office Research, Development and Statistics Directorate.

Walton, J. 1987. "Urban Protest and the Global Political Economy: The IMF Riots." Pp. 364–86 in *The Capitalist City,* edited by M. Smith and J. Feagin. Oxford, England: Blackwell.

Walton, J. and C. Ragin. 1990. "Global and National Sources of Political Protest: Third World Responses to the Debt Crisis." *American Sociological Review* 55:876–90.

Waters, M. 1995. *Globalization.* London, England: Routledge.

Wilson, W. J. 1987. *The Truly Disadvantaged: The Inner City, the Underclass, and Public Policy.* Chicago, IL: University of Chicago Press.

——. 1996. *When Work Disappears: The World of the New Urban Poor.* New York: Random House.

Yanich, D. 2001. "Location, Location, Location: Urban and Suburban Crime on Local TV News." *Journal of Urban Affairs* 23:221–41.

Zimring, F. E. and G. Hawkins. 1997. *Crime Is Not the Problem: Lethal Violence in America.* New York: Oxford University Press.

WORK-RELATED SOCIAL PROBLEMS

TERESA A. SULLIVAN

University of Texas

S ocial problems related to work are among the most durable and important social problems because work is the principal source of income for individuals and families throughout the world. In fact, the theory and conceptualization of social problems owe much to social thought on issues that face workers in the labor market.

CONCEPTUALIZING WORK AS A SOCIAL PROBLEM

In his germinal work on social problems, C. Wright Mills used a work-related problem to show the difference between an individual's "trouble" and a social problem. In *The Sociological Imagination* (1959), Mills discusses unemployment as an example of a situation that is distressing and difficult for the individual, but is not necessarily attributable solely to shortcomings in the individual's abilities or character. Instead, unemployment varies in predictable ways. Unemployment rates vary, for example, according to the business cycle, region, industry, and demographic characteristics of the

workers. These variations do not seem to be explained by changes in the motivation, attitudes, or skills of the individuals who are unemployed.

There is no question that unemployment is distressing to the individual and is associated with a variety of additional problems that stem from both the lack of income and the loss of work-related status. Unemployed workers experience greater levels of mental and physical illness, higher risk of substance abuse, increased levels of family tension and violence, and a variety of financial consequences, including diminished levels of living, increased debt, and a higher risk of bankruptcy (Sullivan et al. 2000). For the unemployed individual, unemployment is a "trouble" and potentially the threshold to a series of negative events. The more prolonged the period of unemployment is, the greater the likelihood of negative events. "Troubles," however, even if widely shared, do not necessarily constitute a social problem. A social problem arises from a structural dislocation in a social institution.

Mills recognized a battle in political and popular opinion, during the Great Depression of the 1930s, over the origins of the widespread unemployment experienced throughout the industrialized countries. Some editorial writers favored an individualistic explanation, arguing that jobs were available but the unemployed workers were either unable or unwilling to take those jobs. The unemployed were, in effect, accused of being greedy because they were unwilling to work for the prevailing wage. By implication, such explanations relegated unemployment to "troubles," a private misfortune of individuals but not a subject for public policy. Indeed, there was a strong implication that the unemployment resulted from character flaws of the unemployed, such as laziness or a lack of ambition.

Others argued, by contrast, that the unemployment was so widespread that it must be systematic, originating from a structural source. Social scientists offered differing structural explanations for the unemployment. The economist Maynard Keynes, for example, explained the systematic aspect of unemployment with such economic variables as effective demand, deflation, and savings rates. Marxist theorists argued that the high unemployment rate was a result of the internal workings of capitalism. What the social science explanations had in common, however, was the implication that the source of widespread unemployment was structural—that is, it was beyond the ability of the individuals to affect, and so constituted a social problem. A further implication of social problems is that their solution must be addressed at a level of aggregation larger than the individual. The more structural, social problems-based explanations of unemployment were ultimately more influential and led to the development of social policies, such as the unemployment compensation system, to alleviate the impact of unemployment.

The very conceptualization of a phenomenon as a social problem may have its own policy effects. During the 1930s there was great controversy over exactly how many workers were unemployed. The larger the number, the more plausible the structural explanation would be, but there was no reliable source, public or private, for unemployment data. The U.S. government's development of measures of unemployment, which began in 1937, arose from the perceived need to understand and monitor unemployment through a direct empirical measure. Once Congress began to legislate some measures to alleviate unemployment, the data system became even more important as a way to monitor how well the new policies worked.

CLASSES OF EXPLANATION

Even for social scientists who generally accept the social problems perspective, the approaches to studying unemployment and other work-related social problems vary a great deal. An important difference lies in the level of analysis that is used in the studies. Initially these differing levels of analysis may appear to echo the competing individual-versus-structural arguments that dominated the political debate over unemployment. This apparent similarity is misleading, however.

Microlevel analysis is based upon data on individual workers. Occasionally politicians continue to imply that the unemployed are basically lazy, improvident, or gaming the system, but the fairly crude individualistic explanations of the 1930s have become increasingly rare. Today when social scientists use individual level or microdata, they are trying to explain the differential experience of workers in the labor market. This is quite different from an explanation that blames the victims for their unemployment. Instead, social scientists who analyze individual-level data try to identify the workers who are at higher risk of unemployment or other work-related social problems. These higher risks, in turn, often originate in structural arrangements. Thus, the use of microdata can be consistent with a social problems perspective.

The individual worker characteristics that are usually analyzed include education and training, geographic location and mobility, age, race, and gender, and attitudes or opinions. Some of these characteristics are associated with disadvantage because of social problems that are not directly work-related, but intersect with the realm of work. A worker may be poorly educated, for example, because a better education was not available or was too expensive too pursue. Race and gender may be associated with unemployment because of residual discrimination in the labor market. The human capital theory in economics and the more recent social capital theory in sociology and political science analyze characteristics that might leave some workers isolated from the networks that provide preferred jobs. Thus, an analysis based on the individual worker does not necessarily entail an explanation that blames workers for their own plight.

Structural explanations, by contrast, look to social, cultural, and organizational sources for the labor market problems (for an example, see Korpi 2002). The explanatory variables are more often couched in terms of aggregated or group variables. Thus, a structuralist might look to such issues as union activity, firm competitiveness, levels of bureaucratic authority, technological innovation, and occupational composition. High rates of layoff, for example, may be studied within the framework of profit margins, competitiveness of an industry, and weak unionization. Such analyses easily accommodate a social problems perspective and may point to more direct policy interventions.

In addition, analysts who use the social problems perspective may mix the analytic levels in their studies. Thus, the relatively high unemployment rates of young black women result from structural features such as labor market discrimination and greater incidence of layoffs, while their voluntary exit from seasonal or temporary work is associated with their family characteristics (Reid 2002).

ECONOMIC DEVELOPMENT AND WORK-RELATED SOCIAL PROBLEMS

Which work-related social problems are important or salient within a society varies with the general level of economic development, the division of labor within the society, the power relationships among societies, and the social stratification system within the society. To take the extreme example, in a hunter-gatherer society the principal work-related issues related to how abundantly the environment provided foodstuffs. Membership in the tribe guaranteed job security, because everyone of an age to contribute had a role in securing food and shelter. In a medieval society where most people were peasants whose work was determined by tradition and family status, the principal work-related problems turned

on how the feudal lord behaved. That there would be a role for every individual, probably in agriculture, was a given, and job security was not the principal issue. Job mobility was tightly regulated within the feudal society, and only a relatively few urban dwellers or clergy could escape from doing the same work that their parents had done.

In an advanced industrial society, the situation is much more complex, with workers affected by many different occupational specialties, different industries, complex global relationships, and interrelated actions of the government, firms, and impersonal market forces. It is now rare for individuals to gain their work identity principally through custom, tradition, or family inheritance. Instead, most workers compete within a labor market, and true labor markets have become more common throughout the world. Thus, in the United States, in Canada, in Australia, and in the European Union, but also in other parts of the world, the central work-related issue of the twenty-first century is job security.

SECTORAL TRANSFORMATION OF WORK

The complexity of the modern labor market was accomplished through the transformation of many economies from primarily extractive to primarily industrial and finally to primarily service-producing. Every society needs agricultural products, human-made goods and tools, and services. The sectoral transformation refers to the *changing proportions* of the working force that is devoted to these tasks. Until the early modern period, every society relied principally on extractive industries, and most workers were engaged in horticulture, livestock production, fishing, or mining, with a few workers in skilled trades as builders or artificers.

In the early modern period, industrialization brought the factory system and wide-scale employment in manufacturing. Rapid population growth and urbanization accompanied the era of industrialization, but the transformation was uneven. Western Europe and later the United States became leaders in manufacturing, with a persistently large agricultural sector. Because Western Europe and the United States experienced the demographic transition—declining mortality rates and high fertilityrates—during this period, farmers could replace themselves with children on the farm and still send additional sons and daughters to the cities to work in factories. In addition, immigration furnished additional potential factory workers to the large cities of the United States.

In early industrialization, the colonies and other less developed areas of the world served as major markets for manufactured goods but were themselves principally producers of agricultural products and minerals. Since World War II, the former colonies and many other countries have become industrialized, and the accompanying work-related issues of industrialization have developed in them. Even sending out many family members to seek work may no longer be an effective strategy for survival (Gonzalez de la Rocha 2001). As it happens, the modern demographic transition affected Asia, Latin America, and Africa after World War II, with resulting rapid population growth to fuel the growth of cities and the development of factories (Bloom and Brender 1993). As we see below, the export of manufacturing jobs from the advanced countries to the newly developing countries became another source of job insecurity in the advanced countries.

Industrialization typically changes the nature of work by dissolving the old work relationships, which were often embedded in customary and familial arrangements, and creating new, distinct relationships between an employer and an individual worker. This relationship could be personal or even familial, but could also be coldly impersonal. Typically, the larger the workplace is, the more impersonal the relationship is likely to be. Larger workplaces tend to become more bureaucratically organized, with specialized managers and multiple levels of supervision. As workplaces grow larger and more complex, management may view labor abstractly as one more factor of production. Although maintaining the quality of labor is essential to maintaining the quality of the product, managers look to reduce their labor costs whenever possible. Thus, effective managers seek to maximize the quality of labor while minimizing its costs.

Manufacturing technology made it possible for managers to view "labor" abstractly because the technology eroded the importance of the individual,

skilled worker. Factory machinery typically reduced the level of skill needed to perform many manufacturing jobs. In the early stages of industrialization, skilled craft workers played a major role in developing the new factories, designing the machinery, and ensuring the quality of the finished product. But as industrial technology improved, machines often took over the more skilled parts of the craftworker's job. In textiles, for example, machines replaced the skills of weavers, spinners, and other workers, and textile work became a famous example of an industry whose workers were principally machine tenders (Blauner 1964). One indication of how technology had transformed work was that these factory workers were often referred to as "hands." Because it took the boss relatively little time to teach a new worker to tend the machines, factory workers came to be viewed as interchangeable cogs.

Marx referred to the "reserve army of unemployed," by which he meant the many urban residents, some of whom were recently displaced from rural areas, who were available for hire in the new factory system. Many of these unemployed workers would be willing to work for slightly lower wages than the factory workers who were already employed, and so their existence exerted a continuous downward pressure on wages. Arbitrary firing was commonplace because the costs of turnover were low: the boss could always replace the factory hand with another worker, who could be trained in a short period of time. Thus, the social problem of job insecurity resulted from all of these influences: the transformation to manufacturing, the substitution of machine energy for worker skill, the excess supply of labor, and the relatively powerless position of the individual worker.

Under these conditions, early factory owners were able to demand very long hours of work from labor, often in appalling working conditions and at relatively low wages. Workers who expressed dissatisfaction could be fired immediately, with no recourse. Job security was achieved only at the price of immediate compliance and obedience.

Eventually, the long hours and hazardous conditions themselves became identified as problems. In addition, the low pay often forced families to send all of their members, even the youngest, into the labor market to earn enough to keep the family supplied with necessities. Thus, by the turn of the twentieth century, issues such as family instability were indirectly work-related social problems, and child labor was a directly work-related social problem. Gonzalez de la Rocha (2001) described this type of situation in modern-day Guadalajara, Mexico.

These social problems, however, were in some ways subordinate to the primary issue of work instability that had been introduced by the factory system. In response to the reality of work instability, workers and legislators developed measures to provide due process to individual workers and to respect the workers' right to organize. States and to some extent the federal government developed laws and policies to regulate the length of the workday, the minimum working age, compensation for overtime, and the general safety of the workplace. Unions, in particular, sought to protect the job security of their members. Although companies could still lay workers off, collective bargaining agreements typically specified which workers would be laid off first—usually protecting workers with greater seniority.

In the early stages of industrialization, the reserve army came to the cities where the factories were located. This process slowed and then stopped. By the middle of the twentieth century in the United States, both population growth and immigration had slowed dramatically. For a variety of reasons, including the effect of unions and government policy, the unemployment rate was relatively low (Kenworthy 2002). This was also the time when manufacturing leaders began to conceptualize the "reserve army" on a national basis. There were large labor forces available in the less industrialized cities of the South and Southwest, where prevailing wages were considerably lower than in the North and East. In addition, these parts of the country were said to have "favorable business climates," an expression that often referred to an absence of unions, the availability of tax breaks, and less regulation of health and safety. Many older factories in the North and East closed and new factories opened, with lower wage bills, to take advantage of the "cheap labor."

By the late twentieth century, the expansion of industrialization to additional countries in Asia, the Caribbean, Eastern Europe, and Africa opened an additional opportunity for managers to reduce the costs of manufacturing labor by exporting manufacturing jobs. In effect, managers can now shop globally for the cheapest labor (Adler 2000). From the perspective of the original country, this problem is sometimes called the runaway shop. But local elites and even local workers often welcome the runaway shops as a source of additional jobs and further economic development. For workers in manufacturing, however, job security can be threatened by potential replacements worldwide who are willing to work for lower wages.

The runaway shops point to ways that institutional arrangements may affect unemployment. The wages that workers are willing to accept are not the only variable that attracts runaway shops; owners and managers also look for "flexible" labor markets. Labor markets can be characterized as relatively "flexible," in terms of how easy it is for an employer to hire or discharge workers, or as relatively "rigid," in terms of how difficult it is to do either of these things because of payroll taxes, required fringe benefits, legally enforced employment rights, and so on.

DiPrete et al. (2001) examined how unemployment varies between France and Sweden. Both countries have a welfare system that is more extensive than that of the United States, but France was considered to have a more "rigid" labor market than Sweden's in terms of the costs employers pay when they lay off a worker. France has had an unemployment rate that reaches new heights with each economic shock. Sweden, by contrast, tended to have a cyclic unemployment rate that rose and fell with the business cycle, more like that of the United States. These authors argue that the Swedish unemployed were more likely to become reemployed, in part because of active labor market-related government policies. French workers, especially those who were older and less educated, were less likely to be reemployed. One influence on this result is French policies that provide older and more experienced workers with generous early retirement provisions.

The final stage of the sectoral transformation is the movement to a service economy. Both the increased productivity of the latest manufacturing technology and the transfer of manufacturing to Asia, Africa, and Latin America have freed up more American and European workers to provide services. The majority of workers in the United States now provide services rather than manufactured goods. There is a long tradition of self-employment among some service workers (e.g., professionals such as attorneys, physicians, accountants), and other service workers conceive of themselves as independent contractors. For these workers, job security, in the sense of having a job, may not be a problem. But many other service workers are employed within large organizations where their job security may be no greater than that of factory workers. In particular, they may have no employment rights and be subject to layoff or unemployment without warning.

THE JOB SECURITY PARADOX

A paradoxical effect of industrialization was that the individual worker became less important to management at the same time that the job became more important to the individual. The individuals became less important to the manager if their job skills could be replaced by the application of technology and if other potential workers with similar qualifications could be had for the same (or preferably lower) wages.

The job, however, became more important to the individual because markets determined the distribution not only of labor but also of all commodities and services. A farm family might subsist to a large extent on what they could raise to eat and clothes they made for themselves. In the cities, however, all the needs of life had to be purchased, and money was required to purchase them. The job, as the source of the money, was essential, and most families had only their work-related income. Unemployment meant that the family was deprived of income and ultimately of food, clothing, and shelter. Indeed, the first aspect of unemployment relief legislated in Europe, Canada, and the United States was typically the provision either of direct cash support or of goods and services in kind (e.g., Food Stamps, Medicaid). The unemployed rarely have other resources readily available. One recent study

in the United States indicated that one-third of unemployed workers are unable to replace even as much as 10 percent of their income loss through savings or assets (Gruber 2001).

In the rural community, many services were bartered. Someone who became ill or injured might expect to receive care from family members or neighbors as part of the general exchange of favors within the community. In the city, however, such services often had to be purchased. And because the family often had to send all of its adult members into the labor force to earn a living, there were fewer family members available for caregiving to younger and older members; thus, these types of care also entered the market economy.

But the job became more important for other reasons as well. Jobs became a major way in which the government interacted with citizens. Social security systems were closely tied to a worker's job history, and taxes on income inevitably involved the employer as well as the employee. For the government to provide unemployment compensation or to help workers injured on the job, the government had to become more closely involved with employers. In most Western countries, employers now bear some responsibility for ensuring that a person is legally eligible to work.

Moreover, in the United States, jobs became the principal source of access to expensive medical care. The provision of fringe benefits, such as medical insurance and a private pension, has become an important aspect of work. "Good jobs" become defined as those that provide fringe benefits, and the fringe benefits in turn tie workers more closely to their jobs. Workers with a preexisting medical condition, for example, may have difficulties in getting comparable coverage from a new employer and so may wish to stay with their current employer as long as possible (Kapur 1998). Losing one of these jobs means not only a loss of income but also potentially the loss of health insurance and perhaps the loss of pension benefits. There have been many reports of a relationship between illness and unemployment (Fergusson, Horwood, and Woodward 2001; Novo, Hammarstrom, and Janlert 2001), although the direction of causality is sometimes confounded. A person who is chronically ill, for example, may have more difficulty in securing steady employment.

There is finally the intangible aspect of job security that is tied to a person's identity and sense of belonging (Hodson 2001). "What do you do?" is one of the most frequently asked questions when two strangers meet. Social esteem and prestige are closely tied to one's work (Newman 2000). Losing a job, or looking for a job without finding one, means that this identity is lost. One of the most damaging aspects of a layoff for many workers is this loss of status. In a study of downsized workers at two large firms, Koeber (2002) discovered that workers experienced substantial shifts in the subjective meanings they attached to work and to being workers. Yang (2002) described how unemployed Korean men tried to save face following their job loss. Avison (2001) examined the mental health consequences of unemployment for both the workers and their spouses. He found that unemployed women were at higher risk of disorders, especially anxiety disorders, but unemployed men were more prone to substance abuse and depression.

Moreover, as jobs grow in general social importance, there are fewer alternatives to work that are considered a respectable way for adults to spend their time. Retired workers often find their lives dislocated and they feel "at loose ends" because they do not have a job to report to. But being retired is at least a respectable status. Some workers who have been unemployed for a long time and are too discouraged to look for work appear to report themselves in social surveys as "retired," apparently in an effort to disguise their unemployment. Although unemployed workers do spend more time in household tasks, they tend to end this additional work once they are reemployed (Strom 2002b). Housewives and stay-at-home mothers often complain that their efforts are devalued even though the family would find the replacement of their services very expensive (Bianchi et al. 2000). Even volunteer work, although accorded some respect, is not always regarded as "real" work.

The loss of prestige and status that accompanies unemployment often generates its own set of difficulties (Starrin, Jonsson, and Rantakeisu 2001). The unemployed are more likely to be depressed, to be physically ill, and to experience family difficulties. One study in Sweden has shown that even accident risks for children rise if their parents are unemployed (Strom 2002a). Where an entire community has experienced widespread unemployment—for example, through the closing of a major local employer—there are often significant dislocations, an increase in crime, and eventually widespread apathy and discouragement, in addition to whatever privations are experienced through the lack of income. Crime may become the alternative career for the unemployed (Baron 2001). Communities with high levels of unemployment decline in other ways as well, often losing population and government services as their tax bases shrink (Barnett and Mencken 2002).

Thus, while many aspects of the industrial and postindustrial society made workers less important to bosses, these same aspects also made the jobs more important to the workers. As jobs became more important to individuals, the absence of work or unemployment became more important as well. The social significance of unemployment, layoffs, and other forms of job loss became much more important. Thus, in many ways unemployment was the master social problem related to work. But as the section below discusses, other social problems were associated with those who had an employment relationship.

Job Insecurity: The Master Social Problem

As the preceding discussion suggests, the key work-related social problem is a lack of job security. The most aggravated form of job insecurity is unemployment. In national statistical systems, unemployment is usually defined as the active search for work by someone who does not work at all. In the United States, working even 1 hour in a week for pay, or 15 hours unpaid in a family business, is sufficient to define a person as employed rather than unemployed, even if the worker spent all the rest of the week looking for a full-time job.

TYPES OF UNEMPLOYMENT

There are several ways to become unemployed. Young people coming to the labor market for the first time, or people returning to the labor market after schooling or for other reasons, will typically search for work for some period of time before locating a job. This unemployment is characterized as entrant or reentrant unemployment. Frictional unemployment is the unemployment that results from short job searches, either entering the market or reentering it, and frictional unemployment is rarely seen as an important issue. If the average length of time to find a job is fairly long—as it is, for example, during a recession when unemployment generally rises—then this type of unemployment is seen as more significant.

Another type of unemployment is that experienced by job leavers. These are people who have voluntarily left their last job and are looking for a new job. These workers may have quit because they did not like their previous job, or they might have moved to another city with a spouse or have a lead on a promising new job. Unemployment among job leavers is also discounted as a social problem, on the supposition that their job search is voluntary. People who quit are typically not eligible for unemployment compensation, partly from this sort of reasoning. But this supposition could be incorrect if on their previous job they were effectively forced to resign. Employers, for example, frequently prefer to offer an employee the opportunity to resign rather than be fired. The resignation is not as stigmatizing, and the employer's tax for unemployment compensation will not be increased if employees quit.

The final type of unemployment, and the type that creates the greatest concern, is that of job losers. Some people lose their jobs because they are discharged for cause—that is, their work or their behavior is not satisfactory. But job losers are more frequently part of a layoff that may involve many thousands of workers at a time. In the United States, the federal government tracks mass layoffs. Layoffs were once confined to manufacturing industries, but since the 1980s layoffs have become increasingly common in white-collar occupations, including lower and middle management levels (Li 2002). A layoff may affect all workers with a low level of seniority, all workers of a given occupational level, or all workers within a division or plant. A very large layoff will have an immediate negative effect on the surrounding community, not only because of the job losers themselves but also because of the lost multiplier effect of their spending in the local community.

Unemployment is tracked by time period. It is well known that there will be a temporary rise in unemployment at some times of the year. At the beginning of the summer, for example, college and high school students out of school look for work, and there is a rise in the unemployment rate. This type of unemployment is called seasonal unemployment and is not viewed as serious; in fact, in the United States the officially reported unemployment rates are seasonally adjusted to remove these effects. But the seasonally adjusted unemployment rate, and especially the rate for the job losers, is carefully watched over a longer time period. The unemployment rate is one indicator of the business cycle, with the unemployment rate typically rising during recessions and declining during periods of prosperity. In the United States, the Bureau of Labor Statistics releases the unemployment rate on the first Friday of every month, and the stock market, politicians, and editorial writers often react to news of the rate.

Unemployment is also tracked by geographic area. Relatively economically depressed areas will have high rates of unemployment, and chronic high rates of unemployment in turn stimulate migration and other adjustments by the unemployed (Boyd 2002). Within a metropolitan area, unemployment rates tend to be highest in neighborhoods with a high degree of disorganization, so that unemployment becomes part of a nexus of poverty, crime, and economic isolation.

Finally, unemployment is tracked by demographic group. In general, there is a variation in unemployment by age, although the pattern differs somewhat among countries (Sackmann 2001). The young, especially teenagers, often have high unemployment rates, which may be discounted because they are thought to be entrants into the labor market. Because of their experiences with widespread unemployment, younger workers may have lower expectations for job security (Bridges 2001). One result in the workplace may be a lack of solidarity between the older workers, who have greater expectations for job security, and the younger workers, whose expectations are lower (Beaud and Pialoux 2001).

A more enduring problem is that unemployment varies systematically by racial and ethnic group. In the United States, it is a durable finding that the black unemployment rate is about twice that of majority whites, with Hispanic unemployment rates falling between the two. This difference in unemployment reflects, among other things, the discrimination that historically limited blacks to relatively few jobs. Today this differential may also reflect continued segregation into inner-city urban neighborhoods, the legacy of inadequate public education, poor public transportation, and lack of access to networks of friends and family who have news of job openings (Granovetter 1995; Wilson 1997).

One source of the disadvantage of minority workers in employment might be an issue of social capital, namely, their relatively isolated networks. Quite a lot of evidence indicates the value of networks in the job search process. Zippay (2001) discovered that social network contacts were more successful than job training in the reemployment of a random sample of laid-off steelworkers. Given that many minority workers remain residentially segregated, it seems reasonable that they may not have access to job networks that are as effective as those of workers with more social capital. Dohan (2002) argues, for example, that transnational social networks help to explain the greater labor market attachment of Mexican immigrants to the United States, compared with that of native-born Mexican Americans.

The relationship between unemployment and gender is complex. Typically, there are more women than men among the entrants, reentrants, and job leavers, the groups that are considered to have a less serious unemployment problem. When the economy is doing well, women often make up the majority of the unemployed. Indeed, when there is general prosperity, some adults who were not working are attracted into the labor market; because women are still less likely than men to work, the available labor supply that can be attracted to work is disproportionately female. On the other hand, job losers are more likely to be male, and during a recession, males tend to be the majority of the unemployed. Unemployed women should not be discounted in terms of social problems, however, because they are often important earners to their families; for a single-parent family, the unemployment of the single mother is a serious matter indeed.

In addition to what is called "open unemployment," or the type of unemployment that the government periodically measures, there is also the phenomenon of the "discouraged worker." The discouraged workers have no jobs, but they have stopped looking for work because they believe that there is no work available. Although a mass layoff usually produces an increased unemployment rate in a community, the phenomenon of discouraged workers may mean that the measured unemployment rate will drop even if there has been no increase in the numbers employed. Because the measurement of discouragement involves collecting relatively "softer" data, such as attitudes and beliefs about employment, it has been controversial among labor statisticians. It seems likely, however, that the discouraged worker is at least as likely as the unemployed worker to suffer the negative consequences of being without a job.

Underemployment

Workers are excluded from the measurement of unemployment if they work only one hour for pay. As a result, many workers who experience difficulties in the labor market are invisible from public analysis and commentary (Fullsack 2001; Lester and McCain 2001). This issue was initially raised in developing countries, where it was variously called "disguised unemployment" or "underemployment." This term referred to the use of low workers, especially in agriculture, in positions of low marginal productivity. Subsequently, the analysis of underemployment expanded to developed countries, where three dimensions of underemployment have generally been analyzed (Clogg 1979; Clogg and Sullivan 1983; Lester and McCain 2001; Sullivan 1978).

The first dimension, and the one classically alluded to in the literature, is involuntary part-time or seasonal employment (Tilly 1996). Most part-time workers choose this work schedule, and they are called the voluntarily part-time. Their reasons for preferring part-time work vary, but typical reasons include commitments to family or to school. Other part-time workers are involuntarily part-time because they would prefer full-time work and are unable to find it, or they have had a full-time job and their hours of work have been cut back to a part-time schedule. Workers who were previously unemployed appear to be more prone to involuntary part-time work (Caputo and Cianni 2001). The proportion of all workers who are involuntarily part-time varies with the business cycle, and thus appears to be genuinely linked to unemployment. This type of underemployment may also contain an element of discouragement in that the worker does not seek a full-time job in the belief that full-time work is not available or perhaps in the hope that the part-time job will become full-time.

Seasonal workers may be employed full-time during part of the year, but then are unable to find work in other seasons of the year. Seasonal work is common in some localities, such as resort locations, and it is also common in some industries. In retail commerce, for example, there is a sharp increase in employment around the end-of-the-year holidays, and these workers are then released as soon as the holiday sales end. When the seasonal worker would like additional work during the rest of the year, this arrangement could be termed underemployment.

Part-time and part-year workers have relatively low earnings because of their work schedules. A different type of underemployment affects workers who are full-time, but whose pay rate is so low as to be below some socially defined normative wage. Examples of this normative wage include the legal minimum wage, official poverty levels, or minimum budgets for a family of a certain size.

Although perhaps not technically underemployed, workers reemployed following a job displacement, such as a plant closing, are of current interest (U.S. Bureau of Labor Statistics 2000). Typically, at least one-third of these displaced workers are unable to earn at the same levels they had earned on their previous jobs. Many studies in the United States have indicated that they experience serious downward mobility in terms of the wage rate they are able to command in their new jobs, although one study in Germany indicated small earnings losses (Couch 2001).

A final form of underemployment is the mismatch of skills and occupation. Well-educated workers who are unable to find jobs commensurate with their education level may be said to be mismatched, which can be considered a form of underemployment even if the worker is full-time and the wage rate is above the normative minimum. Mismatch represents a potential loss of productivity to the society, and it may be associated with negative consequences for the mismatched worker (de Witte and Batenburg 2001).

The principal obstacle to regular measurement of underemployment is the belief that in a formally free labor market, workers are free to choose to work and free to leave their jobs. From this perspective, underemployed workers have "chosen" their involuntary part-time, or low-paying, or low-skilled jobs, and the quality of their jobs is an inappropriate object for public policy. Recent efforts to measure underemployment have been done principally by researchers who reanalyze available government statistics (see, e.g., Slack and Jensen 2002).

Implicit Job Insecurity

Even workers who are adequately employed, in terms of work schedule, pay rate, and skill use, may nevertheless worry about and fear job insecurity. This fear in itself may be used by managers to spur greater work from their employees, for fear of being the next to go in a corporate downsizing (Gordon 1996). The rounds of downsizing in the early 1990s, which for the first time reached a large number of formerly safe white-collar workers, had the effect of reminding many workers that their jobs might not be secure in the long run (Quadagno et al. 2001).

The prevalence of downsizing forced managers to become more strategic in determining which of their employees were "core," or indispensable to the company, and which workers were more expendable. Outsourcing was one strategy followed in which some specialized functions of the company were contracted to other firms, and the firm's own specialists were laid off. Janitorial work, for example, could be outsourced to a specialized cleaning company, allowing the layoff of janitors who were no longer considered core employees. Eventually, even those workers whose function was central to the company's mission were divided into the critical and the expendable. As round after round of downsizing occurred, many companies reduced their payrolls to the critical core workers, who then began to work very long schedules, often incurring substantial overtime to make up for their missing colleagues. For fear of being moved into a more vulnerable situation themselves, these employees tend to work their long hours without much protest. In effect, the downsized workers serve as a "reserve army."

Many companies, needing additional labor at least when business was brisk, developed a range of tactics for keeping additional workers on call (Fox and Sugiman 1999). The temporary service industry is one result of these developments, because outsourcing temporary increases in labor demand to these services has become common. Temporary workers, who were once limited to clerical work and relatively rare in the economy, are now found in many occupational specialties, and the temporary service industry is rapidly expanding (Henson 1996). Large employers have developed their own internal temporary service facilities.

In addition, some workers who were previously on the payroll have been redeployed as "independent contractors," brought into a company to complete specific tasks within a specific time frame. In many cases, the temporary workers and independent contractors are denied fringe benefits, especially health benefits. The contract employees have limited job security (until the end of their contracts), but the temporary workers have no security at all. Again, while some workers voluntarily embrace these new types of work, others are forced into them and the consequent fluctuations in income that result. One term for this group of workers is the contingent workforce (Barker and Christensen 1998; U.S. Bureau of Labor Statistics 1999).

These developments have led to multiple tiers of employment within a single workplace, with variations in salary and the security of work schedule even for workers who do the same kind of work. An issue of great interest is how much the vulnerable lower tier of employment will overlap with employees who are female, from racial or ethnic minorities, or disabled (Edin and Lein 1997; Smith 1998).

Analysts have argued that the multiple-tier construct now applies more generally in the labor force (see, for example, Beck, Horan, and Tolbert 1978). Within a single industry, more successful firms are more likely to provide secure and attractive employment, with the less successful firms resorting to more frequent layoffs when work is slack. Furthermore, some industries may be "core," often by virtue of oligopolistic organization, and able to provide relatively more steady employment to their preferred workers. Other industries may be more "peripheral," perhaps because of more local or global competition, or because their products have more unsteady demand. The weaker position of these industries translates into weaker job security for their employees (Averitt 1968).

These multiple tiers have been noted for years in the labor markets of developing countries. Workers who are associated with multinational firms are more likely to have relatively high-paid jobs, while those associated with indigenous firms may earn less. And because of rapid population growth and migration, many developing countries also have a large casual labor market with workers who eke out a living doing odd jobs, petty retail, or other economically marginal tasks.

Various theoretical formulations have been advanced to explain these dichotomous structures, but the common element is that workers doing similar jobs may nevertheless have very different work experiences and rewards. Even workers in the preferred categories may not rest easy in their job security. Recent developments in American corporations such as Enron have resulted in the loss of jobs and pensions for employees who previously would have been considered among the most privileged of core workers.

Responses to Job Insecurity

If job insecurity is the principal social problem that affects workers in one way or another, there are nevertheless tactics that individual workers can pursue to reduce their vulnerability within the labor market. Historically, workers have sought monopoly over desired skills or strong worker organizations to redress the balance of power within the workplace. In addition, in democratic regimes workers have sought through their elected representatives and through litigation to secure employment rights and to regulate the workplace.

THE ROLE OF SKILL

One defense an individual worker can have against job insecurity is to have a skill or knowledge that is in high demand but not in high supply. Workers with high levels of skill have traditionally sought ways to encourage a high demand for their work while excluding additional people from eligibility to pursue the work. In medieval times, the craft guilds served this purpose. Relatively few young people were admitted as apprentices, and only the apprentices could hope to eventually master the craft and become full members of the guild.

The professions now serve a similar function for many knowledge occupations, and they have often been successful in getting legal recognition as the sole incumbents of their jobs. Physicians, for example, must pass a licensing exam before receiving the legal right to practice medicine, and persons who attempt to do the work of a physician may be prosecuted for practicing medicine without a license. To get into the schools to gain the knowledge necessary for licensure, however, is difficult; there are relatively few such schools and they are expensive and difficult to enter. Thus, physicians have ensured a limited supply of additional physicians and have worked legally to prevent other occupations from doing the work of a physician. Their monopoly over medical knowledge has been eroded by other occupations (e.g., chiropractors, nurse practitioners, pharmacists) and by the wider availability of medical information through the Internet, but physicians still maintain substantial occupational control.

Another advantage for the professions is that they are often able to keep the most interesting parts of the jobs for themselves while relegating the routine, messy, or dirty parts of the work to other occupations. In hospitals, for example, physicians delegate the tasks of immediate patient care to nurses, nursing assistants, and other occupations. In comparison with other occupational groups, professionals are able to retain a substantial amount of autonomy over their work. Even when they are employed in organizations, where some of these perquisites are limited, professionals tend to have more autonomous and interesting jobs than other workers.

In some countries and in some regions, unions of skilled workers may also play a similar role by limiting the number of young people who may become apprentices and by defining some work as the unique province of their occupation.

The Role of Organization

Strong organization can substitute for monopoly of skill in giving workers some additional control on the job. In contrast with the unions of skilled workers, industrial unions such as the CIO (Congress of Industrial Organizations) in the United States organized groups of semiskilled or even unskilled workers into collective bargaining units. Because of the threat of strikes and other work actions, unions have been able to preserve jobs and wage levels for their workers.

Unionization rates are declining throughout the Western world, however, and managers have developed many tools to erode the effectiveness of collective bargaining. Sometimes the union contract can protect relatively few workers, usually those with the most seniority. Unions such as the United Mine Workers have deliberately accepted greatly improved mining equipment because it improved productivity and wage levels, even though ultimately the mines would employ fewer workers. Unions face collective problems of runaway shops, wage givebacks, and threats of layoff just as individual workers do.

One advantage that unions retain, however, is that they can give a political voice to workers through their lobbying and other efforts. Especially in Europe, organized labor has retained a substantial political voice. This political voice may be expressed in general strikes as well as at the ballot box.

Social Movements

A number of social movements have arisen from the social problems associated with work. In the early factory era, the plight of workers was able to mobilize many sympathizers, and eventually policy makers became convinced that changes were necessary. The early campaigns against child labor and long work days are two examples; these movements in turn may have been instrumental in the later movements for women's suffrage. Workers waged a long battle to earn the rights to unionize and to bargain collectively, and the unions in turn became important players in later social movements, including the civil rights movement.

The civil rights movement in turn identified work-related issues, especially racial discrimination and occupational segregation, as persistent work-related issues. The women's movement similarly focused on a number of work-related issues, including the exclusion of women from certain jobs and apprenticeships, unequal work-related pensions for women, and above all, equal pay for equal work. Later, feminists also argued for better child care and other family-friendly benefits to reduce the conflicts between work and family (Hochschild 1997; Nippert-Eng 1996).

Social Policy

Both workers' organizations and broader social movements petitioned legislators to pass laws that improve the lot of workers. Since the Great Depression, legislated work benefits have become an important counterweight to persisting job insecurity. Social security, workers' compensation, unemployment compensation, occupational safety and health regulations, and antidiscrimination laws are some of the measures that resulted. European nations and Canada and Australia have gone quite a bit further than the United States in providing income supports, guaranteed maternity leave, and similar worker benefits.

The development of the laws also opens another avenue of action, which is litigation to clarify the legislation and to demand enforcement. Both the civil rights movement and the women's movement have been successful in using lawsuits to underscore important legal provisions.

These social policies have incited a strong and well-organized opposition from employers, who argue that such regulations increase the cost of creating a job and encourage the duality between "good jobs" (that provide full benefits) and "bad jobs" (that are unregulated because they are outsourced or temporary, or because they are paid in cash and not

recorded) (Kalleberg, Reskin, and Hudson 2000). The term *rigid* labor market is used to describe markets that have relatively more of these regulations affecting work and jobs. A substantial rollback of the social policy directed toward workers would mark a further increase in work instability, the cardinal social problem related to work. By contrast, there is a substantial set of proposed reforms that could enhance work life (Osterman 1999).

CHANGING WORK IDENTITY

A final possibility is that workers' identities will be more disassociated from their work, or at least from a particular employer (Bowes and Goodnow 1996). Workers will view themselves as independent actors, free to move from employer to employer and less committed to a particular job, occupation, or industry (Baker and Aldrich 1996). Some observers believe that there is already a difference between generations of workers in terms of their commitment to work, such that younger workers are less committed than the retirees whom they are replacing (Dohm 2000). Rather than a general decline in the work ethic, this change in identity instead involves a withdrawal of loyalty from the employer. In the process, however, the worker may also fail to develop bonds of attachment with coworkers, making effective work organizations less likely and leaving the individuals atomized in the labor market.

The Future of Work

A number of factors discussed in the chapter have the potential to escalate job insecurity. Advanced technology, globalization, and changes in the characteristic organization of workplaces each play a role in reducing the significance of the individual worker and thus the worker's value to the firm. Knowledge and skill, worker organization, social movements, and influence on government policy remain some of the ways in which workers may seek to redress this tendency (Bluestone and Harrison 2000).

On the other hand, the increased productivity permitted by advanced technology could instead become the means for shortening the workday or the work year. Employers could redesign jobs to provide greater security and to make jobs more varied and interesting. In return, the workers might find a renewed sense of loyalty to their employers.

Which of these paths is followed depends upon many factors, including the level of regulation exercised by government agencies, the choices employers make in terms of job design, and the roles played by unions and workers themselves.

Even if job instability continues unabated, governments could move to provide more support for unemployed or underemployed workers. Job training or retraining, medical care in lieu of health insurance, and income supports are examples of assistance that could be offered to alleviate the impact of job-related social problems. These options, however, require a political will and taxpayer funding.

REFERENCES

Adler, William M. 2000. *Mollie's Job: A Story of Life and Work on the Global Assembly Line.* New York: Scribner.

Averitt, Robert T. 1968. *The Dual Economy: The Dynamics of American Industrial Structure.* New York: Norton.

Avison, William R. 2001. "Unemployment and Its Consequences for Mental Health." Pp. 177–200 in *Restructuring Work and the Life Course,* edited by Victor W. Marshall, Walter R. Heinz, Helga Kruger, and Anil Verma. Ontario, Canada: University of Toronto Press.

Baker, Ted and Howard E. Aldrich. 1996. "Prometheus Stretches: Building Identity and Cumulative Knowledge in Multiemployer Careers." Pp. 132–49 in *The Boundaryless Career: A New Employment Principle for a New Organizational Era,* edited by Michael B. Arthur and Denise M. Rousseau. New York: Oxford University Press.

Barker, Kathleen and Kathleen Christensen. 1998. *Contingent Work.* Ithaca, NY: Industrial Relations Press.

Barnett, Cynthia and F. Carson Mencken. 2002. "Social Disorganization Theory and the Contextual Nature of Crime in Nonmetropolitan Counties." *Rural Sociology* 67:372–93.

Baron, Stephen W. 2001. "Street Youth Labour Market Experiences and Crime." *La Revue Canadienne de Sociologie et d'Anthropologie/The Canadian Review of Sociology and Anthropology* 38:189–215.

Beaud, Stephane and Michel Pialoux. 2001. "Between 'Mate' and 'Scab': The Contradictory Inheritance of French Workers in the Postfordist Factory." Translated by Richard Nice and Loic Wacquant. *Ethnography* 2:323–55.

Beck, E. M., Patrick M. Horan, and Charles M. Tolbert II. 1978. "Stratification in a Dual Economy: A Sectoral Model of Earnings Determination." *American Sociological Review* 43:704–20.

Bianchi, Suzanne M., Melissa A. Milkie, Liana C. Sayer, and John P. Robinson. 2000. "Is Anyone Doing the Housework? Trends in the Gender Division of Household Labor." *Social Forces* 79:191–228.

Blauner, Robert. 1964. *Alienation and Freedom.* Chicago, IL: University of Chicago Press.

Bloom, David E. and Adi Brender. 1993. "Labor and the Emerging World Economy." *Population Bulletin* 48, 2 (October).

Bluestone, Barry and Bennett Harrison. 2000. *Growing Prosperity: The Battle for Growth with Equity in the Twenty-First Century.* Boston, MA: Houghton Mifflin.

Bowes, J. M. and J. J. Goodnow. 1996. "Work for Home, School, or Labor Force: The Nature and Sources of Changes in Understanding." *Psychological Bulletin* 119:300–21.

Boyd, Robert L. 2002. "A 'Migration of Despair': Unemployment, the Search for Work, and Migration to Farms during the Great Depression." *Social Science Quarterly* 83:554–67.

Bridges, William P. 2001. "Age and the Labor Market: Trends in Employment Security and Employment Institutions." Pp. 319–52 in *Sourcebook of Labor Markets: Evolving Structures and Processes,* edited by Ivar Berg and Arne L. Kalleberg. New York: Kluwer Academic/Plenum.

Caputo, Richard K. and Mary Cianni. 2001. "Correlates of Voluntary vs. Involuntary Part-Time Employment among U.S. Women." *Gender Work and Organization* 8:311–25.

Clogg, Clifford C. 1979. *Measuring Underemployment.* New York: Academic Press.

Clogg, Clifford C. and Teresa A. Sullivan. 1983. "Labor Force Composition and Underemployment Trends, 1969-1980." *Social Indicators Research* 12:117–52.

Couch, Kenneth A. 2001. "Earnings Losses and Unemployment of Displaced Workers in Germany." *Industrial and Labor Relations Review* 54:559–72.

De Witte, Marco and Ronald Batenburg. 2001. "The Dutch Labour Market Since 1971: Trends in

Overeducation and Displacement." Pp. 45–60 in *Restructuring Work and the Life Course,* edited by Victor W. Marshall, Walter R. Heinz, Helga Kruger, and Anil Verma. Ontario, Canada: University of Toronto Press.

DiPrete, Thomas A., Dominique Goux, Eric Maurin, and Michael Tahlin. 2001. "Institutional Determinants of Employment Chances: The Structure of Unemployment in France and Sweden." *European Sociological Review* 17:233–54.

Dohan, Daniel. 2002. "Making Cents in the Barrios: The Institutional Roots of Joblessness in Mexican America." *Ethnography* 3:177–200.

Dohm, Arlene. 2000. "Gauging the Labor Force Effects of Retiring Baby Boomers." *Monthly Labor Review* 123:17–25.

Edin, Kathryn and Laura Lein. 1997. *Making Ends Meet: How Single Mothers Survive Welfare and Low-Wage Work.* New York: Russell Sage.

Fergusson, David M., L. John Horwood, and Lilanne J. Woodward. 2001. "Unemployment and Psychosocial Adjustment in Young Adults: Causation or Selection?" *Social Science and Medicine* 53:305–20.

Fox, Bonnie and Pamela Sugiman. 1999. "Flexible Work, Flexible Workers: The Restructuring of Clerical Work in a Large Telecommunications Company." *Studies in Political Economy* 60:59–84.

Fullsack, Manfred. 2001. "Official Figures and Unofficial Realities: Employment Rates and Their Significance in Russia." *Europe-Asia Studies* 53:613–25.

Gonzalez de la Rocha, Mercedes. 2001. "From the Resources of Poverty to the Poverty of Resources? The Erosion of a Survival Model." *Latin American Perspectives* 28:72–100.

Gordon, David M. 1996. *Fat and Mean: The Corporate Squeeze of Working Americans and the Myth of Managerial Downsizing.* New York: Free Press.

Granovetter, Mark. 1995. *Getting a Job: A Study of Contacts and Careers.* 2nd ed. Chicago, IL: University of Chicago Press.

Gruber, Jonathan. 2001. "The Wealth of the Unemployed." *Industrial and Labor Relations Review* 55:79–94.

Henson, Kevin D. 1996. *Just a Temp.* Philadelphia, PA: Temple University Press.

Hochschild, Arlie R. 1997. *The Time Bind.* New York: Metropolitan Books.

Hodson, Randy. 2001. *Dignity at Work.* New York: Cambridge University Press.

Kalleberg, Arne L., Barbara F. Reskin, and Ken Hudson. 2000. "Bad Jobs in America: Standard and Nonstandard Employment Relations and Job Quality

in the United States." *American Sociological Review* 65:256–78.

Kapur, Kanicka. 1998. "The Impact of Health on Job Mobility: A Measure of Job Lock." *Industrial and Labor Relations Review* 51:282–97.

Kenworthy, Lane. 2002. "Corporatism and Unemployment in the 1980s and 1990s." *American Sociological Review* 67:367–88.

Koeber, Charles. 2002. "Corporate Restructuring, Downsizing, and the Middle Class: The Process and Meaning of Worker Displacement in the 'New' Economy." *Qualitative Sociology* 35:217–46.

Korpi, Walter. 2002. "The Great Trough in Unemployment: A Long-Term View of Unemployment, Inflation, Strikes, and the Profit/Wage Ratio." *Politics and Society* 30:365–426.

Lester, Bijou Yang and Roger A. McCain. 2001. "An Equity-Based Redefinition of Underemployment and Unemployment and Some Measurements." *Review of Social Economy* 59:133–59.

Li, Yaojun. 2002. "Falling Off the Ladder? Professional and Managerial Career Trajectories and Unemployment Experiences." *European Sociological Review* 18:253–70.

Mills, C. Wright. 1959. *The Sociological Imagination.* New York: Free Press.

Newman, Katherine. 2000. *No Shame in My Game.* New York: Vintage.

Nippert-Eng, Christena E. 1996. *Home and Work: Negotiating Boundaries through Everyday Life.* Chicago, IL: University of Chicago Press.

Novo, Mehmed, Anne Hammarstrom, and Urban Janlert. 2001. "Do High Levels of Unemployment Influence the Health of Those Who Are Not Unemployed? A Gendered Comparison and Young Men and Women during Boom and Recession." *Social Science and Medicine* 53:293–303.

Osterman, Paul. 1999. *Securing Prosperity: The American Labor Market: How It Has Changed and What to Do About It.* Princeton, NJ: Princeton University Press.

Quadragno, Jill, David MacPherson, Jennifer Reid Keene, and Lori Paprham. 2001. "Downsizing and the Life-Course Consequences of Job Loss: The Effect of Age and Gender on Employment and Income Security." Pp. 303–18 in *Restructuring Work and the Life Course,* edited by Victor W. Marshall, Walter R. Heinz, Helga Kruger, and Anil Verma. Ontario, Canada: University of Toronto Press.

Reid, Lori L. 2002. "Occupational Segregation, Human Capital, and Motherhood: Black Women's Higher Exit Rates from Full-Time Employment." *Gender & Society* 16:728–47.

Sackmann, Reinhold. 2001. "Age and Labour-Market Changes in International Comparison." *European Sociological Review* 17:373–87.

Slack, Tim and Leif Jensen. 2002. "Race, Ethnicity, and Underemployment in Nonmetropolitan America: A 30-Year Profile." *Rural Sociology* 67:208–33.

Smith, Vicki. 1998. "The Fractured World of the Temporary Worker: Power, Participation, and Fragmentation in the Contemporary Workplace." *Social Problems* 45:411–30.

Starrin, Bengt, Leif R. Jonsson, and Ulla Rantakeisu. 2001. "Sense of Coherence during Unemployment." *International Journal of Social Welfare* 10:107–16.

Strom, Sara. 2002a. "Keep Out of the Reach of Children: Parental Unemployment and Children's Accident Risks in Sweden 1991–1993." *International Journal of Social Welfare* 11:40–52.

——. 2002b. "Unemployment and Gendered Divisions of Domestic Labor." *Acta Sociologica* 45:89–106.

Sullivan, Teresa A. 1978. *Marginal Workers, Marginal Jobs: The Underutilization of American Workers.* Austin, TX: University of Texas Press.

Sullivan, Teresa A., Elizabeth Warren, and Jay L. Westbrook. 2000. *The Fragile Middle Class: Americans in Debt.* New Haven, CT: Yale University Press.

Tilly, Chris. 1996. *Half a Job: Bad and Good Part-Time Jobs in a Changing Labor Market.* Philadelphia, PA: Temple University Press.

U.S. Bureau of Labor Statistics. 1999. "Contingent and Alternative Employment Arrangements, February 1999." *USDL* 99-362 (December 21).

——. 2000. "Worker Displacement during the Late 1990s." *USDL* 00-223 (August 9).

Wilson, William Julius. 1997. *When Work Disappears: The World of the New Urban Poor.* Reprint ed. New York: Vintage.

Yang, Sungeum. 2002. "'Chaemyoun-Saving (Face Saving)' due to Korean Job Loss: Listening to Men's Voices." *Journal of Comparative Family Studies* 33:73–95.

Zippay, Allison. 2001. "The Role of Social Capital in Reclaiming Human Capital: A Longitudinal Study of Occupational Mobility among Displaced Steelworkers." *Journal of Sociology and Social Welfare* 28:99–119.

THE MEDIA AND SOCIAL PROBLEMS

DOUGLAS KELLNER

University of California, Los Angeles

The media provide access to and construct social problems for large numbers of audiences in many parts of the world and in turn themselves have become a social problem in view of their multiple and complex effects, many negative. The media have been blamed by a wide spectrum of theorists and critics for promoting violence and sexism, racism, homophobia, ageism, and other oppressive phenomena. Social problems connected with the media also involve allegedly harmful media influence on children and youth, pornography and the degradation of women and sexuality, advertising manipulation, and the promotion of excessive consumerism and materialism.

Empirical research on media effects in these areas has been mixed and highly contested. Many studies have affirmed that media have negative social effects and help reproduce a number of social problems, while other studies assert skepticism toward claims of negative media effects or attempt to confirm positive aspects of the media.[1] Empirical studies are often funded by institutions that have interests in escaping or deflecting criticism, or they are constrained by bias and limitations of various kinds. Moreover, dominant theories of the media are equally contested on whether the media promote serious social problems or have a more benign influence.

Conflicting theories and research into media effects have intensified debates globally about media as a social problem. Research into media effects and linking the media with social problems emerged for the most part in the United States following the rise of broadcasting and mass media in the 1920s and 1930s (Czitrom 1983), but now the debate and literature is international in scope (McQuail 1994). Likewise, in an increasingly interconnected world, there are widespread concerns about the media and national culture and the ways that global media inform politics, economics, and social and everyday life. Some critical research has focused on the political economy and ownership of the media, often perceiving corporate control of the media by ever fewer corporations as a major global social problem. Other studies in the past decades have researched the impact of global media on national cultures, attacking the cultural imperialism of Western media conglomerates or creeping Americanization of global media and consumer culture (Schiller 1971; Tunstall 1977). Other scholars see a growing pluralization of world media sources and hybridization of global and local cultures, with an expanding literature exploring the ways that global media artifacts are received and used in local contexts (García Canclini 1995; Lull 1995). This literature is divided into research into how specific media or artifacts have promoted oppression in local or national contexts, or even globally, and studies that celebrate the democratizing or pluralizing effects of global media.

In this chapter, I sort out a vast literature on the media and social problems, delineate what I consider key issues and positions, and indicate some of the ways in which the media construct and address social problems and can be seen themselves as a social problem. This will involve, first, analysis of the media, morality, and violence, followed by a section on the politics of representation and debates over how the media contribute to class, race, gender, sexual, and other forms of oppression. Then, I take up media and democracy, setting out the position that corporate ownership and the political economy of the media constitute a social problem in which corporate media undermine democracy. I explore this latter issue with a study of the media in the United States over the past two decades and how corporate media have failed to address crucial social problems and have themselves become a social problem. Finally, I discuss how the Internet and new media can provide alternatives to the corporate media, and attempt to provide some hope that more democratic media and societies can be produced that will address social problems being ignored and intensified in the current era of corporate and conservative hegemony.

The Media, Morality, and Violence

During the 1930s, the Frankfurt School coined the term "culture industry" to signify the process of the industrialization of mass-produced culture and the commercial imperatives that drove the system. The critical theorists analyzed all mass-mediated cultural artifacts within the context of industrial production, in which the commodities of the culture industries exhibited the same features as other products of mass production: commodification, standardization, and massification. The culture industries had the specific function, however, of providing ideological legitimation of the existing capitalist societies and of integrating individuals into their way of life (see Horkheimer and Adorno 1972; Kellner, 1989).

In their theories of the culture industries and critiques of mass culture, the Frankfurt School were among the first social theorists perceiving the importance of the media in the reproduction of contemporary societies. In their view, the media stand in the center of leisure activity, are important agents of socialization and mediators of political reality, and should thus be seen as major institutions of contemporary societies with a variety of economic, political, cultural, and social effects.

The media are also perceived as a social problem for the Frankfurt School in that they produce a mass society that undermines individuality, democracy, and the salutary aspects of high culture. The classical view of Adorno and Horkheimer on the media and morality was that the media were purveyors of bourgeois and capitalist values, which promoted the dominant ideology, constructing viewers as passive consumers of dominant norms and consumer behavior. On Adorno and Horkheimer's model of the cultural industries, the standardized formats of mass-produced media genres imposed predictable experiences on audiences and helped produce a homogenized mass consciousness and society.

As communication studies began emerging in the 1930s and 1940s, and as theorists noted the power of propaganda in World War II, a wide range of studies began appearing of the social effects of the media, promoting debate over the media and social problems and the media as a social problem. Some of the first empirical studies of the effects of film, for instance, criticized the cinema for promoting immorality, juvenile delinquency, and violence. The Motion Picture Research Council funded the Payne Foundation to undertake detailed empirical studies of the impact of films on everyday life and social behavior. Ten volumes were eventually published and a book, *Our Movie-Made Children* (Forman 1933), sensationalized the Payne findings, triggering debates about the media and how they inflamed social problems like crime, youth problems, sexual promiscuity, and what was perceived as undesirable social behavior (see Jowett 1976).

The first models of mass communication built on studies of propaganda, film influence, advertising, and other media studies, assuming a direct and powerful influence of media on the audience. This model became known as the "bullet," or "hypodermic," theory, asserting that the media directly shape thought and behavior and thus induce social problems like crime and violence, rebellious social behavior, mindless consumption, or mass political behavior (see Lasswell 1927 and the presentation of the model in DeFleur and Ball-Rokeach 1989). The propaganda role of the media in World Wars I and II and growing concern about the social roles of film, advertising, and other media promoted debate about how the media were becoming a social problem and were intensifying a wide range of other problems, ranging from crime to growing teen pregnancies.

This model of powerful and direct media effects was questioned in *The People's Choice* (1944) by Paul Lazarsfeld and his colleagues Bernard Berelson and Hazel Gaulet, who in a study of the influence of the media on voters determined that it was "opinion leaders" who were the primary influence in voting behavior, while the media exerted a "secondary" influence. Lazersfeld and Elihu Katz expanded this model in *Personal Influence: The Part Played by People in the Flow of Mass Communication* (1955). Their "two-step flow" model claimed that opinion leaders are the primary influence in determining consumer and political choice, as well as attitudes and values. This model holds that the media do not have direct influence on behavior, but are mediated by primary groups and personal influence, thus in effect denying that the media themselves are a social problem because they merely report on issues and reinforce behavior already dominant in a society.[2]

Yet both conservatives and left-liberal media critics continued to argue that the media had harmful social effects and promoted social problems. Growing juvenile delinquency in the 1950s was blamed on comic books (see Wertham 1996), and rock and roll was broadly attacked for having a wide range of subversive effects (Grossberg 1992). In the 1960s, many different studies of the media and violence appeared in many countries in response to growing violence in society and more permissive public media that increased representations of implicit sex and violence in film, television, and other media.

On the media and violence, some literature continued to assume that violent representations in the media directly cause social problems. A more sophisticated social ecology approach to violence and the media, however, was developed by George Gerbner (2003) and his colleagues in the Annenberg School of Communication. Gerbner's group has studied the "cultural environment" of violence in the media, tracking increases in representations of violence and delineating "message systems" that depict who exercises violence, who is the victim, and what messages are associated with media violence. A "cultivation analysis" studies effects of violence and concludes that heavy consumers of media violence exhibit a "mean world syndrome," with effects that range from depression, to fearful individuals voting for right-wing law and order politicians, to the exhibition of violent behavior.

Another approach to violence and the media is found in the work of Eysenck and Nias (1978), who argue that recurrent representations of violence in the media desensitize audiences to violent behavior and actions. The expansion of youth violence in many parts of the world and media exploitation of sensational instances of teen killings in the United States, Britain, France, Germany, and elsewhere intensified the focus on media and violence and the ways that rap music, video and computer games, television and film, and other types of youth culture have promoted violence.[3]

In addition to seeing the media as a social problem because of growing media and societal violence, from the 1960s to the present, left-liberal and conservative media critics coalesced in arguing that mainstream media promote excessive consumerism and commodification. This view is argued in sociological terms in the work of Daniel Bell, who asserts in *The Cultural Contradictions of Capitalism* (1978) that a sensate-hedonistic culture exhibited in popular media and promoted by capitalist corporations was undermining core traditional values and producing an increasingly amoral society. Bell called for a return to tradition and religion to counter this social trend that saw media culture as undermining morality, the work ethic, and traditional values.

In *Amusing Ourselves to Death* (1986), Neil Postman argued that popular media culture has become a major force of socialization and was subverting traditional literacy skills, thus undermining education. Postman criticized the negative social effects of the media and called for educators and citizens to intensify critique of the media. Extolling the virtues of book culture and literacy, Postman called for educational reform to counter the nefarious effects of media and consumer culture.

Indeed, there is by now a long tradition of studies that have discussed children and media such as television (see Luke 1990). Critics like Postman (1986) argue that excessive TV viewing stunts cognitive growth, creates shortened attention spans, and habituates youth to fragmented, segmented, and imagistic cultural experiences and that thus television and other electronic media are a social problem for children. Defenders stress the educational benefits of some television, suggest that it is merely harmless entertainment, or argue that audiences construct their own meanings from popular media (Fiske 1989, 1993).

Negative depictions of the media and consumerism, youth hedonism, excessive materialism, and growing violence were contested by British cultural studies that claimed that the media were being scapegoated for a wide range of social problems. In *Policing the Crisis* (Hall et al. 1978), Stuart Hall and colleagues at the Birmingham Centre for Contemporary Cultural Studies analyzed what they took to be a media-induced "moral panic" about mugging and youth violence. The Birmingham group argued for an active audience that was able to critically dissect and make use of media material, arguing against the media manipulation perspective. Rooted in a classic article by Stuart Hall titled "Encoding and Decoding" (1980), British cultural studies began studying how individuals and different groups read television news and magazines, engaged in consumption, and made use of a broad range of media. In *Everyday Television: 'Nationwide,'* Charlotte Brunsdon and David Morley (1978) studied how different audiences consumed TV news; Ien Ang (1985) and Tamar Liebes and Elihu Katz (1990) investigated how varying audiences in Holland, Israel, and elsewhere consumed and made use of the U.S. TV series *Dallas;* and John Fiske (1989,

1993) wrote a series of books celebrating the active audience and consumer in a wide range of domains by audiences in many countries.

Yet critics working within British cultural studies, individuals in a wide range of social movements, and academics from a variety of fields and positions began criticizing the media from the 1960s and to the present for promoting sexism, racism, homophobia, and other oppressive social phenomena. There was intense focus on the politics of representation, discriminating between negative and positive representations of major social groups and harmful and beneficial media effects, debates that coalesced under the rubric of the politics of representation.

The Media and the Politics of Representation

The groundbreaking work of critical media theorists like the Frankfurt School, British cultural studies, and French structuralism and poststructuralism revealed that culture is a social construct, intrinsically linked to the vicissitudes of the social and historically specific milieu in which it is conceived, and that gender, race, class, sexuality, and other dimensions of social life are socially constructed in part via media representations (see Durham and Kellner 2001). Media and cultural studies have been engaged in critical interrogations of the politics of representation, which draw upon feminist approaches and multicultural theories to analyze fully the functions of gender, class, race, ethnicity, nationality, sexual preference, and so on in the media. The social dimensions of media constructions are perceived by cultural studies as being vitally constitutive of audiences who appropriate and use texts.

While earlier British cultural studies engaged the progressive and oppositional potential of working class and then youth culture, under the pressure of the social movements of the 1960s and 1970s, many adopted a feminist dimension, paid greater attention to race, ethnicity, and nationality, and concentrated on sexuality. During this period, assorted discourses of race, gender, sex, nationality, and so on circulated in response to social struggles and movements, and were taken up in cultural studies to critically engage the politics of representation.[4] An increasingly complex, culturally hybrid, and diasporic global culture and networked society calls for sophisticated understandings of the interplay of representations, politics, and the forms of media, and theorists cited in this section were groundbreakers in offering new perspectives on these problematics.

Laura Mulvey's essay "Visual Pleasure and Narrative Cinema" (1992) contends that the cinematic apparatus legitimates and perpetuates a patriarchal order in which the object of the look is female and the subject of the look is male. At the time of its publication, Mulvey's article offered a radical tool for analyzing the representation of sexual difference and desire in cinema. The article was taken up by a range of feminist and other critics who attacked sexism and the objectification of women and sexuality in the media and the ways that the camera induces spectators to assume certain subject positions. Yet Doane (1982) argued that focus on the male gaze defocused attention on the female spectator and offered an excessively monolithic model of the cinematic apparatus, and Richard Dyer (1982) discussed the complex ways that male spectators and gays negotiated the viewing of visual representations.

Many gay and lesbian theorists, however, decried the ways that media representations promoted homophobia by presenting negative representations of gay sexuality. Larry Gross's "Out of the Mainstream: Sexual Minorities and the Mass Media" (1989) argues that corporate media culture defines and frames sexuality in ways that marginalize gays and lesbians and "symbolically annihilate" their lives. Stereotypic depiction of lesbians and gay men as "abnormal, and the suppression of positive or even 'unexceptional' portrayals, serve to maintain and police the boundaries of the moral order" (p. 136), in Gross's view. He argues for alternative representations—a call that has to a certain degree been heard and answered by gay and lesbian media producers coming to prominence in the contemporary era (see also Gross and Woods 1999).

A variety of critics of color have engaged racist representations in film, television, and other domains of media culture. Herman Gray (1995), for example, scrutinizes the related trajectory of black representation on network television in an analysis that takes into account the structures and conventions of the medium as well as the sociopolitical conditions of textual production. Gray's examination of race and representation highlights the articulations between contemporary or recent representations of blacks and much earlier depictions. He argues that "our contemporary moment continues to be shaped discursively by representations of race and ethnicity that began in the formative years of television" (p. 73). Contemporary cultural production is still in dialogue with these earliest moments, he writes, and provides regressive as well as progressive aspects of this engagement. Importantly, Gray identifies certain turning points in television's representation of blackness, situating these "signal moments" within the cultural and political contexts in which they were generated. His analysis brings us to a confrontation with the possibilities of mass cultural texts engaging the politics of difference in a complex and meaningful way.

Many critics emphasized the importance of connecting representations of gender, race, class, sexuality, and other subject positions to disclose how the media present socially derogatory representations of subordinate groups. bell hooks (1992) has been among the first and most prolific African American feminist scholars to call attention to the interlockings of race, class, gender, and additional markers of identity in the constitution of subjectivity. Early in her career, she challenged feminists to recognize and confront the ways in which race and class inscribe women's (and men's) experiences. In "Eating the Other" (1992), hooks explores cultural constructions of the "Other" as an object of desire, tying such positioning to consumerism and commodification as well as to issues of racial domination and subordination. Cautioning against the seductiveness of celebrating "Otherness," hooks uses various media cultural artifacts—clothing catalogs, films, rap music—to debate issues of cultural appropriation versus cultural appreciation, and to uncover the personal and political crosscurrents at work in mass media representation.

Critics also have stressed the need for incorporating perspectives and voices of individuals from a variety of global sites in debating issues of contemporary media and society. Chandra Mohanty (1991) raises issues of nation, identity, and power in her often-cited essay, "Under Western Eyes." Mohanty challenges the appropriation and coding of "Third World women" in Western feminist scholarship, reminding us that the third world is more complex, diverse, and multiform than dominant constructions allow. Even the supposedly oppositional discourses of feminism often end up being reductive and ahistorical in terms of what Mohanty calls "Third World difference." Mohanty, like hooks, poses an important challenge to the notion that the category of "woman" can be considered without acknowledging class, ethnic, and racial locations. Her objection is to "the elision . . . between 'women' as a discursively constructed group and 'women' as material subjects of their own history" (p. 56). "Women" in this discourse are constructed as objects, victims, and dependent, rather than as subjects of struggle and resistance in concrete historical conditions.[5]

Media representations thus often construct women and their social problems as victims and objects, and mainstream media rarely present positive representations of women's movements or collective forms of struggle, rather focusing at best on women as individual examples of specific social problems like rape or domestic violence, or, more positively, as individual exemplars of heroism or noble values. In arguing for historically and culturally grounded understandings of women's multiple experiences and resistances, Mohanty presents important theoretical and methodological issues that challenge hegemonies and asymmetries of power in critical cultural studies as well as in mainstream scholarship. Mohanty's work also emphasizes that social and political changes have implications far beyond a single nation's borders.

Just as Mulvey, hooks, and Gray recognize the multilayered and overdetermined character of racial and gendered oppression in and by the media in English-speaking countries, Néstor García Canclini (1995) grapples with the theoretical consequences of the decentering of the nation-state and the impact of postmodern, postnational, and global cultures on Latin American cultural production. In critical media studies, Latin America's "Third World" status of economic dependency on the United States led to theories of "cultural imperialism" wherein the United States was perceived to have a hegemonic and monolithically destructive impact on the indigenous cultural production of its neighbors to the south. European scholars have also dissected the transnational flow of television, film, and other media on various national cultures and the ways that U.S. media corporations like Disney and other transnational media corporations have come to dominate many national cultures, to undermine local cultures, and to have a wide range of harmful cultural and media effects (Mattelart 1979; Mattelart and Mattelart 1998).

Yet Latin American scholars and others also identify globalization as a force calling for fresh research perspectives; new technologies and new markets have impacts that are not simply oppressive, they argue, but rather make way for local and regional cultural production that has progressive potential. In his 1995 book *Hybrid Cultures: Strategies for Entering and Leaving Modernity,* García Canclini describes the far-reaching synthesis of modern and traditional culture in Latin America, and the way that postmodern global culture is complexifying the situation. In the essay "Hybrid Cultures, Oblique Powers," while still taking into account the exercise of power between "first" and "third" world nations, García Canclini argues that the mass media have not erased traditional Latin American forms of cultural expression; rather, he claims that they have contributed to a cultural reconfiguration that has displaced established modes of thinking about culture. This transformation, however, is tied to other social shifts, including the expansion of metropolitan areas, the decrease in collective public action, and the unfinished projects of political change in many Latin American countries. The mass media constitute a new kind of public sphere as they simulate the integration of a disintegrated society. Contrasting media culture with traditional symbols of modernity—monuments and museums—García Canclini engages the central question of how the new, dense networks of economic and ideological crossings, and the deterritorializations and hybridities born of them, reconfigure power relations.

Focus on the politics of representation thus calls attention to the fact that culture is produced within relationships of domination and subordination and tends to reproduce or resist existing structures of power. Such a perspective also provides tools for cultural studies whereby the critic can denounce aspects of media forms and artifacts that reproduce class, gender, racial, and diverse modes of domination and positively valorize aspects that subvert existing types of domination, or depict resistance and movements against them.

Issues of the politics of representation and violence and the media intersect in the impassioned debates over pornography. For a school of feminism and cultural conservatives, pornography and violence against women are one of the most problematic aspects of media culture. Antiporn feminists argue that pornography objectifies women, that the industry dangerously exploits them, and that pornography promotes violence against women and debases sexuality. Prosex feminists and defenders of pornography, by contrast, argue that pornography exhibits a tabooed array of sexuality, provokes fantasy, and awakens desire, and can be used by consumers in gratifying ways.[6]

Hence, while there is widespread agreement that the media construct and provide access to social problems and that their representations are an important part of the social world, there is heated debate over whether the media have positive or negative social effects. Many critics argue that one-sided pro or con positions tended to be simplistic and reductive and that contextual analysis needs to be made on specific media effects of certain technologies or artifacts on specific audiences (Kellner 1995, 2003). This position also asserts that in general, media have contradictory and ambiguous effects and that in many cases it is impossible to accurately discern or distinguish positive or negative features that are often interconnected.

Likewise, there are equally heated debates over whether the media promote or inhibit democracy. In the following sections, I contextualize the debate over media and democracy in terms of the nature and vicissitudes of democracy in a global world. This involves engaging the changing patterns of political economy of the media, expanding the roles of the media in political life, the rise of technologies like the Internet, and the ways that global corporate media constitute a major social problem that also, paradoxically, points to possible solutions.

THE MEDIA AND DEMOCRACY

In classical democratic theory, the press and then the broadcast media were to provide information, ideas, and debate concerning issues of public significance in order to promote a democratic public sphere (Keane 1991). The dual democratic functions of the press were to provide a check against excessive power and to inform the people concerning the major issues of public interest in order to allow their knowledgeable participation in public life. A free press was vitally necessary to maintain a democratic society, and it is often claimed by champions of democracy that freedom of the press is one of the features that defines the superiority of democratic societies over competing social systems.

This concept of a free press was also extended to the broadcast media that were assigned a series of democratic responsibilities. In countries like Britain, which developed a public service model of broadcasting, radio and then television were considered part of the public sector with important duties to reproduce the national culture and provide forums of information and debate for their citizens (Tracey 1998). Even in the United States, where a private industry model of broadcasting came to dominate, in the Federal Communications Act of 1934 and subsequent legislation and court decisions, broadcasting was to serve the "public interest, convenience, and necessity," ascribing certain democratic functions to the media, until the overthrow of these strictures in the 1980s and 1990s.[7]

In Western concepts of democracy, broadcasting was thus initially conceived as a public utility, with the airwaves established as part of the public domain, subject to regulation by the government to ensure that broadcasting would meet its democratic responsibilities. Yet during the two centuries of the democratic revolutions, and constant tensions between the forces of capitalism and democracy, political and corporate powers often came to dominate the media, and over the past several decades, forces of deregulation have expanded private corporate control of dominant media. During the era of laissez-faire deregulation pursued in England by Thatcher and her successors and in the United States by the Reagan administration and subsequent regimes, much of the broadcasting regulatory apparatus was dismantled, and giant corporations took over key broadcast media, or became increasingly powerful. In Europe and then in many different countries, starting with the Thatcher administration in the late 1970s, country after country deregulated its media, allowed a proliferation of private media corporations to compete with largely state-run or state-financed public broadcasting, and thus increased the range of corporate media organizations, which weakened public service broadcasting, replacing it with a market model.

In the era of intensifying globalization of the 1990s and into the new millennium, market models of broadcasting generally emerged as dominant in many parts of the world, and a series of global mergers took place that consolidated media ownership into ever fewer hands. The result has been that a shrinking number of giant global media corporations have controlled a widening range of media in corporate conglomerates that control the press, broadcasting, film, music, and other forms of popular entertainment, as well as the most accessed Internet sites. Media have been increasingly organized on a business model, and competition between proliferating commercialized media have provided an impetus to replace news with entertainment, to generate a tabloidization of news, and to pursue profits and sensationalism rather than public enlightenment and democracy.[8]

Many scholars have sketched out and criticized the consequences of media deregulation and the triumph of a market model for democracy over the past decades (see notes 7-8). Expanded concentration of power in the hands of corporate groups who control powerful media conglomerates have in the view of many undermined democracy, and many indicate increasing corporate control of the media as a serious social problem. If corporate media promote their own interests and agendas, they do not serve their democratic purposes of informing the people and allowing the public to engage in informed civic debate and thus to participate in democratic dialogue and decision making. Moreover, if the media corporations utilize their powerful instruments of communication and information to advance their own corporate interests and those of politicians and policies that they favor, then the media have lost their democratic functions of serving to debate issues of sociopolitical interest and importance and to serve as a critical watchdog against excessive corporate government power and questionable policies. Moreover, the media do not address significant social problems if these issues threaten corporate power or dominant economic interests, and by undermining democracy and not engaging the significant social problems of the era, the corporate media themselves become a social problem, requiring a democratic media politics.

In the view of many media critics, once the corporate media surrendered their responsibilities to serve the public and provide a forum for democratic debate and to address significant issues of common concern, they have largely promoted the growth of corporate and state power and undermined democracy. This results in the ignoring of crucial social problems by corporate media and the advancing of corporate agendas. For Jurgen Habermas, the problem was rooted in the transition from the liberal public sphere grounded in democratic public institutions to a corporate-controlled media of late capitalism.

For Habermas, during the era of the Enlightenment and eighteenth-century democratic revolutions, public spheres emerged where individuals could discuss and debate issues of common concern. In his influential study *The Structural Transformation of the Public Sphere* ([1962] 1989), Habermas contrasted various forms of an active, participatory public sphere in the heroic era of liberal democracy with the more privatized forms of spectator politics in a bureaucratic industrial society in which the media and elites controlled the public sphere. The book delineates the historical genesis of the bourgeois public sphere, followed by an account of the structural change of the public sphere in the contemporary era with the rise of state capitalism, culture industries, and the increasingly powerful positions of economic corporations and big business in public life. On this account, big economic and governmental organizations took over the public sphere, while citizens were content to become primarily consumers of goods, services, political administration, and spectacle.

The classical liberal public sphere was a location where criticism of the state and existing society could circulate. The institutions and sites of the eighteenth-century democratic public sphere included newspapers, journals, and a press independent from state ownership and control, coffeehouses where individuals read newspapers and engaged in political discussion, literary salons where ideas and criticism were produced, and public assemblies, which were the sites of political oratory and debate. During the nineteenth century, the working class developed its own oppositional public spheres in union halls, party cells and meeting places, saloons, and institutions of working-class culture. With the rise of Social Democracy and other working-class movements in Europe and the United States, an alternative press, radical cultural organizations, and the strike, sit-in, and political insurrection emerged as sites and forms of an oppositional public sphere.

Habermas describes a transition from the liberal public sphere that originated in the Enlightenment and the American and French revolutions to a media-dominated public sphere in the current era of what he calls "welfare state capitalism and mass democracy." This historical transformation is grounded in Horkheimer and Adorno's (1972) analysis of the culture industry, in which giant corporations have taken over the public sphere and transformed it from a sphere of rational debate into one of manipulative consumption and passivity. In this transformation, "public opinion" shifts from rational consensus emerging from debate, discussion, and reflection to the manufactured opinion of polls and political and media elites. Rational debate and consensus have thus been replaced by managed discussion and manipulation by the machinations of advertising and political consulting agencies. As Habermas (1989) argued: "Publicity loses its critical function in favor of a staged display; even arguments are transmuted into symbols to which again one can not respond by arguing but only by identifying with them" (p. 206).

For Habermas, the function of the media has thus been transformed from facilitating rational discourse and debate within the public sphere into shaping, constructing, and limiting public discourse to those themes validated and approved by media corporations. Hence, the interconnection between a sphere of public debate and individual participation has been fractured and transmuted into that of a realm of political information and spectacle, in which citizen-consumers ingest and passively absorb media materials. "Citizens" thus become spectators of media presentations and discourse that mold public opinion, reducing consumer-citizens to objects of news, information, and political manipulation. In Habermas's (1989) words: "Inasmuch as the mass media today strip away the literary husks from the kind of bourgeois self-interpretation and utilize them as marketable forms for the public services provided in a culture of consumers, the original meaning is reversed" (p. 171).

Habermas has been criticized for idealizing the bourgeois public sphere and failing to articulate the important democratic functions of alternative public spheres organized by labor, oppositional political groups, women, and other forces not adequately represented in the liberal public sphere. Nonetheless, his concept of a public sphere can serve as a normative ideal of a space in which individuals can freely discuss issues of common concern and organize to implement reforms and social change. Moreover, it can function as a standpoint for critique that indicates dangers to democracy and the failure of the media to address significant social problems, if they are indeed ignored.[9]

GLOBALIZATION AND THE TRIUMPH OF CORPORATE MEDIA

Today's public spheres include the print and broadcast media, computer databases, Web sites, and Internet discussion groups, utilized by social movements, local citizens' organizations, subcultures, political interest groups, and individuals who use listservs, Weblogs, or other instruments to serve various political causes.[10] With the rise of contemporary media and computer society, it is through the print and broadcast media, computers, and various multimedia technologies that political hegemony has been forged over the past two decades (Kellner 1990, 1995, 2003a). During the past several decades, the dominant media of information and communication have become largely "corporate media," first, because they are owned by big corporations like NBC/RCA/General Electric, Murdoch's News Corporation, Bertelsmann, ABC/Disney, Sony, and AOL/Time Warner. Second, these media conglomerates express the corporate point of view and advance the agendas of the organizations that own them and the politicians whom they support and in turn who pursue the interests of the media conglomerates in governmental institutions.

During the era of new liberalism, the most powerful corporate forces have tightened their control of both the state and the media in the interests of aggressively promoting a probusiness agenda at the expense of other social groups. The consequences of the triumph of neoliberalism and its program of deregulation, tax breaks for the wealthy, military buildup, cutback of social programs, and the widening of class divisions are increasingly evident in the new millennium. As the new century unfolds, globalized societies confront the specter of ever-increasing corporate and military power, worsening social conditions for the vast majority, and sporadic mixtures of massive apathy and explosive conflict. In this conjuncture, the corporate media continue to play a major role in managing consumer demand, producing thought and behavior congruent with the system of corporate capitalism, and creating people's sense of political events and issues. Since the media continue to become an ever greater political power and social force, it is all the more important to carry out sustained theoretical reflections on the social functions and effects of the corporate media, analyzing their threats to democracy, and seeing the corporate media as a social problem.

The corporate media form a system and interact and overlap with each other.[11] During the 1980s and 1990s, television networks in the United States amalgamated with other major sectors of the cultural industries and corporate capital, including mergers between CBS and Westinghouse; MCA and Seagram's; Time Warner and Turner Communications; ABC, Capital Cities, and Disney; and NBC, General Electric, and Microsoft. In 1999, CBS merged with the entertainment colossus Viacom in a $38 billion megamerger. Dwarfing all previous information/entertainment corporation combinations, Time Warner and America Online (AOL) proposed a $163.4 billion amalgamation in January 2000, which was approved a year later. This union brought together two huge corporations involved in television, film, magazines, newspapers, books, information databases, computers, and other media,

suggesting a coming synthesis of media and computer culture, of entertainment and information in a new infotainment society.

The fact that "new media" Internet service provider and portal AOL was the majority shareholder in the deal seemed to point to the triumph of the new online Internet culture over the old media culture. The merger itself called attention to escalating synergy among information and entertainment industries and old and new media in the form of the networked economy and cyberculture. Yet the dramatic decline in the AOL Time Warner stock price and corporate battles for control of the giant corporation illustrated the tensions between old and new media and the instabilities and uncertainties at the heart of global capitalism (see Kellner 2003a).

In Europe also there have been growing mergers of media corporations, the rise and decline of media giants like Vivendi and Bertelsmann, and the emergence of new conglomerates to take the place of declining media empires. In France, the Dassault group, headed by a right-wing politician who controlled a media empire, has taken over the weekly *Express* and 14 other acquisitions, while another French conservative group headed by Jean-Luc Lagardere, an associate of Jacques Chirac, is France's biggest publisher, controls the magazine market, and is attempting to expand into telecommunications (Ramonet 2002). In Italy, Silvio Berlusconi owns the three main private television channels, and as prime minister now also controls state television, while in Spain, the Prisa company controls major newspaper and other publications, as well as radio and television networks.

There have also been massive mergers in the telecommunications industry, as well as between cable and satellite industries with major entertainment and corporate conglomerates. By 2003, 10 gigantic multinational corporations, including AOL Time Warner, Disney/ABC, General Electric-NBC, Viacom-CBS, News Corporation, Vivendi, Sony, Bertelsmann, AT&T, and Liberty Media controlled most of the production of information and entertainment throughout the globe.[12] The result is less competition and diversity and more corporate control of newspapers and journalism, television, radio, film, and other media of information and entertainment.

The corporate media, communications, and information industries are frantically scrambling to provide delivery for a wealth of services. These will include increased Internet access, wireless cellular telephones, and satellite personal communication devices, which will facilitate video, film, entertainment, and information on demand, as well as Internet shopping and more unsavory services like pornography and gambling. Consequently, the fusions of the immense infotainment conglomerates disclose a synergy between information technologies and multimedia, which combine entertainment and information, undermining distinctions between these domains and producing powerful new social forces.

The neoliberal deregulation agenda of the 1980s and 1990s attempted to remove all major structural constraints on the broadcasting business in terms of ownership, licenses, and business practices. Furthermore, it eliminated public service requirements and restraints on advertising and programming in many countries, thus allowing television networks, for instance, to increase advertising, cut back on documentaries and public service programming, and use children's programs to dramatize commercial toys, eliminating the regulation of children's television that restricted advertising and forbid children's shows based on commercial toys. Deregulation contributed massively to the concentration, conglomeratization, and commercialization of the mainstream media and to the collapse of the telecommunication industry that cost over half a million people their jobs in 2002 and contributed to around $2 trillion of the $7 trillion lost on the U.S. stock market the same year (see Starr 2002).

Consequently, neoliberal deregulation of the media dramatically redefined the relationships between government and broadcasting and attempted to undo decades of regulatory guidelines and policies. As a result, during the past two decades, there has been a significant reduction of news, documentary, and public affairs broadcasting. The trend toward sensationalism has been intensified with "reality programming" (i.e., tabloid journalism of the sort found in the New York *Daily News* and *Post* or British tabloids that obsess over scandals of leading politicians or the Royals). Tabloid journalism ranges from Geraldo Rivera's "exposés" of

satanism and live drug busts, to the gruesome murder of the week, or series dedicated to tabloid-style crime and sex scandals.

In general, from the 1990s through the present, political broadcast journalism thus turned toward a tabloid-style journalism and media spectacle and away from analysis, criticism, and genuine investigative reporting that engaged social problems (see Kellner 2003a). Deregulation also led to dramatic conglomerate takeovers of radio stations and curtailment of radio news operations. In practice, this meant major cutting back of local news, thus depriving communities that did not have a local daily newspaper of news concerning their areas. Previously, it was radio that was the voice of these communities, but with the takeover of local radio stations by corporate conglomerates, local news and public affairs were often cut back significantly and even sometimes eliminated completely. During the 1990s and into the new millennium, consolidation and commercialization of radio continued to intensify, with a small number of firms buying up more and more local radio stations and imposing standardized Top 40 music formats and nationally syndicated and mostly conservative talk radio shows. Moreover, 2002 *Extra!* surveys indicate that National Public Radio continued to be dominated by white voices, while community radio was under attack from corporate and public radio takeovers.[13]

Other studies during the first decade of broadcasting deregulation indicated an increased amount of commercial interruptions, dramatically deteriorating children's television, large cutbacks in news and public affairs programming, and a more conservative corporate climate at the networks where individuals feared for their jobs in a period of "bottom-line" corporate firing (see Kellner 1990). Furthermore, right-wing pressure groups used a variety of strategies to push and keep network news coverage on the right track. For instance, the Accuracy in Media group carried out campaigns against programs with a perceived "liberal bias" and demanded, and sometimes received, free time to answer supposedly "liberal" programs. Lawsuits by General William Westmoreland against a CBS Vietnam documentary, and by Israeli General Ariel Sharon against *Time* magazine, discouraged the media from criticizing conservative politicians. Although Westmoreland and Sharon lost their cases, the lawsuits had a chilling effect constraining the corporate media against undertaking critical reporting against individuals, corporations, or groups who might sue them.[14]

During Gulf War I of 1991 and the Afghanistan war following the September 11, 2001 terror attacks, the broadcasting networks and press were subject to unprecedented pressure to conform to the views of the respective wars advanced by the Bush administration in question and the Pentagon (see Kellner 1992, 2003b). This pool system that restricted access to the battlefield and that produced censorship of reporters' stories and images followed the British attempt to control news during the Falkland-Malvinas war in the early 1980s (Kellner 1992). On this model, press pools sharply restrict access to the actual battlefields, and the government and military do everything possible to control the flow of images, news, and information. In the 2003 Iraq war, by contrast, the Pentagon allowed "embedded" reporters to travel with troops, but on the whole the media identified with the military and there was little critical reporting (see Kellner, forthcoming).

In addition, during Gulf Wars I and II, as well as during the Afghanistan war, there were organized campaigns to mobilize audiences against networks or papers that criticized U.S. policy, that documented civilian casualties, or that in any way were seen as aiding and abetting the enemy (Kellner 2003b). The result is that during war, the press and broadcasting institutions in the United States are little more than cheerleaders for the military effort and instruments of propaganda for the state. Moreover, not only are news programs slanted toward the hegemonic positions of corporate and government elites, but discussion shows also are dominated by conservative discourses. Although there has been a proliferation of television political discussion shows over the past decade with the rise of 24-hour cable news television, one wonders if the public interest is served by the composition of these corporate media talk shows, which almost always are limited to mainstream representatives of the two major political parties, or other white male, establishment figures, with the predominance of commentators markedly conservative.[15]

Thus, in the past 25 years, while there has been an increase in news and discussion programming in the United States, there has been less of the liberal and socially critical documentaries of the previous decades, and the dominant political discourse has been largely conservative. Moreover, the corporate media have increasingly served as propaganda instruments for the state and big corporations on a global scale (Schiller 1990). For instance, while during the Vietnam era the press was notoriously critical of the U.S. military intervention, during the crisis in the Gulf and Gulf War I, as well as the subsequent Iraq war of 2003, the U.S. corporate media advanced the agenda of the Bush administrations and the Pentagon while failing to adequately inform the public or to debate the issues involved. Instead of serving as a forum for public debate, the corporate media served instead as a propaganda organ for the state, the military, and defense industries, contributing to a further centralization of state, corporate, and military power and growing manipulation and indoctrination of the public. Indeed, in most countries during Gulf War I, various national media corporations followed the framing, images, and discourses of U.S. media like CNN (Kellner 1992).

On the whole, corporate-controlled media promote the interests of conservative parties and economic interests. Globally, the Rupert Murdoch-owned News Corporation has disseminated aggressively right-wing politics, and in Italy, media baron Silvio Berlusconi became prime minister with the aid of his media empire behind him, despite a series of business scandals that could have landed him in jail. As an intense debate over Iraq unfolded in February 2003, the Murdoch press solidly backed the Bush and Blair prointervention line and criticized opponents of the then pending and soon-to-come military assault on Iraq.[16]

In general, the decline of documentaries, public affairs programming, and political discussion helped produce a less informed electorate, more susceptible to political manipulation. Democracy requires vigorous public debate of key issues of importance and an informed electorate, able to make intelligent decisions and to participate in politics. Corporate control of the media meant that corporations could use the media to aggressively promote their own interests and to cut back on the criticism of corporate abuses that were expanding from the 1970s to the present. The tabloidization of news and intense competition between various media meant that the corporate media ignored social problems and focused on scandal and tabloid entertainment rather than issues of serious public concern.

The 1990s was an era of escalating social problems caused by globalization and the abuses of corporate capitalism, key issues like the environment and ecological problems, a crisis in public health, growing inequality between rich and poor, and dangerous corporate practices that would eventually generate global economic crises in the early 2000s. It was an era of neoliberalism in which not only were the media deregulated, but so too were corporate practices, financial markets, and the global economy. The media tended to celebrate the "new economy" and the period of economic boom and growing affluency while overlooking the dangers of an overinflated stock market, an unregulated economy, and the growing divisions between haves and have-nots. During this period, the corporate media thus neglected social problems in favor of celebrating the capitalist economy and technological revolution. The media also overlooked the growth of terrorism, dangerous consequences of the division between the haves and have-nots in the global economy, and growing ecological problems.

In the 2000s, corporate control of the mainstream media has intensified with ever fewer corporations controlling more and more media outlets. In the United States, the Bush administration is pushing an increasingly deregulatory agenda, despite the corporate scandals of 2001–2002, which included many corporations in the telecommunications sector. In June 2003, the FCC passed rules allowing corporations to own a higher percentage of local media, opening the door for more mergers and consolidation. During the same period, the British House of Lords attempted to block a similar deregulatory agenda being promoted by the Labour Party.[17] Hence, struggles over media regulation and consolidation continue while the biggest media conglomerates globally increase their control of print and broadcasting outlets, whereby the Internet becomes more important as an instrument of alternative ideas and democratic debate.

THE INTERNET AND THE PROSPECTS FOR DEMOCRATIC MEDIA

The only way that a democratic social order can be preserved is for the mainstream media to assume their democratic functions of critically discussing all issues of public concern and social problems from a variety of viewpoints and fostering vigorous public debate. The democratic imperative that the press and broadcasting provide a variety of views on issues of public interest and controversy has been increasingly sacrificed, as has their responsibility to serve as a check against excessive government or corporate power and corruption. As I have documented, many critics have argued that over the past decades, a wide range of social problems have not been adequately addressed and that the corporate media themselves have become a major social problem and have blocked social progress while advancing the interests of corporate institutions and conservative politics. To remedy this situation, first of all there must be a revitalization of the media reform movement and a recognition of the importance of media politics in the struggle for democratization and the creation of a just society, and support and development of alternative media.[18] Democratizing the media system will require development of a vigorous reform movement and recognition for all progressive social movements of the importance of invigorating the media system for forward-looking social change and addressing urgent social problems and issues. This process will involve sustained critique of the corporate media, calls for reregulation, and the revitalization of public television, cultivation of community and public radio, improved public access television, an expansion of investigative and public service journalism, and full democratic utilization of the Internet. Since giant and conglomeratized corporations control the mainstream press, broadcasting, and other major institutions of culture and communication, there is little hope that the corporate media will be democratized without major pressure or increased government regulation of a sort that is not on the horizon in the present moment in most parts of the world.

The Internet, by contrast, provides potential for a democratic revitalization of the media. The Internet makes accessible more information available to a greater number of people, more easily, and from a wider array of sources than any instrument of information and communication in history. It is constantly astonishing to discover the extensive array of material available, articulating every conceivable point of view and providing news, opinion, and sources of a striking variety and diversity. Moreover, the Internet allows two-way communication and democratic participation in public dialogue, activity that is essential to producing a vital democracy.

One of the major contradictions of the current era is that for the wired world at least, and increasingly the public at large, the information environment is expanding, consisting of a broad spectrum of radio and television broadcasting networks; print media and publications; and the global village of the Internet, which itself contains the most varied and extensive sources of information and entertainment ever assembled in a single medium. The Internet can send disparate types and sources of information and images instantly throughout the world and is increasingly being used by a variety of oppositional groups (see Kellner 1999; Best and Kellner 2001; Kahn and Kellner 2003). Yet it is also true that thanks to media mergers of the past decade, fewer hands control the dominant media outlets, which can be utilized by powerful corporate and political interests for specific partisan ends, as I document in this chapter. To be sure, much of the world is not yet wired, many people do not even read, and different inhabitants in various parts of the globe receive their information and culture in very dissimilar ways through varying sources, media, and forms. Thus, the type and quality of information vary tremendously, depending on an individual's access and ability to properly interpret and contextualize it.

Democracy, however, requires informed citizens and access to information, and thus the viability of democracy is dependent on citizens seeking out crucial information, having the ability to access and appraise it, and to engage in public conversations about issues of importance. Democratic media reform and alternative media are thus crucial to revitalizing and even preserving the democratic project in the face of powerful corporate and political forces. How media can be democratized and what alternative media can be developed will, of course, be different in various parts of the world, but without a democratic media politics and alternative media, democracy itself cannot survive in a vigorous form, nor will a wide range of social problems be engaged or even addressed.

NOTES

1. For overviews of the literature on media effects, see Klapper (1960) and McQuail (1994). For a reader who presents cases for conflicting positions concerning positive and negative effects of a wide range of media, see Barbour (1994).

2. For an excellent critique of the two-flow paradigm, see Gitlin (1978).

3. See the studies depicting both sides of the debate on contemporary media and alleged harmful or beneficial effects in Barbour (1994) and in Dines and Humez (2003).

4. For examples of studies of the politics of representation, see Gilroy (1991), McRobbie (1994), and texts collected in Durham and Kellner (2001).

5. See the commentary and expansion of her now classic study, "Under Western Eyes," in Mohanty (2003).

6. See the broad array of the pro and con perspectives on pornography in Dines and Humez (2003).

7. See the discussion of the media and democracy in Kellner (1990, chaps. 2 and 3); on the Federal Communications Act of 1934 and the battle for democratic media in the 1930s, see McChesney (1993).

8. On media consolidation and its impact over the past two decades, see Herman and Chomsky (1988), Bagdikian (1997), Schiller (1990), Kellner (1990), and McChesney (2000).

9. On the influence of Habermas's concept of the public sphere, see the studies in Calhoun (1992) and Kellner (2000).

10. On new public spheres and technopolitics, see Kellner (1999), Best and Kellner (2001), and Kahn and Kellner (2003).

11. See Horkheimer and Adorno (1972) and the studies of the structure and impact of contemporary culture industry in McChesney (2000) and Best and Kellner (2001).

12. See the charts on media mergers and concentration in Croteau and Hoynes (2001:75ff.) and in *The Nation* (January 7, 2002) with analysis by Mark Crispin Miller, "What's Wrong with This Picture?"

13. See the reports "White Noise: Voices of Color Scarce on Urban Public Radio" and "No Community Voices Wanted." *Extra!* (September–October 2002). William Safire (2003) cites a Gannett report that indicates

that in 1996, the largest two radio chains owned 115 stations, but by 2003 they owned more than 1,400; a handful of radio company owners used to generate only 20 percent of industry revenue, while today the top five take in 55 percent of all money spent on local radio and the number of station owners has plummeted by a third.

14. For a detailed study of the effects of deregulation on media culture in the 1990s, see McChesney (2000).

15. A 2002 study carried out by a nonpartisan German-based media analysis firm Media Tenor indicated that the three major U.S. network news operations at ABC, CBS, and NBC used news sources that were 92 percent white, 85 percent male, and, where party affiliation was identifiable, 75 percent Republican. Big business had 35 times more representatives than labor; Latinos, Asian Americans, and Arab Americans were almost invisible; "experts" came from primarily elite institutions and rarely nongovernmental organizations; and the established political party and executive branch was strongly favored. Fairness and Accuracy in Writing, "Power Sources: On Party, Gender, Race and Class, TV News Looks to the Most Powerful Groups." *Extra!* (May/June 2002).

16. "Their Master's Voice," *The Guardian* (February 12, 2003). Murdoch owns more than 175 publications on three continents and *The Guardian* documented how leading editors of his media chains duplicated the prointervention stance he took in an interview published in the Australian magazine *The Bulletin.*

17. See Dan Levine, "Bad to Worse. FCC Approves Even More Media Consolidation," *In These Times,* June 6, 2003, and Matt Wells, "Putnam Forces Block on Predatory Media Barons," *The Guardian,* July 3, 2003. Yet in a surprising court decision, a U.S. federal appeals court issued an order blocking the FCC action; see Stephen LaBaton, "U.S. Court Blocks Plan to Ease Rule on Media Owners," *New York Times,* September 4, 2003.

18. For more detailed proposals for democratizing the media and producing alternative media and politics, see Kellner (1990, 1999); McChesney (1997, 2000); Best and Kellner (2001); Jeffrey Chester and Gary O. Larson, "A 12-Step Program for Media Democracy," *The Nation* (July 23, 2002), and McChesney and Nichols (2002).

REFERENCES

Ang, Ien. 1985. *Watching Dallas.* London: Routledge.

Bagdikian, Ben. 1997. *The Media Monopoly.* 6th ed. Boston, MA: Beacon.

Barbour, William, ed. 1994. *Mass Media: Opposing Viewpoints.* San Diego, CA: Greenhaven.

Bell, Daniel. 1978. *The Cultural Contradictions of Capitalism.* New York: Basic Books.

Best, Steven and Douglas Kellner. 2001. *The Postmodern Adventure: Science, Technology, and Cultural Studies at the Third Millennium.* New York: Guilford.

Brunsdon, Charlotte and David Morley. 1978. *Everyday Television: 'Nationwide.'* London, England: British Film Institute.

Calhoun, Craig, ed. 1992. *Habermas and the Public Sphere.* Cambridge, MA: MIT Press.

Croteau, David and Williams Hoynes. 2001. *The Business of Media: Corporate Media and the Public Interest.* Thousand Oaks, CA: Pine Forge.

Czitrom, Daniel J. 1983. *Media and the American Mind.* Chapel Hill, NC: University of North Carolina Press.

DeFleur, M. L. and S. Ball-Rokeach. 1989. *Theories of Mass Communication.* New York: Longman.

Dines, Gail and Jean M. Humez, eds. 2003. *Gender, Race, and Class in Media.* London, England: Sage.

Doane, Mary Ann. 1982. "Film and the Masquerade: Theorizing the Female Spectator." *Screen* 23:74–87.

Durham, Meenakshi Gigi and Douglas Kellner, eds. 2001. *Media and Cultural Studies: KeyWorks.* Malden, MA: Blackwell.

Dyer, Richard. 1982. "Don't Look Now: The Male Pin-Up." *Screen* 23:61–73.

Eysenck, N. J. and D. K. B. Nias. 1979. *Sex, Violence and the Media.* London: Scientific Book Club.

Fiske, John. 1989. *Understanding Popular Culture.* Boston, MA: Unwin Hyman.

———. 1993. *Power Plays, Power Works.* New York: Verso.

Forman, H. J. [1933] 1972. *Our Movie-Made Children.* New York: Ayer.

García Canclini, Néstor. 1995. *Hybrid Cultures: Strategies for Entering and Leaving Modernity.* Translated by Christopher L. Chiappari and Silvia L. Lopez. Minneapolis, MN: University of Minnesota Press.

Gerbner, George. 2003. "Television Violence: At a Time of Turmoil and Terror." Pp. 339–348 in *Gender, Race, and Class in Media,* edited by Gail Dines and Jean M. Humez. London, England: Sage.

Gilroy, Paul. 1991. *There Ain't No Black in the Union Jack.* Chicago, IL: University of Chicago Press.

Gitlin, Todd. 1978. "Media Sociology: The Dominant Paradigm." *Theory and Society* 6:205–24.

Gray, Herman. 1995. *Watching Race: Television and the Struggle for "Blackness."* Minneapolis, MN: University of Minnesota Press.

Gross, Larry. 1989. "Out of the Mainstream: Sexual Minorities and the Mass Media." Pp. 130–49 in *Remote Control: Television, Audiences and Cultural Power,* edited by Ellen Seiter. New York: Routledge.

Gross, Larry and James D. Woods. 1999. "Introduction: Being Gay in American Media and Society." Pp. 3-22 in *The Columbia Reader on Lesbians and Gay Men in Media, Society, and Politics,* edited by Larry Gross and James D. Woods. New York: Columbia University Press.

Grossberg, Lawrence. 1992. *We Gotta Get Out of this Place.* New York: Routledge.

Habermas, Jurgen. [1962] 1989. *The Structural Transformation of the Public Sphere.* Cambridge, MA: MIT Press.

Hall, Stuart. 1980. "Encoding and Decoding." Pp. 128–38 in *Culture, Media, Language,* edited by Stuart Hall, Dorothy Hobson, Andrew Lowe, and Paul Willis. London, England: Hutchinson.

Hall, Stuart, Charles Critcher, Tony Jefferson, John Clarke, and Brian Robert. 1978. *Policing the Crisis: Mugging, the State, and Law and Order.* London, England: Macmillan.

Herman, Edward and Noam Chomsky. 1988. *Manufacturing Consent: The Political Economy of the Mass Media.* New York: Pantheon.

hooks, bell. 1992. *Black Looks: Race and Representation.* Boston, MA: South End.

Horkheimer, Max and T. W. Adorno. 1972. *Dialectic of Enlightenment.* New York: Seabury.

Jowett, Garth. 1976. *Film: The Democratic Art.* Boston, MA: Little, Brown.

Kahn, Richard and Douglas Kellner. 2003. "Internet Subcultures and Oppositional Politics." In *The Post-Subcultures Reader*, edited by D. Muggleton. London, England: Berg.

Katz, Elihu and Paul F. Lazarsfeld. 1955. *Personal Influence: The Part Played by People in the Flow of Mass Communication.* Glencoe, IL: Free Press.

Keane, John. 1991. *The Media and Democracy.* Cambridge, England: Polity Press.

Kellner, Douglas. 1989. *Critical Theory, Marxism, and Modernity.* Cambridge, England: Polity Press.

——. 1990. *Television and the Crisis of Democracy.* Boulder, CO: Westview.

——. 1992. *The Persian Gulf TV War.* Boulder, CO: Westview.

——. 1995. *Media Culture.* London, England: Routledge.

——. 1999. "Globalization From Below? Toward a Radical Democratic Technopolitics." *Angelaki* 4:101–13.

——. 2000. "Habermas, the Public Sphere, and Democracy: A Critical Intervention." Pp. 76-98 in *Perspectives on Habermas,* edited by Lewis Hahn. Chicago, IL: Open Court.

——. 2003a. *Media Spectacle.* New York and London: Routledge.

——. 2003b. *September 11 and Terror War: The Dangers of the Bush Legacy.* Lanham, MD: Rowman & Littlefield.

——. Forthcoming. "9/11, Spectacles of Terror, and Media Manipulation: A Critique of Jihadist and Bush Media Politics." Available at www.gseis.ucla.edu/faculty/kellner/kellner.html.

Klapper, J. 1960. *The Effects of Mass Communication.* New York: Free Press.

Lasswell, Harold. 1927. *Propaganda Technique in the Modern World.* New York: Knopf.

Lazarsfeld, Paul, Bernard Berelson, and Hazel Gaulet. 1944. *The People's Choice.* New York: Duell, Sloan & Pierce.

Liebes, Tamar and Elihu Katz. 1990. *The Export of Meaning: Cross-Cultural Readings of Dallas.* New York: Oxford University Press.

Luke, Carmen. 1990. *TV and Your Child.* London, England: Angus & Robertson.

Lull, James. 1995. *Media, Communication, Culture: A Global Approach.* Cambridge, England: Polity Press.

Mattelart, Armand. 1979. *Multinational Corporations and the Control of Culture.* Brighton, England: Harvester.

Mattelart, Armand and Michelle Mattelart. 1998. *Theories of Communication.* London, England: Sage.

McChesney, Robert. 1993. *Telecommunications, Mass Media, and Democracy: The Battle for the Control of U.S. Broadcasting, 1928–1935.* New York: Oxford University Press.

——. 1997. *Corporate Media and the Threat to Democracy.* New York: Seven Stories.

——. 2000. *Rich Media, Poor Democracy.* New York: New Press.

McChesney, Robert and John Nichols. 2002. *Our Media, Not Theirs: The Democratic Struggle Against Corporate Media.* New York: Seven Stories.

McQuail, Dennis. 1994. *Mass Communication Theory.* London, England: Sage.

McRobbie, Angela. 1994. *Postmodernism and Popular Culture.* New York: Routledge.

Mohanty, Chandra Talpade. 1991. "Under Western Eyes: Feminist Scholarship and Colonial Discourse." Pp. 51-80 in *Third World Women and the Politics of Feminism,* edited by C. T. Mohanty, A. Russo, and L. Torres. Bloomington, IN: Indiana University Press.

——. 2003. "'Under Western Eyes' Revisited: Feminist Solidarity through Anticapitalist Struggles." *Signs* 28:1–29.

Mulvey, Laura. 1992. "Visual Pleasure and Narrative Cinema." Pp. 22–45 in *The Sexual Subject: A Screen Reader in Sexuality*, edited by Mandy Merck. New York and London: Routledge.

Postman, Neil. 1986. *Amusing Ourselves to Death: Public Discourse in the Age of Show Business*. New York: Viking.

Ramonet, Ignacio. 2002. "A Less Free Press." *Le Monde diplomatique* (December). Available at www.mondediplo.com/200212/01/press.

Safire, William. 2003. "On Media Giantism." *New York Times,* January 20.

Schiller, Herbert I. 1971. *Mass Communications and the American Empire*. Boston, MA: Beacon Press.

———. 1990. *Culture, Inc.* New York: Oxford University Press.

Starr, Paul. 2002. "The Great Telecom Implosion." *The American Prospect,* September 9, 2002, pp. 20–4.

Tracey, Michael. 1998. *Decline and Fall of Public Service Broadcasting*. Oxford, England: Oxford University Press.

Tunstall, Jeremy. 1977. *The Media Are American*. New York: Columbia University Press.

Wertham, Fredric. 1996. *Seduction of the Innocent*. New York: Amerreon.

CONSUMPTION AS A SOCIAL PROBLEM

DOUGLAS J. GOODMAN

University of Puget Sound

Consumption is a problem. One of the most interesting aspects of our consumer culture is that this statement really requires no argument. Consumer culture itself proclaims consumption to be a problem. For example, we are inundated with advertising that attacks the absurdity of advertising, people buy books that condemn consumption, and, indeed, as I argue below, we often consume products that express our disdain for consumption.

This chapter starts with an examination of the contradictions of Western, mainly United States, consumer culture—its contradictions with the demands of production, with bourgeois culture, and the contradictions in the view of the consumer. All of these are themselves social problems, but what makes consumption an especially interesting case is that these contradictions have been transformed into further reasons to consume. Consumer culture has managed the trick of presenting more consumption as the solution to the problems of consumption. The second part of this chapter traces how this has happened, because it is important to look at the history of the "consumption of

anticonsumption" in the United States before turning to its present international manifestation.

The contradictions associated with the globalization of consumer culture are the focus of the final section. At the transnational level, a new contradiction has emerged between consumer culture's Americanized homogenization and its production of a heterogeneity of hybrid forms and invented traditions. I argue that this contradiction has also provided an impetus to more consumption.

Contradictions Between Consumer Culture and Capitalist Production

A capitalist economic system requires, by definition, the accumulation of capital that is then consistently and rationally invested in production. Capitalism was able to emerge because it was originally linked to a culture that emphasized self-control, delayed gratification, and rational planning in the pursuit of clearly defined goals. However, a culture structured around production has, to a large extent, been transformed into a culture structured around consumption, and this is hardly a culture of self-control and delayed gratification. A culture that once saw work as a moral end in itself now sees work only as a means toward more consumption (Schor 2000).

The French social theorist Roland Barthes (1990) notes the difference between what capitalism requires of those who produce and those who consume—even though they are usually the same person. "Calculating, industrial society is obliged to form consumers who don't calculate; if clothing's producers and consumers had the same consciousness, clothing would be bought (and produced) only at the very slow rate of its dilapidation; [clothes f]ashion, like all fashions, depends on a disparity of two consciousnesses, each foreign to the other" (p. xi).

Capitalist production still requires self-restraint, discipline, and frugality in our work, but our consumer culture promotes just the opposite. Daniel Bell, in *The Cultural Contradictions of Capitalism* (1976), argued that the only solution to this contradiction is for us to become fragmented, to have one set of values at work and another when we consume. As Bell puts it, "One is to be straight by day, and a swinger at night" (p. 72). But Bell did not believe that this fragmentation would be sustainable. The industrialized world would soon enter a crisis because the capitalist economy is contradicted by a consumer culture that is focused on hedonism and novelty. Consumer culture's pursuit of the new and improved and rejection of all that is old-fashioned and passé has infected a culture that now rejects all traditions and that accepts new values with an ironic stance that degenerates into bitter attack once they are no longer fashionable. We have lost all overriding values motivating us to work—only the desire for more consumption. But Bell believed that this value cannot get us through an economic downturn in the way that a work ethic could.

More than 25 years later, Bell's analysis appears to be absolutely correct. Capitalism seems even more riven by this contradiction than ever. However, his prediction appears to be absolutely wrong: the disjunction continues and even worsens, but it does not appear to be bringing us any closer to a cultural crisis. Indeed, I argue below that our very fragmentation now fuels our consumption as we purchase commodities that promise a lost wholeness.

Contradictions Between Consumer and Bourgeois Culture

Those, such as Marxists and the aristocracy, who see themselves as outside of consumer culture have always had an animosity toward it. Marxists have argued that consumer culture rests on the exploitation of workers (Sklair 1995). Even where it seems to benefit the workers, that benefit is only a device to "buy off" their revolt and delay the triumph of the popular will (Marcuse 1965). Those who see themselves as part of an aristocratic tradition advance a more elitist condemnation (Gronow 1997). Consumer culture is, for them, a contradiction in terms. Nothing that can be popularly consumed could be a true culture. The aristocratic critique believes that the triumph of consumerism is the triumph of the popular will, and this is precisely what they do not like.

Because consumer culture became identified with bourgeois culture, the disdain of consumer culture by both Marxists and aristocrats is usually combined with a rejection of the bourgeoisie. Nevertheless, even though bourgeois culture is deeply intertwined with consumption, bourgeois culture has roots that preceded consumer culture (Schudson 1998), and despite the best efforts of modern advertising, bourgeois culture is still not entirely comfortable with the centrality of consumption. Consequently, we see a contradiction between consumer culture and the bourgeois culture out of which the former emerged. Bourgeois culture was related to the Christian, especially Protestant, religion (Weber 2002). Its early emphasis was on sacrifice and self-restraint. Identity and personal satisfaction were to be found in a career or vocation. In addition, it included a sense of family and community that encompassed but extended beyond the self-reliant individual (Ashcraft 1972).

All of these traits are inimical to consumer culture. Rather than sacrifice and self-restraint, hedonism and luxurious indulgence are emphasized. Consumer culture presents identity as being infinitely transformable with the purchase of new products (Halter 2000), and even on the production side, people are encouraged to be flexible, mobile, and transitory rather than devoting themselves to a lifelong vocation (Hage and Powers 1992). Finally, consumer culture emphasizes the individual over the community. It may take coordinated groups to produce objects, but these objects are usually consumed by individuals.

Consumer culture grew out of bourgeois culture, but parent and progeny are often at odds and there is little hope that there will ever be a complete reconciliation between bourgeois culture and its "prodigal son." A bourgeois critique of consumer culture has persisted and helps to explain the long sociological neglect of consumption as a serious subject of study (Ritzer, Goodman, and Wiedenhoft 2001). And even ordinary shoppers are often subject to self-contempt because their consumption is so indulgent and unrestrained.

Michael Schudson (1998) lists three bourgeois objections to consumer culture. The first he calls the Puritan objection, which criticizes the pursuit of material goods because it takes away from the spiritual. The second he calls Quaker, and it objects to the frivolity and indulgence that are not compatible with a life of simplicity and self-restraint. Finally, there is the objection that he calls republican, which believes that consumer culture has undermined the community, leading to political complacency and the lack of civic engagement.

There is a long history of bourgeois anticonsumption sentiments (Breen 1993; Horowitz 1985). Indeed, consumer culture has always developed in tandem with its own critique. We consume, but we often feel guilty about it. The belief that consumer culture is not compatible with spirituality, simplicity, and community is a strong part of our bourgeois heritage. The feeling that virtue lies in thrift and self-restraint, and sin in consumption, is still present, even when it has lost its religious roots. But just as our fragmentation fuels more consumption, so does our guilt and loss of spiritual meaning. Advertisers have found ways to use this guilt to get us to consume more. As I describe below, we buy objects that promise spirituality, simplicity, and community.

THE CONSUMER AS SOVEREIGN AND AS DUPE

The demands of capitalist production and its relation with bourgeois culture do not exhaust the contradictions of consumer culture. There is also a strong contradiction in regard to the rationality, autonomy, and power of the consumer. On the one hand, the consumer is sovereign. The consumer's rational choices determine the direction of the economy. Everything is designed with the intent (albeit often failing) of pleasing the consumer. The rich and powerful of our society must listen to the consumers' voice and try to discern their fleeting whims. On the other hand, the consumer is often portrayed as nothing but a dupe, subject to uncontrolled impulses and manipulated by the most transparent tricks.

Probably the first thing that we think of in terms of manipulating the consumer is advertising. Billions of dollars are spent on advertising every year, and very little of it is of the informational variety that the assumption of a rational consumer would expect. Advertising is increasingly pervasive. In 1880, only $30 million was spent on advertising in the United States; 30 years later, it had increased to $600 million (Durning 1992), and today it is in excess of $200 billion in the United States and over $300 billion worldwide (Cardona 2002). Every day, North Americans are exposed to an estimated 12 billion display ads, 3 million radio commercials, and more than 200,000 TV commercials. Not only are ads plastered on billboards, shown between breaks on TV shows, popped up on our computer screens, and placed beside text in our newspapers, but they are also beamed into classrooms, played in elevators, featured as props in movies, placed above the urinal in men's bathrooms, made part of athletes' uniforms, and displayed in every place and in every manner that human ingenuity can devise. We seem to be currently engaged in a grand experiment to see just how much of our society can be given over to the economic system, and perhaps the riskiest part stems from the constant exposure of people—from cradle to grave, from waking to sleeping—to advertising.

Examining advertising makes it clear that the concept of a consumer culture includes much more than a direct relation between individuals and the objects they consume. To a large extent, that relation is mediated by the meanings attached to the objects. Of course, all cultures have attached traditional meanings to objects, but our culture is so flooded with a constant stream of new (and improved) products that they long ago exceeded all traditional meanings. Many objects depend, at least initially, on the meanings produced by advertising. Whatever its initial aim, advertising does more than sell products. It is an integral part of consumer culture. It not only attaches meanings to commodities but also to the people who purchase and use them.

> The advertising in the women's magazines, the house-and-home periodicals, and sophisticated journals like the *New Yorker* was to teach people how to dress, furnish a home, buy the right wines—in short, the styles of life appropriate to the new statuses. Though at first the changes were primarily in manners, dress, taste, and food habits, sooner or later they began to affect more basic patterns: the structure of authority in the family, the role of children and young adults as independent consumers in the society, the patterns of morals, and the different meanings of achievement in the society. (Bell 1976:69)

Indeed, the meanings produced by a consumer culture extend even to the personality of the consumer. It is not just a motorcycle or a white ball gown that one purchases, but the identity that goes with it. One becomes a biker or a debutante. Identities become commodities to buy, and like other commodities, there are competing identities on the market. As a 1991 cover of *Cosmopolitan* declared: "By changing the way you look . . . you can create a new you!"

One of the early leaders in advertising, Helen Woodward (1926), stated the attraction of the purchasable identity: "To those who cannot change their whole lives or occupations, even a new line in a dress is often a relief. The woman who is tired of her husband or her home or a job feels some lifting of the weight of life from seeing a straight line change into a bouffant, or a gray pass into beige. Most people do not have the courage or the understanding to make deeper changes" (p. 345).

It is in this sense that consumer culture and advertising contain a strong dose of idealism. We are more attached to the ideal meaning of the object and to the ideal identity represented by the object than the object itself. This is the phenomenon that Raymond Williams (1976) refers to when he writes that advertising is proof that people in modern capitalist societies are not materialist. "If we were sensibly materialist, in that part of our living in which

we use things, we should find most advertising to be of an insane irrelevance" (p. 26). It is not that we are tricked by the meanings that advertisements deliver. To a large degree, it is the meaning—the advertising, the brand, the logo, the Nike swoosh, the Polo pony—that is wanted, especially by the young. The actual commodity is just the convenient carrier of that meaning.

The idea that we wear the logo, not the clothes, drink the advertising, not the soda, and drive the image, not the car has seemed to many to prove that we are being manipulated. Advertisers, it has been argued, create desires that consumers obediently express as if they were their own. This has been called the *hypodermic theory* of advertising—ads inject us with false needs (Key 1972). According to this theory, the desire to consume is largely the product of the manipulations of advertisers on an unsuspecting public. A passive public is duped into spending money on things they do not need.

Vance Packard's *The Hidden Persuaders* (1957) was an early and influential example of this viewpoint, arguing that our minds are controlled by the hidden, subliminal messages contained in advertising. Packard's interviews with advertisers revealed their rather disturbing attitude toward the general public.

> Typically they see us as bundles of daydreams, misty hidden yearnings, guilt complexes, irrational emotional blockages. We are image lovers given to impulsive and compulsive acts. We annoy them with our seemingly senseless quirks, but we please them with our growing docility in responding to their manipulation of symbols that stir us to action. (P. 12)

Another influential book attacking consumer culture was Stuart Ewen's *Captains of Consciousness* (1976). He argued that consumer society is a gigantic fraud, a conspiracy to manipulate the public and sell people items they do not need. Whereas those who controlled society were once captains of industry, society is now controlled through the manipulations of advertising by captains of consciousness.

These books have been followed by a steady succession of anticonsumption books, including most recently *The Overspent American: Upscaling, Downshifting, and the New Consumer* (1998) by Juliet Schor; *No Logo: Taking Aim at the Brand*

Name Bullies (2000) by Naomi Klein; *Culture Jam: How to Reverse America's Suicidal Consumer Binge—And Why We Must* by Kalle Lasn (2000); and *Shoveling Fuel for a Runaway Train: Errant Economists, Shameful Spenders, and a Plan to Stop Them All* by Brian Czech (2002)—not to mention the magazines such as *Ad Cult* and *AdBusters*.

Of course, it is easy enough to dismiss this hypodermic theory by pointing to advertising's spectacular failures. New products with substantial advertising are introduced every day and the vast majority of them fail. One of the most cited examples is the huge amount spent introducing and marketing the Edsel car, which became a laughable flop (Larrabee 1957).

Furthermore, it has been argued that the creation and control of meaning is not a one-way process. Advertisers may create saleable meanings for the new commodities, but consumers often create meanings of their own (Abercrombie 1994; Fiske 1989). For example, hippies took the American flag and unpatriotically used it as clothing, punks took the safety pin and used it as bodily adornment, rap DJs took the turntable and turned it into a creative instrument. None of these uses were intended or even imagined by those who created and marketed the products. Advertisers may often have the first word on meanings, and there is no disputing the power of that position, but consumers sometimes have the last word. Rather than simply a conduit for the producers' meanings, consumer objects are often a site of struggle over meaning.

Despite this, few can doubt that advertising is aimed at controlling our behavior, and we must suspect that it is fairly successful. Otherwise, why would corporations continue to spend billions of dollars on it? Nevertheless, most people, although they often feel disdain for advertising, are not ready to revolt against the "captains of consciousness" and their "hidden persuaders." Perhaps this is because the sort of control that advertising exerts is not one that is experienced as disagreeable. It is not a rigid, constraining control, but exactly its opposite. It manipulates us toward unrestraint in spending. It encourages us to enjoy forbidden pleasures, to break the old rules of thrift and self-discipline. One might say that it is controlling us to go out of control, at least where consuming is concerned. Controlling us

to be, in a sense, out of control is a contradiction, but it is one that is easy to avoid examining too closely. Despite the contradiction, it is easy to think of this control as freedom and this manipulation as power.

What the vast amount of advertising really sells is consumer culture itself. Even if advertising fails to sell a particular product, the ads still sell the meanings and values of a consumer culture. As Christopher Lasch (1994) writes, "The importance of advertising is not that it invariably succeeds in its immediate purpose, much less that it lobotomizes the consumer into a state of passive acquiescence, but simply that it surrounds people with images of the good life in which happiness depends on consumption. The ubiquity of such images leaves little space for competing conceptions of the good life" (p. 1387).

What advertising constantly sells is the idea that there is a product to solve each of life's problems. That the good life, the attractive personality, the appropriate taste can be purchased along with the object that we are told represents it. However, this promise is constantly broken. One of our first great disappointments is the discovery that buying that special toy does not bring us the infinite fun portrayed on television (Gunter and Furnham 1998). Neither, we soon discover, does buying those clothes gain us social acceptance. Our first car does not translate into freedom, and buying a beer does not surround us with beautiful members of the opposite sex. We buy the commodities, but the good life does not follow.

The authors of *Beyond the Limits* explain why, despite our continued dissatisfaction, we continue to consume.

> People don't need enormous cars, they need respect. They don't need closets full of clothes, they need to feel attractive and they need excitement and variety and beauty. People don't need electronic equipment; they need something worthwhile to do with their lives. People need identity, community, challenge, acknowledgment, love, and joy. To try to fill these needs with material things is to set up an unquenchable appetite for false solutions to real and never-satisfied problems. The resulting psychological emptiness is one of the major forces behind the desire for material growth. (Meadows, Meadows, and Randers 1992:216)

The greatest contradiction that consumer culture has had to face is not an economic system that values both the accumulation of capital and consumer extravagance, nor its contradiction with the bourgeois ethics out of which it emerged, nor the contradiction between the rational and irrational consumer. The greatest contradiction that consumer culture has had to deal with is that it does not deliver on its own promises.

THE CONSUMPTION OF ANTICONSUMPTION

Whatever the problem, advertising has tried to position a product as its solution. Not simply the personal problems of halitosis, shyness, unattractiveness, but also social problems such as oppression or inequality. For example, advertising has always portrayed itself as on the side of liberation, especially from everything old and traditional. This usually takes the form of a liberation from old commodities in favor of new and improved commodities, but there has sometimes been an actual political component. For example, advertisements for cigarettes were early public proclamations for women's equality. A leading advertiser of the 1920s described an advertising-inspired parade where, with the support of a prominent feminist, some young women lit "torches of freedom" (i.e., cigarettes) "as a protest against woman's inequality" (Ewen 1976:161). Gender inequality could be solved by buying the right brand of cigarettes, the right toys for little girls, the right suit for the businesswoman.

By the middle of the 1950s, consumer culture and advertising were increasingly seen as part of the problem rather than as solutions. A common theme of popular magazine articles, movies, and sermons, as well as of academic writing, was the problem of conformity, of consumerism, and the loss of the work ethic. It shows the protean ingenuity of consumer culture that advertising was able to present even this problem as solvable by more consumption. Because this innovation was so important to the spread of consumer culture, I examine it in detail.

Hip Consumerism

Thomas Frank, in *The Conquest of Cool* (1997), has described the changes in advertising as one of the most important processes behind the counterculture of the 1960s. Frank's main thesis is that the counterculture received its impetus from the momentous transformation that advertising underwent in the early 1960s. Advertising made the hatred of consumer culture one of its own themes and presented the consumer as a rebel against the "establishment" and conformity.

The counterculture of the 1960s was deeply critical of consumer culture. One of the founding documents of the counterculture, the Port Huron Statement, condemned marketing techniques intended to "create pseudo-needs in consumers" and to make "wasteful 'planned obsolescence' . . . a permanent feature of business strategy" (Miller 1987:339). However, many on both the left and right have commented on the deep connections between consumer culture and the counterculture of the 1960s. Both promulgated a doctrine of hedonism, liberation, and continual transgression. Frank (1997) makes sense of this contradiction by demonstrating that consumer culture was itself critical of consumer culture, and the counterculture was, to a large extent, a reflection of that.

> The central theme that gives coherence to American advertising of both the early and late sixties is this: Consumer culture is a gigantic fraud. It demands that you act like everyone else, that you restrain yourself, that you fit in with the crowd, when you are in fact an individual. Consumer culture lies and seeks to sell you shoddy products that will fall apart or be out of style in a few years; but you crave authenticity and are too smart to fall for that Madison Avenue stuff (your neighbors may not be). Above all, consumer culture fosters conventions that are repressive and unfulfilling; but with the help of hip trends you can smash through those, create a new world in which people can be themselves, pretense has vanished, and healthy appetites are liberated from the stultifying mores of the past. (P. 136)

In other words, consumer culture presented consumption as a solution to its own problems.

The generally accepted story of the relation between the 1960s counterculture and consumer culture is that the latter co-opted the former. In the beginning, the story goes, there was an authentic counterculture, which was in opposition to capitalism and corporate culture. However, this authentic movement either sold out or was effectively mimicked by a mass-produced counterfeit culture of groovy, psychedelic products that captured the youth market and subverted the real counterculture's threat. Frank (1997) contends that the mass-produced counterfeit culture was "not so much evidence of co-optation, but rather evidence of the counterculture's roots in consumer culture" (p. 27).

Of course, few would deny the connection between the counterculture and the popular music and "rebel" celebrities of consumer culture. Furthermore, the role of television and popular magazines in advertising the "summer of love" and the entire hippie phenomenon is unquestioned. Frank's argument goes further than this to claim that it was in the heart of the beast, in advertising itself, that the first changes occurred that triggered the counterculture and the hippie movement. "The changes here were, if anything, even more remarkable, more significant, and took place slightly earlier than those in music and youth culture" (p. 27).

Frank's study of advertising in the late 1950s and early 1960s shows that it was developing its own counterculture. A new generation of advertisers was growing tired of the repetitive, "scientific" ads of the 1950s and was finding success with ads that were ironic, rebellious, and that attacked or made fun of consumer culture itself.

In 1960, the advertising company Doyle Dane Bernbach launched a campaign that was to define hip consumerism. It was for the Volkswagen beetle. It is no accident that the commodity most identified with the 1960s counterculture is the Volkswagen.

Most car advertising before the 1960s was a beautiful fantasy of some sort: a verdant green countryside, elegantly dressed models, and gleaming metal; or a racetrack, skimpily dressed models and more gleaming metal. Its photography grabbed you, and its text labored powerfully to extol the virtues of the car. The Volkswagen ad, in contrast, was simple, not flashy; self-deprecating, not self-congratulatory; and funny, not serious. It was the opposite of advertising as everyone knew it. One of the first ads was a full page of mostly white space with a small picture of the car in the upper corner, a small headline toward the bottom saying "Think Small," and a couple of paragraphs that described how strange the car was.

Most significantly, the ads made fun of the product, advertising, and consumer culture. It was the ads that first called the car a beetle, and said that the station wagon "looked like a shoebox." But it was at consumer culture itself that the ads aimed their sharpest barbs. They ridiculed the use of cars as status symbols. They poked fun at dealers' sales tactics. They pilloried the faddishness and planned obsolescence of the fashionable commodity.

These new ads were extremely successful and initiated a revolt in advertising against the hard sell that still dominated the industry. In this "revolution," the new generation of advertisers saw the emerging counterculture "not as an enemy to be undermined or a threat to consumer culture but as a hopeful sign, a symbolic ally in their own struggles against the mountains of dead-weight procedure and hierarchy that had accumulated over the years" (Frank 1997:9). This partnership changed consumer culture.

> Almost no American car manufacturers were still using the idealized, white-family-at-play motif by that year [1965]. And with the exception of luxury lines (Cadillac, Lincoln, Chrysler), virtually every car being marketed in America introduced its 1966 model year as an implement of nonconformity, of instant youthfulness, of mockery toward traditional Detroit-suckers, or of distinction from the mass society herd. . . . The critique of mass society leveled by the American automakers was noticeably different from that of Volkswagen and Volvo. The ads of the Big Three automakers were not concerned with evading planned obsolescence, but with discovering for annual style changes a more compelling meaning. Where Volkswagen and Volvo emphasized authenticity and durability, Detroit stressed escape, excitement, carnival, nonconformity, and individualism. It is a cleavage that goes to the heart of the commercial revolution of the sixties: every brand claimed to be bored, disgusted, and alienated, but for some these meant the never-changing Volkswagen and blue jeans; they steered others toward the Pontiac Breakaway and the Peacock Revolution. (Frank 1997:156–7)

What we see then is not the emergence of a movement that opposed consumer culture and was then co-opted and defeated by it, but rather a change within consumer culture itself. In the 1960s, consumer culture entered a new phase, which Frank calls "hip consumerism." It is now more resistant to criticisms, because it is able to transform those very criticisms into reasons to consume. Hip consumerism uses the ambivalence, the contradictions, and the disappointments due to advertising's constantly broken promises as further inducements to buy more. The protests against manipulation, conformity, and loss of meaning are transformed into reasons to consume. Disgust with consumerism is turned into the fuel that feeds consumerism because we express our disgust with consumer culture through consumption.

Advertising no longer sells a commodity so much as a rebellious stance. For example, Benetton's ads have not used pictures of its products since 1989. Instead their ads feature shocking images of AIDS victims, racism, war, and death row inmates. Oliviero Toscani, Benetton's head of advertising, sees these as a criticism of consumer culture. "The advertising industry has corrupted society. It persuades people that they are respected for what they consume, that they are only worth what they possess" (Tinic 1997:325). This is not the head of the politburo speaking, but the head of advertising at a major international company.

Hip consumers are anticonsumption, but they have been taught to express their attitudes through what they buy. They are rebels, but they have been taught to rebel against last year's fashions and especially to rebel against the old-fashioned Puritanism and frugality of their parents. They crave traditions and are willing to buy the latest tradition. They want authenticity and will pay for its simulation.

What changed during the sixties, it now seems, were the strategies of consumerism, the ideology by which business explained its domination of the national life. Now products existed to facilitate our rebellion against the soul-deadening world of products, to put us in touch with our authentic selves, to distinguish us from the mass-produced herd, to express our outrage at the stifling world of economic necessity. (Frank 1997:229)

Hip consumerism has become the latest and strongest version of consumer culture. Both the critique of consumption and the solution to the problems of consumption are now contained within consumer culture. In other words, consumer culture presents itself as a problem that only more consumption can solve. Ads that incorporate ironic attacks on consumer culture are themselves protected from those attacks because they have positioned themselves on the side of the skeptical viewer.

Advertisements that promote rebellion, mock authority, and promise a mass-produced nonconformity are now ubiquitous. For example, one of the main targets of the counterculture's and feminist's critique of consumer culture was the cosmetics industry, which was taken to be the epitome of artificiality and conformity to mass-produced standards of beauty. However, hip consumerism has revamped these commodities as signs of ironic artificiality, defiance, and nonconformity. A case in point, one company, significantly named Urban Decay, offers cosmetics with names like Plague, Demise, Rat, Roach, and Asphyxia.

New Age Consumerism

In addition to buying to express nonconformity and rebellion, consumers also buy to express an interest in living a simple life, a concern about the environment, and a declaration of spirituality. For instance, those who seek the simple life can choose among over 100 models of sleeping bags. They can peruse the ads in *Real Simple,* "the magazine devoted to simplifying your life." They can buy an SUV to get off-road and closer to nature. They can furnish their home with the latest craze in traditional crafts. They can, if they possess the money, have custom-made, one-of-a-kind clothes fashioned for them out of hand-spun fabric.

We can call this variant of the hip consumer, the New Age consumer. An article by Sam Binkley (forthcoming) discusses one of the most important documents of the change from hip consumption to New Age consumption, the *Whole Earth Catalog.* This strange mix of a Sears Roebuck catalog and opinionated *Consumer Reports* put together by dropouts from the counterculture used its lists of commodities to carry the sixties' rebellious spirit into the spiritual environmentalism that characterizes the New Age consumer.

The hip consumer responds to the contradictions of consumer culture through consumption that emphasizes artifice, irony, and nonconformity. The New Age consumer responds to these same contradictions also with consumption, but they prefer commodities that represent a noncommercial and more spiritual life. The New Age consumer prefers boutiques to national chains, gentrified neighborhood centers to shopping malls. However, even the mall-based chain store can be sold to the New Age consumer if it is properly marketed, as Anita Roddick proved when she introduced the environmentally friendly, politically correct, and eminently hip chain, the Body Shop.

New Age consumers demonstrate through their consumption that they are earth-friendly, socially responsible, enlightened global citizens in tune with nature. They prefer natural wood, natural fibers, natural ingredients, organic food, and herbal body care products. All of these are sold as remedies for the problems of consumer culture.

Kimberly Lau provides an interesting case of New Age consumerism in her study of *New Age Capitalism* (2000). She covers a number of examples, including the spread of yoga and macrobiotic diets, but most germane is her examination of the marketing of aromatherapy. In it we see many of the attributes of hip consumption that Frank described, but with a New Age twist.

Horst Rechelbacher, founder of Aveda, introduced aromatherapy to the American public in 1978. Since Aveda's success, others have followed suit, including specialty stores such as the Body Shop, Garden Botanika, and H2O. In addition, noncosmetic but hip retailers such as the Gap, The Limited, Eddie Bauer, Urban Outfitters, Banana Republic, Pier 1 Imports, and The Nature Company have all introduced aromatherapy products. Lau (2000:34) estimates the sale of aromatherapy products to be $300 million to $500 million, with an annual growth rate of approximately 30 percent.

Lau describes three characteristics of the aromatherapy advertising campaign that appeal to the New Age consumer: (1) it is presented as eco-friendly; (2) it is a remedy for the psychic ills of modern civilization; and (3) it is able to function as a hip consumer's status symbol.

As Lau (2000) informs us, "[E]veryone from aromatherapists to essential oil suppliers and aroma researchers praises the earth-friendly nature of aromatherapy, but no one articulates the precise nature of its environmentalism" (pp. 39–40). Finding no evidence for its ecological beneficence, Lau can only surmise the following formula: "[T]he association seems as simple as plants = green = earth-friendly" (p. 40).

In addition, aromatherapy is associated with ancient and contemporary cultures that are portrayed as unsullied by the problems of modern consumer culture. It is variously associated with the ancient practices of Egypt, Greece, Rome, India, and China. In addition, Aveda advertises that some of its ingredients are obtained from the Yawanawa, who live in the rainforests of western Brazil. Lau (2000) sees this identification of aromatherapy with ancient and nonindustrialized cultures as "part of an attempt to counter modernity and the techno-industrial capitalist system it signifies" (p. 30). In other words, it positions this product outside of consumer culture, as an alternative and even an antidote.[1]

Of course, this alternative to consumer culture can only be consumed by those able to afford it. This allows Aveda products, like most hip commodities, to function both as a status symbol and as an anti-status symbol. It represents both the material resources to buy expensive body care products and a criticism of Western materialism.

> Aveda makes available for purchase the idea of participating in cultural critique, of living according to ancient philosophies, of living an alternative lifestyle. . . . Consumption becomes a mode of addressing social, political, and cultural disenchantment, although the very processes enabling consumption are what characterize modernity, itself the cause of the disenchantment being critiqued. (Lau 2000:133)

Furthermore, all the New Age commodities discussed by Lau claim to remedy the fragmentation that Bell predicted would destroy consumer culture. Reconnecting mind, body, and spirit is a primary theme of these products. They are all, at least in name, holistic. Here too, the contradictions of our consumer culture function as another reason to consume.

Not only do these products turn anticonsumption into a reason for more consumption, but it is arguable that they co-opt any real opposition to consumer culture.

> Each product comes with a tag, an address, a lifestyle. The act of purchase locates the individual within a tribe, and in this way, fashion functions to regulate lifestyles and produce the belief that every consumer choice is a free choice, a way in which individuals invent themselves. Such practices can co-opt self-identifying groups into the consumer cycle, even those who may be politically and ethically opposed to it—for example, those targeted by the new niche markets in anti-fashions, eco-sensitive clothing, and products from recycled materials. (Finkelstein 1995:232)

Consumption as a Culture

The social problem of consumption involves much more than just the act of consuming. We live today in a consumer culture. To say that we are a consumer culture means that our central shared values have to do with consumption. Accordingly, a consumer culture has effects far beyond actual consumption and its associated advertising. The shared concepts and values of a culture help people to relate their individual lives to larger themes. Because of this, a culture tends to change all other institutions into something compatible with its values.

Historically, most cultures have been centered on a set of religious values and concepts. Alternatively, a few cultures have found their values and concepts in secular intellectual and aesthetic movements, usually called "high" culture. This is the type of culture that one refers to when speaking of the arts, manners, or education. A consumer culture is distinct from either of these.

This is not to say that religion and high culture have disappeared from our society, but they have become instances of consumer culture. People still have religion, but increasingly, they "shop around" for the right religion and choose one that fits their lifestyle. Religion is not a tradition that we are inextricably embedded in; instead it is chosen, consumed, and sometimes discarded, returned, or exchanged like any other commodity.

Similarly, high culture has simply become a niche market in a consumer culture. People who go to opera and art museums are a marketing cluster group who also buy Italian espresso machines, BMW convertibles, and Hugo Boss clothes. For the rest of us, high culture is what we listen to while we are on hold waiting for customer service. It is what we pass on our way to the museum gift shop. It is what we buy to match our living room. Even where high culture is not simply a commodity, it functions more and more like a commodity, with an emphasis on the new, the latest, the attention-getting, the controversial, the shocking.

The same sort of transformation happens in higher education, where students are more and more treated like consumers and the mission of the school is increasingly shaped by its attempts to market itself to its target audience. Similarly, news becomes entertainment, and history is turned into theme parks. Indeed it seems that every human expression, from art to sex to outrage, is either sold as a commodity or used to sell a commodity. It is this consumer culture that is now spreading over the entire world.

CONSUMPTION AS AN INTERNATIONAL SOCIAL PROBLEM

That consumer culture is becoming a global phenomenon seems increasingly difficult to deny. A global consumer culture is connected to the international flow of goods, money, people, information, and services that has been called globalization. The international and cross-border "diffusion of practices, values and technology" (Albrow 1997:88) has resulted in a compression of time and space (Giddens 1990; Harvey 1989) that encourages not only economic but also cultural interdependence. The borders that once separated cultures have become so permeable that "there are no absolute political, social or cultural boundaries unbreached by global flows" (Kelly 1999:240).

To be sure, analysts have challenged the magnitude and, indeed, valence of globalization's effects. But whether globalization is good (Friedman 1999; Ohmae 1990) or bad (Gilpin 2000; Mittleman 2000), strong (Appadurai 1996; Hobsbawm 1997) or feeble (Hirschman 1982; Hirst and Thompson 1996), there can be little doubt that the world is becoming increasingly interconnected and that this has enormous cultural implications. Just as with globalization itself, these cultural implications are also open to various interpretations. Some see globalization as leading to the creation of heterogeneous local cultures, others as an Americanized homogeneity, still others as leading to hybrids of the local and the global, the new and the old. I argue next that all of these are happening in globalization and that there is evidence to point to a global consumer culture as an explanation for the increasing presence of what appears to be a contradiction.

Clearly, there are multiple forces at work in globalization—economic, political, institutional, technological—but undoubtedly the most obvious form that globalization assumes is as a global consumer culture.

> Few expressions of globalization are so visible, widespread and pervasive as the worldwide proliferation of internationally traded consumer brands, the global ascendancy of popular cultural icons and artifacts, and the simultaneous communication of events by satellite broadcasts to hundreds of millions of people at a time on all continents. The most public symbols of globalization consist of Coca-Cola, Madonna and the news on CNN. (Held et al. 1999:327)

Steger (2002:36) cites Nike sneakers on Amazonian Indians, Texaco baseball caps on sub-Saharan youths, and Chicago Bulls sweatshirts on Palestinians. In such descriptions it is easy to see a homogenized—even Americanized—consumer culture spreading throughout the world by creating standardized tastes and desires. And, in fact, this homogenized world is often precisely what the advertising for consumption promises, as in the McDonald's ad, "It's what everyone around the world keeps saying—It's MacTime," or when Pepsi wants to teach the world to sing in perfect harmony.

Nevertheless, the question over whether globalization increases cultural homogeneity by establishing common codes and practices or whether it increases a heterogeneity of newly emerging differences seems now, to many analysts, to have been answered. Globalization does both. Globalization appears to make people more different but in a similar way. It creates a mixed system, where people are homogenized into similar individuals, ethnicities, and nations who want different things. It creates what Roland Robertson (1995) has called *glocalization.*

Glocalization

According to Robertson (2001), "globalization is not an all-encompassing process of homogenization but a complex mixture of homogenization and heterogenization" (p. 199). There is an interpenetration of the global and the local that creates a difference-within-sameness. Robertson (1995) points out that a global culture can bolster, revive, or even create a local culture. Indeed, he argues that "what is called local is in large degree constructed on a trans- or super-local basis" (p. 26). The local is not opposed to the global; rather it is an aspect of the global. Consequently, the homogeneity of global cultural flows will be matched by the heterogeneity of their reception, appropriation, and response. It is this that characterizes glocalization.

Glocalization is related to delocalization—what Scholte (2000) calls deterritorialization. According to Scholte, the defining characteristic of our global culture is that relations between people are no longer dependent on a territorial location, territorial distance, or territorial borders. Instead, we now inhabit a new supraterritorial space along with the preexisting territorial space. The idea of glocalization is that our relation to the territorial locality is changed by the supraterritorial global context. Transnational forces undermine our bond to a fixed local culture, its unquestioned traditions, and stable identities. As Cowen (2002) says, "[I]ndividuals are liberated from the tyranny of place more than ever before" (p. 4).

Not only is delocalization caused by supraterritorial forces, but people themselves are more mobile and prone to cross borders (Mittleman 2000:58–73). Many of a locale's residents did not grow up in that locality, and they bring other traditions to this new place. In addition, indigenous locals travel, interact, and return, thereby transforming their cultures. These processes are so prevalent that a number of cities are dominated by cosmopolitan elites and immigrant neighborhoods. Sassen (1991) describes these as global cities.

These processes lead to a cultural form that is referred to as "hybridization" (Pieterse 1995) or "creolization" (Hannerz 1992). Zwingle (2000) describes "sitting in a coffee shop in London drinking Italian espresso served by an Algerian waiter to the strains of the Beach Boys singing 'I wish they all could be California girls'" (p. 153). Pieterse (1995) describes "Thai boxing by Moroccan girls in Amsterdam, Asian rap in London, Irish bagels, Chinese tacos and Mardi Gras Indians in the United States" (p. 53). We regularly see these hybrids in music, novels, restaurants, paintings, crafts, and so on. The hybrid form pervades both high and popular culture and even "traditional" culture.

In fact, much of what we take to be local and traditional is a hybrid. Glocalization is connected to delocalization through the creation or re-creation of the local traditions in a way that conforms to global forces. Robertson (1995) notes the "increasingly global 'institutionalization' of the expectation and construction of local particularism. Not merely is variety continuously produced and reproduced in the contemporary world, that variety is an aspect of the very dynamics which a considerable number of commentators interpret as homogenization" (p. 38). In an earlier work, Robertson (1992) explains that "the contemporary concerns with civilizational and societal (as well as ethnic) uniqueness—as expressed via such motifs as identity, tradition and indigenization—largely rests on globally diffused ideas" (p. 130).

This is not to say that delocalization leads directly to heterogeneous glocalization; it could lead to the complete global homogenization that so many critics fear. Robertson's theory of glocalization is not purely theoretical. Robertson (1995) calls this "an empirical problem." "It is not a question of either homogenization or heterogenization, but rather of the ways in which both of these two tendencies have become features of life across much of the late-twentieth-century world. In this perspective the problem becomes that of spelling out the ways in which homogenizing and heterogenizing tendencies are mutually implicative" (p. 27).

This means that, on the one hand, we cannot ignore the powerful forces of homogenization that are at work and simply trust to an inevitable glocalization to provide heterogeneity. On the other hand, we need to further analyze why transnational forces and delocalization do tend to heterogeneous glocalization, at least to the extent that they do.

The reason for heterogeneous glocalization is that one of the primary forces propelling globalization is consumer culture. A global consumer culture encourages glocalization because the local provides a valuable resource for our supralocal exchanges and therefore leads to increased heterogeneity of content along with homogeneity of form. Robertson (1995) recognizes this.

> To a considerable extent micromarketing—or, in the more comprehensive phrase, glocalization—involves the construction of increasingly differentiated consumers, the "invention" of "consumer traditions" (of which tourism, arguably the biggest "industry" of the contemporary world, is undoubtedly the most clear-cut example). To put it very simply, diversity sells. From the consumer's point of view it can be a significant basis of cultural capital formation (Bourdieu, 1984). This, it should be emphasized, is not its only function. The proliferation of, for example, "ethnic" supermarkets in California and elsewhere does to a large extent cater not so much to difference for the sake of difference, but to the desire for the familiar and/or to nostalgic wishes. (P. 29)

The anthropologist Ulf Hannerz (1992) also notes the similarity between glocalization and the niche markets created by consumer culture.

> If one tendency is to homogenize and reach as widely as possible with the same product, there is again the alternative of seeking competitive advantage through distinctiveness, in a particular market segment. The scenario of global homogenization rather too much ignores this alternative, but since it is so often preoccupied with the commodities of popular culture, it is reasonable to make the observation that much of what the entrepreneurs of popular culture in the Third World are doing these days seems to involve carving out such niches. (Pp. 237–8)

This should not be a surprise, since the very term *glocalization* began as "one of the main marketing buzzwords of the beginning of the nineties" (Tulloch 1991:134). Global culture seems to be precisely tracking the trend among consumer goods that marketers have already recognized. Although there are some global brands, one business analyst observed that this "does not mean that there is a global consumer for companies to target. International cultural differences are by no means disappearing and, in the late twentieth century, individualism is as strong a world force as internationalism. Consumer goods are becoming more, rather than less, focused on the individual" (Fitzgerald 1997:742). However, the individuals focused on by global marketing are, as one business leader put it, "heteroconsumers": "People who've become increasingly alike and indistinct from one another, and yet have simultaneously varied and multiple preferences" (Levitt 1988:8).

Not only do traditions become glocalized as an "invention of tradition" (Hobsbawm and Ranger 1983) to appeal to the consumer tastes of tourists, but identity itself becomes a form of consumption shaped by a global consumer culture.

> Every social and cultural movement is a consumer or at least must define itself in relation to the world of goods as a non-consumer. Consumption within the bounds of the world system is always a consumption of identity, canalized by a negotiation between self-definition and the array of possibilities offered by the capitalist market. (Friedman 1994:104)

Thus, there is indeed greater heterogeneity, but it is in the context of and, to a large extent, in response to the homogeneity of a consumer culture. As Jonathan Friedman (1994) points out, "[W]hat appears as disorganization and often real disorder is not any the less systemic and systematic" (p. 211). Global consumer culture creates what Wilk (1995) calls "global systems of common difference." Again, this seems to be recognized by consumer advertising. An AT&T ad says, "What makes us all the same is that we're all different" (quoted in Wilk 1995).

McDonaldization as Heterogeneity and Homogeneity

Because *McDonaldization* (Ritzer 2000) has become a widely used term for the globalization of consumer culture, it is useful to employ it to examine the interplay of heterogeneity and homogeneity. First, however, it is necessary to clearly define what is meant by McDonaldization. It is not simply the spread of a particular restaurant chain. Instead it is the spread of the processes of efficiency, calculability, predictability, and control that McDonald's successfully introduced into consumption. The idea of McDonaldization is that these processes are coming to dominate more economic and cultural sectors as well as spreading globally.

Although McDonaldization refers to much more than the restaurant chain, it is instructive to begin with a focus on the heterogenizing aspects of McDonald's itself. We see within the homogeneity of McDonald's (the vanguard of McDonaldization) four types of heterogeneity.

First, McDonald's in a non-American setting provides a cheap and easily accessible tourist experience. Stephenson (1989) describes the experience of Dutch patrons where a local McDonald's provides "a kind of instant emigration that occurs the moment one walks through the doors, where Dutch rules rather obviously don't apply and where there are few adults around to enforce any that might" (p. 227).

Second, when McDonald's is accepted as a local institution, it creates a new heterogeneous hybrid locality. The literature is rife with descriptions of tourists to the United States from other countries who are surprised to see a McDonald's here. Watson's (1997) collection is full of descriptions of the acceptance of McDonald's as a local phenomenon in East Asian countries. This is indicative not of the power of the local but of the power of McDonald's to re-create the local. As Ritzer (2001) points out, "Its impact is far greater if it infiltrates a local culture and becomes a part of it than if it remains perceived as an American phenomenon superimposed on a local setting" (p. 171).

Third, the chain varies its menu to adapt to particular localities. In India, McDonald's outlets serve Vegetable McNuggets and Maharaja Macs made with mutton. In Turkey, they offer a chilled yogurt drink. In Italy, espresso and cold pasta. Teriyaki burgers are on the menu in Japan, Taiwan, and Hong Kong (along with red bean sundaes). The main sandwich in the Netherlands is a vegetarian burger; in Norway it is McLaks (a grilled salmon sandwich); in Germany, frankfurters; in Uruguay, a poached egg hamburger called the McHuevo.

Finally, the process of McDonaldization is adopted by indigenous competitors of McDonald's to create a local variety of fast food. Ritzer (2001) mentions Russkoye Bistro in Russia, Ronghua

Chicken and Xiangfei Roast Chicken in China, Mos Burger in Japan, and Uncle Joe's Hamburger in Korea. Ritzer (2001) writes that "it is not the existence of American chains (and other new means of consumption) in other countries that is the most important indicator of the spread of McDonaldization, but rather the existence of indigenous clones of those McDonaldized enterprises" (p. 170).

We see then that, on the one hand, McDonald's itself becomes more heterogeneous by adapting to the local, and, on the other hand, McDonaldization promotes heterogeneity in the locality by creating a tourist experience, a hybrid local, and by promoting McDonaldized local competitors. Nevertheless, as glocalization would predict, along with this increased heterogeneity of product and locality comes an increased homogeneity of process—of calculability, efficiency, predictability, and control.

THE CONTRADICTIONS OF GLOBAL CONSUMER CULTURE

We see in global consumer culture the same contradictions that we outlined above. Of course, as capitalism has spread, we see also the spread of its contradiction between a calculating, rational, frugal producer and an impulsive, irrational, prodigal consumer. In addition, even though many of these countries don't have a Protestant tradition or a bourgeois culture, we nevertheless see a contradiction between their traditional ethos and the impulses of a consumer culture. This often takes the form of a generational difference in developing countries.

> In each nation, there remains a significant population segment who have lived through underdevelopment, whose collective memories of material deprivation and thrifty ways are still fresh. Their moral/ideological position on savings has made them resistant to the rapid expansion of consumerism. In addition, this group often sees the arrival of consumerist culture as the consequence of the penetration and contamination of traditional cultural practices by "Western," particularly American, cultures. Thus, the moral debate on consumption has often been characterized as a "generational conflict," supposedly between the deprived generation who embody thrift as a traditional value and the affluent and fast-spending, "Westernised" generation. (Beng-Huat 2000:8)

We also see the same contradictory view of the consumer. On the one hand, the spread of consumer culture is driven primarily by the choices made by those who live in the invaded territory. The consumer is the sovereign director of globalizing consumer culture. On the other hand, as Wilk (1994) writes, "it is clear that people are not making completely free choices about goods. They are not merely absorbing foreign goods into their existing modes of consumption, and making free strategic choices in the global marketplace. Third world consumers are subject to various forms of coercion, both economic and ideological" (p. 81).

These contradictions of global consumer culture are also resolved through the consumption of anticonsumption. Just as in Western culture, others are encouraged to consume in order to represent their belief in anticonsumption traditions, their disdain of advertisers' attempts to control them, or their rebellion.

We certainly see some of the same aspects of hip consumerism in response to the globalization of consumer culture. For example, marketers in Eastern Europe have introduced a new product labeled "Ordinary Laundry Detergent" as a hip response to the heavy promotion of Tide as cleaning "better than ordinary laundry detergent" (Money and Colton 2000:190). However, most characteristic of the response to the contradictions of global consumption has been what Robertson (1992) calls a "willful nostalgia." Woodruff and Drake (1998) report, for example, that "Czech made" soft drinks promise to relieve the stress of the urban, cosmopolitan life that is associated with such global products as Coke and Pepsi. The cosmetics company Shiseido emphasizes its Japanese origins even outside of Japan and advertises an image of Japanese mystique, luxury, and exoticism (Schutte and Ciarlante 1998). The makers of French chocolates emphasize a nostalgic other of tropical cocoa jungles, but also the craft tradition of handmade chocolates (Terrio 1996).

We even see this willful nostalgia being used by McDonald's itself. The McDonald's in Singapore offers a "kampong" burger. Beng-Huat (2000) tells us that "kampong refers to the villages in which most Singaporeans lived prior to being resettled into high-rise public housing estates, a time which is remembered nostalgically as the 'good old days' when life was much more relaxed and community more organic than today's high-stress living in a globalised economy" (pp. 195–6).

Of course, nostalgia has been an important part of the empire building and nation building of the past few centuries (Anderson 1991), but in comparison to this politically driven nostalgia, the consumer-driven nostalgia is more focused on the particular and even the marginal as a resource for producing products and tourist experiences for a transnational capitalism that is oriented to niche markets interested in the exotic and the authentic. Robertson (1992:159) is quick to point out that this politically driven nostalgia has not been supplanted (and that is so much clearer in the post-September 11 world), but nevertheless, the politically driven nostalgia is embedded in or, at least, intertwined with consumer-driven nostalgia. There is a consumerist demand for and a production of nostalgia that is ready at hand when political crises have need of it.

Along with these familiar contradictions, we see also the highlighting of a new one, the contradiction outlined above between heterogeneity and homogeneity. In reaction to the new contradiction, people are encouraged to consume in order to resist a homogenizing globalization that is usually and most effectively presented as Americanization.

The Consumption of Anti-Americanization

Before I describe the way in which anti-Americanization is used to spur consumption, I should point out that America first spurred consumption as a symbol for rebellion rather than as a symbol of homogeneous conformity. Schutte and Ciarlante (1998:195) describe Coca-Cola, Levi's, and Marlboro as symbols of individualism and freedom. Yoshimi (2000) describes American consumer goods as "symbols of 'emancipation' and 'resistance'" (p. 202). According to Beng-Huat (2000), "American products have been used to express resistance to local repressions" (p. 16). Humphrey (1995) says that Western consumer goods represented "resistance to the regime" (p. 57) in the Soviet Union, and this continued in the post-Communist Russia with Chevrolet

successfully selling cars to Russians with a "Born in the U.S.A." campaign (Money and Colton 2000:189).

Despite the use of images portraying American products as symbols of emancipation and resistance, quite the opposite symbolization has often occurred. This has emerged naturally enough from the contradictions of global consumer culture listed above. There has been a condemnation of the unbridled consumer both as not rational enough and as not traditional enough (Sachs 1998). Furthermore, the image of the sovereign consumer that consumer culture introduced has often been used as the basis for criticizing the manipulated consumer. It was not long before both nations and local entrepreneurs saw the advantage to be gained in portraying globalization, or more usually Americanization, as the enemy. Appadurai (1996) notes the benefits of "posing global commoditization (or capitalism, or some other such external enemy) as more real than the threat of its own hegemonic strategies" (p. 32). Beng-Huat (2000) describes the "moral panic" created by the South Korean government and media against an Americanized consumer culture.

Of course, these moral crusades have not diminished consumption in South Korea or in any other culture. Instead, as I describe below, these antiglobalization attitudes function like the anticonsumption attitudes described in the first part of this chapter. They fuel more consumption. This might be suspected, since, as many analysts have noted, the United States is "the home of opposition and resistance to globalization, in spite of the widely held view that globalization is an American project. In fact, it has by now become appropriate to talk of the globalization of anti-globalism" (Robertson 2001:459).

McDonaldization in France

Let us return again to McDonald's and look at its reception in France as an exemplary case of the consumption of anti-Americanization. McDonald's was, for the French, identified with America, and the French relation with American culture has been, to say the least, ambiguous. France is well known for having rejected American culture in the 1960s and 1970s, only to embrace it by the mid-1980s (Kuisel

1993). Even though McDonald's was introduced into France in 1972 in the period of supposed American rejection, it nevertheless benefited from this American association because many saw McDonald's as a kind of "reverse snobbery" (Fantasia 1995:227). This was true even among the upper class, as evidenced by the fact that a haute couture fashion show served a buffet of McDonald's food during this period. Even more recently, Fantasia's (1995) research shows that French teenagers are attracted to McDonald's because of what they perceive as the American characteristics of informality, brashness, brightness, and playfulness (pp. 218–27).

Along with McDonald's there was an accompanying spread of McDonaldization among the French food industry. In the beginning, these French fast-food restaurants tried to benefit from the association of fast food with America with such names as Magic Burger, B'Burger, Manhattan Burger, Katy's Burger, Love Burger, and Kiss Burger (Fantasia 1995:206). In addition, their look and food products were copied from the American model. Indeed, Fantasia (1995:206) reports that French-owned hamburger places far outnumbered American-owned ones. More important than the food and the look, the restaurants copied the processes of McDonaldization: its efficiency, calculability, predictability, and control.

Of course, McDonald's identification with America has not been solely to its benefit. The very thing that has made McDonald's so popular has also made it the target of antiglobalization activists. French McDonald's have been sites of protest as well as of vandalism and bombing. The case of Jose Bove, who destroyed a half-built McDonald's in protest of a WTO ruling, has become a cause célèbre with support from tens of thousands of protestors as well as political leaders (Antonio and Bonanno 2000:56). More recently, those protesting the invasion/liberation of Iraq have burned a Ronald McDonald statue in Ecuador, smashed McDonald's windows in Paris, and scaled a McDonald's sign in South Korea.

Nevertheless, despite the opposition to McDonald's, McDonaldization has continued apace and increasingly acquired a French twist. French fast food quickly moved from American food and look to traditional French foods such as croissants and sandwiches on brioche or baguettes. Despite their now identifiably French names, products, and looks, these food outlets follow the same standardized, mechanized, and efficient practices that McDonald's introduced. However, they market themselves as a French, that is, non-American, fast food. In a minor reverse incursion, a few of these French fast-food places (e.g., Pret a Manger) have invaded America, drawing upon the French identification with fine food to help sell their McDonaldized products.

More important than this reverse incursion is the fact that the French fast-food places have used the rejection of McDonald's and of Americanization to sell their own products. In other words, the rejection of McDonald's has been used to promote the spread of McDonaldization. France provides us with a clear example of the increase in heterogeneity—of products, look, national identification—along with the increased homogenization of process.

This is not merely an economic phenomenon. As Chua Beng-Huat (2000) describes in the case of Singapore, the state is deeply involved:

> Consumption expansion thus tends to lead to some level of global homogenization of culture among consumers; an effect that gives rise to negative responses to globalisation. As consumer goods are always also cultural goods, expansion of consumption of imported products and services often gives rise to an exaggerated sense of "panic," of cultural "invasion" which, supposedly, if left unchecked will result in the demise of the local culture. Critics, including the state, thus inveigh against specific "foreign" targets, such as "Americanisation" or "Japanisation," and take upon themselves to promote "local" culture as ballast against the "foreign" cultural invasions. The desire of the state to involve itself in such ideological critique is obvious. Homogenisation of culture globally is antithetical to the idea of the "uniqueness" of nationalist sentiments and, therefore, is potentially threatening to the hold of the nation-state on its citizens. Emphasising the "national" as "local" differences is in the interests of the nation-state as an act of self-preservation. Hence, existing alongside embracing the arrival of capital is a cultural/moral critique of both the commodification of social life and the "cultural imperialism" of the countries from which the goods originate. (Pp. 183–4)

We see a similar effect in the marketing of such soft drinks as Mecca Cola and Qibla Cola, which target the European Muslim community and position themselves as an expression of anti-Americanization (Hundley 2003). The idea is that individuals are to express their contempt for America and its associated consumer society through the consumption of products that are produced, packaged, and marketed in a way that is deeply dependent on American consumer culture. In addition, although not so strongly anti-American, the Japanese create a national identity that is presented as distinct from others, especially Americans, and which is tied to what Yoshino (1999) calls a cultural marketplace. Likewise, Foster (2002) describes the people of Papua New Guinea as using consumption to create a local identity in opposition to the identity attached to global brands. As one final example, Johnston (2001) describes an ad for a flavored milk drink in New Zealand that is strongly critical of American culture, but which uses a musical rap form to express it. In these and many other cases, the spread of consumer culture is supported by the rejection of consumer culture represented as Americanization.

In the context of globalization, the consumption of anticonsumption is given a new twist. As discussed in the first part of this chapter, we have been encouraged to buy in order to establish our individuality in a mass-produced culture; to express our disgust with consumption by more consumption; to purchase the latest improved traditions. Now people are encouraged to buy to express their rejection of homogenized Americanization. Our disgust with the homogenized Americanization of McDonald's is used to expand the underlying process of McDonaldization. Our disgust with global consumer culture is used to strengthen and spread it.

Consumption is, by its own declarations, a social problem. Consumption is experienced as a mix of pleasure and guilt, anticipation and fear, desire and trepidation. We both love and hate our consumer culture, and our guilt, fear, trepidation, and hate involve us in this culture just as deeply as does our love.

Far from creating a crisis, the problems of consumer culture have made it more resilient. This is because our dissatisfaction with the culture is expressed through more consumption. Consumption has become our model for dissent, our model for freedom, our model for political activity. All alternatives to consumer culture—the simple life, the spiritual, the traditional, the local—become variant consumer fantasies. Consumption is a social problem and it is offered as its own solution.

NOTE

1. It is not necessary to invoke ancient and nonindustrialized cultures. Possamai (2002) describes how New Age consumers invoke science fiction and fantasy stories to position commodities outside of consumer culture.

REFERENCES

Abercrombie, Nicholas. 1994. "Authority and Consumer Society." In *The Authority of the Consumer,* edited by R. Keat, N. Whiteley, and N. Abercrombie. New York: Routledge.

Albrow, Martin. 1997. *The Global Age.* Stanford, CA: Stanford University Press.

Anderson, Benedict. 1991. *Imagined Communities: Reflections on the Origin and Spread of Nationalism.* New York: Verso.

Antonio, Robert J. and Alessandro Bonanno. 2000. "A New Global Capitalism? From 'Americanism' and 'Fordism' to 'Americanization-Globalization.'" *American Studies* 41:33–77.

Appadurai, Arjun. 1996. *Modernity at Large: Cultural Dimensions of Globalization.* Minneapolis, MN: University of Minnesota Press.

Ashcraft, Richard. 1972. "Marx and Weber on Liberalism as Bourgeois Ideology." *Comparative Studies in Society and History* 14:130–68.

Barthes, Roland. 1990. *The Fashion System.* Translated by Matthew Ward and Richard Howard. Berkeley, CA: University of California Press.

Bell, Daniel. 1976. *The Cultural Contradictions of Capitalism.* New York: Basic Books.

Beng-Huat, Chua. 2000. "Consuming Asians: Ideas and Issues." Pp. 1–34 in *Consumption in Asia Lifestyles and Identities,* edited by Chua Beng-Huat. New York: Routledge.

Binkley, Sam. Forthcoming. "The Seers of Menlo Park: The Discourse of Heroic Consumption in the *Whole Earth Catalog.*" *Journal of Consumer Culture.*

Breen, T. H. 1993. "The Meaning of Things: Interpreting the Consumer Economy in the Eighteenth Century."

Pp. 249–60 in *Consumption and the World of Goods,* edited by J. Brewer and R. Porter. New York: Routledge.

Cardona, Mercedes. 2002. "U.S. Will See Modest Boost in Ad Spending." *Advertising Age* 73:22–3.

Cowen, Tyler. 2002. *Creative Destruction: How Globalization Is Changing the World's Cultures.* Princeton, NJ: Princeton University Press.

Czech, Brian. 2002. *Shoveling Fuel for a Runaway Train: Errant Economists, Shameful Spenders, and a Plan to Stop Them All.* Berkeley, CA: University of California Press.

Durning, Alan. 1992. *How Much Is Enough? The Consumer Society and the Future of the Earth.* New York: Norton.

Ewen, Stuart. 1976. *Captains of Consciousness: Advertising and the Social Roots of the Consumer Culture.* New York: McGraw-Hill.

Fantasia, Rick. 1995. "Fast Food in France." *Theory and Society* 24:201–43.

Finkelstein, Joanne. 1995. "The Anemic World of the High Consumer: Fashion and Cultural Formation." In *Worlds Apart: Modernity through the Prism of the Local,* edited by D. Miller. New York: Routledge.

Fiske, John. 1989. *Reading the Popular.* Boston, MA: Unwin Hyman.

Fitzgerald, Niall. 1997. "Harnessing the Potential of Globalization for the Consumer and Citizen." *International Affairs* 73:739–46.

Foster, Robert. 2002. *Materializing the Nation: Commodities, Consumption, and Media in Papua New Guinea.* Bloomington, IN: Indiana University Press.

Frank, Thomas. 1997. *The Conquest of Cool: Business Culture, Counterculture, and the Rise of Hip Consumerism.* Chicago, IL: University of Chicago Press.

Friedman, Jonathan. 1994. *Global Identity and Global Processes.* Thousand Oaks, CA: Sage.

Friedman, Thomas. 1999. *The Lexus and the Olive Tree.* New York: Farrar, Straus, Giroux.

Giddens, Anthony. 1990. *The Consequences of Modernity.* Stanford, CA: Stanford University Press.

Gilpin, Robert. 2000. *The Challenge of Global Capitalism.* Princeton, NJ: Princeton University Press.

Gronow, Jukka. 1997. *The Sociology of Taste.* New York: Routledge.

Gunter, Barrie and Adrian Furnham. 1998. *Children as Consumers: A Psychological Analysis of the Young People's Market.* New York: Routledge.

Hage, Gerald and Charles Powers. 1992. *Post-Industrial Lives: Roles and Relationships in the 21st Century.* Thousand Oaks, CA: Sage.

Halter, Marilyn. 2000. *Shopping for Identity: The Marketing of Ethnicity.* New York: Schocken.

Hannerz, Ulf. 1992. *Cultural Complexity: Studies in the Social Organization of Meaning.* New York: Columbia University Press.

Harvey, David. 1989. *The Condition of Postmodernity.* Oxford, England: Blackwell.

Held, David, A. McGrew, D. Goldblatt, and J. Perraton. 1999. *Global Transformations: Politics, Economics and Culture.* Stanford, CA: Stanford University Press.

Hirschman, A. O. 1982. "Rival Interpretations of Market Society: Civilizing, Destructive, or Feeble?" *Journal of Economic Literature* 20:1463–84.

Hirst, Paul and Grahame Thompson. 1996. *Globalization in Question: The International Economy and the Possibilities of Governance.* Cambridge, MA: Polity Press.

Hobsbawm, Eric. 1997. "The Future of the State." In *Social Futures, Global Visions,* edited by Cynthia Hewitt de Alcantara. Oxford, England: Blackwell.

Hobsbawn, Eric and T. Ranger, eds. 1983. *The Invention of Tradition.* Cambridge, England: Cambridge University Press.

Horowitz, Daniel. 1985. *The Morality of Spending: Attitudes toward the Consumer Society in America, 1875–1940.* Chicago, IL: Elephant Press.

Humphrey, Caroline. 1995. "Worlds Apart: Creating a Culture of Disillusionment: Consumption in Moscow, a Chronicle of Changing Times." Pp. 43–68 in *Worlds Apart: Modernity through the Prism of the Local,* edited by D. Miller. New York: Routledge.

Hundley, Tom. 2003. "Foreign Cola Knockoffs Offer Anti-American Political Flavor." *Chicago Tribune,* February 2, p. B1.

Johnston, Jessica. 2001. "The Battle for Local Identity: An Ethnographic Description of Local/Global Tensions in a New Zealand Advertisement." *Journal of Popular Culture* 35:193–205.

Kelly, John. 1999. "Time and the Global: Against the Homogeneous, Empty Communities in Contemporary Social Theory." In *Globalization and Identity: Dialectics of Flow and Closure,* edited by B. Meyer and P. Geschiere. Oxford, England: Blackwell.

Key, Wilson B. 1972. *Subliminal Seduction.* New York: Signet.

Klein, Naomi. 2000. *No Logo: Taking Aim at the Brand Name Bullies.* Toronto, Canada: Knopf Canada.

Kuisel, Richard. 1993. *Seducing the French: The Dilemma of Americanization.* Berkeley, CA: University of California Press.

Larrabee, Eric. 1957. "The Edsel and How It Got That Way." *Harper's* 123 (1):123–46.

Lasch, Christopher. 1994. "The Culture of Consumption." In *Encyclopedia of Social History,* edited by P. Stearns. New York: Garland.

Lasn, Kalle. 2000. *Culture Jam: How to Reverse America's Suicidal Consumer Binge—And Why We Must.* New York: Quill.

Lau, Kimberly. 2000. *New Age Capitalism: Making Money East of Eden.* Philadelphia, PA: University of Pennsylvania Press.

Levitt, Theodore. 1988. "The Pluralization of Consumption." *Harvard Business Review* 2:7–8.

Marcuse, Herbert. 1965. "Repressive Tolerance." In *Critique of Pure Tolerance,* edited by B. Moore, R. Wolff, and H. Marcuse. Boston, MA: Beacon Press.

Meadows, Donella H., Dennis Meadows, and Jorgen Randers. 1992. *Beyond the Limits.* Post Mills, VT: Chelsea Green.

Miller, Jim. 1987. *Democracy Is in the Streets: From Port Huron to the Siege of Chicago.* New York: Simon & Schuster.

Mittleman, James. 2000. *The Globalization Syndrome: Transformation and Resistance.* Princeton, NJ: Princeton University Press.

Money, R. Bruce and Deborah Colton. 2000. "Global Advertising." *Journal of World Business* 35:189–205.

Ohmae, Kenichi. 1990. *Borderless World.* New York: Harper.

Packard, Vance. 1957. *The Hidden Persuaders.* New York: D. McKay.

Pieterse, Jan N. 1995. "Globalization as Hybridization." In *Global Modernities,* edited by Mike Featherstone, Scott Lash, and Roland Robertson. London, England: Sage.

Possamai, Adam. 2002. "Cultural Consumption of History and Popular Culture in Alternative Spiritualities." *Journal of Consumer Culture* 2:197–218.

Ritzer, George. 2000. *The McDonaldization of Society.* Thousand Oaks, CA: Pine Forge.

———. 2001. "Globalization Theory: Lessons from the Exportation of McDonaldization and the New Means of Consumption." In *Explorations in the Sociology of Consumption: Fast Food, Credit Cards and Casino,* edited by G. Ritzer. Thousand Oaks, CA: Sage.

Ritzer, George, Douglas Goodman, and Wendy Wiedenhoft. 2001. "Theories of Consumption." In *Handbook of Social Theory,* edited by G. Ritzer and B. Smart. Thousand Oaks, CA: Sage.

Robertson, Roland. 1992. *Globalization: Social Theory and Global Culture.* London, England: Sage.

———. 1995. "Glocalization: Time-Space and Homogeneity-Heterogeneity." Pp. 25–44 in *Global Modernities,* edited by M. Featherstone, S. Lash, and R. Robertson. London, England: Sage.

———. 2001. "Globalization Theory 2000+: Major Problematics." Pp. 458–71 in *Handbook of Social Theory*, edited by G. Ritzer and B. Smart. London, England: Sage.

Sachs, Jeffrey. 1998. "Unlocking the Mysteries of Globalization." *Foreign Policy* 110:58–64.

Sassen, S. 1991. *The Global City: New York, London, Tokyo.* Princeton, NJ: Princeton University Press.

Scholte, Jan Aart. 2000. *Globalization: A Critical Introduction.* New York: St. Martin's Press.

Schor, Juliet. 1998. *The Overspent American: Upscaling, Downshifting, and the New Consumer.* New York: Basic Books.

———. 2000. "The New Politics of Consumption." Pp. 3–36 in *Do Americans Shop Too Much?* edited by J. Schor. Boston, MA: Beacon Press.

Schudson, Michael. 1998. "Delectable Materialism: Second Thoughts on Consumer Culture." In *Ethics of Consumption: The Good Life, Justice, and Global Stewardship,* edited by D. Crocker and T. Linden. Lanham, MD: Rowman & Littlefield.

Schutte, Hellmut and Deanna Ciarlante, eds. 1998. *Consumer Behavior in Asia.* New York: New York University Press.

Sklair, Leslie. 1995. *Sociology of the Global System.* 2nd ed. Baltimore, MD: Johns Hopkins University Press.

Steger, Manfred. 2002. *Globalism: The New Market Ideology.* Lanham, MD: Rowman & Littlefield.

Stephenson, Peter H. 1989. "Going to McDonald's in Leiden: Reflections on the Concept of Self and Society in the Netherlands." *ETHOS: Journal of the Society for Psychological Anthropology* 17:226–47.

Terrio, Susan J. 1996. "Crafting *Grand Cru* Chocolates in Contemporary France." *American Anthropologist* 98:67–79.

Tinic, Serra A. 1997. "United Colors and Untied Meanings: Benetton and the Commodification of Social Issues." *Journal of Communication* 47:3–25.

Tulloch, Sara, compiler. 1991. *The Oxford Dictionary of New Words.* Oxford, England: Oxford University Press.

Watson, James. 1997. *Golden Arches East: McDonald's in East Asia.* Stanford, CA: Stanford University Press.

Weber, Max. 2002. *Protestant Ethics and the Spirit of Capitalism.* Translated by Stephen Kahlberg. Los Angeles, CA: Roxbury.

Wilk, Richard. 1994. "Consumer Goods as Dialogue about Development." *Culture and History* 7:79–100.

———. 1995. "Learning to Be Local in Belize: Global Systems of Common Difference." Pp. 110–33 in

Worlds Apart: Modernity through the Prism of the Local, edited by D. Miller. New York: Routledge.

Williams, Raymond. 1976. *Keywords: A Vocabulary of Culture and Society.* New York: Oxford University Press.

Woodruff, David and James Drake. 1998. "Ready to Shop until They Drop." *Business Week*, June 22, p. 104.

Woodward, Helen. 1926. *Through Many Windows.* New York: Harper & Brothers.

Yoshimi, Shunya. 2000. "Consuming 'America': From Symbol to System." Pp. 111–34 in *Consumption in Asia Lifestyles and Identities,* edited by Chua Beng-Huat. New York: Routledge.

Yoshino, Kosaku. 1999. "Rethinking Theories of Nationalism: Japan's Nationalism in a Marketplace Perspective." Pp. 8–28 in *Consuming Ethnicity and Nationalism: Asian Experiences,* edited by K. Yoshino. Honolulu, HI: University of Hawaii Press.

Zwingle, Erla. 2000. "A World Together." Pp. 153–64 in *Globalization,* edited by K. Sjursen. New York: H. W. Wilson.

FAMILY PROBLEMS IN GLOBAL PERSPECTIVE

FELIX M. BERARDO

University of Florida

CONSTANCE L. SHEHAN

University of Florida

Developing a systematic global view and assessment of family problems is a challenging endeavor. Problems of data availability and access are among several obstacles encountered. As one might suspect, for example, countries exhibit considerable variability in the types and quality of information gathered with respect to internal and external factors associated with family systems (Settles 2000). Compounding these difficulties is a lack of consensus regarding definitions of family and social problem. Nevertheless, there have been a few courageous attempts. An early example was Goode's *World Revolution and Family Patterns* (1963), a work published four decades ago, in which he sought to describe and interpret the main changes in family patterns that have occurred over the past half-century in Japan, China, India, the West, sub-Saharan Africa, and the Arab countries.

Goode's major thesis was that throughout the world, industrialization and urbanization were affecting all human societies, including their family systems, though at different rates of speed. Hence, "the trend in one family trait may differ from one society to another—for example, the divorce rate or illegitimacy rate might be dropping in one society but rising in another" (p. 2). His analysis led him to conclude that the overall trend seemed to be toward a *conjugal* family pattern, which involves fewer kinship ties and a greater emphasis on the "nuclear" family unit. However, he also noted that certain ideological and value changes are partially independent of industrialization and have had some effect on familial and societal changes. Among the trends he detected were the shift "from the arbitrary power of elders toward personal freedom for the young, from cold marriages based on economic arrangements to unions based on the youngsters' right of choice, from rigidly maintained class barriers between children to an open class system, from the subjugation of the wife to equalitarianism and companionship in marriage, and from the repression of children's emotions to permissiveness" (pp. 6–7).

In this chapter, we concentrate on a number of family problems as part of a wider set of issues discussed in this handbook. We begin with a rather common definition of social problems. We opted to select a specific definition in order to avoid lengthy discussions and disagreements over the concept itself. We could have chosen several others. Current social problems textbooks were examined, with a focus on the chapters on families in particular, noting the major problems selected for coverage. This gave us some idea of what people writing in this area considered to be the major family-related issues currently being emphasized and also being researched by social analysts. We, of course, faced the same limitations and obstacles in our search of relevant cross-cultural literature and data so well detailed by Goode.

DEFINING SOCIAL PROBLEMS

Scholars have long struggled with the development of adequate social scientific definitions of the family, and assessing its role as a reactor to as well as instigator of social change (Vincent 1966). A similar situation is evident with respect to social problems. For example, Dallos and McLaughlin (1993) note that numerous questions have been raised about how and by whom social problems get defined, and that "unproblematic" definitions are not easily arrived at. Moreover, they go on to observe that

> certain private troubles seem to become fully-fledged social problems more "easily" than others and they also remain in the public domain more readily than others. In the course of their social construction all take on a particular public stereotypical representation. Furthermore, there is a tendency in our society to "rediscover" social problems. Many social problems . . . seem to be rediscovered and reconstituted generationally and it is important to realize that social problems have their own "forgotten" definitional history. Such definitional issues have important consequences for those attempting to ascertain the exact nature and extent of a particular social problem and for those devising appropriate levels and types of intervention. (Pp. 4–5)

Any examination of family problems will inevitably encounter its multifaceted connections with other societal institutions. They are inextricably intertwined and for that reason difficult to unravel.

Behavior comes to eventually be defined as a social problem after progressing through a number of stages (Blackman 1989:9–25). Initially, the behavior changes from being primarily a taboo topic to one that is openly discussed. In this process, alternative perceptions regarding the people affected arise. The actions of interest groups, the media, and others create greater public awareness of the problem. Further awareness occurs in the next stage, where efforts are made to involve legislative and judicial action regarding the problem. In the third stage, government policy is created and programs are designed to address the problem. In the final stage, increased recognition of the issue produces greater understanding and changes cultural attitudes and expectations about family relationships. Within and across cultures, these stages in the emergence of social problems occur. However, they do so at different points in time. In the process, definitions of the family become an issue.

DEFINING THE FAMILY

While all known societies have family-like groups, vast social changes occurring around the globe have triggered wide variations in family forms and functions. This diversity has made it increasingly difficult to define the term *family* itself. Social scientists as well as politicians and others often debate the parameters of this basic social unit, revealing conflicting views over the recognition of legitimate family structures and relationships. The traditional definition used by the U.S. Census Bureau limits *family* to two or more persons related by blood, marriage, or adoption. A broad spectrum of demographic changes that have occurred over the past several decades challenges the appropriateness of this traditional definition. We adopt a definition offered by Yorburg (2002), who sees

> *families* as groups related by marriage, birth, adoption, or *mutual definition*. If people define themselves as a

family, they *are* a family. Mutual definition is an essential feature because if people feel they belong to a family group, if they have a deep, personal, emotional involvement (negative or positive) with this group, and if their identity is defined by the group, then we must accept them as a family. They are families even if their relationships are not recognized by tradition, law, or custom. (P. 26)

This approach accepts the notion that *family* is a social construction, and therefore its definition is not limited to that posed by the political, religious, or other institutional systems. It allows for variant shades of meaning, allegiance, and authority, as well as encompassing differential membership in kinship systems.

SOCIAL CHANGE AND FAMILY PROBLEMS: THE ROLE OF WOMEN

Bruce et al. (1995) have noted several worldwide trends affecting families, including unwed motherhood, rising divorce rates, smaller households, and the feminization of poverty. They call particular attention to the rising role played by women throughout the world in providing economic support to family members. Families are becoming increasingly dependent on mothers' paid work. Indeed, social scientists generally agree that the rising economic status of women, along with shifts in the gender-based division of labor, has played a major role in triggering many worldwide changes in the family.

Significant shifts in the world economy have greatly altered women's labor force participation in recent years. Their entry into the workforce is increasing all over the world (United Nations 2000). In all regions except northern Africa and western Asia, at least one-third of the workforce is female. However, their participation rates are still lower than men's. Also, women are disproportionately engaged in nonstandard forms of work, such as temporary and casual employment, part-time jobs, home-based work, self-employment, and working in microenterprises. Nevertheless, as they have achieved more control over their fertility, they have been able to respond to expanding opportunities for education and employment that have come with economic growth and the expansion of the service sector. In many parts of the globe, attitudes toward women's employment have become more favorable, and public policies on family and child care, part-time employment, maternity benefits, and parental and maternal leave have become more supportive. Policies with respect to micro and small enterprises, including funding and credit programs specifically designed to promote women's entrepreneurship, have also played a role.

Bruce et al. (1995) cite many places around the globe where women's economic contributions have become increasingly important to family welfare, including the United States. In a very real sense, the changing roles of women are redefining family relationships, and this ongoing process must be factored into the evolving and shifting international perceptions of family problems.

MATE SELECTION AND FAMILY FORMATION

Historically, marriages have come about primarily through three approaches to securing a spouse: marriage by capture or by arrangement or as a result of free choice (Ingoldsby 1995). Of these, bride capture was relatively rare, whereas the practice of arranged marriages was widespread. In the typical case, parents, sometimes assisted by relatives or professional matchmakers, effect the choosing of the marital partner. However, over time a number of factors, including a spreading democratic ethos and accompanying equalitarian norms in gender relations, the weakening of the power of kinship groups, and the rise of individualism, have spurred a growing acceptance of free choice in mate selection. In the United States, for example, couples generally ignore traditional endogamous rules, instead emphasizing romantic love as the primary prerequisite to marriage. In some places, a mixture of approaches to mate selection has been observed.

> Among the Igbo in Nigeria, for example, about 55 percent of the marriages are arranged, while the remaining 45 percent are in free-choice unions. Most of the latter are younger, indicating a move from arranged to free choice, which we see occurring throughout the world today. . . . As the Igbo move to free mate choice based on love, their various arranged practices are falling into disfavor. (Ingoldsby 1995:151)

Societies undergoing the transition to a more open mate selection system often experience at least temporary strains between generations as the youngest cohort ignore or violate traditional customs and expectations in choosing a marital partner. Thus, in China and Japan, individual choice is on the rise, along with related changes in family formation. In the case of Japan, for example, "many young Japanese are dispensing with tradition. No longer compelled to live by their parents' mores, many are staying single longer and conceiving children before getting married" (Kashiwase 2002:1–4).

Arranged marriages have by no means disappeared, and in some locations it remains the most common method of bringing couples together (Ingoldsby 1995). Globally, however, trends seem to favor a more open and individually oriented mate selection system based upon affection and love. As this trend progresses, tensions arise and generations have to develop acceptable accommodations to these changing norms of family formation.

CHANGING PATTERNS OF CHILDBEARING: FERTILITY

Countries around the world are undergoing various phases of the demographic transition—from high to low mortality and fertility—reflecting economic transformations and advances in medicine and health technology, along with family planning. This is especially noticeable across Asia, where birth and death rates have been declining for decades (East-West Center 2002). For example, Japan, India, South Korea, and China have all experienced noticeable reductions in fertility rates. The Chinese government rewards couples who voluntarily have only one child and punishes those who violate the policy with financial penalties and mandatory abortions. Because of its success in dramatically reducing fertility, there is growing fear that today's young couples will have few children to care for them in old age. India has brought down its birthrate primarily through female sterilization and the use of contraceptive methods. More women in England and Wales now enter the labor force and remain there during their reproductive years. They are postponing childbearing to pursue careers, and are having fewer children than ever before (United Nations 2000).

Japan is illustrative of countries in which the changing status of women has played a significant role in reducing childbearing. Over the past half-century, there has been a significant increase in the proportion of women enrolled in colleges and universities, and now their numbers are about the same as men. Most now work before marriage. "These single working women typically live at home with their parents, have plenty of spending money because they pay little or no rent, and feel little pressure to rush into marriage" (East-West Center 2002:19). Hence, a rising average age at first marriage has accounted for about half of Japan's fertility decline over the past 25 years. When Japanese women do marry, they are now more likely to remain in the labor force. Work responsibilities are apt to conflict with household and child-rearing responsibilities, and this often results in reduced fertility patterns. Interestingly, the sharp reduction in family size has led to a significant lowering of expectations among mothers that they will be supported by their children in old age.

Fertility rates are declining around the world, but large differences among countries remain. The average number of children women have is as high as seven in many countries. Large numbers of children can result from a number of factors, including a tradition of early marriage, the prevalence of polygyny, government population policies, son preference, the subordination of women to men in decisions regarding reproduction, and poverty (in which children can serve as economic assets). Bearing and caring for large numbers of children puts considerable strain on women's health, time, and economy. About 60,000 women die each year in pregnancy and childbirth. For every woman who dies, approximately 30 more incur injuries, infections, and disabilities (Seager 1997). These are usually untreated and unspoken of, but can be humiliating, painful, debilitating, and long-lasting. Maternal mortality rates vary by class, race, and the comparative status of women. Most maternal deaths are in the poor world. An estimated 1 in 13 women in sub-Saharan Africa dies of causes related to pregnancy and childbirth, compared with 1 in 3,200 in Europe, 1 in 3,300 in the United States, and 1 in 7,300 in Canada (Seager 1997).

In many countries, women are engaged in childbearing for most of their adult years. In most of the world, women want fewer children than do their male partners, and women want to exercise more control over their fertility. Many lack knowledge of available contraceptive methods, or lack access to or ability to afford them. Men typically dominate in reproductive decisions. In Nigeria, for instance, 88 percent of the men surveyed and 78 percent of the women said that men's views were more influential in family decisions. For instance, an early 1990s survey of family size preferences in Africa showed that in Niger, husbands said the ideal number of children was 13, while wives said 9.

OUT-OF-WEDLOCK BIRTHS

Women's average age at first childbirth has increased in most developed and less developed countries over the last 20 years. Though the proportion of adolescent women giving birth is generally declining, it remains high. This is particularly true in sub-Saharan Africa: in Ghana, Kenya, and Senegal, for example, half or more of all first births are to women aged 20 and under. In Ecuador and Indonesia, close to half of all first births are to adolescents (Bruce et al. 1995:6). As the cultural desirability of early marriage has receded, the consequences of adolescent childbearing have become increasingly unfavorable. Current evidence from a variety of settings reveals that women who conceive children at a young age and out of the socially accepted sequence have poor economic prospects (Seager 1997).

Sexually active, unmarried adolescents account for a large portion of the unmet need for contraception and safe abortion services in many countries, yet adolescent girls lack effective access to, or power to use, contraception. In Latin America, typically no more than one-fifth of sexually active adolescent girls report using contraception at first intercourse, and only 20 percent to 70 percent of unmarried adolescents report using a contraceptive method during their most recent sexual encounter (Seager 1977). Nonconsensual sex plays a significant role in adolescent pregnancy in developed and less developed countries alike. More than two-thirds of the respondents in a sample of adolescent mothers in Seattle, Washington, reported that they had been sexually abused, and 44 percent had been victims of forced intercourse at some point in their lives. Nearly half of sexually active schoolgirls in Kenya report that their first intercourse was forced or that they were "tricked" into it (Bruce et al. 1995:38).

Many Japanese women are now conceiving before marrying. Of all first births recorded in 2000, 26 percent were to premaritally pregnant women, double what it was 20 years ago. Moreover, premarital conceptions have risen even more rapidly among younger women—58 percent among those aged 20 to 24. Among first births to teen mothers, more than four-fifths were conceived out of wedlock (Kashiwase 2002:1, 4). There has also been an increase in the number of out-of-wedlock births in the United States. By the late 1990s, more than 25 percent of white births, 41 percent of Hispanic births, and 70 percent of black births involved mothers who were not legally married (Smith 1999; Teachman, Tedrow, and Crowder 2000; Ventura et al. 2000). Birthrates for teens aged 15 to 19 have generally declined since the late 1950s. In spite of this decline, the teen fertility rate in the United States is considerably higher than that for other developed countries. During the 1990s, the drop in rates was especially large for black teens. The factors accounting for this downward trend include decreased sexual activity reflecting changing attitudes toward premarital sex, increases in condom use, and adoptions of recently available forms of hormonal contraception that are implanted or injected (Ventura, Matthews, and Hamilton 2001).

CONTRACEPTION AND ABORTION

The use, acceptance, and promotion of manufactured contraceptives have increased substantially worldwide, and this is regarded as one of the great social revolutions of modern times. Globally, 57 percent of women now report using some type of contraception. The highest rates of use are found in East Asia (dominated by China), followed by industrialized Western countries. The lowest rates are found in Africa. Typically, international data are available only for married women of childbearing age (15 to 44). There are virtually no international data available on contraceptive use by unmarried women. Contraception is nearly always the woman's responsibility. Most men take limited responsibility, and in most countries, male contraceptives (condoms) and male sterilization are rarely used. While men dominate childbearing decisions, they are rarely targeted by reproductive planning programs or contraceptive research. The importance of this issue can be seen in the prevalence of abortion.

There are an estimated 25 million to 30 million legal abortions around the world each year. Worldwide, more than one out of every five pregnancies ends in abortion. Approximately 35 out of every 1,000 of the world's women have abortions each year (Painter 1999). Most nations permit abortion, although under varying degrees of restriction, including gestational timing limits, performance by licensed physicians only, mandatory waiting periods, and parental notification or consent for teenagers. Some nations (such as the United States) restrict government funding for abortion, which puts it beyond the reach of the poor. In much of Eastern Europe, state subsidies for abortions have been dropped or limited and the price of abortions has skyrocketed. Abortion rates vary widely around the world. Western Europe has the lowest rate (11 per 1,000 women), while Eastern Europe has the highest (90 per 1,000). Because access to modern contraceptive methods has been limited in this region, abortion has been the primary method of limiting family size. In England and Wales, the official abortion rate is 15.6 per 1,000 women, compared with 22.9 in the United States.

Over the past decade, the number of medically induced abortions that were performed in the United States dropped, to slightly more than 1.3 million. It has been estimated that over 40 percent of women in the United States will have at least one abortion by the time they reach age 45 (Alan Guttmacher Institute 2001). Nearly all the women who are at risk of an unintended pregnancy use a contraceptive method. In fact, the majority of women who have abortions reported that they were using a contraceptive method during the month they became pregnant. Just under half of the 6.3 million pregnancies that occur each year in the United States are unplanned (Alan Guttmacher Institute 2001).

Unsafe Abortion

Each year, 20 million women around the world choose to terminate their pregnancies illegally. "Globally, one unsafe abortion takes place for every seven births" (World Health Organization 2000). Many of these abortions are unsafe because they are performed by unskilled persons using hazardous techniques in unsanitary conditions. The World Health Organization estimates that 19 out of every 20 unsafe abortions take place in the developing regions of the world. Approximately 10 million take place in Asia, another 5 million occur in Africa; Latin America and the Caribbean account for around 4 million, while in Europe the figure approaches 1 million. "Contrary to common belief, most women seeking abortion are not unmarried teenagers. Rather, they are married, live in stable relationships with a partner, and already have several children. They use abortion to limit family size or space births" (World Health Organization 2000:4). However, the situation in the United States is different in regard to the most common marital status and age of women who terminate their pregnancies through abortion: two-thirds of all abortions involve unmarried women but only one-fifth involve teenagers (Alan Guttmacher Institute 2001).

The struggle over abortion rights is not just, or even primarily, a struggle over morality. It is a struggle about women's autonomy. The extent to which women can or cannot control their reproductive choices affects their choices in other spheres: their participation in the economy, education, the household, and in the political and civic arena (Seager 1997). It is increasingly recognized that "enabling women and families to choose whether, when, and how often to have children is central to safe motherhood" (cited in World Health Organization 2000:5). Preventing families from having such control over their fertility limits personal freedoms and aspirations and often reduces the ability of families to improve economically.

DIVORCE

Among the major global trends in family patterns has been a pervasive rise in divorce rates (Bruce et al. 1995; Goode 1993). Historically, there has been considerable variation in divorce rates within and between countries.[1] This often reflects major shifts in their economies as well as the effects of wars. These trends are also influenced by government policies, such as no-fault legislation (Yorburg 2002). In Chile, Malta, and the Philippines, among a handful of other—mostly Catholic—states, divorce remains illegal. In Ireland, divorce was made legal only in 1996. In many countries, divorce is mostly a man's prerogative. In some, especially Islamic states, women are not allowed to initiate divorce. Worldwide divorce laws are generally becoming more liberal, but in several countries, a conservative religious resurgence threatens to restrict women's rights both in marriage and divorce (United Nations 2000). These global patterns also show that "a growing proportion of divorces involved couples with young children, increasing the likelihood that marital dissolution will lead to single parenthood" (Bruce et al. 1995:15).

Currently, divorce is widespread in industrial societies as well as less developed countries. Though the rate varies considerably, it has increased in every country. For example, the rate more than doubled since 1970 in Canada, France, Greece, the Netherlands, the United Kingdom, and former East Germany (Bruce 1995:15). In the United States, roughly 1 out of 5 to 6 marriages now fail, compared with 4 out of 10 in Britain. While the reasons for this are many and complex, it appears that "[w]here women have higher status—higher levels of education and occupational prestige, and where they have independent means of income . . . that they are allowed to keep—birth rates are lower, household size is smaller, the average age at first marriage is higher, and the divorce rate increases" (Yorburg 2002:64). There also is growing evidence that higher divorce rates are associated with women's labor force and political participation (Greenstein and Davis 2002).

A number of reasons have been offered to account for the recent rise in divorce rates throughout the industrialized world (Yorburg 2002:190–2), including unrealistic expectations, more alternatives to satisfy one's social and physical needs, diminishing traditional institutional controls, changing values regarding divorce and single status, new standards with respect to marital happiness and success, and an emphasis on individualism. While changed social conditions and newer standards are evolving at different paces in industrialized countries, nevertheless, they all contribute to the current instability of contemporary marriages. Divorce rates in the United States today are two to three times as high as rates in other industrialized countries such as Sweden, Canada, France, and the United Kingdom. Russia has the highest divorce rate, while some of the lowest rates are in Greece, Portugal, Italy, and Spain. Similarly, low rates can be found in Bulgaria, Croatia, Poland, and Slovenia. Religious and traditional values may account, in part, for low dissolution rates. For example, such marital dissolutions are relatively rare in the Muslim world, though this too is slowly changing.

Does a High Divorce Rate Indicate a Social Problem?

Goode's (1993) analysis led him to conclude that changing divorce patterns create widespread social problems. Moreover,

> Divorce becomes a problem even when the rates themselves are not extremely high by world standards, for the absolute numbers of people involved are so much greater. Its consequences are a problem because people define it so and that perception arises both because of the inevitable rising social support burden, and because people actually know someone who has been affected by divorce. They are also a problem because more people take longer before remarriage, and there is an increase in mother-headed families. (Pp. 21–2)

However, whether high divorce rates should be considered a social problem depends in part on one's ideological or political perspective. From a liberal or progressive standpoint, divorce is often considered necessary and, indeed, preferable to remaining in an unhappy marriage, especially in the case of wives (and their children) suffering from an abusive relationship. Hence, liberals tend to favor a relaxation of divorce laws. Those with a conservative bent, on the other hand, view rising dissolution rates as signifying a selfish attitude that places individual needs and desires above marital and familial obligations (Maciones 2002:343). Thus, conservatives are in favor of making it more difficult to terminate marriage, for example, by tightening divorce legislation. It is not known what the upper limit for divorce rates is before they become a threat to societal stability. Some have suggested that with a high remarriage rate, such as the case in the United States, a strong family system can be maintained.

Consequences of Divorce

Political debate aside, there is sufficient evidence that divorce has a number of negative consequences, particularly for women and children, and hence is of concern to the larger community and society. With divorce,

> Mother-headed families become a higher percentage of all households with children. The payment of non-custodial parents are usually not enough to support the children, even when those parents can afford them—and some parents cannot. Custodial mothers are much more likely than others to be in the work force. Since for various reasons they command lower wages, and often must work part time (for adequate day-care facilities are lacking), they are more likely to be economically deprived. In most countries, even if they worked full time, they would still be in a precarious financial position. In countries with a genuine welfare system they create a large tax burden. Cohabitation continues to increase, and in several countries a majority of marriages are preceded by cohabitation, which itself is much more prone to dissolution than is legal marriage. (Goode 1993:321)

Studies of the children of divorce show initial high levels of negative emotional responses to their parents' separation. Compared with children in intact families, they are likely to suffer significantly more behavioral and psychological problems. Although most children eventually learn to adjust to their new situation, a divorce can have long-lasting effects. Adults whose parents were divorced are more likely to also become divorced or seek psychological counseling than those reared in intact families. Children reared in intact but conflict-ridden marriages may suffer similar consequences. There is evidence that many of a child's difficulties initiate well prior to parental divorce as they are exposed to a home atmosphere filled with tension and conflict built up within the family.

> The debate about the effects divorce has on children is an emotional one, and unfounded claims abound on all sides of the issue. At this point it seems fair to say that the scientific research points to two conclusions. When there are intense and persistent conflicts in the family or one parent is abusive, either sexually, physically, or verbally, the children are likely to be better off after a divorce. However, when the partners are merely frustrated or unfulfilled, evidence indicates that the children are more likely to be harmed than injured by a divorce. (Coleman and Kerbo 2002:43–4)

WIDOWHOOD

Given that women usually have a longer life expectancy than men, that they are usually younger—sometimes considerably younger—than the men they marry, and that they have a much lower remarriage rate than men, it is a demographic certainty that a far greater proportion of them will be left without a spouse. The number of widows is not insignificant. In India alone in 1991 there were 30 million, constituting 10 percent of the female population. In less developed countries in which spousal age differences are large and married fertility continues late in life, such as in Bangladesh, Ghana, Morocco, Nigeria, and Sudan, widows are often left with dependent children to support (Bruce et al. 1995:34–9).

Among the industrialized nations, the probability of mortality before middle age has been declining, and increasingly widowhood is being postponed to the later stages of the family life cycle. Moreover, in most advanced societies, women constitute a preponderance of the widowed population, especially at the older ages. In the United States, for example, 85 percent of widowed persons are women. And among people 65 years of age or over, roughly half the women compared with 14 percent of the men have lost a spouse (Berardo and Berardo 2000).

Widowhood among women age 60 or over is most prevalent in northern Africa and central Asia, where nearly 60 percent of women in this age group have lost their husbands. In other parts of Asia, roughly half of the women aged 60 or over are widowed because of large age differences between spouses (United Nations 2000). The lowest prevalence of female survivors is found in Latin America and the Caribbean, where over one-third of the women aged 60 and over have lost their husbands through death. This is thought to be due, in part, to women in informal unions referring to themselves as single rather than widowed after their spouse dies.

In some parts of the world, wars have left large numbers of widows with dependent children. This situation has been observed in Afghanistan and regions of the Middle East in the last decade. For example, a study in rural Cambodia found that fully 20 percent of the households were headed by widows. An analysis of data from Vietnam revealed that more than one-fifth of women aged 35 to 54 (who were in their twenties and thirties during the Vietnam War) were widows.

Widowhood can and often does have serious financial consequences for women, who may lose property as well as spousal income when their husband dies. In much of sub-Saharan Africa, widows often do not inherit from their husbands, regardless of the age and number of their common children, or the closeness of the marriage. After a husband's demise, it is not uncommon for his kin to remove key possessions. In some parts of India, a widow is seen as being the "cause" of her husband's death and is treated as a "stranger" by her former in-laws. Though she may remain in the family compound, she must sleep and eat in a segregated space and provide for herself and her children. In upper-caste communities, she is prohibited from working for wages, making the pursuit of a livelihood difficult, if not impossible.

Restrictions on residence, ownership, and employment place female survivors in a situation of acute dependency on economic support from others, yet such support may not be forthcoming from members of her family or from in-laws. The economic deprivation and vulnerability of widows is reflected in their high morbidity and mortality rates compared with their counterparts among married women. In India, mortality rates are 86 percent higher among widows than among married women.

In Bangladesh, there is a measurable increase in the deaths of women following the demise of their husband if they do not have sons to provide for them and protect their rights. Even in societies where the extended family has been able to provide contact, companionship, and physical care, the overall availability of such assistance is declining due to such factors as geographical mobility of family members, reductions in family size, the spread of individualism, and decreasing emphasis on the value of families (Yorburg 2002:220).

Human behaviors generally are guided by the dominant prescriptions and proscriptions embedded in particular societies, and this is reflected in wide cross-cultural variations among those who have lost a spouse through death (Lopata 1996). For example, the situation of Hindu widows in India has undergone numerous changes, ranging from extremely harsh treatment in the past to slow but steady improvement in the modern era. The custom of suttee—the wife's self-immolation on her husband's funeral pyre—has long been outlawed but periodically reappears, especially in rural areas. Even today, widows in that highly patriarchal, patrilineal, and patrilocal society experience isolation and a loss of status. Their remarriage rate is very low. Widows often face a difficult life that is influenced by vestiges of patriarchal and religious dogma and exacerbated by economic problems that force them to become dependent on sons, in-laws, and others. Widowers, by contrast, are encouraged to remarry soon and add progeny to the patriarchal line. Israel is another place where the society and religion are strongly patriarchal and women lose status in widowhood. Jewish mourning rituals "tend to isolate the widow and tie her to the past rather than providing means of creating a new life" (Lopata 1996:29). Moreover, women who lose husbands through civilian causes of death encounter greater difficulties than do those whose husbands are killed in the military. War widows and their families receive preferential treatment through government policies that give them special recognition, numerous benefits, and many more alternatives for improving their status and prestige than is possible in more traditional societies. Remarriage, for example, is a much more acceptable alternative for women in Israel than it is in India.

All societies are undergoing various degrees of transition. Korea is a society whose transitional problems are dramatically reflected in the situation of widows. Earlier in Korean history, widowhood resulted in a loss of status, and remarriage generally was prohibited. Husbands tended to be much older than their wives and to have a higher mortality rate, and a large number were killed in wars. Moreover, widowers remarried, whereas most widows remained single. All these factors contributed to a widening ratio of widows to widowers over the years. Under the impact of modernization, including increased urbanization and industrialization, Korean society is being transformed, and with it the conditions surrounding the status of widowhood. This transformation includes a shift from authoritarian societal and familial systems in a primarily rural environment toward systems based on more equalitarian norms. Widows began to move to cities, and this had advantages and disadvantages. On the one hand, they could accompany their sons and take advantage of urban services and the possibility of new friendships. On the other hand, the move removes them from their extended families and neighborhood friends and communal supports in their rural villages. Living with a son in the city strained the daughter-in-law relationship. In addition, being distanced from the relatively stable and integrated life of their villages and lacking friendship networks in their new environment often left them vulnerable to loneliness, especially in the case of the elderly widowed. Presumably, succeeding generations with greater personal resources will encounter fewer adaptational requirements.

While survivors face certain common problems and role strains both within and outside the immediate family, it is difficult to specify a normative course of adjustment. This is the case because in many societies, such as the United States, the widowed are a heterogeneous group characterized by wide differences in social and psychological characteristics. It also is due to the fact that spousal loss evokes such a panorama of emotional and behavioral responses from the survivors, depending on factors such as the timing and circumstances of the spouse's death. For example, a wife whose husband was killed in a military battle will respond differently than she would if he had committed suicide or suffered a long terminal illness. Many other antecedent conditions, such as the quality of the marital relationship, affect the bereavement reactions and coping strategies of survivors. Moreover,

> The difficult and sometimes devastating transition to widowhood or widowerhood necessitates a reintegration of roles suitable to a new status. If children are present, parental death precipitates a reorganization of the family as a social system. Roles and status positions must be shifted, values reoriented, and personal and family time restructured. The potential for role strains and interpersonal conflicts become evident as relationships are lost, added, or redefined. Loneliness becomes a major problem. In many modern societies this adaptive process proceeds with few or no guidelines. (Berardo and Berardo 2000:3255)

Because their role is often not clearly defined, many survivors exhibit considerable anxiety over the ambiguous nature of their new status. Hence, their adaptation may be unnecessarily difficult due to the absence of social support or programs designed to enhance the recovery process (Berardo and Berardo 2003).

DOMESTIC VIOLENCE

All family systems rest in varying degrees on force or the threat of force as a means of social control or member compliance (Goode 1971). While most societal socialization stresses nonviolence and peaceful resolution of conflict as the norm, family violence is quite pervasive.

In fact, domestic violence exists virtually everywhere in the world and among all racial, social class, and age groups. Wife beating, physical punishment of children, and fighting between siblings occur in many societies and with considerable frequency. Other forms of family violence, such as infanticide, patricide, and killing of the aged, occur rarely (Levinson 1989). Adult women are most likely to be the victims and are more likely than any other category of family members to suffer severe and debilitating injuries (Tjaden and Thoennes 2000; U.S. Department of Health and Human Services 2002). Cross-cultural evidence suggests that wife beating is more likely to occur and more likely to be frequent in societies in which men control the family wealth and adults often solve conflicts by resorting to physical violence.... Family violence does not occur in societies in which family life is characterized by cooperation, commitment, sharing, and equality. While these factors do not ensure that wives will not be beaten or children physically punished, it is clear that if they guide family relationships, family violence will be less frequent. (Levinson 1989:104)

It is difficult to compare the incidence of child abuse and wife abuse across cultures because of the absence of precise data on such behavior other than in the United States and some other Western countries. Another difficulty is posed by the lack of consistency in the definitions of abuse and violence. Behaviors that might be seen as abusive in one society could be viewed as normal in another society (Gelles and Cornell 1985:32). Hence, researchers rarely can isolate just one central factor that universally explains abuse or violence. However, it is clear that traditional patriarchal relationships are more apt to involve physical violence and sexual exploitation. Many cultures hold that men have the right to control their wives' behavior and that women who challenge them may be punished. In such places as Bangladesh, Cambodia, India, Mexico, Nigeria, Pakistan, Papua New Guinea, Tanzania, and Zimbabwe, studies find that violence is frequently employed as physical punishment. On the other hand, "in societies with little or no family violence, women and men share in decision making, marriage is monogamous, women have some control over economic resources, and divorce, while relatively infrequent, can be initiated by either sex" (Yorburg 2002:116). Domestic violence is at its most extreme when women leave or attempt to leave abusive relationships (United Nations 2000).

It appears that child and spousal abuse are more common in Western, industrialized nations such as the United States, Great Britain, Germany, and France. Their existence in developing nations seems to be grounded more in the disorganization resulting from modernization. Other countries such as those in Scandinavia exhibit little in the way of child or wife maltreatment, which has been attributed to greater social stability as well as the widespread use of contraceptives, which leads to reduced family size, acceptance of abortion, and supportive mechanisms for working women with children. Again, it must be pointed out that because of cultural differences, factors that explain domestic violence in one country may not do so in others (Gelles and Cornell 1983).

It is important to note that intimate partner abuse is not universal. A number of small-scale societies have been identified in which domestic violence is virtually absent. This suggests that domestic relations can be organized such that partner abuse is minimized (Population Information Program 1999:7). Moreover, legal statutes can be revised and domestic programs initiated that are designed to better protect victims of abuse. Such actions can also increase the social costs to the perpetrators and, it is hoped, influence cultural values, which shift social attitudes toward greater equalitarianism in the status and treatment of women inside and outside the family (Population Information Program 1999:38).

THE AGING FAMILY

A number of potential family problems are associated with the aging populations around the world. Several developed countries, including Italy, Greece, Sweden, Belgium, Spain, Japan, Germany, the United Kingdom, and France, currently have more than one-fifth of their populations aged 60 and over. The ratio of women to men varies dramatically by age, with the disparity becoming most marked among the oldest. At the oldest ages, there is an especially noticeable increase in the female elderly, making aging largely a "woman's issue" (Blair 2000). That trend poses particular dilemmas regarding the autonomy of elderly family members as well as the demands of the caretaker role and its related stresses. Since cultures have traditionally assigned women to the caretaking role, the movement of large numbers of them into the labor force exacerbates the problems of elder care.

Like many other industrialized nations, the United States is experiencing the aging of its population due to declining fertility rates and increasing longevity. A half century ago, about 8 percent of its citizens were 65 years of age or older; today the figure is 13 percent. This rise in the older population will accelerate during the second and third decades of the twenty-first century, as the members of the baby boom generation begin to join its ranks (Lee and Haaga 2002). Another example is Asia, where population aging is taking place much more rapidly than in Western countries, and where the number of people age 65 and over is expected to grow dramatically over the next half century. Japan has the oldest population in Asia and is the most rapidly aging population in the world. Currently at 17 percent, its 65 or older segment is projected to increase to 28 percent by 2025. In Germany, for this same time frame, the figures are 16 and 23 percent, respectively.

These demographic trends pose a number of challenges for families and societies. They affect the economy as a whole and raise numerous policy issues that touch upon such matters as generational conflict over the allocation of financial resources, the maintenance of age-specific support programs, social insurance and health care programs, and pressures to relieve families via residential care facilities or reliable alternatives to institutional care. Longer life expectancy may pose difficulties for younger adults trying to meet the societal expectations regarding filial responsibility. In many countries, the family support system for the elderly is weakening or on the decline:

> In countries where fertility has been low for decades, the elderly have few adult children to provide support, and many of these children have moved away from their family homes. Marriage rates have dropped sharply in some countries, and women are entering the work force in increasing numbers. Middle-aged women, the traditional caregivers, are likely to have less time than they did in the past to care for elderly family members. Increasing exposure to the West may also be introducing new ideas about marriage, family, and individualism—ideas that clash with the traditional sense of responsibility for the elderly. (East-West Center 2002:87)

In several countries, for example, in Japan, South Korea, and Taiwan, the proportion of elderly residing with their adult children has significantly dropped, and that trend is expected to continue. There is a growing awareness in the United States, in Britain, in Asia, and elsewhere of the need for

developing "social policies which recognize the central role of the family and seek to support or relieve informal carers by working explicitly in partnership with them" (Dallos and McLaughlin 1993:139). In recognition of that need, many countries are now providing adult day care along with other support services designed to help adult children care for elderly parents (East-West Center 2002:87).

CONCLUSION

Patterns of marriage and family relationships and structures are continuously evolving in response to social changes manifested in other societal institutions, particularly economic systems. This process of evolution is evident in several emergent trends around the globe, though occurring at different points in time across societies. Among these are the spread of contraceptive knowledge and accessibility, rising rates of cohabitation, the movement toward more open-mate selection systems, a delayed age at first marriage, reductions in family size, the continued flow of women into the paid labor force and their expanded role as economic providers for families, the increasing number of dual-earner families, rising divorce rates, and a growing surplus of elderly women as a result of extended life expectancy.

The Family Decline Debate

Decades before *World Revolution and Family Patterns* was published, a long-standing debate, which continues to this day, was whether these and other changes (for example, the decrease in traditional nuclear households, a historical decline in fertility, a continuously high divorce rate, changing family structures through divorce and remarriage, the rise in dual worker families, expanding equalitarianism, and increasing nonmarital cohabitation) were leading to family disorganization and decay (Popenoe 1995). Others challenged such assertions, pointing instead to the family's "remarkable resiliency and ability to adapt to environmental flux" by reorganizing its structures and relationships (Berardo 1987).

Vincent (1966) noted some time ago that "[s]ince the earliest writing available, changes occurring in the institution of the family have been used and interpreted to support either an optimistic or a pessimistic premise concerning social change, and the pessimists have consistently outnumbered the optimists" (p. 31). This may still be so, even though, as is often the case in debates, the truth probably lies somewhere closer to the middle. As Berardo (1987) points out: "The fact is that the family, like other institutions, is in a perpetual state of evolution rather than dissolution. It interfaces with those institutions in a panorama of complex transactions; sometimes as an independent variable, other times as a dependent variable, perhaps most often as an intervening variable. Its ability to mediate, translate, and incorporate social change in the process of socializing its members is one of its major strengths" (p. 427). A similar observation is made by Bruce et al. (1995): "Families are as adaptable as they are diverse, reconfiguring themselves over their life cycles and evolving to accommodate the myriad pressures of the external world. But while families have always been characterized by change, there is strong evidence that they are changing faster than ever before" (p. 1). The long-standing controversy and associated rhetoric over the presumed decline of the family is important, insofar as which group—the pessimists or the optimists—gains influence in defining what is and what is not a family problem in terms of their particular ideological stance. For example, in recent years, certain political groups, claiming a concern with family values,

> have been reasserting a preference for two-parent families by citing sociological, psychological and economic findings that show advantages of the greater income and social power of these families. The Communitarian Network has been particularly effective in presenting the two-parent nuclear family of western nineteenth and twentieth centuries as a universal truth while denying they propose a narrow definition of family. (Settles 2000:186)

Though we cannot pursue these issues further here, it is worth noting that several United Nations-sponsored conferences during the 1990s were dedicated to examining many commonly accepted beliefs and dominant myths about the family within the context of its changing forms and functions around the world. Taking advantage of data gathered over the past two decades, Bruce et al. (1995:2) report five global trends:

1. Families and households have gotten smaller.

2. The burden on working-age parents supporting the younger and older dependents has increased.

3. Women's average age at first marriage and childbirth has risen.

4. The proportion of female-headed households has increased.

5. Women's participation in the formal labor market has increased at the same time that men's has declined, shifting the balance of economic responsibility in families.

These trends are profoundly altering the patterns of contact and sharing in families.

Social movements and their agendas, such as that occurring with respect to civil rights and feminism, also are playing a significant role in this process. The feminist movement, with its emphasis on greater gender equity in all spheres of life, is especially noticeable. Worldwide, women are assuming a pivotal role in redefining marriage and family relationships and the complex interface of family units with the larger societal organizations. Their changing status is influencing the various potential family problems noted or discussed in this chapter.

Families are our most vulnerable and at the same time most adaptable social units. Despite their recognized resiliency, however, families increasingly will need assistance in coping with the problems we have highlighted here. This will require, among other things, shifts in societal attitudes and policies with respect to family change and diversity. One has to recognize that today's families operate within the context of an increasingly complex milieu. They are experiencing considerable stress. Consequently, if they are to meet their responsibilities, they will need positive collaboration from others. Specifically, it is imperative that policy makers and the public develop a greater awareness of the interconnections between social institutions and families. What is required is a greater sensitivity to family needs and the development, implementation, and refinement of human resource policies designed to meet those needs. The family/work nexus is illustrative here. Most children today have working parents who must struggle to balance the often competing demands of home and job. Given the dramatic rise in dual-earner families, it is essential that other institutions fully recognize the ramifications of that trend and respond with supportive policies. Indeed, it is in their best interest to do so. If such goals are to be achieved, however, there must be a conscientious effort to depoliticize family issues for the common good.

Policy development must begin with an understanding of the widespread diversity of families around the globe—that an abstraction like "the family" is just that, an abstraction. The variations in family forms are real and different. Human resource programs in the public and private sectors based on notions of homogeneity are doomed to fall short of their objectives. Moreover, they can be effective only by recognizing that social and technological changes influence variant family structures, relationships, and values in different ways.

What is needed then is a collaborative interinstitutional effort to assist families. A concerted effort to bolster family units, whatever their form, recognizes the interdependence of social structures in shaping human societies. It is especially during periods of rapid transition that the need for supportive collaboration becomes apparent and imperative.

NOTE

1. It is necessary to point out that various methods for calculating a divorce rate produce different and often misleading results. Some figures reflect the number of divorces in relation to the number of marriages annually; others calculate the rate as the number of divorces per 1,000 population; still others use the number of divorces divided by the number of married women, and so on. A common cliché derived from such calculations and promulgated through the media and by some scholars is that one in every two marriages ends in divorce. More realistic estimates range from one in five to only one in eight unions will eventually be terminated by divorce ("One in Two? Not True" 1987; Yorburg 2002:192).

REFERENCES

Alan Guttmacher Institute. 2001. "Minors and the Right to Consent to Health Care." *The Guttmacher Report on Public Policy* 3:4–9.

Berardo, F. M. 1987 "The American Family: A Commentary." *Journal of Family Issues* 8:426–8.

Berardo, F. M. and D. H. Berardo. 2000. "Widowhood." Pp. 3255–61 in *Encyclopedia of Sociology*. Vol. 3. 2nd ed., edited by Edgar F. Borgatta and Rhonda J. V. Montgomery. New York: Macmillan Reference USA.

———. 2003. "Widowhood." Pp. 1707–12 in *International Encyclopedia of Marriage and Family*. Vol. 4. 2nd ed., edited by James J. Ponzetti Jr. New York: Macmillan Reference USA.

Blackman, J. 1989 *Intimate Violence: A Study of Injustice*. New York: Columbia University Press.

Blair, C. 2000. *Growing Old in America*. Farmington Hills, MI: Gale Group.

Bruce, J., C. B. Lloyd, A. Leonard, P. Engle, and N. Duffy. 1995. *Family in Focus: New Perspective on Mothers, Fathers, and Children*. New York: Population Council.

Coleman, J. W. and H. R. Kerbo. 2002. *Social Problems*. 8th ed. Upper Saddle River, NJ: Prentice Hall.

Dallos, R. and E. McLaughlin, eds. 1993. *Social Problems and the Family*. Newbury Park, CA: Sage.

East-West Center. 2002. *The Future of Population in Asia*. Honolulu, HI: Author.

Gelles, R. and C. P. Cornell, eds. 1983. *International Perspective on Family Violence*. Lexington, MA: D. C. Heath.

———. 1985. *Intimate Violence in Families*. Beverly Hills, CA: Sage.

Goode, W. J. 1963. *World Revolution and Family Patterns*. New York: Free Press.

———. 1971. "Force and Violence in the Family." *Journal of Marriage and the Family* 33:624–36.

———. 1993. *World Changes in Divorce Patterns*. New Haven, CT: Yale University Press.

Greenstein, T. and S. Davis. 2002. "Cross-National Variations in Divorce: Effects of Women's Prestige and Labor-Force Participation." Presented at annual meeting of the American Sociological Association, Chicago, IL.

Ingoldsby, B. 1995. "Mate Selection and Marriage." Pp. 143–57 in *Families in Multi-Cultural Perspective*, edited by B. Ingoldsby and S. Smith. New York: Guilford.

Kashiwase, H. 2002. "Shotgun Weddings a Sign of the Times in Japan." *Population Today* 30:1, 4.

Lee, R. and J. Haaga. 2002. "Government Spending in Older America." *Reports on America.* Washington, DC: Population Reference Bureau 3 (1).

Levinson, D. 1989. *Family Violence in Cross-Cultural Perspective: Frontiers of Anthropology.* Vol. 1. Newbury Park, CA: Sage.

Lopata, H. Z. 1996. *Current Widowhood: Myths and Realities.* Thousand Oaks, CA: Sage.

Macionis, J. 2002. *Social Problems.* Upper Saddle River, NJ: Prentice Hall.

"One in Two? Not True" 1987. *Time,* July 13, p. 21.

Painter, Kim. 1999. "A Global Abortion View." *USA Today,* January 21, p. 8D.

Popenoe, D. 1995. "American Family Decline, 1960–1990." *Journal of Marriage and the Family* 55:527–55.

Population Information Program, The Johns Hopkins University School of Public Health. 1999. "Ending Violence against Women." *Population Reports* 27 (4):1–43.

Seager, J. 1997. *The State of Women in the World Atlas.* New ed. New York: Penguin.

Settles, B. 2000. "Sociology of the Family: Global Advances and Challenges." Pp. 173–96 in *The International Handbook of Sociology,* edited by S. Quan and A. Sales. Thousand Oaks, CA: Sage.

Smith, T. W. 1999. *The Emerging 21st Century Family.* Chicago, IL: National Opinion Research Center.

Teachman, J., L. Tedrow, and K. Crowder. 2000. "The Changing Demography of America's Families." *Journal of Marriage and the Family* 62:1234–46.

Tjaden, P. and N. Thoennes. 2000. *Extent, Nature, and Consequences of Intimate Partner Violence: Findings from the National Violence against Women Survey.* Washington, DC: Institute of Justice and Centers for Disease Control and Prevention.

United Nations. 2000. *The World's Women 2000: Trends and Statistics.* New York: Author.

U.S. Department of Health and Human Services. 2002. *Women's Health USA 2002.* Rockville, MD: Author.

Ventura, S. J., J. A. Martin, S. C. Curtin, R. J. Matthews, and M. M. Parks. 2000. "Births: Final Data for 1998." *National Vital Statistics Report* 48. Hyattsville, MD: National Center for Health Statistics.

Ventura, S. J., T. J. Matthews, and B. Hamilton. 2001. "Births to Teenagers in the United States, 1940–2000." *National Vital Statistics Report* 49. Hyattsville, MD: National Center for Health Statistics.

Vincent, Clark E. 1966. "*Familia Spongia:* The Adaptive Function." *Journal of Marriage and the Family* 28:29–36.

World Health Organization. 2000. "Unsafe Abortion—A Major Public Health Problem." *Safe Motherhood* 28 (1). Geneva, Switzerland: Author.

Yorburg, B. 2002. *Family Realities: A Global View.* Upper Saddle River, NJ: Prentice Hall.

Racial and Ethnic Educational Inequality in Global Perspective

Caroline Hodges Persell

New York University

Richard Arum

New York University

Kathryn Seufert

New York University

One of the most enduring patterns of social life observed by social scientists has been the relationship between social characteristics and various life chances. In particular, researchers have well documented the extent to which educational outcomes are frequently related to the social class and gender of individuals. Education may thus be seen as both a barometer of other social problems, such as poverty and gender stratification, and a mechanism potentially capable of reducing or intensifying these social divisions. Less studied than social class and gender in a

Authors' Note: We would like to thank Lisa M. Stulberg and Jean Yeung for their thoughtful suggestions. We also thank Caren Arbeit, Allegra Blackburn-Dwyer, Sarah Damaske, Zhongyu Fang, Rita Kohli, and Ghislain Potriquet, members of the NYU sociology graduate seminar in Education and Inequality Spring 2003, for their most helpful comments on an earlier draft of this chapter, and especially Chris Choi and Josipa Roksa for their extensive comments.

comparative manner is the relationship between race/ethnicity and educational outcomes, the focus of this chapter. There are several reasons for this research gap.

One primary obstacle responsible for the absence of systematic comparative research on race/ethnicity and education is the very serious difficulty of defining and measuring racial and ethnic groups. While "biologists, geneticists, and physical anthropologists, among others, long ago reached a common understanding that race is not a 'scientific' concept rooted in discernible biological differences," race remains an "extremely important and highly contested social" concept (Omi 2001:243). The social concept of *race* is used here to describe visible physical characteristics that have been imbued with social meanings and evaluations. *Ethnicity* is used to refer to cultural, linguistic, and religious characteristics that again have social meanings and evaluations imputed to them. Key features of racial and ethnic classification are (1) who has the power to define a person or group in certain racial/ethnic terms, and (2) what are the implications of being defined in those ways. Some of the problems with these terms include decisions about whose definitions are used to conduct research. Are "official" governmental definitions used, and if so, with what implications? Or are the groups' own self-definitions used? What is the relationship between "state definitions and popular consciousness," as Omi (2001:254) ponders? What groups are recognized in official policies?

Even if decisions can be reached about whose definitions of race/ethnicity are used, there are further complexities, for example, of heterogeneity and hybridity (Omi 2001). Within any "given" racial/ethnic group there may be variations in social class, gender, historical situation, geographical location, and other factors. Furthermore, in many societies interracial and interethnic marriages are increasing, with the result that larger numbers of people define themselves in terms of mixtures of various racial and ethnic groups. This not only affects racial/ethnic classification but may also affect educational outcomes.

The relationship between race and ethnicity is sometimes coterminous, but often not. Both are sometimes highly correlated with social class or geographical segregation, but not perfectly. One may not explain the other. Such relationships underscore the importance of good controls in research. Race/ethnicity is often related explicitly to issues of immigration and citizenship. Factors pertaining to immigration include issues of timing, selection and entry barriers, purpose of migration, and terms of incorporation. Immigration status needs to be considered in relation to educational attainment. Are immigrants granted citizenship? If not, do they receive the same social benefits and services as citizens, including education? How is their status related to educational outcomes?

In addition, the relative absence of comparative data and the political sensitivity of the subject in a number of countries also limit research. Unlike some of the notable comparative studies of social class (see below), there is no large-scale systematic collection of racial/ethnic data in many nations. As one example, neither race nor ethnicity was measured in the 40-nation Third International Mathematics and Science Study (TIMSS). Existing studies may compare one single nation with another or compare a relatively small number of nations (e.g., Clifton 1997; Darity and Nembhard 2000). One of the reasons for the relative dearth of data may be the politically sensitive nature of racial/ethnic record keeping and data collection in a number of countries. As Clifton (1997) has noted, "[I]n many countries the discussion of ethnic differences in education is controversial" (p. 550). There are also issues of racial record keeping (Omi 2001:255). Controversies abound in many societies, with some arguing for the elimination of all racial/ethnic categories and record keeping, while others stress that such categories are essential for assessing progress toward social justice of groups that have historically faced discrimination.

Finally, it is likely that research has been hampered by a lack of a clear consensus as to how one defines equality in education. Equality may be interpreted as "equality of opportunity" or "equality of results" (Coleman 1968; Uekawa 2000:6). Moreover, equality may be measured at many different levels, including in a classroom, a school, a school district, a political jurisdiction, or a nation-state. Furthermore, equality does not necessarily result from effective or efficient education. Finally, equality may be grounded in opposing organizational principles, such as meritocracy or egalitarianism.

Although difficulties facing researchers in this area are thus far from trivial, citizens and scholars alike also intuitively recognize that race and ethnicity are, more often than not, at the core of both educational inequality and imperatives for policy reform aimed at ameliorating these existing patterns. Given the importance of this topic, in this chapter we review comparative research that leads to the development of an analytic framework for future systematic study of this subject. The chapter proceeds specifically as follows: First, we briefly review what is known from related research on the associations of class, gender, and educational inequality. Second, we advance a conceptual framework for analyzing race/ethnicity and educational outcomes that springs off this prior research, and illustrate its utility with research on education in settings as diverse as Brazil, Israel, Japan, South Africa, and other countries. We conclude the chapter by discussing the substantive implications of our approach for future research and policy reforms intended to address racial and ethnic inequalities in education.

COMPARATIVE RESEARCH ON SOCIAL CLASS AND EDUCATIONAL OUTCOMES

Comparative research on associations between social class and educational outcomes is well developed in terms of both the formulation of "middle range" theoretical hypotheses and empirical measurement. There are both intellectual and institutional reasons for this. In terms of academic interests, modern sociology developed in Europe around debates over the conceptualization of social class and the extent and manner by which this societal differentiation structured contemporary social organization (Durkheim [1893] 1984; Weber 1968). Sociologists at the beginning of the twentieth century focused on the degree to which education was used both as an exclusionary mechanism providing occupational closure and as a vehicle that could facilitate vertical social mobility through schools by "sorting and selecting" individuals for advancement (Sorokin [1927] 1964; Weber 1946). Institutionally,

since the Second World War, social stratification researchers have been at the forefront of the development and statistical analysis of national probability social surveys, and—given the degree to which researchers were interested in assessing mobility rates cross-nationally—they created organizational vehicles (such as the International Sociology Association's Research Committee 28 on Social Stratification and Social Mobility) to facilitate international collaboration in establishing comparable measurement and analytical methods.

In an excellent review of developments in this area, Treiman and Ganzeboom (2000) have described four distinct "generations" of comparative stratification research (see also Ganzeboom, Treiman, and Ultee 1991). In the first phase of research, a large number of national datasets were generated that allowed for cross-national comparisons in rates of occupational mobility between generations (e.g., Lipset and Bendix 1959). In the second generation of research, pioneering work by Blau and Duncan (1967) introduced path analysis into sociological methods and shifted the focus of inquiry to distinguishing between intergenerational occupational mobility associated with educational attainment, and direct inheritance of occupational position through other mechanisms. A third period of research returned to the analysis of intergenerational occupational mobility, but with the use of more sophisticated statistical techniques that allowed scholars to distinguish between structural mobility (i.e., changes in the occupational structure over time) and other forms of mobility that occurred independently of this occupational upgrading (e.g., Erikson and Goldthorpe 1992). In the last decade, a "fourth generation" of research has developed that has focused on the extent to which institutional variation across countries has affected both intergenerational mobility and associations between social class and educational attainment. The two seminal projects in this area have been cross-national in character and were organized by Yossi Shavit and his colleagues. In the early 1990s, Shavit worked with Hans-Peter Blossfeld to organize a collaborative project identifying changes over time in the relationship between parents' class background and individuals' educational attainment. In the 13 countries studied, only two (Sweden and Netherlands) demonstrated any historic decline in the magnitude of associations between class background and the likelihood of individuals successfully completing educational transitions (Shavit and Blossfeld 1993). Following the publication of this study, Yossi Shavit worked with Walter Müller, an early architect of the CASMIN (Comparative Analysis of Social Mobility in Industrial Nations) project, to examine associations between educational achievement and occupational attainment in a similar large set of advanced economies. Shavit and Müller (1998) found stronger benefits of educational attainment in countries with greater standardization of curriculum and specialization in terms of occupational subject matter. In addition to projects by Shavit and associates, a large number of other researchers have explicitly attempted to extend this comparative stratification framework to a broader range of countries, including once neglected societies in the developing world (for noteworthy examples of this research and related reviews, see Buchmann and Hannum 2001; Ganzeboom and Treiman 1993, 1997; Rijken 1999; Uekawa 2000).

Given the well-developed state of this related research area, what can be learned in terms of potential theoretical hypotheses that might be extended into a comparative examination of associations between education and race/ethnicity? While race and ethnicity are social phenomena that are distinctly different in character from economic class, Weber's work ([1921] 1968) reminds us that race, ethnicity, and class at times operate in a similar fashion, as they are at the core simply competing dimensions through which societal groups organize struggles over access to, and control of, scarce resources. Our reading of prior research on the relationship between social class and educational attainment suggests six distinct hypotheses that could be explicitly considered in comparative research on race/ethnicity and education:

1. A *modernization thesis* suggests that as societies develop economically, pressures for rationalization and increased efficiency in allocation of human resources will diminish traditional forms of discrimination (Parsons 1970; Treiman 1970).

2. A *reproduction thesis* maintains that since dominant groups control allocation decisions, both within education and between education and the labor market, no declines in associations between class, race, and ethnic inequalities will occur without prior related changes in political power (Bourdieu 1973; Bowles and Gintis 1976; Collins 1971).

3. A *maximum maintained inequality thesis* holds that reduced inequalities found in educational attainment only occur when dominant groups interested in educational consumption at a given level have been completely saturated in their appetites (Raftery and Hout 1990).

4. A *state-centered thesis* views the state as a relatively autonomous entity that develops as a political compromise between groups and at times (particularly if left-labor, socialist, or democratic-socialist parties are influential) will work to mediate group conflict in society by reducing inequalities in both education and labor market outcomes (e.g., Katznelson and Weir 1985).

5. An *educational standardization thesis* maintains that as national school systems are more standardized and regulated, returns to education will be significantly higher—the effects of this tendency on inequality between groups would be related to the extent to which subordinate social groups have access to educational attainment (Shavit and Müller 1998).

6. A *curriculum specialization thesis* suggests that greater specialization and differentiation in curriculum, particularly occupationally oriented programs, are associated with greater economic rewards for individuals—again the effects of this differentiation on inequalities between groups would be related to the sorting and tracking of individuals into different programs based on ascribed characteristics (Shavit and Müller 1998).

These six hypotheses suggest three large classes of variables to include in a theoretical model of relationships between race/ethnicity and education, specifically (1) relationships between social groups within a society, (2) the nature and role of the state, including the level of economic development, and (3) variations within the institution of education. Applying these competing hypotheses to the issue of race/ethnicity and education would not only be useful in guiding initial comparative research efforts on the topic, but as important, would also serve both to inform stratification research focused on social class and to facilitate the development of educational policy intended to reduce inequalities. For example, appreciating the degree to which standardization and specialization of curriculum are associated with racial/ethnic inequality in educational outcomes abroad would be critical in guiding policy-makers' decisions regarding such reforms in any particular country.

COMPARATIVE RESEARCH ON GENDER AND EDUCATIONAL OUTCOMES

Racial/ethnic inequalities in educational outcomes may more closely resemble inequalities by gender than they do inequalities by class, because gender and race both reflect ways that meanings are attributed to physical characteristics, and policies may be based on those characteristics. Existing comparative research on gender and educational equity identifies a number of important issues, questions, and hypotheses for the study of racial/ethnic equity in education. These may be discussed in terms of the degree of overall gender stratification in a society, national characteristics, and specific educational policies and practices.

Degree of Gender Stratification

Bradley and Ramirez (1996) analyzed the social correlates of the expansion of women's share of higher education from 1965 to 1985. In a multivariate analysis of 90 nations, they found several factors that were significantly related to gains in women's share, including the size of the higher education gender gap in 1965. Countries with bigger gender gaps in 1965 made larger gains by 1985, perhaps, they suggest, because of the increasing prevalence of a strong, transnational norm of relative gender parity. They also found that countries with systems of higher education founded since 1965 had greater increases in women's share of higher education than countries with older systems. Level of economic development in 1965 had a strong positive effect on the growth in women's share of higher education in economically developing countries, but not in more developed countries. The authority of the state had

positive and significant effects on the growth in women's share of higher education in economically developing countries, but not in more developed ones. Finally, having a population that was 80 percent or more Islamic was negatively related to increasing women's share of higher education in economically developing countries. Their models explain more than half the variance in developing countries and just under half the variance in more economically developed countries.[1]

Bradley and Ramirez's study identifies both structural and ideological characteristics of countries that are related to gender gains in higher education, as well as contingent effects based on the level of economic development. To what degree are literacy and universal access to education official state goals? Are such goals part of a country's conception of what it is to be "a modern state," as Meyer, Ramirez, and Soysal (1992) and Ramirez and Boli (1987) suggest? LeTendre, Naumowicz, and Johnson (2000) note an important contingent relationship here, with their observation that countries outside the core (i.e., developing nations) are more likely to be influenced by transnational norms of universalism (whether by gender or race/ethnicity) than are core nations, which tend to be more influenced by internal considerations.

National ideologies about gender affect educational parity along such a dimension, and raise similar questions about racial/ethnic ideologies. For example, patriarchal ideologies and practices are related to low rates of educational parity by gender, raising the question of whether racial/ethnic ideologies are related to educational equality by race/ethnicity. What is the state's role in affirming or challenging ideologies of racial/ethnic supremacy? What is the relationship between such ideologies and educational policies?

National Characteristics

National characteristics include both structural and ideological features. For example, Persell et al. (1999) found that structurally, the percentage of a population in agriculture was the single biggest factor correlated with gender disparities in educational access (p. 411). Living in a rural rather than an urban area decreased girls' chances of attending school. Are racial/ethnic disparities also affected by the percentage in agriculture and the percentage who are urban dwellers in a country? If so, through what mechanisms? Is the power of the central state to enforce more universalistic criteria weaker in rural areas compared with urban ones?

Another structural characteristic of states is the existence of a nonagricultural labor market and the degree to which opportunities in that labor market are related to educational attainment and achievement. If economic modernization has occurred and both of these conditions exist, does education offer the same economic opportunities for all individuals in the society? Opportunities for women in the labor market are related to their educational attainment and achievement, leading us to expect that equal economic opportunities for all racial/ethnic groups would be related to the more equal educational attainment and achievement of children of all races/ethnicities. For low-income families especially, sending children to school when few economic opportunities are seen to result from schooling may be an economic strain, particularly if education is not free.

Educational Policies and Practices

Like state policies, educational policies and practices have structural and ideological dimensions that may affect outcomes. Equal access to educational opportunities and resources is a key threshold condition, but not a sufficient one for analyzing equality. Access alone does not address the issues of attendance and dropout rates that may affect educational achievement and attainment. Studies of gender equity in education suggest the important distinction between access per se and the actual content of the education received, as well as its consequences. Simply going to school may be a necessary condition, but the character of educational practices in schools, treatment by teachers, the curriculum students study, and the way curriculum relates to students' lives may affect what and how individuals learn. For example, single-sex secondary schools may foster the academic achievement and educational attainment of women (Powers 1995). Are there any parallels with the existence of schools for racial/ethnic minorities? What role do schools in

general play in promulgating or opposing racial/ethnic ideologies?

Gender process theorists see gender as more mutable and variable in different contexts, and they direct attention to educational institutions as arenas within which gender is constructed. They see much of this engendering activity as occurring through peer relations and activities that lie largely beyond the control of school authorities. Transposed to the realm of racial/ethnic relations, process theory directs attention to educational institutions as arenas within which race/ethnicity is constructed, perhaps in opposition to formal school ideologies.

PROPOSED FRAMEWORK FOR STUDYING RACE/ETHNICITY AND EDUCATIONAL OUTCOMES IN GLOBAL PERSPECTIVE

Using theory and research on class and gender educational inequality as a springboard, our aim in this section is to delineate a framework for analyzing racial/ethnic educational inequality cross-nationally, and illustrate it with research from some diverse countries. An outline of the major elements in the framework appears in Table 16.1.

Racial/Ethnic Relationships

The first element stresses the importance of taking a historical perspective on the relations between dominant and dominated racial/ethnic groups in a country. Attention needs to be paid to what stigmatized racial/ethnic groups have been identified in a country, on what basis, when, under what circumstances, and by whom. What are their numbers relative to dominant groups? In some countries, no data on racial groups is collected. Perhaps in response to the apartheid regime's statutory definitions of racial groups, South Africa replaced it with a "deracialized" regime in 1993. One consequence is that national educational statistics are no longer collected on a racial basis (Fedderke, De Kadt, and Luiz 2000), and it is no longer possible to use data collected by the state to compare historically relevant racial groups in terms of educational expenditures, teacher qualifications, or pupil-teacher ratios,

Table 16.1   Elements to Include in a Model of Racial/Ethnic Inequality in Education

I.   Racial/ethnic intergroup relationships, historically and today
     These relationships might vary within a country from one area or city to another, as well as between countries.
     A. Identification of racial/ethnic groups
         1. What are they? Who decides?
         2. What is the relative size of various groups?
         3. Possibilities for "passing"
     B. Degree of racial/ethnic stratification
         1. Relative political power
         2. Overlap with economic inequality
         3. Extent of social integration
             a. Extent of geographical segregation
             b. Extent to which associations in civil society are racially/ethnically integrated
             c. Rates of intergroup marriage
     C. How dominant group(s) perceive and treat subordinate group(s)
         1. Is a subordinate group perceived as culturally, politically, or religiously threatening?
         2. Degree of stigmatization of subordinate groups
     D. Interaction between racial/ethnic inequality and gender inequalities
     E. Citizenship and immigrant status
         1. How easily citizenship is granted
         2. To what degree immigration is encouraged
         3. Racial/ethnic characteristics of immigrants
     F. Responses of subordinated racial/ethnic groups to their position
         1. Group identity
         2. Separatist/oppositional orientation
         3. Social movements
         4. Regime change
         5. Assimilationist orientation
II. National characteristics and policies
     A. Demographic characteristics
         1. Population size
         2. Population density
         3. Ethnic/racial diversity
     B. Economic features
         1. Level of development
         2. Percentage in agriculture
         3. Percentage urbanized
         4. Degree of economic inequality
         5. Place in the world system
         6. Type of political economy
     C. Political system
         1. Nature of the state
         2. State power
     D. State policies
         1. Regarding racial/ethnic groups
         2. Regarding immigration
         3. Regarding citizenship
     E. Cultural policies and practices
         1. Ideologies regarding racial/ethnic groups
         2. "Official languages" and language minorities

(Continued)

Table 16.1 Continued

III. Educational characteristics and policies
    A. National educational policies (regarding racial/ethnic differences, curriculum, tests, language, teacher qualifications)
        1. Degree to which there is a centrally organized system
        2. Degree to which national policy is enacted
        3. Degree to which national policy is implemented
    B. Structural features within educational systems
        1. Tracking
        2. School expenditures
        3. Degree of racial/ethnic segregation
        4. Degree of class segregation
        5. Degree of gender segregation
    C. Instructional elements
        1. Teachers' qualifications
        2. Teachers' expectations
        3. Instructional strategies used by teachers
        4. Peer relations

to see whether there are fewer inequities in such resources in the postapartheid regime. In Brazil in 1970, the nation's then ruling military junta barred the collection of racial data, "asserting that race was not a meaningful concept for social measurement. The resulting information void, coupled with government censorship, diminished public discussion of racial issues, but it did not substantially reduce racial inequalities. When racial data were collected again in the 1980 census, they revealed lower socioeconomic status for those with darker skin" (American Sociological Association 2002:5; Fernandes 1999; Telles 2002).

The historical relationships between different groups need to be analyzed, including the degree to which boundaries are institutionalized and strictly enforced, and whether relations between groups have taken on castelike features. Castelike relations are characterized by membership being permanently determined by birth, social and occupational roles being determined by caste, not by education and ability, and one's permanent position being changeable only by emigration or by passing, as Ogbu (1978) notes. The ease or difficulty with which subordinate group members may "pass" as members of the dominant group is an empirical question, as is the degree to which assimilation is an option. For example, historically, was there slavery based on race or ethnicity? If so, did a complex ideology of racial inferiority develop to justify slavery? Was the abolition of slavery followed by a caste society based on race/ethnicity? How institutionalized were castes in terms of law, social institutions, social distance, segregation, and ideologies? How long did they exist?

Drawing upon the theoretical and empirical work of John Ogbu (1978, 1994), Fischer et al. (1996) argue that a group's social location in society is related to their test scores and educational achievement. Racial/ethnic groups that are subordinated and stigmatized in a society due to conquest or capture or because of the conditions under which they immigrated are likely to perform less well on "intelligence" tests and in school because of three processes: socioeconomic deprivation, group segregation, and stigmatization. First, there is a greater chance that the children of low-status racial/ethnic groups will grow up in poverty, plagued by low incomes, high unemployment in the neighborhood, with little or no wealth, poorer health, and lower parental education. Second, members of subordinated racial/ethnic groups are likely to be segregated from other groups in society. Racial/ethnic "ghettoes" concentrate and intensify disadvantages. They also receive fewer government services and opportunities. This means that children who otherwise might do well in school must deal with higher concentrations of social problems and reduced resources and opportunities. Third, being a member of a subordinated group in society brings with it cultural stigmatization, or in some sense a "spoiled" identity. This can lead to self-doubt, and even self-hate, or to an oppositional stance toward values and behaviors associated with the dominant group (Fordham 1988, 1993, 1996).

Clearly, the extent to which historical domination led to castelike relations is very likely to be related to the extent of racial/ethnic stratification over time. This feature refers to the *relative status* of various racial/ethnic groups on such key indicators as economic, political, and social status. Various researchers (Blau et al. 2001; Peterson and Krivo 1999; Roscigno 1999) have suggested ways to measure the degree of economic racial inequality. The extent to which political power is shared is another key dimension to measure, as is the extent of social integration. The case of South Africa is particularly interesting in this respect. It underwent political/racial regime change in 1993, which has established relative political equality. However, considerable economic and social inequality remains, and racial/ethnic inequalities in education persist.

Social integration might be measured by the degree of racial/ethnic geographical segregation, the extent to which social institutions are integrated, and rates of intergroup marriage, for instance. A high degree of geographical segregation weakens the possibility that social capital extending beyond the members of one's own group will develop, and increases the possibility that subcultural distinctiveness may develop (Massey and Denton 1993). In India, Varshney (2002) found that some cities had a high degree of ethnic integration in their economic exchanges and civic associations, while others had very little. Those with more integration were much less likely to experience serious ethnic strife between Hindus and Muslims. Rates of intergroup marriage are another indicator of intergroup social stratification. Relational measures such as these could be used to describe the degree and nature of racial/ethnic inequality over time in a city, region, or country.

Few researchers have yet explored in any systematic or large-scale way the degree to which race/ethnicity overlaps with or interacts with gender inequality. In the United States, the high rates of unemployment and imprisonment among subordinated African American males, their decreasing marriage rates, and the growing proportions of low-income or impoverished female-headed minority families have been noted by Wilson (1998) and others as part of the concentration of disadvantage, suggesting some ways gender inequalities may interact with class and race. In many highly agricultural and rural countries, the much lower rates of educating girls are correlated with higher birthrates and more poverty. If rural residence is correlated with race/ethnicity, as it was in the apartheid regime of South Africa, that is another way gender and class inequalities may interact with race/ethnicity. Further possible interactions need to be explored.

Citizenship and immigration status become especially relevant when they are related to race/ethnicity. Countries have often established quotas on either immigration or citizenship (by allowing guest workers only temporary status) that may or may not be related to the racial/ethnic composition of immigrants. The state of Israel reveals how complex the interrelationships between race/ethnicity and nationality can be. Israeli society has undergone dramatic changes since its inception in terms of demographic composition, economic modernization, educational structure, and even geographical borders. Excluding the occupied territories of Gaza and the West Bank, Israeli society is primarily divided ethnically between Arab Israelis (about 20%) and Jewish Israelis (80%)—with the former group divided among Muslims, Christians, and Druse, and the latter divided between Sephardic Jews with Spanish, African, and Middle Eastern origins, and Ashkenazic Jews with largely Western, Central, and Eastern European roots. In recent years, significant numbers of "guest workers" have also arrived from Asia and elsewhere to replace Palestinian workers excluded from participation in the Israeli economy during recent ethnic unrest.

The history and current status of how dominant groups perceive and treat subordinate groups may be related to the groups' relative size, conditions and purposes of early contact, and the degree of inequality between them. If subordinated groups are viewed as somehow "threatening," whether because of their numbers, culture, or behaviors, that is likely to affect how they are treated, specifically with respect to the amounts of separation, social control, and stigmatization they experience. Processes of domination involve both symbolic and coercive social control. Symbolic social control is evident in the formulation of legitimating ideologies, processes of stigmatization, and legal definitions of group differences that favor dominant groups. Examples of coercive social control include physical separation, discrimination, and the use of police or other agents of violence. Historically, extensive caste systems involving racial/ethnic separation and control were evident in India, South Africa, and the United States. South Africa became a unified country in 1910, and it operated a racial caste system until 1994. The apartheid regime statutorily defined racial groups (also called "racial estates") and legally imposed racial segregation when it created four "independent" "homelands" (or bantustans) from 1976 through the early 1980s (Fedderke et al. 2000:277).

Given the history of racial/ethnic relations in a country, another variable that may affect the educational consequences of those social relationships is the responses of subordinated racial/ethnic groups to their treatment. Do members of dominated groups develop a group identity, or are they caught up in ideologies of individualism and assimilation? Are there competing responses within a given racial/ethnic group, with some favoring assimilation and others taking an oppositional or even a separatist position? For example, among U.S. blacks, nationalist, Africanist, and various separatist ideologies began developing in the early nineteenth century (Moses 1978, cited in Shujaa 1996). Attention needs to be paid to social movements that work for structural and cultural change. Some oppositional movements were successful—for example, the independence movements in India, Africa, and other postcolonial countries; racial regime change in South Africa and Zimbabwe (using different means)—while others may have achieved at least some changes—for example, the civil rights movement in the United States and the movement in India to abolish the caste system. Historical racial/ethnic relations occur within different national contexts, the second major element in the framework.

National Characteristics and Policies

One basic question is whether a nation's demographic characteristics and level of economic development affect racial/ethnic group equity. The modernization thesis suggests that the level of development or GNP per capita is related to the degree of racial/ethnic educational inequality in a country. However, some research suggests that such features may not make much difference. In a study of 12 countries where they "could find data of a reasonable quality that measure the gap between economically subaltern and dominant groups," Darity and Nembhard (2000) found there was

> pronounced intergroup inequality . . . in countries with both large populations (India, United States, Brazil, and Japan) and small populations (Belize, Trinidad and Tobago, Israel, and New Zealand) . . . [i]n higher-income countries (Australia, Canada, Japan, and the United States), as well as in lower-income countries (India, Belize, and South Africa); and in countries with high growth rates (Malaysia, Japan, Belize, and India), as well as in countries with low or negative growth rates (South Africa and New Zealand). Finally, pronounced intergroup inequality was apparent in countries with high levels of general inequality (Brazil, South Africa, and Malaysia), as well as in countries with low levels of general inequality (Canada, India, Australia, and Israel). (P. 308)

In short, they found that "economic disparity correlated with race and ethnicity is present and looks remarkably similar across a wide range of nations" (p. 308). In addition, they noted that "subaltern groups frequently are numerical minorities, but in some cases, they constitute a majority or plurality of the population" (p. 308).

While neither the level of modernization nor a number of other national characteristics was found to be related to the degree of racial/ethnic inequality, these factors may still need to be controlled in any large-scale comparison of nations. At least four other national characteristics may be important, including position in the world system, state power, state policies, and cultural ideologies in a country.

The location of a country in the world-system does affect minority educational policies, according to LeTendre et al. (2000:651). Specifically,

LeTendre and others suggest that peripheral nations may be more susceptible to international pressures for adhering to human rights standards, while core nations may be affected more by internal pressures. Japan, a core nation, may be an example of a country that pays little attention to human rights standards in its treatment of Koreans. On the other hand, the apartheid regime in South Africa may ultimately have been influenced by cultural and economic interactions (including boycotts) with other countries in the world.

The nature of the state (liberal democratic or relatively more autocratic) may not necessarily predict relative equality among racial/ethnic groups. Whatever the state characteristics, they are mediated through state power and policies. Some strong, relatively autocratic regimes (e.g., contemporary Singapore) have official policies of racial/ethnic equality, or maintain that race is immaterial (Brazil). We are inclined to believe that the type of state may be less important than the degree of state power and the nature of state policies regarding racial/ethnic groups.

South Africa, under the apartheid regime, used the power of a strong autocratic state controlled by whites to enforce a policy of racial separation and inequality. In 1993, South Africa experienced a bloodless racial and political regime change that overthrew its racial caste system (apartheid) and replaced it with a "deracialized" regime. However, state power for enforcing the official policy now may be considerably less because it is shared among all racial/ethnic groups. State power may depend on the political, economic, and cultural resources that a state controls, the degree to which the state is relatively highly centralized (France, Israel) or more decentralized (United States, South Africa), the relative power of states and markets, and the relative power of the central state relative to regional governing bodies.

State policies about race and ethnicity need to be considered. For example, despite the presence of cultural and ethnic diversity in Japan, the government maintains an ideology that Japan is an "ethnically homogeneous nation-state" (Akiba 2000:609). Japan does not fully embrace and recognize cultural minorities (Motani 2002), but generally maintains an assimilation policy regarding minority racial and ethnic groups (Akiba 2000; Motani 2002). In the case of Koreans in Japan, Akiba (2000) describes Japan's policy as assimilation, but legal separation. Singapore, a country with 76.7 percent Chinese, 14 percent Malays, and 7.9 percent Indians, has made the goal of racial/ethnic equality part of its explicit state policy (Kang 2001). Brazil abandoned its policy of refusing to collect data on racial groups, despite its desire to see itself as a racial democracy. Now, "[t]he three main categories for skin color listed on the census are white, black and brown," but Brazilians use more than 300 words and phrases to describe their skin color (Easterbrook 2002). The case of Brazil also illustrates that while state policy is one level of analysis, the issue of policy enactment remains. In 1994, Telles wrote that there is "virtually no state intervention in racial affairs." He went on to note that there is a 1951 law that makes racial discrimination illegal, but it is rarely used (p. 46). Legislation in 1989 specifically made discrimination in employment, housing, and other areas based on race illegal (Bureau of Democracy 2000), but it is not clear how often this law is used. As Telles (1994) explains, "No doubt one reason for the lack of state intervention is the widely held ideology that supports the illusion that race does not significantly affect life chances" (p. 49). Moreover, Guimaraes (2001) insists that race discrimination is both denied and confused with class discrimination, which permits racism as a system to function in Brazil. Furthermore, "Culture, rather than race, is used as a justification for social inequalities" (Guimaraes 2001). Analyses need to go beyond simply describing state racial/ethnic policies to consider how they are implemented.

State policies also bear directly on decisions about immigration and citizenship. Countries that wish to increase their populations, such as Argentina, Canada, and Israel, have generally had liberal immigration and naturalization policies. While Israel admits all Jews who seek to enter the country (although the definition of who is a Jew is debated), some immigrants have racial/ethnic characteristics seen as setting them apart. A country like the United States has had a highly variable policy concerning immigration, with the flow of immigrants growing or shrinking depending on economic conditions and needs and the levels of "nativism" expressed (see Higham 1963). Another set of countries (England, France, Netherlands) retains relationships with former colonies (in the Caribbean, Africa, India, Pakistan, and Indonesia, for instance). Those colonial ties are related to immigration policies and have led to the admission of increasing numbers of persons seen as racially and/or ethnically different. Still other countries have had very restrictive policies of granting citizenship (e.g., Switzerland, Germany), although they rely on temporary guest workers from poorer lands who can be exported when labor markets contract. As these examples suggest, citizenship has possibly complex interrelations with racial/ethnic differentiation. We expect that when immigration status and citizenship are related to segregation, other forms of stratification, stigmatization, and social controls, they will also be related to differential educational outcomes.

State cultural policies, particularly those dealing with the designation of "official languages" and the treatment of language minorities, are also likely to affect educational outcomes, because such policies may interact with educational policies and practices. South Africa recognizes 11 official languages, but Afrikaans is still very important for political and economic activities and English is important for international communication. Thus, some languages are more "useful" than others. In Singapore, even though the official language of instruction is English and there are four official languages, there appear to be advantages for Chinese children taught by Chinese teachers who may speak Chinese with them in school (Kang 2001). In Japan, the first language of most Koreans in Japan is Japanese (Motani 2002). In Korean ethnic schools, students are mainly instructed in Korean, although the curriculum and quality of the schools are similar to those of Japanese schools (Motani 2002). However, considerably more emphasis is placed on Korean language, history, and geography than in Japanese schools.

State policies can clearly privilege the language(s) of one or more groups over those of others. Such policies are compounded in many countries with the legacy of colonialism. What happens, for example, when African countries, which may be fragmented into multiple language groups (e.g., 5 in Zimbabwe, 11 in South Africa), adopt the language of a former colonial power? Is there ambivalence between the cultural hegemony of Western Europe, on the one hand, and the practicality of having a common language that favors no single internal ethnic/tribal group?

A number of state characteristics and policies thus need to be included in any effort to study racial/ethnic educational inequalities cross-nationally. State-level features and policies in turn need to be analyzed in relation to educational systems, policies, and practices.

Educational Characteristics and Policies

The contours of the educational system in a country, the nature of national educational policies, the structure of educational institutions, and instructional elements all need to be considered. Does a country have a nationally organized system of education, and does it encompass elementary, secondary, and higher education? A key aspect is how it is financed. Does education depend largely upon national financial support? If fiscal responsibility is shared, what are the relative proportions provided by national, state or provincial, and local levels of government? How large a private educational sector is there? Is it run on a for-profit or nonprofit basis?

The case of South Africa underscores the importance of how educational systems are financed. Until 1995, education was not compulsory for blacks in South Africa. Under apartheid, families were charged school fees for public schooling, a policy that clearly discriminated against black South Africans who were disproportionately poor, as well as other low-income persons, and contributed to the unequal educational legacy today. Control over educational finance remains within the jurisdiction of provinces in South Africa (Murray 1997:377). As in the United States, school districts have variable tax bases. Provincial governments use financing formulas that make flat grant allocations to each district regardless of need. Consequently, large disparities exist between provinces in terms of per capita expenditures in public ordinary schools. Because of the decentralized educational policy, where there are large regional disparities, it is difficult to equalize educational expenditures either within or across those regional units. Given the extensive degree of geographical racial/ethnic segregation within South Africa, such a policy affects racial/ethnic opportunities.

At the level of state racial/ethnic educational policy, it is important to consider both historical and contemporary state policies. In historical terms, were there state policies excluding certain racial/ethnic groups from education? Or were they treated differently or exposed to separate and perhaps unequal educations? One of the key features LeTendre and his colleagues identify is the degree of autonomy groups are granted to develop distinctive school systems that transmit their culture and language in the face of "global trends toward isomorphism in schools" (LeTendre et al. 2000:650). They note the tension between independence for groups and the national push toward unity and assimilation, and observe in the United States that ethnicity grounded in religion has received more legal recognition, with corresponding group independence (e.g., in the case of the Amish or Hutterites), than ethnicity grounded in language and cultural differences other than religion (e.g., in the case of Hispanics or Native Americans), although such independence has not been achieved without a struggle. A state policy designed to "agglomerate and assimilate" racial/ethnic minorities (LeTendre et al. 2000:651) leaves little room for preserving cultural distinctiveness or other aspects of racial/ethnic identity. Do separate schools have consequences for the status attainment of members of smaller linguistic communities? How, if at all, are such problems handled?

The case of Koreans in Japan is an instructive example of how state educational policy may affect the educational achievement and attainment of members of a distinct ethnic group. Although less than 1 percent of Japan's population is non-Japanese, in 2000 Koreans were the second largest national ethnic minority group in Japan, following the Chinese. Koreans in Japan are a remnant of Japan's colonial history. Japan annexed Korea in 1910 and controlled the nation until 1945 (Akiba 2000; Motani 2002). The Japanese government suppressed Korean language and culture, and Koreans were required to learn Japanese language and traditions, while excluding Korean language and history. Following World War II, approximately one-fourth of the earlier number of Korean residents remained in Japan. In 1945, after the end of Japanese colonial rule, Koreans in Japan set up many "ethnic" schools. In 1946, there were 539 Korean schools serving approximately 41,000 students (Akiba 2000). These schools were supposed to adhere to a Japanese curriculum. In 1948, the ministry of education in Japan decided that Koreans must have a Japanese public education, and many Korean "ethnic" schools closed between 1948 and 1955 (Akiba 2000; Motani 2002). In 1965, Japan and Korea signed the San Francisco Treaty, which stated that all Korean students in Japan should enroll in Japanese public schools (Motani 2002). Many Koreans were angered by the treaty and perceived the Japanese government as acting to suppress Korean language, culture, and ethnic identity (Motani 2002). Consequently, many Koreans resisted the treaty requirements.

Currently, while more than 100 Korean ethnic schools are operating in Japan (Motani 2002), more than 85 percent of Korean students in Japan are enrolled in Japanese schools (Akiba 2000). Japan "allows" Koreans to operate their own schools, but does not recognize most Korean schools as regular schools (Akiba 2000; Motani 2002). Instead, Korean ethnic schools are generally placed in the government's "nonacademic" school category. This puts Korean ethnic school students at a disadvantage with respect to higher education, because regular school graduates may automatically apply to institutions of higher education, while graduates of other schools may not (Motani 2002). Many graduates of Korean ethnic schools must also graduate from a Japanese school or pass a national exam in order to apply to a university. Moreover, Japan uses competitive, standardized national exams for entrance into high schools and universities. Korean students who have fewer cultural and language differences generally perform better on the national exams (Akiba 2000) than those who are more culturally distinct. This leads many Korean parents to perceive studying Korean language and culture as a "barrier to academic success" for their children (Akiba 2000:607). Due to these disadvantages, many Korean students choose not to enroll in Korean ethnic schools (Motani 2002). Clearly, any cross-national comparison of racial/ethnic educational equality needs to consider the nature of such national educational policies.

Simply having educational policies, however, reveals little about how they are enacted or implemented. For example, in South Africa, "[a] discourse of human rights and anti-discrimination has . . . formally come to underpin education policy, to replace the apartheid discourse of the past. However, a careful analysis of education policy provisions reveals that there are few substantive policy guidelines and few specific programmes to deal with 'race,' equity and human rights, particularly policy and programmes which can inform practice and relationships at school level" (Kruss 2001:45). Kruss developed a typology of four different contexts and the responses within them to the new educational policy framework, while noting that there may be other responses as well. The four situations reveal some of the complexities of enacting educational policies and the varieties of responses policies can elicit, highlighting how difficult it is to make general statements about policy at the national level. The four situations show the weight of the apartheid past, in terms of discourses, ideological frameworks, assumptions, beliefs, educational practices, and resources and advantages. "Without clear programmatic directives to develop school-level policy, we find that new forms of discrimination have emerged, in many schools now based on culture, language, ethnicity and, more explicitly, on class instead of race" (Kruss 2001:58). Kruss's work shows both formal and informal reactions in schools to desegregation or other educational policies, and stresses the importance of understanding not only stated policies but their implementation.

Policy contains both structural and content components. Is education organized in relatively similar structures throughout a country? Do the same age groupings occur everywhere? Is education segregated by anything other than age, and if so, what? Do all children attend the same type of educational structures? Is there mandatory education, and if so, to what age, and is it enforced? Do all children experience the same curriculum throughout a country? Why or why not? At what point does curricular differentiation begin, on what basis, and what forms does it take?

The importance of differences in educational structure and content for racial/ethnic educational equality is illustrated by Israel. There, significant waves of immigration were followed by dramatic changes in the educational system to address these changes, with vocational education introduced into secondary schools historically to provide curriculum for low-performing Sephardic immigrants (Ayalon 1994; Shavit 1984), and a more recent expansion of higher education occurring to increase access for less able students (Yogev 2000). In addition, Arab Israelis have faced a segregated education system with significantly lower levels of educational resources. Interestingly, however, while Israeli Jews in general have had greater educational attainment, Arab Israelis have historically fared surprisingly well in terms of access to higher education—at times even surpassing tertiary attendance rates found among certain Sephardic Jewish ethnic groups. This ethnic variation has been understood primarily in terms of state educational policy: Arab Israelis' educational experiences, unlike Sephardic schooling, involved little exposure to secondary vocational education that operated to divert students from higher educational enrollment (Shavit 1990).

Instructional variations may also affect racial/ethnic educational equality. Do all children have similarly qualified teachers? If not, on what basis do differences occur? In South Africa before 1994, race rather than class was the biggest determinant of educational opportunities (Fedderke et al. 2000:262). By 1993, whites were receiving seven times the amount of per pupil educational expenditures spent on blacks and twice the amount spent on coloreds and Asians (Fedderke et al. 2000:270–1). Unequal expenditures were related to pupil-teacher ratios and teacher qualifications as well. White students were seldom in classes with more than 24 pupils per teacher, while the best black pupil-teacher ratio, in private schools, was 32 (Fedderke et al. 2000:263). In terms of teacher qualifications, whites were also more likely to have highly qualified teachers (i.e., those with tertiary-level qualifications). Consequently, by 1994, vast racial differences in educational attainment were evident. In the United States, low-income and minority children are much less likely to have teachers who are certified in the subjects they are teaching (Haycock 1998; Ingersoll 2002).

In class, do all teachers use similar instructional strategies? Do all children experience similar teacher expectations? If not, on what basis do differences occur? In the United States, teachers have generally lower expectations for African American students (Farkas et al. 1990; Ferguson 1998). In what ways do the peers of schoolchildren differ? In the United States, minority students are much more likely to attend schools with larger proportions of low-income children than are white children (Bidwell and Kasarda 1975). How does that affect the social relationships that occur in schools?

We expect that the degree of racial/ethnic inequality, the nature of national policies, and variations in educational policies and experiences will affect the degree of racial/ethnic educational inequality (resources received, graduation rates, achievement) that exists in a country. Educational outcomes in selected countries are consistent with this expectation. At the end of the South African apartheid regime, vast racial differences in educational attainment were evident. The South African government has increased government expenditures on black children's education in South Africa since 1994, but the quality and content of black education has not changed substantially, according to some reports (Nkabinde 1997, cited in Murray 1997:378). As U.S. researchers have found, improved achievement seems to depend on how increased expenditures are spent, and whether they change teacher qualifications, professional development, and instructional strategies (Darling-Hammond 1995; Ferguson 1991; Gamoran, Secada, and Marrett 2000; Wenglinsky 1997), as well as upon larger social and economic contexts (Ainsworth 2002; Roscigno 1999). Nevertheless, growing numbers of black students are graduating from college or technical institutes in South Africa. This number doubled in the past decade, as did the number receiving educational honors, according to the South African Institute of Race Relations (Rossouw 2001). Enrollments in that time period shifted away from historically black universities to historically white ones. In certain fields of study such as education, languages, public administration, and social welfare, blacks outnumber whites, but in others they lost ground, including engineering, architecture, medicine, commerce, mathematics, science, and computer science (Rossouw 2001).

In Brazil, "the Non-White (black and mulatto) population shows an educational attainment significantly inferior to that of the white population" (Fernandes 1999:23). Nonwhites encounter the largest barrier to educational access in the lowest grades and in higher education (Fernandes 1999). In her study of age cohorts in Brazil over an 81-year period ending in 1988, Fernandes (1999) found that race had become increasingly important over the years in determining educational outcomes. In 2002, less than 1 percent of students and professors at the University of Brasilia were black and mulatto (Easterbrook 2002). Efforts to change the situation in higher education are under way. The state of Rio de Janeiro passed a law in 2002 requiring its two public universities to reserve 40 percent of their freshman slots for black and mulatto students, and the Brazilian Congress was considering a proposal to require race-based quotas at all 53 federal universities (Easterbrook 2002). Further research is needed to assess whether such changes in educational policy, in isolation from other efforts to achieve racial/ethnic equality, can effect lasting changes in educational attainment.

In Japan, with more and more Korean students enrolling in Japanese schools, there is a "move toward complete assimilation" (Akiba 2000:601). Nevertheless, ethnic gaps in educational attainment persist. Although there are no national data on Korean students' academic performance in Japan, a 1990 study in Kyoto found that 89.7 percent of Koreans attended school beyond the compulsory level, compared with the city average of 95.3 percent (Okano and Tsuchiya 1999). In Israel, differential achievement among Ashkenazic and Sephardic Jews remains, with Palestinians occupying a middle ground between them. In the United States, a black-white test score gap persists (Jencks and Phillips 1998), as well as racial gaps in other more general indicators of achievement and attainment.

Further study of the interplay among the major elements in the framework proposed here is needed. It requires that governments, it is hoped with some inputs from their populations, will collect and analyze data on racial/ethnic groups. More work is needed to identify exactly how the three major elements in this framework are related to each other, how educational policies and practices in a country vary according to the degree of racial/ethnic stratification in it, to what degree national characteristics and policies can affect educational policies and practices, and whether educational policies and practices can mediate or overcome racial/ethnic inequalities in a society. More work is needed to identify what national characteristics and policies are necessary for reducing inequalities.

IMPLICATIONS

What implications for future research can be drawn from the framework proposed here? Many studies examining racial/ethnic inequalities in education emphasize more microlevel factors, such as family background, schools, neighborhoods, and communities. While these microlevel variables are undoubtedly important, such a focus often ignores key macrolevel factors, including the degree of racial and ethnic stratification historically and today, national characteristics, and state educational policies. The framework proposed here encourages future researchers to include such macrolevel factors when examining racial and ethnic inequalities in education cross-nationally.

The research reviewed demonstrates the importance of considering each category in future research. First, the history of racial/ethnic relations in a country appears to have lingering consequences in such countries as Israel, Japan, Brazil, South Africa, and the United States. The historical, and continuing, degree of power inequality, physical and cultural separation, and economic inequality between racial/ethnic groups are major factors affecting educational outcomes. Without state and educational policies that work systematically to mitigate such continuing effects, they are likely to continue to shape educational outcomes. Even with changes in state policy, as in South Africa, the weight of historical disadvantages continues.

Second, national characteristics related to economic development—whether degree of class stratification or level of modernization—seem to have little or no major independent effects on the way race/ethnicity is related to education in the countries examined here, although such factors may need to be considered and controlled. State policies may contribute to increasing racial/ethnic disparities in educational outcomes or do little to mitigate them.

The case of Japan suggests that state policy contributes to maintaining or increasing racial/ethnic inequalities. Regime change by itself, however, may not be enough, as the example of South Africa suggests, nor is formal adoption of a state policy embracing a commitment to equality by itself a sufficient lever for achieving relatively equal racial/ethnic educational outcomes. Despite major changes in government policies, the funding and implementation of those policies have been sufficiently uneven and incomplete in the face of deeply structured historical patterns of racial disadvantage to achieve educational equality in South Africa. South Africa might learn from Brazil's attempts at deracialization that such a policy in the face of vastly different racial outcomes may obscure the importance of race for educational and other outcomes.

Third, state educational policies may contribute, directly or indirectly, to the maintenance or intensification of unequal racial/ethnic educational outcomes, as in Israel's policy of segregated education and the introduction of vocational secondary education. In general, the distribution of educational resources, whether financial, symbolic, or instructional, is an important consideration for future research. There are many examples in which ethnic groups do not receive the same financial resources, and they may be denied symbolic equality as well. In South Africa, the persistence of a decentralized system of funding for education means that geographically concentrated racial/ethnic groups receive vastly different financial resources, which in turn affect teacher qualifications and other educational resources. Japan's educational policy of refusing to accept the credentials of culturally and ethnically distinctive schools plays an important role in creating unequal educational opportunities for Koreans in Japan. The creation or maintenance of separate schools or distinct curricular tracks for different racial/ethnic groups, by virtue of state educational policy, contributes to unequal social status at least and perhaps to vastly different subsequent educational opportunities, such as access to higher education. Sorokin's ([1927] 1964) insight, that the role of schools in social mobility is determined by particular political institutional formulations, rather than simply economic development or democracy more generally, is supported.

Much of the research we reviewed does not include the subjective responses of members of various racial/ethnic groups to state and educational policies. Some research on South Africa and Japan suggests the possibility of varied responses, including assimilation into a prevailing middle-class ethos in some South African schools, opposition in the case of other South African schools, and a forced choice between assimilation or ethnic identity among Koreans in Japan. Systematic responses of racial and ethnic groups to such policies seems a fruitful dimension to include in future research.

Relationships between race/ethnicity and education are influenced in different ways by varied and complex factors. There may be regional variations in how state or educational policies are implemented, such as localized funding or curriculum, suggesting little uniformity even within the same country. Clearly, this cautions against overly simplistic generalizations about a given nation's state or educational policies, and how such policies may affect the relationship between race/ethnicity and education. There is a good possibility that state and educational policies may operate in "contextually contingent ways," as Charles and Bradley (2002) note about gender inequality in higher education.

Beyond the proposed framework outlined here, there are a number of practical considerations for future research on racial/ethnic inequalities in education. One central concern is the sensitivity of racial/ethnic issues in many countries. As shown, the importance of data on race/ethnicity may be doubted in some countries for various reasons, and collecting data on race/ethnicity may be perceived as perpetuating racial/ethnic inequalities. Without such data, however, persisting inequalities may be ignored. We argue, therefore, that data collection on race/ethnicity and education is vital to documenting the persistence or lessening of racial/ethnic inequalities in education. Whenever possible, researchers should collect such data while being aware of the sensitive nature of racial/ethnic issues in many countries. Finally, another necessary consideration for future research on racial/ethnic inequalities in education is the creation of comparative research teams composed of racially/ethnically and nationally mixed researchers, given the importance of contextual contingencies in studying racial/ethnic educational inequalities.

Documenting racial/ethnic educational inequalities and framing further research on them in terms of racial/ethnic relations, political and economic contexts and policies, and educational policies and practices, as well as the possible interactions among these three sets of factors, should contribute to policy-relevant knowledge that could be used to reduce such inequalities and some of the social problems associated with them.

NOTE

1. This paragraph is from Persell et al.'s discussion of Bradley and Ramirez (1996:413–14).

REFERENCES

Ainsworth, J. W. 2002. "Why Does It Take a Village? The Mediation of Neighborhood Effects on Educational Achievement." *Social Forces* 81:117–52.

Akiba, M. 2000. "Educational Policy for Korean Students in Japan." *International Journal of Educational Research* 33:601–609.

American Sociological Association. 2002. *Statement of the American Sociological Association on the Importance of Collecting Data and Doing Scientific Research on Race.* Adopted by the Elected Council of the ASA on August 9, 2002.

Ayalon, H. 1994. "Monopolizing Knowledge? The Ethnic Composition and Curriculum of Israeli High Schools." *Sociology of Education* 67:264–76.

Bidwell, C. E. and J. D. Kasarda. 1975. "School District Organization and Student Achievement." *American Sociological Review* 40:55–70.

Blau, J. R., V. L. Lamb, E. Stearns, and L. Pellerin. 2001. "Cosmopolitan Environments and Adolescents' Gains in Social Studies." *Sociology of Education* 74:121–38.

Blau, P. and O. D. D. Duncan. 1967. *The American Occupational Structure.* New York: Wiley.

Bourdieu, P. 1973. "Cultural Reproduction and Social Reproduction." In *Knowledge, Education, and Cultural Change,* edited by R. Brown. London, England: Tavistock.

Bowles, S. and H. Gintis. 1976. *Schooling in Capitalist America.* New York: Basic Books.

Bradley, K. and F. O. Ramirez. 1996. "World Polity and Gender Parity: Women's Share of Higher Education, 1965–1985." *Research in Sociology of Education and Socialization* 11:63–91.

Buchmann, C. and E. Hannum. 2001. "Education and Stratification in Developing Countries: A Review of Theories and Research." *Annual Review of Sociology* 27:77–102.

Bureau of Democracy, Human Rights, and Labor, U.S. Department of State. 2002. *Country Reports on Human Rights Practices in 1999: Brazil.* Washington, DC: Author.

Charles, M. and K. Bradley. 2002. "Equal but Separate? A Cross-National Study of Sex Segregation in Higher Education." *American Sociological Review* 67:573–99.

Clifton, R. A. 1997. Race and Ethnicity in Education. Pp. 550–55 in *International Encyclopedia of the Sociology of Education,* edited by L. J. Saha. Oxford, England: Pergamon.

Coleman, J. S. 1968. "The Concept of Equality of Educational Opportunity." *Harvard Educational Review* 38:7–22.

Collins, R. 1971. "Functional and Conflict Theories of Educational Stratification." *American Sociological Review* 36:1002–19.

Darity, W., Jr. and J. G. Nembhard. 2000. "Racial and Ethnic Economic Inequality: The International Record." Pp. 308–11 in *Cross-National Comparisons of Racial and Ethnic Economic Inequality* 90(2), AEA Papers and Proceedings.

Darling-Hammond, L. 1995. "Inequality and Access to Knowledge." Pp. 465–83 in *Handbook of Research on Multicultural Education,* edited by J. A. Banks and C. A. M. Banks. New York: Simon & Schuster Macmillan.

Durkheim, E. [1893] 1984. *The Division of Labor in Society.* New York: Free Press.

Easterbrook, M. 2002. "Brazil Considers Quotas to Bridge Racial Divide in Higher Education: The Only Problem with the Proposed Policy Would Be Deciding Who Is Black." *Chronicle of Higher Education,* March 1.

Erikson, R. and J. Goldthorpe. 1992. *The Constant Flux: A Study in Class Mobility in Industrial Societies.* Oxford, England: Clarendon.

Farkas, G., R. P. Grobe, D. Sheehan, and Y. Shuan. 1990. "Cultural Resources and School Success: Gender, Ethnicity, and Poverty Groups within an Urban School District." *American Sociological Review* 55:127–42.

Fedderke, J. W., R. De Kadt, and J. M. Luiz. 2000. "Uneducating South Africa: The Failure to Address the 1910–1993 Legacy." *International Review of Education* 46:257–81.

Ferguson, R. F. 1991. "Racial Patterns in How School and Teacher Quality Affect Achievement and Earnings." *Challenge: A Journal of Research on Black Men* 2 (1):3–35.

——. 1998. "Teachers' Perceptions and Expectations and the Black-White Test Score Gap." Pp. 273–317 in *The Black-White Test Score Gap,* edited by C. Jencks and M. Phillips. Washington, DC: Brookings Institution Press.

Fernandes, D. C. 1999. "Educational Stratification, Race and Socioeconomic Development in Brazil." Unpublished Ph.D. dissertation, Department of Sociology, University of Wisconsin, Madison, WI.

Fischer, C., M. Hout, M. S. Jankowski, S. R. Lucas, A. Swidler, and K. Voss. 1996. *Inequality by Design.* Princeton, NJ: Princeton University Press.

Fordham, S. 1988. "Racelessness as a Factor in Black Students' School Success: Pragmatic Strategy or Pyrrhic Victory?" *Harvard Educational Review* 58:54–84.

——. 1993. "'Those Loud Black Girls': (Black) Women, Silence, and Gender 'Passing' in the Academy." *Anthropology & Education Quarterly* 24:3–32.

——. 1996. *Blacked Out: Dilemmas of Race, Identity, and Success at Capital High.* Chicago, IL: University of Chicago.

Gamoran, A., W. G. Secada, and C. B. Marrett. 2000. "The Organizational Context of Teaching and Learning." Pp. 37–63 in *Handbook of the Sociology of Education,* edited by M. T. Hallinan. New York: Kluwer Academic/Plenum.

Ganzeboom, H. and D. Treiman. 1993. "Preliminary Results on Educational Expansion and Educational Achievement in Comparative Perspectives." In *Solidarity of Generations: Demographics, Economics and Social Change, and Its Consequences,* edited by H. A. Becker and P. L. Hermkens. Amsterdam, The Netherlands: Thesis Publishers.

——. 1997. *Occupational Status Attainment in Comparative Perspective.* Paper presented at the ISA Research Committee on Social Stratification and Social Mobility, May 18–20, Tel Aviv, Israel.

Ganzeboom, H., D. Treiman, and W. Ultee. 1991. "Comparative Intergenerational Stratification Research: Three Generations and Beyond." *Annual Review of Sociology* 17:277–302.

Guimaraes, A. S. 2001. "Race, Class and Color: Behind Brazil's 'Racial Democracy.'" *NACLA Report on the Americas* 34 (Abstract):38–9.

Haycock, K. 1998. "Good Teaching Matters . . . A Lot." *Thinking K–16* 3 (2):3–14.

Higham, J. 1963. *Strangers in the Land: Patterns of American Nativism, 1860–1925.* New York: Atheneum.

Ingersoll, R. M. 2002. *Out-of-Field Teaching, Educational Inequality, and the Organization of Schools*. Seattle, WA: Center for the Study of Teaching and Policy, University of Washington.

Jencks, C. and M. Phillips, eds. 1998. *The Black-White Test Score Gap*. Washington, DC: Brookings Institution Press.

Kang, T. 2001. "Post-Secondary Aspiration Formation and Outcomes of Female 'Normal' Students in Singapore." Unpublished Ph.D. dissertation, New York University, New York.

Katznelson, I. and M. Weir. 1985. *Schooling for All: Class, Race and the Decline of the Democratic Ideal*. Berkeley, CA: University of California Press.

Kruss, G. 2001. "Towards Human Rights in South African Schools: An Agenda for Research and Practice." *Race Ethnicity and Education* 4 (1):45–62.

LeTendre, G., D. Naumowicz, and B. Johnson. 2000. "The 'Problem' of Minority Education in an International Perspective." *International Journal of Educational Research* 33:577–655.

Lipset, S. and R. Bendix. 1959. *Social Mobility in Industrial Society*. Berkeley, CA: University of California Press.

Massey, D. and N. A. Denton. 1993. *American Apartheid: Segregation and the Making of the Underclass*. Cambridge, MA: Harvard University Press.

Meyer, J. W., F. O. Ramirez, and Y. N. Soysal. 1992. "World Expansion of Mass Education, 1870–1980." *Sociology of Education* 65:128–49.

Moses, W. 1978. *The Golden Age of African American Nationalism: 1850–1925*. New York: Oxford University Press.

Motani, Y. 2002. "Toward a More Just Educational Policy for Minorities in Japan: The Case of Korean Ethnic Schools." *Comparative Education* 38:225–37.

Murray, G. 1997. "Opportunity-to-Learn Issues Common to South Africa and the United States." *Journal of Negro Education* 66:376–82.

Nkabinde, Z. P. 1997. *An Analysis of Educational Challenges in the New South Africa*. Lanham, MD: University Press of America.

Ogbu, J. U. 1978. *Minority Education and Caste: The American System in Cross-Cultural Perspective*. New York: Academic Press.

——. 1994. "Racial Stratification and Education in the United States: Why Inequality Persists." *Teachers College Record* 96:264–98.

Okano, K. and M. Tsuchiya. 1999. *Education in Contemporary Japan*. Cambridge, England: Cambridge University Press.

Omi, M. A. 2001. "The Changing Meaning of Race." Pp. 243–63 in *America Becoming*, Vol. 1, edited by N. J. Smelser, W. J. Wilson, and F. Mitchell. Washington, DC: National Academy Press.

Parsons, T. 1970. "Equality and Inequality in Modern Society, or Social Stratification Revisited." In *Social Stratification*, edited by E. O. Lauman. Indianapolis, IN: Bobbs-Merrill.

Persell, C. H., C. James, T. Kang, and K. Snyder. 1999. "Gender and Education in Global Perspective." Pp. 407–40 in *Handbook of the Sociology of Gender*, edited by J. S. Chafetz. New York: Kluwer Academic/Plenum.

Peterson, R. D. and L. J. Krivo. 1999. "Racial Segregation, the Concentration of Disadvantage, and Black and White Homicide Victimization." *Sociological Forum* 14:465–93.

Powers, M. H. 1995. "Factors That Influence the Educational Attainment Levels of Women Students at the University Of Malawi, Africa." Unpublished Ph.D. dissertation, Indiana University.

Raftery, A. and M. Hout. 1990. *Maximally Maintained Inequality: Expansion, Reform and Opportunity in Irish Education, 1921–1975*. Paper presented at the ISA Research Committee on Social Stratification and Social Mobility, Madrid, Spain.

Ramirez, F. O. and J. Boli. 1987. "The Political Construction of Mass Schooling: European Origins and Worldwide Institutionalization." *Sociology of Education* 60:2–17.

Rijken, S. 1999. *Educational Expansion and Status Attainment: A Cross-National and Over-Time Comparison*. Amsterdam, The Netherlands: Interuniversity Center for Social Science Theory and Methodology.

Roscigno, V. J. 1999. "The Black-White Achievement Gap, Family-School Links, and the Importance of Place." *Sociological Inquiry* 69:159–86.

Rossouw, H. 2001. "Number of Black Graduates in South Africa Doubled in Past Decade, Report Says." *Chronicle of Higher Education*, December 18. Retrieved from chronicle.com/;daily/2001/12/2001121806n.htm.

Shavit, Y. 1984. "Tracking and Ethnicity in Israeli Secondary Education." *American Sociological Review* 49:210–20.

——. 1990. "Segregation, Tracking, and the Educational Attainment of Minorities: Arabs and Oriental Jews in Israel." *American Sociological Review* 55: 115–26.

Shavit, Y. and H.-P. Blossfeld. 1993. *Persistent Inequality: Changing Educational Attainment in Thirteen Countries*. Boulder, CO: Westview Press.

Shavit, Y. and W. Müller, eds. 1998. *From School to Work: A Comparative Study of Educational Qualifications and Occupational Destinations.* Oxford, England: Oxford University Press.

Shujaa, M. J., ed. 1996. *Beyond Desegregation: The Politics of Quality in African American Schooling.* Thousand Oaks, CA: Corwin.

Sorokin, P. [1927] 1964. *Social and Cultural Mobility.* New York: Free Press.

Telles, E. 1994. "Industrialization and Racial Inequality in Employment: The Brazilian Example." *American Sociological Review* 59:46–63.

——. 2002. "Racial Ambiguity among the Brazilian Population." *Ethnic and Racial Studies* 25:415–41.

Treiman, D. 1970. "Industrialization and Social Stratification." In *Social Stratification,* edited by E. O. Lauman. Indianapolis, IN: Bobbs-Merrill.

Treiman, D. and H. Ganzeboom. 2000. "The Fourth Generation of Comparative Stratification Research." Pp. 123–50 in *The International Handbook of Sociology,* edited by S. Quah and A. Sales. Thousand Oaks, CA: Sage.

Uekawa, K. 2000. *Making Equality in 40 National Education Systems.* Chicago, IL: University of Chicago.

Varshney, A. 2002. *Ethnic Conflict and Civic Life.* New Haven, CT: Yale University Press.

Weber, M. [1921] 1968. *Economy and Society.* Berkeley, CA: University of California Press.

——. 1946. "The Rationalization of Education and Training." Translated by H. H. Gerth and C. W. Mills. In *Max Weber: Essays in Sociology.* Oxford, England: Oxford University Press.

Wenglinsky, H. 1997. "How Money Matters: The Effect of School District Spending on Academic Achievement." *Sociology of Education* 70:221–37.

Wilson, W. J. 1998. "The Role of the Environment in the Black-White Test Score Gap." Pp. 501–10 in *The Black-White Test Score Gap,* edited by C. Jencks and M. Phillips. Washington, DC: Brookings Institution Press.

Yogev, A. 2000. "The Stratification of Israeli Universities: Implications for Higher Education Policy." *Higher Education* 40:183–201.

HEALTH AS A SOCIAL PROBLEM

WILLIAM C. COCKERHAM

University of Alabama, Birmingham

At this time in history it is a well-established fact that many health problems have social origins and connections. We know that diseases are not always exclusively biological; rather, their onset and course are often instigated and abetted by living conditions and behavior. Health becomes a social problem when the social aspects of people's lives cause them to become sick or undermine their capacity for longevity. The key variable in this situation is social class, since people in the upper social strata generally maintain good health until quite late in life. It therefore becomes most important to understand what social factors cause health to deteriorate earlier among those at the bottom of society (Robert and House 2000; Wermuth 2003).

Whereas health itself is a social problem because it is spread unevenly throughout society, the provision of health care can be a similar problem when costs and lack of availability act as barriers to medical treatment. This situation is reviewed for the United States, as it is the only major country without some form of national health insurance providing universal health care coverage to its population. However, the focus of the chapter is on the unequal social distribution of health in societies generally, since this condition precedes problems in obtaining health care and promotes the differential need for such care. Consequently, it is the primary purpose of this chapter to review current research findings in a global context and identify the major social causes of health and illness.

HEALTH: AGENCY VERSUS STRUCTURE

Health behavior, like other forms of social behavior, is affected by the dialectical relationship between agency and structure. Agency is the ability of actors to choose their behavior, while structure refers to regularities in social interaction (e.g., institutions, roles), systematic social relationships (e.g., status, class), and access to resources that constrain or empower choices. The interplay of agency and structure are particularly obvious with respect to health lifestyles. Health lifestyles are collective patterns of health-related behavior based on choices from options that are available to people according to their life chances (Cockerham 2000a). Life chances are a form of structure in that they are, as Max Weber (1978; Dahrendorf 1979) suggests, the structural probabilities people have in life to obtain satisfaction for their needs, wants, and desires, and are largely determined by their socioeconomic situation. The behaviors that are generated from health lifestyle choices are typically shaped by the person's life chances and can have either positive or negative consequences for his or her health.

This is not to say that people often deliberately choose behavior that harms their health, but some people do engage in risk behavior that opens the door to that possibility. Negative health lifestyles like smoking, taking drugs, heavy alcohol use, eating high-fat and unbalanced diets, regularly subjecting oneself to highly stressful situations, not getting enough relaxation and rest, not using automobile seat belts, and so on promote health problems through illness or injury. The research literature is clear that these activities can be harmful. Yet people do these things because of addiction, ignorance, thoughtlessness, or denial. When it comes to health lifestyle choices, either positive or negative, people at the top of society typically make the healthiest choices and have the resources to support their decision. Those at the bottom have greater socioeconomic constraints on their choices and may even find there is little choice available. Poor health lifestyles and their adverse outcomes accompany negative social conditions. We see this situation, for example, in the case of smoking and AIDS.

Smoking

It is common knowledge that smoking tobacco is bad for your health. There is strong evidence linking smoking to the risk of heart disease, atherosclerosis, stroke, lung and other cancers, emphysema and other respiratory diseases, liver disease, and other health problems, thereby making it the lifestyle practice with the largest number of negative consequences for health (Jarvis and Wardle 1999; Rogers and Powell-Griner 1991; Ross and Wu 1995). In the United States, smoking causes a man to lose more than 13 years of life on average and a woman 14.5 years (Centers for Disease Control 2002). Some 440,000 people die each year from smoking-related causes.

Although the proportion of smokers in Western countries has substantially decreased as awareness of the effects of smoking on the body became generally known, some people nevertheless choose to smoke—with the decision to smoke or not smoke an exercise of agency. That is, the decision to smoke is a choice. But is that choice independent of structure? The answer is that it is not. Structure intervenes in this decision as distinct differences persist between specific population groups, suggesting that decisions about smoking are not entirely an individual matter. Social structural factors like gender, race, and social class influence these outcomes. For example, men are more likely than women to smoke, but among smokers they are also more likely to quit. As for nonsmokers, white men are more likely to be in this category than black men, black women slightly more likely than white women, the well-educated more likely than the less-educated, and persons in the upper social strata more likely than those in the lower strata (Cockerham 2004). In Great Britain, Andrew Adonis and Stephen Pollard (1997) find that smoking is largely a habit of the poor, as nearly three times as many people in unskilled occupations smoke as do those with professional jobs. A similar situation exists in the United States, where adults with less than a high school education were nearly three times as likely to smoke as those with a bachelor's or higher degree (Center for Health Statistics 2002).

So there is a social pattern to smoking, which indicates that smoking is not a random, individual decision completely independent of structural influences. As Martin Jarvis and Jane Wardle (1999) observe, smoking, along with drinking and drug use, are individual risk behaviors that involve an element of personal choice. However, smoking and other risk behaviors have not been viewed in a broad social context as much as they have been characterized as situations of individual responsibility. The reasoning goes that if people wish to avoid the negative effects of smoking on their health, they should not smoke; if they choose to smoke, what happens to them physiologically is no one else's fault but their own. This victim-blaming approach, state Jarvis and Wardle (1999:241), is not helpful, as it fails to account for the underlying reasons why disadvantaged people are drawn to poor health habits like smoking and the nature of the social conditions that reinforce this behavior.

The social factors identified by Jarvis and Wardle (1999) that induce people to smoke are adverse socioeconomic conditions, deprivation, and stressful circumstances. "This illustrates what might be proposed as a general law of Western society," conclude Jarvis and Wardle, "namely, that any marker of disadvantage that can be envisaged, whether personal, material or cultural, is likely to have an independent association with cigarette smoking" (p. 242). Growing up in a household where one or both parents smoke, having a smoking partner, and socializing with smokers regularly are other reasons that invoke smoking in a social context. These situations are also more likely toward the bottom of the social scale. Of course, some affluent people likewise smoke and the reasons for doing so may be different than those listed above—although stress is a likely culprit for everybody. Smoking among the affluent does not change the fact that this behavior is unusual at the higher levels of society and that the smoking habit is concentrated among lower strata groups, especially the lower class.

AIDS

Another health problem that would seem to be largely a matter of agency or choice is HIV/AIDS. AIDS destroys a person's immune system against infection, causing that individual to become sick and often die from a variety of cancers and viruses, or pneumonia. AIDS is a virus itself—the human immunodeficiency virus (HIV)—that is primarily transmitted through sexual intercourse or intravenous drug use (by sharing contaminated needles). Blood transfusions or infection of prenatal infants by their infected mothers are other methods of transmission. With the exception of infants and unsuspecting blood transfusion recipients, choice with regard to sexual risks and IV drug use that would allow a virus into the blood stream is a factor in the transmission of AIDS. After all, why would someone choose to risk exposure to AIDS if they could avoid it by taking precautions (using condoms) or staying away from the social networks and sex partners where AIDS is prevalent? Except for people in a position of powerlessness in a sexual or IV

drug-using relationship, it would seem that some choice is involved. But, as I discuss, structural conditions operate as well.

In the beginning of the AIDS epidemic, in the mid-1980s, infected persons were principally homosexual white males in the West and heterosexual couples in Africa, where the illness originated and is believed to have passed to humans through the blood of infected chimpanzees killed for food. However, in the United States, where AIDS mortality is now declining, the magnitude of the epidemic shifted to African Americans and Hispanics. In 1985, there were more than twice as many AIDS cases reported among non-Hispanic white men as among non-Hispanic black men; by 1997, blacks surpassed whites in the total number of new cases annually and had the highest overall rates per capita of any racial group. The most recent figures for mid-2000 for males show non-Hispanic blacks maintaining the highest rate of 117 cases per 100,000 resident population, followed by Hispanics at 48.8, American Indians/ Native Alaskans at 16.7, non-Hispanic whites at 15.1, and Asians/Pacific Islanders at 8.2. The rates for females are 48.0 cases per 100,000 for non-Hispanic blacks, 13.4 for Hispanics, 7.6 for American Indians/Native Alaskans, 2.2 for non-Hispanic whites, and 1.9 for Asians/Pacific Islanders. AIDS now stalks the African American community as it does no other, with the somewhat distant exception of Hispanics.

When it comes to mortality from AIDS, black men and women are again especially affected, as are Hispanic men. As shown in Table 17.1, black males have the highest mortality rates for AIDS. Table 17.1 shows that black male AIDS mortality was 26.2 per 100,000 resident population in 1987 and the rate increased to 90.4 by 1995. Preliminary data for 1999 show the rate to have decreased to 37.0, which remains the highest by far of any gender or racial group. The next highest mortality rate belongs to black females, who are usually infected through IV drug use with contaminated needles or by sexual intercourse with bisexual or IV drug-using men who have AIDS. Table 17.1 shows the rates for black women as 4.6 per 100,000 in 1987, 24.7 in 1995, and 13.3 in 1999. Next are Hispanic males with rates of 18.8 in 1987, 42.0 in 1995, and 11.3 in 1999. The mortality rates for white non-Hispanic males have

Table 17.1   Mortality Rates for AIDS by Sex and Race, United States, 1987, 1995, 1999

	(Deaths per 100,000 Resident Population)		
Males	*1987*	*1995*	*1999*[a]
Non-Hispanic White	10.7	18.0	4.0
Black	26.2	90.4	37.0
American Indian/Native Alaskan	*	11.6	5.0
Asian/Pacific Islander	2.5	6.3	1.4
Hispanic	18.8	42.0	11.3
Females	*1987*	*1995*	*1999*[a]
Non-Hispanic White	0.5	0.8	0.7
Black	4.6	24.7	13.3
American Indian/Native Alaskan	*	*	*
Asian/Pacific Islander	*	0.7	*
Hispanic	2.1	9.0	

Source: National Center for Health Statistics (2001).

Note: * = less than 20 deaths
a. Preliminary data for 1999

declined from a high of 18.0 in 1995 to 4.0 in 1999. Among males, Table 17.1 shows that the lowest rates for males are among Asians/Pacific Islanders, while female AIDS mortality has been negligible among non-Hispanic whites, American Indians/Native Alaskans, and Asians/Pacific Islanders.

The shift in AIDS cases and mortality from non-Hispanic whites to African Americans and also to Hispanic males points to a pattern that is associated more with socioeconomic than biological factors, as each of these two racial minority groups contains a large proportion of the poor in American society. Some 46.4 percent of all blacks and 51.3 percent of all Hispanics in the United States are poor or near poor, compared with 22.2 percent of the non-Hispanic white population (National Center for Health Statistics 2002). A major reason blacks have the highest rates of AIDS and other sexually transmitted diseases is the "intraracial network effect" (Laumann and Youm 2001). Blacks are highly segregated from the other racial/ethnic groups in American society, and the high number of sexual contacts between an infected black core and its periphery of yet uninfected black sexual partners

tends to contain the infections within the black population. Entrenched poverty, joblessness, low incomes, minimal access to health care, and a reluctance to seek treatment for sexually transmitted diseases because of the social stigma attached to them are other major factors.

Even though life expectancy has improved for people in all social classes in the United States and most other countries during the twentieth century, the examples of smoking and AIDS illustrate the penalty for being socially and economically disadvantaged: higher morbidity and mortality in virtually every society. Mortality for the lower classes remains proportionately greater than that of higher social strata, and this gap refuses to disappear. While the last century witnessed a worldwide epidemiological transition from acute to chronic diseases as the major causes of mortality, there was not a corresponding social transition. Whereas communicable diseases killed off the poor in much greater numbers than the affluent in past historical periods, chronic diseases like heart disease and cancer now continue the same pattern. In fact, mortality from both acute and chronic diseases is now greater among the poor than the nonpoor—although members of all social classes eventually die from something. The affluent just stay healthier longer, and this fact demonstrates the strong relationship between social class position and health.

SOCIAL CLASS AND HEALTH

Regardless of the country a person lives in, class position is a major determinant of health and life expectancy (Braveman and Tarimo 2002; Cockerham 2004; Lahelma 2000; Link and Phelan 2000; Mirowsky, Ross, and Reynolds 2000; Mulatu and Schooler 2002; Robert and House 2000). This finding holds true for all but a few diseases and throughout the life span, although differences narrow somewhat at the oldest ages (Beckett 2000; Robert and House 1994; Winkleby et al. 1992). Typically, class membership is determined by a person's socioeconomic status as measured by his or her income, occupation, and education. Income, in relation to health, reflects differences in spending power, housing, diet, and access to medical care; occupation represents status, job responsibility, physical activity, and health risks associated with work; and education indicates a person's skills for acquiring positive social, psychological, and economic resources (Winkelby et al. 1992).

Education is the strongest single socioeconomic predictor of a person's level of health, although income and occupation are important. Well-educated people are usually the best informed about health matters and most cognizant of the need to live in a healthy manner and obtain professional health services when needed. The well-educated, in contrast to the less-educated, are more likely to have fulfilling, subjectively rewarding jobs, higher incomes, less economic hardship, and a stronger sense of control over their lives and their health (Ross and Wu 1995). They are also more likely to live a healthy lifestyle by exercising, abstaining from smoking, eating nutritious food, and consuming only moderate amounts of alcohol (Cockerham, Rütten, and Abel 1997). The relationship between education and health is strongest in adulthood, as the less-educated have increasingly more sickness and disability and die sooner than the well-educated (Arber 1993; House et al. 1994). While

there may be some convergence between health and class in old age, surviving cohorts of lower-class elderly are significantly smaller than their middle- and upper-class counterparts.

The relationship between class and health not only consists of the advantages of higher socioeconomic status in guiding health behavior and acquiring medical care, but also the disadvantages associated with the health effects of poverty, racism, chronic and acute stressors, lack of social support, unhealthy living conditions, rundown neighborhoods, poor sanitation, enhanced likelihood of exposure to environmental pollution, lessened access to health care, and greater prevalence of crime, violence, AIDS, heart disease, schizophrenia, and various other physical and mental illnesses. To be poor by definition is to have less of the good things—including health—produced by society.

Race and Gender

Race. The powerful role of class in shaping health is illustrated by the number of studies showing that class generally overrides race and gender in determining health status. This is seen in research in the United States showing that differences in health and life expectancy between races are largely explained by socioeconomic factors (Braithwaite and Taylor 1992; Krieger et al. 1993; Lillie-Blanton and LaVeist 1996; Robert and House 2000; Rogers et al. 1996; Schoenbaum and Waidmann 1997; Williams and Collins 1995). A major reason for this outcome, as noted, is that African Americans and Hispanics are generally overrepresented in the lower class and the lower class has the worst health regardless of race. This is especially true in studies of the health of African Americans, who have the worst overall health profile of any racial/ethnic group in the United States. Being poor means having significantly less opportunity to be healthy, but the biological aspects of race are not terribly important in this context unless social factors like prejudice and discrimination intervene to link race with poverty and lock individuals into the lower class.

This is not to claim that race is entirely meaningless when it comes to disease, as genetic research shows a few notable differences. For example, a gene variation usually absent in whites and Hispanics but found in African Americans increases the risk of developing a rare type of abnormal cardiac rhythm or heartbeat that can be fatal (Splawski et al. 2002). Sickle cell anemia is also more prevalent among people of African origin. Swedes, conversely, are prone to develop an iron metabolism disorder (hemochromatosis) that is absent or rare in Chinese and Indians. However, overall racial differences in health are largely displayed along class lines.

Gender. As for gender, class differences in health are markedly noticeable for men and at least moderately so for women (McDonough et al. 1999; Nettleton 1995; Robert and House 2000). Men generally experience health, illness, and mortality according to their class position (Marmot 1996; Marmot, Shipley, and Rose 1984). We know that socioeconomic disadvantages also harm women's health, but the strength of the social class gradient in relation to that of men has not been as conclusive, although there is evidence it exists (McDonough, Walters, and Strohschein 2002). Most of the research on class and gender has focused on men rather than women, so less is known about the situation for women. However, Peggy McDonough et al. (1999) found in the United States that the link between social class and mortality is similar for both men and women, and research in North America and Western Europe shows the same pattern (Arber 1989; Pappas et al. 1993; Wilkinson 1996). In Britain, recent research, for example, shows significantly greater morbidity among both men and women who are the most socially disadvantaged (Cooper 2002).

Additionally, the health experiences of women differ from those of men in that women are usually sick more often but live longer—some five to seven years longer on average (Arber and Thomas 2001). Some researchers challenge this assessment and argue that the health of men and women is more similar than assumed, but varies at different ages and in relation to different afflictions (Walters, McDonough, and Strohschein 2002). Nevertheless, the conventional view still holds that women do indeed experience more ill health compared to men and the situation requires considerably more

investigation if this conclusion is to be changed. Socioeconomic inequalities in women's health are also more pronounced if they additionally have to cope with lower wages and less job opportunities than men, and being a single parent and sole provider for a household (Annandale 1998; Lahelma, Arber, et al. 2002; McDonough et al. 2002; Moss 2002; Nettleton 1995). Inequality in women's health is even more pronounced in South Asian countries like Bangladesh and Nepal, where men live longer than women. The social devaluation of women, along with nutritional deprivation and lessened access to medical care, has helped curtail the natural longevity of women in these countries (Braveman and Tarimo 2002; Cockerham 2004).

As for health lifestyles, we know that women typically eat healthier diets and smoke and drink less alcohol than men, but exercise far less (Calnan 1987; Cockerham et al. 1997). Smoking and alcohol consumption are more important determinants of health for men than women, but body weight and physical inactivity are more important for women (Denton and Walters 1999). Social class, however, intervenes in this pattern as people in higher social strata, regardless of gender, participate more in leisure-time exercise, eat healthier foods, and smoke and drink less (Blaxter 1990; Reid 1998). While gender is an important lifestyle variable in that women generally seem to take better care of their health than men and live longer as well through a combination of social and biological factors, differences in health and longevity nonetheless exist between women of different social strata.

Class and Health in the United States

As elsewhere in the world, socioeconomic status is one of the strongest and most consistent predictors of health and longevity in the United States. Traditionally, the poor have had the worst health and shortest lives. For example, rates of coronary heart disease—the nation's leading killer—have declined for all Americans, but the decrease has been greatest for the upper and middle classes (Cockerham 2004). Heart disease is now more concentrated among the poor because of greater obesity, smoking, and stress, along with less leisure-time exercise, poorer diets, and higher levels of blood pressure. Studies of exercise, for instance, show that men with the lowest level of education have the steepest decline in physical activity as adults (Grzywacz and Marks 2001). Other research shows greater stress, inadequate diets and housing, and more alcohol abuse and smoking among the poor in the United States (Link and Phelan 2000; Mirowsky et al. 2000; Ross and Wu 1995). Residents of disadvantaged neighborhoods characterized by danger, crime, incivility, and limitations on outdoor physical activity have also been found to have worse self-reported health and physical functioning and more chronic health problems than people living in more advantaged neighborhoods (Ross and Mirowsky 2001).

Fifty years ago, coronary heart disease was associated with an affluent way of life (i.e., rich diets, smoking, well-paid but stressful jobs). However, as the affluent began to practice healthier lifestyles and routinely seek preventive care in the form of medical checkups and drugs to reduce high blood pressure and harmful low-density lipoprotein cholesterol levels, heart disease was postponed until later in life or avoided altogether. Preventive health care has never been a trait of help-seeking among the lower classes, who typically wait to visit physicians until they feel bad, are less likely to have a regular physician, and are more likely to go to a hospital emergency room when sick (Cockerham 2004).

Historically, the lower class has not received the same quality of medical care available to the classes above it because they lacked the money or health insurance to pay for care in the American fee-for-service system. Disadvantaged patients relied on charity care or teaching hospitals. A considerable portion of the literature in medical sociology in the 1950s and 1960s documented the problems of the poor in obtaining quality medical care. The situation changed in the mid-1960s with the passage of two federally sponsored health insurance programs: Medicare to cover all persons over age 65 and Medicaid for people with low incomes. Medicaid is a welfare program in which the federal government shares the costs of health care services for the poor with the various states. The passage of Medicare and Medicaid legislation over the strong opposition of organized medicine marked a turning point in medical politics as the federal government emerged as a dominant factor in health care delivery.

Medicare and Medicaid not only established the precedent of the federal government's involvement in health care administration, but the programs also provided needed insurance to cover services for the old and those living in poverty where these services were not covered before. Prior to this time, the upper class visited physicians for care more often than the other social classes, followed by the middle and working classes, with the lower class at the rear. The pattern changed temporarily in the late 1960s, with the upper class seeing doctors the least and the middle class seeing them the most. However, as the lower class began taking advantage of the new health insurance programs, they replaced the middle class as the strata seeing doctors the most. This is appropriate because they have the worst health problems overall, but indications are that they should visit doctors even more often because they still tend to delay in seeking care until their health conditions worsen (Cockerham 2004). Part of the delay stems from the lack of treatment facilities in poor neighborhoods (Robert and House 2000).

Although health care has become more accessible for the poor in the United States, equity has not been achieved. In a free market system lacking national health insurance covering the general population, those persons who are socially disadvantaged are also medically disadvantaged when it comes to obtaining quality care. The United States has a two-track system of medical care consisting of a private and public track. The public track is a system of welfare medicine supported by public health insurance. The urban poor have traditionally been dependent on public hospitals and clinics, and this situation has not changed. Often these facilities are underfinanced, understaffed, and overcrowded with patients. Few such hospitals and clinics exist in inner-city areas or neighborhoods populated by the poor. The rural poor also have problems of access, as doctors and hospitals may not be available where they live.

The problems of access, high costs, and the availability of quality care are compounded by the large percentage of Americans without health insurance. In 2001, some 18.1 percent of the population between the ages of 18 and 64 years did not have health insurance coverage. This includes 40.1 percent of all Hispanics in this age group, followed by 22.8 percent of all non-Hispanic blacks and

13.5 percent of all non-Hispanic whites. Only about half (49.7%) of all Hispanics have private health insurance compared with 61.9 percent of blacks and 80 percent of whites. People without health insurance are typically the near-poor, whose annual family income is less than $25,000, which is often too much money to allow them to qualify for Medicaid, or, in the case of some Hispanics, they are illegal migrants. Nevertheless, they live in very disadvantaged circumstances and obtaining medical care is difficult. Health in the United States remains one of the nation's most important social problems.

Class and Health in Great Britain

Class differences in mortality have been observed in Britain since the first Registrar-General's Occupational Analysis of 1851 and have continued into the twenty-first century. A negative gradient in mortality by social class—the lower the class, the higher the mortality—has been evident from the beginning. This gradient has persisted even though life expectancy for all classes has continued to improve through the years. The social class-mortality gradient exists for infants, as well as children and adults. It reflects not only differences in mortality but in injury and morbidity as well (Reid 1998). Earlier in the twentieth century, heart disease was an exception to the general pattern in that the affluent were much more prone to heart disease and other circulatory disorders than manual workers. By 1971, as in the United States, the situation had reversed itself, with heart ailments far greater among those at the bottom of society (Coleman and Salt 1992). Consequently, the epidemiological transition in Britain from acute to chronic diseases as the major causes of mortality did not alleviate the health circumstances of the poor. Heart disease shifted more strongly into their ranks than ever before.

Why? Again the answer is differences in living conditions and class-based health lifestyles like alcohol use, smoking, diet, and exercise—especially leisure-time exercise unaccompanied by the stress and strain of manual labor and deadlines, quotas, demands, and schedules for physical outputs mandated by others. More judicious use of physician services, particularly preventive care by the affluent, were also important. Britain, however, is of special interest in studies of class and health because the country established equity in health care delivery. Since 1948, Britain has had a national health service providing the lower classes with medical care similar to that of people higher on the social scale. The British government employs the majority of physicians and other health workers and owns most of the nation's health care facilities. Services are essentially free to those who use them, and the care provided is generally paid for out of government tax revenues.

A major assumption was that the provision of quality care to all classes would improve levels of health throughout society, as poverty would no longer be a barrier for someone requiring professional medical treatment. Health did improve for all social classes. However, in 1980, the British public was surprised by the government-sponsored Black Report, which disclosed that the lower class still had significantly worse health, disability, and life expectancy than the classes above them. Prior to this time, it had widely been thought that British society was becoming more egalitarian and longevity more equal among the different classes. But the Black Report showed this was clearly not the situation. The report blamed class differences in health on socioeconomic conditions, such as poor living quarters, overcrowding, work accidents, exposure to dampness and cold, and unhealthy lifestyle practices, such as smoking, drinking, and poor nutrition.

Current studies in Britain show that—despite the continued upward trend in life expectancy—the highest strata not only live longer than the lowest, but the gap is widening (Annandale 1998; Reid 1998; Shaw, Dorling, and Smith 1999). That is, the upper class has even greater longevity than it did in the recent past, despite improvement for all classes. A government report shows, for example, that differences in longevity for the two highest classes in relation to the two lowest increased from 3.7 years in 1977–81 to 4.7 years in 1987–91 for males and from 2.1 years to 3.4 years for females during the same period (Drever and Whitehead 1997). From the early to the mid-1980s, males in the two highest classes had gained an additional 1.0 year of life expectancy over men in the two lowest classes, while upper strata women had added an additional 1.3 years. And this had taken place in a country providing equitable health care to all.

Other research shows that the gap in levels of morbidity also widened between the employed and unemployed during the same period, with the unemployed showing increasingly greater amounts of sickness (Lahelma et al. 2000). In addition to a shorter life expectancy, the lower classes still have higher infant mortality, more chronic disability, more absence from work due to illness, and higher ratios of risk behavior like obesity, lack of exercise, and smoking.

Class and Health in Canada, Australia, and Western Europe

The link between class and health in Western society is a universal finding. Studies conducted in Canada, Australia, and Western Europe—all in countries with national health insurance coverage—confirm the pattern noted in Britain and the United States. Canadian studies show that lower socioeconomic groups have the worst health and shortest life spans (Frohlich and Mustard 1996; Humphries and Doorslaer 2000; McDonough et al. 2002), and Australian research shows the same pattern (Lupton 2000). The same situation exists in Western Europe generally (Kunst et al. 1998), including not only Britain (Adonis and Pollard 1998; Arber 1993; Arber and Thomas 2000; Borooah 1999; Chandola 2000; Marmot 1996; Reid 1998; Wilkinson 1996), as previously discussed, but also Britain and Finland (Lahelma et al. 2000; Lahelma, Arber, et al. 2002), France (Orfali 2000), France and Spain (Lostao et al. 2001), Spain (Regidor et al. 2002), Germany (Knesebeck and Siegrist 2000; Mielck et al. 2000), Italy (Piperno and DiOrio 1990), and even the highly egalitarian Nordic countries of Denmark, Norway, Sweden, and Finland (Hemström 1999, 2000; Lahelma 2000; Lahelma, Kivela, et al. 2002; Sundquist and Johansson 1997).

The Nordic countries represent a unique case because they are relatively similar in terms of history, culture, language, geographical location, economies, and social structure (Lahelma, Kivela, et al. 2002). They all have high standards of living and extensive state welfare systems providing universal benefits for health, education, and social security for young and old. Moreover, there is an emphasis on gender equality, full employment, and a relatively even distribution of income. Yet even in these countries, Lahelma, Kivela, and their colleagues (2002), along with other scholars (Hemström 1999, 2000), find persistent socioeconomic inequities in levels of health among women as well as men. Germany represents another special situation in that the country was formerly divided between a capitalist West and communist East. Despite the fact that both parts of Germany experienced different political, economic, and social systems for 45 years (1945–1990), upper socioeconomic groups in East Germany as well as in West Germany have better health compared with people below them on the social ladder (Mielck et al. 2000).

EXPLANATIONS OF THE CLASS-HEALTH RELATIONSHIP

It is obvious from the prior discussion that health is a social problem largely because of class inequities and the living conditions associated with these inequities. Health, like class, is stratified from top to bottom along socioeconomic lines. Major explanations for this relationship include the following.

The Social Gradient in Mortality

A British project providing strong evidence of class differences in mortality is the Whitehall Studies conducted by Michael Marmot and his colleagues. Some 17,000 male civil government employees, classified according to their job, were interviewed about their health practices in the late 1960s. These men were between 40 and 64 years of age at the time. In the first study, Marmot et al. (1984) examined the mortality rates for these men and found that regardless of the cause of death, those with the highest occupational rank had the lowest mortality and the percentages increased the lower the job position. What was particularly interesting was that the highest status men (senior administrators) had lower mortality than the next highest (professional/executives) and so on down the line until the bottom of the status hierarchy was reached, where mortality was the highest. Marmot (1996) was surprised that the pattern of class differences in deaths among the civil servants paralleled society as a whole, since the jobs were all stable, provided pensions, and presumably were free of occupational hazards. The difference between the top and bottom grades of the civil service was in fact three times greater than the top and bottom social classes in national mortality data.

Marmot et al. (1991) conducted a second study to recheck their results and found that, as in the first study, each group had worse health and higher mortality than the one just above it in the status hierarchy. As Marmot (1996) later stated: "In the higher grades of the civil service there is no poverty, yet those who are near the top have worse health than those at the top and the gradient continues all the way down" (p. 48). These findings led to the formulation of a social gradient theory of mortality. This theory holds that the highest social strata (the upper class) lives longer than the next highest (the upper middle class), which lives longer than the next highest (the lower middle class), and so on down the social ladder—forming a gradient from high to low. The exact reasons for this gradient are not yet known, but some studies suggest that the gradient results from class differences in self-esteem and stress (Evans, Barer, and Marmor 1994), income inequality (Wilkinson 1996), deprivation over the life course (Power and Hertzman 1997), or health lifestyles and social support (Cockerham, Hattori, and Yamori 2000), or some combination thereof.

While there are questions whether the social gradient theory can also be used to explain health differences between rich and poor countries or geographical areas within countries, the theory holds up relatively well with respect to class differences. That is, the social gradient exists as depicted. Moreover, the research upon which it is based suggests that medical care alone cannot counter the adverse effects of lower-class position on health. The Whitehall studies demonstrate that the lower a person is on the social scale, the less healthy that person is likely to be and the sooner he or she can expect to die. Conversely, the higher one is on the social ladder, the better are one's prospects for health and longevity than those of people in the class below.

Relative Income

Another influential explanation emerging from research in Britain is Richard Wilkinson's (1992,

1996) relative income theory. Wilkinson focuses on the health of whole societies, rather than individuals, because when it comes to practical politics and public policies, he maintains that it is the health of whole societies that is most important. He suggests that relative position in a social hierarchy can be determined by relative income, and that the psychosocial effects of the different social positions in a society have health consequences. Stress, poor social networks, low self-esteem, depression, anxiety, insecurity, and loss of a sense of control are reduced and social cohesion is enhanced—when income levels are more equal. Consequently, Wilkinson claims that relative levels of income *within* a society therefore have more significant effects on health and mortality than the society's absolute level of wealth. That is, what matters the most in determining health and mortality is not how wealthy a society is overall, but how evenly wealth is distributed among its members. Countries with the longest life expectancy may not have the most wealth; instead, the best health and greatest longevity is found in those nations with the smallest differences in income levels and smallest proportion of the total population living in poverty. This is seen in countries like the United States, for example, that have wide disparities in income and lower life expectancies than countries like Sweden, where income is more evenly distributed and life expectancy is higher.

Several studies initially supported Wilkinson's thesis, including those with data on mortality in U.S. metropolitan areas (Lynch et al. 1998) and states (Kawachi et al. 1997). But the most recent studies do not support his position. One problem is that cash income may bear little relation to material and psychosocial well-being in subsistence agricultural economies, where many goods and services are obtained directly from the environment and barter is common (Ellison 2002). This situation limits the utility of relative income theory to rich countries. But new studies conducted with data from countries with high per capita income have likewise failed to find a significant association between income inequality and health (Gravelle, Wildman, and Sutton 2002; Lynch et al. 2001). Other research determined that the association between income distribution and variations in health is modest if people living in poverty are excluded (Judge, Mulligan, and Benzeval 1998). There is research that also failed to find a greater slope in the social gradient when income and mortality differences in a population widen (Ellison 2002; Power and Hertzman 1997), and there are statistical questions about what income equality actually measures in relation to health (Ellison 2002; Gravelle et al. 2002). The evidence is now mounting that the income inequality thesis does not explain differences in health between countries, with the possible exception of child and infant mortality, nor are its effects the same in all countries (Lynch et al. 2001).

Social Causation/Social Selection

Another approach to explaining health inequality is the social causation/social selection debate. The social causation explanation maintains that the lower class is subjected to greater socioeconomic adversity as a result of a deprived life situation and has to cope with this deprivation with fewer resources. Thus, adversity and the stresses associated with it affects the lower class more severely than it does the classes above it, and their health is more impaired as a result. The social selection explanation holds that there is more illness in the lower class because chronically sick persons tend to "drift" downward in the social structure (the "drift" hypothesis), or conversely, healthy individuals in the lower class tend to be upwardly mobile, thereby leaving behind a "residue" of ill persons (the "residue" hypothesis).

Poor health can limit the upward social mobility of people as they lack the health to improve their situation in life and dwell in a more or less permanent sick role, or poor health can cause them to drift downward in the social structure as they find it difficult to maintain their position in society. However, most ill persons are most likely not especially mobile, either up or down. Essentially, they stay where they are. When the question is whether class position affects health (social causation) or health causes class position (social selection), the strongest evidence is on the side of social causation (Marmot et al. 1991). This evidence suggests that class position contributes more to the onset of poor health than poor health causes class position. But the two

explanations are not mutually exclusive in which one explanation is completely wrong and the other totally correct (Annandale 1998; Lahelma 2000; Macintyre 1997). There are undoubtedly situations where sickness locks a person into the lower class or causes downward movement in society. Nevertheless, class position and the health lifestyles and living environment associated with it are the most powerful social factors bringing about poor health.

HEALTH IN THE FORMER SOCIALIST AND DEVELOPING COUNTRIES

Thus far this chapter has largely focused on the relationship between health and society in affluent Western countries. This relationship is perhaps most apparent in countries where there are relatively high standards of living and social factors like class position play a particularly obvious role in promoting or harming health. Most of the research literature and theories about the health/society link likewise reflect conditions in industrialized countries (Gilbert and Walker 2002). Elsewhere in the world, health is also a social problem. The concluding part of this chapter briefly reviews the situation in the former socialist countries of Europe and developing countries where health today is especially problematic.

Former Socialist Countries

The socialist regimes of the former Soviet Union and Eastern Europe came crashing down in 1989–91 largely because of economic failures. Much earlier, however, in the mid-1960s, life expectancy had already starting falling in these countries. This rise in mortality is, in fact, one of the major crises of the late twentieth century, second perhaps only to the AIDS epidemic. This is a surprising development and without precedent in modern history, as nowhere else has health worsened so seriously in peacetime among industrialized nations. Ironically, the former socialist countries espoused a communist ideology of socioeconomic inequality that theoretically should have promoted health for all of their citizens. Yet the reverse occurred and life expectancy fell dramatically for men, while longevity for women typically stagnated instead of rising, as it did in the West.

Infectious diseases, environmental pollution, and genetic maladaptations have not been the primary causes of the decrease in life expectancy, nor has poor-quality health care been the main culprit (Cockerham 1997, 1999, 2000b; Hertzman 1995; Marmot 1996). Virtually all sources agree that increases in cardiovascular diseases are responsible for the change in mortality patterns, while alcohol-related accidents and poisonings are also of major importance (Cockerham 1997, 1999, 2000b; Dmitrieva 2001; Marmot 1996; Tulchinsky and Varavikova 1996). Are social factors responsible? The answer is yes. These factors are stress, health policy, and especially health lifestyles.

Stress has probably been an important contributing variable in this situation, but its exact role has not been determined because of a lack of direct evidence linking cardiovascular mortality in the former socialist states to chronically stressful socioeconomic and psychological conditions. This is not to say that stress is not important; rather, its effects have not been documented. The stress explanation is also undermined by the fact that the Czech Republic reversed its rise in male mortality in the mid-1980s despite sharing the same stressful circumstances with its socialist neighbors.

A policy failure to address chronic diseases is another likely contributing factor, as the Soviet-style health care delivery system lacked the flexibility administratively and structurally to adjust to health problems that could not be handled by the mass measures successful in controlling infectious ailments (Field 2000). The strongest evidence identifies negative health lifestyles as the primary social determinant of the decline in life expectancy (Adevi et al. 1997; Cockerham 1997, 1999, 2000b; Janečková 2001; Ostrowska 2001; Steptoe and Wardle 2001). The lifestyle pattern is one of excessive alcohol consumption, heavy smoking, high-fat diets, and lack of health-promoting exercise. Heavy alcohol use is especially noteworthy among Russian men, as adult males compose 25 percent of the population but drink 90 percent of all alcohol consumed.

The social nature of the mortality crisis is underscored by the fact that these lifestyle practices are especially characteristic of middle-age, working-class males. This social group, not surprisingly, is largely responsible for the decline in male longevity. Social class is once again important, yet in the former socialist countries it is the health lifestyles of the working class—not so much the lower class—causing premature deaths from heart disease and alcohol-related incidents. The epicenter of the downturn in life expectancy during the Soviet period and today is Russia, where 2000 figures show Russian males living 58.9 years on average, some 5.1 years less than in 1965. Russian women lived 71.8 years in 2000 compared with 72.1 years in 1965. Only 76.2 percent of Russian men and 91.3 percent of women currently reach the age of 50 years. Elsewhere, in countries like the Czech Republic, Poland, and Hungary, the situation has improved or is improving, but in Russia and many other former socialist states, problems remain.

Developing Countries

Inequities in health are even more striking in developing countries characterized by extensive poverty, such as those in South Asia and Africa. Modern medical care is an unaffordable luxury for many urban dwellers and virtually nonexistent in rural areas. In such countries, health policy is usually oriented toward just meeting basic needs, such as treating the sick, rather than prevention or the expansion of specialized services. Whereas levels of health are much worse in some countries than in others, life expectancy in developing nations has generally improved (Gallagher, Stewart, and Stratton 2000; Kuate-Defo and Diallo 2002). Widespread use of immunizations and the effective treatment of diarrhea with oral fluids have saved millions of lives. Nevertheless, the low levels of health and life expectancy are appalling by Western standards. Overall life expectancy in 2000 in Mozambique was 31.3 years, Zambia 33 years, Burundi 33.4 years, Central African Republic 34.1 years, Somalia 35.1 years, and Uganda 35.7 years.

Much of the blame for low life expectancy in Africa south of the Sahara is due to the massive AIDS epidemic. Of the over 23 million people with HIV worldwide, some 95 percent of the total live in developing countries and 70 percent are in sub-Saharan Africa (Gilbert and Walker 2002). In some African countries, 20 percent to 35 percent of the total population is HIV-infected as the virus spreads through society affecting people from all walks of life largely through heterosexual intercourse. For example, about one in eight of all adults between the ages of 15 and 49 years are infected in South Africa. The majority are women, who are especially disadvantaged throughout Africa by poverty, a heavy workload, lack of access to health services, and low social status and decision-making power (Berhane et al. 2001).

AIDS is not the only problem, however, as communicable diseases are more prevalent in developing countries despite the epidemiological transition to chronic illnesses. Africa's burden of disease is still marked by very high communicable disease morbidity, including high rates of tuberculosis, malaria, and other infectious diseases. As H. van Rensburg and Charles Ngwena (2001) explain: "Africa's health status, burden of disease, and health care needs are conspicuously shaped by poverty, malnutrition, infectious diseases, armed conflict, drought, famine, inadequate access to primary and secondary education, lack of safe water, sanitation, and a range of socioeconomic factors propelling inequitable distribution of resources" (p. 369). Poverty underlies most of the social conditions promoting poor health (Gilbert and Walker 2002). About half of the entire population of Africa south of the Sahara lives in poverty. In countries like Niger, where over 90 percent of the population lives on $2 a day or less and the government spends three times more on international debt repayment than health and education, prospects for improvement in health care delivery are poor (Rensberg and Ngwena 2001).

Class is still important in determining the health of people in developing societies, as the upper classes live the longest, with the class gradient much steeper and even smaller at the top than in industrialized nations. In both low-income and middle-income countries, including not only African nations but countries in Asia (i.e., Thailand and Indonesia) and Latin America (i.e., Dominican Republic, Venezuela, Brazil, and Mexico), wide gaps in health and health care exist between socioeconomic strata (Braveman and Tarimo 2002). Roberto Castro (2001), for example, documents

socioeconomic differences in health problems in Mexico, and Everardo Nuñes (2001) describes health inequities in Brazil, where over 30 percent of the population lives in poverty.

CONCLUSION

This chapter has shown that inequalities in health exist globally and are based on a number of factors, especially social class but also race and gender. Health becomes a social problem when particular segments of the population are deprived of healthy living conditions and adequate health care. Although people are living longer today than ever before in most countries of the world, there are indications that disparities in health are increasing between social strata on a global basis just as economic inequalities are widening (Braveman and Tarimo 2002). As Lahelma (2001:88) points out, egalitarian policies need to be implemented that aim at improving the health of the most disadvantaged groups, reducing the gaps between other strata, and improving the overall level of health of the population as a whole. This will take time, money, and commitment to the goals. But presently there is little progress in this direction on a worldwide scale, and health remains a major global social problem.

REFERENCES

Adevi, O., G. Chellaraji, E. Goldstein, A. Preker, and D. Ringold. 1997. "Health Status during the Transition in Central and Eastern Europe: Development in Reverse?" *Health Policy and Planning* 12:132–45.

Adonis, A. and S. Pollard. 1997. *A Class Act: The Myth of Britain's Classless Society.* London, England: Penguin.

Annandale, E. 1998. *The Sociology of Health and Medicine.* Oxford, England: Polity Press.

Arber, S. 1989. "Gender and Class Inequities in Health: Understanding the Differentials." Pp. 250–79 in *Health Inequalities in European Countries,* edited by A. Fox. Aldershot, England: Gower.

———. 1993. "Chronic Illness over the Life Course: Class Inequalities among Men and Women in Britain." Pp. 39–64 in *Medical Sociology: Research on Chronic Illness,* edited by T. Abel, U. Gerhardt, J. Siegrist, and W. Heuvel. Bonn, Germany: Informationszentrum Sozialwissenschaften.

Arber, S. and H. Thomas. 2000. "From Women's Health to a Gender Analysis of Health." Pp. 94–113 in *The Blackwell Companion to Medical Sociology,* edited by W. Cockerham. Oxford, England: Blackwell.

Beckett, M. 2000. "Converging Health Inequalities in Later Life—An Artifact of Mortality Selection?" *Journal of Health and Social Behavior* 41:106–19.

Berhane, Y., Y. Gossaye, M. Emmelin, and U. Hogberg. 2001. "Women's Health in a Rural Setting in Societal Transition in Ethiopia." *Social Science & Medicine* 53:1525–39.

Blaxter, M. 1990. *Health and Lifestyles.* London, England: Tavistock.

Borooah, V. 1999. "Occupational Class and Probability of Long-Term Limiting Illness." *Social Science & Medicine* 49:253–66.

Braithwaite, R. and S. Taylor, eds. 1992. *Health Issues in the Black Community.* San Francisco, CA: Jossey-Bass.

Braveman, P. and E. Tarimo. 2002. "Social Inequalities in Health within Countries: Not Only an Issue for Affluent Nations." *Social Science & Medicine* 54:1621–35.

Calnan, M. 1987. *Health & Illness: The Lay Perspective.* London, England: Tavistock.

Castro, R. 2001. "Medical Sociology in Mexico." Pp. 214–32 in *The Blackwell Companion to Medical Sociology,* edited by W. Cockerham. Oxford, England: Blackwell.

Center for Health Statistics. 2002. *Health, United States, 2002.* Washington, DC: U.S. Government Printing Office.

Centers for Disease Control and Prevention. 2002. "Annual Smoking-Attributable Mortality, Years of Potential Life Lost, and Economic Costs—United States, 1995–1999." *Morbidity & Mortality Weekly Report* 51:300–302.

Chandola, T. 2000. "Social Class Differences in Mortality Using the New UK National Statistics Socio-Economic Classification." *Social Science & Medicine* 50:641–49.

Cockerham, W. 1997. "The Social Determinants of the Decline in Life Expectancy in Russia and Eastern Europe: A Lifestyle Explanation." *Journal of Health and Social Behavior* 38:117–30.

——. 1999. *Health and Social Change in Russia and Eastern Europe.* London, England: Routledge.

——. 2000a. "The Sociology of Health Behavior and Health Lifestyles." Pp. 159–71 in *Handbook of Health Behavior.* 5th ed., edited by C. Bird, P. Conrad, and A. Fremont. Upper Saddle River, NJ: Prentice Hall.

——. 2000b. "Health Lifestyles in Russia." *Social Science & Medicine* 51:1313-24.

——. 2004. *Medical Sociology.* 9th ed. Upper Saddle River, NJ: Prentice Hall.

Cockerham, W., H. Hattori, and Y. Yamori. 2000. "The Social Gradient in Life Expectancy: The Contrary Case of Okinawa in Japan." *Social Science & Medicine* 51:115–22.

Cockerham, W., A. Rütten, and T. Abel. 1997. "Conceptualizing Health Lifestyles: Moving beyond Weber." *Sociological Quarterly* 38:601–22.

Coleman, D. and J. Salt. 1992. *The British Population: Patterns, Trends, and Processes.* Oxford, England: Oxford University Press.

Cooper, H. 2002. "Investigating Socio-Economic Explanations for Gender and Ethnic Inequalities in Health." *Social Science & Medicine* 54:693–706.

Dahrendorf, R. 1979. *Life Chances.* Chicago, IL: University of Chicago Press.

Denton, M. and V. Walters. 1999. "Gender Differences in Structural and Behavioral Determinants of Health: An Analysis of the Social Production of Health." *Social Science & Medicine* 48:1221–35.

Dmitrieva, E. 2001. "The Russian Health Care Experiment: Transition of the Health Care System and Rethinking the Sociology of Medicine." Pp. 320–33 in *The Blackwell Companion to Medical Sociology,* edited by W. Cockerham. Oxford, England: Blackwell.

Drever, F. and M. Whitehead. 1997. *Health Inequalities: Decennial Supplement.* London, England: HMSO.

Ellison, G. 2002. "Letting the Gini out of the Bottle? Challenges Facing the Relative Income Hypothesis." *Social Science and Medicine* 54:561–76.

Evans, R., M. Barer, and T. Marmor, eds. 1994. *Why Are Some People Healthy and Others Not?* New York: Aldine DeGruyter.

Field, M. 2000. "The Health and Demographic Crisis in Post-Soviet Russia: A Two-Phase Development." Pp. 11–42 in *Russia's Torn Safety Nets,* edited by M. Field and J. Twigg. New York: St. Martin's.

Frohlich, N. and C. Mustard. 1996. "A Regional Comparison and Health Indices in a Canadian Province." *Social Science & Medicine* 42:1273–81.

Gallagher, E., T. Stewart, and T. Stratton. 2000. "The Sociology of Health in Developing Countries." Pp. 389–97 in *Handbook of Medical Sociology.* 5th ed., edited by C. Bird, P. Conrad, and A. Fremont. Upper Saddle River, NJ: Prentice Hall.

Gilbert, L. and L. Walker. 2000. "Treading the Path of Least Resistance: HIV/AIDS and Social Inequality—A

South African Case Study." *Social Science and Medicine* 54:1093–110.

Gravelle, H., J. Wildman, and M. Sutton. 2002. "Income, Income Inequality and Health: What Can We Learn from Aggregate Data?" *Social Science & Medicine* 54:577–89.

Grzywacz, J. and N. Marks. 2001. "Social Inequalities and Exercise during Adulthood: Toward an Ecological Perspective." *Journal of Health and Social Behavior* 42:202–20.

Haywood, M., E. Crimmins, T. Miles, and Y. Yang. 2000. "The Significance of Socioeconomic Status in Explaining the Racial Gap in Chronic Health Conditions." *American Sociological Review* 65:910–30.

Hemström, Ö. 1999. "Explaining Differential Rates of Mortality Decline for Swedish Men and Women: A Time-Series Analysis." *Social Science & Medicine* 49:1759–77.

——. 2000. "Society, Health, and Health Care in Sweden." Pp. 298–318 in *The Blackwell Companion to Medical Sociology,* edited by W. Cockerham. Oxford, England: Blackwell.

Hertzman, C. 1995. *Environment and Health in Central and Eastern Europe.* Washington, DC: World Bank.

House, J., J. Lepkowski, A. Kinney, R. Mero, R. Kessler, and A. Herzog. 1994. "The Social Stratification of Aging and Health." *Journal of Health and Social Behavior* 35:213–34.

Humphries, K. and E. Doorslaer. 2000. "Income-Related Health Inequality in Canada." *Social Science & Medicine* 50:663–71.

Janeèková, H. 2001. "Transformation of the Health Care System in the Czech Republic—A Sociological Perspective." Pp. 367–74 in *The Blackwell Companion to Medical Sociology,* edited by W. Cockerham. Oxford, England: Blackwell.

Jarvis, M. and J. Wardle. 1999. "Social Patterning of Individual Health Behaviours: The Case of Cigarette Smoking." Pp. 240–55 in *Social Determinants of Health,* edited by M. Marmot and R. Wilkinson. Oxford, England: Oxford University Press.

Judge, K., J. Mulligan, and M. Benzeval. 1998. "Income Inequality and Population Health." *Social Science & Medicine* 46:567–79.

Kawachi, I., B. Kennedy, K. Lochner, and D. Prothrow-Stith. 1997. "Social Capital, Income Inequality, and Mortality." *American Journal of Public Health* 87:1491–98.

Knesebeck, O. and J. Johannes Siegrist. 2000. "Medical Sociology in Germany." Pp. 287–97 in *The Blackwell Companion to Medical Sociology,* edited by W. Cockerham. Oxford, England: Blackwell.

Krieger, N., D. Rowley, A. Herman, B. Avery, and M. Phillips. 1993. "Racism, Sexism, and Social Class: Implications for Studies of Health, Disease, and Well-Being." *American Journal of Preventive Medicine* 9:82–122.

Kuate-Defo, B. and K. Diallo. 2002. "Geography of Child Mortality Clustering within African Families." *Health & Place* 8:93–117.

Kunst, A., F. Groenhof, J. Mackenbach, and the EU Working Group on Socioeconomic Inequalities in Health. 1998. "Mortality by Occupational Class among Men in 11 European Countries." *Social Science & Medicine* 46:1459–76.

Lahelma, E. 2000. "Health and Social Stratification." Pp. 64–93 in *The Blackwell Companion to Medical Sociology,* edited by W. Cockerham. Oxford, England: Blackwell.

Lahelma, E., S. Arber, K. Kivelä, and E. Roos. 2002. "Multiple Roles and Health among British and Finnish Women: The Influence of Socioeconomic Circumstances." *Social Science & Medicine* 54:727–40.

Lahelma, E., S. Arber, O. Rahkonen, and K. Silventoinen. 2000. "Widening or Narrowing Inequalities in Health? Comparing Britain and Finland from the 1980s to the 1990s." *Sociology of Health & Illness* 22:110–36.

Lahelma, E., K. Kivelä, E. Roos, T. Tuominen, E. Dahl, F. Diderichsen, J. Elstad, I. Lissau, O. Lundberg, O. Rahkonen, N. Rasmussen, and M. Yngwe. 2002. "Analysing Changes in Health Inequalities in the Nordic Welfare States." *Social Science & Medicine* 55:609–25.

Laumann, E. and Y. Youm. 2001. "Racial/Ethnic Group Differences in the Prevalence of Sexually Transmitted Diseases in the United States: A Network Explanation." Pp. 327–438 in *Sex, Love, and Health in America,* edited by E. Laumann and R. Michael. Chicago, IL: University of Chicago Press.

Lillie-Blanton, M. and T. LaVeist. 1996. "Race/Ethnicity, the Social Environment, and Health." *Social Science & Medicine* 36:441–50.

Link, B. and J. Phelan. 2000. "Evaluating the Fundamental Cause Explanation for Social Disparities in Health." Pp. 47–67 in *Handbook of Medical Sociology.* 5th ed., edited by C. Bird, P. Conrad, and A. Fremont. Upper Saddle River, NJ: Prentice Hall.

Lostao, L., E. Regidor, P. Aïach, and V. Domínguez. 2001. "Social Inequalities in Ischaemic Heart and

Cerebrovascular Disease Mortality in Men: Spain and France, 1980–1982 and 1988–1990." *Social Science & Medicine* 52:1879–87.

Lupton, D. 2000. "Health, Illness, and Social Policy in Australia." Pp. 441–55 in *The Blackwell Companion to Medical Sociology,* edited by W. Cockerham. Oxford, England: Blackwell.

Lynch, J., G. Kaplan, E. Pamuk, R. Cohen, K. Heck, J. Balfour, and I. Yen. 1998. "Income Inequality and Mortality in Metropolitan Areas of the United States." *American Journal of Public Health* 88:1071–80.

Lynch, J., G. Smith, M. Hillemeier, M. Shaw, T. Raghunathan, and G. Kaplan. 2001. "Income Inequality, the Psychosocial Environment, and Health: Comparisons of Wealthy Nations." *Lancet* 358:194–200.

Macintyre, S. 1997. "The Black Report and Beyond: What Are the Issues?" *Social Science & Medicine* 44:723–45.

Marmot, M. 1996. "The Social Pattern of Health and Disease." Pp. 42–67 in *Health and Social Organization,* edited by D. Blane, E. Brunner, and R. Wilkinson. London, England: Routledge.

Marmot, M., M. Shipley, and G. Rose. 1984. "Inequalities in Death—Specific Explanations of a General Pattern." *Lancet* 83:1003–06.

Marmot, M., G. Smith, S. Stansfeld, C. Patel, F. North, J. Head, I. White, E. Brunner, and A. Feeney. 1991. "Health Inequalities among British Civil Servants: The Whitehall II Study." *Lancet* 337:1387–93.

McDonough, P., V. Walters, and L. Strohschein. 2002. "Chronic Stress and the Social Patterning of Women's Health in Canada." *Social Science & Medicine* 54:767–82.

McDonough, P., D. Williams, J. House, and G. Duncan. 1999. "Gender and the Socioeconomic Gradient in Mortality." *Journal of Health and Social Behavior* 40:17–31.

Mielck, A., A. Cavelaars, U. Helmert, K. Martin, O. Winkelhake, and A. Kunst. 2000. "Comparison of Health Inequalities between East and West Germany." *European Journal of Public Health* 10:262-7.

Mirowsky, J., C. Ross, and J. Reynolds. 2000. "Links between Social Status and Health Status." Pp. 47–67 in *Handbook of Medical Sociology.* 5th ed., edited by C. Bird, P. Conrad, and A. Fremont. Upper Saddle River, NJ: Prentice Hall.

Moss, N. 2002. "Gender Equity and Socioeconomic Inequality: A Framework for the Patterning of Women's Health." *Social Science and Medicine* 54:649–61.

Mulatu, M. and C. Schooler. 2002. "Causal Connections between Socio-Economic Status and Health: Reciprocal Effects and Mediating Mechanisms." *Journal of Health and Social Behavior* 43:22–41.

National Center for Health Statistics. 2001. *Health, United States, 2001.* Washington, DC: U.S. Government Printing Office.

———. 2002. *Health, United States, 2002.* Washington, DC: U.S. Government Printing Office.

Nettleton, S. 1995. *The Sociology of Health and Illness.* Oxford, England: Polity Press.

Nuñes, E. 2001. "Social Science and Health in Brazil." Pp. 233–44 in *The Blackwell Companion to Medical Sociology,* edited by W. Cockerham. Oxford, England: Blackwell.

Orfali, K. 2000. "The French Paradoxes." Pp. 263–86 in *The Blackwell Companion to Medical Sociology,* edited by W. Cockerham. Oxford, England: Blackwell.

Ostrowska, N. 2001. "In and Out of Communism: The Macrosocial Context of Health in Poland." Pp. 334–46 in *The Blackwell Companion to Medical Sociology,* edited by W. Cockerham. Oxford, England: Blackwell.

Pappas, G., S. Queen, W. Hadden, and G. Fisher. 1993. "The Increasing Disparity in Mortality between Socioeconomic Groups in the United States, 1960 and 1986." *New England Journal of Medicine* 87:811–16.

Piperno, A. and F. DiOrio. 1990. "Social Differences in Health and Utilization of Health Services in Italy." *Social Science & Medicine* 31:305–12.

Power, C. and C. Hertzman. 1997. "Social and Behavioral Pathways Linking Early Life and Adult Disease." *British Medical Bulletin* 53:210–21.

Regidor, E., J. Gutierrez-Fisac, V. Domínguez, M. Calle, and P. Navarro. 2002. "Comparing Social Inequalities in Health in Spain: 1987 and 1995/97." *Social Science & Medicine* 54:1323–32.

Reid, I. 1998. *Class in Britain.* Cambridge, England: Polity Press.

Rensberg, H., van and C. Ngwena. 2001. "Health and Health Care in South Africa against an African Background." Pp. 365–91 in *The Blackwell Companion to Medical Sociology,* edited by W. Cockerham. Oxford, England: Blackwell.

Robert, S. and J. House. 1994. "SES and Health over the Life Course." Pp. 253–74 in *Aging and Quality of Life,* edited by P. Abeles, H. Gift, and M. Ory. New York: Springer.

———. 2000. "Socioeconomic Inequalities in Health: An Enduring Sociological Problem." Pp. 79–96 in *Handbook of Medical Sociology.* 5th ed., edited by

C. Bird, P. Conrad, and A. Fremont. Upper Saddle River, NJ: Prentice Hall.

Rogers, R., R. Hummer, C. Nam, and K. Peters. 1996. "Demographic, Socioeconomic, and Behavioral Factors Affecting Ethnic Mortality by Cause." *Social Forces* 74:1419–38.

Rogers, R. and E. Powell-Griner. 1991. "Life Expectancies of Cigarette Smokers and Nonsmokers in the United States." *Social Science & Medicine* 32:1151–9.

Ross, C. and J. Mirowsky. 2001. "Neighborhood Disadvantage, Disorder, and Health." *Journal of Health and Social Behavior* 42:258–76.

Ross, C. and C. Wu. 1995. "The Links between Education and Health." *American Sociological Review* 60:719–45.

Schoenbaum, M. and T. Waidmann. 1997. "Race, Socioeconomic Status, and Health: Accounting for Race Differences in Health." *Journal of Gerontology* 52B:61–73.

Shaw, M., D. Dorling, and G. Smith. 1999. "Poverty, Social Exclusion, and Minorities." Pp. 211–39 in *Social Determinants of Health,* edited by M. Marmot and R. Wilkinson. Oxford, England: Oxford University Press.

Splawski, I., K. Timothy, M. Tateyama, C. Clancy, A. Malhotra, A. Beggs, F. Cappuccio, G. Sagnella, R. Kass, and M. Keating. 2002. "Variant of SCN5A Sodium Channel Implicated in Risk of Cardiac Arrhythmia." *Science* 297:1333–6.

Steptoe, A. and J. Wardle. 2001. "Health Behaviour, Risk Awareness and Emotional Well-Being in Students from Eastern Europe and Western Europe." *Social Science & Medicine* 53:1621–30.

Sundquist, J. and S. Johansson. 1997. "Indicators of Socio-Economic Position and Their Relation to Mortality in Sweden." *Social Science & Medicine* 45:1757–66.

Tulchinsky, T. and E. Varavikova. 1996. "Addressing the Epidemiologic Transition in the Former Soviet Union: Strategies for Health System and Public Health Reform in Russia." *American Journal of Public Health* 86:313–20.

Walters, V., P. McDonough, and L. Strohschein. 2002. "The Influence of Work, Household Structure, and Social, Personal and Material Resources on Gender Differences in Health: An Analysis of the 1994 Canadian National Population Health Survey." *Social Science & Medicine* 54:677–92.

Weber, M. 1978. *Economy and Society.* 2 vols. Edited and translated by G. Roth and C. Wittch. Berkeley, CA: University of California Press.

Wermuth, L. 2003. *Global Inequality and Human Needs: Health and Illness in an Increasingly Unequal World.* Boston, MA: Allyn & Bacon.

Wilkinson, R. 1992. "Income Distribution and Life Expectancy." *British Medical Journal* 304:165–68.

——. 1996. *Unhealthy Societies: The Afflictions of Inequality.* London, England: Routledge.

Williams, D. and C. Collins. 1995. "U.S. Socioeconomic and Racial Differences in Health: Patterns and Explanations." *Annual Review of Sociology* 21:349–86.

Winkleby, M., D. Jatulis, E. Frank, and S. Fortman. 1992. "Socioeconomic Status and Health: How Education, Income, and Occupation Contribute to Risk Factors for Cardiovascular Disease." *American Journal of Public Health* 82:816–20.

HOW MEDICAL CARE SYSTEMS BECOME SOCIAL PROBLEMS

ANDREW TWADDLE

University of Missouri, Columbia

Medical care has been an important social concern as far back as we have history. People have always wanted to forestall death, prevent disease, illness, and sickness, and find cures for their afflictions. Among the earliest specialized skills to be developed were the shaman, the "witch doctor," the "medicine person." Every known society makes some provision for responding to sickness, almost always by designating certain persons as healers and having a body of specialized knowledge that could be transmitted from one designated healer to another. As we entered the modern era, medical care became emblematic not just of the need to respond to disease and death but of modern science. It could be said that medicine replaced religion, physicians replaced priests, and hospitals replaced cathedrals, not just in their centrality to the society but in the amount of wealth they consumed.

In recent years, we have witnessed a call for the reform of medical care to reduce its cost to the society and its alleged inefficiencies. It is interesting that such critiques of medical care systems are almost a worldwide phenomenon. They are remarkably similar in content and rhetoric from country to country irrespective of the way in which the country itself or its medical care system is organized. I here consider the nature of the problems that these calls for reform seek to solve, the nature of the solutions being offered, and what all that might say about social problems in larger societies.

In this chapter, I define medical care systems vis-à-vis health problems and medical care. As part of that process, I distinguish democratic, professional, and market models for system organization. I then specify some criteria for a well-functioning system that set an internationally agreed-upon standard to assess when systems are problems. As part of that step, we identify major trends of the twentieth century that have made medical care systems in developed countries more problematic. Then I look at trends in the United States, Sweden, India, the third world, and transnational comparisons of medical care systems. Finally, I offer a brief discussion of medical care systems as social problems.

HEALTH PROBLEMS, MEDICAL CARE, AND MEDICAL CARE SYSTEMS

Perhaps the best way to focus on medical care systems is to first identify two related subjects that are excluded from this analysis: health problems and medical care, both of which are better suited to the chapter in this volume contributed by Professor Cockerham.

Health Problems

By health problems, I mean the events that befall individuals that fall within the jurisdiction of the medical care system. Mark Field (1982) called them the "five Ds"—death, disease, disability, discomfort, and dissatisfaction. I have referred to them as disease (physiological events that reduce capacities or reduce life expectancy), illness (subjective body state perceptions and/or feelings of competence), and sickness (social definition of health identity based on participation in the social order).[1] These are problems that people face that lead them to seek out healers, people with special competence in combating health problems.

While medical care and medical care systems are ways of dealing with health problems, the problems themselves are not part of the system but the "target"—to use Mark Field's term—*of* the system.

Medical Care

Medical care is a clinical activity focused on the diagnosis and treatment of disease. It is what takes place when a person who is symptomatic encounters a health care professional. There is a considerable social science literature on the professions of medicine and nursing, and a smaller literature on other health care professions. There are also studies on health care utilization, professional-patient interaction, technical quality, and quality of care, all of which are socially structured.

Medical care is an activity *directed toward individuals* with health problems. It takes place *within* a variety of systems. While medical care systems can influence the distribution and frequency of some practices, the content of medical care is recognizable regardless of the system within which it is practiced. It is not in itself a part of the system.

Medical Care Systems

It is when we look at the organizations developed to provide medical care in response to health problems and the ways in which they are connected that we can talk of a *system* of medical care. The idea of a system is a set of interconnected components. Field (1982) wrote about the health system as having several such components, some sociological and some cultural. He saw the sociological components as personnel (who must be recruited, trained, and allocated) using technologies (that must be developed through research) to provide services (that must be organized) to address problems of mortality and morbidity. We might make a partial list as follows:

Personnel—physicians, chiropractors, nurses, physical therapists, social workers, laboratory technicians, ward managers, pharmacists, and others in the more than 2,000 occupational titles found in the medical care system as well as others that might be found in other systems such as shamans, faith healers, Christian Science practitioners; and so forth.

Organizations—colleges, universities (especially medical, nursing, and health-related profession faculties) that select, screen, and train personnel; hospitals and clinics; laboratories; pharmaceutical companies; medical equipment manufacturers; and so forth.

Technologies—stethoscopes, drugs, heart-lung machines, x-ray machines, endoscopes, and a vast array of other equipment used in the diagnosis and treatment of disease; drugs, hypnosis, biofeedback, and other techniques used to combat illness; occupational therapies, prostheses, and other techniques used to combat sickness.

Regulation—legislatures, accreditation agencies, licensing boards, disciplinary boards, public health inspections, and other agencies designed to regulate the system and assure quality.

There are many ways in which these components can be organized. Field, for example, delineated five

Facet	Democratic	Professional	Market
Definition	Decision making by citizens or representatives accountable to the citizenry	Decision making by experts with special training and credentials based on abstract knowledge	Decision making by consumers under conditions where there are a large number of providers acting independently and perfect knowledge of price and quality
Dominant actors	Political parties, politicians, civil servants	Professionals	Business interests
Dominant value	Equity/equality	Effectiveness/quality	Efficiency
Dominant goals	Preservation and extension of democracy, influence in decision making	Enhancement of knowledge, improvement of technique and capacity, application to problems within domain of expertise	Profit
Mode of regulation or control	Elections, opposition parties	Socialization, ethical standards, informal sanctions, formal sanctions imposed by colleagues	Competition

Figure 18.1   Modes of Medical Care Organization

types of medical care systems: anomic (e.g., nineteenth-century United States and Europe), pluralistic (e.g., twentieth-century United States), insurance/social security (e.g., France, Japan, Canada), national health service (e.g., U.K.), and socialized (e.g., Soviet Union).

Another approach has been to classify health systems by types designating their founding architects: Beveridge (U.K.), Bismark (Germany), and Semenko (USSR). The first of these is a national health system in which the national government collects taxes, provides the infrastructure, and employs the personnel (directly in the case of specialist, indirectly by contract for primary care). The second is a social insurance system in which people are required to purchase health insurance to purchase care in a private "market." The last is a state-provided system that disappeared with the collapse of the Soviet Union.

Yet another has been to characterize societies according to level of development, capitalist versus socialist economies, and degree of Western medicine vis-à-vis other practices (Roemer 1977), or along a continuum of the degree to which the market organizes economic activity.

The approach I follow in this chapter is one developed in conjunction with a study of medical care reform in Sweden (Twaddle 1999) and used in a recent collaborative study of medical care reform in 20 countries (Twaddle 2002). In this formulation, there are three different ways in which human services, including medical care, can be organized. Each differs in the kinds of people who dominate the system and make the key decisions, the kinds of values central to those who dominate the system, the goals of the system, and the most important means of social control used to regulate the system. I have called these types democratic, professional, and market (see Figure 18.1).

Democratic Systems

A democratic system is one in which decision making is done by citizens or their representatives. The important feature is that decision makers are accountable to the citizens. In such a system, political parties, politicians, and civil servants are the key decision makers, with the former having responsibility for policy considerations and the latter for administration. A democratic system tends to place greater weight on the value of equality and equity, and the exercise of the democratic process itself is a dominant goal. There is great concern under such systems for there to be broad, even universal, access to medical care. The main mode of regulation is through elections and the activity of opposition parties.

Professional Systems

A professional system is one in which decision making is done by experts who have special training and credentials based on abstract knowledge. The key decision makers are professionals, in the case of medical care almost exclusively physicians. Professionals tend to emphasize the value of effectiveness or quality. Medical care in such systems tends to emphasize state-of-the-art technology and the skillful application of knowledge to the patients who are treated in the system. The dominant goals of a professional system tend to be the enhancement of knowledge and improving capacities in diagnosis and treatment. The main mode of regulation is the socialization of professionals, the use of informal sanctions, and rarely the use of formal sanctions imposed by colleagues when there are extreme instances of poor quality practice.

Market Systems

A market system is one in which decision making is done by customers who make choices from available services based on conditions where there are a large number of independent providers and transparency regarding price and quality. In such a system, medical care is seen as a commodity not substantially different from clothing, automobiles, laundry detergent, or any other of a myriad of things people purchase in their daily lives. In a market system, business interests dominate, the core value is efficiency, and the dominant goal is profit. The mode of regulation is competition.

* * *

A few brief comments may be in order here. First, a kind of atomistic market system could be said to have characterized Europe and North America during most of the seventeenth to nineteenth centuries.

Second, toward the end of the nineteenth century, the professions, particularly medicine, managed to gain control of their work and achieve a substantial degree of autonomy in the selection, training, and discipline of members of the profession as well as the social and economic terms of "delivering" medical care (Freidson 1972a; Starr 1982; Twaddle and Hessler 1987). The professions characterized their work in direct opposition to the market. Medical care was not a commodity. Patients were vulnerable to exploitation and lacked the knowledge to know when they were getting good or poor service. Hence, it was important that the professional-patient relationship be governed by ethical norms that were strikingly in opposition to the caveat emptor of the marketplace. To be a professional was to accept a fiduciary relationship vis-à-vis the patient. The patient must be able to trust the physician to diagnose and treat according to the needs of the patient, not the profitability of procedures.

Third, during the twentieth century, most medical care systems in the developed world were organized along democratic lines. Professionals were left in control of clinical decisions (diagnosis and treatment), but the organization of an increasingly large and expensive system was transferred to political authorities. In every developed nation, with the conspicuous exception of the United States, national health insurance or national health systems were created, beginning in the 1920s, but with the greatest activity in the 1950s to 1970s (Twaddle 2002). One effect was a substantial broadening of access to medical care to larger segments of national populations.

Fourth, beginning in the United States in the late 1940s, not-for-profit prepaid group practices, such as Kaiser-Permanente in Portland, Oregon, demonstrated that they could deliver high-quality medical care at a lower cost than was the case for the general population, most of whom were covered by indemnity insurance plans. They did this not by practicing more aggressive preventive medicine (erroneously being designated as health maintenance organizations or HMOs) but by providing care in the least expensive setting suited to the case.

Fifth, beginning in the United States in the 1960s, as an unintended consequence of the passage of Medicare, investor-owned, for-profit corporations entered into health care delivery, starting with the nursing home sector. By the year 2000, a large portion of the U.S. medical care system was owned by such corporations. These corporations bought or built large numbers of hospitals and organized them into systems to reduce duplication of services, control costs, and increase profits. Many expanded into other countries, with the result that there are corporate medical care systems that are truly transnational in scope.

Sixth, in a very short period around 1980, only partly in response to rapidly rising medical care costs, a seemingly unified global effort was made in countries with democratic systems or professional systems to introduce "market mechanisms" into the medical care systems. The most widespread of these originated in the United Kingdom and tried to separate "purchasers" and "sellers" of medical care, creating competition in the public sector. Another was the use of U.S.-initiated diagnosis-related groups (DRGs) to account for and reimburse medical expenses. It has been claimed that medical care is inefficient and that competition, markets, and privatization will make it more efficient. In every instance, these reforms were initiated by the internationally exposed business elites.[2]

Seventh, we should note two limits of the democratic-professional-market classification. On the one hand, these are ideal types that have value for focusing discussion, but they are not found in pure form anywhere. Some aspects of all three types can be found in most systems. On the other hand, there are some historical systems that cannot be accounted for in this typology, such as the old Soviet system, or what may be an emerging monopolistic system. When there is a monopoly, either of an undemocratic state or a corporate monopoly, public accountability disappears, possibly compromising efficiency, effectiveness, and equity.

Medical care systems are important in their own right in providing health care to a population. It is not only possible, but demonstrable, that a society can have a favorable profile of health problems and excellent medical care provided in a system that yields poor mortality and morbidity outcomes (viz., the United States). It is also possible to have a less favorable profile of health problems, poorly resourced medical care, and still have an excellent system that yields good mortality and morbidity outcomes (viz., Cuba).

How Can Medical Care Be a Social Problem?

A first approach to this question may be to identify features of a well-functioning medical care system. In the public health literature, there is a reasonable consensus on several such features. A good medical care system provides services that are

- *Available.* The kinds of technology and treatment that people need are present in locations where people can reach them. Adequate availability differs with the type of service under consideration, most important the frequency and speed with which it is needed. The distribution of personnel is a major issue here.
- *Accessible.* It is not enough that services be present; people in need must be able to make use of them. That is, there should be no significant barriers to prevent services from being employed where needed. Plant architecture, charges for services, personnel attitudes, working hours, and screening procedures may all make service less accessible.
- *Acceptable.* Medical services should be provided in a manner that does not offend the values or scruples of the population. They should be of types that seem reasonable, provided under conditions that preserve the dignity and self-respect of patients. They should help solve health problems rather than worsen them.
- *Relevant.* Services should be of a type that meets the needs of people they are intended to serve and that are appropriate to the kinds of health problems they have.

- *Affordable.* The society must be able to absorb the cost of services. The system must be designed so as not to bankrupt the larger systems it ostensibly supports.
- *Flexible.* Services should be adaptable to individual needs, local conditions, and changes in the populations being served.

A system that fails to provide services that meet these criteria—to some degree not easy to specify—will be seen by at least some members of that society as being a problem requiring collective action.

In the developed world, there have been some trends that have led to medical care systems being considered more problematic than in the past. We can argue that this is not despite, but largely because of, the rapid growth of knowledge and technological capacity in the system (see Figure 18.2).

If we go back to the beginning of the twentieth century, we find that most medical care was of poor quality relative to the state of medical knowledge. The germ theory of disease, synthesized and demonstrated in the 1870s by Pasteur and others, was still not incorporated into medical practice. In different ways in different countries, steps were taken, generally at the instigation of those physicians who were university trained and some economic elites, to create a system of medical education with the following characteristics: affiliation with universities, systematic training in core biophysical sciences, supervised clinical training, and licensing examinations for graduates as a condition for entering practice.

The establishment of modern medical education had a number of sequels: an explosion of knowledge and demand for medical care, increasing work pressures on practitioners, expanding technology, consolidation of medical practice in hospitals and clinics, specialization and rationalization of work (which is fragmentation of services from the patient's perspective), and rapidly increasing costs of medical care.[3]

Whereas one could argue that there was a "crisis of competence" at the beginning of the twentieth century, there was a dual "crisis of alienation" and a "fiscal crisis" by the 1970s. The crisis of alienation refers to the loss of control by patients and the growing autonomy of the medical profession *within the physician-patient relationship.* The knowledge gap between the professional and patient had grown enormously; the professional-patient encounter had shifted from the home of the patient to the reception; the terms of payment had become less negotiable; and the social class gap between physician and patient had grown to a point where it was difficult for the average physician to understand the social circumstances of the average patient.

The fiscal crisis stemmed from the enormous infrastructure of medicine, the massive investments in technology, the overspecialization of physicians, and the inefficient use of services. By the end of the 1970s, double-digit inflation of medical care costs was all but universal in the developed world. The cost of medical care was rising at a rate far in excess of the economies of the countries it ostensibly served. By the 1980s, virtually every developed nation was searching for a way to "cap" the rise in medical care expenditures. How they went about this varied, but all faced the prospect of a medical care system—however it was organized and financed—that could bankrupt the country. Let us consider a few examples.

The United States of America

The United States has often been referred to as an "outlier," a country that does not fit the general pattern of the developed world with reference to medical care. As compared with the rest of that world, it has the least developed social welfare sector, preferring a residual approach to welfare rather than an institutional approach.[4] It is the only developed country without a national system of health insurance and one of the few without a national health system. This is largely the result of a deep-seated cultural distrust of government. It has led to both higher than average levels of mortality and the most expensive medical care system in the world, what Wessen (2002) has called an ethic of "live free and die."

The Fiscal Crisis

One important characteristic of the way in which medical care was financed in the United States is that it is tied to employment. During World War II,

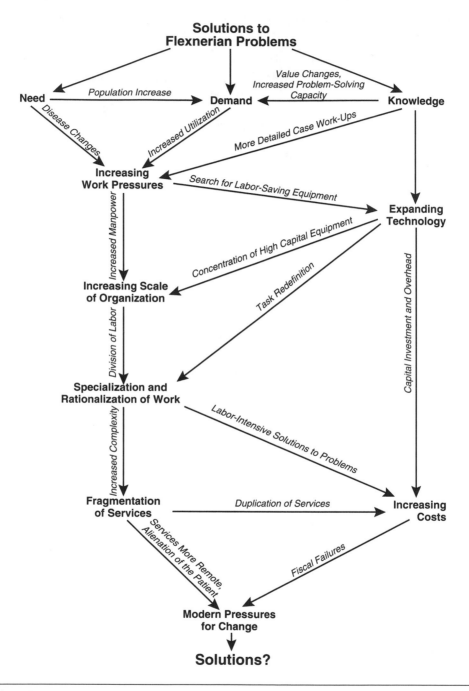

Figure 18.2   Trends in Medicine Affecting the Physician–Patient Relationship

industry was faced with trying to attract employees at a time when wages were not allowed to increase. They did so by offering expanded benefits, most centrally health insurance (Fein 1986).

The model in Figure 18.2 was initially developed in the context of the U.S. system. By the 1960s, the United States had the highest infant mortality and the lowest life expectancy of any developed country. It was partly in response that the National Institutes of Health were created and there was an enormous infusion of money into medical research.

The cost of medical care in the 1970s was increasing at a rate of approximately 15 percent per year, with the gross national product increasing at less than 3 percent. The cost of the medical care system per capita in 1997 was 2.3 times the median for the OECD (Organization for Economic Cooperation and Development) and 1.5 times that of the next most expensive system. Looked at another way, the United States spent about 4 percent of the gross national product on medical care at the close of World War II, 5.2 percent in 1960, 12.5 percent in 1990, and 13.5 percent by 1997 (Wessen 2002). Some estimates for 2001 put the percentage above 15.

As an attempt to control costs under Medicare, utilization review was established in hospitals. It had little impact on length of stay or the overall rise in medical care costs. By the 1970s, there were several attempts at the federal level to find some way of holding down medical expenditures. During the 1970s, there was an attempt to require "certificates of need" wherein hospitals would have to demonstrate a need for new investments before they could qualify for federal or state funds (Starr 1982). This also failed, as the boards of review tended to be composed of hospital administrators who would not turn down applications lest their own be compromised. There were other efforts to control costs, but none worked, largely because the United States had an atomistic system of medical care. Each unit stood on its own, making its own decisions, rising or falling on its ability to attract resources. There was little to no integration, leading to the charge that medical care was a "nonsystem."

In the meantime, corporations were increasingly concerned that the rise of medical care costs were an increasing burden to the cost of doing business. The cost of providing health insurance was eating into profits. The Washington Business Group on Health was founded in 1974 to support cost containment, including utilization review, Professional Service Review Organizations, and Health Systems Agencies, just as the Reagan administration was moving to dismantle them in a program of deregulation (Navarro 1994; Starr 1982). By the 1980s, this group was pushing quietly behind the scenes for the national government to take over health insurance to get it off the corporate budgets.

Insurance companies were also looking for ways to contain costs. They had not liked fee-for-service reimbursement for a long time (Freidson 1972b), and many preferred a system of capitation (where physicians are paid according to the number of patients registered in their practices) or by salary. They had taken initiatives to enter into agreements with physicians to provide care at lower rates to their customers, creating lists of "preferred providers" who would be on an approved list for people insured with that company. There were efforts to link primary care physicians with specific specialists as well (e.g., Himmelstein and Woolhandler 1993).

The unique approach taken in the United States was to organize medical care under the control of "private" insurance companies, what has been called *managed care*. This came about through the convergence of two initially separate developments: the creation of prepaid group practice and the emergence of investor-owned, for-profit medical care.

Prepaid Group Practice

At the close of World War II, Kaiser Industries, which had experience in providing medical care to workers who were on large projects isolated from urban centers,[5] decided to offer a plan to the public. They would hire a group of physicians and build a hospital in Portland, Oregon. People could subscribe to their service through their employers and receive comprehensive medical care for a single flat fee for the year. Enrolled patients not only got primary care; referrals to specialists also took place within the group practice, and hospital care was given by the Kaiser hospital. If the patient needed care the group could not provide, the patient would be referred outside the system at no additional out-of-pocket expense.

Kaiser Permanente quickly demonstrated that they could reduce the cost of medical care by about 40 percent as compared with the national average. Research directed at assessing quality of care has assessed claims that prepaid group practice is either of lower or higher quality as compared with fee-for-service practices. The result is that there seems to be no difference.

That model was extremely controversial among physicians, many of whom saw group practice as communism and suspected that Kaiser Permanente was withholding needed services (e.g., Mahoney 1973). The supporters of Kaiser Permanente claimed that they provided more aggressive preventive medicine, resulting in prepaid group practices being called health maintenance organizations (HMOs).[6]

The Nixon administration tried to promote HMOs as a way of capping costs. Enrollment increased over the next decade, but not to the degree that the government had hoped, reaching only 4 percent of the population by the early 1980s.

A few points are essential to understand subsequent historical developments. First, HMOs developed as *self-insured* systems of medical care delivery. Their patient populations were not the clients of commercial insurance companies. Second, they were offered as one alternative to employees. Kaiser Permanente *required employers to offer other options,* ensuring that nobody was forced into the HMO. Third, the HMO was originally a *not-for-profit* system of health care delivery. With that, let us explore the other major trend.

Investor-Owned, For-Profit Organizations

A much stronger move, however, was the emergence of *investor-owned, for-profit medical care organizations* (IOFPO). One consequence of the enactment of Medicare in 1965 was that nursing homes could be profitable while providing a decent level of care as "extended care facilities," providing up to 90 days of posthospital care. This created an environment where corporations entered the field and expanded to the ownership of hospitals. This movement resulted in the development of a number of huge corporations that owned chains of hospitals, often concentrated into regions where they could rationalize care in ways a more atomistic system could not.

Investor-owned, for-profit systems made decisions according to the profit potential of medical care, not on the basis of patient needs. They changed hospitals from physicians' workshops (where independent physicians admitted patients and strongly influenced policy) to places were physicians had to work within corporate rules.[7] Physicians lost autonomy and many saw corporate medicine as a threat to the profession, reducing medicine to a commodity to be marketed in the same manner as automobiles or clothing.[8]

From the end of World War II until the late 1980s, the proportion of the population with health insurance expanded to nearly 90 percent. During the economic crisis of the 1980s, businesses began to downsize, and many workers lost their jobs. Many others changed from full-time to part-time work. In both instances, they became uninsured. The percentage of the population with health insurance dropped. For the first time, a population that has always had economic security in the face of disease felt itself vulnerable, generating agitation for a political response to what was seen as a medical care crisis. The Jesse Jackson campaign of 1988 took national health insurance as a core proposal, and the Dukakis campaign advocated the right of everyone to have "basic health insurance" (Navarro 1994).

It was in the 1992 campaign that the issue came to a head. Polls indicated that approximately two-thirds of the U.S. population supported some form of national health program guaranteeing health insurance for everyone (Navarro 1994). The Clinton campaign made national health insurance its centerpiece, arguably creating his margin of victory. When the commission chaired by Hillary Clinton issued a report that (1) threatened the profits of the insurance companies and (2) failed to provide relief to corporations, the Business Round Table announced its opposition and the plan failed in Congress.[9]

Managed Care

With the failure of the Clinton Health Plan, the insurance companies moved to take control of the medical care system through the imposition of "managed care." In essence, the insurance companies, with the collaboration of employers, stopped writing indemnity insurance policies[10] and wrote new policies in which they limited coverage to physicians with whom they had a contract and set requirements that they approve in advance any expensive tests, referrals, or treatments.[11] The companies had promised the employers that they could reduce the cost of medical care by reducing "unnecessary" care and monitoring to see that the most efficient practices were used.

Managed care, the commercial control of medical care activity, has been controversial. First off, it has not resulted in a reduction of medical care costs. Instead, the cost of the system has increased at the same rate as was the case before the imposition of managed care. Increasingly, employers are coming to the conclusion that managed care has not been a solution to their cost problem. Physicians and other health professionals have been unhappy with managed care because it has infringed on clinical decision making, undermined patient trust in physicians, and undermined ethical control of patient care. Patients are unhappy because it has made the system more bureaucratic and less responsive to their needs. Insurance company executives are very happy with managed care. It has greatly increased corporate profits and the salaries of CEOs.

Indeed, this seems to be the new alignment on health policy regarding managed care. On the one side are the patients and professionals; on the other, the insurance companies. Employers tend to side with the insurance industry, but inconsistently. At issue is whether medicine will be (1) a professional activity where decisions are made by trained experts acting ethically on behalf of their patients or (2) a business, where profit potential will constrain and occasionally override professional judgement.[12]

Not on the table in the United States is the option of having a democratically controlled system where bodies accountable to the public organize medical care facilities and allocate resources, leaving clinical judgment to professionals. However, there is a "single payer" movement that seems to be slowly gathering strength. How influential it will become remains to be seen.

The problems of the U.S. system focus most sharply on accessibility and acceptability. With regard to accessibility, there has been a shift in economic activity that has resulted in secure full-time employment being reduced in favor of part-time work with no benefits. Since 1993, approximately 1.5 million people have lost their health insurance each year. Those who get medical care tend to get high-quality services, but too many cannot get care except at the threshold of death. Increasingly, people are finding it unacceptable for insurance clerks to participate in clinical decisions. In both these problems, the United States is unique on the world scene. The cost of medical care continues to increase rapidly. It is an intensely important problem, currently led by the increase in the cost of pharmaceuticals. The fiscal crisis remains unabated, a problem we share with many other countries.

Given that democratic control of the system has never been a large factor in the United States, it is not surprising that the system is poor with regard to equity. Where services are available and accessible, they tend to be of high quality, that is to say, effective. The private health insurance system is expensive and inefficient. Americans get less service for a higher price than any other people on the planet.

Sweden[13]

Whereas the United States is arguably the least developed welfare state in the developed world, Sweden is arguably the most highly developed. They had a provision for public medicine as early as the 1600s and public hospitals as early as the 1700s. The current system developed with the rapid expansion of the welfare state between 1950 and the early 1970s. In essence, it is a county-based system where the 26 counties own the hospitals, hire the medical staff, and raise the taxes to finance the system. The national government sets standards and oversees quality. Prior to the early 1980s, it could also control the allocation of technology and personnel (Sidel and Sidel 1983). The main problem with the Swedish medical care system as of 1980 was that it was overspecialized (only 14% of physicians were in primary care compared with 41% in the United States) and too focused on hospitals. The cost of the system was high even when the cost of discrete units of service were low.[14] That problem was being addressed with a program to expand primary care.

In the 1980s, Sweden undertook a number of reforms. In 1982, all responsibility for medical care was decentralized to the counties, which were given much more latitude in organizing services. Private practice expanded, and technologies that had been limited to regional hospitals moved down to the county hospital level. Both increased the cost of the system.[15] To counter this, there was a reform in 1984 (the "Dagmar Reform") that replaced fee-for-service reimbursement of private practice in favor of bloc grants to counties. The number of private physicians dropped by three-fifths in one year.

In 1991, there was a reform that transferred responsibility for care of the aged from the counties to the municipalities, a change that resulted in a sharp drop in the quality of care for the aged.[16] A successful part of that reform was a stipulation that municipalities were responsible for the medical care of "bed blockers" (hospital patients whose medical care is complete and who need a nursing home placement). It very much speeded the transfer of patients to nursing homes.

Another problem was that there were long waiting lists for treatment for certain conditions in the large cities. In 1992, an agreement was reached that if patients with those conditions were not treated by their own county within three months, they could seek care in any other county and their county would have to pay for it. Waiting lists all but melted away.

A short-lived reform was one that provided for each Swede to register with a physician who would be a point of service. It also allowed private physicians to compete freely with the public sector in providing that service. The number of private physicians increased, the cost of primary care expanded very rapidly, and the reform was repealed a year later by the next government.

An important experiment was carried out by the Federation of County Councils. Several counties were encouraged to undertake "market reforms" (largely introducing competition into the public sector), and several others were encouraged to find ways to cut costs in the context of a budget-driven system. After a few years, they made an assessment and found that the budget-driven systems were all more

successful in reducing costs (Landstingsförbundet 1995).

The overall thrust of all these reforms was to reduce national control of the system and to increase the influence of market forces. While those promoting reforms claimed that the system would be more efficient if more privatized and market controlled, there was no evidence to support that view. Indeed, the problems the system faced could be more easily solved because there were political units with the power to make decisions. A stronger case could be made that the faltering economy could no longer afford to have a comprehensive medical care system, but medical care was one of the few areas where the percentage of GDP spent was shrinking. The explanation for the reforms was ultimately political.

Beginning in the early 1970s, the employers and the right-wing party began a campaign to roll back the welfare state. They worked to frame the debate by providing "educational" materials to the schools. Neoliberal economic arguments were developed and promoted. Employers unilaterally withdrew from the accord that regulated labor-management negotiations. In the meantime, the Social Democrats were weakened by internal disputes over centralization and a neoliberal finance minister who prioritized inflation control over employment security. They alienated their base in the labor movement. In 1991, a right-of-center government attempted a major assault on the welfare state, only to be rebuffed in the next election.

The challenge to the welfare state, in which medical care was the centerpiece, came from the internationally exposed economic elites, who were seeking ways to maximize profits, mostly by becoming more competitive in international trade. They sought to reduce taxes, which required reducing the welfare state.

If we refer to the criteria listed above, Sweden seems to be performing at a high level. The full range of services is available in the system. Access is universal. The organization of services is acceptable to almost all Swedes (although there are some problems for immigrants who are not used to bureaucratic systems). Great strides have been made toward development of a more adequate primary care sector. While there is some disagreement, the consensus seems to be that primary care is now adequate to meet national needs. Costs are once again increasing, however, and some way will have to be found to bring them under control by regulating the allocation of technology and personnel. The one complaint that seems to be shared by a large minority is that the system lacks flexibility. It is too rigid to adapt easily to different local conditions and individual needs when those are unusual.

India[17]

India is the fifth largest economy in the world and the second most populous country after the People's Republic of China. Until 1947, it was a British colony, achieving independence through a nonviolent mass campaign led by Mohandas Gandhi. It is a multiethnic society with a large number of religious and cultural groups. With its vast geographic area and diversity, it is far from homogeneous in its resources or medical care needs (World Bank 2001).

As was the case with all European colonies, the British created a medical care system to protect the colonists from the diseases in the colonies. These services were not accessible to the "native" population, with the exception of a small elite group. According to Banerji (1979), "Not only were the masses denied access to the western system of medicine, but this system contributed to the decay and degeneration of the preexisting indigenous systems." The result was a worsening of access to curative services on the part of most Indians.

According to Baru (2002), the history of the medical care system in postcolonial India can be divided into three broad periods: (1) a period of growth and expansion from independence until the oil shock in the late 1970s, (2) a period from the late 1970s through the 1980s, when there were cutbacks on public spending and concessions to the private sector, and (3) the more recent influence of loans from the International Monetary Fund (IMF) and the World Bank.

The Indian medical care system, along with much of its public organization, is stamped with its colonial history. In the case of India, the medical care system was shaped by a commission that created a plan for medical services while the transition to independence was under way. The Bhore

Commission (Government of India 1946) noted that the population of India was mostly poor and in need of basic services. They proposed a system based on state investment in an environment where private capital was quite limited. Baru noted that even the large corporate interests supported state sponsorship of education and health care. Private physicians did not oppose a public system as along as professional autonomy was not compromised. The result, according to Baru (2002), was that

> [t]he Bhore Commission accommodated the interests of the professional bodies by not taking measures to eliminate private interests both within and outside the health service system. Thus, even at the time of independence a substantial percentage of doctors were practicing in the private sector as individual practitioners, but the number of institutions was very small. (P. 271)

Not only is the private sector by far the largest in India, but the bulk of public medical care is provided not by the national government but by the states. Indeed, the public sector has struggled with inadequate funding throughout the past half century. In spite of efforts to expand public services, the system is more than 70 percent private; there are vast differences from state to state in the services available in the public sector; and the bulk of public investment in medical care has been in preventive, rather than curative services. The result is that the bulk of the population has not had access to more than very limited curative medical care.

Up to the late 1970s, there was expansion of medical services. With the "oil shock" of the 1970s—when the newly formed OPEC countries curtailed oil production and raised prices—the cost of virtually everything increased. The country had to curtail its public services, and there was a retrenchment of medical care, affecting both the volume and distribution of health care. There were cutbacks in the public sector, which resulted in a reduction of preventive medicine and primary care. At the same time, opportunities were opened for private investment in medical services, resulting in a small expansion of specialized medicine, nursing homes, and hospitals. Most of these were small, proprietary, and in many cases owned and staffed by unqualified physicians.

The largest expansion was in the arena of pharmaceuticals, medical equipment, and private insurance. Companies from outside India, particularly the United States, became more important players in the medical care economy. Medical care services for the wealthy and the middle class expanded. Those for the poor, still the bulk of India's population, contracted.

To cope with shrinking resources for public health, India turned to the IMF and the World Bank for development loans. Those agencies imposed a "structural adjustment" program. This consisted, in part, of requiring that India shift from directly providing services by governments (mostly states) in favor of contracting services out to the private sector, and instituting user fees. The program was designed to strengthen the secondary (specialized) level of care. The contracting agents are states, reducing the decision-making capacity of the state. The stated goal of "structural adjustment" is to reduce the public sector and to privatize. It is pursued rigidly and dogmatically by the IMF, and somewhat more pragmatically by the World Bank.

The consequences of these trends are not fully known, as the last wave of reform is quite recent. At a minimum, it has damaged primary care, not least because the linkages with the secondary and tertiary levels of care have been compromised and privatization has reduced availability and accessibility. A two-tier system of health care, one for the rich and one for the poor, has been supported. It seems likely, but not proven, that infant and maternal mortality will increase and disability will become more prevalent.

Third World

While the first world, ranging from the United States to Sweden, has little problem with the availability of services, the same cannot be said of India or the third world, where economic development is low. There, the services the first world takes for granted are either totally unavailable or available to only a very small part of the population. Furthermore, the first world has taken steps to make the provision of medical care more difficult for poorer "developing" countries.

Much of the third world consists of countries that were at one time European colonies. The colonial powers brought Western medicine with them, but with a limited mission: to protect the colonists from the diseases found in the colonies.[18] Physicians were imported and hospitals constructed for the Europeans. To varying degrees, the "native" elites were allowed to use Western medical facilities as well, but the general population was excluded (Alubo 1995; DeCraemer and Fox 1975; Fox 1994). When countries achieved independence, they most often retained the medical care system that had been created by the colonists. That is, the system served the elites, not the masses, with the added complication that in most cases, few, if any, native physicians had been trained.

To complicate matters, these countries had little money and poor prospects of developing a growing economy. Growth in the medical care sector, as in others, was slow and often not well targeted to the needs of the population. Most developing countries faced causes of death and sickness in the form of waterborne disease. There was a need for public health programs to establish a clean water supply. Yet the main investment was in high-technology medicine such as cardiac intensive care units. Only a small proportion of the population, the economic elites, survived long enough to take advantage of such technology.[19]

Nevertheless, with the urging of the World Health Organization's "Health for All by the Year 2000" campaign, there had been some development of primary care and public health. These programs made some progress in reducing mortality until the IMF entered the scene with their "structural adjustment program."

The IMF was created at the end of World War II to stabilize the exchange of currencies. It has evolved over time into the most important source of development funding for the third world. Its policies are set by a committee of first world bankers, dominated by the United States. The appointments to the board by the Reagan and George H. W. Bush administrations pushed a neoliberal economic program— supporting the dismantling of public programs, privatization, and opening the economy to competition from outside the country.

While most economists believe that there are conditions under which such a program can be beneficial, the IMF has pushed this program across the board, whether or not those conditions have been met (e.g., Stiglitz 2002). The result has often been that public health programs have been seriously weakened, and publicly financed medical care has been reduced. Especially unfortunate has been the fact that all this happened at the time the AIDS epidemic developed. African nations were unable to respond in meaningful ways, with the result that sub-Saharan Africa has very high levels of HIV infection and high mortality from AIDS, especially among women and children (Pearce 2000; Turshen 1999).[20]

For much of Africa, medical care systems are in a state of collapse. The problem is that medical care is unavailable to most people. Where it is available, it is often not accessible to those not part of the economic and political elite. The absence of public health systems that could address the most central needs of the population means that the systems often lack relevance. The system is low in equity, low on quality, and low on efficiency. It does not do a good job of reducing excess deaths, preventing disease, or treating disease.

Transnational Trends

A recent study has compared health care reforms in 20 countries (Twaddle 2002). It found that there was an all but universal change from democratically and professionally organized systems toward market systems. Furthermore, that change took place within a very short time period around 1980.

There were a large number of specific reforms across the countries studied, but only nine that were reported by a majority of countries. These included an ideology of equity or equality, expansion of health insurance or movement toward a national health system, and a move toward more universal coverage. All of these are democratic reforms and all were predominantly pre-1980. Post-1980, we find a dominant ideology of efficiency, a shift from public to private insurance coverage or provision of services, a focus on competition, incentives, "productivity," and choice, reduction of benefits to patients and/or cost shifting by requiring patients to

pick up more of the cost of services, and a focus on cost containment and/or rationing of care. All of these are market reforms. Decentralization was a widespread reform, but it could not be identified with markets, professions, or democracy, as it served different interests in different places.

Clearly, market reform is not limited to the United States. Indeed one of the most widely imitated reforms in the world was an initiative of the Thatcher government in the United Kingdom. They tried to create a stronger market within the public sector by separating "purchasers" of medical care (the public authorities who decide how tax revenues will be spent) and the "providers" of care (hospitals, clinics, physicians, etc.). The idea was that instead of having a set of providers who are funded year after year, they should be made independent of the state to compete for the state funds (Ham 1996; Hunter 2002; Light 1992, 1995). Variants of that reform can be found in Israel (Gross and Anson 2002), Sweden (Twaddle 1999, 2002), the Central European countries (Oreskovic 2002), Russia (Field 2002), and Argentina (Belmartino 2002).

Market reforms have caused considerable ferment, generally posing threats to professional interests and to quality of care. There is a growing consensus among health care researchers that market reforms have no documented benefits to patients and much is placed at risk: having professionals who will place the needs of patients first, and having reduced barriers to diagnosis and treatment even after one has access to the system being the most important. Indeed, market reforms are primarily a mechanism for corporate interests to extract profits from the medical care system (Evans 1997).

Indeed, the reform movement seems to be an initiative of internationally exposed economic elites.[21] Their agenda is not specifically to reform medical care, but to organize their economies to be more responsive to their interests. They want to reduce the cost of labor, reduce taxes, and improve their ability to market goods in other countries. Part of that agenda is to reduce the size and cost of the welfare state, at the heart of which, in most countries, is the medical care system. These elites are coordinated transnationally through such organizations as the World Economic Forum,[22] and others.

WHEN MEDICAL CARE
SYSTEMS BECOME SOCIAL PROBLEMS

In general, medical care is seen as a good thing. The problem is having care that is available, accessible, acceptable, relevant, affordable, and flexible. When a system fails to operate in ways that meet these criteria, it becomes a social problem.

1. By far the most widespread problem is affordability. Medical care systems throughout the world are increasing in cost at a rate in excess of the growth of the world economy and the economies of respective nations. Virtually every society has an interest in controlling costs, if for no other reason than to prevent medical care from bankrupting the society. While this issue may not resonate with the general public in all societies, it is clearly one that concerns those with responsibility for the social provision of medical services.[23]

To those affected, or those who think they may be affected, accessibility has great salience. In the developed world, availability necessarily implies rationing. To allow all forms of service to be available locally unleashes a cost spiral that is unsustainable. What is needed is a way to locate services where people can reach them when needed without duplication at the local level. The United States has the greatest problem with duplication, as hospitals compete to attract staff who want to have the latest techniques at their personal disposal. Sweden, prior to 1982, did the best job of allocating specialists and technology through a system of regional, county, and local hospitals with national regulation of which specialties and technologies could be located at each level. In the developing world, availability is the core issue as societies cannot afford (or are politically blocked by the first world) to provide services.

Accessibility is of even greater public salience to those affected or potentially affected. Most important here is the cost barrier, greater in the United States than in any other developed country. Private health insurance is failing to provide widespread access to medical care. The percentage of the population with private insurance has been declining. The middle class is increasingly threatened with the loss of health insurance. Those with modest incomes, especially the aged, are increasingly faced with choices among food, housing, and medicines. Public insurance is limited to a small part of the population in need and is often inadequate to meet all the costs of medical care. There is slowly gathering momentum behind a movement to create universal health coverage, although opposition in the business community is still substantial.

The other criteria seem to be less salient to the general public, although they can be important to specific groups.

It is seldom that acceptability becomes an issue. There is debate in developed countries about the use of aggressive medical care for terminally diseased people, but this is more a medical care than a system issue. Several years ago, India instituted a compulsory sterilization program that resulted in the collapse of the government. This, however, was a matter of policy and not the nature of the system. Where acceptability of the system becomes an issue, it tends to be with reference to the adequacy of coverage—that is, accessibility.

Relevance tends to be an issue in the first world with reference to the mix of primary versus specialized care and hospital versus ambulatory care. Sweden created a system that was much too specialized and much too focused on hospital care, and had to take steps to shift toward primary care outside the hospital. That they could do that is one of the reasons they reduced the cost of the system during the 1980s and early 1990s. The elite control of medical care in the developing world also creates problems of relevance, as the system is designed to meet the needs of a very small sociopolitical cadre rather than the general population.

Flexibility is an increasing issue. Managed care in the United States makes the system less able to adapt to the needs of individual patients, especially when they fall outside the average. Hospital care is inherently less flexible than ambulatory care. In most of the world, it is the hospital and the hospital clinics that get the brunt of criticism for being inflexible.

2. The form of a system has an impact on the kinds of problems the system needs to address.

Professional systems tend to be focused on technology, making it available and accessible. Physicians and other professionals are trained to want to practice with knowledge and skill, leading to services that are of high quality and guided by ethical norms. A system left to the control of professionals, however, tends to be highly specialized, maldistributed, and plagued with runaway inflation. Physicians are trained to meet patient needs regardless of cost. They tend to prefer living in some places rather than others. There is always a problem with the geographic distribution of services when it is under professional control.

Market systems tend to prioritize profits. There is a tendency toward greater cost control as a means of maximizing profits. The usual manner of accomplishing this is through restriction of services to those that are profitable. Services that are inherently expensive will be contained. The downside is that there is a tendency to encroach on clinical decision making in ways that professionals see as unethical and a maldistribution of services to those who have the resources to pay.

Democratic systems tend to work toward universal coverage, seeing that nobody is left without access to care. Services tend to be better distributed and of high-average quality. Cost control tends to be better than in professional systems and more equitable than in market systems. They may, depending on the political decisions made, constrain research more than other systems, and they restrict the income-producing potential of the system for private interests.

However the system is organized, it is seen as a problem for some part of the society. The most satisfactory systems seem to provide for professional control of the clinical decisions while providing democratic control over the shape of the system. The market has no demonstrated value in the organization of medical services, although it may be appropriate for the manufacture of equipment, patent medicines, and the like. The issue of distribution seems critical, as it is the effectiveness of the system across the whole society that seems to have the greatest impact on public health.

Underlying all of these considerations is the impact of elite economic interests on the shaping of medical care systems. In the first world, the internationally exposed corporations in the developed world have mounted a campaign to reduce the welfare state. The infrastructure that has supported the development of both publicly supported medical care systems and the expansion of private health insurance systems has been challenged by a sector of the economy seeking to maximize profits, even at the expense of other economic interests in their own societies. Those same interests control international development funding and threaten health care systems in the developing and third world by devolution of the public sectors and unleashing horrendous epidemics.

All this is to say that underlying the social problems of medical care systems is the larger and more pernicious social problem of monopoly capitalism.

NOTES

1. The distinctions among disease, illness, and sickness correspond to the World Health Organization's declaration in its constitution that "health is not the mere absence of disease but a state of complete physical, psychological, and social well being." The distinctions are most fully described in Twaddle and Nordenfelt (1994), which can be obtained free of charge by writing Tema H, Universitet I Linköping, Linköping, Sweden.

2. That is, businesses that see their major competition coming from businesses outside their own country.

3. These are spelled out in more detail in my textbook with Richard Hessler (1987) and in my two books on health care reform (1999, 2002).

4. Institutional systems target the whole population as beneficiaries (Medicare and social security are examples in the United States), while residual systems target an "underclass" (Medicaid and most of what Americans call "welfare" is of this type).

5. Kaiser had constructed several large dams and during the war was a major shipbuilder, with a plant on Vancouver Island. They had created a hospital and a group practice of physicians to provide medical care to the workers.

6. In fact, they did neither. What was different was that Kaiser Permanente had an integrated system in which the hospital could operate at a loss balanced out by a surplus in the ambulatory care clinics. They provided each service in the least expensive possible setting. At that time, most indemnity insurance had a perverse incentive

to hospitalize patients, as that was the only place they would have insurance coverage. Given the current popularity of the HMO designation, I adopt it here with the caveat that I recognize its inadequacy.

7. In a television program on the IOFPO hospitals in Dallas, broadcast by a major network some years ago, an emergency room physician was questioned about the policy of not treating patients without evidence of health insurance and whether this was not a violation of medical ethics. His response was that medical ethics was often in conflict with corporate policy.

8. There are a number of editorials in the *New England Journal of Medicine* that spoke to that issue in the 1980s and 1990s. On the IOFPO movement, see Gray (1991).

9. On the failure of the Clinton Health Plan, see Kelly (1998), Navarro (1994), and Skocpol (1997).

10. Policies that indemnify holders against loss by paying whatever the physician or hospital charges less deductibles and copays.

11. To have people without expert training or a fiduciary relationship with the patient entering into clinical decisions is unique on the world scene. The democratic control of medical care in countries with "socialized" systems has been limited to allocation of resources, not clinical decision making.

12. This division was clearly the case in legislative hearings in the state of Missouri on a bill to regulate managed care (Wieman 1999).

13. This section draws heavily from Twaddle (1999).

14. That is, a hospital day or a specific service was relatively cheap in Sweden when compared with other countries. What drove up the cost was that too much was done in expensive settings when cheaper—outside the hospital—settings would do as well.

15. Hollingsworth, Hage, and Hanneman (1990) found that to control the cost of medical care, the state must be able to control the allocation of technology and personnel.

16. The idea behind this reform was to unify medical care services (a county responsibility) with social services (a municipal responsibility).

17. Unless otherwise noted, the information in this section comes from Baru (2002) and World Bank (2001).

18. This was the period when departments and schools of "tropical medicine" were created in European universities with the mission of protecting their nationals abroad.

19. These assertions come from decades of conversations with colleagues from Africa in the fields of medical sociology and public health.

20. Unlike in the United States, AIDS in sub-Saharan Africa is a disease of the well-educated heterosexual population. It disproportionally affects those with the training needed to further development. The major reservoir is prostitutes who service males who are away from their families.

21. This is best documented in Sweden, but available evidence suggests the same is true in the other countries studied.

22. This is an organization of CEOs of corporations that do a billion Swiss francs of business a year, pay more than $25,000 in dues each year and a four-figure conference fee. It operates in secrecy. Nothing said by anyone in the meetings can be reported. A few plenary sessions are open to the press. The meeting consists of seminars designed to generate a consensus on "how to make the world a better place." The consensus is taken back to the several countries by the most powerful people in the respective economies. This would explain why such similar reforms take place in such dissimilar societies almost simultaneously.

23. Political ideology is also a factor, as cost control provides a vehicle for the dismantling of a key component of the welfare state.

REFERENCES

Alubo, S. Ogoh. 1995. *Medical Professionalism and State Power in Nigeria.* Jos, Nigeria: Center for Development Studies.

Banerji, D. 1979. "Place of the Indigenous and the Western Systems of Medicine in the Health Services of India." *International Journal of Health Services* 9:511–19.

Baru, Rama. 2002. "Health Sector Reform: The Indian Experience." Pp. 267–81 in *Health Care Reform around the World*, edited by Andrew Twaddle. Westport, CT: Auburn House.

Belmartino, Susanna. 2002. "Health Care Reform in Argentina." Pp. 221–40 in *Health Care Reform around the World*, edited by Andrew Twaddle. Westport, CT: Auburn House.

DeCraemer, Willy and Reneé C. Fox. 1975. *The Emerging Physician.* Stanford, CA: Hoover Institution.

Evans, Robert G. 1997. "Going for the Gold: The Redistributive Agenda behind Market Based Health Care Reform." *Journal of Health Politics, Policy and Law* 22:427-65.

Fein, Rashi. 1986. *Medical Care, Medical Costs: The Search for a Health Insurance Policy.* Cambridge, MA: Harvard University Press.

Field, Mark. 1982. "The Health Care System and the Polity: A Contemporary American Dialectic." *Social Science and Medicine,* 14A:397–413.

——— 2002. "The Inelasticity of Institutional Patterns: An Impediment to Health Care Reform in Post-Communist Russia." Pp. 160–78 in *Health Care Reform around the World*, edited by Andrew Twaddle. Westport, CT: Auburn House.

Fox, Reneé C. 1994. *In the Belgian Chateau: The Spirit and Culture of a European Society in an Age of Change.* Chicago, IL: Ivan R. Dee.

Freidson, Eliot. 1972a. *Profession of Medicine.* New York: Dodd Mead.

———. 1972b. "The Organization of Medical Practice." In *Handbook of Medical Sociology,* edited by H. Freeman, S. Levine, and L. Reeder. Englewood Cliffs, NJ: Prentice Hall.

Government of India. 1946. *Report of the Health Survey and Development Committee (Bhore Committee).* Vols. 1 and 4. Delhi: Manager of Publications.

Gray, Bradford. 1991. *The Profit Motive and Patient Care: The Changing Accountability of Doctors and Hospitals.* Cambridge, MA: Harvard University Press.

Gross, Revital and Ofra Anson. 2002. "Health Care Reform in Israel." Pp. 198–218 in *Health Care Reform around the World*, edited by Andrew Twaddle. Westport, CT: Auburn House.

Ham, Chrisopher. 1996. "Learning from the Tigers: Stakeholder Health Care." *Lancet* 347:951-3.

Himmelstein, D. and S. Woolhandler. 1993. *Managed Competition: A Grimm Fairy Tale.* Cambridge, MA: Harvard University Center for National Health Program Studies.

Hollingsworth, J. Rogers, J. Hage, and R. Hanneman. 1990. *State Intervention in Medical Care: Consequences for Britain, France, Sweden, and the United States.* Ithaca, NY: Cornell University Press.

Hunter, David. 2002. "Health System Reforms: The United Kingdom Experience." Pp. 37–57 in *Health Care Reform around the World*, edited by Andrew Twaddle. Westport, CT: Auburn House.

Kelly, Shawn. 1998. "A Sociohistorical Analysis of the Role of Interest Groups in Shaping National Health Insurance Reform." Unpublished doctoral dissertation. University of Missouri, Columbia.

Landstingsförbundet. 1995. *Vad ska man kall det som händer in Mora?—och andra frågor om styrmodeler.* Stockholm, Sweden: Author.

Light, Donald. 1992. "Radical Experiment: Transforming Britain's National Health System to Interlocking Markets." *Journal of Public Health Policy* 13:146–55.

———. 1995. "Equity and Efficiency in Medical Care." *Social Science and Medicine* 35:465–70.

Mahoney, A. R. 1973. "Factors Affecting Physician's Choice of Group or Independent Practice." *Inquiry* 10:9–18.

Navarro, Vicente. 1994. *The Politics of Health Policy: The US Reforms, 1980–1994.* Cambridge, MA: Blackwell.

Oreskovic, Stipe. 2002. "Introducing Compulsory Health Insurance in Central Europe." Pp. 121–40 in *Health Care Reform around the World*, edited by Andrew Twaddle. Westport, CT: Auburn House.

Pearce, Ibatola. 2000. "Death and Maternity in Nigeria." Pp. 1–26 in *African Women's Health,* edited by M. Turshen. Brunswick, NJ: Rutgers University Press.

Roemer, Milton. 1977. *Comparative National Policies on Health Care.* New York: Dekker.

Sidel, Victor and Sidel, Ruth. 1983. *A Healthy State.* New York: Praeger.

Skocpol, Theda. 1997. *Boomerang: Health Care Reform and the Turn Against Government.* New York: Norton.

Starr, Paul. 1982. *The Social Transformation of American Medicine.* New York: Basic Books.

Stiglitz, Joseph. 2002. *Globalization and Its Discontents.* New York: Norton.

Turshen, Meredeth. 1999. *Privatizing Health Services in Africa.* Brunswick, NJ: Rutgers University Press.

Twaddle, Andrew. 1999. *Health Care Reform in Sweden 1980–1994.* Westport, CT: Auburn House.

———, ed. 2002. *Health Care Reform around the World.* Westport, CT: Auburn House.

Twaddle, Andrew and Richard Hessler. 1987. *A Sociology of Health.* New York: Macmillan.

Twaddle, Andrew and Leonard Nordenfelt. 1994. *Disease, Illness and Sickness: Three Central Concepts in the Theory of Health.* Linköping, Sweden: Tema H, Universitet I Linköping.

Wesson, Albert. 2002. "The United States: Live Free and Die?" Pp. 97–120 in *Health Care Reform around the World*, edited by Andrew Twaddle. Westport, CT: Auburn House.

Wieman, Jennifer. 1999. "Professions, Patients and Profits: Testimony before the Missouri Joint Interim Committee on Managed Care." Unpublished undergraduate honors thesis, Department of Sociology, University of Missouri, Columbia, MO.

World Bank. 2001. *India, Raising the Sights: Better Health Systems for India's Poor.* Washington, DC: Health, Nutrition, Population Sector Unit, South Asia Region, the World Bank.

AIDS AS A SOCIAL PROBLEM

The Creation of Social Pariahs
in the Management of an Epidemic

BRONWEN LICHTENSTEIN

University of Alabama

AIDS (acquired immune deficiency syndrome) was viewed as a social problem[1] as soon as epidemiologic reports about a "gay plague" appeared in the United States. Like other sexually transmitted diseases, AIDS was associated with people "who had the misfortune to fit into rather distinct classes of outcasts and social pariahs" (Shilts 1987). The first social pariah to be named in the AIDS epidemic was the white, gay man whose lifestyle was assumed to be an efficient conduit for HIV (human immunodeficiency virus) transmission. AIDS, in fact, was known as the "gay white man's disease" well past the time when the accuracy of this characterization should have been questioned, and certainly past the time when heterosexual citizens in developing countries were being infected at an alarming rate. This chapter will address the concept of AIDS as a social problem along two dimensions: first, in its creation of social pariahs through discourse about who was infected and, second, in the subsequent problems of this representation for responding to the epidemic.

My approach to AIDS as a social problem will center on the understanding of disease as a socially constructed phenomenon. In this conceptualization, AIDS is not just a virus that afflicts hapless individuals at random but is the product of social and economic forces that help determine how, when, and where particular persons are infected. To paraphrase Robin Gorna (1996), AIDS has nothing to do with being an equal-opportunity virus, even though it has been presented as such in the media and in health promotion materials. Like many other infectious diseases, HIV/AIDS affects certain people more than others. In the United States, it affects minorities more than whites. Around the globe, HIV/AIDS affects those who are poor or disenfranchised. As stated by the late Jonathan Mann, former director of the World Health Organization's Global Program for HIV/AIDS, inequality through poverty, discrimination, or marginalization is the central societal lesion underlying AIDS and ill health worldwide (Mann 1993).

Neither of the popularized conceptualizations (AIDS as a disease of socially deviant risk groups or AIDS as an equal opportunity disease) has explicitly acknowledged the structural factors underlying the HIV risk for disadvantaged or marginalized members of society. The "social fault lines theory" (Bateson and Goldsby 1988), however, underlies much of the current sociological literature on HIV/AIDS, although as Mann (1993) has noted, societies try hard to ignore it. My approach to AIDS as a social problem will illustrate how structural factors give rise to differential HIV infection patterns. I will present three archetypes (icons) of HIV/AIDS ("the gay white man," "the injection drug user," and "the African prostitute") for analysis. These three perspectives will illustrate the links between stigmatizing iconography and the management of an epidemic.

Definitions

HIV/AIDS

HIV infection is a syndrome that takes the form of opportunistic diseases such as Kaposi's sarcoma, Pneumocystis carinii pneumonia (PCP), cytomegalovirus (CMV), toxoplasmosis, and the virulent forms of thrush, herpes, and hives. HIV infection can be transmitted through unprotected sexual intercourse, contaminated hypodermic needles, and untreated blood products. HIV infection has a latency period of 5 to 15 years but is usually fatal if an untreated infection has progressed to AIDS. Antiretroviral medicines developed for the treatment of HIV infection can significantly prolong the life of "people with HIV" (PWH). HIV infection may be deadly in societies in which lifesaving medicines are unavailable and chronic (manageable) in wealthy nations in which antiviral regimens are the standard of medical care.

Iconography

Iconography is the study of societal understandings about icons, that is, how groups of people are presented, created, and reproduced through pictorial, textual, or media representations. The formal definition of iconography stems from the concept of icons as images, statues, figures, pictures, or representations. In the HIV/AIDS epidemic, these icons are public images of those who become HIV-positive (Gilman 1988). This chapter will investigate the ways in which iconography serves to reveal compelling but rarely stated frameworks around which meanings and understandings are organized. Iconography may be thought of in this context as a study in attributions to images that are particularly relevant to HIV/AIDS on broad societal levels. Following Gilman (1988), this approach recognizes the extraordinary power the images have to reflect (and shape) society's responses to individuals suffering from disease.

Naming a New Disease and Its Icons

The first cases of HIV infection were documented in 1979 among gay men in the United States. AIDS was classified as a new disease as soon as scientists had determined its incidence and origins. The spread of HIV infection around the globe ended the complacency that had existed after the virtual elimination of such diseases as syphilis, smallpox, poliomyelitis, cholera, and yellow fever in their epidemic forms (Lichtenstein 1996a). The appearance of a deadly new disease renewed fears about human susceptibility and led to a search for viral and human culprits in an attempt to control the spread of infection.

HIV/AIDS was dubbed the "gay plague" because the first people known to be afflicted were men from self-defined gay communities in San Francisco, Los Angeles, and New York (Altman 1986). The Centers for Disease Control and Prevention (CDC) specifically linked the "homosexual lifestyle" to an emerging epidemic of pneumonia, Kaposi's sarcoma, and wasting disease associated with gay men (Treichler 1988a). The association of an epidemic with a lifestyle set the scene for the way HIV/AIDS was perceived and managed in the United States. The scientific community initially labeled the new disease "gay-related immune deficiency," or GRID. The syndrome was later and more neutrally renamed AIDS, but the link between male homosexuality and AIDS was firmly established as an epidemiologic entity (AIDS became "HIV infection" or "HIV/AIDS" once the difference between asymptomatic and symptomatic stages emerged). This first-world conceptualization of the new epidemic as a gay man's disease continued even after it was known that AIDS afflicted heterosexual populations in sub-Saharan Africa. Most Western literature about HIV/AIDS focused on the idea of male homosexuality as a locus of the epidemic, whether as an assumption or as a point of argument.

Concern about the sexual behavior of gay men was expressed through political vilification, media hyperbole, and sociobehavioral interventions. While moral concern centered on the nature of same-sex activity and the perceived threat to health and social order, sociobehavioral interventions were predicated on the notion that sexual behavior could (or should) be changed (Rushing 1995). Like syphilis before it, HIV/AIDS soon emerged as a "sexual" epidemic in terms of its politics and management. This meant that HIV/AIDS was viewed in terms of social deviance rather than as a public health threat that needed immediate attention (Shilts 1987). In the early days of the epidemic in the United States, this response was evident from the Reagan administration's refusal to address HIV/AIDS as an urgent public health issue (Perrow and Guillen 1990). The government's refusal meant that HIV prevention was given low priority in the public health sector.

The management of AIDS focused on "risk groups" as a means of tracing, monitoring, and controlling the spread of disease. The initial investigation of HIV infection by epidemiologists meant that the new disease was constructed in terms of a risk group iconography of social or sexual deviance. The CDC initially used this construction in public health surveillance and case reports (Oppenheimer 1988). The epidemiologic emphasis was instrumental in HIV/AIDS becoming known as the epidemic of the 4 H's: Homosexuals, Haitians, Heroin addicts, and Hemophiliacs (Treichler 1988a). The use of risk groups as the explicit basis of surveillance reports ceased after 1993, but the data were still organized according to modes of transmission that are commonly associated with risky behavior. HIV/AIDS therefore continued to be associated with sexual and social deviance.

AN EPIDEMIC OF INEQUALITY

The United States

In the United States, the demography of HIV/AIDS has undergone substantial change since the early days of the epidemic. While white middle-class men in major urban areas in the Northeast and Pacific West were among the first to be afflicted, HIV infection is now associated with ethnicity and poverty. African Americans and Hispanics account for 54 percent and 19 percent of new infections in the United States, respectively, even though they make up only 12 percent and 9 percent of the population (CDC 2002a; U.S. Census Bureau 2001). This epidemiologic pattern is similar to other sexually transmitted infections (STI) such as syphilis, gonorrhea, chlamydia, and genital herpes (CDC 2001a), all of which disproportionately affect minorities.

Most new infections occur in the southeastern states. African Americans in particular are at risk of HIV transmission. In Alabama, for example, 72 percent of new cases occurs among African Americans, who represent 26 percent of the state population (Alabama Department of Public Health 2002). Similar patterns occur in Mississippi, Georgia, Florida, and South Carolina (CDC 2001b). The gap between the number of infected men and women is narrowing for African Americans, meaning that the AIDS iconography of the gay white man in the 1980s is no longer a primary referent in the 21st century. Women in the Southeast account for one-third to one-half of new infections (CDC 2001b). This development suggests that HIV/AIDS among African Americans is developing a "Type II" (non-Western) demographic pattern that is often associated with HIV transmission in developing countries.

The structural dimensions of HIV/AIDS in the United States are evident in social problems that afflict the poor and disenfranchised. In Brown and Wiesman's (1993) study of low-income women in the United States, for example, housing instability was a primary indicator of HIV risk, while other factors such as "man sharing" (partner concurrency) in communities where there is an imbalance in the ratio of men to women through death or imprisonment were indicators of HIV risk for African Americans

(Campbell 1999). Sexual relationships involving an element of financial exchange are also common and are linked to man sharing, drug use, and poverty (Lichtenstein 2000). Sexual networks involving partner concurrency and commodification are efficient conduits for STI because transmission can occur at multiple points in a community in a relatively short period of time (Laumann et al. 1994). African Americans are also vulnerable to HIV transmission because of homophily (black-on-black sexual relations), meaning that infection becomes "pooled" and therefore self-reproducing within members of a community (Pfingst 2002).

Inequality Around the Globe

The emergence of ethnic and poverty-related disparities outlined above is consistent with HIV transmission patterns across the globe. Bloor (1995) has noted that HIV/AIDS is socially patterned in terms of who is most at risk of HIV transmission, both locally and on a global scale (i.e., some societies or groups are more vulnerable than others). Mann's (1993) assessment of this social patterning is that it is characterized by poverty, political upheaval, and social systems in which women in particular lack equality. Many of the recent public health reports on HIV/AIDS are concerned with issues of discrimination and poverty (e.g., UNAIDS 2000). The following section addresses the social patterning of HIV/AIDS in terms of gender and poverty, the two main issues that appear in these reports.

Women

Women now outnumber men in HIV incidence. Biological factors, such as being the receptive partner, place women at greater risk of HIV infection than men (Caldwell and Caldwell 1993), as does their subordinate position in society (Mann 1993). The links between women's biology, social status, and HIV/AIDS are evident in the infection rates of girls who are sold into prostitution in Thailand and who exchange sex in Africa, India, and other countries in which women lack economic and social equality (UNAIDS 2000). Mann (1993) has argued that women who are unable to make life decisions

with regard to marriage, property distribution, or income are often rendered powerless in their sexual lives; thus, they become susceptible to HIV and other diseases through the double jeopardy of biology and sex discrimination.

Mann (1993) has further noted that reforms of laws governing property and divorce may be more important in helping to prevent HIV infection than increasing the distribution of brochures or condoms. Condoms may not be a useful HIV prevention tool for women for a variety of reasons, such as the fact that only men can use them or because men perceive them to be a threat to masculinity or as a sign of being unfaithful (Crosby et al. 2000). The prevalence of rape is also a potent factor in HIV risk for women (Epstein 2002), as is unequal access to education (UNAIDS 2000). Lichtenstein (2002) has documented the way in which domestic abuse victims are at risk of HIV transmission through nondisclosure and lack of condom use by infected men who use sexual coercion and violence to control their partners. The fact that women are becoming infected with HIV/AIDS at higher rates than men around the globe has prompted Mann (1993) to conclude that not only does gender discrimination play a role in health care for women but also that ipso facto, male-dominated societies are a threat to public health.

Men

Structural factors affect men's risk of HIV transmission as well. HIV transmission in sub-Saharan Africa has been fostered, in part, by the shift from agrarian to capitalist forms of economy, which has resulted in large-scale migration across regions of the African continent and the disruption of traditional patterns of work and kinship. This development has separated men from their families and relocated them in industrial towns and cities in which prostitution or contingent relationships are common (Epstein 2002). War, famine, and poverty affect men's as well as women's HIV risk through the social dislocation caused by troop movements and recruitment (particularly of young boys) for military purposes. Hankins, Friedman, Zafar, and Strathdee (2002) have reported that ethnic patterns of recruitment into the Ugandan National Liberation

Army after the overthrow of Idi Amin in 1979 correlated positively with geospatial patterns of HIV transmission and that infectious diseases (including HIV/AIDS) can spread quickly in battlefield medical settings.

In parts of Europe (e.g., Edinburgh, Scotland) as well as in the United States, structural factors involving men's HIV risk include urban decay and post–World War II changes that eliminated employment and housing opportunities. In one notable example, the geographical distribution of HIV infection associated with intravenous drug use in New York was linked to the slum clearance and forced relocation that concentrated poverty in overcrowded southern parts of the Bronx (Wallace 1988). In Russia, an increase in injection drug-related HIV infection, particularly among men, has been associated with social upheaval and economic hardship in the post-Soviet era (UNAIDS 2001). The relationship between community disruption, risk behavior, and HIV transmission is located firmly within these sociostructural explanations of the epidemic.

Poverty

Structural factors play a critical role in HIV transmission. While in secular and relatively well-to-do countries (e.g., Britain, Canada, the Netherlands, Germany, Norway, Australia, and New Zealand) the epidemic is said to be contained by virtue of a well-funded and coordinated response (Davis and Lichtenstein 1996), heavily populated countries in which poverty is endemic or that are beset by wars and social dislocation (e.g., Bosnia, Russia, Bangladesh, Sri Lanka, and Ethiopia) have seen an exponential increase in HIV/AIDS that threatens these nations' ability to function (Epstein 2002; UNAIDS 2000). HIV/AIDS has also become a key indicator of social class. This factor is particularly salient in poor nations but also in industrialized countries where there is a considerable wealth gap between rich and poor, and whose health systems are similarly stratified (e.g., the United States) (Smith 1999).

In the case of more egalitarian countries, especially those with national harm-reduction strategies such as needle exchange for injection drug users

(e.g., in Europe, Canada, and Australasia), new cases of HIV infection in heterosexual populations often occur through immigration from countries with high rates of HIV infection or through the sex tourism associated with such countries (Gorna 1996; New Zealand Ministry of Health 2001). The citizens of "sex trade" countries (e.g., Thailand and Kampuchea) are often impoverished, indicating that the movement of populations through travel, immigration, and trade is also socially patterned and that international sex tourism (like other tourism) is part of the economic interface between rich and poor. Another factor relates to refugees from war-torn countries who may suffer from infectious and other diseases. In New Zealand, 40 percent of all new HIV infections over the past five years have occurred among immigrants, particularly those with refugee status (New Zealand Ministry of Health 2001).

Table 19.1 lists the HIV/AIDS rates for 28 countries. The seroprevalence rate in each country is presented together with the main modes of HIV transmission: men who have sex with men (MSM), injection drug use (IDU), and heterosexual (HET). The countries were selected because they are representative of their regions or because the HIV/AIDS data are available in published public health reports.

The table has been organized into four main categories to represent the geospacial distribution of HIV/AIDS. First, there are the industrialized countries whose epidemics are stable or contained (e.g., in Europe, North America, and Australasia). Second, there are the countries that are characterized by a rapid increase in HIV transmission, poverty, political upheaval, and underfunded health systems (e.g., in sub-Saharan Africa, Southeast Asia, and some Caribbean nations). Third, there are the countries whose more recent epidemics began after the collapse of communism or through isolation from their neighbors (e.g., the former Soviet Republics and China, respectively). These countries are experiencing a rapid increase in HIV transmission. The fourth category consists of a small number of high-prevalence countries that have reduced HIV transmission through aggressive public health interventions (e.g., Uganda and Thailand). The table also shows that in general, heterosexual transmission is common in high-prevalence countries; same-sex activity (and to a lesser extent, IDU) is associated with HIV transmission in the West; and injection drug use is associated with HIV transmission in the former Soviet Republics.

Table 19.1 is a beginning point for understanding how the course of the epidemic is shaped by political and socioeconomic factors. The highest HIV transmission rates are in developing countries, particularly in sub-Saharan Africa, the Caribbean, and Southeast Asia. HIV transmission has largely been confined to the group of origin (e.g., middle-class gay men) in wealthier countries, especially those with comprehensive HIV-prevention strategies where needle exchange and targeted funding have proven to be effective (Lichtenstein 1996b). In other countries, cultural disincentives for condom use (e.g., in pronatalist societies), gender discrimination (Mann 1993), and practices such as polygyny or child sex (Gould 1993) are examples of how sociocultural factors ("practices") intersect with HIV transmission.

For Crimp (1988), the point that social factors shape the course of HIV/AIDS and its outcomes is crucial to dispelling the myth of an equal-opportunity disease. In presenting the views of Delaporte (1986), Gould (1993), Mann (1993), Farmer (1999), and others, Crimp (1988) asserts that "AIDS [like other diseases] does not exist apart from the practices that conceptualize it, represent it, and respond to it. We know AIDS only in and through those practices" (p. 3). The following section will discuss how HIV/AIDS exists within a framework of social practices that have given rise to AIDS archetypes (iconography), with a corresponding effect on the management of a public health crisis. The discussion will center on the AIDS iconography of gay men, injection drug users, and African women as representative of the three main "risk groups" identified in the surveillance data in Table 19.1.

AIDS ICONOGRAPHY IN THE MANAGEMENT OF A "SEXUAL" DISEASE

Gay Men

The Iconography

HIV/AIDS is characterized by blame of the afflicted. Sander Gilman (1988) has argued that blame is meted out to the victims of disease in an attempt to isolate those we designate ill. In the case of the gay man, isolation came about, in the scientific sense, through nineteenth-century medicalization in which the homosexual was cast as a subspecies, an abnormal sexual variant (Foucault 1978). The struggle for gay rights in the 1960s was in part a challenge to the medical-scientific discourse that had constructed gay men and women as mentally ill or deficient. The AIDS epidemic again presented homosexuality in terms of disease and as a societal threat. In effect, the categorization of the homosexual as a subspecies in the nineteenth century (a notion captured by gays and reworked to become an "identity" in the 1970s) turned full circle once gay men were classified as "AIDS patients" and "AIDS carriers." Even psychopathology was reintroduced, this time appearing as depression or dementia in the later stages of AIDS (Leibowitz 1985). In contrast to the nineteenth century, however, this iconography has had a unifying effect on the gay community in terms of political action.

The restigmatization of gay men during the HIV/AIDS epidemic was in part the result of an epidemiology that linked high STI rates among gay men to HIV risk. Altman (1986) has noted that the success of the gay movement in claiming legitimacy for its "lifestyle" probably distorted early research on HIV/AIDS because researchers looked for lifestyle factors that could explain the outbreak of HIV infection instead of assuming that the culprit was a specific organism that could also infect heterosexuals. Words such as "immune overload," "immune fatigue," and "life in the fast lane" were used to describe the environment in which AIDS flourished (Treichler 1988a). Misleading perceptions about AIDS arose from the extravagant metaphors that eschewed reason and fanned public fear about "other" lifestyles. Leibowitz (1985) has noted, "The homosexual lifestyle was so blatantly on display to the general public, so closely scrutinized, that it is likely that we will never have been informed with such technic-phantasmal complacency as to how 'other people' live their lives" (p. 3). This negative publicity made the gay man the first AIDS icon and an example of how other icons would be constructed in terms of blame and "otherness."

Table 19.1   HIV/AIDS Prevalence among Adults and Adolescents in Selected Countries, 2002

	% TOTAL POPULATION	% MODE OF TRANSMISSION*		
		MSM	IDU	HET
CATEGORY ONE				
NORTH AMERICA				
Canada**	0.30	69	11	11
United States	0.61	48	33	12
WESTERN EUROPE				
Germany**	0.10	64	14	8
Britain**	0.11	63	8	21
Netherlands**	0.20	67	11	16
France**	0.38	53	21	15
Spain**	0.58	14	65	13
ASIA				
Japan	>0.01	17	0.5	34
AUSTRALASIA				
New Zealand**	0.10	77	2	15
Australia	0.15	84	3	6
CATEGORY TWO				
AFRICA (Sub-Saharan)				
Malawi	15.96	0	0	89
South Africa	20.10	n.d. (mainly heterosexual)		
Zimbabwe	33.70	n.d. (mainly heterosexual)		
Botswana	38.80	n.d. (mainly heterosexual)		
ASIA		n.d. (mainly heterosexual)		
Cambodia	2.70	n.d. (mainly heterosexual)		
India	0.80 (underestimate)	n.d. (mainly heterosexual)		
CARIBBEAN & SOUTH AMERICA				
Haiti	6.10	(unknown 79)		18
Bermuda	3.50	3	1	90
Guyana	2.70	3	0	92
Belize	2.00	13	<1	41
CATEGORY THREE				
EASTERN EUROPE***				
Lithuania	0.10	87	7	19
Poland**	0.10	25	50	15
Russian Federation	0.90	26	6	16
Ukraine	0.96	1	79	17
ASIA				
China	0.10 (underestimate)	1	39	23
CATEGORY FOUR				
Uganda	5.70	n.d. (mainly heterosexual)		
Thailand	1.80	1	5	83

Source: UNAIDS (2002).

Note: *MSM* = Men who have sex with men; *IDU* = Injection drug use; *HET* = heterosexual transmission; n.d. = no data.

*Totals do not add up to 100 percent because of the number of infections in "Unknown" or other categories (e.g., perinatal, blood transfusion, blood product).

**National needle exchange (NEP) or harm-reduction programs for IDU. Some of these programs (e.g. in Spain and Poland) were recently introduced in response to sudden increases in IDU-related infractions.

***Totals for Eastern Europe do not reflect the increase in new IDU-related HIV infections.

The Response

In the United States, the gay community mobilized in support of AIDS care for the afflicted and for HIV prevention programs. AIDS iconography ("the AIDS patient as a special case") was used as a political tool by gay organizations such as the AIDS Coalition to Unleash Power (ACTUP) to demand health services for PWH (Kramer 1990). At the time, the U.S. government was suspected of refusing to respond to the epidemic because of what Shilts (1987), Altman (1986), and Kramer (1990) have described as a trenchant antagonism toward homosexuality and the "inherent" immorality of gays. Kramer (1990), for example, believed that a stigmatizing AIDS iconography was "behind the U.S. government's torpid, fitful, fragmented [response, that was] riven with prejudice against those afflicted with the virus" (p. 26).

In further explaining the formal sector response, organizational analysts Perrow and Guillen (1990) have drawn attention to the fragmented nature of health care in the United States and to the nation's historic inability to respond quickly to a public health crisis. Panem (1988) has documented how large-scale federal funding was allocated in 1985 only after the epidemic had threatened the health of heterosexuals. By this time, the gay community's care and prevention programs had become a model for responding to HIV/AIDS. Gay activists had also turned their attention to the rapid development of medicines for HIV disease, using their status as AIDS icons to give weight to their demands (Burkett 1995). The antiviral medicines for treating HIV disease were fast-tracked through the Food and Drug Administration in the 1990s on the basis of this political activism.

The self-help model of gay men and women in the United States has been adopted on a global scale. In Britain, for example, the Terrance Higgins Trust (THT; a London-based gay community group) provided help to PWH along the same lines as in the United States (Lichtenstein 1996a). This action took place against a backdrop of denial by the Thatcher government, which had made no secret of its disapproval of homosexuality and which initially offered little in the way of funds for prevention and care

(Weeks 1989). Only after heterosexuals were thought to be at threat of infection did Mrs. Thatcher delegate the job of AIDS policy to the deputy prime minister, who then created a "period of wartime emergency" in 1986 (Berridge and Strong 1992). The government's response built on the gay community model, eventually incorporating its principles and operations into the formal health sector.

Britain's response to HIV/AIDS occurred in three stages. Weeks (1989) has called these stages (1) dawning awareness (1981–1985), (2) crisis management (1986–1987), and (3) normalization (1988 onward). During the first phase, gay organizations worked to meet the needs of infected persons on a voluntary basis. In the second stage, parliament underwrote Britain's response to HIV/AIDS by empowering certain individuals to direct policy or to allocate large sums of money to community agencies and existing health authorities. In the third stage, political control of AIDS policy reverted to government agencies for integration into the health system as described above (Street 1993). This integration of services occurred at the same time that AIDS was being reconceptualized as a chronic disease in terms of its clinical management (Berridge and Strong 1992).

Britain's three-phase response is similar to that of Europe, Canada, and New Zealand and to some degree reflects the political and organizational structures of these countries (Australia's case was different in that the government took control of the epidemic in its early stages). These Western countries, with their focus on containment and favorable political structures, appear to have fared better than the United States with its plethora of competing, heterogeneous organizations and programs over which no one individual or voice has had effective control (Perrow and Guillen 1990). For example, Britain's HIV epidemic is still mostly confined to gay men, and the total seroprevalence rate remains relatively low at 0.11 percent of the population (compared with 0.61 percent for the United States). On a national basis, harm-reduction programs for IDU, among other measures, have been instrumental in HIV prevention in Britain (Henderson 1993). The iconography of AIDS in Britain, therefore, has been used with some success by the gay community and public health authorities as a rationale for targeted interventions and for limiting the spread of HIV/AIDS.

Injection Drug Users (IDU)

The Iconography

In the United States, people labeled "drug abusers" have been the targets of a moral crusade since the early twentieth century (Kandall 1996). IDU in particular have been singled out for their presumed sociopathology. The image of the IDU is of the urban, high-risk male living a shadowy existence; he is also associated with crime and ethnicity in the popular imagination (Lichtenstein 1996c). IDU have been presented as a bridge to the heterosexual population for HIV transmission and are therefore viewed as sexually dangerous as well as criminal. This representation has placed IDU in an invidious position in relation to HIV prevention because they are often regarded as too unworthy or too unreliable for HIV prevention in the United States, even though harm-reduction programs for this population have worked in other countries (UNAIDS 2001).

The iconography of the IDU intersects with ethnicity and race. Gilman (1988) has argued that this association stems from the iconography of syphilis and other STI in which disease is associated with minority status. The imagery is constructed around a stereotype that in the United States often centers on the "hypersexuality" of African Americans. An illustration of this imagery is the drug-addicted African American woman who engages in prostitution or who barters sex at crack houses (Kemp 2002; Murphy and Rosenbaum 1997). Kemp (2002) refers to this representation as a "controlling image" because it assumes that drug-using African American women are hypersexual disease-bearers. The iconography also involves African American men, for example, the HIV-positive sports icon Magic Johnson (a former superstar of U.S. basketball), who is said to have been infected by having sex with thousands of women (King 1993). The publicity surrounding Magic Johnson's confession about his HIV status prompted King to argue that his hypermasculine stance helped to promote myths about African American hypersexuality and other constructions.

Gilman (1988) writes that prior to the AIDS epidemic, the association between race and STI culminated in the Tuskegee experiment (1932–1972), where it was assumed that black men had greater immunity to syphilis and where they were observed without treatment, sometimes until they died. (Smith in King 1993) argued that the creation of images about hypersexual, drug-addicted African Americans allows the problem of HIV infection and its devastating effects on minority communities to be viewed and dismissed through the selective lens of bigotry. For Kemp (2002), the conflation of social deviance with HIV infection under the rubric of personal responsibility helps to conceal the class-based nature of HIV/AIDS in the United States. The focus on ethnicity and risk behavior (particularly illicit drug use) therefore reveals a modern form of stigmatization that can be justified in terms of beliefs about "personal responsibility," even as it ignores the structural basis for disparities in HIV risk, particularly in communities of color. While this justification is understandable in terms of the personal havoc wreaked through addiction, imprisonment, and adverse familial effects, the stigmatizing iconography has relegated IDU to an illegal, shadowy existence outside the realm of proactive HIV prevention in which IDU themselves might become full participants.

The Response

America's "War on Drugs" has shaped the iconography of the IDU. This policy has portrayed injection drug use as a problem of blacks or Hispanics in large cities such as Miami or New York (Sills 1994). The imagery has not only hampered HIV prevention efforts, but those moral leaders and lawmakers in the United States who have responded to the War on Drugs have been particularly fierce in raising barriers to HIV prevention for IDU, their sexual partners, and their children (Cohen 1999; Gould 1993). This response includes some African American leaders who have also opposed needle exchange programs, believing them to be a genocidal plot to destroy black communities through accepting illicit drug use as fact (Cohen 1999). However, there is little doubt that the politicization of needle exchange and the refusal of the U.S. federal government to fund harm-reduction programs has increased HIV transmission in minority communities. The CDC estimates that IDU is now the direct or indirect cause of 33 percent of all new cases of HIV/AIDS in the United States, with most of these infections occurring among African Americans (CDC 2001b).

The refusal to provide federal funding for needle exchange in the United States has resulted in programs being established in a piecemeal fashion in only 81 cities, mostly in the Pacific West and the Northeast (CDC 2001b). In a *Washington Post* article entitled "Scarcely a Dent in the AIDS Menace," Rene Sanchez (1994) noted that the problems inherent in a lack of federal funding were reflected in one city-sponsored program in Washington, D.C., that was so restrictive as to be a "complete flop." Other U.S. needle exchanges have been similarly hampered by moral, fiscal, and political concerns. Hurley and Jolley (1997) have documented that many of the 55 needle exchange programs established in U.S. cities by 1994 operated illegally, with tenuous funding, and on a limited scale. The authors concluded that needle exchange remains controversial in the United States despite sufficient evidence about its efficacy in HIV prevention.

National needle exchange programs have been established in a number of other countries, especially in Europe (Hurley and Jolley 1997). Most of these programs were introduced without the moral furor that occurred in the United States. Britain is one nation where such programs were given official, if quiet, sanction once the government realized that the HIV/AIDS epidemic demanded a departure from the U.S.-style War on Drugs (Henderson 1993). The HIV prevalence in IDU in Britain has remained low (8 percent of the total infections), and other countries with needle exchange have reported similar success. These countries include Canada (11 percent of the total), the Netherlands (11 percent), Australia (3 percent), and New Zealand (2.4 percent) (Australian Annual Surveillance Report 2001; CDC 2001b; European Centre for the Epidemiological

Monitoring of AIDS 1999; New Zealand Ministry of Health 2001). The CDC has noted the special case of Poland, where a national needle exchange program successfully limited the number of new infections in IDU and prevented HIV from gaining a foothold in the general population (CDC 2001b). HIV prevalence also remains low in countries such as the Czech Republic, Hungary, and Slovenia, where well-designed HIV/AIDS programs, including needle exchange, were established more recently on a national basis (CDC 2001b).

The countries mounting a strong response to HIV prevention for IDU have several factors in common. First, they rejected the "War on Drugs" rhetoric that characterized the U.S. response. Second, they had a tradition of government intervention in public health crises. To illustrate, the Netherlands, an innovator in health reforms, established the world's first needle exchange program in 1984. This program provided a model for other countries (American Civil Liberties Union 2001). The British government followed the Netherlands' example by taking a U-turn in existing drug policy and by approaching harm reduction as a government responsibility rather than as a social problem to be criminalized (Henderson 1993). In New Zealand, Australia, and Canada, the iconography of IDU as a public health threat led the government to allocate funds to community groups, which then supplied clients with clean needles and HIV prevention materials, including condoms (Davis and Lichtenstein 1996). The AIDS iconography of the IDU as "socially disreputable" and "criminal" was tempered by this approach so that injection drug use became partially decriminalized in the interests of protecting the public health.

The iconography of the IDU as criminal has masked the role of social change as an important element in promoting illicit drug use. The World Health Organization has noted the case of former Soviet countries (e.g., Belarus, Ukraine, Russia, Bulgaria, and Romania) as examples of the syndemic of social change, illicit drug use, and HIV/AIDS. The CDC has defined "syndemic" as two or more factors interacting synergistically and contributing to an excess burden of disease in a population (CDC 2002b). The transition to capitalism in these countries has been marked by a recent and rapid spread of drug trafficking, proximity to drug supply routes, widespread unemployment, economic dislocation, and political instability (UNAIDS 2001). There are also fewer government services, high inflation, endemic corruption, and widening disparities between the rich and poor. A particularly dramatic example of the effects of social change on HIV transmission has been in the Ukraine. There, 47 cases of HIV infection in 1994 had risen to 24,000 by 1998, with an estimated 79 percent of these infections occurring in IDU (see Table 19.1). This example underscores the importance of understanding how the effects of political change are often expressed synergistically through risk taking, ill health, criminality, and other social problems.

The African "Eve"

The Iconography

Much of the scientific and public speculation about the origins of HIV/AIDS has centered on the African subcontinent. From the outset, Dr. Robert Gallo (codiscoverer of HIV) stated that he could not conceive of AIDS coming from anywhere else but Africa (Treichler 1988a). The Africa theory is now widely accepted in the scientific literature (Connor and Kingman 1988; Leibowitz 1985), especially after it was linked to a single species of African ape (see Feng et al. 1999). However, the idea of sexually transmitted disease as "New World" in origin predated this latest discovery. Gilman (1988) and Fee (1988) have noted that understandings about STI and Africa began during colonial times when syphilis was linked with African slavery. They also note that while the Europeans had infected colonized people with STI, blame was attributed to the non-Europeans in the racist ideology of the times. Gilman (1988) has argued that such attributions about STI are very much in line with Western notions that blacks are inherently different and have a fundamentally different relationship to disease. Blame has also been attributed to women as "natural reservoirs" of such disease, particularly in colonized countries (Kehoe 1992).

The AIDS epidemic in Africa has been defined as heterosexual, or Type II in epidemiologic terms

(Smallman-Raynor, Cliff, and Haggett 1992). For this reason, and in the tradition of the STI epidemics, attributions of blame have again centered on women. Treichler (1988a) has noted that "African women, whose exotic bodies, sexual practices, or who knows what, are seen to be so radically different from those of [other] women that anything could happen in them" (p. 46). The "African Eve" icon has emerged from this conceptualization as sexually promiscuous and often a prostitute. This iconography is perpetuated in common lore, but also in HIV surveillance that focuses mainly on women as sentinel populations (i.e., pregnant women, female sex workers). This gendered approach has identified the problem of women's greater HIV risk, but the lack of surveillance data for men reinforces the notion of women being the locus of disease and perpetuates largely unexamined assumptions about heterosexuality being the only mode of HIV transmission in Africa.

Most attributions about women as AIDS vectors center on prostitutes who have sex with migrant workers and truckers or women who engage in "commodity" or "survival sex" (see Barnett and Blaikie 1992; Gould 1993). African women have sometimes been labeled "pervasive vectors" and a "major reservoir of the AIDS virus" because of the "literally hundreds of contacts they have a year" (Packard and Epstein 1992; Treichler 1988b). Certain types of African women (notably those from the non-clitoridectomizing Haya tribe of Northwest Tanzania) are said to be so interested in sex that they constitute a disproportionate number of Nairobi's sex workers (Caldwell and Caldwell 1993). The African woman's alleged promiscuity and high-STI rates have helped cast her as the female, heterosexual equivalent of the gay male "fast-laner." This focus on female promiscuity has proven a distraction from investigating the broader mechanisms of HIV/AIDS in Africa or men's roles in HIV transmission and thus provided little predictive power for understanding the scope of the epidemic.

The Response

Popular beliefs about the sexual dangerousness of women have had unfortunate results. These results include HIV-positive women in South Africa being kept in hospital against their will, ostensibly to protect their partners from infection (Raletsemo 1995). On a social level, women are perceived as "vaginas waiting to infect men" (Patton 1994). A particularly tragic outcome of the epidemic is that young female children who are orphaned by HIV/AIDS turn to prostitution as the only means of supporting themselves and their siblings (Gould 1993). At the same time, older infected men seek virgins or young girls for sexual intercourse as protection from disease, thus bringing the virus into the next generation (UNAIDS 2000). These practices not only expose women to HIV risk at an early age, but the sexual commodification of girls is being naturalized by the events surrounding maternal death and orphanhood.

The emphasis on women's sexuality has given rise to extreme comments about female AIDS vectors. For example, a Zimbabwe MP, Chief Mutoko, is reported to have said,

> If a pregnant woman is found to have AIDS, she should be killed so that the AIDS ends there with her. . . . You should not only terminate the pregnancy because the woman would still continue to spread the AIDS. (*The Press* 1994:4)

Chief Mutoko made this statement despite belonging to a male elite that routinely has access to a retinue of *femmes libres* ("tokens of esteem") as a class privilege (Gould 1993). In a similar vein, influential men in Mozambique resist the idea of issuing condoms to women because to do so would promote promiscuity and disrespect of men (Epstein 2002). These perspectives ignore the gendered hierarchy of HIV transmission and the fact that HIV infection has often passed from social elites (powerful men) to the lower classes (female consorts) in what Gould (1993) refers to as "the hierarchical diffusion of the virus in Africa" (p. 83).

The notion that African women are natural reservoirs of STI/HIV infection has also been promulgated through studies of female prostitution and other forms of sexual exchange. Packard and Epstein (1992) have argued that this first-world construction in the scientific literature reflects the Western tendency to look for deviance in an African

setting. This conceptualization means that the behavior of African prostitutes has been described, quantified, and analyzed in a manner similar to that of gay men in the United States. To reiterate Leibowitz (1985), this focus illustrates how the sexuality of an AIDS icon provides a legitimized and often titillating insight into how "other people" live their lives. The heterosexual man (often the silent partner in the HIV/AIDS epidemic) avoids this scrutiny. Indeed, prevalence statistics for men are rarely listed in AIDS reports (see UNAIDS 2002).

A social problems perspective on the female vector theory of AIDS in Africa is that cultural practices, poverty, and economic factors contribute to the high rates of HIV infection in the region. For example, polygamy, widow sharing (which requires a woman to marry her late husband's brother), and "dry sex" are considered to be important factors in HIV transmission. A lack of circumcision among sub-Saharan African men has been associated with higher HIV infection rates in the region, particularly in the presence of genital ulcer disease (GUD) (Caldwell and Caldwell 1993; Connor and Kingman 1988; Leibowitz 1985). The politics of gender inequality also mean that impoverished women are likely to be at risk by having sex with older, wealthier men ("age mixing") in exchange for food or money (Epstein 2002). These sexual exchanges often occur in depopulated rural areas because of out-migration of men to industrial cities in South Africa, or in regions characterized by war and famine.

Several recent studies and reports have suggested that violence against women has become a critical element of HIV risk in Africa (Epstein 2001; Hankins et al. 2002; UNAIDS 2000). This violence is part of greater problems relating to poverty as well as to war and civil unrest. Two examples of violence-related HIV risk include the "jack rolling" of women (seemingly random rape and robbery) by youth in urban slums in Johannesburg (Gould 1993) and the rape of female refugees in refugee camps in war-torn countries of Africa and elsewhere (Hankins et al. 2002). Violence has also been directed toward HIV-positive women because of assumptions about their promiscuity or because of a heightened stigma (UNAIDS 2000). The iconography of African women as AIDS vectors masks the power structures that give rise to discriminatory practices and differentials in HIV risk and offers a reminder of the synergy between inequality and disease.

HIV/AIDS IN THE TWENTY-FIRST CENTURY

The Iconography

The creation of social pariahs in the AIDS epidemic was an alarmist response to an emerging health crisis. This iconography emerged from existing ideas about the role of sexual deviance in the transmission of STI. AIDS as a social problem was first defined by its specificity (e.g., gay men and IDU in the developed world and "the female prostitute" in Africa). However, recent developments suggest that AIDS iconography is becoming more unified in the twenty-first century. For example, "ethnicity" is now a defining feature of HIV risk across the globe, meaning that there is a conflation of race and risk behavior in understandings about HIV transmission. This conflation is evident in the focus on HIV transmission in developing countries, particularly in sub-Saharan Africa and Asia. In the United States and other countries with majority white populations, the trend toward conflation is evident in STI/HIV surveillance statistics and in HIV prevention funding that is increasingly targeted to minority populations.

Delaporte's (1986) analysis of responses to the cholera epidemic in eighteenth-century France provides a model for further understanding the iconography of HIV/AIDS. Delaporte noted that cholera disproportionately afflicted working-class citizens in Paris, leading to the widespread belief that they were the source of contagion. Attributions of blame included accusing the poor of being thieves and revolutionaries who were spreading disease in a plot to overthrow the French ruling classes. Public health responses included quarantine for the afflicted in hospitals outside city areas and marking the doors of victims who had died. At the heart of the problem were the overcrowding and unsanitary conditions that ensured that the poor had a higher susceptibility to disease. The newly coined "germ theory" of the nineteenth century later provided a scientific explanation for cholera as an infectious rather than iatrogenic agent (i.e., due to environmental factors rather than to sin or social inferiority). This explanation led to a revolution in public health in the development of modern-day sewers and treated drinking water that ended the outbreaks of cholera in industrialized nations. Attributions of blame for the poor as disease bearers in the cholera epidemic soon disappeared, suggesting that such blame motifs occur in the absence of a cure or adequate measures of control.

Delaporte's theory that diseases are produced through harmful or discriminatory practices has been the basis of theorizing by Crimp (1988) and other community AIDS activists. For these activists, the public attitudes and laws that drive homosexuality underground, or that prevent the funding of needle exchange, have provided a fertile ground for HIV transmission. Two related factors are at work. Gilman (1988) has noted that the desire to create a *cordon sanitaire* between infected persons and others becomes a matter of urgency. A stigmatizing iconography is necessary in order to justify this distance on moral grounds. Furthermore, the iconography exists only for as long as it is useful or relevant. In the case of the STI epidemics, a stigmatizing iconography persisted in the interests of controlling sexuality and in the absence of a cure (Brandt 1988). This imagery, which focused on "good-time girls" and female prostitutes, largely vanished from public view in the United States and in other Western nations once a cure (penicillin) was found in 1943.

The reemergence of a stigmatizing iconography in the HIV/AIDS epidemic indicates the persistence of STI-related images but also the concerns of moral entrepreneurs and the "worried well" during the time of plague (Lichtenstein 1996c). If the responses to other epidemics are any guide, the stigma of HIV/AIDS will diminish over time because there will no longer be a compelling need to flee from the specter of death (i.e., if a cure is found or as HIV infection becomes less fatal, as in the case of syphilis). HIV/AIDS may become just another STI, which, although stigmatized, can be managed by "passing" or concealing it from other people (Goffman 1963). This historical precedent suggests that the iconography of HIV/AIDS will change over time. I propose three discrete stages to take account of this type of development. A linear path may follow from Stage 1 to Stage 3 or may vary depending on international patterns in the epidemiology of HIV/AIDS. The stages are (1) *personalization,* in which the disease is viewed as a potential threat to everyone; (2) *externalization,* in which the sense of personal threat diminishes if the disease is seen to afflict a particular segment of society; and (3) *habituation,* in which HIV/AIDS becomes "just another disease" in terms of its treatment and perceptions about its normality. These stages are outlined below.

In the first stage, *personalization,* explanations are urgently sought for the sudden appearance of the disease, its level of contagion, and the means by which it is spread (i.e., through ports of entry or immigration). In the case of HIV/AIDS, there was an immediate search for "risk groups" to determine the threat to society. The public gained a semblance of control over its panic, in part through a defining set of images about PWH. In terms of Gilman's (1988) concept of creating barriers to the threat of contagion, this iconography later resulted in the involuntary detention of HIV-positive Haitians who attempted to immigrate to the United States and in the segregation of PWH from other patients in U.S. hospitals. Other countries also followed this example, as in the case of the quarantine of PWH in Cuba and the compulsory hospital confinement of infected women in South Africa.

In the second stage, *externalization,* AIDS is seen as more of an external threat to the majority, and iconography becomes less compelling as a mechanism for HIV control. In the United States, this stage occurred after HIV/AIDS was understood to afflict "other" types of people and societies more clearly and after antiviral medicines transformed HIV/AIDS into a more manageable disease. This second stage has been reached in most industrialized countries, where a diminishing sense of personal threat means that safer-sex guidelines are often being ignored, even by people deemed at high risk of infection (CDC 2001a). However, this externalization is not the case in developing countries, particularly those in sub-Saharan Africa, where the number of infections continues to escalate and where categories of HIV risk are being expanded to take account of the scale of the tragedy.

The third stage, *habituation,* will relegate HIV/AIDS to a minor health concern if a vaccine is developed or a cure is found. In the West, this development will mean that HIV/AIDS will become part of the hidden epidemic of STI (Eng and Butler 1997) in which "passing" (Goffman 1963) is considered normative. Stage 3 may be reached by developed nations during the twenty-first century. However, based on present projections in the global epidemiology of AIDS, developing countries may progress slowly, if at all. For example, Stage 2 may not be reached in some sub-Saharan countries in the foreseeable future if antiviral medicines remain unavailable to the public or if so many people are infected that it becomes impossible for overburdened and underfunded health systems to offer HIV prevention to reduce the level of infection in their societies. Nevertheless, the waxing and waning of all epidemics throughout human history (e.g., leprosy, bubonic plague, cholera, yellow fever, influenza) suggests that a staged response will eventually take place, even as it involves a catastrophic loss of life.

The Epidemiology

Further outbreaks of HIV/AIDS in the twenty-first century depend upon sexual cultures, war, famine, drug routes, and political unrest, as well as access to antiretroviral medicines and treated blood supplies. Recent trends in HIV transmission indicate that large population centers (the former USSR, China, and India) will become epicenters of HIV infection in the twenty-first century (Bogaarts 1996; UNAIDS 2001). China, for example, stands on the brink of an explosive AIDS epidemic, mainly through injection drug use and illegal schemes to sell untreated blood in rural areas (*New York Times* 2002b). Southeast Asian countries such as Indonesia and Kampuchea also face the rapid spread of HIV infections among heterosexuals, indicating a generalizing epidemic rather than one that is confined to sentinel populations engaging in injection drug use and same-sex activity. Table 19.2 depicts "New Wave" epidemics in Asia and the former Soviet republics based on twenty-first century projections in UNAIDS reports. The table also

Table 19.2   Twenty-First Century Growth Projections for "New" Versus "Old" Epidemics Based on HIV
Prevalence Data from 1994–1999 and UNAIDS Reports*

"New Wave" Regions		
Very high growth	*Moderate to high*	*Low to moderate*
Asia		
China, Malaysia, Nepal, Singapore	India, Burma (Myanmar), Thailand (declining)	Bhutan, Kampuchea, Indonesia, Korea, Laos, Mongolia, The Philippines, Pakistan, Sri Lanka, Vietnam
Former Soviet Republics		
Belarus, Bulgaria, Estonia, Georgia, Latvia, Moldova, Romania, Russia, Ukraine	Lithuania	Armenia, Azerbaijan, Kyrgyzstan, Tajikstan, Turkmenistan, Uzbekistan
"Older Epidemic" Regions**		
Caribbean, Central, and South America		
None	Haiti, Panama	Barbados, Bahamas, Belize, Bolivia, Chile, Costa Rica, Cuba, Dominican Republic, Ecuador, El Salvador, Grenada, Guadeloupe, Guyana, Honduras, Jamaica, Martinique, Paraguay, Peru, Trinidad, Tobago, Uruguay, Virgin Islands
None	Angola, Botswana, Cameroon, Central African Republic, Congo, Equatorial Guinea, Ethiopia, Gabon, Ghana, Guinea, Guinea Bissau, Côte d'Ivoire, Kenya, Madagascar, Malawi, Mali, Mozambique, Namibia, Niger, Nigeria, Rwanda, South Africa, Tanzania, Togo, Zaire, Zambia, Zimbabwe	Benin, Burkina Faso, Burundi, Chad, Gambia, Liberia

Source: UNAIDS Surveillance and Reports (2002).

*The table does not include 28 mostly Islamic countries with insufficient data. The table also does not include countries in Western and Central Europe, Australasia, and North America with stable infection rates.

**The once exponential increase in HIV prevalence in these "Older Epidemic" countries has slowed, as indicated by the absence of a "Very High Growth" category in this table. The "Older Epidemic" regions listed here are characterized by a generalized spread into urban and rural populations.

depicts "Older Epidemics" in non-Western regions that are continuing to grow.

Table 19.2 shows that HIV prevalence is not only increasing in Africa and Asia but also across a large swath of the Northern Hemisphere once considered to be at minimal risk. For some countries, the AIDS epidemic is "rising so fast that it is a threat to global stability" (*New York Times* 2002a). HIV prevalence is expected to triple over the next eight years in the "new-wave" countries, which also account for more than 40 percent of the world's population. Experience has shown that the enormity of these newer epidemics depends on how quickly and effectively HIV prevention takes place among sentinel groups (Carael 2002) and how much access the newly infected have to antiviral medicines and other forms of treatment (Farmer 1999).

CONCLUSION

This chapter has indicated that HIV/AIDS is socially patterned and that marginality plays an important role in HIV transmission. HIV risk has been well documented in terms of individualized behavior ("risk behaviors"), but the view that disease is produced through structural inequality offers a broader view of the synergy between individual behavior, social structure, and disease. This structuralist perspective offers a unique opportunity for developing an impetus to change laws, attitudes, and practices in order to protect the public health. The countries that have changed or introduced legislation in the AIDS era to meet this public health threat have usually succeeded in limiting the spread of HIV/AIDS. Nations that have lacked the political will or resources for HIV prevention may face economic and social ruin, particularly in AIDS-ravaged countries in sub-Saharan Africa. The path of HIV transmission around the globe will depend on whether societies perceive HIV/AIDS to be an intractable social problem, like poverty or crime, or whether AIDS as a "special case" will prevail in the interests of humanity. This question will be answered by how much AIDS is perceived as a threat in the twenty-first century and whether the disproportionate suffering of some citizens and countries will continue to be tolerated on a global scale.

NOTE

1. The social inequality perspective of this chapter is offered as a counterpoint to popular stereotypes of HIV-positive people as irresponsible or deviant. This is not to suggest that personal factors have no role in becoming infected or that irresponsibility cannot play a role in infecting others. However, the "personal responsibility" mantra of modern times has created a geography of blame that has not occurred in nonsexual epidemics, such as influenza. I take the view of Farmer (1999), who argues that the idea of personal agency is highly exaggerated and is tantamount to blaming the victim. In this view, not only do individualistic notions of personal responsibility fail to acknowledge how AIDS has become an epidemic of powerlessness, ethnicity, and poverty, but they are flawed because the harmful effects of inequality on disease patterns remain unchallenged and intact.

REFERENCES

Alabama Department of Public Health. 2002. *HIV/AIDS Surveillance Statistics.* Montgomery, AL: HIV/AIDS Surveillance Branch.

Altman, D. 1986. *AIDS in the Mind of America.* New York: Anchor Books/Doubleday.

American Civil Liberties Union. 2001. "Drug Policy: Fact Sheet on Needle Exchange Programs." Retrieved from http://www.aclu.org/issues/ drugpolicy/syringe/ _exchange_facts.html.

Australian Annual Surveillance Report. 2001. HIV/AIDS: *Viral Hepatitis and Sexually Transmissible Infections in Australia.* Sydney, New South Wales: National Centre in HIV Epidemiology and Clinical Research, University of New South Wales.

Barnett, T. and P. Blaikie, eds. 1992. *AIDS in Africa: Its Present and Future Impact.* New York: Guildorm.

Bateson, M. C. and R. Goldsby. 1988. *Thinking AIDS: The Social Response to the Biological Threat.* Reading, MA: Addison-Wesley.

Berridge, V. and P. Strong. 1993. "AIDS Policies in the United Kingdom: A Preliminary Analysis." In *AIDS: The Making of a Chronic Disease,* edited by E. Fee and D. Fox. Berkeley, CA: University of California Press.

Bloor, M. 1995. *The Sociology of HIV Transmission.* London, England: Sage.

Bogaarts, J. 1996. "Global Trends in AIDS Mortality." *Population and Development Review* 22 (1):21–45.

Brandt, A. M. 1988. "AIDS: From Social History to Social Policy." Pp. 147–71 in *AIDS: The Burdens of History,* edited by E. Fee and D. M. Fox. Berkeley, CA: University of California Press.

Brown, V. and G. Weismann. 1993. "Women and Men Injection Drug Users: An Updated Look at Gender Differences and Risk Factors." Pp. 147–94 in *Handbook of Risk of AIDS: Injection Drug Users and Sexual Partners,* edited by B. Brown and G. Beschner. Westport, CT: Greenwood.

Burkett, E. 1995. *The Gravest Show on Earth: America in the Age of AIDS.* Boston, MA: Houghton Mifflin.

Caldwell, J. C. and P. Caldwell. 1993. "The Nature and Limits of the Sub-Saharan African AIDS

Epidemic: Evidence from Geographic and Other Patterns." *Population and Development Review* 19 (4):817–48.

Campbell, C. 1999. *Women, Families, and HIV/AIDS: A Sociological Perspective on the Epidemic in America.* New York: Cambridge University Press.

Carael, M. 2002. "Dynamics of HIV Epidemics." Paper presented at the 10th International Congress on Infectious Diseases, March 11–14, Singapore.

Centers for Disease Control and Prevention. 2001a. *Sexually Transmitted Disease Surveillance.* Atlanta, GA: Department of Health and Human Services.

——. 2001b. *Report on HIV/AIDS.* Atlanta, GA: Department of Health and Human Services.

——. 2002a. *HIV/AIDS Update: A Glance at the HIV Epidemic.* Atlanta, GA: Department of Health and Human Services.

——. 2002b. "Syndemics Overview: What is a Syndemic?" Atlanta, GA: Department of Health and Human Services. Retrieved from http://www.cdc.gov/syndemics/overview-definition.htm.

Cohen, C. J. 1999. *The Boundaries of Blackness: AIDS and the Breakdown of Black Politics.* Chicago, IL: Chicago University Press.

Connor, S. and S. Kingman. 1988. *The Search for a Virus: The Scientific Discovery of AIDS and the Quest for a Cure.* London, England: Penguin Books.

Crimp, D. 1988. "Cultural Analysis/Cultural Activism." Pp. 257–76 in *Cultural Analysis, Cultural Activism,* edited by D. Crimp. Cambridge, MA: MIT and October Magazine Ltd.

Crosby, R. A., R. J. DiClemente, G. M. Wingood, B. K. Sionean Cobb, and K. Harrington. 2000. "Correlates of Unprotected Vaginal Sex among African American Female Adolescents: Importance of Relationship Dynamics." *Archives of Pediatrics and Adolescent Medicine* 154 (9):893–99.

Davis, P. and B. Lichtenstein. 1996. "AIDS, Sexuality and the Social Order in New Zealand." Pp. 1–10 in *Intimate Details and Vital Statistics: AIDS, Sexuality and the Social Order in New Zealand,* edited by P. Davis. Auckland, New Zealand: Auckland University Press.

Delaporte, F. 1986. *Disease and Civilization: The Cholera in Paris, 1832.* Cambridge, MA: MIT Press.

Eng, T. R. and W. T. Butler, eds. 1997. *The Hidden Epidemic: Confronting Sexually Transmitted Diseases.* Committee on Prevention and Control of Sexually Transmitted Diseases of the Institute of Medicine. Washington, DC: National Academy Press.

Epstein, H. 2001. "AIDS: The Lessons of Uganda." *The New York Review of Books,* July 5.

——. 2002. "The Hidden Cause of AIDS." *The New York Review of Books,* May 9.

European Centre for the Epidemiological Monitoring of AIDS. 1999. "HIV/AIDS Surveillance in Europe." Report No. 61, June 20. Retrieved from http://www.ceses.org/aidssurv.

Farmer, P. 1999. *Infections and Inequalities: The Modern Plagues.* Berkeley, CA: University of California Press.

Fee, E. 1988. "Sin Versus Science: Venereal Disease in Twentieth Century Baltimore." Pp. 121–46 in *AIDS: The Burdens of History,* edited by E. Fee and D. Fox. Berkeley, CA: University of California Press.

Feng, G., E. Bailes, D. L. Robertson, Y. Chen, C. M. Rodenburg, S. F. Michael, L. B. Cummins, L. O. Arthur, M. Peeters, G. M. Shaw, P. M. Sharp, and B. H. Hahn. 1999. "Origin of HIV-1 in the Chimpanzee Pan Troglodytes Troglodytes." *Nature* 397:436–41.

Foucault, M. 1978. *The History of Sexuality: An Introduction,* vol. 1. New York: Random House.

Gilman, S. 1988. "AIDS and Syphilis: The Iconography of Disease." Pp. 87–107 in *AIDS: Cultural Analysis, Cultural Activism,* edited by D. Crimp. Cambridge, MA: MIT and October Magazine Ltd.

Goffman, E. 1963. *Stigma: Notes on the Management of a Spoiled Identity.* New York: Touchstone.

Gorna, R. 1996. *Vamps, Virgins and Victims: How Can Women Fight AIDS?* London, England: Cassell.

Gould, P. 1993. *The Slow Plague: A Geography of the AIDS Epidemic.* Cambridge, MA: Blackwell.

Hankins, C. A., S. R. Friedman, T. Zafar, and S. A. Strathdee. 2002. "Transmission and Prevention of HIV and STD in War Settings: Implications for Current and Future Armed Conflicts." Paper presented at the 97th American Sociological Association Meeting, August 16–19, Chicago, IL.

Henderson, S. 1993. "Luvdup and De-Elited." Pp. 119–30 in *AIDS: Facing the Second Decade,* edited by P. Aggleton, P. Davies, and G. Hart. London, England: Falmer.

Hurley, S. F. and D. Jolley. 1997. "Effectiveness of Needle-Exchange Programmes for Prevention of HIV Infection." *Lancet* 349:1797–1800.

Kandall, S. R. 1996. *Substance and Shadow: Women and Addiction in the United States.* Cambridge, MA: Harvard University Press.

Kehoe, J. 1992. "Medicine, Sexuality, and Imperialism: British Medical Discourses Surrounding Venereal

Disease in New Zealand and Japan: A Socio-Historical and Comparative Study." Ph.D. Dissertation, Department of Sociology, Victoria University, Wellington, New Zealand.

Kemp, Q. 2002. "A Black Feminist Perspective on Poor African American Women Who Are at Risk for HIV/AIDS." Paper presented at the 97th American Sociological Association Meeting, August 16–19, Chicago, IL.

King, S. 1993. "The Politics of the Body and the Body Politic: Magic Johnson and the Ideology of AIDS." *Sociology of Sport* 10:270–85.

Kramer, L. 1990. *Reports from the Holocaust: The Making of an AIDS Activist.* New York: Penguin Books.

Laumann, E. O., J. H. Gagnon, R. T. Michael, and S. Michaels. 1994. *The Social Organization of Sexuality: Sexual Practices in the United States.* Chicago, IL: University of Chicago Press.

Leibowitz, J. 1985. *A Strange Virus of Unknown Origin.* New York: Ballantine Books.

Lichtenstein, B. 1996a. "The Iconography of Eve: Epidemiologic Discourse in New Zealand's Organizational Response to HIV/AIDS." Ph.D. dissertation, Department of Sociology, University of Canterbury, Christchurch, New Zealand.

———. 1996b. "Needle Exchange: New Zealand's Experience." *American Journal of Public Health* 86:1319.

———. 1996c. "Icons of AIDS: The Media and Popular Culture." Pp. 66–80 in *Intimate Details and Vital Statistics,* edited by P. Davis. Auckland, New Zealand: Auckland University Press.

———. 2000. "HIV Risk and Healthcare Attitudes Among Detained Adolescents in Alabama." *AIDS Patient Care and STDs* 14 (3):113–24.

———. 2002. "They're Not Out There After All: HIV-Positive Women and the Myth of Promiscuity." Paper presented at the 97th American Sociological Association Meeting, August 16–19, Chicago, IL.

Mann, J. 1993. "The Global Effects of AIDS." *Green Left,* April 28, pp. 14–16.

Murphy, S. B., and M. Rosenbaum. 1997. "Two Women Who Used Cocaine Too Much: Class, Race, Gender and Crack." Pp. 98–112 in *Crack in America: Demon Drugs and Social Justice,* edited by C. Reinarman and H. G. Levine. Berkeley, CA: University of California Press.

New York Times. 2002a. "AIDS as a Threat to Global Stability." October 5. Retrieved from http//www. naplesnews.com/02/10/perspectrive/d825240a/htm.

———. 2002b. "Annan Warns China of an AIDS Epidemic." October 15. Retrieved from http//query.nytimes. com/search/full-page?res=9FO4EFDC1E3AF936-A25753CIA9649C8B63.

New Zealand Ministry of Health. 2001. *AIDS New Zealand,* Issue 48.

Oppenheimer, G. M. 1988. "In the Eye of the Storm: The Epidemiological Construction of AIDS." Pp. 267–300 in *AIDS: The Burdens of History,* edited by E. Fee and D. M. Fox. Berkeley, CA: University of California Press.

Packard, R. and P. Epstein. 1992. "Medical Research on AIDS in Africa: An Historical Perspective." In *AIDS: The Making of a Chronic Disease,* edited by E. Fee and D. Fox. Berkeley, CA: University of California Press.

Panem, S. 1988. *The AIDS Bureaucracy.* Cambridge, MA: Harvard University Press.

Patton, C. 1994. *Last Served? Gendering the HIV Pandemic.* London, England: Taylor and Francis.

Perrow, C. and M. Guillen. 1990. *The AIDS Disaster: The Failure of Organizations in New York and the Nation.* New Haven, CT: Yale University Press.

Pfingst, L. 2002. "Do Sociodemographic Characteristics of Sex Partners Account for Differences in Self-Reported History of Sexually Transmitted Disease between Blacks and Whites?" Paper presented at the American Sociological Association Meeting, August 16–19, Chicago, IL.

The Press. 1994. "Kill Pregnant AIDS Sufferers, Says MP," August 16–19, p. 4. Christchurch, New Zealand.

Raletsemo, G. 1995. *Living in South Africa with AIDS: A Personal Story. Women Alive Advocacy.* Retrieved from http//www.thebody.com/wa/summer95/soafrica/ html.

Rushing, W. A. 1995. *The AIDS Epidemic: Social Dimensions of an Infectious Disease.* Boulder, CO: Westview.

Sanchez, R. 1994. "Scarcely a Dent in the AIDS Menace." *Washington Post,* April 18, pp. A1, A8.

Shilts, R. 1987. *And the Band Played On.* New York: Penguin Books.

Sills, Y. G. 1994. "The AIDS Pandemic." *Social Perspectives.* Westport, CT: Greenwood.

Smallman-Raynor, M., A. Cliff, and P. Haggett. 1992. *Atlas of AIDS.* Oxford, England: Blackwell.

Smith, D. B. 1999. *Health Care Divided: Race and Healing a Nation.* Ann Arbor, MI: University of Michigan Press.

Street, J. 1993. "A Fall in Interest? British AIDS Policy, 1986–1990." In *AIDS and Contemporary History,* edited by V. Berridge and P. Strong. Cambridge, England: Cambridge University Press.

Treichler, P. A. 1988a. "AIDS, Homophobia, and Biomedical Discourse: An Epidemic of Signification." Pp. 31–70 in *AIDS: Cultural Analysis, Cultural Activism,* edited by D. Crimp. Cambridge, MA: MIT and October Magazine Ltd.

——. 1988b. "AIDS, Gender and Biomedical Discourse: Current Contests for Meaning." Pp. 190–226 in *AIDS: The Burdens of History,* edited by E. Fee and D. Fox. Berkeley, CA: University of California Press.

UNAIDS. Joint United Nations Programme on HIV/AIDS. 2000. "Report on the Global HIV/AIDS Epidemic, June 2000." Geneva, Switzerland: World Health Organization. Retrieved from http://www.unaids.org/epidemic-update/report.

——. 2001. "AIDS Epidemic Update." Geneva, Switzerland: World Health Organization. Retrieved from http://www.unaids.org/epidemicupdate/report dec01/index.html.

——. 2002. "Epidemiological Fact Sheets on HIV/AIDS and Sexually Transmitted Infections: 2002 Update." Geneva, Switzerland: World Health Organization. Retrieved from http://www.unaids.org/hivaidsinfor/statistics/fact_sheets.

U.S. Census Bureau. 2001. *Census 2000: Population by Race and Hispanic or Latino Origin for the United States.* Washington, DC: U.S. Department of Commerce.

Wallace, R. 1988. "A Synergism of Plagues: Planned Shrinkage, Contagious Housing Construction, and AIDS in the Bronx." *Environmental Research* 47:1–33.

Weeks, J. 1989. *Sex, Politics and Society.* London, England: Longman.

War, Militarism, and National Security

Ian Roxborough

State University of New York, Stony Brook

War has been a scourge of humankind throughout history. In the twentieth century, well over 100 million people died as a result of war[1] (Sivard 1996:18–19). Yet for some people, war is not first and foremost a social problem. Traditionally, rulers have seen war as an instrument of policy, a means to attain the goals of the state. As "the last argument of kings," war has historically been a normal part of statecraft. For nineteenth-century military theorist Carl von Clausewitz ([1832] 1976), war was simply the continuation of politics by other means. That war caused great suffering was not to be denied, but as an inevitable element of normal international politics, war could not in unequivocal terms be described as a social problem.

In a world of sovereign states, the rulers of each state are forced to concern themselves with the security problems inherent in international anarchy. Since no state can ever be sure that it will never be attacked by hostile military forces, all states are under compulsion to maintain defense establishments sufficiently robust to deter aggression. The security dilemma is dynamic. One state's efforts to increase its security by building up its armed forces generally prompt neighboring states to do likewise. Thus, whatever else might be a contributing factor, the risk of war is inherent in a world of sovereign states.

What Does It Mean to Say That War Is a Social Problem?

The belief that war was inevitable and "natural" began to change during the Enlightenment with the development of a critique of war as a purely irrational activity. These philosophical critiques, by philosophers such as Montesquieu, Rousseau, and Kant and by political economists such as Thomas Paine and Adam Smith, however, had little impact until the transformation of European and North American society created the kind of mass public that would take a moral cause and transform it into a social movement. This was to occur with the rise of the business and commercial classes and a large stratum of professionals in the middle of the nineteenth century. A few decades later, organized labor would add its weight to emerging peace movements. War became a social problem when the expansion of the political sphere in Western Europe and the United States and the transmutation of Enlightenment critique into proposals for public policy suggested ways of abolishing or ameliorating war (Howard 2000).

The first peace society was founded in London in 1816 by a Quaker. An international peace convention met in London in 1843, and such meetings continued to be a regular feature of the European and North American scene. By 1900, there were 425 peace organizations in existence. In 1910, Andrew Carnegie established his Endowment for International Peace with a fund of $10 million to promote the study of the causes of war (Howard 1978).

However, countervailing forces were also at work in Europe and North America. As Michael Howard (1978) points out, "the wave of the 'Peace Movement,' which by the middle of the [nineteenth] century seemed to be gathering such irresistible momentum, was met head on by an equally strong current of bellicose nationalism" (p. 47). By the end of the nineteenth century, both Europe and the United States were bellicose, and in some ways very militaristic, societies (Gillis 1989). An inflated spirit of patriotism and xenophobia "fuelled an alarmingly intensive arms race [that] could not be laid at the door of the old aristocracy" (Howard 1978:61).

Contemporary discussions of war as a social problem derive from this European and North American intellectual heritage. The twin features of this heritage—the Enlightenment concern to limit or abolish war and the remarkable bellicosity of those societies—define the parameters of modern thinking about war.

We are accustomed to thinking of war and peace as a fairly simple dichotomy. A moment's reflection, however, suggests that the boundary between war and peace is often fuzzy and porous. Moreover, in times of peace, preparations for war continue and have a major impact on society. To some degree or other, war is never very far away. J. David Singer (2000) has argued that all nations are somewhere along the road to war:

> First, every country socializes its children to think in terms of "we" and "they". . . . Second, almost every state has an army. . . . Third, to encourage us to salute the flag, sing the anthem, pay for the armed forces and their equipment, deliver our young people to the tender mercy of the military, tolerate a lot of secrecy, and accept lethal doses of toxicity in the air, water, and soil, we are often pushed along into a hostile frame of mind. Thus we are all moving, at different rates, down the road to war. (P. 20)

THE COSTS OF WAR

Individual Costs

There is little good to say about war: over the centuries, it has brought untold death, suffering, and destruction. Death, while the most obvious and most easily measurable cost of war, is by no means the only cost. There are also wounds and disfigurement, disease, hunger, loss of property and livelihood, torture, and rape. The pain of war extends from the actual combatants to those civilians caught up in the fighting (Grimsley and Rogers 2002). Increasingly, in the twentieth century, with the emergence of "total" or unlimited warfare, civilians have borne many of the direct costs of war (Chickering and Forster 2000; Sivard 1996; Winter 1995; Winter and Siva 2000). Large numbers of people are forced to flee their homes and become refugees, often living in miserable, disease-ridden camps. The demographic consequences of war are far-reaching (Sillanpaa 2001). War can involve genocide and has done so frequently in the twentieth century. The psychological and emotional scars of war must also be counted among these direct costs (Evans and Ryan 2001; Grossman 1995; Shephard 2001).

On the other hand, war is often experienced as emancipatory and as productive of solidarity. Wars involve, at least for some and perhaps for many, meaningful and valued activity. War is the realm of heroism and self-sacrifice, both among combatants and on the "home front," as well as the realm of great pain and suffering. It can generate feelings of intense comradeship and solidarity. And for some combatants, combat is enjoyable (Ferguson 1999; Junger 1929). For others, war is profitable, either as a means of employment or as a means of enrichment through plunder, exploitation, or through more "normal" business practices. But while some individuals or societies may stand to gain from war, on the whole, the balance sheet is markedly negative.

Collective Costs

The costs to individuals are but part of the balance sheet. There are also the economic costs to societies. This is a subject that has generated some controversy, since it has been argued that war can frequently have a decidedly positive impact on economic growth. This is true only under certain rather restrictive circumstances and assumptions. When an economy is stagnant, war production may act as a Keynesian pump-primer, stimulating an increase in economic activity.

While war might stimulate some economies, as it did for the U.S. economy during the Second World War (where the national product nearly doubled during the war), it ruins many economies and wreaks havoc with the fiscal systems of nearly all governments (Harrison 1998). The costs of war frequently result in economic dislocation, higher taxation, a rundown of assets and reserves, and inflation. The social dislocations brought on by war and its economic costs have their political effects, leading to mass mobilization, strike waves, political radicalization, and sometimes revolution (Haimson and Tilly 1989; Skocpol 1979). War can also lead to an extension of citizenship, to the rise of welfare states, and to greater social equality (Mann 1993; Skocpol 1998).

The stimulus of armed conflict sometimes accelerates technical and scientific research, often with massive long-run benefits to society. The development of medical techniques, radar, satellites, and computers are but some of the many examples that can be adduced to support a case that war has greatly accelerated technical innovation and produced widespread improvements for humankind. But war's contribution must be measured against a counterfactual hypothesis concerning the rate and nature of technical advance in the absence of war's stimulus.

In the absence of a reliable study, it seems reasonable to conclude that the net effect of war is decidedly negative. War is destructive.

Costs of Preparing for War

Besides the costs of war itself, there are the costs of maintaining military establishments in peacetime. Prior to the twentieth century, this has been the major item in government expenditure for the vast majority of states (Mann 1986, 1988; Tilly 1990). With the rise of the complex economies and welfare states of the industrial age, expenditure on the military has come to be a smaller percentage of government budgets, but it still remains a substantial economic cost. The direct cost of military establishments in advanced industrial societies tends to be about 1 or 2 percent of gross domestic product (GDP). The United States spends a larger share, about 3 percent, and in war-prone regions, some states (e.g., Israel, Jordan, Kuwait, Saudi Arabia, Angola, Eritrea) spend about 10 percent or more of GDP on their military (Stockholm International Peace Research Organization [SIPRI] 2001:283–88).

To confine the discussion to deaths incurred and to the purely economic costs of war, however, would be a mistake. War ruins lives in other ways. War can traumatize entire societies. Collective loss and the grief that accompanies it are both individual and collective (Bourne, Liddle, and Whitehead 2000; Lary and MacKinnon 2001; Mosse 1990; Winter 1995).

Militarism

Societies organized for war and societies that live in fear or anticipation of war experience effects that must surely be included in the notion of war as a social problem. President Eisenhower expressed concerns that a military-industrial complex was distorting the process of American politics. The cold war had a wide variety of pernicious effects on American society. The confrontation with the Soviet Union produced a widespread, if at times subdued, hysteria that found expression in many ways and pervaded the culture (Boyer 1994; Fried 1990, 1998; May 1988; Whitfield 1991). Red scares and McCarthyite witch-hunts were but the most visible aspects of a general anxiety and conformism that marked American society in the early decades of the cold war. C. Wright Mills (1956) argued that a "power elite" composed of tightly interlocking groups of businessmen, military officers, and the officers of highly centralized states had come to power in the United States. Harold Lasswell (1941) expressed concerns about the possibility of a global trend toward a "garrison state."

Although a garrison state did not develop in the United States during the cold war (Friedberg 2000), Michael Sherry (1995) has argued that Americans have lived in the shadow of war since the 1930s and that the menace of war has come to pervade everyday language and thought:

> War defined much of the American imagination, as the fear of war penetrated it and the achievements of war anchored it, to the point that Americans routinely declared "war" on all sorts of things that did not involve physical combat at all. This militarization shaped every realm of American life . . . making America a profoundly different nation. (P. x)

Not least, the experience of total war in the first half of the twentieth century led to a moral numbness of Western societies as the bombing of cities from the air reaped a growing harvest of death among enemy civilians (Crane 1993; Sherry 1995).

Militarism, as the term has come to be understood, is largely a state of mind (Vagts 1937). It is not to be equated with the existence of armed forces. Nor is it identical to military intervention in politics. Rather, it is a disposition on the part of a society (or at least large and influential segments of it) to glorify or celebrate martial deeds and martial values. Its most obvious manifestations at the beginning of the twentieth century were the jingoist and patriotic movements that supported arms races and war (Mann 1987). Theodore Roosevelt's description of the Spanish-American war of 1898 as "a splendid little war" and the crowds that cheered the soldiers on their way to war in Europe in 1914 were both expressions of militarism. Militarism as an attitude of mind was fostered with the creation at the end of the nineteenth century of a wide range of societies aimed at lobbying on behalf of increased military spending, of training youth for war (the Boy Scouts being one notable example), and veterans' associations (Boemke, Chickering, and Forster 1999). This militarism and its sustaining organizational structure continue today.

ABOLISHING WAR AND CAUSES OF WAR

The root question, of course, is: What causes war? For those concerned with abolishing war, or at least reducing its incidence and severity, the question of the causes of war is a pressing one. There has been much debate and some research on this issue (for recent representative work, see Brown, Cote, and Lynn-Jones 1998; Kagan 1995; Levy 2001; Midlarsky 1989, 2000; Rotberg and Rabb 1988; Vasquez 2000). We now can make more precise statements about the causes of war than we could a century or so ago; but there is no simple, universal answer to the question. Most scholars now accept that any adequate theory of war causation is likely to be multicausal and that no single theory is likely to explain well all cases (Levy 2001). The bottom line is simply that wars happen, in part at least, because some decision makers believe, correctly or incorrectly, that they have something to gain by going to war.

Economic Causes

Since the time of the physiocrats and economic Liberals such as Adam Smith, it has been argued that countries that trade extensively with each other or invest heavily in each other's economies are unlikely to go to war. This was the core of the arguments put forward at the beginning of the twentieth century by Jean Bloch (1899) and Norman Angell (1911) (see also Gallie 1978; Miller 1986). It has been revived by some theorists of globalization (Brooks 1999). The evidence for this is far from conclusive. Economic interdependence of economies has not generally prevented politicians from initiating war. Indeed, on occasion, economic ties have precipitated war (as in the Japanese decision to attack the United States in 1941; Barnhart 1987). The empirical evidence available to date gives mixed support to the notion that the route to a reduced incidence of war runs through increasing economic linkages (Bremer 2000; Copeland 1996).

For these Liberal thinkers, it was not that war was impossible; it simply wasn't rational because it didn't pay (Angell 1911). The evidence on this, however, fails to consistently support the argument. Even in the twentieth century, invading states have been able to extract enough economic resources to make conquest pay (Kapstein 1992; Liberman 1996).

The argument of thinkers such as Bloch and Angell that the irrationality of modern war would produce its obsolescence was given additional support by the impact of the new industrial technologies, particularly the machine-gun, which had made war immensely costly and would produce a stalemate on the battlefield. The Maxim gun, invented in 1884 and rapidly adopted by European armies, was the first fully automatic infantry weapon and heralded a new age in warfare (Echevarria 2000; Ellis 1975). It was argued that it would be so costly to attack an enemy armed with machine-guns that the opposing sides would lapse into what were, in effect, protracted siege operations. War would be lengthy and would require the mobilization of entire economies and societies. Such an effort would produce widespread hunger and misery and lead to the collapse of governments. War would therefore be impossible.

For their part, the Marxists had a similar analysis, merely substituting the terms of a class analysis of modern society. Although European Marxists such as Lenin and Kautsky believed that capitalist imperialism would lead to war, they believed that the transnational interests of workers as a class would prove to be more important than their identification as citizens of nation-states (Mann 1993). Marxists held it as axiomatic that workers would simply refuse to fight wars initiated by their class enemies. (Marxist thinkers in colonial and underdeveloped areas, such as Mao Zedong, Ho Chi Minh, N. M. Roy, and others, were to develop rather different theories of war. For them, war was necessary for national liberation and had an entirely different meaning than it did for citizens of the imperialist core.) Unlike the Liberals, European Marxists saw certain features of modern society—the immediate interests of armaments manufacturers, the push to expand markets leading to imperialism, and the limited democratization of late-nineteenth-century societies—as factors leading to war. But the working classes of all countries would simply put a stop to war by refusing to fight, and their parliamentary representatives would refuse to support the increased taxation that would be necessary to fuel the war machine.

Nationalism

Both Liberals and Marxists were wrong in their belief that war was obsolete. When war did come in 1914, workers flocked to the colors, eager to play their role as citizens. The nation-state trumped transnational class solidarity (Mann 1993). Nationalism proved a much more potent force than either Liberals or Marxists had imagined. As the fighting dragged on, the First World War introduced total war to the modern world. Bloch's (1899) prophecies proved all too true. Hunger, disease, and misery did, indeed, stalk the world. Entire political systems were broken on the rack of prolonged, industrially based total war. The Russian, German, and Austro-Hungarian empires collapsed. Soviet Communism triumphed in Russia, and revolutionary movements and strike waves swept Europe. The Liberals were right in this: war in the modern world would revolutionize entire societies, bringing turmoil, political upheaval, and massive social dislocation in its wake (Kolko 1994).

What many Liberal and Marxist thinkers had underestimated was the impact of mass nationalism on war. Nationalism both increased the disposition of citizens to fight for their country, thereby increasing the likelihood of war, and, by enabling states to field larger armed forces, contributed to a quantum leap in the lethality and destructiveness of war. When allied to the technology of mature industrialism, the passions of mass politics would produce the total wars of the twentieth century.

The phenomenon was complex. Along with mass nationalism, there was, at the conclusion of the "war to end war," a widespread revulsion against war and an upsurge of pacifistic sentiment. Most notoriously, in the Oxford Union debate of February 1933, a majority voted to refuse under any circumstances to fight for king and country. (Six years later, most of them went to war.)

Torn between differing stances, mass publics are neither inherently militaristic nor inherently pacifistic. Depending on the circumstances, mass publics in the twentieth century have ranged from outbursts of emotional patriotism and militarism to widespread revulsion against war, to a dogged determination to "see it through" and endure to the end (Levy 2001; Reiter and Stam 2002).

Ideology, Religion, and Values

If Enlightenment philosophy suggested that the only intelligible causes of interstate conflict were material ones and that these could best be solved through trade rather than war, then it followed that a prime cause of war must lie in the complex of irrational emotions that led to mass hatred, contempt, or misunderstanding. As with nationalism, Liberal (and Marxist) thought had an impoverished understanding of these "unenlightened" belief systems.

The solution to the passions produced by religious and ideological discord would be long-term: rational schooling and the subordination of the passions to the intellect. Tolerance of diversity and a concern for proper, civilized pursuits would ensue. That Christianity was a gospel of peace was taken as axiomatic. This largely Victorian image has recently been given prominence in two variants: the revelation at the end of the cold war of a substratum of primordial "ethnic conflict" and an enduring "clash of civilizations."

The notion that the world is divided into a small number of discrete "civilizations" characterized by divergent value systems is a plausible notion but one that is difficult to test. In its recent formulation by Samuel Huntington (1996), there is some ambiguity as to what constitutes a civilizational value system. What is lacking is an empirical study of the values actually held by the majority of citizens in a region. Furthermore, it is by no means self-evident that people are actuated by coherent value systems, rather than responding to specific situations by drawing on a toolbox of often contradictory guides to conduct.

Even if the empirical problem of defining the value system were resolved, it would still remain to be shown that such presumed differences of fundamental values were the causes of wars. There can be little doubt that during wars (and during prolonged periods of hostility), negative stereotypes about "the other" are usually developed and often are deeply racist in nature (Dower 1986). Such stereotypes may make the fighting more brutal than it might otherwise have been (Cameron 1994; but cf. also Bergerud 1996 for a contrary view), but to argue that the value differences themselves constitute more than an exacerbating factor in the road to war seems implausible. Cultural differences may make misperception of adversary intentions more likely (May 1973) and so contribute to the likelihood of war, but are in themselves seldom a primary cause of war. (The important exception here are wars of racial conquest, such as the Nazi attempt to subjugate the "inferior" peoples of Eastern Europe and Russia and other genocides in the twentieth century; Bartov and Mack 2001; Naimark 2001).

The end of the cold war witnessed what many commentators (e.g., Kaplan 2002; Peters 1999) described as an upsurge of "ethnic" conflict. With the collapse of the Soviet empire and the removal of the restraints of great power rivalry, long-held and deeply rooted ethnic conflicts resurfaced. They had been merely suppressed for a half century. This analysis, too, like that of a clash of fundamental values, while immensely popular, is by no means unproblematic as an explanation of war (for a general critique, see Brown 2001; Gurr 2000).

Ethnic conflict stems from the identification of the warring parties with supposed communities of inheritance, whether on racial, religious, or other grounds. However, some social scientists (Kakar 1996; Kaufman 2001; Sadowski 1998) argue that ethnic identities and grievances are created, or at least made salient, by contemporary politicians with quite different, nonethnic agendas. War is, after all, a complicated business, and it would be surprising if a single dimension such as ethnicity would adequately explain the diverse motives and issues involved. Whatever the evidence in any particular case about the degree to which the central dimensions of a conflict are deliberately and recently manufactured as "ethnic," such conflicts were widely noted in the early 1990s. Beginning in 1991, the former Republic of Yugoslavia collapsed into a series of warring states. Hundreds of thousands were killed, displaced, tortured, and raped. In Burundi and Rwanda in 1994, ethnic conflict between Tutsis and Hutus resulted in over a million deaths. (See the chapter on "genocide" in this volume.) There is, however, a need for caution in extrapolating from this sudden burst of supposedly "ethnic" conflict into the foreseeable future (Gurr 2000). Frequently, as important as the tensions between ethnic groups was the failure of states to maintain elementary levels of security for their populations. Research on the causes of "state failure" and on what can be done to reverse such trends is still at an embryonic stage (Crocker, Hampson, and Aall 2001; von Hippel 2000; Hirsch and Oakley 1995; Stevenson 1995).

The Security Dilemma, Arms Races, Miscalculations, and Misperceptions

As noted in the introduction to this chapter, in a world of international anarchy, all states face a security problem. This alone is a sufficient explanation of the occurrence of war (Mearsheimer 2001). But there are specific conditions under which the security problem is more or less likely to produce war.

Sometimes the security dilemma triggers arms races that become destabilizing and lead to war, as happened with the outbreak of World War I. The naval rivalry between Britain and Germany, the fears of the German general staff that a modernizing Russia might soon overmatch a smaller Germany, and the belief that the side that got in the first blow would stand a better chance of winning the war all produced an increasingly volatile powder keg in Europe from the 1890s on. Seizing on a relatively trivial incident (the assassination of the Archduke Ferdinand at Sarajevo), the German general staff launched a preemptive war against Russia. The European alliance systems rapidly drew in all the great powers, resulting in general war (Hammond 1993; Kennedy 1980; Miller, Lynn-Jones, and Van Evera 1991). Statistical analysis suggests some mild support for the proposition that arms races do increase the probability of war (Sample 2000).

Pondering the experience of the First World War, some thinkers drew the conclusion, in the 1920s and

1930s, that the risk of war might be reduced by controlling arms races. The most notable efforts were the treaties limiting naval construction in the 1920s and 1930s. While they did not prevent war from coming in 1939, they had some utility in bringing some stability to a volatile international situation (Goldman 1994). Similarly, in the later stages of the cold war (and thereafter), the nuclear forces held by the North Atlantic Treaty Organization (NATO) and the Soviet Union (and now Russia) were closely monitored and held to mutually agreed levels. That these levels were more than enough to destroy all life on earth several times over does not mean that the nuclear arms limitations treaties were of no consequence.

Given the security problem, it is not just arms races that can trigger war. Governments may miscalculate the balance of military power, they may miscalculate the likely response of adversaries, and they may misperceive many aspects of the security environment (Jervis 1976).

States do not always behave as rational, unitary actors. Sometimes the rulers of states act on a non-rational or irrational basis. Governmental decision making is a complex game involving all sorts of coalitions and subordinate actors with goals, interests, and perceptions of their own (Allison and Zelikow 1999; Halperin 1974; Kupchan 1994; Snyder 1991). Agendas from domestic politics are often mixed in with calculations about the security situation. Even when rulers use rational cost-benefit calculations, given the limitations of intelligence about enemy intentions and capabilities, these calculations may be fatally flawed (May 1986, 2000; Murray and Millett 1992; Snyder 1984). Finally, the cognitive belief systems of decision makers must be taken into account in any explanation of decisions for war. The use of analogic reasoning often precludes an examination of mistaken assumptions (Burke and Greenstein 1989; Khong 1992; May 1973; Record 2002; Vertzberger 1990, 1998).

World Systems, Long Cycles, and Hegemony

In a world where some powers are militarily more capable than others and where economic, technical, and military capabilities of states grow unevenly, there will be dynamics in the global system that affect the intensity and frequency of war. Periods when there is a well-established hegemony are likely to be periods of relative peace. As a state begins to lose its hegemony and challengers arise, the global system is likely to collapse into a new round of extensive warfare (Doran 2000; Kugler and Organski 1989; Mearsheimer 2001; Modelski and Thompson 1989; Rasler and Thompson 2000; Thompson 1988).

These dynamics can be traced back at least to the formation of the modern European world system in the sixteenth century (Kennedy 1988). The entire nineteenth century was the century of British global dominance. But by the late nineteenth century, both Germany and the United States had begun to overtake Great Britain as economic powers. The German bid for global hegemony resulted in the two world wars of the first half of the twentieth century and was soundly defeated. The aspirations of the United States toward global dominance were ultimately more successful, though driven by complex and contradictory internal pressures (Iriye 1993; LaFeber 1963; Zimmerman 2002).

American intervention in the European war of 1914 to 1918 was followed by a period of isolation in the 1920s and 1930s. Yet America, as one of the most powerful nations on earth, could hardly remain aloof from the storm clouds gathering in Europe and the Far East, despite large domestic constituencies seeking to avoid entanglements in overseas quarrels. Once committed to world war for a second time, the United States assumed a global stance commensurate with its economic power. The rivalry with the Soviet Union that emerged from the ashes of the Second World War cemented American globalism. By midcentury, the United States was hegemonic in the "free world." The eventual collapse of the Soviet Union then left the United States as the sole superpower (Bacevich 2002; Ikenberry 2002; Kupchan 2002).

In recent years, as American predominance has moved into a new phase, commentators (Held et al. 1999; Kugler and Frost 2001; Roxborough 2002) have pondered the implications of "globalization" for world peace. They tend generally to see two countervailing tendencies: on one hand, the increasing integration of the world through open markets and the Internet is seen as promoting peace, much as Liberal thinkers in the nineteenth century had hoped that international trade and improved communications would abolish war. On the other hand, a "backlash" is anticipated from peoples and states that either reject, or are unable to take advantage of, the most recent phase of globalization. Most analysts see both trends occurring simultaneously (Friedman 1999; Kugler 2001; Johnson 2000). Rejection takes many forms, from a dislike of fast food to a concern that the entire moral order of a society is under threat from the "Great Satan" (for a critique, see Sadowski 1998).

Some writers (such as Barber 1995) believe that the new axis of global conflict will be a contest between the "West," or "McWorld," and a rejectionist jihad, frequently equated with radical Islam. The sting in the tail of globalization is thus held to be the possibility of conflict between the core and parts of the third world. In the wake of the attacks on the Pentagon and the World Trade Center, in 2001, President Bush and his advisers began to talk of a "global war on terrorism," which they thought would last a very long time. In addition to military incursions in Afghanistan and Iraq, American troops were deployed to several countries to help hunt down terrorists. Whether further "regime change" in the name of the war on terrorism would be pursued was an open question. Quite how this new war will evolve remains, at the time of writing, still to be seen.

Democracy and War

Democracies almost never go to war against each other. They may be attacked (or they may attack) nondemocracies, but seldom do democracies initiate war between themselves (Brown, Lynn-Jones, and Miller 1996; Weart 1998). While this finding is quite robust (Levy 2001), it is based on a limited database. After all, depending on the definition, democracies have not been around for very long. It is risky to extrapolate a finding based on a relatively short historical time period into the indefinite future.

Why democracies do not go to war with each other remains, still, largely a matter for speculation. Is it because the electorate is reluctant to pay the cost in lives and material damage that war involves? Or perhaps the open debate in democracies reduces the possibility of miscalculation on the part of decision makers. Or is it that democratic electorates tend to hold more pacifistic values and worldviews because they are accustomed to resolving differences by negotiation? Whatever the causal mechanism involved, the finding that democracies generally don't fight other democracies has a clear policy implication: to reduce the incidence of war in the modern world, democracy should be extended and solidified.

International Norms and Regulations

There has gradually developed a series of norms, conventions, and laws that regulate the behavior of states. There are a large number of international treaties to which most states have subscribed. With the establishment in 1919 of the League of Nations and then in 1945 of the United Nations (UN), institutions for managing international conflict were created. Of course, if a particular state decides to ignore such conventions, it may do so. Nevertheless, to the extent that most states voluntarily abide by international law and convention and to the degree that this proves enduring, those laws, conventions, and norms become more solidly established and have greater power.

The original advocate of global institutions was Immanuel Kant (1795), who believed that an international order conducive to permanent peace could be initiated only when

> [c]ertain governments freely abjured their right to make war on each other; and it would expand only as other governments, observing the benefits . . . which accrued from this initiative sought membership within the bond of mutual non-aggression. (Gallie 1978:20)

He argued that a condition of peace was that

> [t]he individual's rights [would] come to transcend the boundaries of his own nation, being secured—and of course also limited—not by any supernatural authority, but by the mutual recognition, among the confederate states, of their rights and duties vis-à-vis each other's nationals. (Gallie 1978:27)

Kant's solution required widespread democracy and a normative underpinning on the part of the citizenry. This was only to become (partially) the case in the second half of the twentieth century.

The central problem with treaties between states is that there is no enforcement mechanism. As Thomas Hobbes ([1651] 1958) said, "Covenants without the sword are but words" (p. 139). It was partly the search for an enforcement mechanism that led to the creation of the League of Nations in 1919. The central idea was that collective security would be maintained by the collective punishment of transgressors. Eventually, the system foundered as a result of free riding on the part of individual states. Judging that their specific security concerns were best served by turning a blind eye to aggression in some particular instance, individual states failed to act together with others in a true concert of nations.

The establishment of the UN in 1945 was more successful. Always limited, of course, by the realities of great power politics, the UN has nevertheless served as a force for peace in a variety of ways (Doyle 2001; Held et al. 1999; Koivusalo 2002; Martin and Simmons 1998; Ruggie 1996). It has been the arena through which a series of conventions limiting the use of certain kinds of armaments (weapons of mass destruction, land mines) have been created. It has also served as a vehicle for legitimating military intervention to respond to aggression or in the form of peacekeeping and humanitarian missions. By the end of the twentieth century, it had become an established norm that states intending to wage war needed the sanction of the UN to legitimate their actions. Although the UN was seriously underfunded, controlled no military forces of its own, and could be disregarded when states wished, it nevertheless played an important role in creating a body of international law and conventions.

Humanizing the Conduct of War

Besides efforts to abolish or contain war, efforts have been made to humanize the conduct of war (Best 1980). War has always been fought within a normative (that is, cultural) framework. But the inherent escalatory dynamics of war, together with the fact that wars are often fought between culturally dissimilar opponents with different notions about the rules of war, make mutually agreed normative understandings fragile.

At times, perhaps distressingly frequently, war degenerates into a struggle with no restraints on conduct, where all actions, no matter how repulsive, are condoned. But war is always waged by men who have culturally defined notions of what war is and what purposes are to be sought in war. Nearly always, this means the acceptance of some ethical constraints on conduct in war. That such ethical norms are at times more honored in the breach than in the observance does not mean that they have no efficacy. The treatment of prisoners of war, for example, indicates widely held and generally observed moral codes of conduct. Of course, some military organizations (the Japanese in the Second World War, for example) have treated prisoners of war more harshly than international norms dictate. These variations, however, do not alter the fundamental point that normative constraints generally operate in war.

Those who have sought to ameliorate the social problem of war by controlling its conduct have attempted to establish internationally agreed codes of conduct. The first such attempt was the 1864 "Red Cross" convention in Geneva, concerned mainly with the "amelioration of the condition of the wounded on the field of battle." Conferences at the Hague in 1899 and 1907 established what are now the basic rules governing the treatment of prisoners of war, the wounded, and civilians. They also outlawed the use of poison gas and dumdum bullets. Subsequent conventions at Geneva in 1928, 1929, and 1949 further specified these issues, and in 1975, biological weapons were added to the prohibited list.

Rules pertaining to the nonuse of certain classes of weapons have had mixed results. From time to time, the appearance of new weapons, such as poison gas, land mines, submarines, and aircraft, has prompted calls for conventions preventing their use in war. While it is clear that some states have simply ignored such prohibitions and that certain classes of weapons (aircraft and submarines, for example) were so desirable that no state could refrain from using them, it is nevertheless the case that a majority of states have generally abided by the Geneva conventions. While the trend toward the increasing destructiveness of war seems unstoppable, efforts to regulate the conduct of war have met with at least partial success (Best 1980).

Value Change

It is sometimes said that war starts as an idea in the minds of men. This is undoubtedly true in many senses. The language and metaphors of war form part of our everyday discourse. Boys play with war toys. War movies continue to be a popular form of entertainment. Some right-wing groups style themselves militias and arm themselves for what they see as a coming war. Tens of thousands spend much of their leisure time reenacting the Civil War. Certainly, nationalism, patriotism, and "team spirit" are all essential if a modern state is to mobilize its population for war; they are part of the problem of war. Such attitudes are widespread in the populations of modern democracies. Certainly, modern culture celebrates violence in many ways. Yet there are countervailing tendencies.

Some contemporary social scientists (Mueller 1989; Shaw 1991) see an emergence of postmilitary societies and the obsolescence of major war. They see a diffusion of global values (most notably, respect for human rights) as operating to reduce the likelihood of major war, at least among the countries of the industrial core (Held et al. 1999; Shaw 1991). Nineteenth-century Liberal thought was simply ahead of its time; only now are we beginning to see the widespread diffusion of antimilitaristic values.

To explain this, political scientist John Mueller (1989) has used the analogy of dueling. Dueling, he argues, was a way of resolving conflicts about honor that gradually fell out of use. Eventually, it became inconceivable as a way to solve disputes. In much the same way, Mueller argues, war is becoming—at least in the countries of the democratic core—an increasingly unthinkable, and hence obsolete, way of resolving disputes. War will not be abolished; it will fade away.

Unfortunately, even the most parochial citizens of the core can take but little comfort in this. Quite apart from the moral issues attendant on being a spectator to armed conflict in the rest of the world, the pacification of the states of the democratic core will not prevent them from becoming involved militarily with states elsewhere in the world.

Currently, many advocates of world peace hope that social movements and nongovernmental organizations (NGOs) will provide the basis for the spread of values conducive to peace and for protest and opposition to war making. The evidence suggests that on particular issues, such as the banning of land mines, concerted efforts by NGOs seem to have paid off (Maddocks 2002). However, in the absence of specific issues, the impact of these social movements and NGOs is likely to be diffuse and hard to measure.

An objective evaluation of the spread and influence of antiwar values is difficult. There is no denying the growth of popular antiwar sentiment. On the other hand, this has proven both episodic and ineffectual in the past, and the metaphors and phrases of war remain deeply entrenched in modern culture.

There are links between the arguments about democracy, international regimes for mediating conflict, and the spread of pacifistic values. For democracy to produce peace, it is necessary that the citizens of democracies evaluate the costs of war as excessively high. In part, this depends on the valuation of human life, primarily among the citizens of the country concerned, though there may also be some concern for the lives of citizens in adversary societies (Mueller 1994).

Nuclear Armageddon and Contemporary Peace Movements

The nature of war changed fundamentally with the dropping of atomic bombs on Japan in August 1945. Within a few years, humanity had acquired the technical capability to destroy civilization, and perhaps human life as such, in a truly apocalyptic scenario. For 40 years, humankind stood poised on the brink of a war, the destructiveness of which beggared the imagination.

Since the end of the cold war, the immediate threat of nuclear annihilation appears to have receded. The hair-trigger standoff between the United States and the Soviet Union has been ratcheted down, and nuclear stockpiles have been reduced in size and alert status. However, the United States and Russia each retain very considerable nuclear forces on active status. Moreover, Great Britain, France, Israel, China, India, and Pakistan all now have nuclear capabilities, though in greatly varying degrees of sophistication. Other nations may well acquire nuclear capabilities in the not-too-distant future (Lewis and Johnson 1995; Paul et al. 2000; Utgoff 2000).

There remains also, of course, the danger of accidental nuclear war (Blair 1993; Sagan 1993). And since the end of the cold war, there has emerged the new problem of "loose nukes," the danger of nuclear weapons or dirty bombs getting into the hands of a variety of state and nonstate actors (Ford and Schuller 1997).

To the proliferation of nuclear weapons, one must now add the proliferation of the means of waging chemical and biological attack and the increasing proliferation of sophisticated weapons systems such as cruise and ballistic missiles (Falkenrath, Newman, and Thayer 1998; Johnson 1997; Lavoy, Sagan, and Wirtz 2000; Roberts 2000; Tucker 2000). How likely the use of such weapons of mass destruction is cannot be accurately gauged. It does seem plausible, however, that the general shift from mutual deterrence on the part of two responsible and identifiable state actors to a situation with multiple actors, some of which are neither responsible nor identifiable, is fraught with great peril. Insofar as deterrence worked during much of the cold war, it may well become less reliable in coming decades.

War has not been abolished, and this is unlikely to happen in the near future. Some of the proposals for the abolition of war rest on slender empirical evidence. The widely held notion that increasing economic ties reduces the risk of war, for example, has only mixed support (Levy 2001). Some other avenues for policy seem much more promising. It seems fair to say that the most promising ways to promote peace involve the spread and consolidation of democracy throughout the world, the global diffusion of pacifistic values, and a continuing search for more effective international mechanisms for preventing crisis escalation. If we see progress on these dimensions, then perhaps war will disappear from the face of the earth. Meanwhile, as long as some states believe that war is an effective instrument of policy, war will remain with us.

CONTEMPORARY TRENDS IN WAR

The central dynamics of war in the recent period have been (1) the increasing destructiveness of war; (2) the pacification of the democratic core; (3) the migration of war to the third world; (4) the rising importance of irregular warfare, in the form of people's war, struggles for national liberation, terrorism, and low-intensity conflict; and (5) the emergence of the United States as the key hegemonic power.

Increasing Destructiveness of War

With the rise of industrial society and the application of science to war, war has become more destructive, both in actuality and, perhaps more significantly, in potential. More and more civilians are victims of war, and entire societies have been set on a war footing or have become militarized. War has become the business of whole populations and not simply of the soldiers engaged in the actual fighting.

The first half of the century was marked by two world wars, which, directly or indirectly, dragged most of the world into their orbit and caused untold suffering, mocking Liberal expectations that material progress and civilization would usher in a peaceful world. Since 1945, there has been no equivalent global conflict, but with the development of atomic weapons, humanity has had to confront the possibility of destruction on a scale sufficient to destroy civilization.

Whether these trends in the frequency and intensity of war can be extrapolated in a linear manner into the future must be a matter of debate. A long historical optic suggests that there is little linearity in trends in the destructiveness of war. The Thirty Years War (1618–1648) spread mass violence throughout European society. In those parts of Germany where the Thirty Years War was most intense, the population declined by perhaps one-third. For much of the Middle Ages, many regions in Europe were prey to armed mobs, often of demobilized warriors, and the predatory activities of feudal lords.

Yet there were also periods of more or less prolonged peace.

Pacification of the Democratic Core

While war has become more destructive, there are trends in the countries of the democratic core toward demilitarization. During the second half of the twentieth century, war, at least between European states, was for many people simply unthinkable (Kagan 2003; Mueller 1989). There was a tendency to believe that this meant an increasingly peaceful world. This was an illusion. The threat of nuclear annihilation remained ever present, even if its appearance in the public consciousness in the form of protest movements remained episodic. Wars within the third world and wars between the democratic core and the rest of the world showed little sign of abating.

War Moves to the Third World

The geographical locus of war has shifted in the period since the Second World War. For much of the modern period, the global dynamics of war were set primarily by the Europeans (and partly by their North American offspring).

By the middle of the twentieth century, European warfare had become globalized. While the aftermath of the Second World War saw a half century of peace in Europe, that war's vast disruptions spurred national liberation and revolutionary movements throughout much of Asia and imparted a new dynamic: that of people's war (Kolko 1994). Asia, the Middle East, and to some extent parts of Africa now became the geographical loci of war.

During the cold war, much of the actual conflict between the superpowers occurred in the periphery, in places such as Korea, Vietnam, Angola, Afghanistan, and Central America. These were sometimes proxy wars, though large numbers of American, Chinese, and Soviet troops also became casualties. There were also many wars fought in the periphery that had little or nothing to do with cold war issues, and this continues to be the case today. While wars in the third world seldom attract much attention in the Western media—at least as long as Western powers are not directly involved—they have been, and continue to be, the proximate cause of widespread suffering, political instability, and poor economic performance.

There are many causes of war in the third world (Harkavy and Neuman 2001; Neuman and Harkavy 1987), and we need to make some distinctions. First, there are a number of middle-range powers, such as China, India, Pakistan, Iraq, Iran, Syria, Vietnam, and North and South Korea. These typically have large military forces, are capable of fighting conventional wars (and have done so in the last half century), and some of them are armed with nuclear weapons, missiles, and chemical and biological weapons.[2] The zones where they are clustered are potential zones of interstate warfare. Some of these states, notably China and India, are of a size such that they can seriously entertain aspirations of regional hegemony. In those cases where the United States, Russia, and Europe (and in some cases, China) feel that they have security interests involved, international conflict in these war-prone regions always entails a risk that the conflict will be globalized.

War involving these middle-range powers will occur for much the same sorts of reasons that war has broken out between European nations in the last several centuries. Conflicts over scarce resources (Homer-Dixon 1998; Klare 2001), tensions arising from economic interdependence, and straightforward security tensions and miscalculations will all, no doubt, contribute to the emergence of more wars.

There is a second group of third world states where armed conflict is also likely. These are fragile or collapsed states. In parts of Africa and Central Asia, the extent of effective state control over territory varies enormously. State collapse is neither inevitable nor irreversible, but it is currently endemic. When states lose control of their territory, power is effectively devolved, leading to the emergence of warlords and armed predatory bands. The attendant evils of economic destruction, disease, rape, child soldiers, and a culture of endemic violence follow as a matter of course.

Guerrilla and Irregular War

In the third world, the boundaries between war, banditry and piracy, economic entrepreneurialism, crime, and revolutionary guerrilla struggle will often be opaque, shifting, and amorphous. Control over internationally traded commodities—minerals, particularly diamonds, and drugs—finance these war efforts and indeed provide much of the stimulus for war in the first place. War becomes little more than a protection racket on a large scale (Tilly 1985). Mercenary armies will intermingle with local militias, religious fanatics, bandits, and warlords (Silverstein 2000). At times, these conflicts will be fused with ethnic, religious, or nationalist struggles aimed at creating new nation-states or at a revolutionary transformation of society (Beckett 2001; Moran 2001). Nationalist impulses are powerful, particularly among peoples without states, such as the Palestinians and Kurds, and among ethnic groups that aspire to nationhood.

The solution to the endemic nature of irregular armed conflict in these weak states is painfully obvious—more effective government and better economic performance—but the magnitude of the task is daunting. Here, indeed, is a social problem of immense proportions.

There are zones of peace in the third world. Some countries have been blissfully free from massive violence, whether in the form of conventional interstate war or in the form of domestic insurgency and civil war. Indeed some, Costa Rica for example, have managed to survive without an army of any appreciable size. What little research there is on how such zones of peace are created suggests that it is the relative weakness of the military that is responsible (Centeno 2002).

In September 2001, with the attack on the World Trade Center and the Pentagon, the kind of low-intensity, "dirty war" characteristic of the third world came to the United States. The attack focused the attention of Western publics on the issue of terrorism. Of course, terrorism has a long history (Laquer 1999). It was a matter of intense concern to political elites at the end of the nineteenth century. Assassinations of political leaders by nationalists and revolutionaries were a regular occurrence. In one form or another, terrorism has persisted throughout the twentieth century. Sometimes described (like guerrilla warfare) as the "weapon of the weak," it has been employed in a range of nationalist, ethnic, and religious struggles and also as a tool of personal and criminal vendettas. By the 1990s, analysts were beginning to be concerned about the use of weapons of mass destruction by terrorists (Cameron 1999; Hoffman 1998; Lesser et al. 1999; Stern 1999).

The intent of terrorists has usually been coercive. They have aimed to raise the costs to their adversaries and persuade them to change policy. Unaccustomed to the irregular warfare of the third world, Western societies have been torn between treating terrorism as crime and accepting the view of the terrorists themselves that they are engaged in a war.

In the West, we are accustomed to thinking of war as a contest between regularly constituted armed forces. This is a historically relatively new form of armed conflict and far from universal in today's world. Indeed, some commentators, such as Martin van Crefeld (1991, 1997) and Ralph Peters (1999, 2002) have argued that such forms of irregular and people's war will increasingly dominate. If they are right, we will need to rethink many of our basic assumptions about the nature of war and armed forces (Davis and Pereira 2002). The distinctions between war and peace and between war and crime may dissolve or at least become increasingly problematic. In one of history's many ironies, the face of war in the third world may perhaps come to the advanced industrial societies, forcing Western societies increasingly to wage war in "irregular" ways.

Terrorism has now emerged as a serious social problem in the United States in the sense that increasing measures are being taken to counter a widely perceived "threat" of terrorism. The magnitude and exact nature of the threat is entirely unclear; but the measures currently being taken to combat the threat of terrorism certainly constitute a second-order social problem. As in the early days of the cold war, there are concerns about governmental surveillance of citizens, civil liberties, widespread moral panic and hysteria, enforced conformism, and so on. Clearly, any administration would have to devote enormous resources to preparing for further attacks, possibly with weapons of vastly greater destructiveness. The cost to American society of the September 11 attacks must be measured not simply in terms of the lives lost and damage incurred on that day, but in the myriad costs of societal response. If Al-Qaeda sees itself "at war" with America, and if the United States remains committed to a global "war against terrorism," then we have yet another instance of the high cost of war.

The Centrality of the United States

The fifth trend of war in the recent period has been the rise of the United States to global hegemony. With the collapse of the Soviet Union in 1991, the United States became the sole superpower. This was bound to change the global dynamics of war in ways at which (at the time of writing in 2003) one could only begin to guess.

As a status quo power, the United States has fallen into the role of attempting to control the many sources of change and instability inherent in global social change. It has intervened in the form of peacekeeping and humanitarian missions in Somalia (1992–1995), Bosnia (1994–present), Haiti (1994), and Kosovo (1999–present). It has sought to act as creator and enforcer of international norms, particularly with regard to the proliferation of weapons of mass destruction. When the United States (and other powers to a lesser degree) has felt its interests threatened, it has intervened militarily, as in Panama (1989), Afghanistan (2001–present), and Iraq (1990–1991 and 2003–present). These expeditionary wars have largely been aimed at preserving the status quo, particularly in regions of concern to the United States.

The United States has backed its pretension to hegemony with vast military spending. As a large and wealthy country, when it devotes 3 percent of its GDP to the military, this results in 37 percent of all global spending on the military. (SIPRI 2001:277–82). Moreover, the U.S. military is increasingly configured for "expeditionary" operations anywhere in the world.

The United States is now in the position where almost any adjustment in international relations can be seen as a challenge to its global hegemony. But a hegemon will be the focus for much resentment and will likely see the development of counterbalancing coalitions among other states. How it will react to perceived challenges to its dominance will be a central question in the years ahead (Kupchan 2002; Mearsheimer 2001).

Michael Sherry (1995) has discussed how Americans perceived the threat of war in the twentieth century:

War came from outside America to intrude upon their lives and to wrest them from their pacific ways.... And war itself seemed a murky phenomenon.... Regarding military vigilance and action as imperatives imposed upon them by external forces, they rarely acknowledged that their immersion in those imperatives arose also from their own values and ambitions.... In the understandable but simple moral drama they saw, bad guys—Nazies, Japs, Commies, Russians—made them take up arms. (P. ix)

Meant to describe the period of the Second World War and the cold war, Sherry's description remains relevant in the post–cold war world. The temptation toward the moralization and demonization of conflict is ever present to Americans. It can, under the appropriate circumstances, lead to "crusades" aimed at improving the world. For a superpower, such hubris is dangerous.

Conclusion

The 30-year cataclysm of the two world wars, followed immediately by the threat of nuclear annihilation, seemed to have unleashed the destructiveness of war beyond all human control. It made a mockery of efforts to abolish war or to fight a "war to end wars." Yet in the second half of the century, nuclear Armageddon failed to occur. For the states of the democratic core, the immediacy of war—if not its terrible threat—was removed. For the democratic core, the second half of the twentieth century was a "long peace." That this "long peace" was simultaneously a cold war does not detract from the importance of its achievement. The pacification of the democratic core led to hopes that war between great powers was becoming obsolete.

Whether peace would spread from the democratic core to the rest of the world and whether war in the third world would draw in the states of the democratic core were still, at the dawn of the twenty-first century, open questions.

War has not gone away. In large part, it has migrated to parts of the third world, where it thrives, largely unnoticed by the publics of the West. These wars are often brutal, messy, and intractable. They stem from a variety of circumstances. Reducing them all to instances of "ethnic conflict" or various "failures" of development leads to an impoverished understanding of the complexities of human conflict. Outside the democratic core, war continues to be a scourge, and the second horseman of the apocalypse continues his terrible ride.

Notes

1. Statistical estimates such as these, no matter how carefully the data have been collected, contain a large margin of error.

2. In this context, it should be noted that weapons of mass destruction are becoming the weapons of the weak. The constraints on the use of such weapons that have developed in the advanced countries cannot automatically be assumed to be operative in these middle-range powers.

References

Allison, Graham and Philip Zelikow. 1999. *Essence of Decision.* 2nd ed. New York: Addison-Wesley.

Angell, Norman. 1911. *The Great Illusion.* London, England: Heinemann.

Bacevich, Andrew J. 2002. *American Empire.* Cambridge, MA: Harvard University Press.

Barber, Benjamin. 1995. *Jihad vs. McWorld.* New York: Random House.

Barnhart, Michael. 1987. *Japan Prepares for Total War.* Ithaca, NY: Cornell University Press.

Bartov, Omer and Phyllis Mack, eds. 2001. *In God's Name: Genocide and Religion in the Twentieth Century.* New York: Berghahn.

Beckett, Ian F. W. 2001. *Modern Insurgencies and Counter-Insurgencies.* London, England: Routledge.

Bergerud, Eric. 1996. *Touched With Fire: The Land War in the South Pacific.* New York: Penguin.

Best, Geoffrey. 1980. *Humanity in Warfare.* New York: Columbia University Press.

Blair, Bruce G. 1993. *The Logic of Accidental Nuclear War.* Washington, DC: Brookings Institution.

Bloch, I. S. 1899. *The Future of War.* Boston, MA: Ginn and Company.

Boemke, Manfred F., Roger Chickering, and Stig Forster, eds. 1999. *Anticipating Total War: The German and*

American Experiences, 1871–1914. Cambridge, England: Cambridge University Press.

Bourne, John, Peter Liddle, and Ian Whitehead, eds. 2000. *The Great World War, 1914–45: Who Won? Who Lost?* London, England: HarperCollins.

Boyer, Paul. 1994. *By the Bomb's Early Light: American Thought and Culture at the Dawn of the Atomic Age.* Chapel Hill, NC: University of North Carolina Press.

Bremer, Stuart A. 2000. "Who Fights Whom, When, Where and Why?" Pp. 23–36 in *What Do We Know About War?* edited by John A. Vasquez. Lanham, MD: Rowman and Littlefield.

Brooks, Stephen G. 1999. "The Globalization of Production and the Changing Benefits of Conquest." *Journal of Conflict Resolution* 43 (5):646–70.

Brown, Michael. 2001. "Ethnic and Internal Conflicts." Pp. 209–26 in *Turbulent Peace: The Challenges of Managing International Conflict,* edited by Chester Crocker, Fen Osler Hampson, and Pamela Aall. Washington, DC: U.S. Institute of Peace Press.

Brown, Michael, Owen R. Cote, Sean M. Lynn-Jones, and Steven Miller, eds. 1998. *Theories of War and Peace.* Cambridge, MA: MIT Press.

Brown, Michael, Sean M. Lynn-Jones, and Steven E. Miller, eds. 1996. *Debating the Democratic Peace.* Cambridge, MA: MIT Press.

Burke, John P. and Fred I. Greenstein. 1989. *How Presidents Test Reality: Decisions on Vietnam, 1954 and 1965.* New York: Russell Sage.

Cameron, Craig M. 1994. *American Samurai: Myth, Imagination, and the Conduct of Battle in the First Marine Division, 1941–1951.* Cambridge, England: Cambridge University Press.

Cameron, Gavin. 1999. *Nuclear Terrorism.* London, England: Macmillan.

Centeno, Miguel. 2002. *Of Blood and Debt.* University Park, PA: Pennsylvania State University Press.

Chickering, Roger and Stig Forster, eds. 2000. *Great War, Total War: Combat and Mobilization on the Western Front, 1914–1918.* Cambridge, England: Cambridge University Press.

von Clausewitz, Carl. [1832] 1976. *On War.* Edited and Translated by Michael Howard and Peter Paret. Princeton, NJ: Princeton University Press.

Copeland, Dale C. 1996. "Economic Interdependence and War." *International Security* 20 (4):5–41.

Crane, Conrad C. 1993. *Bombs, Cities, and Civilians.* Lawrence, KS: University Press of Kansas.

van Crefeld, Martin. 1991. *The Transformation of War.* New York: Free Press.

——. 1997. "Technology and World War II: Postmodern War?" Pp. 298–314 in *The Oxford History of Modern War,* edited by Charles Townsend. Oxford: Oxford University Press.

Crocker, Chester, Fen Osler Hampson, and Pamela Aall, eds. 2001. *Turbulent Peace: The Challenges of Managing International Conflict.* Washington, DC: United States Institute of Peace Press.

Davis, Diane E. and Anthony W. Pereira, eds. 2003. *Irregular Armed Forces and Their Role in Politics and State Formation.* Cambridge, England: Cambridge University Press.

Doran, Charles F. 2000. "Confronting the Principles of the Power Cycle: Changing Systems Structure, Expectation, and War." Pp. 332–68 in *Handbook of War Studies II,* edited by Manus I. Midlarsky. Ann Arbor, MI: University of Michigan Press.

Dower, John W. 1986. *War Without Mercy.* New York: Pantheon.

Doyle, Michael W. 2001. "War Making and Peace Making: The United Nations' Post–Cold War Record." Pp. 529–60 in *Turbulent Peace: The Challenges of Managing International Conflict,* edited by Chester, Crocker Fen Osler Hampson, and Pamela Aall. Washington, DC: United States Institute of Peace Press.

Echevarria, Antulio J., II. 2000. *After Clausewitz: German Military Thinkers before the Great War.* Lawrence, KS: University Press of Kansas.

Ellis, John. 1975. *The Social History of the Machine Gun.* London, England: Croom Helm.

Evans, Michael and Alan Ryan, eds. 2000. *The Human Face of Warfare.* St. Leondard, Australia: Allen Unwin.

Falkenrath, Richard A., Robert D. Newman, and Bradley A. Thayer, eds. 1998. *America's Achilles' Heel: Nuclear, Biological, and Chemical Terrorism and Covert Attack.* Cambridge, MA: MIT Press.

Ferguson, Niall. 1999. *The Pity of War.* London, England: Allen Lane.

Ford, James L. and C. Richard Schuller. 1997. *Controlling Threats to Nuclear Security.* Washington, DC: National Defense University Press.

Fried, Richard M. 1990. *Nightmare in Red.* Oxford: Oxford University Press.

——. 1998. *The Russians Are Coming! The Russians Are Coming! Pageantry and Patriotism in Cold-War America.* Oxford: Oxford University Press.

Friedberg, Aaron L. 2000. *In the Shadow of the Garrison State.* Princeton, NJ: Princeton University Press.

Friedman, Thomas L. 1999. *The Lexus and the Olive Tree.* New York: Anchor Books.

Gallie, W. B. 1978. *Philosophers of Peace and War.* Cambridge, England: Cambridge University Press.

Gillis, John R., ed. 1989. *The Militarization of the Western World.* New Brunswick, NJ: Rutgers University Press.

Goldman, Emily O. 1994. *Sunken Treaties: Naval Arms Control Between the Wars.* University Park, PA: Pennsylvania State University Press.

Grimsley, Mark and Clifford J. Rogers, eds. 2002. *Civilians in the Path of War.* Lincoln, NE: University of Nebraska Press.

Grossman, David. 1995. *On Killing.* Boston, MA: Little, Brown.

Gurr, Ted Robert, ed. 2000. *Peoples versus States: Minorities at Risk in the New Century.* Washington, DC: United States Institute of Peace Press.

Haimson, Leopold and Charles Tilly, eds. 1989. *Strikes, Wars, and Revolutions in an International Perspective: Strike Waves in the Late Nineteenth and Early Twentieth Centuries.* Cambridge, England: Cambridge University Press.

Halperin, Morton H. 1974. *Bureaucratic Politics and Foreign Policy.* Washington, DC: Brookings Institution.

Hammond, Grant T. 1993. *Plowshares into Swords: Arms Races in International Politics, 1840–1991.* Columbia, SC: University of South Carolina Press.

Harkavy, Robert E. and Stephanie G. Neuman. 2001. *Warfare and the Third World.* New York: Palgrave.

Harrison, Mark, ed. 1998. *The Economics of World War II.* Cambridge, England: Cambridge University Press.

Held, David et al. 1999. *Global Transformations.* Stanford, CA: Stanford University Press.

von Hippel, Karin. 2000. *Democracy by Force: US Military Intervention in the Post–Cold War World.* Cambridge, England: Cambridge University Press.

Hirsch, John L. and Robert B. Oakley. 1995. *Somalia and Operation Restore Hope.* Washington, DC: United States Institute of Peace Press.

Hobbes, Thomas. [1651] 1958. *The Leviathan.* New York: Bobbs Merrill.

Hoffman, Bruce. 1998. *Inside Terrorism.* New York: Columbia University Press.

Homer-Dixon. 1998. "Environmental Scarcities and Violent Conflict: Evidence from Cases." In *Theories of War and Peace,* edited by Michael Brown, Owen R. Cote, Sean M. Lynn-Jones, and Steven Miller. Cambridge, MA: MIT Press.

Howard, Michael. 1978. *War and the Liberal Conscience.* Oxford: Oxford University Press.

———. 2000. *The Invention of Peace.* New Haven, CT: Yale University Press.

Huntington, Samuel P. 1996. *The Clash of Civilizations and the Remaking of World Order.* New York: Simon & Schuster.

Ikenberry, John G., ed. 2002. *American Unrivalled: The Future of the Balance of Power.* Ithaca, NY: Cornell University Press.

Iriye, Akira, ed. 1993. *The Cambridge History of American Foreign Relations,* vol. 3, *The Globalizing of America.* Cambridge, England: Cambridge University Press.

Jervis, Robert. 1976. *Perception and Misperception in International Politics.* Princeton, NJ: Princeton University Press.

Johnson, Chalmers. 2000. *Blowback: The Costs and Consequences of American Empire.* New York: Henry Holt.

Johnson, Stuart E., ed. 1997. *The Niche Threat: Deterring the Use of Chemical and Biological Weapons.* Washington, DC: National Defense University Press.

Junger, Ernst. 1929. *The Storm of Steel.* London, England: Constable.

Kagan, Donald. 1995. *On the Origins of War.* New York: Doubleday.

Kagan, Robert. 2003. *Of Paradise and Power: America and Europe in the New World Order.* New York: Knopf.

Kakar, Sudhir. 1996. *The Colors of Violence: Cultural Identities, Religion, and Conflict.* Chicago, IL: Chicago University Press.

Kant, Immanuel. 1795. *To Perpetual Peace: A Philosophical Sketch.* Translated by Ted Humphrey 1983. Indianapolis, IN: Hackett.

Kaplan, Robert D. 2000. *The Coming Anarchy.* New York: Random House.

Kapstein, Ethan B. 1992. *The Political Economy of International Security.* Columbia, SC: University of South Carolina Press.

Kaufman, Stuart J. 2001. *Modern Hatreds: The Symbolic Politics of Ethnic War.* Ithaca, NY: Cornell University Press.

Kennedy, Paul M. 1980. *The Rise of the Anglo-German Antagonism, 1860–1914.* London, England: Ashfield.

———. 1988. *The Rise and Fall of the Great Powers.* London, England: Unwin Hyman.

Khong, Yuen Foong. 1992. *Analogies at War: Korea, Munich, Dien Bien Phu, and the Vietnam Decisions of 1965.* Princeton, NJ: Princeton University Press.

Klare, Michael T. 2001. *Resource Wars.* New York: Henry Holt.

Koivusalo, Meri. 2002. "The Role of International Organizations: Does the United Nations Still Matter?" Pp. 530–40 in *War or Health?* edited by Ilkka Taipale. London, England: Zed Books.

Kolko, Gabriel. 1994. *Century of War.* New York: New Press.

Kugler, Jacek and A. F. K. Organski. 1989. "The Power Transition: A Retrospective and Prospective Evaluation." Pp. 171–94 in *Handbook of War Studies,* edited by Manus I. Midlarsky. Ann Arbor, MI: University of Michigan Press.

Kugler, Richard L. 2001. "Controlling Chaos: New Axial Strategic Principles." Pp. 75–107 in *The Global Century: Civilization and National Security,* edited by Richard L. Kugler. Washington, DC: National Defense University Press.

Kugler, Richard L. and Ellen Frost, eds. 2001. *The Global Century: Civilization and National Security.* Washington, DC: National Defense University Press.

Kupchan, Charles A. 1994. *The Vulnerability of Empire.* Ithaca, NY: Cornell University Press.

——. 2002. *The End of the American Era.* New York: Knopf.

LaFeber, Walter. 1963. *The New Empire: An Interpretation of American Expansion.* Ithaca NY: Cornell University Press.

Laquer, Walter. 1999. *The New Terrorism.* Oxford: Oxford University Press.

Lary, Diana and Stephen MacKinnon, eds. 2001. *Scars of War: The Impact of Warfare on Modern China.* Vancouver, Canada: UBC Press.

Lasswell, Harold. 1941. "The Garrison State." *American Journal of Sociology* 46 (5):455–68.

Lavoy, Peter R., Scott D. Sagan, and James J. Wirtz, eds. 2000. *Planning the Unthinkable.* Ithaca NY: Cornell University Press.

Lesser, Ian O. et al. 1999. *Countering the New Terrorism.* Santa Monica, CA: RAND.

Levy, Jack S. 2001. "Theories of Interstate and Intrastate War: A Levels-of-Analysis Approach." Pp. 3–27 in *Turbulent Peace: The Challenges of Managing International Conflict,* edited by Chester Crocker, Fen Osler Hampson, and Pamela Aall. Washington, DC: United States Institute of Peace Press.

Lewis, William H. and Stuart E. Johnson, eds. 1995. *Weapons of Mass Destruction: New Perspectives on Counterproliferation.* Washington, DC: National Defense University Press.

Liberman, Peter. 1996. *Does Conquest Pay?* Princeton, NJ: Princeton University Press.

Maddocks, Ian. 2002. "Antipersonnel Landmines." Pp. 65–87 in *War or Health?* edited by Ilkka Taipale. London, England: Zed Books.

Mann, Michael. 1986. *The Sources of Social Power,* vol. 1. Cambridge, England: Cambridge University Press.

——. 1987. "War and Social Theory: Into Battle with Classes, Nations and States." Pp. 54–72 in *The Sociology of War and Peace,* edited by Colin Creighton and Martin Shaw. London, England: Macmillan.

——. 1988. *States, War and Capitalism.* Oxford, England: Blackwell.

——. 1993. *The Sources of Social Power,* vol. 2. Cambridge, England: Cambridge University Press.

Martin, Lisa L. and Beth A. Simmons. 1998. "Theories and Empirical Studies of International Institutions." *International Organization* 52 (4):729–57.

May, Elaine Tyler. 1988. *Homeward Bound: American Families in the Cold War Era.* New York: HarperCollins.

May, Ernest R. 1973. *"Lessons" of the Past.* Oxford: Oxford University Press.

——, ed. 1986. *Knowing One's Enemies: Intelligence Assessment before the Two World Wars.* Princeton, NJ: Princeton University Press.

——. 2000. *Strange Victory: Hitler's Conquest of France.* New York: Hill and Wang.

Mearsheimer, John J. 2001. *The Tragedy of Great Power Politics.* New York: Norton.

Midlarsky, Manus I., ed. 1989. *Handbook of War Studies.* Ann Arbor, MI: University of Michigan Press.

——, ed. 2000. *Handbook of War Studies II.* Ann Arbor, MI: University of Michigan Press.

Miller, J. D. B. 1986. *Norman Angell and the Futility of War.* London, England: Macmillan.

Miller, Steven E., Sean M. Lynn-Jones, and Stephen Van Evera, eds. 1991. *Military Strategy and the Origins of the First World War.* Princeton, NJ: Princeton University Press.

Mills, C. Wright. 1956. *The Power Elite.* Oxford: Oxford University Press.

Modelski, George and William R. Thompson. 1989. "Long Cycles and Global War." Pp. 23–54 in *Handbook of War Studies.* Ann Arbor, MI: University of Michigan Press.

Moran, Daniel. 2001. *Wars of National Liberation.* London, England: Cassell.

Mosse, George L. 1990. *Fallen Soldiers.* Oxford: Oxford University Press.

Mueller, John. 1989. *Retreat from Doomsday: The Obsolescence of Major War.* New York: Basic Books.

——. 1994. *Policy and Opinion in the Gulf War.* Chicago, IL: University of Chicago Press.

Murray, Williamson and Allan R. Millett, eds. 1992. *Calculations: Net Assessment and the Coming of World War II.* New York: Free Press.

Naimark, Norman M. 2001. *Fires of Hatred: Ethnic Cleansing in Twentieth-Century Europe.* Cambridge, MA: Harvard University Press.

Neuman, Stephanie G. and Robert E. Harkavy. 1987. *The Lessons of Recent Wars in the Third World.* Lexington, MA: D. C. Heath.

Paul, T. V., Richard J. Harknett, and James J. Wirtz, eds. 2000. *The Absolute Weapon Revisited.* Ann Arbor, MI: University of Michigan Press.

Peters, Ralph. 1999. *Fighting for the Future.* Mechanicsburg, PA: Stackpole.

——. 2002. *Beyond Terror.* Mechanicsburg, PA: Stackpole.

Rasler, Karen and William R. Thompson. 2000. "Global War and the Political Economy of Structural Change." Pp. 301–31 in *Handbook of War Studies II,* edited by Manus I. Midlarsky. Ann Arbor, MI: University of Michigan Press.

Record, Jeffrey. 2002. *Making War, Thinking History: Munich, Vietnam, and Presidential Uses of Force from Korea to Kosovo.* Annapolis, MD: Naval Institute Press.

Reiter, Dan and Allan C. Stam. 2002. *Democracies at War.* Princeton, NJ: Princeton University Press.

Roberts, Brad, ed. 2000. *Hype or Reality? The "New Terrorism" and Mass Casualty Attacks.* Alexandria, VA: Chemical and Biological Arms Control Institute.

Rotberg, Robert I. and Theodore K. Rabb, eds. 1988. *The Origin and Prevention of Major Wars.* Cambridge, England: Cambridge University Press.

Roxborough, Ian. 2002. "Globalization, Unreason and the Dilemmas of American Military Strategy." *International Sociology* 17 (3):339–59.

Ruggie, John Gerard. 1996. *Winning the Peace.* New York: Columbia University Press.

Sadowski, Yahya. 1998. *The Myth of Global Chaos.* Washington, DC: Brookings Institution.

Sagan, Scott D. 1993. *The Limits of Safety: Organizations, Accidents, and Nuclear Weapons.* Princeton, NJ: Princeton University Press.

Sample, Susan G. 2000. Military Buildups: Arming and War. Pp. 165–96 in *What Do We Know About War?* edited by John A. Vasquez. Lanham, MD: Rowman and Littlefield.

Shaw, Martin. 1991. *Post-Military Society.* Philadelphia, PA: Temple University Press.

Shephard, Ben. 2001. *A War of Nerves: Soldiers and Psychiatrists in the Twentieth Century.* Cambridge, MA: Harvard University Press.

Sherry, Michael S. 1995. *In the Shadow of War: The United States Since the 1930s.* New Haven, CT: Yale University Press.

Sillanpaa, Anna. 2001. "The Effects of Wars on Populations." Pp. 198–207 in *War or Health?* edited by Ilkka Taipale. London, England: Zed Books.

Silverstein, Ken. 2000. *Private Warriors.* London, England: Verso.

Singer, J. David. 2000. "The Etiology of Interstate War: A Natural History Approach." Pp. 3–21 in *What Do We Know About War?* edited by John A. Vasquez. Lanham, MD: Rowman and Littlefield.

Sivard, Ruth Leger. 1996. *World Military and Social Expenditures 1996.* Washington, DC: World Priorities.

Skocpol, Theda. 1979. *States and Social Revolutions.* Cambridge, England: Cambridge University Press.

——, ed. 1998. *Democracy, Revolution, and History.* Ithaca, NY: Cornell University Press.

Snyder, Jack. 1984. *The Ideology of the Offensive: Military Decision Making and the Disasters of 1914.* Ithaca, NY: Cornell University Press.

——. 1991. *The Myths of Empire: Domestic Politics and International Ambition.* Ithaca, NY: Cornell University Press.

Stern, Jessica. 1999. *The Ultimate Terrorists.* Cambridge, MA: Harvard University Press.

Stevenson, Jonathan. 1995. *Losing Magadishu: Testing U.S. Policy in Somalia.* Annapolis, MD: United States Naval Institute Press.

Stockholm International Peace Research Organization. 2001. *SIPRI Yearbook 2001: Armaments, Disarmament and International Security.* Oxford: Oxford University Press.

Thompson, William R. 1988. *On Global War.* Columbia, SC: University of South Carolina Press.

Tilly, Charles. 1985. "War Making and State Making as Organized Crime." Pp. 169–91 in *Bringing the State Back In,* edited by Peter B. Evans, Dietrich Rueschemeyer, and Theda Skocpol. Cambridge, England: Cambridge University Press.

——. 1990. *Coercion, Capital, and European States AD 990–1990.* London, England: Blackwell.

Tucker, Jonathan B. 2000. *Toxic Terror: Assessing Terrorist Use of Chemical and Biological Weapons.* Cambridge, MA: MIT Press.

Utgoff, Victor A., ed. 2000. *The Coming Crisis: Nuclear Proliferation, U.S. Interests, and World Order.* Cambridge, MA: MIT Press.

Vagts, Alfred. 1937. *A History of Militarism.* New York: Norton.

Vasquez, John A., ed. 2000. *What Do We Know About War?* Lanham, MD: Rowman and Littlefield.

Vertzberger, Yaacov Y. I. 1990. *The World in Their Minds: Information Processing, Cognition, and Perception in Foreign Policy Decisionmaking.* Stanford, CA: Stanford University Press.

——. 1998. *Risk Taking and Decisionmaking: Foreign Military Intervention Decisions.* Stanford, CA: Stanford University Press.

Weart, Spencer R. 1998. *Never At War: Why Democracies Will Not Fight One Another.* New Haven, CT: Yale University Press.

Whitfield, Stephen J. 1991. *The Culture of the Cold War.* Baltimore, MD: Johns Hopkins University Press.

Winter, Jay. 1995. *Sites of Memory, Sites of Mourning: The Great War in European Cultural History.* Cambridge, England: Cambridge University Press.

Winter, Jay and Emmanuel Siva, eds. 2000. *War and Remembrance in the Twentieth Century.* Cambridge, England: Cambridge University Press.

Zimmerman, Warren. 2002. *First Great Triumph: How Five Americans Made Their Country a World Power.* New York: Farrar, Straus and Giroux.

Sea Change

The Modern Terrorist Environment in Perspective

Gus Martin

California State University, Dominguez Hills

Today, our fellow citizens, our way of life, our very freedom came under attack in a series of deliberate and deadly terrorist acts. The victims were in airplanes, or in their offices; secretaries, businessmen and women, military and federal workers; moms and dads, friends and neighbors. Thousands of lives were suddenly ended by evil, despicable acts of terror.

President George W. Bush, Address to the Nation, September 11, 2001

Sea changes are marked transformations, representing sweeping conversions from an existing environment to a new order. These conversions often denote turning points in history, such as occurred at the end of the Second World War and after the opening of the Berlin Wall. In the modern era, a sea change in the international terrorist environment gained momentum during the decade of the 1990s and was brought to fruition with the terrorist attacks against the United States on September 11, 2001, on the World Trade Center, in New York City, and the Pentagon, in Washington, D.C. Terrorist typologies, their tactics and targets, and counterterrorist measures have all undergone a fundamental transformation in contradistinction to the terrorist environment of the cold war era.

This chapter examines this sea change in the modern terrorist environment and argues that terrorism in the new millennium is fundamentally distinguishable from the terrorist environment of the cold war era. The crux of this discussion is a contextual analysis of the new environment, beginning with the theoretical foundations for a new conventional wisdom on the nature and quality of modern terrorism. For the purpose of assessing the attributes of this sea change, the definitional debate on terrorism is revisited. This is followed by an assessment of the emergence of the "New Terrorism," discussed within the context of a theoretical construct for distinguishing terrorist environments. An argument is made that the "new" elements of the modern terrorist environment do fundamentally differentiate the New Terrorism from previous environments. Finally, an analysis is made of the immediate future of terrorism in a unipolar world.

THE NEW TERRORISM AND A NEW CONVENTIONAL WISDOM

What is the logic behind terrorist violence? Why do terrorist groups persist when ultimate victory is logically unattainable? Experts have observed that terrorists believe violence is a utilitarian method for achieving their goals, a "product of strategic choice" and a "calculation of cost and benefit" (Crenshaw 1998:7, 16). Research has shown that the decision to engage in politically motivated violence is usually a rational choice and the selection of targets and methods is neither random nor a by-product of crazed delusions (Ross 1996). During the cold war rivalry between the democratic West and communist East, terrorist violence was relatively selective in nature, so that targets provided maximum symbolic capital for the terrorists and casualty rates were modest. However, a fundamental shift occurred in the terrorist environment during the 1990s. Although, as Jenkins (1998:244) noted, terrorists still sought to maximize the symbolic and propaganda value of their attacks, they were no longer constrained by tactical or moralistic prohibitions against the types of weapons that they used nor the number of casualties that they inflicted (Vegar 1998). As the incidence of terrorist attacks declined, the number of casualties per attack increased (Vegar 1998). Sectarian terrorism in particular caused an increasing number of casualties per incident, a trend that will continue and that may escalate as religious terrorists develop the capability to wield weapons of mass destruction.

Before 9-11: Warnings of a New Terrorism

During the decade prior to the September 11, 2001, attack, scholars and practitioners actively debated whether a "New Terrorism" had emerged as the preeminent typology for the international terrorist environment. This debate, which continues (albeit less vigorously), is grounded in the political turmoil of the latter decades of the twentieth century. Warfare during the 1980s and 1990s became increasingly irregular and communal as roving bands of soldiers and paramilitaries committed unspeakable acts of violence in Lebanon, Central America, the Balkans, Liberia, Rwanda, East Timor, and elsewhere. During this period, a new transnational solidarity emerged among Islamic extremists, originating from the *jihad* against the Soviet Army in Afghanistan and perceptions during the Gulf War that Muslim holy sites had been "occupied" by nonbelievers. Religious solidarity inspired the creation of loosely configured networks of like-minded radicals, and as Stern (1999:8–10) explained, evidence suggested that these networks were quite willing to acquire and use weapons of mass destruction.

This emerging environment was interpreted by many experts to herald the beginning of a New Terrorism, although some scholars dissented from this assessment (Johnson 2000). Van Creveld (1996) wrote: "In today's world, the main threat to many states . . . no longer comes from other states. Instead, it comes from small groups and other organizations which are not states" (p. 58). Kushner (1998) noted that the capture in the 1990s of notorious terrorists such as Carlos "signaled the changing of the guard" (p. 13). Laqueur (1999) warned: "The new terrorism is different in character, aiming not at clearly defined political demands but at the destruction of society and the elimination of large sections of the population" (p. 81). Stern (1999) identified several factors that have increased the threat from terrorists' use of weapons of mass destruction, noting ominously,

Such weapons are especially valuable to terrorists seeking to conjure a sense of divine retribution, to display scientific prowess, to kill large numbers of people, to invoke dread, or to retaliate against states that have used these weapons in the past. Terrorists motivated by goals like these rather than traditional political objectives are increasing in number. (P. 8)

These common elements—subnational networking, lethality, religious motivation, and a new morality—are cited as the core attributes of the shift toward a New Terrorism (Tucker 2001).

The New Conventional Wisdom

The era initiated by the September 11, 2001, attack is underscored by transformation toward a new conventional wisdom about the attributes of terrorism, the potential scale of violence emanating from terrorists, and response options available to the world community. Although experts vigorously debated the relative likelihood of terrorists' use of weapons of mass destruction prior to the 9-11 attacks (Roberts 2000), in the post–9-11 era, policymakers and analysts have commented repeatedly on the "changed" international and domestic terrorist environment. The fact of the matter is that the new environment arose in the aftermath of predominant leftist and ethnonational typologies that characterized the "old" terrorist environment of the 1970s and 1980s (Hoffman 1998). Unlike the previous decades, the 1990s were distinguished by new and innovatively configured terrorist networks that were responsible for significant international incidents. These networks and incidents were different from those of previous years and were harbingers of a new era of terrorism.

The policy implications of this transformation began with the declaration of war against terrorism in September 2001, progressed through the challenges of building an international regime of counterterrorist cooperation, and saw the establishment of an unprecedented security culture in the United States (as signified by the creation of the Department of Homeland Security). The threat from the New Terrorism presents an extraordinary challenge for governments and societies during the twenty-first century. This is because modern terrorists "would feel no compunction over killing hundreds of thousands if they had the means to do so" (Laqueur 1999:82). A central characteristic of the emerging terrorist environment is that it is characterized by a "horizontal" organizational arrangement wherein independent cells operate with near autonomy without reporting to a hierarchical command structure. Significantly, many of these new terrorists are motivated by varying admixtures of religion and nationalism that do not fit easily into precepts developed during the heyday of terrorism in the cold war era. Thus, the events of September 11, 2001, poignantly confirmed for experts the need to revisit previous analytical constructs for terrorism and counterterrorism.

A DEBATE REVISITED: DEFINING TERRORISM

Has the evolution in the terrorist environment appreciably affected definitional constructs for terrorism? Have governments and experts concluded that the New Terrorism necessitates a reassessment of the fundamental features of terrorism itself? The answer is no. Although few subjects in the analysis of political violence have stimulated as much debate as establishing a definitional foundation for *terrorism,* the discussion has not been significantly affected by the dawning of the modern environment.

During the course of the definitional debate, "More than a hundred definitions have been offered" (Laqueur 1999:5). Although this issue has been historically important within communities of experts, it continues to be arguably less important for the broader lay community. Many laypersons possess an a priori understanding that terrorism is politically motivated violence directed against minimally defended "soft" nodes, such as civilian or passive military targets. These nodes have symbolic value and are considered to be legitimate targets irrespective of whether they are human or infrastructure. Academic and practitioners' definitions of terrorism tend to incorporate this a priori understanding into a number of empirical constructs that reflect the diversity of opinion on this subject. However, although there is some consensus among experts about what kind of violence constitutes an act of terrorism, there is no unanimity. Thus, it is an accepted reality that for the foreseeable future—and through the course of the current terrorist environment—a multiplicity of definitions will continue to exist among governments, private agencies, and scholars.

There has not been a significant reassessment of official definitions of terrorism during the ascendancy of the New Terrorism. Governments and international associations continue to base their approaches on the quality and source of political violence. Typical definitions include the following examples. The British have defined terrorism as "the use of force for political ends, [which] includes any use of violence for the purpose of putting the public or any section of the public in fear" (Heymann 1998:3) and as "the use or threat, for the purpose of advancing a political, religious or ideological cause, of action which involves serious violence against any person or property" (Whittaker 2001:1). In Germany, terrorism has been described as an "enduringly conducted struggle for political goals, which are intended to be achieved by means of assaults on the life and property of other persons, especially by means of severe crimes" (Office for the Protection of the Constitution). The United States Code defines terrorism as "premeditated, politically motivated violence perpetrated against noncombatant targets by subnational groups or clandestine agents."[1]

Scholars have historically engaged in the definitional debate, often drawing fine distinctions between the types of violence that should be labeled as terrorism. Nevertheless, the New Terrorism has not stimulated a fundamental rapprochement toward the core attributes of terrorist behavior. The following constructs are typical of this scholarly dialogue. Gibbs (1989, as quoted in Hamm 1994) defined terrorism as "illegal violence or threatened violence against human or nonhuman objects" (pp. 178–79), so long as that violence meets additional criteria such as secretive features and unconventional warfare. Hoffman (1998) wrote:

> We come to appreciate that terrorism is . . . ineluctably political in aims and motives . . . violent—or, equally important, threatens violence . . . designed to have far-reaching psychological repercussions beyond the immediate victim or target . . . conducted by an organization with an identifiable chain of command or conspiratorial structure (whose members wear no uniform or identifying insignia) . . . and perpetrated by a subnational group or non-state entity. We may therefore now attempt to define terrorism as the deliberate creation and exploitation of fear through violence or the threat of violence in the pursuit of change. (P. 43)

Cooper (2001) offered the following definition: "Terrorism is the intentional generation of massive fear by human beings for the purpose of securing or maintaining control over other human beings" (p. 883). Whittaker (2001:1) lists the following descriptions of terrorism that have been propounded by experts: Contributes the illegitimate use of force to achieve a political objective when innocent people are targeted (Walter Laqueur); a strategy of violence designed to promote desired outcomes by instilling fear in the public at large (Walter Reich); and the use or threatened use of force designed to bring about political change (Brian Jenkins).

One central issue becomes readily apparent from the foregoing definitional discussion. All of the cited constructs focus on political violence emanating from subnational actors, thus leaving open the definitional question of what constitutes terrorist violence at the state level. This facet of terrorism and terrorist environments has also been extensively explored by experts (Claridge 1996; Sluka 1999). However, neither the New Terrorism debates during the 1990s nor the seminal events of September 11, 2001, have elicited much interest for revisiting definitional approaches for state terrorism. There is consensus among practitioners and scholars that state support for terrorist groups, and direct state involvement in international and domestic terrorism, is a significant component of the international terrorist environment.[2] The field is intermittently active in refining descriptive terminology for certain types of deviant state behavior. For example, the definitional category "rogue state" has been accepted by most experts, although discussion continues on which regimes should be categorized as rogues (Tanter 1999). An indication of the minimal degree of dissention on the subject and the attributes of the definitional consensus is the U.S. Department of State's promulgation of an annual list of defined terrorist states. In 2001, for example, the State Department categorized Cuba, Iran, Iraq, Libya, North Korea, Sudan, and Syria as sponsors of terrorism (U.S. Department of State 2002). Such officially sanctioned designations do, of course, reflect a degree of subjectivity and political bias, but they also suggest

Table 21.1 Terrorist Environments

Terrorist Environment	Foremost Participants	State Sponsorship	Group Autonomy	Counterterrorist Options
Monolithic	Single state sponsor	Strong and direct	Minimal, proxies	Clear options, co-opt sponsor
Strong multipolar	Several state sponsors	Strong and direct	Minimal, proxies	Clear options, co-opt sponsor
Weak multipolar	Dissidents, state sponsors	Insecure	Strong	Problematic and unpredictable
Cell-based	Dissident groups	Weak	Strong	Problematic and unpredictable

useful guidelines for identifying the definitional elements of state terrorism.[3]

UNDERSTANDING THE SEA CHANGE: THE TRANSITION OF TERRORIST ENVIRONMENTS

A clear indication of fundamental change in the terrorist environment is the fact that the preeminent typologies present during the latter quarter of the twentieth century have been supplanted by, or in some respects "updated" by, newer typological constructs (Grosscup 1998). In the new era, the incidence of ideological terrorism emanating from the left and right has become secondary to the incidence of religious terrorism. And although ethnonationalism continues to be a potent motivation for terrorist violence, it is no longer stimulated by ideological rivalries between East and West.

Elements of Terrorist Environments

It is necessary to establish a theoretical construct to identify the distinguishing elements of terrorist environments. The underlying question is whether comparisons of these descriptors provide a useful framework to differentiate terrorist environments at particular periods in recent history.

The term *terrorist environment* is an appellation that describes the interplay between many factors. These include terrorist motivations, terrorist tactics and targets, counterterrorist measures, and other descriptors that define the nature and quality of contemporary political violence. Terrorist environments have historically mirrored contemporary international and domestic political tensions, and the idiosyncratic features of these tensions have concomitantly influenced the type and scale of terrorist violence. Thus, the nature and quality of terrorism is never frozen in time, but undergoes periodic permutation as the overall political environment evolves.

The nature and quality of the New Terrorist environment can be evaluated by associating four factors: the foremost participants, the degree of state sponsorship, the degree of group autonomy, and counterterrorist options. These are foundational factors for determining whether a terrorist environment ought to be classified as monolithic, strong multipolar, weak multipolar, or cell based. Table 21.1 illustrates several constructs of terrorist environments, including the concept of "proxy terrorism."

Transitioning Environments

Twentieth-Century Proxy Wars

Terrorism occurs within the context of contemporary social and political environments. These environments are not static and often vary from time to time and region to region. The modern terrorist environment follows on the heels of an environment engendered by the cold war rivalry between the democratic West and the Soviet Union. During the latter half of the twentieth century, this rivalry was in many respects a series of vicarious confrontations that were fought in the developing world. Each side engaged in proxy wars by arming and supporting sympathetic governments and movements in opposition to the other side's proxies. Examples of these wars include the following:

- Greece, where Soviet-supported Marxist forces fought Western-supported forces during the Greek civil war
- Angola, where the Soviets and Cubans supported the Marxist Popular Movement for the Liberation of Angola (MPLA) against the U.S.- and South-Africa-supported National Union for the Total Independence of Angola (UNITA) movement
- Nicaragua, where U.S.-supported contras waged an insurgency against the Eastern-Bloc-supported Sandinista government
- Afghanistan, where U.S.-supported *mujahideen* insurgents resisted the Soviet invasion

The concept of proxy war led to the Eastern Bloc's adoption of proxy terrorism against the West. Revolutionaries from throughout the world were indoctrinated and trained by the Soviet Union and its allies, with promising prospects being recruited from institutions such as the Patrice Lumumba People's Friendship University in Moscow.[4] Other sympathetic governments commonly provided political and logistical support for terrorist movements during this era, so that proxy terrorism was adopted by a number of regional powers, including North Korea, Libya, Syria, Iraq, and Iran. Terrorist movements occasionally acted in concert or in solidarity with one another, describing themselves as "fronts" in a global war against the West. Regional state sponsors provided training facilities, safe havens, and funding for terrorists from around the world. For example, German terrorists received training from their exiled Palestinian comrades in Lebanon.

The Contemporary Environment

The modern terrorist environment falls primarily within the cell-based construct, with some indication that the weak multipolar environment remains somewhat viable. In comparison, the terrorist environment during the 1970s and 1980s tended to cluster around the monolithic strong multipolar and weak multipolar environments. During the previous era, terrorist groups such as the Abu Nidal Organization regularly operated as proxies for state sponsors, often serving as virtual mercenaries. Other terrorist groups such as the Red Army Faction and the Popular Front for the Liberation of Palestine collaborated with one another out of a sense of international solidarity. Proxy terrorism declined with the end of the cold war rivalry, as regimes recognized that "integration and accommodation with the West offer a more promising road to strength and stability than does confrontation" (Pillar 2001:51). In the modern era, Al-Qaeda exemplifies the cell-based model, and Afghanistan under the Taliban typifies the modern weak multipolar model. These latter cases represent a point of departure from the previous terrorist environment.

Points of Departure

Not all scholars agreed during the 1990s debate that the New Terrorism was in fact a "new" typology. There is some validity to this position, because several points of departure arose during the cold war era in contradistinction to the typical typologies of that era. An examination of these points of departure is instructive because they suggest that elements of the New Terrorism can be found in case studies selected from past conflicts. This is illustrated in the following examples of the Battle of Algiers, the "stateless revolutionaries," and the Afghan Arabs.

The Battle of Algiers. The Battle of Algiers is sometimes cited as the first important case of an urban terrorist campaign waged by dedicated revolutionaries who operationalized a cellular organizational model. Algeria had been a French possession for more than a century before achieving independence in 1962. Algeria's war for independence, led by the National Liberation Front (FLN), was particularly brutal, with atrocities being committed by both sides. In 1957, the city of Algiers became a center of terrorist insurrection and military repression. The terrorists designed a cellular organizational model, and their operational strategy emphasized the complete disruption of French civilian life and government administration in Algiers. A large number of attacks were made against French interests and expatriates, including many bombings

Table 21.2   Stateless Revolutionaries

Political Orientation	Group	Constituency	Adversary	Benefactors	Goals
Secular	Japanese Red Army	Oppressed of the world	Capitalism, imperialism, Zionism	Unclear, maybe PFLP[a]	International revolution
Ethnonationalist	Palestinian nationalists (pre-intifadeh)	Palestinians	Israel	State sponsors	Palestinian nation
Sectarian	Al-Qaeda	Fellow believers	Secular governments, the West	Private finance, state sponsors	Islamic predominance

Source: Martin (2003, chap. 9).

a. PFLP: Popular Front for the Liberation of Palestine, a secular socialist Palestinian revolutionary group.

of civilian targets. In reply, elite French paratroopers were sent into the city to engage in unconventional policing activities to root out the terrorist cells. Torture was officially sanctioned, and many innocent Algerian civilians were caught in the counterterrorist net. In the end, the terrorist cells were eliminated, but the brutal counterterrorist methodology of the paratroopers alienated the Algerian community, thus creating widespread sympathy for the FLN.

The Stateless Revolutionaries. Several terrorist movements adopted a "stateless" operational strategy[5] and operated on an international scale. Some groups had no particular home country that they sought to liberate. Other groups had been driven from the land that they claimed and were forced to relocate to bases in sympathetic countries. There were a number of reasons for the stateless profile. Groups such as the internationalist Japanese Red Army espoused a global ideological agenda that justified terrorist violence on behalf of vague concepts, such as championing "the oppressed" of the world. In contrast, Palestinian nationalists functioned within an operational environment that mandated as a practical matter that they select and attack targets internationally. Palestinian terrorists therefore struck from safe havens across state borders and frequently moved from country to country. Al-Qaeda represents the modern incarnation of the stateless

revolutionaries. The group temporarily found safe haven in Afghanistan before being driven out in late 2001 and has always espoused sectarian internationalist revolution. Table 21.2 describes the activity profiles of several stateless dissident groups (Martin 2003).

The Afghan Arabs. Significant numbers of terrorist cadres have been recruited from among the so-called Afghan Arabs. The Afghan Arabs were volunteers from around the Muslim world who fought during the 10-year war against the 1979 Soviet invasion of Afghanistan. Most of these fighters were drawn from Arab nations and hence were popularly known as Afghan Arabs. The anti-Soviet resistance was armed and supported by the United States, which considered the conflict to be another proxy war against its global rival. However, from the perspective of many native Afghans and the Afghan Arabs, the war took on the attributes of a holy jihad against a godless Communist invader and its puppet government.

After suffering 15,000 fatalities, the Soviet Army withdrew from Afghanistan. Many Afghan Arabs considered themselves to be international mujahideen (holy warriors), and began a global movement on behalf of the faith. For example, Algerians who had fought in Afghanistan also fought in the brutal Algerian insurgency during the 1990s. Afghan Arabs volunteered to fight in Bosnia, where they became renowned for their zeal, military prowess, and cruelty. Afghan Arabs traveled to Muslim communities in the developing world, assisting Muslim groups in their causes by providing technical advice and other support. Afghan Arabs created networks of indoctrinated sympathizers that have participated in several uprisings and terrorist incidents. Osama bin Laden and his compatriots were instrumental in linking together the Afghan Arabs and like-minded Muslim radicals under the loose umbrella of Al-Qaeda.

Convergence: Attributes of the New Terrorism

The New Terrorism evolved from a much-debated theoretical construct during the 1990s to an operationalization of the concept as the predominant typology of the modern terrorist environment. The seminal events of September 11, 2001, symbolize the culmination of a predicted convergence between organizational decentralization, operational asymmetry, religious centrality, and a palpable threat from weapons of mass destruction. Thus, Hoffman's (1997) description of the New Terrorism as a "confluence" of these and other factors was quite prescient. This convergent terrorist environment is a decidedly transnational environment, with cells loosely linked to each other across regions and countries. Al-Qaeda and its progeny deliberately position terrorist operatives and autonomous cells in foreign countries, thus creating an amorphous network that is difficult to identify and counter.

Organizational Decentralization

As predicted by many practitioners and scholars, it has become increasingly rare for terrorist movements and networks to organize themselves in pyramidal configurations. In fact, modern terrorist networks such as Al-Qaeda eschew traditional hierarchical organizational models. They have instead adopted cellular configurations that allow for quasi-autonomous operations. Several theoretical models have been posited to describe organizational and communications networks used by clandestine organizations such as terrorist movements. Typical theories describe the following:

- **Chain networks.** A linear arrangement in which information, people, weapons, or resources move through a series of separate contact points.
- **Hub-and-spoke networks.** A centralized arrangement in which information, people, weapons, or resources move through a single contact point before moving out to other contact points. Thus, a series of single contact points and chain networks can be jointly linked through a single hub.
- **All-channel networks.** A complex arrangement in which information, people, weapons, or resources are interconnected through a series of contact points. This type of network allows for innumerable chain and hub-and-spoke contact points to support the overarching all-channel network.

Operational Asymmetry

Experts have agreed since the 1990s that terrorism will be increasingly used as an "asymmetrical" warfighting strategy to engage the United States and its allies (Lesser 1999:94). Asymmetrical warfare refers to carrying out unconventional, unexpected, and nearly unpredictable acts of political violence against an otherwise unassailable opponent. Although it is in fact not a completely unprecedented practice, the disruptive potential from modern asymmetrical warfare has become a worrisome feature of the New Terrorism. In the modern era, terrorists who adopt asymmetrical methods are actively seeking to acquire and wield new high-yield arsenals, are willing to strike at unanticipated targets, and are adept at experimenting with unique and idiosyncratic tactics. This environment is likely to produce terrorists who will use newly available technologies to attack hitherto unthreatened sectors such as communications nodes. The Internet and other sophisticated communications technologies offer unprecedented opportunities for cyberterrorists (Devost, Houghton, and Pollard 1997).

Religious Centrality

As expected by Laqueur (1996) and other scholars, religious terrorism increased in frequency and global reach in the era of the New Terrorism. Many movements and ethnonationalist groups linked their causes to an underlying spiritual principle, as has been observed in Kashmir, Indonesia, India, Israel, and elsewhere. Transnational religious terrorism is particularly troublesome for victims because,

When terrorists adopt a religious belief system, their worldview becomes one of a struggle between supernatural forces of good and evil. They view themselves as living a righteous life in a manner that fits with their interpretation of God's will. According to religious extremists, those who do not conform to their belief system are opposed to the one true faith. (Martin 2003:30)

Supporters of religious terrorists are convinced of the spiritual purity of the fighters. For example, a Pakistani religious student concluded,

Osama [bin Laden] wants to keep Islam pure from the pollution of the infidels. . . . He believes Islam is the way for all the world. He wants to bring Islam to all the world. (Goldberg 2000:35)

Those who would agree with this student do not hesitate to fight, kill, and die in the name of what they perceive as the fulfillment of God's will.

Weapons of Mass Destruction

The literature has been replete with warnings about terrorists' acquisition of high-yield weapons that are capable of causing catastrophic casualties and damage (Falkenrath, Newman, and Thayer 1998; Laqueur 1999; Stern 1999). These weapons include biological and chemical agents, radiological agents, and nuclear weapons, each of which has been cited by experts as a potential terrorist threat (Cole 1997; Hoffman 1998; Tucker 2000). The events of September 11, 2001, demonstrated that weapons of mass destruction also include unexpected devices deployed in an unprecedented manner, such as fuel-laden airliners used as ballistic missiles. Prior to the era of the New Terrorism, terrorists tended to select focused and relatively surgical targets and used fairly predictable methods. However, the morality of the New Terrorism permits the selection of indiscriminate targets and the adoption of previously unthinkable methods, including the deployment of high-yield weapons against large segments of "enemy" civilian populations. This is particularly true of terrorists motivated by ethnic, racial, or religious hatred (Vegar 1998). Selected targets can now be hit with much more destructive power than in the past; all that is really required

is the will to do so. Terrorists are not necessarily interested in overthrowing governments or forcing them to change policies as their primary objectives. Rather, they often simply wish to inflict significant casualties and thereby terrorize and disrupt societies and large populations.

THE NEW FUTURE: TERRORISM IN A UNIPOLAR WORLD

In February 2001, the United States Commission on National Security/21st Century issued a prescient report assessing the contemporary national security environment. The commission was a 14-member bipartisan committee led by former Democratic Senator Gary Hart and former Republican Senator Warren Rudman, with other members drawn from the military, the media, academia, the executive branch, and former legislators. The commission bluntly warned,

The combination of unconventional weapons proliferation with the persistence of international terrorism will end the relative invulnerability of the U.S. homeland to catastrophic attack. A direct attack against American citizens on American soil is likely over the next quarter century. (U.S. Commission on National Security/21st Century 2001:viii)

Thus, threats from subnational terrorists wielding weapons of mass destruction were identified as priority concerns for national security in the new millennium. Observing that "significant changes must be made in the structures and processes of the U.S. national security apparatus" (U.S. Commission on National Security/21st Century 2001), the Commission recommended "the creation of a new independent National Homeland Security Agency (NHSA) with responsibility for planning, coordinating, and integrating various U.S. government activities involved in homeland security" (United States Commission on National Security/21st Century 2001). These and other findings and recommendations challenged policymakers to fundamentally reevaluate the potential threat to the American homeland.

Confirmation of the New Terrorism

The United States has emerged as the world's only superpower at the beginning of the new millennium. At the same time that its economic predominance is projected to continue to grow, its military superiority has become unassailable. Adversaries have no reasonable expectation that they can successfully challenge the United States and its Western allies in a conventional confrontation. Only unconventional and asymmetrical methods afford anti-Western revolutionaries a measure of war-fighting capability in a unipolar world. From the perspective of modern terrorists, particularly stateless revolutionaries such as Al-Qaeda, this new reality necessitates new creativity in selecting and attacking targets. Terrorists have certainly adapted to this new environment, as attacks by Al-Qaeda and their sympathizers repeatedly demonstrated meticulous planning, impressive patience, and dramatic effectiveness.

The record of terrorist violence in the years immediately preceding and succeeding the recent turn of the century confirms that the New Terrorism is the principal typology of the modern terrorist environment:

- In June 1996, a truck bomb in Dhahran, Saudi Arabia, destroyed a barracks housing U.S. military personnel. Nineteen were killed and about 500 were wounded.
- In August 1998, the U.S. embassies in Dar es Salaam, Tanzania, and Nairobi, Kenya, were bombed. The attacks occurred nearly simultaneously. Hundreds were killed or wounded, most of them Kenyans.
- In October 2000, the U.S. Navy destroyer *Cole* was severely damaged by suicide boat bombers in the port of Aden, Yemen. Seventeen sailors were killed.
- On September 11, 2001, four aircraft were hijacked shortly after takeoff on the East Coast of the United States. One airliner crashed into rural Pennsylvania, two crashed into the Twin Towers of the World Trade Center, in New York City, and one crashed into the Pentagon, in Washington, D.C. Nearly 3,000 people were killed. Suicide terrorist hijackers were responsible for the attack.
- In October 2002, massive explosions struck a tourist area on the Indonesian island of Bali. About 190 people were killed, most of them Australians.
- In November 2002, three suicide bombers destroyed an Israeli-owned resort in Mombassa, Kenya. A nearly simultaneous attack was made against an Israeli airliner using two antiaircraft missiles, which failed to hit their target.

These attacks confirm the expectations of practitioners and scholars who predicted the ascendancy of the New Terrorism. They also exemplify the global scope of the New Terrorism, as well as the painstaking planning and selection of targets typifying terrorist violence in the new era.

A War Unlike Other Wars

Strategists readily concede that the war against terrorism is unlike other wars (Pillar 2001). The new security environment engendered by the attacks of September 11, 2001, is forcing policymakers to design innovative strategies for fighting a global war against terrorism (Posen 2001/2002). For example, war has been declared not only against terrorist organizations but also against terrorist *behavior.* Policymakers realize that the "fronts" in this new war are amorphous and fluid and that covert "shadow wars" must be waged using unconventional methods, coercive diplomacy, and vying for the hearts and minds of constituent groups (de Wijk 2002). This requires creating the capacity to deploy military, paramilitary, and coercive covert assets to far regions of the world (Sarkesian 2002). Strategists have also concluded that counterterrorist financial operations must be designed and continuously upgraded to target bank accounts, private foundations, businesses, and other sources of revenue for terrorist networks (Pillar 2001:92). Thus, for example, accessing the terrorists' financial databases requires a broad-based alliance of governments and private financial institutions.

Measures must also be designed to harden targets, deter attacks, and thwart conspiracies, a process commonly referred to as "antiterrorism." Internal security centers, such as customs checkpoints, law enforcement agencies, and immigration authorities, have become frontline operations in the new war. Other features of the new war necessarily include the following:

- Disrupting transnational terrorist networks. Because this requires operational capacity to track extremist operatives, primary responsibility for this task must logically be delegated to intelligence and law enforcement communities.
- Global surveillance of the terrorists' technologies, including telephones, cell phones, and e-mail. Intelligence agencies specializing in electronic surveillance are the most capable institutions to carry out this mission.

In the United States, homeland security is a priority concern for policymakers. The unprecedented features of the new war have, in their estimation, required a complete reconfiguration of the domestic security community (Carter 2001/2002). In October 2001, the USA Patriot Act[6] was signed into law to enhance the security mission of domestic agencies. In November 2002, the United States Senate passed, and President George W. Bush enacted, the Department of Homeland Security Act of 2002. The outcome has been a revamping of the domestic mission and powers of federal agencies, as well as the consolidation of 22 agencies into an overarching Department of Homeland Security, the third-largest agency in the federal government. Taken together, the USA Patriot Act and Department of Homeland Security Act represent the culmination of a sweeping reassessment of domestic security requisites for prosecuting the war against terrorism.

The New Future

What will be the attributes of the new future for terrorist movements, terrorist violence, and counterterrorist options? Many in the international community have come to understand that after September 11, 2001, governments and societies must adapt to a new security environment and a new future. Because it is in the nature of modern terrorists to be flexible and creative in their methodology, it is reasonable to project that the New Terrorism will define the global terrorist environment into the immediate future. Based on current events and recent expert analyses, several conclusions can be reasonably considered.

First, the fundamental sources of terrorist violence will not change in the near future. Intense expressions of intolerance and resentment will continue to motivate violent extremists to blame entire societies and groups of people for their state of affairs. Second, religious violence will remain a central feature of terrorism for the foreseeable future. Internationally, Al-Qaeda and other religious terrorists have consistently attacked targets that symbolize enemy interests. Domestically, religious terrorists in Pakistan, Israel, Malaysia, the Philippines, and elsewhere have waged campaigns to destabilize their governments, often attacking symbolic foreign interests. Third, weapons of mass destruction will become increasingly available to terrorists. In particular, terrorists with religious worldviews have already demonstrated their desire to acquire and wield these weapons. Fourth, more resources will be allocated to counterterrorist programs. Terrorism has become a global problem, so that international cooperation will become increasingly vital to disrupt and defeat the new terrorists. Fifth, although the "old" terrorism will certainly not disappear, its centrality in the global terrorist environment has ended. Ideological terrorism has all but disappeared in the West. In addition, long-standing ethnonationalist conflicts such as those in Northern Ireland, Sri Lanka, and the Spanish Basque region have come tantalizingly close to some degree of resolution in the new millennium. Sixth, and very importantly, asymmetry will continue to be a central terrorist strategy. They will persist in designing highly creative operational and organizational models, and it is very plausible that information technologies in the hands of terrorists will be used to wage cyberterrorism on a global scale.

CONCLUSION

This chapter has attempted to validate the proposition that a New Terrorism is to be differentiated from, and has supplanted, the terrorist typologies of the cold war era. Taken in perspective, the organizational and operational profiles of terrorist movements such as Al-Qaeda do give credence to warnings from experts in recent years that the New Terrorism is the predominant model for the modern terrorist environment. Past patterns of terrorism arose from international political trends that no longer exist, so that movements motivated by ideologies rooted in the old East-West rivalry have become unviable. In their place have arisen loose cellular networks of religious terrorists who are adept at engaging in global asymmetrical warfare.

Those who engage in terrorism are no longer predominantly ideological or ethnonationalist activists who in their view are waging a secular war on behalf of a particular people or in solidarity with the oppressed of the world. The New Terrorism is motivated by a belief that the "one true faith" must be defended from nonbelievers and apostates. Those who follow this creed believe that fighting, killing, and dying in the name of the cause are not only acceptable but also desirable. Thus, it is from this source of radical activism that a sea change has occurred in the international terrorist environment. Governments and societies must, of necessity, collectively and cooperatively adapt themselves to this new environment.

NOTES

1. From United States Code, 22 U.S.C. 2656f(d). See also 18 U.S.C. 2331 for an official definition of *international terrorism.*

2. For data on state-sanctioned repression and terrorism, see the Web sites of Human Rights Watch at http://www.hrw.org/ and Amnesty International at http://www.amnestyusa.org/.

3. It is particularly important to consider that state terrorism is the most organized, and arguably the most catastrophic, application of terrorist violence. The state controls and has access to resources that are unavailable to dissident terrorists, so that its capacity to commit acts of political violence far exceeds in scale the capacity of violent dissidents.

4. The curriculum at Patrice Lumumba University offered a number of courses in "liberation" studies and Marxist ideology. Many students were actively recruited by the KGB, and some received weapons training. Some Palestinians who later became members of terrorist organizations attended the university, as did recruits from around the world. Ilich Ramirez Sanchez, also known as "Carlos the Jackal," briefly attended Patrice Lumumba University.

5. For a discussion of the "stateless revolutionaries," see Martin (2003), chapter 9.

6. An acronym for the Uniting and Strengthening America by Providing Appropriate Tools Required to

Intercept and Obstruct Terrorism Act, Pub. L. No. 107–56 (2001).

REFERENCES

Carter, Ashton B. 2001/2002. "The Architecture of Government in the Face of Terrorism." *International Security,* Winter, 26:5.

Claridge, David. 1996. "State Terrorism? Applying a Definitional Model." *Terrorism and Political Violence,* Autumn, 8:47.

Cole, Leonard A. 1997. *The Eleventh Plague: The Politics of Biological and Chemical Warfare.* New York: Freeman.

Cooper, H. H. A. 2001. "Terrorism: The Problem of Definition Revisited." *American Behavioral Scientist,* February, 44:6.

Crenshaw, Martha. 1998. "The Logic of Terrorism: Terrorist Behavior as a Product of Strategic Choice." In *Origins of Terrorism: Psychologies, Ideologies, Theologies, States of Mind,* edited by Walter Reich. Washington, DC: Woodrow Wilson.

Department of Homeland Security Act of 2002, Pub. L. No. 107–296 (2002).

Devost, Matthew G., Brian K. Houghton, and Neil Allen Pollard. 1997. "Information Terrorism: Political Violence in the Information Age." *Terrorism and Political Violence,* Spring, 9:72.

de Wijk, Rob. 2002. "The Limits of Military Power." *The Washington Quarterly,* Winter, 25:75.

Falkenrath, Richard A., Robert D. Newman, and Bradley A. Thayer. 1998. *America's Achilles' Heel: Nuclear, Biological, and Chemical Terrorism and Covert Attack.* Cambridge, MA: MIT Press.

Gibbs, J. P. (1989). "Conceptualization of Terrorism." *American Sociological Review* 54:329.

Goldberg, Jeffrey. 2000. "Inside Jihad U.: The Education of a Holy Warrior." *New York Times Magazine,* June 25, p. 32.

Grosscup, Beau. 1998. *The Newest Explosions of Terrorism: Latest Sites of Terrorism in the 1990s and Beyond.* Far Hills, NJ: New Horizon.

Gurr, Ted Robert. 1989. "Political Terrorism: Historical Antecedents and Contemporary Trends." In *Violence in America: Protest, Rebellion, Reform,* vol. 2, edited by Ted Robert Gurr. Newbury Park, CA: Sage.

Hamm, Mark S., ed. 1994. *Hate Crime: International Perspectives on Causes and Control.* Highland Heights, KY: Academy of Criminal Justice Sciences; Cincinnati, OH: Anderson.

Heymann, Philip B. 1998. *Terrorism and America: A Commonsense Strategy for a Democratic Society.* Cambridge, MA: MIT Press.

Hoffman, Bruce. 1997. "The Confluence of International and Domestic Trends in Terrorism." *Terrorism and Political Violence,* Summer, 9:1.

——. 1998. *Inside Terrorism.* New York: Columbia University Press.

Jenkins, Brian M. 1998. "Will Terrorists Go Nuclear? A Reappraisal." In *The Future of Terrorism: Violence in the New Millennium,* edited by Harvey Kushner. Thousand Oaks, CA: Sage.

Johnson, Larry C. 2000. "The Threat of Terrorism Is Overstated." P. 27 in *Terrorism: Opposing Viewpoints,* edited by Laura K. Egendorf. San Diego, CA: Greenhaven.

Kushner, Harvey W. 1998. "The New Terrorism." In *The Future of Terrorism: Violence in the New Millennium,* edited by Harvey Kushner. Thousand Oaks, CA: Sage.

Laqueur, Walter. 1996. "Postmodern Terrorism." *Foreign Affairs,* September/October, 75:24.

——. 1999. *The New Terrorism: Fanaticism and the Arms of Mass Destruction.* New York: Oxford University Press.

Lesser, Ian O. 1999. "Countering the New Terrorism: Implications for Strategy." In *Countering the New Terrorism,* edited by Ian O. Lesser et al. Santa Monica, CA: RAND.

Martin, Gus. 2003. *Understanding Terrorism: Characteristics, Perspectives and Issues.* Thousand Oaks, CA: Sage.

Pillar, Paul R. 2001. *Terrorism and U.S. Foreign Policy.* Washington, DC: Brookings Institution.

Posen, Barry R. 2001/2002. "The Struggle Against Terrorism: Grand Strategy, Strategy, and Tactics." *International Security,* Winter, 26:39.

Roberts, Brad, ed. 2000. *Hype or Reality: The "New Terrorism" and Mass Casualty Attacks.* Alexandria, VA: Free Hand.

Ross, Jeffrey Ian. 1996. "A Model of the Psychological Causes of Oppositional Political Terrorism." *Peace and Conflict: Journal of Peace Psychology* 2 (2):129–41.

Sarkesian, Sam C. 2002. "The New Protracted Conflict: The U.S. Army Special Forces Then and Now." *Orbis,* Spring, 46:247.

Sluka, Jeffrey A., ed. 1999. *Death Squad: The Anthology of State Terror.* Philadelphia, PA: University of Pennsylvania Press.

Stern, Jessica. 1999. *The Ultimate Terrorists.* Cambridge, MA: Harvard University Press.

Tanter, Raymond. 1999. *Rogue Regimes: Terrorism and Proliferation.* New York: St. Martin's.

Tucker, David. 2001. "What Is New About the New Terrorism and How Dangerous Is It?" *Terrorism and Political Violence,* Autumn, 13:3.

Tucker, Jonathan B., ed. 2000. *Toxic Terror: Assessing Terrorist Use of Chemical and Biological Weapons.* Cambridge, MA: MIT Press.

Uniting and Strengthening America by Providing Appropriate Tools Required to Intercept and Obstruct Terrorism Act, Pub. L. No. 107–56 (2001).

U.S. Commission on National Security/21st Century. 2001. *Roadmap for National Security: Imperative for Change.* Washington, DC: Author.

U.S. Department of State. 2002. *Patterns of Global Terrorism 2001.* Washington, DC: Author.

Van Creveld, Martin. 1996. "In the Wake of Terrorism, Modern Armies Prove to Be Dinosaurs of Defense." *New Perspectives Quarterly,* Fall, 13:4.

Vegar, Jose. 1998. "Terrorism's New Breed." *Bulletin of the Atomic Scientists,* March–April, 54:50.

Whittaker, David J., ed. 2001. *The Terrorism Reader.* New York: Routledge.

THE RHETORIC AND REALITY OF "MASS DESTRUCTION"

How Genocide Became an International Social Problem

DAVID NORMAN SMITH

University of Kansas

*G*enocide, a term coined during the Nazi Holocaust in 1944, is perhaps the most popular social-scientific coinage of the past century. Yet the reality it names has been less carefully studied than many far-lesser phenomena. Adopted by the United Nations (UN) in 1948 as a legal concept offering a ground for collective action to avert mass murder, the term genocide has since become a staple of partisan rhetoric—yet until the wake of the Rwandan massacres of 1994, the UN had failed to define even a single instance of post-Holocaust slaughter as genocide. A defining global social problem, genocide has nonetheless flown beneath the radar of international scholarship in most areas of study.

Like the proverbial enigma wrapped in a riddle, genocide has thus remained unknown in many ways. This is not, I contend, simply a function of the very real difficulty of the subject of mass destruction but also reflects the contradictory origin and role of the concept itself. "Genocide," from the start, has been as much a political volleyball as an analytic category. It entered the world as a legal principle crafted to authorize breaches of state sovereignty by the global community. For three centuries, the sovereignty of independent states had been effectively sacrosanct in the Euro-American realm.[1] But the stunning horror of the Holocaust called the old norms into question. A window of opportunity opened, briefly, for humanitarian legislation, and the global institutions of the postwar era—above all the UN—acted swiftly to pass a succession of new laws intended to prevent states from abusing civilians, whether in peace or in war, at home or abroad.

At the Nuremberg War Crimes Tribunal of 1946, the concept of war crimes was enlarged, under the rubric "crimes against humanity," to include not only battlefield crimes but also the political, religious, ethnic, and national persecution of civilians (Ferringer 1989:87). Soon afterward, a flurry of further laws passed. The Convention on the Prevention and Punishment of the Crime of Genocide was ratified by the UN on December 9, 1948; the Universal Declaration of Human Rights passed the next day; the Geneva Conventions were enacted in 1949; and the European Convention on Human Rights followed in 1950 (Donnelly 1995:123; Jackson 1995:68). But the bipolar division of the world during the ensuing Cold War between the United States and the Soviet Union impeded the implementation of these principles. The Genocide Convention, in particular, was effectively paralyzed by the enmity and self-interest of the opposing powers, neither of which (in an era of great power involvement in wars in Vietnam, Cambodia, Afghanistan, Ethiopia, Angola, and Nicaragua) could afford the risk of politically tinged charges of mass murder. With the fall of the Soviet Union in the early 1990s, however, a decisive new phase began, the ultimate tendencies of which remain uncertain. On the one hand, the UN was freed from the Cold War constraints that had inhibited interventions—but so too was the United States.

Interventionism is now clearly on the rise, but with two rival centers of gravity: the international community, represented by the UN, and the United States as the dominant state and potential global hegemon. In this moment of tension and doubt, the legitimation of interventions acquires a new urgency, and genocide acquires a new geopolitical salience. "The abridgement of 'human rights' . . . even by repressive policies would not be sufficient to justify interventions, but clear genocidal activities would be," writes Kratochwil (1995:39–40). Hence, the world's heightened sensitivity to genocide in the wake of mass killings in Rwanda and the former Yugoslavia in the 1990s is as complex politically as it is morally and intellectually.

My aim in what follows is to map these complexities, first by tracing the origin of the normative idea of genocide, then by situating this norm in the interstate framework that gives it political meaning.[2]

GENOCIDE AS THE SPUR TO A NEW LEGAL ORDER

In October 1933, provoked by the persecution of Jews and political dissidents in Germany, the League of Nations convened a special meeting in Madrid to consider strengthening legal protections for minorities. As the French scholar Georges Scelle observed at the time, the ensuing debate revealed a world divided on first principles.

The German delegate, flying the flag of racial "dissimilarity,"[3] defended what Scelle called a *Volkish* "new edition of the imperialist interpretation of the nationality principle," insisting that "states should have the right to maintain ties with ethnically similar elements living beyond their borders," even as they suppress minorities themselves. This provoked an opposite reply from the Dutch delegates, whom Scelle quotes as saying that, given "the indissoluble tie between internal and international public order," the League had a "right of intervention" to preserve peace "even during civil wars" (1934:255–56).

The latter position, Scelle stressed (1934:256), "is both super-statist and monist."[4] The implication was that international law supersedes national German law and that, contrary to the thesis of irreducible racial, moral, and legal "dissimilarities" between peoples, law is both unitary and universal in its ultimate principles.

A Polish contributor to this debate took an even stronger stand in favor of the *superétatique* view. This was the jurist Raphaël Lemkin, who, in 1944, would coin the term genocide and then, four years later, would persuade the UN to adopt the Genocide Convention. Fatefully, however, Lemkin's efforts in 1933 were far less successful. Disturbed by the "alarming increase of barbarity" (Lemkin 1944:xiii) that had accompanied Hitler's rise to power just months earlier—and well aware that Nazi terror could escalate radically if no preventive action were taken—Lemkin proposed a treaty to outlaw the "crime of barbarity," which he defined as "the premeditated destruction of national, racial, religious and social collectivities."[5] But the forces arrayed against this kind of proposal were formidable.[6] The Polish foreign minister, Beck, fearing Hitler's ill will, refused Lemkin's request to travel to Madrid to present his proposal in person. After it was read aloud, Beck accused him of "insulting our German friends." Soon afterward, Lemkin was fired as deputy public prosecutor "for refusing to curb his criticisms of Hitler" (Power 2000:22). The first and best opportunity to tie Hitler's hands had been lost.

At a deeper level, the problem in 1933 was that proposals like Lemkin's cut against the grain of international norms. From 1648 until the Paris peace of 1918, private citizens had been regarded as being "under the exclusive control of States" (Cassese 1988:99–103).[7] This precept was called into question when the excesses of the First World War came to light—above all, the extermination of Armenians and the mass killing of noncombatants—and it was further shaken when anti-Jewish pogroms erupted in Poland at the war's end. But artful diplomacy soon rendered the reforming protocols of the 1919–1921 period moot (Macartney 1934; Sharp 1978). Hence, until the Holocaust, the "sovereign" rights of states continued to be jealously guarded, while citizens and minorities were left to fend for themselves.

The consequences were predictable. Between 1933 and 1939, Germany was allowed to infringe the rights of Jews and radicals on a vast and growing scale, "within view of the whole world" and "without any attempt by Germany at concealment" (Fein 1979:193). All the future Allied Powers sat idly by, shielded by conventional legal norms from any sense of responsibility for German affairs. While "the British were well aware of Nazi violence and discrimination against German Jewry before the war, they operated on the assumption that this anti-Semitism was simply a core feature of Nazism 'and must be accepted as such. As long as the majority of German people supported Nazism and as long as Nazi anti-Semitism was legislative and non-violent, then Britian had no right or obligation to intervene'" (Gannon 1971:277, cited by Fein 1979: 183).[8] This policy became "appeasement" only when Hitler's military exported his terror across national boundaries. Until then, it was just business as usual, protected from critical scrutiny by custom and law.

Later, when Hitler's anti-Jewish policy turned decidedly violent, concern for his civilian victims remained modest. Long after the Jewish Socialist Party of Poland released the first fully authenticated report of Nazi massacres in May 1942—at a time when fewer than 15 percent of the ultimate victims had perished—the Allied Powers consistently refused to take special steps to halt the Holocaust (Feingold 1970; Wyman 1984; Wyman and Medoff 2002; Wyman and Rosenzweig 1996). Not until 1944 did mounting domestic pressure induce the previously indifferent Roosevelt administration to take baby steps to encourage third-party rescue attempts—and even then, with the death camps working overtime, the Allies continued to resist calls to bomb the rail lines leading to the camps (Fein 1979:193). By the time Auschwitz was finally liberated by Soviet troops in 1945, roughly 70 percent of European Jewry had been exterminated—a total of 5.1 to 6.1 million in all (Fein 2001:49). Also slaughtered, and by the same methods, were between 250,000 and a million Gypsies.[9]

"What renders this situation so horrifying," Hayim Fineman of the Labor Zionist Bloc remarked in 1946, "is the fact that this tragedy was not unavoidable. Many of those who are dead might have been alive were it not for the refusal and delays by our own State Department . . . and other agencies" (cited by Hilberg 1967:671). The truth of this comment is plain.[10]

Equally plain is the truth of a remark by the British delegate to the UN that the League of Nations' failure to ban genocide before the war gave the Nazis impunity for peacetime atrocities (Power 2002:52).

The Genocide Convention, in other words, was an afterthought. Crimes of a barbarity hitherto unknown had been committed on a scale hitherto unimagined, under the protective cover, in part, of a venerable but now suspect ideal of inviolable state sovereignty. To respond, the world needed new ideas. Among these, the most influential proved to be Lemkin's concept of genocide, which he introduced in a study of Axis policy (1944) and which was first applied by the Nuremberg tribunal in 1946. "Sovereignty," Lemkin had long believed, "cannot be conceived of as the right to kill millions of innocent people" (cited in Chalk 1994:47). Late in 1946, the UN officially condemned genocide for the first time. Two years later the UN passed the Genocide Convention, which went into effect on January 12, 1951, after 20 nations had signed it. A half century later, the grand total of signatory nations had risen to

130 (Power 2002:54, 59, 64; Ratner and Abrams 2001:27–8).

Since 1951, there have been many opportunities to save lives under the aegis of the Genocide Convention. If the UN had acted with humanitarian resolve, many crimes of states against peoples could have been halted or contained—in Cambodia, Bangladesh, Burundi, Indonesia, East Timor, South Africa, and elsewhere. But the Genocide Convention quickly fell victim to the *realpolitik* of the Forty Years Cold War. The United States refrained from signing the Convention until the eve of the Soviet collapse, and the UN managed to evade the issue even in obvious cases of planned mass slaughter (as in Cambodia). Imperial interest and state sovereignty took precedence over human rights in case after case. When, in 1994, the UN did finally recognize the state-led killing of Tutsis and dissidents in Rwanda as genocide, this came, once again, after the fact. Well over a half-million people had already perished, and the genocide had already ended, halted not by the UN (which had *removed* peacekeepers from Rwanda when the massacres began), but by a largely Tutsi army from neighboring Uganda (Des Forges 1999; Melvern 2000). Once again, genocide was denounced only after it had ended. On balance, the Genocide Convention seemed to be a monument to good intentions gone awry.

Since 1994, however, it has become apparent that imperial interest may be served more by the selective abridgement of state sovereignty than by its unconditional defense. Allegations of actual and potential "mass destruction" have become the rallying cry for an aggressive new interventionism, manifest, above all, in the so-called Bush Doctrine of preemptive intervention to block mass destruction. This gives the Genocide Convention a new profile. Given "a growing consensus among American policymakers that military intervention should be launched to stop genocide," the lesson that many have drawn from the Rwandan debacle is highly activist: "To be more successful, a lower threshold for action would have been required, perhaps authorizing intervention *as soon as the risk of genocide was deemed sufficiently high*" (Kuperman 2002:100; my italics). How and by whom this risk is defined, of course, is the decisive question.

The world, it seems, is impaled on the horns of a dilemma. Minority rights violations of the gravest kind, including vicious state-sponsored massacres, have led many to doubt the tenability of old norms of state sovereignty. And few would challenge the view that peacekeeping forces should restrain genocides whenever possible—by bombing the rails to Auschwitz or disarming Rwandan *génocidaires*. But in an unequal world, the formula of "humanitarian intervention" is susceptible to self-interested manipulation. Powerful states can use the mere appearance of genocidal intent on the part of weaker states—allegedly revealed by their possession of mass-destructive weapons—to infringe their sovereignty, with or without international support.

Genocide, in other words, remains as indelibly political as ever. As a principle of international law and legitimacy, it is a thread in the tapestry of the state system. Hence, to grasp the evolving geopolitics of genocide, we need to understand its role in the evolving nexus of states.

THE ANTINOMIES OF SOVEREIGNTY

The roots of the current tension between state and superstate authorities lie in the remote past, with the simultaneous crystallization, in the early medieval era, of Italian city-states and the "Holy Roman" structures of church and empire. Despite the conflicts between them—which grew acute in the later eleventh century—both the popes and emperors sought, and received, formal recognition from their subject realms for several centuries after Charlemagne was anointed the first *Imperator Romanus* by Pope Leo III in 800 C.E. But as the Italian city-states outgrew their dependence on spiritual and temporal overlords, ritual recognition yielded to a legal doctrine of nonrecognition, which, in turn, laid the ideological groundwork for the ultimate assertion of state sovereignty. The driving forces that led to the affirmation of state sovereignty were, of course, economic and political, not merely ideological. But "sovereignty" is irreducibly an ideological construct and hence requires explanation at this level as well as structurally.

In the early days of the Carolingian empire, the liturgy of king-making included, besides anointment and coronation, the acclamation of the emperor by the nobility (Canning 1996:55–63). This liturgy was thought to confer power upon the ruler constitutively, not simply to acknowledge his preexisting eminence. Over time, as acclamation evolved into the semilegal ritual of *recognitio,* the residually democratic aspect of this ritual (the lingering awareness that the emperor's power derived from the voluntary submission of his subjects) became "grating and disturbing" to the increasingly theocratic rulers. In 1270 C.E., the Frankish kings, the original locus of the empire, excised the recognition ceremony in a vain effort to rid themselves of the "populist" implication that what is recognized today can be renounced tomorrow (Ullmann 1966:147, 202–203). But the risk of recognition and its withdrawal cannot be overcome so easily. When, in the thirteenth and fourteenth centuries, the German-born emperors began to lose their grip on the dynamic commercial cities of coastal Italy (Venice, Genoa, Florence, Pisa, and Milan), French and Italian jurists formulated a new doctrine of the "nonrecognition" of empire (Ercole 1915, 1931; Sereni 1943). Bartolus, the most influential jurist of the age, gave this doctrine its canonical form: "City-states recognize no superiors."[11] At first, this was simply a statement of fact. In the late medieval period, as states gathered strength and structure, the overarching power of the empire clearly waned. But when the empire reasserted its claims—especially in the early 1500s when the Habsburgs united Spain to central Europe under Charles V—the nonrecognition doctrine became a principle of open defiance.[12] Just as the papacy was confronted by the *de facto* nonrecognition of Protestant reformers in the same century, so the empire confronted *de jure* declarations of independence from rising national states. The early-sixteenth-century jurists Suarez, Victoria, and Gentili "denied . . . the claim of the emperor to exercise temporal jurisdiction over princes" (Gross 1948:32). Gentili went further, applying the same principle to the Pope, whose authority, he said, remained valid only for the faithful "who still recognized his rule" (Sereni 1943:64).

In the world of practical politics, this lesson was learned only after a long series of chaotic and bloody conflicts, culminating in the Thirty Years War, which, from 1618 to 1648, drew all of Europe into a maelstrom of antagonisms, old and new. As the ascending forces of capitalism and colonialism and the nation-state called every previous structure and identity into question, violence tore the social fabric at every seam, from class to nation to religion. The Habsburg version of the empire, which had stretched from Spain and Holland to Austria and beyond, was decisively defeated, and its core German territories were bled white. Millions died, and millions more were displaced. It became plain that the old powers were incapable of assuring either peace or security. The leaders of the victorious anti-imperial camp, most notably France and Sweden, proclaimed a new age of national independence, freed from Habsburg overlordship. On this ground, in 1648, the Peace of Westphalia established the legal foundation for a new European order. The principle of this order was the simultaneous independence and interdependence of sovereign states.

The new states no longer recognized the authority of the universal institutions of church and empire. The emperor had been "forced to abandon all pretenses on the field of battle" (Gross 1948:28), and the pope, Innocent X, was left to fulminate vainly against the hubris of states.[13] Where, previously, the pope and the emperor had enjoyed a monopoly of sovereign legitimacy, now states claimed sovereignty for themselves. Instead of recognizing their ostensible superiors, they recognized other states, their avowed equals. And since they no longer deferred to overarching institutions, the only "higher" power they could accept was the emerging international concert of states.

The new state system had begun to assume distinctively modern form in the early sixteenth century. The older roots of this system can be traced far earlier—according to Tilly (1990), to the immediate wake of the Carolingian era in 990 C.E. And in the succeeding half millennium, many steps were taken toward the modern system, particularly in the diplomatic relations among the Italian city-states: the recognition of the rights of foreign merchants and merchandise, the elaboration of a rudimentary system of treaties and embassies, and so on. But the scholarly consensus is that this state system first crystallized in the Buda peace treaty of 1503. Since

1494, a widening circle of wars had broken out, prompted, initially, by a French invasion of Italy (Grewe 2000:13). Of these wars, the most decisive pitted Venice against the Ottoman Empire, with the auxiliary involvement of most of the powers of the day: Portugal, Spain, the papacy, England, Bohemia-Hungary, Poland-Lithuania, and others. The Buda settlement that closed this chapter in European history is widely regarded as the first major multilateral peace settlement of the modern type (Tilly 1990:162). Not long after, jurists began to deduce the latent reality and sovereignty of a body of international law. Thus, Victoria concluded that states cannot "refuse to be bound by international law, the latter having been established by the authority of the whole world" (1532, cited by Gross 1948:32). Gentili held, similarly, that all the world's peoples, "united in the *societas humana,*" are rightly "governed by the *jus gentium,* or international law" (1598, cited by Sereni 1943:64; cf. p. 103f).

The laws of the state system were thus accorded a kind of sovereignty all their own. These laws, of course, did not wield the directly interventionist power of the pope or the emperor, and in this sense the "sovereignty" they embodied was more ideal than real. The actual locus of power had shifted from the commanding heights of the universal institutions to the bold new national states, especially Spain, France, and England. But the vertical tension between states and the system they formed remained plain. However much they might want to deny the disembodied social reality of the international community, the new states were hardheaded enough to grasp that they could not violate its norms with impunity. A dialectic of reciprocal claims to sovereignty bound states not only to each other but also to the larger system of states.

One of the most striking aspects of the Westphalian peace settlement was the fact that the assembled delegates—145 in all, representing every corner of Europe—adopted a virtual constitution, giving all signers the right to intervene to enforce its provisions. One of the subsidiary Westphalian treaties warns aggressors that "all and every one of those concern'd in this Transaction shall be oblig'd to join the injur'd party, and assist him with Counsel and Force to repel the Injury" (Treaty of Münster, cited by Gross 1948:25); and rulers were warned

that any effort to redraw the religious map would be grounds for their overthrow (Tilly 1990:160).

Just about every conflict in this period, whatever its ultimate economic or political roots, ultimately acquired such strong religious overtones that interconfessional toleration soon became a byword for peace. As early as 1555, a Catholic-Lutheran peace treaty signed at the Imperial Diet of Augsburg assigned "each religion its own region" and asked the faithful to resettle among their brethren, to reduce the risk of violence. Just 10 years earlier, sectarian violence in Provence had grown so fierce that a pamphleteer, seeking a word adequate to convey the idea of mass murder, took *massacre* from the butcher's vocabulary.[14] Calvin's successor, Beza, clarified the logic of the new term when he deplored "the savage massacre that the judges at Aix perpetrated . . . not upon one or two individuals but upon the whole population, without distinction of age or sex, burning down their villages as well" (cited by Greengrass 1999:69).

The implication of the charge of massacre was that heresy hunters were moved by genocidal intent. In the sectarian traumas of the ensuing decades, which peaked in 1572 in the St. Bartholomew's Day massacre of Huguenots in Paris, the word massacre became a virtual synonym for genocide, and loomed particularly large in the Protestant vocabulary.

In 1648, after the horror of the Thirty Years War, both Catholics and Protestants resolved to break the cycle of violence. It was in this spirit that the Westphalian envoys agreed to work together to repress future religious atrocities. But the will to intervention soon weakened. The appeal of *raison d'état* and national sovereignty proved too strong. By the end of the sixteenth century, European states had effectively attained the monopoly of legitimate violence in their own territories that Max Weber defined as the core principle of state identity. How states wielded this monopoly—in particular, whether they deployed violence against their own citizens—was their own affair. Hence, in 1758, reviewing a century of experience post-Westphalia, the jurist Vattel was able to conclude that in the concert of European states, "The only universal law is that states have an equal right not to be hindered in their internal affairs" (Philpott 1996:40; cf. Glete 2002). Nonintervention, Vattel argued, is a logical corollary of sovereignty (Onuf 1995:43).

There is a certain irony in the fact that nonintervention was enshrined as a "law" in this way at a moment when the slave trade and colonial empire building were disrupting cultures at an epic pace. It was in the 1750s, for example, that England wrested control over India from its rivals. In the same decade, Portuguese slave traders became so worried over the costs incurred when slaves died en route to the Americas—"the slave is a thing that may die" at any time, one warned—that they forced their African and Brazilian trading partners to assume financial responsibility for all who died on the way (Miller 1988:658ff.). In Europe, however, "nonintervention" remained the order of the day. Wars—between Spain, France, England, and the Netherlands in particular—periodically adjusted the balance of power, but left the great states undisturbed internally.

Everything changed in 1789. The Jacobin and Napoleonic leaders of the French Revolution sought to revise every social relation, not only in France, but across Europe. So profound was the challenge, so great the trauma for every *ancien régime,* that in 1815, when Napoleon was finally defeated, three of his victorious enemies—reactionary Prussia, Russia, and Austria—formed a "Holy Alliance" to make the world safe for monarchy. Their goal was to crush future revolutions. An accord signed in Troppau in 1820 enunciated this clearly:

> States that have undergone a change of government due to revolution, the results of which threaten other states, *ipso facto* cease to be members of the European Alliance. . . . If, owing to such alterations, immediate danger threatens other states, the parties bind themselves, . . . if need be by arms, to return the guilty state into the bosom of the Great Alliance. (Cited by Krasner 1995:243–44)

In effect, the Alliance sought to shield itself from revolutionary interventions by counterrevolutionary interventions. Sovereignty, in its popular form, was viewed as anything but sacred. Like Napoleon, but with an aristocratic bias, the Alliance members sought to render their national monopolies of legitimate violence international. Their formula for achieving this was both legal and military: to withdraw recognition and send in troops.

Britain opposed the interventionism of the Troppau accord, but with little success. In 1821, the Alliance authorized its leading spirit, Metternich, to send Austrian troops into Naples and Piedmont to prop up weak monarchies. Soon after, France won support for an invasion to restore Spanish absolutism. By 1850, antipopular interventions of this kind had become a leading theme in European politics. Between 1815 and 1900, the reactionary powers intervened in the domestic affairs of other states (mainly Spain, Germany, and Italy) 17 times. Sixteen of these interventions occurred before 1850, and in almost every case the motive was to repel popular sovereignty (Leurdijk 1986, cited by Krasner 1995:245–46).

As we saw earlier, there appears to be an elective affinity between interventionism and the idea of genocide. Hence, it is not surprising that in this vortex of uprisings and interventions, hints of the idea of genocide began to circulate widely. The Jacobin terror sparked a wave of criticism and analysis. Gracchus Babeuf, the most egalitarian of French revolutionaries, offered a harsh indictment of Robespierre's "exterminating wheel," which received its animating impulse, he said, from a "system of government" that was also a "system of extermination." This system culminated in the vicious repression of the Vendéan peasant rebels, in outright *"populicide"* ([1794] 1987:96–8). The privileged orders were even more fearful and enraged, responding to the revolution both with conspiracy theories, revealing a streak of paranoia (Cohn [1967] 1996:25–46), and with dark warnings of a genocidal Prometheus unbound. The great Prussian philosopher Hegel spoke for many when, in his *Philosophy of Right* ([1821] 1991), he decried the kind of destructive "fanaticism" that is bent, he wrote, on "demolishing the whole existing social order, eliminating all individuals regarded as suspect by a given order, and annihilating any organization that attempts to rise up anew" (p. 38).

Meanwhile, counterrevolution also inspired intimations of genocide. In 1831, a decade after Hegel's prophecy and Metternich's invasion of Italy, the poet August von Platen, in his fiery *Polenlieder,* called the repression of the Polish revolution by reactionary Russia a case of *Völkersmord*—that is, the outright "murder of a people" (cited by Jonassohn 1998:140; cf. Henry 2001:9f.).

Sovereignty and Humanitarianism

Escalating conflicts, in other words, combined with bureaucratic and technical advances in mass destruction, gave nineteenth-century Europe a dawning awareness of the growing potential for ethnopolitical mass murder. But this awareness faded in the century of British hegemony from 1815 to 1914. The Holy Alliance collapsed in 1825, and although Metternich and his allies remained active, it was ultimately the British-led counteralliance that placed its imprimatur on the age. This gave the dialectic of national and international sovereignty a new impetus, since Britain—which was almost unchallenged in its global dominion for an extraordinarily long period—took a strongly humanitarian and anti-interventionist stance. The brusque cynicism of the Holy Alliance gave way to a Victorian discourse of peace. Rhetoric and reality in this phase were often jarringly discordant, given the scale and brutality of nineteenth-century colonial violence in British India, China, and Jamaica. But a humanitarian ethic took root that was not altogether disingenuous.

Giovanni Arrighi traces this ethic, in part, to the exigencies of free trade capitalism, which could not abide the chaotic disruptions of trade and profit making that accompanied Napoleonic wars and counterrevolutionary machinations. By staking its claim to global legitimacy on the alleged ethical and historical necessity of free markets, Britain put the state system on a new footing:

> The Westphalia system was based on the principle that there was no authority . . . above the inter-state system. Free trade imperialism, in contrast, established the principle that the laws operating within and between states were subject to the higher authority of a new, metaphysical entity—a world market ruled by its own "laws"—allegedly endowed with supernatural powers greater than anything pope and emperor had ever mastered in the medieval system of rule. (Arrighi 1994:55)

Seeking both cultural and military hegemony, Britain became the voice of the market as well as ruler of the seas. In both spheres, it defended the categorical imperative of free trade and the rule of law and the market. "By presenting its world supremacy as the embodiment of this metaphysical entity, the United Kingdom succeeded in expanding its power in the inter-state system well beyond what was warranted by the extent and effectiveness of its coercive apparatus" (Arrighi 1994:55).

The humanitarian ethic has many other roots as well, including, not least, Puritanism.[15] But it is difficult to deny that peace is good for business. Many movements, antislavery as well as antiwar, arose in part on this foundation. Other humanitarian currents arose as well, calling attention to issues of health, mental health, hospital reform, prison reform, and animal protection, among others. And the newborn labor movement extended the circle of humanitarian concerns still further, inspiring poor relief, minimum-wage laws, unemployment and health insurance, factory regulations, limits on child labor, and much else. Almost all such reforms first gained real momentum in this period.

Organized peace campaigns also arose on a large scale for the first time in the nineteenth century. There had been precursor movements,[16] but only when pacifism became profitable did it became widely popular. The initial momentum in favor of generalized peace had come in the eighteenth century, stimulated by growing international trade and the desire to unify Europe against the Ottomans. Vattel, Rousseau, and Kant all took Saint-Pierre's slogan of permanent peace seriously and found an audience for this slogan among the burgeoning commercial classes of the later eighteenth century.

The organized peace movement, like so much else, was an immediate outgrowth of the Napoleonic Wars. The first formal peace groups were founded in the United States in 1815, in Britain in 1816, and in France in 1821. Such groups grew prolifically and ultimately convened major international peace conferences in London (1843), Brussels (1848), Paris (1849), and elsewhere. Now as before, peace was urged on economic as well as on moral grounds. Leading French and British free traders (including Bastiat, Say, Bright, and especially Cobden, who was closely identified with the peace movement) argued that protective tariffs provoke wars. The Brussels conference linked peace to the standardization of weights, measures, and coinage.

By the start of the twentieth century, there were 425 peace organizations worldwide. Crowning this movement were the two Hague Peace Conferences, of which the second (in 1907) produced what appeared to be definitive results. In 1910, in the aptly named *Great Illusion,* the influential peace advocate Norman Angell was sufficiently emboldened to predict "that war had become so destructive of all economic values that nations would never again engage in it" (as paraphrased by Northedge 1967:66).

The ever-greater destructiveness of war, in other words, was increasingly viewed as a legitimate ground for preventive action both by the state system and by international civil society, which began to crystallize in this period. Domestic issues were less likely to attract reforming attention, but the exceptions to this rule were significant. Antislavery campaigns, which were perhaps the most dynamic and deeply rooted of the interventionist movements, were fueled by the conviction that free labor is superior to slavery not only morally but also economically (Smith 2001). Here, as in the antiwar movement, the spur to reform was moral zeal coexisting, uneasily but productively, with the profit motive. A similar duality of altruism and self-interest marked the early minority rights movement as well.

By World War I, the theme of minority rights had begun to emerge from the shade into which it had been willed by diplomats eager to defend state sovereignty. The consensus until then had been that the dominion of states over subjects is immune to outside interference, an inalienable part of their *domaine réservé.*[17] But since Augsburg in 1555, religion had figured as the one grand exception to this rule. And since Westphalia a century later, the rights of religious minorities had become a virtual template for human rights in the later, modern sense. This is true both in terms of the intrinsic moral content of the call for minority rights and also in the ulterior expediency that so often lurked behind this call.

What began as a principle of the truce between Catholics and Protestants soon became a bargaining chip in the relations between Christian Europe and the Ottoman Empire. Beginning in 1615, when Austria concluded a treaty with the Ottomans guaranteeing religious freedom to all those in the Muslim realm "who profess themselves the people of Christ" (cited by Macartney 1934:161), Austria entered into a competition with its French and Russian rivals to be recognized as the protector of Ottoman Christians. In 1649, the new Westphalian ideal of toleration gave France an impetus to renew a long-forgotten medieval pledge to protect Lebanese Christians, and in 1673, France won concessions for Jesuits and Capuchins as well. In 1699, Austria won the right to intervene in Ottoman territory itself—a major break from tradition, which was subsequently reaffirmed in 1718, 1739, and 1791. Russia, jealous of Austrian prerogatives, won concessions for Orthodox believers in treaties negotiated with the Ottomans between 1774 and 1829. In 1853, Russia challenged Ottoman sovereignty so fundamentally that in the ensuing Crimean War, England and France sided with Turkey, resolving that "no State shall claim a protectorate over the subjects of the Sultan"; rather, they said, "the Great Powers shall see to the guarantee of the privileges granted to the Christians without infringing the Sultan's sovereign rights" (cited by Macartney 1934:162–3). When Austria too threatened the use of force to defend Turkish sovereignty, Russia yielded.

At this stage, Western Europe was too concerned about the danger of Russian expansionism to press its advantage against the declining Ottomans. England in particular was firmly resolved to stand with Turkey against Russia. Sovereignty, not interventionism, was the principle of the hour. But the shoe was on the other foot in May 1876 when the Ottomans brutally crushed a revolt by Bulgarian Christians in east Rumelia, killing 15,000 people. British opposition politicians led by Gladstone seized on a current of popular humanitarian outrage, mixed with anti-Islamic bias, to take power away from Disraeli's pro-Turkish government (Saab 1991). Ultimately, the traditional foreign policy elite was able to contain the interventionist impulses catalyzed in this way by the Bulgarian agitation. But the anti-Muslim valence of this agitation strengthened Britain's hand against Ottoman Turkey, which could now be portrayed as a kind of rogue state *avant le lettre*. Turkey, with continuing brutality—often directed against its Armenian minority—gave the world every reason to accept this portrait.

In 1877, just a year after the Bulgarian atrocities, the Turks massacred Armenians as well. The European Powers responded by forcing the Turks to sign a treaty pledging to respect minority rights; but this was soon forgotten by almost everyone involved. In this case, as in others, the threat of humanitarian intervention proved expedient and popular; but Britain and its allies were flexible—many said cynical—about whether they would live up to their threats. They wasted no sympathy on the Turks, but they did not rush to help the Armenians. When it served their interests, they were entirely capable of turning a blind eye to Ottoman misdeeds.

In 1894, pressed on all fronts and worried about growing Russian influence among Christian minorities, the last of the Ottoman sultans, Abdul Hamid, ordered the slaughter of more than 10,000 Armenians by Kurdish death squads, the *Hamidye,* which he armed with repeating rifles (Reid 1992:37). Further violence of this kind simmered on a low boil until the sultanate was overthrown by Young Turk nationalists in 1908, and then flared up again sharply in 1909. This was a portent of dire things to come. In 1915 and 1916, under the cover of war, the Young Turks embarked on mass murder, killing over a million Armenians.

This, scholars agree, is the first indisputable genocide of the modern era.[18] A persecuted ethnic-religious minority was singled out for extermination by a regime capable of acting on its intent. Turkey, pressured for centuries to honor minority rights, chose to reassert its sovereignty over minorities in the most intransigent and definitive way possible.[19] Aware that humanitarian rhetoric often serves self-interest—and knowing that self-interest dictates inaction more often than the reverse—the Young Turks chose to ignore the claims of international law. They believed that the world would ignore their transgressions.

They were right. "Who, after all, speaks today of the annihilation of the Armenians?" This was Hitler's question to his commanders when, on the eve of invading Poland in 1939, he explained why he believed that Germany could take

Lebensraum from the Poles with impunity (cited by Fein 1979:4).

SOVEREIGNTY *IN EXTREMIS*

When states fear the loss of their sovereignty, they can react with extreme nationalism. When they feel humiliated, they can react with extreme violence. Turkey and Germany proved the truth of these propositions in the waning years of Britain's century of dominance.

At least since 1815, Britain's sheer power and the growing influence of its free trade norms had become increasingly oppressive. This was especially true for faltering powers, like the Ottoman Empire, and upstarts, like the German nation, which found themselves blocked and frustrated by Anglo-French priority in capitalist enterprise and the global scramble for empire.[20] A defiantly and romantically protectionist, chauvinist, antibourgeois, antihumanitarian, and authoritarian reaction set in. Universal law and morality were belligerently rejected. Racial-ethnic war was declared a natural necessity. Peace, tolerance, and charity were scorned as the virtues of weaklings and hypocrites.

Ultimately, this antihumanist worldview bore fruit in actual violations of international law and morality and actual ethnonational war and murder. It bears careful scrutiny.

In the Turkish case, we can take the writings of Ziya Gökalp as archetypal. Gökalp, the main Young Turk theorist, was a key figure in the crusade to transform Turkey from the nucleus of a declining empire into a modern state and nation (Akural 1978; Smith 1995). His views changed over time and were never entirely cohesive; but they capture the spirit of Young Turk nationalism.

Gökalp advocated an ethnically Turkish nation, which he opposed to the Ottoman ethnic mélange. "Why is everything Turkish so beautiful and everything Ottoman so ugly?" He imputes to the Turks a "national soul," a "metahistorical" identity. The Turks, he writes, are Nietzsche's supermen, "whiter and more handsome than Aryans." It was thanks to Turkish culture that the Ottomans had never definitively lost to the West—that, indeed, "they expelled the British and the French from the Dardanelles

[and] defeated the British-armed and financed Greeks and Armenians and thus, indirectly, the British also."[21] Nor will Turkey allow universalist ethics to tie its hands: "If there are no higher values than the good of a particular society, then society is not subject to any moral obligations regarding its relations to other societies." The same applies to the claims of individuals: "Do not say 'I have rights'; There is only duty, no right." Sovereignty is elitist, not popular: "Democracy is not the rule of the ignorant masses *(avam)* but of the elite." Indeed, the people are merely "malleable raw material" to be shaped by the ruling "saviors," "heroes" and "geniuses" of the nation—a category, Gökalp wrote in 1915, that includes Talat Pasha and Enver Pasha, who were then presiding over a genocide.[22]

Not welcome in the sacred Turkish circle are the non-Muslim minorities, who had embraced Western values "just like a man who buys ready-made suits." By 1914, Gökalp had concluded "that only a State consisting of one nation can exist." Western culture is "rotten" and will be replaced by a civilization created "by the Turkish race which has not, like other races, been demoralized by alcohol and licentious living, but has been strengthened and rejuvenated in glorious wars." Insults will not go unpunished. "As individuals, we are not vindictive/But we do not forget national revenge."[23]

This is not just nationalism spiced with ethnic pride and prejudice. It is, rather, as Durkheim held with respect to similar German views, a "pathological" reaction to national frustrations in the realm of state pride and sovereignty. Skeptics might doubt, Durkheim adds, that the state is concrete enough "to have made any deep impression upon men's minds," but in fact many people now hold deeply belligerent convictions about states and their rivalries. In the German case, Durkheim says, this belligerence has achieved a kind of "morbid enormity." This, in turn, has inspired a series of vain but enormously destructive attempts to defy the laws of social gravity.

"There is no state so powerful," Durkheim writes, "that it can govern eternally against the wishes of its subjects and force them, by purely external coercion, to submit to its will. There is no state that is not submerged in the vaster milieu formed by the ensemble of other states, that does not, in other words, take part in the great human community to which it is subject and owes its respect. There is a universal conscience and world public opinion, and it is no more possible to escape their empire than to escape the empire of physical laws; for they are forces which react against those who transgress them. A state cannot maintain itself when all humanity is arrayed against it" (1916: 45–6, 7).[24] Germany, however—like Turkey—had proven unwilling to bow to this reality. "To affirm its power more impressively, we shall even find it exciting the whole world against itself, and lightheartedly braving universal anger." International law is scorned, treaty obligations dismissed, individual and minority rights rejected, morality defied, and war exalted. The pivot of this mentality, Durkheim concludes, is the wish "to rise 'above all human forces,' to master them and exercise an absolute sovereignty over them. It was with this word 'sovereignty' that we began our analysis, and it is to this that we must now return and conclude, for it sums up the ideal we are offered" (1916:45).

Like Lemkin three decades later, Durkheim sees the will to unlimited sovereignty as the crux of an irrationalist *raison d'état*. Taking the works of Heinrich Treitschke as the *locus classicus* of this outlook, Durkheim stresses that Treitschke's views are representative of widely held opinions, however far they stray from the reality principle.[25] In actuality, Durkheim says, sovereignty is always relative, a function of relations with other, legally equivalent states. Interdependence is the rule, not sheer independence. States normally depend on each other, on treaties, and on domestic and foreign opinion. "Exaggerate, on the contrary, [state] independence, release it from all limitation and reserve, raise it to an absolute, and then you will grasp Treitschke's idea of the state" (1916:7). This proud and autarkic state refuses to recognize any higher jurisdiction, or even to "permit a contrary will to express itself, for any attempt to apply pressure to it is a denial of its sovereignty. It cannot have even the air of yielding to any kind of exterior constraint, without enfeebling and diminishing itself" (1916:8). For Treitschke, war and weapons decide all truly contested questions, not law.[26] "Without war, the state is inconceivable, and indeed, the fundamental attribute of sovereignty is the right to make war at will" (1916:11). Universal ethical claims are nugatory: For Treitschke, "the

State is not an Academy of Arts. When it sacrifices its power to the ideal aspirations of humanity, it contradicts itself and goes to its ruin." Nor can the state tolerate even the slightest insult. "The State is not a violet, which blooms in the shade; its power should be proudly displayed in the full light of day, and must not permit itself to be challenged, even symbolically. When its flag is insulted, the State's duty is to demand satisfaction, and, if this fails, to declare war" (Treitschke, cited by Durkheim 1916:14, 9).

War, whatever its cause, is sacred and ennobling. "It is war," as Durkheim paraphrases Treitschke, "which compels men to master their natural egoism; it is war which raises them to the majesty of the supreme sacrifice, the sacrifice of self" (1916:12). Sovereignty, monopolized in this way by the German state, is thus denied in principle to all others: "Universal hegemony is an ultimate ideal for the state" (1916:43). So, too, "Germany has never recognized the right of peoples to self-determination" (1916:40). Nor does the German state recognize humanity per se: "For the state humanity is nothing. The state is its own end, and beyond it there is nothing that commands its loyalty" (1916:23). Hence, Africans and Asians should expect no mercy from their colonial rulers: "In those lands," Treitschke says, "he who knows not how to terrorize is lost" (cited by Durkheim 1916:25). Specifically, Treitschke praises "the example of the English, who, over 50 years ago, bound Hindu rebels to the mouths of cannon and then scattered their bodies to the winds" (cited by Durkheim 1916:25).

Analytically, Durkheim finds the Achilles' heel of Treitschke's worldview in his steadfast refusal to accept the reality of the world community and its train of laws, norms, beliefs, institutions, and myths. For Treitschke, physical force is everything, culture evanescent at best. Recalling the example of Steinthal and others, Durkheim says that, formerly, German scholars deserved credit for stressing the "impersonal, anonymous and obscure forces which are not the least important factors in history" (1915:27).[27] So, too, many historians have said that "the state is a result rather than a cause" (1915:34) and that statecraft is a comparatively superficial aspect of social life—yet for Treitschke, the state is power, and power is all.

The problem with Treitschke's perspective is not just that he exaggerates the independence of sovereign states, but, rather, that he misconstrues sovereignty altogether. States are more than merely physical forces. They exist socially and morally; they have legal rights and obligations; they occupy statuses. A nation acquires legal reality as a state when it wins recognition from other states. Recognition is thus "constitutive" in the sense that it gives the nation a legal status that it would not otherwise have; it confers legitimacy, sovereignty, rights, and obligations in the wider state system.[28]

The Treitschkean error, in short, is to exaggerate the state's independence not merely from other states but also from the very web of legal, moral, and social ties that give the state its power in the first place. The state's monopoly of domestic violence, for Durkheim as for Weber, springs from its legitimacy—that is, from public willingness to recognize its claims. Treitschke, and others like him, mistakenly think that the state is so innately powerful that it compels loyalty, when in reality its power is a function of public loyalty. And he wrongly imagines that the German state can thrive even without the recognition and support of the international community. This overvaluation of the state and its power proved fatal to Germany, and its victims, in two world wars.

GENOCIDE AND SOVEREIGNTY

When Durkheim's pamphlet first appeared, it would have been easy to doubt whether *mentalité* is truly as historically significant as he implies. In the aftermath of the Holocaust, however, it is hard to think otherwise. A pathological mentality of "morbid enormity" came to the fore once again, seeking unlimited sovereignty with all the intensity of wounded narcissism. "In the future," Durkheim wrote, "historians and sociologists will have to establish the causes" (1916:46) of this simultaneously aggressive and submissive mentality. But its content, he was certain, was a fetishistic overvaluation of state sovereignty.

Raphaël Lemkin agreed. While his overall account of genocide was multidimensionally sociological—encompassing social structure, institutions, geopolitics, culture, and economics (see Smith 2000)—Lemkin was also mindful of the centrality of intentional actors, from Hitler and Himmler to the *Einsatzgruppen*.[29] To explain the mentality that spurred the systematic murder of Jews, Gypsies, Poles, Serbs, Bolsheviks, the mentally ill, and the infirm, Lemkin invokes a range of psychological tendencies: Treitschkean "exaggerated pride" and self-righteousness, a tendency to "glory" in wartime barbarity, contempt for victims, cynicism, denial, and a cold resolve to follow leaders and orders (1992: 189–235). Lemkin was also sternly determined to stress the connection between this toxic mentality and the issue of sovereignty. State power, ratcheted to dizzying and transgressive heights, was Hitler's end as well as his means. The sacralization of German sovereignty at the expense of other states and nations was central to Nazism.[30] Accordingly, Lemkin's principal aim was to place restraints on the sovereignty of genocidal states, preferably before they took action. Genocide, in this vision, would be a legal cause for intervention by the world community. Sovereignty, in other words, would be self-canceling when it turned cancerous.

This vision is plausible only if international law can be enforced, and that, in turn, requires an effectively institutionalized state system. Lemkin did indeed repose a fair amount of hope in international law and the UN. But he was hardly a legal utopian. On the contrary, Lemkin was keenly aware that international law is highly limited in its potential efficacy. Imperial rivalries, clashing cultures, bureaucratic indecision, corporate venality, and political cowardice all limit the extent to which the world community can act to halt genocide. But the only alternative to a superstate system is reliance on states—and nothing could be more utopian than to count on states to restrain themselves. Hence Lemkin's guarded hope that the world community, despite its severe limits, would accept the call to ethical responsibility in the case of genocide. Hence, also, his dismay when the Universal Declaration of Human Rights (UDHR) was enacted by the UN just one day after the passage of the Genocide Convention.[31]

Many people have found Lemkin's resistance to the UDHR mystifying. But it is, in fact, entirely consistent with his realism about the limits of international law. If the global community is ever to take the fateful step of breaching state sovereignty, the precipitating cause must be overwhelmingly clear and significant. The UN cannot be asked to act in every instance of injustice; such an expectation would gravely dilute its criteria for action and reduce the chance that it would ever act, or act consistently and without prejudice. Yet that is precisely what the human rights charter demanded, Lemkin said:

> The same provisions apply to mass beatings in a concentration camp and to the spanking of a child by its parents. In brief, the dividing line between the crime of Genocide, which changes the course of civilization on one hand, and uncivilized behavior . . . disappears. (Cited by Power 2002:75)

International law could not be expected to eradicate prejudice and discrimination in the myriad forms specified in the human rights charter. "History has tried to achieve this task through a combined travail of revolution and evolution, but never before has a . . . lawyer dreamed . . . of replacing a historical process by fiat"—that, truly, is utopian, and "Utopia belongs to fiction and poetry and not to law" (cited by Power 2002:76). Lemkin was scathing, furthermore, when it was suggested that genocide could be subsumed under the rubric of discrimination. "Genocide," he wrote, "implies destruction, death, annihilation, while discrimination is a regrettable denial of certain opportunities of life. To be unequal is not the same as to be dead" (cited by Power 2002:75).

Drawing a clear line between genocide and other forms of violence and oppression is crucial to Lemkin's intent and, indeed, to the entire enterprise of legislating against action intended to physically destroy an entire social group. It is also pertinent with respect to the analytic and definitional problems that have plagued the comparative study of genocide.

The general assumption in the study of genocide seems to be that, since genocide is a word everyone knows, it must have a coherent meaning. "We have defined genocide," Chalk and Jonassohn (1990) say in a standard work, "because we assume that it is a definable form of human behavior" (pp. 26–7). In reality, however, the word is jural in origin and import, and it cannot be readily applied outside the realm of law. And even in law, major problems arise.

The most often noted problem with the term "genocide" is precisely the one that Lemkin feared: semantic stretch. "Virtually everything but genocide, as Raphaël Lemkin first defined it, is called genocide!" (Fein 1994:95). This is obviously the case in ordinary partisan politics, where charges of genocide have become so routine that they no longer carry much sting. Abortion is called "the genocide of the unborn," the drug trade is called "genocidal" for communities blighted by drug use, the Marxian goal of a classless society is said to be "genocidal" toward the bourgeoisie, and so on.[32] But semantic stretch also informs much of the academic discourse on genocide. Israel Charny, one of the principal figures in the relatively small world of comparative genocide studies, widens the "definitional matrix" to include, in addition to "intentional genocide," mass death resulting from ecological negligence or abuse, "the overuse of force or cruel and inhuman treatment," mass murder "incidental" to the prosecution of war, and "cultural genocide" that destroys culture or language without direct loss of life (1994:76–7). More recently, the anthropologist Nancy Scheper-Hughes suggests the concept of "a genocide continuum" to cover the spectrum of "small wars and invisible genocides" that she says occur in everyday settings (schools, hospitals, clinics, courts, etc.) and that reveal our fatal capacity "to reduce others to nonpersons, to monsters, or to things" by acts of "social exclusion, dehumanization," and so on (2002:369). Leo Kuper, often called the "doyen of genocide studies" (Charny 1994:64; cf. Chalk and Jonassohn 1990:16), also favored a loose definition. Given that the Genocide Convention defines genocide ambiguously as action intended to destroy a group either "in whole or in part," without clarifying the phrase "in part," Kuper extended the category to include "massacres" of relatively small size and uncertain intentionality. This extended the notion of genocide to gray areas

left unclear by the Convention. And though Kuper formally advised against "new definitions of genocide, when there is an internationally recognized definition" (1981:39) affirmed by the Genocide Convention, he nevertheless amended the official definition, in practice, in one basic and quite arbitrary respect, while ignoring other proposed revisions.[33]

The work informed by these wide-angled definitions is well-intentioned and often valuable.[34] But defining genocide this broadly deprives the term of its power and specificity. Scholars, reluctant to omit anything from their taxonomies, have increasingly tended to say that genocide is simply a human universal and constant, found in every corner of the world and in all periods (Jonassohn 1990:415 and 1998:2, 10; Kuper 1981:11). The method this typically inspires is an effort to trawl through history for cases of mass violence, which are then classified under the headings of one typology or another. These typologies and taxonomies can be modestly fruitful in analytic terms,[35] but politically and legally, they have to be handled with great care. The tendency to widen the definitional circle, however morally understandable, tends to convert genocide into a legitimating rhetoric for great power interventionism.

Consider what would happen, for example, if the international community were to define genocide as a "continuum" running from social exclusion to ethnic cleansing. That would justify interventions almost anywhere, on almost any grounds. Several critics of Michael Walzer's famous *Just and Unjust Wars* (1977) have proposed essentially this, saying that even "under ordinary oppression peoples' socially basic human rights are violated . . . systematically enough to . . . justify intervention" (Luban 1980:396; cf. Beitz 1980; Doppelt 1980).[36]

This is extremely dangerous. Indeed, precisely because arguments of this kind are motivated by the best intentions, they offer moral cover for amoral *realpolitik*. That is the predicament faced by human rights nongovernmental organizations (NGOs). They want to see wrongs righted, and they feel pained when the great powers fail to help. But when great powers are asked to intervene, one danger—is that they might intervene. As Weiss and Chopra observe, the main problem with the doctrine of humanitarian intervention is its "vulnerability to abuse"—the fact that "powerful states with ulterior motives would be able to intervene in weaker states on the pretext of protecting human rights" (1995:90).

Currently, given the asymmetry of power between the United States and the rest of the world—the fact, as Michael Mann remarked a decade ago, that "American power is [now] qualitatively greater than anything known in this area of civilization since the Romans" (1990:7)—the danger of this kind of abuse is far greater than ever before. Interventions by the United States and by the UN have both soared in number since 1989 (Gurr and Harff 1994; Knutsen 1997), and the United States is clearly en route to a kind of hegemonic status, with unilateralist tendencies restrained only in part by countervailing global forces. The problem before us, then, is to find ways to prevent genocide and encourage human rights without yielding the mantle of humanitarianism or the legitimate monopoly of global violence to the new hegemon and its legions.

This, of course, is no easy task. Since 1988, as Levene has incisively shown (2001), the great powers have more often permitted or even encouraged genocide than the reverse. The international community has been irresolute at best, and states continue to value sovereignty over solidarity. What then is still possible?

Few would now dispute that genocide is a sufficient ground for genuinely humanitarian intervention,[37] and it appears, at present, that the only body capable of interceding without primarily venal motives is, despite everything, the UN. Grave doubts about the UN's will and power are, of course, apropos. But there appear to be simply no alternatives. So NGOs that hope to prevent future genocides will have to find ways to influence the UN. That, in turn, is likely to require grassroots efforts to sway the UN's member states.

The UN should also be asked to continue to define genocide exactly enough to permit delimited legal action. Otherwise, genocide will remain more a trope than an article of law. Considerations of this kind originally came into play as early as 1948, when the UN chose to omit the idea of "cultural genocide" from the Genocide Convention. It was clear even then that this category is too vague and elastic as to be "susceptible to adequate definition, thereby potentially giving rise to abusive and illegitimate claims of genocide" (Ratner and Abrams 2001:31). More recently, the genocide tribunals in Rwanda and the former Yugoslavia have echoed this point, emphasizing, rightly, that they are "guided by the Convention's primary focus on preventing the physical destruction of groups" (Ratner and Abrams 2001:32–3; cf. Magnarella 2000). Narrow, focused definitions of this kind will remain necessary in the future as well.

What, then, of less-than-genocidal human rights violations? Here, too, I would argue that grassroots action is key. Consider labor rights, for example. Plainly, no government or international body will intervene militarily to assure workers in China, Cameroon, or Burma the right to strike. But cross-border solidarity efforts to provide aid and resources—from the global labor movement, supportive NGOs, and others of goodwill—are an elementary necessity. And if, over time, efforts of this kind succeed in eliciting support from national or international bodies as well, all the better. But it would be highly unrealistic to imagine that action by states or the world community would prove decisive in cases of this type. Only in extreme cases of genocide-like gravity, and then only rarely, can we credibly hope to exert influence at the level of the state system per se.

NOTES

1. See below for details on this and related points.

2. Space limits preclude an account of the various substantive theories of genocide, but for an overview, see Smith (2000). And for details on social-scientific and historical perspectives relevant to the analysis of the only two genocides formally recognized as such by the UN, see Smith (1998, 1996).

3. In the original German reproduced by Scelle this is *Dissimilierung*.

4. Italics deleted.

5. Raphaël Lemkin, "The Evolution of the Genocide Convention," p. 1, reel 2, *Lemkin Papers,* New York Public Library; cited by Power (2002:21). Under the same rubric, Lemkin also sought to ban "oppressive and destructive actions directed against individuals as *members*" of persecuted groups (1944:94, 91; italics mine). For further details, see Lemkin (1933, 1935).

6. This was true, it seems, despite "the universal moral condemnation of Hitlerian politics" that Scelle observed at the Madrid meeting (1934:256).

7. The only formal limitation on this principle was the decision, promulgated at Westphalia in 1648, that states could not violate the religious liberties of their subjects with impunity. This principle, inspired by the universal havoc and ruin of the Thirty Years War, was later ignored more often than it was remembered.

8. Fein (1979:183, cited in Gannon, 1971:277). Here and elsewhere, I have standardized the spelling of the term *anti-semitism,* which often appears in a variety of other forms (e.g., antisemitism, anti-Semitism).

9. Fein (2001:52) cites as her sources here Gabrielle Tyrnauer (1989:v) and Ian Hancock (1994:10).

10. For voluminous detail, see David Wyman's 13-volume documentary appendix (1989–1991) to his classic 1984 study *The Abandonment of the Jews.*

11. *"Civitates superiorem non recognoscentes."* This principle was stated in the mid-fourteenth century. Equally influential was the corollary enunciated by Baldus a generation later, that rulers of cities recognize no superiors (Calasso 1951).

12. Translated into the language of humanism, the same principle appears as the ground for a defense of popular sovereignty—based on the *de facto* nonrecognition of the monarch—in Étienne de La Boétie's classic *Discourse of Voluntary Servitude* ([1555] 1975).

13. Innocent X issued a bull, *Zel domus,* condemning the Westphalian peace as "null, void, invalid, iniquitous, unjust, damnable, reprobate, inane, empty of meaning and effect for all time." Papal hostility to international law, which was seen as a Protestant heresy, remained lively even in the twentieth century. The works of Grotius, for example, which have often been hailed as the intellectual inspiration for the Westphalian treaties, remained on the index of banned books into the last century. See Philpott (1996:42, 59) and the sources he cites, especially Bull (1990) and Maland (1966:161).

14. The pamphlet appeared the year after the Augsburg Diet (1556). *Massacre* originally meant butcher's chopping block; *massacreur* meant butcher's knife.

15. Tergel (1998) credits Troeltsch with the view that we owe the wide diffusion of the ideal of universal human rights to radical Puritans during the Reformation, above all to those who held that "the integrity of inner life should not be subject to interference by the state" (p. 55).

16. Notable, among others, were sects inspired by the Sermon on the Mount (e.g., the Albigenses, Waldenses, Lollards, Hussites, Moravians). Also significant was the Synod of Elne, which propounded the Truce of God in 1027. Individuals of note include Erasmus, Crucé, Penn, Rousseau, Saint-Pierre, Kant, and others.

17. See Heiberg (1994:9ff.).

18. See Melson (1992), Chalk and Jonassohn (1990), and myriad others. The Turkish government denies the genocide vehemently to this day, and most other governments have been too polite to challenge these denials.

19. On February 28, 1915, the Young Turk central committee, Jemiyet, telegraphed its plans to the regional administrators who would implement the genocide. "Jemiyet has decided to free the fatherland from the covetousness of this accursed race . . . to exterminate all Armenians living in Turkey, without allowing a single one to remain alive" (Bey, cited by Fein 1979:15).

20. These could be characterized as situations of national anomie and cognitive dissonance, marked by discrepancies between expected and achieved national statuses and the perceived failure of international norms to reward legitimate national aspirations.

21. See, respectively, Gökalp ([1923] 1968:74); Heyd (1950:161); and Parla (1985:138). Gökalp dreamed of "Turan," Greater Turkey, which, he hoped, the war would bring: "The land of the enemy shall be devastated/ Turkey shall be enlarged and become Turan" (pp. 40, 74).

22. See, respectively, Heyd (1950:58, paraphrasing Gökalp); Parla (1985:68, quoting Gökalp); Heyd (1950:133); and Parla (1985:71, 91).

23. The quoted passages are, respectively, a citation from Gökalp, a paraphrase, and two more citations, all taken from Heyd (1950:78, 131, 78–9, and 58). After the war, Gökalp was tried for complicity in war crimes, but he was deported to Malta before the trial concluded.

24. All citations from this pamphlet are from the French edition of 1916. But the English translation (1915) is quite good and will often be used as a template.

25. Treitschke is for imperial Germany, in other words, what Gökalp was for the Young Turks. The parallel between the two has been stressed by Uriel Heyd—who claims, however, that Durkheim's "appreciation of Treitschke" (!) showed that all three shared cognate views (1950:63). Taha Parla, whose stance toward Gökalp is apologetic, takes comfort in Heyd's implication that "if Gökalp was illiberal, he was not more so than Durkheim

was" (1985:66). Others who have echoed Heyd include Melson (1992:164).

26. Many other writers cite these passages as well. See, for example, Dampierre (1917), who quotes a characteristic line: "War," says Treitschke, "is the form of litigation by which States make their claims valid" (p. 53).

27. For detail on Steinthal's relevance on questions of this kind, see Smith (1997).

28. This was a well-known doctrine in Durkheim's day, dating back to Pufendorf, at least. Le Normand (1899) and Triepel (1899) both defended this view, which is also visible in Weber's notion of recognition as the act constitutive of authority. For an incisive exposition of Pufendorf on this subject, see Ian Hunter (2001). And since Pufendorf was writing just decades after 1648, it is relevant to note that "the idea of an international order founded on or revealed by recognition" (Strang 1996:23) is central to the Westphalian state system.

29. For a good recent statement of the need to learn from both "intentionalist" and "functionalist" accounts of the Holocaust, see Ulrich Herbert (2000).

30. Lemkin, unlike Durkheim, also stressed the extent to which this mentality pivots around the concept of "peoples" arrayed against each other ethnically. Whereas Durkheim's focus is primarily on the state, Lemkin (like most of his successors) focuses on the nation as well as on the state, on nationalism as well as on statism.

31. On December 10, 1948.

32. Most people who call abortion murder would probably accept that there is a difference between multiple murders and the intended destruction of an entire social group. No one, to my knowledge, has yet claimed that feminists seek the destruction of the unborn *in toto*. Nor do many people say that the drug trade owes its existence to a deadly plot against the whole or a majority of a specific group. The wish to have a classless society, meanwhile, could only be validly linked to genocide if the means to this end were mass murder. Some modern dictators, of course, have used Marxist rhetoric to justify the slaughter of their enemies, just as others have used democratic rhetoric. But Marx called only for the abolition of private ownership of the means of production, not for the murder of the owning class. This is no more genocidal in principle than calling for the abolition of slavery.

33. Kuper said that since it would "vitiate" his analysis to exclude cases of mass murder in which the intended victims are political groups—cases that are not covered by the language of the Genocide Convention—he would include such cases in his discussion anyway. This, he seemed to think, did not contravene the established definition. Lawyers, I think, would disagree.

34. Kuper's work, in particular, is incisive and learned, and Scheper-Hughes is the author of a classic study of "the violence of everyday life" in Brazil (1992).

35. See especially Fein (1993) and Chalk and Jonassohn (1990).

36. Walzer's initial premise was that regimes should be considered presumptively legitimate even if repressive, since—until a popular revolt proves otherwise—we have to infer a "fit" between the state and the people. Under pressure from his critics, Walzer reverted to a more Lemkin-like logic, ultimately agreeing that "interventions can be justified whenever a government engages in the massacre or enslavement of its own citizens" (Walzer 1980:217).

37. Remarkably, in 1948, the American Anthropological Association opposed the Universal Declaration of Human Rights *in principle,* objecting that this statement was "conceived only in terms of the values prevalent in the countries of Western Europe and America" (cited by Hinton 2002:2). Clearly, under the cover of a liberal cultural relativism, this approach raised the nonintervention premise to an ethical absolute and allowed state sovereignty to tower over human rights. Few anthropologists today would find this sensible; see, for example, Ferguson (2003).

REFERENCES

Akural, Sabri M. 1978. *Ziya Gökalp.* Doctoral dissertation, University of Indiana.

Angell, Norman. 1910. *The Great Illusion.* New York: G. P. Putnam's Sons.

Arrighi, Giovanni. 1994. *The Long Twentieth Century: Money, Power, and the Origins of Our Times.* London and New York: Verso.

Babeuf, Gracchus. [1794] 1987. *La guerre de la Vendée et le système de dépopulation.* Paris, France: Tallandier.

Beitz, Charles R. 1980. "Nonintervention and Communal Integrity." In *Philosophy and Public Affairs* 9 (4):385–92.

Bull, Hedley. 1990. "The Importance of Grotius in the Study of International Relations." In *Hugo Grotius and International Relations,* edited by Hedley Bull, Benedict Kingsbury, and Adam Roberts. Oxford, England: Clarendon.

Calasso, Francesco. 1951. *I Glossatori e la teoria della Sovranità.* 2nd ed. Milan, Italy: Dott. A. Giuffrè-Editore.

Canning, Joseph. 1996. *A History of Medieval Political Thought, 300–1450.* London, England: Routledge.

Cassese, Antonio. 1988. *International Law in a Divided World.* Oxford, England: Clarendon.

Chalk, Frank. 1994. "Redefining Genocide." Pp. 47–63 in *Genocide: Conceptual and Historical Dimensions,* edited by George J. Andreopoulos. Philadelphia, PA: University of Pennsylvania Press.

Chalk, Frank and Kurt Jonassohn, eds. 1990. *The History and Sociology of Genocide: Analyses and Case Studies.* New Haven, CT: Yale University Press.

Charny, Israel W. 1994. "Toward a Generic Definition of Genocide." Pp. 64–94 in *Genocide: Conceptual and Historical Dimensions,* edited by George J. Andreopoulos. Philadelphia, PA: University of Pennsylvania Press.

Cohn, Norman. [1967] 1996. *Warrant for Genocide: The Myth of the Jewish World Conspiracy and the Protocols of the Elders of Zion.* 2nd ed. London, England: Serif.

Dampierre, Jacques, Marquis de. 1917. *German Imperialism and International Law.* London, England: Constable.

Des Forges, Alison. 2001. *Leave None to Tell the Story: Genocide in Rwanda.* New York: Human Rights Watch.

Donnelly, Jack. 1995. "State Sovereignty and International Intervention." Pp. 115–46 in *Beyond Westphalia?* edited by Gene M. Lyons and Michael Mastanduno. Baltimore, MD: Johns Hopkins University Press.

Doppelt, Gerald. 1980. "Statism without Foundations." In *Philosophy and Public Affairs* 9 (4):399–403.

Durkheim, Émile. 1915. *Germany Over All.* Translated by "J. S." Paris, France: Librairie Armand Colin.

——. 1916. *"L'Allemagne au-dessus de tout": La mentalité allemande et la guerre.* Paris, France: Librairie Armand Colin.

Ercole, Francesco. 1915. "L'Origine Francese di una Nota Formola Bartoliana." *Archivo Storico Italiano,* lxxiii, part ii.

——. 1931. "Sulla Origine Francese e le Vicende in Italia della Formola: 'Rex Superiorem Non Recognoscens est Princeps in Regno Suo.'" *Archivo Storico Italiano,* xvi, ser. vii.

Fein, Helen. 1979. *Accounting for Genocide.* Chicago, IL: University of Chicago Press.

——. 1993. *Genocide: A Sociological Perspective.* Newbury Park, CA: Sage.

——. 1994. "Genocide, Terror, Life Integrity, and War Crimes." Pp. 95–108 in *Genocide: Conceptual and Historical Dimensions,* edited by George J. Andreopoulos. Philadelphia, PA: University of Pennsylvania Press.

——. 2001. "Remembering for the Present." Pp. 43–54 in *Remembering for the Future: The Holocaust in an Age of Genocide,* vol. 1, *History,* edited by Margot Levy, Wendy Whitworth, John K. Roth, and Elisabeth Maxwell. New York: Palgrave.

Feingold, Henry L. 1970. *The Politics of Rescue: The Roosevelt Administration and the Holocaust, 1938–1945.* New Brunswick, NJ: Rutgers University Press.

Ferguson, R. Brian. 2003. "Introduction: Violent Conflict and Control of the State." Pp. 1–58 in *The State, Identity and Violence: Political Disintegration in the Post–Cold War World,* edited by R. Brian Ferguson. London, England: Routledge.

Ferringer, Natalie J. 1980. *Crimes Against Humanity: A Legal Problem in War and Peace.* Doctoral dissertation, University of Virginia.

Gannon, Franklin Reid. 1971. *The British Press and Germany, 1933–1939.* Oxford, England: Clarendon.

Glete, Jan. 2002. *War and the State in Early Modern Europe: Spain, the Dutch Republic and Sweden as Fiscal-Military States, 1500–1660.* London, England: Routledge.

Gökalp, Ziya. [1923] 1968. *The Principles of Turkism.* Leiden, The Netherlands: E. J. Brill.

Greengrass, Mark. 1999. "Hidden Transcripts: Secret Histories and Personal Testimonies of Religious Violence in the French Wars of Religion." Pp. 69–88 in *The Massacre in History,* edited by Mark Levene and Penny Roberts. New York: Bergahn Books.

Grewe, Wilhelm G. 2000. *The Epochs of International Law.* Translated and edited by Michael Byers. New York: Walter de Gruyter.

Gross, Leo. 1948. "The Peace of Westphalia, 1648–1948." In *American Journal of International Law* 42 (1):20–41.

Gurr, Ted Robert and Barbara Harff. 1994. *Ethnic Conflict in World Politics.* Boulder, CO: Westview.

Hancock, Ian. 1994. "Jewish Responses to the Porrajamos (The Romani Holocaust)." Paper presented at the *Remembering for the Future II Conference,* March 13–17, Berlin, Germany.

Hegel, G. W. F. [1821] 1991. *Elements of the Philosophy of Right.* Cambridge, England: Cambridge University Press.

Heiberg, Marianne. 1994. "Introduction." Pp. 3–32 in *Subduing Sovereignty: Sovereignty and the Right to Intervene,* edited by Marianne Heiberg. London, England: Pinter.

Henry, Séan. 2001. *August von Platen in the Discourse of Homosexuality 1821–1935.* Doctoral dissertation, University of Kansas, German Department.

Herbert, Ulrich. 2000. "Extermination Policy: New Answers and Questions about the History of the 'Holocaust' in German Historiography." Pp. 1–52 in *National Socialist Extermination Policies: Contemporary German Perspectives and Controversies,* edited by Ulrich Herbert. New York: Bergahn Books.

Heyd, Uriel. 1950. *Foundations of Turkish Nationalism: The Life and Teachings of Ziya Gökalp.* London, England: Luzac & Co. and Harvill Press.

Hilberg, Raul. [1961] 1967. *The Destruction of the European Jews* (with a new postscript). Chicago, IL: Quadrangle.

Hinton, Alexander Laban. 2002. "The Dark Side of Modernity." Pp. 1–42 in *Annihilating Difference: The Anthropology of Genocide,* edited by Alexander Laban Hinton. Berkeley, CA: University of California Press.

Hunter, Ian. 2001. *Rival Enlightenments: Civil and Metaphysical Philosophy in Early Modern Germany.* Cambridge, England: Cambridge University Press.

Jackson, Robert H. 1995. "International Community beyond the Cold War." Pp. 59–86 in *Beyond Westphalia?* edited by Gene M. Lyons and Michael Mastanduno. Baltimore, MD: Johns Hopkins University Press.

Jonassohn, Kurt. 1990. "Some Consequences of Genocide for the People of the Perpetrator States." Pp. 415–21 in *The History and Sociology of Genocide,* edited by Frank Chalk and Kurt Jonassohn. New Haven, CT: Yale University Press.

Jonassohn, Kurt (with Karin Solveig Björnson). 1998. *Genocide and Gross Human Rights Violations in Comparative Perspective.* New Brunswick, NJ: Transaction.

Knutsen, Torbjørn L. 1997. "Sovereignty and Intervention." Pp. 228–49 in *Beyond Westphalia?* edited by Gene M. Lyons and Michael Mastanduno. Baltimore, MD: Johns Hopkins University Press.

Krasner, Stephen D. 1995. *A History of International Relations Theory.* 2nd ed. Manchester, England: Manchester University Press.

Kratochwil, Friedrich. 1995. "Sovereignty as *Dominium.*" Pp. 21–42 in *Beyond Westphalia?* edited by Gene M. Lyons and Michael Mastanduno. Baltimore, MD: Johns Hopkins University Press.

Kuper, Leo. 1981. *Genocide: Its Political Use in the Twentieth Century.* New Haven, CT: Yale University Press.

Kuperman, Alan J. 2001. *The Limits of Humanitarian Intervention: Genocide in Rwanda.* Washington, DC: Brookings Institution.

La Boétie, Étienne de [1555] 1975. *The Politics of Obedience: The Discourse of Voluntary Servitude.* Translated by Harry Kurz. Montreal, Canada: Black Rose.

Lemkin, Raphael. 1933. "Akte der Barbarei und des Vandalismus als *delicta iuris gentium.*" In *Internationales Anwaltsblatt Vienna,* November.

———. 1935. "Terrorisme: Rapport et Projet de Textes." In *Actes de la Vᵉ Conférence Internationale pour l'Unification du Droit Pénal.* Paris, France: Éditions A. Pedone.

———. 1944. *Axis Rule in Occupied Europe.* Washington, DC: Carnegie Endowment for International Peace.

———. 1992. *Not Guilty? Raphael Lemkin's Thoughts on Nazi Genocide,* edited by Steven L. Jacobs. Lewiston, ME: Edwin Mellen.

Le Normand, René. 1899. *La reconaissance internationale et ses diverses applications.* Paris, France: Imprime Camis.

Leurdijk, J. H. 1986. *Intervention in International Politics.* Leeuwarden, The Netherlands: Eisma B.V.

Levene, Mark. 2001. "Remembering for the Future: Engaging with the Present." Pp. 55–70 in *Remembering for the Future: The Holocaust in an Age of Genocide,* vol. 1, *History,* edited by Margot Levy, Wendy Whitworth, John K. Roth, and Elisabeth Maxwell. New York: Palgrave.

Luban, David. 1980. "The Romance of the Nation-State." *Philosophy and Public Affairs* 9 (4): 393–97.

Macartney, C. A. 1934. *National States and National Minorities.* London, England: Oxford University Press.

Magnarella, Paul J. 2000. *Justice in Africa: Rwanda's Genocide, Its Courts, and the UN Criminal Tribunal.* Aldershot, England: Ashgate.

Maland, David. 1966. *Europe in the Seventeenth Century.* London, England: Macmillan.

Mann, Michael. 1990. "Introduction: Empires with Ends." Pp. 1–11 in *The Rise and Decline of the Nation State,* edited by Michael Mann. Oxford, England: Blackwell.

Melson, Robert. 1992. *Revolution and Genocide: On the Origins of the Armenian Genocide and the Holocaust.* Chicago, IL: University of Chicago Press.

Melvern, Linda. 2000. *A People Betrayed: The Role of the West in Rwanda's Genocide.* London, England: Zed Books.

Miller, Joseph C. 1988. *Way of Death: Merchant Capitalism and the Angolan Slave Trade, 1730–1830.* Madison, WI: University of Wisconsin Press.

Northedge, F. S. 1967. "Peace, War, and Philosophy." Pp. 63–7 in *The Encyclopedia of Philosophy,* vol. 6, edited by Paul Edwards. New York: Macmillan.

Onuf, Nicholas. 1995. "Intervention for the Common Good." Pp. 43–58 in *Beyond Westphalia?* edited by Gene M. Lyons and Michael Mastanduno. Baltimore, MD: Johns Hopkins University Press.

Parla, Taha. 1985. *The Social and Political Thought of Ziya Gökalp, 1876–1924.* Leiden, The Netherlands: E. J. Brill.

Philpott, Daniel. 1996. "On the Cusp of Sovereignty: Lessons from the Sixteenth Century." Pp. 37–62 in *Sovereignty at the Crossroads? Morality and International Politics in the Post–Cold War Era,* edited by Luis E. Lugo. Lanham, MD: Rowman & Littlefield.

Power, Samantha. 2002. *"A Problem from Hell": America and the Age of Genocide.* New York: Basic Books.

Ratner, Steven R. and Jason S. Abrams. 2001. *Accountability for Human Rights Atrocities in International Law.* 2nd ed. New York: Oxford University Press.

Reid, James J. 1992. "Total War, the Annihilation Ethic, and the Armenian Genocide, 1870–1918." Pp. 21–52 in *The Armenian Genocide: History, Politics, Ethics,* edited by Richard G. Hovannisian. New York: St. Martin's.

Saab, Anne Pottinger. 1991. *Reluctant Icon: Gladstone, Bulgaria, and the Working Classes, 1856–1878.* Cambridge, MA: Harvard University Press.

Scelle, Georges. 1934. *Précis de droit des gens: Principes et systematique,* vol. 2, *Droit constitutionnel international.* Paris, France: Librairie du Recueil Sirey.

Scheper-Hughes, Nancy. 1992. *Death Without Weeping: The Violence of Everyday Life in Brazil.* Berkeley, CA: University of California Press.

——. 2002. "Coming to Our Senses." Pp. 348–81 in *Annihilating Difference: The Anthropology of Genocide,* edited by Alexander Laban Hinton. Berkeley, CA: University of California Press.

Sereni, A. P. 1943. *The Italian Conception of International Law.* New York: Columbia University Press.

Shannon, Richard. 1963. *Gladstone and the Bulgarian Agitation, 1876.* London, England: Thomas Nelson.

Sharp, Alan. 1978. "Britain and the Protection of Minorities at the Paris Peace Conference, 1919." Pp. 170–188 in *Minorities in History,* edited by A. C. Hepburn. London, England: Edward Arnold.

Smith, David Norman. 1995. "Ziya Gökalp and Émile Durkheim: Sociology as an Apology for Chauvinism?" In *Durkheimian Studies/Études durkheimiennes* 1 (1), New Series, November, 45–51.

——. 1996. "The Social Construction of Enemies: Jews and the Representation of Evil." In *Sociological Theory* 14 (3):203–40.

——. 1997. "Judeophobia, Myth, and Critique." Pp. 123-54 in *The Seductiveness of Jewish Myth,* edited by S. Daniel Breslauer. Albany, NY: SUNY Press.

——. 1998. "The Psychocultural Roots of Genocide: Legitimacy and Crisis in Rwanda." In *The American Psychologist* 53 (7):743–53.

——. 2000. "Genocide." Pp. 1066–1073 in *Encyclopedia of Sociology,* edited by Edgar F. Borgatta and Rhonda Montgomery. New York: Macmillan.

——. 2001. "Abolitionism and Social Theory: Slavery, 'Wage Slavery,' and the Visibility of Oppression." In *Current Perspectives in Social Theory* 20:143–81.

Strang, David. 1996. "Contested Sovereignty: The Social Construction of Colonial Imperialism." Pp. 22–49 in *State Sovereignty as Social Construct,* edited by Thomas J. Biersteker and Cynthia Weber. Cambridge, England: Cambridge University Press.

Tergel, Alf. 1998. *Human Rights in Cultural and Religious Traditions.* Uppsala, Sweden: Acta Universitatis Upsaliensis.

Tilly, Charles. 1990. *Coercion, Capital, and European States, AD 990–1990.* Cambridge, MA: Blackwell.

Triepel, Heinrich. 1899. *Völkerrecht und Landesrecht.* Leipzig, Germany: C. L. Hirschfeld.

Tyrnauer, Gabrielle. 1989. *Gypsies and the Holocaust: A Bibliography and Introductory Essay.* Montreal, Canada: Interuniversity Centre for European Studies and Montreal Institute of Genocide Studies.

Ullmann, Walter. 1966. *Principles of Government and Politics in the Middle Ages.* New York: Barnes & Noble.

Walzer, Michael. 1977. *Just and Unjust Wars.* New York: Basic Books.

——. 1980. "The Moral Standing of States." In *Philosophy and Public Affairs* 9 (3):209–29.

Weber, Max. [1919] 1946. "Politics as a Vocation." Pp. 77–128 in *From Max Weber,* edited by Hans H. Gerth and C. Wright Mills. New York: Oxford University Press.

Weiss, Thomas G. and Jarat Chopra. 1995. "Sovereignty under Siege." Pp. 87–114 in *Beyond Westphalia?* edited by Gene M. Lyons and Michael Mastanduno. Baltimore, MD: Johns Hopkins University Press.

Wyman, David S. 1984. *The Abandonment of the Jews: America and the Holocaust, 1941–1945.* New York: Pantheon.

——, ed. 1989–1991. *America and the Holocaust: A thirteen-volume set documenting the editor's book The Abandonment of the Jews.* New York: Garland.

Wyman, David S. and Rafael Medoff. 2002. *A Race Against Death: Peter Bergson, America, and the Holocaust.* New York: New Press.

Wyman, David S. and Charles H. Rosenzweig, eds. 1996. *The World Reacts to the Holocaust.* Baltimore, MD: Johns Hopkins University Press.

GLOBALIZATION

JOHN BOLI
Emory University

MICHAEL A. ELLIOTT
Emory University

FRANZISKA BIERI
Emory University

After a decade or so of self-congratulatory neoliberal homilies about the wonderful new world forged by the irresistible *deus ex machina* of globalization, by the late 1990s globalization had become the target of wave upon wave of fist-shaking critics and self-proclaimed champions of the poor and the oppressed. Vivid images of heavy-handed police tactics at the World Trade Organization (WTO) meetings in Seattle, raw street violence in Genoa, the clamorous World Social Forum gatherings in Porto Alegre to challenge global capitalism's annual summit in Davos

(the World Economic Forum)—all this, and much more, have made "antiglobalization" a prominent presence on the world stage. Not a coherent movement but an inchoate array of disparate nongovernmental organizations (NGOs), activists, grassroots organizations, labor unions, anarchists, academics, and numerous other elements, the antiglobalization forces preach a long litany of complaints that have little in common except for one overriding theme: Globalization is the problem, not the solution.[1]

Our purpose here is not to assess the purported sins of globalization. Rather, we will survey the antiglobalization landscape, conducting a kind of ecological analysis of the many species of antiglobalization in the context of a theoretical framework that can help answer several fundamental sociological questions: Why has globalization become the dreadful scourge of the twenty-first century? Why do social movements increasingly express their concerns as problems of globalization? What social processes give rise to these movements, and what is the deeper meaning of the social problems they identify as consequences of globalization?

Our analysis begins with a theoretical framework within which we situate the *globalization problematique.* We use ideas borrowed from Durkheim (2001, 1984), Douglas (1966, 1986), Ellul (1975), and several global cultural analysts (Boli and Thomas 1999; Meyer et al. 1997; Robertson 1992; Thomas et al. 1987) to depict the rising tide of complaints about globalization as efforts to preserve or restore sacred elements at the core of the world moral order. Put another way, globalization is used as an umbrella term covering a panoply of failures of various authoritative or powerful actors in world society—states, intergovernmental organizations (IGOs), corporations, and individuals—to act in accordance with global models specifying the broadly legitimated responsibilities they are expected to assume. In this depiction, globalization itself (as a catch-all concept used in numerous theories-of-everything) could emerge only under particular world-cultural conditions, and its appropriation by moral guardians as the embodiment of evil is a logical consequence of those conditions.

We then conduct our ecological survey, identifying the many species of ills linked to globalization and further elaborating our counterfactual analysis regarding species of ills for which globalization could be, but is not, blamed. This survey has two components: We review the ills themselves and identify the types of victims championed in antiglobalization discourse as well as the presumed villains and heroes in the great struggle between good and evil that globalization has come to represent. Our penultimate section discusses the solutions offered to redeem the sins of globalization, and the conclusion discusses structural conditions that affect the intensity of concern about globalization and speculates briefly about future developments.

THEORIZING THE GLOBALIZATION PROBLEMATIQUE

An important substantive observation for our theoretical analysis is globalization's polymorphous character. Laments about the imprecision of the term are commonplace—it means too many things in too many contexts. For many, globalization is only or essentially economic (Amin 1997; Chase-Dunn 1998; Gereffi and Korzeniewicz 1994; Sklair 2001): rising world trade, expanding foreign investment, global companies, multinode production chains, and the IGOs (mainly the IMF [International Monetary Fund], and GATT [General Agreement on Tariffs and Trade]/WTO) that manage the world economy. Others emphasize political globalization in the form of international law and courts, democratization, the general population of global governance IGOs, the rapidly expanding array of international nongovernmental organizations (INGOs) that constitute global civil society, and so on (Diamond 1993; Keohane and Nye 1989). Still others focus on cultural globalization—values (e.g., human rights and environmentalism), lifestyles (fast-food restaurants, video games, high fashion), media consumption (CNN, Hollywood, and Bollywood), and problematized local cultures and national identities (Appadurai 1990, 1996; Hannerz 1991, 1996; Küng 1998; McLuhan 1989; Smith 1980; Ritzer 1993). The concept has become so elastic that it verges on totality.

This totalistic quality has the interesting consequence of making globalization available as an explanation of almost any observable feature of contemporary world society. It has the added attraction of bringing to the fore the most powerful actors in world society as both engines of global development and potential brakes on global progress. Thus, transnational corporations (TNCs) are often seen as the dynamos powering the globalization dreadnaught, backed up by mighty states (of the capitalist core, the West, or rising Asian countries), and facilitated by the neoliberal programs of the IGOs that manage the world economy (Broad 2002; Mander and Goldsmith 1996; Rodrik 1997; Sklair 2001; Smith and Johnston 2002). States (and, in most accounts, only states) can also inhibit globalization if they are sufficiently strong, misguided, or fanatical.

In any case, globalization is the arena in which the giants of the modern world pit their strength and wiles against one another. The combatants of the globalization arena are daunting in their power, wielding their gleaming technology like master arc welders or time-warped gladiators. The world arena buzzes with the excitement of the splendiferous riches offered by globalization while an undercurrent of grave danger and potentially illimitable catastrophe swirls beneath the arena floor.

A realm of superhuman beings with the capacity for great good and evil, offering rewards beyond imagining to those who do their bidding but threatening by their sheer size and strength, locked as they are in intense competition, to crush the mere mortals who observe in awe their momentous struggles—this is the global morality play it is our pleasure and horror to attend. The play's script is grounded in the global moral order that is a fundamental pillar supporting the broader world-cultural canopy that has crystallized over the past two centuries (Boli 1997). Globalization has become a dominant concern within the global moral order as both the god of peace and prosperity and the beguiling devil that visits humanity with misery and destruction. What has brought globalization to the fore as the central moral dilemma of our time is, thus, the dense organization and institutionalization of world culture and its foundational moral order, particularly over the past 50 years (Boli and Thomas 1999; Meyer et al. 1987; Meyer et al. 1997).

To understand globalization's moral centrality, therefore, we begin with the world moral order.[2] Like all moral orders, the global instance builds on a distinction between the sacred and the profane (Douglas 1966; Durkheim 2001). The sacred is both powerful and dangerous (Ellul 1975), constituting the central locus of authority, value, and meaning in the cultural realm. It commands reverence, deference, respect, and sacrifice. Those subject to the sacred must approach it with care and discipline, never treating it with the instrumentality or casualness that earmark everyday behavior in the realm of the profane.

Weber (1968) argued that rationalization disenchants the world, stripping away the gods and spirits and leaving nothing in their place but emptiness. Here, Weber erred. The world is disenchanted, yes, but not so the cultural complex that has disenchanted it. Rather, as Ellul (1975) argues, the disenchanting forces themselves have generated new forms of sacrality in place of the demoted sacred order. Durkheim (1973) and Goffman (1956) corrected Weber's misunderstanding by showing that rationalized (differentiated) culture embeds sacrality first and foremost in the individual—not in individuals as discrete carbon units, but in "the Individual" as a mythic concept around which a cult of great power has coalesced. The individual is the ultimate source of political authority: Sovereignty resides in the people and is delegated by them to the institutions that govern them. The individual is the ultimate source of (monetarized) value: Individuals labor, harvest, invest, deal, invent, and sell, producing wealth and ever-rising gross national product (GNP)/capita. The individual is the ultimate locus of meaning: Only individuals are capable of deriving meaning from the swirl of life; only individuals can give life the meanings it assumes. For those whose worldview is thoroughly constructed by individualist culture, all this is patently obvious: Only individuals are real, tangible, acting agents. Families, ethnic groups, companies, states, and INGOs are nothing but collections of individuals, convenient fictions without distinctive substance.

But the sacred core of the world moral order is not so simple. Alongside the mythic Individual, collectivities enjoy some degree of sacrality. In line with many historical traditions, the family is not wholly reducible to the sum of its (individual) parts; neither is the village, the clan, or the ethnic group. In rationalized form, "protected classes" of individuals—racial and ethnic minorities, identity groups defined by disability, sexual orientation, and the like, and various other particularistic categories—are moderately reified and sacralized. Yet these collectivities are continually undermined by the highly reified individual, and only one collectivity—the nation—enjoys a sacred status that is at all comparable to that of the individual. The nation provides a major source of identity for individuals as citizens, a consequence of the extensive nation-building efforts of states and private actors that downplay other sources of identity in favor of the national collectivity (Anderson 1991; Bendix 1964). Nations are the primary collective building blocks of world society, managed by states that are presumed to represent the will of their ultimately sovereign citizen-individuals. States are therefore the armed protectors of the sacrality of citizen-individuals, and the assumed (if rarely realized) coincidence of nationhood and state-bounded territory makes the collectivity of citizen-individuals within the territory a sacred entity in its own right.

The mythic Individual is instantiated by each individual person; as such, the world moral order posits a fundamental egalitarianism among these carbon units that was always present in the doctrines of Christendom (a major source of the original version of the moral order). Christendom allotted one and only one soul to every person; the more secularized global order allots one and only one personality (two or more constitute a pathology). Christendom made eternal salvation the ultimate and universal existential issue; the global order makes individual development and self-actualization in this world the primary measure of the "life well lived."

From this dual underpinning of the egalitarian individual and the encompassing nation, the global moral order presents a complex set of derivative categories, mostly collections of individuals who are deemed worthy of special consideration because they suffer inequalities or are excluded from progress and justice. Recent decades have seen a proliferation of these categories, thanks in no small part to the great success of social scientists in discovering new dimensions of inequality and exclusion, and in inventing new properties of (categories of) individuals with respect to which inequality and exclusion can be identified. Thus, the status and well-being of many categories related to disability, illness, cultural background, sexual orientation, and so on are now well ensconced in the global moral order as matters of concern and motivations for action.

Violations and Victims

Moral transgressions violate the sacred. Analyzing violations—heinous deeds—is thus a trustworthy means of identifying the sacred. Heinous deeds have victims, and they can be victims only if they are imbued with sacrality. Lacking sacrality, the object of a deed that causes injury or damage is not a victim, and the deed itself is not heinous. Thus, individual people, as sacred entities, are victims whenever they are the direct objects of injurious or damaging deeds; we call such violations assault, robbery, rape, and murder. The property of individuals, however, is not directly eligible for victim status; one would be quite astonished to read that a convenience store from which goods were burgled in the night was the "victim" of the burglary. The store is not sacred, though it may be valued and treasured by its owner; as an extension of its owner, it is to be protected from harm, but it cannot be victimized. Similarly, the moral order renders nonhumans and most inanimate objects as only weakly sacralized, if at all. A dog shot by a grouchy neighbor is not a victim; a car struck by a drunk driver is not a victim; a massive rock formation destroyed for road construction is not a victim.

Categories of individuals can be victims, and this type of claim is common. Weak or vulnerable categories of people are especially likely to be identified as victims; they may not be inherently more sacred than the strong or the privileged, but violations of their sacrality are more heinous. The aged, the infirm, the very young; "women and children" as, say, civilian victims of warfare (more than civilian men!); ethnic or national minorities with long histories of repression or discrimination; the poor, the uneducated, the marginalized—such categories, when violated, are especially worthy of concern.

Can collective entities as such be victims? Here, the moral order is less clear. In extreme cases such as genocide or severe repression, when the very survival of a group is at stake, collectivities are reified as more than mere aggregates of individuals. Anguish over the collective fate of, for example, the Bosnian Muslims, the Kurds, and the Tibetans has been widespread. In addition, such holistic entities as "Tibetan culture" and the "traditions" of rainforest dwellers are regularly invoked as victims of various types of violations of the moral order. Such usage, however, is far less frequent than the identification of violations of individuals separately or as members of categories.

Alongside human-based entities, nature is also sacred. Numerous forms of the moral violation of nature are commonly lamented. Specifications of nature's sacrality are many, indicated by violations that threaten "endangered" species, "fragile" ecosystems, revered natural places, and so on. A different set of abstractions reflects the sacrality of the nation: Desecrations of historic sites, of totems like the national flag and national monuments, of statues of national leaders, and of war memorials are gravely reprehensible acts. However, strictly national sacred entities and abstractions are only weak candidates for global moral lamentation unless they are conceptualized as elements belonging to humanity as a whole, for example by their appearance on the United Nations Educational, Scientific, and Cultural Organization's World Heritage List (UNESCO 2003). Sacred sites on this list, such as the giant stone Buddhas in Afghanistan that were destroyed by the Taliban, are much more likely to evoke global concern than comparable sites where sacrality is linked only to a particular nation.

The degree of severity attributed to a violation—the amount of horror, fear, disgust, shame, or guilt it evokes—indicates the degree of sacrality of the entity being violated. This principle underscores the derivative sacrality of property, and of nonhuman objects more generally, as compared with persons. Robbery without battery is deemed much less serious than a "brutal" mugging ("At least you weren't hurt!"). A suitcase bomb that destroys the unoccupied offices of a TNC is less shocking than a car bombing that kills a company executive; the extinction of a species through overfishing is much less regrettable than a rampaging rebel group wiping out a pygmy tribe in the Congo.

In the prevailing global moral order, people as individuals and categories are the center of the universe; people's cultures are of considerable concern, their particular nations less so; nature's sites, fauna, and flora deserve variable degrees of reverence and protection, tempered by the logic of resource extraction and exploitation that compels an instrumentally unsympathetic view of nature. At the highest level of abstraction, the global moral order still makes room for a variety of gods, particularly those high gods chartered by "world" religions, but violations even of the high gods are often couched in terms of the sacrality of individuals. For instance, violations of "freedom of religion" imply limitations on the rights of individuals to believe in the god or gods of their choosing, not the victimization of one or another

god. In this sense, even the sacrality of the high gods is increasingly derivative of the sacrality of persons.

Global Movements as the Ritualistic Restoration of Sacrality

Violations threaten the sacred. In the realm of the high gods, violations thereby threaten the miscreant as well because the high god may react punitively. In the "secularized" global moral order that enthrones the individual as the greatest and highest god, however, responses to violations must come from the individual, acting alone or in concert with others. The modern individual is not simply empowered with extensive rights but also saddled with sober responsibilities regarding the moral order. Thus, a responsible world citizen (Boli and Thomas 1997) is to be on the alert for violations of the global moral order and to take action when they occur. Timber companies ravaging the "lungs of the earth" in Brazil or Borneo? Write a protest letter! Indonesian subcontractors demanding 12-hour work shifts of textile workers in poorly ventilated factories? Support the International Labor Rights Fund! Corrupt government officials siphoning development aid to buy villas on the Riviera? Establish Transparency International (as former World Bank officer Peter Eigen did) to expose the corruption and outline reforms that could curb it!

Heroic Redeemers

Transnational social movements (Guidry, Kennedy, and Zald 2000; Keck and Sikkink 1998; Khagram, Riker, and Sikkink 2002; Smith, Chatfield, and Pagnucco 1997) impelled by considerations of equality, justice, liberty, autonomy, self-actualization, empowerment, cultural authenticity, and many other watchwords anchored in the global moral order are the white knights, the rescue squads, the holy redeemers of the contemporary world. They constitute the "conscience of the world" (Willetts 1996); like ubiquitous Quakers, they bear witness to the transgressions of global villains (Wapner 1996; Wapner, Ruiz, and Falk 2000) and preach to the iniquitous (TNCs, states, elites, and interest groups great and small) that they may better their ways. At heart, those who call globalization into question, who see in global structures and processes the source of many ills, who rage against the IMF, lambast Unocal's Burmese pipeline project (EarthRights International 2003), monitor Mattel's Asian factories, or gather signatures petitioning for poor-country debt relief are dedicated above all to restoring the global moral order that has been violated, in their eyes, by these powerful transgressors.[3]

The special property that lifts these critics of globalization to the highest moral plane is their disinterestedness. Self-interested action is legitimate in the moral order—individuals and other actors are entitled to pursue their rights and satisfy their needs and desires—but self-interested action is not virtuous. Virtue adheres in transcendence of the self, transcendence of particularism; the truly virtuous are those who relate to the world as servants of others. Virtuous action is civilized action, the overcoming of primordial drives and instincts that shout of ego and defense and narrow horizons, in favor of the broad perspective, the long sweep, the good of the many. Virtue is selflessness, the willing abandonment of self-interest on behalf of, especially, those who are unable to pursue their own interests effectively. By this logic, those members of the fortunate, comfortable classes of the world who dedicate themselves to righting the wrongs of globalization as activists, organizers, intellectuals, and office staffers become excellent candidates for redeemer status. They work not for themselves, but for those in need of aid, indeed for all of humanity and nature. If they approach their selfless (and often thankless) tasks with substantial doses of humility and unpretentiousness, they may even become paragons of virtue, joining the ranks of such shining global lights as Mohandas Gandhi, Mother Teresa, Martin Luther King Jr., and Jimmy Carter.

The restorative action of the virtuous redeemers, now routinized, rationalized, and expanding across virtually every domain of human endeavor, is ritualistic in the crucial Durkheimian sense (cf. Wuthnow 1987): The redeemers participate in recurring collective action, often of substantial emotional intensity (viz., street demonstrations, confrontations with police), in which the moral order is repeatedly invoked and affirmed such that its preeminent status and, indeed, its ineffable reality become unimpeachable

truths for the redeemers themselves. One obvious result is heightened solidarity among the world-savers, who, armed with the slingshots of their moral invocations and the stones of scientific analysis, data on poverty and disease, and models of socially responsible actors, stand against the Goliaths who threaten to enslave humanity and destroy the planet in the service of the perennial devils of plunder, profit, and power. The more important result is the continual propagation of the global moral order by antiglobalization forces. In this, they are joined by a host of other transnational and national organizations whose routine practices have the same effects—including, ironically enough, many of the targets of antiglobalization rhetoric and mobilization who are seen as major violators of the moral order (more on this below).

Movements against globalization are ritualistic in a more superficial sense as well: The heroic redeemers engage in actions whose efficacy in washing away the sins of the world is so difficult to establish that only great faith can render the actions sensible and meaningful. Definite antiglobalization successes are uncertain and rare. One of the more widely trumpeted victories came against the Organization for Economic Cooperation and Development's (OECD) proposed Multilateral Agreement on Investment (MAI), which evoked vigorous mobilization by a wide range of organizations who felt it would strip developing countries of their capacity to regulate foreign investment (Ayres 2002). Though the MAI was withdrawn in 1998, its proponents only grudgingly admit that anything other than technical and economic considerations led to this decision (Kobrin 1998). On the other hand, movements against big dams, often tied rhetorically to the fight against globalization, have stopped many projects (Khagram 2000), and the demonstrations against the WTO have been effective inasmuch as the WTO has felt compelled to increase its interaction with NGOs, be less restrictive in releasing information to the public, and establish an NGO "room" in its Web site (WTO 2003). Nevertheless, as critics of globalization energetically write letters, prepare policy papers, conduct investigations, lobby at international meetings, send delegates to monitor corporate behavior, and so on, they do so without much tangible evidence that their efforts make a difference. Like supplicants to a mighty and mysterious god, they find vindication more in the conviction that their actions are just, proper, and disinterested—that is, in accord with the global moral order—than in the knowledge that they are making progress toward their immensely ambitious goals.

Globalization's Ambiguity

What makes the attempts to restore the sacred order so numerous and widespread is, above all, the radical ambiguity of globalization's effects (cf. Ellul 1980). Every new job created in a Mattel toy factory in China implies that yet another exploited worker with no union support joins the workforce. Cheaper travel both enables more people to enrich their lives by going abroad and increases the threat of rampant tourism to local cultures. Though the Amungme have been displaced by Freeport McMoRan's mining operations in Irian Jaya (Abrash 2001; CorpWatch 1997), Javanese miners have found the means to put tin roofs on their bamboo houses and feed their children more protein. These examples illustrate the dualistic consequences of every instance of large-scale social development when considered in relation to the global moral order. Globalization brings much that is welcome and much that is deplored—and much that is welcome and deplored at one and the same time.

Such ambiguity inheres not only in globalization processes themselves but also in the complexity and internal inconsistency of the moral order. The Individual that lies at the core of the moral order is both egalitarian and empowered ("agentic," to use an academic term for this mythological aspect). Empowerment demands freedom of action, choice, and orientation, but egalitarianism demands restrictions on that freedom: Nothing is more certain than the inequality and exploitation generated by a totally free market (Polanyi 1944; Roemer 1982, 1988). Make a move toward freedom and equality is at risk; push for equality and freedom declines. Similarly, the pursuit of rationalized progress, as conventionally understood, necessarily entails the disenchantment of traditional cultures and encroachment on the natural habitats of nonhuman species. At a more abstract level, cultural relativism—the principle that every people's culture should be judged from within its own value system and historical circumstances—crashes headlong into the cultural absolutism of doctrines of universal human rights, liberal democracy, elaborately psychologized personhood, and other valued constructs derivative of the global moral order. *In toto,* those who seek to gain purchase as critics of globalization have a virtually unlimited number of handholds ready for the grabbing, thanks to the complexity and contradictions of both globalization processes themselves and the moral order that is also an aspect of globalization. The wondrous puzzle, in fact, is that critics are so selective regarding the range of evils they attribute to globalization. Much more moral outcry is possible.

Counterfactuals: Globalization Not on Trial

Not every human problem is linked to globalization. Consider noise pollution: Do demonstrators railing at the WTO or G8 carry signs demanding "Keep Our Cities Quiet!"? Do we find specialized INGOs charging that TNCs are responsible for traffic accidents or jaywalking? Has any prominent critic made a name for him- or herself by depicting globalization as the root cause of white-collar crime or petty larceny? Divorce rates, psychological disorders, litigiousness, learning disabilities, voter apathy, suicide, and many other purported ills of modern societies are yet to find their global crusaders or make a splash in the ocean of antiglobalization discourse.

One might object that these problems are not decried as ills of globalization because they are not global problems; they are individual, local, or national issues, even though they may be found worldwide. Exactly! This objection overlooks the fact that no problem or transgression is inherently global. Only in the context of an encompassing culture that begins with the conception of the world as a single entity—of a global society and natural environment, of universalistic science and technology, of global systems and global projects, above all of a global moral order—can any social problem become associated with globalization. Prior to the nineteenth century, there were essentially no global problems; in the twenty-first century, interpreting problems globally is routine. But this routinization of the global problematique (Robertson and Chirico 1985) remains an opaque process that is poorly understood. Theories to explain why particular types of social problems are seen as global while most types have yet to be constructed as arenas for global moral combat are notable by their absence. While such theorizing is outside our scope here, this lacuna should be kept in mind as we turn to our ecological survey of the ills of globalization.

DIMENSIONS OF GLOBALIZATION'S ILLS

For convenience, we have grouped the problems attributed to globalization under five rubrics: economic, environmental, cultural, political, and human. We begin with the economic dimension.

Economic Evils

Globalization as an economic phenomenon is roughly synonymous with the worldwide expansion of capitalist markets, financial and investment flows, and production commodity chains and distribution networks. Globalization's champions insist that these processes boost wealth and prosperity worldwide, giving everyone greater access to goods and services and dramatically increasing standards of living (*The Economist* 2001b, 2001c, 2001d; Wolf 1997). The benefits of economic globalization purportedly extend to other dimensions as well; the "new world order" proclaimed after the first Gulf War imagined economic liberalization and global integration creating common interests (via interdependence) and promoting shared liberal values (freedom, democracy, civil rights, the rule of law) that would thereby reduce conflict and promote global solidarity.

Globalization's critics espy instead a capitalist juggernaut of untrammeled exploitation and neo-imperialism, driven by the avarice of wealthy countries, TNCs, and the western-dominated IMF, WTO, and other IGOs that manage the capitalist world economy (ATTAC 1998; International Forum on Globalization [IFG] 1995; Oxfam 1996). The relentless global expansion of capitalism, uneven in its effects and unstable in its cyclical operations, threatens the rights and well-being of individuals and nations. Put another way, it violates important principles of the global moral order, above all the principles of egalitarian individualism and national development—and so, at a deeper level, it violates the sacrality of both the individual and the nation.

Threats to Egalitarian Individualism

Whether driven by greed (as frequently presumed by globalization's critics) or competition (a hollow excuse, in critics' eyes, because of capitalism's inherent tendencies toward monopoly), capitalists at all levels systematically exploit workers. Global capitalists are especially vile because the powerful TNCs they command give them strong leverage over political elites in less developed countries. Capital seeks new production sites with low wages and generous state subsidies; the result is wages that amount to a few dollars for each pair of Reebok running shoes that retail at $100 a pair or each silk blouse that Donna Karan sells at Bloomingdale's for $125. Labor is not being paid the full value of its production. Instead, local subcontractors, global distributors, and the TNCs that control commodity chains rake in the profits (Gereffi and Korzeniewicz 1994). The result is steep inequality, the working masses earning little more than subsistence wages (if that!) while the capitalist few enjoy lives of unconscionable luxury.

Inequality also results from such secondary mechanisms as corruption, fraud, and financial manipulation (additional violations of global moral principles). Local and national politicians demand kickbacks to approve foreign investments, workers are denied overtime pay, financial wizards concoct elaborate schemes to inflate reported profits or swindle investors. The notorious recent scandals involving Enron, WorldCom, Arthur Anderson, and other giant corporations are presumed by antiglobalization activists to be standard operating procedure in both the core and the periphery. Tying together all these violations committed by the juggernaut of capitalism is the umbrella concept of neo-imperialism. The capitalist core, pushing its neoliberal agenda by means of the IMF and WTO, offers loans, investments, and jobs in exchange for compliance with free market reforms that lower tariffs, privatize government functions, and reduce spending on welfare programs. These so-called structural adjustment programs ultimately constitute a scheme to provide more opportunities for profit and expose workers to further exploitation (Amin 1997; Bello 1996; Broad 2002; Klein 2002). When investment occurs in the form of subcontracting, the exploitative machinations of the TNCs are concealed by the direct control of native capitalists and managers, a practice that deflects complaints from the TNCs themselves.

The inequalities that global capitalism generates are inequities because they violate the principles of egalitarian individualism. Regarding egalitarianism, the world moral order does not insist on complete equality of outcomes. However, severe inequalities that leave a large portion of humanity living in deplorable conditions are wholly illegitimate, and theories that explain this deplorable state as the result of capitalist exploitation find many adherents. Where basic needs, such as adequate food and shelter, clean water, and functioning refuse and waste disposal are lacking, the inequalities involved are not simply unjust; they are violations of essential human rights, as spelled out especially in the International Covenant on Economic, Social, and Cultural Rights (United Nations [UN] 1966) and similar conventions of recent decades. At this point, sacralized individualism enters in: These impoverished people are denied the capacity to live with dignity and the opportunity to develop as capable, empowered world and national citizens. To the extent that their impoverishment is due to capitalist exploitation, it is plainly wrong. Everyone should enjoy the just fruits of their labors, but market operations are always distorted in favor of the capitalists.

Global inequalities become inequities by another logic as well. The global moral order is tolerant of inequality only if it is merited, that is, only if equality of opportunity actually obtains. Insofar as disparities in income and wealth are consequences of differences in diligence, persistence, integrity, inventiveness, and the like, they are acceptable and can be useful stimulants to entrepreneurship and innovation. But economic inequalities, especially in the severe form found in world society, necessarily imply great inequality of opportunity both within and among countries. Those oppressed by capitalist exploitation, corruption, fraud, and manipulation are denied opportunities of many sorts: for education, job training, small-business loans, Internet access, and much more. They lack the opportunity to participate in modern, rationalized institutions that would enable them to produce and consume at the level of their more fortunate counterparts in the capitalist core countries. This sweeping violation of egalitarian individualism is a huge affront to the moral sensibilities of responsible world citizens.

Threats to Labor

A good deal of the criticism of globalizing capitalism builds on a less individualized concept of labor, using collective terms such as the working class, peasants, even "the masses." Such formulations are especially prominent with regard to labor issues. Campaigns against sweatshops, for example, reflect a growing concern over the mistreatment of workers as a class in both the core and the periphery (Bonacich and Appelbaum 2000; Featherstone 2002; Klein 2002; Louie 2001; Ross 1997). Some groups worry as well about lower-level white-collar workers (clerical, administrative, data processing, and similar positions), raising concerns about excessive working hours, poor ergonomics, and even restrictive dress codes. To protect labor and prevent abuses, much agitation focuses on legal measures regarding collective labor rights and regulations. Clearly, the well-meaning efforts of the International Labour Organization (ILO) over many decades have been insufficient to ensure labor rights everywhere in the world. Unless worldwide economic practices are improved to guarantee full bargaining rights, the right to strike, labor representation in decision-making processes, and the like, labor, especially in the periphery, will continue to be violated (International Confederation of Free Trade Unions [ICFTU] 2001; International Labor Rights Fund 2003).

Threats to National Development

Following the logic of dependency and world-system arguments (Cardoso and Faletto 1979; Frank 1967, 1979; Galtung 1972; Wallerstein 1979), critics of globalizing capitalism contend that neocolonialism continues to inhibit economic development in the periphery. Foreign direct investment and subcontracting create enclaves of labor-intensive production, often in special economic zones heavily subsidized by peripheral states. Poorly integrated into the respective national economies, these enclaves perpetuate peripheral subordination to the core, whose advanced technology, domination of research and development, and financial resources ensure core control of economic relations (Chase-Dunn 1998; Dixon and Boswell 1996). Through the repatriation of profits from the periphery, TNC managers can pacify core workers and lavishly reward themselves. The result in the periphery is less capital accumulation, lower consumer demand, and uneven development. At the same time, core capitalists have lured peripheral countries to borrow heavily, particularly in periods of economic crisis (e.g., the oil shocks of the 1970s, the Asian meltdown in 1997). The result is crushing debt burdens and austerity programs imposed by the IMF that make life even more difficult for peasants, farmers, and the working classes (Jubilee Movement International 2001).

In more specific terms, the globalization of agribusiness is decried as undercutting the principal means of economic support in many peripheral countries (Shiva 2000a, 2000b). Core-country agriculture is vastly more productive than its counterpart in the periphery; the push for lowered tariffs via the GATT and WTO has exposed peasants using oxen to pull wooden plows to the competition of megafarms using global positioning system (GPS)-guided tractors and miracle-grow fertilizers. This assault on the livelihood of the rural poor is made even worse by extensive dumping of surplus core production in the form of food aid (most infamously under the Public Law 480 program of the United States), which especially undercuts smaller and poorer producers and thus promotes steep inequalities in the agricultural sector.

Finally, the global pharmaceutical and biotechnology industries have become prominent sources of evil profiting from new forms of exploitation. The drug companies operate programs to systematically evaluate the diverse flora of tropical rain forests in search of plants that local peoples have identified as useful in their "traditional" medical treatments. The biotech firms, meanwhile, scour the earth for varieties of crops produced by local peoples through patient centuries of selection and hybridization, seeking to identify the genetic composition and mechanisms involved (Shiva 2000b). Both pharma and biotech then seek patents on these promising innovations so they can profit by licensing them to users—including the local peoples whose knowledge and long labors have made the patents possible (Shiva 1997; Tokar 2001).

All of these threats to national development obviously violate the sacrality of many individuals, as discussed above. They also suggest a more collective concern: They are violations of the sacrality of the nation. If the nation is exploited, its industries undermined, its resources controlled by foreigners, and its capital resources dwindling, it has no hope of succeeding in the pursuit of progress. The state will be weak, corrupted by foreign capital and unable to meet its responsibilities to ensure the welfare and liberties of its people in accordance with the standard world-cultural model of the state (Meyer et al. 1997). The nation will be perpetually poor and vulnerable, not autonomous and truly "developing." This sin of globalization is thus both collective (an assault on the nation) and individual (injuring the nation's citizens), making it a severe violation of the global moral order.

Environmental Excesses

In many accounts, globalization is the bane of the environment. Activists bemoan the destruction caused by globalizing technology, industry, and consumerism (Klein 2002; Sklair 2001), protesting everything from strip mining to offshore oil drilling to nuclear power generation. Air and water pollution, encroachment on natural wonders, destruction of the habitats of plants and animals, acid rain, tropical deforestation, species extinction, and much more are linked to the irresponsible behavior of profit-obsessed global companies and the states that compete for their investments and production facilities.

Dating from the 1960s, the explosion of environmental awareness was an important factor in the emergence of the discourse of globalization because it assumed a single, integrated natural world encompassing the entire planet. Grounded in the Darwinian view that humanity is part and product of nature (Frank et al. 1999), the environmental movement warns that destruction of the environment and excessive use of nonrenewable "natural resources" that cannot be replenished threaten not just nature but also humanity's own welfare and future. Beyond these instrumental concerns, nature is imbued with sacrality in its own right and thereby worthy of protection and preservation. Thus, the "ecological sensibility" (Wapner 1996) to which environmental organizations habitually appeal rests on this dual anchoring in the global moral order: On behalf of sacred individuals and sacred nature, environmental care is both virtuous and necessary.

Threats to Individuals

Globalization threatens individuals environmentally in many ways: Air pollution causes respiratory problems, toxic wastes cripple human cells, and the ozone hole increases skin cancers. Humans suffer directly, and humans suffer from large-scale damage that throws entire ecosystems out of whack. Thus, for environmental critics, the supposed prosperity celebrated by globalization's champions is superficial and shortsighted. If economic development is not tempered by environmental considerations, future generations will face catastrophe (World Commission on Environment and Development 1987). The globalization juggernaut must be brought under control; "sustainable development" that balances economic growth with environmental management is imperative.

Individuals also suffer from the inequalities inherent in environmental problems ("environmental justice" has become an entire scholarly field). The drivers of globalization—TNCs and core states—push their dirty industries and dirty laundry (toxic wastes) on the third world, and the economic inequalities produced by globalization leave poor countries with few resources to cope with their environmental problems (Hofrichter 1993). Thus, the argument goes, the poor get poorer also in environmental terms. At the same time, the poor become guinea pigs for untested adulterations of nature (GMOs, or genetically modified organisms, in the form of seeds and foodstuffs; see Tokar 2001; Shiva 1997, 2000a). Thus, once again, those who suffer most in the environmental realm are the poor, the marginalized, and the defenseless, to whom the

benefits of globalization are completely out of reach.

Threats to Nature

While preserving nature is considered crucial to human welfare, plant and animal species as well as the natural landscape itself are also sacralized, as is evident in such measures as "endangered species" legislation and the list of World Heritage Sites mentioned earlier (many sites are natural rather than cultural places). Globalization's threat to the natural world is incessant and always abhorrent. Consider the horrified reaction in November 2002, when an oil tanker sank off the coast of Spain. Bad enough that local fishermen lost income; still worse, in many eyes, that (economically valueless) fish and birds were also harmed. The more radical forms of environmentalism see no other way to preserve nature's sacrality than the declaration of great swaths of the natural world as entirely off-limits to human presence. Nature is profoundly vulnerable to human incursions; the balance between human sacrality and nature's sacrality must not always tip toward the former.

To preserve nature's sacrality, one of the more radical approaches is the "voluntary simplicity" movement—choosing not to consume resources, indeed, choosing not to be a "consumer" at all. Vegetarianism, veganism, recycling, and reusing are ritualized efforts to restore the sacred nature of nature. Adherents of these practices—whether they are individuals, municipalities, companies, or states—seek to purify themselves as a means of purifying nature, reducing their exploitation of nature's wonders to help ensure long-term ecological health. Activists in global movements promoting these practices hope to steer globalization in directions that will avoid the ultimate collapse of the natural world.

Threats to the Planet

At the broadest level, planet Earth (the "blue planet" of Karliner 1997; "Gaia" of Lovelock 1988) and everything on it are threatened by globalization. If the trajectory of global development—ever more, ever faster, ever higher, ever wider—is not radically curtailed, globalization will bring its own demise. (The parallel to long-lived Marxist scenarios of capitalism sowing the seeds of its own destruction is not entirely accidental.) There is only one "Mother Earth," and we must make every attempt to ward off evil from this sacred goddess. Rescuing the planet means shifting from fossil fuels to renewable energy alternatives, defusing the "population bomb" (Ehrlich's catchy 1971 phrase), shifting to a closed-cycle economy, decommodifying nature, and so on. Radical reorientations are demanded to avoid the coming catastrophe. The horsemen of the looming apocalypse are many and varied: rising ocean levels from global warming, the collapse of food production due to monocultural reliance on genetically engineered grains, unstoppable swarms of insects that have developed resistance to pesticides, and on and on. All this, because globalizing capitalism and technological hubris refuse to accept the "limits to growth" (Meadows, Meadows, and Randers 1993) that are inherent in the carrying capacity of this small, lonely planet.

Cultural Calamities

While the global moral order is fundamentally individualistic, the sacrality of the nation as a holistic collectivity provides a basis for moral championing of distinctiveness and difference ("diversity") in the form of cultural variations across societies. An interesting contradiction is at work here: The global moral order is, in most respects, highly universalistic—it applies everywhere, to each and to all—but it also encompasses the principle of cultural relativism. This principle holds that, ultimately, no culture can be judged except from within its own framework because no culture has a monopoly on truth or righteousness. In its strongest form, the principle implies that all cultures are equally "valid" and, therefore, equally deserving of respect and protection. The contradiction produces much contention in world society, including lengthy debates about whether human rights are indeed universal or are particular to given societies or civilizational arenas. Considerable consensus reigns, however, regarding the desirability of diversity as a general principle. The great variety of cultures is seen as central to the human condition, making life richer and more interesting; accordingly, preservation of that variety is a strongly ensconced moral value. Put

another way, cultural authenticity is highly prized and worthy of protection. The Balinese dance show performed for drunken tourists in a raucous, smoky Kuta Beach bar is a regrettable sham compared with the same movements observed in a remote village where foreigners are rarely seen.

Globalization's threats to cultural diversity and heterogeneity are several. Many of the forces of globalization are strongly homogenizing, producing organizational and structural isomorphism in economic and technical realms, state institutions, educational systems, and the like (Meyer et al. 1997). Every global traveler recognizes the sameness of the world's airports, business hotels, tourist beaches, and fashion styles. For most analysts, globalization is essentially homogenizing—and this is a great threat to distinctive cultures everywhere. A bland, undifferentiated, always-familiar world is on the horizon; no individual culture can stand up to the massive onslaught of culture-leveling globalization.

The most visible and vitriolic critiques of cultural homogenization are less generic. This aspect of globalization is the latest and, one could say, highest form of imperialism: cultural imperialism (Mattelart 1979; Schiller 1976; Smith 1980; for a critique, see Tomlinson 1991). The world is being reshaped in the image of the West, especially the United States. Dressed up in the finery of discourse about "universal values" and "liberal democracy," the Americans and Europeans are imposing their values and ways of life on the rest of the world. In the age of naked imperialism, guns and merchants and priests forced the West's culture on the colonies; now Coca-Cola, McDonald's, Disney, and Vivendi are seducing, brainwashing, manipulating, and forcing their way into every town, village, mayoral office, and presidential palace. National cultures are undermined, often with the willing cooperation of the state and business elites. The pursuit of profit trumps all other considerations, making a mockery of local distinctiveness and rendering cultural authenticity impossible. A bleak future in which all of humanity has been transformed into mindless consumers of tasteless fast foods, violent video games, frivolous Hollywood blockbusters, and mass-produced fashions is in the offing (Klein 2002).

On the flip side, globalization also produces new forms of heterogeneity through massive migration.

While the principle of diversity suggests that this rising heterogeneity would be welcome, the challenge to cultural authenticity that it constitutes also provokes strong negative reactions. This is one area in which most of the opposition to globalization comes not from the left, but from the right, and in the core more than the periphery. Even the most powerful countries are not safe from the impurities of foreign blood, customs, and values. The response is a variety of measures meant to restore the (mythical) purity of the national culture: French critics decry the Muslim invasion, German skinheads attack Turkish immigrants, American conservatives seek to seal the border with Mexico.

Beyond the concern for individual cultures, globalization has also engendered what is increasingly seen as a broad threat to the entire human collectivity: fundamentalisms. Both popular (Barber 1995; Friedman 1999) and scholarly (Lechner 1993; Lewis 2002) accounts depict fundamentalisms as dialectically generated by globalization, partly in reaction to its homogenizing cultural threats and partly as identities justified by the principle of cultural authenticity that provide powerful vehicles of mobilization to compete in global systems. While Huntington's (1996) thesis of clashing civilizational arenas—Christendom versus Islam, or the West against the Rest—has some cachet, and the hot topic of the day (terrorism) is widely seen as Islamic fundamentalism's defiance of the West, broader views see globalization's fostering of many fundamentalisms, both religious and secular (Ellul 1967), as inimical to human civilization as a whole. The extremism associated with moral certainty, intolerance, and dedicated evangelistic fervor can lead to nothing but violence, disorder, and collapse. Here, the principles of cultural relativism and moral universalism collide in spectacular fashion.

Political Pejoratives

Threats to the Nation

The global moral order's incoherent, but nonetheless powerful, embrace of both universalism and particularism (Robertson 1992) is played out in the ethnonationalism conundrum that has intensified in many parts of the world. Because the moral order accords value and the right of protection to distinct cultures, any group that can plausibly claim a shared identity and history is eligible to be considered a "nation." Coupled with the right of national self-determination, one of the pillars of international law, any such group can therefore claim the right to its own state. Globalization heightens this tendency, educating ever more groups with ever more dubious "national" status about the rules of the system and encouraging them to seize the opportunity to mobilize for autonomy. The result is widespread civil war, particularly in weak states where effective centralized authority is problematic. Globalization thus threatens the (often fictive) nation in many independent countries, even while it strengthens the status of would-be nations.

Threats to the State

The state is famously disparaged as being too small for the big things and too big for the small things. The first half of this gibe, for most observers, has become a truism: States are, they hold, overwhelmed by globalization (Sassen 1996; Strange 1998). They have lost control of their economies and are powerless to deal with large-scale environmental problems. Global competition puts constant downward pressure on wages and social spending, while volatile stock and currency markets make a mockery of state economic planning. State sovereignty is in decline, state capacities are insufficient, and power has shifted to global capital and TNCs. In addition, globalization intensifies corruption; state officials have their hands in the deep pockets of investment-eager companies before the latter can even reach for their wallets. States rot from within, becoming little more than private enrichment clubs for those who have clawed their way to the pinnacles of power.

These assertions about globalization's incapacitation of the state are not in themselves of particular moral significance because, unlike the nation, the state is not (*pace* Nietzsche) a repository of sacred value in the global moral order. The state is modeled as a functional, instrumental structure; it is to use rational organization to perform an increasingly broad range of tasks in the centralized management of society. The incapacities of the state become violations of the moral order, however, insofar as they indicate that states are no longer capable of meeting their obligations to their citizens (cf. Boli 2001). If the state does not educate (to create human capital, empower individuals, and promote tolerance), if it does not provide adequate health care (to maintain labor productivity and economic growth), if it does not enforce the law (to maintain the order upon which all other social functions depend), the state is delinquent and, ultimately, illegitimate. Worse still, if the state is so weak that it cannot keep ethnonationalist rebellions in check, it fails even in its most basic responsibility of ensuring the physical integrity of its citizens, who may be forced to flee the country and end up suffering in squalid refugee camps for many years.

But globalization also offers correctives for this disabling of the state. A host of experts, advisers, technicians, consultants, lawyers, and other professionals from NGOs, bilateral aid agencies, IGOs, UN bodies, and the private sector swarm around the state to identify problems, teach global norms, propose solutions, and help manage projects (Chabbott 1999; Finnemore 1993; Meyer et al. 1997). In other words, legions of globalized actors—in this case, largely not associated with the antiglobalization movements or discourse—are ready to rush in to diminish violations of the global moral order and help (or induce) the state to operate in accord with the expectations imposed on it by that order. States must respect and ensure the realization of a large set of human rights; if they cannot or will not do so, world society swings into action (with, of course, highly variable effectiveness).

Threats to Egalitarian Individualism

The incapacitation and corruption of the state purportedly engendered by globalization also imply that the nature of the state itself is perverted, that is, that it does not accord with the deep foundations of the global moral order. States are to operate through principles of universal, egalitarian citizen empowerment; participatory democratic processes are to determine state policies and programs. To the extent that state elites are given to toadying to foreign investors, conspicuously consuming high-status global commodities, peddling influence on behalf of comprador bourgeois interests, and the like,

democracy and the impartial rule of law are shoved aside. Global capital is more interested in stability than democracy, its critics claim, and it props up autocratic regimes by turning a blind eye to abuses of power.[4] Thus, one of the self-evident bases of the good society envisioned in the global moral order—"power to the people" in the form of the universal and egalitarian empowerment of citizens—is gravely imperiled by globalization (Hertz 2002).

Undemocratic countries are subject to a variety of pressures promoting democracy, and waves of national level democratization have repeatedly swept through world society (Loya 2003). At the level of global politics, however, the situation is decidedly less promising. Charges of global elitism in the world economy and of core-country (especially the United States) domination of major IGOs are rampant. A transnational capitalist class (Sklair 2001) controls all the important institutions of global governance and steadfastly opposes any degree of meaningful democratization of those institutions. This global autocracy makes the struggle for national level democracy irrelevant because states are themselves increasingly irrelevant (Strange 1998). Thus, calls for democratization and transparency at the global level, and the construction of democratically structured global institutions that would, in effect, amount to a genuine world state, are common themes of much of the antiglobalization discourse. A global civil society has already been constructed, but it can achieve only so much through moral suasion, consumer boycotts, shaming, and the other familiar mechanisms of informal pressure tactics. If the nation-state is increasingly unable to implement the global moral order, it must be supplanted by a democratic global state that will do so effectively.

Human Harms

Finally, globalization entails risks of injury and incapacitation that strike at the very being of human beings. With the ever-greater speed and intensity of global flows, both ancient and new social ills previously confined to certain locales or regions proliferate rapidly throughout the world. Global transportation systems, production and distribution networks, and information technologies make every point on the planet liable to these human harms.

Threats to the Moral Integrity of the Individual

The global moral order envisions a highly idealized model of the universal Individual: competent, disciplined, industrious, inquisitive, emotionally stable, compassionate, and so on. Anything that interferes with the ability and commitment of individuals to pursue this idealized model is morally suspect. Consciousness-altering drugs are a prime example. Globalization has made the drug trade emphatically worldwide (Schaeffer 1997; Wilson and Zambrano 1994), linking coca-producing Colombian farmers to Russian wholesalers to Chicago street retailers. The global drug trade is a scourge that prevents individual "self-actualization" both directly (through use and addiction) and in countless derivative ways, producing violence, corruption, disease transmission through needle sharing, and drug-financed rebels who challenge weak states in outright civil wars.

Another threat of moral degradation is trafficking in individuals. Slavery was outlawed in the nineteenth century, but it repeatedly rears its ugly head in the global sex trade that traps poor women and children in webs of prostitution and pornography (Williams 1999). A more moderate form is the "mail-order bride," which critics see as a thinly veiled ploy by rich white men to exploit poor, desperate women of color (Coalition Against Trafficking in Women 2003). The global pornography industry, powered by the Internet, poses special threats to children and perpetuates violence against women. Once again, apocalyptic images are painted by energetic crusaders—the assault on individuals' moral fiber is beyond the control of states, the gates of hell are gaping wide. So dire is the problem that a "war" on drugs and pornography is required, and the more tolerant attitude toward drugs and pornography in some developed countries only confirms the fear that, woe unto us, the war is in danger of being lost.

Threats to the Physical Integrity of the Individual

As a highly sacralized entity in world culture, the individual must also be protected from physical harm. Contemporary models of selfhood promote not only a morally sound psyche (free from sin, vice, and dysfunction) but also a healthy body, free from ailment and disease. The articulation of concerns for physical integrity has a longer pedigree than most of the problems discussed here; international conferences focused on cholera, the plague, yellow fever, typhus, and smallpox were held as far back as the latter part of the nineteenth century (Goodman 1971; Howard-Jones 1975). With rapid globalization, however, the problem of infectious and endemic diseases has intensified greatly. At greatest risk are the populations of poor or peripheral countries, where mechanisms to provide universal protection of the individual are most problematic. As the global health system has become highly organized, with strong links to national health care systems, outbreaks of new diseases or ailments are now routinely interpreted as globally threatening, so global machinery swings into action to combat them (as with the drug trade, military metaphors are popular here). The effort to control the spread of HIV (human immunodeficiency virus) was a watershed event that boosted the global response system to unprecedented heights, and the recent example of SARS (severe acute respiratory syndrome) shows how insistent the global system has become regarding universal, coordinated action to protect the physical integrity of all individuals. China has been raked over the coals for its slow and deceptive action; as in several other areas, China is a laggard with respect to enforcement of the global moral order, and it has been duly castigated as such.

The imperative of preserving physical integrity and the principle of global egalitarianism come together with respect to another health-related ill of globalization: the inordinately high price of drugs and medicines offered by global pharma. AIDS (acquired immune deficiency syndrome) treatments have been the focal point of most critical voices in this area, but many other medications priced out of the reach of the truly needy are also at issue. Antiglobalization movements blame global agreements on intellectual property rights and patents (World Health Organization [WHO] 1998) for this transgression, castigating the World Intellectual Property Organization for its unwillingness to relax property rights in limited areas related to individual health. The logic of the complaints is clear: Disregard for the principles of the global moral order cannot be justified by considerations of profit and revenue maximization. Health care (i.e., the physical integrity of the individual) is a human right, not simply an opportunity for high returns on investment.

Threats to the Integrity of the Species

Humanity as a collective entity is less highly reified in the global moral order than the individual or nation, and humanity is often understood as only an aggregate of individuals, but with respect to some issues, it is treated as a transcendent collectivity ("homo sapiens"). Threats to the integrity of the species are constructed as both terrestrial and, at least since the previous era of rapid globalization in the nineteenth century, extraterrestrial. On the earthly plane, cloning and other forms of genetic engineering take center stage. Globalized research and development have opened the door to genetic manipulation and selection that were almost inconceivable before 1950. The issue is posed in terms of purportedly fundamental questions: What does it mean to be a human being? Who are we to be playing God? What calamities await us if we allow genetic design to enter into the most holy realm of human reproduction (Hanson 2001; Tokar 2001)? The ubiquitous issues of inequity and homogeneity are also invoked: Genetic selection could legitimate and revitalize eugenics, leading to discrimination against those with disabilities and diseases; cloning could lead to the eradication of human diversity altogether.

A closely related issue is the creation by artifice of (quasi-)human life, as dramatized in cinematic productions such as *Blade Runner* (1982) and *AI* (2001). The same fundamental questions arise when the drama is generalized to technology as a whole: Like Frankenstein's monster, the products of globalized technology turn on their creators (viz., Chaplin's *Modern Times,* Kubrick's *2001,* Cameron's *Terminator* films). A cottage industry of ethicists and academicians has arisen to worry about these matters, constantly searching for answers anchored in the global moral order, but the rapid pace of global scientific advance often leaves the

moralizers dealing with last year's issues. Explicit antiglobalization activity targeting genetic engineering or technology as a whole is relatively rare, but the threat is clear: Globalization enables evildoers to embark on potentially cataclysmic scientific endeavors, whether the world is ready for them or not.

Finally, a remarkable set of problems linked to globalization, but not yet the theme of antiglobalization petitions or protests, involves extraterrestrial threats to humanity: alien visitors, massive meteors, space-traveling diseases, and so on. Because globalization entails an ever-stronger sense of the Earth as a single, integrated entity, efforts to bound and protect this small, largely defenseless home of *l'humanité entière* from cosmic perils are on the rise. Globalization does not "cause" these cosmic perils, but it leads to worldviews in which, for example, building space-based missile systems to intercept potential collision-course meteors is a reasonable, even necessary, activity.

Many and varied are the ways the world could end, thanks in no small part to the ongoing elaboration of the global moral order and the ever-expanding range of threats that can be identified by inventive scientists and intellectuals. Considering the full panoply of problems and perils associated with globalization, it is a wonder that world society has not long since gone completely under.

SOLUTIONS

All is not lost. The world need not come to an ignoble or catastrophic end. Globalization is not inevitable or unstoppable (Starr 2000); it is not necessarily "out of control" (Hedley 2002). Valiantly battling the evils of the world, redeemers impelled by a sense of extreme urgency to cleanse the world of its sins are everywhere. Taking advantage of the global systems of communication, transportation, and finance that are, in their analyses, themselves part of the problem, the redeemers outline a range of soteriological solutions that should restore the sacred core of the moral order: the individual, the nation, and nature.[5] They seek to ensure that the many rights associated with these sacred entities are respected or guaranteed. This is most explicit in the many calls for democratization, individual empowerment, and citizen participation, which represent attempts to restore or protect the sacrality of the individual. We will show that this logic applies to the principal features of other types of solutions as well.

Democratization

Antiglobalization movements see democratization or democratic control of the villains of globalizing capitalism—global governance IGOs, core capitalist states, and TNCs—as an absolute imperative. Peripheral states are in no less need of democratization, though they are depicted as not only villains but also victims because they are forced to submit to the domination of global capitalism. Chronically disregarding the interests of the common people, the villains promote the narrow interests of the privileged. They shield themselves from the will of the people, resisting demands for transparency and accountability. What is needed, the critics of globalization insist, is broad inclusiveness and participation so the voices of the many will be heard and alternative visions of world order can have a hearing. Vibrant, active, inclusive civil societies at both national and global levels are crucial to restructuring, changing, or abolishing the current system dominated by free market neoliberalism. Individuals everywhere should be empowered as citizens and consumers; whole societies must be mobilized to avoid the perils of unregulated globalization.

Not surprisingly, the globalization critics themselves, and the organizations that stand behind them, are presumed to be essential to democratization. Since 2001, they have gathered in glorious diversity at the World Social Forum (WSF): local women's groups, peasant and labor organizations, environmental, development, and religious movements, and many other types from all sorts of countries. The open-armed inclusiveness of this event is intentional, as it legitimates the WSF as the "voice of the people" in opposition to the elitism of states, IGOs, and TNCs. Inspired and informed by each other in increasingly complex and fluid networks, these global, national, and local groups take democracy into their own hands. They lobby, circulate petitions, sponsor local initiatives on environmental protection or indigenous rights; they swarm to UN and other IGO conferences, take stands on legislation, and mount street protests. From grassroots organizing to transnational networking, they are promoting democratization by practicing it, and they steadfastly insist that democratization is essential if globalization's ills are to be cured.

Empowerment of the Victims

The lion's share of antiglobalization activity is carried out by the privileged and comfortable denizens of the developed countries. Their efforts, no matter how well-meaning or sincere, are hardly enough. Rather, the victims themselves must be empowered. Antiglobalization movements stress "giving voice" to the marginalized, the poor, women, children, indigenous peoples, nature, and so on to counter the hegemonic domination of global neoliberal capitalism. The Third World Network (2003) speaks on behalf of its namesake—the great majority of the world's population—in calling into question many aspects of globalization. The Grameen Bank (Yunus and Jolis 1999) takes practical action to empower the poor through microlending. Women's empowerment is the goal of the World Women's March, the NGO parallel summits at UN conferences on women, human rights and health campaigns opposing female genital mutilation, and so forth. Support is mustered to empower indigenous peoples in their struggles regarding, for example, Newmont Mining's proposed operations in forest reserves in Ghana (Project Underground 2000) and the Enron/Shell pipeline through the Chiquitano forest and "indigenous ancestral homelands" in Bolivia (Amazon Watch 2002).

The WSF (2001:1) reflected this focus on inclusion and empowerment in its Porto Alegre Call for Mobilization: "We are women and men, farmers, workers, unemployed, professionals, students, blacks and indigenous peoples, coming from the South and from the North, committed to struggle for peoples' rights, freedom, security, employment and education." Global civil society provides a forum for the oppressed, a fleet of vehicles propelling them to the seats of power. They shall be empowered; the global moral order demands it.

Awareness

Democratization and empowerment depend on awareness: The ills of globalization must be publicized, alternatives to neoliberalism must be articulated, and consciousness of oppression, exploitation, and injustice must be raised. The masks behind which the villains of globalization hide their machinations must be torn away. Unmasking is the self-appointed task of a great many international and domestic INGOs, which uncover and publicize the villains' irresponsible, selfish, shortsighted behavior. Amnesty International regularly puts the finger on human rights abusers; Transparency International posts lists of highly corrupt states on the Web; CorpWatch monitors TNCs to reveal human rights and environmental violations; AccountAbility audits corporations to ensure that their social responsibility deeds match their words. Global campaigns always make increased awareness a primary goal, whether it be the Infact campaign against Nestlé (1977–1986) and its current "Hall of Shame" list of TNCs (Infact 2003), the alliance fighting against the proposed Free Trade Area of the Americas, or the Jubilee 2000 effort to win debt relief for poor countries (Jubilee Movement International 2001). More traditional consumer awareness campaigns are conducted by organizations pushing for fair (not free) trade and sustainable development, and even by some TNCs that have "seen the light" and become paragons of virtue for the antiglobalization forces (Max Havelaar, the Body Shop, Patagonia, and a few other companies). To guide the awareness efforts, numerous policy and research operations have emerged to articulate alternatives to neoliberal capitalist globalization. The IFG presents elaborate studies and position papers; the Institute for Policy Studies, Economic Policy Institute, and Transnational Institute counter the proglobalization forces with a wide range of documents and press releases.

Awareness, in the activists' view, is crucial for empowerment and mobilization. Awareness enables and motivates the powerless to stand up for themselves, to protect their own sacrality, to push for the respect and protections to which they, as instances of the sacred Individual, are entitled. Awareness will help restore the sacred order; it is necessary to know the word of God to attain salvation.

Rationalizing Regulation of TNCs

Because in many accounts, TNCs are the engines powering globalization's wheels, they are especially problematic. As everyone knows, many TNCs are richer and stronger than most states, and even the most powerful core states are often depicted as little more than sycophantic retainers of their TNC overlords. Hence, the TNCs must be brought under control and reoriented to human, not financial or hierarchical, purposes. The general mechanism for reining in the TNCs is regulation, although this is too formalistic a term in that it suggests legal action to shape TNC behavior but states are not the principal players on this stage. At work is a less formal notion of regulation by which global civil society organizations, acting as watchdogs, nags, monitors, and moral guides, attempt to reform and redeem the sinners.

Knowing that moral exhortation alone is usually ineffective, the guardians of global virtue try to make it costly for firms to pollute, exploit, or discriminate. They assume that negative publicity, especially if systematic and recurring, will create legitimacy and image problems for their targets. If a company is broadly seen as a doer of evil, investors may become leery, suppliers may fear "guilt by association," and consumers may look for alternatives. The possibility of declining sales, profits, and share prices thereby becomes a powerful motivator for companies to embrace "social responsibility" and "corporate ethics." The "Triple Bottom Line" (SustainAbility 2003) that adds social and environmental impacts to conventional financial results becomes an attractive concept, however cynical or manipulative company executives may be about it.

Make no mistake: Corporations have enormous resources and reach, compared with their critics, and antiglobalization groups entirely lack formal political authority. Yet their cultural authority—based on pious invocation of the global moral order, the prestige of scientific evidence, the credentials of their members, their ability to speak on behalf of "all humanity," and the fame of some of their leaders—is not insignificant (Boli 1999). They have been a key factor in the widespread reorientation of TNC rhetoric and, in some domains, of TNC behavior as well.

The specific mechanisms involved are several. First, of course, is the targeting of the TNCs themselves, in terms of both negative publicity and direct contact and lobbying. Activists concentrate on high-profile TNCs with strong brands, such as Nike, Reebok, the Gap, the infamous Kathy Lee Gifford operation, Coca-Cola, and the like. Increasingly, TNCs are willing to meet with their critics and even to establish liaison offices to regularize relationships with them, though much hostility is also evident. Second is the monitoring of company-generated codes of conduct, ethics, or behavior. Many companies have developed in-house codes to which they claim to adhere; Levi Strauss was the first to establish a comprehensive code of conduct for its manufacturing and finishing contractors, in 1991. Similarly, business and industry INGOs have established industry codes to guide their members' practices. In the early 1990s, responding to NGO pressure and the lessons learned from Nike's global problems, Levi Strauss, Reebok, and Liz Claiborne led the way in establishing an apparel industry code, primarily targeting their overseas contractors. While such codes are, strictly speaking, purely voluntary and self-policing, they offer a fulcrum by which globalization critics can gain leverage against the companies if they detect violations.

Third is the creation and promulgation of codes of conduct by INGOs and national organizations. As a way to reduce the exploitation of child labor, for instance, the Clean Clothes Campaign pushes its 1998 "Code of Labor Practices for the Apparel Industry." Rugmark (an INGO) promotes its certification process whereby manufacturers can attest that children are not employed in the making of rugs and carpets. Similarly, the "Ethics on the Label" (*"De l'ethique sur l'etiquette"*) campaign directed at toy manufacturers and other companies for human rights violations in the workplace has urged consumers since 1997 to buy only goods produced under acceptable conditions, thus also informing companies of the sins to be avoided.

A fourth mechanism is general business codes of conduct or ethics that outline social responsibility obligations for TNCs in general. The first general code to gain global recognition was the Sullivan Principles, initiated by Baptist Pastor Leon Sullivan in 1977 to reduce U.S. business activity in South Africa and thereby weaken apartheid (Sethi and Williams 2000). By 1994, 150 American TNCs had adopted the Sullivan Principles. Later efforts include the Coalition for Environmentally Responsible Economies' CERES Principles, developed in 1989 after the Exxon Valdez disaster in Alaska and now endorsed by 50 major companies; Social Accountability 8000 (SA 8000), an endeavor by the Council on Economic Priorities Accreditation Agency from 1997 to assess labor practices, working conditions, and trade; and AA1000, a standards procedure for measuring the social and ethical achievements of companies, developed by Account Ability (an INGO promoting social responsibility and sustainable development) in 1999. A much more highly rationalized program that comes closer to the conventional sense of "regulation" is the ISO 14000 set of standards for environmentally sound organizational practices. Though also voluntary, this program requires companies seeking certification to undergo an intensive review by independent experts and demonstrate conformity with a large number of conditions.

IGOs have also been involved in conduct code development, beginning with the OECD's Guidelines for Multinational Enterprises in 1976, which was followed in 1977 by the ILO Tripartite Declaration of Principles concerning Multinational Enterprises and Social Policy and the UN Conference on Trade and Development's Draft Code of Conduct. An outgrowth of the intensive mobilization by third-world countries in the 1970s to establish a New World Economic Order, New World Information Order, and the like, these early efforts were ineffectual and are largely forgotten. A more recent example that has both inspired some activists and drawn considerable criticism from others is the 1999 Global Compact, largely the creation of UN Secretary-General Kofi Annan, whose nine principles concerning human rights, labor, and the environment envision a "partnership" among states, international organizations, and TNCs to work cooperatively for global improvements. Its anchoring in the global moral order is strikingly evident on the home page for the compact, which prominently quotes Secretary-General Kofi Annan as follows: "Let us choose to unite the power of markets with the authority of universal principles" (UN Global Compact 2003).

We should note that codes of conduct rarely address issues of global economic inequality directly; they deal primarily with issues lumped under the rubric of "human rights" (labor rights, child labor, women and minority issues, etc.) and with environmental matters, though responsibilities toward the local community also show up frequently. A major theme in recent years, though not always explicitly discussed, is sustainable development, which has become a loosely conceived catchall notion that envisions a "balance" between development and environmental concerns. Yet it too has come under fire from globalization's critics, who worry about TNCs and major IGOs adopting the term to disguise their tendency to put much more emphasis on "development" than on "sustainability" (IFG 2002).

Backlash

Predictably enough, champions of neoliberalism and TNC-dominated economic globalization have gone on the offensive against their antiglobalization critics.[6] Leading the charge have been the *Wall Street Journal, The Economist, Forbes, Fortune,* and other major business publications, along with neoconservative think tanks such as the Heritage Foundation, American Enterprise Institute, and Hoover Institution. Officials of the IMF and WTO have also swung into action. The backlash's starting point is simple: The benefits of globalization far outweigh its drawbacks; globalization is a progressive, modernizing force that promises salvation from the world's evils (*The Economist* 2001b). Free markets generate efficiency and the optimal allocation of resources through the principle of comparative advantage. The competitive global economy benefits consumers by producing the best products at the lowest prices. Free markets expand individual freedom and the capacity to choose. Inequality is a consequence not of markets, but of individual variability with regard to self-discipline, entrepreneurship, planning, self-investment, and so on. In any case, the rising tide of global economic development lifts all boats, both those of the more advanced North and those of the developing South. TNCs provide capital and employment opportunities in developing countries that compensate for the lack of indigenous capital; the positive spillover effects of foreign investment gradually pave the way for self-sustaining economic growth. Globalization enhances environmental protection because TNCs are much more aware of and committed to the importance of the environment than are local companies. What is more, free markets produce free polities—economic openness will lead to democratization, not dictatorship. And finally, what is misinterpreted as cultural imperialism is only the result of free individuals freely making choices; if their choices lead to homogenization, what could be more proper?

Directly contrary to globalization's critics, the neoconservative backlash thus bemoans not too much marketization, but too little. Corruption distorts markets, shifting capital and revenues to inefficient uses. Weak law enforcement distorts markets by allowing coercive and manipulative measures to determine business decisions. Government monopolies distort markets by encouraging fiscal irresponsibility, large budget deficits, and excessive indebtedness. If the South suffers in its trading relations, the problem is that trade is not completely free, so disequilibria in global production and consumption still plague the world economy. Economic liberalization has not gone far enough; the universal solution is the total triumph of the market.

Challenges to the Legitimacy of NGOs and Global Civil Society

Besides flooding the world with neoliberal ideology, the defenders of globalization have also launched direct assaults on antiglobalization critics and movements. These protestors, activists, and NGO representatives are not elected by any identifiable constituency—and certainly not by those whom they claim to represent. Neither are they accountable to any constituency; policy proclaimers such as the IFG and CorpWatch can advocate anything they please because they cannot be held responsible for their words or deeds. This lack of accountability, the backlash forces continue, leads antiglobalization activists to endorse policies that would harm the very people they claim to support (arguing, e.g., that forcing subcontractors to pay above-market wages in a given country would only force companies to move their plants elsewhere). Antiglobalizers are even depicted as enemies of the poor (*The Economist* 2001a). Contrary to the pretense they try to maintain, they are hardly the embodiment of virtue, acting selflessly on behalf of the poor and oppressed. They have their own narrow interests, and they often care more about basking in the light of moral righteousness than working toward practicable, meaningful solutions to global problems. Their calls for world democracy, transparency, and accountability ring hollow because they are themselves neither democratic, transparent, nor accountable (International Chamber of Commerce 1998).

Another line of attack relates to expertise and professionalism: Globalization's critics do not understand the issues; they are misinformed, and they have simplistic approaches to complex realities. "The valid criticisms are buried under a heap of error, muddle and deliberate distortion" (*The Economist* 2001e:21). Their accounts of business malpractice are unfair, exaggerated, or false. They are sensationalistic, staging splashy but pointless events to attract members and funding. True experts keep their distance from these irresponsible movements; thus, the critics' data, publications, and analyses are incorrect and unreliable. And, in the end, the antiglobalizers have little to offer in terms of constructive alternatives to neoliberal globalization. They whine and complain but cannot build. Small wonder—for they are themselves by-products, as it were, of globalization itself. Without global information and communication systems, the free movement of people, and the resources that the world economy has generated, globalization's critics would be entirely marginal and invisible.

The Radical Critique: Co-Optation

Antiglobalization movements face criticism not only from globalization's defenders but also from within their own camp. Popular NGOs and global civil society groups are all too willing, the argument goes, to cooperate with the villainous forces of global capitalism. Starr (2000), for example, puts the feet of these movements to the fire for not being anticorporate enough. They are content with superficial reforms, negotiating away the vital changes that must occur if the needs of the many are to take precedence over the needs of the few. Microcredit lending is a debt trap for the poor; antisweatshop campaigns support the capitalist paradigm; and fair trade groups and sustainable development movements reinforce unequal exchange and other systemic evils of capitalism. For Starr, the antiglobalization forces that penetrate to the core of the problems are the anarchists, hackers, and other radical groups who steadfastly refuse to accept the world capitalist system's unrepentant nonchalance toward the moral order.

Agents of the Same Global Moral Order?

The often rancorous conflicts between antiglobalization groups and their neoconservative detractors obscure an important underlying commonality: By and large, the parties to the conflict adhere to the same global moral order. From both sides, the welfare and empowerment of individuals (the holiest of holies) are invoked first and foremost to justify policies and practices. Not even the most myopic defenders of capitalism dare endorse neoliberalism as a means of exploiting workers, keeping the masses in check, or defusing the population bomb through starvation and disease. Their backlash arguments assume the same general goals of rising living standards, better health, more education, cleaner air, and the like that the antiglobalizers argue are inhibited by untrammeled capitalism. The same goes for the sacrality of nature (how often do oil companies place newspaper ads gloating over the devastation of nature in the name of progress?), the nation (does anyone endorse the collapse of societies or cultures?), and various special-protection groups (what right-wing think tank demands increased discrimination against minorities or women?).

Agreement about the content of the global moral order is thus extensive.[7] With regard to some principles, there is significant variation in emphasis: Globalization's critics stress the importance of equality (everyone has the right to a minimum standard of living; excessive wealth is inherently exploitative) while their opponents focus more on freedom (minimizing constraints on individual action is the supreme value; inequalities may result, but in a truly open system they are due to individual characteristics alone). Similarly, some strains of antiglobalization rhetoric downplay individualism in favor of collective entities (the family, village, ethnic group, nation) or public goods (peace, solidarity, local autonomy). On the whole, however, these variations span a quite narrow range. Most of the dimensions of the global moral order are well institutionalized, which implies that most of the debate about globalization's problems are likely to continue along the same tracks that have already been laid.

CONCLUSION

Globalization is, as we have seen, an elastic concept that has been stretched in many directions. Correspondingly, globalization is assailed as the cause of a host of social problems. When the term came into fashion in the 1990s, intellectuals and activists of many sorts latched onto it in a wave of oppositional enthusiasm and imagination not seen since the revival of Marxism 30 years earlier. The irresistible allure of globalization as a master concept for describing and decrying the world's ills reflects both the awesome power of the presumed engines of globalization (TNCs, states, IGOs) and the broad and deep institutionalization of the global moral order in the second half of the twentieth century. Intense commitment to guarding and protecting the entities occupying the sacred core of the moral order—especially the individual, the nation, and nature—has yielded a vast array of organizations and networks that relentlessly seek out violations of the moral order and expose the violators to public scrutiny and pressure.

Increasing cultural complexity and global integration heighten the ambiguous duality of globalization processes, constantly enhancing the opportunities to identify new global problems while also producing increasingly precise information about ever more dimensions of social life that can be used to detect violations of the global moral order. If we had meaningful measures of the globalization problematique (counts of the number of antiglobalization organizations, position papers, press releases, individuals involved, network links), they would surely show exponential growth throughout the 1990s. Whether that growth has continued is less certain

because one aspect of globalization, terrorism, has occupied so much space in the global public realm since the 2001 attacks in the United States. Never before has a single issue so rapidly erupted into the public realm, and the terrorism theme has recast many of the globalization debates in sometimes unlikely ways. But a tour of antiglobalization Web sites should be enough to convince anyone that the current obsession with terrorism has hardly diminished concerns about other problems of globalization. Indeed, other problems have often been reinterpreted to show why solving them would also help to remove the conditions that produce global terrorism.

As long as the world economy continues to become more integrated, global organizations continue to expand their responsibilities for global governance, world communication and transportation systems continue to develop, and global flows of goods, services, cultural products, and people continue to expand, there is every reason to expect the problematization of globalization to expand as well. We should expect further increases in global imagery, world-society thinking, relativized conceptions of "nation" and "culture," and the like by a growing proportion of the world's population. Further elaboration of the theme of the global will be accompanied by further elaboration of the problems of the global.

Of course, unending globalization is not inevitable. Excessive unilateralism in the guise of a "war on terrorism" by the hegemonic world power could undermine global institutions and geopolitical mechanisms that maintain global systems. Too-rapid expansion of the European Union could lead to its collapse and a surge of bugger-thy-neighbor nationalism. Regional integration could produce armed rivalries for the control of vital resources and global domination. Any scenario that produced a substantial degree of "de-globalization" would probably also reduce the construction of globalization as the source of global ills. The significance of the global moral order would thereby give way to particularistic (but still largely similar) moral orders at lower levels, for example, by shifting primacy away from the sacred Individual and nature in favor of particular nations. Even with the great disruptions that these scenarios would entail, though, it seems likely that globalization would eventually make a comeback, as it did so spectacularly after the world wars. We suspect that the globalization problematique is with us for a very long time to come.

Notes

1. Globalization's critics make their homes on both the left and the right ends of the political spectrum; the strangeness of these bedfellows can hardly be overstated. Hard-line conservative isolationists like political gadfly Pat Buchanan object to free trade agreements with the same fervor as the radically liberal consumer advocate supreme, Ralph Nader. Because most antiglobalization activity comes from the left, it will be our focus here, but our arguments are generally applicable to sniping from the right as well.

2. This sketch of the global moral order draws on the discourse of debates regarding globalization and the many formalized declarations of moral concepts and precepts created by states, IGOs, and NGOs in the postwar period. Chief among the latter, of course, is the Universal Declaration of Human Rights; alongside it are literally hundreds of documents at the national, regional, and global levels regarding human rights (Office of the United Nations High Commissioner for Human Rights 2002; University of Minnesota Human Rights Library 2003) and many more documents having less "official" status. We present here a synthesis of the underlying moral order that emerges in these documents and the discourse but do not offer specific references to them.

3. In the terminology of social movement theorists, our analysis of the global moral order treats an important "master frame" (McAdam and Snow 1997; Snow and Benford 1988) that shapes global movements. This frame both motivates and legitimates activists while setting the basic parameters within which both activists and their targets must operate discursively.

4. The counterargument that economic openness and the consequent marketization of the economy create powerful pressures for democratization is not given much credence by critics of globalization. Apart from the uncertain empirical validity of this claim, critics are reflexively suspicious of it because its chief proponents are, once again, neoliberal conservatives strongly allied with global capital or the major global governance IGOs.

5. A particularly thorough document offering solutions to globalization's ills, though mainly dealing with economic issues, is the IFG's (2002) *Alternatives to Economic Globalization.*

6. This section draws especially heavily on the series of articles published by *The Economist* (2001a).

7. Of course, globalization's champions may embrace the global moral order insincerely or deceitfully. Even so, they strengthen it by invoking it, thus bolstering their opponents and increasing the legitimation problems facing sinful TNCs, states, and capitalists. The latter, meanwhile, despite their vast resources, seem powerless to articulate an alternative moral order that would better justify their domination and wealth.

References

Abrash, Abigail. 2001. "The Amungme, Kamoro & Freeport: How Indigenous Papuans Have Resisted the World's Largest Gold and Copper Mine." *Cultural Survival Quarterly* 25 (1):38–43.

Amazon Watch. 2002. "Bolivia's New Gas Projects." Retrieved from http://www.amazonwatch.org.

Amin, Samir. 1997. *Capitalism in the Age of Globalization.* New York: Zed.

Anderson, Benedict. 1991. *Imagined Communities: Reflections on the Origin and Spread of Nationalism.* Rev. ed. London, England: Verso.

Appadurai, Arjun. 1990. "Disjuncture and Difference in the Global Cultural Economy." *Public Culture* 2 (2):2–23.

———. 1996. *Modernity at Large: Cultural Dimensions of Globalization.* Minneapolis, MN: University of Minnesota Press.

ATTAC. 1998. "Platform of the International Movement ATTAC." Retrieved from http://www.attac.org/indexen/index.html.

Ayres, Jeffrey M. 2002. "Transnational Political Processes and Contention against the Global Economy." Pp. 191–205 in *Globalization and Resistance: Transnational Dimensions of Social Movements,* edited by Jackie G. Smith and Hank Johnston. Lanham, MD: Rowan and Littlefield.

Barber, Benjamin. 1995. *Jihad vs. Mcworld.* New York: Times Books.

Bello, Walden. 1996. "Structural Adjustment Programs: 'Success' for Whom?" Pp. 285–93 in *The Case against the Global Economy: And for a Turn toward the Local,* edited by Jerry Mander and Edward Goldsmith. San Francisco, CA: Sierra Club.

Bendix, Reinhard. [1964] 1976. *Nation-Building and Citizenship.* Berkeley, CA: University of California Press.

Boli, John. 1997. "The Moral Order of World Culture and the Operation of World Authority." Revised version of a paper presented at the conference, Institutional Analysis, May 1995, Tucson, Arizona.

——. 1999. "World Authority Structures and Legitimations." Pp. 267–300 in *Constructing World Culture: International Nongovernmental Organizations Since 1875,* edited by John Boli and George M. Thomas. Stanford, CA: Stanford University Press.

——. 2001. "Sovereignty from a World-Polity Perspective." Pp. 53–82 in *Problematic Sovereignty: Contested Rules and Political Possibilities,* edited by Stephen D. Krasner. New York: Columbia University Press.

Boli, John and George M. Thomas. 1997. "World Culture in the World Polity: A Century of International Non-Governmental Organization." *American Sociological Review* 62 (2):171–90.

——, eds. 1999. *Constructing World Culture: International Nongovernmental Organizations since 1875.* Stanford, CA: Stanford University Press.

Bonacich, Edna and Richard. P. Appelbaum. 2000. *Behind the Label: Inequality in the Los Angeles Apparel Industry.* Berkeley, CA: University of California Press.

Broad, Robin, ed. 2002. *Global Backlash: Citizen Initiatives for a Just World Economy.* New York: Rowan and Littlefield.

Cardoso, Fernando H. and Enzo Faletto. 1979. *Dependency and Development in Latin America.* Berkeley, CA: University of California Press.

Chabbott, Colette. 1999. "Development INGOs." Pp. 222–48 in *Constructing World Culture: International Nongovernmental Organizations Since 1875,* edited by John Boli and George M. Thomas. Stanford, CA: Stanford University Press.

Chase-Dunn, Christopher K. 1998. *Global Formation: Structures of the World Economy.* Lanham, MD: Rowan and Littlefield.

Coalition Against Trafficking in Women. 2003. "An Introduction to CATW." Retrieved from http://www.catwinternational.org/about/index.html.

CorpWatch. 1997. "Global Gold Rush: The Story of Freeport-McMoRan in Indonesia." Retrieved from http://www.corpwatch.org/issues/PID.jsp?articleid=965.

Diamond, Larry. 1993. "The Globalization of Democracy." Pp. 31–69 in *Global Transformation and the Third World,* edited by Robert O. Slater, Barry M. Schutz, and Steven R. Dorr. Boulder, CO: Lynne Rienner.

Dixon, William J. and Terry Boswell. 1996. "Dependency, Disarticulation, and Denominator Effects: Another Look at Foreign Capital Penetration." *American Journal of Sociology* 102 (2):534–62.

Douglas, Mary. 1966. *Purity and Danger.* London, England: Routledge & Kegan Paul.

——. 1986. *How Institutions Think.* Syracuse, NY: Syracuse University Press.

Durkheim, Emile. 1973. "Individualism and the Intellectuals." Pp. 43–57 in *Emile Durkheim on Morality and Society,* edited by Robert N. Bellah. Chicago, IL: University of Chicago Press.

——. 1984. *The Division of Labor in Society.* New York: Free Press.

——. 2001. *The Elementary Forms of Religious Life.* New York: Oxford University Press.

EarthRights International. 2003. "The Situation in Burma." Retrieved from http://www.earthrights.org/burma.shtml.

The Economist. 2001a. "Globalisation and Its Critics: A Survey of Globalisation." September 29, pp. 1–30.

——. 2001b. "Is Globalisation Doomed?" September 29, p. 14.

——. 2001c. "Profits over People." September 29, pp. 5–9.

——. 2001d. "Grinding the Poor." September 29, pp. 10–13.

——. 2001e. "A Plague of Finance." September 29, p. 21.

Ehrlich, Paul R. 1971. *The Population Bomb.* New York: Ballantine.

Ellul, Jacques. 1967. *The Political Illusion.* New York: Knopf.

——. 1975. *The New Demons.* New York: Seabury.

——. 1980. *The Technological System.* New York: Continuum.

Featherstone, Liza. 2002. *Students Against Sweatshops.* New York: Verso.

Finnemore, Martha. 1993. "International Organizations as Teachers of Norms: The United Nations Educational, Scientific, and Cultural Organization and Science Policy." *International Organization* 47 (4):565–97.

Frank, Andre Gunder. 1967. *Capitalism and Underdevelopment in Latin America; Historical Studies of Chile and Brazil.* New York: Monthly Review.

——. 1979. *Dependent Accumulation and Underdevelopment.* New York: Monthly Review.

Frank, David J., Ann Hironaka, John W. Meyer, Evan Schofer, and Nancy B. Tuma. 1999. "The Rationalization and Organization of Nature in World Culture." Pp. 81–99 in *Constructing World Culture: International Nongovernmental Organizations Since 1875,* edited by John Boli and George M. Thomas. Stanford, CA: Stanford University Press.

Friedman, Thomas L. 1999. *The Lexus and the Olive Tree.* New York: Farrar, Straus, Giroux.

Galtung, Johan. 1972. "A Structural Theory of Imperialism." *African Review* 1 (4):93–138.

Gereffi, Gary and Miguel Korzeniewicz, eds. 1994. *Commodity Chains and Global Capitalism.* Westport, CT: Greenwood.

Goffman, Erving. 1956. "The Nature of Deference and Demeanor." *American Anthropologist* 58 (3):473–502.

Goodman, Neville M. 1971. *International Health Organizations and Their Work.* London, England: Churchill Livingstone.

Guidry, John A., Michael D. Kennedy, and Mayer N. Zald, eds. 2000. *Globalizations and Social Movements: Culture, Power, and the Transnational Public Sphere.* Ann Arbor, MI: University of Michigan Press.

Hannerz, Ulf. 1996. *Transnational Connections: Culture, People, Places.* London, England: Routledge.

———. 1991. "Scenarios for Peripheral Cultures." Pp. 107–28 in *Culture, Globalization and the World-System,* edited by Anthony D. King. Binghamton, NY: Dept. of Art and Art History, State University of New York.

Hanson, Mark J., ed. 2001. *Claiming Power over Life: Religion and Biotechnology Policy.* Washington, DC: Georgetown University Press.

Hedley, R. Alan. 2002. *Running Out of Control: Dilemmas of Globalization.* Bloomfield, CT: Kumarian.

Hertz, Noreena. 2002. *The Silent Takeover: Global Capitalism and the Death of Democracy.* New York: Free Press.

Hofrichter, Richard, ed. 1993. *Toxic Struggles: The Theory and Practice of Environmental Justice.* Philadelphia, PA: New Society Publishers.

Howard-Jones, Norman. 1975. *The Scientific Background of the International Sanitary Conferences, 1851–1938.* Geneva, Switzerland: World Health Organization.

Huntington, Samuel P. 1996. *The Clash of Civilizations and the Remaking of World Order.* New York: Simon & Schuster.

Infact. 2003. "Infact's Hall of Shame Campaign." Retrieved from http://www.infact.org.

International Chamber of Commerce. 1998. "The Geneva Business Declaration." Statement by Helmut O. Maucher, ICC President, September 24. Geneva: Author.

International Confederation of Free Trade Unions (ICFTU). 2001. *A Trade Union Guide to Globalization.* Brussels, Belgium: Author.

International Forum on Globalization (IFG). 1995. "IFG Position Statement." Retrieved from http://www.ifg.org/about/statemnt.htm.

———. 2002. *Alternatives to Economic Globalization: A Better World is Possible.* San Francisco, CA: Barrett-Koehler.

International Labor Rights Fund. 2003. "About the International Labor Rights Fund." Retrieved from http://www.laborrights.org/.

Jubilee Movement International. 2001. "Statement of the Jubilee Movement International for Economic and Social Justice." Retrieved from http://www.jubilee2000uk.org/jmi/jmi-policies/statement_bamako_english.htm.

Karliner, Joshua. 1997. "Grassroots Globalization: Reclaiming the Blue Planet." Chap. 7 in *The Corporate Planet: Ecology and Politics in the Age of Globalization,* edited by Joshua Karliner. San Francisco, CA: Sierra Club.

Keck, Margaret E. and Kathryn Sikkink. 1998. *Activists without Borders: Advocacy Networks in International Politics.* Ithaca, NY: Cornell University Press.

Keohane, Robert O. and Joseph S. Nye. 1989. *Power and Interdependence.* New York: HarperCollins.

Khagram, Sanjeev. 2000. "Toward Democratic Governance for Sustainable Development: Transnational Civil Society Organizing around Big Dams." Pp. 83–114 in *The Third Force: The Rise of Transnational Civil Society,* edited by Ann M. Florini. Washington, DC: Carnegie Endowment for International Peace.

Khagram, Sanjeev, James V., Riker, and Kathryn Sikkink. 2002. *Restructuring World Politics: Transnational Social Movements, Networks, and Norms.* Minneapolis, MN: University of Minnesota Press.

Klein, Naomi. 2002. *No Space. No Choice. No Jobs. No Logo.* New York: Picador USA.

Kobrin, Stephen Jay. 1998. "The MAI and the Clash of Globalizations." *Foreign Policy,* Fall, 112:97–109.

Küng, Hans. 1998. *A Global Ethic for Global Politics and Economics.* Oxford: Oxford University Press.

Lechner, Frank J. 1993. "Global Fundamentalism." Pp. 19–36 in *A Future for Religion? New Paradigms for Social Analysis,* edited by William H. Swatos Jr. Newbury Park, CA: Sage.

Lewis, Bernard. 2002. *What Went Wrong? Western Impact and Middle Eastern Response.* Oxford: Oxford University Press.

Louie, Miriam Ching Yoon. 2001. *Sweatshop Warriors: Immigrant Women Workers Take On the Global Factory.* Cambridge, MA: South End.

Lovelock, James E. (1988). *The Ages of Gaia.* New York: W. W. Norton.

Loya, Thomas A. (2003). *Global Pro-Democracy Movements.* Unpublished doctoral dissertation, Emory University, Dept. of Sociology.

Mander, Jerry and Edward Goldsmith. 1996. *The Case against the Global Economy: And for a Turn Toward the Local.* San Francisco, CA: Sierra Club.

Mattelart, Armand. 1979. *Multinational Corporations and the Control of Culture: The Ideological Apparatuses of Imperialism.* Sussex, England: Harvester.

McAdam, Doug and David S. Snow, eds. 1997. *Social Movements: Readings on Their Emergence, Mobilization, and Dynamics.* Los Angeles, CA: Roxbury.

McLuhan, Marshall. 1989. *The Global Village: Transformations in World Life and Media in the 21st Century.* New York: Oxford University Press.

Meadows, Donella, Dennis L. Meadows, and Jörgen Randers. 1993. *Beyond the Limits: Confronting Global Collapse, Envisioning a Sustainable Future.* White River Junction, VT: Chelsea Green.

Meyer, John W., John Boli, and George M. Thomas. 1987. "Ontology and Rationalization in the Western Cultural Account." Pp. 12–37 in *Institutional Structure: Constituting State, Society, and the Individual,* edited by George M. Thomas, John W. Meyer, Francisco O. Ramirez, and John Boli. Newbury Park, CA: Sage.

Meyer, John W., John Boli, George M. Thomas, and Francisco O. Ramirez. 1997. "World Society and the Nation-State." *American Journal of Sociology* 103 (1):144–81.

Office of the United Nations High Commissioner for Human Rights. 2002. *Human Rights: A Compilation of International Instruments,* 2 vols. New York: United Nations.

Oxfam International. 1996. "Oxfam International's Mission Statement." Retrieved from http://www.oxfam.org/eng/about_strat_mission.htm.

Polanyi, Karl. 1944. *The Great Transformation: The Political and Economic Origins of Our Time.* Boston, MA: Beacon.

Project Underground. 2000. "Goldmining in Ghana Destroys Livelihoods, Health and the Environment." Retrieved from http://www.moles.org/Project Underground/drillbits/5_19/4.html.

Ritzer, George. 1993. *The McDonaldization of Society: The Changing Character of Contemporary Social Life.* Newbury Park, CA: Pine Forge.

Robertson, Roland. 1992. *Globalization: Social Theory and Global Culture.* Newbury Park, CA: Sage.

Robertson, Roland and Joann Chirico. 1985. "Humanity, Globalization, and Worldwide Religious Resurgence: A Theoretical Exploration." *Sociological Analysis* 46 (3):219–42.

Rodrik, Dani. 1997. *Has Globalization Gone Too Far?* Washington, DC: Institute for International Economics.

Roemer, John. E. 1982. *A General Theory of Exploitation and Class.* Cambridge, MA: Harvard University Press.

——. 1988. *Free to Lose: An Introduction to Marxist Economic Philosophy.* Cambridge, MA: Harvard University Press.

Ross, Andrew, ed. 1997. *No Sweat: Fashion, Free Trade, and the Rights of Garment Workers.* New York: Verso.

Sassen, Saskia. 1996. *Losing Control? Sovereignty in an Age of Globalization.* New York: Columbia University Press.

Schaeffer, Robert K. 1997. *Understanding Globalization: The Social Consequences of Political, Economic, and Environmental Change.* Lanham, MD: Rowman and Littlefield.

Schiller, Herbert. 1976. *Communication and Cultural Domination.* White Plains, NY: International Arts and Sciences Press.

Sethi, S. Prakash and Oliver F. Williams. 2000. *Economic Imperatives and Ethical Values in Global Business: The South African Experience and International Codes Today.* Boston, MA: Kluwer.

Shiva, Vandana. 1997. *Biopiracy: The Plunder of Nature and Knowledge.* Boston, MA: South End.

——. 2000a. *Seeds of Suicide: The Ecological and Human Costs of Globalisation of Agriculture.* New Delhi, India: Research Foundation for Science, Technology, and Ecology.

——. 2000b. *Stolen Harvest: The Hijacking of the Global Food Supply.* Cambridge, MA: South End.

Sklair, Leslie. 2001. *The Transnational Capitalist Class.* Oxford, England: Blackwell.

Smith, Anthony. 1980. *The Geopolitics of Information: How Western Culture Dominates the World.* New York: Oxford University Press.

Smith, Jackie G., Charles Chatfield, and Ron Pagnucco, eds. 1997. *Transnational Social Movements and Global Politics: Solidarity Beyond the State.* Syracuse, NY: Syracuse University Press.

Smith, Jackie G. and Hank Johnston, eds. 2002. *Globalization and Resistance: Transnational Dimensions of Social Movements.* Lanham, MD: Rowan and Littlefield.

Snow, David and Robert Benford. 1988. "Ideology, Frame Resonance, and Participant Mobilization." *International Social Movement Research* 1:197–217.

Starr, Amory. 2000. *Naming the Enemy: Anti-Corporate Movements Confront Globalization.* New York: Zed.

Strange, Susan. 1998. *Mad Money: When Markets Outgrow Governments.* Ann Arbor, MI: University of Michigan Press.

SustainAbility. 2003. "What Is the Triple Bottom Line?" Retrieved from http://www.sustainability.com/philosophy/triple-bottom/tbl-intro.asp.

Third World Network. 2003. "Introduction." Retrieved from http://www.twnside.org.sg/twnintro.htm.

Thomas, George M., John W. Meyer, Francisco O. Ramirez, and John Boli. 1987. *Institutional Structure: Constituting State, Society, and the Individual.* Newbury Park, CA: Sage.

Tokar, Brian, ed. 2001. *Redesigning Life? The Worldwide Challenge to Genetic Engineering.* New York: Zed.

Tomlinson, John. 1991. *Cultural Imperialism.* Baltimore, MD: Johns Hopkins University Press.

United Nations (UN). 1966. *International Covenant on Economic, Social, and Cultural Rights.* GA resolution 2200 A (XXI). New York: Author.

United Nations Educational, Scientific, and Cultural Organization (UNESCO). 2003. "The World Heritage List." Retrieved from http://whc.unesco.org/heritage.htm.

United Nations Global Compact. 2003. "UN Global Compact." Retrieved from http://www.unglobalcompact.org/Portal/.

University of Minnesota Human Rights Library. 2003. "International Human Rights Instruments." Retrieved from http://www1.umn.edu/humanrts/instree/ainstls1.htm.

Wallerstein, Immanuel. 1979. *The Capitalist World-Economy: Essays.* Cambridge, England: Cambridge University Press.

Wapner, Paul Kevin. 1996. *Environmental Activism and World Civic Politics.* Albany, NY: State University of New York Press.

Wapner, Paul Kevin, Lester Edwin J. Ruiz, and Richard Falk, eds. 2000. *Principled World Politics: The Challenge of Normative International Relations.* Lanham, MD: Rowman and Littlefield.

Weber, Max. 1968. *Economy and Society: An Outline of Interpretive Sociology,* 2 vols. New York: Bedminster.

Willetts, Peter, ed. 1996. *The Conscience of the World: The Influence of Non-Governmental Organisations in the UN System.* Washington, DC: Brookings Institution.

Williams, Phil, ed. 1999. *Illegal Immigration and Commercial Sex: The New Slave Trade.* Portland, OR: Frank Cass.

Wilson, Suzanne M. and Marta Zambrano. 1994. "Cocaine Commodity Chains and Drug Politics: A Transnational Approach." Pp. 297–315 in *Commodity Chains and Global Capitalism,* edited by Gary Gereffi and Miguel Korzeniewicz. Westport, CT: Greenwood.

Wolf, Martin. 1997. "Why This Hatred of the Market?" Retrieved from http://mondediplo.com/1997/05/globalisation3155.

World Commission on Environment and Development. 1987. *From One Earth to One World: An Overview.* Oxford: Oxford University Press.

World Health Organization (WHO). 1998. "Globalization and Access to Drugs: Perspectives on the WTO/TRIPS Agreement." Retrieved from http://www.who.int/medicines/library/dap/who-dap-98-9-rev/who-dap-98-9.htm.

World Social Forum (WSF). 2001. "Porto Alegre Call for Mobilization." Retrieved from http://www.globalsolidarity.org/porto_eng.html.

World Trade Organization (WTO). 2003. "Nongovernmental Organizations (NGOs)." Retrieved from http://www.wto.org/english/forums_e/ngo_e/ngo_e.htm.

Wuthnow, Robert. 1987. *Meaning and Moral Order: Explorations in Cultural Analysis.* Berkeley, CA: University of California Press.

Yunus, Muhammad and Alan Jolis. 1999. *Banker to the Poor: Micro-Lending and the Battle against World Poverty.* New York: Public Affairs.

TECHNOLOGY AND SOCIAL PROBLEMS

FRANK WEBSTER

City University, London

MARK ERICKSON

Aston University, Birmingham

At the outset, we would make three important observations. The first may be obvious, but it is crucial: the relationship between technology and social problems is contingent on place. While just about everyone in the North has ready access to a landline phone and the majority now even possess mobiles, the majority of the current population of the world will never even get to use a telephone. Similarly, there is a good deal of talk about the rapid uptake on the Internet and e-mail in affluent societies. This technology's diffusion is the fastest in human history, much more rapid than electricity, the motorcar, and even television. It is a safe bet that readers of this chapter use e-mail as a matter of daily routine, scarcely able to imagine how they conduct business without it. Indeed, in North America, well over 30 percent of people now have access to the Internet (and a much higher proportion of households are wired), though the technology only became available in the 1990s. But in Africa today, scarcely 2 in 1,000 are able to connect to the Internet—a figure that worsens dramatically if the Cape is excluded from calculation (Glasius, Kaldor, and Anheier 2002:281–85). Thus, the globe is sharply divided into zones of technological saturation and technological paucity. We want at the outset to identify this as being a significant social and global problem: the uneven economic and technological development of the world.

Second, we need to note that providing precise definitions of *technology* is elusive. The commonsense conception of technology—machinery and tools that carry out tasks on our behalf—may exclude things we would probably also want to call technology. For instance, is computer software technology, or should we reserve the term for hardware alone? This is not simply a problem for social scientists, who are used to dealing with concepts that at times appear to defy hard and fast definition. Politicians and legislators also have difficulties: in 1993, the inventor of the PGP (Pretty Good Privacy) encryption software was investigated by the Federal Bureau of Investigation for exporting a weapon after posting a copy of PGP on an Internet bulletin board. But is an idea that generates a computer programme to be categorized in the same way as an Armalite rifle? Does "technology" encompass them both? In what follows, will we not only face problems of defining technology in terms of what we should include and exclude but also the fact that many scholars argue that we cannot readily disentangle technology from its social context, nor even from the context of the knowledge that leads to its inception, that is, science. We will revisit these issues later in this chapter when we consider more theoretical understandings of technology. For the time being, suffice it to say that we need to bear in mind the contingent nature of technology and the breadth of phenomena, artifacts, and thought encompassed by the term itself. The concept of technology has fuzzy boundaries that will make absolute definition and identification difficult.

Third, as societies become more technological, the possibilities emerge for especially complex relationships between social problems and technology. However, we need to be cautious here: the saturation of our society with so much technology and the dramatic technological changes that Western industrial societies have undergone in recent centuries can make it appear as if the relationship between technology and social problems is exclusive to our own time. The relationship of humans to technology, the possibilities technology creates for us, and the problems that emerge from this are not new questions for social scientists and philosophers, as the work of Lewis Mumford (1934, 1971) shows. Furthermore, we are by no means the first generation to consider technology as being problematical: Ned Ludd and his followers roamed the industrializing landscape of early-nineteenth-century England, smashing machines that they saw as responsible for their loss of jobs and livelihoods. These machine breakers, Luddites, paid dearly for their actions: new laws were enacted by Parliament, and at York in 1813, 17 were publicly hanged for their crimes (Grint and Woolgar 1997:46; Reid 1986).

So, we need to exercise caution in our use of the concept of technology and need to note that our own location on the globe and in a specific history will affect our understanding of technology's relationship to social problems.

TECHNOLOGY AND SOCIAL PROBLEMS

What is the relation between technology and social problems? At first take, technology seems related to social problems only as a solution. This is so because technologies are artifacts that allow people to achieve goals. In this light, once a social problem is identified and the decision taken to address the problem, then appropriate technologies can be sought to achieve that end. For instance, in the United Kingdom, unruly behaviour at football grounds, usually associated with young and aggressive men, was a cause for concern amongst politicians, soccer's management bodies, supporters, as well as the police during the 1970s and 1980s. The remarkable growth of closed circuit television surveillance (CCTV) and use by law enforcers of camcorders at and around football stadiums have been the technological answers to this social problem. There has been a radical decline in disturbances on the terraces because those involved can be sure they will be filmed, identified, and in due course arrested and punished. Thus, a technological solution to the problem of violence at and around football grounds was developed. To be sure, not all technological solutions to social problems are successful, but those that do work are legion and, possibly for that reason, frequently go unobserved—from hip replacements that make the incapacitated (and usually elderly) able to walk again, to the refrigerator that keeps food fresh and thereby extends its use, to electronic tags that allow criminals to be released from overcrowded prisons while still being under supervision.

Of course, much hinges here on what is meant by a *social problem* and how it comes about that it is targeted for eradication. Sociologists, as well as other critics, have long insisted that a social problem is not a given, and this means that there are hard questions to be asked about who defines what as a problem to which technologies may be applied. Even as regards the example given above, there may be some who consider fighting between fans at football grounds as unproblematic since it is largely contained conflict that is victimless (save for those who attend the games). There may be many who watch ice hockey as much for the entertainment of opponents hitting one another, rather than the puck, with their sticks. So, much depends on who conceives and what gets labeled a social problem.

Nevertheless, if we can leave to one side this matter of definition, then it remains the case that technology is generally regarded as an answer to problems. The goals for which technologies are created may be novel (e.g., recording music), or they can allow us to do things long imagined but hitherto unattainable (e.g., real-time transmission across vast distances), though for the most part technologies make more efficient established ways (e.g., improving the quality and durability of music recordings). Occasionally, technologies are invented without a clear purpose (e.g., the telephone), and more frequently, technologies are adapted by users in ways the designers did not envisage initially (e.g., text messaging with mobile phones). As a general rule, however, technologies help us meet goals, and as such they are welcomed as important, even privileged, means of overcoming social problems.

Technology as Beneficent

Regarded in this way, technology may be regarded as being of quite unrivalled beneficence to society. From it have come radical and continuous improvements in health (cheaper and more plentiful food, better medical interventions), in opportunities to travel (the railway engine, the airplane), and in access to knowledge (the paperback revolution, the photocopier). If one accepts that malnutrition and illness are to be avoided, that immobility is restrictive and cramping, and that ignorance is an anathema that can be fought by advances in publishing, then technology has manifestly been an important means of addressing these social problems.

In point of fact, technology may be seen to be contributing to the alleviation of social problems in two ways. The first, mentioned above, is the more

direct, in being a "technical fix" applied more or less directly to a perceived problem. For example, elderly people living alone may be seen to be vulnerable to falls, in which circumstances they may need to call for assistance. A technical fix may involve the production of portable alarms that attach to their wrists. It is easy enough to think of instances such as this in which technology responds to a social problem.[1]

However, a less direct but surely even more significant contribution of technology comes from its capacity to continuously increase living standards. This view is that technology is the dynamo driving the generation of wealth, alleviating suffering and allowing, through time, ordinary people to enjoy everyday luxuries such as holidays, leisure pursuits, and physically undemanding employment. Bluntly put, technological innovation contributes to an increase in human happiness by virtue of its ability to provide *more*. This is less directly a contribution to the solution of social problems than is the technical fix, but it is of enormous moment since technology's capacity to increase wealth is the requisite for alleviating human misery and freedom from want. Its premise is that poverty is the most oppressive social problem there may be and that technology, in raising living standards, mitigates and even removes the condition. In support of it is the well-grounded finding that affluent people are happier than are poor. Seen in this way, it is not surprising that the utopian tradition has long held to the mediaeval idyll of the Land of Cockayne, a land of idleness and luxury that relies on there being material abundance always available and freedom from imposed labour (Davis 1981).

This perception of technology has exercised enormous influence in social thought. Indeed, it has often been a favoured way of understanding history. In these terms, the most consequential feature of human history is the Industrial Revolution, a process that began in the mid-eighteenth century and has continued unceasingly ever since (Hobsbawm 1968). It marked a break with century upon century of unchanging ways of life, caused enormous upheaval and dislocation, yet brought with it sustained improvements in standards of life. As David Landes (1969) observed, the Industrial Revolution "changed man's way of life more than anything since the discovery of fire: the Englishman of 1750 was closer in material things to Caesar's legionnaires than to his own great-grandchildren" (p. 5). Moreover, it is misleading to see the Industrial Revolution as a one-off event. More accurate is to conceive it as a process, which introduced profound changes in ways of life, accelerated change itself, and made change itself routine. Nonetheless, one ought not to underestimate the shock of the Industrial Revolution itself. Historians refer to the "Fall of the Roman Empire" as of enormous consequence in world history, and indeed it is. But we need to remember that this took place over six centuries and, more importantly, had little impact on habitual ways of life compared to the industrialisation process. Today, we are but three or four centuries beyond the Industrial Revolution's commencement, yet the changes in how we live are scarcely comparable to those of our preindustrial ancestors. For instance, our life expectations are today almost double; it is confidently expected nowadays that children will outlive their parents (yet in 1800, only about one in four children survived infancy; Plumb 1950:13), and we are surrounded with affordable comforts and luxuries inconceivable to our predecessors. So much are we now beneficiaries of everyday opulence that we "can hardly understand the keenness with which a fur coat, a good fire on the hearth, a soft bed, a glass of wine, were . . . enjoyed" in mediaeval times (Huizinga 1924:9).

There are numerous dimensions to the Industrial Revolution, but at its heart was technology (Landes 1969). This brought mechanisation (and later automation) of production, the harnessing of inanimate energy (steam, later oil and electricity), and radical improvements in the getting and working of raw materials (for example, in metallurgy and chemistry). And from this combination came a cornucopia of products and processes that have continued to transform everyday life.

It was conventional amongst social scientists in the 1950s and 1960s to emphasise the confluence of modernisation, industrialisation, and technological innovation (Aron 1967). The likes of Talcott Parsons (1966) and Walt Rostow (1960) charted stages of development that (while they expanded their analyses to consider changes in the division of labour, shifts in how people related one to another, and the emergence of new social divisions) put technology at the centre of their accounts. The presumption was that a technological society was a superior form and that the wealth emanating from its development was to be welcomed precisely because it meliorated the conditions of the majority. Accordingly, the leading societies, those to be emulated, were the likes of Western Europe and especially the United States of America. There was an often explicit doctrine of progress underpinning such accounts. Many thinkers went even further to suggest that a "logic of industrialism" (Kerr et al. 1960) was driving even ideologically polarised nations such as the Soviet Union and the United States along the same developmental path, one that because of the "imperatives of technology" required much the same sorts of factory systems, bureaucracies, education, and hierarchies based on levels of expertise (Galbraith 1967).

The radicalisation of social science in the late 1960s led to a sustained assault on the perceived conservatism of this argument (Frank 1969; Webster 1990). Many of these criticisms were to the point, yet it is noticeable that the viewpoint did not disappear. Indeed, it has returned in recent decades with the suggestion that we are experiencing the emergence of an "information society." It is worth spending some time on the thought of the major conceiver of the information society, Daniel Bell (b. 1919), because it is at once an influential strain of social science thinking and one that is underpinned by an insistence that technology is the foundation of social change and improvement. Bell's argument in *The Coming of Post-Industrial Society* (1973) is that we may understand change in terms of transitions from preindustrial, through industrial, to postindustrial society by tracking where people are employed. In preindustrial society, the vast majority of people worked on the land, compelled by the exigencies of nature to labour long hours at subsistence level. The Agricultural Revolution in seventeenth- and eighteenth-century England manifested in innovations in breeding cattle and crop rotation and enclosures, and led to increased production from the land such that people could be fed without all having to work there. This released them to move (and be moved) to the growing towns where they could find employment as industrial workers in the burgeoning factories. The Agricultural Revolution never ceased, such that over the years, farming—thanks to ongoing technical developments such as battery production, chemical fertilisers, the combine harvester, the tractor, and, more recently, genetically modified crops—has made astonishing leaps in output without needing many people to work the land. In the United Kingdom today, for instance, only about 3 percent of the workforce now work in agriculture, though these few produce over half the nation's food (and it need scarcely be said that this is an enormously greater volume than that produced in the eighteenth century, when just about everyone worked on the land).

The central point is that technological innovation on the land means that we receive much more output for less input. This translates into a requirement for few farm workers but plentiful food to support a workforce that is employed elsewhere. It was in the nineteenth century that the industrial society came into being, identified by Bell in terms of where most people made their livelihoods (cf. Kumar 1978, chap. 6). The argument is that once there was sufficient output from the land to ensure they could be fed, then industrialisation could take off since workers could be ensured of adequate food supplies. However, Bell develops his argument to insist that the same process of technical rationalisation continues in industry itself: ongoing technological innovation leading to massive increases in output per worker. In his view, this ethos of "more for less" means that the society further enriches itself. What happens then, however, is that as wealth accumulates from the development of the assembly line, automation, and new product and process production, it becomes possible for new needs to be fulfilled by spending this wealth. For instance, education and pensions become affordable as wealth increases, as, sooner or later, does education up to the age of 21 or 22 and retirement at an earlier age than 65. This in turn generates employment in particular kinds of work, which consumes wealth in providing services of one sort or another. The beauty of this theory is that so long as additional wealth continues to be generated from industry and industrialised agriculture, then people may continue to create needs that in being met, stimulate service employment. For instance, entertainers, sports instructors, and psychotherapists are all characteristics of an affluent society, though doubtless these are nowadays seen as essential to many people.

Ultimately, the theory goes, just about everyone will be employed in services (which have the advantage of being immune, by and large, from substitution by technology) because technology will take over the bulk of agriculture and industry at the same time as it ensures continued increases in wealth. It appears that neither individuals nor societies ever become incapable of spending their wealth, since each can create an infinity of new needs: a shorter working week, personal trainers, lifelong education facilities, and so on. At a certain point, we enter a postindustrial society, since while the wealth generated by industry continues unabated, most people will work in the service industries. These, adds Bell, are much more desirable and satisfying than other forms of work, since they are "people-to-people" activities, the major element of which is information (consider the teacher educating her charges, the scriptwriter with his story, the journalist with her angle) rather than machine operation or working with and against the elements. Accordingly, a postindustrial society is an "information society" and much more appealing than what went before.

What we would emphasise here is the current popularity of Bell's vision of how change has come about and where it is going (Webster 2002, chap. 3). For example, in recent years Francis Fukuyama (b. 1953) has produced his influential "end of history" thesis (Fukuyama 1992). Simply, this argues that the capitalist West has triumphed over the communist alternatives because of its capacity to outproduce it. Though Fukuyama's praise is for "liberal capitalism," at base it is the same as that offered by Bell in that its central proposition is that technological innovation is what really counts and the open market economies are the means by which technology advances most propitiously. Thus, Fukuyama notes that "the unfolding of technologically driven economic modernization creates strong incentives for developed countries to accept the basic terms of the universal capitalist economic culture" (pp. 96–7). In this view, the West won the cold war because it could most effectively make available the consumer goods such as television, compact disc players, and video recorders. When Fukuyama refers to the "victory of the VCR," he is ploughing a similar track to that of Daniel Bell: technology is the major expression of change. Not surprisingly, he too embraces a convergence theory of development. Revealingly, Fukuyama's more recent work follows a similar line of technology determining the form of human society: biotechnology is changing our attitude toward the world we live in and toward ourselves as human beings (Fukuyama 2002).

In all such thinking, the fulcrum of change is technology or, to use Bell's terminology, a guiding principle of "more for less." Productivity is the key to development, and this stems from advances in technology. Without greater output from fewer people, then a service society, and all that accompanies it, is unthinkable. As Bell observes, this is not a novel interpretation of history: his understanding draws on Max Weber's (1864–1920) notion of instrumental action (efficiency expressed by minimum investment for maximum return), which, says Bell, is most often expressed in technological form, and, further back, in Henri St.-Simon's (1760–1825) celebration of the emergence of engineers and other technicians (Taylor 1976).

It has to be said that Max Weber was famously glum about the future, however much more efficient it would come to be (Turner 2000, chaps. 4–5). But the theory of postindustrialism slews off pessimism, insisting that productivity increases mean that social problems can be identified and addressed. Furthermore, Bell observes that many social problems that are identified in postindustrial society would have been ignored, or not even imagined, in previous epochs. It fits logically with his thesis that only an affluent society can be concerned about, say, the environment or the quality of working life. During the nineteenth and twentieth centuries, for instance, scarcely anyone objected to the waste tips and belching smoke from collieries and manufacturing centres (one of these tips, after heavy rain, slipped and overwhelmed a school in 1966 at Aberfan in Glamorgan, claiming the lives of almost 150 children). The mining towns of North East England and South Wales had a Klondike character—housing was assembled next to the place of work at cheapest cost with little regard for those who had to live there (Beynon and Austrin 1994). In Bell's view, this was because, at that time, an "economising" ethic predominated, which sought maximum return on investment irrespective of the harm done to the natural or human environment (during the late

nineteenth century, no less than one in five or six miners were injured underground every year, and several thousand were killed there annually; Benson 1980:41).

By the late twentieth century, such are the needs that may be addressed by a "post-scarcity" or "post-materialist" society (Inglehart 1990) that a "socialising" ethos—which prioritises the "communal" elements of life—comes to prevail, one that urges shorter working hours and concern for the conditions of labour and can express a desire to maintain an "unspoilt" environment. That is, only affluent societies can imagine certain matters as social problems: until they attain a given level of wealth, they are caught in the strictures of imposed conditions. A thought experiment demonstrates this point readily enough: imagine, if one can, a worker in the nineteenth century needing paid annual holidays of six weeks (the current norm in Western Europe, though a good deal less in the United States) or yearning for the weekend breaks that adorn our newspaper supplements. In truth, the concept of holidays, beyond the occasional feast day, is an outcome of advanced industrial societies that provide the wealth to pay for them as well as the technologies and organisational techniques to make them affordable (notably the package tour; Urry 2002). Similarly, it is salutary to be reminded that poverty, perceived as a social problem that might be remedied, is a product of the modern age. Of course, there have long been the poor and destitute, but as the biblical adage puts it, "The poor are always with us." It was only in the early nineteenth century that poverty was "discovered" and imagined as something that might be removed by effective social policies (Himmelfarb 1984; Inglis 1971).

Daniel Bell's orthodox sociology finds an echo in much Marxian thinking about technology and its connections with social problems. It is generally acknowledged that Marxian analysis locates the cause of social problems in the unequal class relations that characterise capitalist societies. The familiar advocacy is that transformation of capitalism is required to solve social problems. However, a closer look at Marxian accounts reveals that this is by no means the case as regards technology. Recurrently in the writings of Marx and Engels, as well as in many followers, there is an insistence that a prerequisite of reform is a certain level of technological development. That is, in the Marxian tradition, one encounters time and again the claim that a foundation for all else is a given technological base. This being so, it carries the necessary presumption that technology per se is an essential contributor to solving social problems. This much is clear in Marx's well-known distinction between the "realm of freedom" and the "realm of necessity" and his argument that "the true realm of freedom . . . can blossom forth only with this realm of necessity as its basis" (Marx, as cited in McLellan 1977:496–7). Marx's insistence that politics could not be meaningfully addressed until a certain sufficiency was attained—here we encounter the (in)famous base/superstructure division that runs through most Marxian analysis (Gouldner 1980)—is evident in his claim, in *The German Ideology* (1848), that "the development of productive forces . . . is an absolutely necessary practical premise, because without it privation, want, is merely made general, and with want the struggle for necessities would begin again" (Marx and Engels 1976:49). This amounts to arguing that until one is fed adequately, sheltered securely, and able to have adequate time away from work, meaningful politics are impossible. Certain social problems must be addressed as a prelude to the class struggle.

It is because of this similarity in argument that Daniel Bell's work was received even by sympathisers as "fairly familiar Marxist stuff" (Schonfield 1969:20) and even as "apolitical Marxism" by Seymour Martin Lipset (1981:22), and it is surely why he could identify 1960s Soviet accounts of the "Scientific Technological Revolution" (Dahrendorf et al. 1977; Gouré et al. 1973) as consonant with his own vision of postindustrial society (Bell 1973:106–12). The common thread is the assumption that technology is a foundational principle for social life and something that addresses problems such as the arduous physical demands of labour and inadequacy of food supply, which must be solved prior to engagement in politics. We can also identify echoes of Herbert Marcuse in Bell's thesis. Marcuse (1968) represents a strong trend in Marxian thinking toward an idealized future of a leisure society:

Within the advanced societies the continued application of scientific rationality would have reached a terminal point with the mechanization of all socially necessary labour. Further progress would mean the break, the turn of quantity into quality. It would open the possibility of an essentially new human reality—namely the existence of free time on the basis of fulfilled vital needs. (Pp. 230–31)

Similarly, it should not be surprising that André Gorz (b. 1920), an influential contemporary voice within the Marxian tradition, has called for socialism to be constructed around "leisure," which is founded on the plentitude produced by advanced technologies. Urging that the Left revoke its commitment to struggle as workers, Gorz (1982) advocates the goal of "winning power no longer to function as a worker" (p. 67). In his view, technology now meets "primary needs" (p. 97), so socialism should be conceived as freedom from work so long as conditions of life are ensured. With basic needs satisfied by technology, socialism may be constructed in "leisure" activities in what Gorz, recalling Marx's distinction between "necessity" and "freedom," calls the "sphere of autonomous activity" (p. 93).

Theoretical Knowledge

If technology is perceived, apparently consensually, as the prerequisite of any desirable society because it ameliorates the most basic of social problems, then there is also an important change in the character of technological development that needs to be appreciated. This involves the central role of *theory,* by which is meant knowledge that is abstract, generalisable, and codified. It is abstract in that it is not of direct applicability to a given situation and generalisable in so far as it has relevance beyond particular circumstances, and it is presented in things such as books, articles, television, and educational courses. Theoretical knowledge has come to play a key role in contemporary society, in marked contrast to earlier epochs when practical and situated knowledge were predominant. If one considers, for instance, the makers of the Industrial Revolution, it is clear that these were what Daniel

Bell (1973) has referred to as "talented tinkerers" who were "indifferent to science and the fundamental laws underlying their investigations" (p. 20). Abraham Darby's development of the blast furnace, George Stephenson's railway locomotive, James Watt's steam engines, Matthew Boulton's engineering innovations, and any number of other inventions from around 1750 to 1850 were the products of feet-on-the-ground innovators and entrepreneurs, people who faced practical problems to which they reacted with practical solutions. Though by the end of the nineteenth century, science-based technologies were shaping the course of industry, it remained the case that just a century ago,

> Vast areas of human life continued to be ruled by little more than experience, experiment, skill, trained common sense and, at most, the systematic diffusion of knowledge about the best available practices and techniques. This was plainly the case in farming, building and medicine, and indeed over a vast range of activities which supplied human beings with their needs and luxuries. (Hobsbawm 1994:525)

In contrast, today, innovations start from known principles (though these principles may be understood only by a minority of experts). These theoretical principles, entered in texts, are the starting point, for instance, of the advances of the Human Genome Project and of the physics and mathematics that are the foundation of modern computing and electronic engineering. Areas as diverse as aeronautics, plastics, medicine, and pharmaceuticals illustrate realms in which theoretical knowledge is fundamental to life today.

Moreover, theoretical knowledge's primacy is not limited to leading-edge technological innovations. Indeed, it is hard to think of any technological applications in which theory is not a prerequisite of development. For instance, road repair, house construction, sewerage disposal, or motorcar manufacture are each premised on known theoretical principles of material durability, structural laws, toxins, energy consumption, and much more. This knowledge is formalised in texts and transmitted especially through the educational process, which, through specialisation, means that most people are ignorant of the theoretical knowledge outside of their own expertise. Nonetheless, no one today can be unaware of the profound importance of this theory for what one might conceive as everyday technologies, such as microwave ovens, compact disc players, and digital clocks. It is correct, of course, to perceive the architect, water engineer, and mechanic to be practical people. Indeed they are: but one ought not to overlook the fact that theoretical knowledge has been absorbed by these practitioners and in turn integrated into their practical work (and often supplemented by smart technologies of testing, measurement, and design that have incorporated theoretical knowledge).

The primacy of theoretical knowledge nowadays reaches far beyond science and technology. Consider, for instance, politics, and one may appreciate that theoretical knowledge is at the core of much policy and debate about social problems. To be sure, politics is the "art of the possible," and it must be able to respond to contingencies, yet wherever one looks, be it transport, environment, or the economy, one encounters a central role ascribed to theory (cost-benefit analysis models, concepts of environmental sustainability, theses on the relationship between inflation and employment). In all such areas, criteria that distinguish theoretical knowledge (abstraction, generalisability, codification) are satisfied. This theoretical knowledge may lack the law-like character of nuclear physics or biochemistry, but it does operate on similar grounds, and it is hard to deny that it permeates enormous amounts of contemporary life.

There are several important consequences of this rise to prominence of theoretical knowledge. First, if it is the case that "the theorists (have been) in the driving seat . . . telling the practitioners what they were to look for and should find in the light of their theories" (Hobsbawm 1994:534–55), then this provides considerably enhanced control over social problems than hitherto. With theory leading, there comes necessarily an enhanced command over affairs. For instance, known demographic patterns can be modeled into the future based on fertility rates, life expectancy, morbidity, and so on, thereby allowing for long-term planning of solutions to anticipated problems. Again, traffic growth and its flows and energy consumption can be mapped and measured, projected forward, and integrated with other forms of transportation in such a way as to foresee problems such as bottlenecks, noise pollution, and accident rates—and planners and policymakers can make necessary adjustments to best plan transport networks. Similarly, environmental conditions may be tracked and projected in terms of "What if?" scenarios, to which appropriate measures may be taken to thwart the worst consequences of a particular tendency. Second, the prominence of theory places greater emphasis on its codification and transmission across the generations, which, in turn, raises the significance of education and the credentials that are issued. It is remarkable, in this light, to note that in all advanced societies, something like one-third of each age-group will participate in higher education. It is to be expected that the products of such education systems will emerge both better equipped and more willing to tackle social problems in the future. Third, and related, is the diminishing role of belief in fate (Giddens 1991, chap. 4). As people become aware of and informed by theoretical knowledge, so will resignation to destiny decline. This is, of course, a long-term trend, but it is something markedly evident nowadays in, for example, the refusal to accept that age necessarily removes one's capacity to participate fully in society (one sees instances of this in middle-aged women giving birth, in questioning why retirement should be mandatory at age 65, and in insistence that sex relations may be continued into old age). It is a tendency most manifest in the emergence of genetic engineering, where "nature" is contested in anything from reproduction of the species to production of fruits. At one time, problems of poverty might have been explained fatalistically as the "will of God," while wars might have been accounted for in terms of "man's brutality to man" and pregnancy put down to "luck." But such views are increasingly unacceptable in an age in which theoretical knowledge is dominant and in which technical solutions can be applied or, if not ready to hand, designed.

Summary

In sum, we may say that technology resolves social problems in at least three ways:

1. By direct intervention in providing technical fix solutions

2. Through raising living standards and thereby mitigating the problems associated with poverty that have bedeviled human history

3. By its being more capable of conscious application through the primacy of theoretical knowledge in the modern world

Such argument will have no truck with those who counter our highly technological society with an idyllic past. Accompanying the undoubted weakening of community bonds (Nisbet 1972:47–106), a long-term effect of industrialisation, has been a refrain of idealisation of preindustrial life. Ever since the Romantic poets such as Wordsworth and Coleridge (and even before), there has been a strain of thought that counterposes the industrial life (dirty, dishonest, unhealthy, and fraught) with that of rural ways (harmonious, rooted, stable, and healthy). It may be an especially virulent mode of thought in England that finds expression in a retrospective nostalgia for a disappearing "golden age" that is being destroyed by invasive technologies—the power station, the automobile, the factory, and the urban sprawl (Newby 1979)—but it has to be emphasised that it is a myth. While this myth of ruralism may bring comfort to today's car-owning commuter (who will typically earn his living in the nearby town or city), who enjoys his whitewashed cottage (suitably installed with central heating, carpets, electricity, and similar high-tech conveniences), it bears little relation to the lives of real country dwellers who lived prior to modernity. If people hung together more assiduously in villages and hamlets in agrarian times, and they surely were more communal than we are today, then it was because of what Raymond Williams (1973) termed a "mutuality of the oppressed," because life for most was nasty, brutish, and short, and cooperation was a condition of survival.

We have referred earlier in this chapter to the low life expectations of most people for most of the time (until the nineteenth century, it was but 40 years for as far back in human history we can go, and it has about doubled over the last century for people in affluent societies). Before industrialisation, people were subject to the vagaries of plague, pestilence, and tempestuous weather in ways that are hard to imagine today (for instance, the Black Death in the mid-fourteenth century swept across Europe as a pandemic, killing almost half the entire British population, and numerous other outbreaks of plague continued well into the eighteenth century; Cannon 2002:753). They were oppressed by the forces of nature against which they had to do continual battle, whether it was married women who endured multiple pregnancies because the technological means of birth control were unknown or at best rudimentary, whether it was against sudden crop failure or diseased animals, whether it was the search for potable water and the maladies of human waste, whether it was seeing many of their infants fail to survive, or whether it was simply a chronic lack of nourishment. It has been technological innovation and the industrialisation that is its accompaniment that have alleviated these circumstances.

TECHNOLOGY AS A SOCIAL PROBLEM

But can one accept the forgoing? It is surely unpersuasive given the apparently enormous number of cases in which technology appears to be a manifest cause of social problems. A litany of cases comes to mind. For instance, arguably the major issue facing the world today is environmental damage (Brundtland 1987), notably global warming and the associated climatic shifts and potentially catastrophic floods that will accompany this. Profligate use of gasoline, inappropriate use of solid fuels, and CFCs (chlorofluorocarbons) are some of the causes of this predicament. As sobering is the issue of nuclear power, the disposal of the waste from which is extraordinarily complex, time dependent, and risky (Patterson 1976). Following the disaster at Chernobyl in Ukraine in 1986, no one will need much reminding of the social problems emanating from nuclear power production. Again, consider the issue of nvCJD (new variant Creutzfeldt-Jacob disease, a neurological condition for which there is no cure), which has killed scores of humans in recent years and has been linked to their eating cattle contaminated by BSE (bovine spongiform encephalopathy) during the 1980s and 1990s in Europe. The cause of BSE has been traced to the technology of feeding cattle with the remains of other animals, surely another instance where technology creates social problems.

Moreover, technologies can appear advantageous to some but may cause social problems for others. For example, if a new technology is introduced into the workplace and this requires fewer employees than before, then social problems—unemployment, anxiety, and dislocation—are clearly imposed on some even if the majority are beneficiaries. Indeed, one could go further to suggest that many workplace technologies have resulted in a decline in the autonomy of those who must work with them—machine pacing and intrusive monitoring of performance are some of the maladies frequently complained about by those who work in factories and indeed many offices (Noble 1984). Such practices lead to stress, industrial injuries, alienation, and anomie, and the deleterious effects of increased technology in workplaces may outweigh the positive increases in efficiency and production, particularly if a long-term view is taken (Bradley et al. 2000, chap. 5).

It helps understanding the role of technologies in creating social problems by distinguishing between anticipated and unanticipated consequences of their development. An anticipated social problem might involve the introduction of a technology that leads to there being less work available. For example, the spread of computerisation in the newspaper industry led to the demise of the established printer. The technology here contributed to a social problem that might have been addressed in various ways (retraining, early retirements, freeze on new recruitment, etc.), but it is evident that the problem was foreseen by many commentators (Martin 1981). An unanticipated consequence is one where the introduction of the technology produces an effect far away from the intended sphere of influence (Tenner 1996). For example, the development of modern birth control technologies had an intended consequence in allowing women to control reproduction and was effective in allowing people to choose when and how many children to have. However, few would have expected that a problem would later emerge in Western Europe of a decline in the younger elements of the population, which exacerbates a serious problem of long-term care of the older generation and, in the longer term, to problems of maintaining population levels. Relatedly, medical technologies help lengthen the life span, and this is usually regarded as a very positive development. But an unanticipated consequence of greater longevity is major pressure on pension funds that were designed on a different actuarial basis. In addition, with more and more people living into and beyond their 80s and supported by improved medical technologies that keep them going, there comes the problem of providing the care they tend to require as they grow frail. With fewer people available in the younger generations and increased geographical spread, we face serious, but unexpected, difficulties posed by the prolongation of life.

There are many other examples of unanticipated consequences of technological development. For example, the spread of the private car has been, for many, a very great benefit, allowing options to travel securely and pleasurably. Today, the vast majority of homes in the United Kingdom own a motor car. However, an unanticipated consequence of this has been the problem of social exclusion of significant minorities. The elderly who may not be able to drive on health grounds, the poor who cannot afford cars, and car-less women are frequently excluded from many activities because of this, particularly as public transport has declined precisely because of preferences given to private transport. Transport, indeed, is littered with examples of technologies introduced with clear goals in mind, but one finds unexpected social problems arising as a result, amongst which noise, road accidents, and physical pollution loom large. For instance, the remarkable rise in airplane travel has meant cheap and fast transit for many people, but the location of airports and the emissions from planes, especially those on short haul, create serious social problems (Royal Commission on Environmental Pollution 2002). All advanced societies have undergone major road-building programmes in recent decades, the main reasons for which are to alleviate the stress on the existing network. But frequently, the new roads attract additional traffic and, in turn, create further problems of congestion and pollution. The London arterial motorway, the M25, is a byword for this in England, as is the Paris ring road in France. Again, the positioning of closed circuit television cameras on street corners has been intended to ensure that deviants are apprehended and the law abiding can go their way unmolested, yet an unanticipated consequence has been a distinct expansion of "big brother" in towns and cities, and concerns about privacy have been voiced because of heightened surveillance (Norris and Armstrong 1999). And how can one fail to observe that the increased availability of cheap food, courtesy of high-tech farming, convenience food availability, and more sedentary lifestyles have contributed untowardly to the massive social problem— what has been called a "global epidemic"—of obesity, where some 60 percent of adults in the United States are overweight or obese and suffer in consequence high rates of coronary disease and other maladies?

On the ground, of course, divisions between what can be anticipated and what cannot may be blurred because of difficulties of seeing far into the future and predicting effects in complex situations. A characteristic response is to carry out "risk assessments" that attempt to identify the pros and cons of technological innovations (perhaps cheaper production but fewer employees; more jobs but an unsightly production centre; greater yields but more susceptibility to disease). These can be highly complex matters involving public inquiries and considerable research provision (e.g., agreeing on the sites of power stations or airports), but they are also a part of everyday life, where people endeavour to weigh the range of social effects of technological innovations in order to control them more effectively (Beck 1992). Not infrequently such a "risk assessment" can conclude that a technology will lead to social problems, but these may be addressed by additional technological fixes. For instance, the availability of motorcars may lead to unacceptable congestion in urban areas, which, in turn, can be answered by the introduction of bicycle and bus lanes and disincentives introduced to reduce the appeal of automobile traffic, such as the tolls being introduced in London in 2003 (the collection of which relies on sophisticated computer and satellite technologies that will scan car registration numbers and bill accordingly).

A common response to the accusation that technology can create social problems is to argue that it is a neutral phenomenon that can be used either positively or negatively. This use/abuse approach is remarkably widespread in discussions of technology and society relationships. There is clearly something in this, in that one may readily think of instances where the principle is operative. For instance, one may use an automobile to help rob a bank or speed one to one's grandchildren, a computer to access pornography or to organise for good causes. The corollary of such an argument is that technology per se cannot cause social problems because technology itself is itself apart from the social realm: it is only when social interventions are made that the issue of benefits as opposed to disbenefits comes into play. An enormous amount of discussion of technology and the future adopts the use/abuse approach, one evidenced in arguments that suggest alternatives of utopia or dystopia depending on social choices in the development of ICTs (information and communication technologies), genetic engineering, and other advanced technologies. Scenarios of either "big brother" or "information for all," a "leisure society" or mass unemployment, and the establishment of "electronic communities" or a life of social isolation are frequently portrayed in such discussions.

The use/abuse approach sits comfortably with the view, reviewed above, that technology is fundamentally beneficent. In these terms, so long as it is used wisely, technology signifies progress. To this degree, technology may be regarded, even by critics of the status quo, as a positive development, as something that might be regarded as a legacy waiting for more appropriate social policies to be put in place. This sort of thinking is evident in much Marxian thinking, which perceives technology as a "base," as the foundation upon which socialism may be built, though it has been developed by capitalist forces (Webster and Robins 1986, chap. 4). Technology here is a necessary but neutral inheritance that will be put to good use when social policies change. Insofar as radicals embrace technology in this way, they share the same use/abuse approach of more conservative commentators on technological innovation.

A major difficulty with this view is that while technology is said to be neutral, it is also insisted that it is essential to the modern social world. To the degree that it sees technology as foundational to society, it is technologically determinist, something that subordinates the social to a secondary role and must also think in terms of technology "impacting" on society as though it were an external force (MacKenzie 1998). The use/abuse vision of technology sharply separates technology and the social,

suggesting that the latter plays a role in shaping the technology's applications, but this only after an essentially asocial technology has been developed. The problem here is that it is evident that technologies are influenced by social relationships before and during their development. For instance, research and development decisions prioritise some and relegate other proposals. The huge spending of powerful nations on defence has been a major reason why some of the most virtuoso computer communications technologies were found in the military and space domains. The relative paucity of investment in research on alternative energies is surely the reason why they are so underdeveloped. Or take the homes in which people live, an everyday technology if ever there was one, yet vital to us all. Can anyone who has ever ridden a train or coach through a city, from the centre to the suburbs, be unaware of the values that are integrated into the architecture of homes? Size of plot, style of building, number of rooms, type of brickwork (or other), proximity to other houses and to roadways, and even the location of garages speak volumes about social values, aesthetic, class, and culture. Bluntly put, the use/abuse approach to technology is oversimplistic, suggesting too straightforward a role for social choices while acceding to the view that technology is the fundamental determinant of how we live. Seen from this point of view, technology may not create social problems simply due to unfortunate abuses, but because social values and priorities have already found a place *inside* a technological development (MacKenzie and Wajcman 1999).

This leads on to more radical theories of technological innovation. Here, we encounter a characteristic emphasis on power, interests, and control as decisive features of technology's development (Dickson 1974). Radical thinkers typically draw attention to the import of markets in developing technologies (e.g., consumer electronic goods meet high-level demand for home music systems, and most recent innovations there build upon the enormous success of the television), to corporate power (e.g., in dominating technological development through patents or through their capacity to provide the necessary capital to see technologies through to successful implementation), and to political stakeholders (notably the defence industry). Such approaches regard technology as profoundly influenced by the current organisation of society, which may, for a variety of reasons, introduce technologies that create or exacerbate particular social problems precisely because they have incorporated social values from the outset (Noble 1983). For instance, it has been observed that technologies aimed at the shop floor have been guided, for the most part, by distrust of the workforce. It is hard to think of technologies that have been designed with the goal of empowerment and ennoblement of the worker (though a case may be made for the Apple Mac). Rather, the aim has been to maximise output and reduce costs, to which ends the goal has been to diminish the role of the worker. Again, it is hard to see the motorcar as merely a neutral technology that may be used and abused when one reflects on the ways in which it tends to consolidate the intensely private mode of life of the Western world. That is, the typical car is designed to be privately owned, to accommodate the modern nuclear family (four seats, though with plenty of cars developed to reflect other social values—the sports car, the executive car, the "about-town" car). Above all, perhaps, the car is antipathetic to shared forms of transport, as witnessed in the decline in train and bus services over the years. Finally, consider the intimate role a great deal of technological development has had with the military. It cannot be surprising that, for instance, the leading-edge ICTs are found in the arms industry, in a battery of weapons from spy satellites to digitalised infantry, where the development of "information warfare" has been enormously stimulated by a "revolution in military affairs" (Cohen 1996; Robins and Webster 1999, chap. 7).

More radical still are approaches to technology that are informed by ecological insights (Pepper 1996). At the outset, an ecological point of view would comment on the anthropocentric orientation of most technological change (Leopold 1949). This presupposes that the human species is the centrepiece of the world and that it has a right to do what it will to the earth and other species, so long as humanity benefits. Such hubris has resulted in extinction of many other species and in crises as diverse as overfishing and desertification. From such a perspective, technology, guided by anthropocentric values, results in major problems for the sustainability of other life forms alongside humans and even for the survival of life itself. Here, we may also draw a distinction between ecocentric as opposed to technocentric positions. The latter evokes the technologist's conviction that what matters above all is control of the environment in pursuit of advantage to humans. However, an ecocentric approach proclaims that humans are part of nature and that they should act accordingly. As such, technologies are to be developed that are in harmony with and respectful of nature. These are likely to be small scale and uncomplicated in design, far removed from the large-scale and centralising technologies characteristic of the advanced societies.

Such critical approaches to technology, though they encompass a range of opinion, share a refusal to see technology as an autonomous, asocial phenomenon (Winner 1977). Necessarily, then, they refuse any straightforward depiction of technology as the answer to social problems. Indeed, they frequently regard technology, insofar as it expresses sectional interests or power, as contributing to and even creating social problems. It is noticeable that such critical approaches have come from campaigners, in recent years, most clearly the environmental movements. From such quarters have been high-profile critiques, for example, of the oil industry and its technologies, which can pollute the environment and arguably squander nonrenewable energy resources.

What these critiques share is an insistence that it is untenable to distinguish sharply between technology and the social realm. Inside academe, this has been taken up and extended to be presented as various versions of *social constructionism.* Less engaged than the environmental or political critics of technology, constructionism shares the view that the social is a constitutive part of technology. When it comes to considering questions of technology and social problems, it follows that the constructivist position refuses to accept the implied binary division. Perhaps the most widely cited version is Bruno Latour's (1996) actor network theory, which, attempting to break with such oppositions, approaches human and nonhuman elements as *actants* in networks of relationships. While conceptually persuasive and capable of producing richly impressive case studies of technological development, such an approach has difficulties in addressing large-scale and structural questions (Winner 1993).

WHAT IS TECHNOLOGY?

These debates about the neutrality or otherwise of technology and its relationship to the social realm lead us back to a crucial issue: just what is technology, and how do we relate to it? The pervasiveness of technology in advanced industrial societies may lead to, paradoxically, a hiding of technology in that we become so used to being surrounded by it and so inured to its everyday influences that it can become difficult to identify what technology actually is. Some commentators endeavour to explain this difficulty in "seeing" technology by reference to large-scale changes in societies themselves. The concepts of "technoscience" and "technoscientific society" are pertinent here.

We start this section by noting that it is generally difficult in contemporary society to distinguish science from technology: when we look at technological objects in our lives, we often think of science. Likewise, when we think of science, we often think of the technology that science engenders. This conflation and fusion of science and technology has been called "technoscience" by some commentators (Aronowitz and DiFazio 1994; Haraway 1997; Latour 1987), and it is connected to the growth of theoretical knowledge, of which science is a considerable element, to which we referred above. The identification of the conflation of science and technology is the starting point for a range of different perspectives on technoscience.

Latour (1987) and Aronowitz and DiFazio (1994), whilst approaching this topic from very different perspectives (broadly, social constructionism and critical theory), agree that the distinguishing feature of technoscience is the conflation of science and technology, where we simply cannot separate science from technology, and vice versa. Aronowitz and DiFazio take a broad structural look at technoscience, focusing on workplaces, noting that it is the state of affairs that results when science becomes inextricably linked with the technology it has created, where "work cannot be separated from its

mechanical aspects, which, in the light of the drift of the field, seem to dominate all so-called intellectual problems" (p. 51). This is an echo of the work of Jürgen Habermas (1971), who describes the emergence of a technocratic consciousness in advanced industrial societies: it is this consciousness that promotes the application of technical solutions to social problems regardless of the appropriateness of such strategies.

In contrast, Latour (1987) identifies technoscience in society as a whole, rather than just in the world of work. For Latour, when we see particular pieces of technology, or particular effects of technology—say, the PC (personal computer) sitting on your desk—we will see science as the driving force behind them, even when there is no clear link between the technology and scientific knowledge. He acknowledges that this conception of technoscience might expand to include all interest groups and ideologies. But Latour refuses such expansion, insisting instead that understanding of technoscience should be based on identifying the *networks* of knowledges, interests, and actors involved in a *particular* production. Thus, each instance of technoscience is to be judged on its own terms: Latour's technoscience is a concept to allow us to analyse the microworld surrounding a technology: how does *this* object come into being in *this* way and at *this* time? Where Aronowitz and DiFazio see technoscience as an all-pervading "ideology" that has similar effects in different places, Latour's technoscience is subject and place specific.

As well as describing the inseparableness of the objects of technology from the practice and knowledge of science, technoscience can also designate a state of affairs (a time and place, in this case Western industrial societies in the early twenty-first century) where intellectual problems of the day become increasingly dominated by technical considerations and, often, solutions. This is what Haraway (1997) does:

> This discourse takes shape from the material, social, and literary technologies that bind us together as entities within the region of historical hyperspace called technoscience. *Hyper* means "over" or "beyond," in the sense of "overshooting" or "extravagance." Thus, technoscience indicates a time-space modality that is

extravagant, that overshoots passages through naked or unmarked history. Technoscience extravagantly exceeds the distinction between science and technology as well as those between nature and society, subjects and objects, and the natural and artificial that structured the imaginary time called modernity. (P. 3)

Technoscience is thus both an object of inquiry and a context in which our inquiry can be located, and technoscience "exceeds" science and technology: it is bigger than the sum of its parts. Furthermore, technoscience is also a language and a grammar that we are using to describe the world around us and our selves within the world. If we follow Haraway's understanding of technoscience, we will find it resists being broken down into constituent components: we will not find it possible to look at an object in contemporary industrial society and see what is "scientific" about it and what is "technological." Indeed, Haraway would want to go further and say that we cannot identify "objects" in contradistinction to "subjects" and that such distinctions have been rendered meaningless by our changing relationships to artifacts and nonhuman actors. This is not simply due to the fusing together of science and technology; it is also due to the changing shape of our language and grammar of meaning. Our lives are now described by technoscientific language, and our meanings are constructed around technoscientific viewpoints on the world. We cannot extricate ourselves from this form of life, this technoculture. Thus, for many contemporary observers, social problems, technology, and (scientific) knowledge become inextricably linked.

CONCLUSION

So, how might we conclude this discussion of technology and social problems? It can be agreed that the preeminence of theoretical knowledge has led to enhanced control over technological development, and therefore the capability and purposefulness of technology have been enormously increased, though this is by no means to say that technology's consequences can all be foreseen. It is also surely clear that the positing of linear relationships between technology and society are unpersuasive. Though it is commonplace to think so (Winner 1997), the notion that technology solves social problems is a half-truth that is countered by the charge, also half true, that technology creates social problems. The difficulty with such thinking is that both types assume that technology and society are independent of one another, though—at least with the argument that technology is the privileged answer to social problems—technology is also presumed to be foundational, and thereby determining, of social relations.

It is therefore important that we consider how we might best conceive technology and society relationships. There are various proposals here, ranging from those that evoke technology as but a tool of the powerful to deep ecology adherents who would emphasise a profoundly anti-ecological outlook driving modern technology's search for control over the earth. There appears now to be a consensus that some form of social constructionism must be endorsed (though there are multiple versions of this), if for no other reason than that technology cannot be removed from social circumstances that give it meaning, shape its applications, and guide its development. The concept of technoscience is a response to this situation, one that starts from the inseparability of technology, science, and society. From such perspectives, to ask plainly what is technology's connection with social problems is misdirected. Much more complicated and nuanced analyses are required that reject cause-effect relations and move away from thinking about technology, science, and society as autonomous entities. However, whichever of these approaches is adopted, each carries with it the risk that technologies come to be regarded as "just another social relationship." While social constructionism frees up the imagination and effectively counters technological determinism, it is hard to agree that technologies can be regarded in quite the same way as, say, friendship relations in a local pub. Technologies have a materiality and durability that is absent in most social relationships. Any adequate attempt to understand the technology and social problems nexus must come to terms with this.

NOTE

1. Yet once again our definition of what constitutes a social problem here can confuse us. We could present this example in terms that see technology as the problem. The

individuation of society that has been facilitated by technology has led to the emergence of societies that have diminished forms of community and result in the isolation and vulnerability for senior citizens that call for portable alarms.

REFERENCES

Aron, Raymond. 1967. *The Industrial Society.* London, England: Weidenfeld and Nicolson.

Aronowitz, Stanley and William DiFazio. 1994. *The Jobless Future: Sci-Tech and the Dogma of Work.* Minneapolis, MN: Minnesota University Press.

Beck, Ulrich. 1992. *Risk Society.* London, England: Sage.

Bell, Daniel. 1973. *The Coming of Post-Industrial Society: A Venture in Social Forecasting.* London, England: Peregrine.

Benson, John. 1980. *British Coalminers in the Nineteenth Century.* Dublin, Ireland: Gill and Macmillan.

Beynon, Huw and Terry Austrin. 1994. *Masters and Servants: Class and Patronage in the Making of a Labour Organisation.* London, England: Rivers Oram.

Bradley, Harriet, Mark Erickson, Carol Stephenson, and Steve Williams. 2000. *Myths at Work.* Cambridge, England: Polity.

Brundtland, Gro Harlem. 1987. *Our Common Future: World Commission on Environment and Development.* Oxford: Oxford University Press.

Cannon, John, ed. 2002. *Oxford Companion to British History.* Oxford: Oxford University Press.

Cohen, Elliot A. 1996. "A Revolution in Warfare." *Foreign Affairs* 75 (2):37–54.

Dahrendorf, Ralph et al. 1977. *Scientific-Technological Revolution: Social Aspects.* London, England: Sage.

Davis, J. C. 1981. *Utopia and the Ideal Society: A Study of English Utopian Writing, 1516–1700.* Cambridge, England: Cambridge University Press.

Dickson, David. 1974. *Alternative Technology and the Politics of Technical Change.* London, England: Fontana.

Frank, André Gundar. 1969. *Capitalism and Under-development in Latin America: Historical Studies of Chile and Brazil.* New York: Monthly Review Press.

Fukuyama, Francis. 1992. *The End of History and the Last Man.* London, England: Hamish Hamilton.

——. 2002. *Our Posthuman Future: Consequences of the Biotechnology Revolution.* London, England: Profile Books.

Galbraith, John Kenneth. 1967. *The New Industrial State.* Harmonsworth, England: Penguin.

Giddens, Anthony. 1991. *Modernity and Self-Identity: Self and Society in the Late Modern Age.* Cambridge, England: Polity.

Glasius, Marlies, Mary Kaldor, and Helmut Anheier, eds. 2002. *Global Civil Society 2002.* Oxford: Oxford University Press.

Gorz, André. 1982. *Farewell to the Working Class: An Essay on Post-Industrial Socialism.* London, England: Pluto.

Gouldner, Alvin. 1980. *The Two Marxisms: Contradictions and Anomalies in the Development of Theory.* London, England: Macmillan.

Gouré, L. et al. 1973. *Convergence of Communism and Capitalism: The Soviet View.* Miami, FL: University of Miami, Miami Center for Advanced International Affairs.

Grint, Keith and Steve Woolgar. 1997. *The Machine at Work.* Cambridge, England: Polity.

Habermas, Jurgen. 1971. *Towards a Rational Society: Student Protest, Science, Politics.* Boston, MA: Beacon.

Haraway, Donna J. 1997. *Modest_Witness@Second_Millennium. FemaleMan©_Meets_OncoMouse™: Feminism and Technoscience.* London, England: Routledge.

Himmelfarb, Gertrude. 1984. *The Idea of Poverty: England in the Early Industrial Age.* London, England: Faber and Faber.

Hobsbawm, Eric J. 1968. *Industry and Empire: An Economic History of Britain Since 1750.* Harmonds-worth, England: Penguin.

——. 1994. *Age of Extremes: The Short Twentieth Century.* London, England: Michael Joseph.

Huizinga, Johan. 1924. *The Waning of the Middle Ages.* Harmondsworth, England: Penguin.

Inglehart, Ronald. 1990. *Culture Shift in Advanced Industrial Society.* Princeton, NJ: Princeton University Press.

Inglis, Brian. 1971. *Poverty and the Industrial Revolution.* London, England: Hodder and Stoughton.

Kerr, Clark et al. 1960. *Industrialism and Industrial Man.* Cambridge, MA: Harvard University Press.

Kumar, Krishan. 1978. *Prophecy and Progress: The Sociology of Industrial and Post-Industrial Society.* London, England: Allen Lane.

Landes, David S. 1969. *The Unbound Prometheus: Technological Change and Industrial Development in Western Europe from 1750 to the Present.* New York: Cambridge University Press

Latour, Bruno. 1987. *Science in Action.* Cambridge, MA: Harvard University Press.

——. 1996. *Aramis, or, The Love of Technology.* Cambridge, MA: Harvard University Press.

Leopold, Aldo. 1949. *A Sand County Almanac and Sketches Here and There.* Oxford: Oxford University Press.

Lipset, Seymour Martin. 1981. "Whatever Happened to the Proletariat? An Historic Mission Unfulfilled." *Encounter,* June, 56:18–34.

MacKenzie, Donald. 1998. *Knowing Machines: Essays on Technical Change.* Cambridge, MA: MIT Press.

MacKenzie, Donald and Judy Wajcman, eds. 1999. *The Social Shaping of Technology.* 2nd ed. Buckingham, England: Open University Press.

Marcuse, Herbert. 1968. *One Dimensional Man.* London, England: Sphere Books.

Martin, Roderick. 1981. *New Technology and Industrial Relations in Fleet Street.* Oxford, England: Clarendon.

Marx, Karl and Frederick Engels. 1976. *Collected Works,* vol 5. London, England: Lawrence and Wishart.

McLellan, David, ed. 1977. *Karl Marx: Selected Writings.* Oxford: Oxford University Press.

Mumford, Lewis. 1934. *Technics and Civilization.* London, England: Routledge & Kegan Paul.

——. 1971. *The Pentagon of Power.* London, England: Secker & Warburg.

Newby, Howard. 1979. *Green and Pleasant Land? Social Change in Rural England.* Harmondsworth, England: Penguin.

Nisbet, Robert. 1972. *The Sociological Tradition.* London, England: Heinemann.

Noble, David F. 1983. "Present Tense Technology." *Democracy* 4 (Parts 1–3):8–24, 70–82, 71–93.

——. 1984. *Forces of Production: A Social History of Industrial Automation.* New York: Oxford University Press.

Norris, Clive and Gary Armstrong. 1999. *The Maximum Surveillance Society: The Rise of CCTV.* Oxford, England: Berg.

Parsons, Talcott. 1966. *Societies: Evolutionary and Comparative Perspectives.* Englewood Cliffs, NJ: Prentice Hall.

Patterson, Walter. 1976. *Nuclear Power.* Harmondsworth, England: Penguin.

Pepper, David. 1996. *Modern Environmentalism.* London, England: Routledge.

Plumb, J. H. 1950. *England in the Eighteenth Century.* Harmondsworth, England: Penguin.

Reid, Robert. 1986. *Land of Lost Content: The Luddite Revolt, 1812.* London, England: Heinemann.

Robins, Kevin and Frank Webster. 1999. *Times of the Technoculture: From the Information Society to Virtual Life.* London, England: Routledge.

Rostow, Walter. 1960. *The Stages of Economic Growth: A Non-Communist Manifesto.* Cambridge, England: Cambridge University Press.

Royal Commission on Environmental Pollution. 2002. *The Environmental Effects of Civil Aircraft in Flight.* London, England: Author.

Schonfield, Andrew. 1969. "Thinking about the Future." *Encounter* 32 (2):15–26.

Taylor, Keith, ed. 1976. *Henri Saint-Simon, 1760–1825: Selected Writings on Science, Industry, and Social Organisation.* London, England: Croom Helm.

Tenner, Edward. 1996. *Why Things Bite Back: Predicting the Problems of Progress.* London, England: Fourth Estate.

Turner, Stephen, ed. 2000. *The Cambridge Companion to Weber.* Cambridge, England: Cambridge University Press.

Urry, John. 2002. *The Tourist Gaze.* 2nd ed. London, England: Sage.

Webster, Andrew. 1990. *Introduction to the Sociology of Development.* 2nd ed. London, England: Macmillan.

Webster, Frank. 2002. *Theories of the Information Society.* 2nd ed. London, England: Routledge.

Webster, Frank and Kevin Robins. 1986. *Information Technology: A Luddite Analysis.* Norwood, NJ: Ablex.

Williams, Raymond. 1973. *The Country and the City.* London, England: Chatto and Windus.

Winner, Langdon. 1977. *Autonomous Technology: Technics-out-of-Control in Political Thought.* Cambridge, MA: MIT Press.

——. 1993. "Social Constructionism: Opening the Black Box and Finding It Empty." *Science as Culture* 3 (16):427–52.

——. 1997. "Technology Today: Utopia or Dystopia?" *Social Research* 64 (3):989–1017.

THE INTERNET AS A GLOBAL SOCIAL PROBLEM

GILI S. DRORI

Stanford University

With helicopters hovering above and armored vehicles patrolling the streets, police forces in protective gear were trying to keep peace in the streets of Naples, Italy. Naples, known more for its scenery than for its political activism, was swamped with antiglobalization protesters coming to demonstrate against the meeting of the Global Forum, the United-Nations-led transnational policy forum. These protesters challenged a variety of traditional Global Forum agenda items, from citizen representation to governance reforms to corporate involvement. Yet the agenda of the Third Global Forum's Naples 2001 meeting was devoted to the single theme of "e-governance." On this meeting's program was the initiative to harness the Internet revolution to improve public administration through increasing transparency and accountability. Antiglobalization protesters, on the other hand, were holding banners proclaiming that

the Internet Age is only exacerbating global inequalities, a result of greedy corporate leaders and failed international aid policies. How did the Internet, or in its alternative label, the *global digital divide,* become such an explosive policy issue, drawing people into street demonstrations and conference halls? What is the aura, or mystique, of the Internet and of high-tech that has led to the definition of the Internet as a global social problem? These issues are at the core of this chapter.

In this chapter, I review a range of issues relating to the global digital divide and specifically to global disparities in access to the Internet.[1] In addition to the general questions, I also ask: what are the various proposals to address this newly conceived social problem? What do these discussions imply about current global social priorities? And what are the related research tasks for social scientists? After a short review of global trends in

Author's Note: I thank John Meyer, Francisco Ramirez, Hilton Obenzinger, and Evan Schofer, as well as the members of Stanford University's comparative workshop, for their thoughtful comments on earlier drafts of this paper.

Internet diffusion and of global gaps in its current use, the sections of this chapter follow the order of these questions.

INTERNET DEVELOPMENT AND DIFFUSION

The "Internet revolution" of the late 1990s made such terms as "e-commerce" and "dot com" into household words and let us dream that tomorrow's technology was already here. Internet development built upon the few decades of innovative computer technology, making progress by creating faster, cheaper, and more capable communications through a shared and open network.

The first steps toward a global open network of electronic information exchange were made in DARPA[2] laboratories in the early 1960s, marked by the move from a conceptual "galactic network" to the 1968 development of ARPANET[3] and later the introduction of "internetting."[4] These experimentations with open-architecture networking[5] and with various protocols to meet the requirements made by such openness resulted in the Internet. For the following two decades, the network grew, while still maintaining its elite character: after the first host-to-host message was sent in October 1969 from Leonard Klienrock's laboratory at MIT to Elizabeth (Jake) Feinler in the Stanford Research Institute (SRI), all the joining hosts were academic institutions or major research and development (R&D) labs. These pioneering networks offered data-sharing capabilities and electronic mail to their respective community members yet did not reach beyond their institutional boundaries. Only in 1984/1985 did network members, namely NSFNET and the British JANET, explicitly aspire to serve the entire higher-education community. Then, NSF's conditioning of its sponsorship on "the connection must be made available to ALL qualified users on campus,"[6] combined with DARPA's founding of the Internet Activities Board (IAB), extended the reaches of this technology. Finally, Tim Berners-Lee's 1989 development of the basic concept of the World Wide Web while at the European Organization for Nuclear Research (CERN), backed by the 1993 introduction of Mosaic,[7] led to the launching of the World Wide Web Consortium in 1994.[8] This groundbreaking project, developing a global hypertext platform for information sharing, made the Internet into an information and communication bridge across businesses, peoples, and governments the world over. Today, the World Wide Web is an expansive network, still based on the pioneering ideals of open architecture and open protocol yet also commercializing the initial sponsorship of government and academic institutions. Clearly, more recent technological advances, moving from character-based language into graphical interface and from command structure into "point-and-click" control, popularized the Internet, making it more comprehensible and welcoming to the general population.

The Internet quickly came to be the fastest-growing information and communication technology ever. The number of Web sites grew from 200 in June 1993 to 20 million such sites in late 2000 (United Nations Development Programme [UNDP] 2001:32), with estimates of as many as 2 million Web pages added daily (Lake in DiMaggio et al. 2001:308); the number of Internet users around the world grew from 16 million in 1995 to over 500 million in 2001, and was estimated to reach 655 million in 2002 (UNDP 2001:25 and International Telecommunications Union [ITU] updates[9]); the number of e-mail accounts grew from about 15 million worldwide in the early 1990s to 569 million at the end of 1999 (Compaine 2001:325); the number of Internet hosts[10] worldwide doubled in the two years 1999 to 2001[11] and grew tenfold[12] in OECD[13] member states between 1990 and 2000 (UNDP 2002:189); and the number of countries connected to the Internet grew from 8 in 1988 to 214 in 2000 (ITU 2001:1). The Internet system itself is also increasingly more robust: "In 2001 more information can be sent over a single cable in a second than in 1997 was sent over the entire Internet in a month" (UNDP 2001:30). And international Internet capacity reached the remarkable level of some 300 Gbit/s[14] in 2001, almost five times greater than its capacity in 1999, so it now exceeds international telephone circuit capacity (ITU 2001:3). Last, such advancement in technology also means cheaper access to it: for example, the cost of one megabit of computer memory dropped from $US 5,257 in 1970 to 17 US¢ in 1999 (UNDP 2001:2, 33), and Internet dial-up costs[15] reached their lowest rate ever in 2002 to an average of $US 45 for 30 hours of dial-up access in OECD countries (ITU 2001:3).

The rate of diffusion of the Internet is like no other communication technology before it. The Internet was the quickest technology to ever be adopted by American households, faster than cell phones and personal computers and much faster than other household products such as the microwave, VCR, electricity, and the telephone (see Compaine 2001:322; Norris 2001:33). Thus, "It took television 13 years and the telephone 75 years to acquire 50 million users," while "it took the internet [only] five years" (Main 2001:85).

In summary, the Internet appeared on the field of communication technology in the early 1990s and quickly changed all parameters of technology diffusion. Most dramatically, the Internet made unprecedented leaps in terms of accessibility and affordability, making this technological diffusion faster to spread and lower in cost than all communication and household technologies before it. The Internet, then, quickly lowered the barriers to communication technology: during its short life, Internet technology has enabled more people to have access to more information at a lower cost than imagined, or planned, by its conceivers. Nevertheless, numerous barriers still prohibit most of humanity from gaining access to this newest communication technology.

FALLING THROUGH THE NET[16]

Even with such changes in access to, and cost of, communication brought about by the Internet during the 1990s, this information and communication technology still left many people worldwide not linked to this network. So, despite the Internet's dramatic global diffusion, only 5 percent of the world's population is now "on-line" (ITU 2001:1). In addition, countries and world regions still differ greatly in their Internet capacities. For example, more than 97 percent of all Internet hosts are located in developed countries, which are home to only 16 percent of the world's population (UNDP 2001:40). By comparison, in 2000, 35 of the least-developed countries, which are home to a half billion people, accounted for only 1 percent of on-line users (Norris

2001:45). This comparison between the share of global population and the share of the global on-line population is the most striking evidence of the global divide in access to the Internet. This great gap between the relative shares exists when considering both levels of industrialization (see Figure 25.1) and regional location (see Figure 25.2).[17] These data reveal that the only three world regions where the share of global on-line population is greater than the share of global population are Scandinavia, North America, and Western Europe—regions that account for 66 percent of the global on-line population while accounting for only 13 percent of the number of countries and 14 percent of total world population.

This North-South divide in Internet access extends also to Internet capacity: global regions and countries are clearly divided by the varying ability of local networks to serve multiple users and to transfer great data quantities. For example, the whole continent of Africa has less bandwidth[18] than the city of Sao Paulo, Brazil, while all of Latin America's bandwidth is roughly equal to that of the city of Seoul, South Korea (UNDP 2001:3). In countries and regions lacking such capacity, Internet connections are less efficient and, by definition, less available. In this sense, varying levels of Internet capacity set barriers before Internet users in developing countries and in marginal regions: their network is overloaded, if not overwhelmed, not because of a large number of users or great amounts of data transferred, but rather due to a low capacity to serve those users. It is, then, the local network's capacity that prohibits people's full-fledged use of the Internet, if it is available at all.

Another related major barrier to universal access to Internet technology is the cost of the required hardware and connection. Mainly due to income differentials, Internet technology is beyond the reach of most of humanity. In other words, most of humanity, hardly able to afford basic life necessities such as food, clothing, and medication, can certainly not meet the expense of purchasing the necessary technological tools[19] or paying the connection fees.[20] For example, in the United States, the cost of a single personal computer (PC) equals one-tenth of the gross domestic product (GDP) per capita, while in Zimbabwe the cost of a PC equals about 10 times the GDP per capita (Main 2001:94). Thus, with

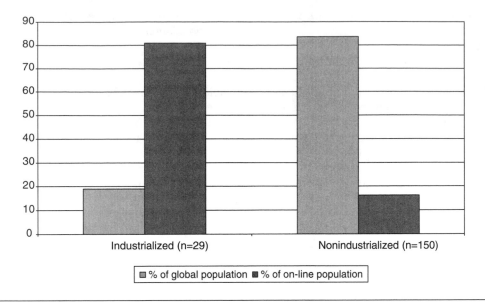

Figure 25.1   Global Internet Users, by Industrialization

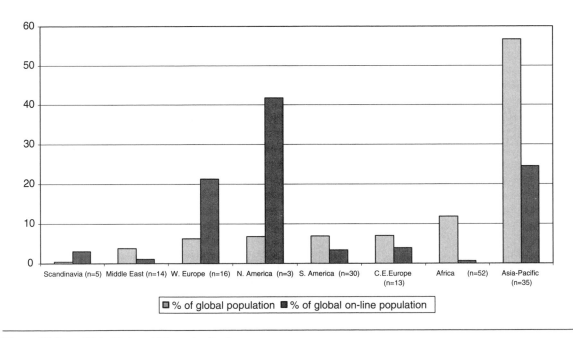

Figure 25.2   Global Internet Users, by Region

average annual income in countries with low human development equaling $US 1200, owning the cheapest Pentium III computer, costing about $US 700 in January 2001 (UNDP 2001:35, 144), is still a distant dream for most of humanity. After all, half of humanity has never even made a single phone call (World Bank 2000); hence, there are real doubts about the ability of these people to be able to use a phone system, let alone a PC, as a gateway to the Internet.

In addition to this Internet gap between developed and developing countries, great digital disparity exists also among the Western, affluent nations. Even within the group of OECD member nations, the difference among countries is dramatic: in the year 2000, for example, the number of Internet hosts per 1000 people in Finland, the United States, and Norway was 200.2, 179.1, and 193.6, respectively, whereas the ratios in other OECD member countries, such as Japan, Germany, and South Korea, were merely 49.0, 41.2, and 4.8, respectively (UNDP 2001:48). Similarly, the cost differentials in Internet dial-up costs among OECD countries ranged from about $US 90 per 30 hours in June 2000 in Belgium to $US 13 in Canada (ITU 2001:3). These differences reveal the extent of variation in Internet access, capacity, and cost even within this exclusive group of economically advanced and technologically sophisticated countries. Moreover, while Scandinavian countries rank highest in all per capita measures of Internet use, having 51.5 percent of their population on-line (NUA 2000 data in Norris 2001:47), the United States is clearly the leader: 79 percent of all Internet hosts, 59 percent of all electronic mailboxes, 54 percent of all on-line shoppers, and 38 percent of all Internet users are American. These differences among Western countries highlight the distinction between relative and absolute Internet capacity: per capita ratios and growth rates in Internet access are high in all Western countries, indicating a solid Internet basis and a rapid rate of change in Internet access across the West, yet the United States remains the distant leader because of its overwhelming absolute dominance of the Internet field. In this sense, the rapid expansion of the Internet may give the impression that "Internet laggers" may be catching up to their leaders at an astounding rate, yet currently the United States is still by far the global leader in Internet capacity and use.

These global divides in Internet capacity between the global North and South and among the wealthy Northern countries are layered over intranational disparities; in other words, as much as Internet gaps are obvious cross-nationally, similar gaps exist within nations, along social class and regional boundaries. In India, residents of the state of Uttar Pradesh, the province that is home to the technology hub Bangalore, have 68 times more Internet connections than residents of the state of Maharashtra, the home of the city of Mumbai, which is the financial and commercial capital of India and the most urbanized of the Indian states (UNDP 2001:41). This gap is even more evident when we compare Uttar Pradesh with poorer and more marginal states within India. In other places, such intranational divides in Internet access follow income divides. For example, in Israel, a nation categorized as a global hub of Internet technology and dot.com activity (UNDP 2001:45), only 19 percent of Israeli households in the lowest income percentile have computers, while in the highest income percentile, the rate of computer ownership is 92 percent (Ackerman 2001). Even in the United States, where the number of Internet users grows by more than 30 percent annually, Internet access is far from reaching all walks of life equally: only 12 percent of Americans are expected to be "e-connected" by the year 2005 (UNDP 2001:35), and currently, the disparity among American users is widening along income and resources divides (OECD 2000:86).[21]

These intranational digital divides map landscapes of urbanity (Graham 2002) and cultural capital. Even in the era of open-networking technologies, social capital is still being reproduced and social closure maintained: the disadvantaged, previously marked by their distance from the economic and cultural core (as manifested by lower income, less education, and fewer social connections than those of members of the local social elite), are currently distanced from the high-tech core and its networking nodes. These intranational divides reflect, perpetuate, and magnify the global digital divide to define layers of technological exclusion, or marginality. In other words, the global elite is leaving behind the rest of humanity, the heterogeneous group of the global "have-nots," as a result of deepening global divides.

Most important, these divides—global and national, regional and local, urban and rural—clearly identify the parameters of modern technological exclusion. Digital marginality is distinctly related to parameters of education, wealth, and professional skills, as well as to health standards and political participation. The profile of the average Internet user is a citizen of an OECD country, white, male, with professional skills and an advanced degree, younger than 35, from an urban center, and a speaker of English. A similar profile defines the average Chinese Internet user: in China, 70 percent of Internet users completed tertiary education, 84 percent are under age 35, 70 percent are male, and the residents of only two cities, Shanghai and Beijing, account for more than 60 percent of all Chinese Internet users (UNDP 2001:40). This profile, worldwide and in China, reflects the persistent connection between social characteristics and, in this case, Internet access. Even while the share of Americans[22] among on-line users worldwide dropped from 70 to 38 percent between 1995 and 2000 (Norris 2001:45), signaling the expansion of the Internet to other nationalities and other global social groups, the basic characteristics of the on-line population are still strikingly biased toward elite features: the on-line population worldwide is still unique in terms of its human resources, racial and gender composition, and social standing.

Some dimensions of the Internet divide seem, nevertheless, to be closing more quickly than others. Specifically, it seems that the divide quickest to narrow is the gender gap, marking the difference between men and women in access to the Internet. In the United States, for example, women's share among Internet users jumped from 38 percent in 1996 to 51 percent in 2000, and in Thailand from 35 percent to 49 percent in the single year 1999 to 2000 (UNDP 2000:40). This narrowing of the gender gap and the persistence of the other social dimensions of the digital divide (along racial, income, and ethnic boundaries) suggest, though, that this gender parity "catch-up" is occurring among the privileged social groups. In other words, within the elite (which tends to be the wealthy, urban, and educated group), women are closing the Internet gap with men; it is doubtful, however, whether such a catch-up is occurring within other social classes.

Interesting in particular is the intersection of the national-level dynamics of the gendered Internet divide with the global dimension. Such intersection yields more dramatic, while similar, results: it is in the poorest, least-educated, and more marginalized societies that women have the smallest share of Internet users compared with men. For example, in Ethiopia, Senegal, and Zambia women's share of Internet users is 14 percent, 17 percent, and 36 percent, respectively, and in the Arab world, women's share of Internet users is only 4 percent (Bridges.org 2002). In developing countries, where women's rights are particularly breached, women's shares of the e-connected population are extremely low; and the poorer the country is, the more distant women are from this frontier technology. In this regard, it seems, global marginality intersects with local marginality to deepen global disparities.

In summary, while the world is clearly more "wired," persistent patterns of technological marginality remain; moreover, on some social dimensions, the patterns of technological marginality are growing. Such patterns follow the contours of location, social capital, age, gender, and race. Furthermore, they are magnified yet further by the global dimension of each such social resource. Together, these layers of social divides define, if not determine, the differential access to the Internet, or technological marginality. Yet what is the allure, or appeal, of technological marginality that allowed it to rise over other dimensions of social inequality to become a call for action? How did this global Internet divide come to be conceived as a social problem requiring social attention?

CONCEIVING OF THE INTERNET GAP AS A SOCIAL PROBLEM

The Internet revolution, powered by rapid globalization, also exposed and magnified the major restructuring brought about by globalization pressures. Global Internet diffusion refocused discussions on the issue of the consequences of globalization, assessing the role of social arrangements and organizations in determining the trends and the outcomes of this technology globalization process. So, in the debates raging on the outcomes of globalization for democratization, poverty alleviation, and health care (among other issues), Internet globalization added a technological dimension to the discussions of growing global disparities. The imagery of the Internet in such discussions has, basically, two faces: technological capacity is conceived as (1) the new human capital criterion or as (2) a new form of Western imperialism.[23]

On one hand, the Internet is conceived as a hopeful vehicle for information diffusion and thus for all the social benefits that rely on greater access to free and open information sources. In this postindustrial era, when knowledge is a most precious commodity, the capacity to access the frontiers of knowledge defines the new human capital: greater prospects await those who acquire access to, and proficiency with, the Internet. Also, for developing countries, the Internet as a gateway into the information society serves as an attractive "leap-frogging" development strategy,[24] and thus barriers to its diffusion should be eliminated. Specifically, this mode of communication allows for global integration without the buildup of costly infrastructure: patients in Africa can access medical information from Scandinavia; Asian students can study in American on-line universities; and British researchers can access documents in Indian archives. In this sense, virtual institutions (hospital, university, and library) create global connections, correcting "market imperfections" in information distribution and institutional linkages. And through these connections, the Internet also provides a voice for marginalized populations to communicate their agendas and to reach widely scattered populations: Saudi dissident groups discuss their vision of a new Saudi Arabia on-line; American labor unionists communicate their strategies to local unions in Latin America through e-mail; and environmental international nongovernmental organizations (INGOs) monitor violations through e-postings by indigenous tribes from around the world. The Internet, then, serves as a community builder, allowing otherwise scattered people to communicate freely. This vision is summarized in numerous policy documents: the

Internet, they claim, sets the basis for global integration and thus development.[25]

The alternative perspective on global Internet diffusion came to label the Internet revolution as "e-mperialism," referring to an electronic form of imperialism. Here, the claim is that the Internet, through the control of its content by Westerners, is a vehicle for penetration of Western ideas and ideals. From hardware[26] to software,[27] the Internet is diffusing Western logic. And with its growing importance for global integration, the Internet is forcing indigenous cultures to surrender to its mechanics and thus to its logic. In this sense, the Internet is the most powerful, most integrated form of Western domination, combining economic pressures with cultural oppression (see Hall 1999). From this perspective, Internet gaps perpetuate already existing, and widening, development gaps. Also, such technological gaps, because they follow the contours of Western dominance, contribute to the persistent marginalization of non-Western cultures, movements, and regimes. In other words, the emerging "knowledge caste system" both reflects existing power relations (based, for example, on colonial imbalances) and maintains this global social arrangement (based, for example, on trade imbalances).

Both perspectives on global Internet diffusion, much like other discussions of global social issues,[28] conceive of the Internet divide as a problem. The two perspectives—the hopeful modernization and the condemning world system perspectives—differ, however, on what is the core problem and thus where its remedy lies. From the first perspective, Internet gaps expose market imperfections in technology diffusion, and they result in ever-growing development gaps; the remedy lies, then, in the liberalization of globalization to the extent that the Internet, and other technologies, can freely diffuse worldwide. From the second perspective, the problem lies in the persistence of social divides, in this case global and technological in nature; the remedy is, therefore, the end of Western domination over indigenous economies and cultures worldwide. Therefore, these two perspectives, while coming from distinct theoretical and policy angles, differ only a little in their perception of the Internet gap as a social problem: while the perspectives argue over the root cause—is it due to market imperfections or to social power relations?—they share an understanding that Internet diffusion is indeed a global, development-oriented social problem. This common perception made its way into the policy guidelines of various institutions, regardless of their stand on globalization, development, or technology issues. For example, the World Bank, emphasizing that the Internet has become a prerequisite for integration into the world economy and thus for economic development, argues that there exists a strong correlation between Internet capacity and foreign direct investment (World Bank 2000). Hence, argue its proglobalization experts, any lag in Internet connectivity results in further economic marginalization, for nations as well as for individuals. The same is true for the relationship between Internet connectivity and other dimensions of social development: inability to employ this technology for learning leaves already marginalized countries behind in terms of access to health information, educational resources, and political mobilization.

In summary, both perspectives see the Internet as a hopeful vehicle for global integration—either through access to useful information sources or as a voice for the disenfranchised. Therefore, both perspectives see the lack of access to this resource, or the Internet divide, as a problem of global integration. Why, then, despite their very different approaches to the social role of the Internet, do both perspectives still conceive of its diffusion path as a social problem? What is their related definition of a social problem? And what are the themes that inspire their approach to Internet gaps as a social problem?

UNDERLYING THEMES

The conceptualization of the global Internet divide as a social problem is rooted in Western, now global, culture and its emphasis on the ideals of progress and justice.[29] Modern sensitivities call for the achievement of progress[30] and justice.[31] The differential diffusion of Internet capacity is therefore defined as a gap by our hope for development and our standard of equality. And it is by these criteria—of development and of equality—that the differential access to the Internet came to be defined as a

social problem. In this sense, the identification of the global digital divide is much like the definition of, and criteria for, other social problems, such as education (Chabbott and Ramirez 2000) or the environment (Frank, Hironaka, and Schofer 2000). The common thread among these social concerns is that the definition of a global social problem is that which hinders the achievement of development and justice.

What are, then, the depictions of development and of justice? And how is the Internet interwoven with the depictions of these social goals? First, technology in general and Internet technology in particular are seen as instrumental for the achievement of national development. The Internet is conceived as a linkage mechanism or as a resource for global economic, cultural, and political integration. Such integration into the wider world has two tracks: a literal track, whereby the Internet connects people and countries to others as a mode of exchange of commodities and knowledge, and an abstract track, whereby the Internet connects people and countries to others by exchanging ideas and norms. Through either track of integration, it is assumed that the more integrated countries and people are, the more prosperous and more modern they will become. Most technology policies, therefore, refer to the Internet as a strategic resource, or a means, for development. In general, the effects of the Internet on development are mediated by the role of Internet technology as a tool of integration.[32]

Three things regarding the definition of development emerge from this taken-for-granted social role of Internet technology. First, discussions of Internet diffusion address this technology in a purely instrumental, or technical, manner. The Internet is seen as predominantly a means for enhancing modern-style development and not as a general cultural framework; in this sense, the Internet is not perceived as a Western cultural framework but rather as a means toward Western goals. Second, the Internet, because it came into the discourse of developmentalism[33] only in the late 1990s, was influenced by the policy fashions of the time and the related expansion of the definition of development from purely economic terms to broader social goals. For this reason,[34] Internet technology is perceived as affecting democratization and political participation, empowerment and rights, and health care delivery, in addition to economic prosperity.[35] Last, the belief that the Internet and development are intertwined is a taken-for-granted postulation, operating as an example of the myth of the endless utility of technological advancement (see Sarewitz 1996). This belief is not substantiated by empirical evidence demonstrating such a positive association between Internet capacity and any goals of development; not even UNDP (2001) and World Bank (2000) proclamations of such relationships offer more than anecdotal evidence of local high-tech booms, such as in India and Israel. Such anecdotal tales support the myth of the utility of technology in general and of the groundbreaking Internet technology in particular.

The second social goal interwoven with perceptions of the Internet is social justice. Justice is an accepted global norm, based on universalistic notions that human status and the related rights, privileges, and duties extend worldwide, beyond nationality, territoriality, race, gender, or other social divides. The Internet, perceived as a cutting-edge technology on which developmental benefits depend, is defined as yet another right and privilege that should be accessible for humans worldwide. The Internet is to be diffused worldwide as a basic human right; and like all human rights, it should diffuse worldwide without barriers. Specifically, the Internet's ability to empower social groups and to offer a voice for the socially marginalized, as well as its ability to bypass governmental censorship and open information channels, is also a means for the delivery of other human rights, such as the right of self-determination. This perception is sometimes made more strategic and utilitarian: because a variety of developmental benefits hinge on access to Internet technology, any barrier to the Internet is also a barrier to development. But at the same time, the broader approach to the Internet as a global social problem maintains that the universal access to this new social resource is required.

This powerful and persistent taken-for-granted belief in information and communication technology (ICT) as a means for development and for justice sets the basis for the mystique of high-tech in policy circles and in the public's opinion. Had the Internet (and ICT in general) gotten the reputation as godless entertainment—as does television, for example—it would not benefit from such broad support. Yet the mystique of ICT does not come solely from its utility, even while conceptualization and images of utility clearly mediate this process. New ICT is regarded with the same high esteem as, for example, the pharmaceutical industry;[36] however, the direct benefits from pharmaceutical advances and proliferation to global audiences are obvious and proven. Overall, then, the mystique of technology in general, while divorced from the proven performance or utility of each particular technology, is the source of the Internet's global diffusion. It is also a source for defining any diffusion barriers as a social problem, in this case, the social problem of the global digital divide.

In summary, social perception of the Internet technology frames it as both a means and a right. This perception is anchored in the modern ideals of progress and justice. Because of the reign of developmentalism (or the ideal of progress) and the premium on equality and justice, any inequality and cause of inequality are conceived as problems, for both social fabric and economic development. The global gap in Internet access is, clearly, such a dimension of inequality and a cause for further inequality, and is thus defined as a social problem. As illustrated in Figure 25.3, as technology is "filtered" through our normative "screens" of progress and justice, the utility of such technology is assessed and defined as means of progress and the rightful claim for justice. Any barrier to access to such technology is, then, a cause for conceiving of this technology as a global social problem, even if such barriers are a mere reflection of persistent social, nontechnological barriers. Here, again, the mystique of high-tech propels it as a social problem further than other social resources that are also influenced by our desire for development and our concern with inequality. For example, recent "education for all" global initiatives do not enjoy the intense public attention, nor the catchy title, given to the global digital divide, from front-page coverage in central newspapers to street demonstrations. It seems, then, that the global digital divide is accompanied by a missionary tone, promoting the proliferation of Internet technology in terms of modern-day salvation, namely progress and justice.

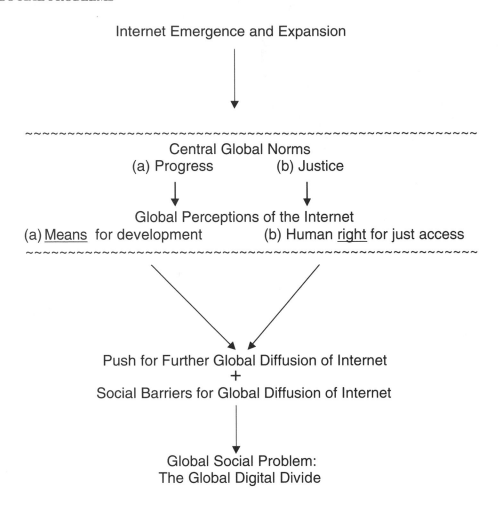

Internet Emergence and Expansion

~~~~~~

Central Global Norms
(a) Progress   (b) Justice

Global Perceptions of the Internet
(a) Means for development   (b) Human right for just access

~~~~~~

Push for Further Global Diffusion of Internet
+
Social Barriers for Global Diffusion of Internet

Global Social Problem:
The Global Digital Divide

Figure 25.3   Conceiving of the Internet as a Global Social Problem: The Process

Contributing to this social commotion around the global digital divide are the "experts" who are growing in numbers as well as in social reverence. The definition of the Internet gap as a social problem is consolidated through the work of professionals and the growing number of organizations that are seen as expert, or professional, voices. Together, development professionals and other "moral entrepreneurs" solidify the concern with global gaps, particularly technology gaps. And international organizations, offering learned or scientized agendas and the resources for their implementation, institutionalize the definition of the Internet gap as a social problem, both by calling attention to its existence and offering prescribed policy remedies to it. One such locus of expertise and moral entrepreneurship, as mentioned earlier, is the Global Forum: in its Naples 2001 meeting, the interest in governance focused on the application of Internet technologies to the promotion of e-governance. Similarly, UNDP's 2001 *Human Development Report,* focusing on technological disparities, supports the institutionalization of the global digital divide as a global social problem and raises the Internet to higher consciousness as a core issue in development policymaking. Most important, through its texts and dense descriptions of trends, social effects, and policy implications, UNDP defines this as an urgent social matter and anchors it in developmentalism. Other international organizations take this social role even when the issues or remedies do not relate directly to their core agendas. For example, the Union of International Associations (UIA),[37] while having *none* of its members list the global digital divide among their main goals or themes, posts elaborate texts about it as a global social problem. In its detailed directories, UIA describes not only the global digital divide as a global social problem but also its many layered dimensions: computer illiteracy, elitist control of information technology, lack of Internet access, and informational obstacles to world trade are listed among its "world problems," while among its remedial strategies, UIA lists increasing Internet access, using the Internet for development, providing public computer centers, and connecting schools to the Internet.[38] Overall, then, such expert-supported (not to say initiated) perception of this newly fashioned social divide consolidates a global social movement of sorts and imprints social policy and action worldwide, adding the missionary tone of developmentalism to an otherwise technical agenda.

A CALL FOR POLICY AND ACTION: FROM TECH CAPACITY TO SOCIAL AGENDA

Worldwide policies are initiated, and action is taken to address the issue of differential Internet capacity. Conceiving of social policy to remedy this Internet gap came in parallel, if not as a response, to its definition as a social problem. And even in the short duration of its public attention, the framing of the global Internet gap as a social problem changed the policy response from focusing on technical capacity to addressing a wide social agenda.

Solutions to the technical dimension of this problem looked more like corporate strategy and state planning than like social reforms. For example, for high-tech corporations to locate production sites outside the United States, they relied on reviews of various countries' ICT capacities, and this led to governments addressing their nations' relative technology capacity rankings. Governments regarded the ICT gap as a national human capital problem, addressed mostly through higher-education reforms to respond to human resources needs of potential foreign direct investors. Such is the case of Intel's entry into Costa Rica in 1998: the combination of two development strategies (human capital and foreign direct investment) and the combination of two national forces (the Costa Rican government and a private sector foundation) transformed the image of Costa Rica from a "banana republic" to "Silicon Valley South" and lured Intel to establish a local plant there. Throughout this process of strategizing national and corporate developments, high-tech is repeatedly framed as a capacity measure: technical education is declared a national human capital (Kendall 2002). Other governments also labored to make their countries attractive to corporate ICT expansion and through it to have their goals of national economic development benefit from ICT globalization.[39] For example, governments worldwide invested heavily in creating ICT hubs and in identifying such hubs as "Silicon-Valley-like." This desire to link with, even imitate, Silicon Valley's success is most apparent in the choice of names for the new ICT hubs: Israel's "Silicon Wadi"[40] and Cambridge's (United Kingdom) "Silicon fen" make the references to the Mecca of ICT prosperity, the American Silicon Valley, rather obvious.[41]

Governments worldwide rushed to integrate their countries' interests into the corporate, yet global, strategizing. Such strategizing reflects a global division of labor: it allocates corporate headquarters and venture capital to core countries (primarily the United States and Scandinavia), whereas R&D and production units are located in the semiperiphery (India, Taiwan, Israel, and Ireland, but also Brazil and South Africa). All these semiperipheral ICT hubs also have strong diasporic contacts to Silicon Valley, the global ICT capital (see Saxenian 2000).

The Indian government, hoping to capitalize on the success of its high-tech diaspora (or "brain drain"), initiated a special bond issuance to nonresident Indians. Similarly, the government of Israel was quick to establish an economic attaché to Silicon Valley in an effort to use the "Israeli tribe" in Silicon Valley to strengthen its home ICT sector. Overall, corporate and governmental labor planning is what guides the approach toward global differences in Internet capacity.

Despite the dominance of the econocentric themes set by the "Washington consensus" institutions, current formulations of ICT policy—whether national, international, or transnational—clearly reflect an additional tone. As the dedication of the Naples 2001 meeting of the Third Global Forum to e-governance implies, the Internet is now considered within a broader range of social consequences, in addition to economic benefits of dot.com advances. The consequences of Internet capacity (and hence ramifications of the lack of such capacity) are recognized as ranging from income to democratization to health, and from agriculture to education to law. It is now understood, therefore, that policy decisions regarding the Internet gap should address infrastructural issues (from education to civil engineering); immigration and "brain drain" issues (from "push" forces for migrants to incentives for returning nationals); racial, ethnic, and gender policies (from support and integration to cultural preservation); as well as the initial impetus toward economic and financial planning (from tax breaks to socially responsible corporations to encouraging foreign direct investment).

With this transition from a labor-planning approach to a social agenda approach also came public policies to tackle these connections between the Internet gap and its various social consequences. To provide Internet access to low-income populations, the Brazilian government, for example, funds a university-sponsored project to produce cheap yet powerful PCs, priced at about $300. Similarly, to bypass the costly buildup of line telephone connections, technology for wireless Internet access was developed, partly with Indian governmental support (UNDP 2001:98). This technology, now available in numerous developing countries, offers publicly funded alternatives to the profitability considerations of multinationals.

The precise timing of the transition in policy themes regarding the Internet gap is difficult to identify, mostly because of the short time period that has passed since the Internet revolution. Despite this difficulty, the change in tone is clear: the Internet gap ceased to be a matter of corporate strategy and human resource planning and became a wide-scale social concern. In some sense, the change of tone regarding global Internet disparities parallels recent amendments to other social policy issues: a move away from a focus solely on economic development as the ultimate social goal and toward a broad understanding of what social development means, including parameters of social justice. Addressing the Internet gap became, then, a cause of global civil advocacy.

In terms of public policy, however, there exist a variety of paths for closing the Internet gap, without a single such solution emerging as the preferred model for success. Governments, therefore, struggle to adjudicate among such diverging policy paths as promoting industry-university R&D cooperation, sponsoring programs to expand access (such as computers in all schools and libraries), or encouraging privatization of communication markets. It is also unclear from these public policies whether the social problem of the Internet gap is a problem of social inequality or of technology. In other words, it is unclear whether the proposed "solutions" lie (1) in encouraging social equality on multiple social dimensions or (2) in making technology diffusion more efficient. In this sense, policies are undecided and vague as to whether the measures taken to remedy the problem should (1) promote expanded access to the Internet, as with other social resources, by tackling social barriers or (2) support the technical advancement of the Internet to ease its proliferation. Overall, therefore, policies that address the digital divide lack focus in their conceptualization of the Internet's role as well as in their proposed measures to close the gap in access to it.

The Global Internet Divide as a Platform for Social Research

The lack of focus on the part of policies to close the Internet gap calls for further social research and assessment on this issue. In fact, current policy "solutions" do not even identify whether the root of this gap is social or technical in nature. Here, social science research can offer great help by investigating potential tracks of policy, assessing policy effectiveness, and offering deeper understanding of social priorities. Specifically, social science research can assist by addressing the following research directions.

Identify trends on multiple indicators of capacity, access, and cost. Currently, consensus exists in the literature neither on indicators (and their quality) nor on trends (convergence or divergence, widening or closing of the gap), despite a growing availability of cross-national measures of ICT capacity.

Identify the characteristics of the Internet divide and its trajectory, pointing to specific outcomes of this global technology divide. In this research direction, the global Internet gap is seen as both a dependent variable (or an outcome) and an independent variable (or a source) of social conditions. In such analyses, the role of various social institutions (governments, corporations, nongovernmental organizations, and social movements) should be considered. And such analyses may also reflect the various "levels" of the Internet divide: global, global-regional, national, and intranational regional.

Consider the institutional features of such trends of expansion, specifically decoupling among various dimensions of ICT policy and trends of cross-national isomorphism. Studies of science globalization suggest that these institutional features are prevalent in the particular social fields of science and technology diffusion: encouraged to do so by international science-and-development organizations, countries rush to adopt some science practices (such as establishing agencies for science-and-technology policy coordination) yet fail to follow up such policy initiatives with actual scientific work (expanding science education programs in school or sponsoring more R&D), thus establishing a decoupled, or fragmented, national science field (see Drori et al. 2003). Applied specifically to the case of ICT globalization, the puzzle is not the trend of Internet expansion per se, but rather the correspondence (1) among types of ICT or (2) between policy initiatives and policy results.

Offer policy assessment of the role of ICT in the achievement of social progress worldwide. Here,

social scientists should contemplate, among other issues, the role of the state and intergovernmental organizations in technology globalization. Specifically, assessment is needed on whether public policy offers better solutions to the problem of the global digital divide than, for example, social networks (such as the case of diasporic communities). Another issue to consider is the role that the private sector can, and should, take in global technology diffusion.

CONCLUDING COMMENTS

The Naples antiglobalization riots of 2001 clearly dramatized global concern with the digital divide. Violent and vocal as they were, these riots gave the impression that there are two sides to this debate, presumably con and pro, on the issue of global Internet disparities. This is, however, greatly misleading: actually, all are in complete agreement. Even among the warring sides of the globalization debate, there is a clear agreement on the fact that a great gap exists between countries and between world regions in access to information and communication technology. And all agree that such a gap in access and use of the Internet is harmful to humanity because it impedes social development and perpetuates global injustices. In this sense, all "sides" agree about the ultimate goal of Internet proliferation, namely, more equitable and far-reaching social development. The point of disagreement is, surprisingly, only on the *means* to achieve such a goal: should the world unite around neoliberal themes and let market forces guide the process of Internet globalization, or rather, should technology diffusion be guided by direct social policy to bridge the technology gap?

In this sense, global discussions of the Internet gap and of the broader issue of the global digital divide add only a few issues to the existing list of issues and policies of global development and technology. As has been the case for a long while, policy discussions revolve around the means to achieve an undisputed social goal, and disagreements arise along ideological divides. In all such discussions, the dominant discursive themes are, as mentioned earlier, progress and justice; in all such discussions, technology, here the Internet, is conceived as a means for achieving these undisputed social goals. This brings up the question: what's new about Internet technology? Is the Internet a revolutionary technology deserving special policies and a fresh approach? Or is it merely the latest in a series of modern technologies directed at boosting development? Clearly, the rapid rate of Internet diffusion sets it apart from any other human technology. Nevertheless, some comparisons are made between the Internet and early modern communication technology, such as the telegraph (Standage 1998). Both these "old" and "new" communication technologies enable individuals and businesses to expedite relations and contacts, thus altering human perception of time and space by condensing these dimensions. In this sense, the Internet is also comparable to breakthroughs in transportation technology, such as the railroad: similar to the pattern of communication technologies, the railroad connected places that were previously far apart, creating nodes of contacts and establishing hubs for the network.

If these similarities among the various technologies are significant, they have implications for the trajectory of the current gap in global Internet capacity; if Internet diffusion is to follow the path of old ICTs, then one can expect a growing diversification of the on-line population and hence a narrowing of the access gap over time. Moreover, considering the rapid rate of Internet diffusion, the narrowing of this "new" technology gap may be quicker than the rate of "old" technologies. This "normalization hypothesis" emphasizes the inevitable closing of social access gaps over time.[42] Its proponents often accuse the media of mythologizing a social gap that is soon to be closed, like technology divides before it (Powell 2001). The opposing view of this diffusion trajectory notes that while the rapid narrowing of the Internet gap may be the view from the United States, clearly the pace of technology adoption is much slower in other world regions, even among other OECD or European Union countries.[43]

These persistent international gaps in capacity, even among the affluent countries, raise the question of the Internet's contribution to solving problems of development. Specifically, are ICTs more crucial to development than other technologies, such as health-related, agricultural, or civil engineering

technology? This is of particular importance in poor and developing countries that face the frustrating dilemma of adjudicating among urgent social problems and among dwindling public funds. While great emphasis has been put on the Internet as the key to providing new-age social and economic development and while great funds are allocated to address this social gap, there is no clear evidence that greater Internet capacity yields development to help countries in making these decisions.

The most important dimension of the global Internet divide is, in my opinion, the problem of layered inequality: global divides layered upon national differences; national upon regional; regional upon racial, ethnic, and gender divides, as well as upon education, age, and language skill characteristics. Socially marginalized groups are now also disenfranchised from this new technological frontier; the poor in developing countries, and especially those in rural areas or women and minorities in these countries, are at a great (social) distance from the presumably boundaryless technology of the Internet. This layered inaccessibility of the Internet clearly perpetuates previously existing social inequality; "virtual" (or on-line) inequalities come to reflect "real-life" inequalities (Luke 1998). But more important, this layered inaccessibility of the Internet also works to further expand inequality, adding dimensions of inequality (digital upon income and education) and of social differentiation (transnational upon urban/rural and male/female).

This layered inequality is clearly not "virtual"; rather, it is solidified, or materialized, through the institutionalization of global ICT hubs. Such hubs, only 46 locations worldwide, are local enclaves (regions within nations); specifically, all these global technology hubs, other than the two small nations of Israel and Singapore, trace the boundaries of global cities (see UNDP 2001:45; also Hillner 2000).[44] These technology hubs/global cities are separate from their national context, revealing patterns of global elitism; they identify horizontal networks of manufacturing, as well as trace patterns of consumption, culture, and standard of living. They, therefore, have more in common with other technology hubs from around the world than with their own nations and neighboring cities. For example, while Bangalore is identified as one such global ICT hub,

India ranks at the lower global end of UNDP's 2001 technology achievement index: simultaneously, Bangalore is a global center for ICT activity, and India's general population has an average 5.1 years of education and an adult literacy rate of only 44 percent (UNDP 2001:3). The geography of high-tech identifies cities, rather than nations and global regions, as centers of activity. In this sense, the global digital divide extends global social gaps to new dimensions and forms a new geography of global, transnational social inequality. This form of transnational elitism, or "e-litism," challenges the accepted notions of social order and affiliation: national sovereignty, national identity, and national cohesion are left to be reconsidered.

Notes

1. The global digital divide refers to global disparities in access to information and communication technology (ICT). In this chapter, I focus specifically on one such ICT, namely the Internet. This focus simplified the arguments: it avoids the collapsing of various ICTs (from telephones to satellite to PCs), as well as various dimensions of these technologies (from infrastructural issues such as electricity and technological literacy, to period-specific issues such as the dating of the technology's birth, to utilization issues such as cost) onto a single cast.

2. Defense Advanced Research Projects Agency, the central R&D organization of the American Department of Defense.

3. The first network operating with Interface Message Processors (IMPs).

4. For a more detailed history of the development of the Internet, naming the various scientists involved in its various stages of progress, see The Internet Society's narratives, at http://www.isoc.org/internet/history/brief.shtml.

5. Meaning that the network is linking multiple independent networks through an arbitrary design and does not force a protocol or technology upon them.

6. Quoted in the Internet Society's narrative of the development of the Internet; see http://www.isoc.org/internet/history/brief.shtml#Initial_Concepts.

7. The first popular graphic interface for the World Wide Web.

8. See Berners-Lee's (1999) tale of the invention of the World Wide Web.

9. ITU updates are available on http://www.itu.int/ITU-D/ict/statistics/at_glance/Internet01.pdf and http://www.itu.int/ITU-D/ict/statistics/at_glance/KeyTelecom99.html.

10. Meaning an independent Internet node with an Internet Protocol (IP) address. Hosts are labeled by a 32-byte numerical sequence (sectioned into 4 groups, divided by periods); they appear as, for example, 01.23.456.789. Each host also has a URL (Uniform, or Universal, Resource Locator) Internet address, used in hypertext, which are the familiar "http://www.," and so forth, addresses.

For clarification of other Internet terms, see any one of the various Internet glossaries listed on http://www.isoc.org/internet/links/glossaries.shtml.

11. From 72,004,971 to 141,382,198; see http://www.itu.int/ITU-D/ict/statistics/at_glance.

12. From 9.1 per 1,000 people to 98.1.

13. Organization for Economic Cooperation and Development, which groups 30 developed countries that share commitments to democratic government and market economy.

14. Gigabytes per second, a measure of capacity of data transfer per unit of time for digital systems. See also Endnote 10.

15. Comprising both ISP price (fee collected by the Internet service provider for access through its service) and phone charges (for accessing the ISP).

16. This figure of speech, portraying the "escape" of potential users despite the increasing density of this communication network and its reaches, has been used repeatedly to describe the failure of the digital revolution to reach the general population. It became prevalent after being offered as the title of a series of reports by the U.S. National Telecommunications and Information Administration: the 1995 report was titled "Falling through the Net: A Survey of the 'Have-Nots' in Rural and Urban America," and the 1999 report was titled "Falling through the Net: Defining the Digital Divide."

17. Data for these Figures are adapted from Norris (2001:46).

18. Bandwidth measures the capacity of the network to transmit data within a fixed time unit; for example, for digital systems, it quantifies the number of bytes per second. It thus appraises the ability of the network to operate multiple major tasks: to serve multiple users, to transfer great amounts of data, and to execute these tasks simultaneously. Again, for clarification of other Internet terms, see any one of the various Internet glossaries listed on http://www.isoc.org/internet/links/glossaries.shtml.

19. Meaning purchasing both a PC to serve as a gateway to the Internet and also all the networking gear.

20. Fees such as the cost of a telephone call to access the ISP and the subscription fee to the ISP.

21. The impact of intranational factors on the global Internet divide is implied in the finding that even countries that are similar in global standing and resources (such as Britain and Luxembourg or Malaysia and Vietnam) differ greatly in the rate of Internet diffusion to their population (see Norris 2001:66, 79). For a preliminary comparative investigation of the national characteristics that explain this Internet gap among otherwise similar countries, see Drori and Jang (2003).

22. Noted to be still marked as highly educated, wealthy, male, and from an urban center.

23. As discussed in depth later in this chapter, the globalization of technology and the resulting global digital divide have an impact on a whole host of social issues: technological diffusion—and divides—shape the prospects of democratization, health, and agriculture advances, governance social welfare reforms, as well as industrialization and trade. The breadth of the social consequences of global technological diffusion and divides therefore stands in sharp contrast to the limited scope of the current discussions of this process, as revealed in this section. This juxtaposition exposes the gap between imagery and perception, on one hand, and real effects, on the other.

24. Suggesting that developing countries can catch up with developed countries by skipping over developmental stages.

25. Offering a typical policy proclamation, a World Bank document declares, "A global society is emerging with pervasive information capacities that make it substantially different from an industrial society; much more competitive, more democratic, less centralized, less stable, more able to address individual needs and friendlier to the environment" (World Bank, cited in Main 2001:95).

26. Through, for example, the Latin-character-based features of computer keyboards.

27. Through the Internet's insidious reliance on English as its core language.

28. For example, the special issue of *Social Problems* (Vol. 48, No. 4, 2001) devoted to globalization and social problems considers a great variety of issues—inequality, environmental policies in the World Bank, migration flows, and female genital cutting—as social problems.

29. For extensive discussions of these twin pillars of Western, now global, society, see Meyer, Boli, and Thomas (1987) and Meyer, Thomas, and Ramirez (1997).

30. Taken to mean collective development, or accumulation of resources, measured mainly in economic terms.

31. Interpreted as fairness and equality in terms of access to social resources, if not in terms of outcomes.

32. Like the public approach toward scientific advances (see Drori et al. 2003), the perception of utility is mixed with a fear of its destructive consequences. This is clearly the underlying tone in the discussion of "genetically modified food or FrankenFood"; it also applied to the mixing of the Internet's empowering benefits with the fear of its invasive and omnipresent penetration. This is an expression of the "good vs. bad" debate in regard to technological progress.

33. For descriptions of the discursive regime of developmentalism and analyses of its constitution and its effects, see Escobar (1983, 1995) and Ferguson (1990).

34. And therefore unlike policies of science, education, or earlier technologies, which were embedded in a narrowly conceived discourse of development.

35. Although I emphasize the subordination of the Internet discussions to developmentalism, these discursive regimes are, in fact, mutually supportive. The faith in the benefits of technology is one of the main factors shaping developmentalism and its policy plans (Escobar 1995:32, 35–6).

36. The evenhanded approach to both the Internet and pharmaceutical advances as critical for human development is evident in, for example, the approach of the UNDP. UNDP's *Human Development Report of 2001,* titled "Making New Technologies Work for Human Development," focuses solely on information technologies and pharmaceutical developments as the critical knowledge-based advances required for improving human conditions worldwide.

37. UIA is an international association of all transnational organizations. Its directories list organizations by their core themes or goals and by their national locations and offer biographical and contact information about each member organization. Such directories have served to map various global organizational fields, from development to population control to science, both governmental and nongovernmental (see Boli and Thomas 1999; Diehl 1997).

38. See http://www.db.uia.org/scripts/sweb.dll.

39. In all such governmental policy statements, ICT globalization is referred to as attracting foreign direct investment. In the heydays of the "Washington consensus," this label obviously became more palatable to development strategists.

40. *Wadi* is the Israeli Arab language word for a creek, which also sounds like "valley."

41. The crisis of the American high-tech sector, or the "dot.com bust," exposes the myth-like features of this fascination with Silicon-Valley-styled development. It seems that countries worldwide rushed to imitate American high-tech and to connect themselves to this global Internet core, while much of its development is now claimed to be overestimated, or inflated. The motivation for such imitation is therefore not necessarily the actual performance of

Internet investments in terms of development, but rather the taken-for-granted belief that the Internet is the source for development.

42. See Resnick (1998); Schement (2001:305); Norris (2001:70–6).

43. This opposition to the "normalization thesis" does not, however, claim that Internet technology is any different than previous ICTs.

44. On the issue of global cities and their dislocation from their national, geopolitical, and cultural context, see Sassen (2001).

REFERENCES

Ackerman, Gwen. 2001. "Israel's Internet Don Quixote." *Jerusalem Post* (Digital Israel Section), June 5. Also available at http://www.jpost.com/Editions/2001/06/03/Digital/Digital.27401.html>.

Berners-Lee, Tim with Mark Fischetti. 1999. *Weaving the Web: The Original Design and Ultimate Destiny of the World Wide Web by Its Inventor.* San Francisco, CA: Harper.

Boli, John and George M. Thomas, eds. 1999. *Constructing World Culture: International Nongovernmental Organizations Since 1875.* Stanford, CA: Stanford University Press.

Bridges.Org. 2000. Retrieved from http://www.bridges.org/spanning/chpt2.html.

Chabbott, Colette and Francisco O. Ramirez. 2000. "Development and Education." Pp. 163–87 in *Handbook of Sociology of Education,* edited by M. T. Hallinan. New York: Kluwer.

Compaine, Benjamin M. 2001. "Declare the War Won." Pp. 315–35 in *The Digital Divide: Facing a Crisis or Creating a Myth?* edited by Benjamin M. Compaine. Cambridge, MA: MIT Press.

Diehl, Paul F., ed. 1997. *The Politics of Global Governance: International Organizations in an Interdependent World.* Boulder, CO: Lynne Rienner.

DiMaggio, Paul, Eszter Hargittai, W. Russell Neuman, and John P. Robinson. 2001. "Social Implications of the Internet." *Annual Review of Sociology* 27: 307–36.

Drori, Gili S. and Yong Suk Jang. 2003. "The Global Digital Divide: A Sociological Assessment of Trends and Causes." *Social Science Computer Review* 21 (3):144–61.

Drori, Gili S., John W. Meyer, Francisco O. Ramirez, and Evan Schofer. 2003. *Science in the Modern World Polity: Institutionalization and Globalization.* Stanford, CA: Stanford University Press.

Escobar, Arturo. 1983. *Power, Knowledge, and Discourse as Domination: The Formation of Development Discourse, 1945–1955.* Paris, France: UNESCO.

——. 1995. *Encountering Development: The Making and Unmaking of the Third World.* Princeton, NJ: Princeton University Press.

Ferguson, James. 1990. *The Anti-Politics Machine: "Development," Depoliticization, and Bureaucratic Power in Lesotho.* Cambridge, England: Cambridge University Press.

Frank, David J., Ann Hironaka, and Evan Schofer. 2000. "Environmental Protection as a Global Institution." *American Sociological Review* 65:122–27.

Graham, S. 2002. "Bridging Urban Digital Divides? Urban Polarization and Information and Communication Technology." *Urban Studies* 39 (1):33–56.

Hall, M. 1999. "Virtual Colonialism." *Journal of Material Culture* 4 (1):39–55.

Hillner, Jennifer. 2000. "Venture Capitals." *Wired* Issue 8.07, 7 August. Retrieved from http://www.wired.com/wired/archive/8.07/silicon.html.

International Telecommunications Union (ITU). 2001. "Numbering Cyberspace: Recent Trends in the Internet World." Telecommunication Indicators Update, January/February/March 2001. Retrieved from http://www.itu.int/ITU-D/ict/statistics.

Kendall, Megan. 2002. *A Whale in a Swimming Pool: High Technology as a Strategy for National Development in Costa Rica.* Unpublished undergraduate honors thesis, Stanford University, CA.

Luke, Timothy W. 1998. "The Politics of Digital Inequality: Access, Capacity and Distribution in Cyberspace." Pp. 120–42 in *The Politics of Cyberspace,* edited by Chris Toulouse and Timothy W. Luke. New York and London: Routledge.

Main, Linda. 2001. "The Global Information Infrastructure: Empowerment or Imperialism?" *Third World Development* 22 (1):83–97.

Meyer, John W., John Boli, and George Thomas. 1987. "Ontology and Rationalization in the Western Cultural Account." Pp. 12–37 in *Institutional Structure: Constituting State, Society, and the Individual,* edited by George M. Thomas, John W. Meyer, Francisco O. Ramirez, and John Boli. Newbury Park, CA: Sage.

Meyer, John W., John Boli, George Thomas, and Francisco O. Ramirez. 1997. "World Society and the Nation-State." *American Journal of Sociology* 103:144–81.

Norris, Pipa. 2001. *Digital Divide: Civic Engagement, Information Poverty, and the Internet Worldwide.*

Cambridge, England: Cambridge University Press.

Organization for Economic Cooperation and Development. 2000. *Information Technology Outlook.* Paris, France: Author.

Powell, Adam Clayton, III. 2001. "Falling for the Gap: Whatever Happened to the Digital Divide?" Pp. 309–14 in *The Digital Divide: Facing a Crisis or Creating a Myth?* edited by Benjamin M. Compaine. Cambridge, MA: MIT Press.

Resnick, David. 1998. "Politics on the Internet: The Normalization of Cyberspace." Pp. 48–68 in *The Politics of Cyberspace,* edited by Chris Toulouse and Timothy W. Luke. New York: Routledge.

Sarewitz, Daniel. 1996. *Frontiers of Illusion: Science, Technology, and the Politics of Progress.* Philadelphia, PA: Temple University Press.

Sassen, Saskia. 2001. *The Global City: New York, London, Tokyo.* Princeton, NJ: Princeton University Press.

Saxenian, AnnaLee. 2000. "The Bangalore Boom: From Brain Drain to Brain Circulation?" In *Bridging the Digital Divide: Lessons from India,* edited by Kenneth Kenniston and Deepak Kumar. Bangalore, India: National Institute of Advanced Study.

Schement, Jorge Reina. 2001. "Of Gaps by Which Democracy We Measure." Pp. 303–307 in *The Digital Divide: Facing a Crisis or Creating a Myth?* edited by Benjamin M. Compaine. Cambridge, MA: MIT Press.

Standage, Tom. 1998. *The Victorian Internet.* New York: Walker.

United Nations Development Programme. 2001. *Human Development Report 2001: Making New Technologies Work for Human Development.* New York: Author.

——. 2002. *Human Development Report 2001: Deepening Democracy in a Fragmented World.* New York: Author.

World Bank. 2000. *World Development Indicators* [CD-Rom]. Retrieved from http://www.worldbank.org/data/wdi/index.htm.

RISK

JOHN TULLOCH

Cardiff University and Charles Sturt University

*R*isk is an endemic term in international media and communication systems. A short Google Web search at the time of writing gives me, among many other examples, the following: "Mapping malaria risk in Africa," "Millions of Eritreans risk famine. The crops are failing," "14.5 million people in southern Africa at risk of starvation, half of them in Zimbabwe," "A *Generation at Risk* reveals the staggering dimensions of the AIDS epidemic in sub-Saharan Africa," "Millions at risk in Afghan crisis," "The risk of inadvertent nuclear use between India and Pakistan," "Asia-Pacific countries at risk from mismanaged oceans," "Most of Southeast Asia's reefs at risk from overfishing, pollution," "Europe at risk from hepatitis outbreak," "Mothers and newborns at risk in Kosovo crisis," "Russia's nuclear risk: securing the world's largest stockpile of nuclear warheads in the former Soviet Union," "Australia at high risk of attack. . . . TERRORISM STRIKES HOME" "The ozone hole above Antarctica has divided into two parts," "Scientists worry about global warming impacts on Antarctica's emperor penguins as their population drops 50 percent due to warming trend reducing sea ice," "Earth crash. Documenting the collapse of a dying planet. Researchers find trash floating across world's oceans . . . warn Antarctica is at particular risk for the disruption of non-native species."

Potential tourists frequently search the Web for risk information. So, if I seek out "risk" in Argentina on Google, I read that car accidents are the leading cause of death to travellers, 60 percent of country areas have endemic Chagas's Disease "associated with sleeping in adobe-style huts and houses that harbour the night-bit triatomid (assassin) bug," cholera is active in the country, the human prevalence of Echinococcosis is among the highest reported worldwide, drinking water outside main cities may be contaminated, hepatitis B associated with unsafe sex is a risk to tourists, Leishmaniasis (associated with sandfly bites) is a risk in the northern third of the country, malaria "is year-round in country areas," typhoid fever vaccination is "recommended for travellers venturing outside of tourist areas," and there is a "potential risk of yellow fever in northeastern forested areas." Similarly, concerning Australia, I read that motor vehicle accidents are the leading cause of death among travellers under 55, and I am warned about snakes and spiders (especially the deadly funnel web), saltwater crocodile risks in the Northern Territory, Dengue Fever in Northern Queensland and Torres Strait Islands (with areas of "greatest risk along the coast from Carnavon to Port Darwin to Towns Peak"), giardiasis, which is "endemic in Tasmania and poses a risk to visitors," hepatitis A "endemic at low levels," marine hazards ("the box jellyfish, the most dangerous jellyfish in the world, and also the sea wasp are found in northern coastal waters"), Queensland tick typhus, which "has been reported in travellers to northern beaches of Sydney Harbour," and that "outbreaks of Australian encephalitis . . . occur annually," particularly in Western Australia, Victoria, and South Australia.

Even a quick glance at these different Web constructions of risk begins to indicate different rhetorical postures according to the genre that I have searched for: for example, the cataclysmic language of environmentalist risk ("documenting the collapse of a dying planet"), the humanitarian focus on huge numbers in "third world" famine stories ("14.5 million people in southern Africa at risk of starvation"), and the more "controlled" genre of tourist risk communication (which attempts to domesticate potential "wild zones," while leaving spaces like Kosovo to a different genre of "post-conflict recovery" risk discourse). And there are, of course, many other areas of risk communication discourse, such as financial risk and risk management, health risk, terrorism and "weapons of mass destruction," and so on.

It would take a different study to explore the rhetorical differences in public communication constructions of risk discourse. For example, it is immediately apparent that the tourist risk communication genre offers a map and a chronology, positioning the potential tourist in a position of individual agency that does not exist in environmentalist risk rhetoric ("Severe air pollution exists in Santiago, especially during the winter months, May through August"). When and where to travel is then seen as a matter of choice insofar as, my Google site also tells me, "On a conceptual level risk characterization is very simple, consisting of the bringing together of two risk components, *hazard* and *exposure*. Risk assessment is bringing together the probabilities of hazard and exposure to produce an understanding of the likelihood of some type of adverse outcome." Put simply, if, as a tourist, you do not want the risk of dying

within minutes from the sting of an Australia box jellyfish *(hazard),* avoid swimming outside protective nets *(exposure)* in the ocean in northern Australia during the summer months.

But my emphasis in this chapter is less on the differences within public discourses of risk and, rather, on *differences in academic risk discourse where commentators observe that public risk communication is endemic* to the extent of becoming the "new public sphere" and a defining mark of "late-" or "post-" or "risk-" modernity itself.

Over the last decade, risk discourse has become an increasingly salient issue in social scientific research, and here the "very simple" definitions of risk (as in public risk discourse above) have increasingly been put at stake. In a recent article, Asa Boholm notes the vast recent proliferation of risk research in European and U.S research organizations, in new peer-reviewed journals, in conferences, in an increasing flow of books on the topic of risk, and in contributions on risk research from a range of disciplines including geography, economics, sociology, political science, and psychology (Boholm 2002).

Quite apart from the rush of recent books on "risk society" itself, the potency of the *concept* of risk is also indicated by the fact that even in recent books that foreground a different name for current modernity, as in David Lyons's *Surveillence Society: Monitoring Everyday Life* (2001), Jock Young's *The Exclusive Society* (1999), or Frank Furedi's *Culture of Fear: Risk-Taking and the Morality of Low Expectation* (2002), risk plays a central role.

RISK AGENDA
SETTING: DEFINING THE FIELD

Like Boholm, a number of commentators emphasise the different development of risk-defining research in the United States and Europe. In *Risk in the Modern Age,* Maurie J. Cohen (2000) describes two "schools" of risk research: on one hand, the American school, stressing "pragmatism over ideology," with a tendency to site-specific empirical case studies as "social problems" and with "an insufficiently robust theoretical core that could link it to broader sociological and social scientific currents"

(p. 15), and on the other, the European work associated with "the emergence of Green Parties in many European countries, most particularly . . . in Germany, and further prompted by wider sociological interest in 'new social movements'" (particularly noting here the influence of Ulrich Beck's "risk society" work; p. 13). Cohen argues that this European work is "grounded in a much stronger theoretical tradition" that draws heavily "on the sociology of science and sociology of scientific knowledge . . . characterized by a strong social constructivist perspective. Inherent in this view is an emphasis on social interpretation and the dismissal of biophysical facts" (p. 13).

But Cohen's U.S./European "school" dichotomy is clearly only one way of representing the current research field. Piet Strydom (2002), in his book *Risk, Environment and Society,* for example, speaks of Beck and Luhmann as "the two major contemporary theoretical directions in the social scientific field of risk, environment and society" (p. 69) and hardly mentions major U.S. risk scholars, for example, from the Harvard Center for Risk Analysis. Yet it is the case that Beck's work in Europe and John D. Graham's Harvard group research has been very influential, and in a longer account, I would want to compare symptomatic books such as Beck's *Risk Society* and Graham and Wiener's *Risk vs. Risk: Tradeoffs in Protecting Health and the Environment* (1995) to examine not only the differences of critical assumption but also potentials for synergy that Cohen is looking for.

So, on one hand, we note that there is much that is typical of current *U.S.-modernity* underpinning *Risk vs. Risk,* including the emphasis of the importance of "market demand for risk reduction" (Graham and Wiener 1995:40); an undiminished (compared with Beck) belief in scientific research and technological change in playing "perhaps the fundamental role . . . in risk reduction" (Graham and Wiener 1995:39); and consequently a continuing emphasis on the leading role of "quantitative factors estimated by technocrats" such as the Harvard risk researchers themselves (Graham and Wiener 1995:270). It is clear from the optimistic hope in *Risk vs. Risk* that science will produce a "risk-superior" state ("reducing overall risk rather than trading one kind for another"; Graham and

Wiener 1995:2–3). The Harvard research is positioned within what Beck describes as "industrial modernity," where science's traditional grand narratives have not been overquestioned and where the social problems associated with risk research are seen as "side effects," especially of the lack of a "holistic" approach to risk by "decision makers."

Yet on the other hand, we should also note the strongly cognitivist thrust of *both* Beck *and* Graham/Wiener. In fact, Graham and Wiener's (1995) emphasis on "values and ethics that vary from community to community and person to person" as "essential foundations of democratic pluralism" (p. 270) is not wholly different from Beck's, even if embedded in a reformist rather than cataclysmic politics. Both "schools" are here moving (if only cautiously) toward what Strydom (2002) calls "new public sphere" discourses of risk communication (p. 163).

Still, there is only so far one can go with these U.S./European binaries or indeed the attempts to find synergies between them. Cohen (2000) pins some of his hopes for "mutually beneficial" interaction on the fact that within the "European" field of risk research, "There are indications that . . . so-called strong constructivism is giving way to a . . . critical or ontological realism that combines sociological and scientific epistemologies" (p. 15). Thus, an important recent exploration of risk communication via what he calls a "pragmatic-realist constructivism on a weak naturalistic basis" is Strydom's *Risk, Environment and Society* (Strydom 2002:152; see also New 1995; Rosa 1998). On the other hand, Alan Irwin (2001) has also been important in going beyond the realist/constructivist divide via the notion of "actively-generated co-construction" that "captures the dual process of the social and the natural being varyingly constructed within environmentally-related practices and particular contexts" (p. 173).

But while sharing Cohen's interest in a nonrelativist involvement between different traditions, my own direction here is different from his. I don't want to privilege one or other epistemological position in risk research (Tulloch 1999) nor indeed simply "U.S." and "European" risk research. In fact, I prefer to examine current research not via the convergence of two "schools," but via "mutually beneficial" *difference,* drawing as much on the critiques of Beck for his lack of engagement with "lay" knowledge and everyday life (Wynne 1996), affect (Hetherington 1998), aesthetics (Lash 1996), and particularly communication and media (Cottle 1998; Tulloch and Lupton 2001) as on more general cultural studies critiques of Harvard-style risk communication in the American context (Fiske 1990; Sullivan et al. 1994).

In particular, I share Strydom's emphasis on *risk communication* as a more positive way ahead in accessing in the public sphere, "the *multiplicity* of competing and conflicting contributions to public communication," each examined "in the discursive process in the medium in which they are related to one another in the working out of the politics of risk" (Strydom 2002:84). *Risk theory,* no less than the broader public sphere, needs to be seen as part of that "fluid social space of competing and conflictual communicative structures" (Strydom 2002:107), adopting different cognitive positions and cultural models. So, I want here to begin to examine current and recent risk research projects on their own terms, discursively, with some sense of their cultural and cognitive assumptions and their relative gains, weaknesses, and outcomes, especially in relation to risk communication. In particular, I want to draw on Strydom's emphasis *on a new public sphere* based on "an immense increase in the importance of public communication and the discursive organization of society," to focus on recent research on the "transfer effects" (Strydom 2002:69) between what Boholm calls different "knowledge modes" (i.e., on risk communication in its systemic sense).

Risk and Safety: Mediating Knowledge Modes

To provide a map for what follows, I will look first at a current research article by Asa Boholm, reporting potentially carcinogenic electromagnetic fields in new Volvo cars, to illustrate a "nuanced realist position" (Boholm 2002:10) on risk and safety problems.

For Boholm, risk is about meaning construction within specific expert-political, mediated, and everyday contexts, and it is this dynamic of relationships that makes her want to "move from on the one hand the broad sociological meta-perspectives offered by Anthony Giddens and Ulrich Beck, or on the other hand the methodological individualism characteristic of much of the current research on risk within psychology, economics and to some extent political science" (especially in the United State) in search of "more nuanced ethnographic and context specific accounts . . . which problematize structural dimensions such as shared meaning systems and institutional settings" (Boholm 2002:1–2).

This leads Boholm directly to focus on expert/lay *"translation"* (i.e., on *risk communication* as a contested public sphere between shared meaning systems). Her Volvo cars example illustrates both the importance of the media in providing the public with cognitive shortcuts or schemata and people's "everyday" alternatives in managing new uncertainty (Boholm 2002:16).

Boholm provides a useful template, which I will use to organise the case studies of this chapter. She argues for an analytical distinction between three basic modes of knowledge communication about risks:

1. *Everyday experience* where information is *disseminated through the small talk and gossip of ordinary life* about locally and temporally situated matters. "Risks are not dealt with as isolated 'things' but as matters [of food, transportation, household safety matters, children, the neighbourhood, local traffic, etc.] that threaten taken for granted interpersonally negotiated states of safety" (Boholm 2002:17).

2. *Science-driven scenarios* where results *and controversies emanating from science and technology* are framed as the likelihood of undesirable events. "This mode structures information by defining risk objects, objects at risk and a causal link" (Boholm 2002:17) and tends to be probabilistic in its communicative mode, though generally requiring translation via media.

3. *Collective narratives* about *risk events,* such as the Chernobyl nuclear reactor breakdown or the September 11, 2001, terrorist attack on America, where comments by experts (e.g., scientists, ministers, etc.) and counterexperts (e.g., Greenpeace and other nongovernmental organizations offering alternative priorities) are *communicated through*

news media via systematic dramaturgical structures, which can become labelling epitomes for subsequent events (Boholm 2002:17).

As Boholm recognises, these three knowledge modes are useful heuristic devices rather than separate categories. But given that all three modes of knowledge will often interact, "How is information/knowledge translated from one experience mode to another?" And how are socially constructed risks (such as Chernobyl) and a scientific abstract model "translated to an experience-near category that is imbued with social meanings" in everyday life? (Boholm 2002:18). These are issues of risk communication as a new public sphere, which I will explore further via recent case studies in risk that relate to Boholm's three knowledge modes.

SCIENCE-DRIVEN SCENARIOS

I will look first at two very different case studies examining the "translation" between science-driven scenarios and "personal, local experience" (Boholm 2002:16).

The Case of American Airbags

The first case study assumes the importance of "accurate" translation of expert knowledge to the public. Harvard Center for Risk Analysis (HCRA) Director John D. Graham's "Technological Danger Without Stigma: The Case of Automobile Airbags" (2001) notes the recent research-led "generalized knowledge" of unexpected risk of injury and death, especially to small women and children, in 60 million U.S. vehicles. Uncertainty is not a socially systemic or ontological category for Graham, as it is for Beck or Giddens, but rather a specifically situated problem of individual psychological processes tied in to media representation. Graham's position in writing this piece is as the politically (and positively) involved "tradeoff" risk expert of his earlier *Risk vs. Risk* book, responding to the available new technologies of design (such as powered, depowered, and "smart" airbags) and concerned that this may be "a case study of a technology that has not been stigmatized adequately for the larger public good" (Graham 2001:243). Thus, the key relationship

between beneficial science-driven expert knowledge and different public values of *Risk vs. Risk* is still central here.

In this case study, the "uncertainty" of risk communication is seen to lie not among the research experts (as in Beck), but with public responses, given that unlike Boholm's Volvo example, there was no public outrage at all to media coverage of the new findings. In exploring this conundrum, Graham (2001) initially uses psychological risk-perception models to score public responses to various risks, which predict that although "public outrage against airbags may not be as virulent as the reaction to nuclear power or pesticides, [it] *should* be substantial" (p. 244). This is then supported by his risk-and-benefit theory that "where risk is [media-visually] identifiable and benefit is statistical, [it] has been predicted to produce public reactions that will stigmatize a technology—even if the ratio of risk to benefit is low from an actuarial perspective" (p. 244).

Lurking still in much U.S. risk communication research is the tendency to a linear-flow model where authentic "expert" knowledge is compromised for a relatively "passive" receiver by the "media-as-problem" (usually because of its "sensationalism," "irresponsibility," "misrepresentation of the facts of science," etc.). There is more than a hint of this in Graham's (2001) account:

> The media has publicized some of the dangers of airbags with sensationalist vigor . . . as well as sizzling prime-time TV coverage on American Broadcasting Company's *48 hours* and *Dateline NBC*. Particularly juicy for the mass media were indications that both government and industry knew about possible dangers to children for twenty years but did little to warn parents when airbags came into the fleet in large numbers in the 1990s. (P. 245)

We note Graham's media adjectives of "sensationalist," "sizzling," and "juicy," which are almost inconceivable usages in recent media/cultural studies. Yet the fact is that there has *not yet been public outrage* in the United States about the well-publicised airbag findings, and Graham sets out to hypothesise why this is the case. He offers three possible explanations.

In relation to the first two, public ignorance and personal optimism linked to an assumption of other people's irresponsible behaviours, Graham (2001) believes that the exposure of "unsettling facts" that "airbags kill more young children than they save" and that "the risk-benefit ratio for airbags is unfavourable—at least for belted occupants—at low and moderate impact speeds" (p. 250), as well as knowledge about different airbag speed/impact ratios in Australia and parts of Europe, may change public attitudes. In the case of his third explanation about "on-screen benefits" justifying perceived risks, Graham specifically supports "a rationalist perspective [which] seems implausible to some social scientists but is beginning to demand a new hearing" (p. 251). And yet he still worries about continuing media influence on this "cost/benefit" rationalism:

> Television portrayals of airbag deployment create an image of a soft, cuddly, billowing bag that insulates the motorist from harsh and sinister crash forces. Even the disturbing deaths of children are frequently misperceived by people as a consequence of inadvertent suffocation rather than severe brain or spinal cord injury. (P. 252)

It is clear from the weight that Graham gives throughout his article to "unsettling facts" that may well change the public attitude to U.S. airbags, as well as his discussion of the "cuddly" airbag "on-screen," that he gives significant weight to his hypothesis "that people don't have enough information about the risks of airbags, conveyed in a sufficiently compelling fashion [by the media and other opinion leaders], to engender significant concern" (Graham 2001:254). There is, in other words, not *enough* research information flowing through the public sphere.

Graham's research is hypothesis driven, primarily quantitative, and within its own critical assumptions, powerfully conceived. Yet there is still—in relation to Boholm's "inherently dynamic relational order of meaningful connections" between object of risk (airbags), object at risk (children and small women), and evaluation of outcomes—a continuing emphasis in this Harvard risk research on the *knowledgeable expert* (as clinician, educator, or elected official), on the *media's failure* to convey science "in a sufficiently compelling fashion," and on a *misconceived public* whose behaviours need changing by way of opinion leaders and by *better risk communication* transparently conveying "unsettling" research facts in the public sphere.

The Politics of Genetically Modified Food

Unlike Graham's airbag research, recent researchers from Lancaster, Sussex, and Cardiff Universities with an Economic and Social Research Council (ESRC) funded project on genetically modified (GM) food began with Beck's assumption that *scientific uncertainty is ubiquitous* in "risk society," that in this societal context the *public does not misconceive* science and technology, and that there is a need for new, more democratic institutions of *policy codetermination.* Thus, whereas Graham and the Harvard group tend toward an individualistic benefit/risk rationalist perspective that focuses on individual decision making and behaviour change within a "risk-superior" scenario, the ESRC group immediately established a societal/ethical emphasis on cooperative decision making. Graham's phalanx of expert/political change agents disappears from view, and now it is the *experts,* not the car-driving or GM-food-eating public, whose behaviours need to change. "This would require politicians and scientific advisors to make significant changes to their ways of making decisions. Not least it would require a sharing of power over the process and possible outcomes" (ESRC Programme 1999:4).

Under the heading "inaccurate characterisation of public perceptions," the ESRC team (1999) approaches the media and notions of public ignorance:

> Government officials and politicians often express frustration at the "inaccurate and emotional" reactions of the public in the GM debates. Often campaign groups and the media are singled out as the villains of the piece, guilty of spreading hysteria through stories that are based on half-truths or unproven speculation. But . . . there is much evidence to suggest that the assumption of public ignorance is wrong on a number of fronts. . . . [P]eople . . . want to know. . . . Is the technology needed? Who stands to gain and lose from it? How are ethical issues considered? (P. 9)

Like the Harvard researchers, the ESRC group emphasises the "variety of different values" within public opinion, but the outcomes of these assumptions are very different for the two research groups. Given past British experience with BSE ("mad cow disease"), the ESRC team (1999) points out, "It seems both reasonable and rational to many people to harbour doubts about the reliability of regulatory science" (p. 8); and then, given the British government's apparently strong support for GM food technology, it was not an implausible step for many to assume that "it has also sided with the industry. For many, this undermines the government's independence. . . . Independence and trust become key issues in determining people's attitudes to the technology" (pp. 8, 9).

Two particular criteria underpin the ESRC team's entire document on GM food and risk. First, there is a reflexive emphasis on *both* "expert" and "lay" framing assumptions. Second, there is a focus on ethics, widespread public participation, and the precautionary principle in a world where there is *no "sound science" available* to make "balanced" decisions. Various publics' wide *ownership* of right and wrong decisions would replace the expert-led "knowledge" of scientific grand narratives.

Consequently, whereas Graham's recent emphasis is on defusing uncertainty as more expert advice gets conveyed by better media means to an, as yet, only partially comprehending public, the ESRC team has a primary policy focus on how to make the government a more "intelligent customer" for "a wider range of advice." Thus, whereas Graham's paper is fundamentally hypothetical ("Why no outrage about airbags?"), based on earlier psychological models of risk perception and Harvard's own quantitative research data, the ESRC team's report is qualitative, political-ethical (about power sharing and transparency), and methodological in that it explores a variety of methods of "deliberative and inclusionary processes" (DIPs) in decision making on contentious issues such as GM foods. These DIP methods include the focus group, citizens' juries, in-depth groups, consensus conferences, stakeholder decision analysis, and deliberative polling. "The central aim of all the methods is to capture value through the creation of small public spaces where people can discuss particular subjects, both with each other and with decision makers" (ESRC Programme 1999:215). These small but proliferating nuclei of an emerging public sphere would establish the legitimacy of governance, insofar as political trust would, as Strydom (2002) says, "depend not only on participatory and expressive rights, but also on general access to deliberative processes" (p. 138).

As regards science/media/everyday interfaces, the ESRC group (1999) argues,

> What we are just beginning to realise, is that there are many "publics" in society, and that any given individual may move in and out of a number of bonding groups. The lesson here is that many messages are needed to help different cultural solidarities come to terms with GM futures. (P. 19)

The case studies of car airbags and the politics of GM food indicate the need for a further issue to be added to Boholm's questions about heuristic knowledge modes. That is, what are the *critical frames* underpinning the theories of risk communication employed to answer her questions about "translating" from one knowledge mode to another in creating a public sphere? According to which model of communication "flow" we use, the ethicized or hypothesised relationship between "science," "the media," and "publics" will appear very differently, with wide differences as to what the "risks" to be "communicated" really are.

MEDIA NARRATIVES ABOUT RISK EVENTS

As Boholm notes, *media risk events* about major environmental disasters, civil disorder, or terrorist attacks appear from time to time as international collective event narratives where, as it were, the world stops and watches. An interesting pattern emerges in the two case studies I look at next, first by the Swedish Centre for Public Sector Research (CEFOS) group and second by Van Loon in his recent book, *Risk and Technological Culture* (2002), both of which relate visual images and cultural intuition via a *nonlogorational* model of risk communication.

Risk Events, Visual Images, and Cultural Intuition

The CEFOS team's research on media images of Chernobyl 10 years after the meltdown, on the film *Erin Brockovich,* and on the Swedish Hallandsas Tunnel crisis are part of an ongoing risk-media project. In the (early) Chernobyl piece, Boholm (1998) combines concepts from symbolic anthropology, semiotics, and cultural studies in trying to detect "stereotypical themes of imagery, which indicate highly conventionalised understandings of various aspects of the meanings to be drawn from the accident, and which are conveyed by the photographic material" (p. 139). And yet images of child victims caught by the camera, staring directly and sadly into the camera, or two older sisters standing in front of their house and also looking at the camera, or a little girl happily smiling into the camera with her mother and grandmother in a radioactive village take us beyond the stereotype to new cognitive "shortcuts" about body control.

The accident at Chernobyl brutally forced people in the Ukraine, without any aid of culturally available symbols, to reconsider their own mortality as well as the perception of their own bodies, being unable to fulfil their projects for life as parents, husbands, mothers, and children. These are the images of Chernobyl and its aftermath, projected as a "theatre of mortified flesh" and "bodies that gaze" (Boholm 1998:138).

The CEFOS team have taken this work on visual media knowledge transfer further in their article "From Vision to Catastrophe," on the Hallandsas Tunnel case in southern Sweden. Here, they work from within the field of stigma and "socially amplified hazards" research (Flynn, Slovic, and Kunreuther 2001; Kasperson, Jhaveri, and Kasperson 2001) in examining "risk understanding as intuitive and non-probabilistic" (Ferreira, Boholm, and Lofstedt 2001:284). Drawing also on Roland Barthes's notion of the "glance," they argue for a relationship between newspaper images that rely on the viewer's *existing* knowledge (like the conjuncture of "the dairy farm as an integrated whole," including farmers, cows, pasture, and milk) and the image-glance that "reveals the fundamental deviation from any supposed steady state" (Ferreira et al. 2001:290). Thus, in the Hallandsas Tunnel example, a set of newspaper images showing a close-up of a deformed, dead cow; a man squatting and pointing to a stream of polluted water; a farmer dumping milk into a urine reservoir; and a family posing next to their drinking well act together as a new "testimony of disorder" (Ferreira et al. 2001):

> The kind of photographs that "witness" the collapse of dairy farm imagery do not rely on notions of rationality . . . but in the relation between how the imagery of order is culturally constructed and how its disruption is visualized. . . . Like the mixing of water and poison, the mixing of milk and urine . . . plays upon one of the strongest "taboos" in every society. . . . The theory of rational choice . . . overlooks the fact that choices are made according to available alternatives that are themselves symbolic constructs. . . . The argument forwarded here is that stigma (its mark and visibility) . . . is *implicated* from already existing ideas about how the world is socially constructed. (Pp. 291, 295, 297)

Thus, as water (or milk) breaks its contextual boundaries and transgresses into other visual contexts, a putative hazard "flow" becomes "a main feature of risk events" (Ferreira et al. 2001:297). Once it has achieved a certain level of emotional power, the metaphoric image may then "structure and condition the interpretation of new events. . . . [I]t could be expected that future tunnel projects in Sweden would be, if not stigmatized, at least much more debatable and problematic than they have been hitherto" in just the same way as stereotypes of seawater pollution "will 'recall' an imagery of marine life in danger and endow new instances of pollution with emotional power" (Ferreira et al. 2001:299).

What the CEFOS team is attempting with an anthropological account of risk and stigma is nothing less than a media image theory for Beck's (1992) somewhat throwaway comment in *Risk Society:*

> What eludes sensory perception becomes socially available to "experience" in media pictures and reports. Pictures of tree-skeletons, worm-infested fish, dead seals (whose living images have been engraved on human hearts) condense and concretize what is otherwise ungraspable in everyday life. (P. 100)

And as in Ferreira's *Erin Brockovich* analysis, there is the sense that the "metaphor of packing and decoding information [that] excels in rhetoric and knowledge transfer" must be abandoned since "it deals poorly with the expression of emotions, the sharing of feelings, the impact of visual forms."

Ferreira prefers a "tuning fork" metaphor for her new public sphere of risk communication, since when "struck, it emits vibrations" (Ferreira 2003). People as tuning forks share the same cultural frequencies and begin to resonate with the same intuitive vibrations.

Images and Media Hybridities: The Rodney King Risk Event

The CEFOS team's *image-event* public sphere focus on the relationship between intuitive understandings, scientific-technical explanations, pre-existing cultural "resonances" (in contrast to logorational/lingusitic talk), and risk ambiguity is taken further within a systematic theory of risk and the media by Joost Van Loon.

Like Boholm, Van Loon is interested in examining residual cultural and collective media narratives about major events (like the September 11, 2001, terrorist attacks in the United States), which "can be used to label other events" (Boholm 2002:11). Thus, Van Loon (2002) argues, vis-à-vis the World Trade Center attacks,

> The label "terrorism" is a crucial element of the *logos* of the warfare state. It is a rather fluid category that can be applied to a wide range of activities usually directed against the state apparatus. . . . [U]rban disorders or "riots" [for example] share with terrorism a space of violent pathogenecity. (P. 169)

Van Loon begins his account of the international television image-event beating of Rodney King in Los Angeles by noting that while we need to reject the empiricist notion of media images that "seeing is believing," we must nevertheless take account of "the strong intuitive sense that the videotape [of King's bashing by police officers in Los Angeles] *does* show excessive violence under the colour/collar of authority" (Van Loon 2002:178). Drawing on Deleuze and Guattari, Van Loon argues that *media hybridities generate violence* and that different hybrid forms engender different forms of

violence (Van Loon 2002:179–80). In the case of the King beating, there were several: First, the hybridity between the camcorder-videotape and legal discourse. Here, Van Loon (2002) explains how the almost all-white jury could acquit the white policemen despite the evidence of the video:

> Legal discourse only recognises its own constitutions as valid as a result of which notions of truth and justice tend to be perceived as completely internal to its own discursive formations. . . . Legal discourse requires interpretations based on binary specificity: something is or is not. (P. 180)

In contrast, the King videotape was blurred, having an arbitrary beginning and ending point and lacking singularity of perspective. Thus the legal procedures *enframed* the videotape of the beating in their own way: (1) manipulating the images by sharpening, enlarging, mapping, and freeze-framing (for example of King's tilted leg, which the defence attorney argued indicated threatening behaviour), thus creating a *hyperreality* "that could not be seen by the untrained eye of the lay audience" (Van Loon 2002:180) and (2) fragmenting the tape into still images, stopping the flow of aggressive action by police and stretching the time between action and interpretation, so that police officers could be asked

> [To] retrospectively insert their reflections into the event, as if . . . they were conscious of their own actions. . . . Reasonability was already inscribed into the event from the outset by the very media hybridity through which it was formed. (Van Loon 2002:181)

Here, we see in Van Loon, Luhmann's (1989) emphasis on society as a set of autonomous "autopoetic" systems (legal, scientific, political, economic, media, etc.) that "expertly" frame the public sphere.

Second, though, beyond Luhmann's self-referential expert legal "autopoesis," things "*did not make any sense*" to wider publics. This is because most people were "cast" by another media hybridity. Instead of the "*camcorder + videotape + litigation* hybrid," they encountered the "... *+ camcorder + videotape + broadcasting + ...* hybrid" (Van Loon 2002:181). Within *this* discursive convention, the ambiguity of the videotape was not a problem at all, first, because its "blurred images, lack of voice-over and absence of editing intensified the sense of authenticity with which it emerged as an unmediated reality"; second, because "the absence of clarity and singularity helped the TV medium to take a step back. . . . The metanarrative of news coverage is the story that places two perspectives in opposition to another and allows itself to wither away from binary contestation" (Van Loon 2002:181). This smooth merging of videotape and news broadcast conventions *realized* a different form of violence from that of the acquittal among different publics. This is the "active audience" aspect of Van Loon's media hybridities, where he focuses on different potential readings (by those who have experienced violence at the hands of members of the Los Angeles Police Department, by police supporters, and by whites similar to the jurors) as "situated sensibilities" (Van Loon 2002:182).

> The third hybridity is a meta-hybridity between the first and the second. The trial was being broadcast itself, and in the news coverage of the trial, images of the beating were also appropriated to situate the verdict. For many people, the . . . incompatibility within the medium hybrid produced a final and most violent clash between symbolic and indexical violence that in turn materialized into new embodied constellations that we associate with the 1992 LA riots. (Van Loon 2002:182)

Here the "risk communication" of *different* "expert" hybridities is fundamental in constructing an explosive public event in Los Angeles.

What is new about Van Loon's work is that he has further developed Beck's notion of a *risk society "turn"* in popular consciousness, in which the earlier resort of publics to the expertise of instrumental rationality is no longer automatic. In the same way that in the Rodney King case, the hybrid "expert" risk events "opened up much larger questions about social inclusion, risk, the role of the media, as well as camcorders and countersurveillance," so the "risk society thesis suggests that we may have arrived at a point where we are no longer able to carelessly inhabit technologies, because we now anticipate risks everywhere, regardless of the increasing investments in safety technology and security concepts" (Van Loon, 2002:183, 195). The

communication of risk hybridities *becomes the new public sphere.*

Other orders or risks that Van Loon sees as marking the risk society "turn" from the *logos* of state-reduced risk to the *nomos* of a "flow of deviations and irreducibility" (Van Loon 2002:159) include issues of hazardous waste disposal, cyber-risk, and health risk (in which he includes "emergent viruses" such as HIV/AIDS and Ebola, and the reemergence of nearly forgotten lethal diseases such as tuberculosis, cholera, and bubonic plague).

It is here, in the collision between Giddens's different forms of expertise; in the overlap between Beck's industrial and risk modernities; in the tension between Luhmann's "autopoesis" of sovereign, self-referential systems and Deleuze and Guattari's symbiotic "assemblages" of different information-processing systems; and in the move (via their theory of hybridities) toward Strydom's new public sphere of risk communication as a discursive democratic activity of "competing, contradictory and conflicting rationality claims" (Strydom 2000:155), that Van Loon now positions media studies' long-term project of "resistance" discourse.

Van Loon's (2002) HIV example of the "various gay and lesbian movements [that] were able to travel alongside highly nomadic HIV, mobilizing public concern . . . and as a result accumulate both financial, social, political, symbolic and cultural capital within the newly formed networks of AIDS concern" (p. 83) illustrates his argument of the way in which assemblages emerge out of the everyday, which is such a feature of the risk society "turn" and brings us to the third of Boholm's three modes of knowledge transfer. Here, I will look at one final piece of current risk research under Boholm's "everyday experience" heading.

EVERYDAY EXPERIENCE

A feature of many of the major risk theorists mentioned above (e.g., Beck, Luhmann, Strydom) is that when they speak about risks and the "everyday," they tend to focus on new social movements such as Beck's example of the German Green Party and Strydom's ecological citizens. Yet we should remember that for most people most of the time, quotidian everyday life is not taken up with new solidarity groupings. We should also recall the ESRC group's point that "any given individual may move in and out of a number of bonding groups (ESRC Programme 1999:19) and Boholm's argument that in everyday life, "Risks are not dealt with as isolated 'things,' but as matters that threaten taken for granted interpersonally negotiated states of safety" (Boholm 2002:17).

In their current research, Tulloch and Lupton (2003) are, like Van Loon, drawing closely on Beck's risk society thesis. But unlike Van Loon, they move directly away from the "Eurocentric," technoscientific centering of Beck's analysis, partly because a major research programme they conducted in Australia found little empirical support for Beck's environmentally focused "cataclysmic democracy of risk" thesis. What it *did* find was that many of the building blocks of Beck's "industrial modernity," such as class, race/ethnicity, and gender, remained major ingredients of their Australian interviewees' "risk biographies."

This in itself is not a particular problem for Beck's thesis, which allows for an "overlap" between "industrial" (or "class") modernity and risk modernity. But given Strydom's (2002) "new public sphere" view that "Beck gains access to the new epoch" starting "from the most prominent public debate" (pp. 57–8), a major problem for Tulloch and Lupton was the tiny minority in the Australian research who prioritised techoscientific risk in their litany of everyday risk concerns.

In their book, *Risk and Everyday Life* (2003), Tulloch and Lupton agree with commentators who contend that in Beck's work, "Broad tendential speculations are advanced about infrastructural and organisational processes that have little grounding in the actual processes of institutional and everyday life" (Alexander 1996:134). They also agree with Lash and Wynne's (1992:7) view that the development of a questioning of expert knowledges blurs the boundaries between the "private" and the "public," for while risks may be debated at the level of expertise and public accountability, they are managed by most individuals at the level of the local, the private, the everyday, and the intimate. It is here, Tulloch and Lupton argue, that fine-grained empirical analysis that is able to explore people's ideas and

experiences of risk (and risk communication) may prove useful.

Tulloch and Lupton thus make two specific moves in their extension and critique of the risk society thesis. First, they examine the ways in which people conceptualize risk and see it as affecting them as part of the risk hybridities and border crossings of their everyday lives. This focuses on the private/public sphere overlap. Tulloch and Lupton's study (2003) revealed, for example, three major discourses employed by interviewees to describe the pleasures and benefits of *voluntary* risk taking via discourses of self-improvement; of emotional engagement drawing on a neo-Romantic ideal of the body/self allowed to extend itself beyond the conventionalising strictures of culture; and a third discourse of control, which in some way counters that of emotional engagement in privileging control over one's emotions and bodily responses as a valued aspect of engaging in risky public activities.

Second, Tulloch and Lupton (2003) drew on the "risky underemployment" rather than technoscientific "cataclysmic democracy" aspect of Beck's risk-society analysis to conduct detailed empirical work in the United Kingdom. For Beck (1992), the "risks accompanying . . . underemployment [that] compete with the partial freedom and sovereignty gained [by employees] in being able to arrange their own lives" (p. 148) are not clearly managed and mobilized by solidarity groups. Instead, the uncertainty of work risks must be managed by another central development of risk society: the risk biographies of individualization.

But there is, Tulloch and Lupton (2003) argue, a deep "hybridity" within Beck's own thesis: between the "new" public sphere of "afraid" citizens and his privatized "model of everyday life, which puts the ego at its centre." Tulloch and Lupton argue that Beck cannot be accused, in principle, of omitting the importance in his theory of the "everyday" and its situated, local negotiation. Indeed, Beck (1992) argues for the importance of focusing attention on how individualization "can be understood as a change of life situations and biographical patterns" (p. 128). What he can be criticized for, though, is allowing the individual-everyday to drop out of *both* his theory of a new public sphere *and* his (lack of empirical) method, except as monological categories (social movements, etc.) within his concept of a new subpolitics. Using Beck's notion of risk biography as a methodological device, Tulloch and Lupton argue for a revision of Beck's theory via fine-grained analyses of the ways in which reflexivity and individualization are experienced as part of personal biographies (yet still structured via such categories as age, class, ethnicity, sexual preference, and gender) and how *media* negotiation by individuals often reflects personal positioning within a new public sphere of "risky underemployment" and risk communication. For example, they note distinct differences between high-tech and car-worker interviewees in Oxfordshire, England, in terms of the richness and proactivity of their media use (including the Internet) across a range of perceived hazards, from GM food to unemployment.

In some respects, this research, with its evidence that high-tech professionals maintain a strong sense of identity and control in going beyond the job-for-life syndrome and seeing themselves as secure in their "new knowledge" competences, supports Strydom's (2002) emphasis on a "new form of class conflict" (p. 162). But Strydom's "new class" analysis is still based on the technoscientific risk emphasis of Beck's work. Whereas because Lupton and Tulloch's research has examined, via self-reflexive biographies, interviewees' perceptions of a wide range of risks—environmental, employment related, familial, personal, lifestyle, health, fear of crime, and so on—no such dichotomised culturally constituted cognitive "class" structures appeared, at least not in relation to "science" and the definition of nature. What was apparent was that as Beck and others also argue, binarised *social-public risk positions* are still perceived and that in the case of both "high-tech" and "traditional" workers, this understanding of "two nations" persisted most virulently in relation to fear of crime. So that whereas two different Cowley car workers (threatened with imminent loss of jobs after the BMW "walkout") would agree over their interpretation of the workings of international corporations, they might disagree over adequate public responses to GM food and similarly agree/disagree with individual interviewees in the high-tech sector. But something that nearly all interviewees agreed upon was the major potential for crime (invading the high-tech professionals'

secluded Oxfordshire villages or the car workers' comfortable suburban districts) as the new "knowledge economy" created a world of mobile, contract-employed "knowledge haves" and the increasingly underemployed "knowledge have-nots." Here, indeed, it was culturally constituted cognitive structures that determined the "class" positions, but ones arising from Beck's world of "risky underemployment" far more than from his "catastrophic democracy of risk" (which is where Strydom's ecological citizens come from). In this rather common perception, fear of crime was seen as the growing dystopia of a public sphere of risk talk based on an increasing inability of "us" and the "other" to talk at all.

CONCLUSION

Risk communication is an endemic aspect of current life, and some commentators argue that is the defining "public sphere" aspect of late modernity. I began with a selection of risk communications from a Web site to indicate both their ubiquity and their different rhetorical modes and gestures in terms of positioning agency. However, that has not been my focus in this chapter. Rather, I have begun with that ubiquity of public risk discourse to indicate why so many academics, in a variety of disciplines, now theorise (and empirically examine) risk.

I have looked here at a series of recent or current empirical risk research projects to examine the development of some key issues of theory and substance (democratization, media impact, everyday risk communication) that emerged from "foundation" academic risk texts, discussing the work of Beck in Germany and Graham/Wiener in the United States. I focused particularly on recent studies that raise issues of media and risk communication as central issues, particularly in the light of Strydom's recent equation of risk communication as the new public sphere. I have used a "case study" approach to allow for some analysis of differences in current risk research internationally, while trying to give space for their own (sometimes competing) cognitive positions.

Boholm provides a useful template of modes of knowledge transfer (everyday experience, science-driven scenarios, media collective narratives) in the construction of a public sphere of risk communication, as well as useful empirical work examining different "everyday" schemata responding to issues of trust and risk in the car industry. Continuing car safety and risk issues, Graham hypothesises why there is not *more* uncertainty about airbags in U.S. cars, given well-publicised research findings indicating the risk to children and smaller women from airbags. Arguing that there is still an implicit tendency in Graham's work to construct the media as "problem" and publics as "lacking" in understanding "unsettling facts," I moved in two directions: (1) to a British study that positions "lack" among scientists and politicians, calling for a more ethical, transparent, and democratically inclusive approach to risk decision making and (2) to approaches that focus directly on media and risk communication; the Swedish CEFOS work on risk events, visual images, and cultural resonance; and Van Loon's theorisation (extending Beck and Luhmann) of media assemblages, hybridity, and the "violence" of any discursive judgement (or "transfer" between knowledge modes). In Van Loon's work, Boholm's modes of knowledge transfer shift from template to interactive, *anti* autopoetic discursive (risk communication) modes, and thus closer to Strydom's (2002) notion of a more democratic risk society where "a struggle between social movements, the state, industry, science and so forth . . . is fought out via the media and plays off before the observing public" (p. 135). Thus "competing, contradictory and conflicting rationality claims . . . engage in a reciprocal critique" (p. 155). Finally, Lupton and Tulloch's Australian/British research brings media back to the everyday, and a sense of new "class" perceptions in relation not to world environmental catastrophe, but to very localised fear of crime. In emphasizing the pleasures of voluntary risk taking, it also reminds us that the strongly cognitive emphasis of both Beck and Graham/Wiener needs augmenting with research about the emotive and pleasurable aspects of risk taking and its public communication.

REFERENCES

Alexander, J. 1996. "Critical Reflections on 'Reflexive Modernization.'" *Theory, Culture & Society* 13:133–38.

Beck, U., ed. 1992. *Risk Society: Towards a New Modernity.* London, England: Sage.

Boholm, A. 1998. "Visual Images and Risk Messages: Commemorating Chernobyl." *Risk Decision and Policy* 3 (2):125–43.

———. 2002. "The Cultural Nature of Risk: Can There Be an Anthropology of Uncertainty?" *Ethnos: Journal of Anthropology* 68 (2):1–21.

Cohen, M. J. 2000. "Environmental Sociology, Social Theory and Risk: An Introductory Discussion." Pp. 3–31 in *Risk in the Modern Age: Social Theory, Science and Environmental Decision-Making,* edited by M. J. Cohen. Basingstoke: Macmillan.

Cottle, S. 1998. "Ulrich Beck, 'A Risk Society' and the Media: A Catastrophic View." *European Journal of Communication* 13 (1):5–32.

Economic and Social Research Council Environmental Change Programme (ESRC). 1999. *The Politics of GM Food: Risk, Science and Public Trust.* Special Briefing No. 5. University of Sussex, England.

Ferreira, C. 2003. "Risk, Transparency and Cover Up: Media Narratives and Cultural Resonance." Unpublished manuscript, CEFOS, University of Goteborg, Sweden.

Ferreira, C., A. Boholm, and R. Lofstedt. 2001. "From Vision to Catastrophe: A Risk Event in Search of Images." Pp. 283–99 in *Risk, Media and Stigma: Understanding Public Challenges to Modern Science and Technology,* edited by J. Flynn, P. Slovic, and H. Kunreuther. London, England: Earthscan.

Fiske, J. 1990. *Introduction to Communication Studies.* 2nd ed. London, England: Routledge.

Flynn, J., P. Slovic, and H. Kunreuther, eds. 2001. *Risk, Media and Stigma: Understanding Public Challenges to Modern Science and Technology.* London, England: Earthscan.

Furedi, F. 2002. *Culture of Fear: Risk-Taking and the Morality of Low Expectation.* London, England: Continuum.

Graham, J. 2001. "Technological Danger without Stigma: The Case of Automobile Airbags." Pp. 24–55 in *Risk, Media and Stigma: Understanding Public Challenges to Modern Science and Technology,* edited by J. Flynn, P. Slovic, and H. Kunreuther. London, England: Earthscan.

Graham, J. D. and J. B. Wiener, eds. 1995. *Risk vs. Risk: Tradeoffs in Protecting Health and the Environment.* Cambridge, MA: Harvard University Press.

Hetherington, K. 1998. *Expressions of Identity: Space, Performance, Politics.* London, England: Sage.

Irwin, A. 2001. *Sociology and the Environment: A Critical Introduction to Society, Nature and Knowledge.* Cambridge: Polity.

Kasperson, R. E., H. Jhaveri, and J. Kasperson, 2001. "Stigma and the Social Amplification of Risk: Towards a Framework of Risk Analysis." Pp. 9–27 in *Risk, Media and Stigma: Understanding Public Challenges to Modern Science and Technology,* edited by J. Flynn, P. Slovic, and H. Kunreuther. London, England: Earthscan.

Lash, S. 2000. "Risk Culture." Pp. 47-62 in *The Risk Society and Beyond: Critical Issues of Social Theory,* edited by B. Adam, U. Beck, and J. Van Loon. London, England: Sage.

Lash, S. and B. Wynne. 1992. "Introduction." Pp. 1–8 in *Risk Society: Towards a New Modernity,* edited by U. Beck. Sage: London.

Luhmann, N. 1989. *Ecological Communication.* Cambridge, MA: Polity.

Lyons, D. 2001. *Surveillence Society: Monitoring Everyday Life.* Buckingham, England: Open University.

New, C. 1995. "Sociology and the Case for Realism." *Sociological Review* 808–26.

Rosa, E. A. 1998. "Metatheoretical Foundations for Post-Normal Risk." *Journal of Risk Research* 1 (1):15–44.

Strydom, P. 2002. *Risk, Environment and Society: Ongoing Debates, Current Issues and Future Projects.* Buckingham, England: Open University.

Sullivan, T., J. Hartley, D. Saunders, M. Montgomery, and J. Fiske. 1994. *Key Concepts in Communication and Cultural Studies.* 2nd ed. London, England: Routledge.

Tulloch, J. 1999. "Fear of Crime and the Media." Pp. 34–58 in *Risk and Sociocultural Theory: New Directions and Perspectives,* edited by D. Lupton. Cambridge, England: Cambridge University Press.

Tulloch, J. and D. Lupton. 2001. "Risk, the Mass Media and Personal Biography: Revisiting Beck's 'Knowledge, Media and Information Society.'" *European Journal of Cultural Studies* 4 (1):5–7.

——. 2003. *Risk and Everyday Life.* London, England: Sage.

Van Loon, J. 2002. *Risk and Technological Culture: Towards a Sociology of Virulence.* London, England: Routledge.

Wynne, B. 1996. "'May the Sheep Safely Graze?' A Reflexive View of the Expert-Lay Knowledge Divide." In *Risk, Environment and Modernity: Towards a New Ecology,* edited by S. Lash, B. Szerzynski, and B. Wynne. London, England: Sage.

Young, J. 1999. *The Exclusive Society: Social Exclusion, Crime and Difference in Late Modernity.* London, England: Sage.

CRIME

MICHAEL TONRY

Cambridge University

Crime is a congeries of social problems that are best thought of together but generally are not. A short list would include criminal harms, fear of crime, victimization, and collateral effects. The meanings of the first three are self-evident. By "collateral effects," I mean the unintended or incidental effects of crime and punishment on offenders, victims, and their families; their immediate communities; and the larger community.

The crime-preventive effects of punishment are a good thing, but they are purchased at a high cost in state resources and human suffering and have many unintended and undesirable consequences. Many are collateral, such as the psychological effects on children of having their mothers sent to prison or the living-standard effects of the family's loss of an imprisoned parent's income. Some are direct, such as the multiple harms done to people sent to prison and to the people who work in them as guards and in other roles. Some are indirect, such as public goods foregone when, for example, a state spends money on prison operations rather than on higher education.

This is a handbook of "social problems." It may be useful if I spell out what I mean by that term. Among many possibilities, two primary conceptions contend. The first, top-down, latches on to "social" and focuses on the processes and meanings that cause some phenomena to be characterized as problems. This is not nonsensical. Homosexuality, drug use, prostitution, or heresy are in one sense "problems" only if that is how they are conceived, and whether and to what extent they are varies with time and place. However, that a practice such as prostitution is lawful or widely accepted as socially acceptable does not mean that it does not cause social harm. Alcohol use is an example of a lawful and socially accepted practice that nonetheless has behavioral, health, and economic consequences that are widely seen as harmful.

The second, bottom-up, conception focuses on "problems" and looks at harms or social disadvantages associated with social practices. It tries to measure them, understand their causes, and look for ways they can be eliminated, reduced, or ameliorated.

This top-down/bottom-up difference in conceptions can easily be overstated. Social problems necessarily are socially constructed. Nonetheless, for crime, at least, the bottom-up conception that begins with harms and disadvantages suffered by

465

human beings is the more useful. Many forms of violence and takings of others' property are regarded as crimes in most societies. Focusing on them empirically and building understanding upwards sheds more light than does focusing on how and why particular behaviors come to be seen as problems.

This does not mean that the flowering of a set of harms into a "social problem" is not an important occurrence. Until recognition and description by doctors of the abused-child syndrome in the 1960s (Kempe et al. 1962) or the emergence of heightened concern about violence against women in the 1970s (e.g., Walker 1979), child and spousal abuse were regarded as small-scale problems but quickly came to be seen as vastly bigger. Whether they did become vastly bigger is an open question. Heightened attention led to creation of new reporting and data-recording systems, to changes in laws and practices in the criminal justice and social welfare systems, and to increases in the number and influence of advocacy groups.

These developments, among many other effects, led to vastly greater reporting and recording of information about possible or alleged incidents of abuse. Whether the steep increase in the 1980s and 1990s in official estimates of the number of incidents of child abuse resulted wholly from increased reporting is unknowable, but there is wide agreement that most of it did (Garbarino 1989). Likewise for domestic violence. No one doubts that much of the apparent increase in the 1980s and 1990s shown by police data resulted from changes in citizen reporting and police recording of incidents (Blumstein and Beck 1999).

The social construction of phenomena into social problems has important consequences. Whether or not child and spouse abuse became more common in the 1980s and 1990s, characterizing them that way led to enormous increases in political attention and investment of public resources in efforts to address them.

Nonetheless, to understand the dimensions of phenomena that are constructed into social problems, we need first to understand their prevalence and incidence. To understand crime-writ-large as a social problem, we need to see the subject whole— as criminal harms, fear, victimization, collateral effects, and state responses. Otherwise, a complicated set of interrelated harms and disadvantages disappears from view.

In the contemporary United States, for example, crime is conceived of primarily as criminal harms. This has had a number of unfortunate effects. First, crime is seen primarily as a problem caused by criminals who deliberately choose to harm others. So seen, it seems natural to focus policy responses on criminals' bad motives or characters and to punish them, and to base prevention approaches primarily on efforts to incapacitate and deter offenders. As a result, the severity of penalties and the prison population in the United States ratcheted up continuously for 30 years beginning in 1972. In most Western countries, imprisonment rates were broadly stable or grew a little during most of that period, followed by modest increases in a number of countries in the late 1990s. By 2000, the number of people in American prisons per 100,000 population (the rate was around 700 per 100,000) was 5 to 12 times higher than in other Western countries (Tonry 2001).

Second, if the crime problem is understood primarily as the immoral behavior of individuals, there is little reason to invest heavily in treatment programs. Criminals don't deserve to have their immoral behavior rewarded. And in any case, there's no reason to suppose that treatment programs will prevent crime any better than do deterrent and incapacitative strategies. As a result, rehabilitation programs withered away in prison and community settings beginning in the mid-1970s, and probation and parole redefined their core missions from treatment and support to control and surveillance. Many Western governments, especially in Germany, the Netherlands, and Scandinavia, make much larger investments in treatment and educational programs for offenders than occurs in the United States (Albrecht 2001). There is ample evidence that many well-run programs can reduce future offending (Gaes et al. 1999), so the American failure to invest in them means that less crime is prevented that at reasonable expense could be and that victims and offenders both suffer unnecessarily.

Third, if crime is primarily the result of criminals' immoral choices, there's little reason to invest in crime prevention efforts outside the criminal justice system. Most Western countries, including notably Belgium, Denmark, England, France, the Netherlands, and Sweden, have established major crime prevention agencies that develop programs of developmental, community, and situational prevention (Tonry and Farrington 1995). There is no comparable American agency.

John Bright (1992) of England's Crime Concern, a government-supported private crime prevention agency, explained why. He spent six months in the United States learning about American crime prevention approaches and interviewing public officials. Many were so committed to the idea that crime is best understood as private immorality and should be dealt with as such, that they simply had little interest in other approaches to crime prevention. This, Bright speculated, was because adoption of other approaches would obscure emphasis on offenders' immorality.

Similar reasons might be given for why American antidrug efforts focus primarily on law enforcement approaches rather than, as countries as diverse as Italy, the Netherlands, Spain, and Switzerland do, on public health approaches that emphasize treatment and reduction of harms to drug users and the community (MacCoun and Reuter 2001).

Failure to invest more money and energy in prevention is unfortunate because there is substantial evidence that many developmental and situational crime prevention programs are effective (Tonry and Farrington 1995). Developmental prevention programs identify factors in children's lives that put them at particular risk of becoming involved in crime, drug use, or other forms of antisocial behavior, and attempt to reduce the influence of those factors (Tremblay and Craig 1995). Situational prevention programs attempt to redesign products, buildings, and processes to make them less vulnerable to crime (Clarke 1995). Cost-benefit analyses show that developmental programs in particular are considerably more cost-effective crime preventatives than are harsher punishments (Greenwood et al. 1996).

Fourth, if policymakers focus primarily on offenders, there is little reason to think about victims or others who are affected by crime and responses to it. Victims' rights and interests, for example, received little attention in the United States until the 1980s, and even today, the principal programs for

victims are funded not from general government revenues, but from fines and other financial penalties paid by offenders. And programs remain much less comprehensive than in other countries. In England, for example, a state-funded program called Victim Support has since the 1960s organized visits and support from volunteers for most victims of nontrivial crimes (Bright 1992).

But other people who are affected by crime and its consequences have also been overlooked. These include offenders, who are stigmatized when they are convicted or sent to prison. Offenders sent to prison may lose their jobs or families, become socialized into deviant values, and emerge from prison with a shorter life expectancy and lower annual and lifetime earnings than other people. If a large proportion of young men are sent to prison, they aren't available as partners for young women or as workers (Hagan and Dinovitzer 1999). Partners and children are affected by what happens to offenders, and if offenders are concentrated, as they are, in particular neighborhoods, then the neighborhood will be damaged as a functioning social organism (Clear et al., Forthcoming; Clear, Rose, and Ryder 2001; Fagan, Forthcoming).

So, those are some reasons why, if we want to understand crime as a social problem, we need to look at it as a whole and not simply in terms of bad acts of bad people. This is not a new idea. More than 200 years ago, Jeremy Bentham (1789), the utilitarian theorist, argued that the only justifiable policies for dealing with crime were those that minimized human suffering or maximized human satisfaction, taking everybody, including offenders, into account. He concluded that punishments cannot be justified if on balance they cause more harm than they prevent.

CRIMINAL HARMS

Crime is a pervasive phenomenon in industrialized Western societies. A core set of behaviors—killings (murders and manslaughters), inflicting significant injuries (various kinds of assaults), forcible or abusive sexual relations (rape), stealing (theft or larceny, and if by force or threat of force, robbery), serious cheating (fraud), entering property with bad motive (burglary)—is everywhere counted as

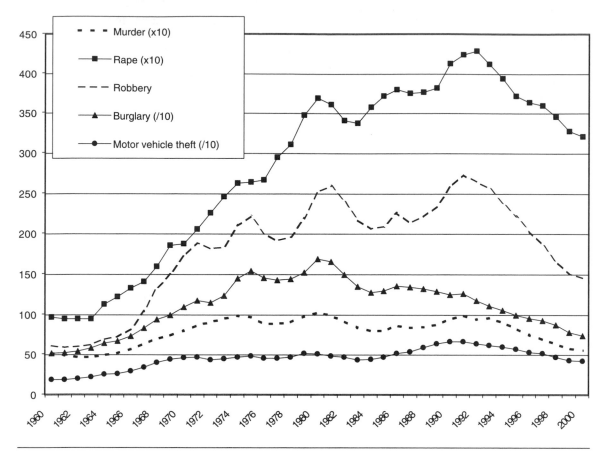

Figure 27.1 Reported Crime Rates, United States 1960–2000 (per 100,000 Population), Murder, Rape, Robbery, Burglary, and Motor Vehicle Theft

serious crime. Drug dealing and trafficking are regarded as serious crimes in most places, as is procuring for prostitution. Behaviors commonly regarded as less serious crimes include shoplifting, drug use and possession, gambling, prostitution, and driving under the influence of drugs or alcohol (DUI). In some non-Western countries, some consensual sexual acts such as homosexual relations, adultery, and sexual intercourse outside marriage are considered serious crimes, as are heretical religious beliefs. In some Asian countries, notably in China and Southeast Asia, various political and cultural activities are counted as serious crimes. In this chapter, I attend almost exclusively to the core set of commonly recognized serious crimes, and I don't

discuss organized crime, transnational crime, or gangs. What distinguishes these groups is not the kinds of crimes they commit—garden variety violent, property, and drug crimes mostly—but the threats that their organizations present. I also don't discuss white-collar crime or political crime.

In most Western countries, violent and property crime rates have been falling or stable from the early 1990s through the beginning of the new century. Figure 27.1 illustrates this for the United States. It is based on data collected from police departments and published by the Federal Bureau of Investigation (FBI) in the Uniform Crime Reports (UCR). It shows reported crime rates for 1960 through 2000 for murder, rape, robbery, burglary, and motor

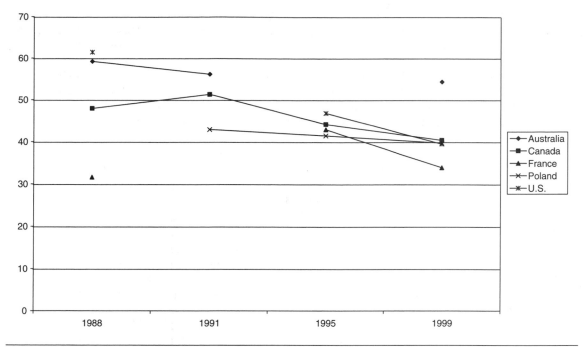

Figure 27.2   Trends in Crime as Measured by the ICVS, 1988, 1991, 1995, 1999

vehicle theft. Because my interest here is in crime trends rather than in absolute levels, some rates have been multiplied or divided by 10 so that they can all be shown in one figure. Rates for all offenses peaked around 1980 and again in 1990, and since then have fallen steadily.

A similar pattern, though typically with the peak slightly later, characterizes most Western countries (Lamon 2002). This can be shown using official police data from individual countries, but it is difficult to make cross-national comparisons. That is because offenses are defined differently in different countries and statistical recording systems vary substantially. Consequently, when official data from two countries are compared, it is very difficult to know whether the same things are being measured in both. To remedy this, the International Crime Victims Survey (ICVS) is administered approximately every 4 years in a sizeable and increasing number of countries. Because the ICVS uses the same questions, the same definitions of crimes, and the same data collection method in each country,

it is the most credible source of comparative knowledge of victimization trends (Nieuwbeerta 2002). Figure 27.2, drawn from ICVS data, shows overall victimization trends for five diverse countries (Australia, Canada, France, Poland, and the United States) for selected years between 1988 and 1999. Rates fell in all five countries—continuously for the United States and from the mid-90s for all.

This section discusses the harms caused by major categories of crime and recent trends in their occurrence. Harms vary from clear and unambiguous to unclear and disputed.

The harms caused by violent crimes, and therefore why they are everywhere taken seriously, are self-evident. They cause or threaten death, pain, or sexual violation and attendant adverse consequences to their victims, and vicarious suffering for victims' loved ones.

The harms caused by property crimes are sometimes more uncertain. Many losses suffered by businesses from shoplifting or other thefts are regarded as costs of doing business and are taken into account in setting prices. A business that experiences less theft than it expected will, in a sense, receive a windfall. It has made customers pay more than they otherwise would have had theft losses not been overestimated. An insured private citizen may benefit from losing property in a theft. Many insurance policies provide "replacement cost coverage," which means that theft of a two-year-old television will result in purchase of a new one. This may provide a collateral benefit to the economy since it provides demand for new products, and since insurance premiums are actuarially calculated, the cost of the new television has been taken into account in setting the premium. Many victims, of course, lack insurance or have policies that make them pay part of the loss. There are also ancillary harms caused by thefts such as the inconvenience of being without something and having to take the time to replace it. Finally, thefts are unethical acts and undermine people's senses of confidence and security.

The harms caused by other crimes are even harder to characterize. For drug crimes, for example, it is hard to know whether drug use or drug law enforcement causes the greater harm (Nadelmann 1992). Many argue that the effects of use of drugs other than alcohol are relatively modest—some adverse health effects, some reduction in workforce participation, and some reductions in responsible parenting and citizenship—compared with the effects of drug law enforcement. Because drugs are illegal, they must be purchased from people willing to accept the risks of breaking the law, and prices are much higher as a result. Illegal drugs must be purchased under dangerous circumstances, and there are no assurances that they are what they are represented to be or that they are not contaminated. Many addicted users sell drugs, work as prostitutes, or commit burglaries or street crimes in order to buy drugs at artificially high prices. Police tactics in drug law enforcement raise difficult civil liberties questions. And the police, court, and correctional costs of handling drug offenders in the United States total many billions of dollars (Office of National Drug Control Policy 2002). Many people, however, think of drug use primarily as a moral issue and that the kinds of costs and consequences described above are regrettable, but in the end necessary.

One last crime, DUI, illustrates why many crimes raise difficult policy dilemmas. No one questions that alcohol is much the most costly abused drug in the United States. Its abuse causes hundreds of thousands of deaths of users per year, leads to billions of dollars per year in lost economic productivity, and contributes annually to tens of thousands of motor vehicle accidents each year that lead to hundreds of thousands of injuries and 10,000 to 20,000 deaths. Yet alcohol use and sale remain legal, and the criminal justice system response is a combination of mass media consciousness-raising campaigns, small-scale mandatory jail term policies for DUI recidivists, and (usually, though not always, short) prison sentences for DUI-caused deaths. Americans clearly feel much more ambivalently toward alcohol than toward marijuana, heroin, or Ecstasy.

The differing kinds of harms that various crimes threaten illustrate why scholars study the social construction of crimes. For some kinds of property crimes, for example, plausible arguments exist that they cause relatively little economic harm, and yet they are everywhere made criminal. Conversely, plausible arguments exist that many violations of environmental laws cause very great social and economic harm, and yet they are seldom criminally prosecuted and less often result in prison sentences. The different ways the criminal law and the criminal justice system handle alcohol and marijuana provide even starker examples of how historical, economic and social class, and ideological influences shape how America addresses objectively parallel social problems.

VICTIMIZATION

The data on American crime trends shown in Figure 27.1 are from the UCR that the FBI annually compiles. The FBI data have been available since the late 1920s. There are, however, a number of well-known problems with police data. They are underinclusive. Many crimes are never reported to the police, often because they are not serious or because victims believe the police can do nothing about them. Some crimes are reported to the police, but they do not enter the FBI data because the police do not record them; sometimes because they don't believe the crime occurred; sometimes because they don't think it was serious; and sometimes for reasons of inefficiency or official policy.

Victimization surveys were invented in the 1960s to serve as a second source of crime trends and to learn about crimes that are either not reported to the police or are not recorded by them. Since 1973, the U.S. Bureau of the Census, on behalf of the U.S. Bureau of Justice Statistics (BJS), has surveyed 40,000 to 60,000 households every six months to learn about crimes committed against household members. The sample of households is selected so that it is representative of the overall U.S. population. The survey is called the National Crime Victimization Survey (NCVS).

Victimization surveys are carried out in many countries, though no other country has conducted surveys so often or over so long a period, and no other uses anywhere near so large a sample. In recent years, the British, Dutch, Finnish, and Netherlands surveys have been administered on an annual basis, and the British survey will soon incorporate a much larger sample. In this chapter, I mostly refer to the NCVS because it is the largest and most sophisticated, and the ICVS because it includes data from many Western countries. The ICVS also in some years includes less developed and developing countries (Nieuwbeerta 2002, chaps. 4–7; Zvecic and del Frate 1995).

Police data on recorded crimes and victimization data are not exactly different measures of the same thing. Partly this is because many events that people consider crime victimizations are never reported to the police. More important, though, it is because many crimes do not have easily identifiable individual victims. This is true not only of white-collar and organized crime but also of drug crimes, many "morals" crimes (prostitution, illegal gambling, pornography), traffic crimes, and vandalism. Such actions are defined as crimes because legislators believe they cause damage to the community. In addition, businesses are the victims of many property crimes, including shoplifting, burglary, and embezzlement. Not having individual victims, none of these categories of crime are measured by victimization surveys.

Figure 27.3 shows NCVS victimization rates for six crimes for the period 1980 through 2000. As in Figure 27.1, some rates have been divided by 10 so they can all be shown in one figure. The patterns parallel those from UCR data shown in Figure 27.1. Reported victimization for all six offenses declined from around the early to mid-1990s, some from peaks (e.g., auto theft and assault), and others as extensions of long-term downward trends (e.g., rape, burglary, theft). Figure 27.2, presenting comparative data from five countries, shows that similar victimization trends characterize most countries.

Victimization surveys can be done in many ways, including face-to-face interviews, telephone interviews, Internet questionnaires, and self-completed paper questionnaires. Each has advantages and disadvantages. In the NCVS, most interviews are face-to-face or by telephone. In the ICVS, most are by telephone.

Having one-on-one encounters, whether in person or over the phone, provides the opportunity to ask not only about crime but also about other subjects. The NCVS confines its questions to crime victimization and very closely related subjects, such as fear of crime and whether and why crimes are reported to the police. The ICVS and the British Crime Survey (BCS) (Kershaw et al. 2001), the largest national victimization survey outside the United States, ask questions about a much wider range of subjects, including confidence in the police, courts, and other agencies; opinions about sentencing; and actions taken to prevent crime, such as installation of burglar alarms, staying in at night, and other self-protective measures. The next section discusses fear of crime. This one mentions a few other findings.

First, the BCS (e.g., Kershaw et al. 2001) and the NCVS (Rennison 2002) show that crime victimization is not equally spread. In English-speaking countries, men are more likely to be victimized by crime than are women, blacks than whites, Hispanics than non-Hispanics, and city dwellers than suburbanites and people living in small towns and rural areas. These patterns hold true overall and are even more pronounced for violent crimes.

Second, victimization is not randomly distributed by age. Both for violent crime and for theft, the most common property crime, in the United States, 16- to 19-year-olds have the highest victimization rates, followed by 12- to 15-year-olds and 20- to 24-year-olds.

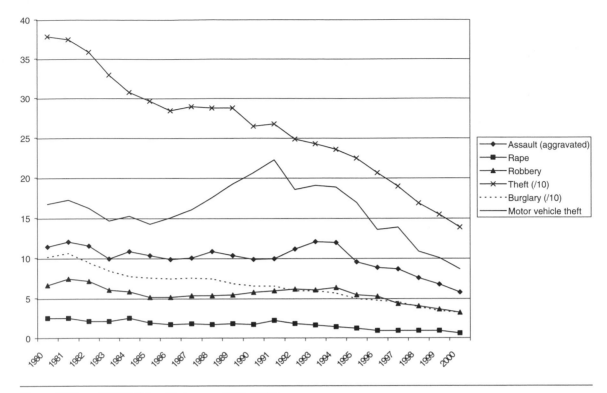

Figure 27.3   NCVS Crime Estimates, 1980–2000

The elderly, though the group most fearful about crime, have much the lowest likelihood of victimization (Rennison 2002).

Third, there are pronounced income patterns in crime victimization. Victimization risks are inversely correlated with income. The NCVS, for example, divides its respondents into seven household income bands from under $7,000 to over $75,000. The risk of violent crime victimization is highest for the lowest-income group and drops successively in each higher band. The violent risk for the lowest income group (7 percent are victimized) is 2.5 times that of the highest group (3 percent). For theft, victimization rates are highest for the lowest-income group and then decrease through the fifth group, after which they stabilize (Rennison 2002).

Fourth, approximately half of all crimes are reported to the police. Though the broad patterns of findings from all representative victimization surveys are similar, I use ICVS results for illustration (Mayhew and van Dijk 1997, fig. 9, table 4). Results from a 1996 survey of 11 industrialized countries showed that, on average, 50 percent of victimizations were reported to the police. Swedish and Swiss respondents were at the high end, reporting 57 to 58 percent of victimizations to the police, and France and Northern Ireland were at the low end, reporting 47 to 48 percent. There were three principal reasons why crimes were not reported. Much the most common was that the crime wasn't serious enough or nothing was lost. The second most common was that people "solved it themselves" or it was otherwise just not appropriate to call the police. The third was that the "police could do nothing." The three most common reasons for not reporting in the United States in 2001 were similar: "reported to another [that is, not police] official," "private or personal matter," "object recovered; offender unsuccessful," and "not important enough" (BJS 2003, table 3.43).

American crime reporting rates are somewhat lower. In 2001, NCVS respondents indicated that they had reported 49 percent of violent crimes to the police and 37 percent of property crimes. Ordinary theft was the least likely crime to be reported (30 percent of the time), and auto theft the most likely (82 percent). Violent crimes, depending on what they were, were reported to the police 40 to 55 percent of the time (Rennison 2002:10).

FEAR

Fear of crime in recent decades has worried policymakers almost as much as crime itself. There are several reasons for this. First, public opinion research in the 1990s showed that fear of crime remained high even though crime rates fell steadily. Ordinary citizens cannot be presumed to know much about crime statistics, but in the 1990s, the decline in crime rates was so great and received so much attention in both newspapers and television news shows that few people could not have heard. Why might fear of crime have remained persistently high? One reason might be that rates, though lower, remained above some absolute level that causes widespread fear. Another might be that politicians often in the 1980s and 1990s ran on "tough on crime" platforms, and the campaigning and related media attention created a false impression of a growing crime problem in people's minds. Whatever the reason, if citizens are fearful, policymakers are concerned that voters will hold them responsible.

A second reason why policymakers worry about high levels of fear of crime is that it weakens neighborhoods and communities. If people are fearful, they won't go out as often or at particular times, for example, at night. If they are fearful in the communities where they live, they are likely to go elsewhere for recreation and shopping, and their own neighborhoods will deteriorate.

Researchers evaluating police-patrolling experiments in the 1970s (police in cars versus on foot, one- versus two-officer police cars, high-visibility versus low-visibility patrolling) found that most of the experiments had no effects on crime rates but that more visible policing, especially foot patrol, reduced fear of crime (Sherman 1992). If fear of crime undermines communities and neighborhoods, the lesson was that more visible policing will reduce fear and some of the time, at least, strengthen neighborhoods.

The NCVS does not devote much attention to fear of crime. The closest proxy questions ask people whether they believe crime is increasing, decreasing, or staying about the same. People who think crime is getting worse will be more likely to be fearful, or to be more fearful, than people who think crime is decreasing. The Gallup Poll asked a representative sample of Americans this in 2001, when American crime rates had been falling for a decade. Overall, 41 percent thought crime rates higher, and 43 percent thought them lower. The breakdowns, however, are striking. Women (49 percent) were much more likely than men (33 percent) to think crime rates were higher, blacks (56 percent) than whites (40 percent), high school dropouts (54 percent) than people with graduate training (16 percent), and people who earned less than $20,000 (57 percent) than people who earned more than $75,000 (24 percent) (BJS 2003, table 2.38). The ICVS shows the same patterns in other countries (Nieuwbeerta 2002, chaps. 17–19).

Fear is based on information, whether true or false, and therefore often on stereotypes. People know about society in general from the mass media but know about their own communities and neighborhoods from personal experience. One consequence is that we tend to think things are worse elsewhere than where we live. In 2001, for example, a representative sample of Americans was asked whether crime nationally was better, worse, or about the same. Forty-one percent said there was more crime, 43 percent said there was less, and 10 percent said about the same. When the same question was asked about "your own area," 26 percent said there was more crime, 52 percent said there was less, and 18 percent said it was about the same (BJS 2003, tables 2.38., 2.41).

The ICVS asks more questions about fear than does the NCVS. Its data offer a fuller picture. There are substantial national differences in the pervasiveness of fear of crime. In the most recent (2000) survey, 35 percent of respondents from Poland and Australia said they felt unsafe on streets in their neighborhoods at night, compared with around

15 percent in Canada, Sweden, and the United States (Wittebrood 2002, fig. 1). The average rate for 16 countries was 23 percent. The cross-national fear-of-crime findings on men versus women, majority versus minority residents, and rural versus urban respondents parallel those for the NCVS. Probably not surprisingly, people who have been victims of violence or of burglary are more fearful on the streets and at home than are people who have not been victims.

Victims' Burdens

Only in the past 30 years have collateral effects of crime and punishment received much attention from policymakers, researchers, and policy analysts. State systems of prosecution, trial, and punishment began to take shape hundreds of years ago, in part to bring crime within the province of the organized state and thereby to forestall vigilantism and private revenge. Crimes came to be seen as offenses against the state. The victim might have an important role to play as witness, but the legal action set the state against the defendant. A widespread conceptualization formed that the fundamental issue in a criminal case is whether the state can satisfactorily demonstrate, usually by proof beyond a reasonable doubt, that the defendant committed a crime and accordingly that the state has authority to deprive him of life, liberty, or property.

That image, though it is fundamentally important in a society that values individual liberty, does not allow much of a role for the victim. As a result, few governments had programs to help victims of crime deal with physical, emotional, and financial consequences of their victimization. Because the trial pitted the state against the defendant, pretrial procedures and trials were organized around the interests and convenience of the lawyers and the defendant. Thus, if the trial were continued many times, the victim might time after time take a day off work to testify at a trial only to find that it had been rescheduled. Similarly, because the victim was not a party to the prosecution, courts generally lacked authority to order offenders to pay restitution to victims.

To remedy these things, beginning in the 1970s, a number of initiatives occurred. Initially in a small number of American jurisdictions, but by the 1990s in most jurisdictions, courts and prosecutors established victim and witness offices. Their job was to help victims understand the court process, notify them when they had to appear in court and of changes in schedule, and sometimes to help arrange transportation to the courthouse.

By the early 1980s, the "victims' rights" movement took shape and pressed a variety of claims: for victim restitution as part of the offender's sentence, for a right to testify in trials and sentencing and parole hearings, for the preparation of a "victim impact statement" in every case, for a right to be notified when "their" offender had a release hearing or was released, and eventually for enactment of a "Victim's Bill of Rights" as an amendment to the U.S. Constitution. The constitutional amendment never passed, but many states enacted victims' bills of rights and established many of the proposed victims' policies.

The federal Victims of Crime Act passed in 1984 and set up a Federal Crime Victims Fund that receives moneys paid by federal offenders as fines and as explicit victim compensation penalties. It also receives money forfeited by federal offenders, and, as many white-collar and drug defendants forfeit large amounts, the fund in the 1990s contained hundreds of millions of dollars. Much of this is paid out to states according to formulas and is supposed to be spent to fund state programs that address crime victims' needs. Otherwise, crime victims receive only whatever services and funds are available under general state and federal welfare programs. These are typically not generous in the United States, and crime victims are treated no better than anyone else who qualifies for help.

Victims of crime in other countries benefit both from state-funded services and support, such as that provided by England's Victim Support, and also from general state welfare and medical programs. As these are typically more generous and better funded than such programs in the United States, victims in other Western countries are better treated.

Crime causes emotional and physical suffering for victims. It also imposes financial costs, including lost earnings, out-of-pocket expenditures for medical and mental health care, the value of lost money or property, and costs of replacement and repair of lost or damaged property. Some efforts have been made to estimate these things, among other costs of crime and punishment. I discuss this in the next section.

COLLATERAL COSTS

A cost-benefit literature on the costs of crime emerged in the 1980s. Much imagination was invested in calculating the costs of crime and the criminal justice system, but no one thought to take the offender and his costs and suffering into account. The principal aim was to calculate whether "prison works" in the sense that the economic value of crimes prevented through locking people up outweighed the costs of operating the criminal justice system, including the prisons.

The earliest article, by Edwin Zedlewski of the U.S. National Institute of Justice, concluded that for one average prisoner, "A year in prison [at] total social costs of $25,000" would produce a saving of "$430,000 in [reduced] crime costs" (Zedlewski 1987:3–4). Zedlewski assumed that each person locked up would commit 173 crimes per year if at liberty. His article provoked a fierce response (e.g., Zimring and Hawkins 1988). Should the costs of the police be included in the calculation, since every society has a police force? Should crime prevention costs, from burglar alarms to private security firms' fees, be included? Were the estimates of the numbers of crimes prevented per locked-up offender accurate or even remotely plausible? Should both incapacitative and deterrent effects be predicted, or only incapacitative effects?

Gradually, over time, the estimation techniques improved, and general agreements were reached about what should be taken into account. The most striking development, and the most influential, was a series of estimates of victims' direct out-of-pocket expenses, their pain and suffering, and their risk of death that were provided by economist Mark Cohen (1988:546). For most crimes, the intangible costs of pain and suffering and risk of death far outweighed out-of-pocket costs. For rape, direct costs totaled $4,617, intangible costs $46,441. For personal robbery, direct costs totaled $1,114, intangible costs $11,480; for assault, it was $422 and $11,606.

Cohen developed these estimates by adapting data from jury awards in tort (accident) cases and applying them to economic analyses of crime.

This was a cockamamie thing to do. Only very serious accidents result in jury awards (most are settled), and he was thus using data on the most serious accidents to estimate the costs of average crimes. Jury awards are inflated to include attorneys' fees (a third to a half of the total). Cohen's inflated estimates, however, soon became widely used. This is probably because they were the only ones around.

Whether Cohen's estimates are plausible, however, is not the point. What is important is what is missing. Nowhere in this literature, including even in vigorous critiques of its quality and value (Zimring and Hawkins 1995, chap. 7), did anyone take account of offenders. A prison sentence entails pain and suffering by the offender. During the period behind walls, he is denied liberty, deprived of the company of loved ones, and exposed to the dangers and degradations of prison life. When he is released, he will be stigmatized and face numerous obstacles to resuming a normal life. These range from ineligibility for many professions, inability to vote, and employer resistance to employing ex-cons. He will after prison have lower life chances, life expectancy, and lifetime earnings than if he'd not spent time in prison. His family also will have suffered, economically, socially, and psychologically, if it survived intact.

Social scientists did little better than economists in relation to the effects of punishment on offenders. My 1995 *Malign Neglect* was one of the first calls for attention to collateral effects of imprisonment for prisoners, their families, and their communities. When, in 1997, I commissioned an essay from John Hagan and Robin Dinovitzer (1999) on the collateral effects of punishment, they had to report that the literature was fragmentary and fugitive, though they did their best to pull it together. On many important subjects—for examples, the effects of a parent's imprisonment on children's development and well-being or the effects of imprisonment on offenders' later health and life expectancy—there was no respectable social science literature. The inattention is beginning to end, and work is beginning to appear on the effects of imprisonment on prisoners' communities (Clear et al. 2001; Fagan, Forthcoming) and on collateral costs more generally (Mauer and Chesney-Lind 2002).

Social workers and health care workers, of course, have long known about the collateral effects of imprisonment for prisoners and their families. When parents who formerly supported the family go to prison, families must often apply for food stamps and income support. When caregivers, usually mothers, go to prison, child care agencies must arrange foster care or placements with responsible relatives. When children raised in broken and impoverished homes fail in school, participate in gangs or drug abuse, and manifest mental health problems, state agencies must respond. Such consequences were known and, however inadequately, addressed by care providers, however little systematic attention they received from academics. The Hagan and Donovitzer essay (1999) surveys the literatures on these subjects. I mention four somewhat less well-known literatures in the next few paragraphs.

First, both quantitative and qualitative literatures show that imprisonment reduces offenders' job prospects and their average and lifetime earnings (Fagan and Freeman 1999). Insofar as ex-prisoners support partners and children, they too experience reduced standards of living and often lesser life chances than they would otherwise have had. Reduced job prospects should be no surprise. Prisoners lose their jobs when they go to prison. When they come out, they bear the stigma of being ex-cons and find that many employers do not want to hire them at all, or only for low-pay dead-end jobs. Self-esteem and self-confidence plummet for many, and planning for the future becomes difficult. That family break-up, social failure, and mental health problems follow should be no surprise. These in their turn make prospects of good jobs and good earnings worse.

Second, as sociologist William Julius Wilson (1987) showed, though few researchers have followed this up, imprisonment impedes family formation and thereby undermines communities and increases the number of children raised in disadvantaged single-parent families. Wilson calculated, from census data, the number of "marriageable males" per 100 women of the same age and race in urban neighborhoods. By this, he meant employed men. He learned that the number of marriageable

(employed) young black men for every 100 young black women had declined steadily throughout the 1970s and 1980s and was lowest for young blacks among all age-and-race combinations. A principal reason for this is that since the late 1980s, nearly a third of young black men are at any time in prison or jail or on probation or parole. In other words, because so many more black men were sent to prison in the 1970s and 1980s and suffered the stigma of being ex-convicts afterwards, there were simply fewer attractive potential marriage partners around for young urban black women than in earlier times. Chances of formation of two-parent families declined.

Third, sociologist Todd Clear and others (Clear et al., Forthcoming; Clear et al. 2001) have studied the effects on communities when large numbers of young men are removed and sent to prison. Clear found something surprising. That removal of young men reduces the number of potential partners for women and reduces the number of potential workers is not surprising. What Clear and his colleagues found, and more recently Jeffrey Fagan (Forthcoming) has confirmed, is that sending many young men to prison increases crime rates in the community. To laypeople, this should be counterintuitive. After all, people are sent to prison because they have committed crimes, so surely removal of criminals from a community should decrease crime rates. Instead, what Clear and colleagues and Fagan found, was that neighborhoods from which very large numbers of offenders were sent to prison experienced higher crime rates. The reasons were that removal of so many young men fundamentally undermined community cohesion—things fell apart—and that above some critical number, men who amass criminal records become positive role models for youth when there are so few or no conventional role models at all. Stating the last point differently, when many or most men in a community acquire prison records, going to prison stops being stigmatizing and prison stops serving even potentially as a deterrent to crime. Crime rates rise in a community as a result.

Fourth, in the United States, a country in which many millions of people have been convicted of felonies, disenfranchisement laws have greatly reduced voting and other participation in democratic and economic institutions (Fellner and Mauer 1998). These laws vary from state to state. In some, people are barred from voting while in prison. In others, though, they are barred if they've ever had a felony conviction. Thus, in the 2000 presidential election in Florida, which George Bush won by a whisker, hundreds of thousands of state residents, mostly black men, were unable to vote because of their felony convictions. Demographic voting patterns (black people and poorer people tend to vote for Democrats) suggest that Bush would have lost the Florida election and therefore the presidency if Florida had not had a felon disenfranchisement law.

Felons, however, are in many states disqualified from other activities open to other citizens. These include occupational exclusion laws that forbid felons from becoming lawyers, barbers, or teachers. And they include laws that make felons ineligible for some educational and social service benefits. And federal law makes many felons who are immigrants vulnerable to deportation.

CONCLUSIONS

Crime thus is not one social problem, but many. In this chapter, I have identified and discussed some of the effects of crime that most people would consider social problems. These include the suffering, economic costs, and undesirable collateral effects of crime for victims, offenders, and communities. That is phrased in general terms. When we become more specific, hundreds of social problems appear that warrant analysis, understanding, and policy solutions. Most of them damage people's lives in ways that could be avoided or ameliorated. The life chances of children are diminished when they lose their parents or when their material conditions of life greatly worsen. The life expectancies of adults are lessened when, because they are ex-prisoners, they cannot get good jobs or earn adequate incomes, and because of that their self-esteem and hopes for the future plummet, and with that their mental and physical health.

There are many ways to address social problems associated with crime. One is to establish policies and programs aimed at remedying direct and collateral effects of crime.

Victims' programs, social work programs aimed at disadvantaged households and at-risk children, and parenting skills programs in prison exemplify the wide range of possible remedies. Or we can reduce the intrusiveness and severity of American crime and drug control policies and thereby make many of the collateral effects of crime less common and less likely.

REFERENCES

Albrecht, Hans-Jörg. 2001. "Post-Adjudication Dispositions in Comparative Perspective." Pp. 293–330 in *Sentencing and Sanctions in Western Countries,* edited by Michael Tonry and Richard Frase. New York: Oxford University Press.

Bentham, Jeremy. 1789. *Introduction to the Principles of Morals and Legislation.* Reprinted in 1948, as edited by Wilfred Harrison. Oxford: Oxford University Press.

Blumstein, Alfred and Allen Beck. 1999. "Population Growth in U.S. Prisons, 1980–1996." Pp. 17–62 in *Crime and Justice: A Review of Research,* vol. 26, *Prisons,* edited by Michael Tonry and Joan Petersilia. Chicago, IL: University of Chicago Press.

Bright, John. 1992. *Crime Prevention in America.* Chicago, IL: University of Illinois at Chicago.

Clarke, Ronald. 1995. "Situational Crime Prevention." Pp. 91–150 in *Crime and Justice: A Review of Research,* vol. 19, *Building a Safer Society— Strategic Approaches to Crime Prevention,* edited by Michael Tonry and David P. Farrington. Chicago, IL: University of Chicago Press.

Clear, Todd R., Dina R. Rose, and Judith A. Ryder. 2001. "Incarceration and the Community: The Problem of Removing and Returning Prisoners." *Crime and Delinquency* 47:335–51.

Clear, Todd R., Dina R. Rose, Elin Waring, and Kristen Scully. Forthcoming. "Coercive Mobility and Crime: A Preliminary Examination of Concentrated Incarceration and Social Disorganization." *Journal of Quantitative Criminology.*

Cohen, Mark A. 1988. "Pain, Suffering, and Jury Awards: A Study of the Cost of Crime to Victims." *Law and Society Review* 2 (3):537–55.

Fagan, Jeffrey. Forthcoming. "Crime, Law, and the Community Dynamics of Incarceration in New York City." In *The Future of Imprisonment,* edited by Michael Tonry. New York: Oxford University Press.

Fagan, Jeffrey and Richard B. Freeman. 1999. "Crime and Work." In *Crime and Justice: A Review of Research,* vol. 25, edited by Michael Tonry. Chicago, IL: University of Chicago Press.

Fellner, Jamie and Marc Mauer. 1998. *Losing the Vote: The Impact of Felony Disenfranchisement Laws in the United States.* New York: Human Rights Watch.

Gaes, Gerald, Timothy Flanagan, Laurence Motiuk, and Lynn Stewart. 1999. "Adult Correctional Treatment." Pp. 361–426 in *Crime and Justice: A Review of Research,* vol. 26, *Prisons,* edited by Michael Tonry and Joan Petersilia. Chicago, IL: University of Chicago Press.

Garbarino, James. 1989. "The Incidence and Prevalence of Child Maltreatment." Pp. 219–62 in *Family Violence,* edited by Lloyd Ohlin and Michael Tonry. Chicago, IL: University of Chicago Press.

Greenwood, Peter W., C. Peter Rydell, James Chiesa, and Karyn Model. 1996. *Diverting Children from a Life of Crime: Measuring Costs and Benefits.* Santa Monica, CA: RAND.

Hagan, John, and Rachel Dinovitzer. 1999. "Collateral Consequences of Imprisonment for Children, Communities, and Prisoners." Pp. 121–62 in *Crime and Justice: A Review of Research,* vol. 26, *Prisons,* edited by Michael Tonry and Joan Petersilia. Chicago, IL: University of Chicago Press.

Kempe, C. Henry, Frederic N. Silverman, Brandt F. Steele, William Droegemuller, and Henry K. Silver. 1962. "The Battered Child Syndrome." *Journal of the American Medical Association* 181:17–24.

Kershaw, Chris, Natalie Chivite-Matthews, Carys Thomas, and Rebecca Aust. 2001. *The 2001 British Crime Survey, First Results, England and Wales.* London: Home Office, Research, Statistics, and Development Directorate.

Lamon, Philippe. 2002. "Crime Trends in Thirteen Industrialized Countries." In *Crime Victimization in Comparative Perspective,* edited by Paul Nieuwbeerta. The Hague, The Netherlands: Boom Juridische Uitgevers.

MacCoun, Robert and Peter Reuter. 2001. *Drug War Heresies: Learning from Other Vices, Times, and Places.* Cambridge, England: Cambridge University Press.

Mauer, Marc and Meda Chesney-Lind, eds. 2002. *Invisible Punishment: The Collateral Consequences of Mass Imprisonment.* New York: New Press.

Mayhew, Pat and Jan J. M. van Dijk. 1997. *Criminal Victimisation in Eleven Industrialised Countries.* The Hague, The Netherlands: Netherlands Ministry of Justice, Research and Documentation Center.

Nadelmann, Ethan. 1992. "Thinking Seriously about Alternatives to Drug Prohibition." *Daedalus* 121:87–132.

Nieuwbeerta, Paul, ed. 2002. *Crime Victimization in Comparative Perspective.* The Hague, The Netherlands: Boom Juridische Uitgevers.

Office on National Drug Control Policy. 2002. *National Drug Control Policy.* Washington, DC: U.S. Government Printing Office.

Rennison, Callie. 2002. *Criminal Victimization 2001.* Washington, DC: U.S. Department of Justice, Bureau of Justice Statistics.

Sherman, Lawrence W. 1992. "Attacking Crime: Police and Crime Control." Pp. 159–230 in *Modern Policing,* edited by Michael Tonry and Norval Morris. Chicago, IL: University of Chicago Press.

Tonry, Michael. 1995. *Malign Neglect: Race, Crime, and Punishment in America.* New York: Oxford University Press.

———. 2001. "Punishment Policies and Patterns in Western Countries." Pp. 3–28 in *Sentencing and Sanctions in Western Countries,* edited by Michael Tonry and Richard S. Frase. New York: Oxford University Press.

Tonry, Michael and David P. Farrington. 1995. "Strategic Approaches to Crime Prevention." Pp. 1–20 in *Crime and Justice: A Review of Research,* vol. 19, *Building a Safer Society—Strategic Approaches to Crime Prevention,* edited by Michael Tonry and David P. Farrington. Chicago, IL: University of Chicago Press.

Tremblay, Richard and Wendy Craig. 1995. "Developmental Crime Prevention." Pp. 151–236 in *Crime and Justice: A Review of Research,* vol. 19, *Building a Safer Society—Strategic Approaches to Crime Prevention,* edited by Michael Tonry and David P. Farrington. Chicago, IL: University of Chicago Press.

U.S. Bureau of Justice Statistics. 2003. *Sourcebook of Criminal Justice Statistics, 2001.* Washington, DC: U.S. Department of Justice, Bureau of Justice Statistics.

Walker, Lenore. 1979. *The Battered Woman.* New York: Harper & Row.

Wilson, William Julius. 1987. *The Truly Disadvantaged.* Chicago, IL: University of Chicago Press.

Wittebrood, Karin. 2002. "Fear of Crime and Victimization in Western Industrialized Countries." In *Crime Victimization in Comparative Perspective,* edited by Paul Nieuwbeerta. The Hague, The Netherlands: Boom Juridische Uitgevers.

Zedlewski, Edwin W. 1987. *Making Confinement Decisions.* Washington, DC: U.S. Department of Justice, National Institute of Justice.

Zimring, Franklin E. and Gordon Hawkins. 1988. "The New Mathematics of Imprisonment." *Crime and Delinquency* 34:425–36.

——. 1995. *Incapacitation: Penal Confinement and the Restraint of Crime.* New York: Oxford University Press.

Zvecic, Ugljesa and Anna Alvazzi del Frate. 1995. *Criminal Victimisation in the Developing World.* Rome, Italy: United Nations International Crime and Justice Institute.

JUVENILE DELINQUENCY

MARK C. STAFFORD

University of Texas at Austin

This chapter is mainly about juvenile delinquency in the United States. However, to gain a broader understanding of the central issues, considerable attention also is given to delinquency outside the United States. After some preliminary considerations involving the meaning of the term *delinquency* and legal reactions to juvenile offenders both in and outside the United States, the chapter turns to a discussion of the amount and distribution of delinquency in the United States, including its demographic correlates and trends. The chapter focuses next on delinquency outside the United States, with comparisons to U.S. delinquency. The last part of the chapter considers theories about the causes of juvenile delinquency, both individual level and aggregate level theories.

PRELIMINARY CONSIDERATIONS

Juvenile delinquency is lawbreaking by juveniles, which in the United States and many other countries makes it subject to juvenile court jurisdiction. States establish the age range for juvenile court jurisdiction in the United States, but the minimum age in most states is 7, and the maximum age is 17. In contrast, juvenile court jurisdiction in Austria extends only from ages 14 to 18 (Edelbacher and Fenz 2002). Children under age 14 cannot be held responsible for their lawbreaking, even for serious offenses. Hong Kong distinguishes between "juveniles" and "young offenders." Whereas juveniles range from ages 7 to 15, young offenders range from 16 to 20. Even then, no one under age 14 can be imprisoned, and a person aged 16 to 20 can be imprisoned only if a court is "certain that there are no other suitable methods of dealing with the person" (Traver 2002:219). Indian boys above age 16 are treated as adults, but Indian girls are still treated as juveniles until age 19 (Sharma 1996). Many countries do not have separate courts for juveniles and adults. For example, adult courts double as juvenile courts in Namibia, although a person under age 18 can have parental assistance in criminal proceedings (Schulz 2002).

In the United States and many other countries, juvenile delinquency is not limited to criminal offenses, such as robbery, burglary, and theft, which are illegal for both juveniles and adults. Juvenile delinquency also includes status offenses that are illegal only for juveniles, examples being runaway and truancy. In India, a juvenile can be adjudicated as a delinquent for such status offenses as waywardness, incorrigibility, and habitual disobedience (Chakreborty 2002). In contrast, German law does not designate status offenses (Albrecht 2002), nor does Sweden (Winterdyk 2002a).

There is considerable variation among countries in legal reactions to juvenile offenders. They are treated more leniently than adult offenders in most countries. However, five countries, including the United States, allow capital punishment for juveniles convicted of committing serious offenses (the others being Bangladesh, Barbados, Iran, and Pakistan: Winterdyk 2002a). Other countries allow corporal punishment (e.g., Bolivia, Honduras, Sudan, Zimbabwe, and Singapore).

Many U.S. states recently have changed their juvenile codes to de-emphasize rehabilitation and more strongly emphasize punishment, justice, deterrence, and accountability (Snyder and Sickmund 1999). For example, the purpose of the 1996 Texas Juvenile Justice Code (chap. 51.01) was mainly to "provide for the protection of the public and public safety." Consistent with that purpose, the code was first, to "promote the concept of punishment for criminal acts" and second, to rehabilitate. Although identifying rehabilitation as at least a secondary purpose, the code revealed a weak commitment by linking it to accountability: "to provide treatment, training, and rehabilitation that emphasizes the accountability and responsibility of both the parent and the child for the child's conduct." That weak commitment is inconsistent with judicial interpretations of earlier (pre-1960) Texas juvenile justice codes, which said that the purpose of the juvenile justice system was "not one of punishment, but . . . protection of the child for its own good . . . not . . . to convict and punish juveniles but to guide and direct them." However, it is consistent with a new "culture of control" in other countries, including Britain, making the "practice of rehabilitation . . . increasingly inscribed in a framework of risk rather than a framework of welfare. . . . Rehabilitation is thus represented as a targeted intervention inculcating self-controls, reducing danger,

[and] enhancing the security of the public" (Garland 2001:176).

JUVENILE DELINQUENCY IN THE UNITED STATES

How much lawbreaking in the United States is attributable to juveniles? In 2000, there were approximately 9 million arrests in the United States, and about 17 percent (1.5 million) of them involved juveniles (Federal Bureau of Investigation [FBI] 2001:226). That figure is interpretable by comparing it to the percentage of the U.S. population composed of juveniles. Since in most states, juvenile court jurisdiction extends from ages 7 to 17, the relevant figure is the percentage of the population in that age range. That figure was 15.9 percent in 2000 (U.S. Census Bureau 2001), so juveniles were only slightly more likely than adults (proportionately speaking) to have been arrested.

Table 28.1 shows the percentage of U.S. arrests involving juveniles, by type of offense, for 2000. The data are from the FBI's Uniform Crime Reports, which publishes arrest data for eight serious index offenses (top panel in the table) and less serious nonindex offenses (bottom panel). Juveniles were neither more nor less likely than adults to have been arrested for serious violent offenses. However, there was variation by type of violent offense, with juveniles more likely than adults to have been arrested for robbery (accounting for 25 percent of the arrests). Juveniles also were more likely than adults to have been arrested for serious property offenses, especially arson (the other property offenses being burglary, larceny-theft, and motor vehicle theft).

The first two nonindex offenses in Table 28.1, curfew/loitering and runaway, are status offenses (illegal only for juveniles), which is why 100 percent of the arrests involved juveniles. In addition, juveniles were more likely than adults to have been arrested for vandalism, disorderly conduct, liquor law violations, weapons violations, and other (nonaggravated) assaults; and they were less likely than adults to have been arrested for drug abuse, vagrancy, drunkenness, and driving under the influence. The figures for drug abuse, drunkenness, and driving under the influence are contrary to popular

Table 28.1   Percentage of U.S. Arrests Involving Juveniles, by Type of Offense, 2000

Type of Offense	Percentage
Violent offenses	15.9
Murder	9.3
Rape	16.4
Robbery	25.3
Aggravated assault	13.9
Property offenses	32.0
Burglary	33.0
Larceny-theft	31.2
Motor vehicle theft	34.3
Arson	52.8
Curfew and loitering	100.0
Runaway	100.0
Vandalism	40.6
Disorderly conduct	25.9
Liquor law violations	23.3
Weapons: carrying, possessing	23.6
Other assaults	18.0
Drug abuse	12.9
Vagrancy	9.3
Drunkenness	3.4
Driving under the influence	1.4

Source: FBI (2001:226).

Table 28.2   Percentage of U.S. High School Seniors in 2000 Reporting Delinquency in Past 12 Months, by Type of Offense

Type of Offense	Percentage
Arguing/fighting with parents	88.8
Theft under $50	30.5
Shoplifting	28.7
Trespass into house/building	22.7
Group fighting	19.7
Vandalism at school	13.5
Theft over $50	12.5
Serious fight in school/work	12.3
Hurt someone badly	11.9
Vandalism at work	7.2
Auto theft	5.2
Theft of car part	5.1
Hit instructor/supervisor	2.9
Arson	2.8
Armed robbery	2.8
Been arrested	9.1
Alcohol	73.2
Marijuana/hashish	36.5
Stimulants	10.5
Hallucinogens	8.7
Sedatives	6.3
Tranquilizers	5.7
Cocaine	4.5
Crack cocaine	2.2
Steroids	1.7
Heroin	1.5

Source: Maguire and Pastore (2001).

beliefs that alcohol and other drug abuse are more juvenile than adult problems in the United States. Except for liquor law violations, adults and not juveniles were more likely to have been arrested for alcohol and other drug offenses.

Many offenders avoid arrest. Many offenses go undetected, and even when detected, the police may exercise bias in arresting offenders. For these reasons, researchers sometimes question juveniles themselves to obtain estimates of their lawbreaking. The data from these "self-report surveys" are collected by questionnaires or interviews, which ask such questions as: "During the past 12 months [or some other period, such as the past 6 months], how often have you . . . [a description of some offense, such as 'used marijuana']." One of the most comprehensive self-report surveys in the United States is conducted by University of Michigan researchers, who have sampled high school seniors throughout the nation since 1975. Table 28.2 shows the percentage of seniors in 2000 that reported committing various offenses at least once during the past year.

The nonalcohol/nondrug offenses most commonly reported were arguing with parents, which is a status offense, followed by theft under $50, shoplifting, and breaking into a house or building (see top panel in Table 28.2). Although a higher percentage reported committing minor rather than serious offenses, a fairly high percentage reported committing serious offenses as well: about 12 percent reported having been involved in a serious fight at school or work and hurt someone badly. Only a small percentage of seniors reported committing the most serious offenses: arson and armed robbery (2.8 percent for each offense).

Self-report surveys tend to reveal that virtually all U.S. juveniles commit delinquency at some time. In contrast, only 9 percent of seniors reported having been arrested during the past year, suggesting that arrest data for a particular year may underestimate the number of juvenile offenders by as much as 90 percent.

About 73 percent of the 2000 seniors reported alcohol use during the past year, and 37 percent reported marijuana or hashish use (see bottom panel in Table 28.2). The next highest percentages were for stimulants, hallucinogens, sedatives, and tranquilizers. Despite recent media attention on juvenile cocaine use in the United States, less than 5 percent of seniors reported either cocaine or crack use during the past year. Even smaller percentages reported use of steroids or heroin. Rohypnol, the "date rape" drug, was added to the survey only recently and has never been used by more than about 1 percent of U.S. high school seniors (Johnston, O'Malley, and Bachman 2000:28).

Demographic Correlates of Juvenile Delinquency in the United States

U.S. arrest rates increase rapidly during the teenage years, peak at about age 18, and then decrease (Empey, Stafford, and Hay 1999), although the peak age is higher for violent offenses than for property offenses (Jensen and Rojek 1998). For murder, the arrest rate for 18-year-olds in 2000 was 15 times greater than the arrest rate for 13- to 14-year-olds; and for rape, robbery, and aggravated assault, the arrest rates at age 18 were 2 to 3 times greater than the arrest rates at ages 13 to 14 (FBI 2001:226; U.S. Census Bureau 2001). The arrest ratios for 18-year-olds to 13- to 14-year-olds for burglary, larceny-theft, motor vehicle theft, and arson were smaller, with none exceeding 2 to 1. The age pattern in self-reported data is similar to that in arrest data, with self-reported delinquency tending to increase during the teenage years and the peak age varying by offense.

Males accounted for approximately 72 percent of all arrests of juveniles in the United States in 2000 (FBI 2001:225). Females accounted for a majority of juvenile arrests only for runaway and prostitution. Although self-reported delinquency is also higher for males than for females, the gap between males and females is less than that in arrest data. Moreover, the ratio of male-to-female self-reported

delinquency has been decreasing over time, especially for serious offenses (Jensen and Rojek 1998).

The public and the mass media often depict juvenile delinquency in the United States as committed disproportionately by lower-class juveniles. Uniform Crime Reports does not provide data on the social class of arrested juveniles. However, many researchers have collected their own data on the relationship between social class and arrests (Tittle and Meier 1990). Some studies have shown that lower-class juveniles are overrepresented in arrests, while others have not. Even though there appears to be a slight tendency for lower-class juveniles to be overrepresented in arrests, the social class differences in arrests are not nearly as large as age and gender differences. The same holds for the relationship between social class and self-reported delinquency. There is only a weak relationship between social class and self-reported delinquency, although there is evidence of more serious, repetitive delinquency among lower-class juveniles (Farnworth et al. 1994; Tittle and Meier 1990).

Black juveniles tend to have higher arrest rates than white juveniles, especially for serious offenses (Empey et al. 1999). However, there are much smaller black-white differences in self-reported data than in arrest data (Elliott 1994; Hindelang, Hirschi, and Weis 1981).

Migrant status is associated with race and ethnicity, and it has long been believed that juvenile delinquency in the United States is more likely to be committed by foreign-born than native-born juveniles (e.g., Waters 1999). However, contrary to such beliefs, foreign-born juveniles generally do not commit more delinquency. For example, the first waves of Laotian, Cambodian, and Vietnamese immigrants committed relatively little delinquency, although there were increases in successive waves (Waters 1999:61). Mexican immigrants came to the United States primarily in two separate waves, one in the early 1900s and the other later in the 1900s. There is no systematic evidence that delinquency rates were high among juveniles in the first wave. There was considerable gang delinquency among Mexican-American juveniles in the second wave in the 1970s and 1980s, especially in large California cities; but the relevant data lack accurate information about immigration status.

Trends in Juvenile Delinquency in the United States

Except for burglary, there were increases from 1975 to the mid-1990s in U.S. juvenile arrest rates for the index offenses of murder, rape, robbery, aggravated assault, larceny-theft, and motor vehicle theft; and the increases were greater for the violent offenses than for the property offenses (Stafford and Kyckelhahn 2002). There was a 132 percent increase from 1975 to 1994 in the juvenile arrest rate for murder, a 58 percent increase for rape, a 26 percent increase for robbery, and a 134 percent increase for aggravated assault. In contrast, there was a 13 percent increase from 1975 to 1994 in the juvenile arrest rate for the index offense of larceny-theft and a 33 percent increase for motor vehicle theft. The juvenile arrest rate for burglary decreased 42 percent from 1975 to 1994 (arson, although an index offense, is not considered because Uniform Crime Reports did not report arson arrests over the entire period).

Since 1994, the juvenile arrest rate has decreased for every index offense, including burglary. Indeed, by the end of the 1990s, the juvenile arrest rate for most index offenses—murder, rape, robbery, burglary, larceny-theft, and motor vehicle theft—was close to its lowest, if not the lowest, since 1975.

The increases in juvenile arrests for violent offenses from 1975 to 1994 corresponded to increasing public concern about youth violence, especially murder and aggravated assault. Zimring (1998:35–6) reports that the murder arrest rates for juveniles aged 13 to 17 and adults aged 18 to 34 moved together, remaining virtually unchanged, from the mid-1970s to the mid-1980s. Then the "under-18 rate takes off from 1985–1993 in a pattern that diverges from the homicide rates in the stable, older age group" (Zimring 1998:35). Most of the increase in the juvenile arrest rate for murder was attributable to an increase in murders with guns. From the mid-1970s to the mid-1990s, there was no increase in murders without guns. The reason for the increase in murders with guns is unclear. However, the "proportion of homicides committed with guns did not increase among adults, so no general increase in handgun availability seems to explain the sharp increase in youth shootings" (Zimring 1998:35).

Changes in the juvenile arrest rate for aggravated assault roughly mirrored changes in the juvenile arrest rate for murder: little change from the mid-1970s to the mid-1980s, then a large increase from the mid-1980s to the mid-1990s, followed by a decrease (Stafford and Kyckelhahn 2002; Zimring 1998). The similarity in the trends is consistent with a belief that aggravated assault is the nonlethal equivalent of murder. However, Zimring (1998:39) reports evidence that is inconsistent with that belief. Although the adult arrest rate for aggravated assault increased, as did the juvenile arrest rate for aggravated assault, from the mid-1980s to the mid-1990s, the adult arrest rate for murder decreased during that period, which is opposite from the trend for juveniles. What accounted for the large increases in the arrest rate for aggravated assault from the mid-1980s to the mid-1990s, for both juveniles and adults? According to Zimring (1998:39–40), the answer is a change in police practices. Since about 1980, the police in the U.S. have classified a higher percentage of assaults as aggravated rather than simple.

Changes in police practices cast doubts on interpretations of trends in arrest data, making it difficult to determine the extent to which the trends are functions of changes in juvenile delinquency or changes in the behavior of the police. Since the data in self-report surveys are not affected by changing police practices, it is useful to examine trends in self-reports of juvenile delinquency and compare them with trends in arrest data.

Table 28.3 reports percentage changes in self-reported nonalcohol/nondrug offenses by high school seniors from 1975 to 2000. Like arrests of juveniles in the United States, there were increases from 1975 to 1985 (Column 1 of Table 28.3) and 1985 to 1995 (Column 2 of Table 28.3) in the percentage of seniors that reported committing many of the offenses. Moreover, like juvenile arrests, there was a decrease in the percentage of seniors that reported committing many of the offenses from the mid-1990s to 2000 (Column 3 of Table 28.3). However, unlike juvenile arrests, the increases from the mid-1970s to the mid-1990s were not considerably greater for violent offenses than for property offenses. Indeed, for four of the violent offenses (group fighting, serious fight in school/work, hitting an instructor/supervisor, and armed robbery), there

Table 28.3   Percentage Changes in Reported Delinquency by High School Seniors, 1975–2000, by Type of Offense

Type of Offense	Percentage Change			
	1975–1985	*1985–1995*	*1995–2000*	*1975–2000*
Arguing/fighting with parents	1.1	1.5	–1.6	1.0
Theft under $50	–7.1	4.3	–2.9	–5.9
Shoplifting	–24.5	12.8	–4.0	–18.2
Trespass into house/building	–6.8	–10.3	–3.4	–19.2
Group fighting	18.4	–9.7	5.9	13.2
Vandalism at school	7.8	1.4	–3.6	5.5
Theft over $50	25.0	32.9	34.4	123.2
Serious fight at school/work	24.7	–18.7	–16.9	–15.8
Hurt someone badly	21.1	7.0	–3.3	25.3
Vandalism at work	7.8	12.7	16.1	41.2
Auto theft	43.6	–14.3	8.3	33.3
Theft of car part	19.6	–23.9	0.0	–8.9
Hit instructor/supervisor	0.0	0.0	–6.5	–6.5
Arson	11.8	31.6	12.0	64.7
Armed robbery	29.6	0.0	–20.0	3.7

Source: McGarrell and Flanagan (1985); Maguire and Pastore (1995, 2001).

was either no change or a decrease in the percentage of seniors that reported committing them from 1985 to 1995 (hurting someone badly being the exception). Then, while there was a decrease from 1995 to 2000 in the percentage of seniors that reported committing most of the violent offenses, as there was with juvenile arrests for violent offenses, there was in increase in the percentage that reported committing some of the property offenses, which is contrary to the trend for juvenile arrests for property offenses. In addition to differences between arrests and self-reports of juvenile delinquency in the directions of the trends, the magnitudes of the changes over time (both increases and decreases) were not nearly as great for self-reported delinquency as they were for arrests.

As for self-reports of alcohol and other illegal drug use by high school seniors (figures not shown here), there have been many decreases in use after peaks in the late 1970s (Johnston, O'Malley, and Bachman 1994:78–9; Pastore and Maguire 2000:236–7). Alcohol use increased from 1975 to 1979 but has decreased since then. Similarly, marijuana use peaked in 1979, but it decreased from 1980 to 1992. Marijuana use has increased since

1992, but current use is still less than it was in 1979. The peak year for cocaine use was 1985, but there was decreased use until 1993, when it increased. Questions about steroid use have been included in the University of Michigan survey of high school seniors only since 1989. Although steroid use decreased from 1989 to 1992, it has increased since then. However, it is still the case that only a small percentage of high school seniors report use of steroids (Johnston et al. 2000:4). Questions about crystal methamphetamine ("ice") also were added to the survey in 1989, and questions about Rohypnol (the "date rape" drug) were added in 1996. Each year, about 1 percent of high school seniors reported use of these drugs (Johnston et al. 2000:20, 28).

JUVENILE DELINQUENCY OUTSIDE THE UNITED STATES

Data on juvenile delinquency outside the United States are often poor, with the notable exceptions of Canada, Australia, Western European countries, and a few others. Many countries do not collect systematic data on delinquency. Among the countries that do, the data are often incomplete because of faulty record keeping. Consequently, estimates of delinquency outside the United States tend to be crude.

As in the United States, juveniles in Germany, England and Wales, India, Hong Kong, and Canada are more likely to commit minor than serious offenses (Albrecht 2002; Gelsthorpe and Kemp 2002; Sharma 1996; Traver 2002; Winterdyk 2002b). Juveniles outside the United States also are more likely to commit property offenses than violent offenses (Albrecht 2002; Edelbacher and Fenz 2002; Gelsthorpe and Kemp 2002; Herczog and Irk 2002; Mishra 1991; Sharma 1996; Walgrave 2002; Yue 2002). For example, a 1998 self-report survey in Belgium revealed that about 25 percent of juveniles committed minor property offenses during the past year, while only about 12 percent committed an act of physical violence or carried a gun (Walgrave 2002). Similarly, serious violent offenses are "rare events" for juveniles in Germany, with the highest rates of offending among young adults (Albrecht 2002:179).

Researchers in some countries report high rates of illegal drug use by juveniles, while others do not. For example, according to Winterdyk (2002b), only 4 percent of cases processed in Canadian juvenile courts were drug-related. In contrast, Gelsthorpe and Kemp (2002) conclude that illegal drug use is widespread among juveniles in England and Wales, although this is confined mainly to marijuana.

Demographic Correlates of Juvenile Delinquency Outside the United States

As in the United States, juvenile delinquency outside the United States tends to peak during the teenage years. For example, the peak age range for juvenile offending in China is 14 to 17 (Yue 2002). However, unlike U.S. arrest rates, which peak at about age 18 and then decrease, Indian arrests do not peak until ages 30 to 40 (Mitra 1988). The peak offending age in Belgium is 16 (Walgrave 2002).

Gender is also a strong correlate of juvenile delinquency outside the United States, with much more lawbreaking committed by males than by females. Eighty percent of juvenile offenders processed in youth courts in Canada in 1998 to 1999 were male (Winterdyk 2002b); and in South Africa

in 1996 to 1997, 90 percent of juveniles charged in magistrate's courts were male (Skelton and Potgieter 2002). In China, it has been estimated that males account for 98 percent of delinquency (Yue 2002). Also, as in the United States, the ratio of female-to-male juvenile offending reportedly has been increasing in many other countries, mainly because of large increases in female offending. A partial list of countries with large reported increases in female offending includes South Korea (for violent offenses), Canada (for violent offenses), China (for drug offenses), the Netherlands (for diverse offenses), and Scotland (for diverse offenses) (see chapters in Winterdyk 2002c).

In contrast to the United States, there is evidence of a strong relationship between social class (actually family income) and juvenile delinquency in some other countries. For example, Mitra (1988) has reported that about 70 percent of juveniles apprehended on various charges in India were from low-income families (also see Mishra 1991; Sharma 1996), although a later report by Chakreborty (2002) has put that figure at about 50 percent. According to Yue (2002), more than half of arrested juvenile drug users in parts of China in the mid-1990s were either unemployed or school dropouts, and Farrington (1999) has indicated that the "typical delinquent [in the United Kingdom] . . . tends to be born in a low-income . . . family" (p. 5).

A reliance on official police data casts doubts on most non-U.S. studies of the relationship between social class and juvenile delinquency. Law enforcement officials may be biased against low-income juveniles and thus be more likely to pursue charges against them. If so, the *true* relationship between social class and juvenile delinquency outside the United States might be as weak as it is in the United States. However, it is also possible that there is a stronger relationship between social class and delinquency outside the United States. Poverty may be an important cause of juvenile delinquency outside the United States because of its intensity. In Namibia, where it has been reported that delinquency is strongly related to social class, more than half the population has an annual per capita income of $US 85 or less, and the economic situation for young people is "bleak" (Schulz 2002:373). "In 1999, 16,000 school-leavers were competing for

4,000 new jobs," and due to such limited employment opportunities, "an increasing number of youth will be turning to crime, prostitution, and substance abuse, among other delinquent activities" (Schulz 2002:374). According to Mitra (1988), "Most of the incidents of delinquencies [in India] were the result of economic conditions" (p. 98). Poor children in India, especially those in rural areas, suffer from malnutrition, and only about 30 percent attend school.

Juveniles in many racially and ethnically distinct minority groups in countries outside the United States have high rates of arrest, juvenile court referral, and institutionalization. For example, aboriginal juveniles in South Australia have a juvenile court referral rate that is over five times higher than the rate for other juveniles (Brady 1985). In the Netherlands, juveniles of Moroccan and Antillean descent are overrepresented in the juvenile justice system (Ferwerda 2002); and in India, about 75 percent of institutionalized juvenile offenders are from the lower castes (e.g., Regar, Harijan, Kanjar, Kumhar, Sunar, Jat) (Sharma 1996). Poverty is a shared characteristic of many minority groups. For example, in the Netherlands, there are areas in the middle-sized and large cities that are comparable to slums in the United States with a large number of minorities living in substandard housing and experiencing high unemployment (Ferwerda 2002). Moreover, high delinquency rates for Moroccan and Turkish juveniles in Belgium have been attributed to their low socioeconomic status and educational exclusion (Walgrave 2002).

Not all minority groups have high delinquency rates. They "are in fact very low among some racial [and ethnic] minority groups, for example, Chinese and Japanese in the U.S. and certainly below average in other groups such as Indians and Pakistanis in Britain" (Cox 1985:130).

Little is known about the relationship between migrant status and juvenile delinquency in non-U.S. countries. However, Cox (1985:130) has indicated that first-generation immigrants to Australia committed "very little" delinquency; and although second-generation immigrants committed more delinquency than their parents did, they committed no more delinquency than other Australian juveniles of similar socioeconomic status. However, there were relatively high delinquency rates among Yugoslav, Hungarian, and Vietnamese immigrants to Australia.

Trends in Juvenile Delinquency Outside the United States

It is difficult to draw defensible conclusions about trends in juvenile delinquency in many countries outside the United States. As indicated previously, delinquency data outside the United States are often poor. The quality of the data also may change over time. If based on official data, such as police records, reported trends in delinquency may reflect more than changes in lawbreaking by juveniles. Commenting on the situation in Belgium, Walgrave (2002) has said that reported trends may reflect "the public's changing degrees of tolerance or of confidence in police, to a change in effectiveness in police-record-keeping, [and] to norm erosion . . . [as well as] to real changes in criminality" (p. 51). Any or all of these factors may vary over time.

The data problems notwithstanding, there were reported increases in youth violence in many countries during the past few decades, prompting one researcher to describe the increases as "an international phenomenon" (Winterdyk 2002b:93). For example, rates of Canadian juveniles charged with violent offenses more than doubled from the mid-1980s to the late 1990s, and similar increases in violent offending were found in self-report surveys of Canadian juveniles during the same period (Winterdyk 2002b:72, 93). Violent victimization of Canadian juveniles often occurs in schools, with bullying/intimidation/threats and physical attacks/fights without weapons being the most common violent offenses. Schools have responded by incorporating diverse security measures, including guards, metal detectors, and closed-circuit televisions (Winterdyk 2002b).

According to Edelbacher and Fenz (2002), youth violence also has been increasing in Austria. The violence is directed against women and young children in families, and there are drug-related robberies, gang fights, and violence at soccer games.

Mirroring the trend in the United States, prosecution and arrest rates of juveniles for violent offenses increased in Hong Kong from the mid-1970s to the mid-1990s, when they decreased (Traver 2002:222–23). However, a different picture emerged from surveys in which persons were asked to report their previous victimization experiences. These victimization surveys provided little evidence for an increase in youth violence in Hong Kong from 1979 to 1999 (Traver 2002:225–26). For violent offenses involving single offenders, there was a decrease in the percentage of offenders estimated to be under age 21 (combining "juveniles" and "young offenders"), from a high of 25 percent in 1981 to a low of 12 percent in 1998. For violent offenses involving multiple offenders, there was an increase in the percentage of offenders under age 21, from 24 percent in 1978 to 46 percent in 1994. However, many of the offenses involving multiple offenders were "relatively minor . . . involving local youths extorting lunch money and similarly small sums of money from other, less aggressive youths" (Traver 2002:226).

The increase in the prosecution and arrest rates of juveniles in Hong Kong for violent offenses has been attributed to increased reporting of lawbreaking to legal officials (Traver 2002). The victimization surveys revealed that the percentage of violent crimes reported to the police increased substantially from 1978 through the 1990s, and the increased tendency to report was greatest for offenses committed by offenders under age 21.

While violent offending by juveniles in Canada increased from the mid-1980s to the late 1990s, rates of juveniles charged with property offenses decreased during that period (Winterdyk 2002b). In contrast, in Austria, the percentage of property offenses committed by juveniles increased from 1990 to 1999 (Edelbacher and Fenz 2002). In Hong Kong, there were increases from the mid-1980s to the late 1990s in the prosecution and arrest rates of juveniles for some property offenses (e.g., "shop theft"), and there were decreases for other property offenses (Traver 2002).

Given widespread illegal drug use by juveniles in many countries outside the United States, it is surprising that there are few reports of trends. There are reported increases in both Canada (Winterdyk 2002b) and England and Wales (Gelsthorpe and Kemp 2002). Yue (2002) reports that there also have been increases in China since the late 1980s. Juvenile drug users have not been limited to Southwest China, where access to drugs is easier because of its proximity to the "Golden Triangle; drug using-young people today are found and documented in almost every province in China" (Yue 2002:116). Although traditionally, heroin has been the illegal drug most commonly used by Chinese juveniles, they are now turning to amphetamines, Ecstasy, and other newer types of drugs.

CAUSES OF JUVENILE DELINQUENCY

What causes juvenile delinquency? There are diverse theories that address that question, and those theories can be categorized by whether they are intended to account for individual level variation in delinquency or aggregate level variation. The first type of theory addresses this question: Why do some juveniles commit more delinquency than others? The second type of theory addresses this question: What accounts for variation in delinquency rates among social units, such as neighborhoods or countries?

Individual Level Theories of Juvenile Delinquency

According to Hirschi's (1969) social control theory, weak bonds to conventional society cause juvenile delinquency. Specifically, the likelihood of delinquency will increase to the extent that juveniles are weakly attached to parents and teachers, weakly committed to long-term educational and occupational goals, uninvolved in conventional activities (e.g., studying, playing sports), and do not believe in the moral legitimacy of conventional norms, including laws. According to Hirschi (1969), one of the most important bonds is attachment to parents. If juveniles are not strongly attached to their parents, they will not form strong commitments to conventional goals, nor will they internalize conventional norms; and consequently, there will be little to prevent them from breaking the law. According to Hirschi (1969), "If a person does not care about the wishes and expectations of other people . . . then he is to that extent not bound by the norms. He is free to deviate" (p. 18).

Gottfredson and Hirschi's (1990) self-control theory is a variation of social control theory.

Lawbreaking is said to be a desirable strategy for pursuing self-interests because it provides "immediate, easy, and certain short-term pleasure" (Gottfredson and Hirschi 1990:41). The central question is what constrains lawbreaking. For Gottfredson and Hirschi (1990), the answer is high self-control. People with high self-control will resist the immediate pleasures associated with lawbreaking. Conversely, low self-control people will be impulsive, prone to risk taking, self-centered, and hot tempered, and they will prefer easy gratification and physical rather than mental activities. According to Gottfredson and Hirschi (1990), ineffective child rearing causes low self-control. It is caused by the inability of parents to monitor a child's behavior, recognize norm violations when they occur, and punish those norm violations.

The Gottfredson-Hirschi theory is not limited to juvenile delinquency. It is assumed that low self-control is established in early childhood and once established will remain stable over the life course. Hence, low self-control will cause not only juvenile delinquency but adult crime as well. Moreover, in addition to causing lawbreaking, Gottfredson and Hirschi (1990) say that people with low self-control will "tend to pursue immediate pleasures that are *not* criminal: they will tend to smoke, drink, use drugs, gamble, have children out of wedlock, and engage in illicit sex" (p. 90). Thus, it is a theory of deviance, broadly conceived, to include such things as job and marital instability, accidents, and addictions.

Both social control theory and self-control theory posit that there is no special motivation needed to explain juvenile delinquency; it is assumed that all juveniles are motivated to violate the law and will do so if not restrained (controlled). In contrast, strain theories assume that only some juveniles are motivated to violate the law. According to Cohen (1955) and Cloward and Ohlin (1960), the motivation to commit delinquency stems from blocked goal achievement. According to Cohen (1955), all children want status and acceptance, and lower-class children experience more difficulty than middle- and upper-class children in achieving those goals, especially in school. The reason is that lower-class children have not learned the behaviors necessary for school success, such as self-control (Cohen 1955). Schools are said to be middle-class

institutions that use a "middle-class measuring rod" to judge students, and consequently lower-class children are socialized to fail (Cohen 1955:84–93). According to Cohen (1955), delinquency can be a solution to such failure, and this is especially true of gang delinquency because the gang represents a collection of like-minded peers who grant status and acceptance to one another for lawbreaking.

Cloward and Ohlin's (1960) version of strain theory assumes that all Americans value economic success as characterized by the American Dream. There is a strain toward delinquency among lower-class juveniles because they are denied educational and occupational opportunities to achieve economic success. Consequently, they will turn to illegitimate opportunities when they are available. According to Cloward and Ohlin (1960), income-producing delinquency, such as theft and fraud, is rational and utilitarian and is aimed at achieving economic success. Such offending will occur in neighborhoods with stable adult crime that can provide illegitimate opportunities to achieve economic success. If illegitimate opportunities are unavailable, as is the case in neighborhoods without stable adult crime, the strain toward delinquency will be manifested in petty offending and assaults. Alcohol and other drugs will be used by "double failures," juveniles who have failed to use both legitimate and illegitimate opportunities for economic success.

According to both the Cohen and Cloward-Ohlin versions of strain theory, the strain toward delinquency should be experienced only by lower-class juveniles. The problem is, as indicated previously, that there is a weak relationship between social class and delinquency, at least in the United States. Because of this problem, Agnew (1985, 1992) has proposed a revised version of strain theory, which expands the notion of strain to include not only blocked goal achievement but also maltreatment and other types of adversity, which can be experienced by juveniles in all social classes. He identifies three types of delinquency-producing strain. The first, the *failure to achieve positively valued goals,* includes Cohen's (1955) and Cloward and Ohlin's (1960) blocked-goal achievement. However, it also includes notions of injustice and unfairness. For example, a strain toward delinquency will be caused by a belief that valued resources, such as grades or attention from teachers, are not distributed fairly. The second type of delinquency-producing strain, the *removal of positively valued stimuli,* might result from the death of a parent, the loss of a boyfriend or girlfriend, or suspension from school. The third type is the *presentation of aversive stimuli,* and it includes maltreatment by teachers, abuse from parents, and criminal victimization.

The final individual level theory to be considered is learning theory. An early version of the theory was posited by Sutherland (1939; Sutherland and Cressey 1974:75–7), who claimed that delinquency is learned mainly in primary or intimate groups, such as families and peer groups. Juveniles will commit delinquency to the extent that they have learned techniques for violating the law (e.g., learning how to properly smoke marijuana) and "definitions" (attitudes) favorable to violation of law in excess of "definitions" unfavorable to violation of law. Although delinquency is likely to be learned from association with groups of lawbreakers, it also is possible to learn it from association with law-abiding groups.

Believing that Sutherland did not go far enough in specifying the process by which delinquency is learned, Akers (1985, 1998, 2000; Burgess and Akers 1966) has reformulated it by drawing on learning theory in psychology. According to Akers's (1998:68) social learning theory, the likelihood of delinquency will increase to the extent that juveniles are rewarded for it (e.g., through approval or prestige) or escape punishment for it. The likelihood of committing delinquency will decrease to the extent that juveniles are punished for it or a reward for it is removed or withheld. Although rewards and punishments for delinquency can be nonsocial, as when drug use creates a desired euphoria, most of the learning of delinquency will involve social rewards and punishments, such as acceptance and exclusion.

Aggregate Level Theories of Juvenile Delinquency

In contrast to individual level theories that attempt to explain why some juveniles commit more juvenile delinquency than others, aggregate level theories attempt to account for variation in delinquency rates among social units, such as neighborhoods or countries. To be sure, there are aggregate level versions of some individual level theories. For example, Akers (2000:81–2) has proposed that social learning variables are affected by four dimensions of social structure: (1) *differential social organization,* which refers to the structural correlates of delinquency in a social unit, such as family instability; (2) *differential location in the social structure,* which includes the social class, gender, race/ethnic, and age composition of a social unit; (3) *theoretically defined structural variables,* which refers to variables that have been identified in other theories; and (4) *differential social location,* which refers to the primary and secondary group memberships in a social unit. These dimensions of social structure will affect variation in the learning environments, which, in turn, will affect variation in delinquency rates.

Other aggregate level theories have no individual level versions. One of the more prominent aggregate level theories is social disorganization theory, which can be traced to the work of Shaw and McKay (Shaw 1929; Shaw and McKay 1942) in the first half of the twentieth century but which recently has received renewed attention (e.g., Bursik and Grasmick 1993; Sampson, Raudenbush, and Earls 1997). According to the theory, lower-class neighborhoods are socially disorganized or lack effective social controls. Part of the social disorganization involves ineffective parental control of children. Without effective parental control, delinquent traditions will develop and will be transmitted from one generation to the next, causing high neighborhood delinquency rates.

In another aggregate level theory, Messner and Rosenfeld (1997) have proposed that the effects of poverty on juvenile delinquency (as well as adult crime) will depend on the strength of noneconomic institutions, such as the family and the educational and the political systems. "What is distinctive about the United States," according to Messner and Rosenfeld (1997:69), "is the exaggerated emphasis on monetary success." Given the strong pressure to succeed monetarily, people will formulate wants and desires that are difficult to satisfy by legal means. "This . . . helps [to] explain criminal behavior with an instrumental character that offers monetary rewards" (Messner and Rosenfeld 1997:76). The strong emphasis on monetary success also will weaken noneconomic institutions, and weak noneconomic institutions will increase the effects of poverty on income-producing delinquency. This is why "crime rates are . . . exceptionally high in the United States" (Messner and Rosenfeld 1997:x). When noneconomic institutions are strong, poverty will not cause an increase in income-producing delinquency.

Brief Comments on Tests of the Theories

Tests have produced support for all of the theories, at least to some extent (for an extensive review, see Empey et al. 1999). Key predictors of juvenile delinquency have been found to include attachment to parents, religious beliefs, self-control, school failure, divorce of parents, parental abuse, and association with delinquent peers. However, most of the tests have been based on studies in the United States, Canada, Australia, Britain, and a few other countries. Hence, there is a need for tests in other countries. However, the available evidence suggests that the theories have broad application. To mention only two examples of tests in very different countries, AlRomaih (1993) found evidence to support Hirschi's (1969) social control theory in a sample of juveniles in Saudi Arabia, and Maxwell (2001) reported findings consistent with Agnew's (1985, 1992) version of strain theory from a study of juveniles in the Philippines.

DISCUSSION

Legal distinctions between juvenile delinquency and adult crime stem from a belief that juveniles are different from adults. In particular, a belief that juveniles are more immature than adults and in greater need of nurturance and protection has been used to justify a distinction between juvenile and adult lawbreaking. The *parens patriae* (parent of the country) doctrine, which supported the creation of juvenile courts in the United States in the late 1800s and early 1900s and guided U.S. juvenile justice policies through much of the twentieth century, gave legal officials considerable power to protect juveniles (Stafford 1995). Hence, juveniles were granted *protective rights* out of a belief that they lacked the capacity to care for themselves and make effective choices. However, during the past several decades, juveniles in the United States have been granted fewer protective rights and more *liberating rights*. The shift is associated with a growing belief that juveniles can make choices that are just as effective as those made by adults. Increasingly, it has been believed that juveniles need liberating rights, such as due process in juvenile court and free expression in school. The extension of liberating rights to juveniles in the United States also has been associated with expectations of greater responsibility for them and demands that they be held accountable for their actions. This has led to an increasing de-emphasis on rehabilitation and an increasing emphasis on punishment in many U.S. states.

Unlike the United States, many countries still grant more protective than liberating rights to juveniles and emphasize rehabilitation more than punishment (Winterdyk 2002a). At the same time, recent "moral panic" over increased juvenile delinquency in some countries, especially increased youth violence in some European countries, "has prompted more punitive reactions than rehabilitative approaches" (Winterdyk 2002a:xx). However, this important question largely has been ignored: Has there been improvement in the physical, psychological, and social well-being of juveniles because of a shift from protective rights and rehabilitation to liberating rights and punishment? There is considerable need for research on this question, both in and outside the United States. Until it is addressed carefully, policymakers largely will be operating in the dark about the consequences of different juvenile justice policies.

REFERENCES

Agnew, Robert. 1985. "A Revised Strain Theory of Delinquency." *Social Forces,* September, 64:151–67.
———. 1992. "Foundation for a General Strain Theory of Crime and Delinquency." *Criminology,* February, 30:478–87.
Akers, Ronald L. 1985. *Deviant Behavior: A Social Learning Approach.* 3rd ed. Belmont, CA: Wadsworth.

——. 1998. *Social Learning and Social Structure: A General Theory of Crime and Deviance.* Boston, MA: Northeastern University Press.

——. 2000. *Criminological Theories: Introduction, Evaluation, and Application.* 3rd ed. Los Angeles, CA: Roxbury.

Albrecht, Hans-Jorg. 2002. "Juvenile Crime and Juvenile Law in the Federal Republic of Germany." Pp. 171–205 in *Juvenile Justice Systems: International Perspectives,* edited by John A. Winterdyk. Toronto, Canada: Canadian Scholars' Press.

AlRomaih, Yousef Ahmed. 1993. *Social Control and Delinquency in Saudi Arabia.* Unpublished dissertation, Washington State University.

Brady, Maggie. 1985. "Aboriginal Youth and the Juvenile Justice System." Pp. 112–25 in *Juvenile Delinquency in Australia,* edited by Allan Borowski and James M. Murray. Melbourne, Australia: Methuen.

Burgess, Robert L. and Ronald L. Akers. 1966. "A Differential Association-Reinforcement Theory of Criminal Behavior." *Social Problems,* Fall, 14:128–47.

Bursik, Robert J, Jr. and Harold G. Grasmick. 1993. *Neighborhoods and Crime: The Dimensions of Effective Community Control.* New York: Lexington Books.

Chakreborty, Tapan. 2002. "Juvenile Delinquency and Juvenile Justice in India." Pp. 265–96 in *Juvenile Justice Systems: International Perspectives,* edited by John A. Winterdyk. Toronto, Canada: Canadian Scholars' Press.

Cloward, Richard A. and Lloyd E. Ohlin. 1960. *Delinquency and Opportunity: A Theory of Delinquent Gangs.* New York: Free Press.

Cohen, Albert. 1955. *Delinquent Boys: The Culture of the Gang.* New York: Free Press.

Cox, David R. 1985. "Migrant Youth and Juvenile Delinquency." Pp. 126–39 in *Juvenile Delinquency in Australia,* edited by Allan Borowski and James M. Murray. Melbourne, Australia: Methuen.

Edelbacher, Maximilian and Claudia Fenz. 2002. "Juvenile Justice System: An Austrian Perspective." Pp. 1–27 in *Juvenile Justice Systems: International Perspectives,* edited by John A. Winterdyk. Toronto, Canada: Canadian Scholars' Press.

Elliott, Delbert S. 1994. "Serious Violent Offenders: Onset, Developmental Course, and Termination." *Criminology,* February, 32:1–21.

Empey, LaMar T., Mark C. Stafford, and Carter H. Hay. 1999. 4th ed. *American Delinquency: Its Meaning and Construction.* Belmont, CA: Wadsworth.

Farnworth, Margaret, Terence P. Thornberry, Marvin D. Krohn, and Alan J. Lizotte. 1994. "Measurement in the Study of Class and Delinquency: Integrating Theory and Research." *Journal of Research in Crime and Delinquency,* February, 31:32–61.

Farrington, David P. 1999. "Predicting Persistent Young Offenders." Pp. 3–21 in *Juvenile Delinquency in the United States and the United Kingdom,* edited by Gary L. McDowell and Jinney S. Smith. London, England: Macmillan.

Federal Bureau of Investigation. 2001. *Crime in the United States: Uniform Crime Reports, 2000.* Washington, DC: U.S. Government Printing Office.

Ferwerda, Henk. 2002. "Youth Crime and Juvenile Justice in the Netherlands." Pp. 385–409 in *Juvenile Justice Systems: International Perspectives,* edited by John A. Winterdyk. Toronto, Canada: Canadian Scholars' Press.

Garland, David. 2001. *The Culture of Control: Crime and Social Order in Contemporary Society.* Oxford: Oxford University Press.

Gelsthorpe, Loraine and Vicky Kemp. 2002. "Comparative Juvenile Justice: England and Wales." Pp. 127–69 in *Juvenile Justice Systems: International Perspectives,* edited by John A. Winterdyk. Toronto, Canada: Canadian Scholars' Press.

Gottfredson, Michael R. and Travis Hirschi. 1990. *A General Theory of Crime.* Stanford, CA: Stanford University Press.

Herczog, Maria and Ferenc Irk. 2002. "Comparative Juvenile Justice: An Overview of Hungary." Pp. 235–64 in *Juvenile Justice Systems: International Perspectives,* edited by John A. Winterdyk. Toronto, Canada: Canadian Scholars' Press.

Hindelang, Michael J., Travis Hirschi, and Joseph G. Weis. 1981. *Measuring Delinquency.* Beverly Hills, CA: Sage.

Hirschi, Travis. 1969. *Causes of Delinquency.* Berkeley, CA: University of California Press.

Jensen, Gary F. and Dean G. Rojek. 1998. *Delinquency and Youth Crime.* 3rd ed. Prospect Heights, IL: Waveland.

Johnston, Lloyd D., Patrick M. O'Malley, and Jerald G. Bachman. 1994. *National Survey Results on Drug Use from the Monitoring the Future Study, 1975–1993,* vol. 1, *Secondary School Students.* Rockville, MD: National Institute on Drug Abuse.

——. 2000. *Monitoring the Future: National Results on Adolescent Drug Use, Overview of Key Findings, 1999.* Bethesda, MD: National Institute on Drug Abuse.

Maguire, Kathleen and Ann L Pastore, eds. 1995. *Sourcebook of Criminal Justice Statistics, 1994.*

Washington, DC: U.S. Government Printing Office. Retrieved from http://www.albany.edu/sourcebook.

——, eds. 2001. *Sourcebook of Criminal Justice Statistics, 2001.* Retrieved from http://www.albany. edu/sourcebook.

Maxwell, Sheila Royo. 2001. "A Focus on Familial Strain: Antisocial Behavior and Delinquency in Filipino Society." *Sociological Inquiry,* Summer, 71:265–92.

McGarrell, Edmund F. and Timothy J. Flanagan, eds. 1985. *Sourcebook of Criminal Justice Statistics, 1984.* Washington, DC: U.S. Government Printing Office.

Messner, Steven F. and Richard Rosenfeld. 1997. *Crime and the American Dream.* 2nd ed. Belmont, CA: Wadsworth.

Mishra, B. N. 1991. *Juvenile Delinquency and Justice System.* New Delhi: Ashish Publishing.

Mitra, N. L. 1988. *Juvenile Delinquency and Indian Justice System.* Rajouri Garden, New Delhi: Deep and Deep.

Pastore, Ann L. and Kathleen Maguire, eds. 2000. *Sourcebook of Criminal Justice Statistics, 1999.* Washington, DC: U.S. Government Printing Office.

Sampson, Robert J., Stephen W. Raudenbush, and Felton Earls. 1997. "Neighborhoods and Violent Crime: A Multilevel Study of Collective Efficacy." *Science,* August, 277:918–24.

Schulz, Stefan. 2002. "Juvenile Justice in Namibia: A System in Transition." Pp. 353–84 in *Juvenile Justice Systems: International Perspectives,* edited by John A. Winterdyk. Toronto, Canada: Canadian Scholars' Press.

Sharma, D. D. 1996. *Young Delinquents in India.* Jaipur, India: Printwell.

Shaw, Clifford R. 1929. *Delinquency Areas: A Study of the Geographic Distribution of School Truants, Juvenile Delinquents, and Adult Offenders in Chicago.* Chicago, IL: University of Chicago Press.

Shaw, Clifford R. and Henry D. McKay. 1942. *Juvenile Delinquency and Urban Areas: A Study of Rates of Delinquents in Relation to Differential Characteristics of Local Communities in American Cities.* Chicago, IL: University of Chicago Press.

Skelton, Ann and Hennie Potgieter. 2002. "Juvenile Justice in South Africa." Pp. 477–501 in *Juvenile Justice Systems: International Perspectives,* edited by John A. Winterdyk. Toronto, Canada: Canadian Scholars' Press.

Snyder, Howard N. and Melissa Sickmund. 1999. *Juvenile Offenders and Victims: 1999 National Report.* Washington, DC: Office of Juvenile Justice and Delinquency Prevention.

Stafford, Mark C. 1995. "Children's Legal Rights in the United States." *Marriage and Family Review* 21 (3/4):121–40.

Stafford, Mark and Tracey L. Kyckelhahn. 2002. "Delinquency and Juvenile Justice in the United States." Pp. 529–56 in *Juvenile Justice Systems: International Perspectives,* edited by John A. Winterdyk. Toronto, Canada: Canadian Scholars' Press.

Sutherland, Edwin H. 1939. *Principles of Criminology.* 3rd ed. Philadelphia, PA: Lippincott.

Sutherland, Edwin H. and Donald R. Cressey. 1974. *Criminology.* 9th ed. Philadelphia, PA: Lippincott.

Tittle, Charles R. and Robert F. Meier. 1990. "Specifying the SES/Delinquency Relationship." *Criminology,* May, 28:271–99.

Traver, Harold. 2002. "Juvenile Delinquency in Hong Kong." Pp. 207–34 in *Juvenile Justice Systems: International Perspectives,* edited by John A. Winterdyk. Toronto, Canada: Canadian Scholars' Press.

U.S. Census Bureau. 2001. Retrieved from http://eire. census.gov/popest/archives.

Walgrave, Lode. 2002. "Juvenile Justice in Belgium." Pp. 29–59 in *Juvenile Justice Systems: International Perspectives,* edited by John A. Winterdyk. Toronto, Canada: Canadian Scholars' Press.

Waters, Tony. 1999. *Crime and Immigrant Youth.* Thousand Oaks, CA: Sage.

Winterdyk, John A. 2002a. "Introduction." Pp. xi–xl in *Juvenile Justice Systems: International Perspectives,* edited by John A. Winterdyk. Toronto, Canada: Canadian Scholars' Press.

——. 2002b. "Juvenile Justice and Young Offenders: An Overview of Canada." Pp. 61–102 in *Juvenile Justice Systems: International Perspectives,* edited by John A. Winterdyk. Toronto, Canada: Canadian Scholars' Press.

——, ed. 2002c. *Juvenile Justice Systems: International Perspectives.* Toronto, Canada: Canadian Scholars' Press.

Yue, Liling. 2002. "Youth Justice in China." Pp. 103–26 in *Juvenile Justice Systems: International Perspectives,* edited by John A. Winterdyk. Toronto, Canada: Canadian Scholars' Press.

Zimring, Franklin E. 1998. *American Youth Violence.* Oxford: Oxford University Press.

DRUG USE AS A GLOBAL SOCIAL PROBLEM

ERICH GOODE

University of Maryland

A perusal of scholarly articles, research monographs, and textbooks verifies that the bulk of discussions of social problems focus on a single country—usually the United States. The subject is rarely taught, and the topic is rarely studied, outside the United States. The purpose of such discussions, insofar as other countries are considered, is to assess the impact of social problems on that single country. In fact, the very definition of what a social problem is in the first place has typically been based on a single country as its unit of analysis. For instance, a major theoretical monograph opens with the following question to its readers: "What do you think are the ten most important social problems in the United States today?" (Loseke 1999:3). The worldwide perspective rarely enters into discussions of social problems.

This book represents a departure from the tradition that social problems need be isolated to a single country or society. Our position is that the most significant social problems are international in scope—indeed, global. Hence, a consideration of social problems from a worldwide perspective has become necessary. This is especially the case with respect to drug use. The cocaine used on the streets of Los Angeles was derived from coca plants grown in Peru, Bolivia, and Colombia. The antismoking campaigns launched in the United States have an impact in lowering the consumption of tobacco in Brazil. Recent declines in the consumption of alcohol and alcohol-related automobile fatalities that have taken place in North America are also observed throughout Western Europe. The de facto legalization of small quantities of cannabis products in the Netherlands is being debated nearly everywhere in the world; the country's laissez-faire policy toward the drug has attracted visitors and temporary residents from all over the world. More and more, issues, concerns, conditions—in short, social problems—have assumed global dimensions. Hence, in this chapter, I will examine drug use as an international problem.

The process of globalization has an impact on three different yet interconnected aspects of the drug problem: drug trafficking, drug consumption, and reactions to drug trafficking and drug consumption. Globalization influences the production and sale of illicit drugs because of the development of international networks linking their ultimate source, that is, growers and manufacturers, through smugglers and wholesale traffickers, to the retail, seller-to-user connection. Globalization also influences the consumption of drugs not only through trafficking, that is, the process of delivering the substances to the user, but also as a result of broadcasting role models of drug consumption in global media and other modern means of communication; the spread of conceptions of a recreational youth culture, a lifestyle that certain drugs are seen to enhance; and worldwide economic changes that have fostered the growth of large strata of young people with disposable incomes and recreational time on their hands (United Nations [UN] 2001:19). And the internationalization of reactions to drug trafficking and consumption include antidrug social movement activity, such as antidrug media campaigns, news stories on drug arrests and other police activity, reports of the results of drug surveys, and the doings of drug users; the adoption of treatment programs; subdirectories of the UN; Interpol and other international police agencies; and political and military efforts to eradicate drug trafficking and drugs at their source. Here, we shall examine some of these global networks.

DRUGS, DRUG ABUSE, AND DRUG DEPENDENCE: SOME BASIC DEFINITIONS

The term *drug* may be defined in several ways. Within a medical context, a "drug" is a therapeutic agent physicians use to heal the body; in this sense, penicillin is a drug. Within a legal context, a "drug" is a controlled substance, one whose possession and sale are subject to legal penalties under specified circumstances. Within a psychopharmacological context, a "drug" refers to a substance that is psychoactive, that is, that influences the workings of the mind and has an effect on mood, emotion, and cognitive processes. It is this third definition that I will follow here. Of course, some substances are drugs according to two or even all three of these

definitions. For instance, morphine is used by physicians to block pain, is a controlled substance whose possession and sale outside a medical context are illegal, and is psychoactive. Psychopharmacologically, both alcohol and tobacco, although legal and not used for medicinal purposes, are drugs and hence will be considered as such in this chapter.

Researchers distinguish drug "use" from drug "abuse." Drug *use* is a neutral term that refers to any effectual consumption of a psychoactive substance. In contrast, drug *abuse* is defined in various ways, according to the interests of the observer. Nonetheless, most drug specialists follow the dictionary definition of abuse, that is, "to treat in an injurious, harmful way." Hence, following this definition, drug abuse refers to a level or degree of use of one or more substances that is harmful or that risks a significant measure of harm to the user and/or others. According to this definition, alcoholism is a form of drug abuse, as would be nearly all cigarette smoking. Obviously, abusiveness is a matter of degree; there is no precise cutoff point demarcating "abusive" from "nonabusive" drug use. Nonetheless, as a general rule, the higher the doses and the more frequent the use, the greater the likelihood that it constitutes abuse.

Another crucial distinction is that between use and dependence. "Use" encompasses any and all effectual consumption of psychoactive substances, including experimentation and occasional consumption. In contrast, "dependence" characterizes only the upper reaches of use. Prior to the 1970s, "addiction" referred to a type of dependence on a substance that produces a clear-cut physical withdrawal symptom when use of the drug is abruptly discontinued. Chemically addictive drugs include the narcotics, the sedatives (such as barbiturates), and alcohol, a major sedative. It became clear to researchers that a number of drugs, while not physically addictive, produce a strong pattern of dependence or continued, uncontrollable, harmful use in a substantial proportion of users; cocaine and the amphetamines provide striking examples. Currently, in addition to physical addiction, experts include psychic and behavioral dependence within their scope of drug dependence. *Drug dependence* is defined as the recurrent yearning for a psychoactive substance such that the user seems incapable of discontinuing its use despite its negative consequences. In clear-cut patterns of dependence, the user's life revolves around the acquisition of the drug and getting high, thereby undermining or destroying that which was previously valued, such as academic achievement, job and career, income, house, marriage, family, and children. Again, not all drug use is dependence, and not all physical addiction is psychological dependence, and vice versa (McKim 2003:42–3, 74–103). In fact, within the entire circle of at-least-onetime users, for practically every psychoactive substance (except tobacco), persons who are dependent on the drug constitute a minority. Even regular users are more likely to be casual and infrequent in their consumption than heavy, chronic, or compulsive.

WHAT MAKES DRUG USE A SOCIAL PROBLEM?

Nearly all definitions of social problems are based on at least three elements: a real or imagined condition; the feeling on the part of a segment of the population that that condition is bad, wrong, or undesirable; and the attitude that something can, should, and needs to be done to change that presumably undesirable condition (Loseke 1999:5–7). Lurking behind this seeming agreement, however, looms a major rift in the field.

Social problems have been defined in two starkly different ways, objectively (Manis 1974, 1976) and subjectively (Best 1995:3–10; Loseke 1999:3–21). Objectivism adopts an essentialistic approach: A phenomenon is defined by an inner "essence" that is manifested in measurable, concrete ways. Subjectivism adopts a constructionist approach; here, a phenomenon is defined by how it is conceptualized, regarded, perceived, talked about, defined, dealt with, or reacted to by the relevant members of a society.

Objectivism

The essentialistic approach to social problems is that they exist as an objective condition that harms a substantial number of people, whether in a given society or worldwide. By this definition, *objective* refers to physical, material consequences we can see and lay our hands on. Accordingly, social problems are "measurable and widespread conditions" that harm "living, breathing people" (Loseke 1999:7). This definition holds that these conditions cause harm that can be measured by specific indicators that all unbiased observers agree are undesirable, such as death, illness, injury, incapacitation, hospitalization, loss of productivity, illiteracy, a stunting of potential, monetary cost, or loss to the society. The operational definition of the social problem is the measurable harm a given condition causes. According to this definition, the existence, seriousness, and causes of social problems are decided by experts, persons who have the training and evidence to determine such things (Manis 1976:25). Objectively speaking, for instance, cigarette smoking is a social problem because it kills people; corporate crime is a social problem because people lose money, their health, and sometimes their lives as a result of the greed of executives; racism is a social problem because millions of minority members are denied their full potential as a result of discrimination against them and society loses the full potential of a segment of the population.

Consider drug use and abuse: Objectively, drug use can cause damage to human life. It can kill people, and make it impossible for users to pursue an education, hold down a job, or remain healthy. Caring for or attempting to cure addicts and alcoholics costs society many billions of dollars and diverts money from other important social enterprises. Drug selling is a dangerous activity, not infrequently leading to murder. Whole communities have been held hostage to drug dealers and users; their members live each day in fear that they will be robbed or killed and that their children will get snatched up by lives of addiction and crime. Millions of American workers are dependent on drugs or alcohol—or both; they lose valuable work time to illness and in the case of jobs that require physical coordination, threaten their lives and those of their coworkers. Alcoholism often destroys families and may embitter their members for a lifetime. Thousands of babies are born addicted each year, often prematurely; withdrawal is life threatening to their tiny bodies, and many of them are difficult, problem children when they enter the public school system. Clearly, the problem of drugs and alcohol has an objective dimension; the quality of human life—indeed, its very existence—is often threatened or damaged by the ingestion of psychoactive substances.

Constructionism

The subjective or constructionist definition does not see the social problem as an objective, concrete real-world condition that causes measurable harm to a substantial number of people in a society. Rather, to the constructionist, social problems need not even be based on objectively real conditions at all. This is why constructionists refer to "putative" conditions. According to the constructionist definition, by Best (1995), "The objective status of those conditions is irrelevant" (p. 6). From the constructionist perspective, social problems "are what people view as social problems" (p. 4). The constructionist's perspective sees the social problem as follows:

A product, something that has been produced or constructed through social activities. When activists hold a demonstration to attract attention to some social condition, when investigative reporters publish stories that expose new aspects of the condition, or when legislators introduce bills to do something about the condition, they are constructing a social problem. (P. 6)

The defining ingredient of the social problem, says the constructionist, is a claim about the undesirability of a given condition, real or imagined, leading to widespread concern about that condition, culminating in a certain type of collective action to do something about it. Conditions become social problems only when they are defined as or felt to be problematic—disturbing, undesirable, and in need of a solution or remedy. Objectively, real conditions are not problems until they are constructed as such by the human mind, called into being or constituted by the definitional process, and translated into collective action. Conditions that do not even exist in the material world—such as witches, the ritual murder of tens of thousands of children by Satanist cabals, the theft of and commerce in human body parts, and alien abductions—are social problems if they generate widespread public concern.

Constructionists argue that what makes a given condition a problem is the "collective definition" (Blumer 1971) of a condition as a problem, the degree of felt public concern over a given condition or issue. While there are differences among constructionists, there is a common core to their thinking: Conditions become social problems only when they are defined as or felt to be problematic—disturbing in some way, undesirable, and in need of solution or remedy. Social problems do not exist "objectively" in the same sense that a rock, a frog, or a tree exists; instead, they are constructed by the human mind, called into being or constituted by the definitional process (Schneider 1985; Spector and Kitsuse 1973, 1977). Say Spector and Kitsuse (1973), "The existence of objective conditions does not in itself constitute social problems" (p. 5). Fuller and Myers (1941) go on to state, "Social problems are what people think they are, and if conditions are not defined as social problems by the people involved in them, they are not problems to these people, although they may be problems to outsiders or scientists" (p. 320). More contemporaneously, Spector and Kitsuse (1977) define social problems as "the activities of individuals or groups making assertions of grievances and claims with respect to some putative conditions" (p. 75).

To the constructionist, the subjective dimension of a social problem can be measured, manifested, or indicated in at least the following five ways. First, the organized, collective efforts on the part of some members of a society to protest or change a given condition—in short, "social problems as social movements" (Mauss 1975). Second, the introduction of bills in legislatures to criminalize the behavior and the individuals presumably causing the condition (Becker 1963:135ff.; Gusfield 1963). Third, the ranking of a condition or an issue in the public's rank order of the most serious problems facing the country. Fourth, public discussion of an issue in the media in the form of magazine and newspaper articles and editorials and television news stories, commentary, documentaries, and dramas (Becker 1963:141–43; Ben-Yehuda 1986; Himmelstein 1983:152–54). And fifth, the steps a society takes to deal with, prevent, or remedy the supposed causes or consequences of the condition, in the form of police, prisons, jails, clinics, hospitals, psychiatrists, public education programs, research projects, and so on. Thus, just as to the objectivist, the reality of a social problem can be measured concretely—by death and disease, for instance—to the constructionist, public concern is manifested in what people think, say, or do about a given condition.

It is extremely important to emphasize that the constructionist approach does not argue that because social problems are defined by the social constructionist, they are "just" or "only" constructed—in other words, that they cause no material or objective harm (Best 2000). Social constructions do not deny or contradict objective reality; the two are separate and independent of one another. Conditions may—or may not—exist; they may—or may not—be objectively serious. Saying that problems are constructed does not automatically deny their existence or seriousness; it treats them as an open question. Hence, to say that the drug problem is constructed does not mean that drug abuse does not cause material harm to users and the rest of the society. What is important from the constructionist perspective is to understand what is made of the information of the material world that members of the society process to put together an image and a course of action about a given condition or imputed condition. Likewise, to say that social problems are constituted by claims about supposedly problematic material-world conditions does not mean that those claims are false. Indeed, a claim may be true but not accepted or valorized by the general public, social movement activists, or legislators. The acceptance and implementation of a claim is socially patterned and must be understood as such. A claim about the problemhood of a given condition or putative condition—as well as its acceptance or rejection of that claim—is what the constructionist of social problems investigates, independent of its objective validity. And drug abuse, objectively a serious social problem, also attracts claims that demand systematic investigation.

To determine the objective worldwide problemhood of drug use and abuse, it is necessary to spell out its scope, size, and extent. And to understand how widespread it is on a global scale, it is necessary to understand the forces, factors, or variables that make for one absolutely necessary condition for use: the worldwide distribution of or trafficking in drugs. How do psychoactive substances reach the hands, and bodies, of their eventual consumers?

FACTORS FACILITATING WORLDWIDE DRUG TRAFFICKING

If we are to consider worldwide drug-trafficking patterns, we must make a distinction between legal and illegal drugs. How drugs are distributed depends on a variety of factors, and chief among them is their legal status. The fact is, the distribution patterns of legal products are very different from those of illegal products. Moreover, we can have vastly more confidence in the figures on the sale of legal products, which are taxable and whose transactions are recorded, than on the figures pertaining to the distribution of illicit products, whose transactions are not recorded any place to which the researcher has access.

Tobacco

Of all aspects of the global picture involving the sale of legal products, the marketing of tobacco around the world is probably the most interesting. In 1964, the year of the Surgeon General's Report on Tobacco and Health, 511 billion tobacco cigarettes were sold in the United States, for a per capita sale, among persons age 18 and older, of 4,195. By 1999, only 430 billion were sold, and per capita sales had dropped to 2,136 (Centers for Disease Control [CDC] 1999). In addition, during the 1990s, the news media investigated the tobacco industry and found that its executives had lied about their knowledge of the harm that cigarettes caused; lawsuits began piling up, and the tobacco industry had to pay multi-billion-dollar fines. Clearly, the cigarette companies—and their profits—were in deep trouble. For decades, they had attempted to enter the Asian market, with mixed success; recent developments have spurred them on to redouble their efforts. Half the world's commercially manufactured cigarettes are sold in Asia. But American companies must compete with Asian brands, which tend to be cheaper. In addition, some Asian countries, such as China, severely restrict the sale of American products, promulgating their own brands.

Perhaps the most interesting feature of marketing cigarettes in Asia—aside from how widespread smoking is there—is its sex-graded pattern of smoking. In Asia, an extremely high percentage of men smoke: In the Philippines and Vietnam, 75 percent; in Indonesia, 66 percent; in China and Taiwan, 55 percent; in South Korea, 54 percent; in Japan, 52 percent; and so on (Bartecchi, MacKenzie, and Schrier 1995; Stesser 1993). Brand loyalty is very important to smokers; hence, for the most part, getting men to switch brands is unlikely to be very successful. But a much lower percentage of Asian women than men smoke: In the Philippines, 18 percent; in Vietnam, 4 percent; in Indonesia, 2 percent; in China, 4 percent; in Taiwan, 3 percent; in South Korea, 5 percent; and in Japan, 10 percent. Cambodia's smokers display the sharpest sex gradation in the world; there, 90 percent of the men but only 3 percent of the women smoke (Struck 2000). Hence, to get Asian women hooked on cigarettes became a major goal of the tobacco industry. Campaigns to link smoking to women's liberation (a technique also tried in the United States) are a major thrust of Asian advertising. With chic, fashionably dressed young women advertising and even distributing cigarettes to Asian women, the message is clear: Smoke cigarettes and you will become modern, Western, and liberated. In addition, enticing Asian youngsters to smoke before they adopt a brand became a major objective of American cigarette manufacturers; hence, American cigarette companies have sponsored (as they have in the United States) racing-car teams, athletic events, rock concerts, and fashion shows to appeal to youngsters.

Richard Peto, an Oxford University medical epidemiologist, estimates that between 1990 and 2020, the number of deaths from tobacco-related diseases in Asia will triple; 50 million Chinese now alive, he says, "will eventually die from diseases linked to cigarette smoking" (Shenon 1994:16). If you look at the number of deaths, says Judith Mackay, a British physician, a consultant to the Chinese government helping to develop an antismoking program, "The tobacco problem in Asia is going to dwarf tuberculosis, it's going to dwarf malaria, it's going to dwarf AIDS [acquired immune deficiency syndrome], yet it's being totally ignored" (Shenon 1994:16). Paradoxes such as these intrigue the student of social problems.

Illegal Drugs

The distribution of illegal drugs has been systematically globalized much more recently than for the licit drug markets.[1] Each illicit drug has its own unique source, and each reaches the ultimate customer in a strikingly different way. Moreover, patterns of distribution are labile and shift from year to year, according to law enforcement practices, changes in the weather, and the development of innovations by growers, traffickers, and sellers. In addition, systematic and valid information on trafficking is difficult to come by, and different estimates may contradict one another. Here are two estimates of the countries of origin of cocaine and heroin, one advanced by the UN and the second, by the Abt Associates, under a research contract from a division of the White House, the Office of National Drug Control Policy. The two estimates on cocaine's origins are the same; the estimates on the origins of heroin are very different.

Drug Trafficking: Varying Estimates

As of 2000, according to the estimate provided by the UN in its publication, *Global Illicit Drug Trends 2001,*[2] 70 percent of the illicit global production of opium originates in Afghanistan. Myanmar, formerly known as Burma, accounts for 23 percent of the total. (Since the fields in Afghanistan are considerably more productive, roughly half the global opium poppy cultivation areas are located in Myanmar, and roughly a third are in Afghanistan.) Other Asian countries, mainly Pakistan and the former Soviet republics of central Asia, account for 5 percent of worldwide opium production, and Mexico and Colombia, about 2 percent. Bolivia, Peru, and Colombia account for more or less the entire world's supply of coca; 70 percent of that total originates from Colombia.

In contrast, Abt Associates estimates that 67 percent of the heroin consumed in the United States originates from South America, 23 percent is from Mexico, 6 percent comes from Southwest Asia (Pakistan and Afghanistan), and 2 percent from Southeast Asia (Bruen et al. 2002:1). While it is highly likely that the vast majority of the heroin used in Southwest Asia also originates from

Southwest Asia and the vast majority of the heroin used in Southeast Asia originates from Southeast Asia, and it is also true that most of the world's heroin consumption takes place in Asia, nonetheless, the UN and Abt figures are too divergent to be reconciled. Their divergence underscores the difficulty of accumulating valid information about behavior whose participants wish to conceal. All (or virtually all) the cocaine consumed in the United States, says Abt Associates, originates from Colombia, Peru, and Bolivia (Layne, Johnston, and Rhodes 2002), which is in agreement with the UN's estimates.

All observers agree, however, that the origin and production of most of the other drugs tends to be much more decentralized and hence, more difficult to estimate. More specifically, according to the UN (2001, 2002), the production of herb cannabis (marijuana) is scattered all over the globe. The majority of the marijuana consumed around the world originates either from domestic or intraregional (that is, from one country to a nearby or adjoining country) production. For instance, more than half the marijuana consumed in the United States is grown domestically; this proportion has been increasing for at least three decades (Pollan 1995). However, some overseas commerce in marijuana does take place, for instance, from West and South Africa and Thailand to Europe, and from Colombia and Jamaica to North America. In contrast, the production of resin cannabis (hashish) is more centralized; worldwide, the majority comes from North Africa (mainly Morocco) and western Asia (Afghanistan and Pakistan). Recently, the former Soviet republics of central Asia have begun exporting both leaf and resin cannabis to Europe.

Since the chemical process is relatively simple, the production of, and hence trafficking in, amphetamine and methamphetamine tends to be largely domestic and intraregional, for instance, within the United States; from Mexico to the United States; within Australia; within China; from one country to another in Southeast Asia; among the countries of Eastern Europe; and from one country to another in Western Europe. However, in the late 1990s, several shipments of methamphetamine manufactured in Thailand have been seized in West Europe and the United States. This may prove to be a growing trend.

In contrast, for most of the countries of the world, Western Europe, mainly the Netherlands and Belgium, remains the principal source for Ecstasy (MDMA). However, recently, seizures of Ecstasy in Latin America indicate that clandestine labs have begun to manufacture MDMA domestically. This may presage a large-scale future development.

Three Models of Drug Trafficking

Three "models" of drug trafficking can be delineated: the pure agricultural model, the pure chemical model, and the mixed model. The "pure agricultural" model refers to systems of trafficking that harvest a product that requires little or nothing (aside from drying and separating parts of the plant) in the way of converting it into the ultimate product; it is consumed more or less as grown. Clearly, marijuana offers the best example here. The "pure synthetic" model refers to a chemical product that does not have its origin as an agricultural product at all, but is developed, from beginning to end, in the lab. And the "mixed" model refers to a product that begins as agricultural produce, which is then synthesized or converted into a chemical, eventually becoming what is consumed by the customer. Heroin (which begins as the Oriental poppy or opium plant) and cocaine (which begins as the coca plant) provide paramount examples here. Each of these "models" harbors some variation, of course, depending, in the case of agricultural products, on the hardiness of the plant and hence whether it can be grown locally or must be imported from abroad, and in the case of synthetic products, the complexity and difficulty of the chemical process. The discussion below applies mainly to the "mixed" model, which requires funneling the produce of many farms (raw opium and coca leaves) to a fairly small number of labs, through high-level traffickers and smugglers, fanning out once again from higher-level to lower-level dealers. The other two models present their own special social and economic structures that make generalizing about them a very different proposition.

Factors Facilitating Worldwide Drug Trafficking

Worldwide drug-trafficking patterns have evolved into their present form and continue to develop along certain lines for a complex mix of reasons. Some of these factors are local, such as climate and indigenous cultural patterns, while others can be generalized to settings all over the world. One master principle that has influenced the sale of illicit substances all over the world is the emergence of worldwide networks that link the source of drugs with their ultimate customers. International and intersocietal commerce have existed for thousands of years. However, it was not until late in the twentieth century that the distribution of the currently illicit drugs took on a truly global complexion. Prior to the early 1970s, international drug linkages tended to be fairly simple: Marijuana was imported into the United States from Mexico; opium, grown in Turkey, was processed into heroin in Marseilles and smuggled into New York; and cocaine, produced in labs in Colombia from leaves gathered in Peru and Bolivia, was brought into the United States and Western Europe.

Perhaps the watershed event that transformed drug distribution to its present, global form was the dismantling in 1972 of the "French Connection" heroin-trafficking network by the French police, U.S. federal agents, and officers in the New York Police Department. The cartel had previously supplied 80 percent of the heroin sold in the United States, and its demise generated a drug "panic," creating an enormous, importunate demand for the drug. This opened up an economic opportunity that many daring, unscrupulous entrepreneurs all over the world could not pass up. In the past three decades, the routes through which heroin specifically (and perhaps as a by-product, illegal drugs generally) travel, the number of source countries and the number of countries through which drugs move, and the national and ethnic groups involved in drug trafficking have virtually exploded (Stares 1996:25, 27–8). Since the 1970s, the international drug trade has been transformed from "a cottage industry" to a global enterprise whose profits are greater than three-quarters of the national economies of the world, estimated at between $180 and $300 billion annually (Stares 1996:2). While some of the preconditions for this development existed previously, the conjunction of several key factors made this development possible specifically during the last quarter of the twentieth century. Some of these developments include the following.

The Collapse of the Soviet Union. Authoritarian regimes such as the former Soviet Union

> have generally fared better than open democratic countries in suppressing drug market activity because the state plays a more intrusive and repressive role in almost all aspects of daily life. By contrast, the capacity of liberal democratic states to reduce the availability of drugs is clearly limited by their commitment to the very principles and values upon which they are based. (Stares 1996:74)

While the Soviet Union, its constituent republics, and the Eastern Bloc nations were never completely successful in suppressing crime and, more specifically, illicit drug trafficking, the collapse of the Soviet Union has produced a power vacuum into which has stepped an array of unscrupulous, ruthless actors willing to violate the law to earn a substantial profit. In the Central Asian republics, for instance,

> Thousands of acres have been given over to the cultivation of opium poppies and cannabis.... Hungary and Czechoslovakia have become major transit countries for Asian heroin destined for West Europe.... Polish health officials warned that a dramatic rise in intravenous drug abuse in Warsaw has unleashed criminal networks engaged in drug trafficking. (Flynn 1993:6)

The "unraveling of socialism and the move toward freer trade among industrialized countries has created a fertile environment for international business" (Flynn 1993:6), including, perhaps especially, illicit ones. The collapse of the Iron Curtain has produced "torrents of people, goods, and services . . . pouring across borders. In their midst, drug shipments . . . move with little risk of detection by customs authorities" (Flynn 1993:6). The central Asian republics, especially Turkmenistan, Uzbekistan, and Tajikistan, have become major opium-growing areas for heroin bound for Eastern Europe. Georgia and Kazakhstan have become major leaf-cannabis-growing areas. And Russia, Bulgaria, and Poland have become major amphetamine- and methamphetamine-producing and -distributing countries (UN 2001).

Economic Privatization. Since the collapse of the Soviet Union and the end of the Cold War, economies all over the world have become increasingly privatized, liberalized, and deregulated (Flynn 1993). China has opened "free trade zones" in a number of port cities, in which state control and even monitoring of commerce has been lifted and an extreme version of laissez-faire capitalism now operates. In 1989, Mexico deregulated the trucking industry, liberalizing barriers to entry into the country and permitting free movement into every city, port, and railroad station. Within two years, the number of registered trucks increased 62 percent. Soon after, Chile and Argentina followed suit. In 1991, Mexico allowed private companies to construct and operate their own ports (Stares 1996:56). The creation of the European Union (EU) in 2002 created a single currency for most of Western Europe and free and open trade across national boundaries. The North American Free Trade Agreement (NAFTA) has removed thousands of trade barriers between the United States and Mexico and the United States and Canada. Worldwide economic deregulation has expedited the flow of goods, both licit and illicit, across national borders. It has proved to be a major shot in the arm for the global drug trade.

Money Laundering. Banking is a major worldwide industry. In some countries, banks operate under a principal of extreme secrecy. "Don't ask, don't tell" is their watchword. Clients may deposit bundles of cash totaling millions of dollars, and the bank releases no record of the transaction to the government. Offshore banks, such as those in Aruba and the Cayman Islands, and banks located in tiny European countries, such as Liechtenstein and Luxembourg, as well as those located in Hong Kong, Cyprus, and Panama, offer "financial secrecy and client confidentiality" (Stares 1996:58). Liechtenstein has more post office box corporations (72,000)—a high percentage of them are banks—than people (23,000). The emergence, indeed, the immense expansion, of such banks has permitted traffickers to launder money earned in the illicit drug trade back into the legitimate economy, thereby avoiding official detection, and, in effect, nullifying a major arm of law enforcement.

Globalization. Globalization is both a relatively recent product of political, economic, technological, cultural, and social changes taking place nearly everywhere on earth and an umbrella concept whose material manifestations have enormously accelerated the illicit drug trade during the past quarter century or so. During that time, international commerce, travel, and communication have multiplied exponentially; the huge increase in the worldwide illicit drug trade is one consequence of internationalization.

According to the U.S. Department of Commerce, in 1970, the value of exports from the United States to foreign countries totaled $42 billion; its imports from other countries were valued at $40 billion. In the year 2000, these figures were $782 billion and $1.2 trillion respectively, an increase of roughly 20 times; adjusting for inflation, this represents an increase of four times. According to the International Trade Administration, the number of tourists entering the United States doubled between 1986 (26 million) and 2000 (51 million); each year, the number of persons simply crossing the country's borders (more than 400 million) is greater than the number of its residents (280 million). In 1991, the first Internet browser was released. By 1994, there were 3 million users of the Internet, nearly all of them in the United States. Today, according to the *Computer Industry Almanac,* there are nearly a half billion Internet subscribers worldwide; by 2005, the *Almanac* estimates, there will be over a billion. According to the International Telecommunication Union, international phone traffic, as measured by billions of minutes, increased from 33 in 1990 to 130 in 2002. In the United States, cell phone subscribers increased from 340,000 in 1985 to 109 million in the year 2000. In trade, travel, and communication, the world has become a global village. We have become, in effect, a "borderless" world (Stares 1996:5).

The movement of persons, goods, and messages across national borders has created a superhighway for traffickers to transport drugs from source to using countries. The sheer volume of bodies and freight coming into every country in the world from every other makes it quite literally impossible for officials to monitor and stem the tide of illicit products. Instant communication to and from every point on the globe enables traffickers to convey information on transactions practically without detection. As a result, the drug trade has increasingly become a transnational phenomenon, driven and fashioned in critical ways by transnational forces and transnational actors. Thus the global diffusion of technical expertise and the internationalization of manufacturing have made it possible to cultivate and refine drugs in remote places of the world and still be within reach of distant markets. (Stares 1996:5–6)

The huge worldwide expansion in trade, transportation, and tourism has facilitated trafficking in established drug-using areas and "opened up new areas of the world to exploit" (Stares 1996:6). Huge increases in international travel, the mass media, and telecommunications "have undoubtedly increased the global awareness of drug fashions around the world" (Stares 1996:6).

Globalization permits enormous flexibility with respect to where illicit drugs may be grown or manufactured and how they may be delivered to their ultimate markets. If law enforcement shuts down an operation in a given province or country, entrepreneurs in another province or country quickly move into the economic vacuum. As we saw, the dismantling of the "French Connection" in 1972 created opportunities for growers and traffickers in other areas of the world to provide the opium and heroin necessary to supply American addicts. Whereas in 1972, Turkey supplied 80 percent of the botanical source of heroin used in the United States, today, according to the UN (2001), the worldwide source of heroin is mainly Afghanistan (70 percent) and Burma, now Myanmar (23 percent); and according to Abt Associates (Bruen et al. 2002:1), it is mainly South America (67 percent in the United States specifically) and Mexico (23 percent in the United States).

After "Operation Intercept," when the U.S. border guards searched every car and person entering the country for drugs (1969), the cultivation of homegrown American marijuana increased dramatically (Inciardi 2002:54–5; Pollan 1995). Today, it is well over half the volume of the marijuana consumed in the United States. Observers refer to this phenomenon as the "push down/pop up" factor (Nadelmann 1988:9), that is, whenever drug trafficking is "pushed down" in one area, it "pops up" in another. The reason for this is, of course, the enormous profits that are to be made in the illicit drug

trade and the unlimited supply of people willing to take the legal risk to earn those profits. It is possible that globalization is the single factor most responsible for the enormous expansion in the drug trade during the past three decades. If it were much more burdensome and problematic to move drugs and money across borders, traffickers would not have the same degree of flexibility to adapt to changing legal, political, and economic circumstances around the world.

Poverty. While upper-level drug dealers tend to be wealthy, almost beyond comprehension, the foot soldiers of the drug trade at either end of the distribution spectrum tend to be poor. As the worldwide economic crisis deepens, exacerbating the enormous gap between the industrialized, developed countries of Western Europe, North America, Australia, New Zealand, the Asian "tigers," and a few oil-rich Persian Gulf states and the poorer, developing nations of the world, poverty assumes an increasingly greater role in drug trafficking. At the source end, the opium poppy, from which heroin is derived, and the coca bush, which yields cocaine, tend to be grown by poor peasant farmers cultivating small plots of land, whose livelihood depends on the illicit crop. (Most of the world's opium and coca, it should be said, is grown for the production of legal substances.) Very few substitute crops are capable of growing on most of such land, and practically no other crop can get to a sufficiently nearby market to support the peasant's family at subsistence earnings. This generalization about the poverty of the majority of hands-on growers does not apply to the leaf cannabis or marijuana grown in North America and Europe, since that industry is extremely decentralized, but it does apply to the resin cannabis or hashish that comes from Western Asia. In the middle of the distribution chain, likewise, much (though almost certainly not most) of the illicit drugs smuggled into a country where they are sold are brought across the border by poor couriers ("mules" or "smurfs") who carry them on their person, often by swallowing drug-filled condoms. And at the low-level, seller-to-consumer end, especially in poor neighborhoods, petty street dealers likewise tend to be poor, typically addicts themselves, barely earning enough on their transactions to pay for their own drug habits. There are, of course, middle-class drug dealers who sell directly to consumers, but they tend to take fewer risks because they usually sell to persons they know, in fairly substantial quantities a small number of times, indoors, in places of residence, and in settings in which violence rarely takes place (Dunlap, Johnson, and Manwar 1994:5–6).

To put the matter another way, the poorer an area, society, or community, the greater the likelihood that the production, trafficking, and sale of illegal drugs will flourish. This is because while the affluent are willing to take moderate risks to earn a great deal of money, the poverty-stricken are willing to take much greater risks to earn relatively little money. A small fraction of 1 percent of the wholesale price of heroin and cocaine goes to the grower. For instance, the coca leaf necessary to produce a kilo of cocaine costs $300 in South America. Refined and smuggled into the United States, that kilo sells for $150,000 retail, that is, sold at $100 per unit in one-gram units that are two-thirds pure (Reuter 2001:19). This represents a markup of 500 times. Clearly, it is the major trafficker and wholesaler who earn the lion's share of the illicit drug profits; the industry's foot soldiers take the most risk and earn the least profit. The poor, with little in the way of economic prospects, are most likely to take such risks. Hence, poverty must be counted as a major factor in the production, distribution, and sale of illicit drugs.

Weak or Corrupt Local and Federal Governments. When the central government does not control major areas of a country and when the police and the army cannot enter an area for fear of being shot, they cannot control illegal activity within that country's borders, and drug lords are free to grow botanicals from which drugs are extracted and to distribute and sell them at will. Major territories of Burma (Myanmar) have been under the control of private drug armies for decades. In Colombia, the army cannot enter major territories that are controlled by rebels, who use drug revenues to finance their operations. In Afghanistan, likewise, local tribes, not the federal government, control the extremely rugged, mountainous terrain where most of the world's opium is grown. In Mexico, until the election of the Vincente Fox regime, the corruption of the police and the army was vast and extensive,

reaching up to the president's family. Border assignments were bought and sold with the expectation that an officer would earn substantial sums from bribes by drug dealers in exchange for immunity from arrest. In such weak or corrupt regimes, honest law enforcement is a virtual impossibility, and drug trafficking is able to flourish.

THE PREVALENCE OF DRUG USE

A variety of agencies around the world collect information on the prevalence of drug use. Among them must be counted the Department of Health and Human Services of the U.S. government, the Australian Institute of Health and Welfare, and the British Home Office. In addition, the UN and the European Monitoring Centre for Drugs and Drug Addiction (EMCDD) distribute surveys to health experts on the consumption of illicit substances and collate and tabulate the information they receive. Though not all of these surveys are without flaw, there is nonetheless a wealth of information on drug use around the world.

Surveys on Drug Use

Monitoring the Future (MTF). Researchers find that the earlier drugs are used during the life cycle, statistically speaking, the greater the likelihood that the user will be involved in behavior that will become a problem to the society. In addition, researchers on adolescence believe, young people are not as moderate in their use of drugs and not as capable of dealing with their effects as are adults. Hence, drug use among youth is of special importance to the student of social problems. Every year since 1975, a large, nationally representative sample of 12th graders has been asked about legal and illegal drug use, availability, and attitudes. In the years following, college students and young adults not in college were added to the sample, and in 1991, 8th and 10th graders were added. Respondents are asked about lifetime, annual, 30-day, and daily prevalence for more than a score of drugs. The 2001 survey of schoolchildren was based on a sample of over 44,000 students in 424 schools. The study's methodological limitation is that its samples do not include runaways, school dropouts, and absentees during the day the survey was conducted, and research indicates that these are the adolescents who are most likely to be drug users. Nonetheless, the majority of drug researchers believe that for teenagers, MTF's survey on drug use is the most reliable and valid study on the consumption of psychoactive substances in existence.

In 2001, according to MTF's survey, 27 percent of American 8th graders, 46 percent of 10th graders, and 54 percent of 12th graders had used one or more illicit drugs one or more times during their lives ("lifetime prevalence"); 20 percent, 40 percent, and 49 percent had done so with marijuana; and 15 percent, 23 percent, and 29 percent had done so with any illicit substance aside from marijuana. The percentage using any illicit drug in the past year was 20 percent for 8th graders, 37 percent for 10th graders, and 41 percent for 12th graders. Comparable figures for use in the past 30 days were 12 percent, 23 percent, and 26 percent. All of these figures represent a substantial rise since 1991, when MTF began studying 8th and 10th graders (Johnston, O'Malley, and Bachman 2002). It is clear that a substantial proportion of American teenagers are taking illegal drugs, and a sizable minority among them are taking these drugs on a fairly regular basis.

In addition to MTF's figures on illicit drug use, the use of substances that are legal for adults but illegal for minors should be of concern to the social problems observer. In 2001, 1 out of 10 12th graders (10 percent) smoked half a pack of cigarettes daily, 80 percent had drunk alcohol at least once in their lives, two-thirds (64 percent) had been drunk at least once, half (50 percent) had drunk at least one alcoholic beverage in the past month, and a third (33 percent) had been drunk in the past month. An astounding 30 percent had consumed five or more drinks in a row during the past two weeks; 13 percent of 8th graders and 25 percent of 10th graders said that they had done so (Johnston et al. 2002). In terms of numbers and percentages, it seems that among American teenagers, objectively speaking, alcohol and cigarettes represent an even more substantial problem than is true of the illicit drugs.

National Household Survey on Drug Abuse (NHSDA). Every year, the Substance Abuse and Mental Health Services Administration (SAMHSA), an agency of U.S. federal government, sponsors a drug survey based on a nationally representative sample of the population. Its sample has one major drawback: It does not include people who do not live in a household. Hence, homeless people are excluded, as are teenage runaways, military personnel, inmates in jail, prison, and mental institutions, and obviously, nonrespondents. The federal Office of National Drug Control Policy, which issues a yearly report, estimates that the excluded populations are more than twice as likely to use and abuse psychoactive substances as the general population. Hence, this problem has an impact most specifically on estimates of heroin and crack cocaine addicts. In sum, then, the National Household Drug Survey hugely underestimates the addict population (Fenrich et al. 1999). Hence, the segment of drug users the student of social problems is most interested in is least likely to be counted. In addition, the survey's adolescents (age 12 to 18) are interviewed in the same household at the same time as their parents or caregivers; thus, their answers may be influenced by that fact.

In 2001, according to the National Household Survey on Drug Abuse (SAMHSA 2002b), not quite 4 Americans in 10 had used at least one illicit drug in their lifetimes (39 percent) and 1 in 4 (24 percent) had done so with at least one illegal drug other than marijuana. Marijuana was, of course, the most popular illegal drug; a third (34 percent) had taken it once or more during their lives. Cocaine (11 percent) and LSD (9 percent) followed at a considerable distance. Only marijuana was used during the past month by substantially more than 1 out of 100 Americans (5 percent). The legal drugs were used by vastly more Americans; 29 percent had used tobacco, and 47 percent had drunk alcohol during the past 30 days.

The British Crime Survey (BCS). Since 1994 every two years, and after 2001 every year, the Home Office has conducted a study on drug use in the general population under the auspices of the British Crime Survey, or BCS (Ramsay et al. 2001). In 2000, its sample size was 13,000, and the age range of its respondents ran from 16 to 59. In 2001 and afterward, its sample size will be 40,000. In the year 2000, roughly a third of its sample had used at least one illicit drug once or more in their lives (34 percent); a tenth (11 percent) used during the previous year; and roughly half this latter figure (6 percent) used in the past month. The figures for cannabis were 27 percent, 9 percent, and 6 percent and for cocaine, 5 percent, 2 percent, and 1 percent. In short, most respondents did not use illicit drugs, and of those who did, marijuana was by far the most popular substance.

Australia's National Drug Strategy Household Survey. In 2001, the Australian Institute of Health and Welfare conducted a household survey on drug use. Its sample was 27,000, and its age range was 14 and older. In their lifetimes, 38 percent of Australians used at least one illicit drug. In the past year, 82 percent of Australians used alcohol once or more, 23 percent did so with tobacco, and 17 percent consumed at least one illegal substance. Cannabis was by far the most popular drug, with 13 percent of the population taking it at least once during the past year. The figure for Ecstasy was 3 percent; for amphetamine, 3 percent; for cocaine, 1.3 percent; and for heroin, 0.2 percent. Many of the findings turned up in the Australian study were parallel to those of the BCS.

UN Estimates of Global Drug Use. Estimates of illicit drug use by the populations of member states are requested by the UN Office for Drug Control and Crime Prevention. They are based on local studies, special population group studies, and law enforcement agency assessments. The UN issues these estimates regularly in its publications, *World Drug Reports* and *Global Illicit Drug Trends.* As the UN admits, these estimates are highly variable in quality; the North American and Western European data are fairly accurate, while those in most of the Asian and African countries are little more than "guesstimates." On the basis of the figures it receives, the UN estimates that in 2000, 207 million people used one or more illicit drugs worldwide; this makes up 3 percent of the world's population or 4 percent of the population age 15 and older. Of this number, the vast majority (147 million) used marijuana or other cannabis drugs; 13 million used cocaine; 12.8 million used opiates (mostly heroin);

and 33 million used "amphetamine-type stimulants": amphetamine, methamphetamine, and Ecstasy. The UN's global survey on drug consumption (see Table 29.1) includes the following observations:

- More than 60 percent of the world's heroin users live in Asia, 20 percent in Europe, and 14 percent in North and South America.

- In 2001, there were more than 900,000 registered drug addicts in China, 83 percent of whom used heroin; it is possible that the number of unregistered addicts is even higher. This figure has been growing sharply over the past decade (it was 70,000 in 1990) and is likely to increase well into the twenty-first century.

- Nearly half the people in the world who used cocaine during the past year (6 out of 13 million) live in the United States. In the United States, annual prevalence is 2 percent. The figure for all of South America is slightly less than half the total for the United States (2.8 million), and in Western Europe, only 2.8 million people used cocaine during the previous year.

- Among all countries of the world, the annual prevalence of abuse of amphetamine is greatest in Australia (3.6 percent) and the United Kingdom (3.0 percent); figures for Honduras (2.5 percent), the Philippines (2.2 percent), and New Zealand (2.0 percent) are lower, but substantial nonetheless.

- Of all regions of the world, proportionally speaking, marijuana consumption is greatest in Oceania, where one in five residents (19 percent) used a cannabis product in the past year. This figure is 30 percent for Papua New Guinea, 29 percent for the Micronesian Federal State, 18 percent for Australia, and 15 percent for New Zealand. Cannabis consumption is also high for two African countries, Ghana (22 percent) and Sierra Leone (16 percent), and a Caribbean country, St. Vincent Grenadines (19 percent). The proportion is roughly 1 in 10 for the United States (9 percent) and the United Kingdom (9 percent). Except for Ireland (8 percent), Switzerland (7 percent), and Spain (7 percent), for most countries of Western Europe, the proportion is in the 3 to 5 percent range. Systematic data from Latin America are sparse, though the

Table 29.1   Annual Prevalence, 1998–2000 (Numbers in Millions)

	Opiates		*Cocaine*		*Cannabis*		*Amphetamine*	
	#	%	#	%	#	%	#	%
Oceania	0.14	0.63	0.2	0.9	4.4	18.8	0.6	2.8
West Europe	1.2	0.33	2.8	0.9	20.6	6.4	2.4	0.7
East Europe	2.7	0.99	0.3	0.1	10.5	3.3	0.9	0.3
Asia	6.3	0.26	0.9	0.2	41.6	2.1	22.3	0.9
North America	1.25	0.41	6.3	2.0	20.4	6.6	2.6	0.8
South America	0.34	0.12	2.8	1.0	13.0	4.7	2.2	0.8
Africa	0.95	0.19	0.9	0.2	36.9	8.1	2.4	0.5
Global	12.88	0.31	13.4	0.3	147.4	3.4	33.4	0.8

Source: United Nations Office for Drug Control and Crime Prevention 2002:224, 244, 254, 260.

Note: # is total number of people in the population, in millions, who used the indicated drug; % is percentage of the population age 15 and older who use the indicated drug.

annual prevalence rate for El Salvador is 9 percent and for Honduras, 6 percent.

- More than half the people in the world who have used Ecstasy live in Western Europe. It is especially popular among teenagers and young adults. Among 15- to 20-year-olds living in Oslo, the lifetime prevalence rate is 5 percent (UN 2001, 2002).

The European Monitoring Centre for Drugs and Drug Addiction (EMCDDA). The European Union (EU), a political and economic entity encompassing nearly all the countries of Western Europe along with Greece, has roughly 380 million inhabitants. Each year, its constituent countries report on their population's drug use; health consequences of their drug use; law enforcement measures; illicit drug seizures; prices and purity; national and international strategies to combat illicit drug distribution; diseases caused by drug abuse; and the use and distribution and consequences of the use of synthetic drugs. And each year, the Centre publishes its *Annual Report on the State of the Drugs Problem in the European Union.* As with other surveys, cannabis consumption is higher than for that of any other illicit substance; in most countries, the lifetime prevalence rate is in the 20 to 25 percent range. Amphetamines have been taken once or more by between 1 and 4 percent of the adult population of EU countries, with the exception of the United

Kingdom, where it stands at 1 in 10. Lifetime Ecstasy use is between 0.5 and 4 percent, and cocaine, between 0.5 and 3 percent. As is true elsewhere, less than 1 percent of the adult population of EU countries has even tried heroin (EMCDDA 2001).

The Prevalence of Drug Use: Summary

Only a minority of the population of nearly every country on earth uses illicit drugs. For some countries, however (for instance, Papua New Guinea), this minority is huge—and it may be substantially larger than is indicated by the available surveys; for others (in all likelihood, Saudi Arabia, where drug dealers are executed in public), it is considerably lower. In contrast, the legal drugs, alcohol and tobacco, attract a much higher proportion and number of users and hence, from the point of view of the potential harm they can inflict, constitute a much more serious social problem. Nonetheless, even a small minority of the society is capable of causing significant harm to the rest of the population. Hence, although the issue of the number of users is relevant and important to any student of social problems, ultimately, what counts is how the lives of users intersect with the substances they use, and how that intersection affects the lives of the population at large.

SUBSTANCE ABUSE AS A SOCIAL PROBLEM: PHYSICAL AND ECONOMIC HARM

It is important to stress that by itself, drug use does not constitute a problem for any society. It is only when the consumption of psychoactive substances, from the point of view of the objectivistic approach, produces physical or economic harm or, from the constructionist perspective, attracts societal concern that drug use becomes a problem. Here, I will focus on the kinds of harm caused by the consumption of illicit substances. Drug-related harm can be measured in countless ways. The first and most basic way is, of course, death; secondarily, disease; third, injury; fourth, predatory, criminal, and violent behavior; and fifth, monetary cost to the society.

Drug-Related Harm

United States Centers for Disease Control (CDC). The federal U.S. Centers for Disease Control estimates that roughly 440,000 people die in the United States each year as a result of cigarette smoking. They estimate the figure for alcohol consumption at roughly 100,000, and for all the illicit drugs added together, according to the Robert Wood Johnson Foundation, about 16,000 (Horgan, Skwara, and Strickler 2001:6). Data on the worldwide picture are patchy and incomplete, but they are certainly several times these figures, and very possibly more or less proportionate as well. With respect to magnitude, therefore, it might seem that cigarette smoking is by far the globe's most serious social problem. But drugs cause harm in different ways; by itself, death does not encompass the entire spectrum of harm. For instance, the victims of tobacco tend to be middle-aged to elderly; hence, the number of years of life lost to tobacco per smoker is comparatively smaller. In contrast, since alcohol consumption is implicated in accidental death, homicide, and suicide, as well as disease, its victims tend to be considerably younger, and hence, the number of years lost per victim is considerably greater. Deaths caused by illicit drugs tend to strike younger victims than is true for tobacco and even alcohol; hence, again, the number of years of life lost is correspondingly greater. According to the CDC, smokers lose roughly a decade of life in comparison with nonsmokers. In fact, in the United States, a smoker is less likely to reach the age of 65 than a nonsmoker is to reach the age of 75. As far as monetary harm is concerned, some analysts argue that the cost of cigarette smoking is considerably less than seems to be the case, since smokers tend to die before they collect old-age benefits (in the United States, social security) and hence, society saves more money as a result of their demise than it pays for the increased cost of their medical care (Viscusi 2002:60ff).

Drug Abuse Warning Network (DAWN). Obviously, one major measure of the harm that drugs do, and hence the problemhood of drug use/abuse, is lethal and nonlethal drug "overdoses," that is, untoward effects that result in medical intervention and at the most extreme level, death. The Drug Abuse Warning Network (or DAWN) is a federal data-collection program that tabulates and publishes figures on both nonlethal and lethal untoward drug reactions. With the single exception of admissions to drug treatment programs, DAWN focuses mostly on acute effects, that is to say, those that occur within the time frame of a single episode of use, rather than chronic or long-term effects. Thus, deaths from AIDS, lung cancer, and cirrhosis of the liver do not appear in DAWN's data, while death from administering an overly potent dose of heroin does.

DAWN's data on nonlethal reactions come to the attention of and are tabulated by emergency departments in the country's metropolitan areas; these reactions include unconsciousness, panic reactions, and suicide attempts. Up to four drugs can be mentioned in a given case or "episode." The results are published yearly in the Department of Health and Human Services' publication *Emergency Department Data from the Drug Abuse Warning Network.* At last tally (the year 2001), there were just over 600,000 emergency department (ED) episodes and, at 1.8 drugs per episode, slightly more than a million emergency department drug mentions (SAMHSA 2003a).

In addition, DAWN tallies lethal "overdoses." Medical examiners in all counties in the United States conduct an autopsy in all cases of "nonroutine" deaths. If one or more drugs are detected in the

Table 29.2   Emergency Department (ED) Episodes, 2000

	Percentage of Episodes	*Number of Mentions*
Alcohol-in-combination	34	204,524
Cocaine	29	174,896
Heroine/morphine	16	97,287
Total number of ED episodes		601,776
Total number of drug mentions		1,100,539

Source: Drug Abuse Warning Network (DAWN), Emergency Department Data, 2001.

decedent's body and are believed to have been responsible for (or associated with) the death, they are tabulated as a "drug-induced" death or as having played a "contributing" role in the death. Up to six drugs may be mentioned in drug-related medical examiner (ME) episodes. DAWN issues a yearly volume, *Drug Abuse Warning Network Annual Medical Examiner Data,* tabulating the number of drug-related deaths in metropolitan areas. At last count, 11,000 drug abuse deaths were counted in the United States, and, at 2.5 drugs per episode, there were nearly 29,000 drug mentions (SAMHSA 2003b).

The most important feature of DAWN's ED (emergency department tallies of nonlethal untoward effects) and ME (lethal "overdoses" tallied by medical examiners) cases is that, almost by definition, they represent use at its most abusive level. Relatively few recreational users show up in DAWN's statistics. DAWN's cases tend to be users who take their drug or drugs frequently, heavily, abusively, and chronically. And by definition, they are the users who, objectively speaking, represent the most serious social problem for the society. They are the ones who die, get sick, are most likely to commit crimes against their fellow citizens, require medical intervention and treatment, and on whom a disproportionately large proportion of the government's drug treatment budget is expended.

In the United States at the beginning of the twenty-first century, there are three drugs that stand head and shoulders above all others in causing or being associated with serious untoward drug reactions: heroin, cocaine, and alcohol. For ED or nonlethal untoward reactions, alcohol (in combination with another drug) is mentioned in roughly

one-third (or 34 percent) of all episodes; cocaine is mentioned in about 3 out of 10 episodes (29 percent); and heroin (or morphine) in 16 percent of all cases. Hence, according to one measure of objective problemhood, nonlethal untoward drug effects, alcohol, cocaine, and heroin rank as the top three drugs with respect to causing harm to users. In the latest ME publication, for the year 2000, for lethal drug reactions, cocaine was mentioned in 43 percent of all episodes; heroin/morphine appeared in 39 percent of all ME episodes; and alcohol-in-combination was mentioned in 37 percent of all cases (SAMHSA 2002a). In other words, objectively speaking, three substances—heroin, cocaine, and alcohol—cause or are associated with the lion's share of one important measure of America's drug problem, acute death. No other single drug comes close to these three (although all the other narcotics added together surpass heroin and alcohol in being present in the bodies of drug overdoses). Hence, from the point of view of causing acute deaths, these three drugs are American society's most serious social problems. Tables 29.2 and 29.3 present DAWN's overdose data for ED and ME cases. Epidemiologically, DAWN's ME cases tend to be male rather than female (75 percent vs. 25 percent), older rather than younger (70 percent are age 35 and older, unlike users in general), and disproportionately black (27 percent, as opposed to 13 percent in the U.S. population).

The European Monitoring Centre for Drugs and Drug Addiction. The EMCDDA (2002) estimates that in the EU between the early 1990s and 2000, the number of acute drug-related deaths (alcohol and tobacco excepted) has stabilized at between 7,000 and 8,000. In some countries, such as Greece, the

Table 29.3   Medical Examiner (ME) Reports, 2000, Number of Mentions and Deaths by Drug

	Number of Deaths	*Percentage of Deaths*
Cocaine	4,782	43
Heroin	4,398	39
Alcohol	4,081	37
Total ME mentions	28,846	
Total ME deaths	11,168	

Source: Drug Abuse Warning Network (DAWN), Medical Examiner Data, 2001.

Note: Cocaine includes crack; heroin includes morphine; alcohol cases are counted only when used in combination with another drug.

trend has been upward, while in others, such as France, there has been a decline; but for almost a decade, the trend has been more or less flat. The use of opiates, including heroin, is most strongly associated with drug-related mortality. The Centre reports that the mortality rate for opiate users in the EU is 20 times higher than is true of the general population of the same age. The huge discrepancy is due not only to drug overdoses but also accidents, suicides, AIDS, and other infectious diseases. In addition, opiate users are more likely to take other drugs, and most specifically, depressants and alcohol. Opiate injectors stand a two to four times greater likelihood of dying as compared with noninjectors. Given its strong relationship with death and disease, the Centre defines "problem" drug use as "injecting drug use or long-duration/regular use of opiates, cocaine, and/or amphetamines." According to this definition, problem drug use varied between 7.1 and 7.8 per 1,000 in the population in Italy to between 1.4 and 2.7 in Germany. The Pompidou Group, which monitors drug abuse and its consequences in European countries, tabulates heroin overdose deaths on a year-by-year basis. The country with the highest rate and number on the continent is Norway. In 2001, with only 4.5 million residents, 453 Norwegians died of a heroin overdose, a rate roughly six times that tallied by DAWN in the United States.

ADAM (Arrestee Drug Abuse Monitoring). The conjunction of drug use with criminal behavior represents a major social problem for all societies. Does drug use cause criminal behavior? Or is a criminal lifestyle associated with the use of psychoactive

substances? Or are the drug laws responsible for the link between drug use and criminal behavior? Most researchers believe that although the use of illicit substances does not "initiate" criminal behavior, it tends to "intensify and perpetuate" it (Inciardi 2002:190).

In more than two dozen cities around the United States, a sample of arrestees charged with drug, property, and violent crimes is approached, and each is asked if he or she is willing to be interviewed; 30,000 males and 10,000 females were included in the most recent sample. Over 8 in 10 who are asked agree to be interviewed. These interviewees are then asked if they can be drug tested; again, roughly 80 percent agree. There are no legal consequences of testing positive. This program is referred to as the Arrestee Drug Abuse Monitoring Program, or ADAM. One aspect of ADAM is that the likelihood of testing positive varies according to the half-life of the particular drug. Cocaine and opiates are not detected beyond three days after use; in contrast, marijuana can be detected a week afterward for a casual user, and a month later for a chronic user.

Perhaps ADAM's most noteworthy finding is that men and women who have been arrested for a crime are massively more likely to have recently used psychoactive drugs than is true of the population at large. In 1999, in the median city, roughly two-thirds of ADAM's arrestees tested positive for the presence of one or more drugs (64 percent for males, 67 percent for females). As we saw, only 6 percent of the American population used one or more illicit drugs in the past month; over 10 times as many of ADAM's arrestees tested positive and hence used (depending on the drug) within the past several days.

These figures indicate that drug use and criminal behavior are extremely closely linked. There are four additional crucial points made by ADAM's data: (1) between 1990 and 2000, cocaine declined in popularity; in 1990, in the median city, 45 percent of the male and 49 percent of the female arrestees tested positive for cocaine, but by 2000, these figures had declined to 29 percent and 33 percent; (2) during this same decade, marijuana increased in popularity—from 20 percent (males) and 12 percent (females) for 1990 to 41 percent and 27 percent respectively in 2000; (3) opiates remain a relatively infrequently used drug among arrestees; in 2000, only 6 percent of the males and 8 percent of the females tested positive for any of the opiates, heroin included; and (4) methamphetamine is still not only a relatively rarely used illicit drug (nationally, in the median city, 2 percent of the men and 5 percent of the women tested positive for methamphetamine); its use is highly regionalized, that is, it is used almost not at all in some cities and by as much as a quarter or even a third in others (ADAM statistics from U.S. Department of Justice 2003).

Problem Drug Use in Australia. According to Australia's National Drug Strategy Household Survey (Australian Institute of Health and Welfare 2002), in the past 12 months, 13 percent of Australians said they drove a motor vehicle under the influence of alcohol; males were twice as likely to have done so, 18 percent versus 8 percent; and 4 percent said that they had done so under the influence of illicit drugs. One percent admitted to having "physically abused someone" while under the influence of alcohol, and 5 percent said that they had been physically abused by someone else who was under the influence. Fourteen percent said that they had been "put in fear" by someone under the influence of alcohol, and 9 percent by someone under the influence of an illicit drug. Three percent said that they were sufficiently abused by someone under the influence of either alcohol or an illegal drug as to require hospital admission. The Australian Institute of Health and Welfare estimated that in 1998, there were 17,671 deaths and 185,558 hospital episodes related to illicit drug use. The Institute puts the cost of drug abuse both legal and illegal at slightly above $1 billion: $833 million for tobacco, $145 million for alcohol, and $43 million for illicit drugs. Australia's population is 20 million.

The National Institute on Alcohol Abuse and Alcoholism (NIAAA). Since 1971, every three years or so, the U.S. National Institute on Alcohol Abuse and Alcoholism, a division of the Department of Health and Human Services, has issued summary reports assessing alcohol's impact on health. At this writing, the most recent volume was released in 2000 (NIAAA 2000). To put its findings in perspective, it should be kept in mind that just under half the American population consumes a dozen or more alcoholic drinks a year; approximately 7 percent of the population drinks abusively, according to NIAAA's criteria. Alcohol is used by more people than any other drug, although tobacco is consumed more often. Alcohol is consumed 5 to 10 times as often as is true of all the illicit drugs combined. According to NIAAA's summary of the available data:

- The total cost of alcohol abuse in the United States is $185 billion.
- Roughly 16,000 people annually are killed in automobile accidents caused by the immoderate consumption of alcohol.
- Alcohol alone is involved in substance-related violence in one-quarter of all incidents, a total of 2.7 million acts of violence per year.
- About 900,000 residents of the United States suffer from cirrhosis of the liver, mainly caused by the heavy use of alcohol, and 26,000 die of the disease each year.
- Excess alcohol consumption is related to immune deficiencies, causing a susceptibility to certain infectious diseases, such as tuberculosis, pneumonia, HIV (human immunodeficiency virus), AIDS, and hepatitis.
- Heavy drinkers (those who consumed 29 or more drinks per week) had twice the risk of mental disorder as compared with abstainers.

These highlights do not exhaust NIAAA's list of harms caused by alcohol. Estimates of the total number of people killed by the consumption of alcohol range between 100,000 and 150,000. Human life is undermined, threatened, corrupted, and destroyed by alcohol abuse. NIAAA does point out that moderate alcohol consumption is not only not harmful but may actually confer certain health benefits on the drinker. For some diseases, the morbidity of moderate drinkers is actually lower than that of abstainers, and moderate drinking is far more common than heavy drinking. Nonetheless, as a psychoactive substance, alcohol stands below (albeit far below) tobacco as a major source of death and disease, and stands virtually alone as a source of violence and accidents. By any reasonable objective criteria, immoderate drinking represents a major social problem in the United States.

Drug Use as an Objective Problem: Summary

In 1996, the World Health Organization (WHO) announced that by the early years of the twenty-first century, 10 million people per year worldwide will die of diseases caused by cigarette smoking. With respect to death and disease, objectively speaking, tobacco is the world's number-one drug problem, killing more people than all other drugs combined, and by a considerable margin. At the same time, the consumption of tobacco tends to kill older users, and it is not associated with violence or accidental injury or death (except for fire-related accidents). Objectively speaking, alcohol is the globe's number-two drug problem. Its consumption is associated with death and disease, and accidents and violence; worldwide, the monetary cost of drinking runs into the hundreds of billions of dollars. The consumption of illicit drugs stands far below the legal drugs with respect to medical harm and monetary cost. Nonetheless, the abuse of two drugs, heroin and cocaine, although used far less frequently, causes overdose deaths roughly on a par with alcohol; criminals use illicit drugs at a rate vastly higher than is true of the population at large; and drug-related illnesses include HIV/AIDS, hepatitis, and pneumonia. Unlike the legal drugs, the worldwide distribution of illicit drugs is associated with political corruption and social disorganization, and holding communities, regions, and entire countries hostage to the rapacious greed of ruthless traffickers. Whether drug legalization would be a solution to the chaos caused by the sale and use of illicit drugs

(Nadelmann 1988) is debatable. In short, the consumption of psychoactive substances causes or is associated with a long list of harmful consequences. Objectively speaking, worldwide, drug use is a major social problem, a worthy subject of inquiry to the interested student of social problems.

DRUG USE AND SALE AS A SOCIALLY CONSTRUCTED PROBLEM

From the constructionist perspective, drug use is a problem for the society because a substantial percentage of the population is concerned about it, the media depict it as a problem, the public regards it as a problem, and officials and social movement organizations take steps to deal with it. Constructionists regard assertions of social problemhood by social actors as "claims" that may or may not be valorized by other members of a society. The constructionist perspective is especially relevant to a global approach to drug use as a social problem because public concern and social movement and government claims, as well as concrete steps to deal with drug use and distribution, are communicated worldwide, from one country to another. Claims about the socially problematic nature of specific conditions, drug use included, are diffused cross-nationally (Best 2001).

One of the major emphases of the constructionist approach to social problems is on the discrepancy between the subjective concern generated by certain conditions and the objective harm caused by those conditions. These discrepancies apply from one time period to another and from one condition to another. For instance, when we compare concern with harm historically, the sudden emergence of the imputed problemhood of a certain condition at a particular point in time focuses the researcher's attention on how and why that condition came to be regarded as a social problem but was not so regarded earlier. What produced the upsurge in concern? Why did claims that were ignored or rejected previously come to be valorized today? Likewise, when we compare the enormous public concern surrounding a given condition that is less harmful than another about which there is less concern, observers are forced to ask why. In other words, the constructionist approach problematizes the attribution of problemhood. This discrepancy is not an essential component of the constructionist's definition of a social problem—as we saw, social constructions are not "just" social constructions, but may have an objective referent as well (Best 2000)—but to the constructionist, it is a theoretically interesting and frequent accompaniment.

Along these lines, then, we learn that the effort to define coffee drinking, a relatively benign activity, as a social problem emerged in the 1970s and was to a certain extent and for a period of time successful (Troyer and Markle 1984). Vested interests—specifically the dairy industry—for a time during the 1930s and 1940s successfully albeit briefly managed to define the production, sale, and consumption of margarine as a "menace" and therefore a problem to society (Ball and Lilly 1982). In the 1970s, the criminal victimization of the elderly came to be seen as a major social problem—when, in fact, this has been the segment of the population that is least likely to be victimized by street crime (Fishman 1978). In the 1960s, the physical abuse of children by their parents or caretakers, which had remained a major source of death, injury, and mutilation for millennia, was "discovered," widely recognized as a social problem, and attacked as a pathological condition in need of remedy (Pfohl 1977). In the 1960s and 1970s, after centuries of use and concomitant disease and death, cigarette smoking came to be defined as undesirable, harmful, and deviant, a problem very much in need of correction, control, and elimination (Markle and Troyer 1979; Troyer and Markle 1983). In 1982, while drug abuse among Israeli adolescents remained stable at an extremely low level, national concern over illicit psychoactive drug use developed and lasted for approximately a month, and just as swiftly disappeared (Ben-Yehuda 1986). It was not until the 1970s—after causing millions of deaths on the highway during the course of this century—that drunk driving came to be seen as a major problem facing the country, and movements sprang up to deal with the problem (Gusfield 1981).

In short, a number of relatively harmful conditions have existed for extremely long periods of time without being defined as problems, yet at a particular point in time, as a result of the influence of an array of forces, they come to be seen as troublesome to the society, conditions that are very much in need of remedy. In a like vein, the public has come to be concerned about some relatively benign conditions and fearful of those that either do not exist or that cause very little objective harm. Clearly, then, there is a measure of independence between the objective and the subjective dimensions for certain specific concrete or putative conditions. Moreover, in each case, the process and outcome of defining a given condition as a social problem is sociologically patterned and structured, the elucidation of which is theoretically strategic. Conditions become successfully defined as social problems not at random, nor solely as a result of their objective seriousness, but because specific segments or interest groups are successful at generating, stimulating, or guiding widespread public concern about them. Claims that these conditions are social problems in need of remedy come to be accepted and acted upon. This is the approach that the constructionist of social problems adopts.

This same discrepancy between objective seriousness and subjective concern obtains with drug use as a social problem. For instance, the Australian 2001 National Drug Strategy Household Survey (Australian Institute of Health and Welfare 2002) revealed that only 3 percent of its respondents designated the use of tobacco as the major drug problem in Australia; 8 percent did so for alcohol, and 90 percent did so for illicit drugs. Yet, as we saw, the use of tobacco costs Australian society almost 6 times as much as alcohol and 20 times as much as the use of illegal drugs, and these drugs kill Australians in roughly the same proportions. More or less the same picture prevails for the United States (Horgan et al. 2001:6). Hence, for the analyst of social problems, the question becomes: Why the discrepancy? What generates so much more societal concern over illicit drug use than is true for legal drug use? And why are the members of a society more concerned about drug use at one point in time than at another? And how are such concerns and claims about the harmful effects of drug use diffused across national boundaries?

The study of the global diffusion of claims making about the problemhood of drug use/abuse is in its infancy. Yet the importance of the issue is undeniable. Worldwide, there are more than a billion cigarette smokers; on average, they stand to lose a decade of life because of their use of a harmful chemical substance, nicotine. Yet, in some countries, the claim that smoking is a serious social problem is not publicly valorized, nor do the governments of these nations take steps to curtail this form of abusive addiction. Why have claims of the social problemhood of smoking spread to some countries but not others? Why has the claim that the immoderate consumption of alcohol is harmful and problematic to the society been widely accepted in some countries but virtually ignored in others? Why have some countries been slow to respond to the worldwide challenge of AIDS, while for others, the deadly disease is regarded both publicly and governmentally as a social problem of major dimensions? Why does the U.S. government regard the consumption of marijuana as a threat, a gateway drug, a substance whose use calls for attention, legal intervention, and research demonstrating pathological effects, while the Dutch government has adopted a policy of domestication and tolerance by law enforcement? In short, why do some claims of the social problemhood of drug use and abuse fail to spread to certain countries, or cross-nationally, while others come to be valorized worldwide?

Diffusion of Claims of Social Problemhood

Japan's Antismoking Campaign. The failure of Japan to accept smoking as a serious threat exemplifies the contingencies entailed in the diffusion or nondiffusion of claims of social problemhood. Roughly 30 percent of the Japanese population smokes—half of its men and 10 percent of its women. (In the United States, the figure is substantially lower, roughly one-fourth, and the difference between men and women is small.) And while the smoking rate in the United States has declined since 1964, in Japan, it has risen; between 1950 and the end of the twentieth century, cigarette sales increased five times in Japan, while its population increased only 50 percent (Ayukawa 2001:215). More to the point, the Japanese government has not taken steps to valorize smoking's harmful effects, the population of Japan does not regard smoking as a serious threat to public health, and social

movement organizations' efforts to ban smoking in public places are ineffective. This inaction is all the more remarkable given Japan's acceptance of cultural innovations from abroad, especially from the United States—where smoking has been regarded as a social problem for four decades. The question is, why has the claim that smoking is a major social problem not diffused from the United States to Japan?

The fact is, the monopoly that administers the manufacture, importation, and sale of tobacco, Japan Tobacco, while technically private, is largely owned by a government agency, the ministry of finance. Hence, the Japanese government "has a direct stake in tobacco sales" (Ayukawa 2001:216). In 1985, the Tobacco Enterprise Law was introduced "to strive for the sound development of the tobacco enterprise and to contribute to the stability of income revenue and the sound development of the national economy." In point of fact, the law advocated that the Ministry of Finance "promote tobacco sales in order to increase revenue from tobacco" (Ayukawa 2001:216). In 1999, cigarette taxes generated $8.5 billion in national tax revenues on Japan Tobacco product sales (Struck 2000:31). In contrast, excise taxes on tobacco in the United States, a country with twice Japan's population, earned $5.2 billion. As a result of tobacco's profitability for the Japanese government, antismoking campaigns, including those launched by the ministry of health, have been defeated nearly everywhere. After 1985, warning labels on packages of cigarettes read only "Smoking by minors is prohibited" and "Be careful not to smoke too much as it may do harm to your health," the latter implying that moderate smoking is not harmful. The government feels that the ministry of health "has no right to put medical messages on cigarette packages" (Ayukawa 2001:217). Two massive reports were issued, in 1987 and 1993, by the ministry of health. However, neither was recognized by the government as an official document, and both had to be published privately.

In 1998, Japan was the only industrialized country that broadcast television cigarette commercials, and the government has never put pressure on the networks or cigarette companies to discontinue them. That year, they were withdrawn, possibly because of international embarrassment. Nonetheless, programs often depict characters smoking, a way of introducing "stealth" advertising. Attractive young women distribute cigarettes in public places and even light them for smokers. In 2000, on Respect the Elderly Day, roughly 15 million cigarettes were distributed by Japan Tobacco—to the residents of nursing homes (Struck 2000). Lawsuits by plaintiffs to restrict smoking have been almost universally dismissed. During the late 1980s and early 1990s, lawsuits to force schools to provide nonsmoking lounge and lunch rooms for teachers were dismissed three times, once by Japan's Supreme Court. Since 1979, lawsuits to force the national railway to mandate that half of its cars be nonsmoking, again, have been consistently dismissed; a voluntary decision by the railway to designate 30 percent of its cars as nonsmoking ended the lawsuit. In Japan, not a single family of a deceased smoker has sued a tobacco company (Ayukawa 2001:229). And information about the hazards of smoking, a major weapon in the hands of antismoking groups in the United States, is extremely difficult to obtain in Japan (Ayukawa 2001:225). In short, the public and governmental concern about smoking that prevails in the United States has not diffused to Japan. Efforts to restrict the use of cigarettes have failed partly because of a variety of cultural and structural factors (for instance, unlike the United States, Japan has very few lawyers, and lawsuits, regarded as unseemly and inappropriately confrontational, are extremely rare there) but largely because of the Japanese government's direct involvement in the sale of tobacco. Antismoking social movement activity remains ineffective, and concerns about the threat of smoking have not even remotely reached American levels. It might seem that restricting tobacco consumption in Japan represents a negative case in the diffusion of social problem—in a sense, the failure of globalization.

But we should make a distinction between effort and success. Social movement activity in Japan and in other Asian countries is not so impotent as to be virtually nonexistent. Not only are antismoking campaigns active and ongoing—although, in comparison with the United States, far less effective—they also incorporate successful tactics borrowed from the United States. WHO advisers to the organization's Asian antismoking efforts say that they have evidence on what strategies have worked

in the United States and they apply them to their Asian campaign, for instance, putting antismoking messages on packs of cigarettes. In Thailand, a label on a cigarette pack states that "smoking reduces sexual ability." In Vietnam, cigarette advertising and the handing out of free samples by "cigarette girls" have been banned. Even in China, the world's leader in cigarette sales (1.7 trillion cigarettes sold annually), restrictions on advertising have been put in place. Says Stephen Tamplin, who coordinates the WHO's antismoking campaign in Asia, "We don't underestimate the battle here; it's huge.... But we're encouraged. We think there's renewed interest in tobacco control" (Struck 2000:A21, A31).

Interpol. A contrary case is provided by Interpol, an acronym referring to the International Criminal Police Organization. Interpol is dedicated to the proposition that drug abuse around the world is harmful and should be curtailed or eliminated—in short, that it constitutes a social problem. Founded in 1914, suspended during the Nazi era, and reconstituted in 1946 with its headquarters in Paris, Interpol provides 179 member nations with information on the whereabouts of international criminals, offers seminars on scientific crime detection, and helps national police departments to apprehend criminals. (Interpol's agents do not themselves make arrests.) Its most effective efforts are in combating counterfeiting, forgery, smuggling—and illicit narcotics. One of Interpol's goals is to alert the international community to the threat that drug abuse poses globally, as well as advancing and facilitating what it considers the most effective policy to control illicit drug distribution and use. According to the Web site materials it posts, the mission of Interpol's Drugs Sub-Directorate is as follows:

> [To] enhance co-operation among member countries and to stimulate the exchange of information between [and among] all national and international enforcement bodies concerned with countering the illicit production, traffic and use of narcotic drugs and psychotropic substances. (www.interpol.int)

This includes collecting information, responding to international drug investigation inquiries, collecting relevant intelligence data and disseminating them to member states, identifying international trafficking organizations, and organizing meetings on a regional or worldwide basis on relevant topics.

Among the many avenues Interpol employs to pursue that end is to act "as a clearing-house for the collection, collation, analysis and dissemination of drug-related information." Interpol's Web site mentions four drugs or drug types as specific targets: cannabis, cocaine, heroin, and synthetic drugs. It identifies the major drug-producing and market nations, routes taken to transport illicit substances, techniques of concealment, and figures on the production and seizure of illegal drugs. Although its informational Web site is low-key and focused more or less on communicating relevant objectively determinable drug-related assertions, there is no doubt in the reader's mind that in posting it, Interpol is engaged in a claims-making activity, that is, defining illicit drug use as wrong, harmful, and a worldwide social problem about which readers need to be aware and on which the agency's efforts are focused. Says Interpol about the consumption of heroin: "The abuse of heroin among youth is a serious problem. Children as young as 13 have been found involved in heroin abuse. According to statistics in 1999, heroin overdose has caused more deaths than traffic accidents." Today's youth culture, says Interpol, "demands stimulants—today, recreational use is no longer limited to weekends," a statement that argues that use inevitably becomes abuse and both justifies Interpol's concern over the consumption of psychoactive substances and its communication of that concern to the public. Of morphine-like synthetic drugs, Interpol states that "attempts to separate the analgesic effects from the euphoria-producing effects, which are those associated with compulsive abuse, have been unsuccessful," arguing both that the medical use of such drugs inevitably creeps into recreational street use and that use based on euphoria-seeking inevitably becomes abuse—again, justifying the agency's concern and its claim that illicit drug use is a social problem in need of remedy. Just as globalization characterizes the distribution of both licit and illicit substances, efforts to define drugs as a social problem and to curtail their distribution and their harmful consequences are likewise globalized.

The United Nations. Another case of international cooperation in defining drug abuse as a social problem is provided by the efforts of the UN. The UN sponsors several organizations that have launched campaigns dedicated to the proposition that drug abuse is a major global problem that must be combated through a variety of programs. According to the UN's Web page, the UN Drug Control Programme (UNDC), founded in 1991, "works to educate the world about the dangers of drug abuse," strengthening international action against drug trafficking and drug-related crime "through alternative development projects, crop monitoring and anti-money laundering programmes" (www.undc.org). In addition, UNDC provides statistics on drug use and trafficking and, though its Legal Assistance Programme, helps to draft legislation and train judicial officials and acts as a liaison with international law enforcement partners, such as Interpol. The UN Commission on Narcotic Drugs (CND), established in 1946, "analyzes the world drug abuse situation and develops proposals to strengthen international drug control." The UN's Global Monitoring Programme of Illicit Crops assists member states to provide data on illicit crops and "integrates aerial surveillance, on-the-ground assessment and satellite sensing." These data, says the UN, will enable member states "to eliminate or significantly reduce the cultivation of drug crops" within a few years. Examples of the UN antidrug abuse campaign include the following.

Worldwide, over 40 million people are infected with HIV/AIDS; according to the UN, 1 in 20 were infected through intravenous (IV) drug injection. In partnership with the Brazilian government, the UNDCP has sponsored a peer-educator anti-AIDS educational campaign to "reach out to targeted groups" such as prostitutes, prisoners, adolescents, drug abusers in treatment centers, miners, and truck drivers, delivering the message that the IV use of drugs can lead to diseases such as AIDS. Since 1991, the percentage of AIDS cases reported in Brazil among injecting drug users, according to year of diagnosis, has been cut in half, from 25.5 to 12.4 percent.

The UNDCP has focused on the remote villages in the Nonghet District of Laos, a leading opium producer, for its antidrug campaign. Opium is the primary source of income for 85 percent of the villages of the district; a cash crop makes it possible for the villagers to purchase food during periods of a rice shortage. Addiction among villagers is extremely high. The UNDCP, working on the assumption that poverty is a major reason for opium production, has worked with villagers to help them cultivate rice, corn, vegetables, fruit, and livestock. In addition, it has helped them build irrigation ditches to water their crops and roadways to get crops to market. Drinking water, medicine, and teacher training are also facilitated. The UN's figures show that in the past four years, opium cultivation in the district has declined 78 percent.

The UN Office for Drug Control and Crime Prevention has produced and distributes video spots in which sports figures, including National Basketball Association stars Dikembe Mutombo, a native of Congo, and Vlade Divac, a Yugoslavian; Khodadad Azizi, a soccer player from Iran; and Hidestoshi Nakata, a Japanese soccer player, emphasize the message, "Sports Against Drugs." The video spots are available in 20 languages. The UN hopes that its antidrug message, delivered by revered sports figures, will convince young people to avoid peer pressure to use drugs, avoid sharing needles, use condoms, and become involved in healthful alternative activities.

Global Diffusion of Antidrug Campaigns: A Summary

The campaigns supported by agencies of the UN and Interpol represent global efforts to define drug abuse as a major social problem and reduce or eliminate its incidence as well as the occurrence of some of its most harmful effects. In short, from a constructionist perspective, the UN and Interpol make claims about the problemhood of drug abuse that have successfully diffused cross-nationally, taking root all over the world. Their efforts have alerted officials to the threat posed by drugs and enabled them to take steps to combat that threat. The UN and Interpol antidrug campaigns represent examples of the global diffusion of drug abuse as a social problem. In Japan, social movement activity and the ministry of health's efforts to define smoking as a social problem have been far less successful,

although in Japan, as well as in Asia generally, such efforts are ongoing and occasionally result in small victories.

Conclusions

Social problems are defined in two radically different ways: objectively, that is, by the harm that conditions cause, and subjectively, that is, by the concern that conditions generate, the claims made about them by spokespersons, and the steps proposed or taken to remedy them. The consumption of psychoactive substances, including tobacco, alcohol, and illicit drugs, is a material-world condition that causes or is associated with an array of related social costs. And drug use, likewise, is a phenomenon that attracts public concern, claims of problemhood, and solutions to remedy the putative problem. Although social problems texts nearly always mention drug use as a major problem, the study of social problems from a global perspective is in its infancy. Drug use offers a dramatic case of the value and richness of the global perspective. Worldwide, changes are taking place that render previous approaches obsolete.

A global explosion of youth with disposable income, sufficient time to engage in recreational activities, and a subculture endorsing hedonism has generated the skyrocketing use of a range of psychoactive chemicals that have come to be called "club drugs": methamphetamine, Ecstasy, ketamine, GHB, and rohypnol, to name only a few of the more widely publicized substances. Not only have global changes generated this reservoir of drug-receptive youth, films and other media disseminated around the globe have communicated the message that drug-induced hedonism is a positive value to be pursued. Worldwide networks of traffickers link Tajik farmers with Nigerian middlemen with Dutch business executives, Lao villagers with Chinese smugglers with Hispanic American dealers, and Belgian chemists with affluent, suburban American high school students. What was once a small cottage industry with fairly simple international links has become, in effect, a major multinational corporation with profits running into the hundreds of billions of dollars and an immense payroll of employees in nearly every country of the world.

Definitions of the problemhood of drug abuse, likewise, are diffused worldwide. While some claims of problemhood fail to take hold because of the influence of local factors (as is the case with smoking in Japan), for the most part, messages that drug use is a harmful condition that must be remedied are disseminated worldwide, from social movements in the United States to the Brazilian government, from the UN to every country on earth, from Interpol headquarters in Paris to every one of its member nations, and from the WHO to Africa. The fact is, drug abuse as a social problem can no longer be studied in any way except globally. Our borderless world, which offers all citizens on earth the cultural richness of every other nation, is Janus-faced. Globalization guarantees the flow of people, ideas, and goods across borders, but it has a dark side as well, and one of its nastier spawn is the flood of psychoactive substances, both licit and illicit, around the world. One thing is certain: Globalization is here to stay; we will be dealing with its consequences, for good or ill, for centuries to come. It has become an ineradicable feature of the human condition. Its impact on drug distribution, use, and abuse and proposed solutions to these problems will forever involve the entire world community.

NOTES

1. Peter Reuter (1996) rightfully criticizes several of the estimates I use in this chapter as "flawed," "inconsistent," and produced by means of "inadequate methodologies." I agree with his argument and his conclusions. Unfortunately, no figures on worldwide production or consumption are produced that would satisfy the criteria a serious methodologist is likely to propose. Reuter suggests the data are so bad because they are not the basis of policy decisions by any government. One might also argue that the data are so bad because Reuter's former employer, the RAND corporation, which conducts detailed, systematic estimates on domestic illicit drug distribution, has never been contracted to do a study on global drug production.

2. The UN's *Global Illicit Drug Trends 2002* takes account of the decline in opium production in Afghanistan under the Taliban, which was steep. Now that the Taliban regime has ended, opium production is back up to its previous levels. Hence, I rely on the UN's 2001 report, whose figures reflect current production levels, rather than its 2002 report, which records a temporary and now-terminated situation.

REFERENCES

Australian Institute of Health and Welfare. 2002. *2001 National Drug Strategy Household Survey.* Canberra, Australia: Author.

Ayukawa, Jun. 2001. "The United States and Smoking Problems in Japan." Pp. 215–42 in *How Claims Spread: Cross-National Diffusion of Social Problems,* edited by Joel Best. New York: Aldine de Gruyter.

Ball, Richard J. and J. Robert Lilly. 1982. "The Menace of Margarine: The Rise and Fall of a Social Problem." *Social Problems* 29:488–98.

Bartecchi, Carl E., Thomas D. MacKenzie, and Robert W. Schrier. 1995. "The Global Tobacco Epidemic." *Scientific American*, May, 272:44–51.

Becker, Howard S. 1963. *Outsiders: Studies in the Sociology of Deviance.* Glencoe, IL: Free Press.

Ben-Yehuda, Nachman. 1986. "The Sociology of Moral Panics: Toward a New Synthesis." *Sociological Quarterly* 27:495–513.

Best, Joel, ed. 1995. *Images of Issues: Typifying Contemporary Social Problems.* 2nd ed. New York: Aldine de Gruyter.

——. 2000. "The Apparently Innocuous 'Just,' the Law of Levity, and the Social Problems of Social Construction." *Perspectives on Social Problems* 12:3–14.

——, ed. 2001. *How Claims Spread: Cross-National Diffusion of Social Problems.* New York: Aldine de Gruyter.

Blumer, Herbert. 1971. "Social Problems as Collective Behavior." *Social Problems* 18:298–306.

Bruen, Anne-Marie et al. 2002. *Estimation of Heroin Availability, 1996–2000.* Washington, DC: Office of National Drug Control Policy.

Centers for Disease Control (CDC). 1999. "Trends in Cigarette Smoking." Atlanta, GA: CDC, Epidemiology and Statistics Unit. Unpublished manuscript.

Dunlap, Eloise, Bruce D. Johnson, and Ali Manwar. 1994. "A Successful Crack Dealer: Case Study of a Deviant Career." *Deviant Behavior* 15:1–25.

European Monitoring Centre for Drugs and Drug Addiction (EMCDDA). 2001. *Annual Report on the State of the Drugs Problem in the European Union.* Lisbon, Portugal: Author.

——. 2002. *Annual Report on the State of the Drugs Problem in the European Union and Norway.* Lisbon, Portugal: Author.

Fenrich, Michael et al. 1999. "Validity of Drug Use Reporting in a High-Risk Community Sample: A Comparison of Cocaine and Heroin Survey with Hair Tests." *American Journal of Epidemiology* 149: 955–62.

Fishman, Mark. 1978. "Crime Waves as Ideology." *Social Problems* 25:531–43.

Flynn, Stephen. 1993. "Worldwide Drug Scourge: The Expanding Trade in Illicit Drugs." *Brookings Review,* Winter, 6–11.

Fuller, Richard C. and Richard R. Myers. 1941. "Some Aspects of a Theory of Social Problems." *American Sociological Review* 6:24–32.

Gusfield, Joseph R. 1963. *Symbolic Crusade: Symbolic Politics and the American Temperance Movement.* Urbana, IL: University of Illinois Press.

——. 1981. *The Culture of Public Problems: Drinking-Driving and the Symbolic Order.* Chicago, IL: University of Chicago Press.

Himmelstein, Jerome J. 1983. *The Strange Career of Marihuana: Politics and Ideology of Drug Control in America.* Westport, CT: Greenwood.

Horgan, Constance, Kathleen C. Skwara, and Gail Strickler. 2001. *Substance Abuse: The Nation's Number One Health Problem.* Princeton, NJ: Robert Wood Johnson Foundation.

Inciardi, James A. 2002. *The War on Drugs III.* Boston, MA: Allyn & Bacon.

Johnston, Lloyd D., Patrick M. O'Malley, and Jerald G. Bachman. 2002. *Overview of Key Findings Monitoring the Future, National Results on Adolescent Drug Use.* Bethesda, MD: National Institute on Drug Abuse.

Layne, Mary, Patrick Johnston, and William Rhodes. 2002. *Estimation of Cocaine Availability, 1996–2001.* Washington, DC: Office of Drug Control Policy.

Loseke, Donileen R. 1999. *Thinking about Social Problems: An Introduction to Constructionist Perspectives.* New York: Aldine de Gruyter.

Manis, Jerome J. 1974. "The Concept of Social Problems: Vox Populi and Sociological Analysis." *Social Problems* 21:305–15.

——. 1976. *Analyzing Social Problems.* New York: Praeger.

Markle, Gerald E. and Ronald J. Troyer. 1979. "Smoke Gets in Your Eyes: Cigarette Smoking as Deviant Behavior." *Social Problems* 26:611–25.

Mauss, Armand L. 1975. *Social Problems as Social Movements.* Philadelphia, PA: Lippencott.

McKim, William. 2003. *Drugs and Behavior: An Introduction to Behavioral Pharmacology.* Upper Saddle River, NJ: Prentice Hall.

Nadelmann, Ethan A. 1988. "The Case for Legalization." *The Public Interest* 92:3–31.

National Institute on Alcohol Abuse and Alcoholism (NIAAA). *10th Special Report to the U.S. Congress on Alcohol and Health, Highlights from Current Research.* Rockville, MD: U.S. Department of Health and Human Services, NIAAA.

Pfohl, Stephen J. 1977. "The 'Discovery' of Child Abuse." *Social Problems* 24:310–23.

Pollan, Michael. 1995. "How Pot Has Grown." *The New York Times Magazine,* December 16, 31–5, 44, 50, 56–7.

Ramsay, Malcolm et al. 2001. *Drug Misuse Declared in 2000: Results from the British Crime Survey.* London, England: Home Office Research, Development and Statistics Directorate.

Reuter, Peter. 1996. "The Mismeasure of Illegal Drug Markets: The Implication of Its Irrelevance." Pp. 63–80 in *Exploring the Underground Economy: Studies of Illegal and Unreported Activity,* edited by S. Pozo. Kalamazoo, MI: Upjohn Institute for Employment Research.

——. 2001. "The Limits of Supply-Side Drug Control." *The Milken Institute Review,* First Quarter, 14–23.

Schneider, Joseph W. 1985. "Social Problems Theory." *Annual Review of Sociology* 11:209–29.

Shenon, Philip. 1994. "Asia's Having One Huge Nicotine Fit." *New York Times,* May 15, 1WK, 16WK.

Spector, Malcolm and John I. Kitsuse. 1973. "Social Problems: A Reformulation." *Social Problems* 21: 145–59.

——. 1977. *Constructing Social Problems.* Menlo Park, CA: Cummings.

Stares, Paul. 1996. *Global Habit: The Drug Problem in a Borderless World.* Washington, DC: Brookings Institution.

Stesser, Stan. 1993. "Opium War Redux." *New Yorker,* September 13, pp. 78–89.

Struck, Doug. 2000. *Fighting for Their Lungs and Minds. Washington Post,* September 21, A21, A31.

Substance Abuse and Mental Health Administration (SAMHSA). 2002a. *Mortality Data from the Drug Abuse Warning Network 2000.* Rockville, MD: SAMHSA, Office of Applied Studies.

——. 2002b. *Results from the 2001 National Household Survey on Drug Abuse: Summary of Findings.* Rockville, MD: Author.

——. 2003a. *Detailed Emergency Department Tables from the Drug Abuse Warning Network 2001.* Rockville, MD: SAMHSA, Office of Applied Studies.

——. 2003b. *Mortality Data from the Drug Abuse Warning Network 2001.* Rockville, MD: SAMHSA, Office of Applied Studies.

Troyer, Ronald J. and Gerald E. Markle. 1983. *Cigarettes.* New Brunswick, NJ: Rutgers University Press.

——. 1984. "Coffee Drinking: An Emerging Social Problem?" *Social Problems* 31:403–16.

United Nations, Office for Drug Control and Crime Prevention. 2000. *World Drug Report 2000.* Oxford, UK, & New York: Oxford University Press.

——. 2001. *Global Illicit Drug Trends 2001.* New York: United Nations.

——. 2002. *Global Illicit Drug Trends 2002.* New York: United Nations.

U.S. Department of Justice. 2003. *2000 Arrestee Drug Abuse Monitoring: Annual Report.* Washington, DC: Author.

Viscusi, W. Kip. 2002. *Smoke-Filled Rooms: A Postmortem on the Tobacco Deal.* Chicago, IL: University of Chicago Press.

THE SEXUAL SPECTACLE

Making a Public Culture of Sexual Problems

KEN PLUMMER

University of Essex

There are multiple realities because people differ in their situations and their purposes. The reality an impressionist painter constructs respecting a maritime scene is not that of a sailor or that of an atomic physicist. The reality a destitute black person constructs respecting the nature of poverty has little validity for a conservative political candidate. . . . Every construction of the world is a demanding activity. It can be done well or badly and be right or wrong. To understand that multiple realities are prevalent is liberating, but such understanding in no way suggests that every construction is as good as every other. . . . There is typically little correspondence between the measures people take against political enemies and the harm they do.

Murray Edelman, *Constructing the Political Spectacle* (1988)

In most societies across time and space, it is possible to find sexual violence and rape, sexual representation and erotica, childhood sexualities and abuse, and masturbation and solitary sexual activities. There is usually a whole array of differing kinds of sexualities outside of the prescribed and conventional penis-vagina/marital/heterosexual intercourse. There will also be sterility and infertility, and many diseases that have their links with sexual activity, from HIV to herpes. Some people will sell their sex, and others will buy it. Some people will change their genders. And some people will be unhappy in their sexual relations, will experience excess desire or little desire, and experiment with sexual fetishes of many kinds. Most societies will have versions of all these: but their meanings, rates, causes, and general "social shape" are likely to differ greatly across time and space.[1] And in only some societies at some times will they ever become "social problems." Whilst "sexual problems"—sufferings and stigmas, diseases and difficulties, taboos and tribulations, defilements and dangers—have probably existed throughout all societies throughout history, the idea that sexualities are "social problems" may be a relatively new one. The spectacle of private passions and desires moving from the private realm into the public spheres for a proliferation of critical analyses and debate may be new. In the Western world, at least we can trace the gradual emergence of the public cultures of "social problem sexual talk"—what we might call the "Sexual Spectacle"—to the last 200 years or so.

In this chapter, I do not have space to focus on any one "sexual problem" (some, such as AIDS, sex work, gender, the family, and sexual violence, are indeed looked at elsewhere in this handbook). Rather, my concern is to start an appraisal of the wider and changing contexts in which the spectacle of shifting sexual problems starts to appear, providing a few indicative illustrations.

CONCEIVING THE SEXUAL

Throughout the 1960s and the 1970s, the key text on social problems was generally considered to be Merton and Nisbet's *Contemporary Social Problems,* and one of the preeminent functionalist theorists of the day, Kingsley Davis, wrote the contributions around sexuality.[2] He worked from a baseline that suggested that sex was composed of "unstable and anarchic drives" that needed to be regulated by sexual norms. He saw the family and economic exchange as rendering heterosexual coitus as obligatory within marriage and suggested that social problems were generated through the violation of such norms. Much of his discussion then turned to the functions of premarital sex, extramarital sex, prostitution, and homosexual behavior, mainly in North America.

Davis wrote, though, at the cusp of a change both in ways of thinking about sexuality and indeed in ways of being sexual. Today, for instance, the phrases "premarital sex" and "extramarital sex" sound faintly quaint in Anglo-American society and are rarely spoken of as major social problems (though they are still major concerns in other parts of the world, and there is an emergent coalition "Chastity Movement" in the United States).[3] He

wrote in times that were pre-Madonna, pre-AIDS, pre-cybersex, pre–new reproductive technologies, pre-Viagra, pre-MTV, and before the rise of feminist, lesbian, gay, bisexual, and transgendered movements. "Sex work" was still "prostitution," and "erotica" was still "pornography." The world of "sexual problems" has moved on. And so have ways of thinking about them.

Indeed, from the 1970s onwards, new ways of thinking about sex started to appear. Sociologists John Gagnon and William Simon made the case that sex was not an anarchic, essential, biological drive, as Davis had argued. They claimed it was profoundly social and had no reality of its own. As Gagnon said in a textbook of the mid-1970s: there are "many ways to become, to be, to act, to feel sexual. There is no one human sexuality, but rather a wide variety of sexualities" (Gagnon 1977, preface). Shortly after this, the French historian of ideas Michel Foucault ([1976] 1978) argued,

> [Sexuality] is the name given to a historical construct . . . a great surface network in which the stimulation of bodies, the intensification of pleasures, the incitement to discourse, the formation of knowledge, the strengthening of controls and resistances, are linked to one another, in accordance with a few major strategies of power. (P. 106)

Startlingly challenging conventional wisdom, he attacked the notion that sex had been repressed in the Victorian world and claimed instead that sexuality in this period was a discursive fiction that had actually organized the social problems of the time. New species—such as the homosexual, the pervert, the masturbating child, the Malthusian couple, the hysterical woman—had literally been invented and come into being as organizing motifs for sexual problems and the spread of surveillance and regulation. The body had become a site for disciplinary practices and new technologies. The Sexual Spectacle has been invented. All this was very far removed from Davis's functionalist model.

A further development in this period was the advance of feminist thinking about sexuality. Whereas Davis had presumed the dominance of heterosexuality and "male sexual needs,"[4] feminist theories of sexuality challenged this. Linking sexuality to "compulsory heterosexuality" and patriarchy, power came to assume a key role in the organizing of sexuality, and topics such as sexual violence, abuse, pornography, and genital mutilation came firmly to the forefront (topics largely neglected both by Davis and earlier social problems texts). Some feminists such as Andrea Dworkin and Catherine MacKinnon claimed that sexuality was organized by men for men and denounced both "heterosexuality" and heterosexual intercourse, whilst others such as Gail Rubin saw the creation of a sex hierarchy as a key organizing feature of society (for samples of all these positions, see Jackson and Scott 1996).

This is not the place to review this vast, varied, and now quite sophisticated "new sexualities" literature (Plummer 2002). What is important to grasp is that there has been a major upheaval intellectually in ways of thinking about sexualities. Despite displaying controversies and divisions, all agree that sexuality is no simple biological urge pressing for release. Human sexualities are always socially produced, organized, and patterned through power relations, and open to historical change. Embedded in political systems, economies, religions, and families, they are contingent upon patriarchies, sex hierarchies, and heterosexism. Historically variable, they are culturally transformable. And this new thinking has immediate consequences for thinking about sexual problems. They can no longer be seen as simply the products of thwarted anarchic sex drives and the breakdown of sexual norms; rather, they are generated through these wider social systems.

SEXUALITIES AND THEIR PROBLEMS

Sexuality may be seen as a personal, public, or sociological problem. In the first case, it is experienced as *personal* suffering that needs dealing with: a sexual desire frustrated, a recovery from sexual abuse, or a disease that needs treatment. A *public* sexual problem by contrast is one that is debated within the public spheres and has been turned into an issue that society must deal with. It is much more visible. This would include safer-sex policies around AIDS (Patton 1996); the concern over the Catholic Church and the disclosures of child sexual abuse (Jenkins 1996; Loseke et al. 2003); the recognition of

stalking as a social problem (Kamir 2001); the debates in law around transgendered people's transformed gender identity (Whittle 2002); or the appearance of the so-called sex addict in the early 1980s (Carnes 1984; Irvine 1995). The issue becomes part of the wider civic culture. To complicate matters further, a *sociological* problem shows how the workings of society leads to a sexual phenomenon occurring: how gay hate crimes may be linked to homophobia and heterosexism or how rape may be linked to key elements of patriarchies. There is no necessary linkage between these three kinds of problems (a personal problem may not become a public problem, for example), but there often can be.

Always waiting in the wings, however, are five potential (or putative) problems linked to sexuality, which can be briefly summarized as follows:

1. *Desire.* This is the problem of who and what "turns you on." The classic problem of the nineteenth century—from Krafft-Ebing to Freud—focused upon the nature of our sexual desires. Who do we wish to have sex with ("sexual orientation," as it came to be called) and how often (the problems of addiction and lack of desire)? Traditionally, these have been seen as the problems of men.

2. *Relationships.* This is the problem of how we integrate (or not) our sexual life into our relationships with others. This ranges all the way from not relating (as in masturbation) to situations where the relation is transitory (as in casual sex, and maybe "promiscuity") to those held sacred within stable patterns of relationships, such as the family and the couple (monogamy, etc.). Traditionally, religion has played a major role in structuring this.

3. *Coercion and violence.* This is the problem of handling sexual acts when they are unwanted and often violently imposed. Here, sexuality is experienced as unwanted and coerced. The patterns move from simply disliking sex with a partner who imposes it upon you to more extreme versions of abuse, pressured sex, rape, and even sexual murder. Again, there is usually a strong gender pattern to this, with men predominantly the aggressors.

4. *Reproduction.* This is the problem of sexuality as a means of conceiving children. Here, sexuality is

experienced as a means of having children or not; and the problems it brings in its wake are linked to abortion, infertility, impotence, illegitimacy, being single, and family size. The ideology of pronatalism plays a major role in all this (cf. Peck and Senderowitz 1974).

5. *Disease.* This is the problem of how diseases may be linked and spread through sexual activities. Here, sexuality is linked to diseases of all kinds. Some have conventionally been called the "venereal diseases" or the "sexually transmitted diseases" (from syphilis to herpes); others such as AIDS have been connected more widely; and still others, such as impotence and frigidity, and sex addiction and low drive, have become the province of sexological experts.

All these "problems," then, can be found as personal sufferings. They are experienced as frustrations, fears, anger, pain, loneliness, hysteria, and just plain "common unhappiness" linked to emotional and embodied worlds. Yet these problems are only analytically separable. The problems can be compounded through their interconnections. To take some obvious cases, one person's desires for sex (maybe a sexual turn-on tinged with violence) may coerce another into the sexual experience, during which, through a coital act, a child may be conceived and a disease spread. Prostitution and sex work likewise may act as a "service" to another's desire but at the same time bring risky relationships, violence, and a potential for both an unwanted child and a disease. Inside a marital relationship, desires may be in conflict, sex may be imposed against someone's will, children not conceived when they are desired, and impotency and frigidity generated. Clearly, the problems linked to sexuality are multiple.

Some problems—those of desire and coercive behavior—are often distinctly shaped by gender. Men seem to want sex in more complicated ways and feel it is their right to take it. Other problems—those of wanting relationships and avoiding coercive sex and reproduction—tend more to become the problems of women. Women tend to want relationships and children and fear the abuse of men. Of course, this is an oversimplification, but we do know

enough about the workings of patriarchy across the world to grasp the broad truth of this.

The patterns are also linked to social divisions and inequalities. Iris Marion Young talks about the five faces of oppression and lists them as exploitation, marginalization, powerlessness, cultural imperialism, and violence (Young 1990). All the problems above are open to such processes. Some sexual problems are drenched in exploitation of others' bodies (much sex work, some forced and arranged marriages, indeed many relationships). Some desires can be ignored and marginalized (e.g., those of gays, fetishists, or the transgendered). Some people find themselves in sexual acts where they hold no power (the simple consensual sadomasochistic act often means the masochist does indeed hold power; I am talking more about the elements of sex when it has to be done but is really not desired by one of the doers). Cultural imperialism and sexual problems may be found when certain desires and identities (e.g., Western gay identity) are presumed to be universal or when reproductive strategies differ across societies (e.g., cultural versions of abortion, new reproductive technologies, birth control programs). And violence is universally found in sexualities through abuse, rape, hate crimes, and the like.

Finally, the problems are frequently differentiated through stigmas. Some desires are stigmatized, others not. Much of modern medical science has indeed spent much time sorting out the different desires and dysfunctions of desires and arranging them into a kind of sex hierarchy (Rubin 1984). The nineteenth century was a major period for the creation of all kinds of sexual clinical taxonomies and perversions. Today, some remain totally taboo, pedophilia for instance, whilst others, such as homosexuality, have become significantly more acceptable, removed from the list of medical complaints and incorporated into prime television sitcoms like *Will and Grace!* Likewise, some relationships, such as the family couple, are strongly supported, while others are less accepted (the spinster was long a suspicious character in the past; Jeffreys 1985). Some violence and coercion is accepted: marital rape has only very recently been recognized as a crime in the West, and in many countries throughout the world, all kinds of sexual indignities still seem to be imposed legitimately on women or gays with full approval of the society and its religious leaders. "Having children through coitus" is nearly always the most acceptable reproductive strategy, whilst patterns of sexuality are often condemned. Contraception is often taboo, and indeed, this becomes more and more controversial as we enter the world of new reproductive technologies. Finally, of course, most diseases carry a degree of stigma. There are staggering histories of syphilis that show just how open to social exclusion certain diseases have been in the past; and AIDS (as chapter 19 of this handbook shows) is only the most recent instance of this stigma at work.

CREATING THE SEXUAL SPECTACLE: THE PUBLIC CULTURES OF "SOCIAL PROBLEM SEXUAL TALK"

Despite the considerable array of problems linked to the sexual, what may or may not be seen as a sexual problem is never automatically announced. A common distinction made in theorizing about social problems is that made between *objective problems* and *constructed problems*. The former focuses upon the nature of problems in the social environment: looking for objective indicators. Often, this means examining a condition that is "wrong, widespread, changeable and where a stand is taken that something needs to be done" (Loseke 1999:5–7). The existence of AIDS since 1982 (or earlier) would seem to fit all these criteria. In the past, masturbation, premarital/extramarital sex, and homosexuality may have fit this criterion (indeed, they do regularly feature in social problems textbooks from the past). But what all this makes clear is that in part, social problems also depend upon definitions, categorizations, and judgments. Some people need to say this is a social problem: identify it within a discourse of trouble, animate it into a full-blown language of "trouble," and institutionalize it into rhetorics and practices that show that "something is being done."[5] And it does sometimes mean that "serious" problems can be ignored or minimized whilst relatively trivial ones are elevated.

Constructionist positions, then, look at the groups involved in making the meanings that designate social problems, aware that these meanings change over time and across different groups and that such meanings are always contested. Constructionists look at the ways in which some people and groups—often in social movements, sometimes in governments, frequently in the media—are claims makers and do "social problems work": they make meaningful labels that simplify the world into typifications and rhetorics, providing evidence and arguments, identifying key types of people ("homosexuals," "serial killers," "single mothers," "people with AIDS," "pedophiles"), usually against a moral backdrop that helps identify "trouble" and "enemies." Different claims makers and different moral backgrounds lead to a different sense of what these problems are, and a political language and spectacle emerges (Edelman 1988). Likewise, the success of such claims depends upon the publics and counterpublics (Warner 2002) who can and will hear them. It depends upon the competitions often made amongst claims: probably only a limited number of social problems can be handled at any one time—otherwise society and its members suffer from overload. As Murray Edelman (1988) says,

> There is . . . a competition for attention among the problems that are publicly discussed. As some come to dominate the political news and discussion, others fade from the scene. There seems to be a limit upon the number of issues people notice and worry about regardless of their severity. (P. 20)

It also depends upon the relative power of different members of society to make such claims stick. The Catholic Church, for example, had for a long time enough power to conceal the pedophilia in its midst from public knowledge.

Making Sexual Problems

As we have seen, there is a major difference between "private, personal sexual problems," and "public sexual problems." Whilst the former are highly individual and idiosyncratic, the latter depend upon multiple public spheres[6] in which the issues around them can be animated. Contemporary public spheres would include the arguments of groups such as the new social movements (transgender movements, evangelical movements, gay and lesbian movements, women's movements); the growing mass media (debates on chat shows over sexuality, press scandals, campaigning books and leaflets, "news making"); and educational worlds (debates produced by various public intellectuals and their adversaries). In my book *Telling Sexual Stories* (1995), I have tried to depict the multiple ways in which we have become increasingly the "sexual story telling society." We can now find multiple voices speaking of the sexual life through books, in the press, on television, in conferences, in schools and universities, and through cyberspace. Unlike in the past, when the "sexual truth" and the "real problems of the sexual" were proclaimed from on high absolutely by Popes and Science, talk of the sexual has now become a ceaseless "Tower of Babel" for many. A cacophonous proliferation of sexual stories is to be found across the media, therapy, social movements, and the like; and alongside this, whenever the term "sexual problem" is now designated, many voices clamor to ask: *sexual problem for whom?*

What started to mark out this change in this new culture initially was probably the arrival of a print culture. As Roy Porter and Lesley Hall (1995) comment,

> Print culture brought sex books into prominence. Thereafter people (as before) had sex, and people (unlike previously) had sex books. Some had one, some had the other, some had both. The relations between writing sex books, reading sex books, and having sex—sex in the body, sex on the brain, thought and action, use and abuse—are profoundly enigmatic and subject to Shandyesque regressions. (P. 104)

Increasingly, as print culture grew—and more recently, media cultures in all their forms—so sexual talk and sexual stories became more and more widespread.

Elsewhere, in some detail, I have suggested some of the stages through which this process of problem designation moves:[7]

1. Imagining—visualizing—empathizing
2. Articulating—vocalizing—announcing
3. Inventing identities—becoming storytellers
4. Creating social worlds/communities of support
5. Creating a culture of public problems

Sociologists have long studied these stages and mechanisms through which social problems are socially constructed. They ask "how the dimensions are carved out, how the number of people drawn into concern about these discussions is increased, how a common pool of knowledge begins to develop for the arena participants, and how all these subprocesses increase the visibility of the problem."[8] And one of the key features in this process is the way in which "the human interest story" is placed on the agenda. A "good personal story" will advance a public sexual problems agenda significantly. A contested sexual life story is usually to be found at the heart of the culture of sexual problems.

Thus, a key feature in the contemporary creation of a public culture of sexual problems debates has been the emergence (over a long time period) of what I wish to call "sexual public identity narratives." We regularly encounter them as we watch the news on television, read a newspaper, buy an autobiography, or watch a docudrama. These are moral tales that become attached to the sexualities of concrete individuals and that figure into their commonly perceived identities. When we say "Monica Lewinsky," "O.J. Simpson," or even "Roe versus Wade," we usually evoke symbolically a host of moral issues around sexuality.[9] Such narratives are everywhere, and simply to provide a list of some of the most well-known names is to sense how iconic some have become:

- "O.J. Simpson" speaks of race, violence towards women, and power (Hunt 1999).
- "Polly Klass" and "Megan Kanka" (her name is lent to "Megan's Law") speak of child sexual murder in the United States; in the United Kingdom, there are similar names, such as "Sarah Payne."
- "Mike Tyson" speaks of rape.
- "Rock Hudson" speaks of AIDS.
- "Anita Hill" and "Clarence Thomas" speak of harassment, race, power, and gender (Morrison 1992).
- "Jeffrey Dahmer" speaks of serial murders, cannibalism, and crime victims (Tithecott 1997).

- "Baby M" speaks of parenting, children, infertility, and the new reproduction (Chessler 1988).
- "Bill Clinton" and "Monica Lewinsky" speak of sex, power, harassment, solicitation, and gender.
- "Mary Kaye Latourneau" speaks of underage sex.
- "Matthew Shepard" speaks of homophobia, "fag baiting," hate crimes, and teenage gays (Loffreda 2000).
- "Michael Jackson" speaks of fame and child abuse.
- "John Profumo," "Jeremy Thorpe," and "Edward Kennedy" speak of politics and sexual scandal.
- "John Wayne Bobbitt" and "Lorena Bobbitt" speak of gender wars, abuse, the "power of the penis," pornography, and sexual violence (Kane 1994).
- Pop stars and film stars—such as Elvis Presley, Madonna, Hugh Grant, the Sex Pistols, Eminem, Garry Glitter—all speak to different sexual matters.

To take a most celebrated instance: the Clinton-Lewinsky debacle. Clinton was of course one of the world's most famed and celebrated people at the time of his "misdemeanors," so it is not surprising that the accounts became a media event. But they also provided a major occasion for people all around the world to debate the nature of the intimate life. It was variously described as (1) a feminist project about harassment and sex in the workplace and power and sexuality; (2) a moral project about the decline of family, family standards, relationships, and even sex; (3) a culture wars project about how sexual standards have changed; and (4) a postmodern project about whether sex is really sex and what indeed "counts" for sex.[10]

Public identity narratives are often accompanied by scandals, a major feature of modern media. Often serving as entertainment, they occur when private acts that offend the idealized dominant morality of a community are made public, narrated by the media, and productive of a range of effects from cultural retrenchment through disruption to change.[11] Often, these have only a personal concern: Hugh Grant meets a sex worker, Divine Brown; George Michael is arrested on charges linked to homosexual indecency. Sometimes, they tell us how far our moralities have shifted and changed. For example, the singer George Michael survived in his career after being arrested, a phenomenon that would not have been likely 25 years earlier. Homosexual scandals were then acts that marked out the horrors of homosexuality and led to social exclusion (often imprisonment). Now, homosexual scandal is less striking; though, by contrast today, the English pop star Gary Glitter had his career abruptly ended when arrested on charges of possession of child pornography and child abuse.

Values, Fears, and Moral Regulation

Although sexuality may be seen as a set of practices around the erotic, it also serves major symbolic functions: it is a litmus for many moral panics, public identity narratives, and discourses that tap into a wide range of social anxieties. The ways in which sexual matters become social problems, then, can often provide a guide to the workings of particular cultures. For example, it is now well documented that whilst campaigns against commercialized prostitution in the nineteenth century certainly had real consequences in shifting public health and strengthening women's lives, they also symbolized the controversies over purity, immigration, "dirty women," and "the age of consent" (Walkowitz 1980, 1992). Likewise, attacks on and anxieties on the "slum sex code" and upon young men at "taxi dance halls" in the early twentieth century were often a way of attacking lower-class men and raising social class issues (White 1993). "Perverts" of all kinds seem to have stalked the nineteenth and twentieth centuries, symbolizing an anarchic, nonreproductive, "sick" and dangerous kind of sex. Race often became an issue in battles over rape and lynching. Controversies over pre- and extramarital sex reinforced patterns of the "normal family." In the late twentieth century, AIDS rapidly became the symbol not only of death, but of promiscuity, permissiveness, and perversions: it marked out the good and the bad. And at the start of the twenty-first century, as I write this, a major concern over "pedophile priests in the Catholic Church" has energized controversies around religion, sexuality, homosexuality, and child abuse (Loseke et al. 2003). Hence, whilst instrumentally, these campaigns try to stop a behavior, symbolically, they reassert existing moral orders. Over and over again, we find "sexualities" being used in this way. Paraphrasing Mary Douglas's (1966) terms, we may say that sex often equals dirt and disorder or stuff out of place, and a society needs to purify itself of all this. Sexual problems emerge when there is a perceived threat to social values, be they religious, familial, feminist, or medical. Behind every sexual problem, there is almost certainly a perceived threat to aspects of the moral order and a group of crusaders struggling to define boundaries. It is rendered a spectacle.

John D'Emilio and Estelle Freedman's account of the history of sex in the United States in the last three and a half centuries can also be read as a history of these threats and as a perpetual reworking of the moral order. Cogently, if rapidly, they suggest several key changes and concerns:

> From a family-centered, reproductive sexual system in the colonial era; to a romantic, intimate, yet conflicted sexuality in nineteenth century marriage; to a commercialized sexuality in the modern period, when sexual relations are expected to provide personal identity and individual happiness apart from reproduction. (D'Emilio and Freedman 1988:xii)

The shifts signpost the centrality of the reproductive, then the relational, and finally the recreational values in the sexual order of the United States over time. What is important is that as each of these shifts in meanings change, so the social problems linked to sexualities may change. Thus, the preindustrial colonial era in the United States saw reproduction as key: it held "a central place within the constellation of meanings associated with sexuality" (D'Emilio and Freedman 1988:52). Courtship and marriage were then taken for granted, and whatever went on outside of this had the potential to be identified as social problems. Throughout much of the nineteenth century, as falling reproduction rates were much resisted, we see more and more campaigns against the scourge of birth control. The family remained an unquestioned pivot throughout the nineteenth and the first half of the twentieth centuries and led to anxieties about all kinds of sexualities that could happen outside of it: in utopian communities, extramarital and premarital sex, in "prostitution," and, of course, through "the homosexual." Wider issues of sexual health also started to be raised as sexual authority started to move from priest to doctor: to the likes of Benjamin Rush, Sylvester Graham, and John Kellogg, who were concerned about the desires

of young men along with the problems of masturbation. A new chastity message became prominent with "health" as its organizing theme. Advice literature for women grew alongside marriage manuals for all.[12]

Some Western Sexual Problems from the Past

This is not the space to consider the full range of sexual problems from the past, but a few may be indicative.

Masturbation

Masturbation was at the heart of many moral campaigns in the past. From the mid-eighteenth century onwards, for example, there was a rising concern over masturbation, with a great deal of public hysteria (what today may well be identified as a moral panic and a social problem). In the United Kingdom, key texts of the time were *Onania, or the Heinous Sin of Self-Pollution* (1710) and Tissot's *Onanism, or a Treatise upon the Disorders Produced by Masturbation* (1760). They warned of the major dangers of self-abuse, both on religious grounds and in medical terms (the dangers of losing the seed and the ways in which this weakened the body). The fear over masturbation seems to have grown and grown, with the strong support of quacks, doctors, and clergy. It was nonreproductive sex (Laqueur 2003).

Periodically, there were major fears and panics over masturbation. Alan Hunt (1998), for example, suggests it became a major target to regulate middle-class boys, often in boarding schools and public schools, in nineteenth- and early-twentieth-century Britain. And yet, by the twentieth century, the fears over masturbation had gone rapidly into decline. We now know that most boys and many girls masturbate regularly (and often throughout life), and few would now claim it as a social problem. We no longer hear of masturbation panics and masturbation scandals that were the stuff of social problems in the past. Indeed, in some contemporary sexological works, an almost opposite view has been taken: masturbation now becomes a liberation, a quest for self-pleasuring, a way of functioning well (indeed, if one does not masturbate, a person may be seen to suffer from "masturbatory organic inadequacy"!).[13] In some quarters, it may still remain fairly taboo, and it may not be discussed a great deal, but in general, it is no longer seen as the social problem of "masturbatory insanity," once a rampant social problem in the Western world requiring social interventions from castration to treatment.

Prostitution

As already suggested, prostitution too has served as a tool for illuminating the wider culture of a society: how it comes under attack, the values put forward, the notions of men and women, the links between reformers and prostitutes, and the meanings of vice. As a cultural symbol, it touches on all the evils of the modern world and often is seen to create a contradictory tension between the exploitation of women and the lust of men. Thus, for example, the feminist values of nineteenth-century women led to movements that were for moral reform, chastity, and temperance (Jeffreys 1987). During this first wave of feminism, many women clearly saw their battleground as targeted on male lust. They waged war over prostitution, the age of consent, contraception, and the moral debauchery of men through drink. The evangelical moral reform societies of the nineteenth century gathered power (and were often co-opted by more conservative forces) as women became organized to resist these "sexual problems of men." Indeed, the debates we witnessed in the latter parts of the twentieth century around pornography and sexual violence were largely repeats of debates that were present at the turn of the century: in those days, it was essentially a contest between the social purity movements and the antivice groups who waged war against prostitution, child slavery, pornography, and the double standard and the sex reformers. As Judith Walkowitz (1984), a leading feminist commentator on prostitution in the nineteenth century, commented,

> Begun as a libertarian sanction against the state sanction of male vice, the repeal campaign helped to spawn a hydra-headed assault against sexual deviation of all kinds. The struggle against state regulation evolved into a movement that used the instrument of the state for repressive purposes . . . they extended the meaning of sexuality. By ferreting out new areas of illicit sexual

activity and defining them into existence, a new "technology of power" was created that facilitated control over an ever-widening circle of human activity. (P. 56)

As she comments, in the beginning, women had some control; but as the movements grew, they lost this power, and the movements came to be used for wider ends.

Sex Crimes and Child Molesters

"Sex crimes" are another social problem with an interesting history of anxiety and panic. Sometimes they enter public consciousness and reach levels of mass hysteria; sometimes we are hardly aware of them. And there are of course competing accounts of when and how they start to be noted and taken more seriously. Over half a century ago, the leading criminologist Edwin Sutherland (1950) summarized the passage of sex offence laws. It still cannot be bettered:

> The diffusion of sexual psychopath laws has followed this course: a community is thrown into panic by a few serious sex crimes, which are given nation wide publicity; the community acts in an agitated manner; and all sorts of proposals are made; a committee is then appointed to study the facts and to make recommendations. The committee recommends a sexual psychopath law as the scientific procedure for the control of sex crime. The recommendation is consistent with the trend toward treatment policies in criminal justice in preference to policies of punishment. (P. 142)

Sutherland was writing about the diffusion of such laws around 1937 in the United States. Today, much of his analysis is seen as one possible (and possibly even cyclical) response. Punitive and rehabilitative models come and go: there are periods of silence and periods when it is a great issue.

The feminist writer Jane Caputi, for example, has argued that sex crime starts to appear as a phenomenon with the famous and widely cited "Jack the Ripper" case in the later nineteenth century. It not only generated huge moral anxiety in its day but also signaled "the age of sex crime," when serial killers and mass murderers became more and more common—in reality and in the mythology of the times. For instance, she suggests there were 644 serial sex killings in the United States in 1966, but 4,118 by 1982 (Caputi 1998:1–2). She cites many examples, the "Boston Strangler," "Son of Sam," the "Hillside Strangler," and the "Yorkshire Ripper," as well as films that play to these fears: from the classics of *"M"* and *Psycho* to the more widespread teen slasher films such as the *Halloween* series. Her work outlines the creation of these fiends in the public mind but at the same time examines how this is part of a wider issue of gender violence and aggression.

By contrast, sociologist Philip Jenkins has traced the differential responses to 100 sex crimes from the late nineteenth century to current times. To summarize his argument, he suggests,

> Originating in the Progressive era, the imagery of the malignant sex fiend reached new heights in the decade after World War II, only to be succeeded by a liberal model over the next quarter of a century. More recently, the pendulum has swung back to the predator model: sex offenders are now viewed as being little removed from the worst multiple killers and torturers. And in each era, the prevailing opinion was supported by what appeared at the time to be convincing research. One reality prevailed until it was succeeded by another. (Jenkins 1998:2)

He does not see these stages as evolutionary and necessarily objective: rather, they "have ebbed and flowed—we forget as well as learn" (p. 3). "The nature of sexual threats to children was perceived quite differently in 1915 than in 1930, and the child abuse issue was framed quite differently in 1984 than in 1994" (p. 215). At the heart of his analysis lies vigorous campaigning groups: child savers, feminists, psychiatrists and therapists, religious and moralistic groups, and of course, politicians.

Jenkins (1998) claims that children are at very low risk from homicide, making nonsense of the claims aired frequently in the 1980s, that "many thousands were killed each year by serial murders, pornographers or pedophile rings" (p. 10). Looking at figures in the United States between 1980 and 1994, he concludes that despite the claims made, strangers killed about 54 children per year and about 5 of these victims were involved as part of sexual assaults.

Social Anxieties, Moral Panics, and Culture Wars

In summary, then, sexuality appears to be a major device used to tap into all sorts of social anxieties, to generate panic, and to demarcate boundaries. Studies point to many different sources of these anxieties and boundary mapping, but they include anxieties over gender roles, heterosexuality, and the family; the importance of reproduction and pronatalism; concerns over the role of youth and childhood; race and racialized categories; the divisions between classes and "class fears"; declines in status; fears over the nation-state itself; an overarching sense of moral progress with accompanying fears of decline; the very nature of ethical and religious systems; end-of-century/millennium fears; and even connections to the fear of death (for examples, see Bayer 1981; Bristow 1977; Boyer 1968; Foldy 1997; Friedman 1990; Gamson 1998; Hunt 1998; McClaren 1997; Plummer 1981; Showalter 1990; Stein 2001; Vass 1986; Walkowitz 1992; White 1993; Zurcher 1976).

A major recent way of understanding these anxieties and fears has been through the idea of "moral panics." Many sexual issues have become "moral panics" whereby in Stanley Cohen's (1972) classic formulation,

> A condition, episode, person or group of persons emerges to become defined as a threat to societal values and interests: its nature is presented in a stylized and stereotypical fashion by the mass media; the moral barricades are manned by editors, bishops, politicians and other right thinking people. (P. 9)

Moral panics have traditionally been short-lived and focused: a riot, a drug overdose, a violent crime, a pedophile murder. Yet, and maybe starting with AIDS, such isolated panics became almost pervasive and commonplace. Spreading out and generating higher levels of anxiety, society has become constantly on edge about "problems" (McRobbie and Thornton 1995:560). Moral panics start to signpost persistent ideological struggles over problems constructed on an almost daily basis. There is an "endless overhead narrative of such phenomenon as one panic gives way to another, or one anxiety is displaced across different panics" (Watney 1997:412).

Yet as a strong sense of core values becomes less and less apparent, so the recognition of social problems becomes harder to define even as a more general social anxiety increases. Arguably, in postmodern times, social problems have to become more extreme—or spoken about in extreme language—if they are to be noticed.

The most general level of attack on sexualities is discussed in Murray Davis's intriguing study *Smut* (1983). For him, the world is peopled by Jehovanists (after the Old Testament God) and Gnostics. Jehovanists are the sexophobes who fear all sex whilst dividing it into two main types: "normal," which is bad enough; and "abnormal," which is terrifyingly worse. They live in a dangerous cosmos populated by horrifying sex, and it more or less has dominated the Western world over the past three centuries. In contrast stand the Gnostics, who sanctify sex "as much as Jehovanists condemn them." Nearly all forms of erotica will be condemned by Jehovanists and celebrated by Gnostics (Davis 1983:95, 173).

At an even broader level is the presence in most societies of a wider sense of moral decline, of which sex is a key part: things are getting worse. It is the "decline and fall theory." There is nothing new about this: each generation seems to be able to find this tension at work. Drawing from Adam Smith, Gertrude Himmelfarb (2001) remarks that there always seem to be two systems at work:

> The liberal or loose system is prone to the "vices of levity"—"luxury, wanton and even disorderly mirth, the pursuit of pleasure to some degree of intemperance, the breach of chastity, at least in one of the two sexes, etc." Amongst the people of fashion these vices are treated indulgently. The "common people," on the other hand, committed to the strict or austere system, regard such vices . . . "with the utmost abhorrence" because they—or at least "the wiser and better sort of them"—know that these vices are almost always ruinous to them. . . . A single week's dissipation can undo a poor workman forever. This is why, Smith explained, religious sects generally arise and flourish among the common people, for those sects preach that morality on which their welfare depends.[14] (Pp. 3–4)

More focused, in the early 1990s, James Davison Hunter (1991) presented these clashes in historically more specific terms as a "culture war." Talking exclusively of U.S. culture (though much of it does have broader applicability), he suggests that whereas in the past, the battlegrounds were drawn up *between* religions—Protestant versus Catholic, Catholic versus Jew—now the battlegrounds are being drawn up between those of different moral and political visions, which cut *across* past schisms, suggesting new alignments. On one side are those of religious orthodoxy—Protestant, Jew, Catholic, Buddhist, and Islamic alike—who continue to seek the truth in a fixed authority, usually through a canonical scripture. On the other side are those who look more pragmatically to the shifts in the modern world for clues as to how to live the new moral life. It is a divide between *cultural conservatives/moral traditionalists* and *liberals or cultural progressives*.

In a later book, Hunter (1994) takes his worries further. He sees the United States as being torn apart by a series of moral conflicts, step by step, escalating so that they are not simply culture wars, but "shooting wars." The "debates" become so acrimonious and bitter, with sides talking only at or way past each other, that the next step can only become bloodshed. Most of these conflicts center over the body, as a key symbol of the wider social order; and the "abortion wars" must be seen as their prime exemplar. Here, indeed, are matters of life and death: the notorious abortion clinic bombings vividly demonstrate how culture wars may indeed become shooting wars. He finds advocates on all sides as culpable of seriously debasing public and democratic discussion; even those who claim to be neutral are in fact duplicitous and have their own axes to grind.

New Problems in the Making? Signs of "Sexual Problems" in a Late-Modern World?

One thrust of the constructionist approach is to suggest that there are plural ways of seeing and experiencing the world. Every way of constructing a social problem is also a way of not constructing it. And so whilst it is possible to trot out a list of commonly regarded social problems of our time—pedophilia, sexual violence, teenage sexuality, family decline, sexual addiction, and AIDS would be some—it is also now possible to think afresh about other issues that have not yet been so constructed but may become so in the future. Are there signs of new social problems of sexuality in the making? This is not to deny the importance of the problems already constructed, but it is to suggest alternatives and wider visions as we move into a somewhat different social order, a late-modern or postmodern world.

Whilst there is a continuing debate amongst scholars over the nature of the modern/late-modern/postmodern world, there is very considerable agreement that life in the twenty-first century is not the same as that in the nineteenth and eighteenth centuries. Even though there are many continuities, the pace of change has speeded up, and new processes such as digitalization, cybernetics, and the new reproductive technologies have evolved so rapidly that for many the world has taken on distinctively new forms. These changes and their speed have had a major impact on the ways in which sexualities are organized and the kinds of problems they are generating. Again, there is no space here for a comprehensive analysis, but consider just five of the following processes and their impact upon sexualities.

First, the *commodification* of sexualities.[15] Of course, sex has always been sold; but it would seem that advanced capitalism brings with it the tendency to drive nearly all aspects of sexuality through a market economy. This applies to something as simple as the cost of a wedding to the multiple developments of new billion-dollar markets: a pink economy for the gay world; hostess and massage parlors for the lonely man; and pop music that shrieks sex objects to a youth market, suggesting what they should wear, what they should dance, what drugs to take, how they should do their hair, and even how they should move. Billboards and advertising routinely sell sex, creating an environment that many now refer to as sexualized and pornographic. We live in a commodified environment where sex is sold for everything. Like all commodities, it is rendered more transient and more objectificatory; people own it and possess it. Likewise, major markets develop that make money from sexual accessories, from pornography to Viagra (Marshall 2000; Tiefer 2000). Is this a sign of a new social problem in the making?

Second, the *mediazation of sexualities.* Sex now inhabits the world of the media: it is found in videos, CDs, newspapers, magazines, books, films, and television. As the various media have come to reorganize our sense of place and break down restricted zones of social life, so all ages, genders, and groups have greater accessibility to sexual imagery through which life can be lived. And the imagery is generally much more "extreme" than was permitted in the past: boundaries are constantly being pushed. In the 1940s, censors objected to Jane Russell showing her cleavage (in the film *The Outlaw,* 1943). In the 1950s, Elvis Presley's famous wiggle meant he had to be filmed from the waist up for the Ed Sullivan Show; and a little later, the Rolling Stones were forced to change their lyric "Let's spend the night together" to "Let's spend some time together" on that same show. By the 1970s, we had the Doors and the Sex Pistols. The 1980s brought Madonna with her "Girlie Show" (1993), her record *Erotica,* and her book *Sex.* Effectively, Madonna broke all the seeming taboos of the day, masturbating on popular video, engaging in sadomasochism, and always mixing a raunchy sexuality with religious blasphemy. And as PCs, Walkmen, and mobiles entered the lives of the young, they gained more and more access to sexualities that were formerly forbidden. Sometimes, this went far beyond the boundaries in terms of violence and misogyny that even the most liberal commentators of the past would have accepted (Gamson 1998). Is this a sign of a new social problem in the making?

Closely linked is the process of the *digitalization of sexualities.* More and more sex is to be found not in real life, but in "virtual life" (which could also include the growth of "telephone sex"). Nowadays, many people live much of their sexual lives on-line. A definitive study of this is still awaited, but we do know that large numbers of people use e-mail to make sexual contacts and buy sexual wares; they go into chat rooms to talk about sex, reinvent their sexual personas, and eventually meet others; they pursue all kinds of Web sites that are saturated with every kind of sexual image you are ever likely to want (and not want) to see. And all kinds of new problems have emerged as a result: cyberstalkers, cyber-rape, childhood security, pedophile abductions, the silent spread of masturbation, and multiple new forms of sex: sex chat rooms, tele-operated compu-sex, sex news groups and bulletin boards, e-mail discussion groups, camcorder sex, new forms of pornography and ways of accessing it, cyborg sex, teledildonics, and virtual sex, along with new approaches to the body and emergent "techno-identities" and "techno-cultures." Here, we have a new language that perhaps mirrors new forms of sexualities: cyberporn, cyberqueer, cyberstalking, cyber-rape, cybervictim, cybersex. Although such new forms can result in people meeting in real space for "real sex," there must be vast amounts of what can only be called "virtual sex" taking place in these virtual spaces, and much of this must be linked to masturbatory worlds. Sadie Plant (2000) hints at the worlds before us:

> Technical cyberspace is well advanced: the hardware is fetishized, the software is porn, and vast proportions of the telecommunications system are consumed by erotica. But these are merely the most overt—and perhaps the least interesting—examples of a degeneration of "natural" sex. As hard and wetwares collapse onto soft, far stranger mutations wrack the sexual scene. The simulation of sex converges with the deregulation of the entire sexual economy, the corrosion of its links with reproduction, and the collapse of its specificity: sex disperses into drugs, trance and dance possession; androgyny, hermaphroditism and transexualism become increasingly perceptible; paraphilia, body engineering, queer sex, and what Foucault calls "the slow motions of pleasure and pain" of SM—already high technology sex—proliferate.[16] (P. 461)

Again, we can ask: is this a sign of a new social problem in the making?

Fourth, we have *the individualization of sexualities*. At the heart of many contemporary sexualities is the idea that we are autonomous human beings who can choose the kind of sexual life we are to lead and with whom (be it bisexual, homosexual, heterosexual, polysexual, or monosexual). Sexualities in the late-modern Western world have been shaped within the framework of an individualist ideology. Late-modern sex reflects the death of the one "Grand Narrative of the Personal Life." As Jeffrey Weeks (2000) remarks,

> This is the real mark of what is different about the late twentieth century: those who used to be spoken of are

now struggling in various ways, using different, often hesitant or incoherent languages to speak for themselves. The result is inevitably confusing, but enormously significant. We are here in a world where the imperatives of history, nature and science are being displaced by the norm of sexual choice, and where a master narrative is being displaced by a multiplication of new narratives, each claiming its own truth. (P. 238)

This is a time of increasing sexual "risk" for all society's members, largely because all the old sexual verities have ceased to be. It is a time of growing self-reflexivity, when the very knowledge produced in the world about sexuality helps shape the emergence of that world as people reflect more on who they want to be sexually. As Ulrich Beck (2000) has powerfully put it,

> We live in an age in which the social order of the national state, class, ethnicity and the traditional family is in decline. The ethics of individual self-fulfillment and achievement is the most powerful current in modern society. The choosing, deciding, shaping human being who aspires to be the author of his or her own life, the creator of an individual identity, is the central character of our time. It is the fundamental cause behind changes in the family and the global gender revolution in relation to work and politics. Any attempt to create a new sense of social cohesion has to start from the recognition that individualism, diversity and scepticism are written into Western Culture. (P. 165)

This is not all good news. Indeed, it brings with it the pain of uncertainty and risk, what Zygmunt Bauman (1999) has called *Unsicherheit* (p. 5).[17] More and more people become wary in their intimate lives: they become cautious, do not know what to do, feel trapped in their anxieties and insecurities and incapable of planning their lives, with decisions taken that are drenched in risk. Along with sexual individualism comes "Sexual Unsicherheit." Is this a sign of a new social problem in the making?

A fifth and final example must also be the shifts being brought about by the *technologization of sex*. Since a major way of approaching sexualities is through their reproductive potential, we now seem to have reached an ironic stage in history when much sexuality has no reproductive potential whatsoever (from the wide use of contraception to masturbation and fetishism; from sadomasochism to AIDS education advocacy of "outercourse") at the very same time as much reproductive behavior can be conducted with little or no "sex." Problems of infertility are resolved (partially) through the new reproductive technologies, whilst problems of desire can now lead to any kind of sexual desire being met without the need for reproductive intercourse. Is this a sign of a new social problem in the making?

THE AUTONOMY AND DIFFUSION OF SOCIAL PROBLEMS: DIFFERENT CULTURES AND GLOBALIZATION

I have been suggesting that whilst all societies have personal problems linked to sexuality, only some of these may become part of the multiple public spheres of social problems. My focus so far has been Anglo-American cultures, where there is a full apparatus at work concerned with identifying, animating, and attempting to resolve sexual social problems. Indeed, in these "sexual story-telling cultures," there is a proliferation of such talk and problems. Implicitly, I have also suggested that such problems may not necessarily be connected to the seriousness or gravity of the personal problems, that they are subject to constant change, and that they are bound up with matters of gender and power. I have lightly hinted that the old world of social problems around sexuality may be changing and that new ones—linked to the arrival of a new late modernity—may be in the making.

What of other cultures? Initially, I think it is very important to recognize the relative autonomy of different cultures in their sexual practices, their sexual cultures, and their sexual problems. (Whilst I will later suggest a certain amount of globalization, it is dangerous to presume too much similarity initially.) To briefly sketch some illustrations, we know that in some strongly religious Moslem societies (and Iran seems a central, if changing, case), the degree of surveillance over the lives of children and women on a day-to-day basis makes the possibility of any "norm violations" (from masturbation to homosexuality) difficult indeed. Penalties are severe, and executions are not uncommon for homosexuality. In many

countries, there is little or no choice over who can be a sexual partner. We know that in many very poor countries (those in sub-Saharan Africa are strong cases), the existence of poverty makes talk of some of the sexual issues aired on Westernized television chat shows ("women who love too much," "sexual addiction," the need for Viagra) seem almost obscene. Yet at the same time, there are indeed many issues in these countries—from AIDS to birth control—in which public issues around sexuality are important in saving lives. In cultures torn by civil war, there also seems to be a widespread culture of rape (it is estimated that some 40,000 women were raped in the Bosnian conflict), and in these desperate situations, the whole culture is permeated by a violence that may also shape its sexualities (Allen 1996).

Everywhere, special issues appear. In China, there is the regulation of one-child families (with attendant problems of concealing children and selecting which gender the child should be). In Latin American societies, there is the widespread prominence of machismo shaping sexual worlds, and indeed in some countries, such as Brazil, a seemingly intense eroticization of everyday life. In some African cultures, women's sexual capacities are truly downplayed. In many societies, such as the Sambia studied by Gilbert Herdt, ritualized forms of sexualities and gender focused upon religion or tradition play prominent roles. Many cultures have special roles for cross-gendering sexualities, such as the "lady boys" in Thailand and the *berdache* in Indian cultures (Bolin 1996; Williams 1986). Japan is an interesting case, too. Standing midway between a very strong traditionalism—where sexuality is highly formalized, "wrapped," and controlled—and a new modern Western "freedom" has resulted in recent years in many new social problems, some arriving on television, others being written about in the Western press. Pornography is more commonplace in comics and books, whilst sexuality has become a prominent feature of everyday Internet encounters (Jenkins 2001). Then there are the "honor killings" in some Islamic societies, where women may be punished by death (or raped) for actual (or even perceived) sexual (mis)conducts. Across the world, sexualities take on different forms and generate different problems.

Yet we are also now starting to sense the globalization and *glocalization* of sexualities, in which the world becomes smaller and more interconnected: a major reordering of time and space in sexual relations may be taking place. Talk about "sexual problems" moves across the globe, in the process often becoming transformed and modified by local cultures. Traditional sexual customs become subject to rapid social change. Media and digitalization generate an information age haunted by the spectres of sexuality, from cybersex to cyber-rape. Postmodern values seem to be on the ascendant, giving priorities to ideas of sexual differences and sexual choices. Global capital turns local sex markets into international ones. World sexual cultures become more and more interconnected. "Global chains" connect emigrating mothers, families, children, and workers across the globe. With all this, it should not be surprising to find that long-standing patterns of sexualities become increasingly disturbed and disrupted (Altman 2001; Ehrenreich and Hochschild 2002).

There starts to be a diffusion of social problems across cultures. Joel Best (2001) has written how sociologists have tended to study social problems in a specific culture based on case studies and hence in isolation from their "geographic spread," with little concern for the ways that problems may diffuse across cultures. Yet whereas once problems may have been generated in isolation, increasingly, globalization—not just through world markets but also through media such as film, television, press, and cyberspace—means that they have global repercussions. There are many "potential" global social problems around sexuality, from AIDS to sex trafficking. Slowly, more and more "problems" come to be identified and diffused on a global scale.[18]

The Case of Same-Sex Relations

One issue that has figured prominently in past discussions of social problems is that of homosexuality (or same-sex relations). Since the 1970s, lesbian/gay politics has been firmly placed on the Western agenda. And with the advance of a strong (and increasingly international) lesbian and gay movement, new issues have appeared on the international agenda (Adam, Duyvendak, and Krouwel

1999). Thus, universal lesbian and gay rights, including a universal age of consent and the inclusion of "sexual orientation" in charters of human rights and antidiscrimination laws, along with mandatory training in "multiculturalism" and "gay affirmative action," have become common in many Western contexts. "Registered partnerships," and sometimes marriages, for lesbians and gays, along with the right of lesbians and gays to adopt and have children have become key foci of a growing international lesbian, gay, bisexual, and transgender movement. New antigay crimes such as "hate crimes" have been created and turned into social problems. A major reworking of the claims being made about homosexuality has been happening over the past 30 years: it can no longer be placed easily in a Western list of "problems" or "deviances" (Smith and Wendes 2000).[19]

Yet whilst all of this is going on, there continues to be massive resistance in many countries. For in most countries of Africa, Asia, or Latin America, same-sex relations remain taboo: largely invisible, rarely discussed, officially nonexistent, and embedded in religions, laws, and beliefs that are deeply inimical to it. Even today, homosexuality is illegal in approximately 70 states in the world as well as being subject to the death penalty in 7 (an estimated 200 homosexuals are executed yearly in Iran; Baird 2001:13). Indeed, the partial acceptance of homosexuality in parts of the West is often used as a major example of the West's decadence. And yet at the same time, new "claims" from the West are being increasingly diffused globally. South Africa and then Ecuador became among the first countries to develop antidiscrimination provisions to lesbians and gays in their national constitutions (Baird 2001:12). Issues such as gay and lesbian "registered partnerships," "families of choice," or even "marriages" are issues now being confronted in more and more countries. All the Scandinavian countries now have such partnership laws in place, as do France, Germany, and South Africa. But perhaps most significantly, countries as different as Mexico and Vietnam are now also calling for legal partnerships (Baird 2001:12).[20] Here then, is a prime example of the diffusion (and transformation) of "sexual social problems talk."

The Case of Child Pornography on the Internet

Another instance of globalization at work is the relatively recent arrival of a complex network of worlds linked through the Internet that cater to interests in child pornography and pedophile abuse. By most accounts, this is widespread and much condemned but quite hard to regulate, and has generated extensive public talk as being a problem in much of the Western media.

In his study of child pornography on the Internet, Philip Jenkins[21] shows just how difficult it is to regulate a fragmented global network such as this. Although there are laws in many Western countries (which make possession of pictures of anyone under 18 years of age an imprisonable offence), other, often poorer, countries have much less stringent laws, and at times it seems that the use of young children for prostitution and pornography is almost condoned. Certainly, many of the images found on the Internet have originated in poorer "bandit" countries (the former communist world, Asia, Latin America, and oddly, also Japan), where regulations are minimal. It may be hard to regulate in countries such as the United States or the United Kingdom, but it is almost impossible in other countries. And as Jenkins (2001) comments, "Lacking a global moral consensus, there will always be areas of unevenness, fault lines in moral enforcement, and the child pornographers are likely to survive in these cracks" (p. 203). Here is an instance where the global public sexual social problem talk around these abuses remains very uneven.

Sexual Citizens, Human Rights, and the Global Culture of Sexual Problems Talk

Both the issues of global Internet child pornography and global same-sex relations start to point in the same direction: to the increasingly popular and widespread talk of global human rights, which, along with linked ideas of citizenship, have become the global *lingua franca* of politics, including sexual politics. In these examples, we have both the rights of the child and the rights of lesbians and gays to help frame the public sexual problems talk. Both sets of rights are instances of a newly emerging language that sets out much broader claims about our global sexualities and intimacies, which elsewhere I have suggested could be designated as "intimate citizenship." Here is *a developing global culture of sexual problems talk,* which gives prominence to ideas of human sexual rights and the sexual citizen (cf. Bell and Binnie 2000; Nussbaum 1999; Petchesky 2000; Plummer 2001b, 2003; Richardson 2000; Weeks 1998).

Claims about sexual problems and their resolutions are increasingly spread by major international groupings such as the United Nations, International Human Rights Courts, and internationally sponsored conferences, which often become "missionaries abroad." But in the study of the global cultures of sexual problems, "sexual rights" is, as Rosalind Petchesky (2000) notes, "the newest kid on the block." Petchesky was one many academic activists at the Beijing Women's Conference in 1995 who struggled for a language of sexual rights. Significantly, she says that "prior to 1993 sexuality of any sort or manifestation is absent from international human rights discourse" (p. 82). Sexuality was too dangerous a topic to even consider. When it appeared, it was (and still is) always counterargued by those who always connect sexuality to immorality and dangerous activities: homosexuality, lesbianism, prostitution, pedophilia, incest, and adultery. The full panoply of the "sexual fringe" is evoked over and over again to have their rights denied in general. The Pope, for example, condemns both reproductive and sexual rights by linking them to a "hedonistic mentality unwilling to accept responsibility in matters of sexuality" and "a self centered concept of freedom" (Petchesky 2000:87). Yet hammered out at the Fourth World Conference on Women (FWCW) in Beijing in 1995 as a massive compromise were the following words:

> The human rights of women include their right to have control over and decide freely and responsibly on matters related to their sexuality, including sexual and reproductive health, free of coercion, discrimination and violence. Equal relationships between men and women in matters of sexual relations and reproduction, including full respect for the integrity of the person, require mutual respect, consent and shared responsibility for sexual behavior and its consequences. (Cited in Petchesky 2000:85)

Tucked away in this statement is a new language of respect for sexual differences. New claims, then, are spreading. But as we would expect, new claims bring new enemies and a language of counterattacks, what may be seen as a kind of counterdiffusion. Far from accepting the West's definitions, many countries come to see "the West" as standing for a whole series of problems linked to it. This is the "sexualized society," the "secularized society," the "decadent society." The "bad West" comes increasingly to signify homosexuality, unwanted babies, delinquency and rising crime, unsupervised children and independent women, explicit sexual imagery, pornographication, pop music and MTV, marriage breakdown, and the decline of religious order. We can see this in every area of controversy: from debates around the family (from forced marriages in much of the world to same-sex marriages as a developing argument); from the concern over AIDS to the international worry over sex tourism and prostitution; from the arrival of worldwide "cyberspace" and "cybersex" to the trading in body parts; from the pervasiveness of global media (film, television, video, music, etc.), with their images of the new intimate lifestyles, to the arrival of global social movements (women, gay, transgender, etc.). It is hard for any of these debates to be conducted any longer within splendid national isolation.[22]

MOVING AHEAD

I have suggested that whilst human sexual problems must be diverse and universal, as societies have (post)modernized, not only have the range and scale of these problems developed, so too has talk about them. The Sexual Spectacle has emerged to embrace a public culture of sexual problems talk linked to social anxieties around gender, family, status, change, and morality. The culture of public talk about sexual problems tells us a great deal not just about sexualities but also about the moral fears and crises of the time. This chapter has not attempted to review any one sexual problem in-depth—or the anxieties it provokes—but instead has tried to provide a sense of the mechanisms in which these problems are identified, turned into public issues, and ultimately may become globalized.

At the start of the twenty-first century, there are a lot of putative sexual problems appearing. The worlds of cybersex, mediated sex, individuated choices, new reproductive technologies, and the like bring all kinds of as yet unanticipated problems. At the same time, on a global level, a new language of international human sexual rights is starting to appear. New worlds of sexual problems and their resolutions seem to be in the making; and these will probably run in parallel with older ones. How these problems are "framed" into rhetorics and argumentations will matter a great deal, for such "claims" are not independent of the problems they purport to comment upon. And sometimes the claims themselves may be more of a problem than the very sexualities they analyze.

NOTES

1. A useful compendium on a number of these cultural differences can be found in Robert T. Francoeur (1997). For a brief tour of historical variations, a classic is Vern Bullough (1976), though it has now been greatly superseded by a wide-ranging series of critical anthropological and historical researches such as those found in Lancaster and Leonardo (1997).

2. See Robert King Merton and Robert Nisbet, *Contemporary Social Problems*. It passed through two decades of editions from the original in 1961 to a 4th edition in 1978. Kingsley Davis started writing about sexuality in the 1930s, and in these volumes he writes three chapters: the population crisis, family disorganization, and "sexual behaviour."

3. There are many different groups in the United States that can be placed under the heading of the Chastity Movement. For example, "True Love Waits" is a national college movement that claims around 2.5 million students have signed its pledge since it was formed in 1993. See also the Web site for the National Abstinence Clearinghouse.

4. In a classic critique of the 1970s, Mary McIntosh had challenged Davis's argument around prostitution, which broadly suggested that prostitution was functional because it resolved problems of male sexual needs. McIntosh asked "whose needs?" (see McIntosh 1978, "Who Needs Prostitutes?").

5. I discuss this in my earlier statement on sexual stories (Plummer 1995:126, "Making Stories Happen").

6. The nature of the public sphere was initially outlined in the work of Habermas and then critiqued by Fraser. We need—according to Fraser and others—to

recognise a model of public spheres where there is the "proliferation of a multiplicity of competing publics" (Fraser 1977:77), some of which she sees as "subaltern counterpublics." There are now multiple, hierarchically layered and contested public spheres (e.g., "black public spheres," "gay public spheres," "evangelical Christian public spheres," etc.). Most recently, see the work of Warner (2002). I develop some of these ideas in Plummer (2003).

7. I have called this "the generic process of story telling" (Plummer 1995:125).

8. See Carolyn Wiener (1981:14). Stages of social problems can be unpacked as claims, grounds, and warrants. "A claim is a demand that one party makes upon another" (Spector and Kitsuse 1987:83). There is a distinct parallel between my argument and the statement that social problems are "the activities or groups making assertions of grievances and claims with respect to some putative conditions" (p. 75). The data or grounds lay out the facts or the major narrative for claims. It usually includes definitions, typifying examples, statistics, quasi-theories, or myth debunking. The warrant acts as the bridge that connects them up. This is a pattern in "rhetorical work" that has been outlined by Joel Best (1990) in his discussion of missing children. Here, he suggests a history. In the earliest days, claims are often couched in extreme form with a vocabulary of moral certainty and rectitude, often righteous indignation. There is little evidence adduced, and the audience is seen as either converted or hostile. But later, the rhetorics become more sophisticated: the claims makers adopt a "rhetoric of rationality," make claims from inside, outline reasonable actions, and see their audience as persuadable (p. 42).

9. Public identity narratives basically have the characteristic that they tell the stories of people's lives. The "Who am I?" question is in some ways handled. They tell the story not only in a private sense but also within some part of the public sphere. Hearing the story of a life in public—as we do all the time—sets afloat not just a range of ethical issues but also illustrations about how they can be resolved. I discuss some of this in Plummer (2001a).

10. See Stein et al. (1999), "A Symposium on the Clinton-Lewinsky Affair" (pp. 247–260); see also Hollway and Jefferson (1998); Hunt (1999, chap. 2).

11. This is a slightly simplified definition of that provided by Lull and Hinerman in "The Search for Scandal" (1997:3).

12. On histories of sexuality, see Bland and Doan (1998); Dean (1996); D'Emilio and Freedman (1988); Irvine (1990); Jeffreys (1987); Porter and Hall (1995); Seidman (1992); White (1993).

13. See the tragic yet comical commentaries on this by Szasz (1980:61–9, 75 et seq.) and Comfort (1967).

14. The quote is from Himmelfarb, but she is discussing (sympathetically) the view of Adam Smith. She is citing him too. See Adam Smith (1937:746–7, 748).

15. Some of the next few paragraphs are modified from parts of Plummer (2003, chap. 2).

16. This quote comes from Sadie Plant's "Coming across the Future." It is one of a useful series of articles on cybersex contained in Bell and Kennedy (2000). See also Gray (2001, chap. 11).

17. As he comments, "The most sinister and painful of contemporary troubles can best be collected under the rubric of Unsicherheit—the German term which blends together experiences which need three English terms—uncertainty, insecurity and unsafety" (Bauman 1999:5).

18. Sometimes, this is very specific. Best shows how "Satanism" diffused from the United States to the United Kingdom, and Ferudi has shown how "road rage" diffused from the United Kingdom to the United States (Best 2001: 3–8; Best and Ferudi 2001).

19. Though this is not without its critics, some of whom have recently suggested that this is part of a "dumbing down of deviance," in which sociologists have played a prominent role in relativising and making more acceptable conducts that were once seen as immoral and perverted.

20. Vanessa Baird's (2001) short book provides a summary guide to most countries throughout the world and their response to homosexuality. She draws heavily from the work of Amnesty International, who have produced a major documentation (2001) and a Web site that updates information.

21. Philip Jenkins's book (2001) is the first major book-length study of which I am aware that treats this issue in detail. Curiously, in nearly all of his other works, Jenkins takes a strong constructionist view of social problems. In this book, the constructions around the problem rarely figure, and his focus is much more concerned with the objective characteristics of the problem on a world scale. That he has reached his own limits with this problem area can be sensed from the title of the book: *Beyond Tolerance*.

22. I discuss all this much more fully in my *Intimate Citizenship* (Plummer 2001b, 2003).

REFERENCES

Adam, Barry, J. W. Duyvendak, and A. Krouwel, eds. 1999. *The Global Emergence of Gay and Lesbian Politics*. Philadelphia, PA: Temple University Press.

Allen, Beverly. 1996. *Rape Warfare: The Hidden Genocide in Bosnia-Herzegovina and Croatia*. Minneapolis, MN: University of Minnesota Press.

Altman, Dennis. 2001. *Global Sex.* Chicago, IL: University of Chicago Press.

Amnesty International. 2001. *Crimes of Hate: Conspiracies of Silence.* London, England: Amnesty International.

Baird, Vanessa. 2001. *The No-Nonsense Guide to Sexual Diversity.* London, England: New Internationalist.

Bauman, Zygmunt. 1999. *In Search of Politics.* Cambridge, England: Polity.

Bayer, Ronald. 1981. *Homosexuality and American Psychiatry: The Politics of Diagnosis.* New York: Basic Books.

Beck, Ulrich. 2000. "Living Your Own Life in a Runaway World." In *On the Edge,* edited by Will Hutton and Anthony Giddens. London, England: Cape.

Bell, David and Jon Binnie. 2000. *The Sexual Citizen.* Cambridge, England: Polity.

Bell, David and Barbara M. Kennedy, eds. 2000. *The Cybercultures Reader.* London, England: Routledge.

Best, Joel. 1990. *Threatened Children: Rhetoric and Concern about Child Victims.* Chicago, IL: University of Chicago Press.

——. 2001. *How Claims Spread: Cross National Diffusion of Social Problems.* New York: de Gruyter.

Best, Joel and Frank Ferudi. 2001. "The Evolution of Road Rage in Britain and the United States." Pp. 107–28 in *How Claims Spread: Cross National Diffusion of Social Problems.* New York: de Gruyter.

Bland, Lucy and Laura Doan. 1998. *Sexology Uncensored: The Documents of Sexual Science.* Cambridge, England: Polity.

Bolin, Anne. 1996. "Traversing Gender, Cultural Contexts and Gender Practices." In *Gender Reversals and Gender Culture,* edited by Sandar Ramet. London, England: Routledge.

Boyer, Paul. 1968. *Purity in Print: The Vice Society Movement and Book Censorship in America.* New York: Scribner.

Bristow, Edward J. 1977. *Vice and Vigilance: Purity Movements in Britain Since 1700.* Totowa, NJ: Rowman and Littlefield.

Bullough, Vern. 1976. *Sexual Variance in Society and History.* Chicago, IL: University of Chicago Press.

Caputi, Jane. 1988. *The Age of Sex Crime.* London, England: Women's Press.

Carnes, Patrick. 1984. *The Sexual Addiction.* Minneapolis, MN: CompCare.

Chessler, Phyllis. 1988. *Sacred Bond: The Legacy of Baby M.* New York: First Vintage Books.

Cohen, Stanley. 1972. *Folk Devils and Moral Panics.* Oxford, England: Blackwell.

Comfort, Alex. 1967. *The Anxiety Makers: Some Curious Preoccupations of the Medical Profession.* London, England: Nelson.

Davis, Murray S. 1983. *Smut: Erotic Reality/Obscene Ideology.* Cambridge, England: Cambridge University Press.

Dean, Carolyn J. 1996. *Sexuality and Modern Western Culture.* New York: Twayne.

D'Emilio, John and Estelle Freedman. 1988. *Intimate Matters: A History of Sexuality in America.* New York: Harper & Row.

Douglas, Mary. 1966. *Purity and Danger.* Middlesex, England: Penguin.

Dworkin, Andrea. 1987. *Intercourse.* London, England: Arrow Books.

Edelman, Murray. 1988. *Constructing the Political Spectacle.* Chicago, IL: University of Chicago Press.

Ehrenreich, Barbara and Arlie Russell Hochschild, eds. 2002. *Global Woman: Nannies, Maids and Sex Workers in the New Economy.* New York: Henry Holt, Metropolitan Books.

Foldy, Michael S. 1997. *The Trials of Oscar Wilde: Deviance, Morality and Late Victorian Society.* New Haven, CT: Yale University Press.

Foucault, Michel. [1976] 1978. *The History of Sexuality.* Translated by Robert Hurley. Middlesex, England: Penguin.

Francoeur, Robert T., ed. 1997. *The International Encyclopedia of Sexuality* (3 vols.). New York: Continuum.

Fraser, Nancy. 1997. "Rethinking the Public Sphere." Pp. 69–97 in *Justice Interruptus: Critical Refelections on the "Postsocialist" Condition,* edited by Nancy Fraser. London, England. Routledge.

Friedman, Andrea. 1996. "The Habitats of the Sex Crazed Perverts: Campaigns against Burlesque in the Depression Era in NYC." *Journal of the History of Sexuality* 7 (2):203–37.

Gagnon, John. 1977. *Human Sexualities.* New York: Scott Foresman.

Gamson, Josh. 1990. "Rubber Wars: Struggles over the Condoms in the U.S." *Journal of the History of Sexuality* 1 (2):262–82.

——. 1998. *Freaks Talk Back.* Chicago, IL: University of Chicago Press.

Gray, Chris Hables. 2001. *Cyborg Citizen: Politics in the Posthuman Age.* London, England. Routledge.

Himmelfarb, Gertrude. 2001. *One Nation, Two Cultures.* New York: Vintage.

Hollway, Wendy and Tony Jefferson. 1998. "A Kiss is Just a Kiss." *Sexualities* 1 (4):405–25.

Hunt, Alan. 1998. "The Great Masturbation Panic and the Discourse of Moral Regulation in 19th and Early

Twentieth Century Britain." *Journal of the History of Sexuality* 8 (4):575–615.

Hunt, Darnell M. 1999. *O. J. Simpson: Facts and Fiction.* Cambridge, England: Cambridge University Press.

Hunter, James Davison. 1991. *Culture Wars.* New York: Basic Books.

———. 1994. *Before the Shooting Begins.* New York: Free Press.

Irvine, Janice. 1990. *Disorders of Desire.* Philadelphia, PA: Temple University Press.

———. 1995. "Reinventing Perversion: Sex Addiction and Cultural Anxieties." *Journal of the History of Sexuality* 5 (3).

Jackson, Stevi and Sue Scott. 1996. *Feminism and Sexuality: A Reader.* Edinburgh, Scotland: Edinburgh University Press.

Jeffreys, Sheila. 1985. *The Spinster and Her Enemies.* London, England: Pandora.

———, ed. 1987. *The Sexuality Papers.* London, England: Routledge.

Jenkins, Philip. 1996. *Pedophile and Priests: Anatomy of a Contemporary Crisis.* Oxford: Oxford University Press.

———. 1998. *Moral Panic: Changing Concepts of the Child Molester in Modern America.* New Haven, CT: Yale University Press.

———. 2001. *Beyond Tolerance: Child Pornography on the Internet.* New York: New York University Press.

Kamir, Orit. 2001. *Every Breath You Take: Stalking Narratives and the Law.* Ann Arbor, MI: University of Michigan Press.

Kane, Peter. 1994. *The Bobbitt Case.* New York: Windsor.

Lancaster, Roger N. and Micaela di Leonardo, eds. 1997. *The Gender/Sexuality Reader.* London, England: Routledge.

Laqueur, Thomas W. 2003. *Solitary Sex: A Cultural History of Masturbation.* London: Zone Press.

Loffreda, Beth. 2000. *Losing Matt Shepard: Life and Politics in the Aftermath of Anti-Gay Murder.* New York: New York University Press.

Loseke, Donileen. 1999. *Thinking about Social Problems: An Introduction to Constructionist Perspectives.* New York: Aldine de Gruyter.

Loseke, Donileen et al. 2003. "We Hold These Truths to Be Self Evident: Problems in Pondering the Pedophile Priest Problem." *Sexualities,* February, 6, pp. 6–14.

Lull, James and Stephen Hinerman. 1997. "The Search for Scandal." In *Media Scandals,* edited by James Lull and Stephen Hinerman. Cambridge, England: Polity.

Marshall, Barbara. 2002. "Hard Science: Gendered Constructions of Sexual Dysfunction in the 'Viagra Age.'" *Sexualities* 5 (2):131–58.

McIntosh, Mary. 1978. "Who Needs Prostitutes?" In *Women, Crime and Sexuality,* edited by Carol Smart. London, England: Routledge.

McLaren, Angus. 1997. *The Trials of Masculinity.* Chicago, IL: University of Chicago Press.

McRobbie, Angela and Sarah Thornton. 1995. "Rethinking Moral Panics for Multi-Mediated Social Worlds." *British Journal of Sociology* 46 (4):559–74.

Merton, Robert King and Robert Nisbet, eds. 1971. *Contemporary Social Problems.* 3rd ed. New York: Harcourt Brace and Janovitch.

Morrison, Tony, ed. 1992. *Race-ing, Justice, En-Gendering Power.* New York: Pantheon.

Nussbaum, Martha. 1999. *Sex and Social Justice.* New York: Oxford University Press.

Patton, Cindy. 1996. *Fatal Advice: How Safe Sex Education Went Wrong.* Durham, NC: Duke University Press.

Peck, Ellen and Judith Senderowitz. 1974. *Pronatalism: The Myth of Mom and Apple Pie.* New York: Thomas Y. Cromwell.

Petchesky, Rosalind P. 2000. "Sexual Rights: Inventing a Concept, Mapping an International Practice." Pp. 8–102 in *Framing the Sexual Subject: The Politics of Gender, Sexuality and Power,* edited by Richard Parker, Regina Maria Barbosa, and Peter Aggleton. Berkeley, CA: University of California Press.

Plant, Sadie. 2000. "Coming across the Future." Pp. 460–70 in *The Cybercultures Reader,* edited by David Bell and Barbara M. Kennedy. London, England: Routledge.

Plummer, Ken, ed. 1981. *The Making of the Modern Homosexual.* London, England: Hutchinson.

———. 1995. *Telling Sexual Stories: Power, Change and Social Worlds.* London, England: Routledge.

———. 2001a. *Documents of Life—2: An Introduction to Critical Humanism.* London, England: Sage.

———. 2001b. "The Square of Intimate Citizenship." *Citizenship Studies* 5 (3):237–53.

———, ed. 2002. *Sexualities: Critical Concepts in Sociology* (4 vols.). London, England. Routledge.

———. 2003. *Intimate Citizenship: Private Decisions and Public Dialogues.* Seattle, WA: University of Washington Press.

Porter, Roy and Lesley Hall. 1995. *The Facts of Life: The Creation of Sexual Knowledge in Britain 1650–1950.* New Haven, CT: Yale University Press.

Richardson, Diane. 2000. *Rethinking Sexuality.* London, England: Sage.

Rubin, Gayle. 1984. "Thinking Sex." In *Pleasure and Danger,* edited by Carole S. Vance. London, England: Routledge.

Seidman, Steven. 1992. *Embattled Eros.* London, England: Routledge.

Showalter, Elaine. 1991. *Sexual Anarchy: Gender and Culture at the Fin de Siecle.* London, England: Bloomsbury.

Smith, Adam. 1937. *An Inquiry into the Nature and Causes of the Wealth of Nations.* New York: Modern Library.

Smith, Ralph and Russell R. Windes. 2000. *Progay/Antigay: The Rhetorical War Over Sexuality.* Thousand Oaks, CA: Sage.

Spector, Malcolm and John Kitsuse. 1987. *Constructing Social Problems.* Hawthorn, NY: Aldine de Gruyter.

Stein, Arlene. 2001. *Strangers in Our Midst.* Boston, MA: Beacon.

Stein Arlene et al. 1999. "A Symposium on the Clinton-Lewinsky Affair." *Sexualities* 2 (2):247–60.

Sutherland, Edwin. 1950. "The Diffusion of Sexual Psychopath Laws." *American Journal of Sociology* 56:142–148. Reprinted in Plummer, Ken. 2002. *Sexualities: Critical Concepts in Sociology,* vol. 1, reading 9.

Szasz, Thomas. 1980. *Sex: Facts, Frauds and Follies.* Oxford, England: Blackwell.

Tiefer, Leonore. 2000. "Sexology and the Pharmaceutical Industry: The Threat of Co-Optation." *Journal of Sex Research* 37 (3):273–83.

Tithecott, Richard. 1997. *Of Men and Monsters: Jeffrey Dahmer and the Construction of the Serial Killer.* Madison, WI: University of Wisconsin Press.

Vance, Carole S., ed. 1984. *Pleasure and Danger.* London, England: Routledge.

Vass, Antony. 1986. *AIDS: A Plague in U.S.* Cambridge, England: Venus Academica.

Walkowitz, Judith. 1980. *Prostitution and Victorian Society: Women, Class and the State.* Cambridge, England: Cambridge University Press.

——. 1984. "Male Vice and Female Virtue: Feminism and the Politics of Prostitution in Nineteenth Century Britain." In *Desire: The Politics of Sexuality,* edited by Ann Snitow, Christine Stansell, and Sharon Thompson. London, England: Virago.

——. 1992. *City of Dreadful Delight: Narratives of Sexual Danger in Late Victorian London.* London, England: Virago.

Warner, Michael. 2002. *Publics and Counterpublics.* New York: Zone Books.

Watney, Simon. 1997. *Policing Desire: Pornography, AIDS and the Media.* 3rd ed. London, England: Cassell.

Weeks, Jeffrey. 1998. "'The Sexual Citizen' Theory." *Culture and Society* 15 (3):35–52.

——. 2000. *Making Sexual History.* Oxford, England: Polity.

White, Kevin. 1993. *The First Sexual Revolution: The Emergence of Male Heterosexuality in Modern America.* New York: NYU Press.

Whittle, Stephen. 2002. *Transgender Laws.* London, England: Routledge.

Wiener, Carolyn. 1981. *The Politics of Alcoholism.* New Brunswick, NJ: Transaction.

Williams, Walter. 1986. *The Spirit and the Flesh: Sexual Diversity in American Indian Culture.* Boston, MA: Beacon.

Young, Iris Marion. 1990. *Justice and the Politics of Difference.* Princeton, NJ: Princeton University Press.

Zurcher, Louis et al. 1976. *Citizens for Decency: Anti-Pornography Crusades as Status Defense.* Austin, TX: University of Texas Press.

Modern-Day Folk Devils and the Problem of Children's Presence in the Global Sex Trade

Julia O'Connell Davidson

Nottingham University

O ver the past decade, national and international policymakers, journalists, and academics have identified children's presence in the global sex trade as a growing social problem. However, media coverage and public and political debate on the subject has remained depressingly simplistic. Indeed, the commercial sexual exploitation of children in the contemporary world is often represented as a very straightforward battle between good and evil, and innocence and corruption. On one hand, we are presented with images of sad, pathetic, helpless victims, small children bought and sold as objects, tricked, raped, beaten, and trapped into a modern form of slavery; on the other, the talk is of the vile monsters who abuse and exploit them, the flesh peddlers, traffickers, pimps, and paedophiles, modern-day folk devils who are the very personification of evil. My aim in this chapter is not to suggest that children's presence in the global sex trade is unproblematic, but rather to argue that the problem of child prostitution is embedded in a much more complex and painful reality than that invoked by popular discourse on the subject.

Author's Note: This chapter is based upon one of the theme papers for the Second World Congress against the Commercial Sexual Exploitation of Children (O'Connell Davidson 2001c). The author is particularly indebted to Ola Florin, Hélène Sackstein, Jacqueline Sánchez Taylor, Sun Wen Bin, and Maia Rusakova, for invaluable information and references. The support of Save the Children Sweden, which funded the researching and writing of the original theme paper, and the Economic and Social Research Council of Great Britain, which funded research in the Caribbean that also contributed to the paper (Award No. R000237625), are gratefully acknowledged.

PAEDOPHILIA AND BEYOND

In 1996, government officials from more than 100 countries and representatives of a range of non-governmental organizations (NGOs) came together at the First World Congress against the Commercial Sexual Exploitation of Children in Stockholm to combat what was identified as a fundamental abuse of children's rights. A second such Congress was held in Yokohama, in December 2001. The Declaration and Agenda for Action from the First Congress made it clear that CSEC (commercial sexual exploitation of children) is rooted in a complex mix of economic, political, social, and legal factors and needs to be addressed through a wide range of measures at local, national, and international levels. Though this emphasis on the complexity of CSEC has exerted some influence on debates concerning the sexually exploited child over the past six years, it has remained largely absent from public and policy debate regarding those who commercially sexually exploit children. Instead, there has been a continued tendency (1) to assume that the "demand side" of CSEC consists of "paedophiles" and the criminals who supply them with children to abuse and/or (2) to concentrate on legal and criminal justice aspects of demand.

One immediate and obvious problem with this preoccupation with "paedophiles" is that it is inconsistent with the definition of "children" employed in international debate on CSEC. This debate is informed by the United Nations' Convention on the Rights of the Child, wherein a *child* is defined as a person under the age of 18. Yet *paedophilia* is a clinical diagnostic category with a very specific and limited meaning. According to the American Psychiatric Association's 1995 manual, it refers to a person aged over 16, who "has had repeated, intense, sexually exciting fantasies for a period of at least six months, has had sexual urges or has carried out behaviours involving sexual acts with one or more children (usually under the age of 13)" (cited in Svensson 2000:27). Furthermore, "The fantasies, the sexual urges or behaviours act as considerable impairments in the individual's ability to function socially, professionally or within other important spheres" (cited in Svensson 2000:27). Some of those who conform to this definition pose a very serious risk to children and can be individually responsible for the sexual abuse of large numbers of children. Yet we should also note that to be clinically diagnosed as suffering from paedophilia, an individual need not necessarily have committed any act of child sexual abuse, and we cannot therefore claim that *all* paedophiles sexually exploit children. It would be still more emphatically wrong to claim that all those who do sexually exploit children are paedophiles, and this would remain the case even if the term were more loosely employed to refer to adults with a sexual interest in young children (as it is used in popular parlance).

Those who are involved as third-party beneficiaries of CSEC, for example, are rarely motivated by personal sexual desire or obsessive fantasies. They sexually exploit children for profit, not because their acts of exploitation bring them psychic relief or sexual gratification. Next, there are those who sexually exploit children if and when they find themselves in situations where children are more readily or cheaply available for sexual use than adults, but whose satisfaction does not hinge on the physical or emotional immaturity of the individuals they exploit. There are also adult men who choose young children as sexual partners primarily on the basis of misconceptions about sexual health or because they uncritically accept myths about virgins being able to restore potency, bring luck to new business ventures, and so on. None of these people are driven by sexual fantasies about children per se.

Furthermore, if children are defined as persons under 18 years of age, it is necessary to recognise that few societies completely proscribe adult-child sexual contact. In most countries, it is legal for an adult to marry, cohabit with, or date a person below the age of 18. Meanwhile, most societies attach a good deal of aesthetic and erotic value to youthful bodies. Adults who seek out younger and more attractive sexual partners, including persons under the age of 18, are not necessarily transgressing the socially agreed perimeters of acceptable sexual desires and therefore cannot be automatically described as sexually "deviant" or psychologically "abnormal." To reduce the problem of children's involvement in the global sex trade to a problem of "paedophilia" is thus to grossly oversimplify matters. Though it is important to address the existence of, and harm caused by, those who consistently and consciously seek out young children to abuse, questions about why children are sexually exploited and by whom do not end here. It is also necessary to ask why it is that people who are *not* "paedophiles" sexually exploit children.

Rationalising the Sexual Exploitation of Children

Orlando Patterson (1982) has observed that "human beings have always found naked force or coercion a rather messy, if not downright ugly business, however necessary" (p. 18). Most societies have therefore sought ways in which to clothe the "beastliness" of power, to propound a set of ideas that make coercive power "immediately palatable to those who exercise it" (p. 18). Just as the power of dominant groups in society is typically cloaked or justified by discourses that humanise or deny it, so individuals are usually reluctant to view themselves as abusive, dominating, cruel, or evil. Whether we are talking about acts of genocide, rape, wife beating, or child sexual abuse, the vast majority of people will use force or coercive power against another human being only if and when they can tell themselves it is natural, right, and justifiable to do so, or when they can conceal from themselves the fact that they are exercising such powers. Thus, research has consistently found that very few of those who sexually exploit children consider themselves to be abusive or exploitative, but rather seek to deny, justify, or humanise their sexual use of children.

For example, British and U.S. studies of convicted child sex offenders suggest that such people typically exhibit distorted attitudes and beliefs that allow them to construct children as being in some way responsible for their own abuse, and/or imagine that children are not harmed by sexual contact with adults, and/or that children are able to consent to, or obtain benefits from, sexual encounters with adults (Ward, Hudson, and Keenan 2000). This may involve minimizing the meaning and consequences of abuse (as when the abuser tells himself that "fondling" or oral sex does not really "count" as sex and causes no harm to the child concerned) and/or denying the coercive nature of the abuse (as when the abuser tells himself that the child instigated, invited, or deserved the abuse). The degree of distortion and denial involved can be quite extraordinary. There are even offenders who claim that their sexual contact with a baby was not wrong because the baby invited or consented to the abuse by, for example, smiling and gurgling when the abuser changed its nappy.

Clearly, no existing society's framework of beliefs can support such a stupendous level of self-deception. Those who sexually abuse very young children therefore have to massively distort socially agreed ideas about consent and the powers one human being can legitimately exercise over another, as well as about the proper objects of adult sexual interest and the proper relations between adults and children. Such people often have an extremely fragile hold on their sense of self and experience great psychological stress as they attempt maintain a view of their own actions as justified or harmless. However, those who abuse very small children are in a minority, and there are other forms of child sexual exploitation that are much easier to accommodate within the framework of socially prescribed or tolerated attitudes toward sexuality, age, consent, and the legitimate exercise of power. As the remainder of this chapter sets out to show, the use of children working in prostitution is a case in point. Before turning to questions about who has sex with child prostitutes and how they rationalise their behaviour, however, it is necessary to briefly consider where, how, and why children are present in prostitution.

CHILDREN AND PROSTITUTION: AN OVERVIEW

Sex commerce is a stigmatized activity that generally takes place within a shadow or illegal economy. It is therefore extremely difficult to obtain accurate statistics on any aspect of the global sex trade. Methodological problems are all the more pronounced in relation to children's presence in the sex industry, since even where certain types of prostitution are legally regulated or tolerated, prostitution involving minors is invariably criminalized. Although claims about the numbers of children in prostitution in various regions of the world are often made by groups campaigning against CSEC, such figures are at best "guesstimates" (Ennew 1986). There is, however, a more general body of empirical evidence on the sex trade around the world that allows us to advance certain claims about child prostitution with reasonable certainty. Using the United Nations definition of the child as a person under the age of 18, research shows that children are present in the sex trade of virtually every country of the world but also reveals much variation in terms of their routes into prostitution, as well as in terms of the social organisation of their commercial sexual exploitation.

There are, for example, cases in which children are abducted or tricked by agents (even sometimes sold to agents by parents or guardians), who then transport them to other countries or cities where they are sold into slavery-like conditions within brothel prostitution or forced to prostitute by a pimp. This type of trafficking has received most research attention in South and Southeast Asia (Brown 2000; Human Rights Watch 2000; Pyne 1995) but is also known to occur in Latin America (Sutton 1994), and there is growing concern about women and children being trafficked from poor and developing countries into the United States, Canada, Australia, Japan, and European Union countries (International Organisation for Migration [IOM] 1996a; U.S. Agency for International Development [USAID] 2001; P. Williams 1999). However, not all children who work in prostitution have been trafficked or are subject to the control of a third party (brothel keeper or pimp). Some work independently, soliciting customers from streets, beaches, parks, bars, or other venues, either in their own hometowns or in other cities or tourist resorts they have migrated to of their own volition (Montgomery 1998; O'Connell Davidson and Sánchez Taylor 1996a, 1996b; Silvestre, Rijo, and Bogaert 1994; S. Williams 1999). Indeed, in both affluent and developing countries, many children who sell sex are "runaways," escaping abusive family situations, institutional care, or rural poverty and entering into cash-for-sex exchanges to survive on the streets (Bagley 1999; Brock 1998; Economic and Social Commission for Asia and the Pacific [ESCAP] 2000; Melrose, Barrett, and Brodie 1999; O'Neill and Barberet

2000). Finally, we should note that many thousands of the world's children grow up in communities that are entirely economically dependent upon the sex industry, and enter the sex trade when they reach the age at which they are expected to do (which is usually below the age of 18). So, for example, although some children who work as prostitutes in brothel districts in India and Bangladesh are victims of internal or cross-border trafficking, others are the daughters of female sex workers who already live in brothel communities (Uddin, Sultana, and Mahmud 2001; see also Saeed 2002).

There have been a number of high-profile cases involving the prostitution of young children by "paedophile rings" (see, for example, an account of the case of Andrew Mark Harvey in Lee-Wright 1990), but available research on both trafficking and prostitution suggests that such cases are rare. Many studies show that adolescents are present in the sex trade, and few have found any evidence of preadolescent children being trafficked into or exploited within the mainstream sex industry. So, for instance, recent International Labour Organization (ILO) research found that more than half of a sample of girls trafficked from Nepal to India were under the age of 16 and one-quarter were under the age of 14 when they were trafficked, but notes that "trafficking of girls seldom takes place before the onset of puberty" (Kumar 2001:2). Likewise, a 1992 survey of sex workers in Thailand revealed that one-third had entered prostitution when below the age of 18 and almost one-fifth were between the ages of 13 and 15 when they first started to prostitute, but found nothing to indicate that it is common for prepubertal children to be exploited in the sex trade (Lim 1998). Though cases of CSEC involving preadolescent children are extremely disturbing and clearly warrant our attention and concern, they also appear to be outside the "norms" of the commercial sex industry in the contemporary world.[1] Thus, although there may be a small and largely concealed "market niche" within prostitution involving very young children, research suggests that the vast majority of children in prostitution are aged between 12 and 18 and are integrated into the mainstream prostitution market, serving demand from prostitute users in general rather than clients with a specific, focused interest in prepubertal children.

Existing research also clearly shows that those adolescents already disadvantaged by a range of economic, social, and political factors are the most likely to end up trading sex. So, for example, it is known that children who are affected by cataclysmic events (armed conflict, civil war, ethnic and racial violence, famine, and environmental degradation and disasters) are at particular risk of sexual exploitation by a range of groups: soldiers, including members of peacekeeping forces, staff and caregivers in institutions, humanitarian aid workers, and other refugee and displaced children. Some 10 million out of the world's 21.5 million refugees and other persons of concern are under the age of 18 (United Nations Commission on Human Rights [UNCHR] 2000), and they are made vulnerable to sexual abuse and exploitation by the circumstances in which they are forced to live. Adolescents in particular often have to fend for themselves and may also have to assume adult responsibilities such as caring for siblings, and studies in Bosnia, Liberia, and Colombia suggest that refugee and displaced children between 12 and 18 sometimes trade sex for official papers, privileges for themselves or their relatives, clothes and food, or protection, as well as for cash (Kadjar-Hamouda 1996).

There are also links between poverty, HIV/AIDS, and CSEC. At the end of 1999, UNAIDS estimated that 13.2 million of the world's children aged under 15 had lost their mothers or both parents as a result of AIDS and that 90% of these children lived in sub-Saharan Africa. It is further estimated that "44 million children in the 34 countries hardest hit by HIV/AIDS will have lost one or both parents from all causes, but primarily from AIDS, by 2010" (USAID 2000). The vast majority of children orphaned by AIDS struggle to subsist, often also to support siblings, and are thus highly vulnerable to involvement in commercial or survival sex. At the same time, the HIV/AIDS pandemic fuels a growth in the demand for CSEC (as well as incidence of child rape) in the regions worst affected. Global political and economic inequalities effectively deny people with AIDS in poor countries access to even the most basic health care. It is believed that as a consequence, some HIV-infected men turn in desperation to old myths about the outward transmission of disease, hoping that sex with a young child will cleanse them (see Gender-Aids Forum 2001).

Other tragedies that are less immediate and dramatic, but equally calamitous, also have an impact on children's lives and render them vulnerable to CSEC. Over the past three decades, "The poorest 20 percent of the world's people have seen their share of global income decline from 2.3 percent to 1.4 percent. . . . Meanwhile, the share of the richest 20 percent has risen from 70 percent to 85 percent" (Castells 1996:80–1). This polarisation is occurring both between and within nations and has been exacerbated by the pursuit of neoliberal policies for fiscal discipline and economic restructuring. In the developing world, the policy packages tied to structural adjustment loans have meant cuts to public spending and subsidies, increasing unemployment, and decreasing real wages. The poor, especially women and youth, have been left struggling to survive. These developments have had an enormous impact on patterns of sexual exploitation.

In undermining welfare benefits and minimum-wage levels and cutting the subsidies that made housing, transport, child care, education, and health care more affordable, neoliberal economic reforms in both affluent and developing nations have intensified many of the pressures that lead children to work and live on the streets (Mickelson 2000:272). Whether in Canada, Zambia, Brazil, Romania, or Cambodia, children who live and work on the streets are vulnerable to sexual abuse, violence, and exploitation from several different groups. Though many street children "form strong, supportive and loving bonds with their peers and members of marginal cultures with whom they interact," relationships formed on the streets can often be "transitory and exploitative," and children are thus at risk from fellow street dwellers (Posner 2000:253). Girl children who live and/or work on the streets are vulnerable to recruitment into full-time street or brothel prostitution, but street children may also engage in "survival sex," trading sex for food, clothes, medicine, protection, and/or a place to stay. Finally, street children often report being sexually assaulted by police officers and/or staff in homes, hostels, and prisons in which they are remanded.

At the same time as intensifying poverty and unemployment amongst already vulnerable women and youth, global economic restructuring has also encouraged an expansion of the commercial sex industry. For example, since the 1970s, world financial institutions have encouraged indebted nations in Latin America and Southeast Asia to respond to economic crisis by developing tourism and/or "nontraditional" export industries such as gold, diamonds, and timber. One side effect of such development policies is the creation of highly concentrated, effective demand for prostitution: affluent tourists seeking "entertainment" and predominantly male, migrant workers in isolated mining and logging regions with cash to spend on "recreation." It is unsurprising to find that adolescents as well as adult women, knowing that prostitution is more highly rewarded than any other form of work available to them, will sometimes elect to migrate from impoverished rural areas to prostitute in tourist resorts or mining or logging encampments in the hope of making enough money to support themselves and their families (Fiengold 1998, 2000; Kempadoo 1999; O'Connell Davidson 2001a; Xie 2000).

Having stressed the link between poverty and prostitution, it is important to note that whether we are talking about affluent or developing countries, the relationship between the two is rarely direct or unmediated. As O'Neill and Barberet (2000) observe,

> Economic pressures play major roles in most cases, especially in street prostitution . . . but these economic pressures often result from familial abuse and neglect. Economic need is a result of being run-aways, single mothers, or unskilled workers. Other influences include coercion from pimps . . . and the need to support a drug habit. (P. 127)

Adolescents who have friends or acquaintances working in prostitution, and/or who have previous histories of sexual victimization also appear to be more likely to turn to prostitution as a strategy for survival than are similarly economically disadvantaged children with no such prior histories. So, for example, a study of 50 sex workers in Calgary, Canada, found that 86 percent had entered prostitution before the age of 18 (more than three-quarters began trading sex before 16) and 82 percent had been raped or sexually abused prior to entering prostitution (Bagley 1999). Recent research in Yunnan Province, China, likewise suggests links between

girls' vulnerability to trafficking into the sex trade and the experience of sexual abuse or domestic violence within the home (ESCAP 2000). These points hold good for boys as well as girls who become involved in trading sex (Gibson 1995).

BUYING SEX FROM CHILD PROSTITUTES

Research on the demand for prostitution in general suggests that it comes overwhelmingly (though not exclusively) from men, but surveys reveal much variation between countries as regards how many men admit to prostitute use. For example, around 9 percent of men in Britain (Wellings et al. 1993), 13 percent of men in Finland (Haavio-Mannila and Rotkirch 2000), 14 percent of men in Hong Kong (Family Planning Association, Hong Kong 2000), 39 percent of men in Spain (Leridon, Zesson, and Hubert 1998), and 16 percent of men in the United States (Monto 2000) admit to having paid for sex at some time in their lives. Studies further suggest that certain subsets of the male population of any given country are more likely than others to engage in prostitute use. There is a great deal of historical and contemporary evidence to suggest that groups of men whose work separates them from home for prolonged periods are particularly prone to prostitute use. This is especially the case when their employment is sex segregated and when the work culture is informed by an ethos of machismo. Unsurprisingly, then, prostitute use has historically been and remains common amongst men in the armed forces (Enloe 1993; Euler and Welzer-Lang 2000; Kane 1993; Moon 1997; Sturdevant and Stoltzfus 1992; Tanaka 2002). Seafarers, truckers, and male migrant workers who spend long periods working in poor conditions in isolated regions (for instance, those who work in logging and mining) are three more significant groups in terms of providing demand for prostitution (Antonius-Smits 1999; Siden 2002; Sutton 1994; Verhaert et al. 1993).

Businessmen may not work away from home for prolonged periods, but they often travel a good deal, and in most major cities around the world, sex workers report that foreign and domestic businessmen are amongst their clients (Allison 1994; Lever and Dolnick 2000; Nencel 2001; Ren 1993). Research also indicates that people are far more likely to enter into various forms of sexual-economic exchange whilst on holiday than they are when at home (Kleibe and Wilke 1995). Demand for prostitution does not come only from men who travel or work away from home, however, and in most settings, local men (including police officers; see Anderson and O'Connell Davidson 2002) are amongst those who buy sex. Although the vast majority of those who pay for sex are men, there is also some evidence of demand from women for a variety of sexual-economic exchanges (Haavio-Mannila and Rotkirch 2000; Meisch 1995; Nagel 1997; Sánchez Taylor 2001).

Reliable data on the number or background characteristics of those who buy sex from persons under the age of 18 are much harder to come by. However, a range of studies have shown that all over the world, adolescents can be found working alongside sex workers aged over 18 in mainstream forms of prostitution. For example, girls aged between 12 and 18 years have been found working in brothel districts, tourist areas, mining encampments, ports and truck stops, on the streets, and in a variety of off-street forms of prostitution (Brown 2000; Kelly and Regan 2000; Mayorga and Velasquez 1999; Melrose et al. 1999; O'Connell Davidson 2001a; O'Connell Davidson and Sánchez Taylor 2001; Rusakova 2001; Uddin et al. 2001), and boys under 18 are likewise present in mainstream male prostitution (Aggleton 1999; West 1992). Although research suggests that some clients have a specific interest in sex with young children or virgins, and some deliberately and consciously seek out sex workers who are above the age of 25, most sex buyers simply take their pick of the prostitutes working in any given setting (Anderson and O'Connell Davidson 2002; O'Connell Davidson and Sánchez Taylor 1996a). Price, availability, and sometimes also physical appearance are often more important to the client than whether the prostitute is aged above or below 18.

Viewed globally, it is almost certainly true to say that only a minority of men are regular or habitual prostitute users. Nevertheless, those with experience of prostitute use represent a significant percentage of the world's male population, and in numerical terms, they certainly amount to some millions of men. Because they use or have used prostitutes in a world in which many sex workers are below the age of 18, we can conclude that the numbers of men who have ever paid for sex with minors are also substantial. This should immediately alert us to problems with models of CSEC that construct the men who pay for sex with children as necessarily deviant, abnormal, evil, or monstrous. Instead, we need to ask why this sizeable number of men want to make use of the commercial sex industry and what is it that makes it possible for them to ignore or overlook questions about the age of the prostitutes they exploit?

The Natural-Born Client

In my own interview research with clients (O'Connell Davidson 1997, 1998, 2001b), I have found that they generally draw upon the idea of male sexual "needs" to explain their own prostitute use. Some men view themselves as lacking the physical or social charms necessary to meet these "needs" in noncommercial contexts (they say things like, "When I was younger I could always pick a girl up at a disco or something, but now I'm older and getting a bit thin on top, like, put on a few pounds, they won't look at me"). Because prostitution affords them instant access to a selection of females, they can, as one man put it, get their "sex drive out for the night." Other clients describe their prostitute use as a quick and simple expedient in situations when no other "outlet" is unavailable. There are also clients who have wives or girlfriends from whom they are not physically separated. They tend to explain their prostitute use as a function of rather more specific sexual "needs" that would otherwise go unsatisfied ("I need something that's just purely sexual, just to meet my needs with no complications") or else as a response to their wife/partner's lack of sexual interest in them. Finally, there are clients who say that they use prostitutes as a means of satisfying a "natural" impulse to have sex with as many different females as often as they possibly can.

These attitudes toward male sexuality can hardly be described as extraordinary. Indeed, it is almost universally assumed that men are *by nature* sexually active and subject to strong sexual urges or appetites, whilst women are assumed to be *naturally* sexually passive and receptive, and great value has traditionally been placed upon female sexual purity and continence. These traditional beliefs about gender difference form the basis for the "double standards" that most societies apply to prostitution. When men use prostitutes, they are widely considered to be simply giving in to a "natural" impulse, whereas females who work as prostitutes are generally condemned and vilified as "unnatural" women. Prostitution thus becomes a "necessary evil"— necessary for men who are possessed of strong and biologically given sexual impulses, and evil for women, who should be modest, chaste, dependent, and passive. And so while prostitution may be viewed as distasteful or immoral, it is also considered to perform an important social function, "soaking up" excess male sexual urges that would otherwise lead to rape, marital breakdown, and all kinds of social disorder, and so protecting the virginity and innocence of "good" girls and women. Whether Scandinavian, Italian, Japanese, Indian, or Thai, clients typically accept such ideas (Anderson and O'Connell Davidson 2002).

Most societies socialise their members to believe that there are natural and fundamental differences between male and female sexuality and that men have strong and biologically based sexual "needs" that cannot be left unmet without harm accruing to the individual concerned. And yet human sexual desire is also very much a social matter. People are rarely completely indiscriminate about the social identities of their sexual partners; indeed, they typically care a great deal about the gender and age (often also the race, ethnicity, and class) of those who meet their sexual "needs" and the precise manner in which they meet them. To speak of sex is, as Thomas Laqueur (1995) has noted, to talk about "a great deal else than organs, bodies and pleasures" (p. 155), for sex is not a mere bodily function or physical need. Our erotic life is grounded in the ideas we use to categorize, interpret, and give meaning to human experience and sociality, and specific sexual desires do not, therefore, directly express some fundamental, timeless, or general human *need* for sex.

The story of the "Natural-Born Client" does not describe a biological reality, then. But naturalizing prostitute use through reference to ideas about male

sexuality does allow clients to construct their sexual contact with the prostitute as a "good" or "commodity" that satisfies a perfectly understandable and reasonable demand on the part of the "consumer." This draws attention to an important way in which very ordinary, everyday attitudes and beliefs about the social world can help very "normal" and unremarkable individuals to rationalise the act of buying sex from children working in prostitution.

Commodity Exchange and Moral Indifference

Prostitution involves a market transaction and is usually (but not always) organised and constructed as a commodity exchange like any other. To imagine the prostitute-client transaction as a commodity exchange, clients have to treat sexuality as though it were something that can be detached from the person. The prostitute's sexuality then becomes some *thing* that she can freely choose to sell, and the client's sexuality is also imagined as somehow estranged and divisible from his *real* self. He enters into the exchange merely to "control" his "sex life" or satisfy his "sex drive." One client I interviewed even compared his sexuality to a vehicle that the owner has to maintain, describing his visits to prostitutes as being "a bit like taking your car to the garage to get it serviced . . . you're paying for the services of an expert, someone who really knows what they're doing" (O'Connell Davidson 1997). Thus "sexual needs," which are in reality socially constructed productions of the human imagination, are fetishized, invested with a life of their own, and viewed as an external force driving the client to behave in particular ways.

By telling himself that prostitution is a commodity exchange (he and the prostitute meet freely in the marketplace and voluntarily contract to dispose of their property), the client can avoid thinking of prostitution as involving a human relationship. This means he can overlook certain facts about the prostitute as a person, facts that would often make sexual contact with her illegitimate in terms of the rules and conventions that in noncommercial contexts, he himself would probably endorse. The prostitute may be another man's wife or girlfriend or pregnant by another man. She may have been coerced into prostitution by a husband, boyfriend, or pimp. She may be debt-bonded or subject to other slavery-like practices by a brothel keeper. She may be extremely young. But because his relationship to her is constructed as a commodity exchange, the client does not feel morally compelled to interrogate what lies behind her sexual "consent." She is a seller, he is a buyer, and he can simply think in terms of an exchange of "values," x amount of money for x sexual benefit (and clients do really talk about "value for money").

This makes it possible for men (sometimes also women) who would not dream of asking their own child's teenage friends for sex, let alone think it right to coerce them into having sex, to buy sex from adolescents who work in the sex trade. Because prostitution is contractually organised as a commodity exchange like any other, buyers can tell themselves that their own actions are quite legitimate. They are simply behaving as a sovereign consumer in a free market behaves, and if they do not accept the child's offer, someone else will. This is made explicit in a guidebook written by a sex tourist for sex tourists. The author, Bruce Cassirer, explains how to go about finding brothels in Bangkok where debt-bonded women and children work:

> These are village girls from Burma or China who are barefoot and who knows how old. . . . If the service is good, tip; if extra special, tip more. These girls live here and are *owned* by the hotel. Your tip is their spending money, so let your conscience be your guide. . . . One way to rationalize it is to say, if it's not me then it's the guy behind me, and who's more likely to be the gentler of the two? (Cassirer 1992:180–81; original emphasis)

When men like this buy sex from children, it is perhaps best understood as an act of moral indifference, and it is by no means clear that this is out of kilter with the moral codes that are widely accepted in liberal democratic states. In a book that starts from a consideration of the Holocaust, the British political theorist Norman Geras (1998) asks how we can make sense of "the depressing but widespread fact that so many people do not come to the aid of others under attack, whether fellow citizens or merely other human beings, and also do not come to

the aid of them in dire need or great distress" (p. 26). Geras's idea is that people imagine themselves as parties to a contract of mutual indifference, whereby they do not feel obligated to come to the aid of others who are under grave assault and do not expect others to feel obligated to help them in a similar emergency. Geras goes on to argue that this kind of moral indifference is underwritten by liberal political thought:

> The principal economic formation historically associated with liberalism, defended by liberals—whether confidently or apologetically—today as much as ever, is one in which it has been the norm for the wealth and comfort of some to be obtained through the hardship and poverty of others, and to stand right alongside these. It is a whole mode of collective existence. Not only an economy. A world, a culture, a set of everyday practices. (P. 59)

Prostitution seems to me to be one such everyday practice; a practice that expresses moral indifference and justifies it by invoking the liberal concept of contractual consent. There are very obvious parallels between Cassirer's advice on how to rationalise buying sex from children forced into prostitution and the thought processes followed by those who, for example, continue to buy cheap garments or trainers from retailers whose use of forced or child labour has been widely publicized. His remarks may be offensive and obscene, but they only distinguish him from most "ordinary decent folk" in the sense that he is willing to extend the logic of the contract of mutual indifference to the arena of commercial sex.

The Prostitute as "Other"

Although clients tend to justify and defend their own prostitute use by describing prostitution as a commodity exchange like any other, few really accept that the prostitute's sexuality can be estranged as a "thing" or "commodity" separate from her person. In fact, the reverse is generally true. Habitual clients actually tend to buy into very traditional ideas about gender and sexuality, and about prostitution. They believe, just as strongly as do religious fundamentalists and moral conservatives, that there is a firm and meaningful line of demarcation between "good" and "bad" women, "Madonnas" and "whores." A female who sells sex is considered by most habitual clients to be different from other women, unlike their own wives, sisters, mothers, daughters, or other "respectable" women. The prostitute is somehow outside the imaginary community of good, respectable, heterosexuals— this is why it is acceptable and morally justifiable to use her in ways that "good" women and girls cannot be used.

In this, once again, the client merely accepts and reproduces what is widely socially endorsed. Societies that are distinguished by all manner of economic, political, religious, and cultural differences share a common tendency to legally and socially construct female prostitutes as a separate class of persons, as criminals, deviants, outsiders, a group apart from other good and decent women. As such, they have been, and are, subjected to various forms of surveillance, social control, and discipline and denied many of the basic rights, protections, and freedoms accorded to other citizens. Indeed, female prostitutes represent a group whose human and civil rights have been continuously, routinely, and systematically violated by the states under which they live (Alexander 1997; Bindman 1997; Kempadoo and Doezema 1998).

Because they "agree" to sell their sexuality as a commodity, prostitutes are held to have placed themselves outside the remit of the socially agreed rules that govern sexual life. They are expelled and excluded from the community, and thus the rape, even the murder, of prostitute women does not evoke the same degree of popular outrage as the rape or murder of women who are covered by the rules, and sexual contact with a child is adjudged differently according to whether it takes place within a commercial or a noncommercial context. In fact, the stigma against prostitutes is so great that it overrides a child's status as a child. A child who prostitutes is no longer a child. An Italian sex tourist once described to me how he picked up a 13-year-old girl in the Dominican Republic and took her back to his apartment for sex. He justified his actions by saying that she was already working as a prostitute, and "she was expecting something, and it wasn't a lollipop" (O'Connell Davidson and Sánchez Taylor 1996b:16). Again, clients who reason in this way

are reproducing attitudes that are widely socially endorsed. The idea that children should not be criminalized for their involvement in prostitution is still not universally accepted, either in principle or practice.

Sexualized Racism

Research shows that in many countries of the world, migrants are now overrepresented in the sex trade. In some European Union countries, it is estimated that more than half of those working in prostitution are migrants, and in most of Western Europe, significant numbers of women from a number of African, Latin American, and Southeast Asian countries, as well as from former Soviet Bloc countries, are present in the commercial sex industry (IOM 1996a, 1996b; Tampep 1999; P. Williams 1999). Migrant women and girls also represent a strong presence in the sex industries of many Asian countries. In 1995, there were an estimated 23,000 Thai female sex workers in Japan (Phongpaichit 1999). Vietnamese women and girls are present in the sex trade in Taiwan, China, Macau, Thailand, and Cambodia (Asian Migrant Centre [AMC] 2000; Foggo 2002; Xie 2000). Latin American and Caribbean sex workers migrate within the region and work in the commercial sex sector in Europe and North America (COIN 1992; IOM 1996a, 1996b; Kempadoo 1999). The list could go on. As is the case in other economic sectors, migrant sex workers frequently find themselves working for low pay under exploitative conditions, as the market for commercial sex is often hierarchically stratified along lines of race/ethnicity and nationality. These hierarchies mirror the distribution of power and privilege in the society as a whole. Sex workers who belong to groups that are in general socially devalued and socially, politically, and economically marginalized are also likely to be devalued by clients and socially constructed as the "natural" or "ideal" occupants of the lowliest positions in the sex industry (Anderson and O'Connell Davidson 2002).

Racism, xenophobia, and ideas about caste also contribute to the demand for commercial sex, including CSEC, in the sense that they encourage clients to view "otherised" groups as "natural" prostitutes. So, for example, white Western sex tourists will say that the local women, men, and children they pay for sex in Asia, Africa, the Caribbean, and Latin America are naturally more sexually willing than their white counterparts (Kruhse-Mount Burton 1995; Sánchez Taylor 2001; Seabrook 1996; O'Connell Davidson and Sánchez Taylor 1996a). Though Australian, North American, Western European, and Japanese sex tourists have received the lion's share of research attention, it should also be noted that sex tourism takes place between and within developing countries. In developing countries, the minority who are prospering as a result of economic restructuring find themselves in a position to consume commercial sex, as well as other luxury goods. Thus, we find that Chinese men provide the bulk of demand for Vietnamese women and girls working in tourism resorts on the Vietnam-China border; Jamaican men travel to Cuba to sexually exploit local women and girls; and domestic Indian tourists provide demand for children and women in brothel districts in Goa. Attitudes toward travel and racial/ethnic difference are significant for understanding tourists' propensity to engage in CSEC. The sentiment behind the Japanese adage "Shameless behaviour during a trip is to be scraped off one's mind" (Allison 1994:140) is shared by a great many tourists, whether they hail from Bombay, Beijing, or Birmingham.

Again, clients' beliefs are not aberrant or extraordinary. Most societies are hierarchically stratified along ethnic, racial, or caste lines and/or are deeply xenophobic and promote or tolerate the belief that minority groups are sexually different. When people buy sex from children in prostitution who do not share their own social identities, they can thus easily tell themselves that these children either do not need, or are unworthy of, the care and protection that would be accorded to children "of their own kind."

In short, clients do not have to cognitively distort dominant attitudes toward sexual life very far at all to feel comfortable about using a child prostitute. Popular beliefs about gender, sexuality, race/caste, and prostitution allow the client to tell himself that the child instigated sex (solicited his custom), consented to sex (accepted money or another benefit in exchange), deserved to be sexually used (is just a "dirty" prostitute), and/or was not really harmed by the sexual contact (is not "one of my own kind" and/or has already been sexually used by many others, so what difference can one more violation make?). These observations hold across a range of otherwise very different societies, for the attitudes that encourage people to engage in CSEC (such as the sexual value attached to youthful bodies, the idea of male sexual "need," the stigmatisation of female prostitutes, and the sexualization of groups deemed to be racial/ethnic/caste "inferiors") have very wide currency. To this, we can add that dominant sexual cultures in virtually all contemporary societies are informed by the assumption that gender difference and inequality are natural, rather than socially and politically constructed, and that it is desirable for men to be "masculine" and women to be "feminine."

All over the world, the boundaries of gender are vigorously maintained and violently policed, and this near-universal insistence on gender difference helps to account for ordinary men's involvement in a range of sexually exploitative practices. It also helps to explain why sexual violence and exploitation are often highly visible in settings where men feel that their "masculinity" is at risk (e.g., when they work in exploitative conditions over which they have little control) and/or in settings where the social premium placed on "masculinity" is suddenly raised (e.g., periods of armed conflict). The obsessive attachment to gender difference is relevant to understanding the sexual abuse and exploitation of both male and female children. If men are taught to believe that masculinity is expressed through the act of insertive sex with a passive and receptive partner, then boys, as well as girls, can be used as vehicles for attaining masculinity.

Third-Party Beneficiaries

Child prostitution takes place within a complex and multifaceted "sex sector," which is linked in a variety of ways to both the formal and informal economy in any given country (see Lim 1998). Some of those who derive economic benefits from the sex sector are wealthy and powerful. They can include government and police officials and those who own and control businesses in the leisure and entertainment sector, which often enjoys a symbiotic relationship with the sex industry. Given that minors are often present in the mainstream sex trade, such people can be said to benefit indirectly from CSEC. Large and respectable tourism, mining, logging, and shipping companies might also be said to be indirectly involved in the sex sector in the sense that a flourishing demand for prostitution, including CSEC, is one of the by-products of their main profit-making activities and/or employment policies (such as providing dormitory accommodation for a migrant male workforce instead of housing for the men and their families). However, those who own and control companies are rarely held personally responsible for the social or environmental costs associated with the sectors within which they operate. Indeed, they are often loudly applauded for taking even the smallest of steps to ameliorate the negative side effects of their firms' profit-making activities.

Other third parties benefit from CSEC in more immediate ways. Economic rewards can be obtained from CSEC through a variety of activities, including trafficking children for purposes of sexual exploitation, organising and/or controlling children in prostitution, procuring children, and producing and distributing child pornography for commercial gain. Individuals can also obtain economic rewards from CSEC without actually becoming directly involved in arranging any child's sexual exploitation (corrupt officials can benefit from bribes, bar owners can "turn a blind eye" to CSEC on their premises and benefit from the custom it draws to their establishment, retailers can profit by selling pornographic materials involving persons under the age of 18, and so on). Few of these people dedicate themselves simply and solely to promoting CSEC, and most come to exploit children through their involvement with the sex trade more generally.

It is also important to note that several people, rather than one single individual, are usually implicated in any given child's sexual exploitation. So, for example, a trafficked-child's journey from her home to the brothel, street, or private flat where she ends up being commercially sexually exploited is usually charted by a number of different social actors: those who recruit her (perhaps people who themselves were originally trafficked into prostitution), those who encourage her (perhaps her own friends or relatives), middle agents, corrupt officials,

pimps, or brothel owners. This "division of labour" reduces any sense of responsibility on the part of each individual involved. Those at the start of the chain do not necessarily know or see the end consequences of their actions, whilst those at the end of the chain can blame the people who acted further back down the line for the child's situation. The motives of these different actors are not always identical, and they do not have equal interests in the commercial sex trade. While some rely on that trade as a major source of income, others benefit from their involvement on a "one-off" or irregular basis.

Very often, the action of those who knowingly derive economic benefits from CSEC is informed by the kind of moral indifference that was described above, but people can "buy into" such attitudes to different degrees and for different reasons. Some of those who sexually exploit children for profit are affluent and privileged individuals who are willing to cynically take advantage of the misfortunes of others for their own personal advantage. Often, the children they exploit are of a different racial, ethnic, caste, or national group from their own, and their willingness to tolerate or promote CSEC is partly linked to their racism/xenophobia. European and North American expatriates who allow children to solicit from bars they own in tourist resorts in developing countries, or procure children for tourists, provide a good example of this (see O'Connell Davidson and Sánchez Taylor 2001).

But other third-party beneficiaries of CSEC are far from privileged and powerful. Women and children, as well as men, are involved, and it is not uncommon for an individual "career" in the sex trade to start with selling sex, then progress to organising the prostitution of others. Nor is it unusual for prostitutes, including children in prostitution, to supplement their incomes by procuring or pimping others. Regardless of their age or gender, a good many people's involvement as third-party beneficiaries of the sex trade is precipitated by exactly the same factors that make children vulnerable to commercial sexual exploitation, including poverty, lack of alternative economic opportunity, absence of educational opportunities, domestic violence, drug addiction, and/or a range of exclusionary social practices and policies based on discriminatory beliefs about gender, race, ethnicity, caste, and/or sexuality.

Indeed, the study of Bangladeshi brothel communities mentioned earlier shows that those born into highly stigmatized communities that are entirely economically dependent on prostitution have little sense of what life is like in mainstream society, and no hope of leaving the community. Moreover, "All but the most protected children are routinely caught up in illicit activities from drinking, drug taking and gambling to theft, pimping and extortion" (Uddin et al. 2001:45). In these and other similar communities, adults who are yesterday's exploited children are today exploiting the children who will become tomorrow's exploiters. Such cycles of exploitation have virtually nothing to do with individual morality or criminality, but a great deal to do with the legal and social construction of prostitutes as a separate class of persons and the systematic violation of their human rights. The actions of all those involved as third parties to CSEC are neither identical nor morally equivalent.

PENALIZE THE BUYERS?

Those who are currently involved in campaigns for the abolition of prostitution (whether it involves adult women or children) often argue that prostitution is a form of sexual violence and comparable with slavery in the sense that it involves the objectification of human beings as mere commodities to be bought and sold (Barry 1995; Jeffreys 1997). They therefore call on all states not only to take measures to protect women and girls from prostitution and to criminalize those who organise and profit from prostitution but also to criminalize the men who buy sex:

> Penalize the buyers. The least discussed part of the prostitution and trafficking chain has been the men who buy women for sexual exploitation in prostitution, pornography, sex tourism and mail order bride marketing. We cannot shrug our shoulders and say "men are like this." . . . Rather, our responsibility is to make men change their behaviour by all means available—educational, cultural, and through legislation that penalizes men for the crime of sexual exploitation. (Raymond 2001:9)

Though many policymakers would be reluctant to follow the example set by Sweden, where the buying of sex per se has recently been criminalized (Månsson 2001), the idea that men should be legally punished for buying sex from minors has gained much more widespread support. Again, if we concentrate on CSEC as a problem affecting very young children, such measures may appear eminently reasonable. Why should a man who pays another adult to rape a nine-year-old be treated differently from a man who abducts and rapes a nine-year-old or who rapes his nine-year-old daughter? But the idea of penalizing the buyer is more controversial when adolescents' presence in the sex trade is considered, especially those who are above the age of sexual consent. Is it really possible to obtain a universal consensus on the need to legally construct and punish men who buy sex from 16- or 17-year-olds as child abusers?

Matters are complicated further if we recognise that adolescent males are also amongst those providing *demand* for prostitution (Anderson and O'Connell Davidson 2002; FPA HK 2000; Monto 2000). There are no data available on the age of prostitutes used by child clients. However, given that some boys under 18 are known to use prostitutes in settings where children aged under 18 are present in prostitution, we cannot discount the possibility that children in prostitution may sometimes be exploited by child clients. And still further problems are posed by the phenomenon of children who sexually exploit other children for financial gain, rather than sexual gratification. Poverty and other forms of social exclusion pave the way into this side of the sex trade, just as they are the major routes into prostitution itself.

The moral issues raised by men's use of adolescent prostitutes also appear more complex if we consider the fact that in many parts of the world, there is strong demand for commercial sex from men whose lives are every bit as bleak, violent, and hopeless as those of the women and children they buy sex from. Consider, for instance, the 350,000 men who work in gold mines in South Africa (Campbell 2001). Around 95 percent of these workers are migrants, the vast majority housed in single-sex hostels, with up to 18 men sharing a room. Their living conditions are dirty and overcrowded; there is no space for privacy or quiet; and there are very limited opportunities for wives or family to visit and few opportunities for leisure or relaxation. Their working conditions are equally grim, underground in the heat, often working with noisy machinery for eight hours with infrequent breaks and lack of access to water, in constant fear of fatal, mutilating, or disabling accidents. This is hardly an environment in which it is easy for human beings to fulfill their own emotional needs or indeed even acknowledge that they experience emotions such as fear, loneliness, or sorrow. As one miner explained to Catherine Campbell (2001):

> They told me that in this situation you must know now that you are on the mines you are a man and must be able to face anything without fear. . . . To be called a man serves to encourage and console you time and again. . . . You will hear people saying "a man is a sheep, he does not cry" . . . no matter how hard you hit a sheep or slaughter it you will not hear it cry. . . . So, that is a comparison that whatever pain you can inflict on a man you will not see him cry. (P. 281)

Sex is viewed as necessary to men's health and well-being and a way of demonstrating one's manhood, and it is unsurprising to find that prostitute use, one of the few possibilities for leisure, is common amongst miners in South Africa (also in parts of Latin America where similar conditions exist; see Sutton 1994). If some of the men who live and work in these conditions are indifferent about questions as to why the prostitutes they use are willing to sell sex or questions about the age of the prostitutes they use, then their indifference merely mirrors the indifference that the rest of world feels toward them.

There are other reasons to exercise caution when discussing sanctions against those who sexually exploit children. Consider, for example, the fact that there are places in the world where it is estimated that between 15 and 30 percent of those working in prostitution are under the age of 18 and that up to 75 percent of the male population engage or have engaged in prostitute use (Anderson and O'Connell Davidson 2002; Brown 2000). In such places, proposals to give custodial sentences to anyone who buys sex from a minor could translate into proposals to incarcerate more than half the male population. Custodial sentences would be equally problematic in contexts in which people become involved in the

sex trade as third-party beneficiaries simply because this is their only real possibility for economic survival. Calls for the incarceration of all perpetrators of CSEC do not always or necessarily represent either a realistic or a humane response to the problem.

Feminist abolitionist analyses of prostitution as a social problem may be grounded in a deeper critique of patriarchal power structures, but it is perfectly possible for states to act on calls to penalize the buyer without even beginning to address the power relations that underpin either the supply or demand side of child prostitution. Indeed, an emphasis on punishing those who buy sex from children helps to discursively construct CSEC as a problem of individual morality and to deflect attention from the global and national economic, social, and political inequalities that underpin it. For example, instead of addressing the question of why refugee and displaced children are so often forced to live in such appalling circumstances that prostitution and/or other forms of sexual-economic exchange become their only or best means of subsisting, politicians can speak of their abhorrence for the individual aid workers and peacekeepers who exploit them, and claim to have addressed the problem by disciplining the few "bad apples" in an otherwise healthy barrel.

An emphasis on the morality of the sex buyer also clouds important questions about the more general and widespread social devaluation of poor and abandoned children. Where street children are popularly stereotyped as thieving, manipulative, unnatural, and immoral beings and referred to as "cockroaches" and "vermin," it is very easy for an adult to rationalise acts of sexual abuse against them. They do not count as children, and they are unworthy of care or protection. Brazil is notorious for the prevalence of such attitudes (see Huggins and Mesquita 2000) but is certainly not alone in tolerating the dehumanisation and even murder of street children. Indeed, governments implicitly endorse the idea that poor children are unworthy of care every time they cut the social and welfare spending that might otherwise provide a safety net for such children. The same points need to be made in relation to global economic governance, for in many cases, children are made increasingly vulnerable to commercial sexual exploitation by macroeconomic policies being enforced by the

International Monetary Fund (IMF) to reduce domestic expenditure and increase interest rates (Rhodes 1999).

In short, moral distinctions between those who are directly involved in CSEC as buyers or third parties and those who are not are much finer than many people care to recognise. Clients and nonclients alike inhabit a world in which prostitution is the only thing that stands between millions of people (adult and child) and the absolute indignities implied by poverty; clients and nonclients alike live in a world in which girls and women, sometimes also boys and men, are sexualised, denied access to educational and employment opportunities, and excluded from communities as a consequence of rape or abuse or sexual orientation or sexual choices they have made, or by virtue of their racial or ethnic identities or their status as noncitizens. And together, governments and world financial institutions play a central role in perpetuating the existence of such a world. So long as these facts are accepted, whether out of indifference or resignation, we all of us carry a degree of moral culpability for the phenomenon of CSEC.

There is a final and very important reason to urge caution about calling for extensions of the state's punitive powers with regard to prostitution, adult or child. In most countries of the world, the civil and human rights of females who work in prostitution are routinely, and often grossly, violated. Prostitutes variously face arbitrary detention, deportation, forcible eviction from their dwellings; enforced health checks, including HIV testing; forcible "rehabilitation"; corporal punishment; and even execution. Few states offer prostitutes adequate protection from violent crime or abusive employers, and prostitutes are frequently victims of crimes perpetrated by corrupt law enforcement agents, including rape, beatings, and extortion. The scale and severity of the human rights violations perpetrated against female prostitutes in the contemporary world was recognised in the 1992 general recommendation made by the Convention for the Elimination of All Forms of Discrimination Against Women (CEDAW) to include prostitutes among those who needed to be offered equal protection under the law (Kempadoo and Ghuma 1999:293; see also Alexander 1997).

Since states are amongst those who most consistently violate prostitutes' rights, it would be naive to trust that calls for stronger legal controls over those who exploit children within prostitution will automatically produce desirable outcomes for either prostitute women or teenagers. Indeed, crackdowns on CSEC and trafficking have often had extremely negative consequences for both adults and adolescents working in prostitution, and the numbers of people arrested for sexually exploiting children in prostitution generally pale into insignificance next to the numbers of women and teenagers arrested for prostitution and/or immigration offences. There is a great deal of work to be done in terms of changing attitudes toward prostitution and creating legal and social environments that are protective of female prostitutes' human rights before we can be confident that calls for tighter and more extensive criminalization of CSEC will not continue to have these unintended and undesirable consequences.

Toward a More Complicated and Differentiated Vision of the Problem of CSEC

Questions about childhood, sexuality, and commercial sex can be hugely controversial, and those who campaign against CSEC often attempt to sidestep disagreements by focusing on aspects of abuse and exploitation upon which there is most agreement. In practice, this means keeping the focus firmly on the sexual use of younger children. Thus, we find that public awareness-raising materials produced by children's rights NGOs, through the use of particular images (broken rose buds, discarded toys, small children being led away by large, shadowy male figures) and examples of cases involving children aged between 3 and 12, have tended to stress the sexual exploitation of young children rather than adolescents.

While the impulse to stick to uncontroversial, common ground is understandable, it also carries certain risks. It leads to an emphasis on sexual abuse and CSEC as the violation of childhood "innocence," and in so doing, suggests that a particular model of childhood (as a state of passivity and dependence) can be universalised and extended to cover both young children and adolescents up to the age of 18. The general dangers of a discourse about child sexual abuse and exploitation as the theft, shattering, rape, or betrayal of "innocence" have been incisively discussed by Jenny Kitzinger (1997). This discourse also poses particular problems in relation to our vision of, and response to, those who sexually exploit children, since it allows participants in policy debates to evade the complexity of CSEC as a social problem.

At the time of writing, many people are increasingly concerned about how quickly and easily politicians can reduce complex geopolitical issues to simple fairy tales about "evil" and monstrous Others who must be "smoked out" and exposed to the "infinite justice" of good, liberty-loving democrats. I believe we need to be equally wary of much of the rhetoric surrounding children's involvement in the sex trade. It is becoming commonplace to remark that CSEC is a global problem and to call for greater cooperation between states in order to police it. But CSEC is not an international problem simply because those who exploit children cross national borders to do so. It is also an international problem because the factors that precipitate children's entry into prostitution and increase their vulnerability within it are global, as well as national and local, as indeed are many of the factors that stimulate the demand for prostitution. The discursive reduction of CSEC to a threat posed by child rapists, traffickers, and paedophiles serves to obscure the economic, social, and political realities that underpin the involvement of men, women, and children in commercial sex trade; it also serves to sideline questions about the mass of ordinary people who provide the demand for commercial sex, including commercial sex with persons under the age of 18. It also turns the problem of CSEC into something external to our own societies. And yet in reality, the problem is very much part of *us,* for both the supply and the demand side of the global sex trade are by-products of inequalities and injustices that are routinely tolerated.

Instead of accepting fairy tales about those who commercially sexually exploit children as the essence of all that is most monstrous and evil, we need to work to redress the inequalities that underpin the market for commercial sex. We also need to transform the ordinary, everyday attitudes and beliefs about gender, race, sexuality, age, economic life, and prostitution that make it possible for ordinary people to use but deny, justify, or humanize the powers such inequalities bequeath them.

NOTE

1. This suggests that demand for sex with prepubertal children is not a common or widespread feature of the commercial sex market and that those who have a specific wish to sexually exploit young children generally use alternative structures to access those children. Whilst such structures may in some cases be parasitic on the mainstream commercial sex trade, they can also operate independently of it. For instance, people who conform to the clinical definition of paedophilia sometimes group together to form clubs or networks through which to exchange images of young children being sexually abused or to "share" victims of abuse amongst themselves. Other structures that can be used to secure sexual access to young children include those that allow for the adoption, fostering, and institutional care of children, as well as systems through which rural children are sent to live and work in more affluent households in urban areas. We should also note that in most countries, mechanisms to monitor and protect young children who are brought into the country by a real or supposed relative are woefully inadequate, and it is therefore possible that children are transported in this way and then sold on to abusers. There is a need for more research on this subject, since at present, there is simply no way of knowing how many such structures exist or how many children are affected by them (End Child Prostitution, Pornography and Trafficking in Children for Sexual Purposes [ECPAT] UK 2001).

REFERENCES

Aggleton, P., ed. 1999. *Men Who Sell Sex: International Perspectives on Male Prostitution and HIV/AIDS.* London, England: UCL.

Alexander, P. 1997. "Feminism, Sex Workers' Rights and Human Rights." Pp. 83–97 in *Whores and Other Feminists,* edited by J. Nagle. London, England: Routledge.

Allison, A. 1994. *Nightwork: Sexuality, Pleasure and Corporate Masculinity in a Tokyo Hostess Club.* Chicago, IL: University of Chicago Press.

Anderson, B. and J. O'Connell Davidson. 2002. *Trafficking—A Demand Led Problem?* Stockholm, Sweden: Save the Children Sweden, SIDA, Swedish Ministry of Foreign Affairs.

Antonius-Smits, C. et al. 1999. "Gold and Commercial Sex: Exploring the Link between Small-Scale Gold Mining and Commercial Sex in the Rainforest of Suriname." In *Sun, Sex, and Gold: Tourism and Sex Work in the Caribbean,* edited by K. Kempadoo. Oxford, England: Rowman and Littlefield.

Asian Migrant Centre (AMC). *2000: Asian Migrant Yearbook 2000: Migration Facts, Analysis and Issues in 1999.* Hong Kong: Author.

Bagley, C. 1999. "Child and Adolescent Prostitution in Canada and the Philippines: Comparative Case Studies and Policy Proposals." In *Child Sexual Abuse and Adult Offenders: New Theory and Research,* edited by C. Bagley and M. Kanka. Aldershot, England: Ashgate.

Barry, K. 1995. *The Prostitution of Sexuality.* New York: New York University Press.

Bindman, J. 1997. *Redefining Prostitution as Sex Work on the International Agenda.* London, England: Anti-Slavery International.

Brock, D. 1998. *Making Work, Making Trouble: Prostitution as a Social Problem.* Toronto, Canada: University of Toronto Press.

Brown, L. 2000. *Sex Slaves: The Trafficking of Women in Asia.* London, England: Virago.

Campbell, C. 2001. "'Going Underground and Going After Women': Masculinity and HIV Transmission amongst Black Workers on the Gold Mines." In *Changing Men in Southern Africa,* edited by R. Morrell. London, England: Zed.

Cassirer, B. 1992. *Travel & the Single Male.* Channel Island, CA: TSM.

Castells, M. 1998. *End of Millennium.* Oxford, England: Blackwell.

COIN. 1992. *Viaje al Exterior: Ilusiones y Mentiras (Exportacion de Sexo Organizado).* Santo Domingo, Dominican Republic: Author.

Economic and Social Commission for Asia and the Pacific (ESCAP). 2000. *Sexually Abused and Sexually Exploited Children and Youth in the Greater Mekong Subregion.* New York: United Nations.

End Child Prostitution, Pornography and Trafficking in Children for Sexual Purposes (ECPAT UK). 2001. *The Trafficking of Children into the UK for Sexual Purposes.* London, England: Author.

Enloe, C. 1993. *The Morning After: Sexual Politics at the End of the Cold War.* Berkeley, CA: University of California Press.

Ennew, J. 1986. *The Sexual Exploitation of Children.* Cambridge, England: Polity.

Euler, C. and D. Welzer-Lang. 2000. *Developing Best Professional Practice for Reducing Sexual Abuse, Domestic Violence and Trafficking in Militarised Areas of Peacetime Europe.* The Research Centre on Violence, Abuse and Gender Relations, Leeds Metropolitan University, England.

Family Planning Association, Hong Kong (FPA HK). 2000. *Report on the Youth Sexuality Study, 1996.* Hong Kong: Author.

Fiengold, D. 1998. "Sex, Drugs and the IMF: Some Implications of 'Structural Adjustment' for the Trade in Heroin, Girls and Women in the Upper Mekong Region." *Refuge* 17 (5).

——. 2000. "The Hell of Good Intentions: Some Preliminary Thoughts on Opium in the Political Ecology of the Trade in Girls and Women." In *Where China Meets Southeast Asia: Social and Cultural Change in the Border Regions,* edited by G. Evans, C. Hutton, and K. Eng. Singapore: Institute of Southeast Asian Studies.

Foggo, D. 2002. "It's Like a Sweet Shop: If This Girl's Not Right, Get Another." *Telegraph,* September 15, pp. 12–13.

Gender-Aids Forum. 2001. Retrieved from http://www.hivnet.ch:8000/topics/gender-aids/.

Geras, N. 1998. *The Contract of Mutual Indifference.* Cambridge, England: Polity.

Gibson, B. 1995. *Male Order: Stories from Boys Who Sell Sex.* London, England: Cassell.

Haavio-Mannila, E. and A. Rotkirch. 2000. "Gender Liberalisation and Polarisation: Comparing Sexuality in St. Petersburg, Finland and Sweden." *The Finnish Review of East European Studies* 7 (3–4):4–25.

Huggins, M. and M. Mesquita. 2000. "Civic Invisibility, Marginality and Moral Exclusion: The Murders of Street Youth in Brazil." Pp. 257–82 in *Children on the Streets of the Americas,* edited by R. Mickelson. London, England: Routledge.

Human Rights Watch. 2000. *Owed Justice: Thai Women Trafficked into Debt Bondage in Japan.* New York: Human Rights Watch.

International Organisation for Migration (IOM). 1996a. *Trafficking in Women to Italy for Sexual Exploitation.* Geneva, Switzerland: Author.

——. 1996b. *Trafficking in Women from the Dominican Republic for Sexual Exploitation.* Budapest, Hungary: Author.

Jeffreys, S. 1997. *The Idea of Prostitution.* Melbourne, Australia: Spinifex.

Kadjar-Hamouda, E. 1996. *An End to Silence: A Preliminary Study on Sexual Violence, Abuse and Exploitation of Children Affected by Armed Conflict.* Geneva, Switzerland: NGO Group for the Convention on the Rights of the Child.

Kane, S. 1993. "Prostitution and the Military in Belize: Planning AIDS Intervention in Belize." *Social Science and Medicine* 36 (7):965–79.

Kelly, L. and L. Regan. 2000. *Rhetorics and Realities: Sexual Exploitation of Children in Europe.* London, England: Child and Woman Abuse Studies Unit.

Kempadoo, K., ed. 1999. *Sun, Sex, and Gold: Tourism and Sex Work in the Caribbean.* Oxford, England: Rowman and Littlefield.

Kempadoo, K. and J. Doezema, eds. 1998. *Global Sex Workers: Rights, Resistance and Redefinition.* New York: Routledge.

Kempadoo, K. and R. Ghuma. 1999. "For the Children: Trends in International Policies and Law on Sex Tourism." In *Sun, Sex and Gold: Tourism and Sex Work in the Caribbean,* edited by K. Kempadoo. Lanham, MD: Rowman and Littlefield.

Kitzinger, J. 1997. "Who Are You Kidding? Children, Power and the Struggle against Sexual Abuse." In *Constructing and Reconstructing Childhood: Contemporary Issues in the Sociological Study of Childhood,* edited by A. James and A. Prout. London, England: Falmer.

Kleibe, D. and M. Wilke. 1995. "AIDS and Sex Tourism: Conclusions Drawn from a Study of the Social and Psychological Characteristics of German Sex Tourists." In *AIDS in Europe: The Behavioural Aspect,* vol. 2, *Risk Behaviour and Its Determinants,* edited by D. Friedrich and W. Heckmann. Berlin, Germany: Edition Sigma.

Kruhse-Mount Burton, S. 1995. "Sex Tourism and Traditional Australian Male Identity." In *International Tourism: Identity and Change,* edited by M. Lafabt, J. Allcock, and E. Bruner. London, England: Sage.

Kumar, B. 2001. *Nepal: Trafficking in Girls with Special Reference to Prostitution: A Rapid Assessment.* Geneva, Switzerland: International Labour Organization, International Programme on the Elimination of Child Labour.

Laqueur, T. 1995. "The Social Evil, the Solitary Vice, and Pouring Tea." In *Solitary Pleasures,* edited by Paula Bennett and Vernon Rosario. New York: Routledge.

Lee-Wright, P. 1990. *Child Slaves.* London, England: Earthscan.

Leridon, H., G. Zesson, and M. Hubert. 1998. "The Europeans and Their Sexual Partners." In *Sexual Behaviour and HIV/AIDS in Europe,* edited by M. Hubert, N. Bajos, and T. Sandfort. London, England: UCL.

Lever, J. and D. Dolnick. 2000. "Clients and Call Girls: Seeking Sex and Intimacy." In *Sex for Sale,* edited by R. Weitzer. New York: Routledge.

Lim, L. 1998. *The Sex Sector: The Economic and Social Bases of Prostitution in Southeast Asia.* Geneva, Switzerland: ILO.

Månsson, Sven-Axel. 2001. "Prostitutes' Clients and the Image of Men and Masculinity in Late Modern Society." In *Globalising Men,* edited by B. Pease and K. Pringle. London, England: Zed.

Mayorga, L. and P. Velasquez. 1999. "Bleak Pasts, Bleak Futures: Life Paths of Thirteen Young Prostitutes in Cartagena, Colombia." In *Sun, Sex, and Gold: Tourism and Sex Work in the Caribbean,* edited by K. Kempadoo. Oxford, England: Rowman and Littlefield.

Meisch, L. 1995. "Gringas and Otavalenos: Changing Tourist Relations." *Annals of Tourism Research* 22 (2):441–62.

Melrose, M., D. Barrett, and I. Brodie. 1999: *One Way Street? Retrospectives on Childhood Prostitution.* London, England: Children's Society.

Mickelson, R., ed. 2000. *Children on the Streets of the Americas.* London, England: Routledge.

Montgomery, H. 1998. "Children, Prostitution and Identity: A Case Study from a Tourist Resort in Thailand." In *Global Sex Workers,* edited by K. Kempadoo and J. Doezema. London, England: Routledge.

Monto, M. 2000. "Why Men Seek Out Prostitutes." In *Sex for Sale,* edited by R. Weitzer. New York: Routledge.

Moon, K. 1997. *Sex Among Allies.* New York: Columbia University Press.

Nagel, J., ed. 1997. *Whores and Other Feminists.* London, England: Routledge.

Nencel, L. 2001. *Ethnography and Prostitution in Peru.* London, England: Pluto.

O'Connell Davidson, J. 1997. "Does She Do Queening? Prostitution and Sovereignty." In *Reclaiming Sovereignty,* edited by L. Brace and J. Hoffman. London, England: Cassell.

———. 1998. *Prostitution, Power and Freedom.* Cambridge, England: Polity.

———. 2001a. *Children in the Sex Trade in China.* Stockholm, Sweden: Save the Children Sweden.

———. 2001b. "The Sex Tourist, the Expatriate, His Ex-Wife and Her 'Other': The Politics of Loss, Difference and Desire." *Sexualities* 4 (1):5–24.

———. 2001c. "The Sex Exploiter." Theme paper for the Second World Congress Against the Commercial Sexual Exploitation of Children, December, Yokohama, Japan.

O'Connell Davidson, J. and J. Sánchez Taylor. 1996a. "Child Prostitution: Beyond the Stereotypes." In *Thatcher's Children? Politics, Childhood and Society in the 1980s and 90s,* edited by J. Pilcher and S. Wagg. London, England: Falmer.

———. 1996b. *Child Prostitution and Sex Tourism in the Dominican Republic.* Research paper. Bangkok: ECPAT.

O'Connell Davidson, J. 2001. *Children in the Sex Trade in the Caribbean.* Stockholm, Sweden: Save the Children Sweden.

O'Neill, M. and R. Barberet. 2000. "Victimization and the Social Organisation of Prostitution in England and Spain." In *Sex for Sale,* edited by R. Weitzer. New York: Routledge.

Patterson, O. 1982. *Slavery and Social Death.* Cambridge, MA: Harvard University Press.

Phongpaichit, P. 1999. "Trafficking in People in Thailand." In *Illegal Immigration and Commercial Sex: The New Slave Trade,* edited by P. Williams. London, England: Frank Cass.

Posner, M. 2000. "Hungry Hearts: Runaway and Homeless Youth in the United States." Pp. 247–56 in *Children on the Streets of the Americas,* edited by R. Mickelson. London, England: Routledge.

Pyne, H. H. 1995. "AIDS and Gender Violence: The Enslavement of Burmese Women in the Thai Sex Industry." In *Women's Rights, Human Rights: International Feminist Perspectives,* edited by J. Peters and A. Wolper. New York: Routledge.

Raymond, J. 2001. *Guide to the New UN Trafficking Protocol.* North Amherst, MA: CATW.

Ren, X. 1993. "China." In *Prostitution,* edited by N. Davis. Westport, CT: Greenwood.

Rhodes, D. 1999. *Poverty in East Asia.* Hong Kong: Community Aid Abroad.

Rusakova, M. 2001. *The Commercial Sexual Exploitation of Children in St. Petersburg and North West Russia.* Stockholm, Sweden: Save the Children Sweden.

Saeed, F. 2002. *Taboo! The Hidden Culture of a Red Light Area.* Oxford, England: Oxford University Press.

Sánchez Taylor, J. 2001. "Dollars Are a Girl's Best Friend? Female Tourists' Sexual Behaviour in the Caribbean." *Sociology* 35 (3):749-64.

Seabrook, J. 1996. *Travels in the Skin Trade: Tourism and the Sex Industry.* London, England: Pluto.

Siden, A. 2002. *Warte Mal! Prostitution after the Velvet Revolution.* London, England: Hayward Gallery.

Silvestre, E. J. Rijo, and H. Bogaert. 1994. *La Neo-Prostitucion Infantil en Republica Dominicana.* Santo Domingo, Dominican Republic: UNICEF.

Sturdevant, S. and B. Stoltzfus. 1992: *Let the Good Times Role: Prostitution and the U.S. Military in Asia.* New York: New Press.

Sutton, A. 1994. *Slavery in Brazil.* London, England: Anti-Slavery International.

Svensson, B. 2000. *Victims and Perpetrators: On Sexual Abuse and Treatment.* Stockholm, Sweden: Save the Children Sweden.

Tampep. 1999. *Health, Migration and Sex Work: The Experience of Tampep.* Amsterdam, The Netherlands: A. de Graaf Stichting.

Tanaka, Y. 2002. *Japan's Comfort Women: Sexual Slavery and Prostitution During World War II and the U.S. Occupation.* London, England: Routledge.

Uddin, F., M. Sultana, and S. Mahmud. 2001. Revised and edited by M. Black and H. Goodman. *Childhood in the Red Light Zone: Growing Up in the Daulatdia and Kandapara Brothel Communities of Bangladesh.* Melbourne, Australia: Save the Children.

United Nations Commission on Human Rights (UNCHR). 2000. *Refugee Children and Adolescents: A Progress Report.* Executive Committee of the High Commissioner's Programme.

U.S. Agency for International Development (USAID). 2000. *Children on the Brink.* Washington, DC: Author.

——. 2001. *Trafficking in Persons: USAID's Response.* Washington, DC: Author.

Verhaert, P., P. Van Damme, R. Van Cleempoel, R. Verbist, R. Vranckx, and A. Meheus. 1993. *Sero-Epidemiology Study on Syphilis, Hepatitis B and HIV among Seafarers in Antwerp.* Conference proceedings on Second International Symposium on Maritime Health, Antwerp, Belgium.

Ward, T., S. Hudson, and T. Keenan. 2000. "The Assessment and Treatment of Sexual Offenders against Children." Pp. 349–61 in *Handbook of Offender Assessment and Treatment,* edited by C. Hollin. London, England: Wiley.

Wellings, K., J. Field, A. Johnson, and J. Wadworth, with S. Bradshaw. 1993. *Sexual Behaviour in Britain: The National Survey of Sexual Attitudes and Lifestyles.* Harmondsworth, England: Penguin.

West, D. 1992. *Male Prostitution.* London, England: Duckworth.

Williams, P., ed. 1999. *Illegal Immigration and Commercial Sex: The New Slave Trade.* London, England: Frank Cass.

Williams, S. 1999. "Commercial Sexual Exploitation of Children in Jamaica." University of the West Indies, School of Continuing Studies, Caribbean Child Development Centre, Mona, Kingston, Jamaica. Unpublished report.

Xie Guangmao. 2000. "Women and Social Change along the Vietnam-Guangxi Border." In *Where China Meets Southeast Asia: Social and Cultural Change in the Border Regions,* edited by G. Evans, C. Hutton, and K. Eng. Singapore: Institute of Southeast Asian Studies.

MENTAL ILLNESS AS A SOCIAL PROBLEM

HOWARD B. KAPLAN

Texas A&M University

No human condition is intrinsically problematic in any group. It becomes socially problematic when it is defined as such, whether by the population at large or by some segment of the population that is particularly influential in developing and implementing social policy directed toward forestalling or alleviating the conditions evaluated as undesirable. The condition may be labeled as socially undesirable either because it is intrinsically noxious or has intrinsically distressful consequences.

Mental illness has been defined as such a problematic condition because it is intrinsically distressing, it impedes the proper performance of social roles, whether by the afflicted individual or those with whom the individual interacts, or otherwise has consequences that are deemed dysfunctional for the social system. Not the least of these

consequences are the social costs of providing responses (preventative or therapeutic programs) aimed at forestalling or assuaging the symptoms of mental illness.

Thus, major depression is now said to be the primary cause of disability, and mental disorders account for 4 of the top 10 causes of disability internationally (World Health Organization [WHO] 2001).

Mental illness is socially problematic not only because of its consequences but also in the sense that among the causes are a wide range of social conditions and circumstances. The resolution of the social problem requires that these factors be recognized and taken into account in the formulation of policies aimed at forestalling or assuaging the magnitude of the problem.

Finally, mental illness is socially problematic because of the absence of a broad consensus on the

Author's Note: This work was supported by research grants (R01 DA 02497 and R01 DA 10016) and by a Career Scientist Award (K05 DA 00136) to the author from the National Institute on Drug Abuse.

561

nature of mental illness. Without consensus, it is not possible to gauge the extent of mental illness in the population and therefore to plan for the number and kind of preventative or remedial services that would be required to obviate or relieve the symptoms. Nor would it be possible, in the absence of consensus, to address the causes that form the basis for social planning to prevent or eradicate the conditions that might consensually be defined as mental illness.

In the following pages, we consider in turn these three socially problematic aspects of mental illness: the processes by which states that are designated as mental illness come to be socially defined as problematic; the social causation of the conditions that are socially designated as mental illness; and the social consequences of mental illness.

DEFINING MENTAL ILLNESS AS SOCIALLY PROBLEMATIC

From the social problem perspective, the definition of mental illness is central to two issues. The first issue concerns the socially constructed nature of mental illness and the reality of the referents of the construct. The second issue relates to the prevalence and distribution of cases according to whatever concepts and measures of mental illness have gained favor in the society.

Mental Illness as a Social Construct

At the outset, the distinction must be drawn between the social attribution of mental illness and the phenomena that evoke the attribution. Behaviors, including the communications of thoughts, feelings, and perceptions, may appear universally but be attributed to mental illness only in certain societies. In other societies, the behaviors in question may be attributed to simple malevolence or physical illness. The responses that are signs of mental illness may be incorporated into social roles as appropriate to those roles. The social roles themselves may be defined as deviant, but in those deviant roles, the behaviors may be appropriate to the role. Even in societies in which the concept of mental illness exists, the groups of which the individual is a part may find the attribution of mental illness to be too

threatening to the continuity of the group and so may be normalized or otherwise defined in more acceptable terms, such as "eccentric" rather than "mad." Whether or not certain behaviors or the psychological structures that are inferred from such behaviors will be interpreted as indications of mental illness depends upon the cultural context, including the social identities of the individuals displaying the behaviors.

When and where the concept of mental illness or some functionally equivalent term exists, behavioral manifestations or putative underlying psychological structures that are said to be indicative of mental illness fall within one or more of the following categories:

1. *Severe and Prolonged Subjective Distress.* Whether or not the occurrence of severe and prolonged and subjective distress is understandable in light of an individual's unfortunate life circumstances, the presence of distressful states such as chronic depression or anxiety are often taken to be indicative of mental illness. The affective states are intrinsically undesirable and, furthermore, may have consequences that are socially undesirable, as when chronic depression results in social withdrawal and the concomitant failure to perform normal social roles, and so prevents performance of complementary social roles.

2. *Affective or Cognitive Aberrations.* A wide variety of situationally inappropriate affective and cognitive responses are taken to be indicative of mental illness regardless of the cause of the aberrations. Included under this rubric would be impaired memory functions, sensory distortions, contrary-to-fact beliefs that resist change when confronted with reality, and euphoric responses in situations that are conventionally expected to produce dysphoric or affectively neutral responses. Loss of memory, cognitive confusion, or hallucinations due to a blow to the head or substance abuse would be included, as would delusions or hallucinations that are traceable to severe and prolonged distress and that function more or less effectively to assuage the distress (delusions of persecution may serve the function of justifying one's failure and at the same time signify that the subject is sufficiently important so as to elicit

persecutory responses). Euphoric emotional responses that are inappropriate or disproportionate to the situation, whether due to delusions, hallucinations, or substance abuse, would also be included under this rubric.

3. *Psychogenic Biological States.* Frequently, undesirable physical states are classified under the rubric of mental illness, particularly when they are regarded both as intrinsically undesirable and as traceable to psychogenic antecedents such as severe and prolonged subjective distress. Cases in point are unfortunate outcomes such as hysterical blindness, catatonic states, and psychophysiological disorders.

4. *Psychogenic Behaviors.* Many overt behaviors are said to be indicative of mental illness when they are both intrinsically undesirable and are directly or indirectly caused by prior impairments of cognitive or affective functions, that is, are outcomes of the first two categories of indicators of mental illness. Cases in point include violent behaviors that result from delusional beliefs ("the devil made me do it"), buying sprees that stem from manic disorders, and deviant behaviors that reflect attempts to forestall or assuage distressful feelings of self-derogation, as when substance abuse reflects the attempt to avoid circumstances that give rise to distressful self-feelings and when violence represents the need to attack the validity of conventional standards according to which the person must regard himself or herself as unworthy (Kaplan 1986, 1996).

The conception of mental illness, particularly in contemporary Western cultures, has overwhelmingly been influenced by the dicta of the psychiatric profession. The pronouncements of this group serve as the gold standard for describing what is and what is not mental illness. For the psychiatrist, "mental illness" refers to "a spectrum of syndromes that are classified by clusters of symptoms and behaviors considered clinically meaningful in terms of course, outcome, and response to treatment" (Bruce 1999:37). Arguably, the categorization of forms of mental illness most widely used in the world today takes the form of the American Psychiatric Association's *Diagnostic and Statistic Manual of Mental Disorders (DSM-IV-tr).*

Particular behaviors or cognitive and affective processes are labeled as mental illness by professionals with greater or lesser success depending upon a number of features of the social interaction among the professionals and their acquiescence or resistance to political influence. As Switzer, Dew, and Bromet (1999) observe:

> Numerous examples of the influence of social and political context on the definition and assessment of mental disorders can be found simply by charting the flow of diagnostic categories into and out of the DSM. The recent creation and addition of posttraumatic stress disorder (PTSD) to the DSM was a direct result of concerted post–Vietnam War lobbying efforts by American military veterans. The elimination of homosexuality as a diagnostic category was a result of lobbying by gay and lesbian organizations, changes in prevailing societal attitudes, and the greater willingness on the part of the medical community to acknowledge the lack of empirical evidence that homosexuality reflects psychopathology. (P. 97)

The definition of mental illness as the public and psychiatric profession conceive of it has important implications for setting public policy. The most significant issue stemming from the conceptualization of mental illness is the judgment of the magnitude of the social problem.

Estimating Prevalence of Mental Illness

Surveys in a range of developed countries suggest that more than 25 percent of persons manifest one or more mental (including behavioral) disorder(s) during their lifetimes (Almeida-Filho et al. 1997; Wells et al. 1989; WHO 2001). However, the rates vary from country to country, and so do the estimates of services that will be required to deal with the social problem that is mental illness. We will focus on the United States as a case in point, recognizing the uncertainties in estimating the prevalence of mental disorder(s) there and in other countries (WHO 2001).

Satisfaction of the need for general population data on the prevalence and distribution of various forms of mental illness was facilitated by the development of the Diagnostic Interview Schedule (DIS) (Robins et al. 1981), a research diagnostic interview that could be administered by trained lay interviewers. This instrument was initially used in the Epidemiologic Catchment Area (ECA) study of over 20,000 respondents interviewed in five separate community epidemiological surveys (Robins and Regier 1991).

Since the ECA study was carried out in metropolitan areas, the results do not generalize to the portion of the population living in rural areas. In part, this limitation was addressed by the National Comorbidity Survey (NCS), funded by the National Institute of Mental Health (NIMH), using a sample said to be representative of the entire United States (Kessler et al. 1994). The NCS interview used the Composite International Diagnostic Interview (CIDI), a modified version of the DIS (Robins et al. 1988). Many of the accepted generalizations regarding the distribution of psychiatric disorders in the community are based upon the results of the ECA and NCS studies (Kessler and Zhao 1999). After adjustments were made for methodological differences, the two studies were observed to be similar in disorder-specific or overall prevalence rates.

According to the NCS (Kessler et al. 1994), approximately 50 percent of the sample reported a lifetime history of at least one of the psychiatric disorders surveyed. Approximately 31 percent of the sample reported at least one disorder during the preceding year. The most common single disorder was major depression. When considering broad classes of disorders, addictive disorders and anxiety disorders were more prevalent than mood disorders or other disorders. When considering the year prior to the interview, anxiety disorders were the most prevalent (Kessler and Zhao 1999).

When considering only *severe and persistent mental illness* (including nonaffective psychosis, bipolar disorder, severe forms of major depression, autism, panic disorder, and obsessive-compulsive disorder) or *serious mental illness* (including those disorders that markedly interfere with major life activities), excluding addictive disorders from either definition, the 12-month prevalence rates for these two categories were estimated to be 2.6 percent and 5.4 percent, respectively. The least-inclusive category of serious and persistent mental illness encompassed an estimated 4.8 million afflicted individuals. The more inclusive category of serious mental illness encompassed 10 million individuals. If

institutionalized residents are included, an additional 2.2 million people are estimated to have serious and persistent mental illness, numbering 12.2 million in the total population (Kessler and Zhao 1999).

The mental illnesses that are counted in the general population tend to be concentrated in a relatively small proportion of the population. As Kessler and Zhao (1999) observe,

> Only 21% of all the lifetime disorders occurred to respondents with a lifetime history of just one disorder, which means that the vast majority of lifetime disorders (79%) are comorbid disorders. . . . Close to six out of every ten (58.9%) disorders in the past year, and nearly nine out of ten (89.5%) severe disorders during this time, occurred to the 14% of the sample having a lifetime history of three or more disorders. These results show that . . . the major burden of psychiatric disorder is concentrated in a group of highly comorbid people who constitute about one-sixth of the population. (Pp. 136–37)

Such descriptive epidemiology of the mentally ill is a necessary tool for public advocacy. Arguments could be made regarding the need for mental health services and their location on the basis of the number and kinds of cases that were counted in the population, their distribution according to social characteristics, and their presence in various geographic areas. However, in evaluating the utility, reliability, and validity of concepts and methods employed in the study of mental illness, we must never lose sight of the fact that evaluations in this regard are the outcome of social influence processes and have no worth except insofar as they reflect what is problematic from the perspective of particular socionormative frameworks.

Social Causation of Mental Illness

From a global perspective, it is apparent that the correlates of mental illness are highly variable. Rates of suicide are relatively high in rural areas of China. At the same time, it has been observed that in low- and middle-income countries, poverty in urban areas summarizes a range of stressors that foreshadow or are otherwise associated with psychiatric disorders

(Desjarlais et al. 1995; WHO 2001). Common psychiatric disorders have been observed to be about twice as prevalent among the poor as among the rich in surveys of Brazil, Chile, India, and Zimbabwe (Patel et al. 1999).

Unique concatenations of causes have been postulated for patterns of mental health and illness in different countries, including, for example, the breakdown of traditional forms of social structures in African societies during colonial rule and dislocations stemming from armed conflicts and other disasters in African and Asian societies (Desjarlais et al. 1995).

Variability is observed as well in the forms of psychiatric disorder that are observed transnationally. Thus, the ratio of brief reactive psychoses to schizophrenia may be lower in Europe and North America than in certain underdeveloped societies (Desjarlais et al. 1995). The range of psychosocial factors affecting the onset and stability of various forms of mental illness is perhaps most apparent in the studies conducted in the United States.

The design and implementation of effective public responses to mental illness depends upon an understanding of the causes of the genesis and continuity of mental disorders. While not ignoring the impact of biogenetic, environmental, and other factors, it is widely recognized that social structures and processes exert important influences on the genesis, continuity, and mode of expression of mental disorders. The literature addressing the social causation of mental illness primarily addresses four issues: the effects of social identities on the genesis of mental illness; intervening social stress-related processes; social factors that influence the form or expression of mental illness; and factors that influence the (dis)continuity of mental illness.

Social Identities and Mental Illness

Every person has numerous social identities that specify the rights and obligations incumbent upon that person within a network of social relationships. These identities are frequently considered to be among the more powerful explanatory constructs employed in the study of the social causation of mental illness (Kaplan 1972). The significance of social identities for the genesis of mental illness

may be illustrated with reference to the literature relating to social identities differentiated according to socioeconomic status, race/ethnicity, marital and parental status, and employment/occupational statuses.

Socioeconomic Status (SES). One of the more robust findings in the literature on mental illness is the inverse relationship between SES and mental health status. For example, in a follow-up of a community sample 16 years later, lower-SES subjects were observed to have a greater probability of developing first episodes of depression and anxiety during the intervening years (Murphy et al. 1991). The inverse relationship between SES and prevalence of mental illness observed in the United States has also been observed in countries throughout the world (Desjarlais et al. 1995).

SES influences mental illness through a number of intervening processes. Lower SES increases the number of stressors one experiences and also is associated with paucity of resources that might have mitigated stress (McLeod and Kessler 1990). SES is positively related to occupations characterized by direction, control, and planning; and such occupations are less likely to be associated with depression (Link, Lennon, and Dohrenwend 1993). Poverty, or its correlates, such as being on welfare rolls, is intrinsically stigmatizing and often leads to feelings of self-inefficacy and related dysphoric moods (Goodban 1985; Popkin 1990).

Living in impoverished neighborhoods, in addition to being intrinsically distressing, may exhaust ability to cope with stress, cause the adoption of (mal)adaptive defense mechanisms such as chronic mistrust or suspicion, and erode feelings of having control over one's own destiny, with the result that the residents despair of ever improving their lot, a loss of hope that is reflected in severe depression (Halpern 1993; Massey and Denton 1993; McLeod and Nonnemaker 1999; Wilson 1991).

Race/Ethnicity. Numerous studies report associations between race or ethnicity and mental illness. For example, Hispanics manifest higher prevalence of both mood disorders and active comorbidity compared with non-Hispanic whites (Kessler and Zhao 1999).

Different ethnic and racial groups evoke differential degrees of esteem or derogation in the general population. This translates into internalization of self-concepts that are self-accepting or self-derogating. Intrinsically distressing self-attitudes, in turn, evoke stress-inducing coping patterns (e.g., hypervigilance) and in the extreme, psychopathological responses. Particular racial and ethnicity-based social identities also lead to adverse outcomes in the form of barriers to approximation of consensually valued goals. Failure to achieve such goals, in turn, increases the probability of pathological outcomes (Akbar 1991; Carter 1993; Essed 1991; Kaplan and Marks 1990).

The probability of perceiving personal traits as stigmatizing depends in part upon whether or not the traits in question are normative in the person's immediate social context. Thus, McLeod and Edwards (1995) reported that impoverished Hispanic and American Indian children living in areas where others were of like race and ethnicity had fewer internalizing and externalizing problems than children who lived in areas where other races and ethnicities were prevalent (Tweed et al. 1990).

The influence of race on psychiatric disorder is moderated by gender and SES. Thus, Williams and associates (1992) observed that low-SES African American women have higher rates of substance abuse disorders than low-SES whites. Unexpectedly, however, low-SES white males have higher rates of psychiatric illness than low-SES African Americans. Perhaps "low social status for a white male in a white-dominated culture may be so dissonant from societal expectations that it can produce serious psychological consequences" (Yu and Williams 1999:157). Alternatively, African Americans may have greater access to coping resources that mitigate the adverse effects of stress on mental health (Williams et al. 1997).

Marital and Parental Status. Separated, divorced, or widowed adults have higher rates of psychiatric disorders than married people. The relationship is stronger for certain disorders such as depression. In contrast, never-married people do not differ markedly from married people in lifetime prevalence rates, although they did have higher rates of disorders during the preceding 12 months (Kessler and Zhao 1999; Umberson and Williams 1999).

The relationship frequently observed between being married and the absence of depressive symptomatology may be accounted for in part by the influence of being married on greater perceptions of social support and mastery that, in turn, are inversely related to depressive symptomatology (Marks 1996; Mirowsky and Ross 1989; Ross and Mirowsky 1989; Turner and Marino 1994; Turner and Turner 1999). Mediating the relationship between divorce and adverse mental health status may well be the economic hardship and social isolation that is attendant upon single parenting, consequences that, in turn, increase the likelihood of poor mental health status (Kitson and Morgan 1990). The relationship between marital status and mental illness is a conditional one:

> So important is marital quality for women, in fact, that the current mental health of married women in bad marriages is worse than that of divorced women. The opposite is true of men, though, in whom mental health is better among those in bad marriages than among the divorced. (Kessler and Zhao 1999:143)

Divorce may be more threatening to white women than to African American women because divorce is more likely to carry a stigma among the former group (Gove and Shin 1989). For men, widowhood is more threatening because it requires adaptations that sorely test their sense of self-sufficiency (Umberson, Wortman, and Kessler 1992). Furthermore, perhaps because widowhood is less expected among the young, it has a more adverse effect on mental health status for the young (Gove and Shin 1989).

The relationship between entering into parenthood and adverse consequences for mental health status may be mediated by the negative impact of parenthood on marital quality and (especially for women) the greater responsibilities incumbent upon the new parents, responsibilities that they may not be prepared for (Cowan et al. 1985; Hackel and Ruble 1992; Nock and Kingston 1988). When certain moderating conditions are present (natural resources, child care, and social support), parenthood may be associated with greater mental health (Gove and Geerken 1977; Ross and Huber 1985; Ross, Mirowsky, and Huber 1983). In the absence of such supports, however, for women, demands of family and work place them in a conflict situation that leads to higher levels of depressive symptoms.

Employment and Occupational Status. Homemakers, the disabled, the unemployed, and the retired have higher lifetime prevalence rates of psychiatric disorder than workers and students. For 12-month prevalence rates, workers have better mental health than adults in all other categories (students, homemakers, the unemployed, disabled, and retired) combined (Kessler and Zhao 1999). Indirectly, macrosocial conditions such as the general state of the economy influence individual mental health both by increasing the probability of unemployment and (even for the employed) the perception of poor economic conditions and consequent stressful feelings of job insecurity (Brenner 1987; Catalano, Rook, and Dooley 1986).

Features of the job situation influence mental health. Thus, the experience of close supervision and the presence of job insecurity, as well as low income, affect mental health status for men but not for women (Adelmann 1987; Lennon 1987; Lowe and Northcott 1988; Miller 1980). In contrast, lower substantive complexity of work and the absence of helpful coworkers adversely affected the mental health status of women but not of men (Lowe and Northcott 1988; Miller 1980).

Social identities have consequences that under specified conditions influence mental health status for better or worse. These intervening and moderating factors in large measure reflect social stress-related processes.

Social Stress and Mental Health

The social stress process as it is related to mental illness implicates constructs related to stressful life events and role strain; intrapersonal and interpersonal mechanisms (coping and social support); negative self-feelings (self-derogation); and patterns of mental illness that either express negative self-feelings or serve as more or less effective modes of forestalling, assuaging, or otherwise coping with negative self-feelings and their causes.

Role Strain and Stressful Life Events. In the course of the socialization process, individuals learn to accept, and in varying degrees to value, their social identities and the obligations incumbent upon them when they occupy those identities. At different times in life, different identities and associated role obligations become more or less important. If the person fails to meet the standards that apply to these identities in a particular situation, then he or she will experience distressful self-rejecting feelings. The intensity of the distress experience will depend upon the value placed on the social identities and the associated obligations that the person fails to meet. For example, for highly valued social identities such as parent, how well one nurtures one's children is a salient standard for self-evaluation. The ongoing inability to fulfill role expectations associated with valued social identities is experienced as role strain.

Discrete experiences that have implications for fulfillment of role expectations and the occupancy of (dis)valued social identities represent stressful life events. Directly, events may induce stress by virtue of being intrinsically disvalued. The event reflects the anticipation or current experience of inability to fulfill felt obligations. Less directly, life events may be stress inducing through either of two pathways. First, life events may result in the disruption of the person's normal and characteristic ways of forestalling experiences of adverse life events, or mitigating the intensity and duration of concomitant subjective distress. Second, life events may impose new requirements on individuals, the fulfillment of which is problematic. To the extent that these new expectations are unfulfilled because they require resources that were heretofore adequate but are now inadequate, the person will experience a self-devaluating/stress-inducing sense of failure (Kaplan, Robbins, and Martin 1983).

Illustrations of the stressful effects of chronic role strain and life events associated with particular social identities abound in the literature. Chronic role strains may result, for example, from serving as a caregiver to a mentally ill family member or from conflicts in societal and occupational roles. The strains that an individual experiences as a member of a group containing a mentally ill person (Avison 1999) may be the result of having inadequate resources to fulfill a socially obligatory role or the recognition that in fulfilling the role of caregiver, the person is unable to fulfill the legitimate expectations that are associated with other social positions that the individual occupies simultaneously. For example, the person may be unable to continue being a good mother while expending her energy as a caregiver to a mentally ill husband.

Regarding stressful life events, loss of a job or interruptions in marital status may instigate or exacerbate levels of anxiety and depression (Kessler, House, and Turner 1987). The child who experiences divorce may suffer both poorer parenting and economic adversity following the divorce that contributes to later mental illness (George 1999; Harris, Brown, and Bifulco 1990; Landerman, George, and Blazer 1991).

Men and women respond differentially to life events that have differential evaluative significance. Thus, wives tend to experience psychological distress in response to undesirable/uncontrollable events, while husbands tend to experience psychological distress in association with undesirable/controllable experiences (Thoits 1987). The inability to accomplish roles within their control may be especially threatening to the masculine self-image. Women who experience interpersonal problems are prone to depression, while men appear to be more vulnerable to depression when encountering job stress and income loss, that is, problems relating to the breadwinner role (Kaplan 1970; Kessler and McLeod 1984; Radloff and Rae 1981).

Often, early childhood adversity may have a moderating effect on the experience of later adversity such that individuals who experienced early negative life events may suffer a greater experience of distress when later life events occur (Landerman et al. 1991). Thus, for adults below the age of 30, but not for other adults, current self-rejecting feelings were associated with reports that during childhood, subjects were very much afraid of being punished by their parents and that they received poorer grades than most of the children they knew (Kaplan and Pokorny 1970).

Coping and Social Support. Among individuals who experience equivalent levels of disvalued life circumstances, individuals characterized by certain social identities may possess more or less efficient personal and interpersonal resources to mitigate the experience of the psychological distress that would ordinarily accompany such circumstances. These

resources might include defensive patterns that permit the denial or redefinition of the self-devaluing significance of the circumstances after the fact, or that provide interpersonal resources that counterbalance the distressful self-feelings. For example, women are not only less likely to use effective mechanisms but are also frequently more likely to use dysfunctional mechanisms, such as selective ignoring responses, which in marriage and parenting actually exacerbate stress rather than assuage it (Pearlin and Schooler 1978).

It has been argued that the increase in depressive symptoms observed for subjects in their 60s could be accounted for by increased cognitive disability and consequent decreased ability to cope with stressors (Krause 1999). The inability to cope successfully influences perceived loss of personal control and so increases depression during the sixth decade of life. This process might be mitigated by the presence of strong social support networks.

Social support refers "to the clarity or certainty with which the individual experiences being loved, valued, and able to count on others should the need arise" (Turner and Turner 1999:302). Empirical studies have widely reported a buffering effect of social support. For example, depression is more likely to develop following the experience of stressors among those individuals who lack social support compared with those who possess social support (Henderson 1992).

Negative Self-Feelings. The inability to forestall or assuage the impact of identity-related role strain and adverse life events through the effective use of coping mechanisms and interpersonal resources results in negative self-evaluation and consequent negative self-feelings. Indeed, the stressful nature of particular life circumstances lies in their threats to the self-esteem motive. For example, the inability to exercise discretion on the job, partly reflected in the close supervision the individual is subject to, influences low self-esteem and high levels of anxiety and depression (Kohn and Schooler 1983; Link et al. 1993). Among the antecedents of high self-esteem are beliefs that one has control over one's own life (Mirowsky, Ross, and Van Willigen 1996).

Numerous theories posit the existence of a self-esteem motive that becomes activated in the face of threats to one's positive self-attitudes. Among these theoretical orientations are self-derogation (Kaplan 1972, 1980, 1986) and self-affirmation theory (Steele 1988). Increasingly, from such perspectives, stressors have in large measure been interpreted in terms of their implications as threats to self-evaluation (Thoits 1999). Kaplan and his associates have perhaps been most consistent in viewing the stress process in terms of the self-threatening nature of life circumstances and mental illness as a reflection of more or less functional adaptations to such threats (Kaplan 1972, 1986, 1996; Kaplan, Boyd, and Bloom 1964; Kaplan and Meyerowitz 1970; Kaplan et al. 1983; Lorimor, Kaplan, and Pokorny 1985). Intrinsically disvalued social positions or identities evoke attitudes of social rejection and, consequently, distressful feelings of self-rejection (Williams et al. 1997). If people are emotionally invested in performing the social roles associated with their identities in the social system, the failure to perform these roles appropriately will evoke self-disapproving attitudes and concomitant self-derogation. Such self-contemptuous attitudes frequently are indicative of mental illness or stimulate pathological responses that represent maladaptive attempts to reduce self-contempt and restore self-accepting attitudes (Kaplan 1986; Thoits 1999).

Mental Illness and Self-Derogation. The failure to obviate assaults upon salient self-evaluative standards by social stressors frequently results in severe and prolonged negative self-feelings (low self-esteem). Low self-esteem, in turn, is implicated in the genesis and stability of mental illness. As Thoits (1999) observes,

> It is virtually impossible to develop a theory of the etiology of mental illness without thinking about self and identity issues. Almost all approaches in psychiatry and clinical psychology (with the exception of behaviorism) view individual's mental health as at least partly influenced by positive self-conceptions, high self-esteem, and/or the possession of valued social identities. (P. 345)

From the perspective of self theory (Kaplan 1996), mental illness frequently is the expression of negative self-feelings or consciously or unconsciously

motivated responses that are intended to serve self-protective or self-enhancing ends. As a *reflection of intrinsically distressful self-feelings,* the perception of life circumstances as threatening to salient self-evaluative standards often manifests itself in anxiety, depression, post-traumatic stress disorders (PTSD), and generally, in dysphoric states. A number of psychodynamic models of *anxiety* states focus on threats to the individual's self-acceptance (Eells et al. 1993):

> In Sullivan's theory, an interpersonal context—specifically, the anticipated unfavorable appraisal by significant other—*produces* anxiety. For Horney, anxiety is triggered in the context of an individual's attempts to actualize an idealized self. . . . In Kohut's model, disintegration anxiety occurs when an individual's selfobjects fail to supply self-esteem needs adequately. (P. 118)

While anxious patients are characterized by feelings of vulnerability, *depressed* patients are characterized by feelings of worthlessness (Beck 1976). It is the end result of being unable to think well of one's self in the face of wanting to think well of one's self (Tesser 1986).

Threats to self-evaluation characterize dysphoria in general and PTSD in particular. McNally (1993) states:

> In addition to anxiety and depression, PTSD patients experience other emotional disturbances that suggest alterations in self-representation (Horowitz, 1986). . . . Soldiers who kill noncombatants or participate in atrocities often experience intense guilt about performing acts profoundly inconsistent with their self-concept as a moral being (March, 1990). (P. 73)

From the perspective of many self theories (Kaplan 1996), a number of psychiatric disorders are *consciously or unconsciously motivated* by the need to forestall self-threatening experiences or to assuage the accompanying distressful self-feelings; and, under specified conditions, they actually decrease negative and increase positive self-feelings. Substance (ab)users may experience an increased sense of self-efficacy, increased feelings of power, suppression of self-awareness of unfavorable self-images, and a sense of belonging in groups where substance (ab)use is countenanced (Kaplan 1986). Violence has also been interpreted as a defense against negative self-feelings. Scheff, Retzinger, and Ryan (1989) assert: "Anger can be a protective measure to guard against shame, which is experienced as an attack on self" (p. 188). Psychopaths maintain a sense of superiority and deal with anxiety by focusing upon emotionally neutral, externalized aspects of behavior and by admitting to and describing their socially undesirable traits during the clinical interview (LaBarba 1965).

So pervasive is the view of many psychiatric disorders as functioning to assuage negative self-feelings that much of contemporary psychoanalysis has been characterized "as a mode of investigation for understanding the vicissitudes of self-development and defensive processes that are invoked to protect the self" (Cooper 1993:46). For Epstein (1993), individuals characterized by delusional systems have sacrificed a need to assimilate the data of reality for a need to enhance self-esteem. Similarly, for Laing (1969), schizophrenia is a workable adaptation to an incoherent world, a way of dissociating from unbearable social circumstances.

For Adler (Ansbacher and Ansbacher 1956), the inferiority complex is at the core of neurosis. To conceal their perceived inferiority from others and themselves, neurotics engage in a variety of safeguarding strategies, including the enhancement of their own self-esteem and sense of superiority by deprecating others. At the same time, the failure of such persons is accounted for by those people and circumstances who are the objects of their aggression. Obsessions and phobias, specifically, may serve avoidance functions and so defend against threats to self-esteem (Salzman 1965).

The specific mechanisms underlying the attempts to satisfy the need for self-acceptance via psychiatric disorders may be illustrated with anorexia nervosa, depression, and narcissism. From numerous perspectives (Vitousek and Ewald 1993), anorexia nervosa is frequently perceived as a way of dealing with the distress associated with confirmation of being unworthy through experiences of failure. The preanorexic adolescent comes to believe that losing weight will alleviate distress. The anorexia provides feelings of success, pride, and superiority, as well as increased sense of self-control, and evokes attention and concern from others.

While depression may be an expression of negative self-feelings, at the same time, it may be considered a defense against such feelings (Epstein 1993; Norem and Cantor 1986; Pyszczynski and Greenberg 1987). Adopting a negative self-image provides relief from the person's futile attempts to maintain a positive self-image. The person attempts to control the emotional reaction to self-threatening circumstances rather than to control the occurrence of such circumstances. By keeping expectancies for positive outcomes low, the person minimizes disappointment.

The narcissist "depends on continual infusion of admiration and approval to bolster an uncertain sense of self-worth" (Giddens 1991:172). For Kohut (1971), the grandiose self is interpreted as a defensive structure that helps the child to deal with (whether through minimization or denial) parental disappointments.

Clinical and theoretical formulations of the relationship between negative self-feelings and psychopathology are compatible with the results of longitudinal studies on large in-community populations (Kaplan 1989; Kaplan et al. 1983). For example, analyses of the first three waves of data of a longitudinal study of adolescents suggest that over one or two years, self-derogation anticipates subjective distress and other behavioral responses interpretable as antecedents or reflections of psychopathology. Subjects who were more self-rejecting were significantly more likely to be referred for psychiatric treatment. The same population in young adulthood revealed an association between self-derogation scores in the 7th grade and self-reports 10 years later of several psychopathological patterns during the intervening time. Numerous other studies indicate, as well, that low self-esteem is associated with subsequent reports of psychological distress, other modes of psychopathology, and antisocial behavior (DuBois et al. 1994; Rosenberg, Schooler, and Schoenbach 1989).

These findings have implications for the prevention and treatment of psychiatric disorders. They sensitize policymakers and therapists to the self-devaluing implications of interpersonal arrangements and to the self-enhancing or self-protective functions of pathological patterns, and therefore to the need to forestall self-devaluing circumstances and/or to facilitate more acceptable and effective response patterns than the pathological patterns that for the mentally ill represent the best adaptations available to them. In short, above all, it must be recognized that mental illness frequently serves important functions for the individual and that until alternatives to resolving the individual's needs are provided, mental illness must suffice as an adaptive mechanism of choice.

Form or Expression of Mental Illness

Social factors influence not only the probability of individuals developing some form of mental illness but also the likelihood of developing particular forms of mental illness.

Cultural and Identity-Specific Variability. Cultural variability in the prevalence of mental illness in general or in particular forms of mental illness is apparent in a number of studies (Agbayani-Siewert, Takeuchi, and Pangan 1999). Leighton and Hughes (1961) cite a number of specific constellations of symptoms that are observed in given areas of culture and that appear to reflect culturally patterned beliefs and practices. For example, "Witiko," observed among the Ojibwa Indians, is frequently characterized by the subject's killing and eating members of his own family. He is said to believe himself possessed by a cannibalistic monster (the Witiko), a being that appears in the traditional mythology of the culture.

Wittkower and Dubreuil (1968) also note cultural variations in the patterns of symptoms associated with traditional diagnostic categories. Thus, with regard to schizophrenia, catatonic body rigidity and negativism are said to be relatively common among the Indian population. Relative to the classical picture of schizophrenia observed among Europeans in general, Asiatic schizophrenics are noted as displaying less aggression and more withdrawal, while southern-Italian patients are said to display more aggression and less withdrawal.

Form of mental illness has been observed to vary within the same society according to social identity as well. One of the more robust findings in

psychiatric epidemiology relates to gender-based differences in the forms that psychiatric disorder takes (Rosenfield 1999):

> Females suffer more than males from internalizing disorders, including depression and anxiety, which turn problematic feelings inward against themselves. . . . More often than men, women live with fears in the forms of phobias, panic attacks, and free-floating anxiety states. In contrast, males predominate in externalizing disorders, expressing problematic feelings in outward behavior. They more often have enduring personality traits that are aggressive and antisocial in character, with related problems in forming close, enduring relationships. (P. 210)

Normal Coping and Form of Mental Illness. A number of observations in the literature are congruent with the thesis that forms of mental illness are extrapolations from normal coping mechanisms observed in cultures, subcultures, or in association with particular social identities (Kaplan 1972). As a basis for one investigation, Figelman (1968) postulated that cultural differences exist between Jews and African Americans ("Negroes" was the term used in the original research) with regard to patterns of coping with aggression and that these cultural differences are reflected in variability in patterns of psychopathology. It was expected that Jewish subjects would be more likely than African Americans to manifest affective disorders (involving either depression or hypomanic defenses against depression) since the Jewish subjects would tend to internalize anger, a pattern that is congruent with the Jewish prohibition against the open expression of anger. African Americans would be more likely to manifest paranoid disorders "because the outward expression of aggression permissible in Negro culture allows for the frequent use of projection as a defense" (Figelman 1968:278). As expected, comparisons of Jewish and African American patients indicated that the former were significantly less likely to display paranoid disorders and were significantly more likely to manifest affective disorders than were the African American subjects.

Breen (1968) also contrasts the cultural styles of American Jewish and African American subjects and relates these styles to modes of psychopathology. The American Jewish culture embodies the cohesive, aggression-controlling style, while the African American culture is characterized in terms of the dispersive, aggression-expressing style. In the event there is a schizophrenic break for whatever reason, it is to be expected that the symptomatic expression of the disorder would reflect, in the extreme, certain aspects of the culture in which the schizophrenia was observed. Thus, the Jewish schizophrenic is likely to be diagnosed in terms of varieties of *dependency schizophrenia,* including simple, hebephrenic, and catatonic schizophrenia. In contrast, the African American in the event of a schizophrenic break would be expected to receive a diagnosis of paranoid "because, in his deterioration, the fear of assault that he has always lived with will be exaggerated" (Breen 1968:284). Observations of male schizophrenic patients supported the hypothesis that the Jewish patients would be more likely to receive diagnoses of schizophrenia and that the African American patients would be more likely to receive diagnoses of paranoid. Thus, the findings are in accord with the viewpoint that schizophrenic sympomatology reflects exaggerations of culturally patterned lifestyles for coping with extreme stress (Kaplan 1972). The pattern of differences in expressions of mental illness for males and females noted above are also interpretable as extensions of differential socially sanctioned coping patterns for males and females.

Social policy dedicated to the reduction of mental illness requires consensus on the nature of mental illness. Policymakers must recognize that mental illness is expressed differently in different groups. By focusing on only one kind of expression, much mental illness (by other standards) might go unrecognized and untreated.

Course of Mental Illness

Social factors influence the course of mental illness as well as the onset and form of psychological disorder. The course of the disorder is influenced by whether or not the person comes into treatment, what happens to the person in treatment and following treatment, and other consequences of being diagnosed as mentally ill.

Entry Into Treatment. One estimate suggests that approximately 70 percent of individuals with needs for mental health services (that is, with mental health disorders) do not receive needed services. Furthermore, only 12 to 13 percent of those with mental health disorders receive services from mental health specialists (Howard et al. 1996; Polgar and Morrissey 1999; Regier et al. 1993). While it might be argued that in certain circumstances, the failure to receive mental health care might be salutary, in general it may be presumed that the failure to receive care, whether due to absence of facilities or barriers to the utilization of such care (and other factors that affect motivation to use available systems of care), would have adverse consequences on the course of the illness (Polgar and Morrissey 1999).

Therapeutic Experiences. For those who enter into treatment relationships, the course of treatment will depend upon a number of factors that enter into the treatment experience. For example, race and ethnicity influence the responses of psychiatrically ill individuals to particular therapeutic modalities. Lawson (1986) indicates that Asians and African Americans respond to psychotropic drugs more quickly and with lower doses than whites. Self-derogation is implicated in the degree of posthospitalization adjustment in the community (Harder et al. 1984; Lorimor et al. 1985). Change in self-derogation level and its ability to predict community adjustment was interpreted in terms of reestablishing the patient's belief in his or her own worth during the course of hospitalization (Lorimor et al. 1985).

The level of posthospitalization expectations also influences the course of illness. Thus, outcomes of schizophrenia appear to be more favorable in less developed countries than in more developed countries, where schizophrenia takes more chronic forms (Sartorius et al. 1976), outcomes that may be attributable to the observation that less developed societies tend to have lower expectations for performance by the mentally disordered and place less stigma on them (Hopper 1992; Horwitz 1999; Waxler 1974).

Former mental patients in the community face a number of problems that increase the likelihood of their being returned to mental hospitals. They are discharged into the community, often prematurely, and are faced with hostility, limited opportunities, and inadequate aftercare programs. They assume the social roles of the unemployed and often go onto welfare rolls. The situation is exacerbated with the passage of legislation that results in the mass release of patients without providing for individualized aftercare programs (Gallagher 2002).

Consequences of Labeling. The very fact of labeling particular behaviors or affective and cognitive processes as indicative of mental illness has consequences for the course of the "mental illness" (Link et al. 1987; Link et al. 1989). While being labeled as mentally ill may not in itself cause mental illness, it is reasonable to believe that it contributes to the continuity of mental illness by evoking attitudes of social rejection, foreclosure of social opportunities, and self-derogatory attitudes (Markowitz 1998; Phelan and Link 1999; Rosenfield 1997; Wright, Gronfein, and Owens 2000). Fearfulness and increased social distance are among the consequences of perceiving previously hospitalized mental patients to be dangerous (Link et al. 1987; Martin, Pescosolido, and Tuch 2000). The label of mental illness exacerbates the patient's self-rejecting attitudes since he or she recognizes the stigmatizing implications of the label. The further erosion of self-respect and a sense of mastery exacerbates preexisting symptoms of depression or other disorders and so may be expected to contribute to a relapse in the posttreatment experience of the former patient (Link et al. 1989; Markowitz 2001; Wright et al. 2000). Indeed, stigmatizing aspects of the therapeutic process lead mental patients to resist committing to the patient role and allow themselves to do so only by compartmentalizing their lives on the psychiatric ward into mutually exclusive "therapeutic" and "nontherapeutic" spheres (Kaplan et al. 1964). Furthermore, the patient may adjust to the stigmatized patient role by focusing on the positive aspects of the status, thus stabilizing a career as mentally ill (Kaplan 2000).

This brief review of the social factors implicated in the genesis, form, and continuity of mental illness suggests that mental disorder is in part a *socially caused* problem and that the recognition of the social causes has the potential to be part of the solution to the problem. In the last analysis, the effectiveness of attempts to reduce the scope of the problem of mental illness must rest upon a sound knowledge of the etiology of mental disorders. Successful public health measures cannot be formulated unless it is understood that the environmental conditions with which these programs are concerned are influential in the genesis of psychopathological states.

In evaluating the total current body of knowledge regarding the causes of mental illness, one may take the pessimistic view that this body consists of a mass of largely unrelated and often inconsistent findings derived by dubious methodology, lacking both a unifying conceptual framework and systematic theory; or one may take the more optimistic point of view that great strides have been made in the employment of rigorous methodology, increasing consensus regarding relevant theoretical orientations and a body of observations that await systematic interpretation in the context of systematic theories. For the sake of motivating research efforts toward the goal of understanding the causes of the phenomena grouped under the label of mental illness, it behooves us to accept the more hopeful view and to put forward theoretical frameworks and research agendas that would serve to systematize our understanding.

SOCIAL CONSEQUENCES OF MENTAL ILLNESS

The consequences of mental illness may be thought of as falling into two categories: (1) responses by social groups in which the illness is observed and (2) the functioning of the social systems in which the mentally ill hold membership.

Responses to and consequences of mental illness vary from country to country. Thus, in several developing nations, psychiatric care is not available; and where such care is available, it takes the form of custodially rather than therapeutically oriented mental hospitals. Indeed, it might be said that in several countries, the modal response is not response since they have no mental health policies or programs (Desjarlais et al. 1995; WHO 2001). In Western Europe, in contrast, a de-emphasis on mental hospitalization is apparent. In the eastern Mediterranean region, an integration of mental health services with general health care patterns may be observed. In more developed countries, mental health care systems have moved from a centralized system to one in which policy determination and implementation responsibilities have been transferred to local administration (WHO 2001).

In terms of dysfunctional consequences of mental illness, studies in Europe have indicated that expenditures on mental illness represent an appreciable portion of all health service costs (Meerding et al. 1998; Patel and Knapp 1998). In countries where direct costs are low, indirect costs in terms of loss of productivity nevertheless are estimated to be quite high (Chisholm et al. 2000).

In some reports, the responses to and consequences of patterns of mental disorder throughout the world are paralleled by those in the United States, while in other respects, they diverge markedly.

Responses to Mental Illness

We consider, in turn, the responses of the mentally ill themselves; the primary membership groups of the mentally ill; the general public; professional groups; and groups responsible for the setting and implementation of policies relating to the mentally ill.

The Mentally Ill. How psychiatric disorder is responded to by the individual and by the groups in which the person holds membership is influenced by a number of factors other than the disorder itself. By one estimate, in a national sample, a mere 40 percent of the persons who met the criteria for psychiatric illness received treatment. Help-seeking by the person is preceded and/or precipitated by a number of factors, including the disruptive effects the patient's symptoms have on the functioning of the groups in which the person holds membership; the perception by the person that his or her symptoms are serious; the insistence by others in the social network that the person seek help; the extent to which the symptoms are judged to be bizarre independently of their disruptive nature; the recognition by the individual that these symptoms reflect mental illness; and the actual and perceived availability of therapeutic resources, including the perception of barriers (cost, distance, and stigma) to utilization of the resources (Mechanic 1968; Zola 1964). The perceived availability of resources (including affordability and accessibility), in turn, is influenced by structural and organizational factors, including the actual existence of caregiving resources, transportation to and from the resources, health education programs that permit the potential user to know of the existence of these programs, health insurance systems that influence affordability, referral patterns among the professional community, and related factors (Polgar and Morrissey 1999; Stein and Test 1980).

Having decided that the seeking of help for emotional problems is warranted as a response to self-acknowledgment of signs or symptoms of mental illness, individuals will adopt any of a wide variety of responses, including speaking with relatives; seeking advice from friends; use of nonmedical professionals, including clergy or supervisors; using traditional healers; and, of course, self-referral to psychiatrists or other physicians (Pescosolido, Boyer, and Lubell 1999). Initially, subjective distress instigates help-seeking from family and friends. When seeking professional help, individuals are more likely to turn to physicians than to mental health specialists, although the tendency to seek help from mental health specialists appears to be increasing over the years (Veroff, Kulka, and Douvan 1981).

The precise nature of the source from whom help is sought is influenced by culture, group membership, and social identities. Thus, cultures characterized by collective versus individual orientations may be inhibited from using mental health services rather than membership groups to assuage symptoms of mental illness (Kashima and Triandas 1986); and loss of face to the individual's membership groups may pose an impediment for Asian Americans in making a decision to seek help from mental health professionals for symptoms of mental illness (Ja and Aoki 1993). More religious people will seek help from religious functionaries, and if one's friends are prone to use psychotherapists, the afflicted individual will be more likely to seek help from such a source (Kadushin 1969). Self-identification as mentally ill and use of mental health professionals is more likely to occur among the more educated, women, and younger people (Horwitz 1982).

Membership Group Responses. The tendency of the public to define mental illness in terms of the more psychotic disorders is paralleled by the disposition of family members to deny, rationalize, and otherwise minimize the significance of emotional and cognitive disorientation of another family member. Often, the disorder reaches the attention of the practitioner only after the occurrence of extremely disruptive behavior with which the family cannot cope. The end result is a long delay between onset of symptoms and family influences on seeking help (Clausen and Radke-Yarrow 1955). Having a close family member who is mentally ill is more likely to evoke responses of denial, normalization, and concealment than is having a more distant relative who is afflicted with signs of mental illness (Horwitz 1982).

Responses by primary group members are influenced by their social identities within and outside the family. Thus, care of the mentally ill generally falls to female relatives (Cook 1988; Gamache, Tessler, and Nicholson 1995); and ethnic minorities engage in more informal care, find provision of care less burdensome, and are less likely to rely on professionals than are white families (Horwitz and Reinhard 1995; Jenkins 1988; Lefley 1987).

Public Responses. The disposition of the problem of mental illness depends in large measure on the responses of the general public with regard to the definition of mental illness, attitudes toward the mentally ill, beliefs about the causes and functions of mental illness, attitudes toward modes of treatment, and predispositions to seek help for symptoms. Regarding definition, over the years, there has been an increasing tendency for the general population to adopt the perspective of psychiatrists regarding the kinds of behaviors that could appropriately be labeled mental illness. However, the population is still loathe to (by any great majority) identify a wide range of behaviors as indicative of mental illness. In the cases of the most severe psychiatrically judged disorders (paranoid and simple schizophrenia), the general population comes closer to adopting psychiatric standards (Kaplan 1972).

Regarding attitudes, in the mass media and in public conceptions, mentally ill individuals connote the morally unsavory, dangerous, and unsuccessful (Phelan et al. 1996; Shain and Phillips 1991; Signorelli 1989). The very fact of entering into a helping relationship with a mental health professional or in an institution functioning to provide care increases the stigma attached to the mentally ill person (Phillips 1963). In part, this may be accounted for by the fact that observers may frequently have difficulty in evaluating behavior as symptomatic of serious mental disturbance. However, knowledge that an individual has sought help from a psychiatrist or has become hospitalized serves to reduce any ambiguity and to identify the individual's behavior to the observer as a relatively serious mental disturbance (Kaplan 1972).

Beliefs about the causes and functions of mental illness held by the general public are not unsophisticated. As recently as 35 years ago, the general public appeared to view mental illness as a way of dealing with or as result of difficult current life situations (Elinson, Padilla, and Perkins 1967). Close to 77 percent of the respondents in one study agreed that "although they usually aren't aware of it, many people become mentally ill to avoid the difficult problems of everyday life"; and a like percentage agreed that "mental illness often grows out of a tough situation that a person gets into and cannot handle."

Attitudes toward mode of treatment reflect beliefs in support of the efficacy of psychiatric care and the belief that such care involves diagnosis and treatment primarily by psychotherapeutic methods (Kaplan 1972). Public attitudes toward mental hospitalization appear to reflect ambivalence in the simultaneous expression of at least three motives: to be protected and/or relieved of the annoyance of mentally ill people, to provide proper care for the mentally ill, and to assuage any guilt that results from the recognition that mental hospitalization might be of limited benefit to the patient (Elinson et al. 1967; Kaplan 1972). In response to florid psychiatric symptoms that severely disrupt ongoing group functioning, substantial portions of the population are willing to employ legal coercion to channel individuals with drug abuse problems or those who are symptomatic for schizophrenia into mental health treatment (Pescosolido et al. 1999).

The various responses that the social order makes to mental illness are mutually influential. For example, because mental illness is defined as illness rather than morally reprehensible behavior means that social control mechanisms that are put in place will take the form of the delivery of medical care rather than more overtly punitive responses, such as nontherapeutic incarceration. When people believe that mental illness is caused by stress, the response will be to provide services that forestall or assuage the experience of distress, but when mental illness is thought to be physiologically based, the disorder will be treated by drugs.

Professional Responses. Arguably the most influential framework for conceptualizing and otherwise responding to the phenomenon of mental illness is the medical model (Cockerham 2003). Increasingly, conditions that were once not thought of as medical problems have come to be viewed in this way; that is, deviant behaviors have been medicalized (Conrad and Scheider 1992). Medicalization involves making claims to the general public and legislative authorities by formal medical organizations that the "deviant" behavior is essentially a medical problem, gaining legitimization of the medical interpretation of the behavior from legislative bodies, and institutionalizing the behavior as a medical problem by formal professional recognition of it as such (Conrad and Schneider 1992).

The public has increasingly come to accept the medical specialty of psychiatry as the legitimate arbiter of the nature and proper treatment of the mentally ill. Frequently, psychiatric nosology is interpreted in terms of labeling of deviance, and psychiatric treatment is recognized as serving a social control function (Tausig, Michello, and Subedi 1999).

In support of this interpretation, studies may be cited (Loring and Powell 1988) that indicate a tendency by white male psychiatrists to diagnose African Americans and women differently than white males, controlling on presenting symptoms. "Existing evidence suggests that persons with social characteristics that differ from those of labelers (psychiatrists) are more apt to have deviant behavior labeled as psychiatric disorder" (Tausig et al. 1999:118). That is, individuals who are deviant in some respects are more likely to be labeled as deviant in other respects (Kaplan 2000; Stiles and Kaplan 1996).

Public Policy. Ultimately, the resolution of the social problem of mental illness will depend upon the formulation and implementation of public policies directed toward ameliorating either the putative causes or the adverse consequences for the individual and society. Some suggestions have been made to effect public policy changes at the macrosocial level. For example, Yu and Williams (1999:163) observe, "There is a need for a renewed commitment to reduce the inequalities in societal institutions that appear to be the basic causes of social inequalities in health" (citing Williams and Collins 1995). Since hospitalized patients upon their return to the community frequently become symptomatic again (Mechanic 1999), it would seem that social policy should direct attention to remediation of the environmental circumstances that give rise to or exacerbate the person's disposition to become mentally ill.

Most policies related to mental illness, however, have been directed toward treatment of the mentally disordered. Over time, the form that these services and systems take changes markedly (Polgar and Morrissey 1999):

> In the United States, four cycles of reform have developed and shifted responsibilities for administration of mental health services among governmental and private interests over the past 200 years (Morrissey, Goldman, & Klareman, 1985). These reforms focused on asylums in the early nineteenth century, mental hospitals in the early twentieth century, community mental health centers in the 1960s, and community support systems in the 1980s. A fifth cycle of reform, involving the growth and evolution of managed care, is currently generating important new questions about the organization and utilization of mental health service delivery (Mechanic, Schlesinger, & McAlpine, 1995; Morrissey, Johnsen, Starrett, Calloway, & Polgar, 1996). (P. 463)

Each of these cycles has their own causes and consequences. For example, the noteworthy shift in care of the mentally disordered from the mental hospital to the community was brought about by the confluence of a number of factors, including the deplorable state of the public mental hospital, the availability of psychotropic drugs, the enormous expenses associated with adequate custodial care, the increasing awareness of the number of mentally ill in the community who remained untreated, legal decisions requiring treatment of the mentally ill in the least-restrictive settings, and newly emerging philosophies of treatment promulgating the maintenance of the patient in the community (Tausig et al. 1999).

The influence of the federal government in combating mental illness is apparent in three earlier pieces of legislation. The National Mental Health Act of 1946 led to the establishment of NIMH a few years later. NIMH engaged in intramural research programs on the causes and treatment of mental illness; they promoted research, professional training, and the development of intense treatment programs through grants to education, research, and treatment institutions as well as to state governments in the form of matching grants. The Mental Health Study Act of 1955 permitted the authorization of a nongovernmental study group, the Joint Commission on Mental Health and Illness, to carry out an intensive nationwide analysis of the mental health problem and to formulate recommendations for a national mental health program. The final report of the Joint Commission on Mental Illness and Health (1961) led to the third major legislative act, the Hill-Harris bill of 1963. Of particular interest is Title II of Public Law 88–164, which authorized the granting of $150 million in federal matching grants to states for the construction and establishment of comprehensive community mental health centers. At the very minimum, the centers were to provide inpatient, out-patient, partial hospitalization, emergency, and consultation and educational services. However, the failure of these programs to provide adequate aftercare for patients released into the community ultimately resulted in large numbers of individuals going untreated for their mental illness (Torrey 1997). Many of the untreated population were homeless, and somewhat more than that number were imprisoned or jailed frequently for crimes associated with their mental illness.

These outcomes, along with changes in administrations, led to new policies at the national level (Kirk 1999):

> The Reagan revolution effectively ended NIMH's power to direct and shape mental health services by consolidating 10 federally funded alcohol, drug abuse, and mental health initiatives into a single block grant to each state. . . .

By 1980, the bad press brought about by deinstitutionalization, in tandem with the public preferences for a non-activist federal government, put NIMH into retreat from any bold new services agenda. From the progressive and activist stance of the early reformers, the Institute, along with much of American psychiatry, turned full steam to the safer harbor of biomedicine. . . . The Institute turned increasingly from the community to the laboratory, from social reform to biological science, from concern with social structures to brain chemistry. (Pp. 550–51)

Each of these policy changes has important implications for better or worse care of the mentally ill. Some of the consequences of recent policy trends cannot be anticipated with any certainty. A recent trend in the delivery of mental health services implicates the evolution of managed care systems, a development that many think will have adverse consequences for the care of the mentally ill (Gallagher 2002).

Some policies address specific aspects rather than the total problem. A case in point is the question of civil commitment. The concepts of dangerousness and unpredictability are inextricably linked in the public mind with the concept of mental patients (Hiday 1995; Rosenfield 1997), a stereotype that is reflected in legal procedures for civil commitment that permit enforced treatment of individuals who are determined to pose a danger to themselves, others, or their property. Such procedures exist even in the face of serious questions regarding the possible violation of constitutional rights that is implicit in the civil commitment process (Hiday 1988).

It has been argued that if the goal of policymakers in the United States is to provide an effective health care delivery system for those afflicted with mental disorders, then these policymakers have failed miserably. The system for health care delivery, indeed, has been defined as a "nonsystem" (Cockerham 2003):

> The existing health care delivery system is a conglomerate of health practitioners, agencies, and institutions, all of which operate more or less independently. There often is little or no effective planning or coordination, with the result that has been (1) a duplication of services, which increases the cost of care; (2) a

maldistribution of services, which translates into a relative abundance of resources in affluent urban areas in contrast to limited resources in urban poverty and rural areas; and (3) a lack of comprehensiveness and continuity of care. Moreover, there is no national system of health insurance, and many people cannot afford by themselves to pay for quality medical care. (P. 302)

This assessment, by implication, dictates the major policy issues that require attention in the contemporary United States. However, these issues will be addressed only when political pressure is exerted upon these policymakers to define mental illness as a critical and unresolved social problem. How they are addressed will be determined by balancing diverse and frequently conflicting values, including those related to economic and political self-interest, public safety, civil liberties, and humanitarian concerns.

Individual and Group Functioning

Mental illness has consequences for the functioning of the individual in various social contexts and for the groups in which the individual participates.

Individual Functioning. Independent of the costs in distress suffered by the mentally ill, mental illness has consequences as well for adoption of social roles and for functioning in the social roles that are adopted or assigned. Mental illness also has implications for family formation and dissolution in that individuals with histories of mental illness are more likely to get divorced and less likely to marry, and when marrying, are more likely to do so at an earlier age (Forthofer et al. 1996; Gotlib and McCabe 1990; Mastekaasa 1992). A history of mental illness is associated with a number of adverse consequences for the mentally ill individual. In particular, the history of mental illness is associated with lower levels of occupational, income, and educational attainment (Clark 1994; George 1999; Kessler et al. 1995). Such individuals are also more likely to have unstable work histories (Clark 1994) and to develop work-related disabilities (Broadhead et al. 1990).

Some of the consequences of mental illness may be secondary effects of being labeled mentally ill rather than of the illness itself. The experience of

rejection in response to being labeled as mentally ill anticipates aspects of mental illness, such as depressive affect, even after controlling for earlier depressive symptoms and expectations of rejections (Link et al. 1997).

Group Functioning. Patterns of mental illness have a variety of direct or indirect consequences that have an impact on the functioning of more or less inclusive social groups in which the mentally ill person holds membership. These include the family, the industrial sector, and the more inclusive society. Caring for a mentally ill person places a great strain upon other family members. Family members find themselves bereft of resources to fulfill their roles, and time demands placed upon them put them in conflict situations such that they cannot fill one role except by ignoring another. Insofar as one individual is unable to fulfill his or her appropriate role because of conflicts in time demands, the ability of individuals to fulfill their complementary roles is affected as well. Furthermore, roles that were formerly played by the mentally ill person now must be performed by others in the family, thus placing further burdens on an already overburdened system. Finally, relationships with systems outside the family are adversely affected insofar as the person must necessarily reduce interaction with friendship and neighborhood groups, as well as make adjustments in work performance schedules (Tausig et al. 1999). Furthermore, readjustments are necessary when hospitalized mental patients return to the family (Cook and Pickett 1987; Fisher, Benson, and Tessler 1990; Noh and Avison 1988).

Patterns of mental illness have adverse effects on the workplace as well (Kessler and Zhao 1999):

There is increasing awareness that people with psychiatric disorders have considerably more work loss days than others (Broadhead, Blazer, George, & Kit, 1990; Johnson, Weissman, & Klerman, 1992). Concerns have been raised that psychiatric disorders might also be related to workplace accidents and voluntary job leaving, both of which are very costly for employers. These considerations have led some commentators to argue that employer-sponsored health insurance that offers generous provisions for mental health coverage should be seen as an investment opportunity rather than a cost of doing business (Kessler & Frank, 1997). (P. 145)

Finally, the costs of providing a health care delivery system are provided at the expense of other social needs. In American society, as it may be presumed in other societies, mental illness has been estimated to have enormous direct and indirect costs. Direct costs, counting the treatment of substance abuse, have been estimated to be more than $297 billion in taxpayer dollars and private costs. Added to this are indirect costs in loss of workforce productivity ($79.3 billion per year), exclusive of loss of income from substance abuse and related psychoses, and loss of productivity associated with the homeless mentally ill (Gallagher 2002).

CONCLUSION

We have said that the social costs of mental illness are great, whether considering the costs of the programs put in place to treat the mentally ill or in terms of the loss of human capital in the workplace and family. If mental illness is regarded as socially problematic, then society should be motivated to formulate and implement effective policies toward forestalling or assuaging the adverse effects of mental disorders. Whenever causes of mental disorder are recognized, these policies should be formulated in ways that take those causes into account. The eradication of the social problem, then, requires an understanding of its causes, the design of appropriate interventions based on such understanding that might forestall mental illness or ameliorate its adverse individual and social consequences, and the collective will to implement social policies that define mental illness as a critically important social problem. Lacking scientific understanding, enlightened public policies based on such understanding, or a leadership that defines mental illness as a social problem deserving precedence, mental illness will continue to be a de facto social problem.

REFERENCES

Adelmann, P. K. 1987. "Occupational Complexity, Control, and Personal Income: Their Relation to Psychological Well-Being in Men and Women." *Journal of Applied Psychology* 72:529–37.

Agbayani-Siewert, P., D. T. Takeuchi, and R. W. Pangan. 1999. "Mental Illness in a Multicultural Context." Pp. 19–36 in *Handbook of the Sociology of Mental Health,* edited by Carol S. Aneshensel and Jo C. Phelan. New York: Kluwer/Plenum.

Akbar, N. 1991. "Mental Disorder Among African Americans." Pp. 339–52 in *Black Psychology,* 3rd ed., edited by R. L. Jones. Berkeley, CA: Cobb and Henry.

Almeida-Filho, N., J. Mari, E. Countinho, J. F. Franca, J. Fernandes, S. B. Andreoli, and E. D. Busnello. 1997. "Brazilian Multicentric Study of Psychiatric Morbidity: Methodological Features and Prevalence Estimates." *British Journal of Psychiatry* 171: 524–29.

Ansbacher, H. L. and R. R. Ansbacher. 1956. *The Individual Psychology of Alfred Adler.* New York: Basic Books.

Avison, W. R. 1999. "The Impact of Mental Illness on the Family." Pp. 495–515 in *Handbook of the Sociology of Mental Health,* edited by C. S. Aneshensel and J. C. Phelan. New York: Kluwer/Plenum.

Beck, A. T. 1976. *Cognitive Therapy and the Emotional Disorders.* New York: Meridian.

Breen, M. 1968. "Culture and Schizophrenia: A Study of Negro and Jewish Schizophrenia." *International Journal of Social Psychiatry* 14:282–89.

Brenner, M. H. 1987. "Relation of Economic Change to Swedish Health and Social Well-Being, 1950–1980." *Social Science and Medicine* 25:183–95.

Broadhead, W. E., D. G. Blazer, L. K. George, and C. K. Tse. 1990. "Depression, Disability Days, and Days Lost from Work in a Prospective Epidemiologic Survey." *Journal of the American Medical Association* 264:2524–528.

Bruce, M. L. 1999. "Mental Illness as Psychiatric Disorder." Pp. 37–55 in *Handbook of the Sociology of Mental Health,* edited by Carol S. Aneshensel and Jo C. Phelan. New York: Kluwer/Plenum.

Carter, J. H. 1993. "Racism's Impact on Mental Health." *Journal of the National Medical Association* 86:543–47.

Catalano, R., K. Rook, and D. Dooley. 1986. "Labor Markets and Help Seeking: A Test of the Employment Security Hypothesis." *Journal of Health and Social Behavior* 27:277–87.

Chisholm, D., K. Sekar, K. Kumar, K. Kishore, K. Saeed, S. James, M. Mubbashar, and R. S. Murthy. 2000. "Integration of Mental Health Care into Primary Care: Demonstration Cost-Outcome Study in India and Pakistan." *British Journal of Psychiatry* 176: 581–88.

Clark, R. E. 1994. "Family Costs Associated with Severe Mental Illness and Substance Abuse." *Hospital and Community Psychiatry* 45:808–13.

Clausen, J. A. and M. Radke-Yarrow. 1955. "Introduction: Mental Illness and the Family." *Journal of Social Issues* 11:3–64.

Cockerham, W. C. 2003. *Sociology of Mental Health Disorder.* 6th ed. Upper Saddle River, NJ: Prentice Hall.

Conrad, P. and J. W. Schneider. 1992. *Deviance and Medicalization: From Badness to Sickness* (Expanded ed.). Philadelphia, PA: Temple University Press.

Cook, J. A. 1988. "Who 'Mothers' the Chronically Mentally Ill? *Family Relations* 37:42–9.

Cook, J. A. and Susan A. Pickett. 1987. "Feelings of Burden and Criticalness among Parents Residing with Chronically Mentally Ill Offspring." *Journal of Applied Social Sciences* 12:79–107.

Cooper, S. H. 1993. "The Self Construct in Psychoanalytic Theory: A Comparative View." Pp. 41–67 in *The Self in Emotional Distress: Cognitive and Psychodynamic Perspectives,* edited by Z. V. Segal and S. J. Blatt. New York: Guilford.

Cowan, C. P., P. A. Cowan, G. Heming, E. Garrett, W. S. Coysh, H. Curtis-Boles, and A. J. Boles III. 1985. "Transitions to Parenthood: His, Hers, and Theirs." *Journal of Family Issues* 6:451–81.

Desjarlais, R., L. Eisenberg, B. Good, and A. Kleinman. 1995. *World Mental Health.* New York: Oxford University Press.

DuBois, D. L., R. D. Felner, M. D. Sherman, and C. A. Bull. 1994. "Socioenvironmental Experiences, Self-Esteem, and Emotional/Behavioral Problems in Early Adolescence." *American Journal of Community Psychology* 22 (3):371–97.

Eells, T. D., M. J. Horowitz, C. H. Stinson, and B. Fridhandler. 1993. "Self-Representation in Anxious States of Mind: A Comparison of Psychodynamic Models." Pp. 100–22 in *The Self in Emotional Distress: Cognitive and Psychodynamic Perspectives,* edited by Z. V. Segal and S. J. Blatt. New York: Guilford.

Ellinson, J., E. Padilla, and M. E. Perkins. 1967. *Public Image of Mental Health Services.* New York: Mental Health Materials Center.

Epstein, S. 1993. "Implications of Cognitive-Experiential Self-Theory for Personality and Developmental Psychology." Pp. 399–438 in *Study Lives Through Time: Personality and Development,* edited by D. C. Funder, R. D. Parke, C. Tomlinson-Keasey, and K. Widaman. Washington, DC: American Psychological Association.

Essed, P. 1991. *Understanding Everyday Racism: An Interdisciplinary Theory.* Newbury Park, CA: Sage.

Figelman, M. 1968. "A Comparison of Affective and Paranoid Disorders in Negroes and Jews." *International Journal of Social Psychiatry* 14:277–81.

Fisher, G. A., Paul R. Benson, and Richard C. Tessler. 1990. "Family Response to Mental Illness: Developments Since Deinstitutionalization." Pp. 203–36 in *Research in Community and Mental Health,* vol. 6, edited by J. R. Greenley. Greenwich, CT: JAI.

Forthofer, M. S., R. C. Kessler, A. L. Story, and I. H. Gotlib. 1996. "The Effects of Psychiatric Disorders on the Probability and Timing of First Marriage." *Journal of Health and Social Behavior* 37:121–32.

Gallagher, B. J., III 2002. *The Sociology of Mental Illness.* 4th ed. Upper Saddle River, NJ: Prentice Hall.

Gamache, G., R. C. Tessler, and J. Nicholson. 1995. "Child Care as a Neglected Dimension of Family Burden Research." Pp. 63–90 in *Research in Community and Mental Health,* vol. 8, edited by J. R. Greenley. Greenwich, CT: JAI.

George, L. K. 1999. "Life-Course Perspectives on Mental Health." Pp. 565–83 in *Handbook of the Sociology of Mental Health,* edited by Carol S. Aneshensel and Jo C. Phelan. New York: Kluwer/Plenum.

Giddens, A. 1991. *Modernity and Self-Identity: Self and Society in the Late Modern Age.* Stanford, CA: Stanford University Press.

Goodban, N. 1985. "The Psychological Impact of Being on Welfare." *Social Services Review,* September, 403–22.

Gotlib, I. H. and S. B. McCabe. 1990. "Marriage and Psychopathology." Pp. 226–55 in *The Psychology of Marriage: Basic Issues and Applications,* edited by F. Finchham and T. Bradbury. New York: Guilford.

Gove, W. R. and M. R. Geerken. 1977. "The Effect of Children and Employment on the Mental Health of Married Men and Women." *Social Forces* 55:66–76.

Gove, W. R. and Hee-Choon Shin. 1989. "The Psychological Well-Being of Divorced and Widowed Men and Women." *Journal of Family Issues* 10:122–44.

Hackel, L. S. and D. N. Ruble. 1992. "Changes in the Marital Relationship After the First Baby Is Born: Predicting the Impact of Expectancy Disconfirmation." *Journal of Personality and Social Psychology* 24:122–31.

Halpern, R. 1993. "Poverty and Infant Development." Pp. 73–86 in *Handbook of Infant Mental Health,* edited by C. H. Zeanah Jr. New York: Guilford.

Harder, D. W., J. S. Strauss, R. F. Kokes, and B. A. Ritzler. 1984. "Self-Derogation and Psychopathology."

Genetic Social and General Psychology Monographs 109:223–49.

Harris, T., G. W. Brown, and A. Bifulco. 1990. "Loss of Parent in Childhood and Adult Psychiatric Disorder: A Tentative Overall Model." *Development and Psychopathology* 2:311–28.

Henderson, A. S. 1992. "Social Support and Depression." Pp. 85–92 in *The Meaning and Measurement of Social Support*, edited by H. O. Veiel, F. and U. Baumann. New York: Hemisphere.

Hiday, V. A. 1988. "Civil Commitment: A Review of Empirical Research." *Behavioral Sciences and the Law* 11:651–66.

———. 1995. "The Social Context of Mental Illness and Violence." *Journal of Health and Social Behavior* 36:122–37.

Hopper, K. 1992. "Some Old Questions for the New Cross-Cultural Psychiatry." *Medical Anthropology Quarterly* 7:299–330.

Horowitz, M. J. 1986. *Stress Response Syndromes*. Northvale, NJ: Jason Aronson.

Horwitz, A. V. 1982. *The Social Control of Mental Illness*. New York: Academic Press.

———. 1999. "The Sociological Study of Mental Illness: A Critique and Synthesis of Four Perspectives." Pp. 57–78 in *Handbook of the Sociology of Mental Health*, edited by Carol S. Aneshensel and Jo C. Phelan. New York: Kluwer/Plenum.

Horwitz, A. V. and Susan C. Reinhard. 1995. "Ethnic Differences in Caregiving Duties and Burdens among Parents and Siblings of Persons with Severe Mental Illnesses." *Journal of Health and Social Behavior* 36:138–50.

Howard, K. I., Thomas A. Cornille, John S. Lyons, John T. Vessey, R. J. Lueger, and S. M. Saunders. 1996. "Patterns of Mental Health Service Utilization." *Archives of General Psychiatry* 53: 696–703.

Ja, D. Y. and B. Aoki. 1993. "Substance Abuse Barriers in the Asian-American Community." *Journal of Psychoactive Drugs* 25:61–71.

Jenkins, J. H. 1988. "Conceptions of Schizophrenia as a Problem of Nerves: A Cross-Cultural Comparison of Mexican-Americans and Anglo-Americans." *Social Science and Medicine* 12:1233–243.

Johnson, J., M. M. Weissman, and G. L. Klerman. 1992. "Service Utilization and Social Morbidity Associated with Depressive Symptoms in the Community." *Journal of the American Medical Association* 267: 1479–483.

Kadushin, C. 1969. *Why People Go to Psychiatrists*. New York: Atherton.

Kaplan, H. B. 1970. "Self-Derogation and Adjustment to Recent Life Experiences." *Archives of General Psychiatry* 22:324–31.

———. 1972. *The Sociology of Mental Illness*. New Haven, CT: College and University Press.

———. 1978. "Self-Attitudes and Schizophrenia." Pp. 241–87 in *Phenomenology and Treatment of Schizophrenia*, edited by W. E. Fann, I. Karacan, A. D. Pokorny, and R. L. Williams. New York: Spectrum.

———. 1980. *Deviant Behavior in Defense of Self*. New York: Academic Press.

———. 1986. *Social Psychology of Self-Referent Behavior*. New York and London: Plenum.

———. 1996. "Psychosocial Stress from the Perspective of Self Theory." Pp. 175–244 in *Psychosocial Stress: Perspectives on Structure, Theory, Life-Course, and Methods*, edited by H. B. Kaplan. San Diego, CA: Academic Press.

———. 2000. "Deviant Identity and Self-Attitudes." Pp. 109–14 in *The Encyclopedia of Criminology and Deviant Behavior* (C. D. Bryant, editor-in-chief), vol. 1, *Historical, Conceptual, and Theoretical Issues*, edited by P. Adler, P. Adler, and J. Corzine. Philadelphia, PA: Taylor and Francis.

Kaplan, H. B., I. Boyd, and S. W. Bloom. 1964. "Patient Culture and the Evaluation of Self." *Psychiatry* 27:116–26.

Kaplan, H. B. and J. H. Meyerowitz. 1970. "Social and Psychological Correlates of Drug Abuse: A Comparison of Addict and Non-Addict Populations from the Perspective of Self-Theory." *Social Science & Medicine* 4:203–24.

Kaplan, H. B. and A. D. Pokorny. 1970. "Age-Related Correlates of Self-Derogation: Reports of Childhood Experiences." *British Journal of Psychiatry*.

Kaplan, H. B., C. Robbins, and S. S. Martin. 1983. "Toward the Testing of a General Theory of Deviant Behavior in Longitudinal Perspective: Patterns of Psychopathology." Pp. 26–76 in *Research in Community and Mental Health*, vol. 3, edited by J. R. Greenley. Greenwich, CT: JAI.

Kaplan, M. S. and G. Marks. 1990. "Adverse Effects of Acculturation: Psychological Distress among Mexican American Young Adults." *Social Science and Medicine* 31 (12):1313–339.

Kashima, Y. and H. C. Triandis. 1986. "The Self-Serving Bias in Attributions as a Coping Strategy: A Cross-Cultural Study." *Journal of Cross-Cultural Psychology* 17:83–98.

Kessler, R. C., C. L. Foster, W. B. Saunders, and P. E. Stang. 1995. "Social Consequences of Psychiatric

Disorders, I: Educational Attainment." *American Journal of Psychiatry* 152:1026–32.

Kessler, R. C. and R. G. Frank. 1997. "The Impact of Psychiatric Disorders on Work Loss Days." *Psychological Medicine* 27:861–73.

Kessler, R. C., J. S. House, and J. Blake Turner. 1987. "Unemployment and Health in a Community Sample." *Journal of Health and Social Behavior* 28:51–59.

Kessler, R. C., K. A. McGonagle, S. Zhao, C. B. Nelson, M. Hughes, S. Eshleman, H. U. Whittchen, and K. S. Kendler. 1994. "Lifetime and 12-Month Prevalence of DSM-III-R Psychiatric Disorders in the United States: Results from the National Comorbidity Survey." *Archives of General Psychiatry* 51:8–19.

Kessler, R. C. and J. D. McLeod. 1984. "Sex Differences in Vulnerability to Undesirable Life Events." *American Sociological Review* 49:620–31.

Kessler, R. C. and S. Zhao. 1999. "Overview of the Descriptive Epidemiology of Mental Disorders." Pp. 127–50 in *Handbook of the Sociology of Mental Health*, edited by C. Aneshensel and J. Phelan. New York: Kluwer/Plenum.

Kirk, S. A. 1999. "Instituting Madness: The Evolution of a Federal Agency." Pp. 539–62 in *Handbook of the Sociology of Mental Health*, edited by Carol S. Aneshensel and Jo C. Phelan. New York: Kluwer/Plenum.

Kitson, G. C. and L. A. Morgan. 1990. "The Multiple Consequences of Divorce: A Decade Review." *Journal of Marriage and the Family* 52:913–24.

Kohn, M. L. and C. Schooler. 1983. *Work and Personality: An Inquiry into the Impact of Social Stratification.* Norwood, NJ: Ablex.

Kohut, H. 1971. *The Analysis of the Self.* New York: International University Press.

Krause N. 1999. "Mental Disorder in Late Life: Exploring the Influence of Stress and Socioeconomic Status." Pp. 183–208 in *Handbook of the Sociology of Mental Health*, edited by C. S. Aneshensel and J. C. Phelan. New York: Kluwer/Plenum.

LaBarba, R. C. 1965. "The Psychopath and Anxiety: A Reformulation." *Journal of Individual Psychology* 21:167–70.

Laing, R. D. 1969. *The Divided Self.* New York: Pantheon.

Landerman, R., L. K. George, and D. G. Blazer. 1991. "Adult Vulnerability for Psychiatric Disorders: Interactive Effects of Negative Childhood Experiences and Recent Stress." *Journal of Nervous and Mental Disease* 179:656–63.

Lawson, W. B. 1986. "Racial and Ethnic Factors in Psychiatric Research." *Hospital and Community Psychiatry* 37 (1):50–54.

Lefley, H. P. 1987. "Culture and Mental Illness: The Family Role." Pp. 30–59 in *Families of the Mentally Ill: Coping and Adaptation*, edited by A. Hatfield and H. Lefley. New York: Guilford.

Leighton, A. H. and J. M. Hughes. 1961. "Cultural as Causative of Mental Disorder." Pp. 341–65 in *Causes of Mental Disorders: A Review of Epidemiological Knowledge.* New York: Milbank Memorial Fund.

Lennon, M. C. 1987. "Sex Differences in Distress: The Impact of Gender and Work Roles." *Journal of Health and Social Behavior* 28:290–305.

Link, B. G., F. T. Cullen, J. Frank, and J. F. Wozniak. 1987. "The Social Rejection of Former Mental Patients: Understanding Why Labels Matter." *American Journal of Sociology* 92:1461–500.

Link, B. G., M. C. Lennon, and B. P. Dohrenwend. 1993. "Socioeconomic Status and Depression: The Role of Occupations Involving Direction, Control, and Planning." *American Journal of Sociology* 98: 1351–87.

Link, B. G., E. L. Struening, M. Rahav, J. C. Phelan, and L. Nuttbrock. 1997. "On Stigma and Its Consequences: Evidence from a Longitudinal Study of Men with a Dual Diagnoses of Mental Illness and Substance Abuse." *Journal of Health and Social Behavior* 38:177–90.

Link, B. G., E. Struening, P. E. Shrout, and B. P. Dohrenwend. 1989. "A Modified Labeling Theory Approach to Mental Disorders." *American Sociological Review* 54 (3):400–23.

Lorimor, R. J., H. B. Kaplan, and A. D. Pokorny. 1985. "Self-Degoration and Adjustment in the Community: A Longitudinal Study of Psychiatric Patients." *American Journal of Psychiatry* 142 (12):1442–446.

Loring, M. and B. Powell. 1988. "Gender, Race, and the DSM-III: A Study of Objectivity of Psychiatric Diagnostic Behavior." *Journal of Health and Social Behavior* 29 (1):1–22.

Lowe, G. S. and H. C. Northcott. 1988. "The Impact of Working Conditions, Social Roles, and Personal Characteristics on Gender Differences in Distress." *Work and Occupations* 15:55–77.

March, J. S. 1990. "The Nosology of Posttraumatic Stress Disorder." *Journal of Anxiety Disorders* 4:61-82.

Markowitz, F. E. 1998. "The Effects of Stigma on the Psychological Well-Being and Life Satisfaction of Persons with Mental Illness." *Journal of Health and Social Behavior* 39:335–47.

———. 2001. "Modeling Processes in Recovering from Mental Illness: Relationships Between Symptoms, Life Satisfaction, and Self-Concept." *Journal of Health and Social Behavior* 42:64–79.

Marks, N. F. 1996. "Flying Solo at Midlife: Gender, Marital Status and Psychological Well-Being." *Journal of Marriage and the Family* 58:917–32.

Martin, J. K., B. A. Pescosolido, and S. A. Tuch. 2000. "Of Fear and Loathing: The Role of 'Disturbing Behavior,' Labels, and Causal Attributions in Shaping Public Attitudes Toward Persons with Mental Illness." *Journal of Health and Social Behavior* 41:208–23.

Massey, D. S. and N. A. Denton. 1993. *American Apartheid: Segregation and the Making of the Underclass.* Cambridge, MA: Harvard University Press.

Mastekaasa, A. 1992. "Marriage and Psychological Well-Being: Some Evidence on Selection Into Marriage." *Journal of Marriage and the Family* 54:901–11.

McLeod, J D. and Kevin Edwards. 1995. "Contextual Determinants of Children's Responses to Poverty." *Social Forces* 73:1487–516.

McLeod, J. D. and R. C. Kessler. 1990. "Socioeconomic Status Differences in Vulnerability to Undesirable Life Events." *Journal of Health and Social Behavior* 31:162–72.

McLeod, J. D. and J. M. Nonnemaker. 1999. "Social Stratification and Inequality." Pp. 321–44 in *Handbook of the Sociology of Mental Health,* edited by Carol S. Aneshensel and Jo C. Phelan. New York: Kluwer/Plenum.

McNally, R. J. 1993. "Self-Representation in Post-Traumatic Stress Disorder: A Cognitive Perspective." Pp. 71–91 in *The Self in Emotional Distress: Cognitive and Psychodynamic Perspectives,* edited by Z. V. Segal and S. J. Blatt. New York: Guilford.

Mechanic, D. 1968. *Medical Sociology: A Selective View.* New York: Free Press.

——. 1999. *Mental Health and Social Policy.* 4th ed. Boston, MA: Allyn & Bacon.

Mechanic, D., M. Schlesinger, and D. McAlpine. 1995. "Management of Mental Health and Substance Abuse Services: State of the Art and Early Results." *Milbank Quarterly* 73 (1):19–55.

Meerding, W. J., L. Bonneux, J. J. Polder, M. A. Koopmanschap, and P. J. Van der Mass. 1998. "Demographic and Epidemiological Determinants of Healthcare Costs in the Netherlands: Cost of Illness Study." *British Medical Journal* 317:111–15.

Miller, J. 1980. "Individual and Occupational Determinants of Job Satisfaction: A Focus on Gender Differences." *Sociology of Work and Occupations* 7:337–66.

Mirowsky, J. and C. E. Ross. 1989. *Social Causes of Psychological Distress.* New York: Aldine de Gruyter.

Mirowsky, J., C. E. Ross, and M. Van Willigen. 1996. "Instrumentalism in the Land of Opportunity: Socioeconomic Causes and Emotional Consequences." *Social Psychology Quarterly* 59:322–37.

Morrissey, J., H. Goldman, and L. Klerman. 1985. "Cycles of Reform in the Care of the Chronically Mentally Ill." *Hospital and Community Psychiatry* 36:70–98.

Morrissey, J., M. C. Johnsen, B. E. Starrett, M. O. Calloway, and M. Polgar. 1996. "A Preliminary Evaluation of the Impact of Medicaid Managed Care on Child Mental Heath Services." Paper presented at the American Sociological Association Annual Meeting, New York.

Murphy, J. M., D. C. Olivier, R. R. Monson, A. M. Sobol, E. B. Federman, and A. H. Leighton. 1991. "Depression and Anxiety in Relation to Social Status." *Archives of General Psychiatry* 48:223–29.

Nock, S. L. and P. W. Kingston. 1988. "Time with Children: The Impact of Couples' Work-Time Commitments." *Social Forces* 67:59–85.

Noh, S. and W. R. Avison. 1988. "Spouses of Discharged Psychiatric Patients: Factors Associated with Their Experiences of Burden." *Journal of Marriage and the Family* 50:377–89.

Norem, J. K. and N. Cantor. 1986. "Defensive Pessimism: 'Harnessing' Anxiety as Motivation." *Journal of Personality and Social Psychology* 51:1208–17.

Patel, V., R. Araya, M. de Lima, A. Ludemir, and C. Todd. 1999. "Women, Poverty, and Common Mental Disorders in Four Restructuring Societies." *Social Science and Medicine* 49:1461–471

Patel, V. and M. R. J. Knapp. 1998. "Costs of Mental Health in England." *Mental Health Research Review* 5:4–10.

Pearlin, L. I. and C. Schooler. 1978. "The Structure of Coping." *Journal of Health and Social Behavior* 19:1–21.

Pescosolido, B. A., C. A. Boyer, and K. M. Lubell. 1999. "The Social Dynamics of Responding to Mental Health Problems: Past, Present, and Future Challenges to Understanding Individuals' Use of Services." Pp. 441–60 in *Handbook of the Sociology of Mental Health,* edited by C. S. Aneshensel and J. C. Phelan. New York: Kluwer/Plenum.

Phelan, J. C. and B. G. Link. 1999. "The Labeling Theory of Mental Disorders (I): The Role of Social Contingencies in the Application of Psychiatric Labels." Pp. 139–49 in *A Handbook for the Study of Mental Health: Social Contexts, Theories, and Systems,* edited by A. Horwitz and T. Scheid. Cambridge, England: Cambridge University Press.

Phelan, J. C., B. G. Link, A. Stueve, and B. Pescosolido. 1996. "Have Public Conceptions of Mental Health Changed over the Past Half Century? Does It Matter?" Paper presented at the Annual Meeting of the American Public Health Association, November, New York.

Phillips, D. L. 1963. "Rejection: A Possible Consequence of Seeking Help for Mental Disorders." *American Sociological Review* 28:963–72.

Polgar, M. F. and J. P. Morrissey. 1999. "Mental Health Services and Systems." Pp. 461–79 in *Handbook of the Sociology of Mental Health,* edited by C. S. Aneshensel and J. C. Phelan. New York: Kluwer/Plenum.

Popkin, S. J. 1990. "Welfare: Views from the Bottom." *Social Problems* 37:64–79.

Pyszczynski, T. and J. Greenberg. 1987. "The Role of Self-Focused Attention in the Development, Maintenance, and Exacerbation of Depression." Pp. 307–222 in *Self and Identity: Psychosocial Perspectives,* edited by K. Yardley and T. Honess. New York: Wiley.

Radloff, L. S. and D. S. Rae. 1981. "Components of the Sex Difference in Depression." Pp. 76–95 in *Research in Community and Mental Health,* edited by R. G. Simmons. Greenwich, CT: JAI.

Regier, D. A., W. E. Narrow, D. S. Rae, R. W. Mandersheid, B. Z. Locke, and F. K. Goodwin. 1993. "The de Facto U.S. Mental and Addictive Disorders Service System." *Archives of General Psychiatry* 50:85–94.

Robins, L. N., J. E. Helzer, J. L. Croughan, and K. S. Ratcliff. 1981. "National Institute of Mental Health Diagnostic Interview Schedule: Its History, Characteristics and Validity." *Archives of General Psychiatry* 38:381–89.

Robins, L. N. and D. A. Regier. 1991. *Psychiatric Disorders in America: The Epidemiology Catchment Study.* New York: Free Press.

Robins, L. N., J. Wing, H. U. Wittchen, J. E. Helzer, T. F. Babor, J. Burke, A. Farmer, A. Jablenski, R. Pickens, D. A. Regier, N. Sartorius, and L. H. Towle. 1988. "The Composite International Diagnostic Interview: An Epidemiologic Instrument Suitable for Use in Conjunction with Different Diagnostic Systems and in Different Cultures." *Archives of General Psychiatry* 45:1069–77.

Rosenberg, M., C. Schooler, and C. Schoenbach. 1989. "Self-Esteem and Adolescent Problems: Modeling Reciprocal Effects." *American Sociological Review* 54:1004–18.

Rosenfield, S. 1997. "Labeling Mental Illness: The Effects of Received Services and Perceived Stigma on Life Satisfaction." *American Sociological Review* 62 (4):660–72.

——. 1999. "Splitting the Difference: Gender, the Self, and Mental Health." Pp. 209–24 in *Handbook of the Sociology of Mental Health,* edited by C. S. Aneshensel and J. C. Phelan. New York: Kluwer/ Plenum.

Ross, C. E. and J. Huber. 1985. "Hardship and Depression." *Journal of Health and Social Behavior* 26:312–27.

Ross, C. E. and J. Mirowsky. 1989. "Explaining the Social Patterns of Depression: Control and Problem-Solving or Support and Talking?" *Journal of Health and Social Behavior* 30:206–19.

Ross, C. E., J. Mirowsky, and J. Huber. 1983. "Dividing Work, Sharing Work, and In-Between: Marriage Patterns and Depression." *American Sociological Review* 48:809–23.

Salzman, L. 1965. "Obsessions and Phobias." *Contemporary Psychoanalysis* 2:1–15.

Sartorius, N., A. Jablensky, A. Korten, G. Ernberg, M. Anker, J. E. Cooper, and R. Day. 1976. "Early Manifestations and First-Contact Incidence of Schizophrenia in Different Cultures." *Psychological Medicine* 16:909–28.

Scheff, T. J., S. M. Retzinger, and M. T. Ryan. 1989. "Crime, Violence, and Self-Esteem: Review and Proposals." Pp. 165–99 in *The Social Importance of Self-Esteem,* edited by A. M. Mecca, N. J. Smelser, and J. Vasconcellos. Berkeley, CA: University of California Press.

Shain, R. E. and J. Phillips. 1991. "The Stigma of Mental Illness: Labeling and Stereotyping in the News." Pp. 61–74 in *Risky Business: Communicating Issues of Science, Risk and Public Policy.* New York: Greenwood.

Signorelli, N. 1989. "The Stigma of Mental Illness on Television." *Journal of Broadcasting and Electronic Media* 33:325–31.

Stein, L. I. and M. A. Test. 1980. *Alternatives to Mental Hospital Treatment.* New York: Plenum.

Steele, C. M. 1988. "The Psychology of Self-Affirmation: Sustaining the Integrity of the Self." Pp. 261–302 in *Advances in Experimental Social Psychology,* vol. 21, edited by L. Berkowitz. San Diego, CA: Academic Press.

Stiles, B. L. and H. B. Kaplan. 1996. "Stigma, Deviance, and Negative Social Sanctions." *Social Science Quarterly* 77 (3):685–96.

Switzer, G. E., M. A. Dew, and E. J. Bromet. 1999. "Issues in Mental Health Assessment." Pp. 81–104 in *Handbook of the Sociology of Mental Health,* edited by C. S. Aneshensel and J. C. Phelan. New York: Kluwer/Plenum.

Tausig, M., J. Michello, and S. Subedi. 1999. *A Sociology of Mental Illness.* Upper Saddle River, NJ: Prentice Hall.

Tesser, A. 1986. "Some Effects of Self-Evaluation Maintenance on Cognition and Action." Pp. 435–64 in *Handbook of Motivation and Cognition: Foundations of Social Behavior,* edited by M. Sorrentino and E. T. Higgins. New York: Wiley.

Thoits, P. A. 1987. "Gender and Marital Status Differences in Control and Distress: Common Stress Versus Unique Stress Explanations." *Journal of Health and Social Behavior* 28:7–22.

——. 1999. "Self, Identity, Stress, and Mental Health." Pp. 345–68 in *Handbook of the Sociology of Mental Health,* edited by Carol S. Aneshensel and Jo C. Phelan. New York: Kluwer/Plenum.

Torrey, E. F. 1997. *Out of the Shadows: Confronting America's Mental Illness Crisis.* New York: Wiley.

Turner, R. J. and F. Marino. 1994. "Social Support and Social Structure: A Descriptive Epidemiology." *Journal of Health and Social Behavior* 35:193–212.

Turner, R. J. and J. B. Turner. 1999. "Social Integration and Support." Pp. 301–19 in *Handbook of the Sociology of Mental Health,* edited by C. S. Aneshensel and J. C. Phelan. New York: Kluwer/ Plenum.

Tweed, D. L., H. F. Goldsmith, D. J. Jackson, D. Stiles, D. S. Rae, and M. Kramer. 1990. "Racial Congruity as a Contextual Correlate of Mental Disorder." *American Journal of Orthopsychiatry* 60:392–403.

Umberson, D. and K. Williams. 1999. "Family Status and Mental Health." Pp. 225–53 in *Handbook of the Sociology of Mental Health,* edited by C. S. Aneshensel and J. C. Phelan. New York: Kluwer/ Plenum.

Umberson, D., C. B. Wortman, and R. C. Kessler. 1992. "Widowhood and Depression: Explaining Long-Term Gender Differences in Vulnerability." *Journal of Health and Social Behavior* 33:10–24.

Veroff, I., R. A. Kulka, and E. Douvan. 1981. *Mental Health in America: Patterns of Help-Seeking from 1957 to 1976.* New York: Basic Books.

Vitousek, K. B. and L. S. Ewald. 1993. "Self-Representation in Eating Disorders: A Cognitive Perspective." Pp. 221–57 in *The Self in Emotional Distress: Cognitive and Psychodynamic Perspectives.* New York: Guilford.

Waxler, N. E. 1974. "Culture and Mental Illness: A Social Labeling Perspective." *Journal of Nervous and Mental Disease* 159:379–95.

Wells, J. E., J. A. Bushnell, A. R. Hornblow, P. R. Joyce, and M. A. Oakley-Brown. 1989. "Christchurch Psychiatric Epidemiology Study, Part I: Methodology and Lifetime Prevalence Rates for Specific Psychiatric Disorders." *Australia and New Zealand Journal of Psychiatry* 23:315–26.

Williams, D. R. and C. Collins. 1995. "U.S. Socioeconomic and Racial Differences in Health." *Annual Review of Sociology* 21:349–86.

Williams, D. R., D. T. Takeuchi, and R. K. Adair. 1992. "Socioeconomic Status and Psychiatric Disorder among Blacks and Whites." *Social Forces* 71: 179–94.

Williams, D. R., Yan Yu, J. S. Jackson, and N. B. Anderson. 1997. "Racial Differences in Physical and Mental Health: Socioeconomic Status, Stress and Discrimination." *Journal of Health Psychology* 2:335–51.

Wilson, W. J. 1991. "Studying Inner-City Social Dislocations: The Challenge of Public Agenda Research." *American Sociological Review* 56: 1–14.

Wittkower, E. D. and G. Dubreuil. 1968. "Cultural Factors in Mental Illness." Pp. 279–95 in *The Study of Personality: An Interdisciplinary Appraisal,* edited by Edward Norbeck, Douglass Price-Williams, and William M. McCord. New York: Holt, Rinehart and Winston.

World Health Organization. 2001. *The Mental Illness Report.* Geneva: Author.

Wright, E. R., W. P. Gronfein, and T. J. Owens. 2000. "Deinstitutionalization, Social Rejection, and the Self-Esteem of Former Mental Patients." *Journal of Health and Social Behavior* 441:68–90.

Yu, Yan and D. R. Williams. 1999. "Socioeconomic Status and Mental Health." Pp. 151–66 in *Handbook of the Sociology of Mental Health,* edited by C. S. Aneshensel and J. C. Phelan. New York: Kluwer/Plenum.

Zola, I. 1964. "Illness Behavior of the Working Class." Pp. 351–61 in *Blue Collar World: Studies of the American Worker,* edited by A. Shostak and W. Gomberg. Englewood Cliffs, NJ: Prentice Hall.

DISABILITY AS A GLOBAL ISSUE

GARY L. ALBRECHT

University of Illinois, Chicago

THE GROWING IMPORTANCE OF DISABILITY IN THE WORLD

Disability is a contentious issue in the world because it epitomizes debates over what constitutes a social problem and its effects on the global population. Disability is a universal experience touching all individuals through their bodies, social relationships, government policies, and the political economy. People experience disability in themselves, those around them, and in the society at large (Finkelstein 1993).

Disability occurs across the life course either through episodic events or chronic conditions, such as heart disease, pulmonary conditions, and depression, which generally worsen over time (Albrecht and Levy 1991). If individuals are not disabled now, they will be if they live long enough or happen to be touched by an epidemic, surprised by an accident, violently abused, or caught in a war zone (Guralnik, Fried, and Salive 1996). We see this in our daily lives, in the life courses of our parents and their friends, and in the daily news reports from different parts of the world. On a personal level,

disability is a defining experience giving people renewed meaning and frequently calling out their best, but often altering their self-identities and social roles and the lives of those around them (Bérubé 1997).

Global ethical debates over how to deal with abortion, euthanasia, mental illness, care for the elderly, and the growing worldwide demand for rehabilitation and assistive care reflect in part the impact of disability on our lives and society (Zwi and Yach 2002). Disability calls social values into question because individuals and societies can be judged by how they treat disabled people. In terms of the political economy, disability is often perceived as a "burden" on individual well-being and on national development (Murray and Lopez 1996a). Because of demand, rehabilitation goods and services are a burgeoning industry and area of innovation (Albrecht 1992). By any measure, disability is a personal experience and a social problem with a global reach that differentially affects individuals within and between societies.

Depending on the part of the world being considered, the population studied, measures employed, and reporting mechanisms in place, disability prevalence is reported to be between 2 and 63 percent of the population. In some areas where disability is politically or culturally seen as an embarrassment or where there are virtually no reliable reporting mechanisms, disability, especially related to stigmatized conditions, is seriously underreported. Yet there is substantial evidence that in those instances where untreated conditions such as AIDS are highly prevalent, where work and environmental conditions are unregulated, and where there are ongoing wars and civil disruptions, disability may affect over half the population (Albrecht and Verbrugge 2000). In any case, when true prevalence rates are ascertained, disability consistently emerges as a global social problem.

In this chapter, I will discuss the different ways that disability is defined and conceptualized as a social problem. Second, I will review the epidemiological data on disability in various parts of the world. Third, I will consider how disability is distributed and experienced cross-culturally. Fourth, I will examine the cross-national responses to disability. Finally, I will look to emerging developments in the field.

DISABILITY DEFINITIONS

Disability definitions are hotly contested for numerous personal, scientific, economic, political, and ideological reasons. The *Oxford English Dictionary (OED)* definition of *disability* exemplifies the debate:

Disability: 1 Lack of ability (to do something); inability, incapacity. Now rare. 2 Shortage of money. 3 An instance of lacking ability; now spec. a physical or mental condition (usu. permanent) that limits a person's activities or senses, esp. the ability to work. 4 Incapacity recognized or created by the law; legal disqualification.

Since disability definitions are used for myriad purposes and represent the social construction of a condition, stakeholder groups will often heatedly disagree on the meaning, measurement, or use of the disability concept. Returning to the *OED* definition, disability is used to refer to inability or incapacity

on the part of an individual, the relation of disability to money, a physical or mental condition, or an incapacity as constructed by the law. By this set of definitions, disability is anchored in the individual, is a medical or social condition related to role expectations and being poor, limits the individual's ability to work and earn money, and is constructed by society and its laws.

Critics quickly respond to such definitions that disability does not reside in the individual, but in discrimination imposed by society, in the physical and social environment that limit the individual's ability to be independent, and in the interaction between individuals' impairments and society's responses to them expressed in reduced role expectations, prejudices, unfriendly laws, and discriminatory policies. The lively discourse around disability, then, reflects a wide diversity of experiences, interests, and intended consequences of those stakeholders invested in defining disability.

The United States government has about 50 specific definitions of disability attached to different social programs (Albrecht and Verbrugge 2000; Bickenbach 1993). For instance, the Americans with Disabilities Act of 1990 states:

The term "disability" means, with respect to the individual—(a) a physical or mental impairment that substantially limits one or more of the major life activities of such an individual, (b) a record of such impairment, or being regarded as having such an impairment. (42 USC 12101)

The Internal Revenue Service code reads:

An individual is permanently and totally disabled if he is unable to engage in any substantial gainful activity by reasons of any medical determinable physical or mental impairment which can be expected to result in death or which has lasted or can be expected to last for a continuous period of not less than 12 months. An individual shall not be considered to be permanently disabled unless he furnishes proof of the existence thereof in such form and manner, and at such time, as the Secretary may require. (28 USC & 22(3))

In Great Britain, under the Disability Discrimination Act of 1995,

A disability is defined as either a physical or mental impairment, which has a substantial and long term adverse effect on a person's day-to-day activities. (s. 1 (19)) (Gooding 1996)

In Australia,

Disability is usually conceptualised as a multi-dimensional experience for the person involving organs or body parts, such as impairment of the mobility of joints or bones, or the functional effects on certain activities, for instance lifting or gripping objects with the hand. There may be involvement in a person's participation in aspects of life, such as education, work or leisure. Participation can be facilitated by the provision of assistive technology or environmental modifications. Physical and environmental factors play a significant role in the creation of disability. (Australian Institute of Health and Welfare 2001:8)

There are two major laws relevant to disability in Australia that employ this definition, the Disability Services Act 1986 and the Disability Discrimination Act 1992. In practice, disability is determined in Australia by whether or not the person has a limitation, restriction, or impairment that has lasted or is likely to last for 6 months or more. Such impairments include loss of sight, loss of hearing, incomplete use of feet or legs, and so forth (Australian Institute of Health and Welfare 1997).

In the European Community (EU), there is considerable activity in addressing disability issues at the present, particularly since 2003 is the EU Year of the Disabled. In cross-national studies of disability in the EU, disability was determined by asking individuals whether they had a chronic physical or mental health problem, illness, or disability and whether they were hampered (severely or to some extent) in their daily activities. The EU response to disability focuses on the problem of inclusion versus exclusion of people from society (Gros-Jean and Padieu 1995):

The Commission in its Communication "building an Inclusive Europe," invites the Member States to strengthen their commitment and to promote greater solidarity for more inclusive economies and societies: the challenge is not only to provide a better assistance to those excluded (or at risk of exclusion), but also to actively address the structural barriers to social inclusion thus reducing the incidences of social exclusion. (European Disability Forum 2001:7)

The definitions of disability in developing nations are not so clearly determined. Persons with spinal cord injuries, for example, usually do not have the resources and medical care to survive for years after injury, so not many of them can be counted as disabled in resource-constrained nations. Likewise, in the Brazilian Amazon where malaria is endemic, having serious malaria symptoms does not excuse one from the performance of daily roles, because "everyone has it" (World Resources Institute 1998).

After heated controversy and field testing in many countries around the world, the World Health Assembly (WHO 2001) endorsed the International Classification of Functioning, Disability and Health (ICF). This system of conceptualizing and defining disability is being used worldwide to classify disability. In this system, a person's functioning and disability are conceived as a dynamic interaction between health conditions and environmental and personal factors (WHO 2001:6). Disability, then, is the umbrella term for any or all of an impairment of body structure or function, a limitation of activities, or a restriction in participation. The key components of disability are defined as follows:

- *Body functions* are the physiological functions of body systems (including psychological functions).
- *Body structures* are anatomical parts of the body, such as organs, limbs, and their components.
- *Impairments* are problems in body function and structure, such as significant deviation or loss.
- *Activity* is the execution of a task or action by an individual.
- *Participation* is involvement in a life situation.
- *Activity limitations* are difficulties an individual may have in executing activities.
- *Participation restrictions* are problems an individual may experience in involvement in life situations.
- *Environmental factors* make up the physical, social, and attitudinal environment in which people live and conduct their lives. These are recorded as either facilitators or barriers (both on a 5-point scale) to indicate the effect they have on the person's functioning.

These definitions are the starting points from which ongoing debate continues over disability definitions, disability determination, and what constitutes an appropriate social response to the problem. Criticisms of the precursor to the ICF, the World Health Organization International Classification of Impairments, Disability and Handicaps (ICIDH II), were based on the complaint that the ICIDH II was grounded in the medical model that located disability in the individual, in pathological (abnormal) conditions, and that medical professionals were the only or at least the most qualified persons qualified to deal with disability and its attendant social problems (Grimby, Finnstram, and Jette 1988). Such a conception of disability was found wanting in considerations of the physical and social environment, the experience of disabled persons, empowerment, social discrimination, social values on human life, human rights, and the notion that disability is a normal, natural experience of moving through the life course. The ICF revision is a serious attempt to remedy some of these fundamental problems with the ICIDH II by considering inclusion, participation, the community, and the environment.

Pfeiffer (2001) concisely summarizes the alternate approaches to the medical model in conceptualizing disability. These other models deserve serious consideration when examining disability as a social problem because they directly impact the definition of the problem, where it is situated, what intervention strategies should be considered, and what social policies make the most sense. Pfeiffer points out that there are at least nine alternatives to the medical model of disability:

1. The first is the social constructionist version as found in the United States, which argues that disability is a set of social roles and expectations that have been constructed by the major institutions in society and are defined as problematic.

2. The second, the social model version espoused in the United Kingdom, is Marxist in orientation, often stressing class conflict. According to the social model, disability is a result of power imbalances between disabled people and health and welfare professionals who often make unilateral decisions about social situations not related to their medical expertise. The social model also sees disability as a problem that resides in the environment and is a result of discrimination, often producing dependency.

3. The third position is that impairment and personal experiences are integral components that must be considered in defining and responding to disability.

4. The fourth model is the oppressed minority version of disability, which conceives of disabled people as a minority group, like racial and ethnic groups, who must employ similar strategies to gain human rights and the exercise of full citizenship.

5. The fifth model conceives of disability in terms of the "independent living movement," which defines disabled people as competent and responsible decision makers who should be given resources and have the right to choose how to allocate them to serve their needs.

6. The sixth version is a postmodern approach to understanding disability in historical texts, cross-cultural contexts, and in the deconstruction of the representations of disability to ascertain the fundamental orientations and unstated assumptions that societies have applied to disabled people.

7. The seventh version envisions disability as a universal experience recognizing that we will all be disabled at one time or another or in one form or another.

8. The eighth version presents disability as human variation and should be appreciated as but one characteristic that is shared among human beings.

9. The ninth version emphasizes discrimination based on disability status. The result is that disabled people are prevented from fully engaging in society because of the physical and social barriers placed in their way.

These different approaches to defining and analyzing disability represent the rich discourse that is under way on theoretical, pragmatic, applied, activist, and social policy levels concerning our understanding of the place of disability in society (Barbour 1995; Barnes 1991; Barnes and Mercer 1996).

THE EPIDEMIOLOGY OF DISABILITY

Disability has multiple causes and different prevalency rates in various parts of the world. Coalminers in the United States, for example, for years suffered from "Black Lung" disease and chronic respiratory conditions that often disabled and killed them, before environmental and occupational reforms ameliorated mining conditions. Today, obesity constitutes a major cause of disability in the United States because of the stress that added weight puts on joints and the skeleton and its relation to Type II diabetes, which increases risk for cardiac, vision, renal, and circulatory problems. Diabetes is an epidemic in the United States, a growing problem in industrialized countries, and is even beginning to affect populations in developing countries. In tropical climates, malaria, schistosomiasis, and guinea worm are major causes of disability, while diarrheal diseases are major culprits in developing countries.

The amount and distribution of disability in different areas of the world is contingent on the ways that disability is actually distributed and measured. As we have seen, for example, there are more than 50 ways of measuring disability in the United States, depending on the scientific rationale, political forces, ideology, and end purposes influencing the measurement strategy. To address just some of these measurement issues, there is a group of government officials and academic researchers working on standardizing the questions and protocols used to measure disability in major national surveys undertaken by the Department of Health and Human Services National Health Interview Survey, the Census Bureau, Social Security Administration, and Labor Department. There is also considerable variation in questions and methods used to estimate disability around the world. That is why WHO has put so much effort into developing and encouraging the use of the ICF.

The estimates of disability in the United States range from about 12 to 22 percent, depending on the instruments and methods being used. The Survey of Income and Program Participation (SIPP), for example, produces higher estimates than some other surveys because it uses a broad-based definition of disability. The SIPP definition considers limitations in specific functional activities, activities of daily living (ADLs), and instrumental activities of daily living (IADLs) as well as the use of special aids, the presence of certain conditions related to mental functioning, and questions pertaining to the ability

to work. By these criteria, in 1995, an estimated 20.6 percent of noninstitutionalized civilians (53.9 million people) met the standards for disability as measured by the SIPP.

As expected, disability is not randomly distributed throughout the population. Figure 33.1 illustrates that women and girls are more likely to have disabilities (21.3 percent) than men (19.8 percent).

To understand this difference, it is important to realize that women live longer than men. The disability rates for men and women are fairly close until old age, when at 85 years of age and over, 59.3 percent of women compared with 50.2 percent of men are disabled. Both blacks and Native Americans have higher rates of disability than any other group both for males and females. Asian and Hispanic males and females have less disability than Native Americans, blacks, and whites. Women are more than twice as likely as men to be disabled by arthritis; men and boys are twice as likely as women to be disabled by learning disabilities or mental retardation.

Similar differences are apparent in other countries. In Great Britain, nearly 20 percent of the working-age population is disabled (Disability Rights Commission 2001). In Great Britain, disability rates increase with age. Women 85 years of age or older have higher disability rates than men; but in contrast to the United States, Asian and Asian British people have higher disability rates than the white population. In Australia, slightly more than 20 percent of the population report having a disability. Among people under the age of 65, 15 percent had a disability; of these, 54 percent were male and 46 percent female (Australian Institute of Health and Welfare 2002). As in the United States and Great Britain, disabled people in Australia are more likely to have lower income and less education, be unemployed, and be more socially isolated than the nondisabled population.

In the EU of 14 countries in 2000, Eurostat reports that about 13 percent of the population is disabled, again, with slightly more women than men being disabled (European Disability Forum 2001). Disability was measured by whether respondents reported that they had a "chronical, physical or mental health problem, illness or disability" and "whether they were hampered (severely or to some

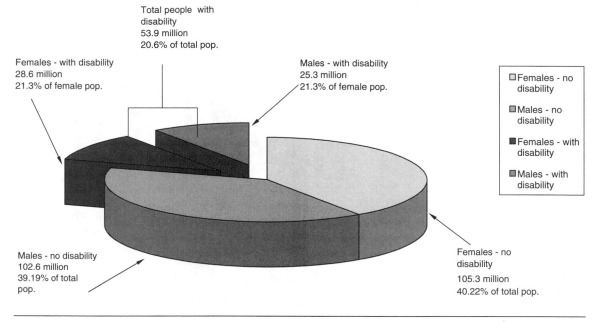

Figure 33.1   Americans With and Without Disabilities, by Gender, 1995

Source: McNeil (1997).

Website: www.census.gov/hhes/www/disable/sipp

Survey: PIPP, 1994–1995

extent) in their daily activities by this problem." As Figure 33.2 indicates, there are significant dispari-ties in disability rates between countries.

For those citizens of these EU nations, the dis-ability rate ranged from 21.1 percent of the Finnish population to only 7.4 percent in Italy. Listed from left to right, the illustrative countries in Figure 33.2 are France, Italy, Greece, Spain, Austria, Finland, and the average for the EU 14 countries. The EU commission reports that the reason for these differ-ences is probably due to different cultural percep-tions, levels of awareness, quality of services provided, and integration of disabled people into society. As in other industrialized nations, disability rates increase with age, and women 85 years of age and older have the highest disability rates. While the European social welfare states seem to provide a more complete safety net for disabled people than most other nations, disabled people in Europe nevertheless experience many forms of exclusion

from society. Reliable national disability statistics are difficult to obtain for developing countries. However, from smaller studies, we know that dis-ability is unevenly distributed in these societies; women are more likely to be disabled than men; dis-ability rates increase with age; and lack of resources, constrained infrastructures, and experience of war contribute to increased disability rates (Hartley and Wirz 2002). For these reasons, disability rates in developing countries are likely to be even greater than those in industrialized nations, regardless of "official" reported statistics.

CROSS-NATIONAL PERSPECTIVES ON DISABILITY

In recent years, disability has become a global concern because the interconnectedness of the world

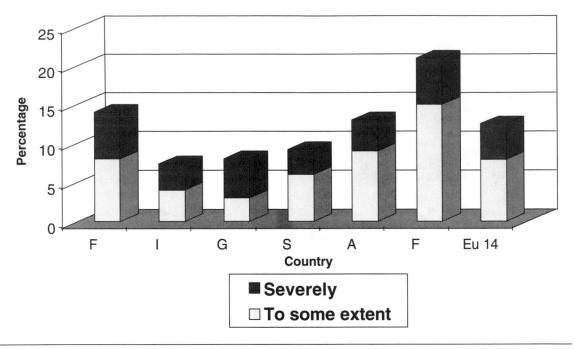

Figure 33.2   Percentage in the EU Severely Hampered to Some Extent, 1996

Source: European Disability Forum (2001).

and the virtual reality of newscasts visually brought disability issues into every life, home, and village. The tradition of hiding disability or ignoring it became impossible as disabled people entered public spaces and demonstrated for their civil rights, and famines, plagues, personal violence, and wars were brought into the public consciousness. Isolationist views of disability were also disrupted when the WHO placed huge energy and political capital into the worldwide ICF project aimed at measuring disability, comparing disability epidemiology within and across societies, and considering its consequences in every nation of the world.

Looking toward the future, the WHO and World Bank, in a collaborative effort, recognized that the burden of disability in emerging and developing countries had serious implications for worldwide economic development, human rights, and quality of life. In 1992, the two agencies launched the Global Burden of Disease Study, conceived to (1) develop internally consistent estimates of mortality from 107 major causes of death for the world and eight geographic regions, (2) estimate the incidence, prevalence, duration, and case fatality for 483 disabling sequelae resulting from those causes of death, (3) ascertain the fractions of mortality and disability attributable to 10 major risk factors, and (4) generate projection scenarios of mortality and disability for the year 2020 (Murray and Lopez 1996a:740). Analyses were undertaken by age, sex, and region of the world. To produce comparable findings across regions, researchers developed a composite measure called the disability-adjusted life year (DALY). This measure was constructed by summing the years of life lost from premature mortality plus years of life with disability, adjusted for severity of disability (Murray and Lopez 1996b). The DALY effort is part of a larger movement among epidemiologists, demographers, and economists to characterize active life years and health-related quality of life. The espoused intervention goals of this work are to produce more healthful environments and encourage more healthful behaviors so that disability can be postponed and compressed into the last years of life.

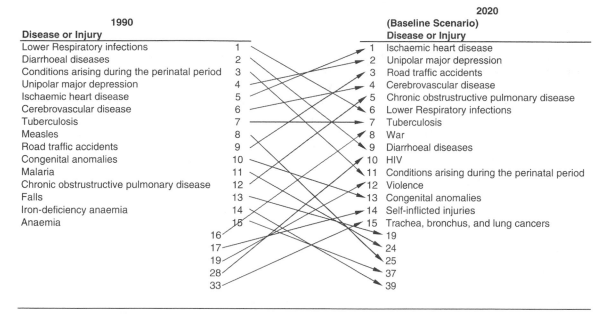

Figure 33.3   Change in Rank Order of DALYs for the 15 Leading Causes, World 1990-2020

Source: Murray and Lopez (1996a), p. 375.

Social policymakers and governments are keenly interested in such work as well, for the outcomes of longer lives and increasing years with disability of individuals in their populations have enormous consequences for the economy and social welfare obligations of the state.

An analysis of the leading causes of DALYs worldwide shows interesting changes over time and considerable differences between regions of the world. The data summarized in Figure 33.3 indicate these worldwide changes estimated through the analysis of multiple data sets and elaborated statistical models.

Across the world, the three leading causes of DALYs in 1990 were lower respiratory infections, diarrheal diseases, and conditions related to the perinatal period. Since this project is sensitive to mental health issues as well as physical conditions, unipolar depression proves to be a leading cause of disability. A more detailed analysis of the data show that an increasing global burden of disease and disability is attributable to obesity and physical inactivity and in Western countries is nearly equal to that of hypertension (Murray and Lopez 1996b). Projecting

to the year 2020, infectious and communicable diseases are expected to be brought increasingly under control with international efforts recently sparked by the Ford, Carter, and Gates Foundations. Therefore, the top five causes of DALYs in 2020 are anticipated to be ischemic heart disease, unipolar major depression, road traffic accidents, and chronic obstructive pulmonary disease. The pulmonary conditions are thought to be the result of this century's epidemic of tobacco-related diseases and air pollution. Extrinsic factors such as road traffic accidents, war, violence, and self-inflicted injuries will add to the disability toll. Now that HIV/AIDS (human immunodeficiency virus (acquired immune deficiency syndrome) is being recognized for the massive problems it produces and given the increased effectiveness of drug "cocktails" in managing the condition and prolonging life, many more people with AIDS will live longer but with disabilities.

There are marked differences between global regions in the prevalence and causes of disability. In general, disability prevalence seems to be highest in sub-Saharan Africa and lowest in market economies (Murray and Lopez 1997). In poorer regions, almost half of the disability is by caused by infectious and childhood diseases and injuries. In these nations, there is a high risk of disability among both the young and old. The disability problem in developing countries is exacerbated as wealthy nations export their high-risk jobs and work conditions. This trend has been exemplified by the recent controversies over work conditions in Nike plants in Vietnam and Indonesia, by the Bhopal chemical accident in India, and the widespread use of migrants working under relatively unregulated work conditions in many industrializing countries. A disproportionate amount of disability is experienced by the poor within and between countries. Even if people have means when they are disability free, the disability experience, discrimination, and social exclusion usually result in loss of jobs, lower wages, decreased support from the community or state, and inadequate health and welfare benefits to meet the needs of disabled people.

CROSS-NATIONAL RESPONSES TO DISABILITY

Responses to disability are shaped by the values and culture of a society, notions of social justice, available resources, and the social welfare systems that are in place. These responses often reflect the compromises that are made between ideals and harsh reality. In laying out the fundamental rights of American citizens, for example, the Bill of Rights asserts that "all men are created equal." The United States Constitution further guarantees that citizens will live in a political economic environment that is characterized by a democratic system in which the rights of the individual are respected and protected. This emphasis on the individual includes the right to vote, freedom of speech, the right to bear arms, representation in government, and freedom of religious belief. These fundamental values expressed in the Bill of Rights and the Constitution are wedded to a capitalist economy that emphasizes and rewards individual effort and theoretically permits persons to acquire education, accumulate personal wealth, and achieve a corresponding rise in social class (Thurow 1996). Thus, in principle, it is ideally possible for any person to become wealthy or president of the United States and for disabled people to live full and

rewarding lives. In fact, this is often not the case for all kinds of reasons.

Through the years, American values have been remarkable for their consistency. In studying values from 1946 to 1976, Williams (1970, 1979) identified five sets of American values and characterized them as follows: (1) competitive achievement and success exemplified through activity, work, and practicality; (2) individual personality and value of the self anchored in ideals of individual freedom, equality, and democracy; (3) progress measured in terms of possession of material things and comfort; (4) humanitarian mores and moral orientation; and (5) nationalism, racism, feelings of group superiority, and an emphasis on isolationism. These values are compatible with earlier observations of American culture. De Tocqueville noted as early as 1877 that individualism promoted social isolationism and withdrawal of Americans from each other (de Tocqueville 1877), and Veblen (1899) observed as early as the nineteenth century that Americans were conspicuous consumers.

Research by Bengston, in California, between 1971 and 1986 indicates that the fundamental values discussed above are unlikely to change over time or across generations (Bengston 1989). In his study, the younger generation expressed higher levels of individualism and lower levels of humanitarianism than their grandparents, but the remarkable conclusion was that values remain relatively constant within and between groups. This conclusion is supported by considerable survey work on American public opinion over the last 50 years (Campbell et al. 1960; Page and Shapiro 1992). While there have been modifications in the expression of these core American values influenced by social and political circumstances over the last 200 years, the underlying values persist. Lipset (1991) notes, for example, that affirmative action was advocated as a compensation action for previous discrimination to allow minorities into the competitive capitalistic system and, second, that America stands out among Western nations in the low level of support it provides for poor and disabled people through its welfare and health care programs. Yet he concludes that these actions have not basically modified the emphases on individual success and equality of opportunity. When taken in concert, these studies and data suggest that the American value system is well defined and stable, stresses individualism and materialism, places emphasis on the individual's work and accomplishments, favors members of the dominant group, and is suspicious of outsiders or those with differences.

One of the deep conflicts in American culture is embedded in the tension between valuing work, individual achievement, and competition in the marketplace, on one hand, and humanitarian activity and a desire to help those in need, on the other. These values and tensions have driven the American approach to dealing with disabled people. For generations, disabled people with all sorts of physical and mental impairments were defined as different, stigmatized, hidden from view, and often placed in institutions (Kurzban and Leary 2001). The state defined disability in terms of people's importance in the political economy of the nation and gave benefits accordingly. The first disability legislation, for example, in the United States was the Pension Act of 1776, which provided compensation for service-connected disability during the Revolutionary War. The second piece of national legislation was the Disabled Seaman's Act of 1798, which gave benefits to merchant seamen who were the economic lifeline of the country. Later legislation provided benefits for veterans of foreign wars and support for injured railroad workers and miners. Workmen's compensation acts were then passed to benefit those who were disabled working in factories essential to manufacturing and transportation industries generated by the Industrial Revolution. Vocational rehabilitation (1916, 1920), social security (1935, 1946), disability insurance in the social security system (1956), and Medicare-Medicaid legislation, expanded health and disability benefits to women, the poor, elderly, and disabled are rather recent components of a disjunctive American welfare and disability system (Albrecht 1992).

The Rehabilitation Act of 1973 and the Americans With Disabilities Act of 1990 and their amendments are the bedrock of a system meant to provide protection, opportunities, care, and services to disabled people. This legislation, taken together, attempts to include disabled people into the larger society by addressing issues of discrimination; access to schools, jobs, and public places; and in helping disabled people live outside institutions. It is important to note, however, that these laws and their interpretations have been vigorously challenged in court by some local governments and private sector employers in an attempt to reduce increases in health and welfare costs. The private sector solution to disability in the United States has consisted of attempts to minimize government programs for disabled people, privatize social security in one form or another, and promote charity. The problem is that charity and gift giving to those in need do not provide an intact safety net for vulnerable populations. David Wagner (2000) points out, for example, that while the United States prides itself on being one of the most generous nations, it provides American citizens with the lowest public benefits of any Western society and has rates of poverty and inequality among the highest in the industrialized world. He argues that independent philanthropy provides a cover for the harshness of America's free market capitalism. Whether his case is overstated or not, privatization of social security investments, heavy reliance on charity, and a cobbled-together, patchwork health and social welfare system do not provide reliable and comprehensive support for the vulnerable elderly and disabled populations, particularly in times of economic hardship.

By contrast, European nations, while also espousing democratic values, are more benign to those in need, have more comprehensive and complete health and welfare systems, manifest less extreme differences in income distribution in society, and have a stronger safety net for the unemployed, poor, women, children, and disabled people (Ardigó 1995). In a comparative study, Evans (1995) examined similarities and differences in public attitudes toward social assistance, full employment, minimum wage legislation, and the general principle of redistribution of income to make inequalities within a country less severe. He compared Australia, Switzerland, the Netherlands, Great Britain, West Germany, Austria, Italy, and Hungary with the United States on all four issues. He discovered that the United States is exceptional in that respondents in national surveys were generally less committed to redistributive welfare policies than respondents in any of the other nations. While he found some social class differences expressed in self-interest (the lower more than the higher social classes support income redistribution across all countries), the more important explanation for differences between the United States and other countries in attitudes toward redistribution of income were American beliefs that inequality is necessary for efficiency, that all Americans have an opportunity to get ahead, and that social position and connections are not important ways of getting ahead.

These attitudes expressing underlying values toward redistribution of income are reflected in actual income distribution in the United States and the major European countries. When comparing earnings dispersion for males over an 18-year period for France, Germany, Italy, Great Britain, Australia, Canada, Sweden, and Japan, Nickell and Bell (1995) found that income dispersion across workers is much larger in the United States than for any other country. Thus, attitudes, values, and actual income dispersion show very consistent patterns cross-nationally when comparing the United States with major European and other industrialized countries. The United States in all instances is more tolerant of inequality. American reformers have focused on these inequalities in calling for the development of a more communitarian approach to social policy (Etzioni 1996), the cultivation of a moral sense (Wilson 1993), and developing a new values framework for reconfiguring American health care (Priester 1992). Regardless of good intentions, the actual public opinion and behavior present a formidable challenge to disabled people. On a national level, increased life expectancy and disability prevalence among the elderly place enormous pressures on health and welfare systems. As in the past, the response of different countries will most likely reflect their underlying value structures, governmental systems, and economic capacities.

Much less is known about treatment of and support for disabled people in developing countries. Across history, some types of disabled people have been stigmatized and isolated more than others. In the tropics, individuals with Hansen's disease (leprosy) were often taken from their communities and placed to live in leprosaria for the rest of their lives. Certainly in the history of slave trade, disabled individuals were not taken as slaves, but left behind as unfit (Patterson 1982). Slavers selected individuals

who were physically strong or who were able to bear "healthy" children. People with serious mental illnesses were often excluded from the community and placed in "madhouses." Today, many people with AIDS in developing countries are not able to afford expensive drug regimens; they spend the last years of their lives disabled and dying in their local communities, where families, volunteers, or missionaries care for them as best they can. Three of the most serious, emergent disabling conditions besides AIDS in contemporary developing countries are injuries due to land mines and war, respiratory conditions due to pollution and tobacco smoking, and traffic accidents as more of the world has cars, buses, and trucks.

Poverty and infrastructures broken by war add to the problem. As a result, disabled people in developing countries most frequently must rely on their families and local communities for support and care. This is a particularly severe problem in places where families have been torn apart due to AIDS or the ravages of war. In these instances, there often is no one to care for disabled people. That is why many think that AIDS is such a threat to countries in Africa and Asia. There are reports that over 20 percent of military and police forces have AIDS and entire villages are so affected by the condition that there is no one to plant crops and harvest them. Survival is an issue. This is why the World Bank and the WHO have been jointly looking at disability as being a barrier to economic development.

IMPLICATIONS AND CONCLUSIONS

Measured by any standard, disability is a global social problem that is becoming more recognized as a threat to personal well-being, the capacities of health and social welfare systems, and the economies of entire communities and nations. Because of the salience of the problem, disability will emerge as a metaphor for other social problems (Smith 2001). For example, degradation of the environment, increases in the human population, and world poverty will be experienced through disabling conditions (Handler and Hasenfeld 1997).

Disability has provided a forum for the development and application of powerful technologies that will benefit large numbers of people (Brandt and Pope 1997). Universal design is a concept that calls for user-friendly physical and social environments that allow persons of all ages and conditions to live public lives, be able to access public institutions, and work in a relatively barrier-free world (Imrie 1996). The technologies developed to implement universal design benefit everyone. Kitchens and bathrooms designed to accommodate disabled people are safer and more convenient for all users. Ramps to houses and buildings provide children, the elderly, and those recuperating from accidents, injuries, or surgery with independence and access to a larger social world. Voice recognition software permits people to access a variety of computing devices, whether they are multitasking or not, in front of a traditional computer. They open up a new world to the visually impaired and those recuperating from illness in their beds. New tactile graphics programs allow students to learn over the Internet using multiple senses, as well as to aid the sensory impaired. New prosthetic and orthotic devices, such as artificial joints, and mobility devices, such as intelligent wheelchairs, make mobility easier for many.

The advocacy of disabled people symbolized by the Americans with Disabilities Act has redefined what it means to be a citizen (Charlton 1998). With rights come responsibilities. Disabled people have demonstrated that they want to be involved in decisions about their own lives and that they want to be responsible for themselves. This breeds a new type of independence. They argue that it is more humane to support people to live independently in the community than it is to exclude them and hide them in institutions. The economic costs are about the same, but the implications for disabled people and the elderly are immense. The public participation of a wide variety of people in social life redefines what it is to be human and a citizen. Disabled people are mobilizing their voices through the vote so that they along with the elderly (two overlapping sets of voters) can exert pressures on society to be more inclusive and to permit more diversity.

Disability raises questions of morality and ethics. On a national level, there is growing evidence that wealthy nations transfer the riskier jobs in their internal labor markets to immigrants or undocumented workers (Aday 2001). In other instances,

entire manufacturing sections of the economy have been exported across borders where costs are low, work conditions are relatively unregulated, and disability risks are high. Examples are dangerous chemical plants that produced the Bhopal disaster in India, shoe-manufacturing plants, and sweatshop clothing and rug-manufacturing factories (Bloomberg News 1998). The question raised is: What is the morality of transferring risk and disability to the disenfranchised?

On an individual level, disability directly challenges notions of personal well-being and quality of life in terms of questions about eugenics, euthanasia, value of human life, and judgments of worth. There are raging debates under way regarding valuation of human life according to "objective" standards such as a person's genetic structure, physical and mental capacity, dependency level, or external judgments of another's quality of life. If these standards were to have been enforced uniformly in the past, there would have not been room in society for the likes of Socrates, Beethoven, Winston Churchill, Franklin Delano Roosevelt, John Fitzgerald Kennedy, Stephen Hawking, and Christopher Reeve (Scotch and Schriner 1997).

On a societal level, disability poses questions of discrimination, stigmatization, and exclusion (Bravemen and Tarimo 2002). There is debate now over what it is to be human, cultured, and a citizen. Who should be included in a society, and who should be excluded? These debates force deep discussions about value and worth. Are people to be judged on their capacity to produce work or income? Is a person's value directly related to how much money he or she has or can earn or the color of their skin, their age, or their gender? What is the value of a poet, a mother, or spiritual leader? These debates are exacerbated by growing research on the personal experience of disabled people. When given the chance to speak, many disabled people speak eloquently to the value of their lives. Even when disabled persons are judged by external observers to not have a very high quality of life, many disabled people report that they do have high-quality lives and that maintaining a balance between body, mind, and spirit is what gives them peace, happiness, and quality of life (Albrecht and Devlieger 1999). These discussions have something to teach others about the meaning of social life. In sum, disability provides us an avenue for reexamining what it means to be a person and a member of society.

REFERENCES

Aday, L. A. 2001. *At Risk in America: The Health and Health Care Needs of Vulnerable Populations in the United States.* 2nd ed. San Francisco, CA: Jossey Bass.

Albrecht, G. L. 1992. *The Disability Business: Rehabilitation in America.* Thousand Oaks, CA: Sage.

Albrecht, G. L. and P. J. Devlieger. 1999. "The Disability Paradox: High Quality of Life against All Odds." *Social Science and Medicine* 48:977–88.

Albrecht, G. L. and J. A. Levy. 1991. "Chronic Illness and Disability as Life Course Events." *Advances in Medical Sociology* 2:3–13.

Albrecht, G. L. and L. M. Verbrugge. 2000. "The Global Emergence of Disability." Pp. 293–307 in *Handbook of Social Studies in Health and Medicine,* edited by G. L. Albrecht, R. Fitzpatrick, and S. C. Scrimshaw. London, England: Sage.

Ardigó, A. 1995. "Public Attitudes and Changes in Health Care Systems: A Confrontation and a Puzzle." Pp. 388–406 in *The Scope of Government,* edited by O. Borre and E. Scarbrough. Oxford: Oxford University Press.

Australian Institute of Health and Welfare. 1997. *Australia's Welfare, 1997.* Canberra, Australia: Australian Government Printing Office.

——. 2001. *Australia's Welfare, 2001.* Canberra, Australia: Australian Government Printing Office.

——. 2002. *Australia's Welfare, 2002.* Canberra, Australia: Australian Government Printing Office.

Barbour, A. B. 1995. *Caring for Patients: A Critique of the Medical Model.* Stanford, CA: Stanford University Press.

Barnes, C. 1991. *Disabled People in Britain and Discrimination.* London, England: Hurst and Company.

Barnes, C. and G. Mercer, eds. 1996. *Exploring the Divide: Illness and Disability.* Leeds, England: Disability Press.

Bengston, V. L. 1989. "The Problem of Generations: Age Group Contrasts, Continuities, and Social Change." In *The Course of Later Life: Research and Reflections,* edited by L. Bengston and L. W. Schaie. New York: Springer.

Bérubé, M. 1997. "The Cultural Representation of People with Disabilities Affects Us All." *Journal of Higher Education,* May 30, p. 124.

Bickenbach, J. 1993. *Physical Disability and Social Policy.* Toronto, Canada: University of Toronto Press.

Bloomberg News. 1998. "Nike Set to Improve Factory Conditions." *Chicago Tribune,* May 13, p. B-4.

Brandt, E., Jr. and A. M. Pope, eds. 1997. *Enabling America.* Washington, DC: National Academy Press.

Bravemen, P. and E. Tarimo. 2002. "Social Inequalities in Health within Countries: Not Only an Issue for Affluent Nations." *Social Science and Medicine* 54:1621–635.

Campbell, A., P. E. Converse, W. E. Miller, and D. E. Stokes. 1960. *The American Voter.* New York: Wiley.

Charlton, J. I. 1998. *Nothing about Us Without Us.* Berkeley, CA: University of California Press.

de Tocqueville, A. 1877. *Democracy in America: Republic of the United States of America and Its Political Institutions.* New York: Barnes.

Disability Rights Commission. 2001. *Disability Rights Commission Briefing, 2001.* London, England: Author.

Etzioni, A. 1996. "The Responsive Community: A Communitarian Perspective." *American Sociological Review* 61:1–11.

European Disability Forum. 2001. *Disability and Social Exclusion in the European Union.* Brussels, Belgium: European Commission.

Evans, G. 1995. "Why Is America Different? Explaining Cross-National Variation in Support for Welfare Distribution." *Working Paper Series* 36:1–28. The University of Oxford, Nuffield College, Centre for Research into Elections and Social Trends, England.

Finkelstein, V. 1993. "The Commonality of Disability." Pp. 9–16 in *Disabling Barriers—Enabling Environments,* edited by J. Swain, V. Finkelstein, S. French, and M. Oliver. London, England: Sage.

Gooding, C. 1996. *Blackstone's Guide to the Disability Discrimination Act of 1995.* London, England: Blackstone.

Grimby, G., J. Finnstram, and A. Jette. 1988. "On the Application of the WHO Handicap Classification in Rehabilitation." *Scandinavian Journal of Rehabilitation Medicine* 20:93–8.

Gros-Jean, C. and C. Padieu. 1995. "Les Exclus: Comment Sortir de l'Approche en Categories?" *Revue Française des Affaires Sociales* 49:5–28.

Guralnik, J. M., L. P. Fried, and M. E. Salive. 1996. "Disability as a Public Health Outcome in the Aging Population." *Annual Review of Public Health* 17:25–46.

Handler, J. F. and Y. Hasenfeld. 1997. *We the Poor People.* New Haven, CT: Yale University Press.

Hartley, S. D. and S. L. Wirz. 2002. "Development of a 'Communication Disability Model' and Its Implication on Service Delivery in Low-Income Countries." *Social Science and Medicine* 54:1543–557.

Imrie, R. 1996. *Disability and the City: International Perspectives.* New York: St. Martin's.

Kurzban, R. and M. R. Leary. 2001. "Evolutionary Origins of Stigmatization: The Functions of Social Exclusion." *Psychological Bulletin* 127:187–208.

Lipset, S. M. 1991. "American Exceptionalism Reaffirmed." In *Is America Different? A New Look at American Exceptionalism,* edited by B. E. Shafer. Oxford, England: Clarendon.

McNeil, John. 1997. Retrieved from http://www.census. gov./hhes/www/disable/sipp.

Murray, C. J. and A. M. Lopez, eds. 1996a. *The Global Burden of Disease.* Boston, MA: Harvard University Press.

——. 1996b. "Evidence-Based Health Policy—Lessons from the Global Burden of Disease Study." *Science* 274:740–43.

——. 1997. "Regional Patterns of Disability-Free Life Expectancy and Disability-Adjusted Life Expectancy: Global Burden of Disease Study." *Lancet* 349:1347–352.

Nickell, S. and B. Bell. 1995. "The Collapse in Demand for the Unskilled and Unemployment across the OECD." *Oxford Review of Economic Policy* 11: 40–62.

Page, B. I. and R. Y. Shapiro. 1992. *The Rational Public: Fifty Years of Trends in American's Policy Preferences.* Chicago, IL: University of Chicago Press.

Patterson, O. 1982. *Slavery and Social Death: A Comparative Study.* Cambridge, MA: Harvard University Press.

Pfeiffer, David. 2001. "The Conceptualization of Disability." Pp. 29–52 in *Exploring Theories and Expanding Methodologies: Where We Are, Where We Need to Go,* edited by S. N. Barnartt and B. M. Altman. Amsterdam, The Netherlands: Elsevier.

Priester, R. 1992. "A Values Framework for Health System Reform." *Health Affairs* 11:84–107.

Scotch, R. K. and K. Schriner. 1997. "Disability as Human Variation: Implications for Policy." *Annals* 549:148–59.

Smith, D. A. 2001. "Editor's Introduction—Globalization and Social Problems." *Social Problems* 48:429–44.

Thurow, L. 1996. *The Future of Capitalism: How Today's Economic Forces Will Shape Tomorrow's World.* London, England: Nicholas Brealey.

Veblen, T. 1899. *The Theory of the Leisure Class.* New York: Macmillan.

Wagner, D. 2000. *What's Love Got to Do With It? A Critical Look at American Charity.* New York: New Press.

Williams, R. 1970. *American Society.* New York: Knopf.

Williams, R. M., Jr. 1979. "Change and Stability in Values and Value Systems: A Sociological Perspective." In *Understanding Human Values,* edited by M. Rokeach. New York: Free Press.

Wilson, J. Q. 1993. "The Moral Sense." *American Political Science Review* 87:1–11.

World Health Organization (WHO). 2001. *International Classification of Functioning, Disability and Health.* Geneva: Author.

World Resources Institute. 1998. *1998–1999 World Resources: A Guide in the Global Environment.* New York: Oxford University Press.

Zwi, A. B. and D. Yach. 2002. "International Health in the 21st Century: Trends and Challenges." *Social Science and Medicine* 54:1615–620.

Corruption as a Global Social Problem

Gary LaFree

University of Maryland

Nancy Morris

University of Maryland

Corruption of public officials exacts a tremendous economic and social toll on societies. It raises the cost of government and encourages wasteful, inefficient projects; it increases cynicism toward politics; it undermines democratic processes and civil society; it diverts scarce resources from worthy projects; it discourages legitimate investors while attracting dishonest con artists; and it increases economic hardship and fiscal difficulties (Elliot 1997; Rose-Ackerman 1999). One of the gravest threats of corruption is a loss of faith in government institutions and judicial systems. In extreme cases, such a loss of faith can encourage popular unrest and vigilantism (Newman 1999:228).

Most observers agree that the opportunity for corruption occurs whenever a public official has discretionary power over some benefit that a private citizen wants or some cost that a citizen wants to avoid (Commonwealth Expert Group 2000:23; Rose-Ackerman 1997:31). Given the breadth of this description, it is hardly surprising that corruption has been around for as long as governments and political institutions have had citizens to influence and regulate. Thus, Noonan (1984) provides examples of efforts to regulate corruption that occurred before biblical times. Kingsley (1944) observed that seats in the English House of Commons during the eighteenth century were characterized by a proprietary nature: "They were a valuable inheritance or a costly acquisition from which proper returns were expected" (p. 26). In the mid-1800s, French social observer Alexis de Tocqueville ([1835] 1969) concluded that corruption was endemic to early American political life. And corruption has remained so common that many observers (Abueva 1966; Leff 1964) have argued that its benefits may actually outweigh its costs. Nevertheless, at the beginning of the twenty-first century, we have witnessed what appears to be a growing worldwide movement to recognize corruption as an important global social problem and to take steps to reduce it.

We begin this review by defining corruption and considering its prevalence among the nations of the world. We then examine research on the causes of corruption, summarizing the most common explanations for corruption and identifying challenges to studying it. Next, we consider the major social, economic, and political consequences of corruption. We close our review by examining several promising methods for combating corruption and offering some predictions about the likely success of these methods.

DEFINING CORRUPTION

According to Peters and Welch (1978), research on corruption has long been hampered by conceptual and operational difficulties. Providing a global definition of corruption is difficult because the precise form that corruption takes is often closely connected to the norms and customs of individual nations (Gardiner 2002; Heidenheimer 1970; Nye 1967). Thus, actions that are perceived as corrupt by those who hold one set of norms may not be so considered by those adhering to a different set of norms. It is therefore unsurprising that we find diverse definitions of corruption in the research literature, ranging from broad guidelines to narrow descriptions. Federal case law in the United States defines corruption as an "offer, payment, promise, or gift that must be intended to induce the recipient to misuse his official position in order to wrongfully direct business to the payer . . . or to obtain preferential legislation or a favorable regulation" (see Colton 2001:899). This definition requires that an action taken by some public official directly benefit some private citizen.

By contrast, the United Nations Crime Prevention and Criminal Justice Division (UN 1997) defines corruption as follows:

> Bribery and any other behavior in relation to persons entrusted with responsibilities in the public or private sector which violates their duties that follow from their status as public official, private employee, independent agent or other relationship of that kind . . . aimed at obtaining undue advantages of any kind for themselves or for others. (P. 7)

Compared with the U.S. definition, this UN definition includes not only improper behavior by public officials but also by "private employees" and "independent agents." Nevertheless, at the heart of both definitions is the assumption that corruption involves the improper use of authority.

Despite the diversity of corruption definitions in the literature, we can identify at least four elements that are common to most discussions of corruption. First, sources (Commonwealth Expert Group 2000:23; Shapiro 1990) generally agree that corruption must involve officials or public agents that occupy positions of trust or authority. This includes politicians, bureaucrats, judges, prosecutors, police, and correctional officers.

Second, most sources agree that corruption can be committed by these public agents only in the course of their official duties. In this regard, corruption is closely related to criminologist Edwin Sutherland's (1949) influential definition of white-collar crime: "crimes by person of high social status in the course of their occupation" (p. 9). However, while white-collar crime includes misdeeds committed by occupants of nongovernmental positions, most definitions of corruption (e.g., Gardiner 2002; Philip 2002) limit it to *public* officials who commit illegal or unethical acts in the course of doing their jobs. This also means that for an act to qualify as corruption, a public agent must be acting in an official capacity. Thus, police officers passing bad checks to stores in such a way that the store employees are unaware that they are dealing with the police would be committing fraud but not corruption.

Notice that this element of corruption encompasses individuals who are using their public positions both to commit illegal acts and to violate informal norms. The commission of illegal acts by public officials acting in a public capacity represents a relatively concrete category. However, the question of what constitutes violation of informal norms is far more complex and relativistic; what is corrupt in one place may be common practice in another, and similarly, what some people view as corrupt may be widely accepted by others (Gardiner 2002; Peters and Welch 1978).

Heidenheimer (1970) emphasizes these distinctions by providing a three-part classification of corruption based in part on public perceptions. *Black* corruption occurs when both public officials and the general public perceive acts to be inappropriate and demand that these acts be punished by law. For example, the widely publicized case of espionage by former CIA employee Aldrich Ames is a clear example of black corruption because his activities were not only considered corrupt by the general public but were also punishable by law. Ames allegedly accepted over $1 million from the KGB for providing the former Soviet Union with information about CIA activities that he acquired through his role as an official for the CIA Directorate of Operations. In return for this payment, Ames provided the KGB with confidential information on U.S. foreign, defense, and security policies; endangered CIA personnel; and compromised several CIA operations (Senate Select Committee on Intelligence 1994).

By contrast, *white* corruption applies to behavior that does not break a specific law and that the general public does not regard as serious enough to warrant formal criminal punishment. For example, it is likely that citizens in some nations may not consider it breaking an informal norm when a public official disregards a traffic violation for a friend or relative. *Grey* corruption occurs when there are legal prohibitions against an act but the public does not support these prohibitions, or when there are no legal prohibitions against an act but the public feels that there should be. According to Heidenheimer, identifying and measuring grey corruption is especially difficult.

Despite the complexities created by including as corruption acts that violate informal norms but not legal statutes, such inclusion also has advantages. Most important, at the present time, nations differ a good deal in terms of the extensiveness of their laws against corruption. Moreover, by including widely

shared informal norms in our definition of corruption, we take into account the fact that legal prohibitions against various forms of corruption are continuing to evolve over time.

Third, most definitions (Philip 2002; Thompson 1993; UN 1997) specify that to qualify as corruption, public officials must receive private gain from their acts. However, the nature of these gains does not have to be monetary, nor does it have to directly benefit the public official. Thompson (1995) distinguishes between *individual* and *institutional* corruption based on the form of the gain received and the manner in which the corruption occurs. In individual corruption, officials derive personal gain in their roles as private citizens, whereas in institutional corruption, officials receive benefits that advance their positions within their organizations or advance their political ideology. Thompson (1993:369) points out that in institutional corruption, the gain that the public official receives is political and is not necessarily illegitimate in itself. Rather, the official's contribution to corruption is filtered through practices that are otherwise legitimate and may even be regular office duties. The most common example of this in U.S. politics is the politician who accepts money from campaign contributors to get elected and then, as a holder of a public office, does favors for them.

And finally, most definitions of corruption (Commonwealth Expert Group 2000; Philip 2002) require that some third party directly benefit from the action taken by the public official. This interpretation excludes officials who commit illegal acts that benefit only themselves, which we would define as criminal or unethical but not as corrupt. And as before, these benefits may involve goods or services, and they may involve positive gains or simply access to goods or services that would otherwise be more difficult or impossible to obtain. For example, in 2002, the Federal Bureau of Investigation issued nearly 90 arrest warrants to city officials in Louisiana for issuing city licenses, vehicle inspections, and city contracts in exchange for bribes (Sayre 2002).

Based on these observations, we define *corruption* as follows:

An abuse of public office that violates formal laws or informal norms, that brings direct or indirect gain to a public official, and that provides a third party with services or resources that would otherwise be more difficult or impossible to obtain.

We can observe that this definition, while distinctive, is closely related to a number of commonly recognized crimes, including bribery, nepotism, misappropriation of public resources for private purposes, embezzlement, extortion, fraud, and influence peddling.

THE RISE OF CORRUPTION AS A GLOBAL SOCIAL PROBLEM

A review of prior research suggests major disagreement about the status of corruption as a social problem before and after the mid-1970s. Prior to that time, corruption was often viewed as a largely benign cultural variation that under certain circumstances was actually beneficial for a given society. Thus, in Robert Merton's (1968) classic work on social theory, he argues that corruption fulfills several positive functions with respect to social integration. Merton draws an analogy between corruption in large U.S. cities and in developing nations and concludes, "In our prevailingly impersonal society, the machine, through its local agents, fulfills the important social function of humanizing and personalizing all manner of assistance to those in need" (p. 128). In other words, Merton claims that city level corruption may allow citizens to cut through impersonal bureaucratic regulations by providing them direct access to public officials who can get problems solved. Similarly, Abueva (1966) argues that corruption may have positive effects on economic development in industrializing societies and is, in any case, unavoidable.

But these conceptions of corruption began to change dramatically after the mid-1970s. The historical events that spurred these changes in the United States were a set of widely publicized cases of bribery by American businesses operating in other nations. In the early 1970s, more than 500 U.S.-based companies were accused of offering bribes to foreign officials in Japan and other countries for preferential treatment in government contracts (Stich 1994). For example, Lockheed, the

giant airline manufacturer, admitted to paying more than \$22 million in bribes to European and Japanese government officials. These widely publicized cases led directly to the congressional passage of the Foreign Corruption Practices Act (FCPA) in 1977 (Colton 2001). The FCPA was designed to combat corruption by Americans doing business in other nations (Heidenheimer 1996). The adoption of the FCPA by the United States and similar legislation in several European nations marked a new level of concern about the importance of corruption in crossnational business deals. While prior U.S. laws had been aimed mostly at curbing corrupt practices within the nation, the FCPA focused instead on transnational corruption, allowing for the prosecution of U.S. companies that engaged in improper practices involving other nations.

The transnational aspect of anticorruption efforts in the United States was pushed further after 1992, during the presidency of Bill Clinton. The Clinton administration aggressively urged other nations to adopt the FCPA and later turned to the Organization for Economic Cooperation and Development (OECD) to secure the cooperation necessary to force compliance (Rosenthal 1989). During the same period, Great Britain expanded its domestic legislation to cover international corruption, thereby requiring the prosecution of corrupt acts committed by British businesspeople or officials abroad (Heidenheimer 1996). Beginning in the early 1990s, the United Nations began to actively condemn corruption and now regularly hosts international conferences on the prevention of corruption (UN 1997). These developments were followed rapidly by the passage of three major international conventions against corruption, which all contain legally binding prohibitions.

First, in 1996, the Organization of American States (OAS) adopted an Inter-American Convention against Corruption. The OAS convention is noteworthy in that it covers a broad range of corruption types and includes signatories from industrializing as well as industrialized nations. Second, in 1997, the OECD passed an Anti-Bribery Convention, which makes bribery abroad a crime and prohibits businesses from treating bribes as legitimate expenses for tax purposes. By 2001, the OECD Convention had been ratified by 33 nations

(Quinones 2001). And finally, in 1999, the Council of Europe adopted a Criminal Law Convention on Corruption that prohibits bribery of domestic and foreign public officials, as well as judges and members of public assemblies. Other international organizations that have been active in developing strong rules against corruption in recent years include the European Union, the Southern African Development Community, and the Economic Community of West African States (Hodess 2001:5).

While the precise reasons for the rising international concern with corruption are no doubt complex, two broad forces that have probably encouraged a growing international interest in corruption are democratization and globalization. The "third wave" (Huntington 1991) of democratization that occurred during the last 30 years of the twentieth century resulted in an unprecedented growth in democratically organized nations. Since the wave of democratization began in 1974, more countries than ever before have attained democracy (at least in the limited sense of constitutionalism and multiparty electoral competition). By 1994, the political watchdog group Freedom House concluded that 60 percent of the world's independent nations could be counted as formal democracies and two-thirds of these as genuine "liberal democracies" (Diamond and Plattner 1995:ix). The collapse of the Soviet Union in 1989 and the rapid rise of new democracies in Latin America in the past three decades represent especially dramatic evidence of these trends.

Democratic governments increase awareness of corruption by breaking up state-run monopolies, by increasing freedom of the press, and by making the conduct of public policy more transparent. Glynn, Kobrinand, and Naim (1997) argue that the growth of democracy has transformed corruption from a mostly regional or national problem into a major global problem:

> In less than a half decade, the worldwide backlash against corruption has swept like a firestorm across the global political landscape. Governments have fallen. Longtime ruling parties have been hounded from office. (P. 7)

Thus, as the number of democracies in the world has increased, so too has public concern about corruption. And as democracy has gained ground around the world, earlier concerns about Western relativism in the definition of corruption have receded (Newman 1999:227).

Heidenheimer (1996) points out that the rapid expansion of the global economy has also increased interest in research on corruption and in efforts to more effectively control it. Glynn et al. (1997) argue that in the emerging postindustrial world, driven increasingly by information technology, tolerating corruption has become more costly. Moreover, as the national and international media have grown more powerful, they more often force political leaders to take responsibility for their actions and the impact their actions have on public policy and government. At the same time, Passas (2000) warns that globalization creates opportunities for corruption and transnational crime by providing new forms of inappropriate conduct (e.g., Internet-related fraud) and new incentives for individuals to take advantage of such opportunities, and by weakening social controls. These changes have raised the concern (Hodess 2001; Wei 2001) that corruption may well reduce or entirely offset any positive influence that globalization may have on international economic development.

SOURCES OF DATA FOR CROSS-NATIONAL STUDIES OF CORRUPTION

Given the difficulties of defining corruption, it is unsurprising that measuring corruption is even more complex. Because definitions of corruption vary according to time, place, and culture, objectively measuring the prevalence of corruption over time and across nations and cultures is an especially difficult task (Johnston 2002). Criminologists generally rely on three main sources of data in the study of criminal or deviant behavior: (1) official, (2) self-report, and (3) victimization. *Official data* are generated by those in charge of controlling or preventing a particular form of criminal or deviant behavior, most typically, the police; *self-report data* are drawn from interviews with actual or potential criminal or deviant offenders; and *victimization data* are collected by surveying individuals about their experiences as victims of crime or deviance.

Collecting corruption data from any of these three sources raises unique challenges.

Because official data are collected by government agencies and because government agencies are most likely to have the considerable resources necessary to pay for data collection, official data are often the most likely to include information collected in a standardized way and over a relatively long period of time. Thus, the United Nations' World Health Organization has collected annual data on homicide from medical examiners in participating countries since 1951 (LaFree 1999; Neapolitan 1997). But for several reasons, official data on corruption pose problems that are more complex than the problems encountered in collecting data on more consistently measured behavior such as homicide. First, compared with other crimes, corruption is less likely to be reported to police and other legal authorities. Second, because corruption is rarely viewed to be as serious as a crime such as homicide, legal systems in most countries spend far less time and resources investigating and prosecuting corruption (Riedel 1990). In general, when less time is spent investigating a particular type of illegal behavior, officials also possess less complete and accurate information about that behavior. And finally, because public officials with the greatest direct knowledge of corruption are often the same individuals who have a vested interest in keeping the practice hidden, obtaining accurate data on corruption from official sources may be especially difficult (Rose-Ackerman 1997). Add to these difficulties the obvious problems of tremendous variation across nations and cultures in terms of (1) how corruption is legally defined, (2) how existing corruption laws are enforced, and (3) how serious a social problem corruption is perceived to be (Rose-Ackerman 1997).

Despite these difficulties, official corruption data could be used much more extensively in cross-national studies. For example, the United States includes two types of crime closely related to corruption (fraud and embezzlement) in its Uniform Crime Reports. Likewise, England and Wales have long included a measure of corruption (fraud) in their Home Office Criminal Statistics Report. The ready availability of official data on corruption, often across many years, suggests that researchers could do much more to exploit these data sources in future research.

Until recently, there were few self-report and victimization surveys aimed at providing information on cross-national comparative corruption. However, this situation is rapidly changing. Early crime victimization surveys were conducted in the United States in the mid-1960s (Sparks 1981) and the Scandinavian countries in the early 1970s (Joutsen 1994). The first major cross-national comparative victimization survey, now called the International Crime Victim Survey (ICVS), was originally carried out in the late 1980s and has now been conducted in 55 nations (Fairchild and Dammer 2001:21; Van Dijk, Mayhew, and Killias 1989).

Since its inception, the ICVS has included questions in its national samples about respondents' experiences with corrupt public officials. Results from the 1999 ICVS indicate that compared with individuals from highly industrialized Western democracies (e.g., United States, England, and Wales), individuals from the transitional democracies of Eastern and Central Europe (e.g., Poland, Ukraine) are substantially more likely to report being confronted by corrupt officials.

In addition, since 1980, the World Values Survey (WVS) has asked large national samples about their tolerance for bribery (Abramson and Inglehart 1995). However, unlike the ICVS, which seeks to measure direct experience of corruption, the WVS asks respondents to react to brief descriptions of corruption (e.g., How justifiable is it for someone to accept a bribe in the course of their duties?).

Transparency International (TI) provides one of the most widely distributed measures of corruption based on interviews. Founded in 1993, TI is an international nongovernmental agency dedicated to detecting and combating corruption. By 2002, TI included 90 independent national chapters around the world (TI 2002). As part of their campaign against corruption, in 1995, TI launched its first comparative corruption measure, the Corruption Perception Index (CPI). By 2002, the CPI included corruption data on 102 nations from all parts of the world.

A major advantage of the CPI is that it creates a composite score based on multiple data sources. For the 2002 version of the CPI, TI (2002) averaged as many as 15 separate sources gathered by nine different institutions (including Freedom House and the World Bank's World Business Survey). The main criterion for inclusion in the CPI is that each source must provide a ranking of nations indicating the overall level of perceived corruption present in each nation (defined as misuse of public office for private gain). All data sources used in the 2002 CPI are businesspeople or country experts. To reduce the possibility of sudden changes in corruption scores due to political scandals, extraordinary media influence, or measurement problems, the CPI averages three years of data from each data source (if available) to produce its corruption averages.

Based on the perception that compared with other forms of corruption, bribery is the activity in which industrializing nations may be more likely to engage, TI supplemented its CPI with a Bribe Payers Index (BPI) in 1999. The BPI polls senior level managers and executives of domestic and foreign companies, chartered accountancies, binational chambers of commerce, national and foreign commercial banks, and commercial law firms operating in 15 "emerging-market" nations (including Argentina, India, Nigeria, and Thailand) about whether leading export companies regularly pay bribes to public officials in the nations in which the surveys are conducted (TI 2002). Thus, the BPI reports levels of bribe paying based on the home nations of the companies doing business in these emerging markets. BPI results for 2002 (TI) show that of the 21 exporting nations in the index, companies headquartered in Australia, Sweden, and Switzerland were perceived to be the least likely to pay bribes (with BPI scores of 8.4 or higher), while companies headquartered in Russia, China, Taiwan, and South Korea were perceived to be the most likely to pay bribes (with BPI scores of 3.9 or lower). U.S. companies were in the middle of the distribution with a BPI score of 5.3 (the same score as Japan).

The World Bank has also conducted two recent surveys that have included self-reported cross-national comparative information on corruption. The World Business Environment Survey (WBES) (World Bank 1997) polled senior level managers of private enterprises in 80 countries about the extent to which they pay bribes to government officials for access to markets. A major finding of the WBES is that compared with large firms, small and medium-sized firms are more likely to admit that they had paid bribes to public officials (Hodess 2001). The results show that managers running smaller firms feel that they are too weak to demand equitable treatment from officials and view bribery as an economic necessity. WBES polls also show that compared with other world regions, East Asia, South Asia, and Africa were the areas where firms were more likely to offer bribes when doing business.

In addition, from 1999 to 2001, the World Bank surveyed 7,011 public officials in 16 countries about the extent of patronage (the selling of public positions) and the effect of patronage on economic and organizational performance (Manning, Mukherjee, and Gokcekus 2000). Results show that as patronage levels in an agency increase, agency performance declines (Hodess 2001). The information provided by the BPI and World Bank polls support the conclusion that more self-report surveys of corruption might be useful, although prior self-report studies of corporate crime (Hollinger and Clark 1983) suggest that such studies are likely to be more valid when limited to the least serious forms of misbehavior.

CROSS-NATIONAL RATES OF CORRUPTION

In the next section, we use the CPI data compiled by Transparency International to compare perceived levels of corruption for 102 nations. The CPI fits squarely under the definition of corruption we developed above, involving public officials in their dealings with private citizens and businesses. In Table 34.1, we rank order CPI scores for all the nations included.

CPI scores range from zero for the most serious perceived levels of corruption to 10 for the least serious levels. The average for the nations included in the 2002 CPI index was 4.6. According to Table 34.1, Finland has the lowest level of perceived corruption (9.7), while Bangladesh is the nation with the highest perceived level of corruption (1.2). We can see at a glance that corruption levels are closely related to world region and level of economic development. Thus, 7 out of the 10 nations perceived to be least corrupt are from Western Europe (Finland,

Table 34.1 Perceived Corruption Among 102 Nations, 2002

Nation	Percentage	Nation	Percentage	Nation	Percentage
Finland	9.7	South Korea	4.5	Georgia	2.4
Denmark	9.5	Greece	4.2	Ukraine	2.4
New Zealand	9.5	Brazil	4.0	Vietnam	2.4
Iceland	9.4	Bulgaria	4.0	Kazakhstan	2.3
Singapore	9.3	Jamaica	4.0	Bolivia	2.2
Sweden	9.3	Peru	4.0	Cameroon	2.2
Canada	9.0	Poland	4.0	Ecuador	2.2
Luxembourg	9.0	Ghana	4.0	Haiti	2.2
The Netherlands	9.0	Croatia	3.8	Moldova	2.1
United Kingdom	8.7	Czech Republic	3.7	Uganda	2.1
Australia	8.6	Latvia	3.7	Azerbaijan	2.0
Norway	8.5	Morocco	3.7	Indonesia	1.9
Switzerland	8.5	Slovak Republic	3.7	Kenya	1.9
Hong Kong	8.2	Sri Lanka	3.7	Angola	1.7
Austria	7.8	Colombia	3.6	Madagascar	1.7
USA	7.7	Mexico	3.6	Paraguay	1.7
Chile	7.5	China	3.5	Nigeria	1.6
Germany	7.3	Dominican Republic	3.5	Bangladesh	1.2
Israel	7.3	Ethiopia	3.5		
Belgium	7.1	Egypt	3.4		
Japan	7.1	El Salvador	3.4		
Spain	7.1	Thailand	3.2		
Ireland	6.9	Turkey	3.2		
Botswana	6.4	Senegal	3.1		
France	6.3	Panama	3.1		
Portugal	6.3	Malawi	2.9		
Slovenia	6.0	Uzbekistan	2.9		
Namibia	5.7	Argentina	2.8		
Estonia	5.6	Côte d'Ivoire	2.7		
Taiwan	5.6	Honduras	2.7		
Italy	5.2	India	2.7		
Uruguay	5.1	Russia	2.7		
Hungary	4.9	Tanzania	2.7		
Malaysia	4.9	Zimbabwe	2.7		
Trinidad & Tobago	4.9	Pakistan	2.6		
Belarus	4.8	Philippines	2.6		
Lithuania	4.8	Romania	2.6		
South Africa	4.8	Zambia	2.6		
Tunisia	4.8	Albania	2.5		
Costa Rica	4.5	Guatemala	2.5		
Jordan	4.5	Nicaragua	2.5		
Mauritius	4.5	Venezuela	2.5		

Source: Transparency International (2002).

Denmark, Iceland, Sweden, the Netherlands, Luxembourg, and Norway), and the 3 exceptions include two Western-style democracies (New Zealand and Canada) and 1 non-Western but highly industrialized Asian nation (Singapore). By contrast, among the 10 nations that have the highest levels of perceived corruption, 5 are from sub-Saharan Africa, 2 are from Asia, 2 are from the former Soviet

Union, and 1 is from Latin America. All 10 nations that show the lowest levels of perceived corruption according to the CPI are also among those classified as "high-income" nations by the World Bank (1999/2000). By contrast, 8 of the 10 nations that have the highest levels of perceived corruption according to the CPI are classified as low income by the World Bank (Bangladesh, Nigeria, Uganda, Indonesia, Kenya, Cameroon, Azerbaijan, and Tanzania), and the remaining 2 nations (Ukraine and Bolivia) are classified as low-middle income.

To provide a more detailed summary of how corruption relates to important national characteristics, we next divided the nations shown in Table 34.1 into three groups based on whether the CPI indicated high levels of corruption (0–3.4), medium levels of corruption (3.5–6.4), or low levels of corruption (6.5–10.0). We then compared corruption levels to six global regions, four income classifications from the World Bank (1999/2000), four Gini index income inequality levels (Deninger and Squire 1996), and three democracy levels based on the index originally developed by Gurr (1974). The results are shown in Table 34.2.

According to Table 34.2, corruption levels are strongly related to world region. The most striking results are the frequency of sub-Saharan African nations in the high-corruption category and the frequency of West European nations in the low-corruption category. More than 70 percent of sub-Saharan African nations in the sample were classified as having high perceived levels of corruption. While much smaller than the sub-Saharan percentage, nearly half the nations of the Americas, Eastern Europe, and Central Asia were also in the high-perceived-corruption category, and more than two-fifths of the Asian nations qualified as high-perceived-corruption nations. By contrast, Western European nations were the least likely to be classified as high-corruption nations. Compared with Western European nations, sub-Saharan African nations were 13 times more likely to be classified as high-corruption nations. At the same time, while nearly three-quarters of West European nations were classified as having low corruption on the CPI, not a single one of the sub-Saharan nations was classified in the low-corruption category.

Table 34.2 also shows that corruption classifications are strongly related to level of economic development. Not a single one of the 28 high-GNP nations was classified as having high levels of perceived corruption. By contrast, not a single one of the 25 low-GNP nations was classified as having low levels of perceived corruption. As we move from high to low levels of GNP, the proportion of nations with high levels of corruption moves from zero to nearly 90 percent. Conversely, as we move from high to low levels of GNP, the proportion of nations with low levels of corruption drops from nearly 80 percent to zero.

The Gini index is a popular measure of income concentration that provides a measure of the gap between the wealthy and the poor in each nation. We created four income inequality categories by classifying nations according to high-Gini index levels (62.3–53.6), upper-middle levels (53.5–39.8), lower-middle levels (39.7–33.1), and low levels (33.0–19.9). Table 34.2 shows that as income inequality increases, so too do levels of perceived corruption. Thus, among the 12 nations that had the highest levels of income inequality, more than two-thirds were classified as high-corruption nations. By contrast, among the 26 nations with the lowest income inequality, less than 40 percent were classified as having low levels of corruption. As we move from the highest to the lowest income inequality levels, the proportion of high corruption countries drops from two-thirds to less than one-third. Conversely, as we move from the highest to the lowest income inequality levels, the proportion of nations classified as low corruption increases from under 10 percent to nearly 40 percent.

To compare corruption with democracy levels, we used an 11-point democracy index (Marshall and Jaggers 2000) that builds on an earlier scale developed by Gurr (1974). This index includes measures such as the competitiveness of the nomination process and the openness of elections in each nation. We divided the index into categories of high levels of democracy (10–8), medium levels (7–4), and low levels (3–0). According to Table 34.2, corruption levels decline as democracy levels rise. Thus, only 22 percent of high-democracy nations have high perceived levels of corruption compared with 70 percent of the medium-democracy and 64 percent

Table 34.2 Cross-National Corruption Levels by Region, Income, Inequality, and Level of Democracy

	Corruption Index[a]							
	High		*Medium*		*Low*		*Total*	
	N	*%*	*N*	*%*	*N*	*%*	*N*	*%*
Region[b]								
Sub-Saharan Africa	12	71	5	29	0	0	17	100
Asia	7	41	5	29	5	29	17	100
Eastern Europe/ Central Asia	9	45	11	55	0	0	20	100
Western Europe	1	5	4	21	14	74	19	100
Middle East/ North Africa	1	20	3	60	1	20	5	100
Americas	11	50	9	39	3	13	23	100
$\Pi^2 = 48.3, p < .001$								
Gross National Product[b]								
High	0	0	6	21	22	79	28	100
Upper middle	4	21	14	74	1	5	19	100
Lower middle	15	54	13	46	0	0	28	100
Low	22	88	3	12	0	0	25	100
$\chi^2 = 98.8, p < .001$								
Inequality (GINI)[c]								
High	8	67	3	25	1	8	12	100
Upper middle	12	48	10	40	3	12	25	100
Lower middle	5	20	12	48	8	32	25	100
Low	8	31	8	31	10	39	26	100
$\chi^2 = 12.8, p < .05$								
Level of Democracy[d]								
High	12	22	22	40	21	38	55	100
Medium	14	70	6	30	0	0	20	100
Low	14	64	7	32	1	4	22	100
$\chi^2 = 25.8, p < .001$								

Sources: a. 2002 Corruption Perception Index, Transparency International (2002).

b. World Bank (1999/2000).

c. GINI Index; Deninger and Squire (1996).

d. Marshall and Jaggers (2000).

of the low-democracy nations. However, nations classified as medium and low on the democracy index have similar levels of perceived corruption. In fact, compared with nations classified as scoring medium on the democracy index, the low-democracy nations were somewhat more likely to have low and medium levels of perceived corruption. In general, these results confirm Montinola and Jackman's (2002) finding of a curvilinear relationship between democracy and corruption levels: corruption levels become somewhat greater as we move from very low democracy levels to medium levels but then decline steeply as we move from medium to high levels of democracy.

SOURCES OF CORRUPTION

The difficulty of obtaining valid cross-national data on corruption has limited the ability of researchers to provide the kind of causal modeling that has become common for other types of crime and deviant behavior. Still, prior research (Mauro 1998; Rose-Ackerman 1978; Tanzi 1998) has identified several processes that are commonly associated with corruption. We can summarize much of this literature by looking at empirical support for the arguments that levels of corruption will be high when (1) the rewards are high and the costs are low and (2) trust in government is low.

Of the two predictions above, the first has no doubt generated the most research. Much of this research has explicitly or implicitly relied on *rational choice perspectives*. Rational choice perspectives originally developed from neoclassical economic theories of crime and assume that individuals are rational human beings who act in ways that maximize their benefits and minimize their costs (Becker 1968; Cornish and Clarke 1986; Paternoster and Simpson 1996). In terms of corruption, benefits and costs can be formal (a promotion or an arrest), informal (an employer's praise or admonition), tangible (monetary rewards or fines), or intangible (the thrill of an act or the moral pangs of guilt). According to Klitgaard (1998), "Corruption is a crime of calculation, not passion. . . . When bribes are large, the chances of being caught small, and the penalties if caught meager, many officials will succumb" (p. 4). The most frequently examined costs of corruption are the legal penalties associated with it; the most common rewards of corruption are the direct financial gains it offers to public officials and to individuals operating in governmental systems that are either monopolistic or highly cumbersome.

Economist Gary Becker's (1968) influential formulation of rational choice theory predicts that corruption (and other crime) is deterred when the penalties for engaging in corrupt acts are increased so that they outweigh the benefits. Thus, the existence of laws criminalizing corruption, the likelihood of detection, and the certainty and severity of punishment should raise the perceived costs of corruption and reduce its occurrence. However,

researchers (Elliot 1997; Myrdal 1968; Rose-Ackerman 1999) point out that in most countries, the conditions for deterring corruption through legal penalties are weak or nonexistent. For example, as of 1995, Taiwan had still not criminalized the payment of bribes, and while Chile had made the payment of bribes a crime, its laws still do not treat receiving bribes as a crime unless it is accompanied by other illegal acts (Rose-Ackerman 1999). In a study in the Asian Pacific, Quah (2001) offers two main reasons for the ineffectiveness of formal, criminal sanctions against corruption. First, in many cases, criminal sanctions are simply not implemented due to a lack of resources or interest. And second, even when sanctions are implemented, the fines are low and imprisonment is unlikely. Nevertheless, there is some indication that increasing the probability of conviction could reduce corruption levels. Using official U.S. criminal justice data, Goel and Rich (1989) find that higher probability of conviction and more severe punishments are significantly related to lower bribery rates at the federal, state, and local levels.

Rose-Ackerman (1997) and others (Klitgaard 1998; Tanzi 1998) have also argued that informal sanctions may reduce corruption levels. While we could identify no prior empirical research that has explicitly tested this assertion with corruption data, there is evidence that informal sanctions may reduce levels of corporate crime. For example, Paternoster and Simpson (1996) found that businesspersons reported that they would be less likely to engage in corporate crime if they faced higher threats of informal sanctions (e.g., loss of the respect of family and friends).

When gauging the costs and benefits of corruption, we must also take into account the level of rewards officials are receiving through legitimate channels. Thus, many researchers (Klitgaard 1998; Mauro 1998; Rose-Ackerman 1999) point out that those public officials who receive low pay face greater rewards for engaging in corruption. Using secondary cross-national data, Van Rijckeghem and Weder (1997) find that civil servants who earn more are less likely to be tempted by corruption. This finding supports the conclusion that low wages for officials encourage corruption. However, the authors also find that it would take very large increases in civil service salaries to significantly reduce corruption levels.

Researchers (Klitgaard 1998; Mauro 1998; Rose-Ackerman 1997; Tanzi 1998) have also noted that bureaucratic monopolies and agencies with extremely cumbersome requirements may increase the likelihood of corruption by raising its rewards to both officials and citizens. Governmental monopolies encourage corruption by creating situations in which public officials have great discretionary power to allocate goods and services (Elliot 1997; Rose-Ackerman 1978). Thus, Klitgaard (1998) notes that corruption is more likely "when an organization or person has monopoly power over a good or service, has the discretion to decide who will receive it and how much that person will get, and is not accountable" (p. 3). Gray and Kaufmann (1998) argue that in highly regulated economies, the profits produced by monopolies can be extremely lucrative and show that individuals and groups seeking access to monopolistic markets are especially likely to engage in corruption.

Other variables that may raise the rewards of corruption are the degree to which regulations are cumbersome and the level of economic competition. Tanzi (1998) argues that extensive, complicated government regulation gives "a kind of monopoly power to the officials who must authorize or inspect the activities" (p. 10). Montinola and Jackman (2002) also argue that the ability of public officials to intervene in the economy may restrict economic competition (see also Bardhan 1997; Mauro 1998; Rose-Ackerman 1978). There is evidence that complicated tax regulations (Tanzi 1998) and harsh trade restrictions (Mauro 1998) are more common in high-corruption societies. By contrast, Ades and Di Tella (1995, 1997) find that high levels of economic openness (measured by the sum of exports and imports as a share of GDP) and high levels of foreign competition (measured as share of imports in GDP) are significantly related to low levels of corruption. Mauro (1998) argues that limited international economic competition typically results in a large amount of domestic profit protected by the state and that this situation increases corruption by raising its monetary benefits for private citizens.

There is also some evidence that the cost-and-benefit caculus proposed by rational choice theorists may work differently in industrialized and industrializing nations. The simple fact that compared with industrialized nations, industrializing nations are characterized by higher rates of poverty supports this conclusion (Gray and Kaufmann 1998; Rose-Ackerman 1999). Because wages as well as accountability in public sector jobs are typically lower in industrializing than in industrialized nations, the benefit of receiving supplemental income from corruption may represent an especially strong temptation in lesser-industrialized nations. There may also be differences between industrialized nations and nations going through rapid economic transitions in terms of the perceived benefits and costs of corruption. Gray and Kaufmann (1998) argue that compared with other nations, nations undergoing rapid economic transition have significantly higher levels of monopoly-related profit because of the unusually large amount of formerly owned state property suddenly put up for sale. The larger value of monopoly profits in transition states, especially under conditions of low public sector wages and low accountability, may significantly increase the rewards of engaging in corruption. This situation may be especially relevant for the "breakaway" republics that formed when the Soviet Union dissolved in 1989. However, much of this discussion is speculative, because few studies have yet provided empirical tests of these predictions.

In addition to variables that affect the costs or benefits of engaging in corruption, high levels of corruption are also frequently linked to low levels of trust in government (Nye 1967). Heidenheimer (1996) cites lack of trust in government as a correlate of corruption and offers Italy as an example. Putnam's (1993) study of civic traditions in Italy revealed that compared with southern Italians, northerners reported higher levels of trust in government and lower levels of perceived corruptness. However, Heidenheimer (1996) points out that compared with residents of other European nations, both residents of northern and southern Italy report low levels of trust in government and high levels of corruption. He concludes that corruption in the Italian political system is a by-product of the general lack of trust among its citizens (Heidenheimer 1996:339).

CONSEQUENCES OF CORRUPTION

Conclusions about the consequences of corruption have gone through three distinct phases during the second half of the twentieth century. First, in the 1960s, researchers generated a lively debate about whether corruption had positive or negative consequences for society. The *culturalists* (Banfield 1958; Myrdal 1968; Wraith and Simpkins 1963) argued that corruption stems from cultural rules that emphasize gift giving and loyalty to family or clan rather than the rule of law, and that these rules were harmful to public interests, stifling economic growth and increasing economic inequality. By openly recognizing that some cultural practices elicited economically harmful or politically destabilizing behavior, the culturalists made a real contribution to research and policy on corruption. However, some culturalists (Banfield 1958; Wraith and Simpkins 1963) developed an overtly moralist tone toward cultural practices that provoked strong objection from critics. This moralist tone is evident in Wraith and Simpkins (1963), who argued that corruption "flourishes as luxuriantly as the bush and weeds which it so resembles, taking the goodness from the soil and suffocating the growth of plants, which have been carefully, and expensively, bred and tended" (p. 12).

The *revisionists* strongly rejected the moral superiority evident in some of the culturalist work on corruption and, more generally, disagreed with the culturalist assumption that corruption had mostly negative consequences for society. They argued instead that corruption could increase economic efficiency, reduce problems of capital formation, and help citizens avoid rigid bureaucratic inflexibility and red tape (Abueva 1966; Bayley 1966; Huntington 1968; Leyes 1965). Thus, Leff (1964) criticizes the culturalists for assuming that in the absence of corruption, officials in industrializing nations would automatically initiate policies that would increase economic development. A more realistic scenario, according to Leff, is that leaders of industrializing nations avoid economic growth policies because they are reluctant to bear the high costs that come with such policies. Similarly, Nye (1967) concludes that corruption contributed positively to the economic development of both the United States and Great Britain.

Second, in the 1970s, before the debate between the culturalists and the revisionists was resolved, both perspectives were increasingly eclipsed by the growing popularity of the neo-Marxist perspective. According to the neo-Marxists (Amin 1974; Wallerstein 1974), corruption was simply a by-product of the international capitalist system. The uneven advance of the global capitalist economy produced a world system of highly industrialized, prosperous "core" nations and lesser-industrialized, economically dependent "peripheral" nations. For the neo-Marxists, corruption required no explanation because it was the inevitable result of capitalist exploitation. This orientation greatly reduced research interest in corruption.

But third, beginning in the 1980s, growing challenges to the neo-Marxist perspective have resulted in a renewed interest in the earlier debates between culturalists and revisionists. Especially important challenges to the neo-Marxist perspective have been the increasing number of nations in Asia and Latin America that began to rapidly industrialize after the 1970s (as opposed to sinking further into poverty) and by the very uneven performance of economies in socialist nations. Moreover, the neo-Marxist perspective did not recognize, let alone explain, the sizable differences in corruption levels among the nations they classified as either core or peripheral. With the decline of the neo-Marxist perspective, we have come full circle, witnessing an increasing interest, once again, in the cultural and revisionist claims about corruption that were popular in the 1960s. But compared with the earlier debate between culturalists and revisionists, recent research on the consequences of corruption has largely rejected the obviously moralistic tone of some earlier culturalist work and has provided far more sophisticated empirical analysis.

In general, these recent empirical studies have added new support to earlier culturalist concerns about the negative impact of corruption on economic and political development. Key conclusions are that corruption reduces economic growth by discouraging private investment (Mauro 1995, 1996), encourages poor management of natural resources (Klitgaard 1998; Johnston 1997), postpones growth-enhancing economic reforms (Abed and Davoodi 2000; Mauro 1998), and increases income inequality and poverty (Gupta, Davoodi, and Alonso-Terme 1998). For example, concentrating on oil-rich Nigeria, Rose-Ackerman (1997) argues that because of extensive corruption, the per capita income of Nigerians stagnated during the same period that the country experienced huge increases in oil exports. Similarly, Johnston (1997) and Wade (1982) show how corruption related to water and irrigation systems reduced economic growth in India and Pakistan.

Corruption may also prevent implementation of economic reforms that might otherwise promote long-term investment and growth. For example, Gray and Kaufmann (1998:8) argue that corruption results in inefficient economic outcomes because it lures talented individuals into corruption-related activities rather than the kinds of entrepreneurial activities that would otherwise stimulate economic growth. Mauro (1998) points out that corruption can also encourage officials to divert public resources into economic markets that make it easier to extract bribes, such as weapons production or large-scale investments. By allocating resources on the basis of the profits to be gained from corruption rather than on fundamental societal needs, corruption distorts government spending and reduces investment in important areas, such as education, which are critical for long-term economic growth.

Recent research (Bardhan 1997; Gray and Kaufmann 1998; Kaufmann and Wei 1999) has also examined the revisionist argument (Huntington 1968; Nye 1967) that corruption increases economic productivity by allowing individuals to cut through bureaucratic red tape. For example, in the 1960s, Leff (1964) argued that corruption stimulates economic growth by providing "speed money" that allows individuals to reduce bureaucratic delays and by encouraging officials who levy bribes to work harder. But recent research by Rose-Ackerman (1999) rejects this argument, claiming that it is unrealistic to expect investors to offer bribes only to avoid inefficient regulations. She claims that the more likely expectation is that investors will pay bribes to avoid any and all state-imposed regulations. Likewise, Gray and Kaufmann (1998) point out that in a highly corrupt environment, public officials may have incentives to increase delays in order to extract even higher bribes.

Also contradicting revisionist claims about the ability of corruption to reduce bureaucratic red tape, Kaufmann and Wei (1999) show that enterprises reporting a greater incidence of bribery were more likely to spend *longer* amounts of time negotiating licenses, obtaining permits, and paying taxes. Moreover, Mauro (1998) and others (Gray and Kaufmann 1998) argue that individuals offering bribes to corrupt officials may actually increase bureaucratic red tape by establishing a custom that halts approval of licenses until a bribe is received. Thus, corrupt practices such as bribes may reduce delays for a few individuals but may nevertheless increase bureaucratic red tape for the economy as a whole (Mauro 1998:685). In support, Mauro (1995) finds that even in countries in which bureaucratic regulations are complex and arguably inefficient, corruption still negatively affects economic growth by reducing long-term private investment.

Corruption may have an especially negative effect on industrializing nations because it exacerbates existing problems. For example, corruption in countries with high levels of inequality often widens the gap between the rich and poor (Rose-Ackerman 1999). While corruption can also slow economic growth in more highly industrialized nations, the consequences are typically less severe (Elliot 1997). Thus, Johnston (1997:69) argues that despite the damaging impact that corruption has on political legitimacy, stable industrialized nations have "long term anti-corruption muscle" because of the extensive set of checks against illegitimate use of power and the separation of public and private sectors.

To summarize then, a growing body of recent research supports the earlier culturalist perspective by showing that the detrimental consequences of corruption for economic development and political legitimacy outweigh its benefits. However, this does not mean that corruption never produces beneficial economic or political consequences. It is possible that corruption can, in selected circumstances, foster economic growth (Braguinsky 1996) and many would argue (Elliot 1997; Heidenheimer and Johnston 2002; Johnston 1997; Rose-Ackerman 1999) that the consequences of corruption are likely to vary by nation depending especially on level of economic development.

COMBATING CORRUPTION

Given the growing interest in corruption as a social problem, it is surprising how little high-quality evaluation research has been done to determine the effectiveness of various intervention efforts. While TI (Hodess 2001) lists over 4,000 books and articles on corruption, almost none of these studies have been carefully evaluated. Instead, the literature is dominated by hundreds of individual case studies and few rigorous experimental interventions.

We can divide prior attempts to combat corruption into two broad categories: motivational and situational. In general, *motivational* approaches seek to reduce the motivation of the would-be offender to commit a corrupt act, while *situational* approaches seek to change the environment to make corruption less likely. Most motivational strategies have taken one of three approaches, either increasing the costs of committing corruption, decreasing the rewards of committing corruption, or increasing the rewards of not committing corruption.

The most common methods of increasing the costs of corruption are to either increase the severity of criminal charges for engaging in corruption or to increase the certainty that these charges will actually be applied. Klitgaard (1998:4) claims that to be successful, anticorruption strategies must quickly identify and punish a few major offenders and corrupt officials. Closely related to the idea of increasing punishment for engaging in corruption is to instead reduce the benefits of corruption. In fact, the OECD's recent Anti-Bribery Convention seeks to do both at the same time: it increases the costs of corruption by making it a crime to engage in bribery in another country, but it also reduces the rewards of corruption by eliminating the practice of allowing those who engage in corrupt practices to deduct bribes as legitimate business expenses. However, the extent to which either of these methods has actually succeeded in reducing corruption is uncertain.

Another popular method for combating corruption is to increase the rewards of engaging in legitimate work. This is most often done by improving the salaries and working conditions of public officials who have positions that facilitate corrupt practices. In many nations, wages of public officials are so low that individuals and their families find it difficult to survive. Moreover, we have seen above that levels of perceived corruption are closely related to national levels of economic development. These considerations make it seem plausible that raising salaries and improving work conditions of employees might in fact reduce corruption levels. However, in the absence of rigorous tests, at present we know little about the extent to which such efforts can in fact be successful at reducing corruption levels.

The other major set of methods for combating corruption focuses on reducing the situational opportunities for engaging in corrupt practices. Perhaps the most obvious methods here are to reduce the power of public monopolies to dispense valued goods and services and to improve the transparency of government dealings with the public. Rose-Ackerman (1978) suggests that competition between politicians and between bureaucrats minimizes corruption in government. If voters can replace politicians, or clients can readily reapply for bureaucratic privileges from different officials, officials have fewer incentives to engage in corruption (Shleifer and Vishny 1993).

In support, a recent study of 66 nations by Montinola and Jackman (2002) found that highly democratic societies had significantly lower levels of perceived corruption. But at the same time, Montinola and Jackman found that nations that first transition to democracy may actually face increasing levels of corruption. The authors note that this pattern highlights the special difficulties faced by nations attempting to establish democracy. If corruption persists or actually gets worse with partial democratization, it may undermine efforts for further democratization. Montinola and Jackman argue (2002:168) that this is exactly what happened to Nigeria in its recent attempts to move toward greater democratization. But the implication of the Montinola and Jackman study is that if transitional nations stay the course, higher levels of democratization will eventually result in much lower levels of corruption.

Another way to reduce situational opportunities for corruption is to increase the transparency and openness of governmental processes. TI (Hodess

2001) argues that "greater transparency in all areas of government practice is probably the most effective single instrument against corruption" (p. 4). The ability of governments to make their dealings more transparent may be boosted by technological changes. Thus, it is an increasingly simple matter for governments to put their records, income statements, and other documentation directly on-line.

Of course, an effective strategy for combating corruption may simultaneously involve both motivational and situational methods. Thus, when the Musevini government in Uganda embarked on an ambitious battle against government corruption in 1986 (Kaufmann 1997), it employed both motivational strategies (e.g., investigating and prosecuting corruption) as well as situational strategies (e.g., reforming the civil service). Similarly, the cleanup of the Philippine tax system in the 1970s and the overhaul of Argentina's social security system both involved not only the immediate firing of corrupt personnel but also attempts to professionalize the remaining staff, adding new regulations and controls, and adopting new incentives and performance assessment systems (Kaufmann 1997).

CONCLUSIONS

We define corruption as an abuse of public office that violates formal laws or informal norms, that brings private gain to a public official, and that provides a third party with services or resources that would otherwise be more difficult or impossible to obtain. Growing democratization and the increasing interconnectedness of the global economy have greatly increased awareness of corruption as a social problem in recent years. However, the difficulty of collecting valid cross-national comparative data on corruption represents a major impediment to scientific study and the development of sound policy. The recent availability of comparative databases such as the one collected by TI represents some progress. Based on data from 102 nations, the TI data show that perceived levels of corruption are highest in the nations of sub-Saharan Africa, the Americas, Eastern Europe, and Central Asia and lowest among nations of Western Europe. Our analyses of the TI data show that high perceived-corruption levels are associated with low-GDP levels, high income-inequality levels, and low levels of democratization. Corruption appears to be most prevalent in situations in which the rewards are high and the costs are low and when trust in government is low. Corruption is encouraged by systems that provide high incentives and little accountability and by governmental systems that are monopolistic and cumbersome.

Early research on corruption was divided between the culturalists, who argued that cultural practices promoting corruption resulted in negative economic and political effects, and the revisionists, who faulted the culturalists for their moralistic tone and argued that corruption often benefited societies by promoting economic development and allowing individuals to avoid bureaucratic red tape. A new wave of empirical research on corruption after the 1980s has supported many of the negative consequences of corruption identified earlier by the culturalists. Efforts to combat corruption have generally emphasized changing the motivation of individual wrongdoers (usually by raising the costs of corruption, reducing the benefits of corruption, or raising the benefits of legitimate behavior) or by reducing the situational opportunities for corruption. Given the growing recognition of corruption as an important social problem, more research that specifically evaluates the success of programs aimed at combating corruption is critical.

Among the varying types of corruption, bribery has probably been the most frequently studied (Hodess 2001; Swamy et al. 1999). However, Thompson (1993) argues that some forms of corruption may be more likely than others to undermine political legitimacy and hence may be more consequential. Future research should provide systematic comparisons of different types of corruption, identifying specific causes and consequences. While the challenges are considerable, researchers also need to do a far better job of examining existing data on corruption and working to develop alternative data sources. For example, analysis of official data on corruption from those countries in which it is routinely collected would be useful, as would the development of self-reported surveys of corrupt practices.

Recognition of the tremendous impact of corruption on the economic, political, and social well-being of societies has grown considerably in recent years. We hope that researchers can take advantage of the current high levels of interest in corruption to begin collecting and analyzing more valid data on corruption and providing a better understanding of the most effective ways of reducing its harmful effects. As we have seen, such efforts are likely to be closely linked to the success of democratic processes worldwide and the viability of an emerging global civil society.

REFERENCES

Abed, G. and H. Davoodi. 2000. *Corruption, Structural Reforms, and Economic Performance in the Transition Economies* (Document No. WP/00/132). Washington, DC: International Monetary Fund.

Abramson, P. and R. Inglehart. 1995. *Value Change in Global Perspective.* Ann Arbor, MI: University of Michigan Press.

Abueva, J. V. 1966. "The Contribution of Nepotism, Spoils, and Graft to Political Development." *East-West Center Review* 3:45–54.

Ades, A. and R. Di Tella. 1995. *Competition and Corruption* (Applied Economics Discussion Paper Series No. 169). Oxford: Oxford University Press.

——. 1997. "The New Economics of Corruption." Pp. 80–99 in *Political Corruption,* edited by P. Heywood. Oxford, England: Blackwell.

Amin, S. 1974. *Accumulation on a World Scale.* New York: Monthly Review.

Banfield, E. 1958. *The Moral Basis of a Backward Society.* New York: Free Press.

Bardhan, P. 1997. "Corruption and Development: A Review of the Issues." *Journal of Economic Literature* 35:1320–346.

Bayley, D. 1966. "The Effects of Corruption in a Developing Nation." *Western Political Quarterly* 19:719–32.

Becker, G. 1968. "Crime and Punishment: An Economic Approach." *Journal of Political Economy* 76:169–217.

Braguinsky, S. 1996. "Corruption and Schumpeterian Growth in Different Economic Environments." *Contemporary Economic Policy* 19:14–25.

Caiden, G., O. P. Dwivedi, and J. Jabbra, eds. 2001. *Where Corruption Lives.* Bloomfield, CT: Kumarian.

Colton, N. 2001. "Foreign Corrupt Practices Acts." *American Criminal Law* 38:891–912.

Commonwealth Expert Group. 2000. *Fighting Corruption: Promoting Good Governance.* London, England: Commonwealth Secretariat.

Cornish, D. and R. Clarke. 1986. *The Reasoning Criminal.* New York: Springer-Verlag.

Deninger, K. and L. Squire. 1996. "A New Data Set: Measuring Income Inequality." *The World Bank Economic Review* 10:565–92.

Diamond, L. and M. F. Plattner. 1995. "Introduction." Pp. ix–xxii in *Economic Reform and Democracy,* edited by L. Diamond and M. F. Plattner. Baltimore, MD: Johns Hopkins University.

Elliot, K. A. 1997. *Corruption and the Global Economy.* Washington, DC: Institute for International Economics.

Fairchild, E. and H. R. Dammer. 2001. *Comparative Criminal Justice Systems.* 2nd ed. Belmont, CA: Wadsworth.

Gardiner, J. 2002. "Defining Corruption." Pp. 25–40 in *Political Corruption: Concepts and Contexts,* edited by A. Heidenheimer and M. Johnston. New Brunswick, NJ: Transaction Publishers.

Glynn, P., S. Kobrinand, and M. Naim. 1997. "The Globalization of Corruption." Pp. 7–27 in *Corruption and the Global Economy,* edited by K. Elliot. Washington, DC: Institute for International Economics.

Goel, R. and D. Rich. 1989. "On the Economic Incentives for Taking Bribes." *Public Choice* 61:269–75.

Gray, C. and D. Kaufmann. 1998. "Corruption and Development." *Finance and Development,* March, pp. 7–10.

Gupta, S., H. Davoodi, and R. Alonso-Terme. 1998. *Does Corruption Affect Income Inequality and Poverty?* (Document No. 98/76). Washington, DC: International Monetary Fund.

Gurr, T. R. 1974. "Persistence and Change in Political Systems, 1800–1971." *American Political Science Review* 68:1482–504.

Heidenheimer, A. J. 1970. *Political Corruption: Readings in Comparative Analysis.* New York: Holt, Rinehart and Winston.

——. 1996. "The Topography of Corruption: Explorations in a Comparative Perspective." *International Social Science Journal* 48 (3):337–48.

Heidenheimer, A. J. and M. Johnston. 2002. *Political Corruption: Concepts and Contexts.* New Brunswick, NJ: Transaction.

Heidenheimer, A. J., M. Johnston, and V. T. Levine, eds. 1989. *Political Corruption: A Handbook.* 2nd ed. New Brunswick, NJ: Transaction.

Heywood, P. 1997. *Political Corruption.* Oxford, England: Blackwell.

Hodess, R. 2001. *Global Corruption Report 2001.* Berlin, Germany: Transparency International.

Hollinger, R. C. and J. P. Clark. 1983. "Deterrence in the Workplace: Perceived Certainty, Perceived

Severity, and Employee Theft." *Social Forces* 62:398–419.

Huntington, S. P. 1968. *Political Order in Changing Societies.* New Haven, CT: Yale University Press.

——. 1991. *The Third Wave: Democratization in the Late Twentieth Century.* Norman, OK: University of Oklahoma Press.

Johnston, M. 1997. "When Politics and Corruption Meet." Pp. 61–81 in *Corruption and the Global Economy,* edited by K. Elliot. Washington, DC: Institute for International Economics.

——. 2002. "Right and Wrong in American Politics: Popular Conceptions of Corruption." Pp. 173–91 in *Political Corruption: Concepts and Contexts,* edited by A. Heidenheimer and M. Johnston. New Brunswick, NJ: Transaction.

Joutsen, M. 1994. "Victimology and Victim Policy in Europe." *The Criminologist* 19:1–3.

Kaufmann, D. 1997. "Corruption: The Facts." *Foreign Policy,* Summer, 114–31.

Kaufmann, D. and S. Wei. 1999. *Does "Grease Money" Speed Up the Wheels of Commerce?* (NBER Working Paper No. 7093, April). Cambridge, MA: National Bureau of Economic Research.

Kingsley, D. J. 1944. *Representative Democracy.* Yellow Springs, OH: Antioch Press.

Klitgaard, R. 1998. "International Cooperation against Corruption." *Finance and Development,* March, pp. 3–6.

LaFree, G. 1999. "Summary and Review of Cross-National Comparative Studies of Homicide." Pp. 125–45 in *Homicide: A Sourcebook of Social Research,* edited by M. D. Smith and M. A. Zahn. Thousand Oaks, CA: Sage.

Leff, N. 1964. "Economic Development through Bureaucratic Corruption." *The American Behavioral Scientist* 8:8–14.

Leyes, C. 1965. "What Is the Problem about Corruption?" *Journal of Modern African Studies* 3:224–5.

Manning, N., R. Mukherjee, and O. Gokcekus. 2000. *Public Officials and Their Institutional Environment: An Analytic Model for Assessing the Impact of Institutional Change on Public Sector Performance* (World Bank Policy Research Working Paper No. 2427). Washington, DC: World Bank.

Marshall, M. G. and K. Jaggers. 2000. "Polity IV Project." Retrieved from http://www.bsos.umd.edu/cidcm/polity.

Mauro, P. 1995. "Corruption and Growth." *Quarterly Journal of Economics* 110:681–712.

——. 1996. *The Effects of Corruption on Growth, Investment, and Government Expenditure* (International Monetary Fund Document No. WP/96/98). Washington, DC: International Monetary Fund.

——. 1998. "Corruption: Causes, Consequences, and Agenda for Further Research." *Finance and Development,* March, pp. 11–14.

Merton, R. K. 1968. *Social Theory and Social Structure.* New York: Free Press.

Montinola, G. R. and R. W. Jackman. 2002. "Sources of Corruption: A Cross-Country Study." *British Journal of Political Science* 32:147–70.

Myrdal, G. 1968. *Asian Drama: An Enquiry into the Poverty of Nations.* New York: Pantheon.

Neapolitan, J. L. 1997. *Cross-National Crime: A Research Review and Sourcebook.* Westport, CT: Greenwood.

Newman, G. 1999. *Global Report on Crime and Justice.* New York: United Nations Office for Drug Control and Crime Prevention.

Noonan, J. 1984. *Bribes.* New York: Macmillan.

Nye, J. S. 1967. "Corruption and Political Development: A Cost-Benefit Analysis." *The American Political Science Review* 61:417–27.

Passas, N. 2000. "Global Anomie, Dysnomie and Economic Crime: Hidden Consequences of Neoliberalism and Globalization in Russia and around the World." *Social Justice* 27:16–44.

Paternoster, R. and S. Simpson. 1996. "Sanction Threats and Appeals to Morality: Testing a Rational Choice Model of Corporate Crime." *Law and Society Review* 30:549–83.

Peters, J. G. and S. Welch. 1978. "Political Corruption in America: A Search for Definitions and a Theory." *American Political Science Review* 78:974–84.

Philip, M. 2002. "Conceptualizing Corruption." Pp. 41–57 in *Political Corruption: Concepts and Contexts,* edited by A. Heidenheimer and M. Johnston. New Brunswick, NJ: Transaction.

Putnam, R. 1993. *Making Democracy Work: Civic Traditions in Modern Italy.* Princeton, NJ: Princeton University Press.

Quah, D. 2001. "Governance and Corruption in West Africa." Pp. 105–19 in *Where Corruption Lives,* edited by G. Caiden, O. P. Dwivedi, and J. Jabbra. Bloomfield, CT: Kumarian.

Quinones, E. 2001. "Implementing the Anti-Bribery Convention: An Update from the OECD." Pp. 197–200 in *Global Corruption Report 2001,* edited by R. Hodess. Berlin, Germany: Transparency International.

Riedel, M. 1990. "Nationwide Homicide Data Sets: An Evaluation of the Uniform Crime Reports and National Center for Health Statistics Data." Pp. 175–205 in *Measuring Crime: Large Scale, Long*

Range Efforts, edited by D. L. MacKenzie, P. J. Baunach, and R. R. Roberg. Albany, NY: State University of New York.

Rose-Ackerman, S. 1978. *Corruption: A Study in Political Economy.* New York: Academic Press.

——. 1997. "The Political Economy of Corruption." Pp. 31–60 in *Corruption and the Global Economy,* edited by K. Elliot. Washington, DC: Institute for International Economics.

——. 1999. *Corruption and Government: Causes, Consequences, and Reform.* New York: Cambridge University Press.

Rosenthal, M. 1989. "An American Attempt to Control International Corruption." Pp. 701–14 in *Political Corruption: A Handbook,* edited by A. J. Heidenheimer, M. Johnston, and V. Levine. New Brunswick, NJ: Transaction Publishers.

Sayre, A. 2002. "U.S. Joins Louisiana Corruption Probe." Retrieved from http://www.miami.com/mld/miami/3956906.htm.

Senate Select Committee on Intelligence. 1994. "An Assessment of the Aldrich H. Ames Case and Its Implications for U.S. Intelligence." Retrieved from http://www.fas.org/irp/congress/1994_rpt/ssci_ames.htm.

Shapiro, S. 1990. "Collaring the Crime, Not the Criminal: Reconsidering the Concept of White-Collar Crime." *American Sociological Review* 55:346–65.

Shleifer, A. and R. W. Vishny. 1993. "Corruption." *Quarterly Journal of Economics* 108:599–617.

Sparks, R. 1981. "Surveys of Victimization: An Optimistic Assessment." *Crime and Justice: An Annual Review of Research,* vol. 3. Chicago, IL: University of Chicago Press.

Stich, R. 1994. *Defrauding America.* Alamo, CA: Diablo Western.

Sutherland, E. 1949. *White Collar Crime.* New York: Holt, Rinehart and Winston.

Swamy, A., S. Knack, Y. Lee, and O. Azfar. 1999. *Gender and Corruption.* Washington, DC: World Bank.

Tanzi, V. 1998. *Corruption around the World: Causes, Consequences, Scope, and Cures* (Document No. WP/98/63). Washington, DC: International Monetary Fund.

Thompson, D. F. 1993. "Mediated Corruption: The Case of the Keating Five." *American Political Science Review* 87:369–81.

——. 1995. *Ethics in Congress: From Individual to Institutional Corruption.* Washington, DC: Brookings.

de Tocqueville, A. [1835] 1969. *Democracy in America.* Translated by H. Reeve. New York: Mentor Books.

Transparency International. (2002). Retrieved from http://www.transparency.org/about_ti/index.html.

United Nations. 1997. "United Nations Action against Corruption and Bribery." Retrieved from http://www.uncjin.org/Documents/Corruption.pdf.

Van Dijk, J., P. Mayhew, and M. Killias. 1989. *Experiences of Crime across the World: Key Findings of the 1989 International Crime Survey.* The Hague, The Netherlands: Ministry of Justice.

Van Rijckeghem and B. Weder. 1997. *Corruption and the Rate of Temptation: Do Low Wages in the Civil Service Cause Corruption?* (Paper No. WP/97/73). Washington, DC: International Monetary Fund.

Wade, R. 1982. "The System of Administrative and Political Corruption: Canal Irrigation in South India." *Journal of Development Studies* 18:287–328.

Wallerstein, I. 1974. *The Modern World-System: Capitalist Agriculture and the Origins of the European World-Economy in the Sixteenth Century.* New York: Academic Press.

Wei, S. 2001. *Corruption and Globalization* (Policy Brief No. 79). Washington, DC: Institute for International Economics.

World Bank. 1997. "World Business Environment Study." Retrieved from http://www.worldbank.org/private-sector/ic/ic_resources.htm.

——. 1999/2000. "World Development Report." Retrieved from www.worldbank.org/wdr/2000/full-report.html.

Wraith, R. and E. Simpkins. 1963. *Corruption in Developing Nations.* London, England: G. Allen.

INDEX

Jette, A., 589
Jha, S. K., 108
Jhaveri, H., 458
Jihad, 356, 361
Job-for-life syndrome, 462
Job insecurity, 199
    advanced technology and, 205
    changes in workplace organization, 205
    corporate downsizing and, 202–203
    excess labor supply, 196
    globalization and, 205
    implicit, 202–203
    independent contractor redeployment, 203
    individual worker powerlessness, 196
    outsourcing and, 202
    responses to, 203
    substitution of machine energy for worker skill, 196
    temporary workers and, 203
    transfer of jobs to developing countries, 196, 197, 198
    transformation to manufacturing, 196
    See also Job security, skill and; Runaway shop
Jobs, access to expensive medical care and, 198
Job security, 195, 198
    immediate compliance and, 196
    See also Job security, skill and
Job security, skill and, 203–205
    limiting numbers of new apprentices, 204
    professional licensing/certification, 204
    role of organization, 204, 205
    social movements, 204–205
    social policy, 205
Job security paradox, 198–199
Johannesburg Earth Summit, 2002, 93
Johansson, M., 114, 116
Johansson, S., 289
Johnsen, M. C., 576
Johnson, A., 547
Johnson, B., 265, 270, 271, 273
Johnson, B. D., 504
Johnson, C., 342
Johnson, D., 127
Johnson, D. G., 80, 81
Johnson, E. "Magic," 324
Johnson, J., 578
Johnson, J. H., 180, 189
Johnson, L. C., 356
Johnson, S. E., 342, 345
Johnson administration, 48
Johnson-Kuhn, J. A., 73
Johnston, H., 390
Johnston, J., 242

Johnston, L. D., 482, 485, 505
Johnston, M., 604, 612, 613
Johnston, P., 500
Joint Commission on Mental Health and Illness, 577
Jolis, A., 405
Jolley, D., 325
Jonassohn, K. 374, 377, 380, 381, 383, 384
Jones, A., 16
Jones, K., 53
Jones, K. L., 149
Jonsson, L. R., 199
Jorgensen, J. J., 146
Joutsen, M., 605
Jowett, G., 210
Joyce, P. R., 563
Jubilee Movement International 2001, 398, 406
Judge, K., 291
Junger, E., 337
Juvenile court jurisdiction, 480, 491
    Austria, 480
    Hong Kong, 480
    India, 480
    U.S. states, 480, 481
Juvenile delinquency, 11, 480–481, 491
    definition, 480
    key predictors, 491
    See also Juvenile delinquency, causes of; Juvenile delinquency, non-U.S.; Juvenile delinquency, U.S.
Juvenile delinquency, causes of, 488–491. *See also* Juvenile delinquency, theories of
Juvenile delinquency, non-U.S., 485–488, 491
    demographic correlates, 486
    minor offenses, 486
    property offenses, 486
    substance abuse, 486
    trends, 487–488
Juvenile delinquency, theories of:
    aggregate-level, 490–491
    individual-level, 488–490
    learning theory and, 490
    self-control theory and, 488–489
    social control theory and, 488, 489, 491
    social disorganization theory, 490
    social learning theory and, 490
    strain theories and, 489–490, 491
    See also Juvenile delinquency, causes of
Juvenile delinquency, U.S., 481–485, 491
    assaults, 481
    avoiding arrest, 482
    demographic correlates, 483
    disorderly conduct, 481

About the Editor

George Ritzer is Distinguished University Professor at the University of Maryland, where he has also been a Distinguished Scholar-Teacher and won a Teaching Excellence Award. He was also awarded the 2000 Distinguished Contributions to Teaching Award by the American Sociological Association. He is perhaps best known for *The McDonaldization of Society* (translated into over a dozen languages) and several related books including *Expressing America: A Critique of the Global Credit Card Society* and *Enchanting a Disenchanted World: Revolutionizing the Means of Consumption.* His latest effort in this domain is *The Globalization of Nothing,* published in late 2003. He is also cofounding editor of the *Journal of Consumer Culture.* And he is well-known for his work in theory and metatheory, including the forthcoming two-volume Encyclopedia of Social Theory (2004).

About the Contributors

Gary L. Albrecht is Professor of Public Health and of Disability and Human Development at the University of Illinois at Chicago. His current work focuses on the quality of life of disabled persons and the political economy of disability. His most recent books are the *Handbook of Social Studies in Health and Medicine* (with Ray Fitzpatrick and Susan Scrimshaw, 2000) and the *Handbook of Disability Studies* (with Katherine Seelman and Michael Bury, 2001), both of which have been released in softback in 2003. He is a Fellow of the American Association for the Advancement of Science (AAAS) and in 2003 a Visiting Fellow at Nuffield College, University of Oxford.

Richard Arum is Associate Professor of Sociology and Chair of the Department of Humanities and Social Sciences in the Professions, New York University. His research on education includes *Judging School Discipline* (2003), and on stratification contributions to *Inequality by Design* (1996). He has published numerous peer-reviewed articles appearing in *American Sociological Review, Criminology, Annual Review of Sociology, International Journal of Sociology,* and *Sociology of Education.*

Salvatore J. Babones is Assistant Professor of Sociology at the University of Pittsburgh. A major thrust of his dissertation, "The International Structure of Income and Its Implications for Economic Growth," is the aggregation of global income distributions at the household level. He is currently working on a study of levels of national income mobility over the past four decades.

Pinar Batur is an Associate Professor of Sociology and the Director of the Urban Studies Program at Vassar College. Her books include *Global Color Line* (1999), edited with Joe Feagin, and *White Racism* (2001), coauthored with Joe Feagin and Hernán Vera. Her research focuses on global racism and antiracist movements.

Felix Berardo's teaching and research interests include family sociology, social gerontology, the sociology of death and survivorship, and the sociology of risk. He has published well over 100 articles in professional journals, and is the author, coauthor, or editor of over a dozen major book-length works. Berardo is former editor of the prestigious *Journal of Marriage and Family,* and is current editor of a monograph series on *Current Perspectives in Family Research,* and deputy editor of the *Journal of Family Issues.* He has served as President of the Florida Council on Family Relations and as Associate Chair and Chair of the Department of Sociology. He has also been elected the President of the University's chapters of two national honor societies, Phi Beta Kappa and Phi Kappa Phi. He is a long-standing member of the local chapter of our national sociology honor society, Alpha Kappa Delta, for whom he formerly served as faculty advisor. Berardo was the recipient of the Arthur Peterson Award in Death Education and has been awarded Fellow status by the Gerontological Society of America and the National Council on Family Relations. His book (with F. Ivan Nye) on *Emerging Conceptual Frameworks in Family Analysis* has been included among a select group of works considered "classics" in family sociology, and has been recognized for its long-lasting impact on the field of family science.

Joel Best is Professor and Chair of the University of Delaware's Department of Sociology and Criminal Justice. He is a former editor of *Social Problems* and a past president of the Society for the Study of Social Problems. His books include *Threatened Children* (1990), *Random Violence* (1999), *Damned Lies and Statistics* (2001), *and Deviance: Career of a Concept* (2004).

Franziska Bieri is a doctoral student in the Department of Sociology at Emory University. Her areas of interest include international social movements and nongovernmental organizations, political sociology, and comparative welfare states. She is currently conducting a study of campaigns against blood diamonds and INGO involvement in the effort to produce an international certification process for conflict-free diamonds.

Tim Blackman is Dean of Social Sciences and Law and Professor of Sociology and Social Policy at the University of Teesside, Middlesbrough, U.K. After completing his Ph.D. at the University of Durham, he worked as a community worker in Belfast, subsequently joining the University of Ulster, where he was active in the community planning movement. In 1990, he moved back to England as Head of Research with Newcastle City Council, later joining Oxford Brookes University before moving to Teesside in 2000. His research interests include regeneration, housing, aging, and public health. He has written widely on these topics and is involved in several regional and local regeneration projects in North East England.

John Boli is Professor and Chair, Department of Sociology, Emory University. His recent books include *The Globalization Reader* (with Frank Lechner) and *Constructing World Culture: International Nongovernmental Organizations Since 1875* (with George M. Thomas). He studies global structures and processes, world culture, transnational corporations, education, citizenship, and state power and authority in the world polity.

William C. Cockerham is Professor of Sociology at the University of Alabama at Birmingham. His most recent publication is *Medical Sociology* (9th ed., 2004), which has been translated into Chinese and Spanish. He currently serves as Vice Chair of the Research Committee on Health Sociology of the International Sociological Association.

Norman K. Denzin (Ph.D., 1966, Sociology, University of Iowa) is Distinguished Professor of Communications, College of Communications Scholar, and Research Professor of Communications, Sociology and Humanities, at the University of Illinois, Urbana-Champaign. He is the author, editor, or coeditor of numerous books, including *Screening Race: Hollywood and a Cinema of Racial Violence; Performing Ethnography;* and *9/11 in American Culture.*

Sonalde Desai is Associate Professor of Sociology at the University of Maryland. She received a B.A. from the University of Bombay, India, and a Ph.D. from Stanford University. Her past work has focused on maternal and child health and gender inequality in developing countries. She is currently working on a book on the growth of the middle classes in India.

Gili Drori teaches in the International Relations Program at Stanford University. Her research interests are the comparative study of science and technology, social development and rationalization, globalization, and governance. She is the coauthor of a newly published book on the globalization of science, its causes and its consequences (*Science in the Modern World Polity: Institutionalization and Globalization*, with John W. Meyer, Francisco O. Ramirez, and Evan Schofer, 2003). She is also the author of several papers and chapters on political change, science and development, and comparative education. Currently, she is writing a book on the global digital divide (forthcoming 2005).

Michael A. Elliott is a doctoral candidate in the Department of Sociology at Emory University. His research interests include processes of historical and contemporary global change, institutional analysis, and social theory. He is currently writing his dissertation on the worldwide development and expansion of human rights ideology.

Mark Erickson is lecturer in Sociology, Aston University Business School. He was educated at Durham University (B.A., 1987; M.A., 1992) and completed his Ph.D. at the University of Sunderland (1996). Prior to his current position, he taught at the universities of Durham, Sunderland, and Birmingham. He is coauthor of *Myths at Work* (with Harriet Brady, Carol Stephenson, and Steve Williams) and is currently completing a book on science and technology.

Joe R. Feagin (Ph.D., Harvard University) is currently the Graduate Research Professor of Sociology at the University of Florida. His teaching and research interests concern the development and structure of institutionalized racial and gender discrimination and oppression in U.S. society. With colleagues, he is currently working on research examining the racial views of white elites, the costs of racism for African Americans, racial barriers in U.S. business networks, and the varieties of discrimination faced by women in the United States. He has published 42 research books and textbooks and more than 150 research articles and book chapters, mostly on issues of urban development, class stratification, discrimination, racism, and sexism. His recent books include *Double Burden: Black Women and Everyday Racism,* coauthored with Yanick St. Jean (M.E. Sharpe, 1998); *Racial and Ethnic Relations,* coauthored with Clairece B. Feagin (7th ed., 2003); *Racist America: Roots, Current Realities, and Future Reparations* (2000); *White Racism: The Basics,* coauthored with Hernán Vera and Pinar Batur (2nd ed., 2001); *The First R: How Children Learn Race and Racism,* coauthored with Debra Van Ausdale (2001); and *Liberation Sociology* (coauthored with Hernán Vera, 2001).

Erich Goode holds a Ph.D. in Sociology from Columbia University, and is Professor Emeritus of Sociology at the State University of New York at Stony Brook, and Visiting Professor of Criminology and Criminal Justice at the University of Maryland at College Park. He is the author of 10 books on a variety of subjects, including *Paranormal Beliefs* (2000) and *Deviance in Everyday Life* (2002). His articles have appeared in scholarly and professional journals, including the *American Journal of*

Sociology, Social Problems, and the *American Journal of Psychiatry,* as well as newspapers and magazines, including the *New York Times,* the *Washington Post,* and the *Chicago Sun-Times.* His areas of socialization are drug use and deviant and criminal behavior. Dr. Goode is the recipient of a Guggenheim fellowship.

Douglas J. Goodman Douglas J. Goodman is an Assistant Professor at the University of Puget Sound in the Department of Comparative Sociology. He was awarded a Mellon Post-Doctoral Fellowship at Wellesley College and an Excellence in Teaching award at the University of Maryland. His publications can be divided into three areas. First are those related to communicating theory to students. These include the three textbooks, *Sociological Theory 6th ed., Modern Sociological Theory 6th ed.* and *Classical Sociological Theory 4th ed.* all co-authored with G. Ritzer, as well as "A Sociological Approach to Social Problems'" (with C. Calhoun & G. Ritzer) *Primus Social Problem* (2000); "The Study of Social Problems," (with G. Ritzer) *Primus Social Problems.* (2000); and "Jacques Lacan: The Imaginary, the Symbolic, the Real," in *Postmodern Social Theory* (1997). Second, are those works on theory addressed more to other theorists and general intellectuals. These include "Dream Kitsch and the Debris of History: An Interview with Martin Jay," *Journal of Consumer Culture* (2003); "Defending the Liberal Arts from the Law," *Law and the Liberal Arts* (2003); "What Collins' *The Sociology of Philosophies* Says About Sociological Theory," *Sociological Theory* (2001); "Postmodern Theory," (with G. Ritzer) *Handbook of Sociological Theory* (2002); "Habermas's Social Theory," (with R. Brown) *Handbook of Social Theory* (2000); and his dissertation, *A Sociology of Freedom.* Finally there are the publications relating to consumer culture. These include, *Consumer Culture: A Reference Handbook* (2003); and "Theories of Consumption," (with G. Ritzer & W. Wiedenhoft) *Handbook of Social Theory* (2000).

Mark Gottdiener is Professor of Sociology and Adjunct Professor of Urban Planning and Architecture at SUNY Buffalo. Prior to this appointment, he was a professor at the University of

California, Riverside, and at the City University in Manhattan. He has also taught as a visiting professor at the Helsinki University of Technology in Finland, the University of Thessaly in Greece, and the National University of Sao Paulo in Brazil.

Gottdiener is the author of 14 books and over 60 published papers. His latest publication is the coedited four-volume standard reference work on semiotics to be published by Sage (UK) later in this year. Prior works are original, groundbreaking cultural studies combining semiotics and political economy, including a book about air travel and air culture, *Life in the Air* (2001), and a second edition of *The Theming of America* (2000). He is currently editor for North America of *Urban Studies* and is on the editorial boards of three other journals, including *Consumption and Culture.*

Gottdiener's main areas of interest are the Henri Lefebvrian New Urban Sociology and the cultural analysis, Socio-Semiotics, both of which he helped to create as approaches in the anglophone academic world to issues of urbanism, tourism, postmodern culture, and contemporary political economy. Currently, he is engaged in grant-supported research on the role of real estate speculation in the multiplication of urban centers in New York, Sao Paulo, London, and Tokyo.

Thomas D. Hall is Lester M. Jones Professor of Sociology, and Chair of the Sociology and Anthropology Department at DePauw University in Greencastle, Indiana. His interests include world-systems analysis, long-term social change, and the evolution of race and ethnic relations. His recent books include *Rise and Demise: Comparing World-Systems* (with Christopher Chase-Dunn, 1997) and *A World-Systems Reader* (2000). He is currently writing, with James V. Fenelon, *Indigenous Peoples and Globalization.*

Howard B. Kaplan, Ph.D., is Regents Professor, Distinguished Professor of Sociology, and Mary Thomas Marshall Professor of Liberal Arts at Texas A&M University. He directs an NIH-funded multigenerational longitudinal study of drug abuse and other deviant adaptations to stress. Among his works are *Patterns of Juvenile Delinquency; Social Psychology of Self-Referent Behavior; Deviant Behavior in Defense of Self; Drugs, Crime, and Other Deviant Adaptations; Social Deviance: Testing a General Theory* (with Robert J. Johnson); and *Organizational Innovation: Studies of Program Change in Community Agencies.*

Douglas Kellner is George Kneller Chair in the Philosophy of Education at UCLA and is the author of many books on social theory, politics, history, and culture, including *Camera Politica: The Politics and Ideology of Contemporary Hollywood Film,* coauthored with Michael Ryan; *Critical Theory, Marxism, and Modernity; Jean Baudrillard: From Marxism to Postmodernism and Beyond; Postmodern Theory: Critical Interrogations* (with Steven Best); *Television and the Crisis of Democracy; The Persian Gulf TV War; Media Culture;* and *The Postmodern Turn* (with Steven Best); *Grand Theft 2000: The Postmodern Adventure: Science, Technology, and Cultural Studies at the Third Millennium* (with Steven Best).

Chigon Kim (Ph.D., SUNY at Buffalo) is Assistant Professor of Sociology at the University of Dayton. His main areas of interest include the impact of sociospatial restructuring on urban communities, labor market change and urban inequality, and comparative analysis of urbanization and urban experience.

Gary LaFree is a Professor in the Department of Criminology and Criminal Justice and a Founding Member of the Democracy Collaborative at the University of Maryland. His recent books include *Losing Legitimacy: Street Crime and the Decline of Social Institutions in America* and *The Changing Nature of Crime in America.* LaFree's current research includes studies of U.S. crime trends by race, the impact of political legitimacy, democratic institutions and economic stress on world homicide rates, and connections between childhood schooling practices and adult criminality. He has just undertaken a large new study on political, economic, and social determinants of global terrorist events.

Bronwen Lichtenstein, Ph.D., is a medical sociologist and research scientist at the University of Alabama. She completed her dissertation on organizational responses to HIV/AIDS in New Zealand in 1996 and then moved to the United States, where she has conducted research on women's health, minority health, STIs, and HIV/AIDS. She is the author of 29 academic articles and has received several grants for research on STIs and HIV/AIDS in both New Zealand and the United States. She was an award-winning writer of fiction in Australia and New Zealand prior to beginning her academic career. Dr. Lichtenstein served as the Chair of the Sociologists' AIDS Network (2001–2002) and has been a member of the Governor of Alabama's HIV/AIDS Commission for Children, Youth, and Adults since 2000.

Yvonna S. Lincoln is Ruth Harrington Chair of Educational Leadership and University Distinguished Professor of Higher Education at Texas A&M University. She is currently the coeditor of *Qualitative Inquiry,* a journal devoted to methodological explorations of qualitative methods, and also coeditor of the of the *Handbook of Qualitative Research,* 1st and 2nd editions. Her research interests include the intellectual histories and origins of the paradigm revolution, and faculty intellectual life more generally, as well as program evaluation and media effects on public perceptions of higher education.

Gus Martin is Associate Professor, Public Administration, School of Business and Public Administration, California State University, Dominguez Hills. He is Chair of Public Administration Department and Coordinator of the Criminal Justice Administration program. He previously sat on the faculty of the Graduate School of Public and International Affairs, University of Pittsburgh. Teaching and research fields of specialization include Administration of Justice, Terrorism and Extremism, Juvenile Justice, Fair Housing, and Urban Affairs. He received an A.B. from Harvard College; J.D. from Duquesne Law School; and Ph.D. from the Graduate School of Public and International Affairs at the University of Pittsburgh. His recent books inclucle *Understanidng Terrorism* (2003) and *The New Era of Terrorism* (forthcoming).

Nancy Morris is a doctoral student in the Department of Criminology and Criminal Justice at the University of Maryland. She received a B.A. in Sociology and B.S. in Political Science from Virginia Tech University, and an M.A. in Criminology

from the University of Maryland. She is currently working on a cross-national study examining variations in levels of social capital and homicide victimization rates. Her current research interests include examining the effects of legitimacy, trust, and social capital on criminal activity and crime rates.

Caroline Hodges Persell is Professor of Sociology at New York University. A past President of the Eastern Sociological Society, she has received grants from the Carnegie Academy for the Scholarship of Teaching and Learning, the National Science Foundation, Danforth Foundation, Fund for the Improvement of Postsecondary Education, and the U.S. Office of Education. She has received a Faculty Development Award from the National Science Foundation and the first Annual Women Educators' Research Award, and was named the first Robin M. Williams Jr. Distinguished Lecturer by the Eastern Sociological Society. Her books include *How Sampling Works* (with Richard Maisel); *Understanding Society: An Introduction to Sociology; Preparing for Power: America's Elite Boarding Schools* (with Peter W. Cookson Jr.); and *Education and Inequality.*

Julia O'Connell Davidson is Professor of Sociology at the University of Nottingham. Over the past decade, the focus of her research and publications has been on prostitution, sex tourism, "trafficking," and children's presence in the sex trade. She is author of *Prostitution, Power and Freedom* (1998).

Ken Plummer is Professor of Sociology at the University of Essex, U.K. His main books are *Sexual Stigma* (1975); *Documents of Life* (1983); *Documents of Life—2* (2001); *Telling Sexual Stories* (1995); and *Intimate Citizenship* (2003); and he has coauthored (with John Macionis) *Sociology: A Global Introduction* (2nd ed., 2002). He has also written numerous articles on sexuality, life stories, symbolic interactionism, and lesbian and gay studies, and edited five collections. He is the founding editor of the journal *Sexualities.*

Ian Roxborough gained his Ph.D. in sociology at the University of Wisconsin–Madison. He taught at the London School of Economics before moving to the State University of New York at Stony Brook in 1990. He is currently working on a book on U.S. military strategy since the end of the cold war.

Kathryn Seufert is a doctoral student in the Department of Sociology a New York University. She received her B.A. in Sociology from Temple University. Her current research interests include stratification, sociology of education, and race and ethnicity.

Constance Shehan is Professor of Sociology at the University of Florida. Her research and teaching interests focus on gender, work, and families. She has published numerous papers about women's employment and domestic labor, focusing on the association between women's work, family roles, and mental health. Dr. Shehan is editor of the *Journal of Family Issues* and author of two recent books, *Marriages and Families* (2nd ed.) and *Through the Eyes of the Child: Revisioning Children as Active Agents of Family Life.*

David Norman Smith has been a member of the sociology faculty at the University of Kansas since 1990. He obtained a Ph.D. from the University of Wisconsin in 1988 and an A.B. in Economics from the University of California Berkeley, in 1974. His writings include books as well as articles on classical and critical theory, antisemitism, authoritarianism, genocide, and the Rwandan genocide of 1994.

Mark Stafford is Professor of Sociology at the University of Texas at Austin. He has published many articles on crime, delinquency, and deviance in such journals as *American Sociological Review, Social Forces, Social Psychology Quarterly,* and *Criminology.* He is one of the authors of the fourth edition of *American Delinquency: Its Meaning and Construction.*

Teresa A. Sullivan is Professor of Sociology and Law at the University of Texas at Austin and the Executive Vice Chancellor for Academic Affairs for the University of Texas System. She has written on labor-based social problems, including unemployment and underemployment, and she has also written on the relationship of consumer debt to layoff and other work-related problems.

Michael Tonry is Professor of Law and Public Policy and Director of the Institute of Criminology, Cambridge, and Sonosky Professor of Law and Public Policy at the University of Minnesota.

John Tulloch is Professor of Cultural Studies and Director of the Centre for Cultural Research into Risk, Charles Sturt University, New South Wales, Australia; and Professor of Media Communication, Cardiff University, Wales. His books and articles on risk include *Television, Risk and AIDS: New Cultural Approaches to Health Communication* (with Deborah Lupton, 1997); *Performing Culture: Stories of Expertise and the Everyday* (1999); *Watching Television: Theories and Method in Audience Analysis* (2000); and *Risk and the Everyday* (2003). Current and recent national competitive grants on risk include "A Risk Society? Australian Perceptions of Risk" (with Deborah Lupton), Australian Research Council Large Grant; and "Risk, Media and Identity in Kosovo: Local/Global Trends in Democratization," Australian Research Council Discovery Grant.

Jonathan Turner is Distinguished Professor of Sociology at the University of California at Riverside. Among his 27 books are 5 devoted to the analysis of social problems. Although his primary area of research is general theory, he has long advocated that theory be useful in assessing and analyzing social problems and public issues.

Andrew Twaddle is Professor Emeritus of Sociology at the University of Missouri, Columbia. His most recent books are *Health Care Reform in Sweden, 1980–1994* (1999) and *Health Care Reform Around the World* (2002). He lives in Boothbay, Maine, and is currently at work on a study of transnational governance of the socioeconomic system and continuing theoretical work on health care.

Frank Webster is Professor of Sociology, City University, London. He was educated at Durham University (B.A., 1972; M.A., 1974) and the LSE (Ph.D., 1978). He was Professor of Sociology at Oxford Brookes University from 1990 to 1998, and at the University of Birmingham from 1999 to 2002. Recent books include *Culture and Politics in the Information Age: A New Politics?* (2001); *The*

Virtual University? Knowledge, Markets and Managements, with Kevin Robins (2002); *Theories of the Information Society* (2nd ed., 2002); *Environmentalism,* 5 volumes, edited with David Pepper and George Revill (2002); *Manuel Castells,* 3 volumes, edited with Basil Dimitriou (2003); *The Information Society Reader,* edited with Ensio Puoskari (2003); and *The Intensification of Surveillance: Crime, Terrorism and Warfare in the Information Age,* edited with Kirstie Ball (2003).

Amy S. Wharton is professor of sociology at Washington State University. She has published several articles on gender inequality at work and is currently completing a book on the sociology of gender. Her current research also includes a study of work, family, and gender in a large, international financial services firm.

Roberta Woods is Assistant Dean of Arts and Social Sciences and Professor of Social Policy at the University of Northumbria, Newcastle Upon Tyne, U.K. She completed her D.Phil. on community development at the University of Ulster, and after a period working in welfare rights returned to Ulster to teach and research in housing and social policy. In 1990, she moved to the University of Newcastle Upon Tyne and was elected to the city council. She subsequently took up a post at Ruskin College, Oxford, returning to North East England in 2000 as an Assistant Dean at Northumbria. Her research interests include governance, housing, and gender studies.

Steven Yearley is Professor and Chair of Sociology at the University of York in England and Senior Research Associate at the Stockholm Environment Institute. He writes on environmental sociology and the sociology of science. Recent books include *Sociology, Environmentalism, Globalization* (1996) and *Making Sense of Science: Social Theory and Science Studies* (2004).